Rick Steves®

FRANCE

Rick Steves & Steve Smith

2015

CONTENTS

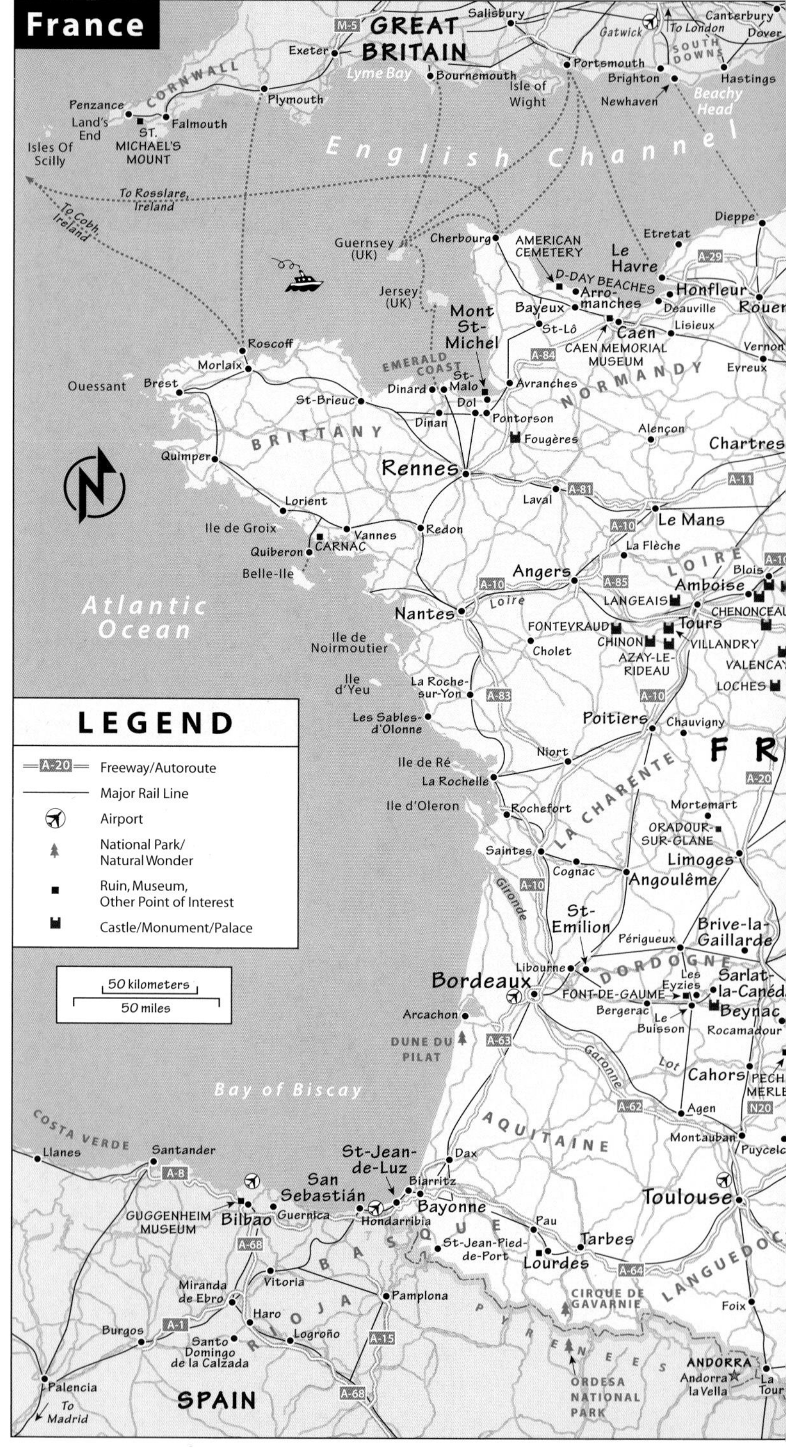

France
GREAT BRITAIN
Salisbury
Exeter
Gatwick
To London
Canterbury
Dover
SOUTH DOWNS
Portsmouth
Brighton
Hastings
Lyme Bay
Bournemouth
Isle of Wight
Newhaven
Beachy Head
CORNWALL
Penzance
Land's End
ST. MICHAEL'S MOUNT
Falmouth
Plymouth
Isles Of Scilly
English Channel
To Rosslare, Ireland
To Cobh, Ireland
Dieppe
Etretat
Guernsey (UK)
Cherbourg
AMERICAN CEMETERY
Le Havre
D-DAY BEACHES
Honfleur
Arromanches
Deauville
Rouen
Jersey (UK)
Mont St-Michel
Bayeux
St-Lô
Caen
Lisieux
CAEN MEMORIAL MUSEUM
Vernon
Evreux
Roscoff
EMERALD COAST
Morlaix
Ouessant
Brest
St-Brieuc
Dinard
St-Malo
Dol
Avranches
NORMANDY
Pontorson
Dinan
BRITTANY
Fougères
Alençon
Chartres
Quimper
Rennes
Laval
Lorient
Le Mans
Ile de Groix
Vannes
Redon
Quiberon
CARNAC
La Flèche
Belle-Ile
LOIRE
Blois
Angers
Amboise
LANGEAIS
Atlantic Ocean
Nantes
Loire
CHENONCEAU
Tours
FONTEVRAUD
Ile de Noirmoutier
Cholet
CHINON
VILLANDRY
AZAY-LE-RIDEAU
Ile d'Yeu
La Roche-sur-Yon
LOCHES
LEGEND
Freeway/Autoroute
Major Rail Line
Airport
National Park/ Natural Wonder
Ruin, Museum, Other Point of Interest
Castle/Monument/Palace
Les Sables-d'Olonne
Poitiers
Chauvigny
Niort
Ile de Ré
La Rochelle
LA CHARENTE
Ile d'Oleron
Rochefort
Mortemart
ORADOUR-SUR-GLANE
Saintes
Limoges
Cognac
Angoulême
Gironde
St-Emilion
Brive-la-Gaillarde
Périgueux
Libourne
DORDOGNE
50 kilometers
50 miles
Bordeaux
Les Eyzies
Sarlat-la-Canéda
FONT-DE-GAUME
Bergerac
Beynac
Arcachon
Le Buisson
Rocamadour
DUNE DU PILAT
Garonne
Lot
Cahors
PECH MERLE
Bay of Biscay
Agen
COSTA VERDE
AQUITAINE
Montauban
Llanes
Santander
St-Jean-de-Luz
Dax
Puycelci
San Sebastián
Biarritz
Toulouse
Bayonne
GUGGENHEIM MUSEUM
Bilbao
Guernica
Hondarribia
BASQUE
Pau
St-Jean-Pied-de-Port
Tarbes
Lourdes
LANGUEDOC
Vitoria
Miranda de Ebro
Pamplona
CIRQUE DE GAVARNIE
Foix
Haro
RIOJA
PYRENEES
Burgos
Santo Domingo de la Calzada
Logroño
ANDORRA
Andorra la Vella
La Tour
Palencia
ORDESA NATIONAL PARK
To Madrid
SPAIN

Channel Tunnel
Ostende
Bruges
To Amsterdam
Düsseldorf
To Berlin
Dunkerque
E-40
Antwerp
Ghent
Calais
FLANDERS
Brussels
A-4
Cologne
Boulogne
E-17
WATERLOO
E-40
Aachen
Bonn
A-16
Lille
E-42
BELGIUM
A-1
Rhine
To Berlin
A-26
E-42
Liège
A-3
Arras
Namur
E-25
A-5
Cambrai
WALLONIE
Cochem
Frankfurt
Abbeville
Aulnoye
A-1
Mosel
Bacharach
A-28
A-16
Amiens
A-26
ARDENNES
Hahn
St-Quentin
Charleville-Mézières
LUXEMBOURG
A-1
Trier
GERMANY
Laon
Beauvais
A-26
Luxembourg City
Mannheim
Senlis
Soissons
Longwy
Heidelberg
CHANTILLY
VERDUN BATTLEFIELD
Thionville
GIVERNY
A-16
de Gaulle
Reims
Saarbrücken
A-1
A-4
Metz
Seine
Epernay
CHAMPAGNE
A-4
A-4
Karlsruhe
A-13
A-4
Paris
DISNEYLAND PARIS
Châlons
A-31
LORRAINE
A-4
Stuttgart
Versailles
A-35
Baden-Baden
Orly
Seine
Nancy
A-10
VAUX-LE-VICOMTE
A-26
St-Dizier
Toul
Strasbourg
A-5
Moselle
VOSGES
ALSACE
FONTAINEBLEAU
BLACK FOREST
A-5
Troyes
A-31
Ribeauvillé
Rhein
A-10
Chaumont
Kaysersberg
A-5
A-6
Colmar
Orléans
Chablis
Laroche
BURGUNDY
LES
Freiburg
Loire
Eguisheim
Auxerre
Culmont
CHAMBORD
Avallon
ABBEY OF FONTENAY
Mulhouse
RONCHAMP
CHEVERNY
GUÉDELON
A-31
VÉZELAY
Belfort
Basel
Semur-en-Auxois
A-3
Zürich
CENTRE
JURA MTNS.
A-36
Vierzon
Sancerre
A-6
A-38
Besançon
SWITZERLAND
Autun
Dijon
Bourges
Châteauneuf-en-Auxois
A-1
Dole
Neuchâtel
Luzern
Nevers
Beaune
Bern
Châteauroux
Le Creusot
Murten
A-71
LA ROCHEPOT
Chalon-sur-Saône
Frasne
A-12
Interlaken
A-2
FRANCE
A-31
Gruyères
Moulins
Brancion
Tournus
Vallorbe
BERNER OBERLAND
Lausanne
Gimmelwald
Cluny
A-1
Lake Geneva
Montreux
Montluçon
Vichy
Mâcon
A-40
Bourg-en-Bresse
Guéret
BEAUJOLAIS
Geneva
A-9
A-40
A-40
Martigny
Zermatt
Lugano
Roanne
Rhône
Lago Maggiore
Clermont-Ferrand
A-72
A-42
Annecy
Chamonix
A-1
SAVOIE
MONT BLANC
Stresa
Lyon
AUVERGNE
Aosta
A-43
A-47
Chambery
Bourg S.M.
A-5
Malpensa
St-Etienne
Vienne
A-43
A-4
Loire
A-41
PIEDMONT
Milan
Dordogne
A-71
A-49
Modane
Po
A-7
Grenoble
A-32
Le Puy-en-Velay
Turin
ITALY
GOUFFRE DE PADIRAC
Lot
Rhône
Valence
A-21
Briançon
Clelles
Rodez
Mende
A-7
Montélimar
Gap
St-Cirq-Lapopie
PROVENCE
Genoa
Cuneo
GORGE DE L'ARDECHE
GORGES DU TARN
Vaison-la-Romaine
To Cinque Terre
PONT DU GARD
Orange
Cordes
Tarn
Millau
Châteauneuf-du-Pape
Digne
Avignon
Uzès
A-10
Albi
A-7
Isle-sur-la-Sorgue
Nîmes
LES BAUX
Roussillon
St-Paul
Menton
Castres
St-Rémy
Vence
MONACO
ROUSSILLON
Arles
Grasse
A-54
LUBERON
GRAND CANYON DU VERDON
Villefranche-sur-Mer
Montpellier
Caunes-Minervois
CAMARGUE
Nice
A-9
Aix-en-Provence
A-8
Antibes
To Bastia, Corsica
Minerve
AIGUES-MORTES
Carcassonne
Béziers
Cannes
Marseille
N97
A-61
COTE D'AZUR
St-Tropez
Narbonne
QUERIBUS & PEYREPERTUSE
LES CALANQUES
Cassis
Toulon
Perpignan
Mediterranean Sea
To Porto Torres, Sardinia
A-9
Collioure
L'Ile-Rousse
To Ajaccio, Corsica
Port Bou
Cadaqués
To Barcelona
Corsica (France)
Figueres

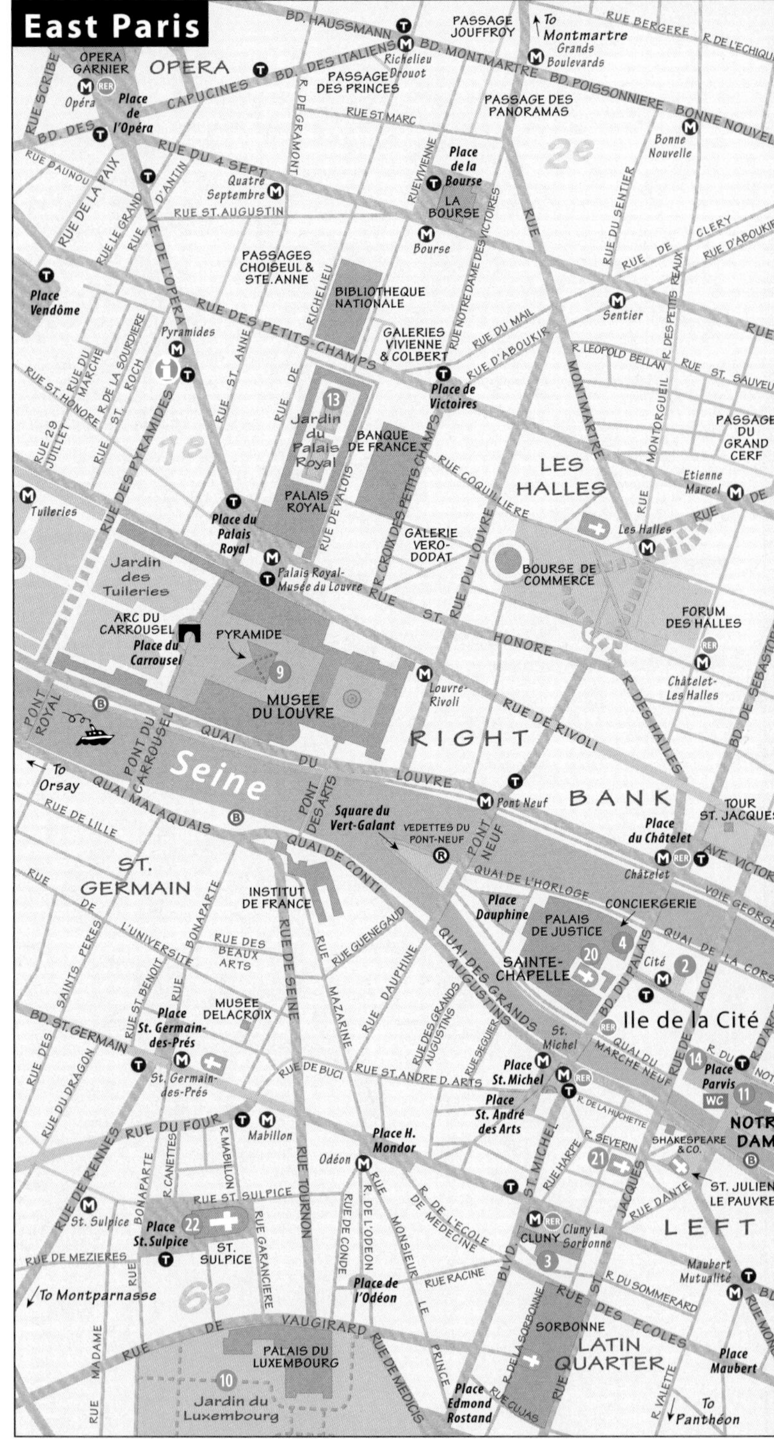
East Paris
BD. HAUSSMANN
PASSAGE JOUFFROY
To Montmartre
Grands Boulevards
RUE BERGERE
R. DE L'ECHIQUIER
OPERA GARNIER
OPERA
Richelieu Drouot
BD. DES ITALIENS
BD. MONTMARTRE
BD. POISSONNIERE
BONNE NOUVELLE
RUE SCRIBE
Opéra
Place de l'Opéra
CAPUCINES
BD. DES
PASSAGE DES PRINCES
R. DE GRAMONT
RUE ST. MARC
PASSAGE DES PANORAMAS
Bonne Nouvelle
2e
RUE DAUNOU
RUE DE LA PAIX
RUE DU 4 SEPT.
Quatre Septembre
D'ANTIN
RUE VIVIENNE
Place de la Bourse
LA BOURSE
RUE ST. AUGUSTIN
RUE LE GRAND
AVE. DE L'OPERA
Bourse
RUE DU SENTIER
RUE DE CLERY
RUE D'ABOUKIR
Place Vendôme
PASSAGES CHOISEUL & STE. ANNE
RICHELIEU
BIBLIOTHEQUE NATIONALE
RUE NOTRE DAME DES VICTOIRES
Sentier
RUE DES PETITS CHAMPS
RUE DU MAIL
R. DES PETITS CARREAUX
Pyramides
GALERIES VIVIENNE & COLBERT
RUE D'ABOUKIR
R. LEOPOLD BELLAN
RUE ST. SAUVEUR
RUE DU MARCHE
R. DE LA SOURDIERE
ST. ROCH
RUE ST. ANNE
RUE DE
RUE ST. HONORE
RUE DES PYRAMIDES
Place de Victoires
13
Jardin du Palais Royal
BANQUE DE FRANCE
RUE 29 JUILLET
1e
MONTMARTRE
MONTORGUEIL
PASSAGE DU GRAND CERF
LES HALLES
RUE COQUILLIERE
Etienne Marcel
Tuileries
Place du Palais Royal
PALAIS ROYAL
RUE DE VALOIS
R. CROIX DES PETITS CHAMPS
GALERIE VERO-DODAT
RUE DU LOUVRE
Les Halles
BOURSE DE COMMERCE
Jardin des Tuileries
Palais Royal-Musée du Louvre
RUE ST. HONORE
FORUM DES HALLES
ARC DU CARROUSEL
Place du Carrousel
PYRAMIDE
9
MUSEE DU LOUVRE
Louvre-Rivoli
RUE DE RIVOLI
Châtelet-Les Halles
BD. DE SEBASTOPOL
R. DES HALLES
PONT ROYAL
PONT DU CARROUSEL
QUAI DU LOUVRE
Seine
RIGHT BANK
To Orsay
QUAI MALAQUAIS
PONT DES ARTS
Square du Vert-Galant
Pont Neuf
PONT NEUF
TOUR ST. JACQUES
RUE DE LILLE
VEDETTES DU PONT-NEUF
Place du Châtelet
Châtelet
AVE. VICTORIA
ST. GERMAIN
QUAI DE CONTI
QUAI DE L'HORLOGE
RUE DE L'UNIVERSITE
INSTITUT DE FRANCE
Place Dauphine
CONCIERGERIE
VOIE GEORGES
PALAIS DE JUSTICE
4
QUAI DE LA CORSE
RUE BONAPARTE
RUE DES BEAUX ARTS
RUE GUENEGAUD
QUAI DES GRANDS AUGUSTINS
SAINTE-CHAPELLE
20
Cité
2
RUE DES SAINTS PERES
RUE ST. BENOIT
MUSEE DELACROIX
RUE DE SEINE
RUE MAZARINE
RUE DAUPHINE
BD. DU PALAIS
RUE DE LA CITE
Ile de la Cité
BD. ST. GERMAIN
Place St. Germain-des-Prés
RUE DES GRANDS AUGUSTINS
St. Michel
QUAI DU MARCHE NEUF
R. D'ARCOLE
RUE DES
St. Germain-des-Prés
RUE DE BUCI
RUE ST. ANDRE D. ARTS
RUE SEGUIER
Place St. Michel
14
R. DU CLOITRE NOTRE
Place Parvis
11
WC
RUE DU DRAGON
RUE DE RENNES
RUE DU FOUR
Mabillon
Place St. André des Arts
R. DE LA HUCHETTE
NOTRE DAME
Place H. Mondor
R. SEVERIN
SHAKESPEARE & CO.
Odéon
R. CANETTES
R. MABILLON
21
ST. JULIEN LE PAUVRE
RUE ST. SULPICE
RUE TOURNON
R. DE L'ODEON
R. DE L'ECOLE DE MEDECINE
ST. MICHEL
RUE HARPE
RUE DANTE
ST. JACQUES
St. Sulpice
Place St. Sulpice
22
ST. SULPICE
RUE GARANCIERE
RUE DE CONDE
RUE MONSIEUR LE PRINCE
CLUNY
Cluny La Sorbonne
LEFT
3
RUE DE MEZIERES
RUE RACINE
BLVD.
R. DU SOMMERARD
Maubert Mutualité
BD.
To Montparnasse
6e
Place de l'Odéon
RUE DES ECOLES
RUE MONGE
RUE DE VAUGIRARD
RUE DE LA SORBONNE
SORBONNE
LATIN QUARTER
Place Maubert
RUE MADAME
PALAIS DU LUXEMBOURG
RUE DE MEDICIS
10
Jardin du Luxembourg
Place Edmond Rostand
RUE CUJAS
R. VALETTE
To Panthéon

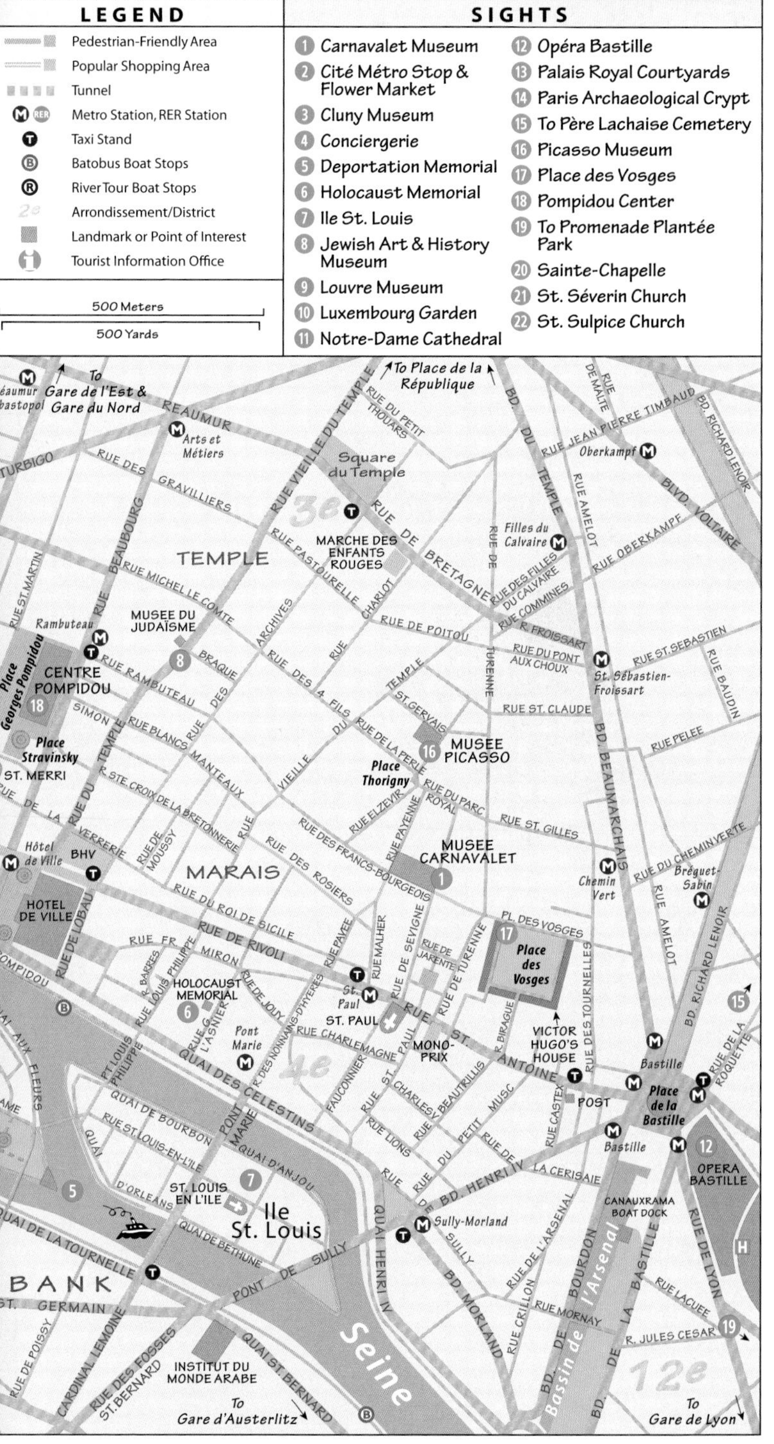
LEGEND
Pedestrian-Friendly Area
Popular Shopping Area
Tunnel
Metro Station, RER Station
Taxi Stand
Batobus Boat Stops
RiverTour Boat Stops
Arrondissement/District
Landmark or Point of Interest
Tourist Information Office
500 Meters
500 Yards
SIGHTS
1 Carnavalet Museum
2 Cité Métro Stop & Flower Market
3 Cluny Museum
4 Conciergerie
5 Deportation Memorial
6 Holocaust Memorial
7 Ile St. Louis
8 Jewish Art & History Museum
9 Louvre Museum
10 Luxembourg Garden
11 Notre-Dame Cathedral
12 Opéra Bastille
13 Palais Royal Courtyards
14 Paris Archaeological Crypt
15 To Père Lachaise Cemetery
16 Picasso Museum
17 Place des Vosges
18 Pompidou Center
19 To Promenade Plantée Park
20 Sainte-Chapelle
21 St. Séverin Church
22 St. Sulpice Church
To Gare de l'Est & Gare du Nord
To Place de la République
Arts et Métiers
Square du Temple
Oberkampf
Filles du Calvaire
TEMPLE
MARCHE DES ENFANTS ROUGES
MUSEE DU JUDAÏSME
Rambuteau
CENTRE POMPIDOU
Place Georges Pompidou
Place Stravinsky
ST. MERRI
St. Sébastien-Froissart
MUSEE PICASSO
Place Thorigny
MUSEE CARNAVALET
Chemin Vert
Bréguet-Sabin
Hôtel de Ville
BHV
HOTEL DE VILLE
MARAIS
Place des Vosges
HOLOCAUST MEMORIAL
St. Paul
ST. PAUL
Pont Marie
MONOPRIX
VICTOR HUGO'S HOUSE
POST
Bastille
Place de la Bastille
OPERA BASTILLE
CANAUXRAMA BOAT DOCK
ST. LOUIS EN L'ILE
Ile St. Louis
Sully-Morland
Bassin de l'Arsenal
BANK
INSTITUT DU MONDE ARABE
Seine
To Gare d'Austerlitz
To Gare de Lyon
3e
4e
12e

West Paris

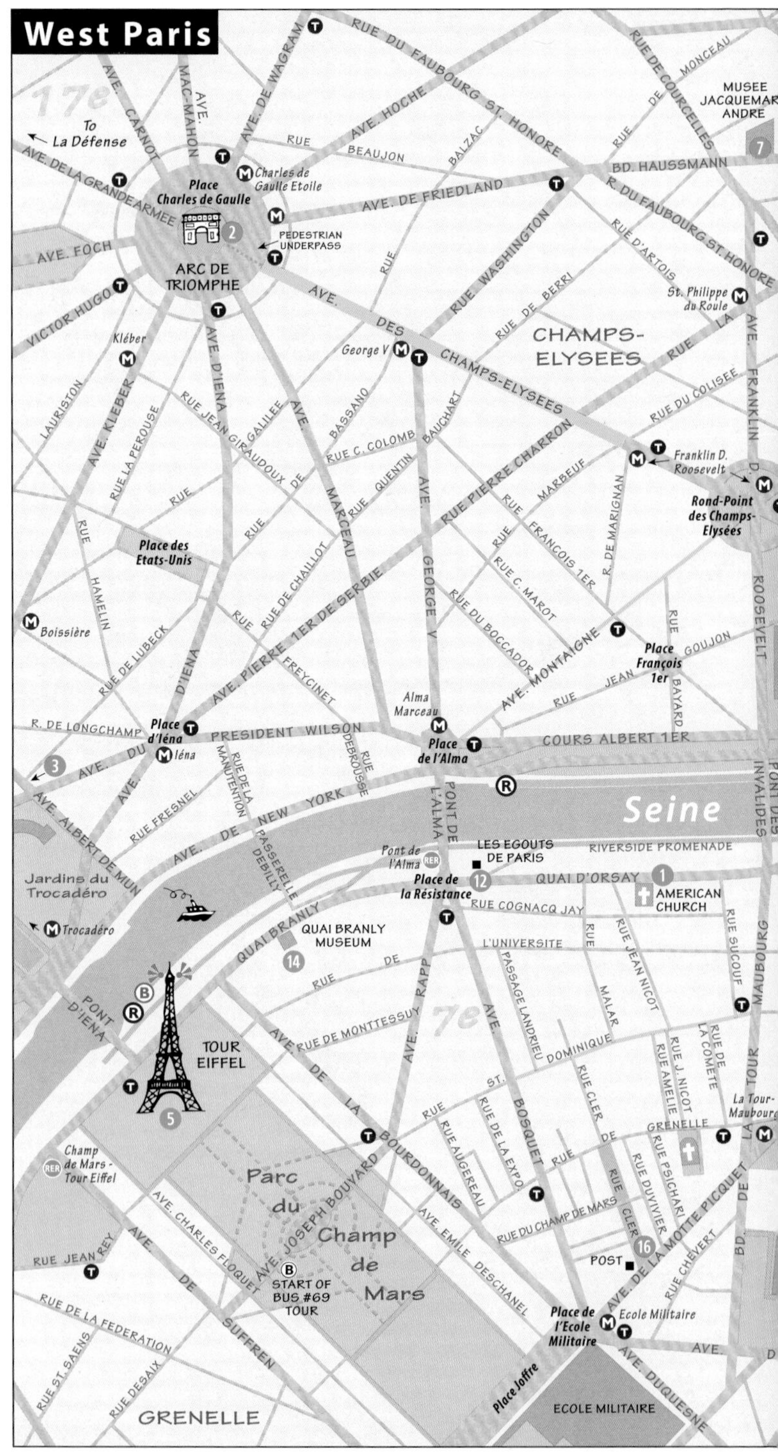

17e
To La Défense
Place Charles de Gaulle
ARC DE TRIOMPHE
Charles de Gaulle Etoile
PEDESTRIAN UNDERPASS
AVE. DE LA GRANDE ARMEE
AVE. FOCH
AVE. CARNOT
AVE. MAC-MAHON
AVE. DE WAGRAM
RUE DU FAUBOURG ST. HONORE
AVE. HOCHE
RUE BEAUJON
BALZAC
RUE DE COURCELLES
RUE DE MONCEAU
MUSEE JACQUEMART ANDRE
BD. HAUSSMANN
AVE. DE FRIEDLAND
R. DU FAUBOURG ST. HONORE
RUE D'ARTOIS
St. Philippe du Roule
RUE WASHINGTON
RUE DE BERRI
CHAMPS-ELYSEES
AVE. DES CHAMPS-ELYSEES
RUE LA BOETIE
AVE. FRANKLIN D. ROOSEVELT
George V
VICTOR HUGO
Kléber
AVE. D'IENA
AVE. KLEBER
LAURISTON
RUE LA PEROUSE
RUE JEAN GIRAUDOUX
GALILEE
BASSANO
RUE C. COLOMB
BAUCHART
RUE DU COLISEE
Franklin D. Roosevelt
Rond-Point des Champs-Elysées
AVE. MARCEAU
RUE QUENTIN
RUE PIERRE CHARRON
MARBEUF
RUE FRANCOIS 1ER
R. DE MARIGNAN
RUE C. MAROT
RUE DU BOCCADOR
AVE. GEORGE V
Place des Etats-Unis
RUE HAMELIN
RUE DE CHAILLOT
AVE. PIERRE 1ER DE SERBIE
RUE FREYCINET
Boissière
RUE DE LUBECK
AVE. MONTAIGNE
Place François 1er
RUE JEAN GOUJON
RUE BAYARD
Alma Marceau
R. DE LONGCHAMP
Place d'Iéna
Iéna
PRESIDENT WILSON
RUE DEBROUSSE
Place de l'Alma
COURS ALBERT 1ER
AVE. DU
RUE DE LA MANUTENTION
RUE FRESNEL
AVE. DE NEW YORK
PASSERELLE DEBILLY
PONT DE L'ALMA
Seine
PONT DES INVALIDES
AVE. ALBERT DE MUN
Jardins du Trocadéro
Trocadéro
Pont de l'Alma
LES EGOUTS DE PARIS
RIVERSIDE PROMENADE
Place de la Résistance
QUAI D'ORSAY
AMERICAN CHURCH
RUE COGNACQ JAY
QUAI BRANLY
QUAI BRANLY MUSEUM
RUE DE L'UNIVERSITE
PASSAGE LANDRIEU
RUE JEAN NICOT
RUE SUCOUF
BD. DE LA TOUR MAUBOURG
PONT D'IENA
AVE. RAPP
RUE DE MONTTESSUY
7e
AVE. BOSQUET
RUE MALAR
RUE ST. DOMINIQUE
RUE J. NICOT
RUE AMELIE
RUE DE LA COMETE
TOUR EIFFEL
AVE. DE LA BOURDONNAIS
RUE CLER
RUE AUGEREAU
RUE DE LA EXPO.
RUE DE GRENELLE
La Tour-Maubourg
RUE PSICHARI
RUE DUVIVIER
Champ de Mars - Tour Eiffel
Parc du Champ de Mars
AVE. JOSEPH BOUVARD
AVE. CHARLES FLOQUET
AVE. EMILE DESCHANEL
RUE DU CHAMP DE MARS
AVE. DE LA MOTTE PICQUET
RUE CHEVERT
POST
RUE JEAN REY
AVE. DE SUFFREN
START OF BUS #69 TOUR
Place de l'Ecole Militaire
Ecole Militaire
RUE DE LA FEDERATION
AVE. DUQUESNE
Place Joffre
ECOLE MILITAIRE
RUE ST. SAENS
RUE DESAIX
GRENELLE

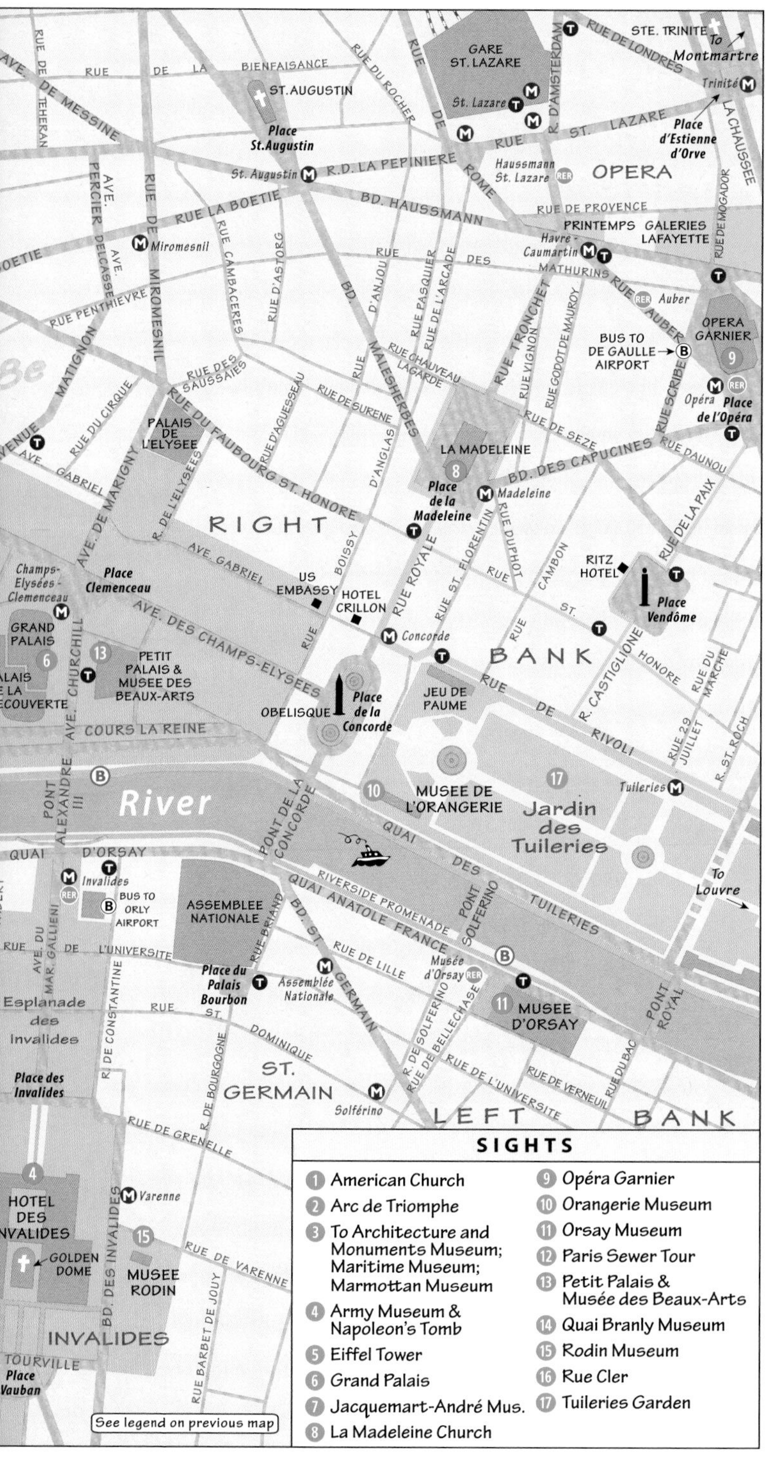

GARE ST. LAZARE
St. Lazare
STE. TRINITE
To Montmartre
Trinité
RUE DE LONDRES
ST. AUGUSTIN
Place St.Augustin
St. Augustin
RUE DE LA BIENFAISANCE
AVE. DE MESSINE
RUE DE TEHERAN
RUE DU ROCHER
RUE DE ROME
R. D'AMSTERDAM
RUE ST. LAZARE
Place d'Estienne d'Orve
LA CHAUSSEE
Haussmann St. Lazare
OPERA
R.D. LA PEPINIERE
BD. HAUSSMANN
RUE DE PROVENCE
PRINTEMPS
GALERIES LAFAYETTE
RUE DE MOGADOR
Havre - Caumartin
RUE DES MATHURINS
RUE LA BOETIE
Miromesnil
AVE. PERCIER
AVE. DELCASSE
RUE DE MIROMESNIL
RUE CAMBACERES
RUE D'ASTORG
BD. MALESHERBES
RUE D'ANJOU
RUE PASQUIER
RUE DE L'ARCADE
RUE AUBER
Auber
OPERA GARNIER
BUS TO DE GAULLE AIRPORT
RUE SCRIBE
Opéra
Place de l'Opéra
RUE PENTHIEVRE
MATIGNON
RUE DES SAUSSAIES
RUE CHAUVEAU LAGARDE
RUE TRONCHET
RUE VIGNON
RUE GODOT DE MAUROY
RUE DE SURENE
RUE D'AGUESSEAU
RUE D'ANGLAS
RUE DE SEZE
RUE DAUNOU
BD. DES CAPUCINES
PALAIS DE L'ELYSEE
RUE DU CIRQUE
RUE DU FAUBOURG ST. HONORE
LA MADELEINE
Place de la Madeleine
Madeleine
RUE DUPHOT
RUE DE LA PAIX
AVE GABRIEL
AVE. DE MARIGNY
R. DE L'ELYSEE
RIGHT BANK
RUE BOISSY D'ANGLAS
RUE ROYALE
RUE ST. FLORENTIN
RUE CAMBON
RITZ HOTEL
Place Vendôme
RUE ST. HONORE
Champs-Elysées-Clemenceau
Place Clemenceau
AVE. GABRIEL
US EMBASSY
HOTEL CRILLON
Concorde
GRAND PALAIS
PETIT PALAIS & MUSEE DES BEAUX-ARTS
AVE. DES CHAMPS-ELYSEES
AVE. CHURCHILL
PALAIS DE LA DECOUVERTE
R. CASTIGLIONE
RUE DU MARCHE
OBELISQUE
Place de la Concorde
JEU DE PAUME
RUE DE RIVOLI
RUE 29 JUILLET
R. ST. ROCH
COURS LA REINE
River
PONT ALEXANDRE III
MUSEE DE L'ORANGERIE
Jardin des Tuileries
Tuileries
PONT DE LA CONCORDE
QUAI DES TUILERIES
QUAI D'ORSAY
To Louvre
Invalides
BUS TO ORLY AIRPORT
ASSEMBLEE NATIONALE
RIVERSIDE PROMENADE
QUAI ANATOLE FRANCE
PONT SOLFERINO
RUE AIME BRIAND
BD. ST. GERMAIN
RUE DE L'UNIVERSITE
AVE. DU MAR. GALLIENI
RUE DE LILLE
Musée d'Orsay
MUSEE D'ORSAY
PONT ROYAL
Place du Palais Bourbon
Assemblée Nationale
Esplanade des Invalides
R. DE CONSTANTINE
RUE ST. DOMINIQUE
R. DE SOLFERINO
RUE DE BELLECHASE
RUE DE VERNEUIL
RUE DU BAC
Place des Invalides
R. DE BOURGOGNE
ST. GERMAIN
Solférino
LEFT BANK
RUE DE GRENELLE
HOTEL DES INVALIDES
GOLDEN DOME
Varenne
BD. DES INVALIDES
RUE DE VARENNE
MUSEE RODIN
RUE BARBET DE JOUY
INVALIDES
TOURVILLE
Place Vauban
See legend on previous map
SIGHTS
1 American Church
2 Arc de Triomphe
3 To Architecture and Monuments Museum; Maritime Museum; Marmottan Museum
4 Army Museum & Napoleon's Tomb
5 Eiffel Tower
6 Grand Palais
7 Jacquemart-André Mus.
8 La Madeleine Church
9 Opéra Garnier
10 Orangerie Museum
11 Orsay Museum
12 Paris Sewer Tour
13 Petit Palais & Musée des Beaux-Arts
14 Quai Branly Museum
15 Rodin Museum
16 Rue Cler
17 Tuileries Garden

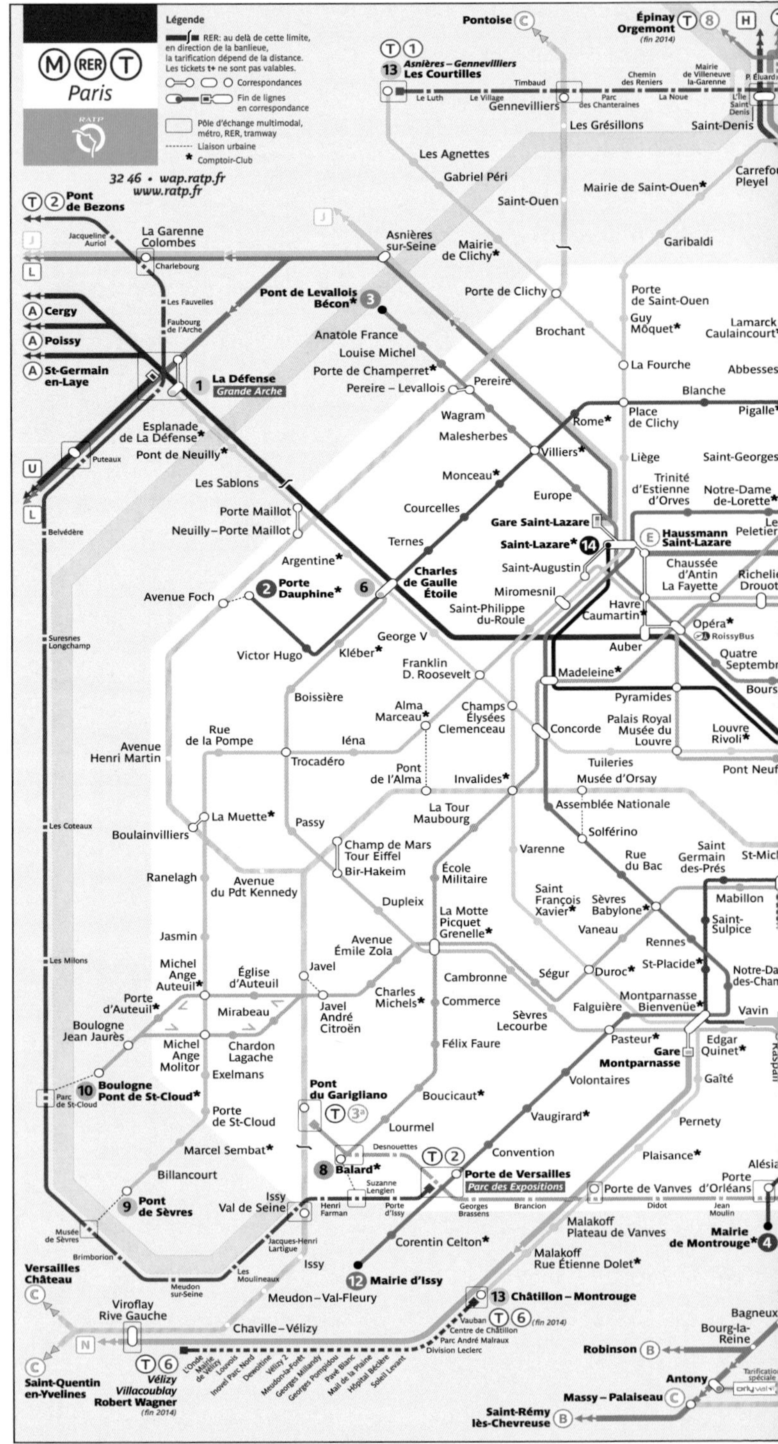
M RER T
Paris
RATP
Légende
RER: au delà de cette limite, en direction de la banlieue, la tarification dépend de la distance. Les tickets t+ ne sont pas valables.
Correspondances
Fin de lignes en correspondance
Pôle d'échange multimodal, métro, RER, tramway
Liaison urbaine
Comptoir-Club
32 46 • wap.ratp.fr
www.ratp.fr
Pontoise
Épinay Orgemont
(fin 2014)
Asnières – Gennevilliers Les Courtilles
Le Luth
Le Village
Timbaud
Gennevilliers
Parc des Chanteraines
Chemin des Reniers
La Noue
Mairie de Villeneuve la-Garenne
L'Île Saint Denis
P. Éluard
Les Grésillons
Saint-Denis
Les Agnettes
Gabriel Péri
Saint-Ouen
Mairie de Saint-Ouen*
Carrefour Pleyel
Pont de Bezons
Jacqueline Auriol
La Garenne Colombes
Charlebourg
Asnières sur-Seine
Mairie de Clichy*
Garibaldi
Les Fauvelles
Faubourg de l'Arche
Pont de Levallois Bécon*
Porte de Clichy
Porte de Saint-Ouen
Guy Môquet*
Lamarck Caulaincourt*
Cergy
Poissy
St-Germain en-Laye
Anatole France
Louise Michel
Porte de Champerret*
Pereire – Levallois
Pereire
Brochant
La Fourche
Abbesses
La Défense
Grande Arche
Blanche
Esplanade de La Défense*
Pont de Neuilly*
Puteaux
Wagram
Malesherbes
Rome*
Place de Clichy
Pigalle*
Villiers*
Liège
Saint-Georges
Monceau*
Trinité d'Estienne d'Orves
Notre-Dame de-Lorette*
Les Sablons
Europe
Courcelles
Porte Maillot
Neuilly – Porte Maillot
Belvédère
Gare Saint-Lazare
Saint-Lazare*
Haussmann Saint-Lazare
Le Peletier
Ternes
Argentine*
Charles de Gaulle Étoile
Saint-Augustin
Chaussée d'Antin La Fayette
Richelieu Drouot
Porte Dauphine*
Avenue Foch
Miromesnil
Havre Caumartin*
Saint-Philippe du-Roule
Opéra*
RoissyBus
George V
Suresnes Longchamp
Victor Hugo
Kléber*
Auber
Quatre Septembre
Franklin D. Roosevelt
Madeleine*
Bourse
Boissière
Pyramides
Alma Marceau*
Champs Élysées Clemenceau
Palais Royal Musée du Louvre
Louvre Rivoli*
Rue de la Pompe
Iéna
Concorde
Avenue Henri Martin
Trocadéro
Tuileries
Pont Neuf
Pont de l'Alma
Invalides*
Musée d'Orsay
La Tour Maubourg
Assemblée Nationale
La Muette*
Passy
Boulainvilliers
Les Coteaux
Solférino
Champ de Mars Tour Eiffel
Bir-Hakeim
Varenne
Rue du Bac
Saint Germain des-Prés
Ranelagh
Avenue du Pdt Kennedy
École Militaire
Saint François Xavier*
Sèvres Babylone*
Mabillon
Dupleix
La Motte Picquet Grenelle*
Vaneau
Saint-Sulpice
Jasmin
Avenue Émile Zola
Rennes
Les Milons
Michel Ange Auteuil*
Église d'Auteuil
Javel
Cambronne
Ségur
Duroc*
St-Placide*
Notre-Dame des-Champs
Porte d'Auteuil*
Mirabeau
Javel André Citroën
Charles Michels*
Commerce
Montparnasse Bienvenüe*
Falguière
Vavin
Boulogne Jean Jaurès
Sèvres Lecourbe
Pasteur*
Edgar Quinet*
Michel Ange Molitor
Chardon Lagache
Félix Faure
Gare Montparnasse
Exelmans
Gaîté
Boulogne Pont de St-Cloud*
Parc de St-Cloud
Volontaires
Pont du Garigliano
Boucicaut*
Porte de St-Cloud
Lourmel
Vaugirard*
Pernety
Marcel Sembat*
Desnouettes
Convention
Plaisance*
Balard*
Porte de Versailles
Parc des Expositions
Alésia
Billancourt
Suzanne Lenglen
Porte de Vanves
Porte d'Orléans
Pont de Sèvres
Issy Val de Seine
Henri Farman
Porte d'Issy
Georges Brassens
Brancion
Didot
Jean Moulin
Musée de Sèvres
Malakoff Plateau de Vanves
Mairie de Montrouge*
Jacques-Henri Lartigue
Corentin Celton*
Brimborion
Malakoff Rue Étienne Dolet*
Versailles Château
Issy
Meudon sur-Seine
Les Moulineaux
Mairie d'Issy
Meudon – Val-Fleury
Châtillon – Montrouge
Viroflay Rive Gauche
Vauban
Centre de Châtillon
Parc André Malraux
Division Leclerc
Bagneux
Chaville – Vélizy
Bourg-la-Reine
Robinson
Saint-Quentin en-Yvelines
Vélizy Villacoublay Robert Wagner
L'Onde
Mairie de Vélizy
Louvois
Inovel Parc Nord
Dewoitine
Vélizy 2
Meudon-la-Forêt
Georges Millandy
Georges Pompidou
Pavé Blanc
Mail de la Plaine
Hôpital Béclère
Soleil Levant
Antony
Tarification spéciale
orlyval
Massy – Palaiseau
Saint-Rémy lès-Chevreuse

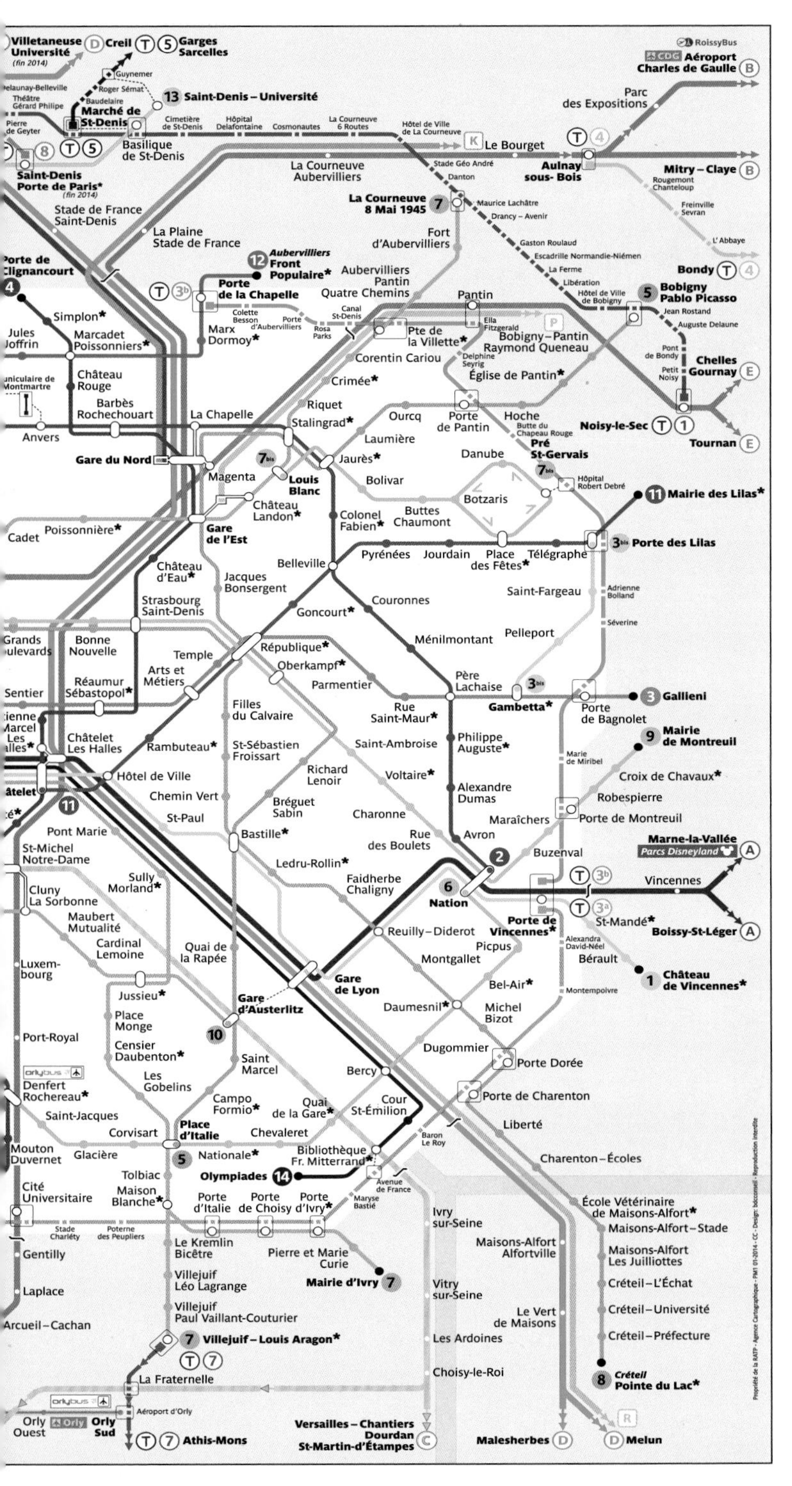

Villetaneuse Université (fin 2014)
Creil
Garges Sarcelles
RoissyBus
Aéroport Charles de Gaulle
Guynemer
Delaunay-Belleville
Roger Sémat
Théâtre Gérard Philipe
Baudelaire
Marché de St-Denis
13 Saint-Denis – Université
Pierre de Geyter
Basilique de St-Denis
Cimetière de St-Denis
Hôpital Delafontaine
Cosmonautes
La Courneuve 6 Routes
Hôtel de Ville de La Courneuve
Parc des Expositions
Le Bourget
Aulnay sous- Bois
Mitry – Claye
Rougemont Chanteloup
Saint-Denis Porte de Paris* (fin 2014)
La Courneuve Aubervilliers
Stade Géo André
Danton
Stade de France Saint-Denis
La Courneuve 8 Mai 1945
Maurice Lachâtre
Drancy – Avenir
Freinville Sevran
La Plaine Stade de France
Fort d'Aubervilliers
Gaston Roulaud
Escadrille Normandie-Niémen
L'Abbaye
Porte de Clignancourt
Aubervilliers Front Populaire*
Aubervilliers Pantin Quatre Chemins
La Ferme
Libération
Bondy
Hôtel de Ville de Bobigny
Bobigny Pablo Picasso
Porte de la Chapelle
Pantin
Jean Rostand
Auguste Delaune
Simplon*
Colette Besson
Porte d'Aubervilliers
Canal St-Denis
Rosa Parks
Ella Fitzgerald
Jules Joffrin
Marcadet Poissonniers*
Marx Dormoy*
Pte de la Villette*
Bobigny – Pantin Raymond Queneau
Pont de Bondy
Chelles Gournay
Petit Noisy
Corentin Cariou
Delphine Seyrig
Funiculaire de Montmartre
Château Rouge
Crimée*
Église de Pantin*
Barbès Rochechouart
Riquet
La Chapelle
Stalingrad*
Ourcq
Porte de Pantin
Hoche
Noisy-le-Sec
Anvers
Laumière
Butte du Chapeau Rouge
Pré St-Gervais
Tournan
Gare du Nord
Jaurès*
Danube
Magenta
Louis Blanc
Bolivar
Hôpital Robert Debré
Mairie des Lilas*
Château Landon*
Botzaris
Poissonnière*
Cadet
Gare de l'Est
Colonel Fabien*
Buttes Chaumont
Porte des Lilas
Pyrénées
Jourdain
Place des Fêtes*
Télégraphe
Château d'Eau*
Jacques Bonsergent
Belleville
Saint-Fargeau
Adrienne Bolland
Strasbourg Saint-Denis
Couronnes
Goncourt*
Séverine
Grands Boulevards
Bonne Nouvelle
Ménilmontant
Pelleport
Temple
République*
Oberkampf*
Arts et Métiers
Parmentier
Père Lachaise
Réaumur Sébastopol*
Sentier
Gambetta*
Gallieni
Porte de Bagnolet
Filles du Calvaire
Rue Saint-Maur*
Mairie de Montreuil
Châtelet Les Halles
Rambuteau*
St-Sébastien Froissart
Saint-Ambroise
Philippe Auguste*
Marie de Miribel
Richard Lenoir
Croix de Chavaux*
Hôtel de Ville
Voltaire*
Châtelet
Chemin Vert
Alexandre Dumas
Robespierre
Bréguet Sabin
St-Paul
Charonne
Porte de Montreuil
Maraîchers
Pont Marie
Bastille*
Rue des Boulets
Avron
St-Michel Notre-Dame
Marne-la-Vallée Parcs Disneyland
Buzenval
Ledru-Rollin*
Sully Morland*
Faidherbe Chaligny
Vincennes
Cluny La Sorbonne
Nation
Maubert Mutualité
Porte de Vincennes*
St-Mandé*
Boissy-St-Léger
Reuilly – Diderot
Cardinal Lemoine
Quai de la Rapée
Picpus
Alexandra David-Néel
Luxembourg
Montgallet
Bérault
Château de Vincennes*
Gare de Lyon
Jussieu*
Bel-Air*
Gare d'Austerlitz
Montempoivre
Place Monge
Daumesnil*
Michel Bizot
Port-Royal
Censier Daubenton*
Dugommier
Saint Marcel
Porte Dorée
Les Gobelins
Bercy
Denfert Rochereau*
Porte de Charenton
Saint-Jacques
Campo Formio*
Quai de la Gare*
Cour St-Émilion
Corvisart
Place d'Italie
Liberté
Chevaleret
Baron Le Roy
Mouton Duvernet
Glacière
Nationale*
Bibliothèque Fr. Mitterrand*
Charenton – Écoles
Tolbiac
Olympiades
Avenue de France
Cité Universitaire
Maison Blanche*
Porte d'Italie
Porte de Choisy
Porte d'Ivry*
Maryse Bastié
École Vétérinaire de Maisons-Alfort*
Ivry sur-Seine
Maisons-Alfort – Stade
Stade Charléty
Poterne des Peupliers
Le Kremlin Bicêtre
Maisons-Alfort Alfortville
Gentilly
Pierre et Marie Curie
Maisons-Alfort Les Juilliottes
Villejuif Léo Lagrange
Mairie d'Ivry
Vitry sur-Seine
Créteil – L'Échat
Laplace
Villejuif Paul Vaillant-Couturier
Créteil – Université
Arcueil – Cachan
Le Vert de Maisons
Villejuif – Louis Aragon*
Les Ardoines
Créteil – Préfecture
Choisy-le-Roi
La Fraternelle
Créteil Pointe du Lac*
orlybus
Aéroport d'Orly
Orly Ouest
Orly
Orly Sud
Athis-Mons
Versailles – Chantiers
Dourdan
St-Martin-d'Étampes
Malesherbes
Melun
Propriété de la RATP - Agence Cartographique - FM1 01-2014 - CC - Design: bdcconseil - Reproduction interdite

PV 314986

France

Bienvenue! You've chosen well. France is Europe's most diverse, tasty, and, in many ways, most exciting country to explore. It's an intriguing cultural bouillabaisse that will challenge your preconceptions and inspire you to think differently.

France is a place of gentle beauty, where the play of light transforms the routine into the exceptional. Here, travelers are treated to a blend of man-made and natural beauty like nowhere else in Europe. With luxuriant forests, forever coastlines, truly grand canyons, and Europe's highest mountain ranges, France has a cover-girl beauty from top to bottom. You'll also discover a dizzying array of artistic and architectural wonders—soaring cathedrals, chandeliered châteaux, and museums filled with the cultural icons of the Western world.

In many ways, France is a yardstick of human achievement. Travelers can trace the whole of European history, from the earliest prehistoric cave paintings to Roman ruins that rival Italy's. In medieval times, France cultivated Romanesque and Gothic architecture, erecting the great cathedrals and basilicas of Notre-Dame, Chartres, Vézelay, and a dozen others. With their innovative designs, French architects set the trends for cities throughout Europe—and with their revolutionary thinking, French philosophers refined modern thought and politics. The châteaux of the Loire Valley and the grand palace of Versailles announced France's emergence as the first European superpower and first modern government. It was France that gave birth to Impressionism and the foundations of modern art. Today's

travelers can gaze dreamy-eyed at water lilies in Claude Monet's Giverny, rejoice amid the sunflowers of Provence that so moved a troubled Vincent van Gogh, and roam the sunny coastlines that inspired Picasso and Matisse. And after all these centuries, France still remains at the forefront of technology, fashion, and—of course—cuisine.

There are two Frances: Paris...and the rest of the country. France's top-down government and cultural energy have always been centered in Paris, resulting in an overwhelming concentration of world-class museums, cutting-edge architecture, and historic monuments. Travelers can spend weeks in France and never leave Paris. Many do.

The other France venerates land, tradition, and a slower pace of life. After Paris, most travelers will be drawn to romantic hill towns and castles, meandering rivers and canals, and oceans of vineyards that carpet this country's landscape. Village life has survived in France better than in most other European countries because France was so slow to urbanize. It was an agricultural country right up until World War II (when a smaller proportion of French citizens lived in cities than Italians did 500 years earlier). And today, even as young people are chasing jobs in the cities, France remains farm country. Everyone venerates the soil *(le terroir)* that brings the flavor to their foods and wines and nourishes a rural life that French people dream about. So although the country's brain resides in Paris, its soul lives in its villages—and that's where you'll feel the real pulse of France.

France offers more diversity than any other nation in Europe; moving from region to region, you feel as if you're crossing into a different country. Paris and the region around it (called Ile de France) is the "island" in the middle that anchors France. To the west are the dramatic D-Day beaches and Tudor-style, thatched-roofed homes of Normandy; to the south lie the river valleys of the Loire and Dordogne, featuring luxurious châteaux, medieval castles, and hill-capping villages. Explore under-the-radar France to the far south, in the Spanish-tinged Languedoc-Roussillon region. Closer to Italy, sun-baked and windswept Provence nurtures Roman ruins and rustic charm, while the Riviera celebrates sunny beaches and yacht-filled harbors. And to the east, travelers encounter Europe's highest snow-capped Alps, the venerable vineyards of Burgundy, and the Germanic villages and cuisine of Alsace.

The forte of French cuisine is its regional diversity. You'll enjoy Swiss-like fondue in the Alps, Italian-style pasta and pesto on the Riviera, Spanish paella in Languedoc-Roussillon, and German sauerkraut mixed with fine wine sauces in the Alsace. *C'est magnifique*—you can taste a good slice of Europe without stepping outside of France.

Each region also produces a wine or other drink that complements its cuisine—such as rich Burgundy wines that go perfectly with *coq au vin,* meaty wines from Languedoc-Roussillon to counter heavy cuisine (such as cassoulet), fruity Côtes du Rhône wines that work well with herb-infused Provençal dishes, and dry whites in Alsace that meld

perfectly with the Germanic cuisine. And in Normandy and Brittany, you'll enjoy apple ciders with crêpes and fresh seafood.

As if that weren't enough, France is also famous for its many pâtés, foie gras, hundreds of different cheeses, sizzling escargots, fresh oysters, *herbes de Provence,* raw meats, fine wine sauces, French fries, duck and lamb dishes, pastries, bonbons, crème brûlée, and sorbets.

L'art de vivre—the art of living—is not just a pleasing expression; it's a building block for a sound life in France. With five weeks of paid vacation, plus every Catholic holiday ever invented, the French are forced to enjoy life. It's no accident that France is home to linger-longer pastimes like café lounging, fine dining, Club Med vacations, barge cruising, and ballooning. You'll run headlong into that mindful approach to life at mealtime. The French insist on the best-quality croissants, mustard, and sparkling water; they don't rush lunch; and an evening's entertainment is usually no more than a lovingly prepared meal with friends.

France demands that the traveler slow down and savor

the finer things; a hurried visitor will miss the *"this is what matters"* barge and blame the French for being lazy. One of your co-authors learned this lesson the hard way while restoring a farm house in Burgundy—and found that it's counterproductive to hurry a project past its "normal pace."

In spite of lavish attention to relaxation, the French are a productive people. French inventors gave us the metric system, pasteurization, high-speed trains, and Concorde airplanes. More importantly, this country rose from the ashes of two debilitating world wars to generate the world's seventh-largest economy. This is thanks in part to determined government intervention that continues today (government spending is 48 percent of GDP). Wine, tourism, telecommunications,

France Almanac

Official Name: It's officially the République Française, but locals, and everyone else, just call it France.

Population: France has nearly 66 million people (more than the combined population of California and Texas). They're a mix of Celtic, Latin, and Teutonic DNA, plus many recent immigrants from around the globe—especially North Africa. Four out of five French are (at least nominally) Roman Catholic. Every French citizen is expected to speak French.

Area: At 215,000 square miles, it's Western Europe's largest nation. (But Texas is still 20 percent bigger.)

Latitude and Longitude: 46°N and 2°E (similar latitude to the states of Washington, North Dakota, and Maine).

Geography: The terrain consists of rolling plains in the north and mountains in the southwest (Pyrenees), southeast (Alps), and south-central (Massif Central). Capping the country on both ends are 1,400 miles of coastline (Mediterranean and Atlantic). The Seine River flows east-west through Paris, the Rhône rumbles north-south 500 miles from the Alps to the Mediterranean, and the Loire travels east-west, roughly dividing the country into north and south. Mont Blanc (15,771 feet) is Western Europe's highest point.

Major Cities: Nearly one in five lives in greater Paris (12 million in the metropolitan area, 2.2 million in the city). Marseille, on the Mediterranean coast, and Lyon, in the southeast, both have about 1.5 million people.

Economy: France's gross domestic product is $2.6 trillion (bigger than California's $2 trillion); the GDP per capita is nearly $40,000 (America's is nearly $52,000). Though the French produce nearly a quarter of the world's wine, they drink much of it themselves. France's free-market economy is tempered by the government, which collects some of Europe's highest taxes (22 percent of GDP—compared to 10 percent in the US) and invests both in industry and social spending (to narrow the income gap between rich and poor). Despite the three-hour lunch stereotypes, the French work as much as their EU neighbors—that is, 20 percent less than Americans (but with greater per-hour productivity).

Government: President François Hollande, elected by popular vote in 2012, heads a socialist government along with president-appointed Prime Minister Manuel Valls. The upper-house Senate (348 seats) is chosen by an electoral college; the National Assembly (577 seats) by popular vote. Though France is a cornerstone of the European Union, many French are Euro-skeptics.

Flag: The Revolution produced the well-known *tricolore,* whose three colors are vertical bands of blue, white, and red.

The Average Jean: The average French person is 39 years old and will live 81 years. This person eats lunch in 22 minutes (four times as fast as 20 years ago) and consumes a glass and a half of wine and a pound of fat a day. The average French citizen pops a bottle of Champagne about every four months. The average worker enjoys five weeks of holiday and vacation a year. A dog is a part of one in three French households; cats are animals non grata.

pharmaceuticals, cars, and Airbus planes are big moneymakers. France is also the European Union's leading agricultural producer and a chief competitor of the US. You'll pass endless wheat farms in the north, dairy farms in the west, vegetable farms and fruit orchards in the south...and vineyards and sunflowers just about everywhere.

With no domestic oil production, France has focused on nuclear power generation, which now accounts for more than 75 percent of the country's electricity production (although renewable energy sources are gaining ground). Electricity is expensive, so the French are careful to turn out lights and conserve—something to remember when you leave your hotel room for the day or evening. Although France's economy may be one of the world's largest, the French remain skeptical about the virtues of capitalism and the work ethic. Business conversation is generally avoided, as it implies a fascination with money that the French find vulgar. (It's considered gauche even to ask what someone does for a living.) In France, CEOs are not glorified as celebrities—chefs are.

The French believe that the economy should support social good, not vice versa. This has produced a cradle-to-grave social security system of which the French are proud. France's poverty rate is half of that in the US, proof to the French that they are on the right track. On the other hand,

if you're considering starting a business in France, think again—taxes are *formidable*. France is routinely plagued with strikes, demonstrations, and slow-downs as workers try to preserve their hard-earned rights in the face of a competitive global economy.

As you travel, you'll find that the most "French" thing about France is the French themselves. Be prepared to embrace (or at least understand) the cultural differences between you and your French hosts. You'll find the French to be reserved in the north and comparatively carefree in the sunny south. Throughout the country, they're more formal than you are. When you enter a store, you'll be greeted not simply with a *"Bonjour,"* but with *"Bonjour, Monsieur* (or *Madame*)." The proper response to the shopkeeper is *"Bonjour, Monsieur* (or *Madame*)." If there are others present, you'd say, *"Bonjour, Messieurs* (or *Mesdames*)"—just to make sure you don't leave anyone out. (For more on the French attitude toward language, see page 16.)

The French are overwhelmingly Catholic but not very devout, and are quick to separate church from state. They are less active churchgoers than Americans, whom they find *très* evangelical. And in France you don't go to church to socialize or to help in charitable deeds (that's what taxes are for). France is also Europe's largest Muslim nation, with well over six million followers (there are twice as many Muslims in France as Protestants). The influx of Muslim immigrants has led to considerable problems of assimilation and remains one of France's thorniest issues to resolve.

The French don't seem particularly athletic—unless you consider tossing little silver balls in the dirt *(pétanque,* a.k.a. *boules)* a sport. A few jog and exercise regularly, and fewer play on recreational teams—though you will find country lanes busy with bike riders hunched over handlebars on weekends. The French are avid sports-watchers. Soccer is king, bike racing is big, and rugby is surprisingly popular for such a refined place. *Le basket* (basketball) is making a move, with a French league and several French NBA stars, including Tony Parker.

Another passion the French share with Americans is their love of movies. They admire Hollywood blockbusters, but they've also carved out their own niche of small-budget romantic comedies and thought-provoking thrillers.

Today's France will challenge many of your preconceptions. The French have a Michelin Guide-certainty in their judgments and are often frank in how they convey their opinions. (Just ask about the best wine to serve with any given course.)

The French see the world differently than we do. The right to bear arms, the death penalty, minuscule paid vacations, and health care as a privilege rather than a basic human

right—these American concepts confound the average Jean. And they don't understand the American need for everyone to be in agreement all the time. Whether it's Iraq, Vietnam, or globalization, the French think it's important to question authority and not blindly submit to it. Blame this aversion to authority on their Revolution hangover.

The French can be a complicated people to understand for hurried travelers. But remember where they've come from: In just a few generations, they've seen two world wars destroy entire cities, villages, landscapes, and their self-respect. They've watched as America replaced them as the world's political and cultural superpower. On the bright side, they've seen their country re-emerge as a global force, with nuclear weapons, a

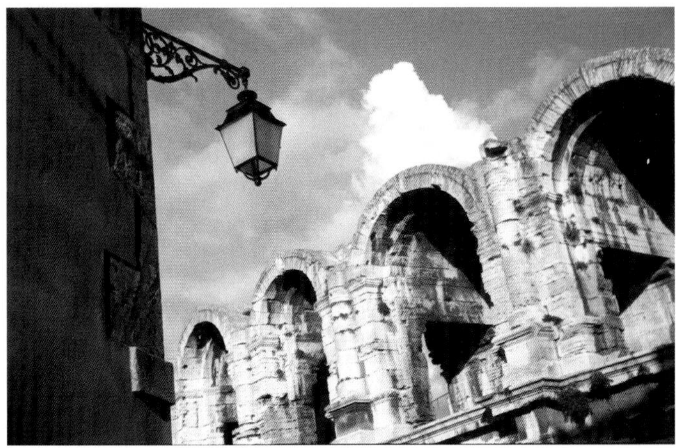

space program, an international spy network, and their own ideas about geopolitics. Like Americans, they're trying to find their place in an increasingly global, multicultural world. Today, they just don't want to be taken for granted. And while the French may—or may not—love your country's politics, this has no bearing on how they will treat you as an individual.

As you travel through this splendid country, come with an appetite to understand and a willingness to experience. Welcome new ideas and give the locals the benefit of your doubt. Accept France on its own terms and don't judge. Above all, slo-o-o-ow down. Spend hours in cafés lingering over un café, make a habit of making unplanned stops, hop on the *art de vivre* barge, and surrender to the play of light as the Impressionists did.

INTRODUCTION

France is a big country by European standards—and would be one of the biggest states if it ever joined the US (unlikely). Geographically, it's a bit smaller than Texas, but has 66 million people (Texas has 26 million) and some 400 different cheeses (Texas has...not that many). *Diversité* is a French forte. This country features three mountain ranges (the Alps, the Pyrenees, and the Massif Central), two coastlines as different as night and day (Atlantic and Mediterranean), cosmopolitan cities (such as Paris, Lyon, Strasbourg, and Nice), and countless sleepy villages. From the Swiss-like Alps to the *molto* Italian Riviera, and from the Spanish Pyrenees to *das* German Alsace, you can stay in France and feel like you've sampled much of Europe—and never be more than a short stroll from a *bon vin rouge*.

This book covers the predictable must-sees while mixing in a healthy dose of Back Door intimacy. Along with seeing the Eiffel Tower, Mont St-Michel, and the French Riviera, you'll take a minivan tour of the D-Day beaches, pedal your way from village to vineyard in the Alsace, marvel at 15,000-year-old cave paintings, and paddle a canoe down the lazy Dordogne River. You'll find a *magnifique* hill-town perch to catch a Provençal sunset, ride Europe's highest mountain lift over the Alps, and touch the quiet Romanesque soul of Burgundian abbeys and villages. You'll learn about each region's key monuments and cities with our thoughtfully presented walking tours and background information. Just as important, you'll meet the intriguing people who run your hotel, bed-and-breakfast, or restaurant. We've also listed our favorite local guides, all well worth the time and money, to help you gain a better understanding of this marvelous country's past and present.

The destinations covered in this book are balanced to include the most interesting cities and intimate villages, from jet-setting

Map Legend

	Viewpoint		Bike Rental/ Bike Route		Winery
	Entrance		Taxi Stand		Pedestrian Zone
	Tourist Info		Tram & Stop		Railway
	Restroom		Bus Stop		Ferry/Boat Route
	Castle		Parking		Airport
	Church		RER Train		Stairs
	Statue/Point of Interest		Tourist Train		Walk/Tour Route
	Park		Batobus Stop		Trail
	Fountain		Métro Stop		

Use this legend to help you navigate the maps in this book.

beach resorts to the traditional heartland. This book is selective, including only the most exciting sights and romantic villages—for example, there are hundreds of beautiful châteaux in the Loire region, but we cover only the top 12. And though there are dozens of Loire towns you could use for a home base, we recommend just the best two.

The best is, of course, only our opinion. But after spending half of our adult lives writing and lecturing about travel, guiding tours, and gaining an appreciation for all things French, we've developed a sixth sense for what touches the traveler's imagination.

ABOUT THIS BOOK

Rick Steves France 2015 is a personal tour guide in your pocket. Better yet, it's actually two tour guides in your pocket: The co-author of this book is Steve Smith. Steve, who has lived in France on several occasions, now travels there annually (as he has since 1986) as a guide, researcher, and devout Francophile. He restored a 300-year-old farmhouse in Burgundy (where he bases himself while updating this book) and today keeps one foot on each side of the Atlantic. Together, Steve and I keep this book current (though, for simplicity, from this point "we" will shed our respective egos and become "I").

This book is organized by destinations. Each destination is a mini-vacation on its own, filled with exciting sights, strollable neighborhoods, affordable places to stay, and memorable places to eat. In the following chapters, you'll find these sections:

Planning Your Time suggests a schedule for how to best use your limited time.

Orientation includes specifics on public transportation, help-

Key to This Book

Updates

This book is updated every year—but things change. For the latest, visit www.ricksteves.com/update.

Abbreviations and Times

I use the following symbols and abbreviations in this book:

Sights are rated:

▲▲▲	Don't miss
▲▲	Try hard to see
▲	Worthwhile if you can make it
No rating	Worth knowing about

Tourist information offices are abbreviated as **TI,** and bathrooms are **WC**s. To categorize accommodations, I use a **Sleep Code** (described on page 1047).

Like Europe, this book uses the **24-hour clock.** It's the same through 12:00 noon, then keeps going: 13:00, 14:00, and so on. For anything over 12, subtract 12 and add p.m. (14:00 is 2:00 p.m.).

When giving **opening times,** I include both peak season and off-season hours if they differ. So if a museum is listed as "May-Oct daily 9:00-16:00," it should be open from 9 a.m. until 4 p.m. from the first day of May until the last day of October (but expect exceptions).

For **transit** or **tour departures,** I first list the frequency, then the duration. So, a train connection listed as "2/hour, 1.5 hours" departs twice each hour and the journey lasts an hour and a half.

ful hints, local tour options, easy-to-read maps, and tourist information.

Sights describes the top attractions and includes their cost and hours.

Self-Guided Walks take you through interesting neighborhoods, pointing out sights and fun stops.

Sleeping describes my favorite hotels, from good-value deals to cushy splurges.

Eating serves up a range of options, from inexpensive cafés to fancy restaurants.

Connections outlines your options for traveling to destinations by train, bus, and plane. In car-friendly regions, I've included route tips for drivers.

France: Past and Present gives you a quick overview of French history, notable citizens, and current political issues.

Practicalities is a traveler's tool kit, with my best travel tips and advice about money, sightseeing, sleeping, eating, staying con-

Top Destinations in France

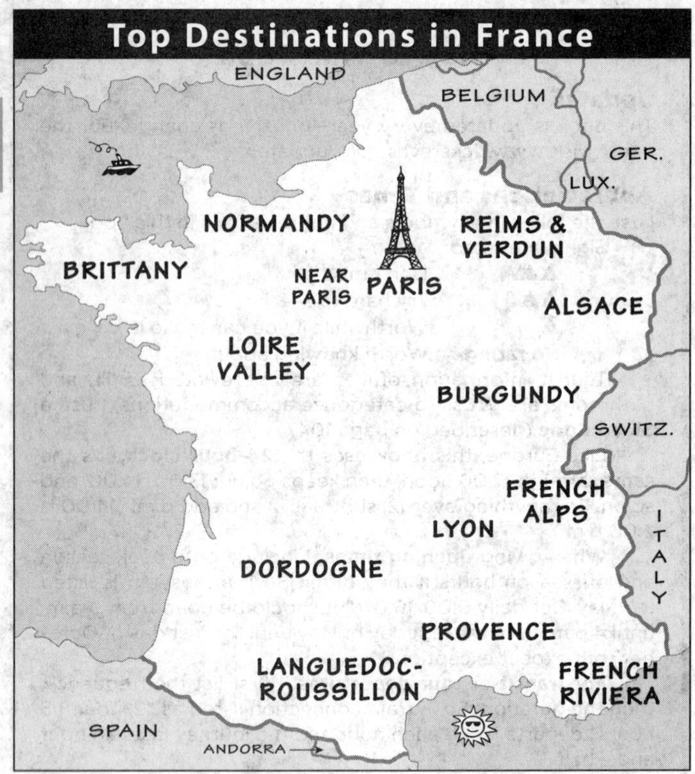

nected, and transportation (trains, buses, car rentals, driving, and flights). There's also a list of recommended books and films.

The **appendix** has nuts-and-bolts information, including useful phone numbers and websites, a festival list, a climate chart, a handy packing checklist, a pronunciation guide for place names, and French survival phrases.

Browse through this book, choose your favorite destinations, and link them up. Then have a *très bon voyage!* Traveling like a temporary local, you'll get the absolute most out of every mile, minute, and dollar. As you visit places I know and love, I'm happy that you'll be meeting some of my favorite French people.

Planning

This section will help you get started planning your trip—with advice on trip costs, when to go, and what you should know before you take off.

Please Tear Up This Book!

There's no point in hauling around a big chapter on Normandy for a day in Provence. That's why I hope you'll rip this book apart. Before your trip, attack this book with a utility knife to create an army of pocket-sized mini-guidebooks—one for each area you visit.

I love the ritual of trimming down the size of guidebooks I'll be using: Fold the pages back until you break the spine, neatly slice apart the sections you want with a utility knife, then pull them out with the gummy edge intact. If you want, finish each one off with some clear, heavy-duty packing tape to smooth and reinforce the spine, or use a heavy-duty stapler along the edge to prevent the first and last pages from coming loose.

To make things even easier, I've created a line of laminated covers with slide-on binders. Every evening, you can make a ritual of swapping out today's pages for tomorrow's. (For more on these binders, see www.ricksteves.com.)

While you may be tempted to keep this book intact as a souvenir of your travels, you'll appreciate even more the footloose freedom of traveling light.

TRAVEL SMART

Your trip to France is like a complex play—it's easier to follow and really appreciate on a second viewing. While no one does the same trip twice to gain that advantage, reading this book in its entirety before your trip accomplishes much the same thing.

Design an itinerary that enables you to visit sights at the best possible times. Note festivals, holidays, market days, specifics on sights, and days when sights are closed or most crowded (all covered in this book). To get between destinations smoothly, read the tips in Practicalities on taking trains and buses, or renting a car and driving. A smart trip is a puzzle—a fun, doable, and worthwhile challenge.

When you're plotting your itinerary, strive for a mix of intense and relaxed stretches. To maximize rootedness, minimize one-night stands. It's worth taking a long drive after dinner (or a train ride with a dinner picnic) to get settled in a town for two nights. Every trip—and every traveler—needs slack time (laundry, picnics, people-watching, and so on). Pace yourself. Assume you will return.

Reread this book as you travel, and visit local tourist information offices (abbreviated as TI in this book). Upon arrival in a new town, lay the groundwork for a smooth departure; get the schedule for the train or bus you'll take when you depart. Drivers can figure out the best route to their next destination.

France at a Glance

These attractions are listed (as in this book) looping counterclockwise around France, starting in Paris and ending in Champagne.

▲▲▲**Paris** World capital of art, fashion, food, literature, and ideas, offering historic monuments, grand boulevards, corner cafés, chic boutiques, cutting-edge architecture, and world-class art galleries, including the Louvre and Orsay.

▲▲**Near Paris** Europe's best palace at Versailles, the awesome cathedral of Chartres, Monet's flowery gardens at Giverny, and a mouse-run amusement park.

▲▲**Normandy** Pastoral mix of sweeping coastlines, half-timbered towns, and intriguing cities, including bustling Rouen (Gothic architecture, Joan of Arc sites), the little romantic port town of Honfleur, historic Bayeux (remarkable tapestry on the Battle of Hastings), stirring D-Day sites and museums, and the almost surreal island abbey of Mont St-Michel.

▲**Brittany** Windswept and rugged, with a forgotten interior, gorgeous coast, Celtic ties, and two notable towns: Dinan (Brittany's best medieval center) and the beach resort of St-Malo.

▲▲**The Loire** Picturesque towns (such as Amboise and Chinon) and hundreds of castles and palaces, including Chenonceau (arcing across its river), the huge Château de Chambord, Villandry (wonderful gardens), lavishly furnished Cheverny, and many more.

▲▲**Dordogne** Prehistoric caves, rock-sculpted villages, lazy canoe rides past medieval castles, and market towns such as pedestrian-friendly Sarlat-la-Canéda, and nearby, for wine lovers, St-Emilion.

▲**Languedoc-Roussillon** Sunny region with a Spanish flair, featuring Albi (fortress-like cathedral and a beautiful Toulouse-Lautrec museum), medieval Carcassonne (walled town with towers, turrets, and cobblestones), remote Cathar castles, and the lovely Mediterranean village of Collioure.

▲▲▲Provence Home to Arles (Van Gogh sights, evocative Roman arena), Avignon (famous bridge and brooding Palace of the Popes), the ancient Roman aqueduct of Pont du Gard, Orange (Roman theater), the beautiful Côtes du Rhone wine road, and rock-top villages such as Les Baux, Roussillon, and Vaison la Romaine.

▲▲▲The French Riviera A string of coastal resorts, including Nice (big city with seafront promenade and art museums), romantic Villefranche-sur-Mer, glitzy Monaco (casino), easygoing Antibes (silky-sandy beaches), and little hilltop Eze-le-Village, with magnificent Mediterranean views.

▲The French Alps Spectacular scenery featuring the drop-dead gorgeous town of Annecy, Mont Blanc (Europe's highest peak), and the world-famous ski resort of Chamonix, with hikes galore and lifts to stunning alpine views.

▲▲Burgundy Aged blend of vineyards and spirituality, with the compact town of Beaune (world-famous vineyards), Fontenay (France's best-preserved medieval abbey), Vézelay (magnificent Romanesque church), the one-of-a-kind medieval castle under construction at Guédelon, Cluny's grand medieval abbey, and the modern-day religious community of Taizé.

▲Lyon Metropolitan city, located between Burgundy and Provence, with an Italianesque old town, two Roman theaters, a terrific Gallo-Roman museum, the stirring French Resistance Center, and delicious cuisine at affordable prices.

▲▲Alsace Franco-Germanic region dotted with wine-road villages, starring half-timbered Colmar and its world-class art, and high-powered Strasbourg and its sensational cathedral.

▲▲Reims and Verdun Champagne-soaked Reims with a historic cathedral and cellars serving the sparkling brew, and nearby Verdun, site of brutal WWI battles, with a compelling, unforgettable memorial.

Update your plans as you travel. Though I encourage you to disconnect from life back home and immerse yourself in the French experience, you can carry a small mobile device (phone, tablet, laptop) to find out tourist information, learn the latest on sights (special events, tour schedules, etc.), book tickets and tours, make reservations, reconfirm hotels, research transportation connections, and keep in touch with your loved ones. If you don't want to bring a pricey device, you can use guest computers at hotels and make phone calls from landlines.

Enjoy the friendliness of the French people. Connect with the culture. Learn a new French expression each day and practice it. Cheer for your favorite bowler at a *boules* match, leave no chair unturned in your quest for the best café, find that perfect hill-town view, and make friends with a waiter (it can happen). Slow down and be open to unexpected experiences. Ask questions—most locals are eager to point you in their idea of the right direction. Keep a notepad in your pocket for noting directions, organizing your thoughts, and confirming prices. Wear your money belt, learn the currency, and figure out how to estimate prices in dollars. Those who expect to travel smart, do.

TRIP COSTS

Five components make up your trip costs: airfare, surface transportation, room and board, sightseeing and entertainment, and shopping and miscellany.

Airfare: Paris and Nice have the most convenient flights from the US. A basic round-trip flight from the US to Paris or Nice can cost, on average, about $1,000 to $2,000 total, depending on where you fly from and when (cheaper in winter). Smaller budget airlines may provide bargain service from several European capitals to many cities in France.

Consider saving time and money in Europe by flying into one city and out of another; for instance, into Nice and out of Paris. Most find the easygoing Mediterranean city of Nice far easier than Paris as a starting point for their trip.

Surface Transportation: For a three-week whirlwind trip of my recommended destinations by public transportation, allow $800 per person. If you'll be renting a car, allow $200 per week, not including tolls, gas, and supplemental insurance. If you'll be keeping the car for three weeks or more, look into leasing, which can save you money on insurance and taxes for trips of this length. Car rentals and leases are cheapest if arranged from the US.

Train passes normally must be purchased outside of Europe but aren't necessarily your best option—you may save money by simply buying tickets as you go. Don't hesitate to consider flying, as budget airlines can be cheaper than taking the train (check www.

skyscanner.com for intra-European flights). Inexpensive flights can get you between Paris and other major cities (such as Nice, Marseille, Strasbourg, Toulouse, Lyon, and Bordeaux). For more on public transportation and car rental, see "Transportation" in the Practicalities chapter.

Room and Board: Outside of Paris, you can thrive in France in 2015 on $150 a day per person for room and board. This allows $15 for breakfast, $20 for lunch, $45 for dinner with drinks, and $70 for lodging (based on two people splitting the cost of a $140 double room). Allow 20 percent more for your days in Paris. Students and tightwads can enjoy France for as little as $60 a day ($30 for a bed, $30 for meals and snacks).

Sightseeing and Entertainment: Figure about $13 per major sight (Louvre-$16, Abbey of Mont St-Michel-$13), $8 for minor ones (climbing church towers), $30 for guided walks, and $25-65 for bus tours and splurge experiences (concerts in Paris' Sainte-Chapelle or a ride on the Chamonix gondola). An overall average of $35 a day works for most people. Don't skimp here. After all, this category is the driving force behind your trip—you came to sightsee, enjoy, and experience France.

Shopping and Miscellany: Figure $5 per ice-cream cone, coffee, or soft drink. Shopping can vary in cost from nearly nothing to a small fortune. Good budget travelers find that this category has little to do with assembling a trip full of lifelong and wonderful memories.

SIGHTSEEING PRIORITIES

So much to see, so little time. How to choose? Depending on the length of your trip, and taking geographic proximity into account, here are my recommended priorities:

3 days: Paris and maybe Versailles
6 days, add: Normandy
8 days, add: Loire
11 days, add: Dordogne, Carcassonne
16 days, add: Provence, the Riviera
19 days, add: Burgundy, Chamonix
22 days, add: Alsace, northern France

This includes nearly everything on the map on page 15. If you don't have time to see it all, prioritize according to your interests. The "France At a Glance" sidebar can help you decide where to go (page 6).

For day-by-day itineraries for a three-week trip, see the sidebars (one for drivers and one for people using trains and buses) in this chapter. Note that a car is especially handy for exploring Normandy, the Dordogne, and Provence.

If you have only a week and it's your first trip to France, do

Whirlwind Three-Week Tour of France by Car

Day	Plan
1	Fly into Paris (save Paris sightseeing for the end of your trip), pick up your car, visit Giverny, and overnight in Honfleur (1 night).
2	Spend today at D-Day sights: Arromanches, American Cemetery, and Pointe du Hoc (and Utah Beach Landing Museum, if you're moving fast). Dinner and overnight in Bayeux (1 night).
3	Bayeux Tapestry and church, Mont St-Michel, sleep on Mont St-Michel (1 night).
4	Spend your morning on Mont St-Michel, then head for châteaux country in the Loire Valley. Tour Chambord, then stay in Amboise (2 nights).
5	Do a day trip, touring Chenonceaux and Cheverny or Chaumont. Save time at the end of the day for Amboise and its sights.
6	Head south to the Dordogne region, stopping en route at Oradour-sur-Glane. End in Sarlat-la-Canéda (2 nights) and browse the town late today.
7	Take a relaxing canoe trip, and tour a prehistoric cave.
8	Head to the Languedoc-Roussillon region, lunch in Albi, and spend the evening in Carcassonne (1 night).
9	Morning in Carcassonne, then on to Provence with a stop at the Pont du Gard aqueduct. Stay in or near Arles (2 nights).
10	All day for Arles and Les Baux.
11	Visit a Provençal hill town such as Roussillon, then depart for the Riviera, staying in Nice, Antibes, or Villefranche-sur-Mer (2 nights).
12	Sightsee in Nice and Monaco.
13	Make the long drive north to the Alps, and sleep in Chamonix (2 nights).
14	If the weather is clear, take the mountain lifts up to Aiguille du Midi and beyond.
15	Allow a half-day for the Alps (in Chamonix or Annecy). Then head for Burgundy, ending in Beaune for wine tasting. Sleep in Beaune (1 night).

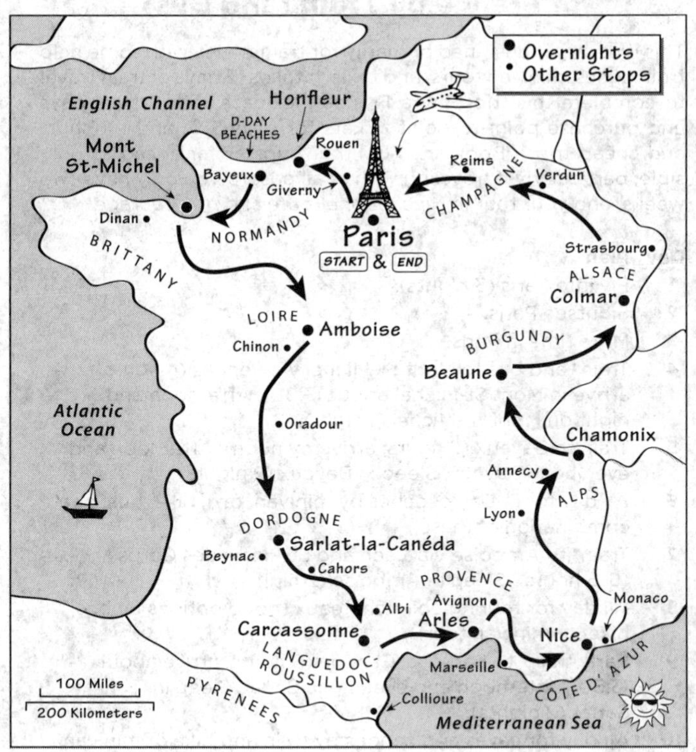

16 Spend the morning in Beaune, then move on to Colmar (2 nights).

17 Enjoy Colmar and the Route du Vin villages.

18 Return to Paris, visiting Verdun or Reims en route. Collapse in Paris hotel (4 nights).

19 Sightsee Paris.

20 More time in Paris.

21 Finish your sightseeing in Paris, and consider side-tripping to Versailles.

Whirlwind Three-Week Tour of France by Train (and Bus)

This itinerary is designed primarily for train travel, with some help from buses, minivan tours, and taxis. It takes 12 days of train travel to complete this trip: Buy a France Flexipass with 9 train days and purchase point-to-point tickets for days 5, 7, and 14 (short and cheap trips). Book any TGV train trips as far ahead as possible, particularly if traveling with a rail pass. If you only have two weeks, end your tour in Nice. *Bonne route* and *bon courage!*

Day	Plan
1	Fly into Paris (3 nights).
2	Sightsee Paris.
3	More time in Paris.
4	Train* and bus to Mont St-Michel via Rennes (4 hours, arrive in Mont St-Michel about 13:00). Afternoon and night on Mont St-Michel (1 night).
5	Train to Bayeux (2 hours, arrive by noon). Afternoon and evening in Bayeux. Sleep in Bayeux (2 nights).
6	All day for D-Day beaches by minivan, taxi, bike, bus, or a combination of these.
7	Train* to Amboise via Caen and St-Pierre des Corps (5-6 hours). Sleep in Amboise (2 nights).
8	All day for touring Loire châteaux (good options by bus, bike, or minivan tour).
9	Early train* to Sarlat-la-Canéda (6 hours, arrive about 13:30). Afternoon and evening in Sarlat. Sleep in Sarlat (2 nights).
10	All day for caves and canoes by train and bike or minivan/taxi tour.

Paris, Normandy, and the Loire. For a more focused 10- to 14-day trip that highlights Paris, Provence, and the Riviera, fly into Paris and out of Nice. After touring Paris, take the TGV train from Paris to Avignon, rent a car there, and drop it in Nice (or use trains, buses, and minivan tours to get around). This trip also works in reverse. Travelers with a little more time could add Burgundy and/or the Alps, which are about halfway between Paris and Provence and easy to explore by car or train.

WHEN TO GO

Late spring and fall are best, with generally good weather and lighter crowds, though summer brings festivals, reliable weather, and long opening hours at sights.

Europeans vacation in July and August, jamming the Riviera,

11 Train or bus to Carcassonne (5.5 hours). Dinner and evening wall walk. Sleep in Carcassonne (1 night).

12 Morning wall walk, then train to Arles (3 hours). Afternoon and evening in Arles. Sleep in Arles (2 nights).

13 Train to Nîmes, then bus to Pont du Gard. Tour Pont du Gard, then bus to Avignon and spend your afternoon/evening there (consider dinner). Train back to Arles (may require reservation).

14 Morning in Arles or Les Baux (by taxi or tour), afternoon train* to Nice via Marseille (4 hours). Sleep in Nice (3 nights).

15 All day for Nice (and maybe Antibes).

16 All day for Villefranche-sur-Mer and Monaco.

17 Morning train* to Annecy (7 hours). Afternoon and evening in Annecy. Sleep in Annecy (1 night).

18 Morning in Annecy, midday train to Chamonix (2 hours), afternoon and evening in Chamonix. Sleep in Chamonix (2 nights).

19 If the weather is clear, take the mountain lifts up to Aiguille du Midi and beyond.

20 Linger in Chamonix or take an early train* to Paris (7 hours) or, closer, Lyon (4 hours). Last afternoon and night in Paris or Lyon. (Or make it a 22-day tour with a night in Burgundy—stay in Beaune, a 6.5-hour train ride from Chamonix—or a 23-day tour with a scenic 6.5-hour train through Switzerland to Colmar, spend two nights there, then take the TGV back to Paris.)

21 Fly home.

* *Indicates TGV train option—book well in advance.*

the Dordogne, and the Alps (worst from mid-July to mid-August), but leaving the rest of the country just lively enough for tourists. And though many French businesses close in August, the traveler hardly notices. May weekends can be busy—many French holidays fall in this month—but June is generally quiet (outside of Paris).

Winter travel is fine for Paris, Nice, and Lyon, but you'll find smaller cities and villages buttoned up tight. Winter weather is gray, noticeably milder in the south (unless the wind is blowing), and colder and wetter in the north. Sights and tourist information offices keep shorter hours, and some tourist activities (such as English-language castle tours) vanish altogether. On the other hand, winter travel allows you to see cities through the lens of a local, as hotels, restaurants, and sights are much calmer. See the climate chart in the appendix for an idea of what to expect from the weather.

Rick Steves Audio Europe

If you're bringing a mobile device, be sure to check out **Rick Steves Audio Europe,** where you can download free audio tours and hours of travel interviews (via the Rick Steves Audio Europe app, www.ricksteves.com/audioeurope, Google Play, or iTunes).

My self-guided **audio tours** are user-friendly, easy-to-follow, fun, and informative, covering the major sights and neighborhoods in Paris (Historic Paris Walk, The Louvre, The Orsay, and Versailles Palace). Compared to live tours, my audio tours are hard to beat: Nobody will stand you up, the quality is reliable, you can take the tour exactly when you like, and they're free.

Rick Steves Audio Europe also offers a far-reaching library of intriguing **travel interviews** with experts from around the globe. The interviews are organized by destination, including many of the places in this book.

What's Blooming When

Thanks to France's relatively mild climate, fields of flowers greet the traveler much of the year:

Mid-April-May: Crops of brilliant yellow colza bloom, mostly in the north (best in Burgundy). Wild red poppies *(coquelicots)* begin sprouting in the south.

June: Red poppies pop up throughout the country. Late in June, lavender blooms begin covering the hills of Provence.

July: Lavender is in full swing in Provence, and sunflowers are awakening. Cities, towns, and villages everywhere overflow with carefully tended flowers.

August-September: Sunflowers flourish north and south.

October: In the latter half of the month, the countryside glistens with fall colors, as most trees are deciduous. Vineyards go for the gold.

KNOW BEFORE YOU GO

Your trip is more likely to go smoothly if you plan ahead. Check this list of things to arrange while you're still at home.

You need a **passport**—but no visa or shots—to travel in France. You may be denied entry into certain European countries if your passport is due to expire within three months of your ticketed date of return. Get it renewed if you'll be cutting it close. It can take up to six weeks to get or renew a passport (for more on passports, see www.travel.state.gov). Pack a photocopy of your passport in your luggage in case the original is lost or stolen.

Book rooms well in advance if you'll be traveling during peak season (spring through fall) or any major holidays (see page 1116).

Call your **debit- and credit-card companies** to let them know the countries you'll be visiting, to ask about fees, request your PIN code (it will be mailed to you), and more. See page 1038 for details.

Do your homework if you want to buy **travel insurance.** Compare the cost of the insurance to the likelihood of your using it and your potential loss if something goes wrong. Also, check whether your existing insurance (health, homeowners, or renters) covers you and your possessions overseas. For more tips, see www.ricksteves.com/insurance.

Consider buying a **rail pass** after researching your options (see page 1091 and www.ricksteves.com/rail for all the specifics).

All **high-speed TGV trains** in France require a seat reservation—book as early as possible, as they fill fast, and some routes use TGV trains almost exclusively. This is especially true if you're traveling with a rail pass, as TGV passholder reservations are limited, and usually sell out well before other seat reservations. If you're taking an overnight train, and you need a *couchette* (overnight bunk)—and you *must* leave on a certain day—consider booking it in advance through a US agent (such as www.raileurope.com). For more on train travel, see the Practicalities chapter.

To avoid long ticket-buying lines at the **Eiffel Tower,** book an entry time three months in advance using its online reservation system (see page 84). Some prehistoric caves in the Dordogne region take online reservations; see page 484. If the greatest cave, Font-de-Gaume, is accepting reservations in 2015 (though it's unlikely), book at least four months in advance. Other sights, such as Avignon's synagogue and some wineries, require that you make an appointment and are noted throughout this book.

If you plan to hire a **local guide,** reserve ahead by email. Popular guides can get booked up. If you want a specific guide, reserve as far ahead as possible (especially important for Paris, D-Day beaches, Burgundy's wine country, and the Riviera).

If you're bringing a **mobile device,** download any apps you might want to use on the road, such as translators, maps, transit schedules and sight-specific audio tours (listed when available in this book). Check out **Rick Steves Audio Europe,** featuring audio tours of major sights in Paris, hours of travel interviews on France, and more (via www.ricksteves.com/audioeurope, iTunes, Google Play, or the Rick Steves Audio Europe app; for details see page 1110).

If you'll be **traveling with children,** read over the list of pre-trip suggestions on page 1056.

Check the **Rick Steves guidebook updates** page for any recent changes to this book (www.ricksteves.com/update).

Because **airline carry-on restrictions** are always changing, visit the Transportation Security Administration's website (www.

The Language Barrier and That French Attitude

You've probably heard that the French are "mean and cold and refuse to speak English." This is an out-of-date preconception left over from the days of Charles de Gaulle. The French are as friendly as any other people, and Parisians no more disagreeable than New Yorkers. Without any doubt, French people speak more English than Americans speak French. Be reasonable in your expectations: French waiters are paid to be efficient, not chatty. And postal clerks are every bit as speedy, cheery, and multilingual as ours are back home.

The biggest error most Americans make when traveling in France is trying to do too much with limited time. This approach is a mistake in the bustling north, and a virtual sin in the laid-back south. Hurried, impatient travelers who miss the subtle pleasures of people-watching from a sun-dappled café often misinterpret French attitudes. With the five weeks of paid vacation and 35- to 39-hour work-week that many French employees consider as nonnegotiable rights, your hosts can't fathom why anyone would rush through their vacation. By slowing your pace and making an effort to understand French culture by living it, you're more likely to have a richer experience.

The French take great pride in their customs, clinging to the sense of their own cultural superiority despite the fact that they're no longer a world superpower. Let's face it: It's tough to keep on smiling when you've been crushed by a Big Mac, Mickey-Moused by Disney, and drowned in Starbucks coffee. Your hosts are cold only if you decide to see them that way. Polite and formal, the French respect the fine points of culture and tradition. Here, strolling down the street with a big grin on your face and saying hello to strangers is a sign of senility, not friendliness (seriously). They think that Americans, while friendly, are hesitant to

tsa.gov) for a list of what you can bring on the plane and for the latest security measures (including screening of electronic devices, which you may be asked to power up).

Traveling as a Temporary Local

We travel all the way to France to enjoy differences—to become temporary locals. You'll experience frustrations. Certain truths that we find "God-given" or "self-evident," such as cold beer, ice in drinks, bottomless cups of coffee, and bigger being better, are suddenly not so true. One of the benefits of travel is the eye-opening realization that there are logical, civil, and even better alternatives.

With a long history rich in human achievement, France is an understandably proud country. To appreciate its people, you need

pursue more serious friendships. Recognize sincerity and look for kindness. Give the French the benefit of the doubt.

Communication difficulties are exaggerated. To hurdle the language barrier, start with the French survival phrases in this book (see the appendix). For a richer experience, bring a small English/French dictionary and/or a phrase book (look for mine, which contains a dictionary and menu decoder), a menu reader, and a good supply of patience. In transactions, a small notepad and pen minimize misunderstandings about prices; have vendors write the price down.

Though many French people speak English—especially those in the tourist trade, and in big cities—you'll get better treatment if you use French pleasantries. If you choose only five phrases, learn and use these: *bonjour* (good day), *pardon* (pardon me), *s'il vous plaît* (please), *merci* (thank you), and *au revoir* (good-bye). The French value politeness. Begin every encounter with "*Bonjour* (or *S'il vous plaît*), *madame* (or *monsieur*)," and end every encounter with "*Au revoir, madame* (or *monsieur*)." When spelling out your name, you'll find that most letters are pronounced very differently in French: *a* is pronounced "ah," *e* is pronounced "eh," and *i* is pronounced "ee." To avoid confusion, say "*a,* Anne," "*e,* euro," and "*i,* Isabelle."

The French are linguistic perfectionists—they take their language (and other languages) seriously. Often they speak more English than they let on. This isn't a tourist-baiting tactic, but timidity on their part about speaking another language less than fluently. If you want them to speak English, say, "*Bonjour, madame* (or *monsieur*). *Parlez-vous anglais?*" They may say *"non,"* but as you continue you'll probably find they speak more English than you speak French.

to celebrate the differences. A willingness to go local ensures that you'll enjoy a full dose of French hospitality.

Europeans generally like Americans. But if there is a negative aspect to the French image of Americans, it's that we are loud, wasteful, ethnocentric, too informal (which can seem disrespectful), and a bit naive.

The French (and Europeans in general) place a high value on speaking quietly in restaurants and on trains. Listen while on the bus or in a restaurant—the place can be packed, but the decibel level is low. Try to adjust your volume accordingly to show respect for the culture.

While the French look bemusedly at some of our Yankee excesses—and worriedly at others—they nearly always afford us individual travelers all the warmth we deserve.

How Was Your Trip?

Were your travels fun, smooth, and meaningful? If you'd like to share your tips, concerns, and discoveries, please fill out the survey at www.ricksteves.com/feedback. To check out readers' hotel and restaurant reviews—or leave one yourself—visit my travel forum at www.ricksteves.com/travel-forum. I value your feedback. Thanks in advance—it helps a lot.

Judging from all the happy feedback I receive from travelers who have used this book, it's safe to assume you'll enjoy a great, affordable vacation—with the finesse of an independent, experienced traveler.

Thanks, and *bon voyage!*

Rick Steves

Back Door Travel Philosophy

From *Rick Steves Europe Through the Back Door*

Travel is intensified living—maximum thrills per minute and one of the last great sources of legal adventure. Travel is freedom. It's recess, and we need it.

Experiencing the real Europe requires catching it by surprise, going casual..."Through the Back Door."

Affording travel is a matter of priorities. (Make do with the old car.) You can eat and sleep—simply, safely, and enjoyably—anywhere in Europe for $125 a day plus transportation costs. In many ways, spending more money only builds a thicker wall between you and what you traveled so far to see. Europe is a cultural carnival, and time after time, you'll find that its best acts are free and the best seats are the cheap ones.

A tight budget forces you to travel close to the ground, meeting and communicating with the people. Never sacrifice sleep, nutrition, safety, or cleanliness to save money. Simply enjoy the local-style alternatives to expensive hotels and restaurants.

Connecting with people carbonates your experience. Extroverts have more fun. If your trip is low on magic moments, kick yourself and make things happen. If you don't enjoy a place, maybe you don't know enough about it. Seek the truth. Recognize tourist traps. Give a culture the benefit of your open mind. See things as different, but not better or worse. Any culture has plenty to share.

Of course, travel, like the world, is a series of hills and valleys. Be fanatically positive and militantly optimistic. If something's not to your liking, change your liking.

Travel can make you a happier American, as well as a citizen of the world. Our Earth is home to seven billion equally precious people. It's humbling to travel and find that other people don't have the "American Dream"—they have their own dreams. Europeans like us, but with all due respect, they wouldn't trade passports.

Thoughtful travel engages us with the world. In tough economic times, it reminds us what is truly important. By broadening perspectives, travel teaches new ways to measure quality of life.

Globetrotting destroys ethnocentricity, helping us understand and appreciate other cultures. Rather than fear the diversity on this planet, celebrate it. Among your most prized souvenirs will be the strands of different cultures you choose to knit into your own character. The world is a cultural yarn shop, and Back Door travelers are weaving the ultimate tapestry. Join in!

PARIS

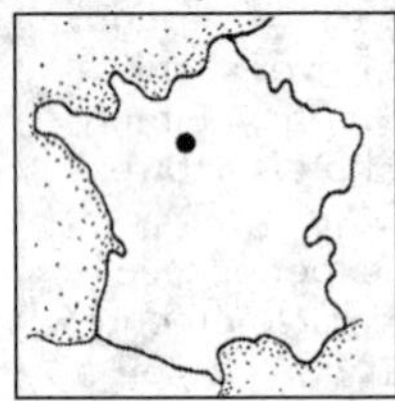

Paris—the City of Light—has been a beacon of culture for centuries. As a world capital of art, fashion, food, literature, and ideas, it stands as a symbol of all the fine things human civilization can offer. Come prepared to celebrate this, rather than judge our cultural differences, and you'll capture the romance and *joie de vivre* that this city exudes.

Paris offers sweeping boulevards, chatty crêpe stands, chic boutiques, and world-class art galleries. Sip decaf with deconstructionists at a sidewalk café, then step into an Impressionist painting in a tree-lined park. Climb Notre-Dame and rub shoulders with the gargoyles. Cruise the Seine, zip to the top of the Eiffel Tower, and saunter down Avenue des Champs-Elysées. Master the Louvre and Orsay museums. Save some after-dark energy for one of the world's most romantic cities.

PLANNING YOUR TIME

I've listed sights in descending order of importance, filling up to seven very busy but doable days in Paris. Therefore, if you have only one day, just do Day 1; for two days, add Day 2; and so on. When planning where to plug in Versailles (see next chapter), keep in mind that the Château is closed on Mondays and especially crowded on Sundays and Tuesdays—try to avoid these days. For other itinerary considerations on a day-by-day basis, check the "Daily Reminder" on page 26.

Day 1: Follow this chapter's Historic Paris Walk. In the afternoon, tour the Louvre. Then enjoy the Trocadéro scene and a twilight ride up the Eiffel Tower.

Day 2: Stroll the Champs-Elysées from the Arc de Triomphe to the Tuileries Garden. Tour the Orsay Museum. In the evening, take a nighttime tour by cruise boat, taxi, bus, or retro-chic Deux Chevaux car.

Day 3: Catch the RER suburban train by 8:00 to arrive early at Versailles. Tour the palace's interior. Then either tour the gardens or return to Paris for more sightseeing.

Day 4: Visit Montmartre and the Sacré-Cœur Basilica. Have lunch on Montmartre. Continue your Impressionist theme by touring the Orangerie. Enjoy dinner on Ile St. Louis, then a floodlit walk by Notre-Dame.

Day 5: Spend the morning in the Rue Cler neighborhood, sampling its market and riverside promenade, then afternoon at the Rodin Museum and the Army Museum.

Day 6: Ride scenic bus #69 to the Marais and tour this neighborhood, including the Picasso Museum and Pompidou Center. In the afternoon, visit the Opéra Garnier, and end your day with rooftop views from the Galeries Lafayette or Printemps department stores.

Day 7: See more in Paris (such as Rue Montorgueil market, Left Bank shopping, Père Lachaise Cemetery, Marmottan or Jacquemart-André museum), or take a day trip to Chartres or Giverny.

PARIS

Orientation to Paris

PARIS: A VERBAL MAP

Central Paris (population 2.2 million) is circled by a ring-road and split in half by the Seine River, which runs east to west. If you were on a boat floating downstream, the Right Bank (Rive Droite) would be on your right, and the Left Bank (Rive Gauche) on your left. The bull's-eye on your map is Notre-Dame, on an island in the middle of the Seine.

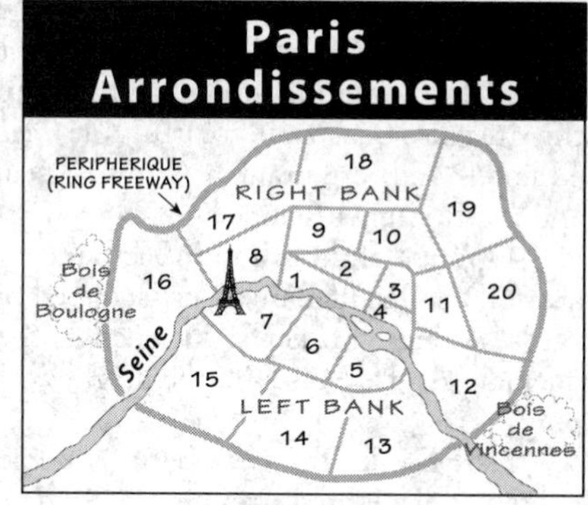

Twenty arrondissements (administrative districts) spiral out from the center, like an escargot shell. If your hotel's zip code is 75007, you know (from the last two digits) that it's in the 7th arrondissement. The city is speckled

with Métro stops, and most Parisians locate addresses by the closest stop. So in Parisian jargon, the Eiffel Tower is on *la Rive Gauche* (the Left Bank) in the *7ème* (7th arrondissement), zip code 75007, Mo: Trocadéro (the nearest Métro stop).

As you're tracking down addresses, these words and pronunciations will help: Métro (may-troh), *place* (plahs; square), *rue* (roo; road), *avenue* (ah-vuh-noo), *boulevard* (boo-luh-var), and *pont* (pohn; bridge).

PARIS BY NEIGHBORHOOD

Paris is a big city, but its major sights cluster in convenient zones. Grouping your sightseeing, walks, dining, and shopping thoughtfully can save you lots of time and money.

Historic Core: This area centers on the Ile de la Cité ("Island of the City"), located in the middle of the Seine. On the Ile de la Cité, you'll find Paris' oldest sights, from Roman ruins to the medieval Notre-Dame and Sainte-Chapelle churches.

Major Museums Neighborhood: Located just west of the historic core, this is where you'll find the Louvre, Orsay, and Orangerie.

Champs-Elysées: The greatest of the many grand, 19th-century boulevards on the Right Bank, the Champs-Elysées runs northwest from Place de la Concorde to the Arc de Triomphe.

Eiffel Tower Neighborhood: Dominated by the Eiffel Tower, this area also boasts the colorful Rue Cler (with many recommended hotels and restaurants), Army Museum and Napoleon's Tomb, and the Rodin Museum.

Opéra Neighborhood: Surrounding the Opéra Garnier, this area on the Right Bank is crisscrossed by a series of grand boulevards. Along with key sights such as the Opéra Garnier and Jacquemart-André Museum, the neighborhood offers high-end shopping.

Left Bank: The Left Bank is home to...the Left Bank. Anchored by the large Luxembourg Garden, the Left Bank is the traditional neighborhood of Paris' intellectual, artistic, and café life. This is also one of Paris' best shopping areas.

Paris Neighborhoods

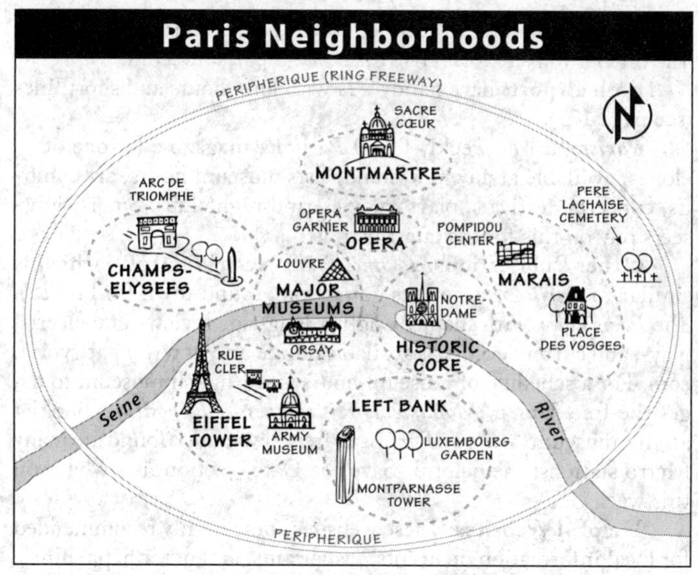

Marais: Stretching eastward to Bastille along Rue de Rivoli/Rue St. Antoine, this neighborhood has lots of recommended restaurants and hotels, shops, the delightful Place des Vosges, and artistic sights such as the Pompidou Center and Picasso Museum. The area is known for its avant-garde boutiques and residents.

Montmartre: This hill, topped by the bulbous white domes of Sacré-Cœur, hovers on the northern fringes of your Paris map. It still retains some of the untamed rural charm that once drew Impressionist painters and turn-of-the-century bohemians.

TOURIST INFORMATION

Paris' TIs can provide useful information but may have long lines. They offer free city maps and, for those who ask, themed booklets on eating, shopping, or walking in Paris (also available online—go to http://en.parisinfo.com and click on "Practical Paris," then "Our Paris Cityguides"). TIs sell Museum Passes and individual tickets to sights (see "Sightseeing Strategies" on page 49).

Paris has several TI locations, including **Pyramides** (daily May-Oct 9:00-19:00, Nov-April 10:00-19:00, 25 Rue des Pyramides—at Pyramides Métro stop between the Louvre and Opéra), **Gare du Nord** (daily 8:00-18:00), **Gare de Lyon** (Mon-Sat 8:00-18:00, closed Sun), and two in **Montmartre** (21 Place du Tertre, daily 10:00-18:00, covers only Montmartre sights and doesn't sell Museum Passes, tel. 01 42 62 21 21; and at the Anvers Métro stop, full-service office, daily 10:00-18:00). In summer, TI kiosks may pop up in the squares in front of Notre-Dame and Hôtel de Ville. The official website for Paris' TIs is www.parisinfo.com.

Both **airports** have handy TIs with long hours and short lines (see page 175).

Pariscope: The weekly €0.50 *Pariscope* magazine (or one of its clones, available at any newsstand) lists museum hours, art exhibits, concerts, festivals, plays, movies, and nightclubs. Smart sightseers rely on this for the latest listings.

Other Publications: *L'Officiel des Spectacles* (€0.50), which is similar to *Pariscope,* also lists goings-on around town (in French). The *Paris Voice,* with snappy English-language reviews of concerts, plays, and current events, is available online only at www.parisvoice.com. For a schedule of museum hours and English museum tours, get the free *Musées, Monuments Historiques, et Expositions* booklet at any museum. *A Nous Paris* is a free newspaper found in many Métro stations; the helpful "Save the Date" section lists what's on this week.

Helpful Websites: These websites come highly recommended for local information on events, restaurants, and other happenings: www.gogoparis.com, www.secretsofparis.com, www.bonjourparis.com, and www.parisbymouth.com.

American Church and Franco-American Center: This interdenominational church—in the Rue Cler neighborhood, facing the river between the Eiffel Tower and Orsay Museum—is a nerve center for the American expat community. For details on worship services, coffee hours, and English/French language exchanges, see the listing within the "Connecting with the Culture" sidebar on page 44.

HELPFUL HINTS

Theft Alert: Thieves thrive near famous monuments and on Métro and RER lines that serve airports and high-profile tourist sights. Beware of pickpockets working busy lines (e.g., at ticket windows at train stations). Pay attention when it's your turn and your back is to the crowd: Keep your bag closed and firmly gripped in front of you. Look out for groups of young girls who swarm around you (be very firm—even forceful—and walk away). Smartphones are a thief magnet anytime, so be aware whenever you're using it or holding it up to take a picture.

In general, it's smart to wear a money belt, put your wallet in your front pocket, loop your day bag over your shoulders, and keep a tight hold on your purse or shopping bag. Muggings are rare, but they do occur. If you're out late, avoid the dark riverfront embankments and any place where the lighting is dim and pedestrian activity is minimal.

Paris has taken action to combat crime by stationing police at monuments, on streets, and on the Métro, and installing security cameras at key sights. You'll go through quick and reassuring airport-like security checks at many major attractions.

ATM Alert: When withdrawing money from a cash machine, use your hand to shield your PIN number from prying eyes. Don't engage with anyone who offers to "help" you use an ATM (which works just like ours do) or warns you that it isn't working properly. If that happens, cancel your operation, take your card, and find a different machine.

Tourist Scams: Be aware of the latest tricks, such as the "found ring" scam (i.e., a con artist pretends to find a ring on the ground that he proclaims is "pure gold" and offers to sell it to you) or the "friendship bracelet" scam (a vendor asks you to help with a demo, makes a bracelet on your arm that you can't easily take off, and then asks you to pay for it).

Distractions by a stranger—often a "salesman," someone asking you to sign a petition, or someone posing as a deaf person to show you a small note to read—can all be tricks that function as a smokescreen for theft. As you try to wriggle away from the pushy stranger, an accomplice picks your pocket.

To all these scammers, simply say "no" firmly (without smiling or apologizing) and step away purposefully. For reports from my readers on the latest scams, go to https://community.ricksteves.com/travel-forum/tourist-scams.

Pedestrian Safety: Parisian drivers are notorious for ignoring pedestrians. Look both ways (many streets are one-way), and be careful of seemingly quiet bus/taxi lanes. Don't assume you have the right of way, even in a crosswalk. When crossing a street, keep your pace constant and don't stop suddenly. By law, drivers are allowed to miss pedestrians by up to just one meter—a little more than three feet (1.5 meters in the countryside). Drivers calculate your speed so they won't hit you, provided you don't alter your route or pace.

Watch out for bicyclists and electric cars. These popular and silent "vehicles" may come at you from unexpected places and directions. Cyclists ride in specially marked bike lanes on wide sidewalks and also have a right to use lanes reserved for buses and taxis. Bikes commonly go against traffic, as many bike paths are on one-way streets. Always look both ways. Paris' popular and cheap short-term electric-car rental program (Autolib') has put many of these small, silent machines on the streets—be careful.

Busy Parisian sidewalks are much like freeways, so conduct yourself as if you were a foot-fueled-car: Stick to your

Daily Reminder

Sunday: Many sights are free on the first Sunday of the month, including the Orsay, Rodin, Picasso, Cluny, Pompidou, Quai Branly, and Delacroix museums. Several sights are free on the first Sunday, but only during the winter, including the Louvre and Arc de Triomphe (both Oct-March) and all the sights at Versailles (Nov-March). These free days at popular sights attract hordes of visitors. Versailles is more crowded than usual on Sunday—but on the upside, the garden's fountains are running (April-Oct).

Look for organ concerts at St. Sulpice and other churches. The American Church often hosts a free concert (usually classical piano and vocals, generally Sept-June at 17:00—but not every week and not in Dec). Luxembourg Garden has puppet shows today.

Most of Paris' stores are closed on Sunday, but shoppers will find relief along the Champs-Elysées, at flea markets, and in the Marais neighborhood's lively Jewish Quarter, where many stores are open. Many recommended restaurants in the Rue Cler neighborhood are closed for dinner.

Monday: These sights are closed today: Orsay, Rodin, Marmottan, Carnavalet, Catacombs, Petit Palais, Victor Hugo's House, Quai Branly, Paris Archaeological Crypt, Deportation Memorial, and Versailles (but the gardens are open April-Oct). The Louvre is far more crowded because of these closings. From October through June, the Army Museum is closed the first Monday of the month, though Napoleon's Tomb remains open. Market streets such as Rue Cler and Rue Mouffetard are dead today. Some banks are closed. It's discount night at many cinemas.

Tuesday: Many sights are closed today, including the Louvre, Orangerie, Cluny, Pompidou, National Maritime, Delacroix, and Architecture and Monuments museums. The Orsay and Versailles are crazy busy today. The fountains at Versailles run

lane, look to the left before passing a slow-moving pedestrian, and if you need to stop, look for a safe place to pull over.

Medical Help: The American Hospital, established by a group of American expat doctors, has English-speaking staff (63 Boulevard Victor Hugo, in Neuilly suburb, Mo: Porte Maillot, then bus #82, tel. 01 46 41 25 25, www.american-hospital.org). **SOS Médecins** (SOS Doctors) is a terrific service that will send a doctor to your hotel room for a reasonable price (most speak some English, house calls to hotels or homes, usually €60-90, tel. 01 47 07 77 77).

Avoiding Lines at Sights: Lines at Paris' major sights can be long. The worthwhile Paris Museum Pass, which covers most sights

today from late May until late June; music (no fountains) fills the gardens on Tuesdays from April to mid-May, and from July through October. Napoleon's Tomb and the Army Museum's WWI and WWII wings are open until 21:00 (April-Sept).

Wednesday: All sights are open, and some have late hours, including the Louvre (until 21:45, last entry 21:00), the Rodin Museum (until 20:45), Sainte-Chapelle (until 21:30 mid-May-mid-Sept), and the Jewish Art and History Museum (until 21:00 during special exhibits only). The weekly *Pariscope* magazine comes out today. Most schools are closed, so kids' sights are busy, and puppet shows play in Luxembourg Garden. Some cinemas offer discounts.

Thursday: All sights are open except the Sewer Tour. Some sights are open late, including the Orsay (until 21:45, last entry 21:00), Marmottan (20:00), the Architecture and Monuments Museum (until 21:00), the Quai Branly (until 21:00), and the Holocaust Memorial (22:00). Some department stores are open late.

Friday: All sights are open except the Sewer Tour. The Louvre is open until 21:45 (last entry 21:00), The Picasso Museum is open until 21:00 on the third Friday of the month (last entry 20:15). Notre-Dame's tower is open until 23:00 (July-Aug), and the Quai Branly closes at 21:00. Afternoon trains and roads leaving Paris are crowded. Restaurants are busy—it's smart to book ahead at popular places.

Saturday: All sights are open except the Jewish Art and History Museum and the Holocaust Memorial. The fountains run at Versailles (April-Oct). Notre-Dame's tower is open until 23:00 (July-Aug), and the Quai Branly is open until 21:00. Department stores are jammed today. Restaurants throughout Paris get packed; reserve in advance if you have a particular place in mind. Luxembourg Garden hosts puppet shows today.

in the city and allows you to skip ticket lines, is sold at museums and monuments, as well as TIs and FNAC stores (no surcharge). Even if you don't buy a Museum Pass, there are other ways to save time in line, such as buying tickets in advance at certain sights. For information on all of these options, see page 49.

Free Wi-Fi: In addition to the Wi-Fi that's likely available at your hotel, you'll find free wireless hotspots at many of Paris' cafés (with a purchase) and at more than 200 public hotspots (including parks, squares, museums, and so on). In a Parisian café, Wi-Fi works just like at home—you order something, then ask the waiter for the Wi-Fi ("wee-fee") password ("*mot de passe*"; moh duh pahs).

Most public parks offer free Wi-Fi (look for purple *Zone Wi-Fi* signs). The one-time registration process is easy: Select the Wi-Fi network (usually called "Paris_WIFI" plus a number), enter your name and email address, check the "*j'accepte*" box, and click "*Me connecter.*" You get two hours per connection. Some convenient hotspots include the park alongside Notre-Dame, Square Viviani (also near Notre-Dame), Place des Vosges (Marais), Champ de Mars park (100 yards south of the Eiffel Tower along Allée Thomy-Thierry), Esplanade des Invalides (along Rue Paul at the north end), the St. Jacques Tower (Mo: Chatelet), and hundreds more.

The Orange network also has many hotspots and offers a free two-hour pass. If you come across one, click "Select Your Pass" to register.

Bookstores: Paris has many English-language bookstores, where you can pick up guidebooks (at nearly double their American prices). Most carry this book. My favorites include **Shakespeare and Company** (some used travel books, Mon-Sat 10:00-23:00, Sun 11:00-23:00, 37 Rue de la Bûcherie, across the river from Notre-Dame, Mo: St. Michel, tel. 01 43 25 40 93); **W. H. Smith** (Mon-Sat 9:00-19:00, Sun 12:30-19:00, 248 Rue de Rivoli, Mo: Concorde, tel. 01 44 77 88 99); and **San Francisco Book Company** (used books only, Mon-Sat 11:00-21:00, Sun 14:00-19:30, 17 Rue Monsieur le Prince, Mo: Odéon, tel. 01 43 29 15 70).

Public WCs: Most public toilets are free. If it's a pay toilet, the price will be clearly indicated. If the toilet is free but there's an attendant, it's polite (but not necessary) to leave a tip of €0.20-0.50. Booth-like toilets on the sidewalks provide both relief and a memory (don't leave small children inside unattended). The restrooms in museums are free and the best you'll find. Bold travelers can walk into any sidewalk café like they own the place and find the toilet downstairs or in the back. Or do as the locals do—order a shot of espresso *(un café)* while standing at the café bar (then use the WC with a clear conscience). Keep toilet paper or tissues with you, as some WCs are poorly stocked.

Parking: Street parking is generally free at night (19:00 to 9:00), all day Sunday, and anytime in August, when many Parisians are on vacation. To pay for streetside parking, you must go to a *tabac* and buy a parking card *(une carte de stationnement)*, sold in €15 and €45 denominations (figure €2-3.60/hour in central Paris). Insert the card into the meter (chip-side in) and punch the desired amount of time, then take the receipt and display it in your windshield. Meters limit street parking to a maximum of two hours. For a longer stay, park for less at an airport (about €10/day) and take public transport or a taxi into the city. Underground lots are numerous in Paris—you'll find them under Ecole Militaire, St. Sulpice Church, Les Invalides, the Bastille, and the Panthéon; all charge about €30-40/day (€60/3 days, €10/day more after that, for locations see www.vincipark.com). Some hotels offer parking for less—ask your hotelier.

Tobacco Stands *(Tabacs)*: These little kiosks—usually just a counter inside a café—are handy and very local. Most sell public-transit tickets, cards for parking meters, postage stamps (though not all sell international postage—to mail something home, use two domestic stamps, or go to a post office), prepaid phone cards, and...oh yeah, cigarettes. To find one of these kiosks, just look for a *Tabac* sign and the red cylinder-shaped symbol above certain cafés. A *tabac* can be a godsend for avoiding long ticket lines at the Métro, especially at the end of the month when ticket booths get crowded with locals buying next month's pass.

Winter Activities: The City of Light sparkles year-round. For background on what to do and see here in winter months, see www.ricksteves.com/pariswinter.

Updates to This Book: For updates to this book, check www.ricksteves.com/update

GETTING AROUND PARIS

Paris is easy to navigate. Your basic choices are Métro (in-city subway), RER (suburban rail tied into the Métro system), public bus, and taxi. (Also consider the hop-on, hop-off bus and boat tours, described under "Tours in Paris," later.)

You can buy tickets and passes at Métro stations and at many *tabacs*. Staffed ticket windows in stations are gradually being phased out in favor of ticket machines, so expect some stations to have only machines and an information desk. Machines accept coins or small bills of €20 or less (none takes American credit cards unless you have a chip-and-PIN card). If a ticket machine is out of order or if you're out of change, buy tickets at a *tabac*.

Public-Transit Tickets: The Métro, RER, and buses all work on the same tickets. You can make as many transfers as you need on a single ticket, except when transferring between the Métro/RER system and the bus system, which requires using an additional ticket. A **single ticket** costs €1.70. To save money, buy a ***carnet*** (kar-nay) of 10 tickets for €13.70 (cheaper for ages 4-10). *Carnets* can be shared among travelers. Kids under four ride free.

Passe Navigo: This chip-embedded card costs a onetime up-front €5 fee (plus another €5 for the required photo; photo booths are in major Métro stations). The weekly *(hebdomadaire)* pass costs €20.40 and covers all forms of transit in central Paris from Monday to Sunday (expiring on Sunday, even if you buy it on, say, a Thursday). A monthly pass that also covers longer trips is available. To use the Navigo, touch the card to the purple pad, wait for the green validation light and the "ding," and you're on your way. For more details, visit www.navigo.fr.

Navigo or *Carnet*? It's hard to beat the *carnet*. Two 10-packs of *carnets*—enough for most travelers staying a week—cost €27.40, are shareable, and don't expire. Though similar in price, the Passe Navigo is more of a hassle to buy, cannot be shared, and only becomes worthwhile for visitors who stay a full week (or more), start their trip early in the week (on a Monday or Tuesday), and use the system a lot.

Other Passes: A handy one-day bus/Métro pass (called **Mobilis**) is available for €6.80. If you are under 26 and in Paris on a Saturday or Sunday, you can buy an unlimited daily transit pass called **Ticket Jeunes Week-end** for the unbeatable price of €3.75. To justify the **Paris Visite** travel card (over *carnets*), you'll have to do lots of traveling, though they do offer minor reductions at minor sights (1 day-€10.85, 2 days-€17.65, 3 days-€24.10, 5 days-€34.70).

By Métro

In Paris, you're never more than a 10-minute walk from a Métro station. Europe's best subway system allows you to hop from sight to sight quickly and cheaply (runs Sun-Thu 5:30-24:30, Fri-Sat 5:30-2:00 in the morning, www.ratp.fr). Learn to use it. Begin by studying the color Métro map at the beginning of this book.

Using the Métro System: To get to your destination, determine the closest "Mo" stop and which line or lines will get you there. The lines are color-coded and numbered, and you can tell their direction by their end-of-the-line stops. For example, the La Défense/Château de Vincennes line, also known as line 1 (yellow), runs between La Défense, on its west end, and Vincennes on its east end. Once in the Métro station, you'll see the color-coded line numbers and/or blue-and-white signs directing you to the train going in your direction (e.g., *direction: La Défense*). Insert your ticket in the automatic turnstile, reclaim your ticket, pass through, and keep it until you exit the system (some stations require you to pass your ticket through a turnstile to exit). The smallest stations are unstaffed and have ticket machines (coins

are essential). Be warned that fare inspectors regularly check for cheaters and accept absolutely no excuses—keep that ticket or pay a minimum fine of €45.

Be prepared to walk significant distances within Métro stations (especially when you transfer). Transfers are free and can be made wherever lines cross, provided you do so within 1.5 hours. When you transfer, follow the appropriately colored line number and end-of-the-line stop to find your next train, or look for orange *correspondance* (connection) signs that lead to your next line.

When you reach your destination, look for the blue-and-white *sortie* signs pointing you to the exit. Before leaving the station, check the helpful *plan du quartier* (map of the neighborhood) to get your bearings. At stops with several *sorties,* you can save time by choosing the best exit.

After you finish the entire ride and exit onto the street, toss or tear your used ticket so you don't confuse it with unused tickets.

Métro Resources: Métro maps are free at Métro stations and included on freebie Paris maps at your hotel. Several good online tools can also help you navigate the public-transit system. The website Metro.paris provides an interactive map of Paris' sights and Métro lines, with a trip-planning feature and information about each sight and station's history (www.metro.paris). The free RATP mobile app (in English, download at www.ratp.fr) and the more user-friendly Kemtro app ($2, www.kemtro.com) can estimate Métro travel times, help you locate the best station exit, and tell you when the next bus will arrive, among other things. Just be careful when using your smartphone in any crowded area, as it can attract thieves.

Beware of Pickpockets: Thieves dig the Métro and RER. Be on guard. If your pocket is picked as you pass through a turnstile, you end up stuck on the wrong side (after the turnstile bar has closed behind you) while the thief gets away. Stand away from Métro doors to avoid being a target for a theft-and-run just before the doors close. Any jostling or commotion—especially when boarding or leaving trains—is likely the sign of a thief or a team of thieves in action. Make any fare inspector show proof of identity (ask locals for help if you're not certain). Keep your bag close, and never show anyone your wallet. For more tips, see page 24.

By RER

The RER (Réseau Express Régionale; air-ay-air) is the suburban arm of the Métro, serving outlying destinations such

Métro Basics

- Save money by buying a *carnet* of tickets or a Passe Navigo.
- Beware of pickpockets, and don't buy tickets from men roaming the stations.
- Find your train by its end-of-the-line stops.
- Insert your ticket into the turnstile, retrieve it, and keep it until the end of your journey.
- Safeguard your belongings: Avoid standing near the train doors with luggage.
- When you're getting off at a stop, the door may open automatically. If it doesn't, open the door by either pushing a square button (green or black) or lifting a metal latch.
- Transfers *(correspondances)* within the Métro and RER system are free.
- Trash or tear used tickets after you complete your ride and leave the station (not before) to avoid confusing them with fresh ones.

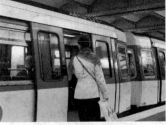

Etiquette

- When your train arrives, board only after everyone leaving the car has made it out the door.
- Avoid using the hinged seats near the doors of some trains when the car is crowded; they take up valuable standing space.
- Always offer your seat to the elderly, those with disabilities, and pregnant women.
- Talk softly in cars. Listen to how quietly Parisians communi-

as Versailles, Disneyland Paris, and the airports. These routes are indicated by thick lines on your subway map and identified by the letters A, B, C, and so on.

Within the city center, the RER works like the Métro and can be speedier if it serves your destination directly, because it makes fewer stops. Métro tickets and the Passe Navigo card are good on the RER when traveling in the city center. You can transfer between the Métro and RER systems with the same ticket. But to travel outside the city (to Versailles or the airport, for example), you'll need a separate, more expensive ticket. Unlike the Métro, not every train stops at every station along the way; check the sign or screen over the platform to see if your destination is listed as a stop (*"toutes les gares"* means it makes all stops along the way), or confirm with a local before you board.

cate (if at all) and follow their lead.

- When standing, hold onto the bar with one hand, leaving room for others while stabilizing yourself so you don't tumble or step on neighboring toes.
- If you find yourself blocking the door at a stop, step out of the car to let others off, then get back on.
- Métro doors close automatically. Don't try to hold open the door for late-boarding passengers.
- On escalators and stairs, keep to the right and pass on the left.
- When leaving a station, hold the door for the person behind you.

Key Words for the Métro and RER

French	Pronounced	English
direction	dee-rek-see-ohn	direction
ligne	leen-yuh	line
correspondance	kor-res-pohn-dahns	connection/transfer
sortie	sor-tee	exit
carnet	kar-nay	discounted set of 10 tickets
Pardon, madame/ monsieur.	par-dohn, mah-dahm/mes-yur	Excuse me, ma'am/ sir.
Je descends.	juh day-sahn	I'm getting off.
Rendez-moi mon porte-monnaie!	rahn-day-mwah mohn port-moh-nay	Give me back my wallet!

For RER trains, you may need to insert your ticket in a turnstile to exit the system.

By City Bus

Paris' excellent bus system is worth figuring out. Buses don't seem as romantic as the famous Métro and are subject to traffic jams, but savvy travelers know that buses can have you swinging through the city like Tarzan in an urban jungle.

Buses require less walking and fewer stairways than the Métro, and you can see Paris unfold as you travel. Bus stops are everywhere, and every stop comes with all the information you need: a good city bus map, route maps showing exactly where each bus that uses this stop goes, a frequency chart and schedule, a *plan du quartier* map of the immediate neighborhood, and a *soirées* map explaining night service, if available (www.ratp.fr). Bus-system

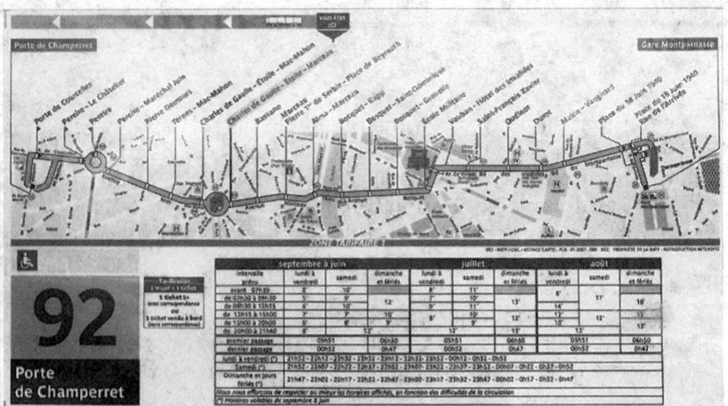

maps are also available in any Métro station (and in the €6.50 *Paris Pratique* map book sold at newsstands). For longer stays, consider buying the €6 *Le Bus* book of bus routes.

Using the Bus System: Buses use the same tickets and passes as the Métro and RER. One Zone 1 ticket buys you a bus ride anywhere in central Paris within the freeway ring road *(le périphérique)*. Use your Métro ticket or buy one on board for €0.30 more, though note that tickets bought on board are *sans correspondance,* which means you can't use them to transfer to another bus. (The ticket system has a few quirks—see "More Bus Tips," below.)

Board your bus through the front door. (Families with strollers can use any doors—the ones in the center of the bus are wider. To open the middle or back doors on long buses, push the green button located by those doors.) Validate your ticket in the machine and reclaim it. With a Passe Navigo, scan it on the purple touchpad. Keep track of what stop is coming up next by following the on-board diagram or listening to recorded announcements. When you're ready to get off, push the red button to signal you want a stop, then exit through the central or rear door. Even if you're not certain you've figured out the system, do some joyriding.

More Bus Tips: Avoid rush hour (Mon-Fri 8:00-9:30 & 17:30-19:30), when buses are jammed and traffic doesn't move. While the Métro shuts down at about 24:30 (Sun-Thu, later Fri-Sat), some buses continue much later (called *Noctilien* lines, www.noctilien.fr). Not all city buses are air-conditioned, so they can become rolling greenhouses on summer days. *Carnet* ticket holders—but not those buying individual tickets on the bus—can transfer from one bus to another on the same ticket (within 1.5 hours, revalidate your ticket

Hop on the Bus, Gus

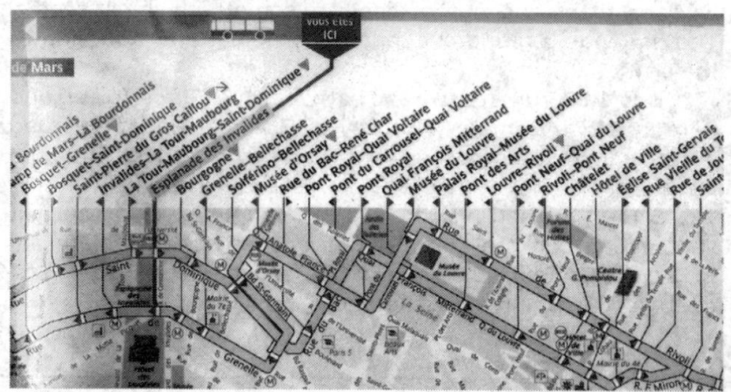

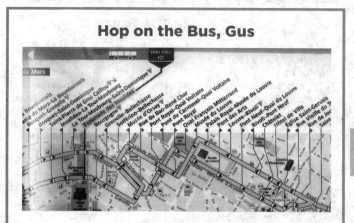

Just like the Métro, every bus stop has a name, and every bus is headed to one end-of-the-line stop or the other. The photo shows the route for bus #69. First, find your stop on the chart. It says "*vous êtes ICI*" ("you are HERE") at Esplanade des Invalides. Next, find your destination stop—let's say Bosquet-Grenelle, located a few stops to the west. Now, find out exactly where to catch the bus going in that direction. On the map showing the bus route, notice the triangle-shaped arrows pointing in the direction the bus is headed. You'll see that Esplanade des Invalides has two different bus stops—one for buses headed east, one for those going west. If you want to go west to Bosquet-Grenelle, head for that street corner to catch the bus. (With so many one-way streets in Paris, it's easy to get on the bus in the wrong direction.) When the bus pulls up, double-check that the sign on the front of the bus has the end-of-the-line stop going in your direction—to "Champ de Mars," in this case.

on the next bus), but you can't do a round-trip or hop on and off on the same line. You can use the same ticket to transfer between buses and tramlines, but you can't transfer between the bus and Métro/RER systems (it'll take two tickets).

For a list of Paris' most scenic and convenient routes, see page 36. I've also listed the handiest bus routes for each recommended hotel neighborhood under "Sleeping in Paris," later.

By Taxi

Parisian taxis are reasonable, especially for couples and families. The meters are tamper-proof. Fares and supplements (described in English on the rear windows) are straightforward and tightly regulated.

A taxi can fit three people comfortably. Cabbies are legally required to accept four passengers, though they don't always like it.

Scenic Buses for Tourists

Of Paris' many bus routes, these are some of the most scenic. They provide a great, cheap, and convenient introduction to the city.

Bus #69 runs east-west between the Eiffel Tower and Père Lachaise Cemetery by way of Rue Cler (recommended hotels and restaurants), Quai d'Orsay, the Louvre, and the Marais (recommended hotels and restaurants).

Bus #87 also links the Marais and Rue Cler areas, but stays mostly on the Left Bank, connecting the Eiffel Tower, St. Sulpice Church, Luxembourg Garden, St. Germain-des-Prés, the Latin Quarter, the Bastille, and Gare de Lyon.

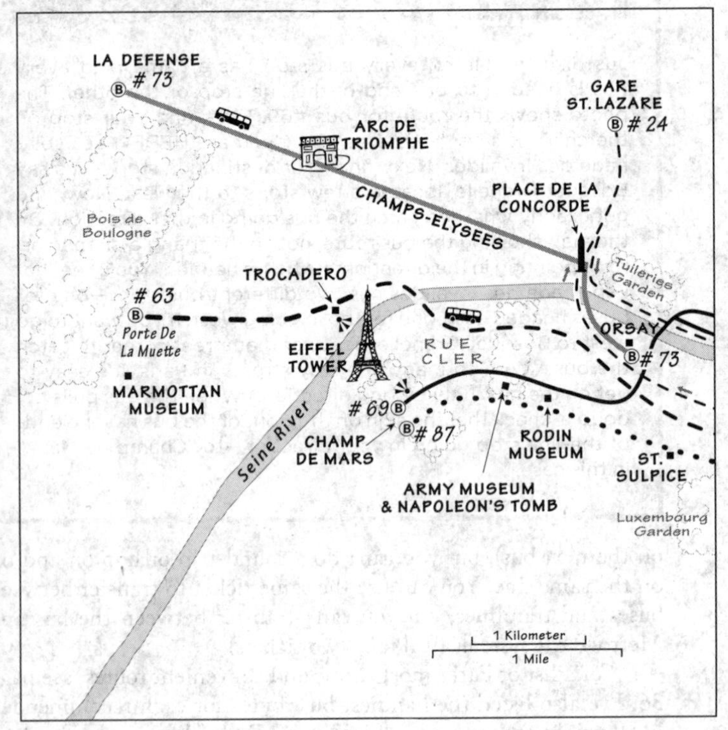

Bus #24 runs east-west along the Seine riverbank from Gare St. Lazare to Madeleine, Place de la Concorde, Orsay Museum, the Louvre, St. Michel, Notre-Dame, and Jardin des Plantes, all the way to Bercy Village (cafés and shops).

Bus #63 is another good east-west route, connecting the Marmottan Museum, Trocadéro (Eiffel Tower), Pont de l'Alma, Orsay Museum, St. Sulpice Church, Luxembourg Garden, Latin Quarter/Panthéon, and Gare de Lyon.

Bus #73 is one of Paris' most scenic lines, starting at the Orsay Museum and running westbound around Place de la Concorde, then up the Champs-Elysées, around the Arc de Triomphe, and down Avenue Charles de Gaulle to La Défense.

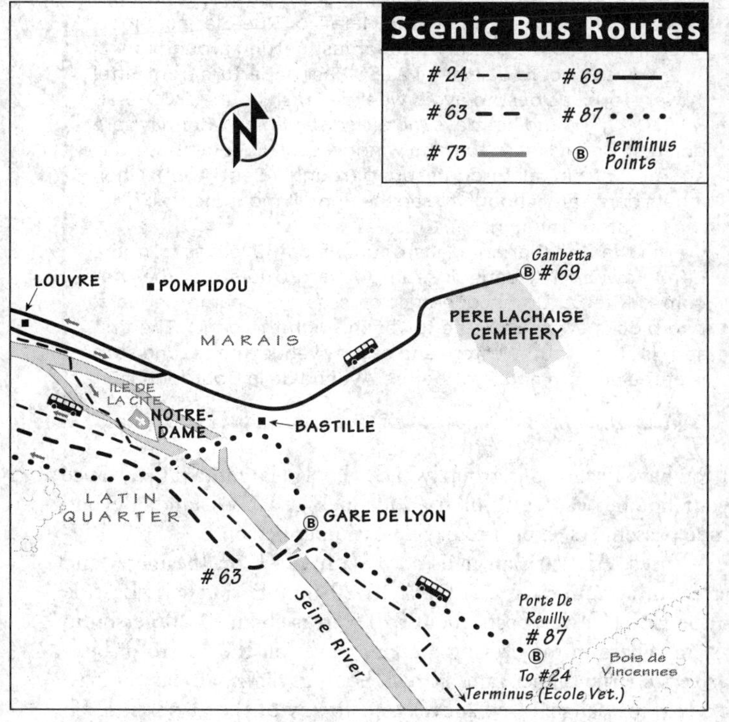

Scenic Bus Route #69

Why pay €25 for a tour company to give you an overview of Paris, when city bus #69 can do it for the cost of a Métro ticket? Get on the bus and settle in for a ride through some of the city's most interesting neighborhoods. Or use this line as a handy way to lace together many of Paris' most important sightseeing districts (you'll need a new ticket each time you board the bus).

Handy line #69 crosses the city east-west, running between the Eiffel Tower and Père Lachaise Cemetery, and passing these great monuments and neighborhoods: Eiffel Tower, Ecole Militaire, Rue Cler, Les Invalides (Army Museum and Napoleon's Tomb), Louvre museum, Ile de la Cité, Ile St. Louis, Hôtel de Ville, Pompidou Center, Marais, Bastille, and Père Lachaise. If you're staying in the Marais or Rue Cler neighborhoods, line #69 is a useful route for just getting around town.

You can board daily until 22:30 (last departure from Eiffel Tower stop). It's best to avoid weekday rush hours (8:00-9:30 & 17:30-19:30) and hot days (no air-conditioning). Sundays are quietest, and it's easy to get a window seat. Evening bus rides are pretty from fall through spring (roughly Sept-April), when it gets dark early enough to see the floodlit monuments before the bus stops running.

In the Rue Cler area, eastbound line #69 leaves from the Eiffel Tower on Avenue Joseph Bouvard (the street that becomes Rue St. Dominique as it crosses the Champ de Mars, two blocks away from the tower through the park). The first stop is at the southwestern end of the avenue; the second stop is at the eastern end (just before Avenue de la Bourdonnais).

PARIS

If you have five in your group, you can book a larger taxi in advance (your hotelier can call), or try your luck at a taxi stand. Beyond three passengers, expect to pay €3 extra per person.

Rates: All Parisian taxis start with €2.60 on the meter and have a minimum charge of €6.86. A 20-minute ride (e.g., Bastille to the Eiffel Tower) costs about €20 (versus about €1.40/person to get anywhere in town using a *carnet* ticket on the Métro or bus). Drivers charge higher rates at rush hour, at night, all day Sunday, for extra passengers (see above), and to any of the airports. Each piece of luggage that goes in the trunk is €1 extra (no fee for the first bag; charge won't appear on the meter, but it is legitimate). To tip, round up to the next euro (at least €0.50). The A, B, or C lights on a taxi's rooftop sign correspond to hourly rates, which vary with the time of day and day of the week (for example, the A rate of €32/hour applies Mon-Sat 10:00-17:00). Tired travelers need not bother with these mostly subtle differences in fares—if you need a cab, take it.

How to Catch *un Taxi:* You can try waving down a taxi, but it's often easier to ask someone for the nearest taxi stand (*"Où est une station de taxi?"*; oo ay ewn stah-see-ohn duh "taxi"). Taxi stands are indicated by a circled "T" on good city maps and on many maps in this book. To order a taxi in English, call the reservation line for the G7 cab company (tel. 01 41 27 66 99), or ask your hotelier for help. When you summon a taxi by phone, the meter starts running as soon as the call is received, often adding €6 or more to the bill. Smartphone users can book a taxi using the cab company's app, which also provides approximate wait times (surcharge similar to booking by phone). To download an app, search for either "Taxi G7" or "Taxis Bleus" (the two major companies, both available in English).

Taxis are tough to find during rush hour, when it's raining, on weekend nights, or on any night after the Métro closes (Sun-Thu at 24:30, later on Fri-Sat). If you need to catch a train or flight early in the morning, book a taxi the day before (especially for weekday departures). Some taxi companies require a €5 reservation fee by credit card for weekday morning rush-hour departures (7:00-10:00) and only have a limited number of reservation spots.

By Bike

Paris is surprisingly easy by bicycle. The city is flat, and riders have access to more than 370 miles of bike lanes and many of the priority lanes for buses and taxis (though be careful on these). You can rent from a bike-rental shop or use the city-operated Vélib' bikes—details are below. All bike-rental shops have good route suggestions. I biked along the river from Notre-Dame to the Eiffel Tower in 15 wonderfully scenic minutes. The new riverside promenade between the Orsay Museum and Pont de l'Alma is magnificent for biking.

Urban bikers will find Paris a breeze. First-timers will get the hang of it quickly enough by following some simple rules. Always stay to the right in your lane, bike single-file, stay off sidewalks, watch out for opening doors on parked cars, signal with your arm before making turns, and use bike paths when available. Obey the traffic laws as if you were driving a car. Parisians use the same road rules as Americans, with two exceptions: When passing vehicles or other bikes, always pass on the left (it's illegal to pass on the right); and where there is no stoplight, always yield to traffic merging from the right, even if you're on a major road and the merging driver is on a side street. You'll find a bell on your bike; use it like a horn to warn pedestrians who don't see you. The TIs have a helpful "Paris à Vélo" map, which shows all the dedicated bike paths. Many other versions are available for sale at newsstand kiosks, some bookstores, and department stores.

Rental Bikes: The following companies rent bikes to individuals, as well as offering organized bike tours (see "Bike Tours," later) and general tips about cycling in Paris. **Bike About Tours** is your best bet for bike rental (€15/day during office hours, €20/24 hours, includes lock and helmet; daily mid-Feb-Dec 9:00-18:00, closed Dec-mid-Feb; shop located near Hôtel de Ville in Vinci parking garage—see map on page 146, Mo: Hôtel de Ville, tel. 06 18 80 84 92, www.bikeabouttours.com, info@bikeabouttours.com. **Fat Tire Bike Tours** has a limited supply of bikes for rent, so call ahead to check availability (€4/hour, €25/24 hours, includes lock and helmet, photo ID and credit-card imprint required for deposit, €2/day rental discount with this book, maximum 2 discounts per book; office open daily 9:00-18:30, May-Aug bike rental only after 11:30 as priority is given to those taking a tour, 24 Rue Edgar Faure—see map on page 84, Mo: Dupleix, tel. 01 56 58 10 54, http://paris.fattirebiketours.com).

Vélib' Bikes: The city's Vélib' program (from *vélo* + *libre* = "bike freedom" or "free bike") gives residents and foreigners alike access to more than 20,000 bikes at nearly 1,500 stations scattered around the city.

While the curbside stations only accept American Express or chip-and-PIN credit cards (see page 1038), any kind of credit card will work if you buy a subscription in advance online at http://en.velib.paris.fr. The subscription process is in English and easy to follow: Click on "Subscriptions and Fees," then scroll down to select the "Short-Term Subscription" you want (€1.70/1 day, €8/7 days, tel. 01 30 79 79 30). Enter your email, choose a PIN number, select your start date, and agree to the terms and conditions. After payment you'll get an ID number. To pick up a bike, go to any bike rack, enter your ID number and PIN at the machine (all have English instructions), select a bike, and away you go! Make sure to pick a bike in working order; if a bike has a problem, locals will turn the seat backwards.

Tours in Paris

To sightsee on your own, download my series of free audio tours that illuminate some of Paris' top sights and neighborhoods, including the Historic Paris Walk, Louvre, Orsay, and Versailles Palace (see sidebar on page 14 for details).

BY BUS

Bus Tours

City Vision offers bus tours of Paris, day and night (advertised in hotel lobbies). I'd consider them only for their nighttime tour (see page 133). During the day, you'll get a better value and more versatility by taking a hop-on, hop-off tour by bus (described next) or Batobus boat (see "By Boat," later), which provide transportation between sights.

Hop-on, Hop-off Bus Tours

Double-decker buses connect Paris' main sights, giving you an easy once-over of the city with a basic pre-recorded commentary, punctuated with vintage French folk songs. You can hop off at any stop, tour a sight, then hop on a later bus. It's dang scenic, but only if you get a top-deck seat and the weather's decent—otherwise, the trip may not be worth it. Because of traffic and stops, these buses can be dreadfully slow. (Busy sightseers will do better using the Métro to connect sights.) On the plus side, because the buses move so slowly, you have time to read my sight descriptions, making this a decent orientation tour.

Of the several different hop-on, hop-off bus companies, **L'OpenTour** is best. They offer frequent service on four routes covering all of central Paris. You can even transfer between routes with one ticket. Look up the various routes and stops either on their website or by picking up a brochure (available at any TI or on one of their bright yellow buses). Their Paris Grand Tour (green route) offers the best introduction and most frequent buses (every 10 minutes). Other routes run a bit less frequently (every 15-30 minutes). You can catch the bus at just about any major sight, such as the Eiffel Tower (look for the Open Bus icon on public transit bus shelters and signs). Buy your tickets from the driver (1 day-€32, 2 days-€36, 3 days-€40, kids 4-11-€16 for 1 or 2 days, allow 2 hours per route, tel. 01 42 66 56 56, www.parislopentour.com). A combo-ticket also covers the Batobus boats, described later (1 day-€41, 2 days-€45, 3 days-€49, kids 4-11-€20 for 2 or 3 days). Also note that L'OpenTour runs night illumination tours (see page 133).

Big Bus Paris runs a fleet of buses around Paris on a route with just 10 stops and recorded narration (1 day-€29, 2 days-€33, kids 4-12-€16, 10 percent cheaper if you book online, tel. 01 53 95 39 53, www.bigbustours.com).

Paris' cheapest "bus tour" is simply to hop on **city bus #69** and enjoy the sights as they roll by (see sidebar on page 35).

BY BOAT

Seine Cruises

Several companies run one-hour boat cruises on the Seine. For the best experience, cruise at twilight or after dark. (To dine while you cruise, see "Dinner Cruises" on page 174.) Two of the companies—Bateaux-Mouches and Bateaux Parisiens—are convenient to the Rue Cler hotels, and both run daily year-round (April-Oct 10:00-22:30, 2-3/hour; Nov-March shorter hours, runs hourly). Some offer discounts for early online bookings.

Bateaux-Mouches, the oldest boat company in Paris, departs from Pont de l'Alma's right bank and has the biggest open-top, double-decker boats (higher up means better views). But this company caters to tour groups, making their boats jammed and noisy (€12.50, kids 4-12-€5.50, tel. 01 42 25 96 10, www.bateaux-mouches.fr).

Bateaux Parisiens has smaller covered boats with handheld audioguides, fewer crowds, and only one deck. It leaves from right in front of the Eiffel Tower (€13, kids 3-12-€5, tel. 01 76 64 14 45, www.bateauxparisiens.com).

Vedettes du Pont Neuf offers essentially the same one-hour tour as the other companies, but starts and ends at Pont Neuf, closer to my recommended hotels in the Marais. The boats feature a live guide whose delivery (in English and French) is as stiff as a recorded narration—and as hard to understand, given the quality of their sound system (€14, €12 if you book direct with this book in 2015, discounts for online bookings, kids 4-12 pay €7, tip requested, nearly 2/hour, daily 10:30-22:30, tel. 01 46 33 98 38, www.vedettesdupontneuf.com).

Hop-on, Hop-off Boat Tour

Batobus allows you to get on and off as often as you like at any of eight popular stops along the Seine. The boats, which make a continuous circuit, stop in this order: Eiffel Tower, Orsay Museum, St. Germain-des-Prés, Notre-Dame, Jardin des Plantes, Hôtel de Ville, the Louvre, and Pont Alexandre III, near the Champs-Elysées (1 day-€15, 2 days-€18, 5 days-€21, April-Aug boats run every

20 minutes 10:00-21:30, Sept-March every 25 minutes 10:00-19:00, 45 minutes one-way, 1.5-hour round-trip, www.batobus.com). If you use this for getting around—sort of a scenic, floating alternative to the Métro—it can be worthwhile, but if you just want a guided boat tour, the Seine cruises described earlier are a better choice. Combo-tickets covering the L'OpenTour hop-on, hop-off buses (described earlier) are available, but skip the one-day ticket, because you'll feel rushed trying to take full advantage of the bus and boat routes in a single day.

Low-Key Cruise on a Tranquil Canal

Canauxrama runs a lazy 2.5-hour cruise on a peaceful canal out of sight of the Seine. Tours start from Place de la Bastille and end at Bassin de la Villette (near Mo: Stalingrad). During the first segment of your trip, you'll pass through a long tunnel (built by order of Napoleon in the early 19th century, when canal boats were vital for industrial transport). Once outside, you glide—not much faster than you can walk—through sleepy Parisian neighborhoods and slowly climb through four double locks as a guide narrates the trip in French and English (adults-€16, kids 12 and under-€8.50, check online for discounts for advance booking, departs at 9:45 and 14:30 across from Opéra Bastille, just below Boulevard de la Bastille, opposite #50—where the canal meets Place de la Bastille, tel. 01 42 39 15 00, www.canauxrama.com). The same tour also goes in the opposite direction, from Bassin de la Villette to Place de la Bastille (usually departs at 9:45 and 14:45). It's OK to bring a picnic on board.

ON FOOT

Walking Tours

Paris Walks offers a variety of two-hour walks, led by British and American guides. Tours are thoughtfully prepared and entertaining. Don't hesitate to stand close to the guide to hear (€12-15, generally 2/day—morning and afternoon, private tours available, family guides and Louvre tours are a specialty, call 01 48 09 21 40 for schedule in English or check printable online schedule at www.paris-walks.com). Tours focus on the Marais (4/week), Montmartre (3/week), medieval Latin Quarter (Mon), Ile de la Cité/Notre-Dame (Mon), the "Two Islands" (Ile de la Cité and Ile St. Louis, Wed), the Revolution (Tue), and Hemingway's Paris (Fri). They also run less-regular tours of Paris' Puces St. Ouen flea market and of the Catacombs, in addition to a WWI tour and a themed walk on the Occupation and Resistance in Paris during the 1940s. Call a day or two ahead to hear the current schedule and starting point. Most tours don't require reservations, but specialty tours—such as

Connecting with the Culture

Paris hosts more visitors than any other city in the world, and with such a robust tourism industry, many travelers feel cut off from the "real life" in the City of Light. Fortunately, Paris offers *beaucoup* ways for you to connect with locals—and thereby make your trip more personal...and more memorable.

Staying with a family is a simple way to experience everyday Parisian life firsthand. Several agencies set up **bed-and-breakfast** stays in private homes (listed on page 154), but other opportunities abound. These get good reviews:

Meeting the French puts travelers in touch with Parisians by organizing dinners in private homes, workplace tours to match your interests/career, and more (tel. 01 42 51 19 80, www.meetingthefrench.com).

Paris Greeter is an all-volunteer organization that connects travelers with English-speaking Parisians who want to share their knowledge of Paris. These volunteer "guides" are not licensed to give historical tours; rather they act as informal companions who can show you "their Paris"—it's like seeing Paris through the eyes of a friend. The tours are free (though donations are welcome), and you must sign up five weeks before your visit (www.greeters.paris).

The American Church and Franco-American Center, an interdenominational church in the Rue Cler neighborhood, offers many services for travelers wanting to connect with Parisian culture. The Thursday evening English/French language exchange (18:00-19:30) is a handy way to meet locals who want to improve their English. It's free and relaxed—just show up. You'll chat with Parisians, who will respond in their best English. English-language worship services are held every Sunday (at 9:00 and 11:00, contemporary service at 13:30). The coffee hour

the Louvre, fashion, or chocolate tours—require advance reservations and prepayment with credit card (deposits aren't refundable).

Context Travel offers "intellectual by design" walking tours geared for serious learners. The tours are led by docents (historians, architects, and academics) and cover both museums and specific neighborhoods. They range from traditional topics such as French art history in the Louvre and the Gothic architecture of Notre-Dame to more thematic explorations like immigration and the changing face of Paris, jazz in the Latin Quarter, and the history of the baguette. It's best to book in advance—groups are limited to six participants and can fill up fast (€60-100/person, admission to sights extra, generally 3 hours, tel. 09 75 18 04 15, US tel. 800-691-6036, www.contexttravel.com). They also offer private tours and excursions outside Paris.

Classic Walks' lowbrow, lighter-on-information but high-on-after each service and the free Sunday concerts (generally Sept-June at 17:00, but not every week and not in Dec) are a good way to meet the very international congregation (church reception open Mon-Sat 9:00-12:00 & 13:00-22:00, Sun 8:30-19:00, 65 Quai d'Orsay, Mo: Invalides, tel. 01 40 62 05 00, www.acparis.org).

Cooking Schools: It's easy to hook up with small cooking schools that provide an unthreatening and personal experience, such as trips to markets (see page 1075 for a list of several schools).

Wine Tasting: Young, enthusiastic Olivier Magny and his team of sommeliers teach fun wine-tasting classes at **Ô Château** wine school/bar near the Louvre, in the 17th-century residence of Madame de Pompadour, King Louis XV's favorite mistress. Olivier's goal is to "take the snob out of wine." At these informal classes, you'll learn the basics of French wine regions, the techniques of tasting, and how to read a French wine label. Classes include Introductory Tasting (€30, 1 hour), Tour de France of Wine (€55, 2 hours), Wine and Cheese lunches (€75, 1.5 hours), Grands Crus tasting (€150, 2 hours), and a wine-tasting dinner (€100, about 2 hours). Register online using code "RS2015" for a 10 percent discount (68 Rue Jean-Jacques Rousseau, Mo: Louvre-Rivoli or Etienne Marcel, tel. 01 44 73 97 80, www.o-chateau.com).

Conversation Swap: Parler Paris is a free-form conversation group organized for native French and English speakers who want to practice in a relaxed environment. In a small group, you'll discuss interesting topics—for the first 45 minutes in French, then for 45 minutes in English. Your first visit is free; after that it's €12 a session (several meetings per week possible, tel. 01 48 42 26 10 or 01 40 27 97 59, www.parlerparlor.com, info@parlerparlor.com).

fun walking tours are run by Fat Tire Bike Tours. Their 3.5-hour Classic Walk covers most major sights (€20, usually at 10:00—see website for days of week; meet at their office at 24 Rue Edgar Faure, Mo: Dupleix, tel. 01 56 58 10 54, http://paris.classicwalks.com). They also offer neighborhood walks of Montmartre, the Marais, and the Latin Quarter, as well as themed walks on the French Revolution (€20, tours run several times a week—see website for details). The company promises a €2 discount on all walks with this book (two-discount maximum per book).

Easy Pass (also operated by Fat Tire Bike) offers skip-the-line interior tours of major sights, including the Louvre, Notre-Dame Tower, Catacombs, Eiffel Tower, Orsay, and Versailles (€40-85/person, includes entry and guided tour). Reservations are required and can be made on their website, by phone, or in person at their Easy Pass office near the Eiffel Tower (daily 9:00-18:00, longer hours in high season, 36 Avenue de la Bourdonnais, Mo: Ecole Militaire, tel. 01 56 58 10 54, http://paris.easypasstours.com). They offer two versions of their Eiffel Tower Easy Pass: one with a guided tour for €59 or one without for €40—handy only if you weren't able to get advance tickets directly from the Eiffel Tower website.

Local Guides

For many, Paris merits hiring a Parisian as a personal guide. **Thierry Gauduchon** is a terrific guide and a gifted teacher (€230/half-day, €450/day, tel. 06 19 07 30 77, tgauduchon@gmail.com). **Sylvie Moreau** also leads good tours in Paris (€200 for 3 hours, €320 for 7 hours, tel. 01 46 07 96 28, mobile 06 87 02 80 67, sylvie.ja.moreau@gmail.com). **Arnaud Servignat** is a fine guide who has taught me much about Paris (private tours starting at €190, also does car tours of the countryside around Paris for a little more, mobile 06 68 80 29 05, www.french-guide.com, arnotour@me.com. **Elisabeth Van Hest** is another likable and very capable guide (€200/half-day, tel. 01 43 41 47 31, mobile 06 77 80 19 89, elisa.guide@gmail.com. **Sylviane Ceneray** is gentle and knowledgeable (€200/half-day, tel. 06 84 48 02 44, www.paris-asyoulikeit.com).

Food Tours

Dig deeper into Paris' food scene on a culinary walking tour. Visit markets, shop at specialty stores, and sample food at locals' favorite eateries.

Friendly Canadian **Rosa Jackson** designs personalized "Edible Paris" itineraries based on your interests and three-hour "food-guru" tours of Paris led by her or one of her two colleagues (unguided itineraries from €125, guided tours—€300 for 1 person, €150/person for 2-3 people, €100/person for 4-6 people, mobile 06 81 67 41 22, www.edible-paris.com, rosa@rosajackson.com.

Paris By Mouth offers more casual and frequent small group tours, with a maximum of seven foodies per group. Tours are organized by location or flavor and led by local food writers (€95/3 hours, includes tastings, www.parisbymouth.com, tasteparisbymouth@gmail.com).

ON WHEELS

Bike Tours

A bike tour is a fun way to see Paris. Two companies—Bike About Tours and Fat Tire Bike Tours—offer tours and bike maps of Paris, and give good advice on cycling routes in the city. Their tour routes cover different areas of the city, so avid cyclists could do both without much repetition.

Run by Christian (American) and Paul (New Zealander), **Bike About Tours** offers easygoing tours with a focus on the eastern half of the city. Their four-hour tours run daily year-round at 10:00 (also at 15:00 June-Sept). You'll meet at the statue of Charlemagne in front of Notre-Dame, then walk to the nearby rental office to get bikes. The tour includes a good back-street visit of the Marais, Rive Gauche outdoor sculpture park, Ile de la Cité, heart of the Latin Quarter (with a lunch break), Louvre, Les Halles, and Pompidou Center. Group tours have a 12-person maximum—reserve online to guarantee a spot, or show up and take your chances (€30, €5 discount with this book, maximum 2 discounts per book, includes helmets upon request, private tours available, see listing on page 39 for contact info). They also offer a day trip by bike to Versailles (€80, see website for details).

Run by a gang of young anglophone expats, **Fat Tire Bike Tours** offers an extensive program of bike, Segway (see below), and walking tours (see Classic Walks listing, earlier). Their young guides run four-hour bike tours of Paris, by day and by night (adults-€30, kids-€28, show this book to get a €4 discount per person, maximum 2 discounts per book, reservations recommended but not required—you can also just show up, especially in off-season). Kid-sized bikes are available, as are tandem attachments that hook on to a parent's bike. On the day tour, you'll pedal with a pack of 10-20 riders, mostly in parks and along bike lanes, with a lunch stop in the Tuileries Garden (tours leave daily rain or shine at 11:00, April-Oct also at 15:00). Livelier night tours follow a route past floodlit monuments and include a boat cruise on the Seine (April-Oct daily at 19:00, less frequent in winter). Both tours meet at the exit of the Dupleix Métro station near the Eiffel Tower; from there you'll walk to the nearby Fat Tire office to pick up bikes (helmets available upon request at no extra charge, for contact info see listing on page 39). They also run bike tours to Versailles and Giverny (reservations required, see website for details).

Segway Tour

Fat Tire offers pricey four-hour **City Segway Tours.** Learn to ride these stand-up motorized scooters while exploring Paris (you'll get the hang of it after about half an hour). These tours take no more than eight people at a time, so reservations are required (must be at least 12 years old or 90 pounds, €90, daily at 9:30, April-Oct also at 14:00 and 18:30, March

and Nov also at 14:00, tel. 01 56 58 10 54, www.citysegwaytours.com).

Pedicab Tour

You'll see **TripUp**'s space-age pedicabs *(cyclopolitains)* everywhere in central Paris. The hard-pedaling, free-spirited drivers (who get some electrical assistance) are happy to either transport you from point A to B or give you a tour at a snail's pace—which is a lovely way to experience Paris (€40-50/hour, confirm approximate price in advance, www.tripup.fr).

Scooter Tour

Left Bank Scooters offers several very small group tours of Paris, plus day trips outside the city. Their tour of Versailles is worth considering for motor scooter enthusiasts: You'll meet in Paris, then ride your scooter to Versailles on quiet roads, following the *route de Versailles* (the same path Louis XIV took to get out there), then do an all-day visit during which you are allowed to drive into the Gardens and down to the Hamlet (€250 for one person, €50 extra for passenger, tel. 06 78 12 04 24, www.leftbankscooters.com). They also do a Paris Highlights tour and a fun night tour of Paris (€150 for one person, €50 extra for passenger). Ask about their private tours of Paris on a vintage bike with sidecar. One person sits behind the guide and another in the sidecar, making this a fun option for kids—or those nervous about piloting their own scooter in the big city (€300 for two people, 3 hours). The company will also deliver rental scooters to daring travelers over age 20 with a valid driver's license (€55-80/day, price depends on size of the scooter's motor and how long you keep it).

Wheelchair Tour

Paris on Wheels provides services for travelers with disabilities, including city wheelchair tours, excursions from Paris, and transportation within the city—a terrific service, as public transportation is not wheelchair-accessible (tel. 06 68 23 74 38, www.parisonwheels.com, derek@parisonwheels.com).

WEEKEND TOUR PACKAGES FOR STUDENTS

Andy Steves (Rick's son) runs **WSA Europe,** offering three-day and longer guided and unguided packages—including accommodations, sightseeing, and unique local experiences—for budget travelers across 11 top European cities, including Paris (from €99, see www.wsaeurope.com for details).

EXCURSIONS FROM PARIS

Most of the local guides listed earlier will do excursion tours from Paris using your rental car. Or consider the following companies, which provide transportation.

Paris Webservices, a reliable outfit, offers many services, including day trips with English-speaking chauffeur-guides in cushy minivans for private groups to several of the destinations covered in this book, including Versailles, Giverny, Burgundy, Normandy, and the Loire (price depends on tour, use promo code "PWS52K15" and show current edition of this book for discounts of 5-10 percent—discount not valid on services they book for you through other companies; tel. 01 45 56 91 67, www.pariswebservices.com, contactpws@pariswebservices.com.

Many companies offer bus tours to regional sights, including all of the day trips described in the next chapter. **City Vision** runs uninspired minivan and bus tours to several popular regional destinations, including the Loire Valley, Champagne region, D-Day beaches, and Mont St-Michel (tel. 01 42 60 30 01, www.pariscityvision.com). Their minivan tours are pricier, but more personal and given in English, and most offer convenient pickup at your hotel (half-day tour about €80/person, day tour about €190/person). Their full-size bus tours are multilingual, mass-marketed, and mediocre at best, but cheaper than the minivan tours—worthwhile for some travelers simply for the ease of transportation to the sights (about €80-170, destinations include Versailles, Giverny, Mont St-Michel, and more).

Sightseeing Strategies

If you plan ahead, you can avoid many of the lines that tourists suffer through in Paris. For most sightseers, the best choice is to buy a Paris Museum Pass. If you decide to forego the pass—or for sights not covered by the pass—you have other options.

PARIS MUSEUM PASS

In Paris there are two classes of sightseers—those with a Paris Museum Pass, and those who stand in line. The pass admits you to many of Paris' most popular sights, allowing you to skip ticket-buying lines. You'll save time and money by getting this pass.

Buying the Pass

The pass pays for itself with four key admissions in two days (for example, the Louvre, Orsay, Sainte-Chapelle, and Versailles), and it lets you skip the ticket line at most sights (2 days-€42, 4 days-€56, 6 days-€69, no youth or senior discounts). It's sold at participating museums, monuments, FNAC department stores, and TIs (even at Paris' airports). Try to avoid buying the pass at a major museum (such as the Louvre), where the supply can be spotty and lines long. It's also not worth the cost or hassle to buy Paris Museum Passes online because you either have to pay dearly to have them shipped to you, or print vouchers and redeem them in person at a Paris TI. For more info, visit www.parismuseumpass.com or call 01 44 61 96 60.

To determine if the pass is a good value for your trip, tally up what you want to see from the list in the next section. And remember, an advantage of the pass is that you skip to the front of most (but not all) lines, which can save hours of waiting, especially in summer. Another key benefit is that you can pop into lesser sights that otherwise might not be worth the expense.

Families: The pass isn't worth buying for children and teens, as most museums are free or discounted for those under age 18 (teenagers may need to show ID as proof of age). If parents have a Museum Pass, kids can usually skip the ticket lines as well. A few places, such as the Arc de Triomphe and Army Museum, require everyone—even passholders—to stand in line to collect your child's free ticket.

What the Paris Museum Pass Covers

Here's a list of key included sights and their admission prices without the pass:

Louvre (€12)	Notre-Dame Tower (€8.50)
Orsay Museum (€11)	Paris Archaeological Crypt (€4)
Orangerie Museum (€8)	Paris Sewer Tour (€4.40)
Sainte-Chapelle (€8.50)	Cluny Museum (€8)
Arc de Triomphe (€9.50)	Pompidou Center (€13)
Rodin Museum (€6-9)	Picasso Museum (€11)
Army Museum (€9.50)	Conciergerie (€8.50)
Panthéon (€7.50)	Versailles (€15-25)

Notable exceptions that are *not* covered by the pass include: the Eiffel Tower, Montparnasse Tower, Marmottan Museum, Opéra Garnier, Notre-Dame Treasury, Jacquemart-André Museum, Grand Palais, Catacombs, Montmartre Museum, Sacré-Cœur's dome, and the ladies of Pigalle.

Using the Pass

The pass is activated the first time you use it—you must write the starting date on the pass.

To use your pass at sights, look for signs designating the entrance for pre-reserved ticket holders. If it's not obvious, boldly walk to the front of the ticket line (after going through security if necessary), hold up your pass, and ask the ticket taker: "*Entrez, pass*?" (ahn-tray pahs). You'll either be allowed to enter at that point, or you'll be directed to a special entrance. For major sights, such as the Louvre and Orsay museums, I've identified passholder entrances on the maps in this book. Don't be shy—some places (Orsay Museum and the Arc de Triomphe, in particular) have long lines in which passholders wait needlessly. At a few sights (including the Louvre, Sainte-Chapelle, Notre-Dame Tower, and Château de Versailles), everyone has to shuffle through the slow-moving baggage-check lines for security—but you still save time by avoiding the ticket line.

Plan carefully to make the most of your pass. First, validate it only when you're ready to tackle the covered sights on consecutive days. Make sure the sights you want to visit will be open (many museums are closed Mon or Tue). The pass provides the best value on days when sights close later, letting you extend your sightseeing day. Take advantage of these late hours. For instance, the Arc de Triomphe and Pompidou Center are always open later, while the Notre-Dame Tower, Sainte-Chapelle, Louvre, Orsay, Rodin, and Napoleon's Tomb have late hours on selected evenings (or at certain times of year). On days that you don't have pass coverage, plan to visit free sights and those not covered by the pass (see page 58 for a list of free sights).

OTHER TICKET-BUYING OPTIONS

If you don't purchase a Paris Museum Pass, or if a sight is not covered by the pass, you have other line-skipping options. For some sights, you can **buy tickets online** at their official website. This is essential at the Eiffel Tower, which isn't covered by the pass and is plagued by long lines in peak season (note that you must choose an entry time when booking). You can also book tickets online for the Orsay, Rodin Museum, Monet's gardens at Giverny, and the Jacquemart-André Museum, as well as for activities like the Bateaux-Mouches cruises and Sainte-Chapelle concerts. Increasingly, other sights are adding this helpful service.

TIs and FNAC department stores sell individual ***"coupe-file"* tickets** (pronounced "koop-feel") for some sights, which allow you to use the Museum Pass entrance (worth the trouble only for the most important sights where lines are longest). TIs sell these tickets for no extra fee, but FNACs add a surcharge of 10-20 percent.

FNAC stores are everywhere, even on the Champs-Elysées (ask your hotelier for the nearest one). Despite the surcharges and often-long lines to buy them, getting *coupe-file* tickets can still be a good idea.

Fat Tire Bike Tours offers **Easy Pass** skip-the-line tickets or tours of major sights, including the Louvre, Notre-Dame Tower, Catacombs, Eiffel Tower, Orsay, and Versailles (for details, see page 45 or visit http://paris.easypasstours.com).

Some sights, such as the Louvre, have **ticket-vending machines** that save time in line. Note that these only accept cash (usually no bills larger than €20) or chip-and-PIN cards (so most American credit cards won't work). At certain sights, including the Louvre and Orsay, **nearby shops** sell tickets, allowing you to avoid the main ticket lines (for details, see the Louvre and Orsay Museum listings).

Historic Paris Walk

This information is distilled from the Historic Paris Walk chapter in *Rick Steves Paris,* by Rick Steves, Steve Smith, and Gene Openshaw. You can download a free Rick Steves audio version of this walk; see page 1110.

You'll start where the city did—on the Ile de la Cité, the island in the Seine River and the physical and historic bull's-eye of your Paris map. The closest Métro stops are Cité, Hôtel de Ville, and St. Michel, each a short walk away.

Allow four hours to do justice to this three-mile self-guided walk, beginning at the Notre-Dame Cathedral and ending at Pont Neuf; just follow the dotted line on the "Historic Paris Walk" map.

▲▲▲Notre-Dame Cathedral

For centuries, the main figure in the Christian pantheon has been Mary, the mother of Jesus. Catholics petition her in times of trouble to gain comfort, and to ask her to convince God to be compassionate with them. The church is dedicated to "Our Lady" *(Notre Dame),* and there she is, cradling God, right in the heart of the facade (circular window in the center), surrounded by the halo of the rose window. Though the church is massive and imposing, it has always stood for the grace and compassion of Mary, the "mother of God."

Imagine the faith of the people who built this cathedral. They broke ground in 1163 with the hope that someday their great-great-great-great-great-great grandchildren might attend the dedication Mass, which finally took place two centuries later, in 1345. Look up the 200-foot-tall bell towers and imagine a tiny medieval community mustering the money and energy for construction. Master masons supervised, but the people did much of the grunt work themselves for free—hauling the huge stones from distant quarries, digging a 30-foot-deep trench to lay the foundation, and treading like rats on a wheel designed to lift the stones up, one by one. This kind of backbreaking, arduous manual labor created the real hunchbacks of Notre-Dame.

Cost and Hours: Cathedral—free, daily 7:45-18:45, Sun until 19:30; **Treasury**—€4, not covered by Museum Pass, Mon-Fri 9:30-18:00, Sat 9:30-18:30, Sun 13:30-18:40; audioguide-€5, free English tours—normally Wed-Thu at 14:00, Sat-Sun at 14:30.

The cathedral hosts **Masses** several times daily (early morning, noon, evening), plus Vespers at 17:45. The international Mass is held Sun at 11:30. Call or check the website for a full schedule. On Good Friday and the first Friday of the month at 15:00, the (physically underwhelming) relic known as Jesus' **Crown of Thorns** (Couronne d'Epines) goes on display (Mo: Cité, Hôtel de Ville, or St. Michel; tel. 01 42 34 56 10, www.notredamedeparis.fr).

Tower Climb: The entrance for Notre-Dame's tower climb is outside the cathedral, along the left side. You can hike to the top of the facade between the towers and then to the top of the south tower (400 steps total) for a gargoyle's-eye view of the cathedral, Seine, and city (€8.50, covered by Museum Pass but no bypass line for passholders; daily April-Sept 10:00-18:30, Fri-Sat until 23:00 in July-Aug, Oct-March 10:00-17:30, last entry 45 minutes before closing; to avoid the worst lines arrive before 10:00 or after 17:00—after 16:00 in winter; tel. 01 53 10 07 00, http://notre-dame-de-paris.monuments-nationaux.fr).

➲ Self-Guided Tour

"Walk this way" toward the front of the cathedral, and view it from the bronze plaque on the ground marked "Point Zero" (30 yards from the central doorway). You're standing at the center of France, the point from which all distances are measured.

Facade: Look at the left doorway, and to the left of the door, find the statue with his head in his hands. The man with the misplaced head is **St. Denis,** the city's first bishop and patron saint. He stands among statues of other early Christians who helped turn pagan Paris into Christian Paris. Sometime in the third century, Denis came here from Italy to convert the Parisii. He settled here on the Ile de la Cité, back when there was a Roman temple on this spot and Christianity was suspect. Denis proved so successful at winning converts that the Romans' pagan priests got worried.

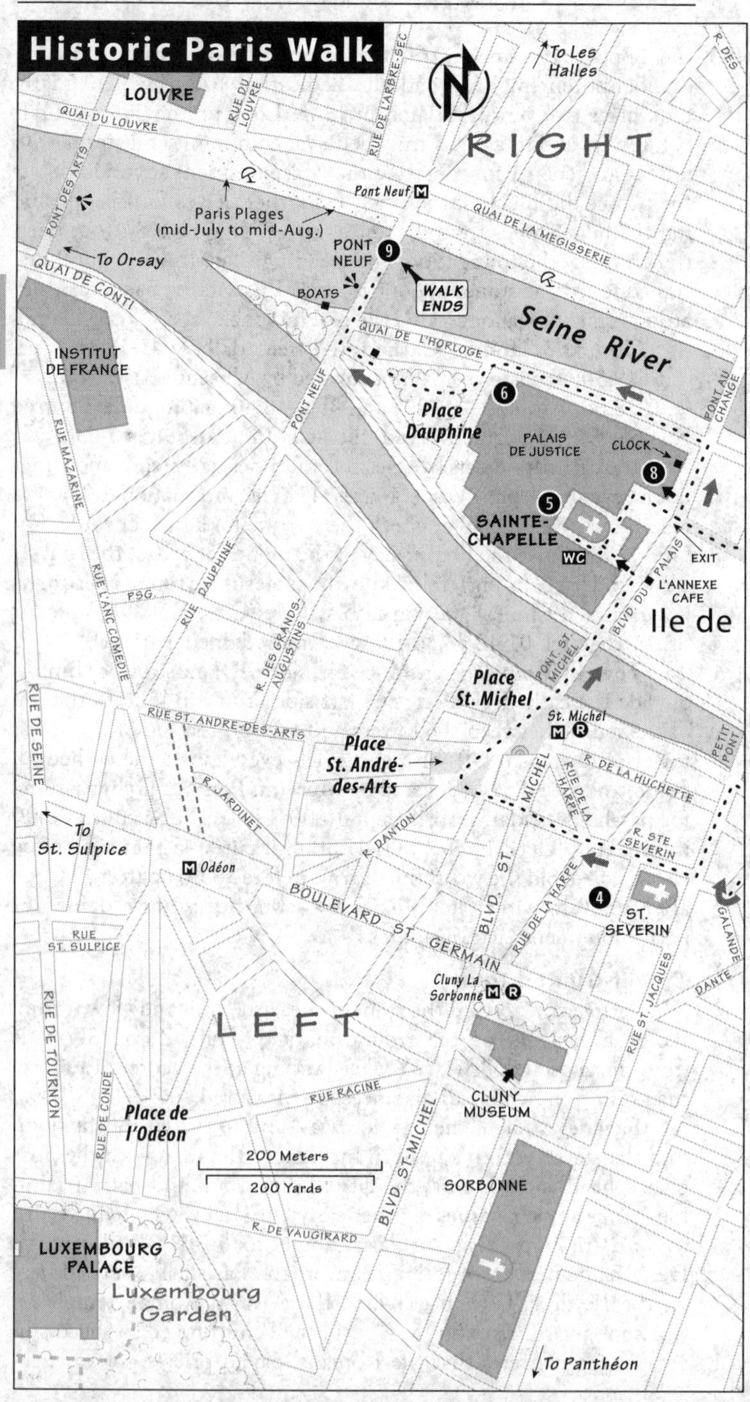

Historic Paris Walk
LOUVRE
QUAI DU LOUVRE
RUE DU LOUVRE
RUE DE L'ARBRE-SEC
To Les Halles
RIGHT
PONT DES ARTS
Paris Plages
(mid-July to mid-Aug.)
Pont Neuf
QUAI DE LA MEGISSERIE
To Orsay
QUAI DE CONTI
PONT NEUF
9
WALK ENDS
BOATS
Seine River
INSTITUT DE FRANCE
QUAI DE L'HORLOGE
PONT NEUF
6
Place Dauphine
PALAIS DE JUSTICE
CLOCK
8
PONT AU CHANGE
5
SAINTE-CHAPELLE
WC
EXIT
L'ANNEXE CAFE
BLVD. DU PALAIS
Ile de
RUE MAZARINE
RUE DAUPHINE
PSG.
RUE L'ANC COMEDIE
R. DES GRANDS-AUGUSTINS
PONT ST. MICHEL
Place St. Michel
St. Michel
RUE DE SEINE
RUE ST. ANDRE-DES-ARTS
Place St. André-des-Arts
R. DE LA HUCHETTE
PETIT PONT
R. JARDINET
MICHEL
RUE DE LA HARPE
To St. Sulpice
R. DANTON
R. STE. SEVERIN
Odéon
BOULEVARD ST. GERMAIN
BLVD. ST.
RUE DE LA HARPE
4
ST. SEVERIN
GALANDE
RUE ST. SULPICE
Cluny La Sorbonne
RUE ST. JACQUES
DANTE
LEFT
RUE DE TOURNON
RUE DE CONDE
RUE RACINE
Place de l'Odéon
CLUNY MUSEUM
200 Meters
200 Yards
BLVD. ST-MICHEL
SORBONNE
R. DE VAUGIRARD
LUXEMBOURG PALACE
Luxembourg Garden
To Panthéon

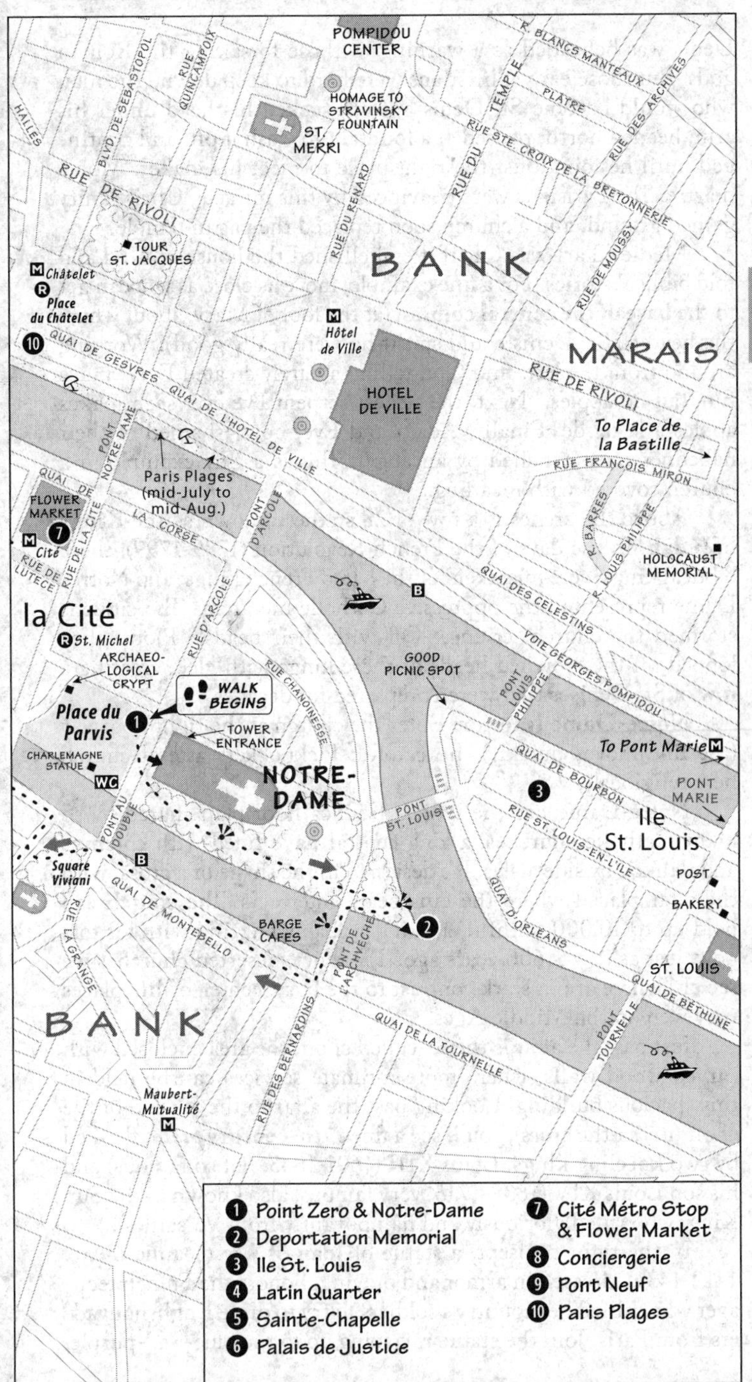
POMPIDOU CENTER
HOMAGE TO STRAVINSKY FOUNTAIN
ST. MERRI
R. BLANCS MANTEAUX
PLATRE
RUE DES ARCHIVES
RUE STE. CROIX DE LA BRETONNERIE
RUE DU TEMPLE
RUE DU RENARD
RUE QUINCAMPOIX
BLVD. DE SEBASTOPOL
HALLES
RUE DE RIVOLI
TOUR ST. JACQUES
Châtelet
Place du Châtelet
BANK
RUE DE MOUSSY
Hôtel de Ville
MARAIS
HOTEL DE VILLE
RUE DE RIVOLI
QUAI DE GESVRES
QUAI DE L'HOTEL DE VILLE
To Place de la Bastille
RUE FRANCOIS MIRON
PONT NOTRE DAME
Paris Plages (mid-July to mid-Aug.)
QUAI DE LA CORSE
FLOWER MARKET
Cité
RUE DE LUTECE
RUE DE LA CITE
PONT D'ARCOLE
R. BARRES
R. LOUIS PHILIPPE
HOLOCAUST MEMORIAL
QUAI DES CELESTINS
RUE D'ARCOLE
la Cité
St. Michel
ARCHAEO-LOGICAL CRYPT
RUE CHANOINESSE
GOOD PICNIC SPOT
VOIE GEORGES POMPIDOU
PONT LOUIS PHILIPPE
WALK BEGINS
Place du Parvis
TOWER ENTRANCE
CHARLEMAGNE STATUE
WC
NOTRE-DAME
To Pont Marie
QUAI DE BOURBON
PONT MARIE
PONT AU DOUBLE
PONT ST. LOUIS
Ile St. Louis
RUE ST. LOUIS-EN-L'ILE
Square Viviani
QUAI DE MONTEBELLO
BARGE CAFES
PONT DE L'ARCHEVECHE
QUAI D'ORLEANS
POST
BAKERY
RUE LA GRANGE
ST. LOUIS
QUAI DE BETHUNE
BANK
RUE DES BERNARDINS
QUAI DE LA TOURNELLE
PONT TOURNELLE
Maubert-Mutualité
1 Point Zero & Notre-Dame
2 Deportation Memorial
3 Ile St. Louis
4 Latin Quarter
5 Sainte-Chapelle
6 Palais de Justice
7 Cité Métro Stop & Flower Market
8 Conciergerie
9 Pont Neuf
10 Paris Plages

Denis was beheaded as a warning to those forsaking the Roman gods. But those early Christians were hard to keep down. The man who would become St. Denis got up, tucked his head under his arm, headed north, paused at a fountain to wash it off, and continued until he found just the right place to meet his maker: Montmartre. The Parisians were convinced by this miracle, Christianity gained ground, and a church soon replaced the pagan temple.

Medieval art was OK if it embellished the house of God and told biblical stories. For a fine example, move as close as you can get to the **base of the central column** (at the foot of Mary, about where the head of St. Denis could spit if he were really good). Working around from the left, find God telling a barely created Eve, "Have fun, but no apples." Next, the sexiest serpent I've ever seen makes apples à la mode. Finally, Adam and Eve, now ashamed of their nakedness, are expelled by an angel. This is a tiny example in a church covered with meaning.

Above the arches is a row of 28 statues, known as the **Kings of Judah.** In the days of the French Revolution (1789-1799), these biblical kings were mistaken for the hated French kings, and Notre-Dame represented the oppressive Catholic hierarchy. The citizens stormed the church, crying, "Off with their heads!" Plop—they lopped off the crowned heads of these kings with glee, creating a row of St. Denises that weren't repaired for decades.

Notre-Dame Interior: Enter the church at the right doorway (the line moves quickly). Be careful: Pickpockets attend church here religiously.

Notre-Dame has the typical basilica floor plan shared by so many Catholic churches: a long central **nave** lined with columns and flanked by side aisles. It's designed in the shape of a cross, with the altar placed where the crossbeam intersects. The church can hold up to 10,000 faithful, and it's probably buzzing with visitors now, just as it was 600 years ago. The quiet, deserted churches we see elsewhere are in stark contrast to the busy, center-of-life places they were in the Middle Ages.

Just past the altar is the so-called choir, the area enclosed with carved-wood walls, where more intimate services can be held in this spacious building. Looking past the altar to the far end of the choir (under the cross), you'll see a fine **17th-century *pietà*,** flanked by two kneeling kings: Louis XIII (1601-1643, not so famous) and his son Louis XIV (1638-1715, very famous, also known as the Sun King, who ruled gloriously and flamboyantly from Versailles).

In the right transept, a statue of **Joan of Arc** (Jeanne d'Arc, 1412-1431), dressed in armor and praying, honors the French teenager who rallied her country's soldiers to try to drive English invaders from Paris. Join the statue in gazing up to the blue-and-purple,

rose-shaped window in the opposite transept—with teeny green Mary and baby Jesus in the center—the only one of the three rose windows still with its original medieval glass.

The back side of the choir walls feature **scenes of the resurrected Jesus** (c. 1350) appearing to his followers, starting with Mary Magdalene. Their starry robes still gleam, thanks to a 19th-century renovation. The niches below these carvings mark the tombs of centuries of archbishops. Just ahead on the right is the **Treasury.** It contains lavish robes, golden reliquaries, and the humble tunic of King (and St.) Louis IX, but it probably isn't worth the entry fee.

Notre-Dame Side View: Back outside, alongside the church you'll notice the **flying buttresses.** These 50-foot stone "beams" that stick out of the church were the key to the complex Gothic architecture. The pointed arches we saw inside cause the weight of the roof to push outward rather than downward. The "flying" buttresses support the roof by pushing back inward.

Picture Quasimodo (the fictional hunchback) limping around along the railed balcony at the base of the roof among the **"gargoyles."** These grotesque beasts sticking out from pillars and buttresses represent souls caught between heaven and earth. They also function as rainspouts (from the same French root word as "gargle") when there are no evil spirits to battle.

The Neo-Gothic 300-foot **spire** is a product of the 1860 reconstruction of the dilapidated old church. Victor Hugo's book *The Hunchback of Notre-Dame* (1831) inspired a young architecture student named Eugène-Emmanuel Viollet-le-Duc to dedicate his career to a major renovation in Gothic style. Find Viollet-le-Duc at the base of the spire among the green apostles and evangelists (visible as you approach the back end of the church). The apostles look outward, blessing the city, while the architect (at top) looks up the spire, marveling at his fine work.

Nearby: The **Paris Archaeological Crypt** is an intriguing 20-minute stop. View Roman ruins from Emperor Augustus' reign (when this island became ground zero in Paris), trace the street plan of the medieval village, and see diagrams of how early Paris grew. It's all thoughtfully explained in English (pick up the floor plan with some background info) and well-presented with videos and touchscreens (€4, covered by Museum Pass, Tue-Sun 10:00-18:00, closed Mon, last entry 30 minutes before closing, enter 100 yards in front of cathedral, tel. 01 55 42 50 10).

• *Behind Notre-Dame, cross the street and enter through the iron gate into the park at the tip of the island. Look for the stairs and head down to reach the...*

Affording Paris' Sights

Paris is an expensive city for tourists, with lots of pricey sights, but—fortunately—lots of freebies, too. Smart, budget-minded travelers begin by buying and getting the most out of a **Paris Museum Pass** (see page 49), then considering these frugal sightseeing options.

Free (or Almost Free) Museums: Many of Paris' famous museums offer free entry on the first Sunday of the month, including the Orsay, Rodin, Cluny, Pompidou Center, Quai Branly, and Delacroix museums, and the Picasso Museum. These sights are free on the first Sunday of off-season months: the Louvre and Arc de Triomphe (both Oct-March) and Versailles (Nov-March). Expect big crowds on free days. Some museums are always free (with the possible exception of special exhibits), including the Carnavalet, Petit Palais, Victor Hugo's House, and Fragonard Perfume Museum. You can usually visit the Orsay Museum for free right when the ticket booth stops selling tickets (Tue-Wed and Fri-Sun at 17:00, Thu at 21:00; they won't let you in much after that). For just €2, the Rodin Museum garden lets you enjoy many of Rodin's finest works in a lovely outdoor setting.

Other Freebies: Many sights don't charge entry, including the Notre-Dame Cathedral, Père Lachaise Cemetery, Deportation Memorial, Holocaust Memorial, Paris *Plages* (summers only), Sacré-Cœur Basilica, St. Sulpice Church (with organ recital), and La Défense mall. Stroll the Left Bank riverside promenade from the Orsay to Pont de l'Alma.

Paris' glorious, entertaining parks are free, *bien sûr.* These

▲Deportation Memorial (Mémorial de la Déportation)

This memorial to the 200,000 French victims of the Nazi concentration camps (1940-1945) draws you into their experience. France was quickly overrun by Nazi Germany, and Paris spent the war years under Nazi occupation. Jews and dissidents were rounded up and deported—many never returned.

Cost and Hours: Free, April-Sept Tue-Sun 10:00-12:30 & 13:30-18:45, Oct-March Tue-Sun 10:00-12:00 & 13:30-17:00 (lunch closure times can vary), closed Mon year-round, may randomly close at other times; at the east tip of the island named Ile de la Cité, behind Notre-Dame and near Ile St. Louis (Mo: Cité); mobile 06 14 67 54 98.

Visiting the Memorial: As you descend the steps, the city around you disappears. Surrounded by walls, you have become a prisoner. Your only freedom is your view of the sky and the tiny glimpse of the river below. Enter the dark, single-file chamber up ahead. Inside, the circular plaque in the floor reads, "They went to the end of the earth and did not return."

include Luxembourg Garden, Champ de Mars (under the Eiffel Tower), Tuileries Garden (between the Louvre and Place de la Concorde), Palais Royal Courtyards, Jardin des Plantes, Parc Monceau, the Promenade Plantée walk, and Versailles' gardens (except when the fountains perform on weekends April-Oct and many Tue).

Reduced Prices: Several sights offer a discount if you enter later in the day, including the Orsay (Tue-Wed and Fri-Sun after 16:30 and Thu after 18:15), the Orangerie (after 17:00), and the Army Museum and Napoleon's Tomb (after 16:00). The Eiffel Tower costs less if you're willing to restrict your visit to the two lower levels—and even less if you're willing to use the stairs.

Free Concerts: Venues offering free or cheap (€6-8) concerts include the American Church, Hôtel des Invalides, St. Sulpice Church, La Madeleine Church, and Notre-Dame Cathedral. For a listing of free concerts, check *Pariscope* magazine (under the "Musique" section) and look for events marked *entrée libre.*

Good-Value Tours: At €15, Paris Walks' tours are a good value. The €12-15 Seine River cruises, best after dark, are also worthwhile. The scenic bus route #69, which costs only the price of a transit ticket, could be the best deal of all.

Pricey...but worth it? Certain big-ticket items—primarily the top of the Eiffel Tower, the Louvre, and Versailles—are expensive and crowded, but offer once-in-a-lifetime experiences. All together they amount to less than the cost of a ticket to Disneyland—only these are real.

The hallway stretching in front of you is lined with 200,000 lighted crystals, one for each French citizen who died. Flickering at the far end is the eternal flame of hope. The tomb of the unknown deportee lies at your feet. Above, the inscription reads, "Dedicated to the living memory of the 200,000 French deportees shrouded by the night and the fog, exterminated in the Nazi concentration camps." The side rooms are filled with triangles—reminiscent of the identification patches inmates were forced to wear—each bearing the name of a concentration camp. Above the exit as you leave is the message you'll find at many other Holocaust sites: "Forgive, but never forget."

• *Back on street level, look across the river (north) to the island called...*

Ile St. Louis

If Ile de la Cité is a tugboat laden with the history of Paris, it's towing this classy little residential dinghy, laden only with high-rent apartments, boutiques, characteristic restaurants, and famous ice-cream shops.

Ile St. Louis wasn't developed until much later than Ile de la Cité (17th century). What was a swampy mess is now harmonious Parisian architecture and one of Paris' most exclusive neighborhoods. If you won't have time to return here for an evening stroll (see page 131), consider taking a brief detour across the pedestrian bridge, Pont St. Louis. It connects the two islands, leading right to Rue St. Louis-en-l'Ile. This spine of the island is lined with appealing shops, reasonably priced restaurants, and a handy grocery. A short stroll takes you to the famous Berthillon ice-cream parlor at #31, which is still family-owned. The ice cream is famous not just because it's good, but because it's made right here on the island. Gelato lovers can comparison-shop by also sampling the (mass-produced-but-who's-complaining) Amorino Gelati at 47 Rue St. Louis-en-l'Ile. This walk is about as peaceful and romantic as Paris gets. When you're finished exploring, loop back to the pedestrian bridge along the park-like quays (walk north to the river and turn left).

• *From the Deportation Memorial, cross the bridge to the Left Bank. All those **padlocks** adorning the railing are akin to lighting candles in a church. Locals and tourists alike honor loved ones by writing a brief message on the lock and attaching it to the railing. You can buy a lock (called* cadenas, *€5) at a nearby bookseller's stall along the river.*

*Turn right after crossing the bridge and walk along the river, toward the front end of Notre-Dame. Stairs detour down to the riverbank if you need a place to picnic. This side view of the church from across the river is one of Europe's great sights and is best from river level. At times, you may find **barges** housing restaurants with great cathedral views docked here.*

*After passing the Pont au Double (the bridge leading to the facade of Notre-Dame), cross the street on your left and find **Shakespeare and Company,** an atmospheric reincarnation of the original 1920s bookshop and a good spot to page through books (37 Rue de la Bûcherie; see page 28). Before returning to the island, walk a block behind Shakespeare and Company, and take a spin through the...*

▲The Latin Quarter

This area's touristy fame relates to its intriguing, artsy, bohemian character. This was perhaps Europe's leading university district in the Middle Ages, when Latin was the language of higher education. The neighborhood's main boulevards (St. Michel and St. Germain) are lined with cafés—once the haunts of great poets and philosophers, now the hangouts of tired tourists. Though still youthful and artsy, much of this area has become a tourist ghetto filled with cheap North African eateries. Exploring a few blocks up or downriver from here gives you a better chance of feeling the pulse of what survives of Paris' classic Left Bank. For colorful wandering and café-sitting, afternoons and evenings are best.

Walking along Rue St. Séverin, you can still see the shadow of the medieval sewer system. The street slopes into a central channel of bricks. In the days before plumbing and toilets, when people still went to the river or neighborhood wells for their water, flushing meant throwing it out the window. At certain times of day, maids on the fourth floor would holler, *"Garde de l'eau!"* ("Watch out for the water!") and heave it into the streets, where it would eventually wash down into the Seine.

Consider a visit to the **Cluny Museum** for its medieval art and unicorn tapestries (see page 93). The **Sorbonne**—the University of Paris' humanities department—is also nearby; visitors can ogle at the famous dome, but they are not allowed to enter the building (two blocks south of the river on Boulevard St. Michel).

Don't miss **Place St. Michel.** This square (facing Pont St. Michel) is the traditional core of the Left Bank's artsy, liberal, hippie, bohemian district of poets, philosophers, and winos. In less commercial times, Place St. Michel was a gathering point for the city's malcontents and misfits. In 1830, 1848, and again in 1871, the citizens took the streets from the government troops, set up barricades *Les Miz*-style, and fought against royalist oppression. During World War II, the locals rose up against their Nazi oppressors (read the plaques under the dragons at the foot of the St. Michel fountain). Even today, whenever there's a student demonstration, it starts here.

• *From Place St. Michel, look across the river and find the prickly steeple of the Sainte-Chapelle church. Head toward it. Cross the river on Pont St. Michel and continue north along the Boulevard du Palais. On your left, you'll see the doorway to Sainte-Chapelle (usually with a line of people).*

Security is strict at the Sainte-Chapelle complex because this is more than a tourist attraction: France's Supreme Court meets to the right of Sainte-Chapelle in the Palais de Justice. Expect a long wait unless you arrive before it opens. First comes the security line (all sharp objects and glass are confiscated). No one can skip this line. Security lines are shortest first thing in the mornings and on weekends (when the courts are closed), and longest around 13:00-14:00 (when staff takes lunch). Once past security, you'll enter the courtyard outside Sainte-Chapelle, where you'll find WCs, information about upcoming church concerts (for details, see page 128), and the ticket-buying line—those with combo-tickets or Museum Passes can skip this lineup. (L'Annexe Café, across the street from the main entry, sells cheap coffee to go—perfect for sipping while you wait in the security line.)

▲▲▲Sainte-Chapelle

This triumph of Gothic church architecture is a cathedral of glass like no other. It was speedily built between 1242 and 1248 for King Louis IX—the only French king who is now a saint—to house the supposed Crown of Thorns. Its architectural harmony is due to the fact that it was completed under the direction of one architect and in only six years—unheard of in Gothic times. In contrast, Notre-Dame took over 200 years.

Cost and Hours: €8.50, €12.50 combo-ticket with Conciergerie, free for those under age 18, covered by Museum Pass; daily March-Oct 9:30-18:00, Wed until 21:30 mid-May-mid-Sept, Nov-Feb 9:00-17:00; last entry 30 minutes before closing, audioguide-€4.50 (€6 for two), 4 Boulevard du Palais, Mo: Cité, tel. 01 53 40 60 80, http://sainte-chapelle.monuments-nationaux.fr.

Visiting the Church: Though the inside is beautiful, the exterior is basically functional. The muscular buttresses hold up the stone roof, so the walls are essentially there to display stained glass. The lacy spire is Neo-Gothic—added in the 19th century. Inside, the layout clearly shows an *ancien régime* approach to worship. The low-ceilinged basement was for staff and other common folks—worshipping under a sky filled with painted fleurs-de-lis, a symbol of the king. Royal Christians worshipped upstairs. The paint job, a 19th-century restoration, helps you imagine how grand this small, painted, jeweled chapel was. (Imagine Notre-Dame painted like this...) Each capital is playfully carved with a different plant's leaves.

Climb the spiral staircase to the Chapelle Haute. Fill the place with choral music, crank up the sunshine, face the top of the altar, and really believe that the Crown of Thorns is there, and this becomes one awesome space.

Fiat lux. "Let there be light." From the first page of the Bible, it's clear: Light is divine. Light shines through stained glass like God's grace shining down to earth. Gothic architects used their new technology to turn dark stone buildings into lanterns of light. The glory of Gothic shines brighter here than in any other church.

There are 15 separate panels of **stained glass** (6,500 square feet—two thirds of it 13th-century original), with more than 1,100 different scenes, mostly from the Bible. These cover the entire Christian history of

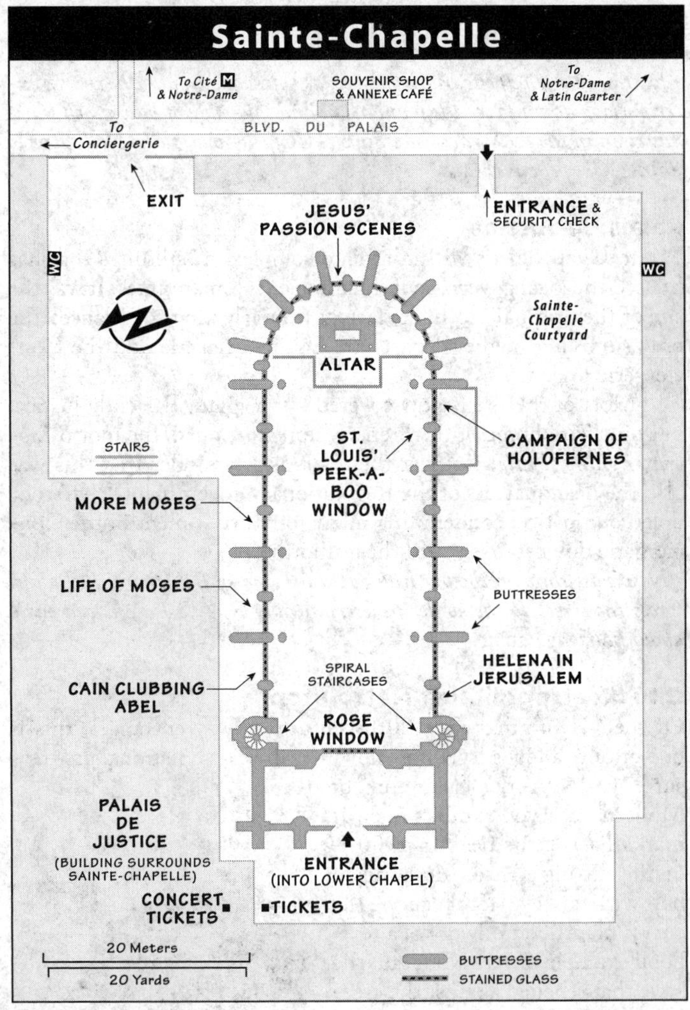

the world, from the Creation in Genesis (first window on the left, as you face the altar), to the coming of Christ (over the altar), to the end of the world (the round "rose"-shaped window at the rear of the church). Each individual scene is interesting, and the whole effect is overwhelming. If you can't read much into the individual windows, you're not alone. (For some tutoring, a little book with color photos is on sale downstairs with the postcards.)

The **altar** was raised up high to better display the Crown of Thorns, the relic around which this chapel was built. The supposed crown cost King Louis more than three times as much as this church. Today, it is kept by the Notre-Dame Treasury (though it's occasionally brought out for display).

• *Exit Sainte-Chapelle. Back outside, as you walk around the church exterior, look down to see the foundation and take note of how much Paris has risen in the 750 years since Sainte-Chapelle was built. Next door to Sainte-Chapelle is the...*

Palais de Justice

Sainte-Chapelle sits within a huge complex of buildings that has housed the local government since ancient Roman times. It was the site of the original Gothic palace of the early kings of France. The only surviving medieval parts are Sainte-Chapelle and the Conciergerie prison.

Most of the site is now covered by the giant Palais de Justice, built in 1776, home of the French Supreme Court. The motto *Liberté, Egalité, Fraternité* over the doors is a reminder that this was also the headquarters of the Revolutionary government. Here they doled out justice, condemning many to imprisonment in the Conciergerie downstairs—or to the guillotine.

• *Now pass through the big iron gate to the noisy Boulevard du Palais. Cross the street to the wide, pedestrian-only Rue de Lutèce and walk about halfway down.*

Cité "Metropolitain" Métro Stop

Of the 141 original early-20th-century subway entrances, this is one of only a few survivors—now preserved as a national art treasure. (New York's Museum of Modern Art even exhibits one.) It marks Paris at its peak in 1900—on the cutting edge of Modernism, but with an eye for beauty. The curvy, plantlike ironwork is a textbook example of Art Nouveau, the style that rebelled against the erector-set squareness of the Industrial Age. Other similar Métro stations in Paris are Abbesses and Porte Dauphine.

The flower and plant market on Place Louis Lépine is a pleasant detour. On Sundays this square flutters with a busy bird market.

• *Pause here to admire the view. Sainte-Chapelle is a pearl in an ugly architectural oyster. Double back to the Palais de Justice, turn right onto Boulevard du Palais, and enter the Conciergerie. It's free with the Museum Pass; passholders can sidestep the bottleneck created by the ticket-buying line.*

▲Conciergerie

Though pretty barren inside, this former prison echoes with history. Positioned next to the courthouse, the Conciergerie was the gloomy prison famous as the last stop for 2,780 victims of the guillotine, including France's last *ancien régime* queen, Marie-Antoinette. Before then, kings had used the building to torture and execute failed assassins. (One of its towers along the river was called "The Babbler," named for the pain-induced sounds that leaked from it.) When the Revolution (1789) toppled the king, the building kept its same function, but without torture. The progressive Revolutionaries proudly unveiled a modern and more humane way to execute people—the guillotine. The Conciergerie was the epicenter of the Reign of Terror—the year-long period of the Revolution (1793-94) during which Revolutionary fervor spiraled out of control and thousands were killed. It was here at the Conciergerie that "enemies of the Revolution" were imprisoned, tried, sentenced, and marched off to Place de la Concorde for decapitation.

Cost and Hours: €8.50, €12.50 combo-ticket with Sainte-Chapelle, covered by Museum Pass, daily 9:30-18:00, last entry 30 minutes before closing, 2 Boulevard du Palais, Mo: Cité, tel. 01 53 40 60 80, http://conciergerie.monuments-nationaux.fr.

Visiting the Conciergerie: Pick up a free map and breeze through the one-way circuit. It's well-described in English. See the spacious, low-ceilinged Hall of Men-at-Arms (Room 1), originally a guards' dining room, with four large fireplaces (look up the chimneys). During the Reign of Terror, this large hall served as a holding tank for the poorest prisoners. Then they were taken upstairs (in an area not open to visitors), where the Revolutionary tribunals grilled scared prisoners on their political correctness. Continue to the raised area at the far end of the room (Room 4, today's bookstore). In Revolutionary days, this was notorious as the walkway of the executioner, who was known affectionately as "Monsieur de Paris."

Upstairs is a memorial room with the names of the 2,780 citizens condemned to death by the guillotine, including ex-King Louis XVI, Charlotte Corday (who murdered the Revolutionary writer Jean-Paul Marat in his bathtub), and—oh, the irony—Maximilien de Robespierre, the head of the Revolution, the man who sent so many to the guillotine.

Just past the courtyard is a re-creation of Marie-Antoinette's cell. On August 12, 1793, the queen was brought here to be tried for her supposed crimes against the people. Imagine the queen spending her last days—separated from her 10-year-old son and now widowed because the king had already been executed. Mannequins, period furniture, and the real cell wallpaper set the scene. The guard stands modestly behind a screen, while the queen psyches herself up with a crucifix. In the glass display case, see her actual crucifix, rug, and small water pitcher. On October 16, 1793, the queen was awakened at 4:00 in the morning and led away. She walked the corridor, stepped onto the cart, and was slowly carried to Place de la Concorde, where she had a date with "Monsieur de Paris."

• *Back outside, turn left on Boulevard du Palais. On the corner is the city's oldest public clock. The mechanism of the present clock is from 1334, and even though the case is Baroque, it keeps on ticking.*

Turn left onto Quai de l'Horloge and walk along the river, past "The Babbler" tower. The bridge up ahead is the Pont Neuf, where we'll end this walk. At the first corner, veer left into a sleepy triangular square called Place Dauphine. It's amazing to find such coziness in the heart of Paris. From the equestrian statue of Henry IV, turn right onto Pont Neuf. Pause at the little nook halfway across.

Pont Neuf and the Seine

This "new bridge" is now Paris' oldest. Built during Henry IV's reign (about 1600), its arches span the widest part of the river. Unlike other bridges, this one never had houses or buildings growing on it. The turrets were originally for vendors and street entertainers. In the days of Henry IV, who promised his peasants "a chicken in every pot every Sunday," this would have been a lively scene. From the bridge, look downstream (west) to see the next bridge, the pedestrian-only Pont des Arts. Ahead on the Right Bank is the long Louvre museum. Beyond that, on the Left Bank, is the Orsay. And what's that tall black tower in the distance?

• *Our walk is finished. From here, you can tour the Seine by boat (the departure point for Seine River cruises offered by Vedettes du Pont Neuf is through the park at the end of the island—see page 42), continue to the Louvre, or (if it's summer) head to the...*

▲Paris *Plages* (Paris Beaches)

The Riviera it's not, but this string of fanciful faux beaches—assembled in summer along a one-mile stretch of the Right Bank of the Seine—is a fun place to stroll, play, and people-watch on a sunny day. Each summer, the Paris city government closes the embankment's highway and trucks in potted palm trees, hammocks, lounge chairs, and 2,000 tons of sand to create colorful urban beaches. You'll also find "beach cafés," climbing walls, prefab pools, trampolines, *boules*, a library, beach volleyball, badminton, and Frisbee areas in three zones: sandy, grassy, and wood-tiled.

(Other less-central areas of town, such as Bassin de la Vilette, have their own *plages*.)

Cost and Hours: Free, mid-July-mid-Aug daily 8:00-24:00, no beach off-season; on Right Bank of Seine, just north of Ile de la Cité, between Pont des Arts and Pont de Sully; for information, go to www.paris.fr, click on "English," then "Visit," then "Highlights."

Sights in Paris

MAJOR MUSEUMS NEIGHBORHOOD

Paris' grandest park, the Tuileries Garden, was once the private property of kings and queens. Today it links the Louvre, Orangerie, and Orsay museums. And across from the Louvre are the tranquil, historic courtyards of the Palais Royal.

▲▲▲Louvre (Musée du Louvre)

This is Europe's oldest, biggest, greatest, and second-most-crowded museum (after the Vatican). Housed in a U-shaped, 16th-century palace (accentuated by a 20th-century glass pyramid), the Louvre is Paris' top museum and one of its key landmarks. It's home to *Mona Lisa, Venus de Milo,* and hall after hall of Greek and Roman masterpieces, medieval jewels, Michelangelo statues, and paintings by the greatest artists from the Renaissance to the Romantics (mid-1800s).

Touring the Louvre can be overwhelming, so be selective. Focus on the Denon wing (south, along the river), with Greek sculptures, Italian paintings (by Raphael and da Vinci), and—of course—French paintings (Neoclassical and Romantic), and the adjoining Sully wing, with Egyptian artifacts and more French paintings. For extra credit, tackle the Richelieu wing (north, away from the river), displaying works from ancient Mesopotamia (today's Iraq), as well as French, Dutch, and Northern art.

Expect Changes: The sprawling Louvre is constantly shuffling its deck. Rooms close, and pieces can be on loan or in restoration. For 2015, a renovation of the pyramid entry may temporarily affect locations of the bag check, guided tour meeting point, and even the entrance itself. Be flexible. If you don't find the artwork you're looking for, ask the nearest guard for its new location.

Cost and Hours: €12, free on first Sun of month Oct-March, covered by Museum Pass, tickets good all day, reentry allowed; Wed-Mon 9:00-18:00, Wed and Fri until 21:45 (except on holi-

Paris at a Glance

▲▲▲Notre-Dame Cathedral Paris' most beloved church, with towers and gargoyles. **Hours:** Cathedral—daily 7:45-18:45, Sun until 19:30; Tower—daily April-Sept 10:00-18:30, Fri-Sat until 23:00 in July-Aug, Oct-March 10:00-17:30. See page 52.

▲▲▲Sainte-Chapelle Gothic cathedral with peerless stained glass. **Hours:** Daily March-Oct 9:30-18:00, Wed until 21:30 mid-May-mid-Sept, Nov-Feb 9:00-17:00. See page 62.

▲▲▲Louvre Europe's oldest and greatest museum, starring *Mona Lisa* and *Venus de Milo*. **Hours:** Wed-Mon 9:00-18:00, Wed and Fri until 21:45, closed Tue. See page 67.

▲▲▲Orsay Museum Europe's greatest Impressionist collection. **Hours:** Tue-Sun 9:30-18:00, Thu until 21:45, closed Mon. See page 76.

▲▲▲Eiffel Tower Paris' soaring exclamation point. **Hours:** Daily mid-June-Aug 9:00-24:45, Sept-mid-June 9:30-23:45. See page 83.

▲▲▲Champs-Elysées Paris' grand boulevard. **Hours:** Always open. See page 99.

▲▲▲Versailles The ultimate royal palace with a Hall of Mirrors, vast gardens, a grand canal, plus a queen's playground. **Hours:** Château April-Oct Tue-Sun 9:00-18:30, Nov-March until 17:30, closed Mon year-round. Trianon/Domaine April-Oct Tue-Sun 12:00-18:30, Nov-March until 17:30, closed Mon year-round. Gardens generally open April-Oct daily 9:00-20:30, Nov-March Tue-Sun 8:00-18:00, closed Mon. See page 195.

▲▲Orangerie Museum Monet's water lilies, plus works by Utrillo, Cézanne, Renoir, Matisse, and Picasso, in a lovely setting. **Hours:** Wed-Mon 9:00-18:00, closed Tue. See page 82.

▲▲Rue Cler Ultimate Parisian market street. **Hours:** Stores open Tue-Sat 8:30-13:00 & 15:00-19:30, Sun 8:30-12:00, dead on Mon. See page 90.

▲▲Army Museum and Napoleon's Tomb The emperor's imposing tomb, flanked by museums of France's wars. **Hours:** Daily 10:00-18:00, July-Aug until 19:00, Nov-March until 17:00; tomb plus WWI and WWII wings open Tue until 21:00 April-Sept; museum (except for tomb) closed first Mon of month Oct-June; Charles de Gaulle exhibit closed Mon year-round. See page 90.

▲▲Rodin Museum Works by the greatest sculptor since Michelangelo, with many statues in a peaceful garden. **Hours:** Tue-Sun 10:00-17:45, Wed until 20:45, closed Mon. See page 91.

▲▲**Marmottan Museum** Untouristy art museum focusing on Monet. **Hours:** Tue-Sun 10:00-18:00, Thu until 20:00, closed Mon. See page 92.

▲▲**Cluny Museum** Medieval art with unicorn tapestries. **Hours:** Wed-Mon 9:15-17:45, closed Tue. See page 93.

▲▲**Arc de Triomphe** Triumphal arch with viewpoint, marking start of Champs-Elysées. **Hours:** Interior—daily April-Sept 10:00-23:00, Oct-March 10:00-22:30. See page 101.

▲▲**Jacquemart-André Museum** Art-strewn mansion. **Hours:** Daily 10:00-18:00, Mon and Sat until 20:30 during special exhibits. See page 107.

▲▲**Picasso Museum** World's largest collection of Picasso's works. **Hours:** Tue-Fri 11:30-18:00, Sat-Sun 9:30-18:00, until 21:00 third Fri of month, closed Mon. See page 111.

▲▲**Pompidou Center** Modern art in colorful building with city views. **Hours:** Wed-Mon 11:00-21:00, closed Tue. See page 114.

▲▲**Sacré-Cœur and Montmartre** White basilica atop Montmartre with spectacular views. **Hours:** Daily 6:00-22:30; dome climb daily May-Sept 9:00-19:00, Oct-April 9:00-17:00. See page 117.

▲**Panthéon** Neoclassical monument celebrating the struggles of the French. **Hours:** Daily 10:00-18:30 in summer, until 18:00 in winter. See page 96.

▲**La Défense and La Grande Arche** The city's own business district and its colossal modern arch. **Hours:** Always open. See page 104.

▲**Opéra Garnier** Grand belle époque theater with a modern ceiling by Chagall. **Hours:** Generally daily 10:00-16:30, mid-July-Aug until 18:00. See page 105.

▲**Carnavalet Museum** Paris' history wrapped up in a 16th-century mansion. **Hours:** Tue-Sun 10:00-18:00, closed Mon. See page 109.

▲**Jewish Art and History Museum** History of Judaism in Europe. **Hours:** Sun 10:00-18:00, Mon-Fri 11:00-18:00, Wed until 21:00 during special exhibits, closed Sat. See page 113.

▲**Père Lachaise Cemetery** Final home of Paris' illustrious dead. **Hours:** Mon-Fri 8:00-18:00, Sat 8:30-18:00, Sun 9:00-18:00, closes at 17:30 in winter. See page 116.

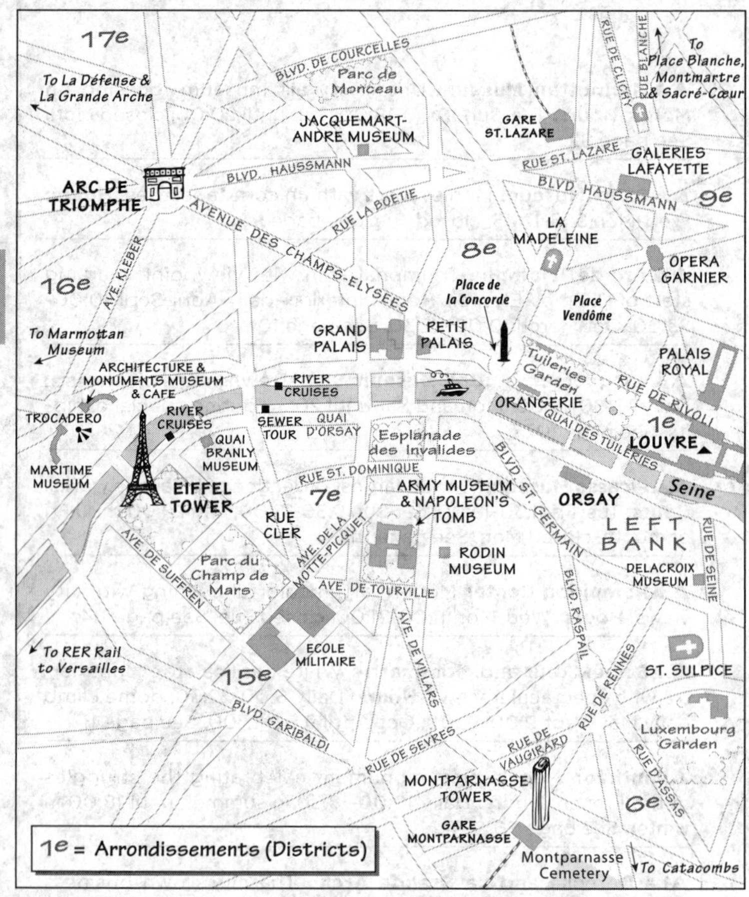

days), closed Tue, galleries start shutting 30 minutes before closing, last entry 45 minutes before closing; several cafés, tel. 01 40 20 53 17, recorded info tel. 01 40 20 51 51, www.louvre.fr.

When to Go: Crowds can be miserably bad on Sun, Mon (the worst day), Wed, and in the morning (arrive 30 minutes before opening to secure a good place in line). Evening visits are quieter, and the glass pyramid glows after dark.

Buying Tickets: Self-serve ticket machines located under the pyramid may be faster to use than the ticket windows (machines accept euro bills, coins, and chip-and-PIN Visa cards). A shop in the underground mall sells tickets to the Louvre, Orsay, and Versailles, plus Museum Passes, for no extra charge (cash only). To find it from the Carrousel du Louvre entrance off Rue de Rivoli (described under "Getting In," next page), turn right after the last escalator down onto Allée de France, and follow *Museum Pass* signs.

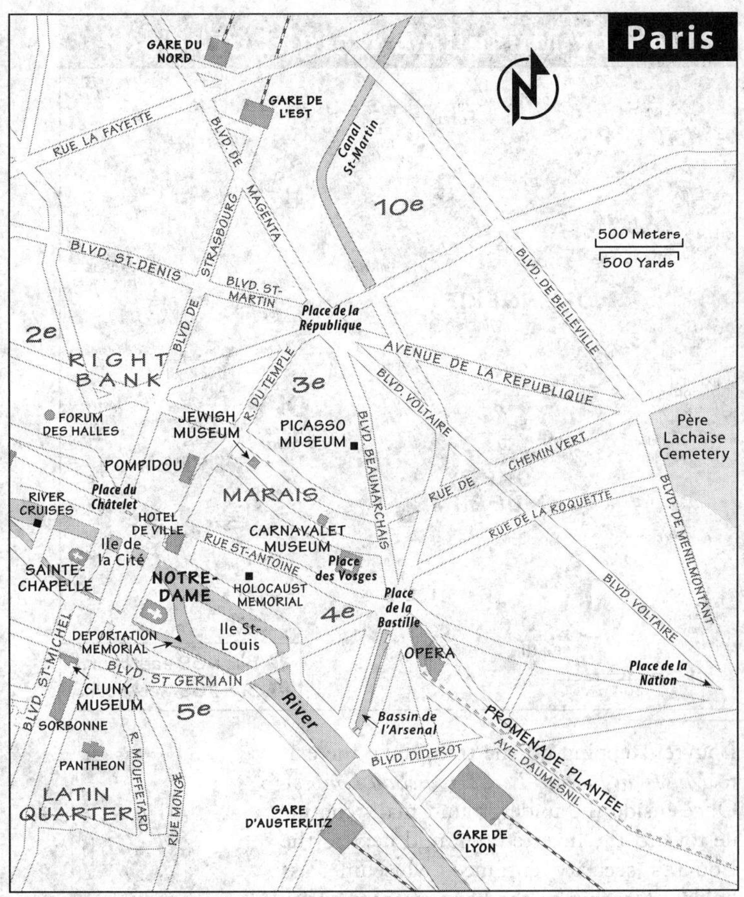

Getting There: It's at the Palais Royal-Musée du Louvre Métro stop. (The old Louvre Métro stop, called Louvre-Rivoli, is farther from the entrance.) Bus #69 also runs past the Louvre.

Getting In: There is no grander entry than through the main entrance at the **pyramid** in the central courtyard, but lines (for security reasons) can be long. Expect some changes during the pyramid's renovation in 2015. Museum Pass holders can use the **group entrance** in the pedestrian passageway (labeled *Pavilion Richelieu*) between the pyramid and Rue de Rivoli. It's under the arches, a few steps north of the pyramid; find the uniformed guard at the security checkpoint entrance, at the down escalator.

Anyone can enter the Louvre from its less crowded **underground entrance,** accessed through the Carrousel du Louvre shopping mall. Enter the mall at 99 Rue de Rivoli (the door with the red awning) or directly from the Métro stop Palais Royal-Musée du

Major Museums Neighborhood

1 Bus #69 eastbound
2 Bus #69 westbound

Louvre (stepping off the train, take the exit to *Musée du Louvre-Le Carrousel du Louvre*). Once inside the underground mall, continue toward the inverted pyramid next to the Louvre's security entrance. Museum Pass holders can skip to the head of the security line.

Tours: Ninety-minute English-language **guided tours** leave twice daily (except the first Sun of the month Oct-March) from the *Accueil des Groupes* area, under the pyramid (normally at 11:00 and 14:00, possibly more often in summer; €12 plus your entry ticket, tour tel. 01 40 20 52 63). **Videoguides** (€5) provide commentary on about 700 masterpieces. Or you can download a free Rick Steves **audio tour** version of the Louvre (see page 14).

Baggage Check: The free *bagagerie* is under the pyramid, behind the Richelieu wing escalator (look for the *visiteurs individuels* sign). Bigger bags must be checked (though they won't take very large bags), and you can also check small bags to lighten your load. The baggage-claim clerk might ask you in French, "Does your bag

Tue-Sun 9:30-18:00, Thu until 21:45, closed Mon, Impressionist galleries start shutting 45 minutes before closing, last entry one hour before closing (45 minutes before on Thu); cafés and a restaurant, tel. 01 40 49 48 14, www.musee-orsay.fr.

Avoiding Lines: The ticket-buying line can be long, but you can skip it with a Museum Pass or an advance ticket. Advance tickets can be purchased online and printed at home (for a small surcharge), or you can buy them in person at FNAC department stores and TIs (see www.musee-orsay.fr). You can also buy tickets and Museum Passes (no markup) at the newspaper kiosk just outside the Orsay (on the steps below the passholder entry—Entrance C), allowing you to skip the ticket-buying line at the museum itself. If you're planning to visit either the Orangerie or the Rodin (and you don't have a Museum Pass), consider starting at one of those museums instead (both of which have shorter lines than the Orsay) and buying an Orsay combo-ticket. You can also avoid lines and crowds by going on Thursday evening when the Orsay is open late.

Getting There: The museum, at 1 Rue de la Légion d'Honneur, sits above the RER-C stop called Musée d'Orsay; the nearest Métro stop is Solférino, three blocks southeast of the Orsay. Bus #69 also stops at the Orsay. From the Louvre, it's a lovely 15-minute walk through the Tuileries Garden and across the pedestrian bridge to the Orsay.

Getting In: As you face the entrance, passholders and ticket holders enter on the right (Entrance C). Ticket purchasers enter on the left (Entrance A). Security checks slow down all entrances.

Tours: Audioguides cost €5. English **guided tours** usually run daily at 11:30 (€6/1.5 hours, none on Sun, tours may also run at 14:30—inquire when you arrive). Or you can download this chapter as a free Rick Steves **audio tour** (see page 1110).

Background

The Impressionist painters rejected camera-like detail for a quick style more suited to capturing the passing moment. Feeling stifled by the rigid rules and stuffy atmosphere of the Academy (the state-funded art school), the Impressionists took as their motto, "Out of the studio, into the open air." They grabbed their berets and scarves and went on excursions to the country, where they set up their easels (and newly invented tubes of premixed paint) on riverbanks and hillsides, or they sketched in cafés and dance halls. Gods, goddesses, nymphs, and fantasy scenes were out; common people and rural landscapes were in.

The quick style and everyday subjects were ridiculed and called childish by the "experts." Rejected by the Salon (where works were exhibited to the buying public), the Impressionists staged their own exhibition in 1874. They brashly took their name from an insult

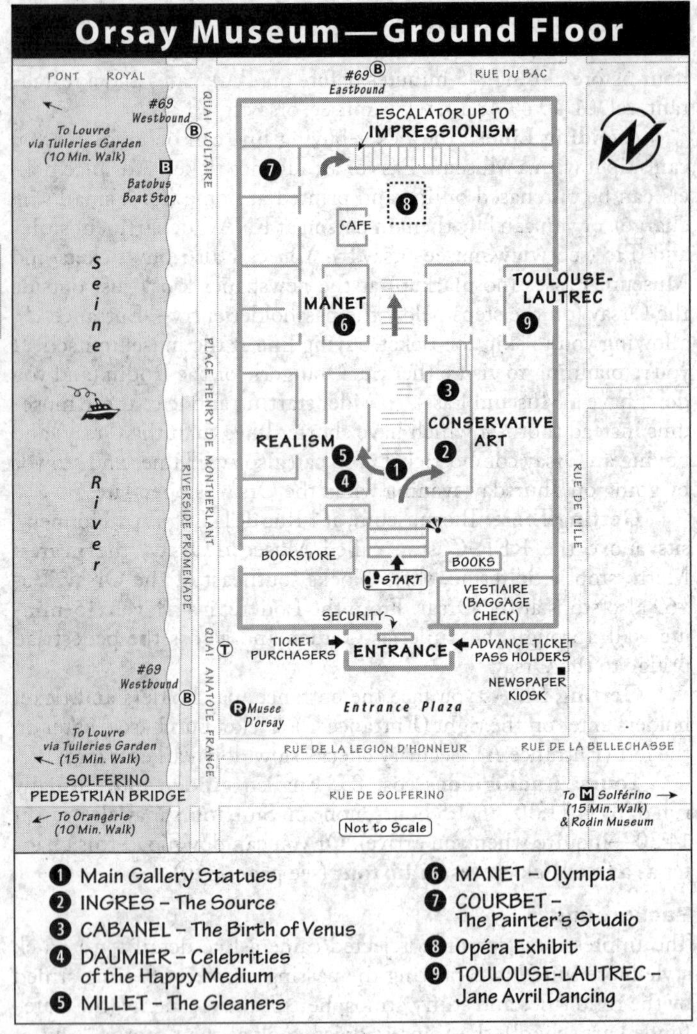

thrown at them by a critic who laughed at one of Monet's "impressions" of a sunrise. During the next decade, they exhibited their own work independently. The public, opposed at first, was slowly won over by the simplicity, the color, and the vibrancy of Impressionist art.

➲ Self-Guided Tour

This former train station, the Gare d'Orsay, barely escaped the wrecking ball in the 1970s, when the French realized it'd be a great place to house the enormous collections of 19th-century art scattered throughout the city.

The ground floor (level 0) houses early 19th-century art, mainly conservative art of the Academy and Salon, plus Realism. On the top floor (not visible from here) is the core of the collection—the Impressionist rooms. If you're pressed for time, go directly there. Remember that the museum rotates its large collection often, so find the latest arrangement on your current Orsay map, and be ready to go with the flow.

Conservative Art to Realism

In the Orsay's first few rooms, you're surrounded by visions of idealized beauty—nude women in languid poses, Greek mythological figures, and anatomically perfect statues. This was the art adored by French academics and the middle-class *(bourgeois)* public.

Alexandre Cabanel's *The Birth of Venus* (*La Naissance de Vénus,* 1863; Room 3) and **Edouard Manet**'s *Olympia* (1863; Room 14) offer two opposing visions of Venus. Cabanel's Venus is a perfect fantasy, an orgasm of beauty. Manet's nude is a Realist's take on the traditional Venus. Manet doesn't gloss over anything. The pose is classic, but the sharp outlines and harsh, contrasting colors are new and shocking. Manet replaced soft-core porn with hard-core art.

Jean-François Millet's *The Gleaners* (*Les Glaneuses,* 1867) shows us three gleaners, the poor women who pick up the meager leftovers after a field has already been harvested for the wealthy. Here he captures the innate dignity of these stocky, tanned women who bend their backs quietly in a large field for their small reward. This is "Realism" in two senses. It's painted "realistically," not prettified. And it's the "real" world—not the fantasy world of Greek myth, but the harsh life of the working poor.

Impressionism

The Impressionist collection is scattered randomly through Rooms 29-36, on the top floor. You'll see Monet hanging next to Renoir, Manet sprinkled among Pissarro, and a few Degas here and a few Degas there. Shadows dance and the displays mingle. Where they're hung is a lot like their brushwork...delightfully sloppy.

In **Edouard Manet**'s *Luncheon on the Grass* (*Le Déjeuner sur l'Herbe,* 1863), you can see that a new revolutionary movement was starting to bud—Impressionism. Notice the background: the messy brushwork of trees and leaves, the play of light on the pond, and the light that filters through the trees onto the woman who stoops in the haze. Also note the strong contrast of colors (white skin, black clothes, green grass).

Edgar Degas blends classical lines and Realist subjects with Impressionist color, spontaneity, and everyday scenes from urban Paris. He loved the unposed "snapshot" effect, catching his models off guard. Dance students, women at work, and café scenes are approached from odd angles that aren't always ideal but make the scenes seem more real. He gives us the backstage view of life. For instance, a dance rehearsal lets Degas capture a behind-the-scenes look at bored, tired, restless dancers (*The Dance Class, La Classe de Danse,* c. 1873-1875). In the painting *In a Café (Dans un Café,* 1875-1876), a weary lady of the evening meets morning with a last, lonely, nail-in-the-coffin drink in the glaring light of a four-in-the-morning café. The pale green drink at the center of the composition is the toxic substance absinthe, which fueled many artists and burned out many more.

Claude Monet, the father of Impressionism, is known for his series of paintings on a single subject. For example, you may see several canvases of the cathedral in Rouen. In 1893, Monet went to Rouen, rented a room across from the cathedral, set up his easel... and waited. He wanted to catch "a series of differing impressions" of the cathedral facade at various times of day and year. He often had several canvases going at once. In all, he did 30 paintings of the cathedral, and each is unique. The time-lapse series shows the sun passing slowly across the sky, creating different-colored light and shadows. The labels next to the art describe the conditions: in gray weather, in the morning, morning sun, full sunlight, and so on.

One of Monet's favorite places to paint was the garden he landscaped at his home in Giverny, west of Paris (and worth a visit, provided you like Monet more than you hate crowds—see the next chapter). The Japanese bridge and the water lilies floating in the pond were his two favorite subjects. As Monet aged and his eyesight failed, he made bigger canvases of smaller subjects. The final water lilies are monumental smudges of thick paint surrounded by paint-splotched clouds that are reflected on the surface of the pond.

Pierre-Auguste Renoir started out as a painter of landscapes, along with Monet, but later veered from the Impressionist's philosophy and painted images that were unabashedly "pretty."

Renoir's best-known work is *Dance at the Moulin de la Galette* (*Bal du Moulin de la Galette,* 1876). On Sunday afternoons, working-class folk would dress up and head for the fields on Butte Montmartre (near Sacré-Cœur basilica) to dance, drink, and eat little crêpes (galettes) till dark. Renoir liked to go there to paint the common Parisians living and loving in the afternoon sun. The sunlight filtering through the trees creates a kaleidoscope of colors, like the 19th-century equivalent of a mirror ball throwing darts of light onto the dancers. The painting glows with bright colors. Even the shadows on the ground, which should be gray or black, are colored a warm blue. Like a photographer who uses a slow shutter speed to show motion, Renoir paints a waltzing blur.

Post-Impressionism

Post-Impressionism—the style that employs Impressionism's bright colors while branching out in new directions—is scattered all around the museum. You'll get a taste of the style with Cézanne, on the top floor, with much more on level 2.

Paul Cézanne brought Impressionism into the 20th century. Bowls of fruit, landscapes, and a few portraits were Cézanne's passion (see *The Card Players, Les Joueurs de Cartes,* 1890-1895). Where the Impressionists built a figure out of a mosaic of individual brushstrokes, Cézanne used blocks of paint to create a more solid, geometrical shape. These chunks are like little "cubes." It's no coincidence that his experiments in reducing forms to their geometric basics inspired the...Cubists. Because of his style (not the content), he is often called the first Modern painter.

Like Michelangelo, Beethoven, Rembrandt, Wayne Newton, and a select handful of others, **Vincent van Gogh** put so much of himself into his work that art and life became one. In the Orsay's collection of paintings (level 2), you'll see both Van Gogh's painting style and his life unfold.

Encouraged by his art-dealer brother, Van Gogh moved to Paris, and *voilà!* The color! He met Monet, drank with Gauguin and Toulouse-Lautrec, and soaked up the Impressionist style. (For example, see how he might build a bristling brown beard using thick strokes of red, yellow, and green side by side.)

But the social life of Paris became too much for the solitary Van Gogh, and he moved to the south of France. At first, in the glow of the bright spring sunshine, he had a period of incredible creativity and happiness. He was overwhelmed by the bright colors, landscape vistas, and common people. It was an Impressionist's dream (see *Midday, La Méridienne,* 1889-90).

But being alone in a strange country began to wear on him. An ugly man, he found it hard to get a date. A painting of his rented bedroom in Arles shows a cramped, bare-bones place (*Van Gogh's Room at Arles, La Chambre de Van Gogh à Arles, 1889*). He invited his friend Gauguin to join him, but after two months together arguing passionately about art, nerves got raw. Van Gogh threatened Gauguin with a razor, which drove his friend back to Paris. In crazed despair, Van Gogh cut off a piece of his own ear.

The people of Arles realized they had a madman on their hands and convinced Vincent to seek help at a mental hospital. The paintings he finished in the peace of the hospital are more meditative—there are fewer bright landscapes and more closed-in scenes with deeper, almost surreal colors.

His final self-portrait shows a man engulfed in a confused background of brushstrokes that swirl and rave (*Self-Portrait, Portrait de l'Artiste,* 1889). But in the midst of this rippling sea of mystery floats a still, detached island of a face. Perhaps his troubled eyes know that in only a few months, he'll take a pistol and put a bullet through his chest.

Nearby are the paintings of **Paul Gauguin,** who got the travel bug early in childhood and grew up wanting to be a sailor. Instead, he became a stockbroker. At the age of 35, he got fed up with it all, quit his job, abandoned his wife (her stern portrait bust may be nearby) and family, and took refuge in his art.

Gauguin traveled to the South Seas in search of the exotic, finally settling on Tahiti. There he found his Garden of Eden. Gauguin's best-known works capture an idyllic Tahitian landscape peopled by exotic women engaged in simple tasks and making music (*Arearea*, 1892). The native girls lounge placidly in unselfconscious innocence (so different from Cabanel's seductive, melodramatic *Venus*). The style is intentionally "primitive," collapsing the three-dimensional landscape into a two-dimensional pattern of bright colors. Gauguin intended that this simple style carry a deep undercurrent of symbolic meaning. He wanted to communicate to his "civilized" colleagues back home that he'd found the paradise he'd always envisioned.

French Sculpture

The open-air mezzanine of level 2 is lined with statues. Stroll the mezzanine, enjoying the works of great French sculptors, including **Auguste Rodin.**

Born of working-class roots and largely self-taught, Rodin combined classical solidity with Impressionist surfaces to become the greatest sculptor since Michelangelo. Like his statue, *The Walking Man* (*L'Homme Qui Marche,* c. 1900), Rodin had one foot in the past, while the other stepped into the future. This muscular, forcefully striding man could be a symbol of Renaissance Man with his classical power. With no mouth or hands, he speaks with his body. But get close and look at the statue's surface. This rough, "unfinished" look reflects light in the same way the rough Impressionist brushwork does, making the statue come alive, never quite at rest in the viewer's eye. Rodin created this statue in a flash of inspiration. He took two unfinished statues—torso and legs—and plunked them together at the waist. You can still see the seam.

Rodin's sculptures capture the groundbreaking spirit of much of the art in the Orsay Museum. With a stable base of 19th-century stone, he launched art into the 20th century.

▲▲Orangerie Museum (Musée de l'Orangerie)

Step out of the tree-lined, sun-dappled Impressionist painting that is the Tuileries Garden, and into the Orangerie (oh-rahn-zheh-ree), a little bijou of select works by Claude Monet and his contemporaries.

Cost and Hours: €8, €5 after 17:00, free for tho[illegible] 18, €16 combo-ticket with Orsay Museum (valid for f[illegible] visit per sight), covered by Museum Pass; Wed-Mon 9:00-18:00, closed Tue, galleries shut down 15 minutes before closing time; audioguide-€5, English guided tours usually Mon and Thu at 14:30 and Sat at 11:00, located in Tuileries Garden near Place de la Concorde (Mo: Concorde or scenic bus #24), 15-minute stroll from the Orsay, tel. 01 44 77 80 07, www.musee-orangerie.fr.

Visiting the Museum: Start with the museum's claim to fame—Monet's water lilies. These eight mammoth-scale paintings are displayed exactly as Monet intended them—surrounding you in oval-shaped rooms—so you feel as though you're immersed in his garden at Giverny.

Working from his home there, Monet built a special studio with skylights and wheeled easels to accommodate the canvases—1,950 square feet in all. Each canvas features a different part of the pond, painted from varying angles at distinct times of day. But the true subject of these works is the play of reflected light off the surface of the pond. The Monet rooms are considered the first art installation, and the blurry canvases signaled the abstract art to come.

Downstairs, in the Walter-Guillaume Collection, you'll see terrific works from artists who bridge the Impressionist and Modernist worlds—Renoir, Cézanne, Utrillo, Matisse, and Picasso. Together they provide a snapshot of what was hot in the world of art collecting, circa 1920.

EIFFEL TOWER AND NEARBY

▲▲▲Eiffel Tower (La Tour Eiffel)

It's crowded, expensive, and there are probably better views in Paris, but visiting this 1,000-foot-tall ornament is worth the trouble. Visitors to Paris may find *Mona Lisa* to be less than expected, but the Eiffel Tower rarely disappoints, even in an era of skyscrapers. This is a once-in-a-lifetime, I've-been-there experience. Making the trip gives you membership in the exclusive society of the quarter of a billion other humans who have made the Eiffel Tower the most visited monument in the modern world.

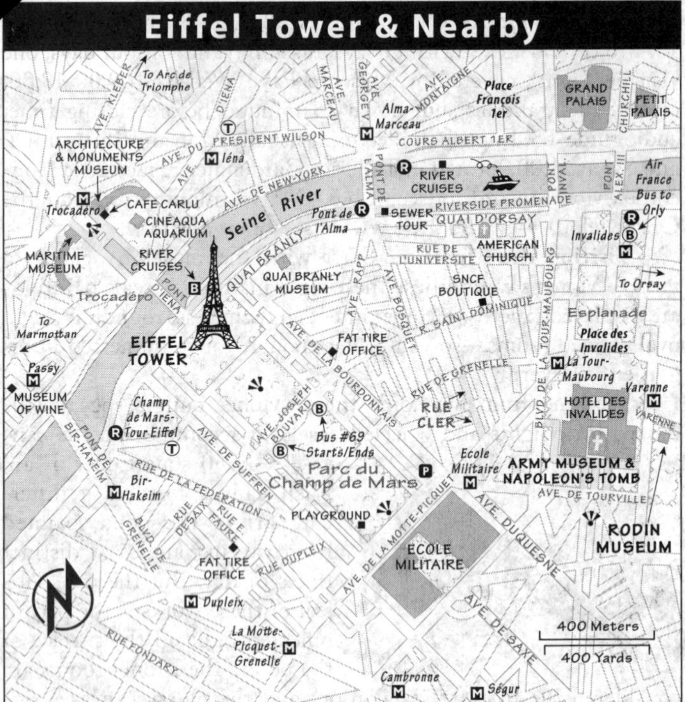

Cost and Hours: €15 all the way to the top, €9 for just the two lower levels, €5 to skip the elevator line and climb the stairs to the first or second level (€4 if you're under age 25), not covered by Museum Pass; daily mid-June-Aug 9:00-24:45, last ascent to top at 23:00 and to lower levels at 24:00 (elevator or stairs); Sept-mid-June 9:30-23:45, last ascent to top at 22:30 and to lower levels at 23:00 (elevator) or at 18:00 (stairs); cafés and great view restaurants, Mo: Bir-Hakeim or Trocadéro, RER: Champ de Mars-Tour Eiffel (all stops about a 10-minute walk away).

Reservations: Frankly, you'd be crazy to show up without a reservation. At www.toureiffel.paris, you can book an entry time (for example, June 12 at 16:30) and skip the initial entry line (the longest)—at no extra cost.

Time slots can fill up months in advance (especially if visiting from April through September). Online ticket sales open up about three months before any given date (at 8:30 Paris time)—and can sell out for that day within hours. Be sure of your date, as reservations are nonrefundable. If there are no reservation slots available, try the website again about a week before your visit—last-minute spots occasionally open up, especially for tickets up to the second level only.

The website is easy, but here are a few tips: When you "Choose a ticket," make sure you select "Lift entrance ticket with access to the summit" if you'd like to go all the way to the top. Then select your date, the number of people in your party, and the time slot (available times show up in green). You must create an account, with a 10-digit mobile phone number as your log-in. (If you don't have one, make up a number, if you must, but make a note of it in case you need to log in again.) Enter the 10 numbers without hyphens, parentheses, or country codes.

After paying with a credit card, you can print your tickets. Follow the printing specifications carefully (white paper, blank on both sides, etc.). If you're on the road, ask your hotel receptionist to help you print out your tickets.

Other Tips for Avoiding Lines: Crowds overwhelm this place much of the year, with one- to two-hour waits to get in (unless it's rainy, when lines can evaporate). Weekends and holidays are worst, but prepare for ridiculous crowds almost any time.

If you don't have a reservation, get in line 30 minutes before the tower opens. Going later is the next-best bet (after 19:00 May-Aug, after 17:00 off-season—after 16:00 in winter as it gets dark by 17:00). When you buy tickets on-site, all members of your party must be with you. To get reduced fares for kids, bring ID.

You can bypass some (but not all) lines if you have a reservation at either of the tower's view restaurants, or you can hike the stairs (shorter lines).

You can buy a reservation time (almost right up to the last minute) for €40 (or a €59 guided tour) through Fat Tire Bikes (see page 40).

When to Go: For the best of all worlds, arrive with enough light to see the views, then stay as it gets dark to see the lights. The views are grand whether you ascend or not. At the top of the hour, a five-minute display features thousands of sparkling lights (best viewed from Place du Trocadéro or the grassy park below).

Getting In: If you have a reservation, arrive at the tower 10 minutes before your entry time, and look for either of the two entrances marked *Visiteurs avec Reservation* (Visitors with Reservation), where attendants scan your ticket and put you on the first available elevator. If you don't have a reservation, follow signs for *Individuels* or *Visiteurs sans Tickets* (avoid lines selling tickets only for *Groupes)*. The stairs entrance—which usually has a shorter line—is at the south pillar (next to Le Jules Verne restaurant entrance).

Pickpockets: Beware. Street thieves plunder awestruck visitors gawking below the tower. And tourists in crowded elevators are like fish in a barrel for predatory pickpockets. *En garde.* There's a police station at the Jules Verne pillar.

Security Check: Bags larger than 19 by 8 by 12 inches are not allowed, but there is no baggage check. All bags are subject to a security search. No knives, glass bottles, or cans are permitted.

Services: Free WCs are at the base of the tower, behind the east pillar. Inside the tower itself, WCs are on all levels, but they're small, with long lines.

Background

The first visitor to the Paris World's Fair in 1889 walked beneath the "arch" formed by the newly built Eiffel Tower and entered the fairgrounds. This event celebrated both the centennial of the French Revolution and France's position as a global superpower. Bridge builder Gustave Eiffel (1832-1923) won the contest to build the fair's centerpiece by beating out rival proposals such as a giant guillotine.

The tower was nothing but a showpiece, with no functional purpose except to demonstrate to the world that France had the wealth, knowledge, and can-do spirit to erect a structure far taller than anything the world had ever seen. The original plan was to dismantle the tower as quickly as it was built after the celebration ended, but it was kept by popular demand.

To a generation hooked on technology, the tower was the marvel of the age, a symbol of progress and human ingenuity. Not all were so impressed, however; many found it a monstrosity. The writer Guy de Maupassant (1850-1893) routinely ate lunch in the tower just so he wouldn't have to look at it.

Visiting the Tower

Delicate and graceful when seen from afar, the Eiffel Tower is massive—even a bit scary—close up. You don't appreciate its size until you walk toward it; like a mountain, it seems so close but takes forever to reach.

The tower, including its antenna, stands 1,063 feet tall, or slightly higher than the 77-story Chrysler Building in New York. Its four support pillars straddle an area of 3.5 acres. Despite the tower's 7,300 tons of metal and 60 tons of paint, it is so well-engineered that it weighs no more per square inch at its base than a linebacker on tiptoes.

There are three observation platforms, at roughly 200, 400, and 900 feet. To get to the top, you need to change elevators at the second level. Note: Some elevators stop on the first level going up. If yours does, don't get off. It's more efficient to see the first floor on the way down. For the hardy, stairs lead from the ground level up to the first and second levels—and rarely have a long line. It's 360 stairs to the first level and another 360 to the second.

If you want to see the entire tower, from top to bottom, then see it...from top to bottom. Ride the elevator to the second level, then immediately line up for the elevator to the top. Enjoy the views on top, then ride back down to the second level. Frolic there for a while and take in some more views. When you're ready, head to the first level by taking the stairs (no line and can take as little as 5 minutes) or lining up for the elevator (but before boarding, ask if the elevator will stop on the first level—some don't). Explore the shops and exhibits on the first level and have a snack. To leave, you can line up for the elevator, but it's quickest and most memorable to take the stairs back down.

The Top: The top level, called *le sommet,* is tiny. (It can close temporarily without warning when it reaches capacity.) You'll find wind and grand, sweeping views. The city lies before you (pick out sights with the help of the panoramic maps). On a good day, you can see for 40 miles. Do a 360-degree tour of Paris. Feeling proud you made it this high? You can celebrate your accomplishment with a glass of champagne from the bar.

Second Level: The second level has the best views because you're closer to the sights, and the monuments are more recognizable. (While the best views are up the short stairway, on the platform without the wire-cage barriers, at busy times much of that zone is taken up by people waiting for the elevator to the top.) The second level has souvenir shops, public telephones to call home, and a small stand-up café.

The world-class Le Jules Verne restaurant is on this level, but you won't see it; access is by a private elevator. The head chef is currently Alain Ducasse, who operates restaurants around the world. One would hope his brand of haute cuisine matches the 400-foot haute of the restaurant.

First Level: The first level has more great views, all well-described by the tower's panoramic displays. By the time you visit, the first level should be entirely remodeled, including a breathtaking glass floor, new eateries, and cinematic presentations about the tower's construction, paint job, place in pop culture, and more. Exhibits all around the first level explore the impact of weather on the tower—how the sun warms the metal, causing the top to expand and lean about five inches away from the sun, or how the tower oscillates slightly in the wind. Because of its lacy design, even the strongest of winds can't blow the tower down, but only cause it to sway back and forth a few inches. In fact, Eiffel designed the tower primarily with wind resistance in mind, wanting a structure seemingly "molded by the action of the wind itself."

The 58 Tour Eiffel restaurant is on this level (also run by chef Alain Ducasse, with more accessible prices). In winter, part of the first level is set up for winter activities (most recently as an ice-skating rink).

After Your Visit: Descend back to earth. From here, consider catching the Bateaux Parisiens boat for a Seine cruise (see page 42) or visiting one of the following nearby sights: the Quai Branly Museum (below), Rue Cler market street (page 90), Army Museum and Napoleon's Tomb (page 90), or Rodin Museum (page 91).

For a final look at the Eiffel Tower, stroll across the river to Place du Trocadéro or to the end of the Champ de Mars and look back for great views. However impressive it may be by day, the tower is an awesome thing to see at twilight, when it becomes engorged with light, and virile Paris lies back and lets night be on top. When darkness fully envelops the city, the tower seems to climax with a spectacular light show at the top of each hour...for five minutes.

Near the Eiffel Tower

▲Quai Branly Museum (Musée du Quai Branly)

This is the best collection I've seen anywhere of so-called Primitive art from Africa, Polynesia, Asia, and America. Because "art illustrates the way in which man organizes and delineates the boundaries of their lands," we gain a better appreciation of a people through their art. The museum is presented in a wild, organic, and strikingly modern building. It's well worth a look if you have a Museum Pass and are near the Eiffel Tower.

After passing the ticket taker, pick up the museum map, then follow a ramp upstream along a projected river of the 1,677 names of the peoples covered in the museum. Masks, statuettes, musical instruments, textiles, clothes, voodoo dolls, and a variety of temporary exhibitions and activities are artfully presented and exquisitely lit. There's no need to follow a route: Wander at whim left and right, and read as much as feels right. Helpful English explanations are posted in most rooms and provide sufficient description for most visitors, though Primitive art lovers will want to rent the audioguide.

Cost and Hours: €9, free on first Sun of the month, covered by Museum Pass; museum—Tue-Sun 11:00-19:00, Thu-Sat until 21:00, closed Mon, ticket office closes one hour before closing; gardens—Tue-Sun 9:15-19:30, Thu-Sat until 21:15, closed Mon; audioguide-€5, 37 Quai Branly, 10-minute walk east (upriver) of Eiffel Tower, along the river (RER: Champ de Mars-Tour Eiffel or Pont de l'Alma), tel. 01 56 61 70 00, www.quaibranly.fr.

Eiffel Tower Views: Even if you skip the museum, drop by its peaceful garden café for fine Eiffel Tower views (closes 30 minutes before museum) and enjoy the intriguing gardens. The pedestrian bridge that crosses the river and runs up to the museum has sensational views of the Eiffel Tower.

National Maritime Museum (Musée National de la Marine)

This fun museum anchors a dazzling collection of ship models, submarine models, torpedoes, cannonballs, *beaucoup* bowsprits, and naval you-name-it. It's a kid-friendly place filled with Pirates of the Caribbean-like ship models, some the size of small cars. Start with the full-sized party barge made for Napoleon in 1810, then look up to see the elaborate stern of the 1694 Réale de France royal galley (don't miss the scale model in the glass case). From here you can follow a more or less chronological display of ship construction, from Roman vessels to modern cruise ships to aircraft carriers. Few English explanations make the free audioguide essential.

Cost and Hours: €8.50, free for those age 26 and under, covered by Museum Pass; Mon and Wed-Fri 11:00-18:00, Sat-Sun 11:00-19:00, closed Tue; includes audioguide, on left side of Place du Trocadéro with your back to Eiffel Tower, tel. 01 53 65 69 69, www.musee-marine.fr.

Architecture and Monuments Museum (Cité de l'Architecture et du Patrimoine)

This museum, on the east side of Place du Trocadéro, takes you through 1,000 years of French architecture, brilliantly displaying full-sized casts and models of some of France's most cherished monuments from the 11th to 21st centuries. Pick up the museum plan, and spend most of your time on the ground floor. Gaze into the eyes of medieval statues and wander under doorways, tympanums, and arches from the abbey of Cluny, Chartres Cathedral, Château de Chambord, and much more. For a good background, you can borrow the English info sheets (available in most rooms), or you can rent an audioguide.

The views from the upper rooms to the Eiffel Tower are sensational, as are those from the terrace of the museum's café, Café Carlu.

Cost and Hours: €8, covered by Museum Pass, Wed-Mon 11:00-19:00, Thu until 21:00, closed Tue, includes audioguide or you can hunt for handheld English explanations, great views from outside tables at on-site Café Carlu (reasonable prices, open same hours as museum and does not require entry into the museum), 1 Place du Trocadéro, Mo: Trocadéro, RER: Champ de Mars-Tour Eiffel, tel. 01 58 51 52 00, www.citechaillot.fr.

Museum of Wine (Musée du Vin)

Step out of urban Paris and into this 15th-century cellar for a musty, atmospheric, wine-fueled experience. The museum displays tools and items used for harvesting and winemaking, collected over the years by the *Confrérie des Echansons*. The role of this order is to protect and promote French wines. Started in 1954, it has thousands of members worldwide. Follow your visit with a wine tasting (€5 for one glass, €25 to taste three wines with a *sommelier*) and/or lunch at the restaurant (open 12:00-15:00, free *apéritif* with lunch if you show this book).

Cost and Hours: €10, €8 with this book, Tue-Sat 10:00-18:00, closed Sun-Mon, free but dry audioguide in English, 5 Square Charles Dickens, Mo: Passy, 15-minute walk from Eiffel Tower, tel. 01 45 25 63 26, www.museeduvinparis.com.

▲Paris Sewer Tour (Les Egouts de Paris)

Discover what happens after you flush. This quick, interesting, and slightly stinky visit (a perfumed hanky helps) takes you along a few hundred yards of water tunnels in the world's first underground sewer system. Pick up the helpful English self-guided tour, then drop down into Jean Valjean's world of tunnels, rats, and manhole covers. (Victor Hugo was friends with the sewer inspector when he wrote *Les Misérables*.) You'll pass well-organized displays with extensive English information explaining the history of water distribution and collection in Paris, from Roman times to the present. The evolution of this amazing network of sewers is surprisingly fascinating. More than 1,500 miles of tunnels carry 317 million gallons of water daily through this underworld. It's the world's longest sewer system—so long, they say, that if it was laid out straight, it would stretch from Paris all the way to Istanbul.

Ask in the gift shop about the slideshow and occasional tours in English. WCs are just beyond the gift shop.

Cost and Hours: €4.40, covered by Museum Pass, May-Sept Sat-Wed 11:00-17:00, Oct-April Sat-Wed 11:00-16:00, closed Thu-Fri, located where Pont de l'Alma greets the Left Bank—on the right side of the bridge as you face the river, Mo: Alma-Marceau, RER: Pont de l'Alma, tel. 01 53 68 27 81.

▲▲Rue Cler

Paris is changing quickly, but a stroll down this market street introduces you to a thriving, traditional Parisian neighborhood and offers insights into the local culture. Although this is a wealthy district, Rue Cler retains a workaday charm still found in most neighborhoods throughout Paris. The street—traffic-free since 1984—is lined with the essential shops—wine, cheese, chocolate, bread—as well as a bank and a post office (market generally open Tue-Sat 8:30-13:00 & 15:00-19:30, Sun 8:30-12:00, dead on Mon). For those learning the fine art of living Parisian-style, Rue Cler provides an excellent classroom. And if you want to assemble the ultimate French picnic, there's no better place.

▲▲Army Musuem and Napoleon's Tomb (Musée de l'Armée)

The Hôtel des Invalides—a former veterans' hospital topped by a golden dome—houses Napoleon's over-the-top-ornate tomb, as

well as Europe's greatest military museum. Visiting the Army Museum's different sections, you can watch the art of war unfold from stone axes to Axis powers.

Cost and Hours: €9.50, €7.50 after 16:00, free for military personnel in uniform, free for kids but they must wait in line for ticket, covered by Museum Pass, temporary exhibits are extra; daily 10:00-18:00, July-Aug until 19:00, Nov-March until 17:00, tomb plus WWI and WWII wings open Tue until 21:00 April-Sept, museum (except for tomb) closed first Mon of month Oct-June, Charles de Gaulle exhibit closed Mon year-round, last tickets sold 30 minutes before closing; videoguide-€6, cafeteria, tel. 01 44 42 38 77 or 08 10 11 33 99, www.musee-armee.fr.

Getting There: The Hôtel des Invalides is at 129 Rue de Grenelle, a 10-minute walk from Rue Cler (Mo: La Tour Maubourg, Varenne, or Invalides). You can also take bus #69 (from the Marais and Rue Cler) or bus #87 (from Rue Cler and Luxembourg Garden area).

Visiting the Museum and Tomb: At the center of the complex, Napoleon Bonaparte lies majestically dead inside several coffins under a grand dome—a goose-bumping pilgrimage for historians. The dome overhead glitters with 26 pounds of thinly pounded gold leaf.

Your visit continues through an impressive range of museums filled with medieval armor, cannons and muskets, Louis XIV-era uniforms and weapons, and Napoleon's horse—stuffed and mounted.

The best section is dedicated to the two World Wars. Walk chronologically through displays on the trench warfare of WWI, the victory parades, France's horrendous losses, and the humiliating Treaty of Versailles that led to WWII.

The WWII rooms use black-and-white photos, maps, videos, and a few artifacts to trace Hitler's rise, the Blitzkrieg that overran France, America's entry into the war, D-Day, the concentration camps, the atomic bomb, the war in the Pacific, and the eventual Allied victory. There's special insight into France's role (the French Resistance), and how it was Charles de Gaulle who actually won the war.

▲▲Rodin Museum (Musée Rodin)

This user-friendly museum is filled with passionate works by the greatest sculptor since Michelangelo. You'll see *The Kiss, The Thinker, The Gates of Hell,* and many more. (Due to ongoing renovations extending into 2015, some rooms may be closed.)

Cost and Hours: €6-9 (depending on temporary exhibits), free for those under age 18, free on first Sun of the month, €2 for garden only (possibly Paris' best deal, as several important works are on display there), €15 combo-ticket with Orsay Museum (valid four days, one visit per sight), both museum and garden covered by Museum Pass; Tue-Sun 10:00-17:45, Wed until 20:45, closed Mon; gardens close at 18:00, Oct-March at 17:00; last entry 30 minutes before closing; audioguide-€6, mandatory baggage check, self-service café in garden, near the Army Museum and Napoleon's Tomb at 79 Rue de Varenne, Mo: Varenne, tel. 01 44 18 61 10, www.musee-rodin.fr.

Visiting the Museum: Auguste Rodin (1840-1917) was a modern Michelangelo, sculpting human figures on an epic scale, revealing through their bodies his deepest thoughts and feelings. Like many of Michelangelo's unfinished works, Rodin's statues rise from the raw stone around them, driven by the life force. With missing limbs and scarred skin, these are prefab classics, making ugliness noble. Rodin's people are always moving restlessly. Even the famous *Thinker* is moving; while he's plopped down solidly, his mind is a million miles away.

Rodin worked with many materials—he chiseled marble (though not often), modeled clay, cast bronze, worked plaster, painted on canvas, and sketched on paper. He often created different versions of the same subject in different media.

Well-displayed in the mansion where the sculptor lived and worked, exhibits trace Rodin's artistic development, explain how his bronze statues were cast, and show some of the studies he created to work up to his masterpiece (the unfinished *Gates of Hell*). Learn about Rodin's tumultuous relationship with his apprentice and lover, Camille Claudel. Mull over what makes his sculptures some of the most evocative since the Renaissance. And stroll the gardens, packed with many of his greatest works (including *The Thinker, Balzac*, the *Burghers of Calais*, and the *Gates of Hell*). The beautiful gardens are ideal for artistic reflection.

▲▲Marmottan Museum (Musée Marmottan Monet)

This intimate, less-touristed mansion on the southwest fringe of urban Paris has the best collection of works by the father of Impressionism, Claude Monet (1840–1926). Fiercely independent and dedicated to his craft, Monet gave courage to the other Impressionists in the face of harsh criticism.

Cost and Hours: €10, not covered by Museum Pass, Tue-

Sun 10:00-18:00, Thu until 20:00, closed Mon, last entry 30 minutes before closing, audioguide-€3, 2 Rue Louis-Boilly, Mo: La Muette, tel. 01 44 96 50 33, www.marmottan.fr.

Visiting the Museum: The museum traces Monet's life chronologically, but in a way that's as rough and fragmented as a Monet canvas. You'll see black-and-white sketches from his youth, his discovery of open-air painting, and the canvas—*Impression: Sunrise*—that gave Impressionism its name. There are portraits of his wives and kids, and his well-known "series" paintings (done at different times of day) of London, Gare St. Lazare, and the Cathedral of Rouen. The museum's highlights are scenes of his garden at Giverny—the rose trellis, the Japanese bridge, and the larger-than-life water lilies.

You'll likely see paintings by Monet's predecessors (Corot, Boudin, Sisley), who pioneered the open-air landscape style that Monet would perfect. The museum also displays works by Monet's contemporaries: fellow Impressionists Degas, Pissarro, Gauguin, and particularly Berthe Morisot, as well as Monet's good friend Pierre-Auguste Renoir, who often worked side by side with Monet, painting the same scene.

The Marmottan also holds Paul Marmottan's eclectic collection of non-Monet objects—period furnishings, a beautifully displayed series of illuminated manuscript drawings, and non-Monet paintings created in the seamless-brushstroke style that Monet rebelled against. A set of medieval illuminated manuscripts lets you appreciate the fine arts of artistic monks before the age of the printing press.

LEFT BANK

Opposite Notre-Dame, on the left bank of the Seine, is the Latin Quarter. (For more information on this neighborhood, see my Historic Paris Walk, earlier.)

▲▲Cluny Museum (Musée National du Moyen Age)

Paris emerged on the world stage in the Middle Ages, the time between ancient Rome and the Renaissance. Europe was awakening from a thousand-year slumber. Trade was booming, people actually owned chairs, and the Renaissance was moving in like a warm front from Italy.

The Cluny is a treasure trove of Middle Ages (Moyen Age) art. Located on the site of a Roman bathhouse, it offers close-up looks at stained glass,

Notre-Dame carvings, fine goldsmithing and jewelry, and rooms of tapestries. The highlights are several original stained-glass windows from Sainte-Chapelle and the exquisite Lady and the Unicorn series of six tapestries: A delicate, as-medieval-as-can-be noble lady introduces a delighted unicorn to the senses of taste, hearing, sight, smell, and touch.

Cost and Hours: €8, free on first Sun of month, covered by Museum Pass; Wed-Mon 9:15-17:45, closed Tue, ticket office closes at 17:15; ticket includes audioguide though passholders must pay €1; near corner of Boulevards St. Michel and St. Germain at 6 Place Paul Painlevé; Mo: Cluny-La Sorbonne, St. Michel, or Odéon; tel. 01 53 73 78 16, www.musee-moyenage.fr.

St. Germain-des-Prés

A church was first built on this site in A.D. 558. The church you see today was constructed in 1163 and is all that's left of a once sprawling and influential monastery. The colorful interior reminds us that medieval churches were originally painted in bright colors. The surrounding area hops at night with venerable cafés, fire-eaters, mimes, and scads of artists.

Cost and Hours: Free, daily 8:00-20:00, Mo: St. Germain-des-Prés.

▲St. Sulpice Church

After it was featured in *The Da Vinci Code,* this grand church became a popular stop for the book's many fans. For pipe-organ enthusiasts, a visit here is one of Europe's great musical treats. The Grand Orgue at St. Sulpice Church has a rich history, with a succession of 12 world-class organists—including Charles-Marie Widor and Marcel Dupré—that goes back 300 years.

Patterned after St. Paul's Cathedral in London, the church has a Neoclassical arcaded facade and two round towers. Inside, in the first chapel on the right, are three murals of fighting angels by Delacroix: *Jacob Wrestling the Angel, Heliodorus Chased from the Temple,* and *The Archangel Michael* (on the ceiling). The fourth chapel on the right has a statue of Joan of Arc and wall plaques listing hundreds from St. Sulpice's congregation who died during World War I. The north transept wall features an Egyptian-style obelisk used as a gnomon (part of a sundial). The last chapel before the exit has a display on the Shroud of Turin.

Cost and Hours: Free, church open daily 7:30-19:30, Mo: St. Sulpice or Mabillon. See www.stsulpice.com for special concerts.

Sunday Organ Recitals: Though the (once-tourable) organ loft is no longer open to visitors, you can hear the organ played at Sunday Mass (10:30-11:30, come appropriately dressed) followed by a high-powered 25-minute recital, usually performed by talented organist Daniel Roth.

Delacroix Museum (Musée National Eugène Delacroix)

This museum for Eugène Delacroix (1798-1863) was once his home and studio. A friend of bohemian artistic greats—including George Sand and Frédéric Chopin—Delacroix is most famous for the flag-waving painting *Liberty Leading the People,* which is displayed at the Louvre, not here.

Cost and Hours: €6, free on first Sun of the month, covered by Museum Pass, Wed-Mon 9:30-17:00, closed Tue, last entry 30 minutes before closing, 6 Rue de Furstenberg, Mo: St. Germain-des-Prés, tel. 01 44 41 86 50, www.musee-delacroix.fr.

▲Luxembourg Garden (Jardin du Luxembourg)

Paris' most beautiful, interesting, and enjoyable garden/park/recreational area, le Jardin du Luxembourg, is a great place to watch Parisians at rest and play. This 60-acre garden, dotted with fountains and statues, is the property of the French Senate, which meets here in the Luxembourg Palace. Although it seems like something out of an espionage thriller, it's a fact that France's secret service *(Générale de la Sécurité Extérieure)* is "secretly" headquartered beneath Luxembourg Garden. (Don't tell anyone.)

Luxembourg Garden has special rules governing its use (for example, where cards can be played, where dogs can be walked, where joggers can run, and when and where music can be played). The brilliant flower beds are completely changed three times a year, and the boxed trees are brought out of the *orangerie* in May. In the southwest corner of the gardens, you can see beehives that have been here since 1872. Honey is made here for the *orangerie.* Close by, check out the apple and pear conservatory, with more than 600 varieties of fruit trees.

Children enjoy the rentable toy sailboats. The park hosts marionette shows several times weekly. Pony rides are available from April through October.

Cost and Hours: Free, daily dawn until dusk, Mo: Odéon, RER: Luxembourg.

Other Parks: If you enjoy Luxembourg Garden and want to see more green spaces, you could visit the more elegant **Parc Monceau** (Mo: Monceau), the colorful **Jardin des Plantes** (Mo: Jussieu or Gare d'Austerlitz, RER: Gare d'Austerlitz), or the hilly and bigger **Parc des Buttes-Chaumont** (Mo: Buttes-Chaumont).

▲Panthéon

This state-capitol-style Neoclassical monument celebrates France's illustrious history and people, balances Foucault's pendulum, and is the final home of many French VIPs.

Cost and Hours: €7.50, free for those under age 18, covered by Museum Pass, daily 10:00-18:30 in summer, until 18:00 in winter, last entry 45 minutes before closing, Mo: Cardinal Lemoine,

tel. 01 44 32 18 00, http://pantheon.monuments-nationaux.fr.

Visiting the Panthéon: Inside the vast building (360 by 280 by 270 feet) are monuments tracing the celebrated struggles of the French people: a beheaded St. Denis (painting on left wall of nave), St. Geneviève saving the fledgling city from Attila the Hun, and scenes of Joan of Arc (left transept).

Foucault's pendulum swings gracefully at the end of a 220-foot cable suspended from the towering dome (under renovation through 2015). It was here in 1851 that the scientist Léon Foucault first demonstrated the rotation of the earth. If the pendulum is back by the time you visit, stand a few minutes and watch its arc (appear to) shift as you and the earth rotate beneath it.

Stairs in the back lead down to the crypt, where a pantheon of greats is buried. Rousseau is along the right wall as you enter, Voltaire faces him across the hall. Also buried here are scientist Marie Curie, Victor Hugo *(Les Misérables, The Hunchback of Notre-Dame)*, Alexandre Dumas *(The Three Musketeers, The Count of Monte Cristo)*, and Louis Braille, who invented the script for the blind.

Montparnasse Tower

This sadly out-of-place 59-story superscraper has one virtue: If you can't make it up the Eiffel Tower, the views from this tower are cheaper, far easier to access, and make for a fair consolation prize. Come early in the day for clearest skies and shortest lines, and be treated to views from a comfortable interior and from up on the rooftop. (Some say it's the very best view in Paris, as you can see the Eiffel Tower clearly...and you can't see the Montparnasse Tower at all.)

Cost and Hours: €14.50, not covered by Museum Pass; April-Sept daily 9:30-23:30; Oct-March Sun-Thu 9:30-22:30; Fri-Sat 9:30-23:00; last entry 30 minutes before closing, dodge tour groups that clog the small elevators, sunset is great but views are disappointing after dark, entrance on Rue de l'Arrivée, Mo: Montparnasse-Bienvenüe—from the Métro, stay inside the station and follow *La Tour* signs; tel. 01 45 38 52 56, www.tourmontparnasse56.com.

Visiting the Tower: Find the view elevator entrance near the skyscraper's main entry (under the awning marked *Paris Tout A 360*). Exit the elevator at the 56th floor, passing the eager photographer (they'll superimpose your group's image with the view). Here you can marvel at the views of *tout Paris* (good even if cloudy), have a drink or a light lunch (OK prices), and peruse the gift shop. Take time to explore every corner of the floor. Exhibits identify highlights of the star-studded vista. Next, climb three flights of steps (behind the photographer) to the open terrace on the 59th floor to enjoy magnificent views in all directions.

Sightseeing Tip: The tower is an efficient stop when combined with a day trip to Chartres, which begins at the Montparnasse train station (see the next chapter for details).

▲Catacombs

Descend 60 feet below the street and walk a one-mile (one-hour) route through tunnels containing the anonymous bones of six million permanent Parisians.

In 1786, health-conscious Parisians looking to relieve congestion and improve the city's sanitary conditions emptied the church cemeteries and moved the bones here, to former limestone quarries. For decades, priests led ceremonial processions of black-veiled, bone-laden carts into the quarries, where the bones were stacked in piles 5 feet high and as much as 80 feet deep. Descend 130 steps and ponder the sign announcing, "Halt, this is the empire of the dead." Shuffle through passageways of skull-studded tibiae, admire 300-year-old sculptures cut into the walls of the catacombs, and see more cheery signs: "Happy is he who is forever faced with the hour of his death and prepares himself for the end every day." Then climb 86 steps to emerge far from where you entered, with white-limestone-covered toes, telling everyone you've been underground gawking at bones. Note to wannabe Hamlets: An attendant checks your bag at the exit for stolen souvenirs.

Cost and Hours: €8, not covered by Museum Pass, Tue-Sun 10:00-17:00, closed Mon; lines are long (figure 1.5 hours of waiting)—arrive by 9:30 to minimize the wait; ticket booth closes at 16:00, come no later than 14:30 or risk not getting in.

Tours and Information: English tours may be offered on Tue and Wed at 12:00 for €4.50. Call ahead or check online to confirm times, show up an hour ahead, go to the front of the line to ask for a ticket, and cross your fingers. If visiting on your own, pick up the free brochure (English version available) for some helpful background. Photos are allowed, but flashes and tripods are not, making most photography hopeless. Tel. 01 43 22 47 63, www.catacombes.paris.fr.

Getting There: 1 Place Denfert-Rochereau. Take the Métro to Denfert-Rochereau, then find the lion in the big traffic circle; if he looked left rather than right, he'd stare right at the green entrance to the Catacombs.

After Your Visit: You'll exit at 36 Rue Rémy Dumoncel, far from where you started. Turn right out of the exit and walk to Avenue du Général Leclerc, where you'll be equidistant from Métro stops Alésia (walk left) and Mouton Duvernet (walk right). Traffic-free Rue Daguerre, a pleasing pedestrian street, is four blocks to the right on Avenue du Général Leclerc (a block from where you entered the Catacombs).

CHAMPS-ELYSEES AND NEARBY

▲▲▲Champs-Elysées

This famous boulevard is Paris' backbone, with its greatest concentration of traffic. From the Arc de Triomphe down Avenue des Champs-Elysées, all of France seems to converge on Place de la Concorde, the city's largest square. And though the Champs-Elysées has become as international as it is Parisian, a walk here is still a must.

Background

In 1667, Louis XIV opened the first section of the street as a short extension of the Tuileries Garden. This year is considered the birth of Paris as a grand city. The Champs-Elysées soon became *the* place to cruise in your carriage. (It still is today; traffic can be gridlocked even at midnight.) One hundred years later, the café scene arrived. From the 1920s until the 1960s, this boulevard was pure elegance; Parisians actually dressed up to come here. It was mainly residences, rich hotels, and cafés. Then, in 1963, the government pumped up the neighborhood's commercial metabolism by bringing in the RER (commuter train). Suburbanites had easy access, and *pfft*—there went the neighborhood.

The *nouveau* Champs-Elysées, revitalized in 1994, has newer benches and lamps, broader sidewalks, all-underground parking, and a fleet of green-suited workers who drive motorized street cleaners. Blink away the modern elements, and it's not hard to imagine the boulevard pre-1963, with only the finest structures lining both sides all the way to the palace gardens.

➲Self-Guided Walk

To reach the top of the Champs-Elysées, take the Métro to the **Arc de Triomphe** (Mo: Charles de Gaulle-Etoile), then saunter down the grand boulevard (Métro stops every few blocks, including George V and Franklin D. Roosevelt). If you plan to tour the Arc de Triomphe (see next listing), do it before starting this walk.

Fancy car dealerships include **Peugeot,** at #136 (showing off its futuristic concept cars, often alongside the classic models), and

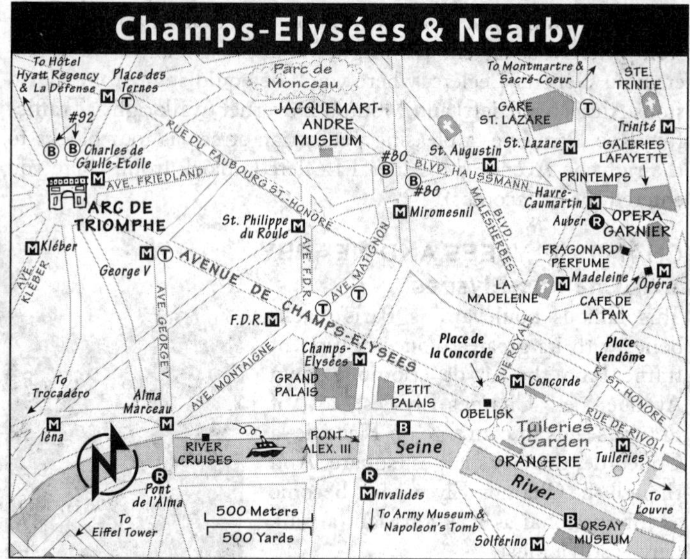

Mercedes-Benz, a block down at #118, where you can pick up a Mercedes bag and perfume to go with your new car. In the 19th century this was an area for horse stables; today, it's the district of garages, limo companies, and car dealerships. If you're serious about selling cars in France, you must have a showroom on the Champs-Elysées.

Next to Mercedes is the famous **Lido,** Paris' largest cabaret (and a multiplex cinema). You can walk all the way into the lobby, passing videos of the show. Paris still offers the kind of burlesque-type spectacles that have been performed here since the 19th century, combining music, comedy, and scantily clad women. Movie-going on the Champs-Elysées provides another kind of fun, with theaters showing the very latest releases. Check to see if there are films you recognize, then look for the showings *(séances)*. A "v.o." *(version originale)* next to the time indicates the film will be shown in its original language; a "v.f." stands for *version française*.

The flagship store of leather-bag maker **Louis Vuitton** may be the largest single-brand luxury store in the world. Step inside. The store insists on providing enough salespeople to treat each customer royally—if there's a line, it means shoppers have overwhelmed the place.

Fouquet's café-restaurant (#99), under the red awning, is a popular spot among French celebrities, serving the most expensive shot of espresso I've found in downtown Paris (€10). Opened in 1899 as a coachman's bistro, Fouquet's gained fame as the hangout of France's WWI biplane fighter pilots—those who weren't shot down by Germany's infamous "Red Baron." It also served as James Joyce's dining room.

Since the early 1900s, Fouquet's has been a favorite of French celebrities. The golden plaques at the entrance honor winners of France's Oscar-like film awards, the Césars (one is cut into the ground at the end of the carpet). There are plaques for Gérard Depardieu, Catherine Deneuve, Yves Montand, Roman Polanski, Juliette Binoche, and several famous Americans (but not Jerry Lewis). More recent winners are shown on the floor just inside.

From posh cafés to stylish shops, monumental sidewalks to glimmering showrooms, the Champs-Elysées is Paris at its most Parisian.

On or near the Champs-Elysées

▲▲Arc de Triomphe

Napoleon had the magnificent Arc de Triomphe commissioned to commemorate his victory at the battle of Austerlitz. There's no triumphal arch bigger (165 feet high, 130 feet wide). And, with 12 converging boulevards, there's no traffic circle more thrilling to experience—either from behind the wheel or on foot (take the underpass).

The foot of the arch is a stage on which the last two centuries of Parisian history have played out—from the funeral of Napoleon to the goose-stepping arrival of the Nazis to the triumphant return of Charles de Gaulle after the Allied liberation. Examine the carvings on the pillars, featuring a mighty Napoleon and excitable Lady Liberty. Pay your respects at the Tomb of the Unknown Soldier. Then climb the 284 steps to the observation deck up top, with sweeping skyline panoramas and a mesmerizing view down onto the traffic that swirls around the arch.

Cost and Hours: Outside and at the base—free, always viewable; steps to rooftop—€9.50, free for those under age 18, free on first Sun of month Oct-March, covered by Museum Pass; daily April-Sept 10:00-23:00, Oct-March 10:00-22:30, last entry 45 minutes before closing; Place Charles de Gaulle, use underpass to reach arch, Mo: Charles de Gaulle-Etoile, tel. 01 55 37 73 77, http://arc-de-triomphe.monuments-nationaux.fr.

Avoiding Lines: Bypass the slooow ticket line with your Museum Pass (though if you have kids, you'll need to line up to get the free tickets for children). Expect another line (that you can't skip) at the entrance to the stairway up the arch. Lines disappear after 17:00—come for sunset.

PARIS

Best Views over the City of Light

Your trip to Paris is played out in the streets, but the brilliance of the City of Light can only be fully appreciated by rising above it all. Invest time to marvel at all the man-made beauty, seen best in the early morning or around sunset. Many of the viewpoints I've listed are free or covered by the Museum Pass; otherwise, expect to pay €8-15. Here are some prime locations for soaking in the views:

Eiffel Tower: It's hard to find a grander view of Paris than from the tower's second level. Go around sunset and stay after dark to see the tower illuminated; or go in the early morning to avoid the midday haze and crowds (not covered by Museum Pass, see page 83).

Arc de Triomphe: Without a doubt, this is the perfect place to see the glamorous Champs-Elysées (if you can manage the 284 steps). It's great during the day, but even greater at night, when the boulevard positively glitters (covered by Museum Pass, see page 101).

Notre-Dame's Tower: This viewpoint is brilliant—it couldn't be more central—but it requires climbing 400 steps and is usually crowded with long lines (try to arrive early or late). Up high on the tower, you'll get an unobstructed view of gargoyles, the river, the Latin Quarter, and the Ile de la Cité (covered by Museum Pass, see page 52).

Steps of Sacré-Cœur: Join the party on Paris' only hilltop. Walk uphill, or take the funicular or Montmartrobus, then hunker down on Sacré-Cœur's steps to enjoy the sunset and territorial

▲Petit Palais (and the Musée des Beaux-Arts)

This free museum displays a broad collection of paintings and sculpture from the 1600s to the 1900s on its ground floor, and an easy-to-appreciate collection of art from Greek antiquities to Art Nouveau in its basement. Though it houses mostly second-tier art, there are a few diamonds in the rough (including pieces by Rembrandt, Courbet, Monet, and the American painter Mary Cassatt). The building itself is impressive, and the museum's classy café merits the detour. If it's raining and your Museum Pass has expired, the Petit Palais is a worthwhile stop.

Cost and Hours: Free, Tue-Sun 10:00-18:00, Thu until 20:00 for temporary exhibitions (fee for those exhibits), closed Mon; audioguide-€5; across from Grand Palais on Avenue Win-

views over Paris. Stay in Montmartre for dinner, then see the view again after dark (free, see page 117).

Galeries Lafayette or Printemps: Take the escalator to the top floor of either department store (they sit side by side) for a stunning overlook of the old Opéra district (free 122).

Montparnasse Tower: The top of this solitary skyscraper has some of the best views in Paris, though they're disappointing after dark. Zip up 56 floors on the elevator, then walk to the rooftop (not covered by Museum Pass, see page 97).

Pompidou Center: Take the escalator up and admire the beautiful cityscape along with the exciting modern art. There may be better views over Paris, but this is the best one from a museum (covered by Museum Pass, see page 114).

Place du Trocadéro and Café Carlu: This is *the* place to see the Eiffel Tower. Come for a look at Monsieur Eiffel's festive creation day or night (when the tower is lit up). Consider starting or ending your Eiffel Tower visit at Place du Trocadéro and having a drink or snack outside at Café Carlu (within the Architecture and Monuments Museum but open to the public). With its privileged spot on Place du Trocadéro, this café offers dramatic views of the Eiffel Tower from its terrace tables (Wed-Mon 11:00-19:00, Thu until 21:00, closed Tue).

Arab World Institute (Institut du Monde Arabe): This building near Ile St. Louis has free views from its terrific roof terrace (Tue-Sun 10:00-18:00, closed Mon, 1 Rue des Fossés Saint-Bernard, Place Mohammed V, Mo: Jussieu, www.imarabe.org).

Bar at Hôtel Hyatt Regency: This otherwise unappealing hotel is noteworthy for its razzle-dazzle 34th-floor bar (Bar la Vue), where you can sip wine and enjoy a stunning Parisian panorama (free elevator but pricey drinks, bar open daily 17:00-24:00, tel. 01 40 68 51 31, www.parisetoile.regency.hyatt.com).

ston Churchill, a looooong block west of Place de la Concorde, Mo: Champs-Elysées Clemenceau; tel. 01 53 43 40 00, www.petitpalais.paris.fr.

Grand Palais

This grand exhibition hall, built for the 1900 World's Fair, is used for temporary exhibits. The building's Industrial Age, erector-set, iron-and-glass exterior is striking, but the steep entry price is only worthwhile if you're interested in any of the exhibitions (each with different hours and costs, located in various parts of the building). Many areas are undergoing renovations, which may still be under way during your visit. Get details on the current schedule from a TI, in *Pariscope,* or from the website.

Cost and Hours: Admission prices and hours vary with each exhibition; major exhibitions usually €11-15, not covered by Museum Pass; generally open daily 10:00-20:00, Wed until 22:00, some parts of building closed Mon, other parts closed Tue, closed between exhibitions; Avenue Winston Churchill, Mo: Champs-Elysées Clemenceau or Franklin D. Roosevelt, tel. 01 44 13 17 17, www.grandpalais.fr.

▲La Défense and La Grande Arche

Though Paris keeps its historic center classic and skyscraper-free, this district, nicknamed "*le petit Manhattan,*" offers an impressive excursion into a side of Paris few tourists see: that of a modern-day economic superpower. La Défense was first conceived more than 60 years ago as a US-style forest of skyscrapers that would accommodate the business needs of the modern world. Today La Défense is a thriving commercial and shopping center, home to 150,000 employees and 55,000 residents.

For an interesting visit, take the Métro to the La Défense Grande Arche stop, follow *Sortie Grande Arche* signs, and climb the steps of La Grande Arche for distant city views. Then stroll gradually downhill among the glass buildings to the Esplanade de la Défense Métro station, and return home from there.

Visiting La Défense: The centerpiece of this ambitious complex is the mammoth **La Grande Arche de la Fraternité.** Inaugurated in 1989 on the 200th anniversary of the French Revolution, it was, like the Revolution, dedicated to human rights and brotherhood. The place is big—Notre-Dame Cathedral could fit under its arch. The "cloud"—a huge canvas canopy under the arch—is an attempt to cut down on the wind-tunnel effect this gigantic building creates.

La Défense is much more than its eye-catching arch. Survey the skyscraping scene from the top of the arch steps. For lunch, join the locals and picnic on the steps; good to-go places are plentiful (and cafés are nearby).

From the arch, wander along the **Esplanade** (a.k.a. "le Parvis"), back toward the city center (and to the next Métro stop). In France, getting a building permit often comes with a requirement to dedicate two percent of the construction cost to art. Hence the Esplanade is a virtual open-air modern art gallery, sporting pieces by Joan Miró (blue, red, and yellow), Alexander Calder (red), and Yaacov Agam (the fountain with colorful stripes and rhythmically dancing spouts), among others. Find a copy of French artist César

Baldaccini's famous thumb in the center (40 feet high). *La Défense de Paris,* the statue that gave the area its name, recalls the 1871 Franco-Prussian war—it's a rare bit of old Paris out here in the 'burbs.

As you descend the Esplanade, notice how the small gardens and *boules* courts (reddish dirt areas) are designed to integrate tradition into this celebration of modern commerce. Note also how the buildings decrease in height and increase in age—the Nexity Tower (closest to central Paris) looks old compared to the other skyscrapers. Dating from the 1960s, it was one of the first buildings at La Défense. Your walk ends at the amusing fountain of Bassin Takis, where you'll find the Esplanade de la Défense Métro station that zips you out of all this modernity and directly back into town.

OPERA NEIGHBORHOOD

The old opera house anchors this neighborhood of broad boulevards and grand architecture. This area is also nirvana for high-end shoppers, with the opulent Galeries Lafayette, the delicate Fragonard Perfume Museum, and the sumptuous shops that line Place Vendôme and Place de la Madeleine. Key Métro stops for this area include Opéra, Madeleine, and Havre Caumartin (RER: Auber).

▲Opéra Garnier

This gleaming grand theater of the belle époque was built for Napoleon III and finished in 1875. For the best exterior view, stand in front of the Opéra Métro stop. From Avenue de l'Opéra, once lined with Paris' most fashionable haunts, the facade suggests "all power to the wealthy." And a shimmering Apollo, holding his lyre high above the building, seems to declare, "This is a temple of the highest arts." But the elitism of this place prompted former President François Mitterrand to have an opera house built for the people in the 1980s, situated symbolically on Place de la Bastille, where the French Revolution started in 1789. This left the Opéra Garnier home only to ballet and occasional concerts.

Cost and Hours: €10, not covered by Museum Pass, erratic hours due to performances and rehearsals, generally daily 10:00-16:30, mid-July-Aug until 18:00, last entry 30 minutes before closing, 8 Rue Scribe, Mo: Opéra, RER: Auber.

Tours: The €5 audioguide gives a good self-guided tour. Guided tours in English run during the summer and off-season on weekends and Wed, usually at 11:30 and 14:30—call to confirm schedule (€13.50, includes entry, 1.5 hours, tel. 01 40 01 17 89 or 08 25 05 44 05).

Visiting the Theater: You'll enter around the left side of the building (as you face the front), across from American Express on Rue Scribe. As you pass the bust of the architect, Monsieur Garnier,

pay your respects and check out the bronze floor plan of the complex etched below. Notice how little space is given to seating.

The building is huge—though the auditorium itself seats only 2,000. The building's massive foundations straddle an underground lake (inspiring the mysterious world of the *Phantom of the Opera*). The real show was before and after the performance, when the elite of Paris—out to see and be seen—strutted their elegant stuff in the extravagant lobbies. Think of the grand marble stairway as a theater. Is it just me, or does the upstairs foyer feel like it belongs at Versailles? As you wander the halls and gawk at the decor, imagine this place in its heyday, filled with beautiful people sharing gossip at the Salon du Glacier.

From the uppermost floor open to the public, visitors can peek from two boxes into the actual red-velvet performance hall. Admire Marc Chagall's colorful ceiling (1964) playfully dancing around the eight-ton chandelier (guided tours take you into the performance hall; you can't enter when they're changing out the stage). Note the box seats next to the stage—the most expensive in the house, with an obstructed view of the stage...but just right if you're here only to be seen. Snoop about to find the side library, information panels describing costume management, and a portrait gallery of famous ballerinas and guests.

Nearby: Across the street, the illustrious Café de la Paix has been a meeting spot for the local glitterati for generations. If you can afford the coffee, this spot offers a delightful break.

Fragonard Perfume Museum

Near Opéra Garnier, this perfume shop masquerades as a museum. Housed in a beautiful 19th-century mansion, it's the best-smelling museum in Paris—and you'll learn a little about how perfume is made, too (ask for the English handout).

Cost and Hours: Free, daily 9:00-17:30, 9 Rue Scribe, Mo: Opéra, RER: Auber, tel. 01 47 42 04 56, www.fragonard.com.

High-End Shopping

This upscale neighborhood hosts some of Paris' best shopping. Even window shoppers can appreciate this as a ▲ "sight." Just behind the Opéra, the **Galeries Lafayette** department store is a magnificent cathedral to consumerism, with a stunning stained-glass dome and a fine rooftop view-terrace. The area between **Place de la Madeleine,** dominated by the Madeleine Church (looking like a Roman temple) and the octagonal **Place Vendôme,** is filled with pricey shops and boutiques, giving travelers a whiff of the exclusive side of Paris (for more on shopping in this area, see page 123).

▲▲Jacquemart-André Museum (Musée Jacquemart-André)

This thoroughly enjoyable museum-mansion (with an elegant café) showcases the lavish home of a wealthy, art-loving, 19th-century Parisian couple. After visiting the Opéra Garnier and wandering Paris' grand boulevards, get inside for an intimate look at the lifestyles of the Parisian rich and fabulous. Edouard André and his wife Nélie Jacquemart—who had no children—spent their lives and fortunes designing, building, and then decorating this sumptuous mansion. What makes the visit so rewarding is the excellent audioguide tour (in English, included with admission, plan on spending an hour with the audioguide). The place is strewn with paintings by Rembrandt, Botticelli, Uccello, Mantegna, Bellini, Boucher, and Fragonard—enough to make a painting gallery famous.

Cost and Hours: €12, not covered by Museum Pass; daily 10:00-18:00, Mon and Sat until 20:30 during special exhibits (which are common); can avoid lines (worst during the first week of special exhibits) by purchasing tickets online (€2 fee), includes audioguide, 158 Boulevard Haussmann, Mo: St. Philippe-du-Roule, bus #80 makes a convenient connection to Ecole Militaire; tel. 01 45 62 11 59, www.musee-jacquemart-andre.com.

After Your Visit: Consider a break in the sumptuous museum tearoom, with delicious cakes and tea (daily 11:45-17:30). From here walk north on Rue de Courcelles to see Paris' most beautiful park, Parc Monceau.

MARAIS NEIGHBORHOOD AND NEARBY

Naturally, when in Paris you want to see the big sights—but to experience the city, you also need to visit a vital neighborhood. The Marais fits the bill, with hip boutiques, busy cafés, trendy art galleries, narrow streets, leafy squares, Jewish bakeries, aristocratic châteaux, nightlife, and real Parisians. It's the perfect setting to appreciate the zest and flair of this great city.

The Marais extends along the Right Bank of the Seine, from the Bastille to the Pompidou Center. The main east-west axis is formed by Rue St. Antoine, Rue des Rosiers (the heart of Paris' Jewish community), and Rue Ste. Croix de la Bretonnerie. The centerpiece of the neighborhood is the stately Place des Vosges. Helpful Métro stops are Bastille, St-Paul, and Hôtel de Ville. The actual Bastille, the prison of Revolution fame, is Paris' most famous nonsight. The building is long gone, and just the square remains.

With more pre-Revolutionary lanes and buildings than anywhere else in town, the Marais is more atmospheric than touristy. It's medieval Paris, and the haunt of the old nobility. During the reign of Henry IV (r. 1589-1610), this area—originally a swamp (*marais*)—became the hometown of the French aristocracy. Big shots built their private mansions (*hôtels*) close to Henry's stylish Place des Vosges.

But in the 19th century, the aristocrats moved elsewhere. The Marais became a working-class quarter, filled with gritty shops, artisans, immigrants, and a Jewish community. Baron Georges-Eugène Haussmann's modernization plan put the Marais in line for the wrecking ball. But then the march of "progress" was halted by one tiny little event—World War I—and the Marais was spared. It limped along as a dirty, working-class zone until the 1960s, when it was transformed and gentrified.

Place des Vosges and West

The following sights are listed roughly in geographical order from east to west, starting at the heart of the Marais.

▲Place des Vosges

Henry IV built this centerpiece of the Marais in 1605 and called it "Place Royal." As he'd hoped, it turned the Marais into Paris' most exclusive neighborhood. Walk to the center, where Louis XIII, on horseback, gestures, "Look at this wonderful square my dad built." He's surrounded by locals enjoying their community park. You'll see children frolicking in the sandbox, lovers warming benches, and pigeons guarding their fountains while trees shade this escape from the glare of the big city (you can refill your water bottle in the center of the square, behind Louis).

Study the architecture: nine pavilions (houses) per side. The two highest—at the front and back—were for the king and queen (but were never used). Warm red brickwork—some real, some fake—is topped with sloped slate roofs, chimneys, and another quaint relic of a bygone era: TV antennas.

The insightful writer **Victor Hugo** lived at #6 from 1832 to 1848. (It's at the southeast corner of the square, marked by the French flag.) This was when he wrote much of his most important work, including his biggest hit, *Les Misérables.* Inside this museum you'll wander through eight plush rooms, enjoy a fine view of the square, and find good WCs (free, fee for optional exhibits, Tue-Sun 10:00-18:00, closed Mon, last entry at 17:40, audioguide-€5, 6 Place des Vosges; Mo: Bastille, St-Paul, or Chemin Vert; tel. 01 42 72 10 16, www.musee-hugo.paris.fr).

Sample the upscale art galleries ringing the square (the best ones are behind Louis). Consider a daring new piece for that blank wall at home. Or consider a pleasant break at one of the recommended eateries on the square.

▲Carnavalet Museum (Musée Carnavalet)

At the Carnavalet Museum, French history unfolds in a series of stills—like a Ken Burns documentary, except you have to walk. The Revolution is the highlight, but you get a good overview of everything—from Louis XIV-period rooms to Napoleon to the belle époque.

Cost and Hours: Free, fee for some temporary (but optional) exhibits, Tue-Sun 10:00-18:00, closed Mon; avoid lunchtime (11:45-14:30), when many rooms may be closed; audioguide-€5, 23 Rue de Sévigné (entrance is off Rue des Francs-Bourgeois), Mo: St-Paul, tel. 01 44 59 58 58, www.carnavalet.paris.fr.

Visiting the Museum: To tour the entire museum is a major course in French history, so focus your energies on the Revolution and beyond. Move quickly through the first half of the museum (pre-Revolution), as you make your way to Room 45, which leads to the Revolution rooms, or skip straight to the Revolution. Explanations are in French only, but many displays are self-explanatory.

No period of history is as charged with the full range of human emotions and actions as the French Revolution: bloodshed, martyrdom, daring speeches, murdered priests, emancipated women, backstabbing former friends—all in the name of government "by, for, and of the people."

You'll see paintings of the Estates-General assembly that

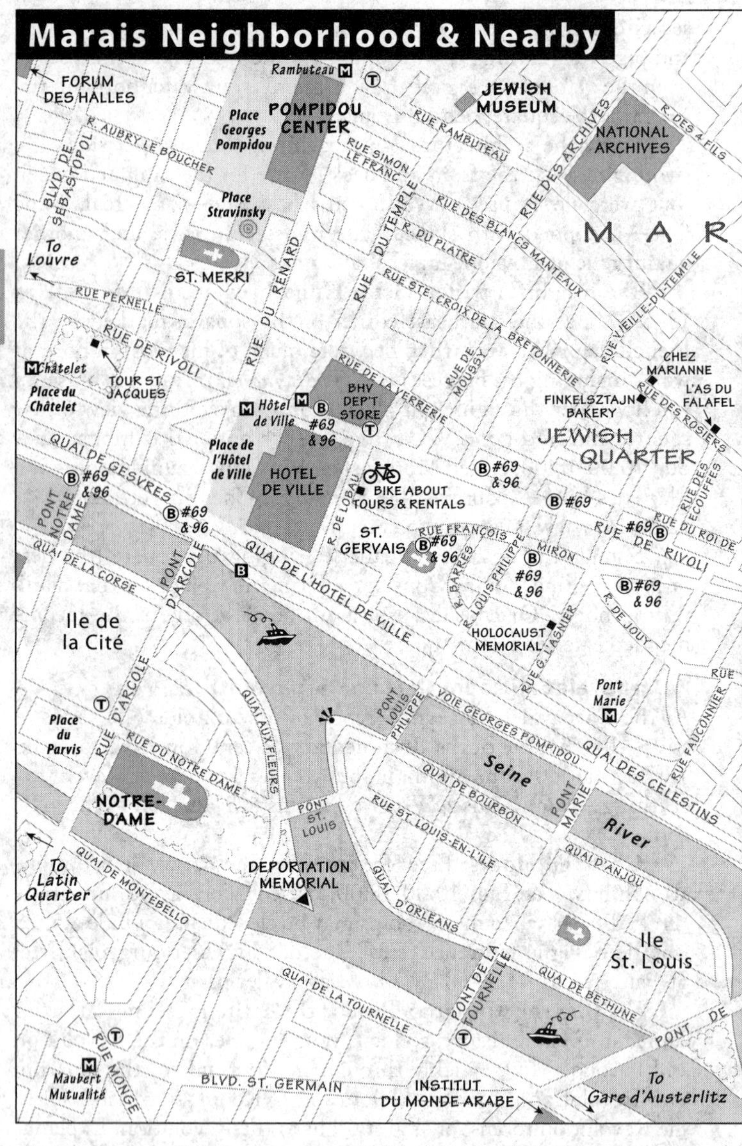

planted the seeds of democracy and a model of the Bastille, the hated prison that was the symbol of oppression. Read the *Declaration ("Tables") of the Rights of Man and the Citizen*. See pictures of the ill-fated King Louis XVI and Queen Marie-Antoinette, and the fate that awaited them—the guillotine. You'll see portraits of all the major players in the Revolutionary spectacle—Maximilien de Robespierre, Georges Danton, Charlotte Corday—as well as

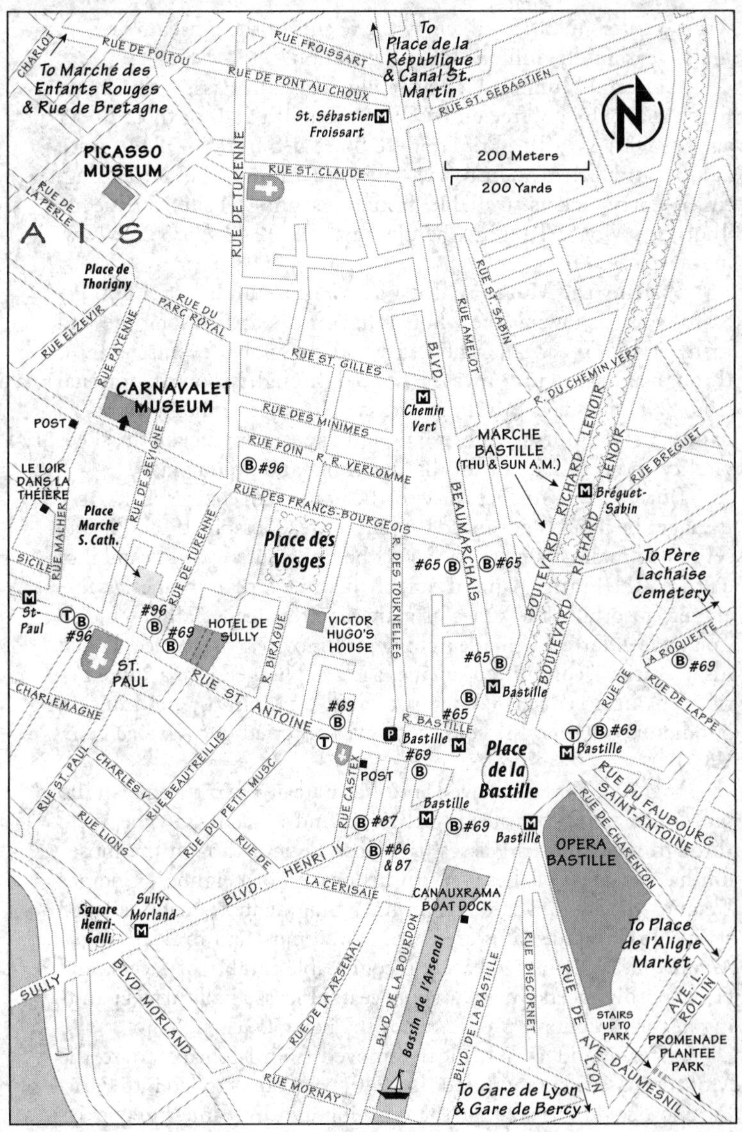

the dashing general who would inherit democracy and turn it into dictatorship...Napoleon Bonaparte.

▲▲Picasso Museum (Musée Picasso)

Whatever you think about Picasso the man, as an artist he was unmatched in the 20th century for his daring and productivity. The Picasso Museum has the world's largest collection of Picasso's work. Visitors in 2015 will enjoy the results of the museum's recent multi-year, multi-million-dollar renovation.

Cost and Hours: €11, covered by Museum Pass, extra charge for special exhibits, free on first Sun of month and for those under age 18 with ID; Tue-Fri 11:30-18:00, Sat-Sun 9:30-18:00, until 21:00 third Fri of month, last entry 45 minutes before closing; timed-entry tickets available from museum website, 5 Rue de Thorigny, Mo: St-Paul or Chemin Vert, tel. 01 42 71 25 21, www.musee-picasso.fr.

Visiting the Museum: The Picasso Museum has over 400 Picasso works, showing the whole range of the artist's long life and many styles. The women he loved and the global events he lived through appear in his canvases, filtered through his own emotional lens. You don't have to admire Picasso's lifestyle or like his modern painting style. But a visit here might make you appreciate the sheer vitality and creativity of this hardworking and unique man.

Born in Spain, Picasso was the son of an art teacher. As a teenager he quickly advanced beyond his teachers. In 1900, Picasso set out to make his mark in Paris, the undisputed world capital of culture. The brash Spaniard quickly became a poor, homesick foreigner, absorbing the styles of many painters (especially Henri de Toulouse-Lautrec) while searching for his own artist's voice. When his best friend committed suicide, Picasso plunged into a "Blue Period," painting emaciated beggars, hard-eyed pimps, and himself, bundled up against the cold, with eyes all cried out (*Autoportrait,* 1901).

In 1904, Picasso moved into his Bateau-Lavoir home/studio on Montmartre, got a steady girlfriend, and suddenly saw the world through rose-colored glasses (the Rose Period, though the museum has very few of these). With his next-door neighbor, Georges Braque, Picasso invented Cubism, a fragmented, "cube"-shaped style. He'd fracture a figure (such as the musician in *Man with a Mandolin,* 1911) into a barely recognizable jumble of facets, and facets within facets. In a few short years, Picasso had turned painting in the direction it would go for the next 50 years.

After World War I, Picasso moved from Montmartre to the Montparnasse neighborhood. In 1940, Nazi tanks rolled into Paris. Picasso decided to stay for the duration and live under gray skies and gray uniforms. The most famous of Picasso's gray-colored war paintings—*Guernica*—chronicled the Spanish Civil War (1936-39). Picasso painted it in Paris, but the work now hangs in Madrid.

At war's end, he left Paris, finding fun in the sun in the south of France. Sixty-five-year-old Pablo Picasso was reborn, enjoying worldwide fame and the love of a beautiful 23-year-old painter named Françoise Gilot. Picasso's Riviera works set the tone for the rest of his life—sunny, lighthearted, childlike, experimenting in new media, and using motifs of the sea. He was fertile to the end, still painting with bright thick colors at age 91.

Rue des Rosiers: Paris' Jewish Quarter

The intersection of Rue des Rosiers and Rue des Ecouffes marks the heart of the small neighborhood that Jews call the Pletzl ("little square"). Once the largest in Western Europe, Paris' Jewish Quarter is much smaller today but is still colorful.

Lively Rue des Ecouffes, named for a bird of prey, is a derogatory nod to the moneychangers' shops that once lined this lane. Rue des Rosiers—the heart of the Jewish Quarter (and named for the roses that once lined the city wall)—has become the epicenter of Marais hipness and fashion, but still features kosher *(cascher)* restaurants and fast-food places selling falafel, *shawarma, kefta,* and other Mediterranean dishes. Bakeries specialize in braided challah, bagels, and strudels. Delis offer gefilte fish, piroshkis, and blintzes. Art galleries exhibit Jewish-themed works, and store windows post flyers for community events. Need a menorah? You'll find one here. You'll likely see Jewish men in yarmulkes, a few bearded Orthodox Jews, and Hasidic Jews with black coat and hat, beard, and earlocks.

Lunch Break: You'll be tempted by kosher pizza and plenty of cheap fast-food joints selling falafel "to go" *(emporter).* Choose from L'As du Falafel (#34), with its bustling New York deli atmosphere, the Sacha Finkelsztajn Yiddish bakery at #27, or Chez Marianne for traditional Jewish meals. (For more options, see page 169).

▲Jewish Art and History Museum (Musée d'Art et Histoire du Judaïsme)

This fine museum, located in a beautifully restored Marais mansion, reconstructs the culture of community through its artistic heritage. It tells the story of Judaism in France and throughout Europe, from the Roman destruction of Jerusalem to the theft of famous artworks during World War II. Displays illustrate the cultural unity maintained by this continually dispersed population. You'll learn about the history of Jewish traditions, from bar mitzvahs to menorahs, and see the exquisite costumes and objects central to daily life. The museum also displays paintings by famous Jewish artists, including Marc Chagall, Amedeo Modigliani, and Chaim Soutine. English explanations posted in many rooms provide sufficient explanation for most; the included audioguide provides greater detail.

Cost and Hours: €8, covered by Museum Pass; Sun 10:00-18:00, Mon-Fri 11:00-18:00, Wed until 21:00 during special exhibits, closed Sat, last entry 45 minutes before closing; includes audioguide, 71 Rue du Temple; Mo: Rambuteau or Hôtel de Ville a few blocks farther away, RER: Châtelet-Les Halles; tel. 01 53 01 86 60, www.mahj.org.

Holocaust Memorial (Mémorial de la Shoah)

This sight, commemorating the lives of the more than 76,000 Jews deported from France in World War II, has several facets: a WWII deportation memorial, a museum on the Holocaust, and a Jewish resource center. Displaying original deportation records, the museum takes you through the history of Jews in Europe and France, from medieval pogroms to the Nazi era. But its focal point is underground, where victims' ashes are buried.

Cost and Hours: Free, Sun-Fri 10:00-18:00, Thu until 22:00, closed Sat and certain Jewish holidays, 17 Rue Geoffroy l'Asnier, tel. 01 42 77 44 72, www.memorialdelashoah.org.

▲▲Pompidou Center (Centre Pompidou)

One of Europe's greatest collections of far-out modern art is housed in the Musée National d'Art Moderne, on the fourth and fifth floors of this colorful exhibition hall. The building itself is "exoskeletal" (like Notre-Dame or a crab), with its functional parts—the pipes, heating ducts, and escalator—on the outside, and the meaty art inside. It's the epitome of Modern architecture, where "form follows function." Created ahead of its time, the 20th-century art in this collection is still waiting for the world to catch up.

Cost and Hours: €13, free on first Sun of month, Museum Pass covers permanent collection and view escalators (but not temporary exhibits), €3 Panorama Ticket lets you ride to the sixth floor for the view (doesn't include museum entry); Wed-Mon 11:00-21:00, closed Tue, ticket counters close at 20:00, arrive after 17:00 to avoid crowds (mainly for special exhibits); audioguide-€5 (rent on ground floor), café on mezzanine, pricey view restaurant on level 6, Mo: Rambuteau or Hôtel de Ville, tel. 01 44 78 12 33, www.centrepompidou.fr.

Visiting the Museum: Buy your ticket (and rent an audioguide if you choose) on the ground floor, then ride up the escalator (or run up the down escalator to get in the proper mood). When you see the view, your opinion of the Pompidou's exterior should improve a good 15 percent. Find the permanent collection—the entrance is either on the fourth or fifth floor (it varies). Enter and show your ticket.

Generally, art from 1905 to 1960 is on the fifth floor, while the fourth floor contains more recent art. But 20th-century art resents being put in chronological order, and the Pompidou's collection is rarely in any neat-and-tidy arrangement. Use the museum's floor plans (posted on the wall) to find select artists.

The 20th century—accelerated by technology and fragmented by war—was exciting and chaotic, and the art reflects the turbulence of that century of change. In this free-flowing and airy museum, you'll come face-to-face with works from the first half of the 20th century, including pieces by Pablo Picasso, Marc Chagall, Henri Matisse, Wassily Kandinsky, Piet Mondrian, Paul Klee, Salvador Dalí, Max Ernst, Jackson Pollock, and many more.

The contemporary collection highlights post-1960 works, including Andy Warhol's pop art. You'll also see fewer traditional canvases or sculptures and lots of mixed-media work, combining painting, sculpture, welding, photography, video, computer programming, new resins, plastics, industrial techniques, and lighting and sound systems. Even skeptics of modern art will find that after so many Madonnas-and-children, a piano smashed to bits and glued to the wall is refreshing.

View from the Pompidou: Ride the escalator for a great city view from the top (ticket or Museum Pass required), and consider a drink at the pricey view-café.

Nearby: The Pompidou Center and the square that fronts it are lively, with lots of people, street theater, and activity inside and out—a perpetual street fair. Kids of any age enjoy the fun, colorful fountain (called *Homage to Stravinsky*) next to the Pompidou Center.

Also nearby is the unique studio of revolutionary sculptor Constantin Brancusi. It's across from (and west of) the Pompidou and is free to visit (Wed-Mon 14:00-18:00, closed Tue, same contact info as Pompidou).

Hôtel de Ville

Looking more like a grand château than a public building, Paris' city hall stands proudly. The Renaissance-style building (built 1533-1628, and reconstructed after a 19th-century fire) displays hundreds of statues of famous Parisians on its facade. Peek from behind the iron fences through the doorways to see elaborate spiral stairways, which are reminiscent of Château de Chambord in the Loire. Playful fountains energize the big, lively square in front.

This spacious stage has seen much of Paris' history. On July 14, 1789, Revolutionaries rallied here on their way to the Bastille. In 1870, it was home to the radical Paris Commune. During World War II, General Charles de Gaulle appeared at the windows to proclaim Paris' liberation from the Nazis. And in 1950, Robert Doisneau snapped a famous black-and-white photo of a kissing couple, with Hôtel de Ville as a romantic backdrop.

Today, this is the symbolic heart of the city of Paris. Demonstrators gather here to speak their minds. Crowds cheer during big soccer games shown on huge TV screens. In summer, the square hosts sand volleyball courts; in winter, a big ice-skating rink. There's often a children's carousel, or *manège.*

East of Place des Vosges

Promenade Plantée Park (Viaduc des Arts)

This two-mile-long, narrow garden walk on an elevated viaduct was once used for train tracks and is now a pleasing place for a refreshing stroll or run (especially for those sleeping in the Marais). Botanists appreciate the well-maintained and varying vegetation. From west (near Opéra Bastille) to east, the first half of the path is elevated until the midway point, the pleasant Jardin de Reuilly (a good stopping point for most, near Mo: Dugommier), then it continues on street level—with separate paths for pedestrians and cyclists—out to Paris' ring road, the *périphérique.*

Cost and Hours: Free, opens Mon-Fri at 8:00, Sat-Sun at 9:00, closes at sunset (17:30 in winter, 20:30 in summer). It runs from Place de la Bastille (Mo: Bastille) along Avenue Daumesnil to St. Mandé (Mo: Michel Bizot) or Porte Dorée, passing within a block of Gare de Lyon.

Getting There: To get to the park from Place de la Bastille (exit the Métro following *Sortie Rue de Lyon* signs), walk a looooong block down Rue de Lyon, hugging the Opéra on your left. Find the low-key entry and steps up the red-brick wall a block after the Opéra.

▲Père Lachaise Cemetery (Cimetière du Père Lachaise)

Littered with the tombstones of many of the city's most illustrious dead, this is your best one-stop look at Paris' fascinating, romantic past residents.

Cost and Hours: Free, Mon-Fri 8:00-18:00, Sat 8:30-18:00, Sun 9:00-18:00, closes at 17:30 in winter, last entry 15 minutes before closing; two blocks from Mo: Gambetta (do not go to Mo: Père Lachaise) and two blocks from bus #69's last stop; tel. 01 55 25 82 10, searchable map available at non-official website: www.pere-lachaise.com.

Visiting the Cemetery: Enclosed by a massive wall and lined with 5,000 trees, the peaceful, car-free lanes and dirt paths of Père Lachaise cemetery encourage park-like meandering. Named for Father *(Père)* La Chaise, whose job was listening to Louis XIV's sins, the cemetery is relatively new, having opened in 1804 to accommodate Paris' expansion. Today, this city of the dead (pop. 70,000) still accepts new residents,

Entertainment in Paris

Paris is brilliant after dark. Save energy from your day's sightseeing and experience the City of Light lit. Whether it's a concert at Sainte-Chapelle, a boat ride on the Seine, a walk in Montmartre, a hike up the Arc de Triomphe, or a late-night café, you'll see Paris at its best.

MUSIC

Jazz and Blues Clubs

With a lively mix of American, French, and international musicians, Paris has been an internationally acclaimed jazz capital since World War II. You'll pay €12-25 to enter a jazz club (may include one drink; if not, expect to pay €5-10 per drink; beer is cheapest). See *Pariscope* magazine under "Musique" for listings, or, even better, the *Paris Voice* website (www.parisvoice.com). You can also check each club's website (all have English versions), or drop by the clubs to check out the calendars posted on their front doors. Music starts after 21:00 in most clubs. Some offer dinner concerts from about 20:30 on. Here are several good bets:

Caveau de la Huchette: This fun, characteristic old jazz/dance club fills an ancient Latin Quarter cellar with live jazz and frenzied dancing every night (admission about €13 on weekdays, €15 on weekends, €6-8 drinks, daily 21:30-2:30 in the morning or later, no reservations needed, buy tickets at the door, 5 Rue de la Huchette, Mo: St. Michel, www.caveaudelahuchette.fr).

Autour de Midi et Minuit: This Old World bistro sits at the foot of Montmartre, above a *cave à jazz*. Eat upstairs if you like, then make your way down to the basement to find bubbling jam sessions Tuesday through Thursday and concerts on Friday and Saturday nights (no cover, €5 minimum drink order Tue-Thu; €18 cover Fri-Sat includes one drink; jam sessions at 21:30, concerts usually at 22:00; no music Sun-Mon; 11 Rue Lepic, Mo: Blanche or Abbesses, tel. 01 55 79 16 48, www.autourdemidi.fr).

Other Venues: For a spot teeming with late-night activity and jazz, go to the two-block-long Rue des Lombards, at Boulevard Sébastopol, midway between the river and the Pompidou Center (Mo: Châtelet). **Au Duc des Lombards** is one of the most popular and respected jazz clubs in Paris, with concerts nightly in a great, plush, 110-seat theater-like setting (admission €20-30, buy online and arrive early for best seats, cheap drinks, shows at 20:00 and 22:00, 42 Rue des Lombards, tel. 01 42 33 22 88, www.ducdeslombards.fr). **Le Sunside,** run for 19 years by Stephane Portet, is just a block away. The club offers two little stages (ground floor and downstairs): "le Sunset" stage tends toward contemporary world jazz; "le Sunside" stage features more traditional and acoustic jazz (concerts range from free to €25, check their website; generally at 20:00, 21:00, and 22:00; 60 Rue des Lombards, tel. 01 40 26 46 60, www.sunset-sunside.com).

For a less pricey—and less central—concert club, try **Utopia.** From the outside it's a hole-in-the-wall, but inside it's filled with devoted fans of rock and folk blues. Though Utopia is officially a private club (and one that permits smoking), you can pay €3 to join for an evening, then pay a reasonable charge for the concert (usually €10 or under, concerts start about 22:00). It's located in the Montparnasse area (79 Rue de l'Ouest, Mo: Pernety, tel. 01 43 22 79 66, www.utopia-cafeconcert.fr).

Old-Time Parisian Cabaret

Au Lapin Agile, a historic little cabaret on Montmartre, tries its best to maintain the atmosphere of the heady days when bohemians would gather here to enjoy wine, song, and sexy jokes. Today, you'll mix in with a few locals and many tourists (the Japanese love the place) for a drink and as many as 10 different performers—mostly singers with a piano. Performers range from sweet and innocent Amélie types to naughty Maurice Chevalier types. And though tourists are welcome, there's no accommodation for English speakers (except on their website), so non-French-speakers will be lost. You sit at carved wooden tables in a dimly lit room, taste the traditional drink (a small brandy with cherries), and are immersed in an old-time Parisian ambience. The soirée covers traditional French standards, love ballads, sea chanteys, and more (€28, €8 drinks, Tue-Sun 21:00-2:00 in the morning, closed Mon, best to reserve ahead, 22 Rue des Saules, tel. 01 46 06 85 87, www.au-lapin-agile.com).

Classical Concerts

For classical music on any night, consult *Pariscope* magazine (check "Concerts Classiques" under "Musique" for listings), and look for posters at tourist-oriented churches. From March through November, these churches regularly host concerts: St. Sulpice, St. Germain-des-Prés, La Madeleine, St. Eustache, St. Julien-le-Pauvre, and Sainte-Chapelle.

Sainte-Chapelle: Enjoy the pleasure of hearing Mozart, Bach, or Vivaldi surrounded by 800 years of stained glass (unheated—bring a sweater). The acoustical quality is surprisingly good. There are usually two concerts per evening, at 19:00 and 20:30; specify which one you want when you buy or reserve your ticket. VIP tickets get you a seat in the first nine rows (€40), Prestige tickets cover the next 15 rows (€30), and Normal tickets are the last five rows (€25). Seats are unassigned within each section, so arrive at least 30 minutes early to get through the security line and snare a good view.

You can book at the box office, by phone, or online. Two different companies present concerts, but the schedule will tell you who to contact for tickets to a particular performance. The small box office (with schedules and tickets) is to the left of the chapel entrance gate (8 Boulevard du Palais, Mo: Cité), or call 01 42 77 65 65 or 06 67 30 65 65 for schedules and reservations. You can leave your message in English—just speak clearly and spell your name. You can check schedules and buy your ticket at www.euromusicproductions.fr.

Flavien from Euromusic offers last-minute discounts with this book when seats are available (limit 2 tickets per book). VIP tickets are discounted to €30, Prestige tickets to €25, and Normal tickets to €16. The offer applies only to Euromusic concerts and must be purchased with cash only at the Sainte-Chapelle ticket booth close to concert time.

Salle Pleyel: This concert hall on the Right Bank hosts world-class artists, from string quartets and visiting orchestras to international opera stars. Tickets range from €10 to €150, depending on the artist and seats you choose, and are usually hard to come by, so it's best to order online in advance (252 Rue du Faubourg St. Honoré, Mo: Ternes, tel. 01 42 56 13 13, www.sallepleyel.fr).

Concerts on the Seine: Enjoy live classical music while cruising past Paris' iconic monuments (€30-40, summer months only, board at Vedettes du Pont Neuf, Square du Vert Galant, tel. 01 42 77 65 65, www.vedettesdupontneuf.com/concerts-en-seine-2/).

Other Venues: Look also for daytime concerts in parks, such as the Luxembourg Garden. Even the Galeries Lafayette department store offers concerts. Many of these concerts are free *(entrée libre),* such as the Sunday atelier concert sponsored by the American Church (generally Sept-June at 17:00 but not every week and not in Dec, 65 Quai d'Orsay, Mo: Invalides, RER: Pont de l'Alma, tel. 01 40 62 05 00, www.acparis.org).

Opera

Paris is home to two well-respected opera venues. The **Opéra Bastille** is the massive modern opera house that dominates Place de la Bastille. Come here for state-of-the-art special effects and modern interpretations of classic ballets and operas. In the spirit of this everyman's opera, unsold seats are available at a big discount to seniors and students 15 minutes before the show. Standing-room-only tickets for €15 are also sold for some performances (Mo: Bastille). The **Opéra Garnier,** Paris' first opera house, hosts opera and ballet performances. Come here for less expensive tickets and grand belle époque decor (Mo: Opéra; generally no performances mid-July-mid-Sept). To get tickets for either opera house, it's easiest to reserve online at www.operadeparis.fr, or call 01 71 25 24 23 outside France or toll tel. 08 92 89 90 90 inside France (office closed Sun). You can also buy your tickets in person either at Opéra Bastille's ticket office (Mon-Sat 14:30-18:30 and an hour before the show, closed Sun) or at Opéra Garnier's ticket office (Mon-Sat 11:30–18:30 and an hour before the show, closed Sun).

FILM

The Open Air Cinema at La Villette (Cinéma en Plein Air) is your chance to relax on the grass and see a movie under the stars with happy Parisians. Films, shown in their original language with French subtitles, start at dusk (free, €7 chair rental, mid-July-Aug Wed-Sun, inside Parc de la Villette complex—enter through main entrance at Cité des Sciences et de l'Industrie, 30 Rue Corentin-Cariou, Mo: Porte de la Villette, www.villette.com).

EVENING MUSEUM VISITS

Various museums are open late on different evenings—called *visites nocturnes*—offering the opportunity for more relaxed, less crowded visits: the Louvre (Wed and Fri until 21:45), Orsay (Thu until 21:45), Rodin (Wed until 20:45), Pompidou Center (Wed-Mon until 21:00), Grand Palais (Wed until 22:00), Holocaust Memorial (Thu until 22:00), Quai Branly (Thu-Sat until 21:00), and Marmottan Museum (Thu until 20:00). Napoleon's Tomb and the Army Museum's WWI and WWII wings are open Tuesdays until 21:00 (April-Sept).

Spectacles in the Gardens: An elaborate sound-and-light show (Les Grandes Eaux Nocturnes) takes place at Versailles (€25, mid-June-mid-July Fri-Sat at 21:00, mid-July-mid-Sept Sat only at 21:00, www.chateauversailles.fr).

NIGHT WALKS

Go for an evening walk to best appreciate the City of Light. Break for ice cream, pause at a café, and enjoy the sidewalk entertainers as you join the post-dinner Parisian parade. Remember to avoid poorly lit areas and stick to main thoroughfares.

Adjust your expectations to the changing times. Paris will always be the City of Light, but it shines a little dimmer these days. In an effort to go green and reduce costs, Paris has toned down the lighting on several monuments, including the Arc de Triomphe and the Louvre's glass pyramid.

▲▲▲Trocadéro and Eiffel Tower

This is one of Paris' most spectacular views at night. Take the Métro to the Trocadéro stop and join the party on Place du Trocadéro for a magnificent view of the glowing Eiffel Tower (see the "Best Views over the City of Light" sidebar on page 102). It's a festival of hawkers, gawkers, drummers, and entertainers.

Walk down the stairs, passing the fountains and rollerbladers, then cross the river to the base of the tower, well worth the effort even if you don't go up (tower open daily mid-June-Aug until 24:45, Sept-mid-June until 23:45).

From the Eiffel Tower you can stroll through the Champ de Mars park past tourists and romantic couples, and take the Métro home (Ecole Militaire stop, across Avenue de la Motte-Picquet from far southeast corner of park). Or there's a handy RER stop (Champ de Mars-Tour Eiffel) two blocks west of the Eiffel Tower on the river.

▲▲Champs-Elysées and the Arc de Triomphe

The Avenue des Champs-Elysées glows after dark. Start at the Arc de Triomphe (observation deck open daily, April-Sept until 23:00, Oct-March until 22:30), then stroll down Paris' lively grand promenade. A right turn on Avenue George V leads to the Bateaux-Mouches river cruises. A movie on the Champs-Elysées is a fun experience (weekly listings in *Pariscope* under "Cinéma"), and a drink or snack at Renault's futuristic car café is a kick (at #53, toll tel. 08 11 88 28 11).

▲Ile St. Louis and Notre-Dame

This stroll features floodlit views of Notre-Dame and a taste of the Latin Quarter. Take the Métro (line 7) to the Pont Marie stop, then cross Pont Marie to Ile St. Louis. Turn right up Rue St. Louis-en-l'Ile, stopping for dinner—or at least a Berthillon ice cream (at #31) or Amorino Gelati (at #47). At the end of Ile St. Louis, cross Pont St. Louis to Ile de la Cité, with a great view of Notre-Dame. Wander to the Left Bank on Quai de l'Archevêché, and drop down to the river for the best floodlit views. From May through September you'll find several moored barges *(péniches)* that operate as bars. Although I wouldn't eat dinner on one of these barges, the atmosphere is great for a drink, often including live music on weekends (daily until 2:00 in the morning, closed Oct-April, live music often Thu-Sun from 21:00). End your walk on Place du Parvis Notre-Dame in front of Notre-Dame (tower open Fri-Sat until 23:00 in July-Aug), or go back across the river to the Latin Quarter.

Open-Air Sculpture Garden

Day or night, this skinny riverfront park dotted with modern art makes for a pleasant walk, but it's especially fun on balmy evenings in the summer, when you may encounter rock and salsa dancing. It's on the Left Bank across from Ile St. Louis, running between the Arab World Institute and Jardin des Plantes (free, music around 20:00, very weather-dependent, Quai St. Bernard, Mo: Cardinal Lemoine plus an 8-minute walk up Rue Cardinal Lemoine toward the river).

AFTER-DARK TOURS

Several companies offer evening tours of Paris. You can take a traditional, mass-produced bus tour for €27 per person, or for a little more (around €100 per couple), take an hour-long, vintage-car tour with a student guide. A pedicab will take you around for €40-50 per hour. Do-it-yourself-ers can save money by hiring a cab for a private tour (around €45 for one hour).

▲Deux Chevaux Car Tours

If rumbling around Paris and sticking your head out of the rolled-back top of a funky old 2CV car *à la* Inspector Clouseau sounds like your kind of fun, consider this. Two enterprising companies have assembled a veritable fleet of these "tin-can" cars for giving tours of Paris day and night: 4 Roues Sous 1 Parapluie (the better choice) and Paris Authentic. Night is best for the tour; skip it in daylight. The informal student-drivers are not professional guides (you're paying for their driving services), though they speak some English. Appreciate the simplicity of the car. It's France's version of the VW "bug" and hasn't been made since 1985. Notice the bare-bones dashboard. Ask your guide to honk the horn, to run the silly little wipers, and to open and close the air vent—*c'est magnifique!*

They'll pick you up and drop you at your hotel or wherever you choose. **4 Roues Sous 1 Parapluie** (4 wheels under 1 umbrella), offers several tours with candy-colored cars and drivers dressed in striped shirts and berets. The Essential Ride lasts 1.5 hours and costs €90 per person for two, €60 per person if you fit three passengers, and €180 if you want the whole backseat to yourself, same price and duration for the Illuminated Paris Ride (tel. 08 00 80 06 31, mobile 06 67 32 26 68, www.4roues-sous-1parapluie.com, info@4roues-sous-1parapluie.com). **Paris Authentic** offers many comparable options with less personal attention (€65/person for 2 people for a 1-hour tour, €50/person for 3 people; €200/couple for a 2-hour tour that includes Montmartre and a bottle of champagne, 10 percent tip appropriate, 23 Rue Jean-Jacques Rousseau, mobile 06 64 50 44 19, www.parisauthentic.com, paris@parisauthentic.com).

Pedicab Tours

Experience the City of Light at an *escargot*'s pace with your private chauffeur pedaling a sleek, human-powered tricycle from TripUp. Call ahead, book online, or flag one down and use our taxi tour (described later) as a road map; they usually work until about 22:00 (€40-50/hour, mobile 06 98 80 69 33, www.tripup.fr, contact@tripup.fr).

▲Nighttime Bus Tours

City Vision's Paris by Night: City Tour connects all the great illuminated sights of Paris with a 100-minute bus tour in 12 languages. The double-decker buses have huge windows, but the most desirable front seats are sometimes reserved for customers who've bought tickets for the overrated Moulin Rouge. Left-side seats are better. Visibility is fine in the rain. These tours are not for everyone. You'll stampede on with a United Nations of tourists, get a set of headphones, dial up your language, and listen to a recorded spiel (which is interesting, but includes an annoyingly bright TV screen and a pitch for the other, more expensive excursions). Uninspired as it is, the ride provides an entertaining overview of the city at its floodlit and scenic best. Bring your city map to stay oriented as you go. You're always on the bus, but the driver slows for photos at viewpoints (€27, kids-€17, 1.75 hours, departs from 2 Rue des Pyramides at 20:00 Nov-March, at 22:00 April-Oct, reserve one day in advance, arrive 30 minutes early to wait in line for best seats, Mo: Pyramides, tel. 01 42 60 30 01, www.pariscityvision.com). City Vision also offers a Paris by Night tour in a small-group minibus, which follows a similar route to the bus tours. They will pick you up and drop you off at your hotel (€60, kids-€47, 2 hours). For all City Vision tours, buy tickets through your hotel (no booking fee, brochures in lobby) or directly at the City Vision office at 214 Rue de Rivoli, across the street from the Tuileries Métro stop.

You can also take a night tour on **L'OpenTour**'s double-decker buses (see page 41) as extensions of their day-tour program (€47 includes day pass and night tour, night tour not sold separately, April-Oct at 22:00, Nov-March at 18:30, depart from 13 Rue Auber, tel. 01 42 66 56 56, www.parisopentour.com).

▲▲▲Do-It-Yourself Floodlit Paris Taxi Tour

I recommend a loop trip that takes about an hour and connects these sights: Notre-Dame, Hôtel de Ville, Ile St. Louis, the Orsay Museum, Esplanade des Invalides, Champ de Mars park at Place Jacques Rueff (five-minute stop), Eiffel Tower from Place du Trocadéro (five-minute stop), Arc de Triomphe, Champs-Elysées, Place de la Concorde, and the Louvre. The trip should cost about €45 (more on Sun). Taxis have a strict meter of €36/hour plus about €1/kilometer. If your cabbie was easy to work with, add a 10 percent tip; if not, tip just 5 percent.

Sleeping in Paris

I've focused most of my recommendations in three safe, handy, and colorful neighborhoods: the village-like Rue Cler (near the Eiffel Tower); the artsy and trendy Marais (near Place de la Bastille); and the historic island of Ile St. Louis (next door to Notre-Dame). Before choosing a hotel, read the descriptions of the neighborhoods closely. Each offers different pros and cons: Your neighborhood is as important as your hotel for the success of your trip.

If you're looking on your own for accommodations (beyond this book's listings), other neighborhoods to consider are the classy Luxembourg Garden neighborhood (on the Left Bank) and the less polished, less central, but less pricey Montmartre neighborhood.

For lower rates or greater selection, look farther away from the river (prices drop proportionately with distance from the Seine), but be prepared to spend more time on the Métro or bus getting to sights. Those staying at least a week can save on meal costs (if not lodging) by renting an apartment. I also list a few bed-and-breakfast agencies, and give suggestions for sleeping near Paris' airports.

Book your accommodations well in advance for Paris—the sooner, the better, especially if you'll be traveling during busy times. In August and at other times when business is slower, some hotels offer lower rates to fill their rooms. Check hotel websites for the best deals. See page 1116 for a list of major holidays and festivals in Paris; for tips on making reservations, see page 1052.

Old, characteristic, budget Parisian hotels have always been cramped. Retrofitted with private bathrooms and elevators (as most are today), they are even more cramped. Hotel elevators are often very small—pack light, or you may need to take your bags up one at a time.

IN THE RUE CLER NEIGHBORHOOD

(7th arrond. Mo: Ecole Militaire, La Tour Maubourg, or Invalides)

Rue Cler, lined with open-air produce stands, is a safe, tidy, village-like pedestrian street. It's so French that when I step out of my hotel in the morning, I feel like I must have been a poodle in a previous life. How such coziness lodged itself between the high-powered government district, the Eiffel Tower, and Les Invalides, I'll never know. This is a neighborhood of wide, tree-lined boulevards,

Sleep Code

Abbreviations **(€1 = about $1.40, country code: 33)**
S = Single, **D** = Double/Twin, **T** = Triple, **Q** = Quad, **b** = bathroom, **s** = shower only, * = French hotel rating system (0-5 stars).

Price Rankings

- **$$$ Higher Priced**—Most rooms €200 or more.
- **$$ Moderately Priced**—Most rooms between €150-200.
- **$ Lower Priced**—Most rooms €150 or less.

Unless otherwise noted, English is spoken, credit cards are accepted, breakfast is not included (but is usually optional), and hotels have elevators, air-conditioning, a guest computer, and Wi-Fi. "Wi-Fi only" means there's no guest computer available. Prices change; verify current rates online or by email. For the best prices, always book directly with the hotel.

stately apartment buildings, and lots of Americans. The American Church and Franco-American Center (see page 24), American Library, American University, and many of my readers call this area home. Hotels here are a fair value, considering the elegance of the neighborhood. And for sightseeing, you're within walking distance of the Eiffel Tower, Army Museum, Quai Branly Museum, Seine River, Champs-Elysées, and Orsay and Rodin museums.

Become a local at a Rue Cler café for breakfast, or join the afternoon crowd for *une bière pression* (a draft beer). On Rue Cler you can eat and browse your way through a street full of cafés, pastry shops, delis, cheese shops, and colorful outdoor produce stalls. Afternoon *boules* (outdoor bowling) on the Esplanade des Invalides is a relaxing spectator sport (look for the dirt area to the upper right as you face the front of Les Invalides; see sidebar on page 1044). The manicured gardens behind the golden dome of the Army Museum are free, peaceful, and filled with flowers (at southwest corner of grounds, closes at about 19:00), and the new riverfront promenade along the Seine is a fine place to walk, run, bike, or just sit and watch the river.

Though hardly a happening nightlife spot, Rue Cler offers many low-impact after-dark activities. Take an evening stroll above the river through the parkway between Pont de l'Alma and Pont des Invalides. For an after-dinner cruise on the Seine, it's a 15-minute walk to the river and the Bateaux-Mouches (see page 42). For a post-dinner cruise on foot, saunter into the Champ de Mars park to admire the glowing Eiffel Tower. For more ideas on nightlife activities here, see page 164.

Breakfast on Rue Cler: For a great Rue Cler start to your day, drop by **Brasserie Aux PTT,** where Rick Steves readers are promised a *deux pour douze* breakfast special (two "American" breakfasts—juice, a big coffee, croissant, bread, ham, and eggs—for €12; closed Sun, opposite 53 Rue Cler, described in more detail on page 158.

Services: There's a large **post office** at the end of Rue Cler on Avenue de la Motte-Picquet and a handy **SNCF Boutique** at 80 Rue St. Dominique (Mon-Sat 8:30-19:30, closed Sun, get there when it opens to avoid a long wait). At both of these offices, take a number and wait your turn. A smaller post office is closer to the Eiffel Tower on Avenue Rapp, one block past Rue St. Dominique toward the river. You can buy your Paris Museum Pass at **Tabac La Cave à Cigares** on Avenue de la Motte-Picquet, across from where Rue Cler ends, or at **Paris Webservices** on 12 Rue de l'Exposition (see "Travel Agency," below).

Markets: Cross the Champ de Mars park to mix it up with bargain-hunters at the twice-weekly open-air market, **Marché Boulevard de Grenelle,** under the Métro, a few blocks southwest of the Champ de Mars park (Wed and Sun 7:00-12:30, between Mo: Dupleix and Mo: La Motte-Picquet-Grenelle). Two minuscule grocery stores, both on Rue de Grenelle, are open until midnight: **Epicerie de la Tour** (at #197) and **Alimentation** (at corner with Rue Cler). **Rue St. Dominique** is the area's boutique-browsing street and well worth a visit if shopping for clothes.

Internet Access: Com Avenue is good (about €5/hour, shareable and multi-use accounts, Mon-Sat 10:00-20:00, closed Sun, 24 Rue du Champ de Mars, tel. 01 45 55 00 07).

Laundry: Launderettes are omnipresent; ask your hotel for the nearest. Here are three handy locations: on Rue Augereau, on Rue Amélie (both between Rue St. Dominique and Rue de Grenelle), and at the southeast corner of Rue Valadon and Rue de Grenelle.

Travel Agency: Contact the helpful staff at **Paris Webservices** to book *"coupe-file"* tickets that allow you to skip the line at key sights, buy the Paris Museum Pass, or for assistance with hotels, transportation, local guides, or excursions (5-10 percent off many services with this book in 2015, use code "PWS52K15" when booking; office open Mon-Sat 8:00-18:00, closed Sun; available by phone daily until 21:00, 12 Rue de l'Exposition, Mo: Ecole Militaire, RER: Pont de l'Alma, tel. 01 45 56 91 67, www.pariswebservices.com, contactpws@pariswebservices.com).

Métro Connections: Key Métro stops are Ecole Militaire, La Tour Maubourg, and Invalides. The useful RER-C line runs from the Pont de l'Alma and Invalides stations, serving Versailles to the southwest; the Marmottan Museum and Auvers-sur-Oise to the northwest; and the Orsay Museum, Latin Quarter (St. Michel stop), and Austerlitz train station to the east.

Bus Routes: Smart travelers take advantage of these bus routes (see map on page 36 for stop locations):

Line #69 runs east along Rue St. Dominique and serves Les Invalides, Orsay, Louvre, Marais, and Père Lachaise Cemetery.

Line #63 runs along the river (the Quai d'Orsay), serving the Latin Quarter along Boulevard St. Germain to the east (ending at Gare de Lyon), and Trocadéro and areas near the Marmottan Museum to the west.

Line #92 runs along Avenue Bosquet, north to the Champs-Elysées and Arc de Triomphe (faster than the Métro) and south to the Montparnasse Tower and Gare Montparnasse.

Line #87 runs from Avenue Joseph Bouvard in the Champ de Mars park up Avenue de la Bourdonnais and serves the Sèvres-Babylone shopping area, St. Sulpice Church, Luxembourg Garden, the Bastille, and Gare de Lyon (also more convenient than Métro for these destinations).

Line #80 runs on Avenue Bosquet, crosses the Champs-Elysées, stops near the Jacquemart-André Museum, and serves Gare St. Lazare.

Line #28 runs on Boulevard de la Tour Maubourg and serves Gare St. Lazare.

Line #42 runs from Avenue Joseph Bouvard in the Champs de Mars park (same stop as #87), crosses the Champs-Elysées at the Rond-Point, then heads to Place de la Concorde, Place de la Madeleine, Opéra Garnier, and finally to Gare du Nord—a long ride to the train station but less tiring than the Métro if you're carrying suitcases.

In the Heart of Rue Cler

Many of my readers stay in the Rue Cler neighborhood. If you want to disappear into Paris, choose a hotel elsewhere. The following hotels are within Camembert-smelling distance of Rue Cler.

$$$ Hôtel Relais Bosquet*** is an exceptionally good hotel in an ideal location, with comfortable public spaces and well-configured rooms that are large by local standards and feature effective darkness blinds. The staff are politely formal and offer a 10 percent discount off the public rate to anyone booking direct with this book in 2015—but you may get better rates by "liking" and booking the hotel through their Facebook page (standard Db-€155-275, bigger Db-€175-295, superior Db-€195-315, extra bed-€30, good €15 breakfast buffet with eggs and sausage, 19 Rue du Champ de Mars, tel. 01 47 05 25 45, www.hotel-paris-bosquet.com, hotel@relaisbosquet.com).

$$$ Hôtel du Cadran***, a well-located *boule* toss from Rue Cler, is daringly modern. You'll find an efficient staff and über-

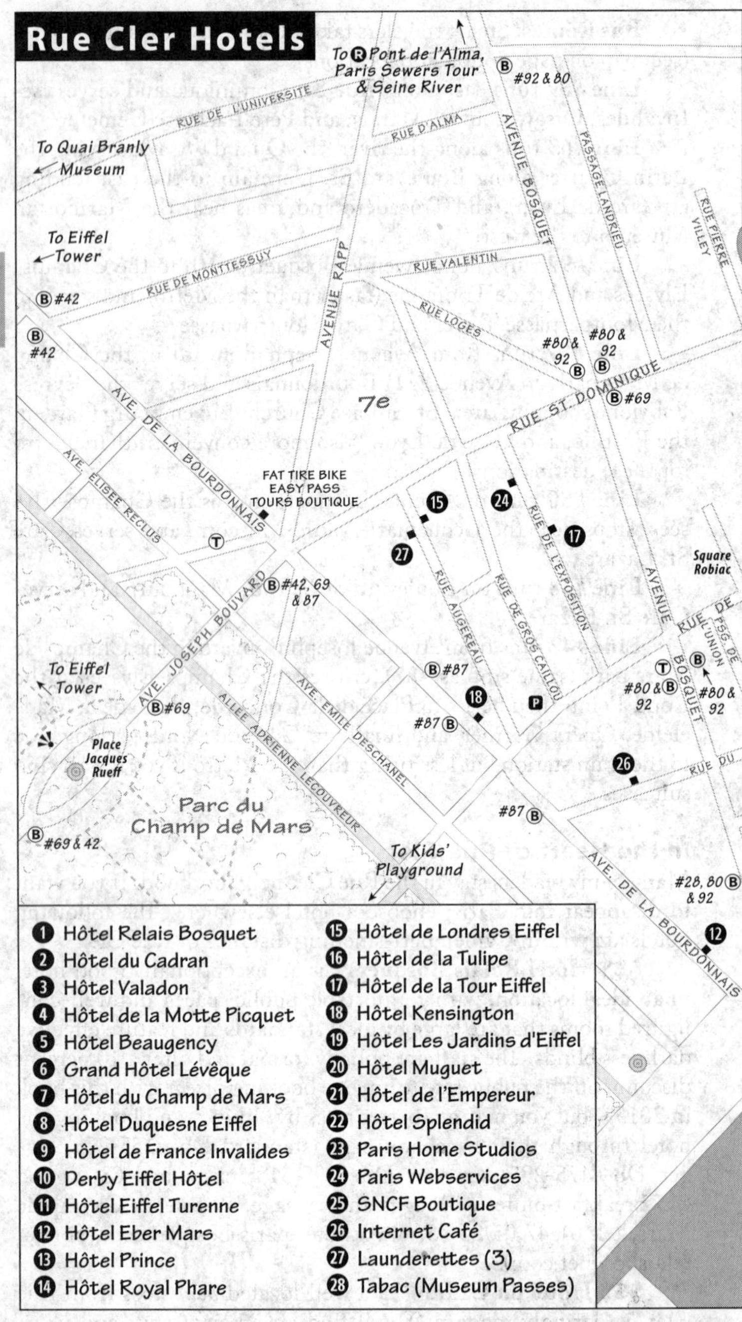
Rue Cler Hotels
To Pont de l'Alma, Paris Sewers Tour & Seine River
#92 & 80
RUE DE L'UNIVERSITE
RUE D'ALMA
To Quai Branly Museum
AVENUE BOSQUET
PASSAGE LANDRIEU
RUE PIERRE VILLEY
To Eiffel Tower
RUE DE MONTTESSUY
AVENUE RAPP
RUE VALENTIN
#42
RUE LOGES
#80 & 92
#80 & 92
RUE ST. DOMINIQUE
#69
7e
AVE. DE LA BOURDONNAIS
AVE. ELISEE RECLUS
FAT TIRE BIKE EASY PASS TOURS BOUTIQUE
RUE DE L'EXPOSITION
Square Robiac
AVE. JOSEPH BOUVARD
#42, 69 & 87
RUE AUGEREAU
RUE DE GROS CAILLOU
RUE DE L'UNION
PSG. DE
To Eiffel Tower
#87
#80 & 92
#80 & 92
#69
ALLEE ADRIENNE LECOUVREUR
AVE. EMILE DESCHANEL
#87
Place Jacques Rueff
RUE DU
Parc du Champ de Mars
#87
#69 & 42
To Kids' Playground
#28, 80 & 92
1 Hôtel Relais Bosquet
2 Hôtel du Cadran
3 Hôtel Valadon
4 Hôtel de la Motte Picquet
5 Hôtel Beaugency
6 Grand Hôtel Lévêque
7 Hôtel du Champ de Mars
8 Hôtel Duquesne Eiffel
9 Hôtel de France Invalides
10 Derby Eiffel Hôtel
11 Hôtel Eiffel Turenne
12 Hôtel Eber Mars
13 Hôtel Prince
14 Hôtel Royal Phare
15 Hôtel de Londres Eiffel
16 Hôtel de la Tulipe
17 Hôtel de la Tour Eiffel
18 Hôtel Kensington
19 Hôtel Les Jardins d'Eiffel
20 Hôtel Muguet
21 Hôtel de l'Empereur
22 Hôtel Splendid
23 Paris Home Studios
24 Paris Webservices
25 SNCF Boutique
26 Internet Café
27 Launderettes (3)
28 Tabac (Museum Passes)

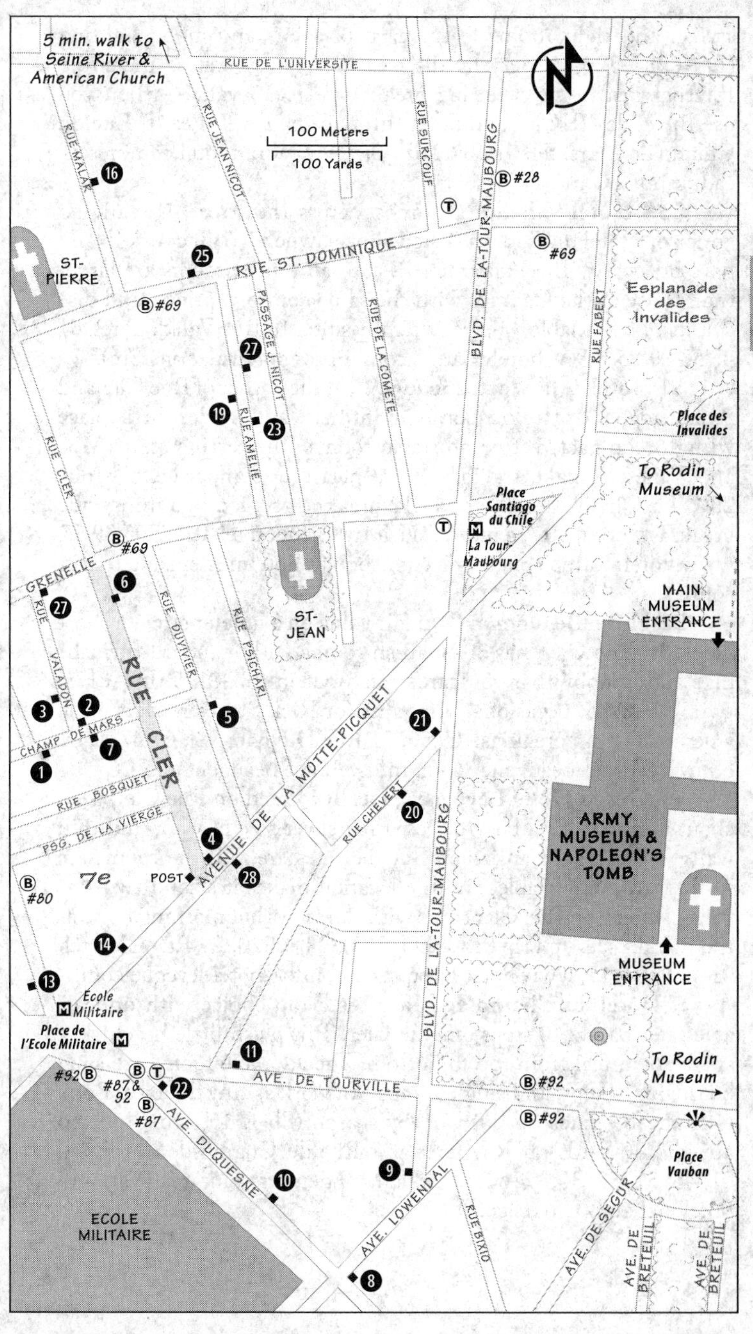

5 min. walk to Seine River & American Church
RUE DE L'UNIVERSITE
100 Meters
100 Yards
RUE MALAR
RUE JEAN NICOT
RUE SURCOUF
BLVD. DE LA-TOUR-MAUBOURG
#28
ST-PIERRE
RUE ST. DOMINIQUE
#69
PASSAGE J. NICOT
RUE DE LA COMETE
RUE FABERT
Esplanade des Invalides
RUE AMELIE
RUE CLER
Place des Invalides
To Rodin Museum
Place Santiago du Chile
La Tour-Maubourg
GRENELLE
RUE VALADON
RUE DUVIVIER
RUE PSICHARI
ST-JEAN
MAIN MUSEUM ENTRANCE
RUE CLER
CHAMP DE MARS
AVENUE DE LA MOTTE-PICQUET
RUE BOSQUET
PSG. DE LA VIERGE
RUE CHEVERT
ARMY MUSEUM & NAPOLEON'S TOMB
7e
POST
#80
MUSEUM ENTRANCE
Ecole Militaire
Place de l'Ecole Militaire
AVE. DE TOURVILLE
#92
#87 & 92
#87
AVE. DUQUESNE
AVE. LOWENDAL
RUE BIXIO
AVE. DE SEGUR
Place Vauban
ECOLE MILITAIRE
AVE. DE BRETEUIL

PARIS

stylish and tight rooms featuring cool colors and mood lighting (Db-€280-320; 5 percent discount off lowest rates, including Internet deals, and free, big breakfast—a €13 value—when you use the code "RICK" and book through their website; 10 Rue du Champ de Mars, tel. 01 40 62 67 00, www.cadranhotel.com, resa@cadranhotel.com).

$$$ Hôtel Valadon***, almost across the street, is really an annex of Hôtel du Cadran (listed above), where you'll check in and have breakfast. The Valadron's 12 cute-and-quiet rooms are larger than those at the Cadran, with the same comfort, prices, and discounts (Tb available, one good family suite, 16 Rue Valadon, tel. 01 47 53 89 85, www.hotelvaladon.com, info@hotelvaladon.com).

$$ Hôtel de la Motte Picquet***, at the corner of Rue Cler and Avenue de la Motte-Picquet, is an intimate and modest little place with 16 compact, yet comfortable rooms. The terrific staff (Moe and Vanessa) make staying here a pleasure (standard Db-€160-230, Tb/Qb-€270-350, good €12 breakfast served in a minuscule breakfast room, 30 Avenue de la Motte-Picquet, tel. 01 47 05 09 57, www.hotelmottepicquetparis.com, book@hotelmottepicquetparis.com).

$$ Hôtel Beaugency***, a fair value on a quieter street a short block off Rue Cler, has 30 smallish rooms with standard furnishings and a lobby that you can stretch out in (Sb-€125, Db-€175, twin Db-€185, occasional discounts for Rick Steves readers—ask when you book, breakfast-€9.50, 21 Rue Duvivier, tel. 01 47 05 01 63, www.hotel-beaugency.com, infos@hotel-beaugency.com).

$$ Grand Hôtel Lévêque**, ideally located on Rue Cler, is all about location. It's a busy place with a sliver-size elevator and thin walls (noise can be an issue). But the rates are fair, the rooms are sufficiently comfortable, and the location makes it a solid two-star value. Rooms on Rue Cler come with fun views but morning noise as the market sets up (Sb-€130, Db-€170, Tb-€220, 29 Rue Cler, tel. 01 47 05 49 15, www.hotel-leveque.com, info@hotel-leveque.com).

$ Hôtel du Champ de Mars** is a top choice with unbeatable rates barely 10 steps off Rue Cler. This plush little hotel has a small-town feel from top to bottom. The adorable rooms are snug but lovingly kept, and single rooms can work as tiny doubles. Book well ahead—rates do not vary by season (Sb-€115, Db-€135, no air-con, 30 yards off Rue Cler at 7 Rue du Champ de Mars, tel. 01 45 51 52 30, www.hotelduchampdemars.com, reservation@hotelduchampdemars.com).

Near Rue Cler, Close to Ecole Militaire Métro Stop

The following listings are a five-minute walk from Rue Cler, near the Ecole Militaire Métro stop or RER: Pont de l'Alma.

$$$ Hôtel Duquesne Eiffel*,** a few blocks farther from the action, is calm, hospitable, and very comfortable. It features handsome rooms (some with terrific Eiffel Tower views), a welcoming lobby, and a big, hot breakfast for €13 (Db-€200-270, price grows with room size, Tb-€220-300, 10 percent less with this book in 2015, 23 Avenue Duquesne, tel. 01 44 42 09 09, www.hde.fr, contact@hde.fr).

$$$ Hôtel de France Invalides** is a fair midrange option away from most other hotels I list. It's run by a brother-sister team (Alain and Marie-Hélène) with a small bar/lounge and 60 well-maintained rooms, some with knockout views of Invalides' golden dome, but no air-conditioning. Rooms on the courtyard are quiet, while those on the Les Invalides side face a large street (Sb-€140, standard Db-€160-300, connecting rooms possible for families, 5 percent discount with this book in 2015, breakfast-€14, 102 Boulevard de la Tour Maubourg, tel. 01 47 05 40 49, www.hoteldefrance.com, contact@hoteldefrance.com).

$$ Derby Eiffel Hôtel*,** a few blocks from the Ecole Militaire Métro stop, has a comfortable lobby and updated rooms (Db-€150-200, Tb-€200-250, 5 Avenue Duquesne, tel. 01 47 05 12 05, www.hotelderbyeiffel.com, derbyeiffelhotel@orange.fr).

$$ Hôtel Eiffel Turenne** is a fair two-star bet with comfortable rooms at OK rates and a lobby with windows on the world. The hotel plans to renovate in 2015, so expect changes from these rates (Sb-€150, Db-€170-220, Tb-€210-250, 20 Avenue de Tourville, tel. 01 47 05 99 92, www.hoteleiffelturenne.com, reservation@hoteleiffelturenne.com).

$$ Hôtel Eber Mars,** a few steps from Champs de Mars park, has comfortable, larger-than-average rooms, an I-try-harder owner, and a sliver elevator (Db without air-con-€120-220, Db with air-con-€160-280, good Tb-€220-300, continental breakfast-€10, 117 Avenue de la Bourdonnais, tel. 01 47 05 42 30, www.hotelebermars.com, reservation@hotelebermars.com).

$ Hôtel Prince,** across from the Ecole Militaire Métro stop, has a spartan lobby and drab halls, but offers good, air-conditioned rooms for the price (Sb-€109, Db-€130, Tb-€150, Wi-Fi only, 66 Avenue Bosquet, tel. 01 47 05 40 90, www.hotel-paris-prince.com, paris@hotel-prince.com).

$ Hôtel Royal Phare,** facing the busy Ecole Militaire Métro stop, is a humble place with 34 unimaginative but perfectly sleepable rooms. Rooms on the courtyard are quietest, with peek-a-boo views of the Eiffel Tower from the fifth floor up (Sb-€100, Db with shower-€115, Db with bath-€125, Tb-€140, breakfast-€7.50, fridges in rooms, no air-con but fans, no Wi-Fi, 40 Avenue de la Motte-Picquet, tel. 01 47 05 57 30, www.hotel-royalphare-paris.com, hotel-royalphare@wanadoo.fr, friendly manager Hocin).

Near Rue Cler, Closer to Rue St. Dominique (and the Seine)

$$$ Hôtel de Londres Eiffel*** is my closest listing to the Eiffel Tower and the Champ de Mars park. Here you get immaculate, warmly decorated rooms (several are connecting for families), snazzy public spaces, and a service-oriented staff. Some rooms are pretty small—request a bigger room. It's less convenient to the Métro (10-minute walk), but very handy to buses #69, #80, #87, and #92, and to RER-C: Pont de l'Alma (Sb-€185, small Db-€220, bigger Db-€240, Db with Eiffel Tower view-€260, Tb-€285, big price swings depending on availability, 1 Rue Augereau, tel. 01 45 51 63 02, www.hotel-paris-londres-eiffel.com, info@londres-eiffel.com, helpful Cédric and Arnaud). The owners also run a good two-star hotel with similar comfort in the cheaper Montparnasse area, **$$ Hôtel Apollon Montparnasse** (Db-€140-170, look for Web deals, 91 Rue de l'Ouest, Mo: Pernety, tel. 01 43 95 62 00, www.paris-hotel-paris.net, info@apollon-montparnasse.com).

$$ Hôtel de la Tulipe***, three blocks from Rue Cler toward the river, has street appeal. The 20 simple rooms surround a seductive, wood-beamed lounge and a small, leafy courtyard (no picnics, please). The owners promise at least a 10 percent discount when you book direct with this book in 2015 (Sb-€170, Db-€190-210, Tb-€230, 4-person apartment-€350, 2-room suite for up to 5 people-€400, continental breakfast-€11, no air-con, no elevator, 33 Rue Malar, tel. 01 45 51 67 21, www.paris-hotel-tulipe.com, hoteldelatulipe@wanadoo.fr).

$ Hôtel de la Tour Eiffel** is a solid two-star value on a quiet street near several of my favorite restaurants. The rooms are well-designed, well-kept, and comfortable. Some rooms have thin walls and none has air-conditioning, but there are six sets of connecting rooms—ideal for families (snug Db-€115, bigger Db-€135-155, Wi-Fi only, 17 Rue de l'Exposition, tel. 01 47 05 14 75, www.hotel-toureiffel.com, hte7@wanadoo.fr).

$ Hôtel Kensington** is a basic budget value close to the Eiffel Tower and run by formal Daniele. It's an unpretentious place with small, modest-but-good-enough rooms (Sb-€79, Db-€99, bigger Db on back side-€122, Eiffel Tower views for those who ask, no air-con, pay guest computer, 79 Avenue de la Bourdonnais, tel. 01 47 05 74 00, www.hotel-kensington.com, hk@hotel-kensington.com).

Near La Tour Maubourg Métro Stop

These listings are within three blocks of the intersection of Avenue de la Motte-Picquet and Boulevard de la Tour Maubourg.

$$$ Hôtel Les Jardins d'Eiffel***, on a quiet street, is a surprisingly big place with professional service, its own parking garage (€24/day), a peaceful patio, and a lobby you can stretch out in. The 80 well-configured rooms—some with partial Eiffel Tower views, some with balconies—offer a bit more space and quiet than other hotels (Db-€170-310, 15 percent Rick Steves discount when you book direct in 2015, check website for discounts, 8 Rue Amélie, tel. 01 47 05 46 21, www.hoteljardinseiffel.com, reservations@hoteljardinseiffel.com).

$$$ Hôtel Muguet*** is a peaceful, immaculate refuge with good rates. This delightful spot offers 43 tasteful rooms with wood furnishings, a greenhouse lounge, and a small garden courtyard. The hands-on manager, Charlene, gives her guests a restful and secure home in Paris (Db-€150-235—more with view, Tb-€235-275, strict cancellation policy: cancel 7 days before arrival or lose deposit, 11 Rue Chevert, tel. 01 47 05 05 93, www.hotelparismuguet.com, muguet@wanadoo.fr).

$$$ Hôtel de l'Empereur** is stylish and delivers smashing views of Invalides from many of its fine rooms. All rooms have queen-size beds, are tastefully designed, and are large by Paris standards (Sb-€140-175, Db-€150-250—more with view, Tb-€225-275, two-room Qb-€300-400, strict cancellation policy: cancel 7 days before arrival or lose deposit, 2 Rue Chevert, tel. 01 45 55 88 02, www.hotelempereurparis.com, contact@hotelempereur.com).

Lesser Values in the Rue Cler Area

Given how fine this area is, this is an acceptable last choice.

$$$ Hôtel Splendid***, at a major intersection near the Ecole Militaire Métro stop, offers adequate comfort with faded furnishings at high prices. Several rooms have a sensational Eiffel Tower view (Sb-€200, standard Db-€240, superior Db with balcony and view-€260, suites-€370, deals for Rick Steves readers, continental breakfast-€12, pay Wi-Fi, small bar, 29 Avenue de Tourville, tel. 01 45 51 29 29, www.hotel-splendid-paris.com, reservation@hotel-splendid-paris.com, helpful Dennis).

IN THE MARAIS NEIGHBORHOOD

Those interested in a more central, diverse, and lively urban locale should make the Marais their Parisian home. Once a forgotten Parisian backwater, the Marais—which runs from the Pompidou Center east to the Bastille (a 15-minute walk)—is now one of Paris' most popular residential, tourist, and shopping areas. This is jumbled, medieval Paris at its finest, where classy stone mansions sit alongside trendy bars, antique shops, and fashion-conscious boutiques. The streets are an intriguing parade of artists, students, tourists, immigrants, and baguette-munching babies in strollers. The Marais is also known as a hub of the Parisian gay and lesbian scene. This area is *sans* doubt livelier and edgier than the Rue Cler area.

In the Marais you have these major sights close at hand: the Carnavalet Museum, Victor Hugo's House, the Jewish Art and History Museum, the Pompidou Center, and the Picasso Museum. You're also a manageable walk from Paris' two islands (Ile St. Louis and Ile de la Cité), home to Notre-Dame and Sainte-Chapelle. The Opéra Bastille, Promenade Plantée park, Place des Vosges (Paris' oldest square), the Jewish Quarter (Rue des Rosiers), the Latin Quarter, and nightlife-packed Rue de Lappe are also walkable. Strolling home (day or night) from Notre-Dame along Ile St. Louis is marvelous.

Most of my recommended hotels are located a few blocks north of the Marais' main east-west drag, Rue St. Antoine/Rue de Rivoli. For those who prefer a quieter home with fewer tourists, I list several hotels in the northern limits of the Marais, near Rue de Bretagne, the appealing commercial spine of this area.

Tourist Information: The nearest TI is at the Pyramides Métro station (daily May-Oct 9:00-19:00, Nov-April 10:00-19:00, 25 Rue des Pyramides).

Services: Most banks and other services are on the main street, Rue de Rivoli, which becomes Rue St. Antoine as it heads east. Marais **post offices** are on Rue Castex and at the corner of Rue Pavée and Rue des Francs-Bourgeois. A busy **SNCF Boutique,** where you can take care of all train needs, is just off Rue St. Antoine at 4 Rue de Turenne (Mon-Fri 8:00-20:30, Sat 10:00-20:30, closed Sun). A quieter SNCF Boutique is nearer Gare de Lyon at 5 Rue de Lyon (Mon-Sat 8:30-18:00, closed Sun). An English language **bookstore** called I Love My Blender is located at 36 Rue du Temple (closed Sun-Mon).

Markets: The Marais has three good farmers' markets close by: the sprawling **Marché de la Bastille,** along Boulevard Richard Lenoir, on the north side of Place de la Bastille (Thu and Sun until 14:30, Mo: Bastille); the **Marché d'Aligre** on Place d'Aligre (Tue-Sat 9:00-14:00, closed Mon, Mo: Ledru-Rollin); and Paris' oldest covered market, the **Marché des Enfants Rouges** at 39 Rue de Bretagne, a 10-minute walk north of Rue de Rivoli (Mo: Filles du Calvaire or Temple). A small **grocery** is open until 23:00 on Rue St. Antoine (near intersection with Rue Castex), and a **Monoprix** with a basement grocery is at 62 Rue St. Antoine near the St-Paul Métro stop. To shop at a Parisian Sears, find the **BHV** department store next to Hôtel de Ville.

Internet Access: Try **Paris CY** (Mon-Sat 10:00-20:00, closed Sun, 8 Rue de Jouy, Mo: St-Paul, tel. 01 42 71 37 37).

Laundry: Launderettes are scattered throughout the Marais; ask your hotelier for the nearest. Here are three you can count on: on Impasse Guéménée (north of Rue St. Antoine), on Rue Ste. Croix de la Bretonnerie (just east of Rue du Temple), and on Rue du Petit Musc (south of Rue St. Antoine).

Métro Connections: Key Métro stops in the Marais are, from east to west: Bastille, St-Paul, and Hôtel de Ville (Sully-Morland, Pont Marie, and Rambuteau stops are also handy). Métro connections are excellent, with direct service to the Louvre, Champs-Elysées, Arc de Triomphe, and La Défense (all on line 1); the Rue Cler area, Place de la Madeleine, and Opéra Garnier/Galeries Lafayette (line 8 from Bastille stop); and four major train stations: Gare de Lyon, Gare du Nord, Gare de l'Est, and Gare d'Austerlitz (all accessible from Bastille stop).

Bus Routes: For stop locations, see the "Marais Hotels" map.

Line #69 on Rue St. Antoine takes you eastbound to Père Lachaise Cemetery and westbound to the Louvre, Orsay, and Rodin museums, plus the Army Museum, ending at the Eiffel Tower.

Line #87 runs down Boulevard Henri IV, crossing Ile St. Louis and serving the Latin Quarter along Boulevard St. Germain, before heading to St. Sulpice Church/Luxembourg Garden, the Eiffel Tower, and the Rue Cler neighborhood to the west. The same line, running in the opposite direction, brings you to Gare de Lyon.

Line #96 runs on Rues Turenne and Rivoli, serves Ile de la Cité and St. Sulpice Church (near Luxembourg Garden), and ends at Gare Montparnasse.

Line #65 runs from Gare de Lyon up Rue de Lyon, around Place de la Bastille, and then up Boulevard Beaumarchais to Gare de l'Est and Gare du Nord.

Line #67 runs from Place d'Italie to the Jardin des Plantes (just south of the Seine), across Ile St. Louis (on Boulevard Henri IV), along Rue de Rivoli past the Louvre, then up to Montmartre.

Taxis: You'll find taxi stands on Place de la Bastille (where Boulevard Richard Lenoir meets the square), on the south side of Rue St. Antoine (in front of St. Paul Church), behind the Hôtel de Ville on Rue du Lobau (where it meets Rue de Rivoli), and a quieter one on the north side of Rue St. Antoine (where it meets Rue Castex).

Near Place des Vosges

(3rd and 4th arrond., Mo: Bastille, St-Paul, or Hôtel de Ville)

$$$ Hôtel le Pavillon de la Reine***,** 15 steps off the beautiful Place des Vosges, merits its stars with top service and comfort and exquisite attention to detail, from its melt-in-your-couch lobby to

Marais Hotels

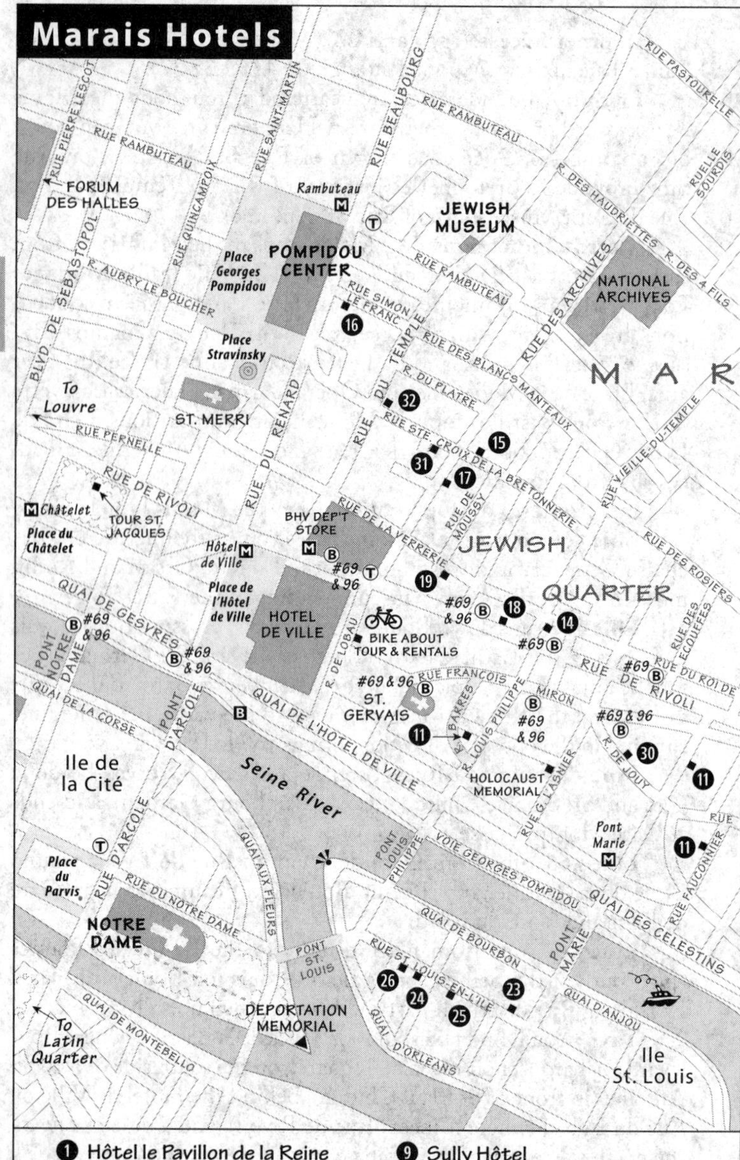

1 Hôtel le Pavillon de la Reine
2 Hôtel St. Paul le Marais
3 Hôtel Castex
4 Hôtel Bastille Spéria
5 Hôtel St. Louis Marais
6 Hôtel du 7ème Art
7 Hôtel de la Place des Vosges
8 Hôtel Jeanne d'Arc
9 Sully Hôtel
10 Hôtel Pratic
11 MIJE Hostels (3)
12 Hôtel Ibis Paris Bastille Opéra
13 Hôtel Daval
14 Hôtel Caron de Beaumarchais
15 Hôtel de la Bretonnerie
16 Hôtel Beaubourg

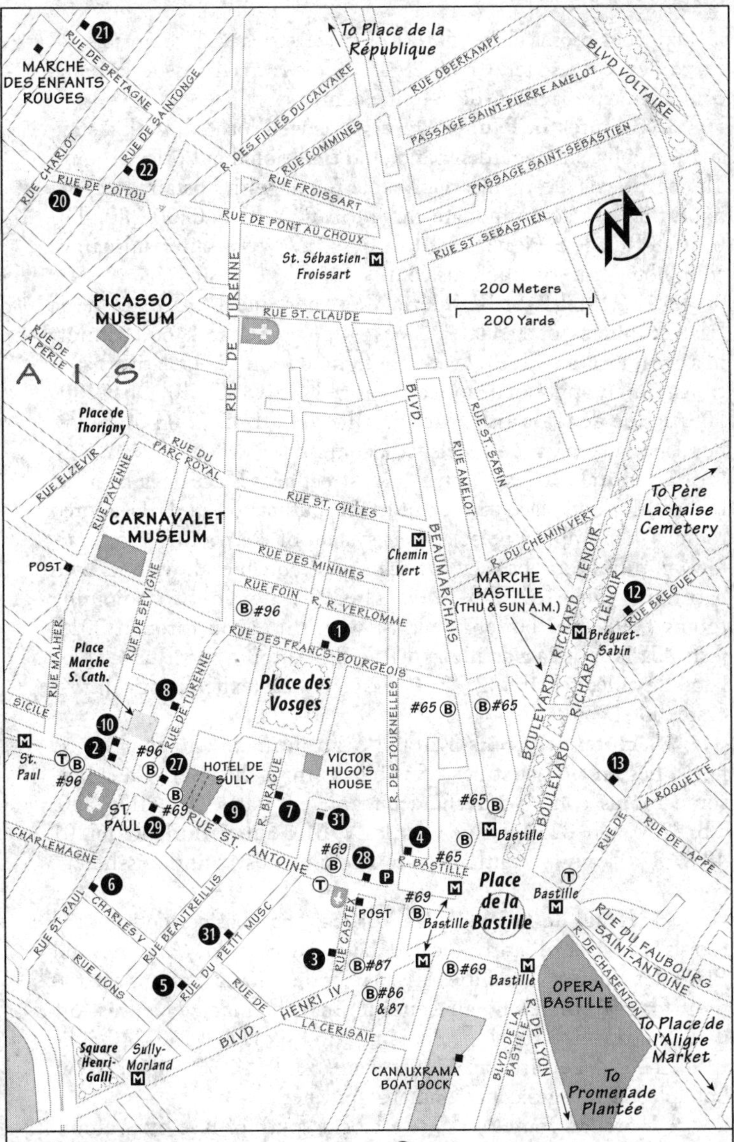

17 D'Win Hôtel
18 Hôtel de Nice
19 Hôtel du Loiret
20 Hôtel Petit Moulin
21 Hôtel du Vieux Saule
22 Hôtel Saintonge
23 Hôtel du Jeu de Paume
24 Hôtel de Lutèce
25 Hôtel des Deux-Iles
26 Hôtel Saint-Louis
27 SNCF Boutique
28 Late-Night Grocery
29 Monoprix (Grocery)
30 Internet Café
31 Launderettes (3)
32 I Love My Blender Book Store

its luxurious rooms (Db-€400-900, price varies with room size, 28 Place des Vosges, tel. 01 40 29 19 19, www.pavillon-de-la-reine.com, contact@pavillon-de-la-reine.com).

$$$ Hôtel St. Paul le Marais* ** is well-located, with a stay-awhile lobby, small garden patio, and traditional but pricey rooms. The best deals are their large double rooms with upstairs sleeping nook that can accommodate three (Sb-€220, Db-€200-280, Tb-€350, 8 Rue de Sevigné, tel. 01 48 04 97 27, www.saintpaulmarais.com, hotel@saintpaulmarais.com).

$$$ Hôtel Bastille Spéria*,** a short block off Place de la Bastille, offers impersonal, business-type service and good comfort in a great location. The 42 well-configured rooms are relatively spacious, simply appointed, and fairly priced (Sb-€180-210, Db-€200-300, 1 Rue de la Bastille, Mo: Bastille, tel. 01 42 72 04 01, www.hotelsperia.com, info@hotelsperia.com).

$$ Hôtel Castex*,** on a quiet street near Place de la Bastille, is a well-located place with comfortable but narrow and tile-floored rooms (that amplify noise). Their system of connecting rooms allows families total privacy between two rooms, each with its own bathroom (Sb-€169, Db-€199, Tb-€239, Qb in two adjoining rooms-€398, free buffet breakfast with this book through 2015, just off Place de la Bastille and Rue St. Antoine at 5 Rue Castex, Mo: Bastille, tel. 01 42 72 31 52, www.castexhotel.com, info@castexhotel.com).

$$ Hôtel St. Louis Marais*,** an intimate and sharp little hotel, lies on a quiet street a few blocks from the river. The handsome rooms come with character and fair rates (Db-€175-230, Tb-€230, Qb-€250, 1 Rue Charles V, Mo: Sully-Morland, tel. 01 48 87 87 04, www.saintlouismarais.com marais@saintlouis-hotels.com).

$$ Hôtel de la Place des Vosges** has basic wood-floored rooms and is brilliantly located between Rue St. Antoine and Place des Vosges. Amenities are sparse, the smallest rooms are too tight for two, there's no air-conditioning, the management is formal, and the elevator skips floors five and six (Db-€150-200, Tb-€190, 12 Rue de Biraque, Mo: St-Paul, tel. 01 42 72 60 46, www.hotelplacedesvosges.com, contact@hpdv.net).

$ Hôtel du 7ème Art,** two blocks south of Rue St. Antoine toward the river, is a young, carefree, Hollywood-nostalgia place with a full-service café-bar and self-service laundry. Its 23 good-value rooms have brown 1970s decor and faded carpets, but the price is fair. The large rooms are American-spacious (small Db-€120, standard Db-€140, large Db-€160-180, extra bed-€20, no elevator, 20 Rue St-Paul, Mo: St-Paul, tel. 01 44 54 85 00, www.paris-hotel-7art.com, reservation@paris-hotel-7art.com).

$ Hôtel Jeanne d'Arc**, a lovely little hotel with thoughtfully appointed rooms, is ideally located for (and very popular with) connoisseurs of the Marais. It's an exceptional value and worth booking way ahead (three months in advance, if possible). Sixth-floor rooms have views, and corner rooms are wonderfully bright in the City of Light but have twin beds only. Rooms on the street can be noisy until the bars close (Sb-€72-98, Db-€120, larger twin Db-€150, Qb suite-€250, no air-con, Wi-Fi only—in lobby, 3 Rue de Jarente, Mo: St-Paul, tel. 01 48 87 62 11, www.hoteljeannedarc.com, information@hoteljeannedarc.com).

$ Sully Hôtel, right on Rue St. Antoine, is a basic, cheap dive run by no-nonsense Monsieur Zeroual. The rooms are frumpy, dimly lit, and can smell of smoke, and the entry is dark and narrow, but the price fits. Two can spring for a triple for more room (Db-€90, Tb-€110, Qb-€120, no elevator, no air-con, Wi-Fi only, 48 Rue St. Antoine, Mo: St-Paul, tel. 01 42 78 49 32, www.sullyhotelparis.com, sullyhotel@orange.fr).

$ Hôtel Pratic, just off the quiet and charming Place du Sainte Catherine, works for travelers who don't mind squeezing sideways to make it past the bed into the bathroom. The half-timbered interior gives this hotel a modest level of charm, but also makes for dark hallways (Sb-€79, Db-€99-157, more for rooms with view of square, no elevator, no air-con, 9 Rue d'Ormesson, tel. 01 48 87 80 47, www.pratichotelparis.com, pratic.hotel@wanadoo.fr).

$ *MIJE Youth Hostels:* The Maison Internationale de la Jeunesse et des Etudiants (MIJE) runs three classy old residences, ideal for budget travelers who are at least 18 years old or traveling with someone who is. Each is well-maintained, with simple, clean, single-sex (unless your group takes a whole room) one- to four-bed rooms for travelers from age 6 to 106. The hostels are **MIJE Fourcy** (biggest and loudest, €11 dinners available with a membership card, 6 Rue de Fourcy, just south of Rue de Rivoli), **MIJE Fauconnier** (no elevator, 11 Rue du Fauconnier), and **MIJE Maubisson** (smallest and quietest, no outdoor terrace, 12 Rue des Barres). None has double beds or air-conditioning, all have private showers in every room—but bring your own towel (all prices per person: Sb-€55, Db-€41, Tb-€36, Qb-€34, includes breakfast, required membership card-€2.50 extra/person, pay Wi-Fi in common areas only, 7-day maximum stay, rooms locked 12:00-15:00, curfew at 1:00 in the morning). They all share the same contact information (tel. 01 42 74 23 45, www.mije.com, info@mije.com) and Métro stop (St-Paul). Reservations are accepted (6 weeks ahead online, 10 days ahead by phone)—though you must show up by noon, or call the morning of arrival to confirm a later arrival time.

East of Boulevard Richard Lenoir

(11th arrond., Mo: Bastille or Bréguet–Sabin)

These cheaper hotels are located a 10-minute walk from Place des Vosges.

$$ Hôtel Ibis Paris Bastille Opéra** is well-run and massive, with 300 reasonably priced, modern, comfortable rooms and a lobby with guest computers and room to roam. Amenities include a dirt-cheap restaurant and private parking (Db-€160, air-con, 15 Rue Breguet, Mo: Bréguet-Sabin, tel. 01 49 29 20 20, www.ibishotel.com, H1399@accor.com.

$ Hôtel Daval,** an unassuming and well-managed place on the wild side of Place de la Bastille, is ideal for night owls. The 23 rooms are small and modest with ship cabin-like bathrooms, but clean and well-maintained, and the rates are good for an air-conditioned place. Ask for a quieter room on the courtyard side (Sb-€98, Db-€110, Tb-€130, Qb-€179, 21 Rue Daval, Mo: Bastille, tel. 01 47 00 51 23, www.hoteldaval.com, hoteldaval@wanadoo.fr).

Near the Pompidou Center

(4th arrond., Mo: St-Paul, Hôtel de Ville, or Rambuteau)

These hotels are farther west, closer to the Pompidou Center than to Place de la Bastille.

$$ Hôtel Caron de Beaumarchais***, on a busy corner, offers 19 pricey but cared-for and character-filled rooms. Its small lobby is cluttered with bits from an elegant 18th-century Marais house (small Db in back-€175, larger Db facing the front-€198, 12 Rue Vieille du Temple, tel. 01 42 72 34 12, www.carondebeaumarchais.com, hotel@carondebeaumarchais.com).

$$ Hôtel de la Bretonnerie***, three blocks from the Hôtel de Ville, makes a fine Marais home. It has a warm, welcoming lobby, helpful staff, and 29 well-appointed, good-value rooms with an antique, open-beam warmth but no air-conditioning (standard "classic" Db-€155, bigger "charming" Db-€185, Db suite-€210, Tb/Qb-€235, between Rue Vieille du Temple and Rue des Archives at 22 Rue Ste. Croix de la Bretonnerie, tel. 01 48 87 77 63, www.bretonnerie.com, hotel@bretonnerie.com).

$$ Hôtel Beaubourg*** is a terrific three-star value on a small street in the shadow of the Pompidou Center. The lounge is inviting, and the 28 plush and traditional rooms are well-appointed and quiet (standard Db-€135-165, bigger twin or king-size Db-€145-175 and worth the extra cost, Db suite with private patio-€190-230, 11 Rue Simon Le Franc, Mo: Rambuteau, tel. 01 42 74 34 24, www.beaubourg-paris-hotel.com, reservation@hotelbeaubourg.com).

$ D'Win Hôtel** is a rare two-star value in the thick of the Marais, with 40 updated and generally spacious rooms, no air-con (but coming soon), and red accents everywhere (Db-€130-140,

Tb-€170, Qb-€200, 20 Rue du Temple, tel. 01 44 54 05 05, www.dwinhotel.com, contact@dwinhotel.com).

$ Hôtel de Nice**, on the Marais' busy main drag, features a turquoise-and-fuchsia "Marie-Antoinette-does-tie-dye" decor. Its narrow halls are littered with paintings and layered with carpets, and its 23 Old World rooms have thoughtful touches and tight bathrooms. Twin rooms, which cost the same as doubles, are larger. Rooms on the street come with some noise (Sb-€85-150, Db-€115-220, Tb-€135-240, reception on second floor, 42 bis Rue de Rivoli, tel. 01 42 78 55 29, www.hoteldenice.com, contact@hoteldenice.com, laissez-faire management).

$ Hôtel du Loiret* is a centrally located and rare Marais budget hotel. It's simple with tight bathrooms, but the rooms are surprisingly sharp considering the price and location (Db-€105, Tb-€150, no air-con, expect some noise, 8 Rue des Mauvais Garçons, tel. 01 48 87 77 00, www.hotel-du-loiret.fr, hotelduloiret@hotmail.com).

Near Rue de Bretagne

(3rd arrond., Mo: Filles du Calvaire or Temple)

These hotels appeal to those wanting quick access to the Marais and a less touristed, quieter neighborhood. Appealing Rue de Bretagne is the soul of this area; it features broad sidewalks hosting a healthy dose of cafés and every kind of shop, plus the lively Marché des Enfants Rouges market area. Allow 15 minutes to walk from these hotels to the heart of the Marais along Rue St. Antoine.

$$$ Hôtel Petit Moulin**** is a plush hideaway designed for the artsy crowd. The extravagant deluxe rooms are a fun splurge (Db-€215-310, deluxe Db-€330-€350, junior suite-€430-450, 29 Rue de Poitou, Mo: St-Sébastien Froissard or Filles du Calvaire, tel. 01 42 74 10 10, www.hotelpetitmoulin.com, contact@hotelpetitmoulin.com).

$$ Hôtel du Vieux Saule*** has 27 simple rooms with little character in a good location. Rooms are tight and modern. Avoid the smoking rooms (Sb-€95-125, Db-€110-165, *supérieure* Db-€145-195, deluxe Db-€180-250, rates vary greatly with season, check online for best deals, small sauna free for guests, 6 Rue de Picardie, Mo: Filles du Calvaire or Temple, tel. 01 42 72 01 14, www.hotelvieuxsaule.com, reserv@hotelvieuxsaule.com).

$$ Hôtel Saintonge*** is a recently renovated, tastefully decorated place in a great location a stone's throw from Rue de Bretagne (Db-€150-170, 16 Rue de Saintonge, Mo: Filles du Calvaire, tel. 01 42 77 91 13, www.saintlouissaintonge.com, saintonge@saintlouis-hotels.com).

ON ILE ST. LOUIS

(4th arrond., Mo: Pont Marie or Sully-Morland)

The peaceful, residential character of this river-wrapped island, with its brilliant location and homemade ice cream, has drawn Americans for decades. There are no budget values here—all of the hotels are three-star or more—though prices are fair considering the level of comfort and killer location. The island's village ambience and proximity to the Marais, Notre-Dame, and the Latin Quarter make this area well worth considering. All of the following hotels are on the island's main drag, Rue St. Louis-en-l'Ile, where I list several restaurants (see page 172). For nearby services, see the Marais neighborhood section; for locations, see the "Marais Hotels" map, earlier.

PARIS

$$$ Hôtel du Jeu de Paume**,** occupying a 17th-century tennis center, is among the most expensive hotels I list in Paris. When you enter its magnificent lobby, you'll understand why. Greet Scoop, *le chien,* then take a spin in the glass elevator for a half-timbered-tree-house experience. The 30 rooms are carefully designed and tasteful, though not particularly spacious (you're paying for the location and public areas). Most rooms face a small garden; all are pin-drop peaceful (Sb-€190-260, standard Db-€290-370, deluxe Db-€460-570, 2-3-room suite-€630-920, breakfast-€18, 54 Rue St. Louis-en-l'Ile, tel. 01 43 26 14 18, www.jeudepaumehotel.com, info@jeudepaumehotel.com).

$$$ Hôtel de Lutèce*** comes with a welcoming wood-paneled lobby and a real fireplace. Rooms at this appealing hotel are handsome, and those on lower floors have high ceilings. Twin rooms are larger and the same price as double rooms. Rooms with bathtubs are on the louder street side, while those with showers are on the courtyard (Db-€250, Tb-€285, 65 Rue St. Louis-en-l'Ile, tel. 01 43 26 23 52, www.hoteldelutece.com, info@hoteldelutece.com).

$$$ Hôtel des Deux-Iles*** has the same owners and slightly lower prices than the Lutèce (listed above), with four single rooms (€210) and a tad less personality—though the room quality is comparable (59 Rue St. Louis-en-l'Ile, tel. 01 43 26 13 35, www.hoteldesdeuxiles.com, info@hoteldesdeuxiles.com).

$$ Hôtel Saint-Louis*** blends character with modern comforts. The well-maintained rooms come with cool stone floors and exposed beams. Rates are reasonable...for the location (Db-€179-199, top-floor Db with micro-balcony-€249, Tb-€289, iPads available for guest in-room use, 75 Rue St. Louis-en-l'Ile, tel. 01 46 34 04 80, www.hotelsaintlouis.com, isle@saintlouis-hotels.com).

AT OR NEAR PARIS' AIRPORTS

At Charles de Gaulle Airport

Both of these places are located outside the T-3 RER stop, and both have restaurants. For locations, see the map on page 176.

$$ Novotel*** is a step up from cookie-cutter airport hotels (Db-€145-200, can rise to €310 for last-minute rooms, tel. 01 49 19 27 27, www.novotel.com, h1014@accor.com).

$ Hôtel Ibis CDG Airport** is huge and offers standard airport accommodations (Db-€100-160, tel. 01 49 19 19 19, www.ibishotel.com, h1404@accor.com).

Near Charles de Gaulle Airport, in Roissy

The small village of **Roissy-en-France** (you'll see signs just before the airport as you come from Paris), which gave its name to the airport (Roissy Charles de Gaulle), has better-value chain hotels with free shuttle service to and from the airport (4/hour, 15 minutes, look for *navettes hôtels* signs to reach these hotels). Hotels have reasonably priced restaurants with long hours, though it's more pleasant to walk into the town, where you'll find a bakery, pizzeria, cafés, and a few restaurants. Most Roissy hotels list specials on their websites.

The following hotels are within walking distance of the town. **$ Hôtel Ibis CDG Paris Nord 2**** is usually cheaper than the Ibis right at the airport (Db-€80-110, 335 Rue de la Belle Etoile, tel. 01 48 17 56 56, www.ibishotel.com, h3299@accor.com). **$ Hôtel Campanile Roissy***** is a decent place to sleep, and you can have a good dinner next door at Hôtel Golden Tulip (Db-€70-130, Allée des Vergers, tel. 01 34 29 80 40, www.campanile-roissy.fr, roissy@campanile.fr). **$$ Hôtel Golden Tulip Paris CDG***** has a fitness center, sauna, and good restaurant for the suburbs (Db-€100-180, 11 Allée des Vergers, tel. 01 34 29 00 00, www.goldentulipcdgvillepinte.com, info@goldentulipcdgvillepinte.com). The cheapest option is **$ B&B Hôtel Roissy CDG***, where many flight attendants stay (Db-€55-60, 17 Allée des Vergers, tel. 01 34 38 55 55, or 02 98 33 75 29, www.hotel-bb.com).

To avoid rush-hour traffic, drivers can consider sleeping north of Paris in either **Auvers-sur-Oise** (30 minutes west of airport) or in the pleasant medieval town of **Senlis** (15 minutes north of airport). In Auvers, **$ Hostellerie du Nord***** is small, friendly, and polished—a treat for those who want to sleep in luxury. It has modern, spacious rooms and a seriously good restaurant that requires reservations (Db-€100-130, suites-€190, *menus* from €60, a block from train station at 6 Rue du Général de Gaulle, tel. 01 30 36 70 74, www.hostelleriedunord.fr). In Senlis, **$ Hôtel Ibis Senlis**** is a few minutes from town (Db-€85-115, Route Nationale A1, tel. 03

44 53 70 50, www.ibishotel.com, h0709@accor.com). If you don't have a car, sleep elsewhere.

Near Orly Airport

Two chain hotels, owned by the same company and very close to the Sud terminal, are your best options near Orly. Both have free shuttles *(navettes)* to the terminal.

$$$ Hôtel Mercure Paris Orly*** provides high comfort for a high price; check their website for discounts (Db-€140-220, book early for better rate, tel. 08 25 80 69 69, www.accorhotel.com, h1246@accor.com).

$ Hôtel Ibis Orly Aéroport** is reasonable and basic (Db-€95-135, tel. 01 56 70 50 60, www.ibishotel.com, h1413@accor.com).

BED-AND-BREAKFASTS

Several agencies can help you go local by staying in a private home in Paris. While prices and quality can range greatly, most rooms have a private bath and run from €80 to €140. Most agency websites allow you to select by neighborhood and most owners won't take bookings for fewer than two nights. To limit stair-climbing, ask whether the building has an elevator. The agencies listed below have a good selection, but there's no good way to check the quality of the rooms as I do with hotels (agencies work with an ever-changing list of owners—each with a few rooms at most). You are at the mercy of whatever information you get from the agency and its website. Buyer beware.

Alcôve & Agapes is the most used B&B resource in Paris, offering a broad selection of addresses throughout the city. Their useful website helps you sort through the options with prices, information about the owners, and helpful photos (tel. 01 44 85 06 05, www.bed-and-breakfast-in-paris.com).

Meeting the French offers several interesting services for travelers wanting to meet the French, including a list of locals who happily rent out their spare rooms to travelers. Most of the hosts are older Parisians with big apartments (tel. 01 42 51 19 80, http://en.meetingthefrench.com).

Good Morning Paris is another source, listing more than 100 properties (tel. 01 47 07 28 29, www.goodmorningparis.fr).

APARTMENT RENTALS

Among the many English-speaking organizations renting apartments in Paris, the following have proven most reliable (also see the list of agencies renting apartments countrywide on page 1054). Their websites are good and essential to understanding your options. Read the rental conditions very carefully.

Paris Perfect has offices in Paris with English-speaking staff who seek the "perfect apartment" for their clients and are selective about what they offer. Their service gets rave reviews. Many units have Eiffel Tower views, and most include free Internet, free local and international phone calls, satellite TV, air-conditioning, and washers and dryers (check their website for rates, 5 percent discount off regular rates for Rick Steves readers, US toll-free tel. 888-520-2087, www.parisperfect.com, reservations@parisperfect.com).

Cobblestone Paris Rentals is a small, American-run outfit offering furnished rentals with a focus on the Marais and central Paris. All apartments offer free Wi-Fi, free international phone calls, and free cable TV. Apartments come stocked with English-language DVDs about Paris, coffee, tea, cooking spices, basic bathroom amenities, and an English-speaking greeter who will give you the lay of the land (two free river cruises for Rick Steves readers who book a stay of five nights or more, www.cobblestoneparis.com, reservations@cobblestoneparis.com).

Home Rental Service has been in business for 20-something years and offers a big selection of apartments throughout Paris with no agency fees (120 Champs-Elysées, tel. 01 42 25 65 40, www.homerental.fr, info@homerental.fr).

Locaflat offers accommodations ranging from studios to five-room apartments, with occasional specials online (63 Avenue de la Motte-Picquet, tel. 01 43 06 78 79, www.locaflat.com, locaflat@gmail.com).

Paris Home is a small outfit with only two little studios, but both are located on Rue Amélie in the heart of the Rue Cler area (see map on page 138). Each has modern furnishings and laundry facilities. Friendly Slim, the owner, is the best part (€690-990/week, no minimum stay, special rates for longer stays, credit cards accepted, free guest computer and US or France telephone calls, free maid service, airport/train station transfers possible, mobile 06 19 03 17 55, www.parishome2000.com, parishome2000@yahoo.fr).

Paris for Rent, a San Francisco-based group, has been renting top-end apartments in Paris for more than a decade (US tel. 866-4-FRANCE, www.parisforrent.com).

Cross-Pollinate is a reputable online booking agency representing B&Bs and apartments in a handful of European cities. Paris listings range from a small studio near the Bastille for €80 per night to a two-bedroom apartment in the Marais for €300 per night. Minimum stays vary from one to seven nights (US tel. 800-270-1190, France tel. 09 75 18 11 10, www.cross-pollinate.com, info@cross-pollinate.com).

Tournights, run by Frederick, rents several apartments around Paris (tel. 01 82 88 38 67, www.tournights.com, info@tournights.com).

Eating in Paris

The Parisian eating scene is kept at a rolling boil. Entire books (and lives) are dedicated to the subject. Paris is France's wine-and-cuisine melting pot. Though it lacks a style of its own (only French onion soup is truly Parisian; otherwise, there is no "Parisian cuisine" to speak of), it draws from the best of France. Paris could hold a gourmet Olympics and import nothing.

My recommendations are centered on the same great neighborhoods listed earlier, under "Sleeping in Paris"; you can come home exhausted after a busy day of sightseeing and find a good selection of restaurants right around the corner. And evening is a fine time to explore any of these delightful neighborhoods, even if you're sleeping elsewhere.

To save piles of euros, go to a bakery for takeout, or stop at a café for lunch. Cafés and brasseries are happy to serve a *plat du jour* (garnished plate of the day, about €13-18) or a chef-like salad (about €10-13) day or night. To save even more, consider picnics (tasty takeout dishes available at charcuteries).

Linger longer over dinner—restaurants expect you to enjoy a full meal. Most restaurants I've listed have set-price *menus* between €20 and €35. In most cases, the few extra euros you pay are well-spent, and open up a variety of better choices. Remember that a service charge is included in the prices (so little or no tipping is expected, although it's polite to round up). Eat early with tourists or late with locals. Before choosing a seat outside, remember that smokers love outdoor tables.

IN THE RUE CLER NEIGHBORHOOD

The Rue Cler neighborhood caters to its residents. Its eateries, while not destination places, have an intimate charm. I've provided a full range of choices—from cozy ma-and-pa diners to small and trendy boutique restaurants to classic, big, boisterous bistros. For all restaurants listed in this area, use the Ecole Militaire Métro stop (unless another station is listed).

On Rue Cler

$ Café du Marché boasts the best seats and prices on Rue Cler. The owner's philosophy: Brasserie on speed—crank out good enough

Good Picnic Spots

Paris is picnic-friendly. Almost any park will do. Many have benches or grassy areas, though some lawns are off-limits—obey the signs. Parks generally close at dusk, so plan your sunset picnics carefully. Hoteliers frown on in-room picnics. Here are some especially scenic areas located near major sights:

Palais Royal: Escape to a peaceful courtyard full of relaxing locals across from the Louvre (Mo: Palais Royal-Musée du Louvre). The nearby Louvre courtyard surrounding the pyramid is less tranquil, but very handy.

Place des Vosges: Relax in an exquisite grassy courtyard in the Marais, surrounded by royal buildings (Mo: Bastille).

Square du Vert-Galant: For great river views, try this little triangular park on the west tip of Ile de la Cité. It's next to the statue of King Henry IV (Mo: Pont Neuf).

Pont des Arts: Munch from a perch on this pedestrian bridge over the Seine (near the Louvre)—it's equipped with benches (Mo: Pont Neuf).

Along the Seine: A grassy parkway runs along the left bank of the Seine between Les Invalides and Pont de l'Alma (Mo: Invalides, near Rue Cler).

Tuileries Garden: Have an Impressionist "Luncheon on the Grass" nestled between the Orsay and Orangerie museums (Mo: Tuileries).

Luxembourg Garden: The classic Paris picnic spot is this expansive Left Bank park (Mo: Odéon).

Les Invalides: Take a break from the Army Museum and Napoleon's Tomb in the gardens behind the complex (Mo: Varenne).

Champ de Mars: The long grassy strip below the Eiffel Tower has breathtaking views of this Paris icon. However, you must eat along the sides of the park, as the central lawn is off-limits (Mo: Ecole Militaire).

Pompidou Center: There's no grass, but the people-watching is unbeatable; try the area by the *Homage to Stravinsky* fountains (Mo: Rambuteau or Hôtel de Ville).

food at great prices to appreciative locals and savvy tourists. It's high-energy, with young waiters who barely have time to smile... *très* Parisian. This place works well if you don't mind a limited selection and want to eat an inexpensive one-course meal among a commotion of people. The chalkboard lists your choices: good, hearty €10 salads or more filling €12-14 *plats du jour*. Arrive before 19:30 to avoid long waits (Mon-Sat 11:00-23:00, Sun 11:00-17:00, at the corner of Rue Cler and Rue du Champ de Mars, 38 Rue Cler, tel. 01 47 05 51 27).

$ Tribeca Italian Restaurant, next door to Café du Marché, has a similar ambience with higher quality and more varied cuisine.

Restaurant Price Code

To help you choose among these listings, I've divided the restaurants into three categories, based on the price for a typical main course.

$$$ Higher Priced—Most main courses €25 or more.
$$ Moderately Priced—Most main courses €15-25.
$ Lower Priced—Most main courses €15 or less.

Choose from family-pleasing Italian dishes or try the roasted Camembert *à la crème* (€11-15 pizzas and pastas, €11 salads, open daily, tel. 01 45 55 12 01, say *bonjour* to helpful manager Paul).

$ Le Petit Cler is an adorable and popular little bistro with long leather booths, a vintage interior, a handful of outdoor tables, and simple, tasty, inexpensive dishes (€9 omelets, €7 soup of the moment, €13-14 salads and *plats,* and sinful *pots de crème,* daily, opens early for dinner, next to Grand Hôtel Lévêque at 29 Rue Cler, tel. 01 45 50 17 50).

$ Café le Roussillon offers a younger, pub-like ambience with good-value food. You'll find design-your-own omelets, fajitas, and easygoing waiters (daily, indoor seating only, at the corner of Rue de Grenelle and Rue Cler, tel. 01 45 51 47 53).

$ Crêperie Ulysée en Gaule offers cheap seats on Rue Cler with crêpes to go. Readers of this book don't have to pay an extra charge to sit if they buy a drink. The family adores its Greek dishes, but their crêpes are your least expensive hot meal on this street (28 Rue Cler, tel. 01 47 05 61 82).

$ Brasserie Aux PTT, a simple traditional café delivering fair-value fare, reminds Parisians of the old days on Rue Cler. Rick Steves diners are promised a free *kir* with their dinner (€12 *plats,* cheap wine, closed Sun, 2-minute walk from most area hotels, opposite 53 Rue Cler, tel. 01 45 51 94 96).

Close to Ecole Militaire

$$ Le Florimond is fun for a special occasion. The setting is warm and welcoming. Locals come for classic French cuisine at fair prices. Friendly English-speaking Laurent, whose playful ties change daily, gracefully serves one small room of tables and loves to give suggestions. The stuffed cabbage and the *confit de canard* are particularly tasty, and the house wine is excellent (€37 *menu,* closed Sun, make reservations two days ahead, 19 Avenue de la Motte-Picquet, tel. 01 45 55 40 38, www.leflorimond.com).

$$ Bistrot Belhara, named for a 35-foot-wave in the Basque region, is a true French dining experience. Watch as chef Thierry peers from his kitchen window to ensure that all is well. He bases his cuisine on what's in season, but the foie gras and *riz au lait de mémé*—his grandma's rice pudding—are delicious any time of year. If you don't know French, the charming Frédéric will translate—and help you choose the perfect wine (€38 *menu,* closed Sun-Mon, reservations smart, a block off Rue Cler at 23 Rue Duvivier, tel. 01 45 51 41 77, www.bistrotbelhara.com).

$$ Café le Bosquet is a contemporary Parisian brasserie where you'll dine for a decent price inside or outside on a broad sidewalk. Come here for standard café fare—salad, French onion soup, *steak-frites,* or a *plat du jour.* Lanky owner "Jeff" offers a three-course meal for €22, and *plats* from €13-19. The escargots are tasty, the house wine is quite good, and the beer is cheap for Paris (closed Sun, free Wi-Fi, corner of Rue du Champ de Mars and Avenue Bosquet, 46 Avenue Bosquet, tel. 01 45 51 38 13, www.bosquetparis.com).

$$ La Terrasse du 7ème is a sprawling, happening café with grand outdoor seating and a living room-like interior with comfy love seats. Located on a corner, it overlooks a busy intersection with a constant parade of people. Chairs are set up facing the street, as a meal here is like dinner theater—and the show is slice-of-life Paris (€16-23 *plats,* good €13 *salade niçoise* or Caesar salad, €8 French onion soup, tasty foie gras, no fixed-price *menu,* daily until at least 24:00, at Ecole Militaire Métro stop, tel. 01 45 55 00 02).

Between Rue de Grenelle and the River, East of Avenue Bosquet

$$$ L'Ami Jean offers authentic Basque specialties in a snug-but-fun, get-to-know-your-neighbor atmosphere with red peppers and Basque stuff hanging from the ceiling. It's not cheap, but the portions are hearty and delicious, and the whole menu changes every two weeks. Parisians detour long distances to savor the gregarious chef's special cuisine and convivial atmosphere. Arrive by 19:30 or reserve ahead (€20 starters, €35 *plats,* €85 eight-course *menu,* closed Sun-Mon, 27 Rue Malar, Mo: La Tour-Maubourg, tel. 01 47 05 86 89, www.lamijean.fr).

$$$ Thoumieux is the neighborhood's grand brasserie, with a classy interior lined with red velvet chairs, chandeliers, and fussy waiters. It's a mini-splurge for most, though designed as an affordable chance to sample renowned chef Jean-François Piège's cuisine: His 10-table restaurant one floor up earned two Michelin stars. Come here for a true brasserie experience (€18-24 starters, €30 *plats,* €12 desserts, daily, 79 Rue St. Dominique, tel. 01 47 05 49 75, www.thoumieux.fr).

$$ Au Petit Tonneau is a small, authentic French bistro with original, time-warp decor, red-checked tablecloths, and carefully prepared food from a limited menu. The place is real, the cuisine is delicious, and the experience is what you came to France for (€39

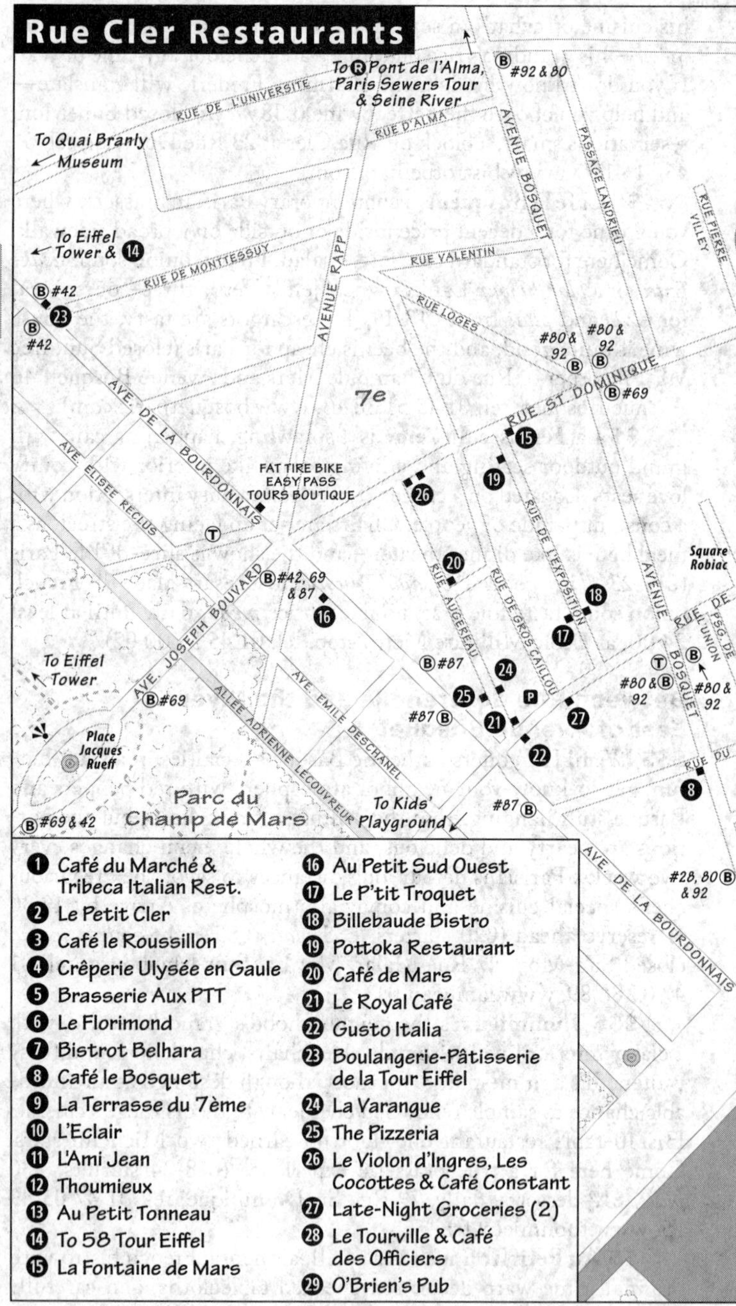
Rue Cler Restaurants
To Ⓡ Pont de l'Alma, Paris Sewers Tour & Seine River
Ⓑ #92 & 80
RUE DE L'UNIVERSITE
RUE D'ALMA
To Quai Branly Museum
AVENUE BOSQUET
PASSAGE LANDRIEU
RUE PIERRE VILLEY
To Eiffel Tower & 14
RUE DE MONTTESSUY
RUE VALENTIN
AVENUE RAPP
RUE LOGES
Ⓑ #42
23
Ⓑ #42
#80 & 92 Ⓑ
#80 & 92 Ⓑ
RUE ST. DOMINIQUE
Ⓑ #69
7e
AVE. DE LA BOURDONNAIS
AVE. ELISEE RECLUS
15
19
26
FAT TIRE BIKE EASY PASS TOURS BOUTIQUE
RUE DE L'EXPOSITION
Square Robiac
20
RUE AUGEREAU
RUE DE GROS CAILLOU
Ⓑ #42, 69 & 87
16
18
17
AVENUE BOSQUET
RUE DE L'UNION
PSG. DE
AVE. JOSEPH BOUVARD
To Eiffel Tower
Ⓑ #87
24
Ⓑ #69
AVE. EMILE DESCHANEL
25
21
27
#80 & 92 Ⓑ
Ⓑ #80 & 92
#87 Ⓑ
ALLEE ADRIENNE LECOUVREUR
Place Jacques Rueff
22
RUE DU
8
Parc du Champ de Mars
To Kids' Playground
#87 Ⓑ
Ⓑ #69 & 42
#28, 80 Ⓑ & 92
AVE. DE LA BOURDONNAIS
1 Café du Marché & Tribeca Italian Rest.
2 Le Petit Cler
3 Café le Roussillon
4 Crêperie Ulysée en Gaule
5 Brasserie Aux PTT
6 Le Florimond
7 Bistrot Belhara
8 Café le Bosquet
9 La Terrasse du 7ème
10 L'Eclair
11 L'Ami Jean
12 Thoumieux
13 Au Petit Tonneau
14 To 58 Tour Eiffel
15 La Fontaine de Mars
16 Au Petit Sud Ouest
17 Le P'tit Troquet
18 Billebaude Bistro
19 Pottoka Restaurant
20 Café de Mars
21 Le Royal Café
22 Gusto Italia
23 Boulangerie-Pâtisserie de la Tour Eiffel
24 La Varangue
25 The Pizzeria
26 Le Violon d'Ingres, Les Cocottes & Café Constant
27 Late-Night Groceries (2)
28 Le Tourville & Café des Officiers
29 O'Brien's Pub

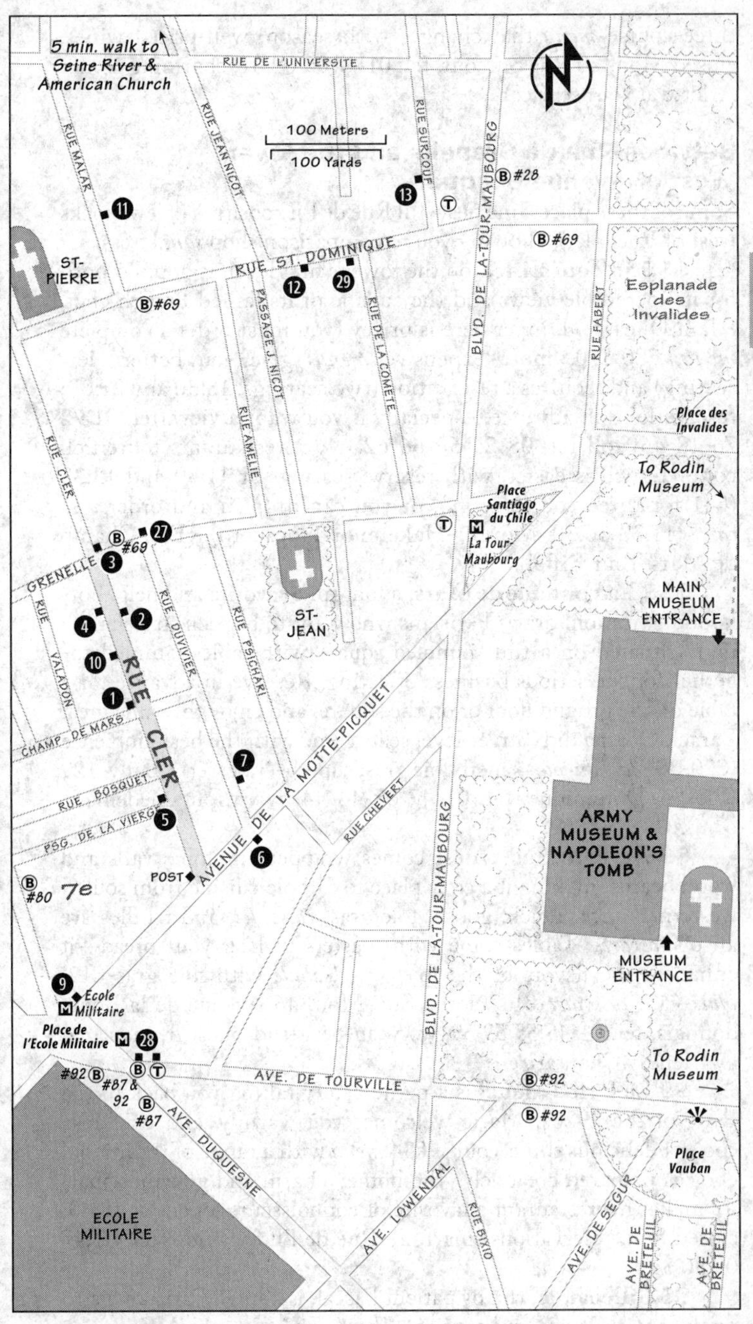
5 min. walk to Seine River & American Church
RUE DE L'UNIVERSITE
100 Meters
100 Yards
RUE MALAR
RUE JEAN NICOT
RUE SURCOUF
BLVD. DE LA-TOUR-MAUBOURG
#28
#69
ST-PIERRE
RUE ST. DOMINIQUE
PASSAGE J. NICOT
RUE DE LA COMETE
RUE FABERT
Esplanade des Invalides
Place des Invalides
RUE CLER
RUE AMELIE
To Rodin Museum
Place Santiago du Chile
La Tour-Maubourg
GRENELLE
#69
RUE DUVIVIER
RUE PSICHARI
ST-JEAN
MAIN MUSEUM ENTRANCE
RUE VALADON
RUE CLER
CHAMP DE MARS
AVENUE DE LA MOTTE-PICQUET
RUE CHEVERT
RUE BOSQUET
PSG. DE LA VIERGE
ARMY MUSEUM & NAPOLEON'S TOMB
POST
#80
7e
BLVD. DE LA-TOUR-MAUBOURG
MUSEUM ENTRANCE
Ecole Militaire
Place de l'Ecole Militaire
To Rodin Museum
AVE. DE TOURVILLE
#92
#87 & 92
#87
#92
AVE. DUQUESNE
Place Vauban
ECOLE MILITAIRE
AVE. LOWENDAL
RUE BIXIO
AVE. DE SEGUR
AVE. DE BRETEUIL
AVE. DE BRETEUIL

three-course *menu* that changes with season, well-priced wines, closed Mon, 20 Rue Surcouf, tel. 01 47 05 09 01, charming owner Arlette at your service).

Between Rue de Grenelle and the River, West of Avenue Bosquet

Some of these places line peaceful Rue de l'Exposition (a few blocks west of Rue Cler), allowing you to comparison shop *sans* stress.

$$$ 58 Tour Eiffel, on the tower's first level, is popular both for its incredible views and the cuisine of its famed French chef, Alain Ducasse. Dinner here is pricey (you must order a complete *menu,* €80-170, more expensive *menus* give you better view seating) and requires a reservation (two seatings: 18:30 and 21:00; reserve long in advance, especially if you want a view, tel. 01 72 76 18 46, toll tel. 08 25 56 66 62, www.restaurants-toureiffel.com). Lunch is easier, with reserve seatings at 11:30 and 13:30 (€41 for three-course *menu*), or you can drop in and order *à la carte* (11:30-16:30, Mo: Bir-Hakeim or Trocadéro, RER: Champ de Mars-Tour Eiffel).

$$$ La Fontaine de Mars, a longtime favorite and neighborhood institution, draws Parisians who want to be seen. It's charmingly situated on a tiny, jumbled square with tables jammed together for the serious business of eating. Reserve in advance for a table on the ground floor or on the square, and enjoy the same meal Barack Obama did. Street-level seats come with the best ambience (€20-30 *plats du jour,* superb foie gras, superb-er desserts, daily, 129 Rue St. Dominique, tel. 01 47 05 46 44, www.fontainedemars.com).

$$ Au Petit Sud Ouest comes wrapped in stone walls and wood beams, making it a cozy place to sample cuisine from southwestern France. Duck, goose, foie gras, *cassoulet,* and truffles are all on *la carte.* Tables come with toasters to heat your bread—it enhances the flavors of the foie gras (*salade* with foie gras-€12, *plats*-€15, *cassoulet*-€16, closed Sun-Mon, 46 Avenue de la Bourdonnais, tel. 01 45 55 59 59, www.au-petit-sud-ouest.fr, managed by friendly Chantal).

$$ Le P'tit Troquet is a petite eatery taking you back to the Paris of the 1920s. Marie welcomes you warmly, and chef José cooks a delicious three-course €34 *menu* with a range of traditional choices prepared creatively. The homey charm and gourmet quality make this restaurant a favorite of connoisseurs (opens at 18:30, closed Sun, reservations smart, 28 Rue de l'Exposition, tel. 01 47 05 80 39).

$$ Billebaude, run by patient Pascal, is a small Parisian bistro popular with locals and tourists. The focus is on what's fresh, including catch-of-the-day fish and meats from the hunt (available in the fall and winter). Chef Sylvain, an avid hunter (as the decor suggests), is determined to deliver quality at a fair price. Try *filet de bar* (sea bass) for your main course and *œufs à la neige* for dessert—but skip this place if you're in a hurry (€35 *menu,* closed Sun-Mon, 29 Rue de l'Exposition, tel. 01 45 55 20 96).

$$ Pottoka's young chef Sébastian Gravé creates a dining experience that changes regularly—attracting locals willing to crowd into this shoebox for a chance to sample his latest creations. Service is friendly, wines are reasonable, and the food is sensational (€22 two-course *menu,* €33 three-course *menu,* book ahead, daily, 4 Rue de l'Exposition, tel. 01 45 51 88 38, www.pottoka.fr).

$$ Café de Mars is a cool place for a fine-quality, reasonably priced meal. It's also comfortable for single diners thanks to a convivial counter (closed Sun, 11 Rue Augereau, tel. 01 45 50 10 90, www.cafedemars.com).

$ Le Royal is a tiny neighborhood fixture offering the cheapest meals in the neighborhood. This humble time-warp place, with prices and decor from another era, comes from an age when cafés sold firewood and served food as an afterthought. Parisians dine here because "it's like eating at home." Gentle Michele and son Guillaume are fine hosts (€6 omelets, €9-12 *plats,* €14 for filling three-course *menu,* daily, 212 Rue de Grenelle, tel. 01 47 53 92 90).

$ Gusto Italia serves up tasty, good-value Italian cuisine in two minuscule places across from each other, each with a few tables outside. Arrive early or plan to wait (€12 salads, €14 pasta, daily, 199 Rue de Grenelle, tel. 01 45 55 00 43).

$ Boulangerie-Pâtisserie de la Tour Eiffel sells inexpensive salads, quiches, and sandwiches, and other traditional café fare. Enjoy the views of the Eiffel Tower (daily, outdoor and indoor seating, one block southeast of the tower at 21 Avenue de la Bourdonnais, tel. 01 47 05 59 81).

$ La Varangue is an entertaining one-man show featuring English-speaking Philippe, who once ran a catering business in Pennsylvania. He now lives upstairs and has found his niche serving a mostly American clientele. The food is cheap and basic, the tables are few, and he opens at 17:30. Norman Rockwell would dig his minuscule dining room—with the traditional kitchen sizzling just over the counter. Try his snails and chocolate cake—but not together (€12 *plats,* €19 *menu,* always a vegetarian option, closed Sun, 27 Rue Augereau, tel. 01 47 05 51 22, www.lavarangue.fr).

$ The Pizzeria across from La Varangue is kid-friendly and cheap (closed Sun, eat in or take out, 28 Rue Augereau, tel. 01 45 55 45 16).

The Constant Lineup

Ever since leaving the venerable Hôtel Crillon, famed chef Christian Constant has made a career of taking the "snoot" out of French cuisine—and making it accessible to people like us. Today you'll find three of his restaurants strung along one block of Rue St. Dominique between Rue Augereau and Rue de l'Exposition. Each is distinct, and each offers a different experience and price range. None of these places is cheap, but they all deliver top-quality cuisine.

$$$ Le Violon d'Ingres, where Christian won his first Michelin star, makes for a good excuse to dress up and dine finely in Paris. Glass doors open onto a chic eating scene, service is formal yet helpful, and the cuisine is what made this restaurateur's reputation (€65-90 *menus,* great-value lunch *menu,* daily, reservations essential, 135 Rue St. Dominique, tel. 01 45 55 15 05, www.maisonconstant.com/violon-ingres).

$$ Les Cocottes attracts a crowd of yuppie Parisians with its creative dishes served in *cocottes*—small iron pots (€15-20 *cocottes,* tasty soups, daily from 18:30, go early as they don't take reservations, 135 Rue St. Dominique).

$$ Café Constant is a cool, two-level place that feels more like a small bistro-wine bar than a café. Delicious and fairly priced dishes are served in a snug setting to a dedicated clientele. Arrive early to get a table downstairs if you can (upstairs seating is a good fallback); the friendly staff speak English (€11 entrées, €16 *plats,* €7 desserts, daily from 19:00, no reservations taken, corner of Rue Augereau and Rue St. Dominique, next to recommended Hôtel de Londres Eiffel, tel. 01 47 53 73 34).

Picnicking near Rue Cler

Picnics with floodlit views of the Eiffel Tower or along the riverside promenade are *très romantique,* and Rue Cler is a festival of food just waiting to be celebrated. For a magical picnic dinner, assemble it in no fewer than five shops on Rue Cler. If they're closed, small, late-night groceries are at 197 Rue de Grenelle (open daily until midnight), as well as where Rues Cler and Grenelle cross.

Nightlife in Rue Cler

This sleepy neighborhood was not made for night owls, but there are a few notable exceptions. The focal point of before- and after-dinner posing occurs along the broad sidewalk at the intersection of Avenues de la Motte-Picquet and Tourville (Mo: Ecole Militaire). **Le Tourville** and **Café des Officiers** gather a sea of outward-facing seats for the important business of people-watching—and fashion-model recruiting.

La Terrasse du 7ème, across the avenue, has a less-pretentious clientele (see listing, earlier). On Rue Cler, **Café du Marché** (listed earlier) attracts a Franco-American café crowd until at least midnight, though the younger-in-spirit **L'Eclair** cocktail café (a few doors down at #32) rocks it until 2:00 in the morning. **Café Roussillon** has a good French pub atmosphere at the corner of Rue de Grenelle and Rue Cler. **O'Brien's Pub** is a relaxed Parisian rendition of an Irish pub, with French men in suits tossing darts and drinking pints (77 Rue St. Dominique, Mo: La Tour Maubourg).

IN THE MARAIS NEIGHBORHOOD

The trendy Marais is filled with diners enjoying good food in colorful and atmospheric eateries. The scene is competitive and changes all the time. I've listed an assortment of eateries—all handy to recommended hotels—that offer good food at decent prices, plus a memorable experience.

On Romantic Place des Vosges

This square offers Old World Marais elegance, a handful of eateries, and an ideal picnic site until dusk, when the park closes (use Bastille or St-Paul Métro stops). Strolling around the arcade after dark is more important than dining here—fanciful art galleries alternate with restaurants and cafés. Choose a restaurant that best fits your mood and budget; most have arcade seating and provide big space heaters to make outdoor dining during colder months an option. Also consider a drink on the square at Café Hugo or a pastry at Carette.

$$ La Place Royale offers a fine location on the square with good seating inside or out. Here you can expect a warm welcome and patient waiters, as owner Arnaud prides himself on service. The cuisine is traditional, well-priced, and served nonstop all day, and the exceptional wine list is reasonable (try the Sancerre white). The €41 *menu* comes with a *kir,* three courses, a half-bottle of wine per person, coffee, and—for Rick Steves readers with this book—a *digestif* that will allow you to linger even longer and savor the setting (€26-41 *menus,* €16 lunch special, daily, 2 bis Place des Vosges, tel. 01 42 78 58 16).

$$ Café Hugo, named for the square's most famous resident, is best for drinks only, but if it's basic café fare you crave, the setting is terrific, with good seating under the arches (daily, 22 Place des Vosges, tel. 01 42 72 64 04).

Near Place des Vosges

$$ Les Bonnes Soeurs, a block from the square, blends modern and traditional fare with contemporary bistro ambience. Isabelle takes good care of her clients and offers portions that are big and inventive. The delicious and filling *pressé de chèvre* starter (a hunk of

Marais Restaurants

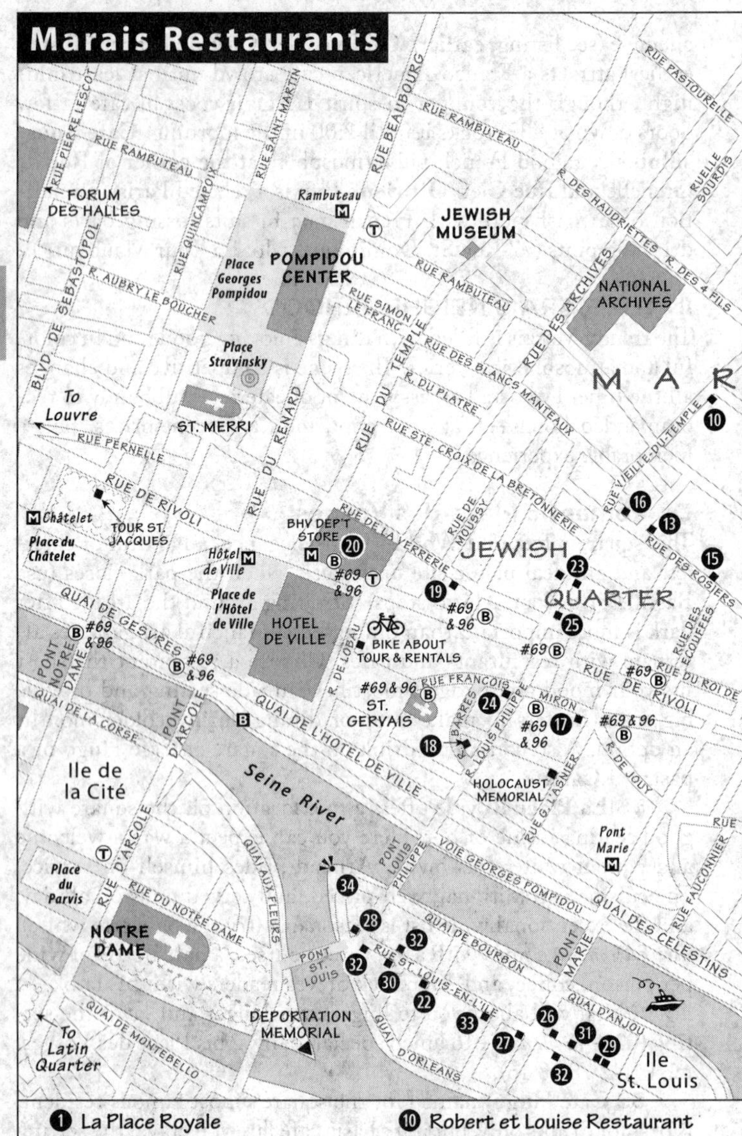

1. La Place Royale
2. Café Hugo
3. Les Bonnes Soeurs
4. Chez Janou
5. Le Petit Marché
6. Café des Musées
7. Brasserie Bofinger
8. Au Temps des Cerises
9. Vin des Pyrénées
10. Robert et Louise Restaurant
11. Breizh Café
12. Place du Marché Ste. Catherine Eateries
13. Chez Marianne
14. Le Loir dans la Théière
15. L'As du Falafel
16. La Droguerie Crêperie
17. Au Bourguignon du Marais

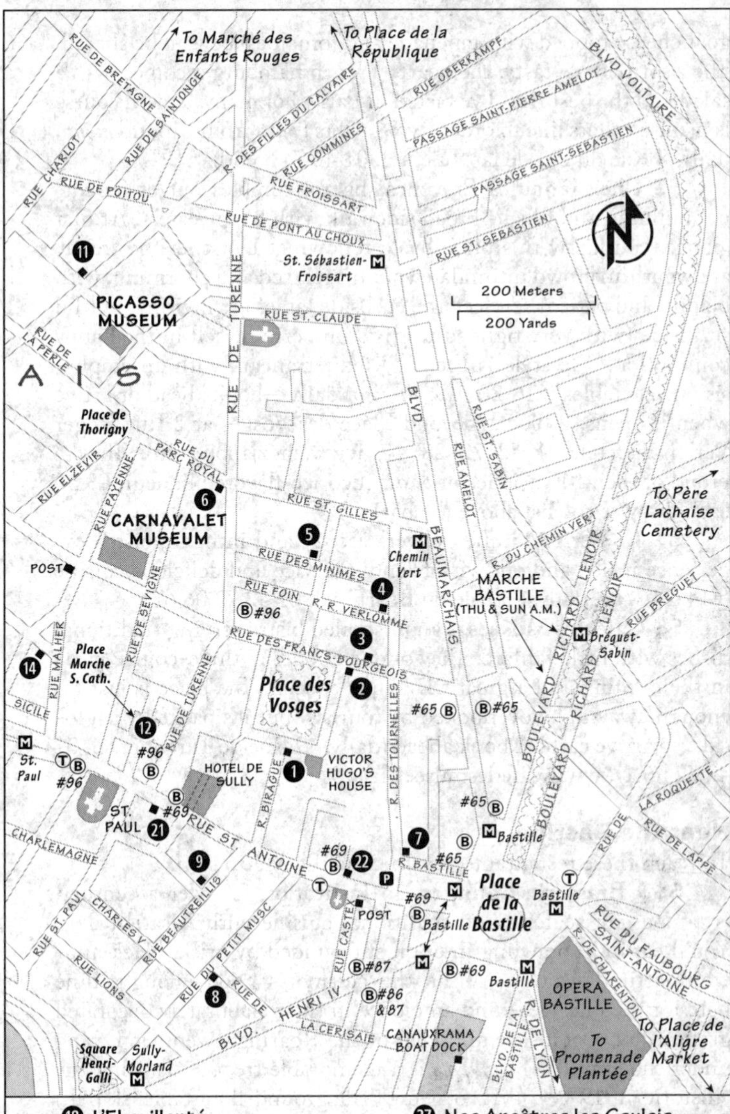

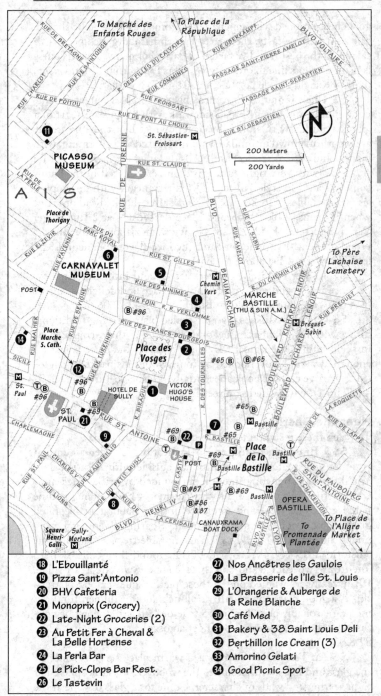

- ⓲ L'Ebouillanté
- ⓳ Pizza Sant'Antonio
- ⓴ BHV Cafeteria
- ㉑ Monoprix (Grocery)
- ㉒ Late-Night Groceries (2)
- ㉓ Au Petit Fer à Cheval & La Belle Hortense
- ㉔ La Perla Bar
- ㉕ Le Pick-Clops Bar Rest.
- ㉖ Le Tastevin
- ㉗ Nos Ancêtres les Gaulois
- ㉘ La Brasserie de l'Ile St. Louis
- ㉙ L'Orangerie & Auberge de la Reine Blanche
- ㉚ Café Med
- ㉛ Bakery & 38 Saint Louis Deli
- ㉜ Berthillon Ice Cream (3)
- ㉝ Amorino Gelati
- ㉞ Good Picnic Spot

goat cheese topped with tapenade and tomatoes) begs to be shared. The risotto is *très* tasty, the hearty French hamburger comes with a salad and the best fries I've tasted in Paris. For many, a main course is plenty; others like to order two starters (*plats* from €16, no *menu*, daily, 8 Rue du Pas de la Mule, tel. 01 42 74 55 80).

$$ Chez Janou, a Provençal bistro, tumbles out of its corner building and fills its broad sidewalk with happy eaters. At first glance, you know this place has a following. Don't let the trendy and youthful crowd intimidate you: It's relaxed and charming, with helpful and patient service. The curbside tables are inviting, but I'd sit inside (with very tight seating) to immerse myself in the happy commotion. The style is French Mediterranean, with an emphasis on vegetables (€16-20 *plats du jour,* daily—book ahead or arrive when it opens, 2 blocks beyond Place des Vosges at 2 Rue Roger Verlomme, tel. 01 42 72 28 41, www.chezjanou.com). They're proud of their 81 varieties of *pastis* (licorice-flavored liqueur, €3.50 each, browse the list above the bar).

$$ Le Petit Marché delivers a cozy and intimate bistro experience inside and out with friendly service and delicious cuisine (€14-24 *plats,* daily, 23 Rue du Béarn, tel. 01 42 72 06 67).

$$ Café des Musées is an unspoiled bistro serving traditional dishes with little fanfare. They offer a good €27 three-course *menu* in the evening and a great €17 lunch special. The place is just far enough away to be overlooked by tourists, but it's packed with locals, so arrive early or book ahead (daily, 49 Rue de Turenne, tel. 01 42 72 96 17, www.cafedesmusees.fr).

Near the Bastille

To reach these restaurants, use the Bastille Métro stop.

$$$ Brasserie Bofinger, an institution for over a century, is famous for seafood and traditional cuisine with Alsatian flair. You'll eat in a sprawling interior, surrounded by brisk, black-and-white-attired waiters. While the cuisine is good enough, dine here for the one-of-a-kind ambience in their elaborately decorated ground-floor rooms, reminiscent of the Roaring Twenties. Eating under the grand 1919 *coupole* is a memorable treat (as is using the "historic" 1919 WC). (If you can't get a ground-floor table, skip it.) Their €29 two-course and €34 three-course *menus* are a fair value. If you've always wanted one of those picturesque seafood platters, this is a good place (open daily for lunch and for dinner, fun kids' menu, reasonably priced wines, 5 Rue de la Bastille, don't be confused by the lesser "Petite" Bofinger across the street, tel. 01 42 72 87 82).

$$ Au Temps des Cerises is a warm place serving wines by the glass and meals with a smile. The woody 1950s atmosphere has tight seating and wads of character. Come for a glass of wine at the small zinc bar and say *bonjour* to Ben (€4-6, try their Viognier), or stay for a tasty dinner (€10 starters, €19 *plats,* good cheap wine, daily, at the corner of Rue du Petit Musc and Rue de la Cerisaie, tel. 01 42 72 08 63).

$$ At **Vin des Pyrénées,** the floor is a mismatch of old tiles, the crowd is a mishmash of loyal locals and visitors, and the chalkboard lists a mélange of authentic offerings. Try the pea soup and *hachis parmentier*—French shepherd's pie (€17-€25 *plats,* €16 two-course lunch special, daily, 25 Rue Beautreillis, tel. 01 42 72 64 94).

In the Heart of the Marais

These are closest to the St-Paul Métro stop.

$$ Robert et Louise (now run by Pascal *et* François) crams tables into a tiny, rustic-as-it-gets interior, warmed by a fireplace grill. The food is red-meat good, well-priced, and popular with tourists (€8 starters, €18 *plats,* €7 desserts, €13 lunch special, closed Mon, dinner only Tue-Wed, 64 Rue du Vieille du Temple, tel. 01 42 78 55 89).

$ Breizh (Brittany) Café is worth the walk. It's a simple Breton joint serving organic crêpes and small rolls made for dipping in rich sauces and salted butter. The crêpes are the best in Paris and run the gamut from traditional ham-cheese-and-egg crêpes to Asian fusion (buckwheat crêpe topped with seaweed butter). They also serve oysters, have a fantastic list of sweet crêpes, and talk about cider like a sommelier would talk about wine. Try a sparkling cider, a Breton cola, or my favorite—*lait ribot,* a buttermilk-like drink (€7-13 dinner crêpes and *plats,* serves nonstop from 12:00 to late, closed Mon-Tue, 109 Rue du Vieille du Temple, tel. 01 42 72 13 77).

$ *On Place du Marché Ste. Catherine:* This small, romantic square, just off Rue St. Antoine, is an international food festival cloaked in extremely Parisian, leafy-square ambience. On a balmy evening, this is a neighborhood favorite, with a handful of restaurants offering mediocre cuisine (you're here for the setting). It's also kid-friendly: Most places serve French hamburgers, and kids can dance around the square while parents breathe. Study the square, and you'll find three French bistros with similar features and menus: **Le Marché, Chez Joséphine,** and **Au Bistrot de la Place** (all open daily with €20-32 *menus* on weekdays, must order *à la carte* on weekends, tight seating on flimsy chairs indoors and out, Chez Joséphine has best chairs).

$ Several hardworking **Asian fast-food eateries,** great for an €8 meal, line Rue St. Antoine.

On Rue des Rosiers in the Jewish Quarter: These places line up along the same street in the heart of the Jewish Quarter.

$$ Chez Marianne is a neighborhood fixture that blends delicious Jewish cuisine with Parisian *élan* and wonderful atmosphere.

Choose from several indoor zones with a cluttered wine shop/deli feeling, or sit outside. You'll select from two dozen *Zakouski* elements to assemble your €14-18 *plat.* Vegetarians will find great options (€12 falafel sandwich—half that if you order it to go, long hours daily, corner of Rue des Rosiers and Rue des Hospitalières-St-Gervais, tel. 01 42 72 18 86). For takeout, pay inside first and get a ticket before you order outside.

$ Le Loir dans la Théière ("The Dormouse in the Teapot") is a cozy, mellow teahouse offering a welcoming ambience for tired travelers (laptops and smartphones are not welcome). It's ideal for lunch and popular for weekend brunch. They offer a daily assortment of creatively filled quiches, and bake up an impressive array of homemade desserts that are proudly displayed in the dining room (€10-14 *plats,* daily 9:00-19:00, 3 Rue des Rosiers, tel. 01 42 72 90 61).

$ L'As du Falafel rules the falafel scene in the Jewish quarter. Monsieur Isaac, the "Ace of Falafel" here since 1979, brags, "I've got the biggest pita on the street...and I fill it up." (Apparently it's Lenny Kravitz's favorite, too.) Your inexpensive meal comes on plastic plates, the €8 "special falafel" is the big hit (€5.50 to go), but many enjoy his lighter chicken version *(poulet grillé)* or the tasty and massive *assiette de falafel* (€10). Wash it down with a cold Maccabee beer. Their takeout service draws a constant crowd (long hours most days except closed Fri evening and all day Sat, air-con, 34 Rue des Rosiers, tel. 01 48 87 63 60).

$ La Droguerie, a hole-in-the-wall crêpe stand a few blocks farther down Rue des Rosiers, has a lighthearted owner. It's a good budget option if falafels don't work for you, but cheap does. Eat as you walk or grab a stool (€5 savory crêpes, daily 12:00-22:00, 56 Rue des Rosiers).

Near Hôtel de Ville

To reach these eateries, use the Hôtel de Ville Métro stop.

$$ Au Bourguignon du Marais is a handsome wine bar/bistro for Burgundy lovers, where excellent wines (Burgundian only, available by the glass) blend with a good selection of well-designed dishes and efficient service. The *œufs en meurette* are mouthwatering, and the *bœuf bourguignon* could feed two (€11-14 starters, €20-30 *plats,* closed Sun-Mon, pleasing indoor and outdoor seating, 52 Rue François Miron, tel. 01 48 87 15 40, run by helpful Mattieu).

$ L'Ebouillanté is a breezy café, romantically situated near the river on a broad, cobbled pedestrian lane behind a church. With great outdoor seating and an artsy, cozy interior, it's perfect for an inexpensive and relaxing tea, snack, or lunch—or for dinner on a warm evening. Their *bricks*—paper-thin Tunisian-inspired pancakes stuffed with what you would typically find in an omelet—

come with a small salad (€15 *bricks,* €13-16 *plats* and big salads, Tue-Sun 12:00-21:30, closed Mon, closes earlier in winter, a block off the river at 6 Rue des Barres, tel. 01 42 71 09 69).

$ Pizza Sant'Antonio is bustling and cheap, serving up €11 pizzas and salads on a fun Marais square (daily, barely off Rue de Rivoli at 1 Rue de la Verrerie, tel. 01 42 77 78 47).

$ BHV Department Store's fifth-floor cafeteria provides nice views, unbeatable prices, and many main courses to choose from, with a salad bar, pizza by the slice, and pasta. It's family-easy with point-and-shoot cafeteria cuisine (Mon-Sat 11:30-18:00, hot food served until 16:00, open later Wed, closed Sun, at intersection of Rue du Temple and Rue de la Verrerie, one block from Hôtel de Ville).

Picnicking in the Marais

Picnic at peaceful Place des Vosges (closes at dusk) or on the Ile St. Louis *quais* (described later). Stretch your euros at the basement supermarket of the **Monoprix** department store (closed Sun, near Place des Vosges on Rue St. Antoine). You'll find small **groceries** open until 23:00 at 48 Rue St. Antoine and on Ile St. Louis.

Nightlife in the Marais

Trendy cafés and bars—popular with gay men—cluster on Rue des Archives and Rue Ste. Croix de la Bretonnerie (closing at about 2:00 in the morning). There's also a line of bars and cafés providing front-row seats for the buff parade on Rue Vieille du Temple, a block north of Rue de Rivoli (the horseshoe-shaped **Au Petit Fer à Cheval** bar-restaurant and the atmospheric **La Belle Hortense** bookstore/wine bar are the focal points of the action). Nearby, Rue des Rosiers bustles with youthful energy, but there are no cafés to observe from. **La Perla** dishes up imitation Tex-Mex and is stuffed with Parisian yuppies in search of the perfect margarita (26 Rue François Miron, tel. 01 42 77 59 40).

$ Le Pick-Clops bar-restaurant is a happy peanuts-and-lots-of-cocktails diner with bright neon, loud colors, and a garish local crowd. It's perfect for immersing yourself in today's Marais world—a little boisterous, a little edgy, a little gay, fun-loving, easygoing... and *sans* tourists. Sit inside on old-fashioned diner stools, or street-side to watch the constant Marais parade. The name means "Steal the Cigarettes"—but you'll pay €11 for your big salad (daily 7:00-24:00, 16 Rue Vieille du Temple, tel. 01 40 29 02 18).

More Options: The best scene for hard-core clubbers is the dizzying array of wacky eateries, bars, and dance halls on **Rue de Lappe.** Just east of the stately Place de la Bastille, it's one of the wildest nightspots in Paris and not for everyone.

The most enjoyable peaceful evening may be simply mentally

donning your floppy "three musketeers" hat and slowly strolling Place des Vosges, window-shopping the art galleries.

ON ILE ST. LOUIS

This romantic and peaceful neighborhood is littered with promising and surprisingly reasonable possibilities; it merits a trip for dinner even if your hotel is elsewhere. Cruise the island's main street for a variety of options, and after dinner, sample Paris' best ice cream and stroll across to Ile de la Cité to see a floodlit Notre-Dame. These recommended spots line the island's main drag, Rue St. Louis-en-l'Ile (see map on page 166; to get here use the Pont Marie Métro stop).

$$$ Le Tastevin is an intimate mother-and-son-run restaurant serving top-notch traditional French cuisine with white-tablecloth, candlelit, gourmet elegance under heavy wooden beams. The romantic setting (and the elegantly romantic Parisian couples enjoying the place) naturally makes you whisper. The *menus* (€33-44 for two courses, €40-67 for three courses) offer a handful of classic choices that change with the season (closed Mon, dinner only Tue, reserve for late-evening dining, fine wine list, 46 Rue St. Louis-en-l'Ile, tel. 01 43 54 17 31, www.letastevin-paris.com, owner Madame Puisieux and her gentle son speak just enough English).

$$$ Nos Ancêtres les Gaulois ("Our Ancestors the Gauls"), famous for its rowdy, medieval-cellar atmosphere, is made for hungry warriors and wenches who like to swill hearty wine. They serve up rustic all-you-can-eat fare with straw baskets of raw veggies and bundles of sausage (cut whatever you like with your dagger), massive plates of pâté, a meat course, and all the wine you can stomach for €40. The food is just food; burping is encouraged. If you want to overeat, drink too much wine, be surrounded by tourists (mostly French), and holler at your friends while receiving smart-aleck buccaneer service, you're home (daily, 39 Rue St. Louis-en-l'Ile, tel. 01 46 33 66 07).

$$ La Brasserie de l'Ile St. Louis is situated at the prow of the island's ship as it faces Ile de la Cité, offering purely Alsatian cuisine (try the *choucroute garnie* or *coq au riesling* for €20), served in a vigorous, Teutonic setting with no-nonsense, slap-it-down service on wine-stained paper tablecloths. This is a good, balmy-evening perch for watching the Ile St. Louis promenade. If it's chilly, the interior is fun for a memorable night out (closed Wed, no reservations, 55 Quai de Bourbon, tel. 01 43 54 02 59).

$$ L'Orangerie is an inviting place with soft lighting and comfortable seating where diners speak in hushed voices so that everyone can appreciate the delicious cuisine and tasteful setting. Patient owner Monika speaks fluent English, and her *gratin d'aubergines* is sinfully good (€27-35 *menus,* closed Mon, 28 Rue St. Louis-en-l'Ile, tel. 01 46 33 93 98).

$ Auberge de la Reine Blanche welcomes diners willing to rub elbows with their neighbors under heaving beams. Earnest owner Michel serves basic, traditional cuisine at reasonable prices. His giant salad can be a beefy meal all by itself (€21-27 *menus*, closed Wed, 30 Rue St. Louis-en-l'Ile, tel. 01 46 33 07 87).

$ Café Med, near the pedestrian bridge to Notre-Dame, is a tiny, cheery *crêperie* with good-value salads, crêpes, and €11 *plats* (€14 and €20 *menus*, daily, limited wine list, 77 Rue St. Louis-en-l'Ile, tel. 01 43 29 73 17). Two similar *crêperies* are just across the street.

Riverside Picnic for Impoverished Romantics

On sunny lunchtimes and balmy evenings, the *quai* on the Left Bank side of Ile St. Louis is lined with locals who have more class than money, spreading out tablecloths and even lighting candles for elegant picnics. And tourists can enjoy the same budget meal. A handy grocery store at #67 on the main drag (open until 22:00, closed Tue) has tabouli and other simple, cheap takeaway dishes for your picnicking pleasure. The bakery a few blocks down at #40 serves quiche and pizza (open until 20:00, closed Sun-Mon), and a gourmet deli and cheese shop—aptly named **38 Saint Louis**—can be found at #38.

Ice-Cream Dessert

Half the people strolling Ile St. Louis are licking an ice-cream cone because this is the home of *les glaces Berthillon* (now sold throughout Paris though still made here on Ile St. Louis). The original **Berthillon** shop, at 31 Rue St. Louis-en-l'Ile, is marked by the line of salivating customers (closed Mon-Tue). For a less famous but satisfying treat, the Italian gelato a block away at **Amorino Gelati** is giving Berthillon competition (no line, bigger portions, easier to see what you want, and they offer little tastes—Berthillon doesn't need to, 47 Rue St. Louis-en-l'Ile, tel. 01 44 07 48 08). Having some of each is not a bad thing.

IN MONTMARTRE, NEAR SACRE-CŒUR

Montmartre can be hit or miss; the top of the hill is extremely touristy, with mindless mobs following guides to cancan shows. But if you walk a few blocks away, you'll find a quieter, more authentic meal at one of the places I've listed below. For locations, see the map on page 118.

The steps in front of Sacré-Cœur are perfect for a picnic with a view, though the spot comes with lots of company. For a quieter setting, consider the park directly behind the church. Along the touristy main drag (near Place du Tertre and just off it), several fun piano bars serve mediocre crêpes and overpriced bistro fare but offer great people-watching. The options become less touristy and more tasty as you escape from the top of the hill.

$$$ Moulin de la Galette lets you dine with Renoir under the historic windmill in a comfortable setting with good prices. Find the old photos scattered about the place (€25 two-course lunch *menu,* €32 three-course *menus,* €28 *plats* for dinner, daily, 83 Rue Lepic, Mo: Abbesses, tel. 01 46 06 84 77, www.lemoulindelagalette.fr).

$$ Restaurant Chez Plumeau, just off jam-packed Place du Tertre, is touristy yet moderately priced, with formal service but great seating on a tiny, characteristic square (elaborate €17 salads, €18-25 *plats,* daily, 4 Place du Calvaire, Mo: Abbesses, tel. 01 46 06 26 29).

$ L'Eté en Pente Douce is a good Montmartre choice, hiding under the generous branches of street trees. Just downhill from the crowds on a classic neighborhood corner, it features cheery indoor and outdoor seating, €10 *plats du jour* and salads, vegetarian options, and good wines (daily, many steps below Sacré-Cœur to the left as you leave, down the stairs below the WC, 23 Rue Muller, Mo: Anvers, tel. 01 42 64 02 67).

DINNER CRUISES

The following companies all offer dinner cruises (reservations required). Bateaux-Mouches and Bateaux Parisiens have the best reputations and the highest prices. They offer multicourse meals and music in aircraft-carrier-size dining rooms with glass tops and good views. For both, proper dress is required—no denim, shorts, or sport shoes; Bateaux-Mouches requires a jacket and tie for men.

Bateaux Parisiens, considered the better of the two, features a lively atmosphere with a singer, band, and dance floor. It leaves from Port de la Bourdonnais, just east of the bridge under the Eiffel Tower. Begin boarding at 19:45, leave at 20:30, and return at 23:00 (€72-155/person, price depends on seating and *menu* option; tel. 01 76 64 14 45, www.bateauxparisiens.com). The middle level is best. Pay the extra euros to get seats next to the windows—it's more romantic and private, with sensational views.

Bateaux-Mouches, started in 1949 and hands-down the most famous, entertains with violin and piano music. You can't miss its sparkling port on the north side of the river at Pont de l'Alma. The boats usually board 19:30-20:15, depart at 20:30, and return at 22:45 (€100-150/person, RER: Pont de l'Alma, tel. 01 42 25 96 10, www.bateaux-mouches.fr).

Le Capitaine Fracasse offers the budget option (€60/person, €90 with wine or champagne; reserve ahead—easy online—or get there early to secure a table; boarding times vary by season and day of week, walk down stairs in the middle of Bir-Hakeim bridge near the Eiffel Tower to Iles aux Cygne, Mo: Bir-Hakeim or RER:

Champ de Mars-Tour Eiffel, tel. 01 46 21 48 15, www.croisiere-paris.com).

Paris Connections

Whether you're aiming to catch a train or plane, budget plenty of time to reach your departure point. Paris is a big, crowded city, and getting across town on time is a goal you'll share with millions of other harried people. Factor in traffic delays and walking time through huge stations and vast terminals. At the airport, expect lines at ticketing, check-in, baggage check, and security points. Always keep your luggage safely near you. Thieves prey on jet-lagged and confused tourists on public transportation.

BY PLANE

Charles de Gaulle Airport

Paris' main airport (airport code: CDG) has three terminals: T-1, T-2, and T-3 (see map). Most flights from the US use T-1 or T-2 (check your ticket, or contact your airline). You can travel between terminals on the free CDGVAL automated shuttle train (departs every 5 minutes, 24/7). Allow 30 minutes to travel between terminals and an hour for total travel time between your gates at T-1 and T-2. All three terminals have access to ground transportation.

When leaving Paris, make sure you know which terminal you are departing from (if it's T-2, you'll also need to know which hall you're leaving from—they're labeled *A* through *F*). Plan to arrive at the airport two to three hours early for an overseas flight, or one to two hours for flights within Europe (particularly on budget airlines, which can have especially long check-in lines). For flight info, dial either 3950 from French landlines (€0.35/minute) or, from the US, dial 011 33 1 70 36 39 50, or visit www.adp.fr.

Services: All terminals have airport information desks (called ADP) and tourist information counters (labeled *Paris Tourisme*), and both are colored bright orange so they're hard to miss. At the Paris Tourisme counters you can get city maps, buy a Paris Museum Pass, and get tickets for the RoissyBus or RER train to Paris—a terrific time- and hassle-saver. You'll also find ATMs *(distributeurs)*, shops, cafés, and bars. The airport offers 15 minutes of free (but slow) Wi-Fi; pay €2 for 30 faster additional minutes. If you are returning home and want a VAT refund, look for tax-refund centers in the check-in area or ask for their location at any ADP information desk.

Terminal 1 (T-1)

This circular terminal has three key floors—arrival *(arrivées)* on the top floor and two floors for departures *(départs)* below. The termi-

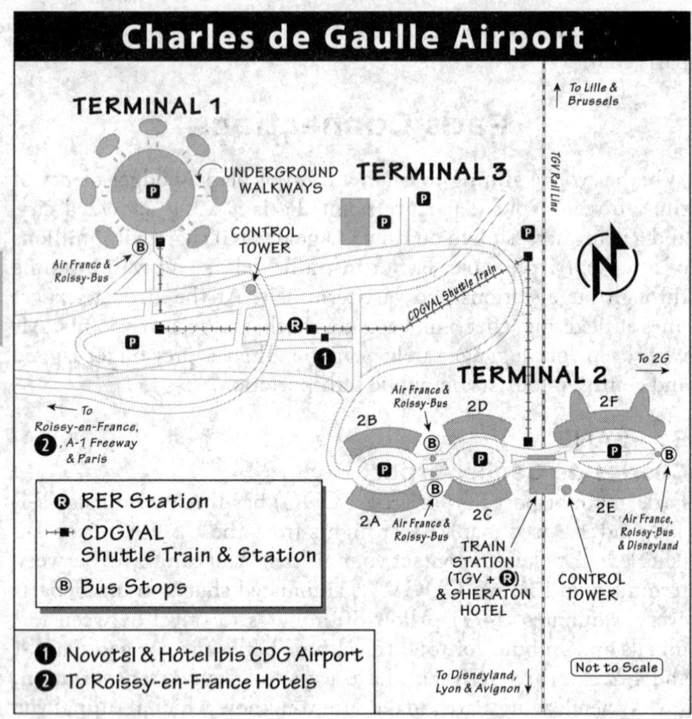

nal's round shape can be confusing—if you feel like you're going around in circles, you probably are.

Arrival Level *(niveau arrivée):* After passing through customs, you'll exit between doors *(porte)* 34 and 36. Nearby are orange ADP information desks with English-speaking staff, a café, a newsstand, and an ATM. Walk counterclockwise around the terminal to find the Paris Tourisme desk (door 6). Walk clockwise to find ground transportation: Air France and RoissyBus (door 34), car rental counters (doors 24-30), and taxis (door 24). To find the Disneyland shuttle bus, follow *CDGVAL* signs to the free CDGVAL shuttle train on floor 1; take it to T-2, then walk to T-2E/F, door 8.

Departure Levels *(niveaux départ):* Scan the departure screen to find out which hall you should go to for check-in. Halls 1-4 are on floor 2, and 5-6 are downstairs on floor 1. Also on floor 1 are the CDGVAL shuttle train, cafés, a post office (La Poste), pharmacy, boutiques, and a handy grocery. Boarding gates and duty-free shopping are located on floor 3, which is only accessible with a boarding pass.

Terminal 2 (T-2)

This long, horseshoe-shaped terminal is divided into six halls, labeled *A* through *F*. If arriving here, prepare for long walks and, in some cases, short train rides to baggage claim and exits. It's a busy place, so take a deep breath and follow signage carefully. The orange airport information desks and Paris Tourisme counters are located near gate 6/8 in each hall. Taxi stops are well-signed. To locate bus stops for Air France and RoissyBus—marked on the map on the previous page—follow *Paris by Bus* signs. For the Disneyland shuttle, follow signs to T-2E/F, door 8.

T-2 has a train station, with RER suburban trains into Paris (described later), as well as longer-distance trains to the rest of France (including high-speed TGV trains). It's located between T-2C/D and T-2E/F, below the Sheraton Hotel (prepare for a long walk to reach your train).

Car-rental offices, post offices, pharmacies, and ATMs are all well-signed. T-2E/F has several duty-free shopping arcades, and other T-2 halls have smaller duty-free shops. You can stash your bags at Baggage du Monde, located above the train station in T-2, but it's pricey (€18 for 12-24 hours, daily 6:00-21:30, tel. 01 34 38 58 90, www.bagagesdumonde.com). Some Paris train stations can store bags for much less.

Getting Between Charles de Gaulle Airport and Paris

Buses, airport vans, commuter trains, and taxis link the airport's terminals with central Paris. If you're traveling with two or more companions, carrying lots of baggage, or are just plain tired, taxis are worth the extra cost. Total travel time to your hotel should be around 1.25 hours by bus and Métro, 1 hour by train and Métro, and 50 minutes by taxi. Keep in mind that, at the airport, using buses (and taxis) requires shorter walks than taking RER trains. Also remember that transfers to Métro lines often involve stairs. For more information, check the "Getting There" tab at www.charlesdegaulleairport.co.uk.

By Bus: RoissyBus makes the 50-minute, non-stop trip to the Opéra Métro stop in central Paris, arriving on Rue Scribe. From there, you can take the Métro to anywhere in the city. To get to the Métro entrance or nearest taxi stand, turn left as you exit the bus and walk counterclockwise around the lavish Opéra building to its front (€11, runs 6:00-23:00, 4/hour until 20:45, 3/hour after that, 50 minutes, buy ticket on bus, tel. 3246, www.ratp.fr/en).

For Rue Cler hotels, take Métro line 8 (direction: Balard) to La Tour Maubourg or Ecole Militaire. For hotels in the Marais neighborhood, take line 8 (direction: Créteil Préfecture) to the Bastille stop. A taxi to any of my listed hotels costs about €12 from here.

Public Transportation to Recommended Hotels

You have many options for traveling between Charles de Gaulle Airport and Paris; which alternative makes the most sense depends on where you're staying and on your budget. Here are my tips for getting to recommended hotels.

Rue Cler Area: The RoissyBus, RER, and "Les Cars" Air France bus all work for Rue Cler hotels—the best solution depends on where in the area your hotel is located. For hotels near the Ecole Militaire and La Tour Maubourg Métro stops, take the RoissyBus directly to the Opéra , then take Métro line 8 (direction: Balard) and get off at your stop. For hotels closer to the river, take RER-B from the airport, change at the St. Michel stop for the RER-C (direction: Versailles Château Rive Gauche or Pontoise), and get off at Pont de l'Alma. The Air France bus works for most hotels in the area but requires a bit more effort—take it to the Arc de Triomphe, walk a few blocks, then grab the #92 city bus and hop off at one of the stops along Avenue Bosquet, shortly after crossing the river (for stop locations near the Arc, see the map on page 100; for stop locations on Avenue Bosquet, see page 138).

Marais and Ile St. Louis: Take "Les Cars" Air France bus (#4) to Gare de Lyon, find the Métro entry near the bus stop, then take a quick trip on Métro line 1 (direction: La Défense). Get off at the Bastille or St. Paul stops for the Marais, or the Hôtel de Ville stop for Ile St. Louis. Or, take the RER-B from the airport to the Châtelet-Les Halles stop and transfer to Métro line 1 (direction: Château de Vincennes; long walk with some stairs in a huge station), and get off at Hôtel de Ville, St. Paul, or Bastille.

"Les Cars" Air France buses run at least twice hourly from 5:45 until 23:00 (tel. 08 92 35 08 20, www.lescarsairfrance.com). **Bus #2** goes to the Etoile stop near the Arc de Triomphe (€17, 45 minutes, see map on page 100) and Porte Maillot (with connections to Beauvais Airport, described later). Once at the Arc de Triomphe, catch city bus #92 (one block away) to the Rue Cler area or city bus #30 to Montmartre. **Bus #4** runs to Gare de Lyon (€17.50, 45 minutes) and the Montparnasse Tower/train station (€17.50, 1 hour). **Bus #3** goes to Orly airport (€21, 1 hour). There is a 10 percent discount for booking your tickets online (be sure to print out your tickets and bring them with you) or pay the driver full price. Round-trip tickets shave roughly 20 percent off the cost of your journey, and groups of four or more are offered an additional discount. See the "Les Cars" website for details.

From Paris to the airport, catch Air France buses at Etoile/Arc de Triomphe (on Avenue Carnot—the non-Champs-Elysées side),

Porte Maillot (on Boulevard Gouvion-St-Cyr—east side of the Palais des Congres), Gare Montparnasse (on Rue du Commandant René Mouchotte—facing the station with the tower behind you, it's around the left side), or Gare de Lyon (look for *Navette-Aéroport* signs, and find the stop on Rue Diderot across from Café Les Deux Savoies).

By Airport Van: The shuttle vans from Charles de Gaulle work like those at home, carrying passengers directly to and from their hotels, with stops along the way to pick up other passengers. Shuttles work best for trips from your hotel to the airport, since they require you to book a precise pickup time in advance—even though you can't ever know exactly when your flight will actually arrive. Airport vans cost about €32 for one person, €46 for two, and €58 for three. While these vans take longer to reach the airport than a taxi does, compared to taxis they're a good value for single travelers and big families. Have your hotelier book at least a day in advance.

Several companies offer shuttle service; I usually just go with the one my hotel normally uses.

Paris Webservices' private car service actually works well from the airport to Paris, because they meet you inside the terminal and wait if you're late. For a one-way trip they charge €80 for up to two people. Booking round-trip costs about €160-180 for up to four people. Rick Steves readers get a 10 percent discount by mentioning promo code "PWS52K15" when you reserve, and showing your driver this book (tel. 01 45 56 91 67, www.pariswebservices.com, contact@pariswebservices.com). They also offer guided tours—see page 49.

By RER: Paris' suburban commuter train is the fastest public transit option for getting between the airport and the city center (€10, 4/hour, 35 minutes to Gare du Nord, runs 5:00-24:00). It runs directly to well-located RER/Métro stations (including Gare du Nord, Châtelet-Les Halles, St. Michel, and Luxembourg); from there, you can hop the Métro to get exactly where you need to go. The RER is handy and cheap, but it can require walking with your luggage through big, crowded stations—especially at Châtelet-Les Halles, where a transfer to the Métro can take 10-15 minutes and may include stairs.

To reach the RER from the airport terminal, follow *Paris by Train* signs, then *RER* signs. (If you're landing at T-1 or T-3, you'll need to take the CDGVAL shuttle to reach the RER station.) The RER station at T-2 is busy with long ticket-window lines (the other airport RER station, located between T-1 and T-2, is quieter). Buy tickets at a Paris Tourisme counter or from the machines at the station to save time (use the green-colored machines labeled *Paris/Ile de France,* coins required, break your bills at an airport shop).

Beware of thieves; wear your money belt, and keep your bags close. For step-by-step instructions on taking the RER into Paris, see www.parisbytrain.com (see the options under "CDG Airport to Paris").

To return to the airport by RER from central Paris, allow plenty of time to get to your departure gate (plan for a 10-minute Métro or bus ride to the closest RER station serving line B, a 15-minute wait for your train, a 30-minute train ride, plus walking time through the stations and airport). Your Métro or bus ticket is not valid on the RER train to the airport; buy the ticket from a clerk or the machines (coins only) at the RER-B station. When you catch your train, make sure the sign over the platform shows *Aéroport Roissy-Charles de Gaulle* as a stop served. (The line splits, so not every line B train serves the airport.) If you're not clear, ask another rider, *"Air-o-por sharl duh gaul?"* Once at the airport, hop out either at T-2 or T-1/3 (where you can connect to T-1 or T-3 on the CDGVAL shuttle).

By Taxi: The 50-minute trip costs about €65. Taxis are less appealing on weekday mornings as traffic into Paris can be bad (in that case, the train is likely a better option). Taxis can carry three people with bags comfortably, and are legally required to accept a fourth passenger for €3 extra (though they may not like it). Larger parties can wait for a larger vehicle. Expect to pay a €1/bag handling fee. Don't take an unauthorized taxi from cabbies greeting you on arrival. Official taxi stands are well-signed.

For trips from Paris to the airport, have your hotel arrange it. Specify that you want a real taxi *(un taxi normal),* not a limo service that costs €20 more (and gives your hotel a kickback). For weekday morning departures (7:00-10:00), reserve at least a day ahead (€5 reservation fee payable by credit card). For more on taxis in Paris, see page 35.

By Car: Car-rental desks are well-signed from the arrival halls. Be prepared for a maze of ramps as you drive away from the lot—get directions from the rental clerks when you do the paperwork.

When returning your car, allow ample time to reach the drop-off lots (at T-1 and T-2), especially if flying out of T-2. Be sure you know your flight's departure hall in T-2 (for example, many Air France and Delta flights for North America leave from T-2E/F). There are separate rental return lots depending on your T-2 departure hall—and imperfect signage can make the return lots especially confusing to navigate.

Getting from Charles de Gaulle Airport to Disneyland Paris

The Val d'Europe (VEA) **Disneyland shuttle bus** leaves from T-2E/F, door 8 (€20, runs every 45 minutes 8:30-20:00ish, 45 minutes, vea-shuttle.co.uk). TGV trains also run to Disneyland from the airport in 10 minutes, but leave less frequently (hourly) and require a shuttle bus ride at the Disneyland end.

Orly Airport

This easy-to-navigate airport (airport code: ORY) feels small, but has all the services you'd expect at a major airport: ATMs and currency exchange, car-rental desks, cafés, shops, post offices, and more (for flight info from French landlines dial 3950, from the US dial 011 33 1 70 36 39 50, www.adp.fr). Orly is good for rental-car pickup and drop-off, as it's closer to Paris and far easier to navigate than Charles de Gaulle Airport.

Orly has two terminals: Ouest (west) and Sud (south). Air France and a few other carriers arrive at Ouest; most others use Sud. At both terminals, arrivals are on the ground level (level 0) and departures are on level 1. You can connect the two terminals with the free Orlyval shuttle train (well-signed) or with any of the shuttle buses that also travel into downtown Paris.

Services: Both terminals have red Paris Tourisme desks where you can get maps of Paris, buy the Paris Museum Pass and tickets for public transit into Paris, and book hotels. There are also orange ADP information desks (near baggage claim) with information on flights, public transit into Paris, and help with other airport-related questions—take advantage of this good information source while you wait for your bags. Both terminals offer 15 minutes of free Wi-Fi (€2/30 minutes of faster Wi-Fi). At the Sud terminal, you can get online for free at McDonald's (departure level).

Getting Between Orly Airport and Paris

Shuttle buses *(navettes)*, the RER, taxis, and airport vans connect Paris with either terminal. Bus stops and taxis are centrally located at arrivals levels and are well-signed.

By Bus: Bus bays are found in the Sud terminal outside exits L and G, and in the Ouest terminal outside exits C, D, and H.

"Les Cars" Air France bus #1 runs to Gare Montparnasse, Invalides, and Etoile Métro stops, all of which have connections to several Métro lines. Upon request, drivers will also stop at the Porte d'Orléans Métro stop. For the Rue Cler neighborhood, take the bus to Invalides, then the Métro to La Tour Maubourg or Ecole Militaire. Buses depart from Ouest arrival level exit B-C or Sud exit L: Look for signs to *navettes* (€12.50 one-way, 4/hour, 40 minutes to Invalides, buy ticket from driver or save 10 percent by booking your tickets online—be sure to print out your tickets and bring them with you). Round-trip tickets save you 20 percent, and groups of four or more are offered an additional discount. See www.lescarsairfrance.com for details.

For the cheapest access to the Marais area, take **tramway line 7** from outside the Sud terminal (direction: Villejuif-Louis Aragon) to the Villejuif Métro station, line 7 (35 minutes, €3.40—plus one Métro ticket—4/hour).

By Bus and RER: The next two options take you to the RER suburban train's line B, with access to the Luxembourg Garden area, Notre-Dame Cathedral, handy Métro line 1 at the Châtelet stop, Gare du Nord, and Charles de Gaulle Airport. The **Orlybus** goes directly to the Denfert-Rochereau Métro and RER-B stations (€7.50, 3/hour, 30 minutes). The pricier but more frequent—and more comfortable—**Orlyval shuttle train** takes you to the Antony RER station, where you can catch the RER-B (€11, 6/hour, 40 minutes, buy ticket before boarding). The Orlyval train is well-signed and leaves from the departure level at both terminals. Once at the RER-B station, take the train in direction: Mitry-Claye or Aéroport Charles de Gaulle to reach central Paris stops.

For access to RER line C, take the bus marked ***Pont de Rungis.*** From the Pont de Rungis station, you can catch the RER-C to Gare d'Austerlitz, St. Michel/Notre-Dame, Musée d'Orsay, Invalides and Pont de l'Alma (€7.50, 4/hour, 35 minutes).

By Taxi: Taxis are outside the Ouest terminal exit B, and to the far right as you leave the Sud terminal at exit M. Allow 30 minutes for a taxi ride into central Paris (about €45 with bags; for more information on airport taxis, see page 177).

By Airport Van: Airport vans are a good means of getting from Paris to the airport, especially for single travelers or families of four or more (too many for most taxis; for information on airport vans, see page 179). From Orly, figure about €23 for one person or €30 for two people (less per person for larger groups and kids).

Getting from Orly Airport to Disneyland Paris

The Val d'Europe (VEA) **shuttle bus to Disneyland** departs from the main bus bays at both terminals (€20, hourly 9:00-19:30, 45 minutes, http://vea-shuttle.co.uk).

Beauvais Airport

Budget airlines such as Ryanair use this small airport, offering dirt-cheap airfares but leaving you 50 miles north of Paris. Still, this airport has direct buses to Paris and is handy for travelers heading to Normandy or Belgium (car rental available). The airport is basic, waiting areas are crowded, and services are sparse, but improvements are gradually on the way (airport code: BVA, airport tel. 08

92 68 20 66—lines open daily 8:00-20:00, www.aeroportbeauvais.com; Ryanair tel. 08 92 78 02 10—lines open Mon-Fri 9:00-19:00, Sat 10:00-17:00, Sun 11:00-17:00; www.ryanair.com).

Getting Between Beauvais Airport and Paris

By Bus: Buses depart from the airport when they're full (about 20 minutes after flights arrive) and take 1.5 hours to reach Paris. Buy your ticket (€17 one-way, €16 online) at the little kiosk to the right as you exit the airport. Buses arrive at Porte Maillot on the west edge of Paris (on Métro line 1 and RER-C). The closest taxi stand is at the Hôtel Hyatt Regency.

Buses heading to Beauvais Airport leave from Porte Maillot about 3.25 hours before scheduled flight departures. Catch the bus in the parking lot on Boulevard Pershing next to the Hyatt Regency. Arrive with enough time to purchase your bus ticket before boarding, or buy online at http://tickets.aeroportbeauvais.com.

By Train: Trains connect Beauvais' city center and Paris' Gare du Nord (20/day, 1.25 hours). To reach Beauvais' train station, take the Beauvais *navette* shuttle bus (€4.50, 6/day, 30 minutes) or local bus #12 (€1, 12/day, 30 minutes).

By Taxi: Cabs run from Beauvais Airport to Beauvais' train station or city center (€15), or to central Paris (allow €150 and 1.25 hours).

Getting from Beauvais Airport to Disneyland Paris

The Val d'Europe (VEA) **shuttle bus to Disneyland** runs from Beauvais via Charles de Gaulle Airport (€25, 2-3/day, 2.5 hours, http://vea-shuttle.co.uk).

Connecting Paris' Airports

"Les Cars" Air France bus #3 directly and conveniently links Charles de Gaulle and Orly airports (€21, stops at Charles de Gaulle T-1 and T-2 and Orly Ouest exit B-C or Sud exit L, roughly 2/hour, 1 hour, 5:45-23:00). See www.lescarsairfrance.com for details.

RER line B connects Charles de Gaulle and Orly but requires a transfer to the Orlyval train. It isn't as easy as the Air France bus mentioned above, though it's faster when there's traffic (€19, 5/hour, 1.5 hours). This line splits at both ends: Heading from Charles de Gaulle to Orly, take trains that serve the Antony stop (direction: St-Rémy-les-Chevreuse), then transfer to Orlyval shuttle train; heading from Orly to Charles de Gaulle, take trains that end at the airport—Aéroport Charles de Gaulle-Roissy, not Mitry-Claye. You can also connect Charles de Gaulle or Orly airports to Beauvais via train. Take the RER-B to Gare du Nord, catch a train to Beauvais, and then a shuttle or local bus to Beauvais Airport (see "Beauvais Airport," earlier).

PARIS

Val d'Europe (VEA) buses run between Beauvais and Charles de Gaulle, en route to Disneyland (€16, 2-3/day, 1-1.5 hours, http://vea-shuttle.co.uk).

Taxis are easiest, but pricey: Between Charles de Gaulle and Orly, it's about €80 and 1 hour; between Charles de Gaulle and Beauvais, €120 and 1 hour; and between Orly and Beauvais, €160 and 1.5 hours.

BY TRAIN

Paris is Europe's rail hub, with six major stations and one minor one, and trains heading in different directions:

- Gare du Nord (northbound trains)
- Gare Montparnasse (west- and southwest-bound trains)
- Gare de Lyon (southeast-bound trains)
- Gare de l'Est (eastbound trains)
- Gare St. Lazare (northwest-bound trains)
- Gare d'Austerlitz (southwest-bound trains)
- Gare de Bercy (smaller station with non-TGV southbound trains)

All six main train stations have banks or currency exchanges, ATMs, train information desks, telephones, cafés, newsstands, and clever pickpockets (pay attention in ticket lines—keep your bag firmly gripped in front of you). Because of security concerns, not all have baggage checks.

Any train station has schedule information, can make reservations, and can sell tickets for any destination. You can save time and stress by buying train tickets or making train reservations at an SNCF Boutique. These small branch offices of the French national rail company are conveniently located throughout Paris, with offices near most of my recommended hotels and museums and at Charles de Gaulle and Orly airports. Arrive when they open to avoid lines (generally open Mon-Sat 8:30-19:00 or 20:00, closed Sun). For a complete list, see www.megacomik.info/boutiquesncf.htm.

Each train station offers two types of rail service: long distance to other cities, called Grandes Lignes (major lines); and suburban service to nearby areas, called Banlieue, Transilien, or RER. You also may see ticket windows identified as *Ile de France.* These are for Transilien trains serving destinations outside Paris in the Ile de France region (usually no more than an hour from Paris). When arriving by Métro, follow signs for *Grandes Lignes-SNCF* to find the main tracks. Métro and RER trains, as well as buses and taxis, are well-marked at every station.

Budget plenty of time before your departure to factor in ticket lines and making your way through large, crowded stations. Paris train stations can be intimidating, but if you slow down, take a

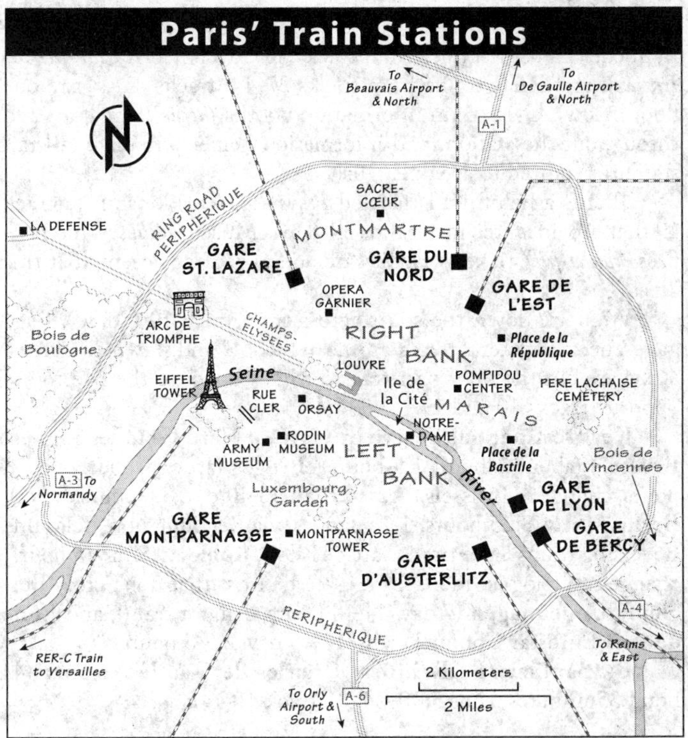

deep breath, and ask for help, you'll find them manageable and efficient. Bring a pad of paper and a pen for clear communication at ticket/info windows. It helps to write down the ticket you want. For instance: "28/05/15 Paris-Nord—>Lyon dep. 18:30." All stations have helpful information booths *(accueil);* the bigger stations have roving helpers, usually wearing red or blue vests. They're capable of answering rail questions more quickly than the staff at the information desks or ticket windows. I make a habit of confirming my track number and departure time with these helpers. To make your trip go more smoothly, be sure to review the many train tips on page 1090.

Gare du Nord

The granddaddy of Paris' train stations serves cities in northern France and international destinations north of Paris, including Copenhagen, Amsterdam (see "To Brussels and Amsterdam by Thalys Train," later), and the Eurostar to London (see "To London by Eurostar Train," also later).

From the Métro, follow *Grandes Lignes* signs (main lines) to reach the tracks at street level. Grandes Lignes trains depart from tracks 2-21 (tracks 20 and 21 are around the corner), suburban Banlieue/Transilien lines from tracks 30-36 (signed *Réseau Ile-de-France*), and RER trains from tracks 37-44 (tracks 41-44 are one floor below). Glass train information booths *(accueil)* are scattered throughout the station, and information-helpers circulate (all rail staff are required to speak English).

There's a helpful TI (labeled *Paris Tourisme*) kiosk near track 19 that provides free maps and sells Paris Museum Passes and fast-pass "*coupe-file*" tickets (credit cards only, no cash accepted at this TI).

WCs are down the stairs across from track 10 (€0.50). Baggage check and rental cars are near track 3 and down the steps. Taxis are out the door past track 3. Steps down to the Métro are opposite tracks 10 and 19.

Key Destinations Served by Gare du Nord Grandes Lignes: Brussels (about 2/hour, 1.5 hours), **Bruges** (at least hourly, 2.5-3 hours, change in Brussels), **Amsterdam** (8-10/day, 3.5 hours direct), **Berlin** (4/day, 8.25 hours, 1-2 changes, via Belgium, non-Belgium-traversing trains leave from Gare de l'Est), **Koblenz** (8/day, 5 hours, change in Cologne, more from Gare de l'Est that don't cross Belgium), **Copenhagen** (7/day, 14-18 hours, 1 night train), and **London** via Eurostar Chunnel train (12-15/day, 2.5-3 hours).

By Banlieue/RER Lines: Charles de Gaulle Airport (4/hour, 35 minutes, runs 5:00-24:00, track 41-44).

Gare Montparnasse

This big, modern station covers three floors, serves lower Normandy and Brittany, and has TGV service to the Loire Valley and southwestern France, as well as suburban service to Chartres.

Baggage check *(consigne)* and WCs are on the mezzanine *(entresol)* level. Most services are provided on the top level (second floor up, Hall 1), where all trains arrive and depart. Trains to Chartres usually depart from tracks 18-24, and the main rail information office *(accueil)* is opposite track 15. As you face the tracks, to the far left and outside are Air France buses to Orly and Charles de Gaulle airports (on Rue du Commandant René Mouchotte). Taxis are to the far right as you face the tracks; also to the right, along track 24 and up the escalator to Hall 2, are car rental desks (except Hertz, which is outside the train station at 15 Rue du Commandant René Mouchotte).

City buses are out front, between the train station and the Montparnasse Tower (down the escalator through the glassy facade). Bus #96 is good for connecting to Marais area hotels, while #92 is ideal for Rue Cler hotels (both easier than the Métro).

Key Destinations Served by Gare Montparnasse: Chartres (14/day, 1 hour), **Amboise** (8/day in 1.5 hours with change in

St-Pierre-des-Corps, requires TGV reservation; non-TGV trains leave from Gare d'Austerlitz), **Pontorson/Mont St-Michel** (3/day, 5.5 hours, via Rennes or Caen), **Dinan** (6/day, 4 hours, change in Rennes and Dol), **Bordeaux** (20/day, 3.5 hours), **Sarlat-la-Canéda** (3/day, 5.5-6.5 hours, change in Libourne or Bordeaux), **Toulouse** (8/day, 5-7 hours, most require change, usually in Bordeaux or Montpellier), **Albi** (4/day, 6.5-9 hours, change in Toulouse), **Tours** (10/day, 1.25 hours), **Madrid** (3/day, 12-14 hours), and **Lisbon** (2/day, 21-24 hours via Irun).

Gare de Lyon

This huge, bewildering station offers TGV and regular service to southeastern France, Italy, Switzerland, and other international destinations.

From the RER or Métro, follow signs for *Grandes Lignes* to reach the street-level platforms (Grandes Lignes and Banlieue lines share the same tracks). Platforms are divided into two areas: Hall 1 (tracks A-N, shaded in light blue) and Hall 2 (tracks 5-23, shaded in yellow). Monitors indicate the hall number well before the track number is posted, so you know in advance which hall your train leaves from. The two halls are connected by a corridor offering many services, including shops and ticket windows for Grandes Lignes and suburban trains *(billets Ile de France).* A TI office is in Hall 1, opposite track M (open Mon-Sat 8:00-18:00, closed Sun, offers free maps and sells Paris Museum Passes and fast-pass *coupe-file* tickets; credit cards only, no cash accepted). Train information booths are opposite tracks A and M in Hall 1 and near track 11 in Hall 2 (others are downstairs). Hall 2 has the best services—including a pharmacy and a good Monop grocery store. You'll find baggage check *(consigne)* in Hall 2 down the ramp, opposite track 17, and in Hall 1, downstairs by track M. Car rental is out the exit past track M (Hall 1).

Don't leave this station without at least taking a peek at the recommended Le Train Bleu Restaurant in Hall 1, up the stairs opposite tracks G-L. Its pricey-but-atmospheric bar/lounge works well as a quiet waiting area—and there's free Wi-Fi. Slip into a red leather couch and time travel back to another era.

Taxi stands are well-signed in front of, and underneath, the station. **"Les Cars" Air France** buses to Gare Montparnasse (easy transfer to Orly Airport) and direct to Charles de Gaulle Airport stop outside the station's main entrance. They are signed *Navette-Aéroport.* To find them, exit Hall 1 with your back to track A. Walk down toward the Café Européen, but don't cross the street. The stop is to the right, on Rue Diderot across from Café Les Deux Savoies (second bus shelter up). Buses normally depart at :15 and :45 after the hour; see "By Bus" on page 177).

Key Destinations Served by Gare de Lyon: Disneyland (RER line A-4 to Marne-la-Vallée-Chessy, at least 3/hour, 45 minutes), **Beaune** (roughly hourly at rush hour but few midday, 2.5 hours, most require change in Dijon; direct trains from Paris' Bercy station take an hour longer), **Dijon** (roughly hourly at rush hour but few midday, 1.5 hours), **Chamonix** (7/day, 5.5-7 hours, some change in Switzerland), **Annecy** (hourly, 4 hours, many with change in Lyon), **Lyon** (at least hourly, 2 hours), **Avignon** (10/day direct, 2.5 hours to Avignon TGV Station, 5/day in 3.5 hours to Avignon *Centre-Ville* Station, more connections with change—3-4 hours), **Arles** (11/day, 2 direct TGVs—4 hours, 9 with change in Avignon—5 hours), **Nice** (hourly, 5.75 hours, may require change, 11.5-hour night train possible out of Gare d'Austerlitz), **Carcassonne** (8/day, 7-8 hours, 1 change, night trains leave from Gare d'Austerlitz), **Zürich** (6/day direct, 4 hours), **Venice** (5/day, 10-12 hours with 1-3 changes; 1 direct overnight, 14 hours, operated by private company Thello—which doesn't accept rail passes, important to reserve ahead at www.thello.com), **Rome** (3/day, 11-16 hours), **Bern** (15/day, 4.5-5.5 hours), **Interlaken** (7/day, 5-6.5 hours, 1-3 changes, 2 more from Gare de l'Est), and **Barcelona** (2/day, 6.5 hours, change in Figueres).

Gare de l'Est

This two-floor station (with underground Métro) serves northeastern France and international destinations east of Paris. It's easy to navigate: All trains depart at street level from tracks 1-30. Check the departure monitors to see which section your train leaves from: Departures marked with a yellow square leave from tracks 2-12, while those marked with a blue square depart from tracks 22-30 (suburban Banlieue trains depart from tracks 13-21). A train information office is opposite track 17, and ticket sales are at each end of the station through the halls opposite tracks 8 and 25. Most other services are down the escalator through the hall opposite tracks 12-20 (baggage lockers, car rental, WC, small grocery store, more shops, and Métro access). There's a post office at track level, near the top of the escalators. Access to taxis and buses is out the front of the station (exit with your back to the tracks).

Key Destinations Served by Gare de l'Est: Colmar (12/day with TGV, 3.5 hours, change in Strasbourg), **Strasbourg** (hourly with TGV, 2.5 hours), **Reims'** Centre Station (12/day with TGV, 45 minutes), **Verdun** (4/day with TGV, 45 minutes; 3 hours by regional train with transfer in Chalôns-en-Champagne), **Interlaken** (2/day, 6.5 hours, 2-3 changes, 7 more from Gare de Lyon), **Zürich** (7/day, 5-6 hours, 1-2 changes, faster direct trains from Gare de Lyon), **Frankfurt** (5 direct/day, 4 hours; 4 more/day with change in Karlsruhe, 4.5 hours), **Vienna** (7/day, 12-17 hours, 1-3 changes),

Prague (5/day, 12-18 hours), **Munich** (6/day, 6 hours, most with 1 change), and **Berlin** (5/day, 8.5 hours, 1-2 changes).

Gare St. Lazare

This compact station serves upper Normandy, including Rouen and Giverny. All trains arrive and depart one floor above street level.

From the Métro, follow signs to *Grandes Lignes* to reach the tracks (long walk). Grandes Lignes to all destinations listed below depart from tracks 23-27; Banlieue trains depart from 1-16. The ticket office and car rental are near track 27. Train information offices *(accueil)* are scattered about the station. This station has no baggage check, but it does have a three-floor shopping mall with a small grocery store, clothing, and more (with your back to the tracks, head a few steps through the halls). Taxis, the Métro, and buses are well-signed.

PARIS

Key Destinations Served by Gare St. Lazare: Giverny (train to Vernon, 8/day Mon-Sat, 6/day Sun, 45 minutes), **Rouen** (nearly hourly, 1.5 hours), **Le Havre** (hourly, 2.25 hours, some change in Rouen), **Honfleur** (13/day, 2-3.5 hours, via Lisieux, Deauville, or Le Havre, then bus), **Bayeux** (9/day, 2.5 hours, some change in Caen), **Caen** (14/day, 2 hours), and **Pontorson/Mont St-Michel** (2/day, 4-5.5 hours, via Caen; more trains from Gare Montparnasse).

Gare d'Austerlitz

This small station provides non-TGV service to the Loire Valley, southwestern France, and Spain. All tracks are at street level. The information booth is opposite track 17, and all ticket sales are in the hall opposite track 10. Baggage check, WCs (with €6 showers that include towel, soap, and the works), and car rental are along the side of the station, opposite track 21. To get to the Métro and RER, you must walk outside and along either side of the station.

Key Destinations Served by Gare d'Austerlitz: Versailles (via RER-C, 4/hour, 35 minutes), **Amboise** (3/day direct in 2 hours, 5/day with transfer in Blois or Les Aubrais-Orléans; faster TGV connection from Gare Montparnasse), **Sarlat-la-Canéda** (1/day, 6.25 hours, requires change to bus in Souillac, 3 more/day via Gare Montparnasse), **Carcassonne** (1 direct night train, 7.5 hours, plus a decent night train via Toulouse, better day trains from Gare de Lyon), and **Cahors** (5/day, 5 hours, at least 1 direct night train; slower trains from Gare Montparnasse).

Gare de Bercy

This smaller station mostly handles southbound non-TGV trains, but some TGV trains do stop here in peak season (Mo: Bercy, one stop east of Gare de Lyon on line 14, exit the Bercy Métro station and it's across the street). Facilities are limited—just a WC and a sandwich-fare takeout café.

Specialty Trains from Paris

To Brussels and Amsterdam by Thalys Train

The pricey Thalys train has the monopoly on the rail route between Paris and Brussels (for a cheaper option, try the Eurolines bus, tel. 08 36 69 52 52, www.eurolines.com). Without a rail pass you'll pay about €160-210 first class, €65-120 second class for the Paris-Amsterdam train (compared to €38-50 by bus), or about €40-70 second class for the Paris-Brussels train (compared to €30 by bus). Even with a rail pass, you need to pay for train reservations (second class-€27-39; first class-€42-62, includes a meal). Book early for best rates (seats are limited in various discount categories, www.thalys.com).

Low-Cost TGV Trains to Southern France

A TGV train called OUIGO (pronounced "we go") offers a direct connection from Disneyland Paris to select cities in southern France at rock-bottom fares with no-frills service. The catch: These trains leave from the Marne-la-Vallée TGV station, an hour from Paris on RER-A. So you can hang at Disneyland Paris before (or after) your trip south and connect with a direct TGV. You must print your own ticket ahead of time, arrive 30 minutes before departure, and validate your ticket. You can't use a rail pass, and you can only bring one carry-on-size bag plus one handbag for free (children's tickets allow you to bring a stroller). Larger or extra luggage is €5/bag if you pay when you buy your ticket. If you just show up without paying in advance, it's €20/bag on the train—yikes. There's no food service on the train (BYO), but children under age 12 pay only €5 for a seat! The website explains it all in easy-to-understand English (www.ouigo.com).

To London by Eurostar Train

The fastest and most convenient way to get from the Eiffel Tower to Big Ben is by rail. Eurostar zips you (and up to 800 others in 18 sleek cars) from downtown Paris to downtown London (1-2/hour, 2.5 hours) faster and more easily than flying. The train goes 190 mph both before and after the English Channel crossing. The actual tunnel crossing is a 20-minute, silent, 100-mile-per-hour nonevent. Your ears won't even pop. Get ready for more high-speed connections: Eurostar's monopoly expired at the

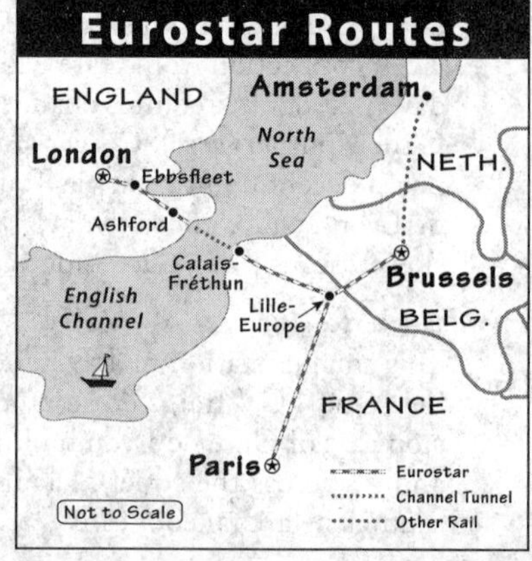

beginning of 2010, and Germany's national railroad is negotiating to run its bullet trains through the Chunnel by 2016.

Eurostar Fares: The Eurostar is not covered by rail passes and always requires a separate, reserved train ticket. Eurostar fares vary depending on how far ahead you reserve, whether you can live with restrictions (refundable vs. non-refundable tickets), and whether you're eligible for any discounts.

A **one-way, full-fare ticket** (with no restrictions on refunds) runs about $210-250 (Standard), $250-330 (Standard Premier), and $410 (Business). **Discounts** can lower fares substantially (figure $60-160 for second class, one-way) for children under 12, youths under 26, seniors 60 or older, adults booking months ahead or traveling round-trip, and rail-pass holders. The early bird gets the best price. If you're ready to commit, you can book tickets as early as 4-9 months in advance.

Buying Eurostar Tickets: Because only the most expensive (full-fare) ticket is fully refundable, don't reserve until you're sure of your plans. But if you wait too long, the cheapest tickets will get bought up.

Once you're confident about the time and date of your crossing, you can check and book tickets by phone or online at www.ricksteves.com/eurostar or www.eurostar.com. Ordering online through Eurostar or major agents offers a print-at-home eticket option. You can also order by phone through Rail Europe at US tel. 800-387-6782 for home delivery before you go, or through Eurostar (French tel. 08 92 35 35 39, priced in euros) and pick up your ticket at the train station. In Europe you can buy your Eurostar ticket at any major train station in any country, at neighborhood SNCF offices, or at any travel agency that handles train tickets (expect a booking fee). You can purchase passholder discount tickets at Eurostar departure stations, through US agents, or by phone with Eurostar, but they may be harder to get at other train stations and travel agencies, and are a discount category that can sell out.

Remember France's time zone is one hour later than Britain's. Times printed on tickets are local times (departure from Paris is French time, arrival in London is British time).

Taking the Eurostar: Eurostar trains depart from and arrive at Paris' Gare du Nord (see page 185). Check in at least 45 minutes in advance for your Eurostar trip. It's very similar to an airport check-in: You pass through airport-like security, fill out a customs form, show your passport to customs officials, and find a TV monitor to locate your departure gate. The currency-exchange booth here has rates about the same as you'll find on the other end. There's a reasonable restaurant before the first check-in point.

Once you start the check-in process, there are only a couple of tiny sandwich-and-coffee counters, and the waiting area can get pretty cramped.

BY BUS

The main bus station is Gare Routière du Paris-Gallieni (28 Avenue du Général de Gaulle, in suburb of Bagnolet, Mo: Gallieni, tel. 01 49 72 51 51). Buses provide cheaper—if less comfortable and more time-consuming—transportation to major European cities. The bus is also the cheapest way to cross the English Channel; book at least two days in advance for the best fares. Eurolines' buses depart from here (tel. 08 36 69 52 52, www.eurolines.com). Look on their website for offices in central Paris.

BY CRUISE SHIP

Ships visiting "Paris" actually call at the industrial city of **Le Havre,** a 2.25-hour train trip north.

Orientation

Le Havre's sprawling port area—harboring industrial, leisure, and cruise ships—stretches along the northern bank of the Seine River. The main **TI** is at the western edge of town, between the marina and the beach (daily July-Aug 9:00-19:00, Sept-June 9:30-12:30 & 14:00-18:30; Wi-Fi, 186 Boulevard Clemenceau, tel. 02 32 74 04 04, www.lehavretourisme.com); additional branches are downtown and at the cruise terminal.

Le Havre's cruise port is located about a mile and a half southwest of the train station at **Pointe de Floride,** which is flanked by two piers: Roger Meunier Pier and Pierre Callet Pier. Both feed into a spacious, modern terminal building with Internet access, a TI, car rental, bike rental, a gift shop, and WCs (www.cruiselehavre.com).

Getting into Le Havre

Most cruise ships provide a **shuttle bus** that takes passengers to various points in Le Havre. If your bus doesn't stop at the train station itself, get off at Les Docks (a shopping and entertainment complex) and walk five minutes north, crossing the harbor canal on the Passerelle Hubert Raoul Duval footbridge.

If there's no shuttle bus, you can take a **taxi** to the train station for about €8.

Getting Between Le Havre and Paris

Trains leave nearly hourly for Paris' St. Lazare station (2.25 hours, €34.50 one-way; may require a change in Rouen, fewer trains on weekends). Most cruise lines offer a "Paris on Your Own" **excur-**

sion, which consists of an un-narrated bus ride from your ship to Paris (generally dropping you near Place de la Concorde), then back again at an appointed time (typically $110-130, compared to $85 for the round-trip train). A 10-hour round-trip **taxi** tour of Paris costs €460.

NEAR PARIS

Versailles • Chartres • Giverny • Disneyland Paris

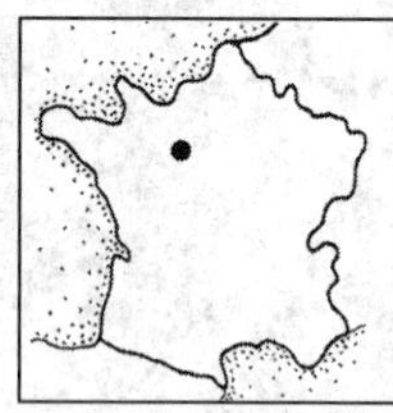

Efficient trains bring dozens of day trips within the grasp of temporary Parisians. Europe's best palace at Versailles, the awesome cathedral of Chartres, the flowery gardens at Giverny that inspired Monet, and a mouse-run amusement park await the traveler looking for a refreshing change from urban Paris.

Versailles

Every king's dream, Versailles (vehr-"sigh") was the residence of French monarchs and the cultural heartbeat of Europe for about 100 years—until the Revolution of 1789 changed all that. The Sun King (Louis XIV) created Versailles, spending freely from the public treasury to turn his dad's hunting lodge into a palace fit for the gods (among whom he counted himself). Louis XV and Louis XVI spent much of the 18th century gilding Louis XIV's lily. In 1837, about 50 years after the royal family was evicted by citizen-protesters, King Louis-Philippe opened the palace as a museum. Today you can visit parts of the huge palace and wander through acres of manicured gardens sprinkled with fountains and studded with statues. Europe's next-best palaces are just Versailles wannabes.

Worth ▲▲▲, Versailles offers three blockbuster sights. The main attraction is the palace itself,

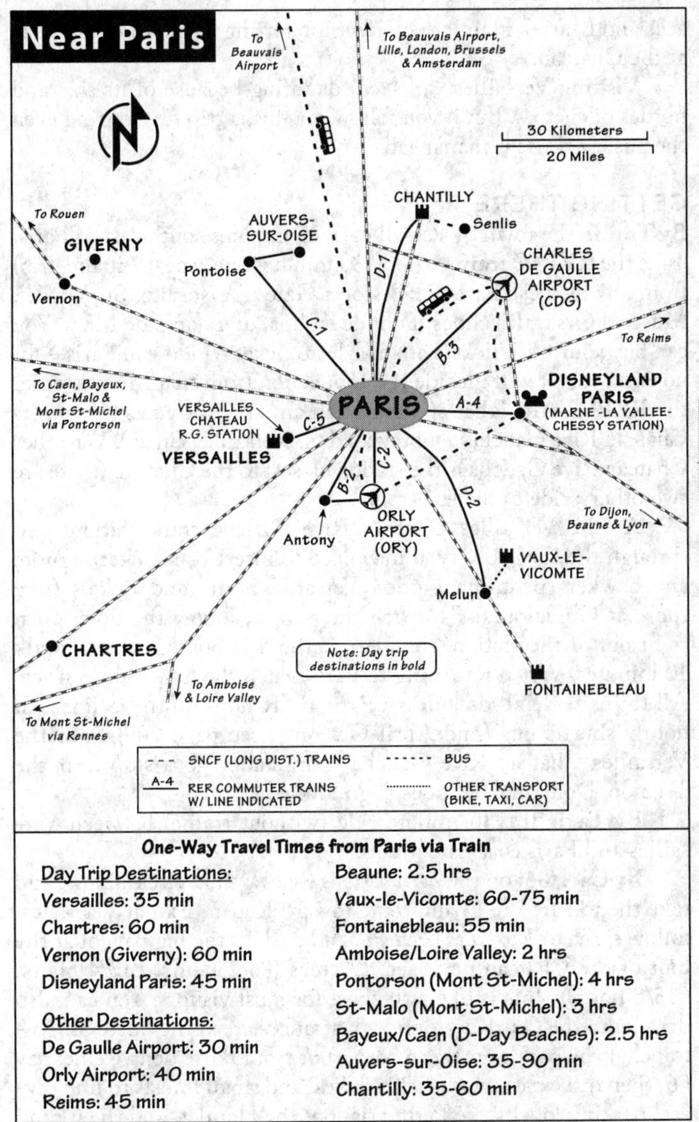

called the **Château.** Here you walk through dozens of lavish, chandeliered rooms once inhabited by Louis XIV and his successors. Next come the expansive **Gardens** behind the palace, a landscaped wonderland dotted with statues and fountains. Finally, at the far end of the Gardens, is the pastoral area called the **Trianon Palaces and Domaine de Marie-Antoinette** (a.k.a. Trianon/Domaine), designed for frolicking blue bloods and featuring several small palaces and Marie's Hamlet—perfect for getting away from the mobs at the Château.

Visiting Versailles can seem daunting because of its size and hordes of visitors. But if you follow my tips, a trip here during even the busiest times is manageable.

GETTING THERE

By Train: The town of Versailles is 35 minutes southwest of Paris. Take the **RER-C train** (4/hour, 35 minutes one-way, €7 round-trip) from any of these Paris RER stops: Gare d'Austerlitz, St. Michel, Musée d'Orsay, Invalides, Pont de l'Alma, or Champ de Mars. You can buy your train tickets at any Métro ticket window in Paris—for no extra cost it will include the connection from that Métro stop to the RER. At the RER station, catch any train listed as "Versailles Château Rive Gauche" (abbreviated to "Versailles Chât"). Versailles Château Rive Gauche is the station closest to the Château (there are two others; ride to the last stop).

At the Versailles Château Rive Gauche train station, exit through the turnstiles (you may need to insert your ticket). Ignore any hawkers peddling guided Versailles tours and tickets (like those at Guidatours). To reach the **palace,** follow the flow: Turn right out of the station, then left at the first boulevard, and walk 10 minutes. When returning to Paris, catch the first train you see: All trains serve all downtown Paris RER stops on the C line. An hourly shuttle bus (mid-April-Oct only; see page 209) links the Versailles Château Rive Gauche train station to a stop near the Trianon/Domaine, but doesn't go to the palace.

By Taxi: The 30-minute ride (without traffic) between Versailles and Paris costs about €60.

By Car: Get on the *périphérique* freeway that circles Paris, and take the toll-free A-13 autoroute toward Rouen. Exit at Versailles, follow signs to *Versailles Château,* and park in the big pay lot at the foot of the Château on Place d'Armes (€6/2 hours, €10/4 hours, €15/8 hours). This is likely the best for most visitors. You can also drive onto the Garden grounds. Entrances are at the Porte St. Antoine (at the park's northern corner) or from Porte de la Reine; pay €6, then drive past wheat fields, lakes, and small forests to find several parking lots by the Petit Trianon, the Hamlet, and the Grand Canal. The car park by the Grand Canal is the most central of these and an easy walk to the Château, but it is tricky to locate and sometimes off limits. You are free to move from one parking lot to another once you're on the grounds.

PLANNING YOUR TIME

Versailles is all about crowd management; a well-planned visit can make or break your experience. Take this advice to heart.

Versailles merits a full sightseeing day and is much more enjoyable with a relaxed, unhurried approach. Here's what I'd do on a first visit:

- Get a pass in advance (explained later, under "Passes").
- Avoid Sundays, Tuesdays, and Saturdays (in that order), when crowds smother the palace interior. Thursdays and Fridays are the best days to visit.
- Leave Paris by 8:00 and arrive at the palace just before it opens at 9:00. Or consider leaving Paris a bit earlier to take advantage of the €10 buffet breakfast at the recommended Hôtel Ibis Versailles (served 7:00-12:00, across from the train station).

- In the morning, tour the Château following my self-guided tour, which hits the highlights. If the line to enter the palace is really long, consider a €7 guided tour to bypass the line (explained later, under "Tours").
- Have a canalside lunch at one of the sandwich kiosks or cafés in the Gardens. Spend the afternoon touring the Gardens, Trianon Palaces, and Domaine de Marie-Antoinette. On weekends from April to October (and many Tuesdays), enjoy the Spectacles in the Gardens (but put up with intense crowds in the Château). Stay for dinner in Versailles town (see recommended restaurants on page 213), or head back to Paris.
- To shorten your visit, focus on the Château and Gardens and skip the Trianon/Domaine, which takes an additional 1.5 hours to see and a 30-minute walk to reach.
- An alternate plan that works well is to visit the Trianon Palaces and Domaine de Marie-Antoinette first (opens at noon), then work your way back through the Gardens to the Château, arriving after the crowds have died down (usually by 14:00, later on Sun). Try to coordinate your arrival so you can catch the shuttle bus from the Versailles Château Rive Gauche train station to the stop near the Grand Trianon (see page 209).

In general, allow 1.5 hours each for the Château, the Gardens, and the Trianon/Domaine. Add another two hours for round-trip transit, plus another hour for lunch, and you're looking at an eight-hour day—at the very least. If you have more time to spend at Versailles, consider one of the following, lesser sights near the palace:

the Equestrian Performance Academy (www.acadequestre.fr) or the King's Vegetable Garden (www.potager-du-roi.fr).

Orientation to Versailles

Cost: Buy either a Paris Museum Pass or a Versailles Le Passeport Pass, both of which give you access to the most important parts of the complex (see "Passes" below). If you don't get a pass, buy individual tickets for each of the three different sections.

The Château: €15, includes audioguide, under 18 free. Covers the famous Hall of Mirrors, the king and queen's living quarters, many lesser rooms, and any temporary exhibitions. For €7 more, you can get a guided tour of the Château—a good deal that also allows you to skip the security line (see "Tours," later). Free on the first Sunday of off-season months (Nov-March).

The Trianon Palaces and Domaine de Marie-Antoinette: €10, no audioguide available, under 18 free. Covers the Grand Trianon and its gardens, the Petit Trianon, the queen's Hamlet, and a smattering of nearby buildings. Free on the first Sunday of off-season months (Nov-March).

The Gardens: Free, except on Spectacle days, when admission is €9 (weekends April-Oct plus many Tue; see "Spectacles in the Gardens," later).

Passes: The following passes can save money and allow you to skip the long ticket-buying lines (but not security checks before entering the palaces). Both passes include the Château audioguide.

The Paris Museum Pass (see page 49) covers the Château and the Trianon/Domaine area (a €25 value) and is the best solution for most. It doesn't include the Gardens on Spectacle days.

The **Le Passeport** pass (€18 for one day, €25 for two days) covers the Château and the Trianon/Domaine area. The price bumps up on Spectacle days (€25 for one day, €30 for two).

Buying Passes and Tickets: Ideally, buy your ticket or pass before arriving at Versailles. You can purchase Versailles tickets at any Paris TI, FNAC department store (small fee), or online at www.chateauversailles.fr (print out your pass/ticket or pick it up near the entrance). If you arrive in Versailles without a pass or a ticket, buy it at the rarely crowded Versailles TI, not far from the train station (€2 service charge, see "Information," next page).

Your last and worst option is to buy a pass or ticket at the usually crowded Château ticket-sales office (to the left as you face the palace). Ticket windows accept American credit cards. Avoid the lines by using the ticket machines at the back of the room (you'll need a chip-and-PIN card or bills).

Hours: The **Château** is open April-Oct Tue-Sun 9:00-18:30, Nov-March Tue-Sun 9:00-17:30; closed Mon year-round.

The **Trianon Palaces and Domaine de Marie-Antoinette** are open April-Oct Tue-Sun 12:00-18:30, Nov-March Tue-Sun 12:00-17:30; closed Mon year-round (off-season only the two Trianon Palaces are open, not the Hamlet or other outlying buildings).

The **Gardens** are open April-Oct daily 9:00-20:30, but may close earlier for special events; Nov-March Tue-Sun 8:00-18:00, closed Mon.

Last entry to all areas is 30 minutes before closing.

Crowd-Beating Strategies: Versailles is packed May-Sept 10:00-13:00, so come early or late. Avoid Sundays, Tuesdays, and Saturdays (in that order), when the place is jammed with a slow shuffle of tourists from open to close. To skip the ticket-buying line, buy tickets or passes in advance, or book a guided tour. Unless you take a guided tour, everyone—including holders of advance tickets and passes—must go through the often slow security checkpoint at the Château's Royal Gate entrance (longest lines 10:00-12:00). Consider seeing the Gardens during mid-morning and the Château in the afternoon, when crowds die down.

Pickpockets: Assume pickpockets are working the tourist crowds.

Information: Before you go, check the excellent website for updates and special events—www.chateauversailles.fr. The palace's general contact number is tel. 01 30 83 78 00. You'll pass the city TI on your walk from the RER station to the palace—it's just past the Pullman Hôtel (daily 9:00-19:00, free Wi-Fi, tel. 01 39 24 88 88). The information office at the Château is to the left as you face the Château (WCs, toll tel. 08 10 81 16 14).

Tours: The 1.5-hour English **guided tour** gives you access to a few extra rooms (the itinerary varies) and lets you skip the long security check line (€22, includes palace entry, at least five tours in English between 9:00 and 15:00 April-Oct; off-season usually only at 9:30 and 14:00). Ignore the tours hawked near the train station (like Guidatours). You can book a tour in advance on the palace's website, or reserve immediately upon arrival at the guided-tours office (to the right of the Château—look for yellow *Visites Conferences* signs). Tours can sell out by 13:00.

A free **audioguide** to the Château is included in your admission. You can download a free Rick Steves audio tour of Versailles; see page 14. Other podcasts and digital tours are available in the "multimedia" section at www.chateauversailles.fr.

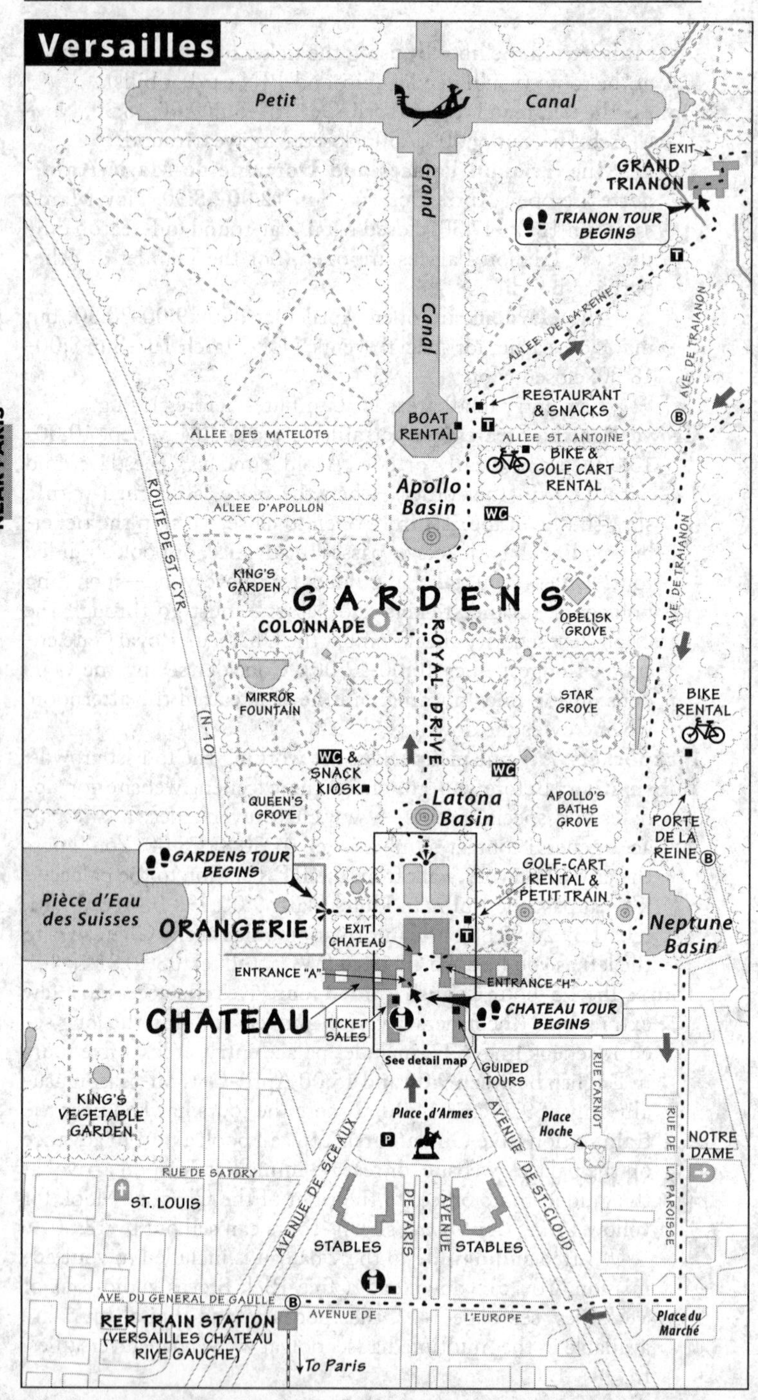
Versailles
Petit
Canal
Grand
Canal
EXIT
GRAND TRIANON
TRIANON TOUR BEGINS
ALLEE DE LA REINE
AVE. DE TRAIANON
RESTAURANT & SNACKS
BOAT RENTAL
ALLEE DES MATELOTS
ALLEE ST. ANTOINE
BIKE & GOLF CART RENTAL
Apollo Basin
WC
ALLEE D'APOLLON
ROUTE DE ST. CYR
KING'S GARDEN
GARDENS
COLONNADE
ROYAL DRIVE
OBELISK GROVE
AVE. DE TRAIANON
MIRROR FOUNTAIN
STAR GROVE
BIKE RENTAL
(N-10)
WC & SNACK KIOSK
WC
QUEEN'S GROVE
Latona Basin
APOLLO'S BATHS GROVE
PORTE DE LA REINE
GARDENS TOUR BEGINS
GOLF-CART RENTAL & PETIT TRAIN
Pièce d'Eau des Suisses
ORANGERIE
EXIT CHATEAU
Neptune Basin
ENTRANCE "A"
ENTRANCE "H"
CHATEAU
TICKET SALES
CHATEAU TOUR BEGINS
See detail map
GUIDED TOURS
RUE CARNOT
KING'S VEGETABLE GARDEN
Place d'Armes
AVENUE DE SCEAUX
AVENUE DE ST-CLOUD
Place Hoche
RUE DE LA PAROISSE
NOTRE DAME
RUE DE SATORY
ST. LOUIS
DE PARIS
AVENUE
STABLES
STABLES
AVE. DU GENERAL DE GAULLE
RER TRAIN STATION (VERSAILLES CHATEAU RIVE GAUCHE)
AVENUE DE
L'EUROPE
Place du Marché
To Paris

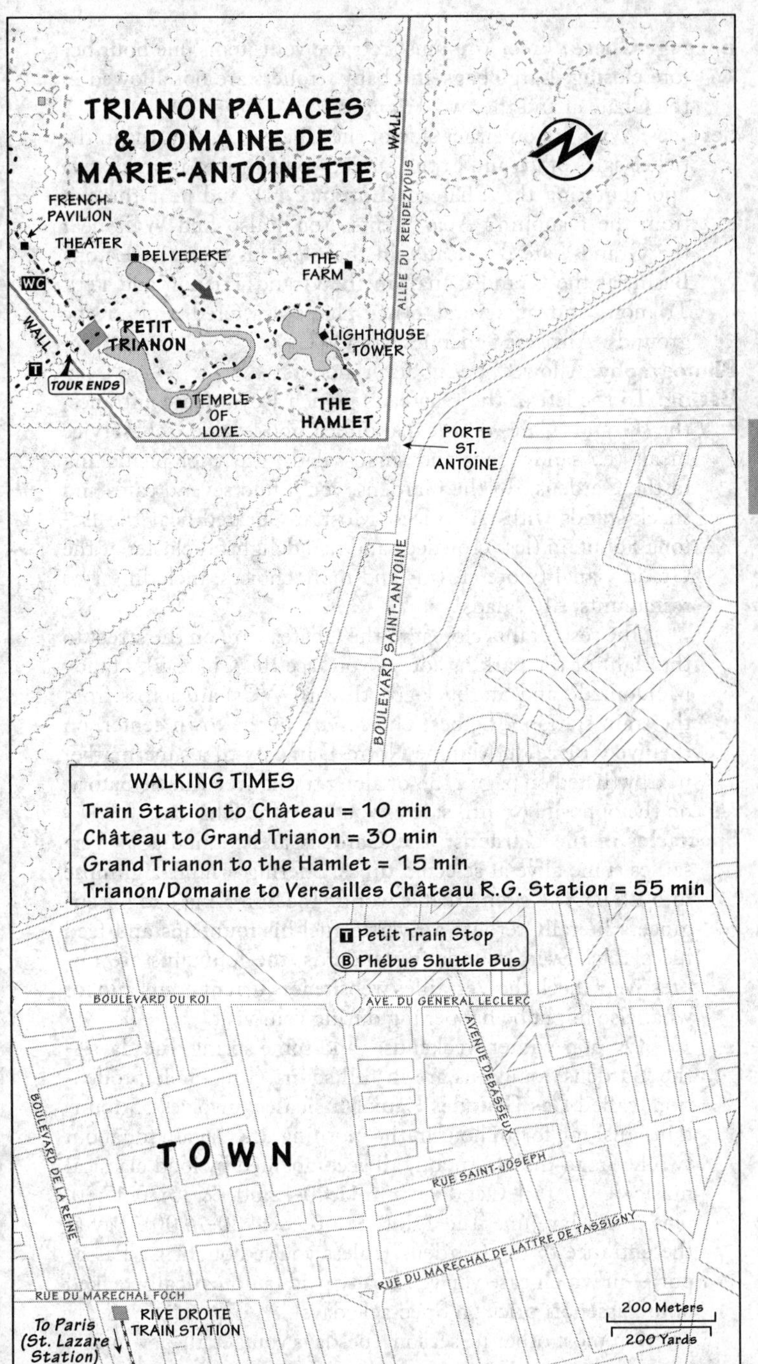
TRIANON PALACES
& DOMAINE DE
MARIE-ANTOINETTE
FRENCH PAVILION
THEATER
BELVEDERE
THE FARM
WC
WALL
PETIT TRIANON
LIGHTHOUSE TOWER
TOUR ENDS
TEMPLE OF LOVE
THE HAMLET
ALLEE DU RENDEZVOUS
PORTE ST. ANTOINE
BOULEVARD SAINT-ANTOINE
WALKING TIMES
Train Station to Château = 10 min
Château to Grand Trianon = 30 min
Grand Trianon to the Hamlet = 15 min
Trianon/Domaine to Versailles Château R.G. Station = 55 min
Petit Train Stop
Phébus Shuttle Bus
BOULEVARD DU ROI
AVE. DU GENERAL LECLERC
AVENUE DEBASSEUX
BOULEVARD DE LA REINE
TOWN
RUE SAINT-JOSEPH
RUE DU MARECHAL DE LATTRE DE TASSIGNY
RUE DU MARECHAL FOCH
RIVE DROITE TRAIN STATION
To Paris (St. Lazare Station)
200 Meters
200 Yards

Baggage Check: Free. You must retrieve your items one hour before closing. Large bags and baby strollers are not allowed in the Château and the two Trianons.

Services: WCs are on either side of the Château courtyard (in the ticket-sales office and in the guided-tours office), immediately upon entering the Château (Entrance H), and near the exit from the Dauphin's Apartments. You'll also find WCs near the Grand Café d'Orléans, in the Gardens near the Latona Basin, at the Grand Canal, in the Grand Trianon and Petit Trianon, and at several other places scattered around the grounds. Any café generally has a WC.

Photography: Allowed, but no flash indoors.

Eating: To the left of the Château's golden Royal Gate entrance, the Grand Café d'Orléans offers good-value self-service meals (€5 sandwiches and small salads, great for picnicking in the Gardens). In the Gardens, you'll find several cafés and snack stands with fair prices. Most are located near the Latona Fountain (less crowded) and in a delightful cluster at the Grand Canal (more crowds and more choices, including two restaurants, €10 salads).

The restaurants closest to the Château are on the street to the right of the parking lot (as you face the Château). Handy McDonald's and Starbucks (both with WCs) are across from the train station. The best choices are in the town center, on the lively Place du Marché Notre-Dame, with a supermarket nearby (listed on page 213), or along traffic-free Rue de Satory, on the opposite (south) side as you leave the Château.

Spectacles in the Gardens: The Gardens and fountains at Versailles come alive at selected times, offering visitors a glimpse into Louis XIV's remarkable world. The Sun King had his engineers literally reroute a river to fuel his fountains and feed his plants. Even by today's standards, the fountains are impressive. Check the Versailles website for current hours and for what else might be happening during your visit.

On non-winter weekends—and some spring Tuesdays—the Gardens' fountains are in full squirt. The whole production, called **Les Grandes Eaux Musicales,** involves 55 fountains gushing for an hour in the morning, then again for about two hours in the afternoon, all accompanied by loud classical music (€9, April-Oct Sat-Sun 11:00-12:00 & 15:30-17:30, plus mid-May-June Tue 11:00-12:00 & 14:30-16:00). Pay at the entrance to the Gardens, unless you've bought Le Passeport—in which case you've already paid (automatically tacked onto Passeport price on Spectacle days).

On most other in-season Tuesdays you get all-day music,

but no water, with the **Les Jardins Musicaux** program (€8, April-mid-May and July-Oct Tue 9:00-18:30).

On certain summer weekend nights you get the big shebang: **Les Grandes Eaux Nocturnes,** which presents whimsical lighted displays leading between gushing fountains and a fireworks show over the largest fountain pool (€25, mid-June-mid-Sept Sat at 21:00, plus mid-June-mid-July Fri at 21:00).

Starring: Luxurious palaces, endless gardens, Louis XIV, Marie-Antoinette, and the *ancien régime*.

OVERVIEW

On this tour, you'll see the Château (the State Apartments of the king and queen as well as the Hall of Mirrors), the landscaped Gardens in the "backyard," and the Trianon Palaces and Domaine de Marie-Antoinette, located at the far end of the Gardens. If your time is limited or you don't enjoy walking, skip the Trianon/Domaine, which is a 30-minute hike from the Château.

This commentary covers the basics. For background, first read the "Kings and Queens and Guillotines" sidebar on page 206. For a detailed room-by-room rundown, consider the guidebook called *The Châteaux, the Gardens, and Trianon* (sold at Versailles).

Self-Guided Tour

THE CHATEAU

• *Stand in the huge courtyard and face the palace. The golden Royal Gate in the center of the courtyard, nearly 260 feet long and decorated with 100,000 gold leaves, is a recent replica of the original. The ticket-sales office is to the left; guided-tour sales are to the right. The entrance to the Château (once you have your ticket or pass) is through the modern concrete-and-glass security checkpoint, marked Entrance A. After passing through security, you spill out into the open-air courtyard on the other side of the golden Royal Gate.*

The section of the palace with the clock is the original château, once a small hunting lodge where little Louis XIV spent his happiest boyhood years. Naturally, the Sun King's private bedroom (the three arched windows beneath the clock) faced the rising sun. The palace and grounds are laid out on an east-west axis.

Once king, Louis XIV expanded the lodge by attaching wings, creating the present U-shape. Later, the long north and

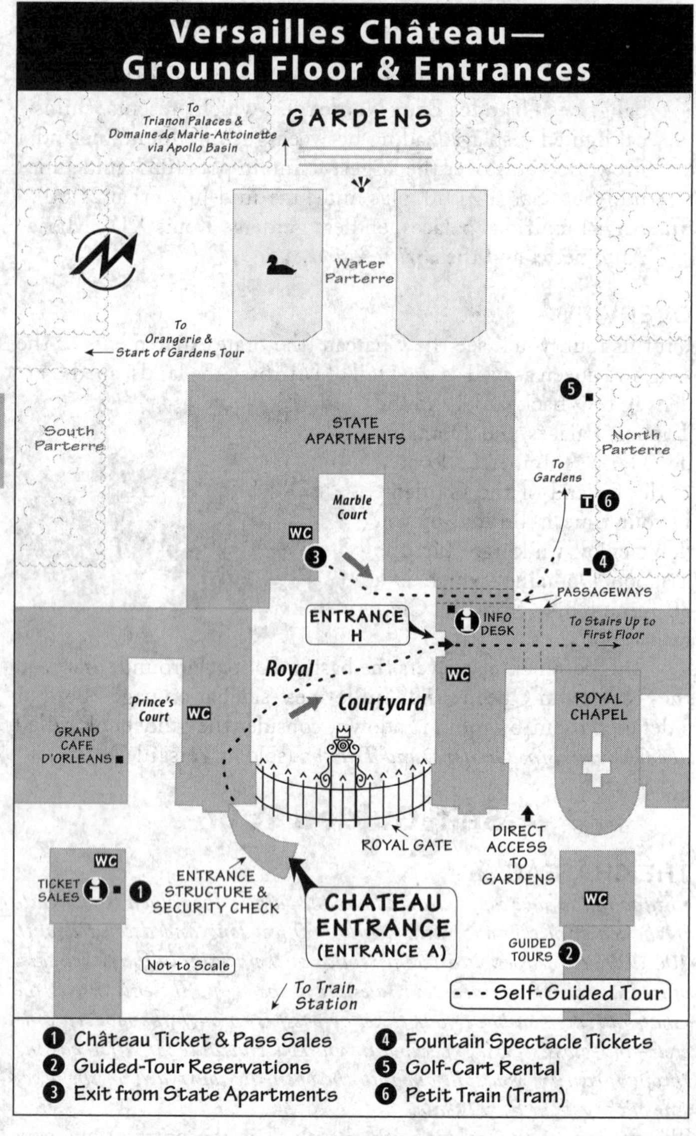

south wings were built. The total cost of the project has been estimated at half of France's entire GNP for one year.

• *Enter the Château from the courtyard at Entrance H—the State Apartments. Inside are an info desk (get a free map), WCs, and free audioguides. Glance through a doorway at the impressive Royal Chapel, which we'll see again upstairs.*

Just follow the flow of crowds. You may pass through a dozen ground-floor rooms with paintings of Louis' XIV, XV, and XVI, and of Versailles at different stages of growth—and may get a peek at the dazzling 700-seat Royal Opera House. (The route and displays change often.) Climb the stairs, passing through more exhibits. Finally, you reach a palatial golden-brown room, with a doorway that overlooks the...

Royal Chapel: Dut-dutta-dah! Every morning at 10:00, the organist and musicians struck up the music, these big golden doors opened, and Louis XIV and his family stepped onto the balcony to attend Mass. While Louis looked down on the golden altar, the lowly nobles on the ground floor knelt with their backs to the altar and looked up—worshipping Louis worshipping God. Important religious ceremonies took place here, including the marriage of young Louis XVI to Marie-Antoinette.

• *Enter the next room, an even more sumptuous space with a fireplace and a colorful painting on the ceiling.*

Hercules Drawing Room: Pleasure ruled. The main suppers, balls, and receptions were held in this room. Picture elegant party-goers in fine silks, wigs, rouge, lipstick, and fake moles (and that's just the men) as they dance to the strains of a string quartet.

On the wall opposite the fireplace is an appropriate painting showing Christ in the middle of a Venetian party. The work—by Paolo Veronese, a gift from the Republic of Venice—was one of Louis XIV's favorites, so the king had the room decorated around it.

• *From here on it's a one-way tour—getting lost is not allowed.*

The King's Wing: The names of the rooms in the King's Wing generally come from the paintings on the ceilings. For instance, the **Venus Room** was the royal make-out space, where couples would cavort beneath the goddess of love, floating on the ceiling. In the **Diana Room,** Louis and his men played pool on a table that stood in the center of the room, while ladies sat surrounding them on Persian-carpet cushions, and music wafted in from next door. Louis was a good pool player, a sore loser, and a king—thus, he rarely lost.

Also known as the Guard Room (as it was the room for Louis' Swiss bodyguards), the red **Mars Room** is decorated with a military flair.

Kings and Queens and Guillotines

- *You could read this on the train ride to Versailles. Relax...the palace is the last stop.*

Come the Revolution, when they line us up and make us stick out our hands, will you have enough calluses to keep them from shooting you? A grim thought, but Versailles raises these kinds of questions. It's the architectural embodiment of the *ancien régime,* a time when society was divided into rulers and the ruled, when you were born to be rich or to be poor. To some it's the pinnacle of civilization; to others, the sign of a civilization in decay. Either way, it remains one of Europe's most impressive sights.

Versailles was the residence of the king and the seat of France's government for 100 years. Louis XIV (r. 1643-1715) moved out of the Louvre in Paris, the previous royal residence, and built an elaborate palace in the forests and swamps of Versailles, 10 miles west. The reasons for the move were partly personal—Louis XIV loved the outdoors and disliked the sniping environs of stuffy Paris—and partly political.

Louis XIV was creating the first modern, centralized state. At Versailles he consolidated his government's scattered ministries so that he could personally control policy. More importantly, he invited France's nobles to Versailles in order to control them. Living a life of almost enforced idleness, the "domesticated" aristocracy couldn't interfere with the way Louis ran things. With 18 million people united under one king (England had only 5.5 million), a booming economy, and a powerful military, France was Europe's number-one power.

Around 1700, Versailles was the cultural heartbeat of Europe, and French culture was at its zenith. Throughout Europe, when you said "the king," you were referring to the French king—Louis XIV. Every king wanted a palace like Versailles. Everyone learned French. French taste in clothes, hairstyles, table manners, theater, music, art, and kissing spread across the Continent. That cultural dominance continued, to some extent, right up to the 20th century.

Louis XIV

At the center of all this was Europe's greatest king. He was a true Renaissance Man, a century after the Renaissance: athletic, good-

The **Mercury Room** may have served as Louis' official (not actual) bedroom, where the Sun King would ritually rise each morning to warm his subjects.

The **Apollo Room** was the grand throne room. Louis held court from a 10-foot-tall, silver-and-gold, canopied throne on a raised platform placed in the center of the room. (Notice the four small metal rings in the ceiling that once supported the canopy.)

looking, a musician, dancer, horseman, statesman, patron of the arts, and lover. For all his grandeur, he was one of history's most polite and approachable kings, a good listener who could put even commoners at ease in his presence.

Louis XIV called himself the Sun King because he gave life and warmth to all he touched. He was also thought of as Apollo, the Greek god of the sun. Versailles became the personal temple of this god on earth, decorated with statues and symbols of Apollo, the sun, and Louis XIV himself. The classical themes throughout underlined the divine right of France's kings and queens to rule without limit.

Louis XIV was a hands-on king who personally ran affairs of state. All decisions were made by him. Nobles, who in other countries were the center of power, became virtual slaves dependent on Louis XIV's generosity. For 70 years he was the perfect embodiment of the absolute monarch. He summed it up best himself with his famous rhyme—*"L'état, c'est moi!"* (lay-tah say-mwah): "The state, that's me!"

Another Louis or Two to Remember

Three kings lived in Versailles during its century of glory. Louis XIV built it and established French dominance. Louis XV, his great-grandson (Louis XIV reigned for 72 years), carried on the tradition and policies, but without the Sun King's flair. During Louis XV's reign (1715-1774), France's power abroad was weakening, and there were rumblings of rebellion from within.

France's monarchy was crumbling, and the time was ripe for a strong leader to reestablish the old feudal order. They didn't get one. Instead, they got Louis XVI (r. 1774-1792), a shy, meek bookworm, the kind of guy who lost sleep over revolutionary graffiti... because it was misspelled. Louis XVI married a sweet girl from the Austrian royal family, Marie-Antoinette, and together they retreated into the idyllic gardens of Versailles while revolutionary fires smoldered.

Even when the king was away, passing courtiers had to bow to the empty throne.

The final room of the King's Wing is the **War Room,** depicting Louis' victories—in marble, gilding, stucco, and paint.

• *Next you'll visit the magnificent...*

Hall of Mirrors

No one had ever seen anything like this hall when it was opened. Mirrors were still a great luxury at the time, and the number and size of these monsters were astounding. The hall is nearly 250 feet long. There are 17 arched mirrors, matched by 17 windows letting in that breathtaking view of the Gardens. The mirrors reflect an age when beautiful people loved to look at themselves. In another age altogether, this is where Germany and the Allies signed the Treaty of Versailles, ending World War I (and, some say, starting World War II).

• *Next up: the queen's half of the palace.*

The Queen's Wing: The King's Wing was mostly ceremonial and used as a series of reception rooms; the Queen's Wing is more intimate. Note: In 2015, some rooms of the Queen's Wing may be closed for renovation.

The **Queen's Bedchamber** was where the queen rendezvoused with her husband. Two queens died here, and this is where 19 princes were born. Louis XIV made a point of sleeping with the queen as often as possible, regardless of whose tiara he tickled earlier in the evening. This room looks just like it did in the days of the last queen, Marie-Antoinette, who substantially redecorated the entire wing. That's her bust over the fireplace, and the double eagle of her native Austria in the corners. The big mahogany chest to the left of the bed held her jewels.

After several more rooms, you'll end up in the **Queen's Guard Room,** where Louis XVI and Marie-Antoinette surrendered to the Revolution, and **Napoleon's coronation room.**

THE GARDENS

Louis XIV was a divine-right ruler. One way he proved it was by controlling nature like a god. These lavish grounds—elaborately planned, pruned, and decorated—showed everyone that Louis was in total command. Louis loved his gardens and, until his last days, presided over their care. He personally led VIPs through them and threw his biggest parties here. With their Greco-Roman themes and incomparable beauty, the Gardens further illustrated his immense power.

Getting Around the Gardens

On Foot: It's a 45-minute walk from the palace, down to the Grand Canal, past the two Trianon palaces, to the Hamlet at the far end of Domaine de Marie-Antoinette. Allow more time if you stop along the way.

By Bike: There's a bike rental station by the Grand Canal. A bike won't save you that much time, and you can't take it inside the grounds of the Trianon/Domaine, but it is fun pedaling around the greatest royal park in all of Europe (about €7/hour or €16/half-day, kid-size bikes and tandems available).

By *Petit Train:* The very slow-moving tram leaves from behind the Château (north side) and makes a one-way loop, stopping at the Petit and Grand Trianons (entry points to Domaine de Marie-Antoinette), then the Grand Canal before returning to the Château (€7.50, round-trip only, free for kids under age 11, 4/hour, runs 10:00-18:00, 11:00-17:00 in winter). Note that you can hop on and off the train and that the one-way loop only goes from the Domaine de Marie-Antoinette to the Grand Canal (not the other way).

By Golf Cart: This makes for a fun drive through the Gardens, but you can't drive it in the Trianon/Domaine, and there are steep late fees. To go out to the Hamlet, sightsee quickly, and get back within your allotted hour, you'll need to rent a cart at the Grand Canal and put the pedal to the metal (€32/hour, €8/15 minutes after that, 4-person limit per cart, rent down by the canal or just behind the Château, near the *petit train* stop).

By Shuttle Bus: Phébus runs an hourly TRI line shuttle bus between Versailles Château Rive Gauche train station and the Trianon/Domaine (shuttle doesn't stop at the Château). It's ideal if you're visiting the Trianon/Domaine first, before the Château. It also works great if you want to return to the station straight from the Trianon/Domaine (€2—or one Métro ticket, mid-April-Oct only, check current schedule for "Ligne TRI" at www.phebus.tm.fr). In 2014, buses departed from Versailles Château Rive Gauche train station at :40 after the hour 8:40-19:40, and from a stop near the Trianon at :07 after the hour 9:07-20:07 (see map on page 200, schedule available at the small Phébus office across from the Versailles Château Rive Gauche train station, near McDonald's).

The Gardens offer a world of royal amusements. The warmth from the Sun King was so great that he could even grow orange trees in chilly France. Louis XIV had 1,000 of these to amaze his visitors. In winter they were kept in the greenhouses (beneath your feet) that surround the courtyard. On sunny days, they were wheeled out in their silver planters and scattered around the grounds.

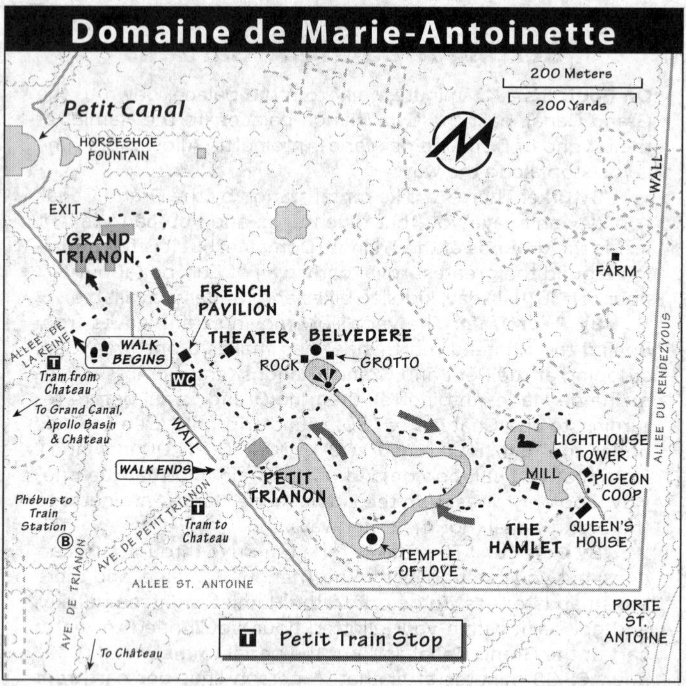

Domaine de Marie-Antoinette

200 Meters
200 Yards
Petit Canal
HORSESHOE FOUNTAIN
EXIT
GRAND TRIANON
FRENCH PAVILION
THEATER
BELVEDERE
ROCK
GROTTO
WALL
FARM
ALLEE DE LA REINE
WALK BEGINS
Tram from Chateau
WC
To Grand Canal, Apollo Basin & Château
WALL
WALK ENDS
PETIT TRIANON
LIGHTHOUSE TOWER
MILL
PIGEON COOP
ALLEE DU RENDEZVOUS
Phébus to Train Station
Tram to Chateau
AVE. DE PETIT TRIANON
AVE. DE TRIANON
TEMPLE OF LOVE
THE HAMLET
QUEEN'S HOUSE
ALLEE ST. ANTOINE
PORTE ST. ANTOINE
Petit Train Stop
To Château

With the palace behind you, it seems as if the grounds stretch out forever. Versailles was laid out along an eight-mile axis that included the grounds, the palace, and the town of Versailles itself, one of the first instances of urban planning since Roman times and a model for future capitals, such as Washington, DC, and Brasilia. A promenade leads from the palace to the Grand Canal, where France's royalty floated up and down in imported Venetian gondolas.

TRIANON PALACES AND DOMAINE DE MARIE-ANTOINETTE

Versailles began as an escape from the pressures of kingship. But in a short time, the Château had become as busy as Paris ever was. Louis XIV needed an escape from his escape and built a smaller palace out in the boonies.

Later, his successors retreated still farther from the Château and French political life, ignoring the real world that was crumbling all around them. They expanded the Trianon area, building a fantasy world of palaces and pleasure gardens—the enclosure called Marie-Antoinette's Domaine.

Grand Trianon: Delicate, pink, and set amid gardens, the Grand Trianon was the perfect summer getaway. This was the king's private residence away from the main palace. Louis XIV usually spent a couple of nights a week here (more in the summer) to escape the sniping politics, strict etiquette, and 24/7 scrutiny of official court life.

Louis XIV built the palace (1670-1688) near the tiny peasant village of Trianon (hence the name) and faced it with blue-and-white ceramic tiles. When those began disintegrating almost immediately, the palace was renovated with pink marble. It's a one-story structure of two wings connected by a colonnade, with gardens in back.

• *To enter the Grand Trianon, you must first pass through a security checkpoint. Pick up the free palace map and follow the one-way route through the rooms.*

The rooms are a complex overlay of furnishings from many different kings, dauphins, and nobles who lived here over the centuries. Louis XIV alone had three different bedrooms. Concentrate on the illustrious time of Louis XIV (1688-1715) and Napoleon Bonaparte (1810-1814). Use your map to find the Mirror Room (Room 3), Louis XIV's Bedchamber (Room 4), the Emperor's Family Drawing Room (Room 9), the Malachite Room (Napoleon's living room; Room 13), and the Cotelle Gallery (Louis' reception hall; Room 16).

Domaine de Marie-Antoinette: Near the Grand Trianon are the French Pavilion (small white building where Marie-Antoinette spent summer evenings with family and a few friends), **Marie-Antoinette's Theater,** and the octagonal **Belvedere** palace.

You'll find the **Hamlet** 10 minutes past the palace. Marie-Antoinette longed for the simple life of a peasant—not the hard labor of real peasants, who sweated and starved around her, but the fairy-tale world of simple country pleasures. She built this complex of 12 thatched-roof buildings fronting a lake as her own private "Normand" village.

Sleep Code

Abbreviations **(€1 = about $1.40, country code: 33)**

S = Single, **D** = Double/Twin, **T** = Triple, **Q** = Quad, **b** = bathroom, **s** = shower only, * = French hotel rating system (0-5 stars).

Price Rankings

$$ Higher Priced—Most rooms more than €110.

$ Lower Priced—Most rooms €110 or less.

Unless otherwise noted, English is spoken, credit cards are accepted, Wi-Fi is free, and breakfast is not included. Prices change; verify current rates online or by email. For the best prices, always book directly with the hotel.

The main building is the Queen's House—actually two buildings connected by a wooden skywalk. It's the only one without a thatched roof. Like any typical peasant farmhouse, it had a billiard room, library, elegant dining hall, and two living rooms.

Once you're done touring the Hamlet, head toward the Petit Trianon (along the way you'll see the white dome of the **Temple of Love**). The gray, cubical **Petit Trianon** is a masterpiece of Neoclassical architecture. It has four distinct facades, each a perfect and harmonious combination of Greek-style columns, windows, and railings. When Louis XVI became king, he gave the building to his bride Marie-Antoinette, who made this her home base. On the lawn outside, she installed a carousel. Despite her bad reputation with the public, Marie-Antoinette was a sweet girl from Vienna who never quite fit in with the fast, sophisticated crowd at Versailles. At the Petit Trianon, she could get away and re-create the charming home life that she remembered from her childhood. Here she played, while in the cafés of faraway Paris, revolutionaries plotted the end of the *ancien régime*.

Town of Versailles

SLEEPING IN VERSAILLES

For a less expensive and more laid-back alternative to Paris, the town of Versailles can be a good overnight stop, especially for drivers. Park in the palace's main lot while looking for a hotel, or leave your car there overnight (see page 196). Get a map of Versailles at your hotel or at the TI.

$$ Hôtel de France*** is in an 18th-century townhouse a peasant's toss from the palace. It offers Old World class, with mostly air-conditioned, traditional rooms, a pleasant courtyard, a bar, and a restaurant (Db-€130, big Db-170, Tb-€220, Wi-Fi, just off parking lot across from Château at 5 Rue Colbert, tel. 01 30 83 92

23, www.hotelfrance-versailles.com, hotel-de-france-versailles@wanadoo.fr).

$ Hôtel le Cheval Rouge***, built in 1676 as Louis XIV's stables, now boards tourists. Tucked into a corner of Place du Marché, this modest hotel has a big courtyard with free parking and sufficiently comfortable rooms connected by long halls (Db-€94-108, Tb/Qb-€135, free breakfast for Rick Steves readers, no air-con, Wi-Fi, 18 Rue André Chénier, tel. 01 39 50 03 03, www.chevalrougeversailles.fr, chevalrouge@sfr.fr).

$ Hôtel Ibis Versailles** offers a good weekend value and modern comfort, with 85 air-conditioned rooms (Mon-Thu Db-€120-135, Fri-Sun Db-€80-105, extra bed-€10, good-value breakfast-€10, guest computer, Wi-Fi, parking-€12, across from RER station at 4 Avenue du Général de Gaulle, tel. 01 39 53 03 30, www.ibishotel.com, h1409@accor.com).

EATING IN VERSAILLES

In the pleasant town center, around Place du Marché Notre-Dame, you'll find a thriving open market (food market Sun, Tue, and Fri mornings until 13:00; clothing market all day Wed-Thu and Sat) and a variety of reasonably priced restaurants, cafés, and a few cobbled lanes. The square—a 15-minute walk from the Château (veer left as you leave the Château)—is lined with colorful and inexpensive eateries with good seating inside and out. Troll the various options or try one of these:

Bistrot du Boucher reeks with fun character inside and has good seating out. They like their meat dishes best here, though you'll find a full menu of choices (€31 for three courses, €23 for two, daily, 12 Rue André Chénier, tel. 01 39 02 12 15).

Au Chien qui Fume is a good choice, with cozy seating inside and out, a playful staff, and reliable, traditional cuisine (€24-30 *menu*, €17 *plats*, closed Sun, 72 Rue de la Paroisse, tel. 01 39 53 14 56).

A la Côte Bretonne is a great bet for crêpes in a friendly, cozy setting. Fluent in English, Yann-Alan and his family have served up the cuisine of their native Brittany region since 1951 (€4-10 crêpes from a fun and creative menu, Tue-Sun 12:00-14:00 & 19:00-22:30, closed Mon, fine indoor and outdoor seating, a few steps off the square on traffic-free Rue des Deux Portes at #12, tel. 01 39 51 18 24).

La Boulangerie has mouthwatering sandwiches, salads, quiches, and more (Tue-Sun until 20:00, closed Mon, 60 Rue de la Paroisse).

Supermarket: A big **Monoprix** is centrally located between the Versailles Château Rive Gauche train station and Place du Marché Notre-Dame (entrances from Avenue de l'Europe and at 5 Rue Georges Clemenceau, Mon-Sat 8:30-21:20, closed Sun).

Chartres

Chartres, about 50 miles southwest of Paris, gives travelers a pleasant break in a lively, midsize town with a thriving, pedestrian-friendly old center. But the big reason to come to Chartres (shar-truh) is to see its famous cathedral—arguably Europe's best example of pure Gothic.

Chartres' old church burned to the ground on June 10, 1194. Some of the children who watched its destruction were actually around to help rebuild the cathedral and attend its dedication Mass in 1260. That's astonishing, considering that other Gothic cathedrals, such as Paris' Notre-Dame, took literally centuries to build. Having been built so quickly, the cathedral has a unity of architecture, statuary, and stained glass that captures the spirit of the Age of Faith like no other church.

PLANNING YOUR TIME

Chartres is an easy day trip from Paris. But with its statues glowing in the setting sun—and with hotels and restaurants much less

expensive than those in the capital—Chartres also makes a worthwhile overnight stop. Dozens of Chartres' most historic buildings are colorfully illuminated at night (May-Sept), adding to the town's after-hours appeal.

If coming just for the day, leave Paris in the morning by train. Chartres is a one-hour ride from Paris' Gare Montparnasse (14/day, about €14 one-way; see page 186 for Gare Montparnasse details). Jot down return times to Paris before you exit the Chartres train station (last train generally departs Chartres around 21:30).

Upon arrival in Chartres, head for the cathedral. Allow an hour to savor the church on your own as you follow my self-guided tour. Then join the excellent cathedral tour led by Malcolm Miller (1.25 hours; tours Mon-Sat at 12:00). Take another hour or two to wander the appealing old city. On Saturday mornings, a small outdoor market sets up a few short blocks from the cathedral on Place Billard.

Orientation to Chartres

TOURIST INFORMATION

At the TI, pick up the English brochure with a good map and basic information on the town and cathedral (Mon-Sat 9:30-18:30, Sun 10:00-17:30, in the historic Maison du Saumon building, 10 Rue de la Poissonnerie, tel. 02 37 18 26 26, www.chartres-tourisme.com). The TI has specifics on cathedral tours with Malcolm Miller, and also rents audioguides for the old town (€5.50, €8.50/double set, about 2 hours). Skip the Chartres Pass, which is sold here.

ARRIVAL IN CHARTRES

Exiting Chartres' train station, you'll see the spires of the cathedral dominating the town. It's a five-minute walk up Avenue Jehan de Beauce to the cathedral (or you can take a taxi for about €7). If arriving by car, you'll have fine views of the cathedral and city as you approach from the A-11 autoroute.

HELPFUL HINTS

Internet Access: For a computer and free Wi-Fi, head to the TI (described earlier), or try the Wi-Fi signal at McDonald's (Place des Epars).

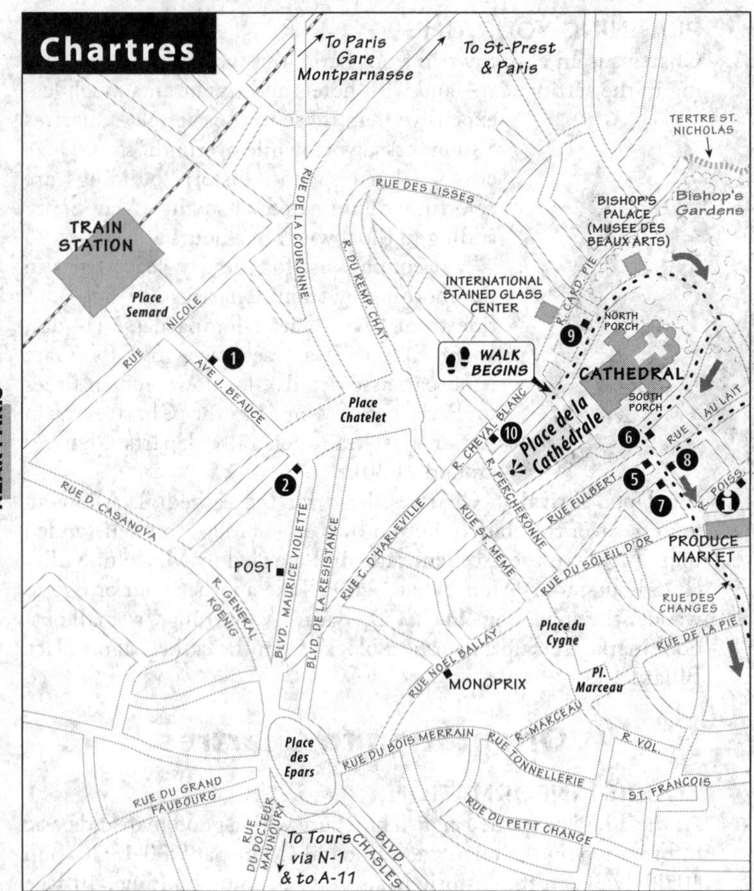

Laundry: The town has several launderettes. The most central is a few blocks from the cathedral (by the TI) at 16a Place de la Poissonnerie (daily 7:00-21:00).

Taxi: If you need to call a taxi, try tel. 02 37 36 00 00.

Sights in Chartres

▲▲▲CHARTRES CATHEDRAL

The church is (at least) the fourth one on this spot dedicated to Mary, the mother of Jesus, who has been venerated here for some 1,700 years. There's even speculation that the pagan Romans dedicated a temple here to a mother-goddess. In earliest times, Mary was honored next to a natural spring of healing waters (not visible today).

In 876, the church acquired the torn veil (or birthing gown) supposedly worn by Mary when she gave birth to Jesus. The

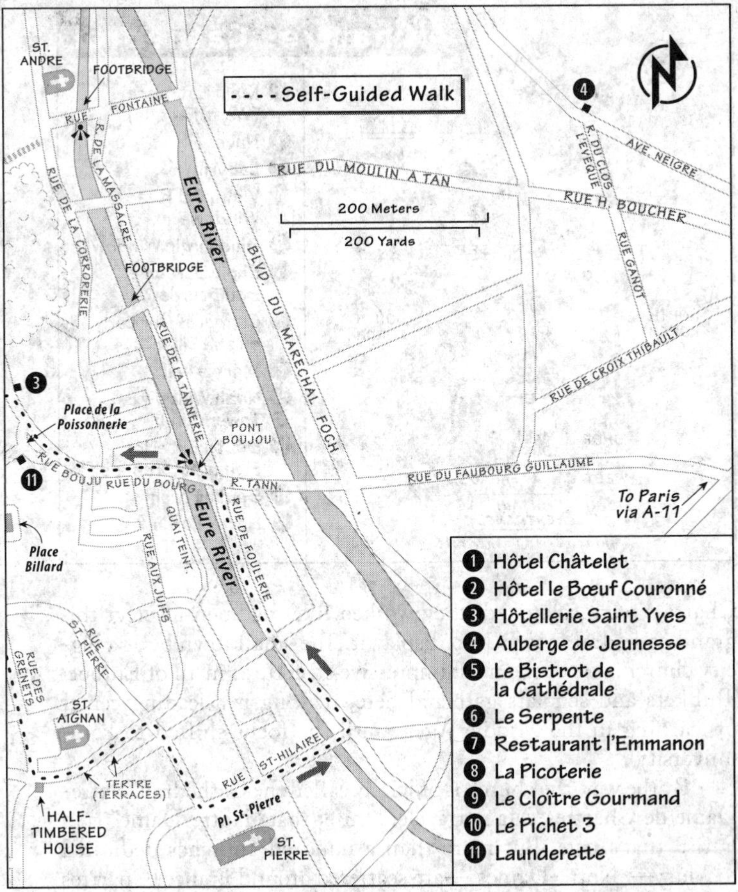

Self-Guided Walk

200 Meters

200 Yards

ST. ANDRE
FOOTBRIDGE
RUE FONTAINE
R. DE LA MASSACRE
RUE DE LA CORRORERIE
FOOTBRIDGE
Eure River
BLVD. DU MARECHAL FOCH
RUE DU MOULIN A TAN
R. DU CLOS L'EVEQUE
AVE. NEIGRE
RUE H. BOUCHER
RUE GANOT
RUE DE CROIX THIBAULT
RUE DE LA TANNERIE
Place de la Poissonnerie
PONT BOUJOU
RUE BOUJU
RUE DU BOURG
R. TANN.
RUE DU FAUBOURG GUILLAUME
To Paris via A-11
QUAI TEINT.
RUE DE FOULERIE
RUE AUX JUIFS
Place Billard
RUE ST. PIERRE
RUE DES GRENETS
ST. AIGNAN
TERTRE (TERRACES)
HALF-TIMBERED HOUSE
RUE ST-HILAIRE
Pl. St. Pierre
ST. PIERRE

1 Hôtel Châtelet
2 Hôtel le Bœuf Couronné
3 Hôtellerie Saint Yves
4 Auberge de Jeunesse
5 Le Bistrot de la Cathédrale
6 Le Serpente
7 Restaurant l'Emmanon
8 La Picoterie
9 Le Cloître Gourmand
10 Le Pichet 3
11 Launderette

2,000-year-old veil (now on display) became the focus of worship at the church. By the 11th century, the cult of saints was strong. And Mary, considered the "Queen of All Saints," was hugely popular. God was enigmatic and scary, but Mary was maternal and accessible, providing a handy go-between for Christians and their Creator. Chartres, a small town of 10,000 with a prized relic, found itself in the big time on the pilgrim circuit.

When the fire of 1194 incinerated the old church, the veil was feared lost. Lo and behold, several days later, townspeople found it miraculously unharmed in the crypt (beneath today's choir). Whether the veil's survival was a miracle or a marketing ploy, the people of

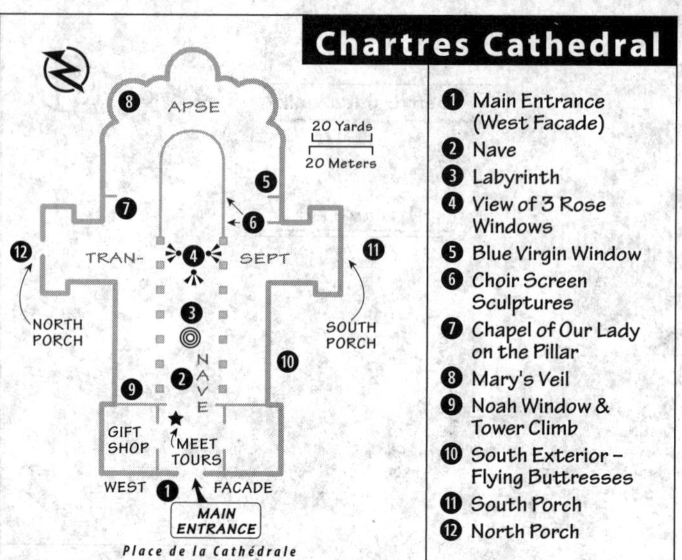

Chartres were so stoked, they worked like madmen to erect this grand cathedral in which to display it. The small town built a big-city church, one of the most impressive structures in all of Europe. Thinkers and scholars gathered here, making it a leading center of learning in the Middle Ages (until the focus shifted to Paris' university).

By the way, the church is officially called the Cathédrale Notre-Dame de Chartres. Many travelers think that "Notre-Dame" is in Paris. That's true. But more than a hundred churches dedicated to Mary—"Notre-Dames"—are scattered around France. Chartres Cathedral is one of them.

Cost: Free, €7.50 to climb the 300-step north tower (free on first Sun of the month and for those under 18).

Hours: Church—daily 8:30-19:30; **tower**—May-Aug Mon-Sat 9:30-12:30 & 14:00-17:30, Sun 14:00-17:30, Sept-April closes daily at 16:30 (entrance inside church after gift shop on left). **Mass** times vary by season: usually Mon-Fri at 9:00 and/or 11:45; Sat at 11:45 and 18:00; Sun at 9:15 (Gregorian), 11:00, and 18:00 (some services held in the crypt). Call or go online to confirm times given here—tel. 02 37 21 59 08 or go to www.diocesechartres.com (click on "*La Cathédrale,*" then "*Infos Pratiques,*" then "*Horaires des Messes*").

Restoration: The interior is undergoing a multiyear restoration. While you'll encounter some scaffolding inside and out, it affects only about 10 percent of the church.

Tours: Malcolm Miller, a fascinating English scholar who moved here 50+ years ago when he was 24, has dedicated his life to studying this cathedral and sharing its wonder through his guided lecture tours. He's slowing down a bit, but his 1.25-hour tours are still riveting even if you've taken my self-guided tour. No reservation is needed; just show up (€10, €5 for students, includes headphones that allow him to speak softly, offered Mon-Sat at 12:00; no tours last half of Aug, Jan-Feb, or if fewer than 12 people show up). Tours begin just inside the church at the *Visites de la Cathédrale* sign. Consult this sign for changes or cancellations. He also offers private tours (tel. 02 37 28 15 58, millerchartres@aol.com). Miller's guidebook provides a detailed look at Chartres' windows, sculpture, and history (sold at cathedral).

You can rent **audioguides** from the gift shop inside the cathedral (near the entrance). Routes include the cathedral (€4.20, 45 minutes), the choir only (€3.20, 25 minutes), or both (€6.20, 70 minutes). **Binoculars** are a big help for studying the cathedral art (rent at souvenir shops around the cathedral).

Boring **crypt tours** take you into the foundations of the previous ninth-century church. The only way to see the crypt, this guided tour in French (with English handout) lets you view remnants of the earlier churches, a modern copy of the old wooden Mary-and-baby statue, and hints of the old well and Roman wall (€3; April-Oct daily at 11:00, 14:15, 15:30, and 16:30 except no 11:00 tour on Sun; late June-mid-Sept also at 17:15; 2/day Nov-March, 30-minute tours start in the cathedral, at the gift shop inside the north tower, tel. 02 37 21 75 02).

➲ **Self-Guided Tour:** Historian Malcolm Miller calls Chartres a picture book of the entire Christian story, told through its statues, stained glass, and architecture. In this "Book of Chartres," the text is the sculpture and windows, and its binding is the architecture. The complete narrative can be read—from Creation to Christ's birth (north side of church), from Christ and his followers up to the present (south entrance), and then to the end of time, when Christ returns as judge (west entrance). The remarkable cohesiveness of the text and the unity of the architecture are due to the fact that nearly the entire church was rebuilt in just 30 years (a blink of an eye for cathedral building).

• *Start outside, taking in the...*

❶ **Main Entrance (West Facade):** Chartres' soaring (if mismatched) steeples announce to pilgrims that they've arrived. Compare the **towers:** The right (south) tower, with a Romanesque stone steeple, survived the fire. The left (north) tower lost its wooden steeple in the fire. In the 1500s, it was topped with the flamboyant Gothic steeple we see today.

• *Enter the church (from a side entrance, if the main one is closed) and wait for your pupils to enlarge.*

❷ **Nave:** The place is huge—the nave is 427 feet long, 20 feet wide, and 120 feet high. Try to picture the church in the Middle Ages—painted in greens, browns, and golds (like colorful St. Aignan Church in the old town). It was full of pilgrims, and was a rough cross between a hostel, a soup kitchen, and a flea market. Taking it all in from the nave, notice that, as was typical in medieval churches, the windows on the darker north side feature Old Testament themes—awaiting the light of Christ's arrival. And the windows on the brighter south side are New Testament.

• *On the floor, midway up the nave, find the...*

❸ **Labyrinth:** The broad, round maze inlaid in black marble on the floor is a spiritual journey. Mazes like this were common in medieval churches. Pilgrims enter from the west rim, by foot or on their knees, and wind inward, meditating, on a metaphorical journey to Jerusalem. About 900 feet later, they hope to meet God in the middle.

• *Walk up the nave to where the transept crosses. As you face the altar, north is to the left.*

❹ **The Rose Windows:** The three big, round "rose" (flower-shaped) windows over the entrances receive sunlight at different times of day. All three are predominantly blue and red, but each has different "petals," and each tells a different part of the Christian story in a kaleidoscope of fragmented images.

The brilliantly restored north rose window charts history from the distant past up to the birth of Jesus. The south rose window, with a similar overall design, tells how the Old Testament prophecies were fulfilled. Christ sits in the center (dressed in blue, with a red background), setting in motion radiating rings of angels, beasts, and instrument-playing apocalyptic elders who labor to bring history to its close.

In the center of the west rose window, a dark Christ rings in history's final Day of Judgment. Around him, winged angels blow their trumpets and the dead rise, face judgment, and are sent to hell or raised to eternal bliss.

• *Now walk around the altar to the right (south) side and find the window with a big, blue Mary (second one from the right).*

❺ **The Blue Virgin Window:** Mary, dressed in blue on a rich red background, cradles Jesus, while the dove of the Holy Spirit descends on her. This very old window (mid-12th century) was the central window behind the altar of the church that burned in 1194. It survived and was reinserted into this frame in the new church around 1230. Mary's glowing dress is an example of the famed "Chartres blue," a sumptuous color made by mixing cobalt oxide into the glass (before cheaper materials were introduced).

• *Now turn around and look behind you.*

❻ **The Choir Screen—Life of Mary:** The choir (enclosed area around the altar where church officials sat) is the heart *(coeur)* of the church. A stone screen rings it with 41 statue groups illustrating Mary's life. The plain windows surrounding the choir date from the 1770s, when the dark mystery of medieval stained glass was replaced by the open light of the French Enlightenment.

• *Do an about-face and find the chapel with Mary on a pillar.*

❼ **Chapel of Our Lady on the Pillar:** A 16th-century statue of Mary and baby—draped in cloth, crowned and sceptered—sits on a 13th-century column in a wonderful carved-wood alcove. This is today's pilgrimage center, built to keep visitors from clogging up the altar area.

• *Double back a bit around the ambulatory, heading toward the back of the church. In the next chapel you encounter (Chapel of the Sacred Heart of Mary), you'll find a gold frame holding a fragment of Mary's venerated veil. These days it's kept—for its safety and preservation—out of the light and behind bulletproof glass.*

❽ **Mary's Veil:** This veil (or tunic) was supposedly worn by Mary when she gave birth to Jesus. In the frenzy surrounding the fire of 1194, the veil mysteriously disappeared, only to reappear three days later (recalling the Resurrection). This was interpreted by church officials and the townsfolk as a sign from Mary that she wanted a new church, and thus the building began.

• *Return to the west end and find the last window on the right (near the tower entrance).*

❾ **The Noah Window and Tower Climb:** Read Chartres' windows in the medieval style: from bottom to top. In the bottom diamond, God tells Noah he'll destroy the earth. Next, Noah hefts an axe to build an ark, while his son hauls wood (diamond #2). Two by two, he loads horses (cloverleaf, above left), purple elephants (cloverleaf, right), and other animals. The psychedelic ark sets sail (diamond #3). Waves cover the earth and drown the wicked (two cloverleafs). The ark survives (diamond #4), and Noah releases a dove. Finally, up near the top (diamond #7), a rainbow (symbolizing God's promise never to bring another flood) arches overhead, God drapes himself over it, and Noah and his family give thanks.

• *To climb the north tower, find the entrance nearby. Then exit the church (through the main entrance or the door in the south transept) to view its south side.*

❿ **South Exterior—Flying Buttresses:** Six flying buttresses (the arches that stick out from the upper walls) push against six pillars lining the nave inside, helping to hold up the heavy stone ceiling and sloped, lead-over-wood roof. The result is a tall cathedral held up by slender pillars buttressed from the outside, allowing the walls to be opened up for stained glass.

⓫ **South Porch:** The three doorways of the south entrance show the world from Christ's time to the present, as Christianity triumphs over persecution. On the center door, Jesus holds a book and raises his arm in blessing. He's a simple, itinerant, bareheaded, barefoot rabbi, but underneath his feet, he tramples symbols of evil: the dragon and lion. Christ is surrounded by his apostles, who spread the good news to a hostile world.

The final triumph comes above the door in the Last Judgment. Christ sits in judgment, raising his hands, while Mary and John beg him to take it easy on poor humankind. Beneath Christ the souls are judged—the righteous on our left, and the wicked on our right, who are thrown into the fiery jaws of hell.

• *Reach the north side by circling around the back end of the church (great views).*

⓬ **North Porch:** In the "Book of Chartres," the north porch is chapter one, from the Creation up to the coming of Christ. Imagine all this painted and covered with gold leaf in preparation for the dedication ceremonies in 1260, when the Chartres generation could finally stand back and watch as their great-grandchildren, carrying candles, entered the cathedral.

OTHER SIGHTS IN CHARTRES

International Stained Glass Center (Centre International du Vitrail)

The low-key glass center (on the north side of cathedral) is worth a visit to learn about the techniques behind the mystery of this fragile but enduring art. Borrow the helpful English booklet (€8 deposit) and take the self-guided tour. A 20-minute video in English describes how glass is made, and a 10-minute French-only video (follow along with the English booklet) explains how it is turned into stained glass. The center offers classes lasting from one to seven days; call ahead or email for topics and dates.

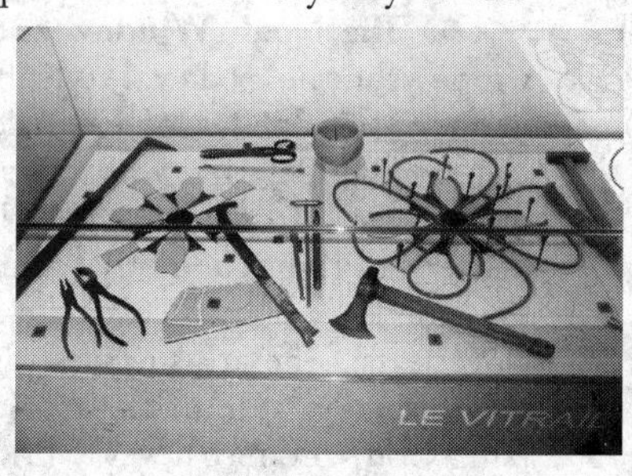

Cost and Hours: €5.50, Mon-Fri 9:30-12:30 & 13:30-18:00, Sat 10:00-12:30 & 14:30-18:00, Sun 14:30-18:00, 5 Rue du Cardinal Pie, 50 yards from cathedral, tel. 02 37 21 65 72, www.centre-vitrail.org, contact@centre-vitrail.org.

Chartres Town

Chartres' old town thrives (except on Sun and Mon) and merits exploration. You can rent an audioguide from the TI, or better, just wander (follow the route shown on the map on page 216).

In medieval times, Chartres was actually two towns—the pilgrims' town around the cathedral, and the industrial town along the river, which was powered by watermills. An easy 45-minute loop takes you around the cathedral, through the old pilgrims' town, down along the once-industrial riverbank, and back to the cathedral. Along the way you'll discover a picnic-perfect park behind the cathedral, see the colorful pedestrian zone, and wander quiet alleys and peaceful lanes.

Sleeping in Chartres

$$ Hôtel Châtelet**,** a block up from the train station, is friendly and comfortable. Don't let the facade fool you—inside is a comfy place with a huge fireplace in the lobby and 40 spotless, spacious, and well-furnished rooms. This hotel may be rated four stars, but it's really a solid three-star place (with three-star prices). Several rooms connect—good for families—and many have partial cathedral views (streetside Db-€105-115, quiet side Db-€120-130, Db with cathedral view-€132-145, add €25/person for Tb and Qb, minibars, air-con, handy and safe parking-€8, 6 Avenue Jehan de Beauce, tel. 02 37 21 78 00, www.hotelchatelet.com, reservation@hotelchatelet.com).

$ Hôtel le Bœuf Couronné** is a vintage two-star hotel, well run by Madame Vinsot, with 18 freshly renovated, good-value rooms and a handy location halfway between the station and cathedral (standard Db-€88, big Db-€124, a few good family rooms, breakfast-€9, no air-con, elevator, guest computer, Wi-Fi, restaurant, parking-€7/day, 15 Place Châtelet, tel. 02 37 18 06 06, www.leboeufcouronne.com, resa@leboeufcouronne.fr).

$ Hôtellerie Saint Yves, which hangs on the hillside just behind the cathedral, delivers well-priced simplicity with 50 spic-and-span rooms in a renovated monastery with meditative garden areas (Sb-€50, Db-€67, Tb-€80, small but workable bathrooms, breakfast-€8, Wi-Fi, TV in the lounge only, 1 Rue Saint Eman, tel. 02 37 88 37 40, www.hotellerie-st-yves.com, contact@hotellerie-st-yves.com).

Hostel: **$ Auberge de Jeunesse,** a 20-minute walk from the historic center, is located in a modern building with good views of the cathedral from its terrace (€14/bunk in 4- to 6-bed dorms, sheet rental-€2.40, dirt cheap meals, Wi-Fi, kitchen access, 23 Avenue Neigre, tel. 02 37 27 64, www.auberge-de-jeunesse-chartres.fr, auberge-jeunesse-chartres@wanadoo.fr).

Eating in Chartres

Dining out in Chartres is a good deal—particularly if you've come from Paris. Troll the places basking in cathedral views, and if it's warm, find a terrace table (several possibilities). Then finish your evening cathedral-side, sipping a hot or cold drink at the recommended Le Serpente.

Le Bistrot de la Cathédrale has the best view terrace—particularly enjoyable on a balmy summer evening—and serves reliable, classic French fare (try the *poule au pot*). The owner has a thing for wine, so the list is good. He also insists on fresh products (*menus* from €23, *plats* from €14, closed Wed, 1 Cloître Notre-Dame, tel. 02 37 36 59 60).

Le Serpente saddles up next door to the cathedral, with view tables on both sides of Rue des Changes, and a teapot collector's interior. Food is basic bistro, and the prices are fair (daily, 2 Cloître Notre-Dame, tel. 02 37 21 68 81).

Restaurant l'Emmanon is one of several places that strings out along pedestrian-friendly Rue des Changes with comfortable indoor and outdoor seating. They are best at €12-15 dinner-size *tartines,* salads, and *plats du jour;* the house wine is a good value (closed Mon, 45 Rue des Changes, tel. 02 37 21 07 05).

La Picoterie serves up a cozy interior and inexpensive fare (omelets, crêpes, salads, and such) with efficient service (daily, 36 Rue des Changes, tel. 02 37 36 14 54).

Le Cloître Gourmand, facing the cathedral's left transept, boasts a small terrace and an intimate, traditional interior. The young chef loves his meat and prides himself on using only the freshest ingredients (€25 *menu,* closed Mon, 21 Cloître Notre-Dame, tel. 02 37 21 49 13).

Le Pichet 3 is run by endearing Marie-Sylvie and Xavier. This local-products shop and cozy bistro makes a fun lunch stop, with cheap homemade soups and a good selection of *plats*—split the pot-au-feu three ways or try the rabbit with plums (€15 *plats,* Thu-Tue 11:00-17:00, closed Wed, 19 Rue du Cheval Blanc, tel. 02 37 21 08 35).

Giverny

Claude Monet's gardens at Giverny are like his paintings—brightly colored patches that are messy but balanced. Flowers were his brushstrokes, a bit untamed and slapdash, but part of a carefully composed design. Monet spent his last (and most creative) years cultivating his garden and his art at Giverny (zhee-vayr-nee), the

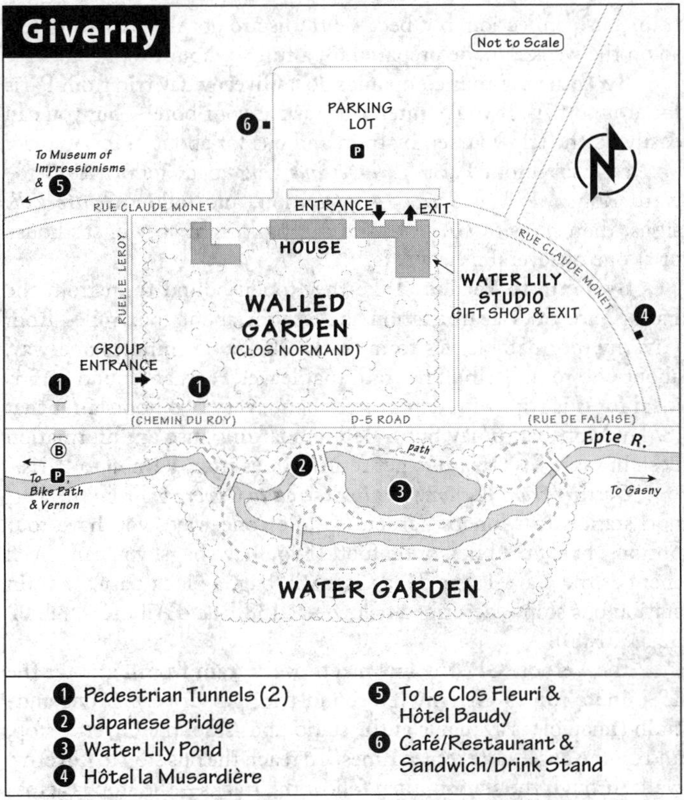

Giverny

Not to Scale

PARKING LOT
P
6
To Museum of Impressionisms & 5
RUE CLAUDE MONET
ENTRANCE
EXIT
HOUSE
RUELLE LEROY
WALLED GARDEN (CLOS NORMAND)
WATER LILY STUDIO
GIFT SHOP & EXIT
RUE CLAUDE MONET
4
GROUP ENTRANCE
1
1
(CHEMIN DU ROY)
D-5 ROAD
(RUE DE FALAISE)
Epte R.
Path
B
To P, Bike Path & Vernon
2
3
To Gasny
WATER GARDEN

1 Pedestrian Tunnels (2)
2 Japanese Bridge
3 Water Lily Pond
4 Hôtel la Musardière
5 To Le Clos Fleuri & Hôtel Baudy
6 Café/Restaurant & Sandwich/Drink Stand

spiritual home of Impressionism. Visiting the Marmottan and/or the Orangerie museums in Paris before your visit here heightens your appreciation of these gardens.

In 1883, middle-aged Claude Monet, his wife Alice, and their eight children from two families settled into this farmhouse, 50 miles west of Paris. Monet, already a famous artist and happiest at home, would spend 40 years in Giverny, traveling less with each passing year. He built a pastoral paradise complete with a Japanese garden and a pond full of floating lilies.

GETTING TO GIVERNY

Drivers can get in and out of Giverny in a half-day with ease. The trip is also doable in a half-day by public transportation with a train/bus connection, but because trains are not frequent (and less so on the weekend), be prepared for a full six-hour excursion.

By Tour: Big tour companies do a Giverny day trip from Paris for around €70. If you're interested, ask at your hotel—but you can easily do the trip yourself by train and bus for about €40.

By Car: From Paris' *périphérique* ring road, follow A-13 toward Rouen, exit at *Sortie 14* to Vernon, and follow *Centre Ville* signs, then signs to *Giverny*. You can park right at Monet's house or at one of several nearby lots.

By Train to Vernon: Take the Rouen-bound train from the Paris Gare St. Lazare station to Vernon, about four miles from Giverny (normally leaves from tracks 20-25, 45 minutes one-way, about €30 round-trip). The train that leaves Paris at around 8:15 is ideal for this trip, with departures about every two hours after that (8/day Mon-Sat, 6/day Sun). Before boarding, use an information desk in Gare St. Lazare to get return times from Vernon to Paris.

Getting from Vernon's Train Station to Giverny: From the Vernon station to Monet's garden (4 miles one-way), you have four options: bus, taxi, bike, or on foot. If you have bags, you can check them at the Café-Tabac de la Gare (€5/bag, a block past the train station bus stop—described below—at 138 Rue d'Albuféra, tel. 02 32 51 01 00).

The Vernon-Giverny **bus** meets every train from Paris for the 15-minute run to Giverny (€8 round-trip, pay driver). A bus-and-train timetable is available at the station bus stop, the Giverny stop, and on the bus—note return times. To reach the bus stop to Giverny, walk through the station, then follow the tracks—the stop is across from the L'Arrivée de Giverny café. Don't dally in the station—the bus leaves soon after your train arrives. During busy times, a line can form while the driver sells tickets and loads the bus.

The bus leaves Giverny from the same stop where it drops you off (near the pedestrian underpass—see map); buses generally run every hour, with the last bus departing at about 19:15 (confirm times by checking schedule upon arrival). Get to the stop at least 15 minutes early to ensure a space. If you miss the return bus and can't wait for the next one, ask a parking attendant, a staffer at Monet's home, or someone at a shop, restaurant, or hotel to call a taxi.

Taxis wait in front of the station in Vernon (allow €14 one-way for up to 3 persons, mobile 06 77 49 32 90 or 06 50 12 21 22).

You can rent a **bike** at L'Arrivée de Giverny, the café opposite the train station (€14, tel. 02 32 21 16 01), and follow a paved bike path *(piste cyclable)* that runs from near Vernon along an abandoned railroad right-of-way (figure about 30 minutes to Giverny). Get the easy-to-follow map to Giverny when you rent your bike, and you're in business.

Hikers can go on **foot** to Giverny (about 1.5 hours one way), following the bike instructions above, and take a bus or taxi back.

Extension to Rouen: Consider combining your morning Giverny visit with an afternoon excursion to nearby Rouen—together they make an efficient, and memorable, day trip from Paris. Note that Rouen's museums are closed on Tuesdays. From Vernon (the halfway point between Rouen and Paris), it's about 40 minutes by train to Rouen; the return trip from Rouen back to Paris takes 70-90 minutes. Plan to arrive at Monet's garden when it opens (at 9:30), so you can be back to the Vernon train station by about 13:00. You'll land in Rouen by 14:00 and have just enough time to see Rouen's cathedral and surrounding medieval quarter. If you leave Rouen around 18:00, you'll pull into Paris about 19:15, having spent a wonderful day sampling rural and urban Normandy.

Sights in Giverny

▲MONET'S GARDEN AND HOUSE

There are two gardens, split by a busy road, plus the house, which displays Monet's prized collection of Japanese prints. The gardens are always flowering with something; they're at their most colorful April through July.

Cost and Hours: €9, not covered by Paris Museum Pass, daily April-Oct 9:30-18:00, closed Nov-March, last entry at 17:30, tel. 02 32 51 90 31, www.fondation-monet.com.

Avoiding Crowds: Though lines may be long and tour groups may trample the flowers, true fans still find magic in the gardens. Minimize crowds by arriving a little before 9:30, when it opens, or come after 16:00 and stay until it closes. Crowds recede briefly during lunch (12:00-13:30), but descend en masse after lunch. The busiest months here are May and June.

If you can't arrive early or late, buy your tickets online (www.fondation-monet.com) or, for a bit more, at any FNAC store in Paris. Another option, if you also plan to visit the Museum of Impressionisms (described later), is to go there first and buy a combo-ticket (*billet couplé*). All of these options allow you to skip the ticket-buying line at Monet's garden and use the group entrance.

Visiting the House and Gardens: After you get in, go directly into the **Walled Garden** (Clos Normand) and work your way around clockwise. Smell the pretty scene. Monet cleared this

land of pine trees and laid out symmetrical beds, split down the middle by a "grand alley" covered with iron trellises of climbing roses. He did his own landscaping, installing flowerbeds of lilies, irises, and clematis, and arbors of climbing roses. In his carefree manner, Monet throws together hollyhocks, daisies, and poppies. The color scheme of each flowerbed contributes to the look of the whole garden.

In the southwest corner of the Walled Garden (near the group entrance), you'll find a pedestrian tunnel that leads under the road to the **Water Garden.** Follow the meandering path to the Japanese bridge, under weeping willows, over the pond filled with water lilies, and past countless scenes that leave artists aching for an easel. Find a bench. Monet landscaped like he painted—he built an Impressionist pattern of blocks of color. After he planted the gardens, he painted them, from every angle, at every time of day, in all kinds of weather.

Back on the main side, continue your visit with a wander through Monet's mildly interesting **home** (pretty furnishings, Japanese prints, old photos, and a room filled with copies of his paintings). The gift shop at the exit is the actual sky-lighted studio where Monet painted his water-lily masterpieces (displayed at the Orangerie Museum in Paris). Many visitors spend more time in this tempting gift shop than in the gardens themselves.

NEARBY SIGHTS

All of Giverny's sights and shops string along Rue Claude Monet, which runs in front of Monet's house.

Museum of Impressionisms (Musée des Impressionnismes)

This bright, modern museum, dedicated to the history of Impressionism and its legacy, houses temporary exhibits of Impressionist art. Check its website for current shows or just drop in. It also has picnic-pleasant gardens in front.

Cost and Hours: €7, daily April-Oct 10:00-18:00, closed Nov-March; to reach it, turn left after leaving Monet's place and walk 200 yards; tel. 02 32 51 94 00, www.mdig.fr.

Vernon

If you have time to kill at Vernon's train station, take a five-minute walk into town and sample the peaceful village. Walk between the tracks and the café across the street from the station, and follow the street as it curves left and becomes Rue d'Albuféra. You'll find a smattering of half-timbered Norman homes near Hôtel de Ville (remember, you're in Normandy) and several good cafés and shops.

Sleeping and Eating in Giverny

$ Hôtel la Musardière** is nestled in the village of Giverny two blocks from Monet's home (exit right when you leave Monet's). Carole welcomes you with 10 sweet rooms that Claude himself would have felt at home in (Sb-€85, Db-€90-100, Tb-€125-140, Qb-€150, breakfast-€11, Wi-Fi) and a reasonable and homey *crêperie*-restaurant with a lovely yard and outdoor tables (€10 crêpes, €26 non-crêpe *menu,* daily with nonstop service, 123 Rue Claude Monet, tel. 02 32 21 03 18, www.lamusardiere.fr, resa@lamusardiere.fr).

$ Le Clos Fleuri is a family-friendly B&B in a modern house with three fine rooms, handy cooking facilities, and a lovely garden. It's a 15-minute walk from Monet's place and is run by charming, English-speaking Danielle, who serves up a generous breakfast (Db-€90 for two or more nights, €100 for one night, cash only, Wi-Fi, 5 Rue de la Dîme, tel. 02 32 21 36 51, www.giverny-leclosfleuri.fr).

Eating: A flowery **café/restaurant** and a **sandwich/drink stand** sit right next to the parking lot across from Monet's home. Enjoy your lunch in the nearby gardens of the Museum of the Impressionisms.

Rose-colored **Hôtel Baudy,** once a hangout for American Impressionists, offers an appropriately pretty setting for lunch or dinner (outdoor tables in front, *menus* from €24, popular with tour groups, daily, 5-minute walk past Museum of Impressionisms at 81 Rue Claude Monet, tel. 02 32 21 10 03). Don't miss a stroll through the artsy gardens behind the restaurant.

Disneyland Paris

Europe's Disneyland is a remake of California's, with most of the same rides and smiles. The main difference is that Mickey Mouse speaks French, and you can buy wine with your lunch. My kids went ducky for it.

Disneyland is easy to get to, and may be worth a day—if Paris is handier than Florida or California.

GETTING THERE

By Train: The slick 45-minute RER trip is the best way to get to Disneyland from downtown Paris. Take RER line A to Marne-la-Vallée-Chessy (check the signs over the platform to be sure Marne-la-Vallée-Chessy is served, because the line splits near the end). Catch it from Paris' Charles de Gaulle-Etoile, Auber, Châtelet-Les Halles, or Gare de Lyon stations (at least 3/hour, drops you 45 minutes later right in the park, about €8 each way). The last train back to Paris leaves shortly after midnight. When returning, remember to use the same RER ticket for your Métro connection in Paris.

By Bus and Train from the Airport: Both of Paris' major airports have direct shuttle buses to Disneyland Paris (€20; from Charles de Gaulle daily 8:30-20:00, every 45 minutes; from Orly daily 9:00-19:30, hourly; 45-minute trip, http://vea-shuttle.co.uk). Fast TGV trains run from Charles de Gaulle to Disneyland in 10 minutes, but leave only hourly.

By Car: Disneyland is about 40 minutes (20 miles) east of Paris on the A-4 autoroute (direction Nancy/Metz, exit #14). Parking is about €15/day at the park.

Overview

The Disneyland Paris Resort is a sprawling complex housing two theme parks (Disneyland Paris and Walt Disney Studios), a few entertainment venues, and several hotels. Opened in 1992, it was the second Disney resort built outside the US (Tokyo was first). With upward of 15 million visitors a year, it quickly became Europe's single leading tourist destination. Mickey has arrived.

Disneyland Paris: This park has a corner on the fun market, with the classic rides and Disney characters you came to see. You'll find familiar favorites wrapped in French packaging, like Space Mountain (a.k.a. *De la Terre à la Lune*) and Pirates of the Caribbean *(Pirates des Caraïbes)*.

Walt Disney Studios: This zone has a Hollywood focus geared for an older crowd, with animation, special effects, and movie magic "rides." The cinema-themed rides include CinéMagique (a slow-motion cruise through film history on a people-mover, mixing film clips, audio-animatronic figures, and live actors); Studio Tram Tour: Behind the Magic (another slow-mo ride, this time mostly outdoors, through a "movie backlot"); and Moteurs... Action! Stunt Show Spectacular (an actual movie sequence is filmed with stunt drivers, audience bit players, and brash MTV-style hosts). The top thrill rides include the Rock 'n' Roller Coaster (which starts out by accelerating from a standstill to 57 miles per hour in less than three seconds, all while Aerosmith tunes blast in your ears) and the Twilight Zone Tower of Terror (which drops passengers from a precarious 200-foot-high perch). Gentler attractions include a re-creation of the parachute jump in *Toy Story* and a *Finding Nemo*-themed ride that whisks you through the ocean current.

Cost: Disneyland Paris and Walt Disney Studios charge the same. You can pay separately for each or buy a combined ticket for both. A one-day pass to either park is about €63 for adults and €53 for kids ages 3-11 (check their website for special offers). Kids under age 3 are free.

A two-day ticket for entry to both parks is about €140 for adults (less for kids); a three-day ticket is about €185. Regular prices are discounted about 25 percent Nov-March, and promotions are offered occasionally (check www.disneylandparis.com).

Hours: Disneyland—daily 10:00-22:00, closes at 20:00 in winter, open later on weekends, until 23:00 mid-May-Aug, hours fluctuate with the seasons—check website for precise times. Walt Disney Studios—daily 10:00-19:00.

Skipping Lines: The free Fastpass system is a worthwhile timesaver for the most popular rides (check map and legend for details; you may have only one Fastpass at a time, so choose wisely). At the ride, check the Fastpass sign to see when you can return and skip the line. Insert your park admission ticket into the Fastpass machine, which spits out a ticket printed with your return time. You'll also save time by buying park tickets in advance (at airport TIs, some Métro stations, or along the Champs-Elysées at the Disney Store).

Avoiding Crowds: Saturday, Sunday, Wednesday, public holidays, and any day in July and August are the most crowded. After dinner, crowds are gone.

Information: Disney brochures are in every Paris hotel. For more info and to make reservations, call 01 60 30 60 53, or try www.disneylandparis.com.

Eating with Mickey: Food is fun and not outrageously priced. (Still, many smuggle in a picnic.) The Disneyland Hotel restaurant Inventions offers an expensive gourmet brunch on Sundays (roughly €60/person) and daily dinners where the most famous Disney characters visit with starstruck eaters.

Sleeping at Disneyland

Most are better off sleeping in the real world (i.e., Paris), though with direct buses and freeways to both airports, Disneyland makes a convenient first- or last-night stop. Seven different Disney-owned hotels offer accommodations at or near the park in all price ranges. Prices are impossible to pin down, as they vary by season and by the package deal you choose (deals that include park entry are usually a better value). To reserve any Disneyland hotel, call 01 60 30 60 53, or check www.disneylandparis.com. The prices you'll be quoted include entry to the park. **Hôtel Santa Fe**** offers a fair midrange value, with frequent shuttle service to the park. Another cheap option is **Davy Crockett's Ranch,** but you'll need a car to stay there. The most expensive is the **Disneyland Hotel******, right at the park entry, about three times the price of the Santa Fe. The **Dream Castle Hotel****** is another higher-end choice, with nearly 400 rooms done up to look like a lavish 17th-century palace (40 Avenue de la Fosse des Pressoirs, tel. 01 64 17 90 00, www.dreamcastle-hotel.com, info@dreamcastle-hotel.com).

NORMANDY

Rouen • Honfleur • Bayeux • D-Day Beaches • Mont St-Michel

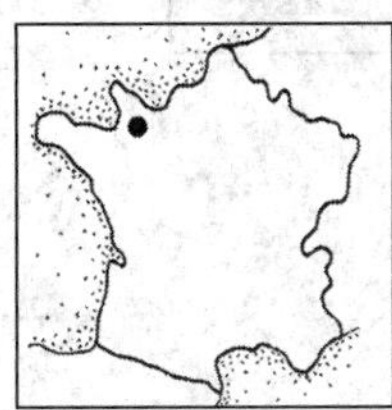

Sweeping coastlines, half-timbered towns, and thatched roofs decorate the rolling green hills of Normandy (Normandie). Parisians call Normandy "the 21st arrondissement." It's their escape—the nearest beach. Brits consider this area close enough for a weekend away (you'll notice that the BBC comes through loud and clear on your car radio).

Despite the peacefulness you sense today, the region's history is filled with war. Normandy was founded by Viking Norsemen who invaded from the north, settled here in the ninth century, and gave the region its name. A couple hundred years later, William the Conqueror invaded England from Normandy. His victory is commemorated in a remarkable tapestry at Bayeux. A few hundred years after that, France's greatest cheerleader, Joan of Arc (Jeanne d'Arc), was convicted of heresy in Rouen and burned at the stake by the English, against whom she rallied France during the Hundred Years' War. And in 1944, Normandy hosted a World War II battle that changed the course of history.

The rugged, rainy coast of Normandy harbors wartime bunkers and enchanting fishing villages like Honfleur. And, on the border it shares with Brittany, the almost surreal island abbey of Mont St-Michel rises serene and majestic, oblivious to the tides of tourists.

PLANNING YOUR TIME

Honfleur, the D-Day beaches, and Mont St-Michel each merit overnight visits. At a minimum, you'll want a full day for the D-Day beaches and a half-day each in Honfleur and on Mont St-Michel. For many, Normandy makes the perfect jet-lag antidote;

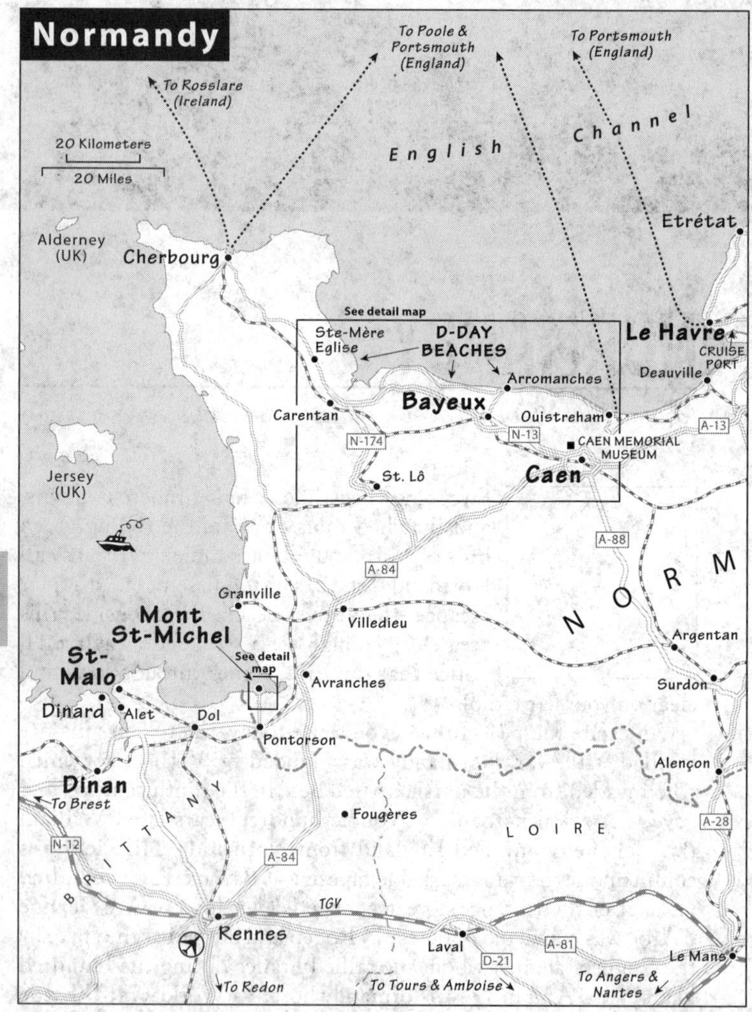

Rouen, which is quick to reach by car or train from either Paris or Beauvais airports, makes a good first stop for your trip.

If you're driving between Paris and Honfleur, Giverny (see previous chapter) or Rouen (covered in this chapter) are easy to visit. By train, they're best as day trips from Paris. The WWII memorial museum in Caen works well as a stop between Honfleur and Bayeux (and the D-Day beaches). Mont St-Michel must be seen early or late to avoid the masses of midday tourists. Dinan, just 45 minutes by car from Mont St-Michel, offers a fine introduction to Brittany (see next chapter). Drivers can enjoy Mont St-Michel as a day trip from Dinan.

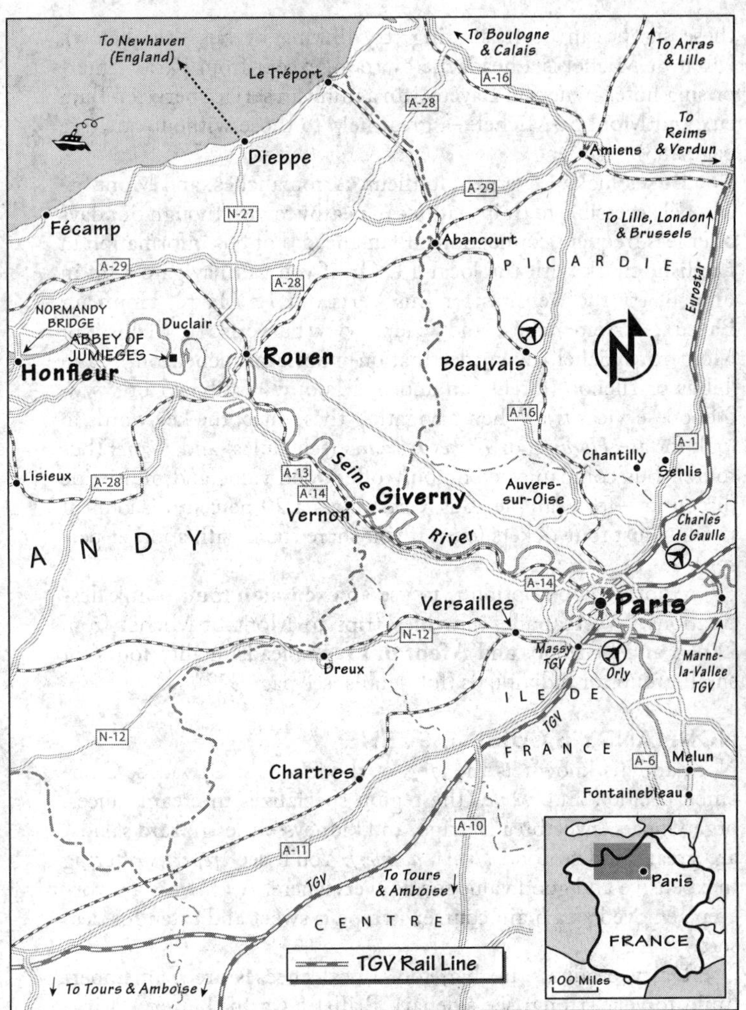

For practical information in English about Normandy, see http://normandy.angloinfo.com or www.normandie-tourisme.fr.

GETTING AROUND NORMANDY

This region is ideal with a **car.** If you're driving into Honfleur from the north, take the impressive but pricey Normandy Bridge (Pont de Normandie, about €5 toll). If you're driving from Mont St-Michel into Brittany, follow my recommended scenic route to the town of St-Malo (see page 348).

Trains from Paris serve Rouen, Caen, Bayeux, Mont St-Michel (via Pontorson or Rennes), and Dinan, though service between these sights can be frustrating (try linking by bus—see below). Mont St-Michel is a headache by train, except from Paris. Enterprising hotel owners in Bayeux run a minivan service between Bayeux and Mont St-Michel—a great help to those without cars (see page 283).

Buses make Giverny, Honfleur, Arromanches, and Mont St-Michel accessible to train stations in nearby towns, though Sundays offer less frequent connections. Plan ahead: For bus information in English, check with the local TI. Or, if you can navigate a bit in French, try the websites for Bus Verts (for Le Havre, Honfleur, Bayeux, Arromanches, and Caen, www.busverts.fr), Keolis (for Mont St-Michel, www.destination-montsaintmichel.com), and Tibus or Illenoo (for Dinan and St-Malo, www.tibus.fr or www.illenoo-services.fr). When navigating these sites, the key words to look for are *Horaires* or *Fiches Horaires* (schedules) and *Lignes* (bus route). Bus companies commonly offer good value and multi-ride discounts—for example, Bus Verts offers a 20 percent discount if you buy just four tickets (even if you share them with another person).

Another good option is to use an **excursion tour** to link destinations. **Westcapades** provides trips to Mont St-Michel from Dinan and St-Malo, and **Afoot in France** leads quality tours for small groups or individuals (for details, see page 332).

NORMANDY'S CUISINE SCENE

Normandy is known as the land of the four C's: Calvados, Camembert, cider, and *crème.* The region specializes in cream sauces, organ meats (sweetbreads, tripe, and kidneys—the "gizzard salads" are great), and seafood *(fruits de mer).* You'll see *crêperies* offering inexpensive and good value meals everywhere. A *galette* is a savory crêpe enjoyed as a main course; a crêpe is sweet and eaten for dessert.

Dairy products are big, too. Local cheeses are Camembert (mild to very strong; see sidebar), Brillat-Savarin (buttery), Livarot (spicy and pungent), Pavé d'Auge (spicy and tangy), and Pont l'Evêque (earthy flavor).

What, no local wine? *Oui,* that's right. Here's how to cope. Fresh, white Muscadet wines are made nearby (in western Loire); they're cheap and match well with much of Normandy's cuisine. But Normandy is famous for its many apple-based beverages. You can't miss the powerful Calvados apple brandy or the Bénédictine brandy (made by local monks). The local dessert, *trou Normand,* is apple sorbet swimming in Calvados. The region also produces three kinds of alcoholic apple ciders: *Cidre* can be *doux* (sweet), *brut* (dry), or *bouché* (sparkling—and the strongest). You'll also find bottles of Pommeau, a tasty blend of apple juice and Calvados (sold in many

Camembert Cheese

This cheap, soft, white, Brie-like cheese is sold all over France (and America) in distinctive, round wooden containers. Camembert has been known for its cheese for 500 years, but local legend has it that today's cheese got its start in the French Revolution, when a priest on the run was taken in by Marie Harel, a Camembert farmer. He repaid the favor by giving her the secret formula from his own hometown—Brie.

From cow to customer, Camembert takes about three weeks to make. High-fat milk from Norman cows is curdled with rennet, ladled into round, five-inch molds, sprinkled with *Penicillium camemberti* bacteria, and left to dry. In the first three days, the cheese goes from the cow's body temperature to room temperature to refrigerator cool (50 degrees).

Two weeks later, the ripened and aged cheese is wrapped in wooden bands and labeled for market. Like wines, Camembert cheese is controlled by government regulations and must bear the "A.O.C." *(Appellation d'Origine Contrôlée)* stamp of approval.

shops), as well as *poiré,* a tasty pear cider. And don't leave Normandy without sampling a *kir Normand,* a mix of crème de cassis and cider. Drivers in Normandy should be on the lookout for *Route du Cidre* signs (with a bright red apple); this tourist trail leads you to small producers of handcrafted cider and brandy.

Remember, restaurants serve only during lunch (11:30-14:00) and dinner (19:00-21:00, later in bigger cities); cafés serve food throughout the day.

Rouen

This 2,000-year-old city mixes Gothic architecture, half-timbered houses, and contemporary bustle like no other place in France. Busy Rouen (roo-ahn) is France's fifth-largest port and Europe's biggest food exporter (mostly wheat and grain). Its cobbled old town is a delight to wander, though the city is pretty quiet at night.

Rouen was a regional capital during Roman times, and France's second-largest city in medieval times (with 40,000 residents—only Paris had more). In the ninth century, the Normans made the town their capital. William the Conqueror called it home before moving to England. Rouen walked a political tightrope between England and France for centuries, and was an English base during the Hundred Years' War. Joan of Arc was burned here (in 1431).

Rouen's historic wealth was built on its wool industry and trade—for centuries, it was the last bridge across the Seine River before the Atlantic. In April of 1944, as America and Britain weakened German control of Normandy prior to the D-Day landings, Allied bombers destroyed 50 percent of Rouen. And though the industrial suburbs were devastated, most of the historic core survived, keeping Rouen a pedestrian haven.

PLANNING YOUR TIME

If you want a dose of a smaller—yet lively—French city, Rouen is an easy day trip from Paris, with convenient train connections to Gare St. Lazare (nearly hourly, 1.5 hours).

Considering the convenient Paris connection and Rouen's handy location in Normandy, drivers can save headaches by taking the train to Rouen and picking up a rental car there (spend a quiet night in Rouen and pick up your car the next morning). Those already in Paris can take an early train to Rouen, stash their bags in the car (leaving it in the secure rental lot at the train station) and visit Rouen before heading out to explore Normandy (for car-rental companies, see "Helpful Hints," later).

Even if you don't have a car, you can visit Rouen on your way from Paris to other Normandy destinations, thanks to the good bus and train service (free daytime bag check available Wed-Mon at the Museum of Fine Arts, closed Tue).

Orientation to Rouen

Although Paris embraces the Seine, Rouen ignores it. The area we're most interested in is bounded by the river to the south, the Museum of Fine Arts (Esplanade Marcel Duchamp) to the north, Rue de la République to the east, and Place du Vieux Marché to the west. It's a 20-minute walk from the train station to the Notre-Dame Cathedral or TI. Everything else of interest is within a 10-minute walk of the cathedral or TI.

TOURIST INFORMATION

Pick up the English map with information on Rouen's museums at the TI, which faces the cathedral. The TI also has €5 audioguide tours covering the cathedral and Rouen's historic center, though this book's self-guided walk is enough for most. They also have free Wi-Fi (for 30 minutes) and a loaner tablet. Ask about sound-and-light shows at the cathedral (generally mid-June-mid-Sept), get details on the new Joan of Arc Museum (open in early 2015), and ask about the Route of the Ancient Abbeys if driving (May-Sept Mon-Sat 9:00-19:00, Sun 9:30-12:30 & 14:00-18:00; Oct-April Mon-Sat 9:30-12:30 & 13:30-18:00, closed Sun; 25 Place de la Cathédrale, tel. 02 32 08 32 40, www.rouentourisme.com). A small office in the TI changes money (closed during lunch year-round).

ARRIVAL IN ROUEN

By Train: Rue Jeanne d'Arc cuts straight down from Rouen's train station through the town center to the Seine River. Day-trippers should **walk** from the station down Rue Jeanne d'Arc toward Rue du Gros Horloge—a busy pedestrian mall in the medieval center (and near the starting point of my self-guided walk). While the station has no baggage storage, you can check bags at the Museum of Fine Arts during open hours for free (10-minute downhill walk from the station, museum described on page 250).

Rouen's **subway** (Métrobus) whisks travelers from under the train station to the Palais de Justice in one stop (€1.50 for 1 hour; descend and buy tickets from machines one level underground, then validate ticket on subway two levels down; subway direction: Technopôle or Georges Braque). Returning to the station, take a subway in direction: Boulingrin and get off at Gare-Rue Verte.

Taxis (to the right as you exit station) will take you to any of my recommended hotels for about €8.

By Car: Finding the city center from the autoroute is tricky—assume you'll get lost for a while. Follow signs for *Centre-Ville* and *Rive Droite* (right bank). You should see signs for *P&R Relais*. These are tram stops outside the center where you can park for free, then hop on a tram (€1.50 each way), avoiding traffic. For day-trippers taking my self-guided walk of Rouen, the parking lot under Place du Vieux Marché is best. Other lots are scattered about the city center and any central spot works (see map on page 242). You can park in street spaces for free overnight (metered 8:00-19:00), or pay for more secure parking in one of many well-signed underground lots (€13/day, €5/3 hours). La Haute Vieille Tour parking garage, between the cathedral and the river, is handy for overnighters. When you get turned around (likely, because of the narrow, one-way streets), aim toward the highest cathedral spires you spot.

When leaving Rouen, head for the riverfront road where autoroute signs will guide you to Paris, or Le Havre and Caen (for D-Day beaches and Honfleur). If you're following the Route of Ancient Abbeys from here, see page 252.

HELPFUL HINTS

Closed Days: Most of Rouen's museums are closed on Tuesday, and many sights also close midday (12:00-14:00). The cathedral doesn't open until 14:00 on Monday and is closed during Mass (usually Tue-Sat at 10:00, July-Aug also at 18:00; Sun and holidays at 8:30, 10:00, and 12:00). The Joan of Arc Church is closed Friday and Sunday mornings, and during Mass.

Market Days: The best open-air market is on Place St. Marc, a few blocks east of St. Maclou Church. It's filled with antiques and other good stuff (all day Tue, Fri, and Sat; on Sun until about 12:30). A smaller market is on Place du Vieux Marché, near the Joan of Arc Church (Tue-Sun until 13:30, closed Mon). The TI has a list of all weekly markets.

Supermarket: Small grocery shops are scattered about the city, and a big **Monoprix** is on Rue du Gros Horloge (groceries at the back, Mon-Sat 8:30-21:00, closed Sun).

Internet Access: The TI offers 30 minutes of free Wi-Fi and has a loaner tablet. Rouen is riddled with Wi-Fi cafés; several are within a few blocks of the train station on Rue Jeanne d'Arc.

English Bookstore: ABC Books has nothing but English-language books—some American, but mostly British (Tue-Sat 10:00-18:00, closed Sun-Mon, just south of St. Ouen Church at 11 Rue des Faulx, tel. 02 35 71 08 67).

Taxi: Call **Les Taxi Blancs** at 02 35 61 20 50 or 02 35 88 50 50.

Car Rental: Agencies with an office in the train station include **Europcar** (tel. 02 35 88 21 20), **Avis** (tel. 02 35 88 60 94), and **Hertz** (tel. 02 35 70 70 71). They have similar hours (normally Mon-Fri 8:00-12:30 & 14:00-19:00, Sat 8:30-12:30 & 14:00-17:00, closed Sun).

SNCF Boutique: For train tickets, visit the SNCF office in town at the corner of Rue aux Juifs and Rue Eugène Boudin (Mon-Sat 10:00-19:00, closed Sun).

Rouen Walk

On this 1.5-hour self-guided walk (see map on page 242), you'll see the essential Rouen sights and experience its pedestrian-friendly streets filled with half-timbered buildings. Remember that many sights are closed midday (12:00-14:00). This walk is designed for day-trippers coming by train, but works just as well for drivers, who should ideally park at or near Place du Vieux Marché (parking garage available).

From Place du Vieux Marché, you'll walk the length of Rue du Gros Horloge to Notre-Dame Cathedral. From there, walk four blocks to the plague cemetery (Aître St. Maclou), loop up to the

The Hundred Years' War (1336-1453)

It would take a hundred years to explain all the causes, battles, and political maneuverings of this century-plus of warfare between France and England, but here goes:

In 1300, before the era of the modern nation-state, the borders between France and England were fuzzy. French-speaking kings had ruled England, English kings owned the south of France, and English merchants dominated trade in the north. Dukes and lords in both countries were aligned more along family lines than by national identity. When the French king died without a male heir (1328), both France and England claimed the crown, and the battle was on.

England invaded the more populous country (1345) and—thanks to skilled archers using armor-penetrating longbows—won big battles at Crécy (1346) and Poitiers (1356). Despite a truce, roving bands of English mercenaries stayed behind and supported themselves by looting French villages. The French responded with guerrilla tactics.

In 1415, the English took still more territory, with Henry V's big victory at Agincourt. But rallied by the heavenly visions of young Joan of Arc, the French slowly drove the invaders out. Paris was liberated in 1436, and when Bordeaux fell to French forces (1453), the fighting ended without a treaty.

church of St. Ouen, and return along Rue de l'Hôpital ending at the Museum of Fine Arts (a 5-minute walk to the train station). The map on page 242 highlights our route.

• *If arriving by train, walk down Rue Jeanne d'Arc and turn right on Rue du Guillaume le Conquérant (notice the Gothic Palace of Justice building across Rue Jeanne d'Arc—we'll get to that later). This takes you to the back door of our starting point...*

Place du Vieux Marché

• *Stand near the entrance of the striking Joan of Arc Church.*

Surrounded by half-timbered buildings, this old market square houses a cute, covered produce and fish market, a park commemorating Joan of Arc's burning, and a modern church named after her. Find the tall aluminum cross, planted in a small garden near the church entry. This marks the spot where Rouen publicly punished and executed people. The pillories stood here, and during the Revolution, the town's guillotine made 800 people "a foot shorter at the top." In 1431, Joan of Arc—only 19 years old—was burned right here. Find her flaming statue facing the cross. As the flames engulfed her, an English soldier said, "Oh my God, we've killed a saint." (Nearly 500 years later, Joan was canonized, and the soldier was proved right.)

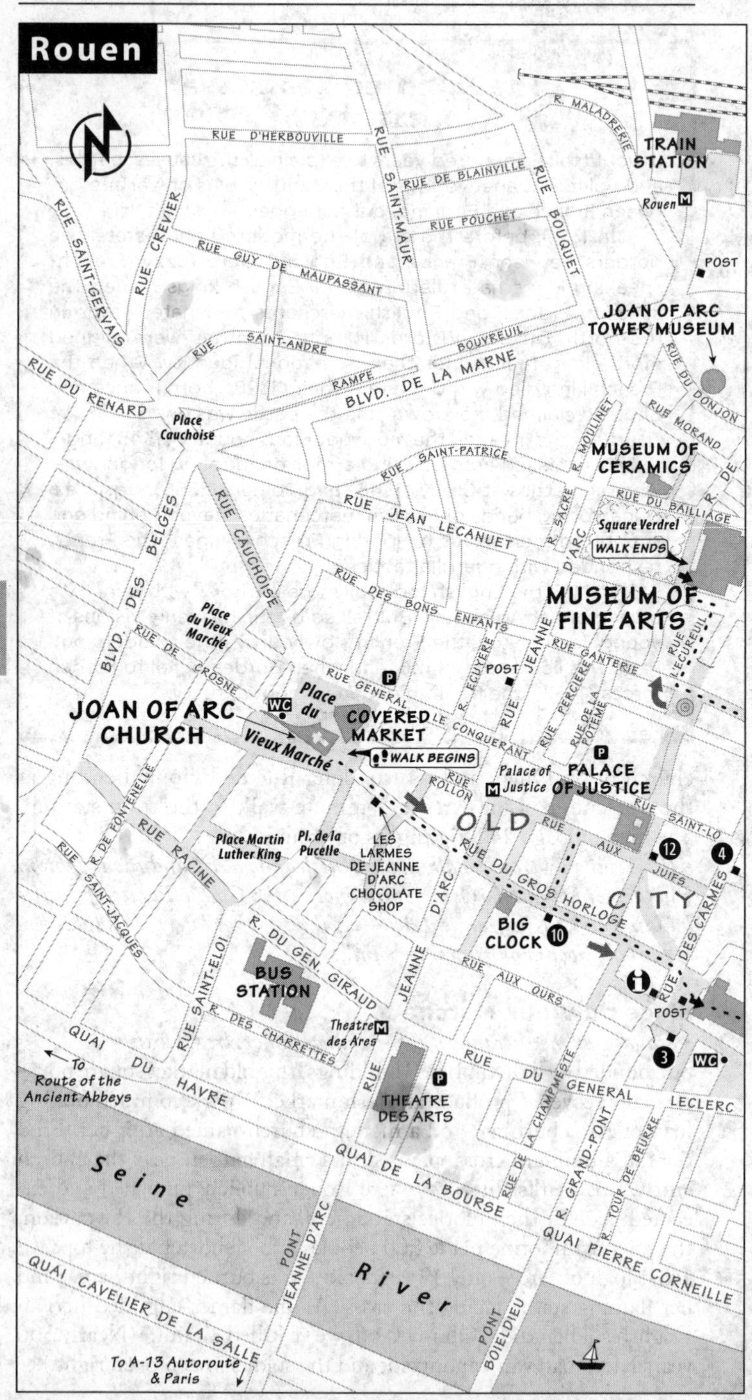
Rouen
Rue d'Herbouville
Rue Saint-Maur
Rue de Blainville
Rue Pouchet
Rue Bouquet
R. Maladrerie
Train Station
Rouen
Post
Rue Saint-Gervais
Rue Crevier
Rue Guy de Maupassant
Rue Saint-André
Rampe Bouvreuil
Blvd. de la Marne
Joan of Arc Tower Museum
Rue du Donjon
Rue Morand
Rue du Renard
Place Cauchoise
Rue Saint-Patrice
R. Moulinet
Museum of Ceramics
Rue du Bailliage
Square Verdrel
Walk Ends
Rue Jean Lecanuet
R. Sacre
Rue Jeanne d'Arc
Rue Cauchoise
Blvd. des Belges
Rue des Bons Enfants
Museum of Fine Arts
Rue l'Ecureuil
Place du Vieux Marché
Rue de Crosne
Rue Ganterie
Rue General le Conquerant
Post
R. Ecuyere
Rue Percière
Rue de la Potème
Joan of Arc Church
Place du Vieux Marché
Covered Market
Walk Begins
Palace of Justice
Palace of Justice
Rue Rollon
Old City
Rue Saint-Lo
Rue aux Juifs
R. de Fontenelle
Rue Racine
Rue Saint-Jacques
Place Martin Luther King
Pl. de la Pucelle
Les Larmes de Jeanne d'Arc Chocolate Shop
Rue du Gros Horloge
Rue des Carmes
Big Clock
R. du Gen. Giraud
Rue aux Ours
Bus Station
Rue Saint-Eloi
R. des Charrettes
Theatre des Arts
Post
Quai du Havre
To Route of the Ancient Abbeys
Rue du General Leclerc
Theatre des Arts
Rue de la Champmeslé
R. Grand-Pont
R. Tour de Beurre
Quai de la Bourse
Quai Pierre Corneille
Seine River
Pont Jeanne d'Arc
Pont Boieldieu
Quai Cavelier de la Salle
To A-13 Autoroute & Paris
Normandy

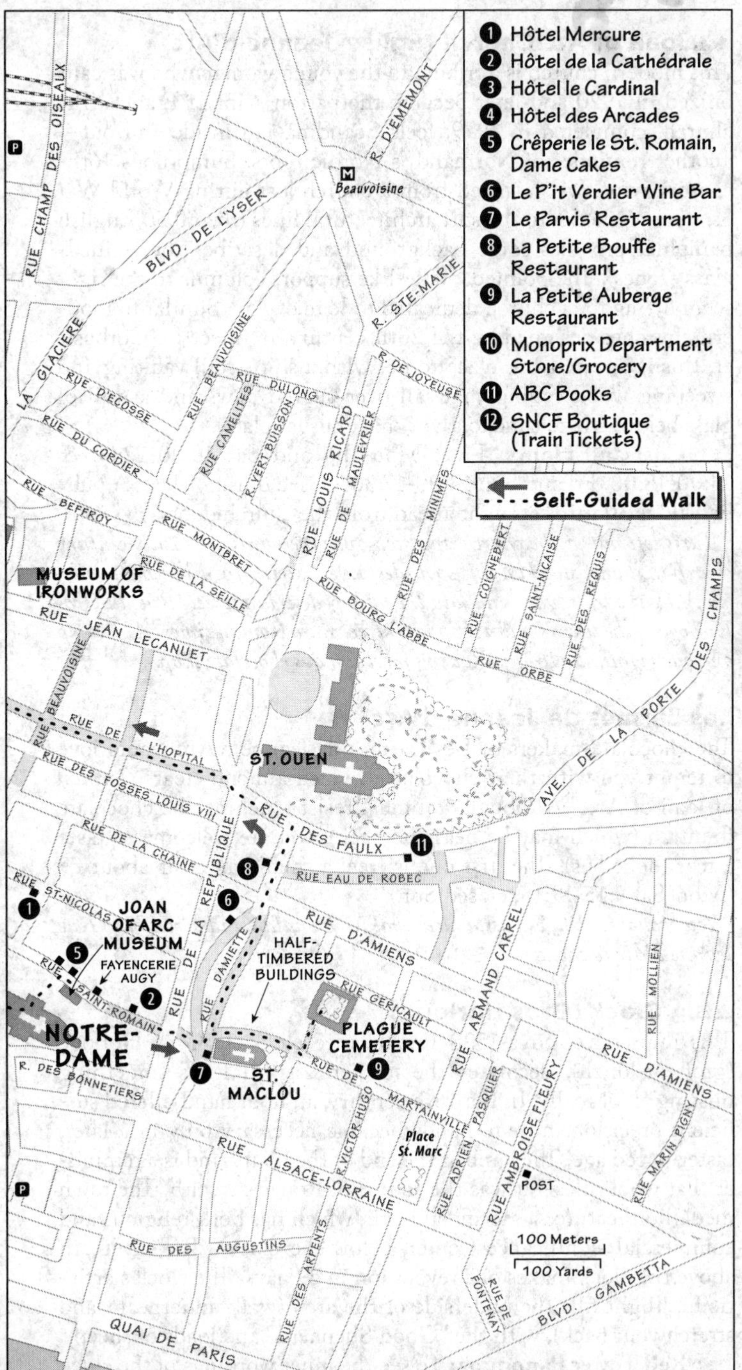

1 Hôtel Mercure
2 Hôtel de la Cathédrale
3 Hôtel le Cardinal
4 Hôtel des Arcades
5 Crêperie le St. Romain, Dame Cakes
6 Le P'it Verdier Wine Bar
7 Le Parvis Restaurant
8 La Petite Bouffe Restaurant
9 La Petite Auberge Restaurant
10 Monoprix Department Store/Grocery
11 ABC Books
12 SNCF Boutique (Train Tickets)
Self-Guided Walk
RUE CHAMP DES OISEAUX
Beauvoisine
R. D'EMEMONT
BLVD. DE L'YSER
R. STE-MARIE
LA GLACIERE
R. DE JOYEUSE
RUE D'ECOSSE
RUE BEAUVOISINE
RUE DULONG
RUE DU CORDIER
RUE CAMELITES
R. VERT BUISSON
RUE LOUIS RICARD
RUE DE MAULEVRIER
RUE BEFFROY
RUE MONTBRET
RUE DES MINIMES
RUE COIGNEBERT
RUE SAINT-NICAISE
RUE DES REQUIS
MUSEUM OF IRONWORKS
RUE DE LA SEILLE
RUE BOURG L'ABBE
RUE JEAN LECANUET
RUE ORBE
AVE. DE LA PORTE DES CHAMPS
RUE BEAUVOISINE
RUE DE L'HOPITAL
ST. OUEN
RUE DES FOSSES LOUIS VIII
RUE DES FAULX
RUE DE LA CHAINE
RUE DE LA REPUBLIQUE
RUE EAU DE ROBEC
RUE ST-NICOLAS
JOAN OF ARC MUSEUM
RUE D'AMIENS
HALF-TIMBERED BUILDINGS
FAYENCERIE AUGY
RUE DAMIETTE
RUE SAINT-ROMAIN
RUE GERICAULT
RUE ARMAND CARREL
RUE MOLLIEN
NOTRE-DAME
PLAGUE CEMETERY
ST. MACLOU
R. DES BONNETIERS
RUE DE MARTAINVILLE
RUE D'AMIENS
RUE VICTOR HUGO
Place St. Marc
RUE ADRIEN PASQUIER
RUE AMBROISE FLEURY
RUE MARIN PIGNY
RUE ALSACE-LORRAINE
POST
RUE DES AUGUSTINS
RUE DES ARPENTS
100 Meters
100 Yards
RUE DE FONTENAY
BLVD. GAMBETTA
QUAI DE PARIS

▲▲Joan of Arc Church (Eglise Jeanne d'Arc)

This modern church is a tribute to the young woman who was canonized in 1920 and later became the patron saint of France. The church, completed in 1979, feels Scandinavian inside and out—another reminder of Normandy's Nordic roots. Sumptuous 16th-century windows, salvaged from a church lost during World War II, were worked into the soft architectural lines (the €0.50 English pamphlet provides some background and describes the stained-glass scenes). The pointed, stake-like support columns to the right seem fitting for a church dedicated to Joan of Arc. Similar to modern churches designed by the 20th-century architect Le Corbusier, this is an uplifting place to be, with a ship's-hull vaulting and sweeping wood ceiling that sail over curved pews and a wall of glass below. Make time to savor this unusual place.

Cost and Hours: Free; Mon-Thu and Sat 10:00-12:00 & 14:00-18:00, Fri and Sun 14:00-17:30; closed during Mass. A public WC is 30 yards straight ahead from the church doors.

• *Turn left out of the church and step over the ruins of a 15th-century church that once stood on this spot (destroyed during the French Revolution). Leave the square and join the busy pedestrian street, Rue du Gros Horloge—the town's main shopping street since Roman times. A block up on your right (at #163) is Rouen's most famous chocolate shop...*

Les Larmes de Jeanne d'Arc

The chocolate-makers of Les Larmes de Jeanne d'Arc would love to tempt you with their chocolate-covered almond "tears *(larmes)* of Joan of Arc." Although you must resist touching the chocolate fountain (which may be near the back), you are welcome to taste a tear (delicious). The first one is free; a small bag costs about €9 (Mon-Sat 9:15-19:15, closed Sun).

• *Your route continues past a medieval McDonald's and across busy Rue Jeanne d'Arc to the...*

▲Big Clock (Gros Horloge)

This impressive, circa-1528 Renaissance clock, le Gros Horloge (groh or-lohzh), decorates the former City Hall. Is something missing? Not really. In the 16th century, an hour hand offered sufficient precision; minute hands became necessary only in a later, faster-paced age. The lamb at the end of the hour hand is a reminder that wool rules—it was the source of Rouen's wealth. The town medallion features a sacrificial lamb, which has both religious and commercial significance (center, below the clock). The silver orb above the clock makes one revolution in 29 days. The clock's artistic highlight fills the underside of the arch (walk underneath and stretch your back), with the "Good Shepherd" and loads of sheep.

Bell Tower Panorama: To see the inner workings of the clock

Joan of Arc
(1412-1431)

The cross-dressing teenager who rallied French soldiers to drive out English invaders was the illiterate daughter of a humble farmer. One summer day, in her dad's garden, 13-year-old Joan heard a heavenly voice accompanied by bright light. It was the first of several saints (including Michael, Margaret, and Catherine) to talk to her during her short life.

In 1429, the young girl was instructed by the voices to save France from the English. Dressed in men's clothing, she traveled to see the king and predicted that the French armies would be defeated near Orléans—as they were. King Charles VII equipped her with an ancient sword and a banner that read "Jesus, Maria," and sent her to rally the troops.

Soon "the Maid" *(la Pucelle)* was bivouacking amid rough soldiers, riding with them into battle, and suffering an arrow wound to the chest—all while liberating the town of Orléans. On July 17, 1429, she held her banner high in the cathedral of Reims as Charles was officially proclaimed king of a resurgent France.

Joan and company next tried to retake Paris (1429), but the English held out. She suffered a crossbow wound through the thigh, and her reputation of invincibility was tarnished. During a battle at Compiègne (1430), she was captured and turned over to the English for £10,000. The English took her to Rouen where she was chained by the neck inside an iron cage, while the local French authorities (allied with the English) plotted against her. The Inquisition—insisting that Joan's voices were "false and diabolical"—tried and sentenced her to death for being a witch and a heretic.

On May 30, 1431, Joan of Arc was tied to a stake on Rouen's old market square (Place du Vieux Marché). She yelled, "Rouen! Rouen! Must I die here?" Then they lit the fire; she fixed her eyes on a crucifix and died chanting, "Jesus, Jesus, Jesus."

After her death, Joan's place in history was slowly rehabilitated. French authorities proclaimed her trial illegal (1455), prominent writers and artists were inspired by her, and the Catholic Church finally beatified (1909) and canonized her (1920) as St. Joan of Arc.

and an extraordinary panorama over Rouen (including a stirring view of the cathedral), climb the clock tower's 100 steps. You'll tour several rooms with the help of a friendly audioguide and learn about life in Rouen when the tower was built. The big bells at the top weigh 1 to 2 tons each and ring on the hour—a deafening experience if you're in the tower. Don't miss the 360-degree view outside from the very top.

Cost and Hours: €6, includes audioguide; April-Oct Tue-Sun

10:00-12:00 & 13:00-19:00; Nov-March Tue-Sun 14:00-18:00; closed Mon year-round, last entry one hour before closing.

• *Walk under le Gros Horloge, then take a one-block detour left on Rue Thouret to see the...*

Palace of Justice (Palais de Justice)

Years of cleaning have removed the grime that once covered this fabulously flamboyantly Gothic building, the former home of Normandy's *parlement* and the largest civil Gothic building in France. The result is striking; think of this as you visit Rouen's other Gothic structures; some are awaiting baths of their own. Pockmarks on the side of the building that faces Rue Jeanne d'Arc are leftovers from bombings during the Normandy invasion. Look for the English-language plaques on the iron fence—they provide some history and describe the damage and tedious repair process.

• *Double back and continue up Rue du Gros Horloge. In a block you'll see a stone plaque dedicated to Cavelier de la Salle (high on the left), who explored the mouth of the Mississippi River, claimed the state of Louisiana for France, and was assassinated in Texas in 1687. Soon you'll reach...*

▲▲Notre-Dame Cathedral (Cathédrale Notre-Dame)

This cathedral is a landmark of art history. You're seeing essentially what Claude Monet saw as he painted 30 different studies of this frilly Gothic facade at various times of the day. Using the physical building only as a rack upon which to hang light, mist, dusk, and shadows, Monet was capturing "impressions." One of the results is in Rouen's Museum of Fine Arts; four others are at the Orsay Museum in Paris. Find the plaque showing two of these paintings (in the corner of the square, about 30 paces to your right if you were exiting the TI).

Cost and Hours: Free, Tue-Sun 8:00-19:00, Mon 14:00-19:00; closed during Mass Tue-Sat at 10:00, July-Aug also at 18:00, Sun and holidays at 8:30, 10:30, and 12:00; also closed Nov-March daily 12:00-14:00.

Cathedral Exterior: There's been a church on this site for more than a thousand years. Charlemagne honored it with a visit in the eighth century before the Vikings sacked it a hundred years later. The building you see today was constructed between the 12th and 14th centuries, though lightning strikes, wars (the cathedral was devastated in WWII fighting), and other destructive forces meant constant rebuilding—which explains the difference in the towers, such as the stones used at each tower's base.

Look up at the elaborate, soaring facade and find the cleaned sections, with bright statues on either side of the central portal—later, we'll meet some of their friends face-to-face inside the cathedral. The facade is another fine Rouen example of Flamboyant Gothic, and the spire, soaring nearly 500 feet high, is awe-inspiring. Why such a big cathedral here? Until the 1700s, Rouen was the second-largest city in France—rich from its wool trade and its booming port. On summer evenings, there may be a colorful sound-and-light show at the cathedral's facade (ask at the TI, starts at dark, which means about 23:00 in June and July).

Walk to the central portal and find a marvelous depiction of the Tree of Jesse. Jesse, King David's father, is shown reclined, resting his head on his hand, looking nonplussed. The tree grows from Jesse's back; the figures that sprout from its branches represent the lineage of Jesus. Compare this happy scene with the many Last Judgments you have seen decorating other church portals.

Cathedral Interior: Look down the center of the **nave.** This is a classic Gothic nave—four stories of pointed-arch arcades, the top filled with windows to help light the interior. Today, the interior is lighter than intended, because the original colored glass (destroyed mostly in World War II) was replaced by clear glass.

Circle counterclockwise around the church along the side aisle. The side chapels and windows have brief descriptions in English, each dedicated to a different saint. These chapels display the changing assortment of styles through the centuries. Look for photos halfway down on the right that show WWII bomb damage to the cathedral.

Passing through an iron gate after the high altar (closed during Mass; may be open on the opposite side even during Mass), you come to several **stone statues.** These figures were lifted from the facade during a cleaning and should eventually be installed in a museum. For us, it's a rare chance to stand toe-to-toe with a saint (weird feeling).

There are several **stone tombs** on your left, dating from when Rouen was the Norman capital. The first tomb is for Rollo, the first duke of Normandy in 933 (and great-great-great-great grandfather of William the Conqueror, seventh duke of Normandy, c. 1028). As the first duke, Rollo was chief of the first gang of Vikings (the original "Normans") who decided to settle here. Called the "Father of Normandy," Rollo died at the age of 80, but he is portrayed on his tomb as if he were 33 (as was the fashion, because Jesus died at that age). Because of later pillage and plunder, only Rollo's femur is inside the tomb.

And speaking of body parts, the next tomb contains the heart of Richard the Lionhearted. (The rest of his body lies in the Abbey of Fontevraud, described on page 438.)

Circle behind the altar. The beautiful **windows** with bold blues and reds are generally from the 13th century. Look back above the entry to see a rare black-and-white rose window (its medieval colored glass is long gone). You'll come to a display for the window dedicated to St. Julien, with pane-by-pane descriptions in English.

Continue a few paces, then look up to the **ceiling** over the nave. Looking directly above Rollo's femur on the opposite side of the apse, you can see the patchwork in the ceiling where the spire crashed through the roof. Perhaps this might be a good time to exit? Pass through the small iron gate, turn right, and leave through the side door (north transept).

Stepping outside, look back at the **facade** over the door. The fine carved tympanum (the area over the door) shows a graphic Last Judgment. Jesus stands between the saved (on the left) and the damned (on the right). Notice the devil grasping a miser, who clutches a bag of coins. Look for the hellish hot tub, where even a bishop (pointy hat) is eternally in hot water. And is it my imagination, or are those saved souls on the far right high-fiving each other?

Most of the facade has been cleaned—blasted with jets of water—but the limestone carving is still black. It's too delicate to survive the hosing. A more expensive laser cleaning has begun, and the result is astonishing.

• *From this courtyard, a gate deposits you on a traffic-free street. Turn right and walk along...*

Rue St. Romain

This appealing street is lined with half-timbered buildings. In a short distance, you can look up through an opening above the entrance to the new Joan of Arc Museum, and gaze back at the cathedral's prickly spire. Made of cast iron in the late 1800s—about the same time Gustave Eiffel was building his tower in Paris—the spire is, at 490 feet, the tallest in France. You can also see the former location of the missing smaller (green) spire—downed in a violent 1999 storm that blew the spire off the roof and sent it crashing to the cathedral floor.

Along the street find the new **Joan of Arc Museum** (L'Historical Jeanne d'Arc), which should open in early 2015. This long overdue museum highlights the mystical person whose fiery death brought such notoriety to Rouen. It's housed in what was once the archbishop's palace next to the cathedral. Check with the TI for the cost and opening hours (which were unavailable when this book was published).

• *Farther down the street, find a shop that shows off a traditional art form in action.*

At **Fayencerie Augy** (at #26), Monsieur Augy and his staff welcome shoppers to browse his studio/gallery/shop and see

Rouen's clay "china" being made the traditional way. First, the clay is molded and fired. Then it's dipped in white enamel, dried, lovingly hand-painted, and fired a second time. Rouen was the first city in France to make faience, earthenware with colored glazes. In the 1700s, the town had 18 factories churning out the popular product (Mon-Sat 9:00-19:00, closed Sun, 26 Rue St. Romain, VAT tax refunds nearly pay for the shipping, www.fayencerie-augy.com). For more faience, visit the local Museum of Ceramics (described later, under "Sights in Rouen").

• *Continue along Rue St. Romain, which (after crossing Rue de la République) leads to the fancy...*

St. Maclou Church

This church's unique, bowed facade is textbook Flamboyant Gothic. Its recent cleaning revealed a brilliant white facade. Notice the flame-like tracery decorating its gable. Because this was built at the very end of the Gothic age—and construction took many years—the doors are from the next age: the Renaissance (c. 1550). Study the graphic Last Judgment above the doors; it was designed when Rouen was riddled with the Black Plague. The bright and airy interior is worth a quick peek.

Cost and Hours: Free, Fri-Mon 10:00-12:00 & 14:00-17:30, closed Tue-Thu.

• *Leaving the church, turn right, and then take another right (giving the little boys on the corner wall a wide berth). Wander past a fine wall of half-timbered buildings fronting Rue Martainville, to the end of St. Maclou Church.*

Half-Timbered Buildings

Because the local stone—a chalky limestone from the cliffs of the Seine River—was of poor quality (your thumbnail is stronger), and because local oak was plentiful, half-timbered buildings became a Rouen specialty from the 14th through 19th century. Cantilevered floors were standard until the early 1500s. These top-heavy designs made sense: City land was limited, property taxes were based on ground-floor square footage, and the cantilevering minimized unsupported spans on upper floors. The oak beams provided the structural skeleton of the building, which was then filled in with a mix of clay, straw, pebbles...or whatever was available.

• *A block farther down on the left, at 186 Rue Martainville, a covered lane leads to the...*

Plague Cemetery (Aître St. Maclou)

During the great plagues of the Middle Ages, as many as two-thirds of the people in this parish died. For the decimated community, dealing with the corpses was an overwhelming task. This half-timbered courtyard (c. 1520) was a mass grave, an ossuary where the bodies were "processed." Bodies would be dumped into the grave (where the well is now) and drenched in liquid lime to help speed decomposition. Later, the bones would be stacked in alcoves above the colonnades that line this courtyard. Notice the ghoulish carvings (c. 1560s) of gravediggers' tools, skulls, crossbones, and characters doing the "dance of death." In this *danse macabre,* Death, the great equalizer, grabs people of all social classes. The place is now an art school. Peek in on the young artists. As you leave, spy the dried black cat (died c. 1520, in tiny glass case to the left of the door). To overcome evil, it was buried during the building's construction.

Cost and Hours: Free, daily mid-March-Oct 8:00-19:00, Nov-mid-March 8:00-18:00.

Nearby: Farther down Rue Martainville, at Place St. Marc, a colorful market blooms Sunday until about 12:30 and all day Tuesday, Friday, and Saturday. If it's not market day, you can double back to the cathedral and Rue du Gros Horloge, or continue with me to explore more of Rouen and find the Museum of Fine Arts (back toward the train station).

• *To reach the museum, turn right upon leaving the boneyard, then right again at the little boys (onto Rue Damiette), and hike up antique row to the vertical St. Ouen Church (a 7th-century abbey turned church in the 15th century, fine park behind). Turn left at the church on Rue des Faulx (an English-language bookstore, ABC Books, is two blocks to the right—see "Helpful Hints," page 240) and cross the busy street (the horseman you see to the right is a short-yet-majestic Napoleon Bonaparte who welcomes visitors to Rouen's city hall).*

Continue down Rue de l'Hôpital's traffic-free lane, which becomes Rue Ganterie (admire the Gothic fountain at Rue Beauvoisine). A right at the modern square on Rue de l'Ecureuil leads you to the ***Museum of Fine Arts*** *and the* ***Museum of Ironworks*** *(both described next, under "Sights in Rouen"). This is the end of our tour. The tower where Joan of Arc was imprisoned (also explained later) is a few blocks uphill, on the way back to the train station.*

Sights in Rouen

The first three museums are within a block of one another, closed on Tuesdays, never crowded, and can all be visited with the same €8 combo-ticket (www.rouen-musees.com).

▲Museum of Fine Arts (Musée des Beaux-Arts)

Paintings from many periods are beautifully displayed in this overlooked two-floor museum, including works by Caravaggio, Peter Paul Rubens, Paolo Veronese, Jan Steen, Velázquez, Théodore

Géricault, Jean-Auguste-Dominique Ingres, Eugène Delacroix, and several Impressionists. With its reasonable entry fee and calm interior, this museum is worth a short visit for the Impressionists and a surgical hit of a few other key artists. The museum café is good for a peaceful break from the action outside.

Cost and Hours: €5, occasional temporary exhibitions cost extra, €8 combo-ticket includes ironworks and ceramics museums; open Wed-Mon 10:00-18:00, 15th-17th-century rooms closed 13:00-14:00, closed Tue; a few blocks below train station at 26 bis Rue Jean Lecanuet, tel. 02 35 71 28 40.

Visiting the Museum: Pick up the essential museum map at the info desk as you enter. Consider a stop in the meditative café to plan your attack.

Climb the stairs to the second floor, where you'll focus your time and savor the lack of crowds. Find the excellent handheld English descriptions in key rooms. The museum is divided into two wings on either side of the main stairway. Turning right when you reach the second floor, you'll find a good collection of works by Géricault (including a small version of *The Raft of the Medusa*) and several small but engaging paintings by Ingres. In the next rooms you'll find scenes inspired by Normandy's landscape—painted by Impressionists Monet, Sisley, and Pissarro—and a handful of paintings from Renoir, Degas, and Corot. Look also for beautiful paintings by Impressionists whose names you may not recognize. Room 2.25 showcases a must-see scene of Rouen's busy port in 1855.

Paintings on the other side of the second floor are devoted to French painters from the 17th and 18th centuries (Boucher, Fragonard, and Poussin) and Italian works, including several by Veronese. A gripping Caravaggio canvas (Room 2.4), depicting the flagellation of Christ, demands attention with its dramatic lighting and realistic faces. Stairs at the rear, near the Caravaggio, lead down to an intriguing collection of works by 16th-century Dutch and Belgian artists and a small room of medieval icons.

On the other side of the ground floor, pass through the bookstore to find a collection of paintings by hometown boy Marcel Duchamp, several colorful Modiglianis, and one grand-scale Delacroix.

Museum of Ironworks (Musée le Secq des Tournelles, a.k.a. Musée de la Ferronnerie)

This deconsecrated church houses iron objects, many of them more than 1,500 years old. Locks, chests, keys, tools, thimbles, coffee grinders, corkscrews, and flatware from centuries ago—virtually anything made of iron is on display. You can duck into the entry area for a glimpse of a medieval iron scene without passing through the turnstile.

Cost and Hours: €3, €8 combo-ticket includes fine arts and ceramics museums, no English explanations—bring a French/English dictionary, Wed-Mon 14:00-18:00, closed Tue, behind Museum of Fine Arts, 2 Rue Jacques Villon, tel. 02 35 88 42 92.

Museum of Ceramics (Musée de la Céramique)

Rouen's famous faience (earthenware), which dates from the 16th to 18th century, fills this fine old mansion. There's not a word of English except in the museum leaflet.

Cost and Hours: €3, €8 combo-ticket includes fine arts and ironworks museums, Wed-Mon 14:00-18:00, closed Tue, 1 Rue Faucon, tel. 02 35 07 31 74.

Joan of Arc Tower (La Tour Jeanne d'Arc)

This massive tower (1204), part of Rouen's brooding castle, was Joan's prison before her untimely death. Cross the deep moat and find three small floors (and 122 spiral steps) covering tidbits of Rouen's and Joan's history, well-described in English. The top floor gives a good peek at an impressive wood substructure but no views.

Cost and Hours: €1.75, Wed-Sat and Mon 10:00-12:30 & 14:00-18:00, Sun 14:00-18:30, closed Tue, one block uphill from the Museum of Fine Arts on Rue du Bouvreuil, tel. 02 35 98 16 21.

NEAR ROUEN

The Route of the Ancient Abbeys (La Route des Anciennes Abbayes)

This route—punctuated with medieval abbeys, apples, cherry trees, and Seine River views—provides a pleasing detour for drivers connecting Rouen and Honfleur or the D-Day beaches (if you're traveling *sans* car, skip it).

From Rouen, follow the Seine along its right bank and track signs for D-982 to Duclair, then follow D-65 to **Jumièges** (the highlight of this route). From near Jumièges you can cross the Seine on the tiny, free-and-frequent car ferry, then connect with the A-13, or continue following the right bank of the Seine and cross at the Pont de Tancarville bridge (free) or the magnificent Normandy Bridge (Pont de Normandie, €5.50, described later). By either route allow 45 minutes from Rouen to Jumièges and another 75 minutes to Honfleur, or two more hours to Bayeux.

Fifteen minutes west of Rouen, drivers can stop to admire the gleaming Romanesque church at the **Abbey of St. Georges de Boscherville** (skip the abbey grounds). This perfectly intact and beautiful church makes for interesting comparisons with the ruined church at Jumièges. The café across from the church is good for meals or drinks.

Farther along the route is the **Abbey of Jumièges,** a spiritual place for lovers of evocative ruins (worth ▲). Founded in A.D. 654 as a Benedictine abbey, it was destroyed by Vikings in the 9th century, then rebuilt by William the Conqueror in the 11th century. This magnificent complex thrived for centuries as Normandy's largest abbey. It was part of a great monastic movement that reestablished civilization in Normandy out of the chaos that followed the fall of Rome (for more about the power of the Benedictines, read about the Cluny Abbey on page 887). The abbey was destroyed during the French Revolution when it was used as a quarry. The abbey has changed little since then.

Today there is no roof to protect the abbey complex, and many walls are entirely gone. But what remains of the abbey's Church of Notre-Dame is awe-inspiring. Study its stark Romanesque facade standing 160 feet high. Stroll down the nave's center; notice the three levels of arches and the soaring rear wall capped by a lantern tower to light the choir. Find a seat in the ruined choir and imagine the church before its destruction. You'll discover brilliant views of the ruins and better appreciate its importance by wandering into the park.

Cost and Hours: €6, helpful English handout and explanations posted, more detailed booklet for sale, daily mid-April-mid-Sept 9:30-18:30, mid-Sept-mid-April 9:30-13:00 & 14:30-17:30, last entry 30 minutes before closing, unnecessary iPad videoguide-€5, tel. 02 35 37 24 02, www.abbayedejumieges.fr). Decent lunch options lie across the street from the abbey.

Sleeping in Rouen

Although I prefer Rouen by day, sleeping here presents you with a mostly tourist-free city (most hotels cater to business travelers). These hotels are perfectly central, within two blocks of Notre-Dame Cathedral. All hotels offer free Wi-Fi unless noted.

$$$ Hôtel Mercure*,** ideally situated a block north of the cathedral, is a concrete business hotel with a professional staff, a stay-awhile lobby and bar, and 125 rooms loaded with modern comforts. Suites come with views of the cathedral, but are pricey and not much bigger than a double. Look for big discounts online (standard Db-€160, "privilege" Db-€200, suite-€290, breakfast-€18, air-con, elevator, guest computer, free Wi-Fi, parking garage-€13/day, 7 Rue Croix de Fer, tel. 02 35 52 69 52, www.mercure.com, h1301@accor.com).

$$$ Hôtel de la Cathédrale** greets travelers with a lovely courtyard and a cozy, wood-beamed lounge/breakfast room. Guest rooms are mostly country-French with basic bathrooms and imperfect sound insulation, but loads of character (Db-€90-120, Tb/Qb-

Sleep Code

Abbreviations **(€1 = $1.40, country code: 33)**

S = Single, **D** = Double/Twin, **T** = Triple, **Q** = Quad, **b** = bathroom, **s** = shower only, * = French hotel rating (0-5 stars)

Price Rankings

$$$ Higher Priced—Most rooms €95 or more.

$$ Moderately Priced—Most rooms between €60-95.

$ Lower Priced—Most rooms €60 or less.

Unless otherwise noted, credit cards are accepted, English is spoken, and Wi-Fi is free. Prices change; verify current rates online or by email. For the best prices, always book directly with the hotel.

€140-160, elevator, guest computer, Wi-Fi, 12 Rue St. Romain, a block from St. Maclou Church, tel. 02 35 71 57 95, www.hotel-de-la-cathedrale.fr, contact@hotel-de-la-cathedrale.fr).

$$ Hôtel le Cardinal** is a solid value with sharp, well-designed rooms, most with point-blank views of the cathedral and all with queen-size beds and modern bathrooms (standard Db-€80-115; €140-160 for fourth-floor rooms—the hotel's largest, with balconies and great cathedral views; non-smoking rooms available, breakfast-€9, elevator, Wi-Fi, 1 Place de la Cathédrale, tel. 02 35 70 24 42, www.cardinal-hotel.fr, hotelcardinal.rouen@wanadoo.fr).

$ Hôtel des Arcades is bare-bones basic, but as cheap and central as it gets (S-€42, Db-€56-62, 52 Rue des Carmes, tel. 02 35 70 10 30, www.hotel-des-arcades.fr, hotel_des_arcades@yahoo.fr).

Eating in Rouen

You can eat well in Rouen at fair prices. Because you're in Normandy, *crêperies* abound. To find the best eating action, prowl the streets between the St. Maclou and St. Ouen churches (Rues Martainville and Damiette) for *crêperies,* wine bars, international cuisine, and traditional restaurants. This is Rouen's liveliest area at night, except for Sunday and Monday, when many places are closed.

Crêperie le St. Romain, between the cathedral and St. Maclou Church, is an excellent budget option. It's run by gentle Mr. Pegis, who serves filling €9-11 crêpes with small salads and offers many good options in a warm setting (tables in the rear are best). The hearty *gatiflette* is delicious (lunch Tue-Sat, dinner Thu-Sat, closed Sun-Mon, 52 Rue St. Romain, tel. 02 35 88 90 36).

Dame Cakes is ideal if it's lunchtime or teatime and you need a Jane Austen fix. The decor is from another, more precious era, and the baked goods are out of this world. Locals adore the tables in the back garden, while tourists eat up the cathedral view from the first-floor room (€12-15 salads and *plats,* garden terrace in back, Mon-Sat 11:00-18:00, closed Sun, 70 Rue St. Romain, tel. 02 35 07 49 31).

Le P'it Verdier is a lively wine bar-café where locals gather for a glass of wine and appetizers in the thick of restaurant row (closed Sun-Mon, 13 Rue Père Adam, tel. 02 35 36 34 43).

Le Parvis, which faces St. Maclou Church, is a good bet for a fine Norman meal featuring homemade cuisine. There's comfortable seating inside and out (€25 two-course *menu,* €30 three-course *menu,* ask about their Bouillabaisse Normand, closed Sun-Mon, 7 Place Barthlémy, tel. 02 35 15 28 80).

La Petite Bouffe is a young-at-heart, appealing, cheery place with tall windows and good prices (€20 three-course *menus,* great choices, inside dining only, closed Sun, 1 Rue des Boucheries St-Ouen, tel. 02 35 98 13 14).

La Petite Auberge, a block off Rue Damiette, is the most traditional place I list. It has an Old World interior, reasonable prices, and it's also open on Sunday (*menus* from €22, closed Mon, 164 Rue Martainville, tel. 02 35 70 80 18).

Rouen Connections

Rouen is well served by trains from Paris and Caen, making Bayeux and the D-Day beaches a snap to reach.

From Rouen by Train to: Paris' Gare St. Lazare (nearly hourly, 1.5 hours), **Bayeux** (14/day, 2.5 hours, change in Caen), **Caen** (14/day, 1.5 hours), **Pontorson/Mont St-Michel** (2/day, 4 hours, change in Caen; more with change in Paris, 7 hours).

By Train and Bus to: Honfleur (6/day Mon-Sat, 3/day Sun, 1-hour train to Le Havre, then easy transfer to 30-minute bus over Normandy Bridge to Honfleur—Le Havre's bus and train stations are adjacent).

Honfleur

Gazing at its cozy harbor lined with skinny, soaring houses, it's easy to overlook the historic importance of Honfleur (ohn-flur). For more than a thousand years, sailors have enjoyed this port's ideal location, where the Seine River greets the English

Channel. William the Conqueror received supplies shipped from Honfleur. Samuel de Champlain sailed from here in 1608 to North America, where he discovered the St. Lawrence River and founded Quebec City. The town was also a favorite of 19th-century Impressionists who were captivated by Honfleur's unusual light—the result of its river-meets-sea setting. Eugène Boudin (boo-dahn) lived and painted in Honfleur, drawing Monet and other creative types from Paris. In some ways, modern art was born in the fine light of idyllic little Honfleur.

Honfleur escaped the bombs of World War II, and today offers a romantic port enclosed on three sides by sprawling outdoor cafés. Long eclipsed by the gargantuan port of Le Havre just across the Seine, Honfleur happily uses its past as a bar stool...and sits on it.

Orientation to Honfleur

Honfleur is popular—expect crowds on weekends and during summer. All of Honfleur's appealing lanes and activities are within a short stroll of its old port (Vieux Bassin). The Seine River flows just east of the center, the hills of the Côte de Grâce form its western limit, and Rue de la République slices north-south through the center to the port. Honfleur has two can't-miss sights—the harbor and Ste. Catherine Church—and a handful of other intriguing monuments. But really, the town itself is its best sight.

TOURIST INFORMATION

The TI is in the glassy public library *(Mediathéque)* on Quai le Paulmier, two blocks from the Vieux Bassin toward Le Havre (July-Aug Mon-Sat 9:30-19:00, Sun 10:00-17:00; Sept-June Mon-Sat 9:30-12:30 & 14:00-18:30, Sun 10:00-12:30 & 14:00-17:00 except closed Sun afternoon Oct-Easter; free WCs inside, pay Internet access, tel. 02 31 89 23 30, www.ot-honfleur.fr). Here you can rent a €3.50 audioguide for a self-guided town walk, or pick up a town map, bus and train schedules, and find information on the D-Day beaches.

Museum Pass: The €10.10 museum pass, sold at the TI and participating museums, covers the Eugène Boudin Museum, Maisons Satie, and the Museums of Old Honfleur (Museum of the Navy and Museum of Ethnography and Norman Popular Art); it more than pays for itself with visits to the Boudin and Satie museums (www.musees-honfleur.fr).

ARRIVAL IN HONFLEUR

By Bus: Get off at the small bus station *(gare routière),* and confirm your departure at the helpful information counter. To reach the

TI and old town, turn right as you exit the station and walk five minutes up Quai le Paulmier. Note that the bus stop on Rue de la République may be more convenient for some accommodations (see map on page 258).

By Car: Follow *Centre-Ville* signs, then find your hotel (easier said than done) and unload your bags (double-parking is OK for a few minutes). Parking is a headache in Honfleur, especially on summer and holiday weekends. Some hotels offer parking...for a price. Otherwise, your hotelier knows where you can park for free. The central Parking du Bassin (across from the TI) is pricey (€2/hour, €14/day). Across the short causeway is Parking du Môle, which is cheaper (only €4/day), but a bit less central. Parking Beaulieu is still farther (take Rue St-Nichol to Rue Guillaume de Beaulieu), but free (see map on page 258 for parking locations). Street parking, metered during the day, is free from 20:00 to 8:00.

HELPFUL HINTS

Market Day: The area around Ste. Catherine Church becomes a colorful open-air market every Saturday (9:00-13:00). A smaller organic-food-only market takes place here on Wednesday mornings, and a flea market takes center stage here the first Sunday of every month and also on Wednesday evenings in summer.

Grocery Store: There's a grocery store near the TI with long hours (daily July-Aug, closed Mon off-season, 16 Quai le Paulmier).

Regional Products with Panache: Visit **Produits Regionaux Gribouille** for any Norman delicacy you can dream up. Say *bonjour* to Monsieur Gribouille (gree-boo-ee), and watch your head—his egg-beater collection hangs from above (Thu-Tue 9:30-13:00 & 14:00-19:00, closed Wed, 16 Rue de l'Homme de Bois, tel. 02 31 89 29 54).

Internet Access: Free Wi-Fi is available at the relaxed **Travel Coffee Shop** (near the recommended La Cour Ste. Catherine B&B) and at several other cafés in town. Ask the TI for a list of cafés with computer terminals and Wi-Fi.

Laundry: Lavomatique is a block behind the TI, toward the port (daily 7:30-21:30, 4 Rue Notre-Dame). You can do your own or ask Madame to do it for you for a small fee.

Taxi: Call mobile 06 18 18 38 38.

Tourist Train: Honfleur's *petit train* toots you up the Côte de Grâce—the hill overlooking the town—and back in about 50 minutes (€6.50, 4/day, more in summer, departs from across gray swivel bridge that leads to Parking du Môle).

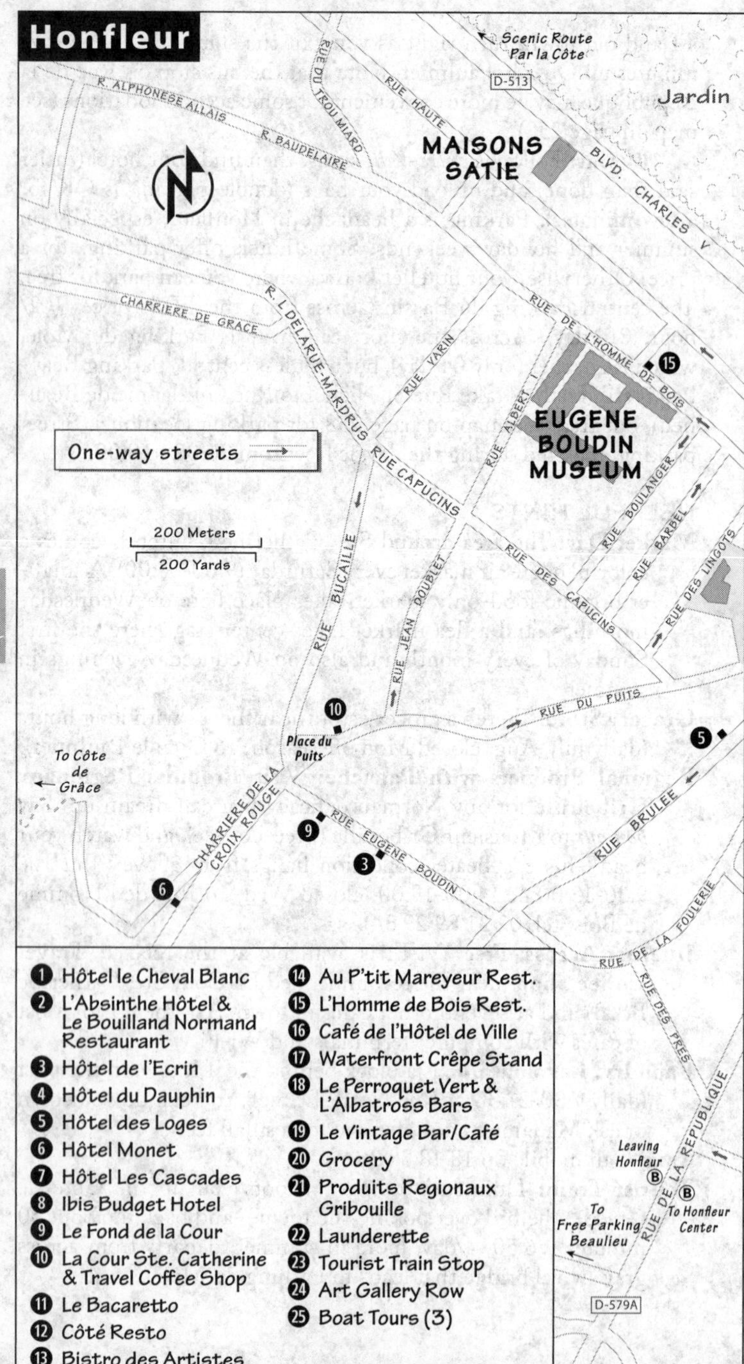
Honfleur
Scenic Route Par la Côte
D-513
Jardin
R. ALPHONESE ALLAIS
R. BAUDELAIRE
RUE DU TROU MIARD
RUE HAUTE
MAISONS SATIE
BLVD. CHARLES V
CHARRIERE DE GRACE
R. L DELARUE-MARDRUS
RUE YARIN
RUE ALBERT I
RUE DE L'HOMME DE BOIS
EUGENE BOUDIN MUSEUM
One-way streets
RUE CAPUCINS
RUE BOULANGER
RUE BARBEL
RUE DES LINGOTS
200 Meters
200 Yards
RUE BUCAILLE
RUE JEAN DOUBLET
RUE DES CAPUCINS
RUE DU PUITS
Place du Puits
To Côte de Grâce
CHARRIERE DE LA CROIX ROUGE
RUE EUGENE BOUDIN
RUE BRULEE
RUE DE LA FOULERIE
RUE DES PRES
RUE DE LA REPUBLIQUE
Leaving Honfleur
To Honfleur Center
To Free Parking Beaulieu
D-579A
NORMANDY
1 Hôtel le Cheval Blanc
2 L'Absinthe Hôtel & Le Bouilland Normand Restaurant
3 Hôtel de l'Ecrin
4 Hôtel du Dauphin
5 Hôtel des Loges
6 Hôtel Monet
7 Hôtel Les Cascades
8 Ibis Budget Hotel
9 Le Fond de la Cour
10 La Cour Ste. Catherine & Travel Coffee Shop
11 Le Bacaretto
12 Côté Resto
13 Bistro des Artistes
14 Au P'tit Mareyeur Rest.
15 L'Homme de Bois Rest.
16 Café de l'Hôtel de Ville
17 Waterfront Crêpe Stand
18 Le Perroquet Vert & L'Albatross Bars
19 Le Vintage Bar/Café
20 Grocery
21 Produits Regionaux Gribouille
22 Launderette
23 Tourist Train Stop
24 Art Gallery Row
25 Boat Tours (3)

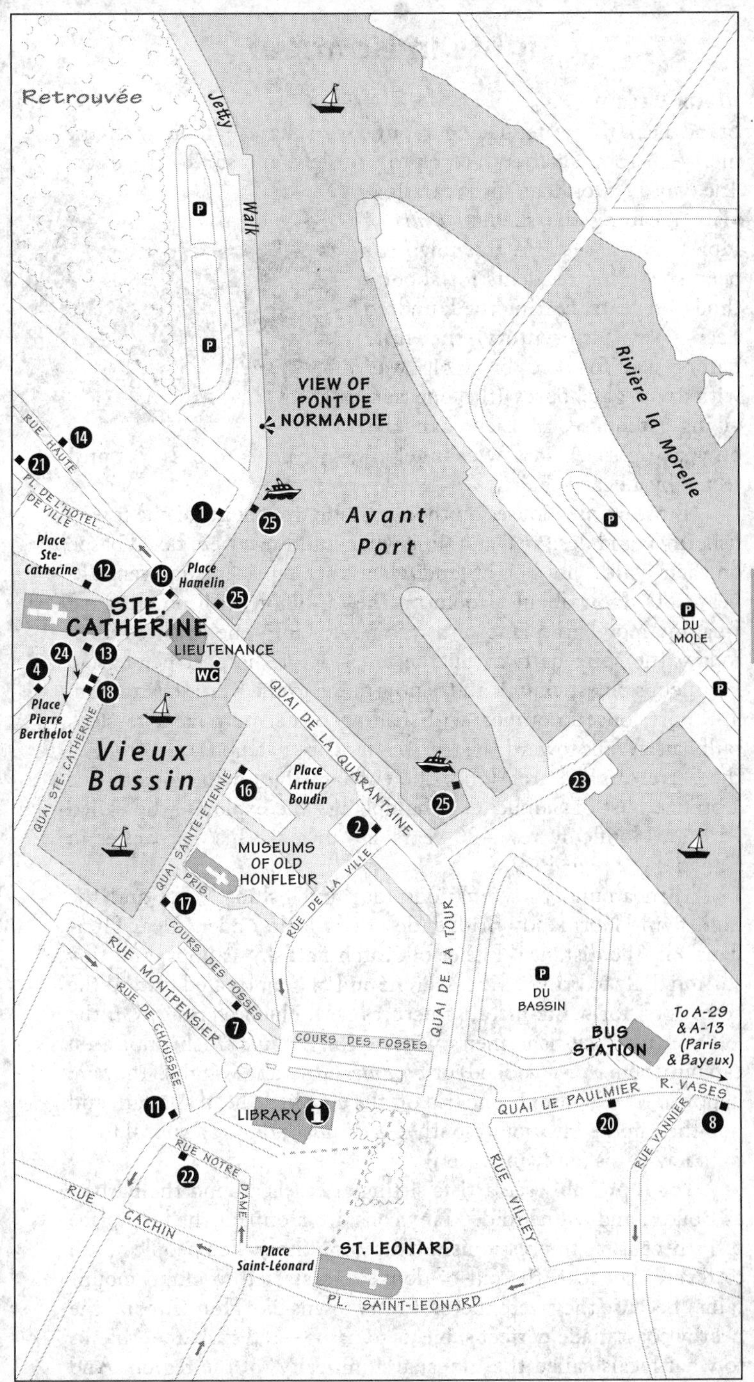

Retrouvée
Jetty
Walk
VIEW OF PONT DE NORMANDIE
Avant Port
Rivière la Morelle
DU MOLE
RUE HAUTE
PL. DE L'HOTEL DE VILLE
Place Ste-Catherine
Place Hamelin
STE. CATHERINE
LIEUTENANCE
WC
Place Pierre Berthelot
QUAI DE LA QUARANTAINE
Vieux Bassin
QUAI STE. CATHERINE
QUAI SAINTE-ETIENNE
Place Arthur Boudin
MUSEUMS OF OLD HONFLEUR
PRIS
RUE DE LA VILLE
QUAI DE LA TOUR
COURS DES FOSSES
RUE MONTPENSIER
RUE DE CHAUSSEE
DU BASSIN
BUS STATION
To A-29 & A-13 (Paris & Bayeux)
COURS DES FOSSES
LIBRARY
QUAI LE PAULMIER
R. VASES
RUE VANNIER
RUE NOTRE DAME
RUE VILLEY
RUE CACHIN
Place Saint-Léonard
ST. LEONARD
PL. SAINT-LEONARD

Sights in Honfleur

Vieux Bassin

Stand near the water facing Honfleur's square harbor, with the merry-go-round across the lock to your left, and survey the town. The word "Honfleur" is Scandinavian, meaning the shelter *(fleur)* of Hon (a Norse settler). This town has been sheltering residents for about a thousand years. During the Hundred Years' War (14th century), the entire harbor was fortified by a big wall with twin gatehouses (the one surviving gatehouse, La Lieutenance, is on your right). A narrow channel allowing boats to pass was protected by a heavy chain.

Those skinny houses on the right side were built for the town's fishermen and designed at a time when buildings were taxed based on their width, not height (and when knee replacements were unheard of). How about a room on the top floor, with no elevator? Imagine moving a piano or a refrigerator into one of these units today. The spire halfway up the left side of the port belongs to Honfleur's oldest church and is now home to the Marine Museum. The port, once crammed with fishing boats, now harbors sleek sailboats. Walk toward the La Lieutenance gatehouse. In front of the barrel-vaulted arch (once the entry to the town), you can see a bronze bust of Samuel de Champlain—the explorer who sailed with an Honfleur crew 400 years ago to make his discoveries in Canada.

Turn around to see various tour and fishing boats and the high-flying Normandy Bridge (described later, under "Near Honfleur") in the distance. Fisherfolk catch flatfish, scallops, and tiny shrimp daily to bring to the Marché au Poisson, located toward the river (look for white metal structures with blue lettering). On the left you may see fishermen's wives selling *crevettes* (shrimp). You can buy them *cuites* (cooked) or *vivantes* (alive and wiggly). They are happy to let you sample one (rip off the cute little head and tail, and pop the middle into your mouth—*délicieuse!*), or buy a cupful to go for a few euros (daily in season).

You'll probably see artists sitting at easels around the harbor, as Boudin and Monet did. Many consider Honfleur the birthplace of 19th-century Impressionism. This was a time when people began to revere, not fear, the out-of-doors, and started to climb mountains "because they were there." Pretty towns like Honfleur and the nearby coast made perfect subjects to paint—and still are—thanks to what locals called the "unusual luminosity" of the region. And with the advent of trains in the late 1800s, artists could travel to the best light like never before. Artists would set up easels along the harbor to catch the light playing on the line of buildings, slate shingles, timbers, geraniums, clouds, and reflections in the water. Monet came here to visit the artist Boudin, a hometown boy, and the battle cry of the Impressionists—"Out of the studio and into the light!"—was born.

If you're an early riser, you can watch what's left of Honfleur's fishing fleet prepare for the day, and you just might experience that famous luminosity.

▲▲Ste. Catherine Church (Eglise Ste. Catherine)

The unusual wood-shingled exterior suggests that this church has a different story to tell than most. Walk inside. You'd swear that if it were turned over, it would float—the legacy of a community of sailors and fishermen, with loads of talented boat-builders and nary a cathedral architect. When workers put up the first nave in 1466, it soon became apparent that more space was needed—so the second was built in 1497. Because it felt too much like a market hall, they added side aisles. Notice the oak pillars, some full-length and others supported by stone bases. Trees come in different sizes, yet each pillar had to be the same thickness. In the last months of World War II, a bomb fell through the roof—but didn't explode. The pipe organ behind you is popular for concerts, and half of the modern pews are designed to flip so that you can face the music. Take a close look at the many medieval instruments carved into the railing below the organ—a 16th-century combo band in wood.

The **church's bell tower** was built away from the church to avoid placing too much stress on the wooden church's roof, and to help minimize fire hazards. Historians consider the structure ugly—I like it. Notice the funky shingled chestnut beams that run from its squat base to support the skinny tower, and find the small, faded wooden sculpture of St. Catherine over the door. Go inside (€2) to appreciate the ancient wood framing and to see a good 15-minute video describing the bell tower's history. The highlights of the tiny museum inside are two wooden sculptures from the bows of two Louis XIII ships. Until recently the bell ringer lived in the bell tower (notice his fireplace behind the video area).

Cost and Hours: Church—free, daily July-Aug 9:00-18:30, Sept-June 9:00-17:15; bell tower—€2, free with ticket to the Eugène Boudin Museum, April-Sept Wed-Mon 10:00-12:00 & 14:00-18:00; closed Oct-March and Tue year-round.

HONFLEUR'S MUSEUMS AND GALLERIES

Eugène Boudin ignited Honfleur's artistic tradition, which still burns today. The town is a popular haunt of artists, many of whom

Eugène Boudin
(1824-1898)

Born in Honfleur, Boudin was the son of a harbor pilot. As an amateur teenage artist, he found work in an art-supply store that catered to famous artists from Paris (such as Jean-Baptiste-Camille Corot and Jean-François Millet) who came to paint the seaside. Boudin studied art in Paris but kept his hometown roots. Thanks to his Paris connections, Boudin's work was exhibited at the Paris salons.

At age 30 Boudin met the teenage Claude Monet. Monet had grown up in nearby Le Havre and, like Boudin, sketched the world around him—beaches, boats, and small-town life. Boudin encouraged him to don a scarf, set up his easel outdoors, and paint the scene exactly as he saw it. Today, we say: "Well, duh!" But "open-air" painting was unorthodox for artists trained to thoroughly study their subjects in the perfect lighting of a controlled studio setting. Boudin didn't teach Monet as much as give him the courage to follow his artistic instincts.

In the 1860s and 1870s, Boudin spent summers at his farm (St. Siméon) on the outskirts of Honfleur, hosting Monet, Edouard Manet, and other hangers-on. They taught Boudin the Impressionist techniques of using bright colors and building a subject with many individual brushstrokes. Boudin adapted those "strokes" to build subjects with "patches" of color. In 1874, Boudin joined the renegade Impressionists at their "revolutionary" exhibition in Paris.

display their works in Honfleur's many art galleries (the best ones are along the streets between Ste. Catherine Church and the port). As you walk around the town visiting the museums, take time to enjoy today's art, too.

Remember, the €10.10 museum pass covers all four museums described below and pays for itself with visits to just the Boudin and Satie museums (pass sold at TI and participating museums).

▲Eugène Boudin Museum

This pleasing little museum has three interesting floors with many paintings of Honfleur and the surrounding countryside. The first floor displays Norman folk costumes, the second floor has the Boudin collection, and the third floor houses the Hambourg/Rachet collection and the Katia Granoff room. The museum will close for an ambitious renovation for several months in early 2015. This work will likely affect the description below—go with the flow.

Cost and Hours: €6.50, €2 extra during special exhibits, covered by museum pass; mid-March-Sept Wed-Mon 10:00-12:00 & 14:00-18:00, closed Tue; Oct-mid-March Wed-Fri and Mon

14:30-17:30, Sat-Sun 10:00-12:00 & 14:30-17:30, closed Tue; €2 English audioguide covers selected works (no English explanations on display—but none needed); elevator, no photos, Rue de l'Homme de Bois, tel. 02 31 89 54 00.

➲ **Self-Guided Tour:** Pick up a map at the ticket counter, tip your beret to Eugène Boudin, and climb the stairs (or take the elevator).

First Floor (Costumes): Monsieur and Madame Louveau (see their photo as you enter) gave Honfleur this quality collection of local traditional costumes. The hats, blouses, and shoes are supported by paintings that place them in an understandable historical and cultural context. Of special interest are the lace bonnets, typical of 19th-century Normandy. You could name a woman's village by her style of bonnet. The dolls are not toys for tots, but marketing tools for traveling clothing merchants—designed to show off the latest fashions. The men's department is in the back of the room.

Second Floor (Boudin Collection and More): Making a right off the stairs leads you into a large room of appealing 20th-century paintings and sculpture, created by artists who produced most of their works while living in Honfleur (special exhibits sometimes occupy this space). A left off the stairs leads through a temporary exhibition hall into the Salle Eugène Boudin, a small gallery of 19th-century paintings. In this room, Boudin's artwork is mixed with that of his colleagues and contemporaries; paintings by Claude Monet and Gustave Courbet are usually displayed. Find the glass display case in the rear titled *Précurseur de l'Impressionisme,* with little pastel drawings, and follow Boudin's art chronologically, as it evolves, from Romanticism through Realism to Impressionism (the heart of this museum).

Upon showing their work in Paris, local artists—such as Eugène Boudin—created enough of a stir that Normandy came into vogue; many Parisian artists (including Monet and other early Impressionists) traveled to Honfleur to dial in to the action. Boudin himself made a big impression on the father of Impressionism by introducing Monet to the practice of painting outside. This collection of Boudin's paintings—which the artist gave to his hometown—shows how his technique developed, from realistic portrayals of subjects (outlines colored in, like a coloring book) to masses of colors catching light (Impressionism). Boudin's beach scenes, showing aristocrats taking a healthy saltwater dip, helped fuel that style. His skies were good enough to earn him the nickname "King of Skies."

Third Floor (Hambourg/Rachet Collection): Follow the steps that lead from the Boudin room to the small Hambourg/Rachet collection (and a smashing painting of Honfleur at twilight).

In 1988, André Hambourg and his wife, Nicole Rachet, donated their art to this museum. The collection is enjoyably Impressionistic, but largely from the mid-20th century.

Third Floor (Salle Katia Granoff): Retrace your steps back to the main stairway to reach the other third-floor room, where you'll find a worthwhile collection of 20th-century works by artists who lived and learned in Honfleur. Find the few paintings by Raoul Dufy (a French Fauvist painter), and compare his imaginative scenes of Normandy with others you've seen. And remember, just because you may not recognize an artist's name doesn't mean that you can't enjoy the work. Be sure to take in the brilliant view of the Normandy Bridge through the windows.

▲Maisons Satie

If Honfleur is over-the-top cute, this remarkable museum, housed in composer Erik Satie's birthplace, is a refreshing burst of witty charm—just like the musical genius it honors. As you wander from room to room with your included audioguide, infrared signals transmit bits of Satie's minimalist music, along with a first-person story (in English). As if you're living as an artist in 1920s Paris, you'll drift past winged pears, strangers in the window, and small girls with green eyes. (If you like what you hear...don't move; the infrared transmission is hypersensitive, and the soundtrack switches every few feet.)

The finale—performed by you—is the *Laboratory of Emotions* pedal-go-round, a self-propelled carousel where your feet create the music (be sure to pedal softly). For a relaxing break, enjoy the 12-minute movie (4/hour, French only) featuring modern dance springing from *Parade,* Satie's collaboration with Pablo Picasso and Jean Cocteau; the Dadaist *Relâche;* and other works. You'll even hear the boos and whistles that greeted these ballets' debuts.

Cost and Hours: €6.10, includes audioguide, covered by museum pass; May-Sept Wed-Mon 10:00-19:00, closed Tue; Oct-Dec and mid-Feb-April Wed-Mon 11:00-18:00, closed Tue; closed Jan-mid-Feb; last entry one hour before closing, 5-minute walk from harbor at 67 Boulevard Charles V, tel. 02 31 89 11 11, www.musees-honfleur.fr.

Museums of Old Honfleur

Two side-by-side folk museums combine to paint a picture of daily life in Honfleur during the time when its ships were king and the city had global significance. The curator creatively supports the artifacts with paintings, making the cultural context clearer. Both museums have loaner handouts with English explanations (more helpful in the Museum of Ethnography).

The **Museum of the Sea** (Musée de la Marine) faces the port and fills Honfleur's oldest church (15th century) with a cool collection of models from fishing boats to naval ships (many of which were constructed in Honfleur's shipyards), marine paraphernalia, and paintings. The **Museum of Ethnography and Norman Popular Art** (Musée d'Ethnographie et d'Art Populaire), located in the old prison and courthouse, re-creates typical rooms from Honfleur's past and crams them with objects of daily life—costumes, furniture, looms, and an antique printing press (€4 each or €5.20 for both, covered by museum pass; both museums open April-Sept Tue-Sun 10:00-12:00 & 14:00-18:30, closed Mon; March and Oct-Nov Tue-Fri 10:00-12:00 & 14:30-17:30, Sat-Sun 10:00-12:00 & 14:00-17:30, closed Mon; closed Dec-Feb).

HONFLEUR WALKS

▲Côte de Grâce Walk

For good exercise and a bird's-eye view of Honfleur and the Normandy Bridge, take the steep 20-minute walk (or quick drive) up to the Côte de Grâce—best in the early morning or at sunset. From Ste. Catherine Church, walk or drive up Rue du Puits, then follow the blue-on-white signs to reach the splendid view over Honfleur at the top of the ramp (benches and information plaque). *Piétons* (walkers) should veer right up La Rampe du Mont Joli; *conducteurs* (drivers) should keep straight. Walkers can continue past the view for about 300 yards to the **Chapel of Notre-Dame de Grâce.** Built in the early 1600s by the mariners and people of Honfleur, the church oozes seafaring mementos. Model boats hang from the ceiling, pictures of boats balance high on the walls, and several stained-glass windows are decorated with images of sailors praying to the Virgin Mary while at sea. Even the holy water basins to the left and right of the entrance are in the shape of seashells. Find the church bells hanging on a wood rack to the right as you leave the church and imagine the racket they could make (daily 8:30-17:15).

Below the chapel, a lookout offers a sweeping view of super-industrial Le Havre, with the Manche (English Channel) to your left and the (just visible) Normandy Bridge to your right.

Jetty/Park Walk

Take a level stroll in Honfleur along the water past the Hôtel le Cheval Blanc to find the mouth of the Seine River and big ships at sea. You'll pass kid-friendly parks carpeted with flowers and grass, and continue past the lock connecting Honfleur to the Seine and the sea. Grand and breezy vistas of the sea and smashing views of the Normandy Bridge reward the diligent walker (allow 20 minutes from the harbor to reach the best views).

NEAR HONFLEUR

Boat Excursions

Boat trips in and around Honfleur depart from various docks between Hôtel le Cheval Blanc and the opposite end of the outer port (Easter-Oct usually about 11:00-17:00). The tour boat *Calypso* takes good 45-minute spins around Honfleur's harbor (€6, mobile 06 71 64 50 46). Other cruises run to the Normandy Bridge (described next), which, unfortunately, means two boring trips through the locks (€9.50/1.5 hours, choose between *Jolie France,* mobile 06 71 64 50 46, or *Les Vedettes Cauchois* near Hôtel le Cheval Blanc, mobile 06 31 89 21 10).

▲Normandy Bridge (Pont de Normandie)

The 1.25-mile-long Normandy Bridge is the longest cable-stayed bridge in the Western world (€5.50 toll each way). This is a key piece of European expressway that links the Atlantic ports from Belgium to Spain. View the bridge from Honfleur (better from an excursion boat or the Jetty Walk described earlier, and best at night, when bridge is floodlit). Also consider visiting the bridge's free Exhibition Hall (under tollbooth on Le Havre side, daily 8:00-19:00). The Seine finishes its winding 500-mile journey here, dropping only 1,500 feet from its source, 450 miles away. The river flows so slowly that, in certain places, a stiff breeze can send it flowing upstream.

▲Etrétat

France's answer to the White Cliffs of Dover, these chalky cliffs soar high above a calm, crescent beach (from Honfleur, it's about 50 minutes by car or 2 hours by bus via Le Havre). Walking trails lead hikers from the small seaside resort of Etrétat along a vertiginous route with sensational views (and crowds of hikers in summer and on weekends). You'll recognize these cliffs—and the arches and stone spire that decorate them—from countless Impressionist paintings, including several at the Eugène Boudin Museum in Honfleur. The small, Coney Island-like town holds plenty of cafés and a **TI** (Place Maurice Guillard, tel. 02 35 27 05 21, www.etretat.net).

Getting There: Etrétat is north of Le Havre. To get here by car, cross the Normandy Bridge and follow A-29, then exit at *sortie Etrétat.* Buses serve Etrétat from Le Havre's *gare routière,* adjacent to the train station (5/day, 1 hour, www.keolis-seine-maritime.com).

Sleeping in Etrétat: **$$$ Hôtel Dormy** makes a nice splurge if the scenery moves you (Db-€140-330, Route du Havre at the edge of Etrétat, tel. 02 35 27 07 88, www.dormy-house.com, info@etretat-hotel.com).

Sleeping in Honfleur

Though Honfleur is popular in summer, it's busiest on weekends and holidays (blame Paris). English is widely spoken (blame vacationing Brits). A few moderate accommodations remain, but most hotels are pretty pricey.

Only two hotels have elevators (Hôtel le Cheval Blanc and Ibis Budget Honfleur), but Hotel Monet has ground-floor rooms. All hotels have free Wi-Fi unless noted.

HOTELS

$$$ Hôtel le Cheval Blanc***, a Best Western, is a waterfront splurge with port views from all of its 35 plush and pricey rooms (many with queen-size beds), plus a rare-in-this-town elevator and a spa, but no air-conditioning—noise can be a problem with windows open (small Db with lesser view-€155, Db with full port view-€180-230, family rooms/suites-€280-435, must cancel by 16:00 the day before or forfeit deposit, Wi-Fi, breakfast-€13, 2 Quai des Passagers, tel. 02 31 81 65 00, www.hotel-honfleur.com, info@hotel-honfleur.com).

$$$ L'Absinthe Hôtel*** offers 11 tastefully restored rooms with king-size beds in two locations. Rooms in the main (reception) section come with wood-beamed decor and Jacuzzi tubs, and share a cozy public lounge with a fireplace (Db-€160-210). Five rooms are located above their next-door restaurant and have port views and four-star, state-of-the-art comfort, including air-conditioning and saunas (Db-€170-200, Db suite-€275; breakfast-€13, private parking-€13, 1 Rue de la Ville, tel. 02 31 89 23 23, www.absinthe.fr, reservation@absinthe.fr).

$$$ Hôtel de l'Ecrin*** is a true Old World refuge. Enter the private courtyard to find a vintage mansion with immaculate gardens around ample grass, a big pool, a sauna and Jacuzzi, and public spaces Eugène Boudin would appreciate. Rooms are *très* traditional —some have four-poster *grand lits* (Db-€120, bigger Db-€145-165, big suites-€200-250, Wi-Fi, free and secure parking, 10 minutes by foot from the harbor at 19 Rue Eugène Boudin, tel. 02 31 14 43 45, www.honfleur.com, hotel.ecrin@honfleur.com).

$$$ Hôtel du Dauphin*** is centrally located, with a colorful lounge/breakfast room, many narrow stairs (normal in Honfleur), and an Escher-esque floor plan. The 30 mostly smallish rooms—some with open-beam ceilings, some with queen- or king-size beds—provide reasonable comfort for the price. If you need a lower floor or bigger bed, request it when you book (Db-€114, Tb-€125-155, Qb-€175, breakfast-€13, Wi-Fi in lobby only, a stone's throw from Ste. Catherine Church at 10 Place Pierre Berthelot, tel. 02 31 89 15 53, www.hoteldudauphin.com, info@hoteldudauphin.com). The same owners also run the **$$$ Hôtel des Loges*****, a few doors up, which offers larger rooms with Wi-Fi, but less personality (same prices). Both hotels offer the first breakfast free for Rick Steves readers in 2015 if you book direct—mention when you reserve and show this book at check-in.

$$ Hôtel Monet**, on the road to the Côte de Grâce and a 10-minute walk down to the port (longer back up), is an overlooked find. This tranquil spot houses 16 mostly tight but good-value rooms facing a courtyard, many with a patio made for picnics. You'll meet welcoming owners Christophe and Sylvie (Db-€65-105, Tb-€80-115, Qb-€95-150, highest rates are for July-Sept, free and easy parking, Wi-Fi, Charrière du Puits, tel. 02 31 89 00 90, www.hotel-monet.fr, contact@hotel-monet-honfleur.com). Reception is closed from 13:00-17:00.

$$ Hôtel Les Cascades, across from the TI and a few blocks from the bus station, delivers basic comfort in a central location at fair prices. The 17 rooms have only double beds (some with two) and the hotel plays second fiddle to its restaurant, so don't expect attentive service (Db-€78, breakfast-€8, 19 Cours des Fossés, tel. 02 31 89 05 83, www.lescascades.com, info@lescascades.com).

$ Ibis Budget Honfleur is modern, efficient, trim, and cheap, with prefab bathrooms and an antiseptically clean ambience (Sb/Db/Tb-€44-66, cheaper off-season, reception is closed 21:00-6:00 but automatic check-in with credit card available 24 hours, elevator, Wi-Fi, across from bus station and main parking lot on Rue des Vases, tel. 08 92 68 07 81, www.ibisbudget.com, h2716-re@accor.com).

CHAMBRES D'HOTES

The TI has a long list of Honfleur's many *chambres d'hôtes* (rooms in private homes), but most are too far from the town center. Those listed here are good values.

$$$ At **Le Fond de la Cour,** British expats Amanda and Craig offer a good mix of accommodations around a peaceful courtyard. There's a large cottage that can sleep six, three apartments with small kitchens, and three standard doubles (Db-€95-130, Tb-€130-160, extra person-€30, short apartment stays possible, standard rooms include English-style breakfast, Wi-Fi, free street parking, private parking-€9/day, 29 Rue Eugène Boudin, tel. 09 62 31 24 30, mobile 06 72 20 72 98, www.lefonddelacour.com, amanda.ferguson@orange.fr).

$$ La Cour Ste. Catherine, kitty-corner to Le Fond de la Cour, is an enchanting bed-and-breakfast run by the open-hearted Madame Giaglis ("call me Liliane") and her big-hearted husband, Monsieur Liliane (a.k.a. Antoine). Their six big, modern rooms—each with firm beds and a separate sitting area—surround a perfectly Norman courtyard with a small terrace, fine plantings, and a cozy lounge area ideal for cool evenings. The rooms are as cheery as the owner—ask about her coffee shop (Db-€90, Db suite-€140, Tb/Qb-€150, extra bed-€30, includes breakfast, small apartments that sleep up to 6 and cottage with kitchen also available, cash only, guest computer, Wi-Fi, free parking in 2015 with this book if reservation made direct, 200 yards up Rue du Puits from Ste. Catherine Church at #74, tel. 02 31 89 42 40, www.coursaintecatherine.com, coursaintecatherine@orange.fr).

Eating in Honfleur

Eat seafood or cream sauces here. It's a tough choice between the irresistible waterfront tables of the many look-alike places lining the harbor and the eateries with good reputations elsewhere in town. Trust my dinner suggestions and consider your hotelier's opinion. It's best to call ahead to reserve at most restaurants in Honfleur (particularly on weekends).

Le Bouilland Normand hides a block off the port on a pleasing square and offers a true Norman experience at reasonable prices. Claire and chef-hubbie Bruno provide quality *Normand* cuisine and enjoy serving travelers. Daily specials complement the classic offerings (€22-30 *menus,* closed Wed, dine inside or out, on Rue de la Ville, tel. 02 31 89 02 41, www.aubouillonnormand.fr).

Le Bacaretto wine bar-café is run by laid-back Hervé, the antithesis of a wine snob. This relaxed and tiny wine-soaked place offers a fine selection of wines by the glass for good prices and a small but appealing assortment of appetizers and *plats du jour* that can make a full meal (closed Wed-Thu, 44 Rue de la Chaussée, tel. 02 31 14 83 11).

Côté Resto saddles up on the left side of Ste. Catherine Church and serves a top selection of seafood in a classy setting. The value is excellent for those in search of a special meal (€24 two-course *menu,* €30 three-course *menu,* great selection, closed Thu, 8 Place Ste. Catherine, tel. 02 31 89 31 33, www.cote-resto-honfleur.com).

Bistro des Artistes is a two-woman operation and the joy of locals (call ahead for a window table). Hardworking Anne-Marie cooks from a select repertoire upstairs while her server takes care of business in the pleasant little dining room. Portions are huge and very homemade; order only one course and maybe a dessert (€18-26 *plats,* closed Wed, 30 Place Berthelot, tel. 02 31 89 95 90).

Au P'tit Mareyeur is whisper-formal, intimate, all about seafood, and a good value. The ground floor and upstairs rooms offer equal comfort and ambience (€35 four-course *menu,* €35 famous Bouillabaisse Honfleuraise, closed Tue-Wed and Jan, 4 Rue Haute, tel. 02 31 98 84 23, mobile 06 84 33 24 03, www.auptitmareyeur.fr, friendly owner Julie speaks some English).

L'Homme de Bois combines way-cozy ambience with authentic Norman cuisine and good prices (€23 three-course *menu* with few choices, €26 *menu* gives more choices, daily, a few outside tables, 30 Rue de l'Homme de Bois, tel. 02 31 89 75 27).

Travel Coffee Shop is an ideal breakfast or lunch option for travelers wanting conversation—in either English or French—and good food at very fair prices (May-Sept 8:00-17:00, closed Wed, April and Oct-Nov Sat-Sun only, closed Dec-March, 6 Place du Puits).

Dining Along the Harbor: If the weather cooperates, slide down to the harbor and table-shop the joints that line the high side. Several places have effective propane heaters. Although the cuisine is mostly mediocre, the setting is uniquely Honfleur—and, on a languid evening, hard to pass up. Take a stroll along the port and compare restaurant views, chair comfort, and menu selection (all of these places look the same to me). If you dine elsewhere, come here for a before- or after-dinner drink—see "Nightlife," below.

Of the harborfront options, **Café de l'Hôtel de Ville** owns the best afternoon sun exposure (and charges for it) and looks across to Honfleur's soaring homes (open daily July-Aug, closed Tue off-season, Place de l'Hôtel de Ville, tel. 02 31 89 07 29).

Breakfast: If it's even close to sunny, skip your hotel breakfast and enjoy ambience for a cheaper price by eating on the port, where several cafés offer *petit déjeuner* (€3-7 for continental fare, €7-13 for more elaborate choices). Morning sun and views are best from the high side of the harbor. If price or companionship matter, head to the Travel Coffee Shop for the best breakfast deal in town (described earlier).

Dessert: Honfleur is ice-cream crazy, with gelato and traditional ice-cream shops on every corner. If you need a Ben & Jerry's ice-cream fix or a scrumptious dessert crêpe, find the **waterfront stand** at the southeast corner of the Vieux Bassin.

Nighttime Food to Go: Order a tasty pizza to go until late from **Il Parasole** (2 Rue Haute, tel. 02 31 98 94 29), and enjoy a picnic dinner with port views a few steps away in front of the La Lieutenance gatehouse.

Nightlife: Nightlife in Honfleur centers on the old port. Several bar/cafés line the high-building side of the port. These two are Honfleur's down-and-dirty watering holes: **L'Albatross** (pub-like with flags, banners, and a loyal following—including me) and **Le Perroquet Vert** (also cool but more existential—"those lights are so...").

Le Vintage, just off the port, is a happening bar/café with live piano and jazz on weekend nights. Casual outdoor seating and a vigorous interior make this a fun choice (closed Tue, 8 Quai des Passagers, tel. 02 31 89 05 28).

Honfleur Connections

There's no direct train service to Honfleur, so you must take a bus to or from a city with rail service. The express PrestoBus—line #39—which links Honfleur with Caen and Le Havre is handy, but runs only two or three times a day. Non-express bus routes also connect Honfleur with Le Havre, Caen, Deauville, and Lisieux—all with direct rail service to Paris. Bus #50 runs between Le Havre, Honfleur, and Lisieux; bus #20 connects Le Havre, Honfleur, Deauville, and Caen. Although train and bus service usually are coordinated, confirm your connection with the helpful staff at Honfleur's bus station (English information desk open Mon-Fri 9:30-12:00 & 13:00-18:00, in summer also Sat-Sun, tel. 02 31 89 28 41, www.busverts.fr). If the station is closed, you can get schedules at the TI. Rail-pass holders will save money by connecting through Deauville, as bus fares increase with distance (Deauville to Honfleur-€2.40, Lisieux to Honfleur-€4.70).

From Honfleur by Bus and/or Train to: Caen (express PrestoBus 2-3/day, 1 hour; more scenic *par la côte* bus #20 4/day direct, 2 hours); **Bayeux** (2-3/day, 1.5 hours; first take PrestoBus to Caen, then 20-minute train to Bayeux, more via scenic bus #20 via the coast to Caen); **Rouen** (6/day Mon-Sat, 3/day Sun, bus-and-train combo involves 30-minute bus ride over Normandy Bridge to Le Havre, then easy transfer to 1-hour train to Rouen); **Paris'** Gare St. Lazare (13/day, 2.5-3.5 hours, by bus to Caen, Lisieux, Deauville, or Le Havre, then train to Paris; buses from Honfleur meet most Paris trains).

Driving Connections: If driving to Rouen, see the Route of the Ancient Abbeys on page 252, and if connecting to the D-Day beaches, consider taking the scenic route "*par la Côte*" to Trouville and pass sea views, thatched hamlets, and stupendous mansions. From Honfleur, drive to the port, pass Hôtel du Cheval Blanc, and stick to this road (D-513) to Trouville, then follow signs for A-13 to Caen.

Bayeux

Only six miles from the D-Day beaches, Bayeux was the first city liberated after the landing. Incredibly, the town was spared the bombs of World War II. After a local chaplain made sure London knew that his city was not a German headquarters and was of no strategic importance, a scheduled bombing raid was canceled—making Bayeux the closest city to the D-Day landing site not destroyed. Even without its famous medieval tapestry and proximity to the D-Day beaches, Bayeux would be worth a visit for its enjoyable town center and awe-inspiring cathedral, beautifully illuminated at night. Bayeux makes an ideal home base for visiting the area's sights, particularly if you lack a car.

Orientation to Bayeux

TOURIST INFORMATION

The TI is on a small bridge two blocks north of the cathedral. Ask for the free *Exploration and Emotion: The Historical Area of the Battle of Normandy* booklet, bus schedules to the beaches, and regional information, and inquire about special events and concerts (TI open July-Aug Mon-Sat 9:00-19:00, Sun 9:00-13:00 & 14:00-18:00; Sept-June, Mon-Sat 9:30-12:30 & 14:00-18:00, Sun 10:00-13:00 & 14:00-18:00, on Pont St. Jean leading to Rue St. Jean, tel. 02 31 51 28 28, www.bessin-normandie.com).

For a **self-guided walking tour,** pick up the map called *Découvrez Vieux Bayeux* at the TI. Follow the bronze plates embedded in the sidewalk, and look for information plaques with English translations that correspond to your map.

Museum Pass: Bayeux's three main museums—the Bayeux Tapestry, Battle of Normandy Memorial Museum, and MAHB—offer combo-tickets that will save you money if you plan to see more than one sight. Combo-tickets covering two sights cost €12; for all three it's €15 (buy it at the first sight you visit).

ARRIVAL IN BAYEUX

By Train and Bus: Trains and buses share the same station (no bag storage). It's a 15-minute walk from the station to the tapestry, and 15 minutes from the tapestry to Place St. Patrice (and several recommended hotels). To reach the tapestry, the cathedral, and the hotels, cross the major street in front of the station and follow Rue de Cremel toward *l'Hôpital*, then turn left on Rue Nesmond. Find signs to the *Tapisserie* or continue on to the cathedral. Taxis are usually waiting at the station. Allow €8 for a taxi from the train station to any recommended hotel or sight in Bayeux, and €22 to

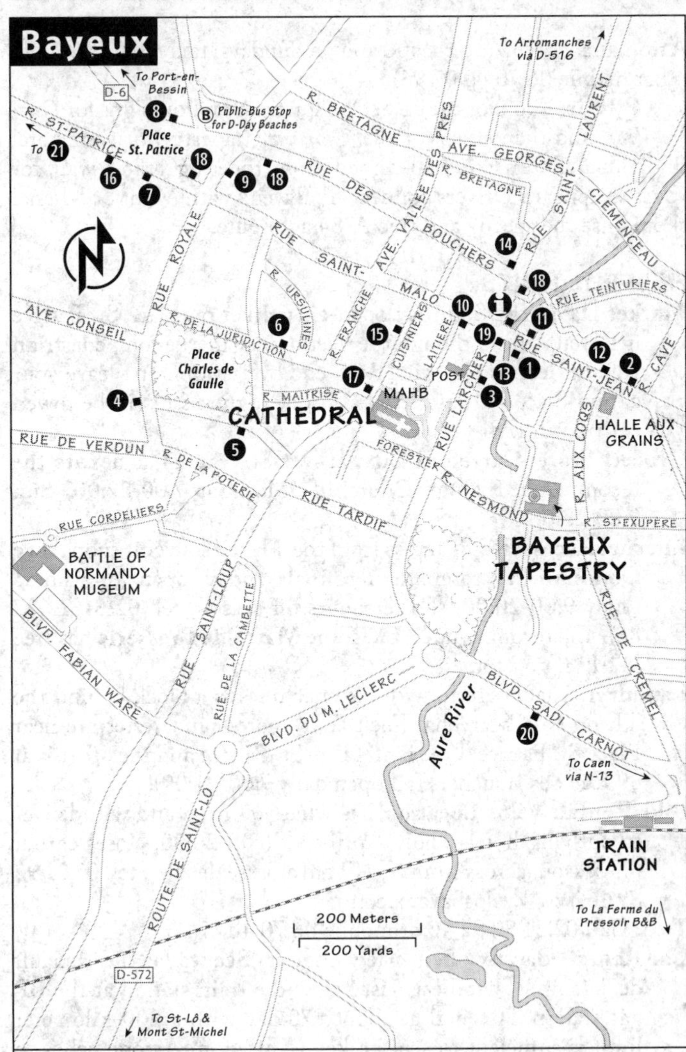

1. Villa Lara, Hôtel Churchill & Carrefour City Grocery
2. Hôtel le Lion d'Or
3. Hôtel Reine Mathilde & Brasserie
4. Le Petit Matin
5. Logis les Remparts B&B
6. Manoir Sainte Victoire
7. Hôtel d'Argouges
8. Hôtel de Sainte Croix
9. Hôtel Mogador
10. Hôtel le Maupassant & Café
11. La Chaumière Deli
12. La Rapière Restaurant
13. Le Volet Qui Penche
14. L'Angle Saint Laurent
15. Le Pommier Restaurant
16. Taverne des Ducs
17. Lace Conservatory
18. Launderettes (3)
19. Bike Rental & Internet Café
20. Scauto Car Rental
21. To Hertz Car Rental

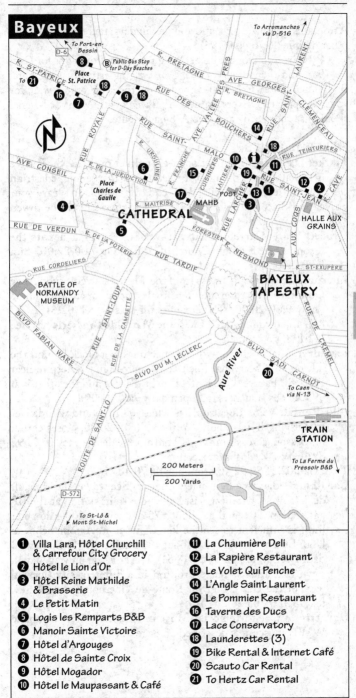

Arromanches (€32 after 19:00 and on Sundays, taxi tel. 02 31 92 92 40 or mobile 06 70 40 07 96).

By Car: Look for the cathedral spires and follow signs for *Centre-Ville,* and then signs for the *Tapisserie* (tapestry) or your hotel (individual hotels are well-signed from the ring road—wait for yours to appear). Drivers connecting Bayeux with Mont St-Michel should use the speedy and free A-84 autoroute.

HELPFUL HINTS

Market Days: The Saturday open-air market on Place St. Patrice is Bayeux's best, though the Wednesday market on pedestrian Rue St. Jean is pleasant. Both end by 13:00. Don't leave your car on Place St. Patrice on a Friday night, as it will be towed early Saturday.

Grocery Store: Carrefour City, at Rue St. Jean 14, is next to the recommended Hôtel Churchill (Mon-Sat 7:00-22:00, Sun 9:00-13:00).

Internet Access: Right across from the TI, the souvenir shop **Aure Commun** has computer terminals and is open long hours (daily 9:00-20:00, shorter hours off-season, tel. 02 31 22 27 86). The recommended **La Reine Mathilde Brasserie** has free Wi-Fi for customers.

Laundry: A launderette with big machines is a block behind the TI, on Rue Maréchal Foch. Two more launderettes are near Place St. Patrice: One is at 4 Rue St. Patrice and the other is at 69 Rue des Bouchers (all open daily 7:00-21:00).

Bike Rental: Vélos Location has what you need and will deliver to outlying hotels (daily April-Oct 8:00-20:30, closes earlier off-season, across from the TI at Impasse de Islet, tel. 02 31 92 89 16, www.velosbayeux.com).

Taxi: Call 02 31 92 92 40 or mobile 06 70 40 07 96.

Car Rental: Bayeux offers a few choices. **Scauto** (at the Renault dealership) is handiest, just below the train station at the BP gas station. A rental at about €70/day with a 200-kilometer limit is sufficient to see the key sights from Arromanches to Utah Beach—you'll drive about 180 kilometers (16 Boulevard Sadi Carnot, tel. 02 31 51 18 51). **Hertz** is the only agency in town that allows you to drop off in a different city (located west of the city center on Route de Cherbourg, off D-613, tel. 02 31 92 03 26).

Day Trip to Caen Memorial Museum: France's most complete WWII museum is described on page 311.

Sights in Bayeux

▲▲▲Bayeux Tapestry (Tapisserie de Bayeux)

Made of wool embroidered onto linen cloth, this historically precious document is a mesmerizing 70-yard-long cartoon. The tapestry tells the story of William the Conqueror's rise from duke of Normandy to king of England, and shows his victory over England's King Harold at the Battle of Hastings in 1066. Long and skinny, the tapestry was designed to hang in the nave of Bayeux's cathedral as a reminder for locals of their ancestor's courage. The terrific museum that houses the tapestry is an unusually good chance to teach your kids about the Middle Ages: Models, mannequins, a movie, and more make it an engaging, fun place to visit.

Cost and Hours: €9, combo-ticket with other Bayeux museums €12 or €15, includes an excellent audioguide for adults and a special kids' version, daily May-Aug 9:00-18:15, March-April and Sept-Oct 9:00-17:45, Nov-Feb 9:30-11:45 & 14:00-17:15—these are first and last entry times, tel. 02 31 51 25 50, www.bayeuxmuseum.com. To avoid crowds, arrive by 9:00 or late in the day.

Film: When buying your ticket, ask when they'll show the English version of the 15-minute battle film (runs every 40 minutes, English times also posted at the base of the steps to the theater).

Visiting the Museum: Your visit has three separate parts that tell the basic story of the Battle of Hastings, provide historical context for the event, and explain how the tapestry was made. At a minimum, allow a full hour to appreciate this important artifact.

Your visit starts with the actual **tapestry,** accompanied by an included audioguide that gives a top-notch, fast-moving, 20-minute scene-by-scene narration complete with period music (if you lose your place, find subtitles in Latin). To keep crowds moving from May through September, the audioguide's pause and rewind functions are disabled, though these are helpful to use off-season. Appreciate the fun details—such as the bare legs in scene 4 or Harold's pouting expressions in various frames—and look for references to places you may have visited (like Dinan). Pay strict attention to scene 23, where Harold takes his oath to William; the importance of keeping one's word is the point of the tapestry. Get close and (almost) feel the tapestry's texture.

Next you'll climb upstairs into a room filled with engaging

Bayeux History—The Battle of Hastings

Because of this pivotal battle, the most memorable date of the Middle Ages is 1066. England's king, Edward the Confessor, was about to die without an heir. The big question: Who would succeed him—Harold, an English nobleman and the king's brother-in-law, or William, duke of Normandy and the king's cousin? Edward chose William, and sent Harold to Normandy to give William the news. On the journey, Harold was captured. To win his release, he promised he would be loyal to William and not contest the decision. To test his loyalty, William sent Harold to battle for him in Brittany. Harold was successful, and William knighted him. To further test his loyalty, William had Harold swear on the relics of the Bayeux cathedral that when Edward died, he would allow William to ascend the throne. Harold returned to England, Edward died...and Harold grabbed the throne.

William, known as William the Bastard, invaded England to claim the throne. Harold met him in southern England at the town of Hastings, where their forces fought a fierce 14-hour battle. Harold was killed, and his Saxon forces were routed. William—now "the Conqueror"—marched to London, claimed his throne, and became king of England (though he spoke no English) as well as duke of Normandy.

The advent of a Norman king of England muddied the political waters and set in motion 400 years of conflict between England and France—not to be resolved until the end of the Hundred Years' War (1453). The Norman conquest of England brought that country into the European mainstream (but still no euros). The Normans established a strong central English government. Historians speculate that had William not succeeded, England would have remained on the fringe of Europe (like Scandinavia), and French culture (and language) would have prevailed in the New World—which would have meant no communication issues for us in France. Hmmm.

exhibits, including a full-size replica of a Viking ship much like the one William used to cross the Channel (Normans inherited their weaponry and seafaring skills from the Norsemen). You'll also see mannequins (find William looking unmoved with his new crown), a replica of the Domesday Book (an inventory of noble's lands as ordered by William), and models of castles (who knew that the Tower of London was a Norman project?). Good explanations outline the events surrounding the invasion and the subsequent creation of the tapestry. Your visit finishes with a 15-minute **film** that ties it all together one last time (in the cinema, skippable if you're pressed for time). You'll exit below, through a *formidable* boutique.

Remember, this is Norman propaganda—the English (the bad guys, referred to as *les goddamns,* after a phrase the French kept hearing them say) are shown with mustaches and long hair; the French (*les* good guys) are clean-cut and clean-shaven—with even the backs of their heads shaved for a better helmet fit.

▲▲Bayeux Cathedral

This massive building, as big as Paris' Notre-Dame, dominates the small town of Bayeux. (Make it a point to see the cathedral after dark, when it's beautifully illuminated.)

Cost and Hours: Free, daily July-Aug 8:30-19:00, Sept-June 8:30-18:00.

Visiting the Cathedral: To start your visit, find the small **square** opposite the front entry (information board about the cathedral in rear corner). Notice the two dark towers—originally Romanesque, they were capped later with tall Gothic spires. The cathedral's west facade is structurally Romanesque, but with a decorative Gothic "curtain" added.

Before entering, head just to the left of the cathedral, find the stairs at the top of a walking lane, and crane your neck up. The little rectangular stone house atop the near tower was the **watchman's home,** from which he'd keep an eye out for incoming English troops during the Hundred Years' War...and for Germans five centuries later (it didn't work—the Germans took the town in 1940). Bayeux was liberated on D-Day plus one: June 7. About the only casualty was the German lookout—shot while doing just that from the window of this stone house.

Now step inside the cathedral. The magnificent view of the **nave** from the top of the steps shows a mix of Romanesque (ground floor) and soaring Gothic (upper floors). Historians believe the Bayeux tapestry originally hung here. Imagine it hanging halfway up the big Romanesque arches. This section is brightly lit by the huge windows above, in the Gothic half of the nave. Try to visualize this scene with the original, richly colored stained glass in all those upper windows. Rare 13th-century stained-glass bits are in the high central window above the altar; the other stained glass is from the 19th and 20th centuries.

Walk down the nave and notice the areas between the big, round **arches.** That busy zigzag patterning characterizes Norman art in France as well as in England. These 11th-century Romanesque arches are decorated with a manic mix of repeated geometric shapes: half-circles, interlocking hatch marks, full circles, and diagonal lines. Notice also the creepy faces eyeing you, especially the ring of devil heads three arches up on the right. Yuck.

Information panels in the side aisles give basic facts about the cathedral (in English). More 13th-century Norman Gothic is in the choir (the fancy area behind the central altar). Here, simple Romanesque carvings lie under Gothic arches with characteristic tall, thin lines adding a graceful verticality to the overall feel of the interior.

For maximum 1066 atmosphere, step into the spooky **crypt** (beneath the central altar), which was used originally as a safe spot for the cathedral's relics. The crypt displays two freestanding columns and bulky capitals with fine Romanesque carving. During a reinforcement of the nave, these two columns were replaced. Workers removed the Gothic veneer and discovered their true inner Romanesque beauty. Orange angel-musicians on other columns add color to this somber room.

River Walk

Join the locals and promenade along the meandering walking path that follows the little Aure River for about 2.5 miles through Bayeux. The path runs both ways from the TI (find the waterwheel behind the TI and keep walking; path marked on city maps).

Lace Conservatory (Conservatoire de la Dentelle)

Notable for its carved 15th-century facade, the Adam and Eve house (find Adam, Eve, and the snake) offers a chance to watch workers design and weave intricate lace, just as artisans did in the 1600s. Enter to the clicking sound of the small wooden bobbins used by the lace-makers, and appreciate the concentration that their work requires. You can also see examples of lace from the past and pick up some nifty souvenirs.

Cost and Hours: Free, Mon-Sat 9:30-12:30 & 14:30-18:00, until 17:00 Mon-Sat, closed Sun, across from cathedral entrance, tel. 02 31 92 73 80, http://dentelledebayeux.free.fr.

MAHB (Musée d'Art et d'Histoire Baron Gérard)

For a break from D-Day and tapestries, MAHB offers a modest review of European art and history in what was once the Bayeux bishop's palace. The core of the museum is a collection of 18th- and 19th-century paintings donated by Baron Henri-Alexandre Gérard more than a century ago. Notable are an early work by neoclassical master Jacques-Louis David—*Le Philosophe (The Philosopher)*—and *Sapho* by Antoine-Jean Gros, a moonlit version of the Greek poetess' death that influenced Géricault and Delacroix. Don't miss the museum's 19th-century courtroom and its elaborate chapel—gushing with early 17th-century "angels" that look like oversexed cherubs.

Cost and Hours: €7, combo-ticket with other Bayeux museums €12 or €15, daily May-Sept 9:30-12:30 & 14:00-18:30, shorter hours off-season, near the cathedral at 37 Rue du Bienvenu, tel. 02 31 92 14 21, www.bayeuxmuseum.com.

▲Battle of Normandy Memorial Museum (Musée Mémorial de la Bataille de Normandie)

This museum provides a manageable overview of WWII's Battle of Normandy. With its many maps and timelines of the epic battle to liberate northern France, it's aimed at military history buffs but is worthwhile for many, especially if you won't be visiting Caen's WWII museum. You'll get a good briefing on the Atlantic Wall (the German fortifications stretching along the coast—useful before visiting Longues-sur-Mer), learn why Normandy was selected as the landing site, understand General Charles de Gaulle's contributions to the invasion, and realize the key role played by aviation. You'll also appreciate the challenges faced by doctors, war correspondents, and civil engineers (who had to clean up after the battles—the gargantuan bulldozer on display looks useful).

Cost and Hours: €6, combo-ticket with other Bayeux museums €12 or €15, daily May-Sept 9:30-18:30, Oct-Dec and mid-Feb-April 10:00-12:30 & 14:00-18:00, closed Jan-mid-Feb, on Bayeux's ring road, 20 minutes on foot from center on Boulevard Fabian Ware, tel. 02 31 51 46 90, www.normandiememoire.com.

Film: A 25-minute film gives a good summary of the Normandy invasion from start to finish (shown in English May-Sept at 10:30, 12:00, 14:00, 15:30, and 17:00; Oct-April at 10:30, 14:45, and 16:15).

Nearby: A right out of the museum leads along a footpath to the **Monument to Reporters,** a grassy walkway lined with white roses and stone monuments listing, by year, the names of reporters who have died in the line of duty from 1944 to today. Some years have been kinder to journalists than others. The path continues to the **British Military Cemetery,** decorated with 4,144 simple gravestones marking the final resting places of these fallen soldiers. The memorial's Latin inscription reads, "In 1944, the British came to free the homeland of William the Conqueror." Interestingly, this cemetery has soldiers' graves from all countries involved in the battle of Normandy (even Germany) except the United States, which requires its soldiers to be buried on US property—such as the American Cemetery at Omaha Beach.

Sleeping in Bayeux

I list hotels in every price range here. Drivers should also see "Sleeping in Arromanches" (page 295). All hotels have free Wi-Fi unless noted.

NEAR THE TAPESTRY

$$$ Villa Lara**** owns the town's most luxurious accommodations smack in the center of Bayeux. The 28 spacious and well-configured rooms all have brilliant views of the cathedral, and a few have small terraces. Helpful owner Rima and her well-trained staff take excellent care of their guests (Db-€260-350, Db suite-€390-520, pricey but excellent breakfast-€22, elevator, Wi-Fi, exercise room, ice machines, comfortable lounges, free and secure parking, between the tapestry museum and TI at 6 Place de Québec, tel. 02 31 21 31 80, www.hotel-villalara.com, info@hotel-villalara.com).

$$$ Hôtel Churchill*,** on a traffic-free street across from the TI, could not be more central. Owners Eric and Patricia are great hosts (ask Eric about his professional soccer career). The hotel has 32 plush-and-pricey rooms with wood furnishings, big beds, and convivial public spaces peppered with historic photos of Bayeux's liberation (small Db-€130, bigger Db-€155, deluxe Db or Tb-€187, Qb-€210, Wi-Fi, 14 Rue St. Jean, tel. 02 31 21 31 80, www.hotel-churchill.fr, info@hotel-churchill.fr).

$$$ Hôtel le Lion d'Or*,** General Eisenhower's favorite hotel in Bayeux, draws a loyal, American and British clientele who love the historic aspect of staying here. It's an Old World place with updated rooms and responsive staff (standard Db-€130-140, bigger Db-€140-175, extra bed-€30, breakfast-€13, no elevator, Wi-Fi, limited but secure parking-€9/day, 71 Rue St. Jean, tel. 02 31 92 06 90, www.liondor-bayeux.fr, info@liondor-bayeux.fr).

$$ Hôtel Reine Mathilde** is a solid, centrally located value with good service. There are 16 sharp rooms above an easygoing brasserie (Db-€85), and six large rooms with three-star comfort in an annex next door (Db-€115-125, Tb-€125-145, Qb-€145-170, breakfast-€9.50, Wi-Fi, one block from the TI at 23 Rue Larcher, tel. 02 31 92 08 13, www.hotel-bayeux-reinemathilde.fr, hotel.reinemathilde@orange.fr).

CHAMBRES D'HOTES NEAR THE CATHEDRAL

$$$ Le Petit Matin, run by friendly Pascal, is a central and handsome five-room bed-and-breakfast with good public spaces, big bathrooms, and a *magnifique* back garden (with play toys) on Place Charles de Gaulle (Db-€100, 9 Rue des Terres, tel. 02 31 10 09 27, www.lepetitmatin.com, lepetitmatin@hotmail.fr).

$$ Logis les Remparts, run by bubbly Christèle, is a delightful, three-room bed-and-breakfast situated above an atmospheric Calvados cider-tasting shop. The rooms are big, comfortable, and homey—one is a huge, two-room suite (Db-€65-90, Tb-€80-110, cash only for payments under €100, breakfast-€7, a few blocks above the cathedral on the park-like Place Charles de Gaulle at 4 Rue Bourbesneur, tel. 02 31 92 50 40, www.lecornu.fr, info@lecornu.fr).

$$ Manoir Sainte Victoire is a classy, 17th-century building with three dolled-up rooms, each dedicated to a different modern artist. The rooms have small kitchenettes and views of the cathedral (Db-€90, includes breakfast, 32 Rue de la Jurisdiction, tel. 02 31 22 74 69, mobile 06 37 36 90 95, www.manoirsaintevictoire.com, contact@manoirsaintevictoire.com).

NEAR PLACE ST. PATRICE

These hotels just off the big Place St. Patrice (easy parking) are a 10-minute walk up Rue St. Martin from the TI (a 15-minute walk to the tapestry).

$$$ Hôtel d'Argouges*** (dar-goozh) is named for its builder, Lord d'Argouges. This tranquil retreat has a mini-château feel with classy public spaces, lovely private gardens, and standard-comfort rooms. The hotel is run by formal Madame Ropartz, who has had every aspect of the hotel renovated (Db-€140-160, Tb-€193, fine family suites-€245, deluxe family-suite-€360 for up to 6—works fine for two couples, extra bed-€15, includes good breakfast, no elevator, secure free parking, just off Place St. Patrice at 21 Rue St. Patrice, tel. 02 31 92 88 86, www.hotel-dargouges.com, info@hotel-dargouges.com).

$$ B&B Hôtel de Sainte Croix offers three big rooms with cavernous bathrooms in a traditional manor home (Db-€94, Tb-€135, Qb-€165, cash only, includes good breakfast, 12 Rue du Marché at Place St. Patrice, mobile 06 08 09 62 69, www.hotel-de-sainte-croix.com, contact@hotel-de-sainte-croix.com, friendly Florence).

$$ Hôtel Mogador** is a simple but good budget value. Choose between wood-beamed rooms on the busy square, or quiet but slightly faded rooms off the street. There are no public areas beyond the small breakfast room and tiny courtyard (Sb-€55, Db-€66, Tb-€77, Qb-€89, breakfast-€9, Wi-Fi, 20 Rue Alain Chartier at Place St. Patrice, tel. 02 31 92 24 58, www.hotelmo.fr, lemogador@gmail.com).

$ Hôtel le Maupassant offers 10 no-star, no-frills rooms with just enough comfort. The rooms are above a central café, and the bartender doubles as the receptionist (S-€35, D-€45, Db-€48, Ts-€75, Wi-Fi, 19 Rue St. Martin, tel. 02 31 92 28 53, h.lemaupassant@orange.fr).

IN THE COUNTRYSIDE NEAR BAYEUX

$$ La Ferme du Pressoir is a lovely, traditional B&B on a big working farm that is immersed in Norman landscapes about 20 minutes south of Bayeux (see map on page 286). If you've ever wanted to stay on a real French farm yet rest in cozy comfort, this is the place. The five rooms are filled with wood furnishings and decorated with bright garden themes. Guests share a kitchenette, and larger groups can stay in a cottage with its own kitchen. The experience is vintage Normandy—and so are the kind owners, Jacques and Odile (Db-€90, Tb-€110, Qb-€130, 5 people-€140, discounts for stays of 3 or more nights, includes good breakfast, tel. 02 41 40 71 07, Le Haut St-Louet, just off A-84, exit at Villers-Bocage, get detailed directions from website, www.bandbnormandie.com, lafermedupressoir@bandbnormandie.com).

Eating in Bayeux

Drivers can also consider the short drive to Arromanches for seaside options (see page 297).

ON OR NEAR RUE ST. JEAN

This traffic-free street is lined with cafés, *crêperies*, and inexpensive dining options.

La Chaumière is the best charcuterie (deli) in town; you'll find salads, quiches, and prepared dishes to go (Tue-Sun open until 19:30, closed for lunch Sun and all day Mon, on Rue St. Jean across from Hôtel Churchill). The grocery store across the street has what you need to complete your picnic.

La Rapière is a lovely, traditional wood-beamed eatery filled with locals enjoying a refined meal and a rare-these-days cheese platter for your finale. The veal with Camembert sauce is memorable (€30-40 *menus,* closed Sun-Mon, 53 Rue St. Jean, tel. 03 31 21 05 45, www.larapiere.net).

Le Volet Qui Penche is a cool, wine-shop-meets-bistro place run by gentle, English-speaking Pierre-Henri. He serves great *charcuterie* and cheese platters and offers a small selection of à la carte items but no wine tastings (€10-12 *plat du jour,* salads, *tartines,* closed Sun, non-stop service on most days making early dinners easy, near the TI at 3 Passage de l'Islet, tel. 03 31 21 98 54).

L'Angle Saint Laurent is a refined and romantic place run by a husband-and-wife team (lovely Caroline speaks English and manages the restaurant, Sébastien cooks). Come here for a special meal of *Normand* specialties done in a contemporary style. The selection is limited, changes often, and is all homemade (€28-38 *menus,* good wine list, closed Sun evening-Mon, 2 Rue des Bouchers, tel. 02 31 92 03 01, www.langlesaintlaurent.com).

La Reine Mathilde Brasserie, an easy-going café, offers bistro fare all day (omelets, big salads, pizza) and has a marvelous outside terrace with cathedral views (daily with nonstop service 12:00-21:00, a block from Rue St. Jean at 23 Rue Larcher).

Le Pommier, with street appeal inside and out, is a good place to sample regional products with clever twists in a relaxed yet refined atmosphere. Owner Thierry mixes old and new in his cuisine and decor and focuses on organic food with no GMOs. His fish and meat dishes are satisfying no matter how he prepares them, and there's a vegetarian *menu* as well—a rarity in meat-loving France (two-course *menu* €21, good three-course *menu* from €25, open daily, 38 Rue des Cuisiniers, tel. 02 31 21 52 10, www.restaurantlepommier.com).

ON PLACE ST. PATRICE

Taverne des Ducs provides big brasserie ambience, efficient and friendly service with English-speaking staff, comfortable seating inside and out, a full range of choices from *la carte*—including French onion soup, *choucroute* (sauerkraut), and all the classics—and set *menus*. Try the cooked oysters with garlic sauce, or the *dos de cabillaud au beurre* (cod in butter sauce). They serve until 23:00 (*menus* from €22, open daily, 41 Rue St. Patrice, tel. 02 31 92 09 88).

Bayeux Connections

From Bayeux by Train to: Paris' Gare St. Lazare (9/day, 2.5 hours, some change in Caen), **Amboise** (2/day, 4.5 hours, change in Caen and Tours' St-Pierre-des-Corps), **Rouen** (14/day, 2.5 hours, change in Caen), **Caen** (20/day, 20 minutes), **Honfleur** (2-3/day, 20-minute train to Caen, then 1-hour PrestoBus—line #39—express bus to Honfleur; more with train to Caen and scenic 2-hour ride on bus #20 via the coast; for bus information, call 02 31 89 28 41, www.busverts.fr), **Pontorson/Mont St-Michel** (3/day, 2 hours to Pontorson, then bus to Mont St-Michel; also consider Hôtel Churchill's faster shuttle van—described below).

By Bus to the D-Day Beaches: Bus Verts du Calvados offers minimal service to D-Day beaches with stops in Bayeux at Place St. Patrice and at the train station (schedules at TI, tel. 08 10 21 42 14, www.busverts.fr). Lines #74/#75 run east to Arromanches and Juno Beach (3-5/day, none on Sun Sept-June; 30 minutes to Arromanches, 50 minutes to Juno Beach), and line #70 runs west to the American Cemetery and Vierville-sur-Mer (3/day in summer, 2/day off-season, none on Sun Sept-June, 35 minutes to American Cemetery, 45 minutes to Vierville-sur-Mer). Because of the schedules, you're usually stuck with either too much or too little time at either sight if you try to take the bus round-trip; consider a taxi one way and a bus the other (for taxi information, see page 274).

By Shuttle Van to Mont St-Michel: The recommended **Hôtel Churchill** runs a shuttle van to Mont St-Michel for €65 per person round-trip (1.5 hours each way; available to the general public, though hotel clients get a small discount). The van leaves Bayeux at 8:30 and returns by 15:00, allowing travelers three hours at Mont St-Michel. The trip is a terrific deal, as you'll get a free tour of Normandy along the way from your knowledgeable driver. For details, see www.hotel-churchill.fr.

D-Day Beaches

The 54 miles of Atlantic coast north of Bayeux—stretching from Utah Beach on the west to Sword Beach on the east—are littered with WWII museums, monuments, cemeteries, and battle remains left in tribute to the courage of the British, Canadian, and American armies that successfully carried out the largest military operation in history: D-Day. (It's called *Jour J* in French—the letters "D" and "J" come from the first letter for the word "day" in either English or French.) It was on these serene beaches, at the crack of dawn on June 6, 1944, that the Allies finally gained a foothold in France, and Nazi Europe was doomed to crumble.

"The first 24 hours of the invasion will be decisive... The fate of Germany depends on the outcome... For the Allies, as well as Germany, it will be the longest day."

—Field Marshal Erwin Rommel to his aide, April 22, 1944 (from *The Longest Day*, by Cornelius Ryan)

June 6, 2014, marked the 70th anniversary of the landings. It was a huge deal here, given how few D-Day veterans are still alive. Locals talk of the last visits of veterans with heartfelt sorrow; they have adored seeing the old soldiers in their villages and fear losing the firsthand accounts of the battles. All along this rambling coast, locals will never forget what the troops and their families sacrificed all those years ago. A warm regard for Americans has survived political disputes, from de Gaulle to "Freedom Fries." This remains particularly friendly soil for Americans—a place where their soldiers are still honored and the image of the US as a force for good has remained largely untarnished.

PLANNING YOUR TIME

I've listed the D-Day sites from east to west, starting with Arromanches (note that several are closed in January). Many prefer to focus on the American sector (west of Arromanches), rather than the British and Canadian sectors (east of Arromanches), which have been overbuilt with resorts, making it harder to envision the events of June 1944. The American sector looks today very much as it would have 70 years ago. For more information on visiting the D-Day beaches, www.normandiememoire.com is a useful resource.

D-Day Sites in One Day

If you only have one day, I'd spend it entirely on the beaches and miss the Caen Memorial Museum. (If you want to squeeze in the museum, visit it on your way to or from the beaches—but remember that the American Cemetery closes at 18:00 mid-April-mid-Sept and at 17:00 the rest of the year—and you need at least 1.5 hours there.) With the exciting sites and museums along the beaches, the Caen Memorial Museum is less important for most.

If you're traveling by car, begin on the cliffs above Arromanches. From there, drive a quarter-mile downhill to the town and visit Port Winston and the D-Day Landing Museum, then continue west to Longues-sur-Mer and tour this site. Spend your afternoon visiting the American Cemetery and its thought-provoking visitors center, walking on the beach at Vierville-sur-Mer, and exploring the Pointe du Hoc Ranger Monument. With an extra half-day, spend it at the Utah Beach sites (to learn about the paratroopers' role in the invasion), then head off to Mont St-Michel or Honfleur.

Canadians will want to start at the Juno Beach Centre and Canadian Cemetery (in Courseulles-sur-Mer, 10 minutes east of Arromanches).

No Car? You can rent a car for a day, or better, take a minivan tour or taxi from Bayeux, or—for a really full day—combine a visit to the Caen Memorial Museum with their guided minivan tour of the beaches (see page 311). Public transport is available, but not practical for more than one sight. Bike riding is dicey as roads are narrow (no bike lanes), there are plenty of blind curves, and traffic is constant.

GETTING AROUND THE D-DAY BEACHES

On Your Own

Though the minivan excursions listed below teach important history lessons—drawing Americans and Canadians out of their cars—**renting a car** is a far less expensive way to visit the beaches, particularly for three or more people (for rental suggestions, see Bayeux's "Helpful Hints" on page 274).

However, if you're staying in Paris and want to make the D-Day beaches a day -trip in a rental car, think twice. A train from Paris to Caen (the most convenient place to pick up a car) takes over two hours. Then you'll face rental paperwork and at least a half-hour drive to your first stop at Arromanches. Just getting to and from the D-Day beaches will take about six hours out of your day. A better alternative is to book a service that will meet you at a train station and drive you to sights (see "By Taxi" and "By Fully Guided Minivan Tour" next). Or take a bus tour that starts in Paris.

Very limited **bus service** links Bayeux, the coastal town of Arromanches, and the most impressive sites of D-Day (see Bus Verts du Calvados information on page 283).

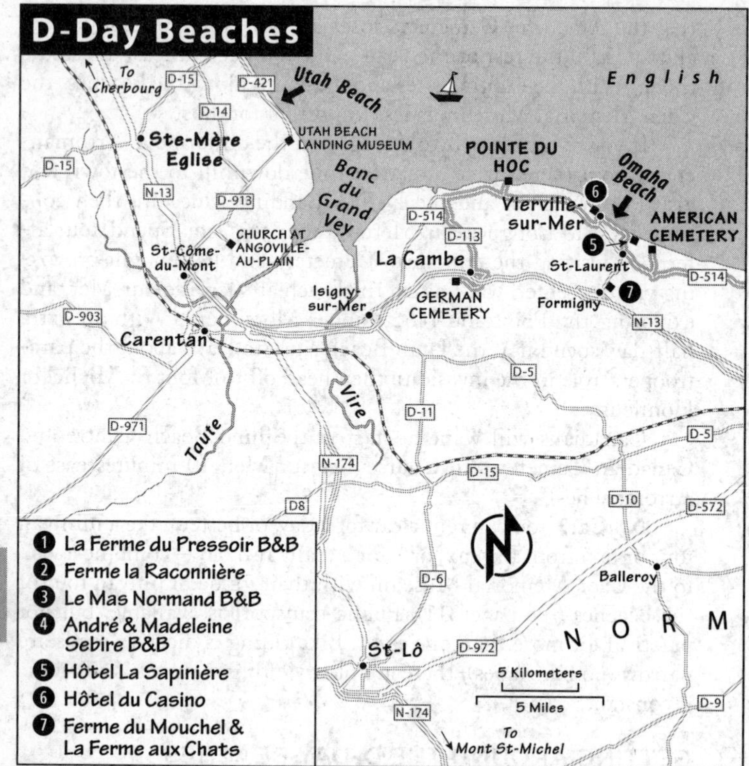

By Taxi

Taxi minivans shuttle up to seven people between the key sites at reasonable rates (which vary depending on how far you go). Allow €240 for an eight-hour taxi day (€300 on Sun) to visit the top Utah and Omaha Beach sites (with no guiding, of course). Figure about €22 each way between Bayeux and Arromanches, €38 between Bayeux and the American Cemetery, and €100 for a 2.5-hour visit to Omaha Beach sites from Bayeux or Arromanches (50 percent surcharge after 19:00 and on Sun, taxi tel. 02 31 92 92 40 or mobile 06 70 40 07 96, www.taxisbayeux.com, taxisbayeux@orange.fr).

Abbeilles Taxis offer D-Day excursions from Caen (€200/5-hour visit, tel. 02 31 52 17 89, www.taxis-abbeilles-caen.com).

By Fully Guided Minivan Tour

An army of small companies offers all-day excursions to the D-Day beaches from Bayeux or nearby. Demand has grown—as has the guide supply to meet it—and today it seems that anyone with passable English wants to guide. Travelers beware. Anyone can get you around the beaches, but effective teaching of the events is another

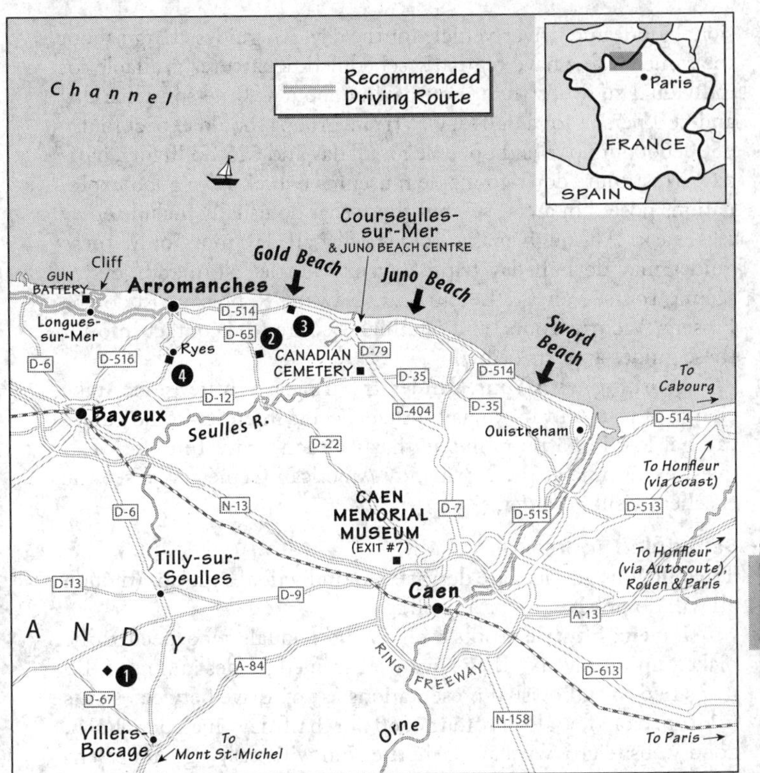

story. You should expect your guide to deliver coherent history lessons and go with you to all sights (and not orient and disperse you).

The tour companies and guides listed in this section are people I trust to take your time seriously. Most deliver riveting commentary about these moving sites. To land one of these top-notch guides, book your tour as far in advance as possible (three months is best), or pray for a last-minute cancellation. The best way to save on the cost is to hire a guide who offers half-day tours or one who is willing to join you in your rental car.

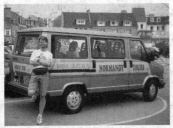

Many tours prefer to pick up in or near Bayeux, and a few levy a small surcharge for a Caen pickup. Many guides skip Arromanches, preferring to focus on sights farther west. While some companies discourage children, others (including Mathias Leclere, Victory Tours, Sylvain Kast, and Edward Robinson) welcome them.

Cost: These tours are pricey because you're hiring a professional guide and driver/vehicle for the day. All guides charge about the same. A few have regularly scheduled departures available for individual sign-ups (figure on paying about €90/person for a day and €60/person for a half-day). Private groups should expect to pay €500-660 for up to eight people for all day and €250-330 for a half-day. Most tours don't go inside museums (which have good explanations posted in any case), but those that do usually include entry fees—ask. Although many guides offer all-day tours only, these guides may do half-day trips: Bayeux Shuttle, Normandy Sightseeing Tours, Vanessa Letourneur, Edward Robinson, Rodolphe Passera, Victory Tours, and Mathias Leclere (the contact info for these guides appears below).

Working with Your Guide: If hiring a private guide, take charge of your tour if you have other specific interests (some guides can get lost in battle minutiae that you don't have time for). Request extra time at the Normandy American Cemetery to see the excellent visitors center.

Scheduled Tours

The following services are designed for individual sign-ups (though all will do private groups as well).

Bayeux Shuttle works well for individuals who need to be picked up in Bayeux. They have well-trained guides and use GPS maps tied to audiovisual presentations as you drive between sights (€110/person for all-day tour, €60 for half-day, includes lunch, good website at www.bayeuxshuttle.com with easy sign-up calendar).

Normandy Sightseeing Tours delivers a French perspective through the voices of its small fleet of licensed guides (€50 for morning tour, €65 for afternoon tour, €95 for day tour), and will pick you up anywhere you like (for a price). Because there are many guides, the quality of their teaching is less consistent (tel. 02 31 51 70 52, www.normandy-sightseeing-tours.com).

The **Caen Memorial Museum** runs a busy program of half-day tours covering the American and Canadian sectors in combination with a visit to the museum. This option works well for those who have limited time (see museum listing on page 311).

Private Tours by Ex-Pats

The following guides offer tours only for private parties. All have their own vehicles; some are happy to ride in your car.

Dale Booth is a fine historian and a riveting storyteller. He leads tours for up to eight people to the American, Canadian, and British sectors using your vehicle or his (tel. 02 33 71 53 76, www.dboothnormandytours.com, dboothholidays@sfr.fr).

Normandy Battle Tours are led by likable, easygoing Stuart Robertson, who is an effective teacher, D-Day author, and historian.

He also owns a bed-and-breakfast near Ste-Mère Eglise and offers combo accommodation/tour packages (tel. 02 33 41 28 34, www.normandybattletours.com, stuart@normandybattletours.com).

D-Day Historian Tours are run by Paul Woodadge, a passionate historian and author who takes your learning seriously. He offers private tours in his minivan. His "Band of Brothers Tour" is excellent (mobile 07 88 02 76 57, www.ddayhistorian.com, paul@ddayhistorian.com).

Eric Le Doux Turnbull of Day Landing Tours is a fine guide with a Scottish background and thorough knowledge and the ability to convey it well (tel. 02 33 30 14 69, www.ddaylandingtours.com, info@ddaylandingtours.com).

Allan Bryson is a calm, sincere guide who prefers picking up clients in Carentan (www.firstnormandybattlefieldtours.com).

D-Day Battle Tours are run by WWII-enthusiast Ellwood von Seibold. He drives a WWII Dodge Command Car and explains events as if you were there (tel. 02 33 94 44 13, mobile 06 32 67 49 15, www.ddaybattletours.com, ellwood@ddaybattletours.com).

Paul de Winter is clean-cut, serious about teaching, has a Ph.D. in military history, and has written a book titled *Defeating Hitler.* History buffs will be happy, but so will others as Paul's delightful wife and driver, Fiona, helps balance the conversation (6-person maximum, www.dewintertours.com, info@dewintertours.com).

Edward Robinson, who is Irish, informal, and chatty (a national trait?), has previously guided for the Caen Memorial Museum and fires important information at you like a machine gun. Taking up to six passengers in his minivan, he tries to get off the beaten track (www.battleofnormandytours.com, edrobinson@battleofnormandytours.com).

Victory Tours is run by friendly Dutchman Roel (pronounced "rule"), who gives half-day and all-day tours. His tours are informal and entertaining, but sufficiently informative for most (departs from Bayeux only and meets Paris trains, tel. 02 31 51 98 14, www.victorytours.com, victorytours@orange.fr).

Michael Phillips brings a gentle, relaxed personal perspective to his tours (British mobile 0780-246-8599, from France dial 00-44/780-246-8599, www.d-daytours.com).

Private Tours by Locals

These capable French natives give a local perspective to the D-Day landings.

Sylvain Kast is a genuinely nice person with good overall knowledge and many French family connections to the war; she's strong in the American sector (mobile 06 17 44 04 46, www.d-day-experience-tours.com).

Countdown to D-Day

1939 On September 1, Adolf Hitler invades the Free City of Danzig (today's Gdańsk, Poland), sparking World War II.

1940 Germany's "Blitzkrieg" ("lightning war") quickly overwhelms France, Nazis goose-step down Avenue des Champs-Elysées, and the country is divided into Occupied France (the north) and Vichy France (the south, ruled by right-wing French). Just like that, nearly the entire Continent is fascist.

1941 The Allies (Britain, the Soviet Union, and others) peck away at the fringes of "fortress Europe." The Soviets repel Hitler's invasion at Moscow, while the Brits (with American aid) battle German U-boats for control of the seas. On December 7, Japan bombs the US naval base at Pearl Harbor, Hawaii. The US enters the war against Japan and its ally, Germany.

1942 Three crucial battles—at Stalingrad, El-Alamein, and Guadalcanal—weaken the German forces and their ally Japan. The victorious tank battle at El-Alamein in the deserts of North Africa soon gives the Allies a jumping-off point (Tunis) for the first assault on the Continent.

1943 More than 150,000 Americans and Brits, under the command of George Patton and Bernard "Monty" Montgomery, land in Sicily and begin working their way north through Italy. Meanwhile, Germany has to fend off tenacious Soviets on their eastern front.

1944 On June 6, 1944, the Allies launch "Operation Overlord," better known as D-Day. The Allies amass three million soldiers and six million tons of *matériel* in England in preparation for the biggest fleet-led invasion in history—across the English Channel to France, then eastward toward Berlin. The Germans, hunkered down in northern France, know an invasion is imminent, but the Allies keep the details top secret.

Vanessa Letourneur is a low-key and likable person who can guide anywhere in Normandy. She worked at the Caen Memorial Museum and offers half-day tours from Bayeux or Caen (mobile 06 98 95 89 45, www.normandypanorama.com).

Mathias Leclere was born four miles from Juno Beach to a family with three centuries of roots in Normandy—he is part of its soil. Mathias is a self-taught historian who leads half-day and full-day tours in his minivan (www.ddayguidedtours.com).

On the night of June 5, more than 180,000 soldiers board ships and planes, not knowing where they are headed until they're under way. Each one carries a note from General Dwight D. Eisenhower: "The tide has turned. The free men of the world are marching together to victory."

At 6:30 on June 6, 1944, Americans spill out of troop transports into the cold waters off a beach in Normandy, code-named Omaha. The weather is bad, seas are rough, and the prep bombing has failed. The soldiers, many seeing their first action, are dazed, confused, and weighed down by heavy packs. Nazi machine guns pin them against the sea. Slowly, they crawl up the beach on their stomachs. More than a thousand die. They hold on until the next wave of transports arrives.

Americans also see action at Utah Beach, while the British and Canadian troops storm Sword, Juno, and Gold. All day long, Allied confusion does battle with German indecision—the Nazis never really counter-attack, thinking D-Day is just a ruse, not the main invasion. By day's end, the Allies have taken all five beaches along the Normandy coast and soon begin building two completely artificial harbors, code-named "Mulberry," providing ports for the reconquest of western Europe. The stage is set for a quick and easy end to the war. Right.

1945 Caen, the modern capital of lower Normandy,Having liberated Paris (August 26, 1944), the Allies' march on Berlin from the west bogs down, hit by poor supply lines, bad weather, and the surprising German counterpunch at the Battle of the Bulge. Finally, in the spring, the Americans and Brits cross the Rhine, Soviet soldiers close in on Berlin, Hitler shoots himself, and—after nearly six long years of war—Europe is free.

Rodolphe Passera speaks fluent English and is a serious student of the Normandy invasion. He works as a guide at the D-Day Landing Museum at Utah Beach and has great energy for teaching. He can join your car or drive you in his Lexus SUV (mobile 06 30 55 63 39, leopardbusinesslanguages@gmail.com).

Bertram Soudrais is a young, flexible, charming, and hard-working guide whose American wife gives him an inside track on Yankee interests (www.executived-daytours.com).

HELPFUL HINTS

Normandy Pass: If you plan to visit several D-Day sites, you can save a few euros by buying the Normandy Pass (€1 added to the full-price admission at your first site). You'll save €1 at most subsequent sites, but the Caen Memorial Museum is not included. The pass is valid for one month and is transferable to anyone.

Good Map: The free and well-done ***Exploration and Emotion: The Historical Area of the Battle of Normandy*** booklet gives succinct reviews of 29 D-Day museums and sites with current opening times. It also mentions driving itineraries that are linked to roadside signposts, helping you understand the significance of the area you are passing through. The map is available at TIs, but you usually need to ask for it (or you can download it yourself from www.normandiememoire.com).

Food Strategies: The D-Day landing sites are rural, and you won't find a grocery on every corner. Pack ahead if you plan to picnic.

Arromanches

This small town was ground zero for the D-Day invasion. Almost overnight, it sprouted the immense harbor, Port Winston, which gave the Allies a foothold in Normandy, allowing them to begin their victorious push to Berlin and end World War II. The postwar period brought a long decline. Only recently has the population of tiny Arromanches finally returned to its June 5, 1944, numbers. Here you'll find a good museum, an evocative beach and bluff, and a touristy-but-fun little town that offers a pleasant cocktail of war memories, cotton candy, and beachfront trinket shops. Arromanches makes a great base for sightseeing (I've listed accommodations under "Sleeping in Arromanches," later). Sit on the seawall after dark and listen to the waves lick the sand while you contemplate the events that took place here 70 years ago.

Orientation to Arromanches

TOURIST INFORMATION

The service-oriented TI has the *Exploration and Emotion* booklet, bus schedules, a photo booklet of area hotels and *chambres d'hôtes*, and helpful Mathilde in charge (daily May-Sept 9:30-18:30, Oct-April 9:30-12:00 & 14:00-17:30, opposite the recommended Hôtel d'Arromanches at 2 Avenue Maréchal Joffre, tel. 02 31 22 36 45, www.ot-arromanches.fr).

ARRIVAL IN ARROMANCHES

The bus stop is located at the top of the town across from the post office. The main parking lot by the museum costs €1.20 per hour (free from 19:00-9:00). For free parking and less traffic, look for the lot between the small grocery store and Ideale Hôtel Mountbatten as you enter Arromanches.

HELPFUL HINTS

ATM: An ATM is across from the museum parking lot.

Groceries: A little **supermarket** is a few blocks above the beach, across from Ideale Hôtel Mountbatten.

Taxi: To get an Arromanches-based **taxi,** call mobile 06 66 62 00 99.

WWII Paraphernalia Store: Arromanches Militaria sells all sorts of D-Day relics (daily 10:00-19:00, 11 Boulevard Gilbert Longuet).

D-Day Sites in Arromanches

In this section, I've linked Arromanches' D-Day sites with some self-guided commentary.

▲▲▲Port Winston Artificial Harbor

Start on the cliffs above the town, overlooking the site of the impressive WWII harbor.

Getting There: Drive two minutes toward Courseulles-sur-Mer and pay €3 to park, or park in Arromanches and walk up. Non-drivers can hike 10 minutes uphill from Arromanches, or take the free white train from the museum to the top of the bluff (runs daily June-Sept, Sat-Sun only Oct-May).

➲ Self-Guided Tour: This commentary will lead you around the site.

• *Find the concrete viewpoint overlooking the town and the beaches and prepare for your briefing. Beyond Arromanches to the left is the American sector, with Omaha Beach and then Utah Beach (notice the sheer cliffs between these two sectors); below and to the right lie the British and Canadian sectors.*

Now get this: Along the beaches below, the Allies arrived in the largest amphibious attack ever, launching the liberation of Western Europe. On D-Day +1—June 7, 1944—17 old ships sailed 100 miles across the English Channel under their own steam to Arromanches. Their crews sank them so that each bow faced the next ship's stern, forming a sea barrier. Then 500 tugboats towed 115 football-field-size cement blocks (called "Phoenixes") across the channel. These were also sunk, creating a four-mile-long breakwater 1.5 miles offshore. Finally, engineers set up seven floating steel "pierheads" with extendable legs; they then linked these to shore with four mile-long floating roads made of concrete pontoons. Soldiers placed 115 anti-aircraft guns on the Phoenixes and pontoons, protecting a port the size of Dover, England. Within just six days of operation, 54,000 vehicles, 326,000 troops, and 110,000 tons of goods had crossed the English Channel. An Allied toehold in Normandy was secure. Eleven months later, Hitler was dead and the war was over.

The **Arromanches 360° Theater** behind you shows a moving film, *Normandy's 100 Days,* encompassing D-Day and the battles to liberate Normandy—about 37,000 Allied and 55,000 German soldiers died and many more were wounded (€5, daily mid-Feb-Dec 10:00-18:00, until 18:30 June-Aug; closed Jan-mid-Feb, 2 shows/hour at :10 and :40 past the hour, 20 minutes, tel. 02 31 06 06 45, www.arromanches360.com).

• *Head down to the town's main parking lot and find the round bulkhead on the seawall, near the D-Day Landing Museum entry. Stand facing the sea.*

The **Prefab Harbor** was created out there by the British. Since it was Churchill's brainchild, it was named Port Winston. Designed to be a temporary harbor (it was used for six months), it was supposed to wash out to sea over time—which is exactly what happened with its twin harbor at Omaha Beach (that one lasted only 12 days, thanks to a terrible storm). If the tide is out, you'll see several rusted floats mired on the sand close in—these supported the pontoon roads. If you stare hard enough at the concrete blocks in the sea to the right, you'll see that one still has what's left of an anti-aircraft gun platform on it.

On the hill beyond the museum, you'll spot a Sherman tank, one of 50,000 deployed during the landings. Behind the museum (not viewable from here) is a section of a pontoon road, an anti-aircraft gun, and a Higgins boat, which was used to ferry 30 soldiers at a time from naval ships to the beaches. If you can, walk down to the beach and wander among the concrete and rusted litter of the battle—and be thankful that all you hear are birds and surf.

▲D-Day Landing Museum (Musée du Débarquement)

The D-Day Landing Museum, facing the harbor, makes a worthwhile 30-45 minute visit and is the only way to get a full appreciation of how the artificial harbor was built. While gazing through windows at the site of this amazing endeavor, you can study helpful models, videos, and photographs illustrating the construction and use of the prefabricated harbor. Those blimp-like objects tethered to the port prevented German planes from getting too close (though the German air force had been made largely irrelevant by this time). Ponder the remarkable undertaking that resulted in this harbor being built in just 12 days, while battles raged. One video

(8 minutes, ground floor) recalls D-Day; the other (15 minutes, upstairs) features the construction of the temporary port—ask for times when it is shown in English.

Cost and Hours: €8, daily May-Aug 9:00-19:00, Sept 9:00-18:00, Oct-Dec and Feb-April 10:00-12:30 & 13:30-17:00, closed Jan, pick up English flier at door, tel. 02 31 22 34 31, www.arromanches-museum.com.

Sleeping in Arromanches

Arromanches, with its pinwheels and seagulls, has a salty beach-town ambience that makes it a fun overnight stop. Park in the town's main lot at the museum (€1.20/hour, free 19:00-9:00). For evening fun, do what most do and head for the small bar at **Restaurant "Le Pappagall"** (see "Eating in Arromanches"), or, for more of a nightclub scene, have a drink at **Pub Marie Celeste,** around the corner on Rue de la Poste. Drivers should also consider my sleeping recommendations near Omaha Beach (see page 304). All hotels have free Wi-Fi unless otherwise noted.

$$$ Hôtel de la Marine*** has a knock-out location with point-blank views to the artificial harbor site from most of its 28 comfortable enough, non-smoking rooms (Db-€116, Tb-€165, Qb-€195, bigger family rooms, elevator, Wi-Fi, view restaurant, Quai du Canada, tel. 02 31 22 34 19, www.hotel-de-la-marine.fr, hotel.de.la.marine@wanadoo.fr).

$$ Hôtel d'Arromanches,** which sits on the main pedestrian drag near the TI, is a good value, with nine mostly small but smartly appointed rooms (some with water views), all up a tight stairway. Here you'll find the cheery, recommended Restaurant "Le Pappagall" and English-speaking Louis at the helm (Db-€70-85, Tb-€96, breakfast-€10, Wi-Fi, 2 Rue Colonel René Michel, tel. 02 31 22 36 26, www.hoteldarromanches.fr, reservation@hoteldarromanches.fr).

$$ Le Mulberry** is an intimate place with nine simple, non-smoking rooms, a small restaurant, and sincere owner Christian. It's a five-minute walk up from the touristy beach, near the town's church, so expect bells to mark the hour until 22:00 (Db-€85-105, Tb-€105-150, includes breakfast, good restaurant, reception closed 13:00-17:00 and after 19:00, a block below the church at 6 Rue Maurice Lihare, tel. 02 31 22 36 05, www.lemulberry.fr, mail@lemulberry.fr).

$$ Ideale Mountbatten Hôtel*,** located a long block up from the water, is an eight-room, two-story, motel-esque place with generously sized, clean, and good-value lodgings, and welcoming owners Sylvie and Laurent. Upstairs rooms have a little view over the sea (Db-€90, Tb-€125-135, includes breakfast, Wi-Fi, easy and free parking, short block below the main post office—PTT—at 20 Boulevard Gilbert Longuet, tel. 02 31 22 59 70, www.hotelarromancheslideal.fr, mountbattenhotel@wanadoo.fr).

IN THE COUNTRYSIDE NEAR ARROMANCHES

$$ Ferme la Raconnière is a 35-room, country-classy oasis buried in farmland with easy car access to Bayeux and Arromanches. It's flawlessly maintained from its wood-beamed, stone-walled rooms to its traditional restaurant (*menus* from €24) and fireplace-cozy lounge/bar (small Db-€70-90, bigger Db-€110-160, Db suites-€180-250, bike rental, service-oriented staff, 4.5 miles southeast from Arromanches in Crépon, tel. 02 31 22 21 73, www.ranconniere.fr, ranconniere@wanadoo.fr).

$$ Le Mas Normand, 10 minutes east of Arromanches in Ver-sur-Mer, is the child of *Provençale* Mylène and *Normand* Christian. Here you get a warm welcome and the best of both worlds: three lovingly decorated, Provence-style rooms wrapped in 18th-century Norman stone. The place is family-friendly with ample grass, a dog, some geese, and no smoking (Db-€75-100, Tb-€130, Qb-€150; ask about their fun, funky and tight *roulotte*—a Gypsy-style trailer; includes breakfast, Wi-Fi; drive to the east end of little Ver-sur-Mer, turn right at Hôtel P'tit Bouchon, take another right where the road makes a "T," and find the sign at 8 Impasse de la Rivière; tel. 02 31 21 97 75, www.lemasnormand.com, lemasnormand@wanadoo.fr). Book well ahead for Christian's twice-weekly home-cooked gourmet dinner, including wine, cider, and coffee (€35/person, requires 4 people, kids' menus available).

$ At **André and Madeleine Sebire**'s B&B, you'll experience a real Norman farm. The hardworking owners offer four modest, homey, and dirt-cheap rooms in the middle of nowhere (Sb-€35, Db-€40, Tb-€45, includes breakfast, 2 miles from Arromanches in the tiny village of Ryes at Ferme du Clos Neuf, tel. 02 31 22 32 34, emmanuelle.sebire@wanadoo.fr, little English spoken). Try these directions: Follow signs into Ryes, then locate the faded green *Chambres d'Hôte* sign opposite the village's lone restaurant. Follow that sign onto Rue de la Forge, cross a tiny bridge, turn right onto Rue de la Tringale, and follow it for a half-mile until you see a small sign on the right to *Le Clos Neuf.* Park near the tractors.

Eating in Arromanches

You'll find cafés, *crêperies,* and shops selling sandwiches to go (ideal for beachfront picnics). The following restaurants are reliable.

Le Mulberry is a good place to dine on homemade recipes at reasonable prices (*menus* from €20, closed Wed, see hotel listing earlier).

Restaurant "Le Pappagall" (French slang for "parakeet") has tasty mussels, filling fish *choucroute,* "*les* feesh and cheeps," salads, and a full offering with fair prices (see Hôtel d'Arromanches listing, earlier).

Hôtel de la Marine allows you to dine or drink in style on the water (*menus* from €21, cool bar with same views, daily, see hotel listing earlier).

Arromanches Connections

From Arromanches by Bus to: Bayeux (bus #74/#75, 3-5/day, none on Sun Sept-June, 30 minutes); **Juno Beach** (bus #74/#75, 20 minutes). The bus stop is near the main post office, four long blocks above the sea (the stop for Bayeux is on the sea side of the street; the stop for Juno Beach is on the post office side).

American D-Day Sites

The American sector, stretching west of Arromanches, is divided between Omaha and Utah beaches. Omaha Beach starts just a few miles west of Arromanches and has the most important sites for visitors, including the American Cemetery and Pointe du Hoc (four miles west of Omaha Beach). Utah Beach sites are farther away (on the road to Cherbourg), but were also critical to the ultimate success of the Normandy invasion. The American Airborne sector covers a broad area behind Utah Beach and centers on Ste-Mère Eglise. You'll see memorials sprouting up all around the countryside.

OMAHA BEACH D-DAY SITES

▲Longues-sur-Mer Gun Battery

Four German casemates (three with guns intact)—built to guard against seaborne attacks—hunker down at the end of a country road. The guns, 300 yards inland, were arranged in a semicircle to maximize the firing range east and west, and are the only original coastal artillery guns remaining in place in the D-Day region. (Much was scrapped after the war, long before people thought of tourism.) This battery, staffed by 194 German soldiers, was more defended than the more famous Pointe du Hoc (described later). The Longues-sur-Mer Battery was a critical link in Hitler's Atlantic Wall defense, which consisted of more than 15,000 structures stretching from Norway to the Pyrenees. The guns could hit targets up to 12 miles away with relatively sharp accuracy if linked to good target information. The Allies had to take them out.

Enter the third bunker you pass. It took seven soldiers to manage each gun, which could be loaded and fired six times per minute (the shells weighed 40 pounds). Outside, climb above the bunker and find the hooks that were used to secure camouflage netting, making it nigh-impossible for bombers to locate them.

A lone observation bunker (look for the low-lying concrete bunker roof just before the cliffs) was designed to direct the firing; field telephones connected the bunker to the gun batteries by underground wires. Walk to the observation bunker to appreciate the strategic view over the channel. You'll pass other bunker (*encuvement*) and mortar (*mortier*) sites. From here you can walk along the glorious *Sentier du Littoral* (coastal path) above the cliffs and see Arromanches in the distance, then walk the road back to your car. You can also drive five minutes down to the water on the small road past the site's parking lot.

The WWI Russian cannon near the parking lot's info kiosk looks like a Tinkertoy compared to those up the short trail.

Cost and Hours: Free and always open. The €5 booklet is helpful, but skip the €4 tour.

Getting There: You'll find the guns 10 minutes west of Arromanches on D-514. Follow *Port en Bessin* signs; once in Longues-sur-Mer, follow *Batterie* signs; turn right at the town's only traffic light.

▲▲▲WWII Normandy American Cemetery and Memorial

"Soldiers' graves are the greatest preachers of peace."
—Albert Schweitzer

Crowning a bluff just above Omaha Beach and the eye of the D-Day storm, 9,387 brilliant white-marble crosses and Stars of David glow in memory of Americans who gave their lives to free Europe on the beaches below. You'll want to spend at least 1.5 hours at this stirring site.

Cost and Hours: Free, daily mid-April-mid-Sept 9:00-18:00, mid-Sept-mid-April 9:00-17:00, tel. 02 31 51 62 00, www.abmc.gov. Park carefully, as break-ins have been a problem. You'll find good WCs and water fountains at the parking lot. Guided tours are offered a few times a day in high season (11:00 and 14:00 in 2014)—call ahead for times.

Getting There: The cemetery is just east of St-Laurent-sur-

Mer and northwest of Bayeux in Colleville-sur-Mer. From route D-514, directional signs will point the way.

➲ **Self-Guided Tour:** Your visit begins at the impressive **visitors center.** Pass security, pick up the handout, sign the register, and allow time to appreciate the superb displays. On the arrival floor, computer terminals provide access to a database containing the story of each US serviceman who died in Normandy.

Descend one level, where you'll learn about the invasion preparations and the immense logistical challenges they presented. The heart of the center tells the stories of the brave individuals who gave their lives to liberate people they could not know, and shows the few possessions they died with (about 25,000 Americans died in the battle for Normandy). This adds a personal touch to the D-Day landings and prepares visitors for the fields of white crosses and Stars of David outside. The pressure on these men to succeed in this battle is palpable. There are a manageable number of display cases, a few moving videos (including an interview with Dwight Eisenhower), and a must-see 16-minute film (cushy theater chairs, on the half-hour, you can enter late).

A lineup of informational plaques provides a worthwhile and succinct overview of key events from September 1939 to June 5, 1944. Starting with June 6, 1944, the plaques present the progress of the landings in three-hour increments. Amazingly, Omaha Beach was secured within six hours of the landings.

A path from the visitors center leads to a bluff overlooking the piece of Normandy **beach** called "that embattled shore—portal of freedom." It's quiet and peaceful today, but the horrific carnage of June 6, 1944, is hard to forget. An orientation table looks over the sea. Nearby, steps climb down to the beautiful beach below. A walk on the beach is a powerful experience and a must if you are sans both car and tour. Visitors with cars can drive to the beach at Vierville-sur-Mer (see next listing).

In the **cemetery,** you'll find a striking memorial with a soaring statue representing the spirit of American youth. Around the statue, giant reliefs of the Battle of Normandy and the Battle of Europe are etched on the walls. Behind is the semicircular Garden of the Missing, with the names of 1,557 soldiers who were never found. A small metal button next to the name indicates one whose body was eventually found—there aren't many.

Finally, wander through the peaceful and poignant sea of headstones. Notice the names, home states, and dates of death (but no birth dates)

inscribed on each. Dog-tag numbers are etched into the lower backs of the crosses. During the campaign, the dead were buried in temporary cemeteries throughout various parts of Normandy. After the war, the families of the soldiers could decide whether their loved ones should remain with their comrades or be brought home (61 percent opted for repatriation).

A disproportionate number of officers are buried here, including General Theodore Roosevelt, Jr., who insisted on joining the invasion despite having a weak heart—he died from a heart attack one month after D-Day (Ted's grave—and his brother Quentin's—lie along the sea, about 150 yards down, in the second grouping of graves just after the row 27 marker—look for the gold lettering). Families knew that these officers would want to be buried alongside the men with whom they fought. Also buried here are two of the Niland brothers, now famous from *Saving Private Ryan* (in the middle of the cemetery, just before the circular chapel, turn right just after the letter "F"; theirs are the ninth and tenth crosses down).

France has given the US permanent free use of this 172-acre site. It is immaculately maintained by the American Battle Monuments Commission.

▲Vierville-sur-Mer and Omaha Beach

This essential detour for drivers allows direct access onto Omaha Beach. From the American Cemetery, drive west along D-514 into St-Laurent, then take a one-way loop drive along the beach, following *Vierville s/Mer par la Côte* signs on D-517. As you drop down toward the beach, WWII junkies should stop at the **Omaha Beach Museum** (Musée Memorial d'Omaha Beach) parking lot. Outside the museum, you'll see a rusted metal object with several legs, called a "Czech hedgehog"—thousands of these were placed on the beaches by the Germans to foil the Allies' advance. Find the American 155mm "Long Tom" gun nearby, and keep this image in mind for your stop at Pointe du Hoc (this artillery piece is similar in size to the German guns that were targeted by US Army Rangers at that site). The Sherman tank is one of the best examples of the type that attacked the D-Day beaches. The museum itself is skippable (€6.20, daily mid-May-mid-Sept 9:30-19:00, shorter hours off-season, closed mid-Nov-mid-Feb, tel. 02 31 21 97 44, www.musee-memorial-omaha.com, good 20-minute film).

A right turn along the water leads to **Le Ruquet** (where the road ends), a good place to appreciate the challenges that American soldiers faced on D-Day. The small German bunker and embedded gun protected this point, which offered the easiest access inland from Omaha Beach. It was here that the Americans would establish their first road inland.

Find your way out to the **beach** and stroll to the right to better understand the assignment that American forces were handed on June 6: You're wasted from a lack of sleep and nervous anticipation. Now you get seasick too, as you're about to land in a small, flat-bottomed boat, cheek-to-jowl with 29 other soldiers. Your water-soaked pack feels like a boulder, and your gun feels even heavier. The boat's front ramp drops open, and you run for your life for 500 yards through water and sand onto this open beach, dodging bullets from above (the landings had to occur at low tide so that mines would be visible).

Omaha Beach witnessed by far the most **intense battles** of any along the D-Day beaches—although the war planners thought Utah Beach would be more deadly. The hills above were heavily fortified with machine gun and mortar nests. (The aerial, naval, and supporting rocket fire that the Allies poured onto the German defenses failed to put them out of commission.) A single German machine gun could fire 1,200 rounds a minute. That's right—1,200. It's amazing that anyone survived. The highest casualty rates in Normandy occurred here at Omaha Beach, nicknamed "Bloody Omaha." Though there are no accurate figures for D-Day, it is estimated that on the first day of the campaign, the Allies suffered 10,500 casualties (killed, wounded, and missing)—6,000 of whom were Americans. Estimates for Omaha Beach casualties range from 2,500 to 4,800 killed and wounded on that day, many of whom drowned after being wounded. But thanks to an overwhelming effort and huge support from the US and Royal navies, 34,000 Americans would land on the beach by day's end.

If the tide's out, you'll notice some remains of rusted metal objects. Omaha Beach was littered with obstacles to disrupt the landings. Thousands of metal poles and Czech hedgehogs, miles of barbed wire, and more than six million mines were scattered along these beaches. At least 150,000 tons of metal were taken from the beaches after World War II, and they still didn't get it all. They never will.

If your stomach is grumbling, **Hôtel La Sapinière's** airy and reasonable café is a short walk away (just west of the American Cemetery; see page 304).

Back in your car, retrace your route along the beach (look for worthwhile information boards along the sea) and hug the coast past the flags heading toward the Pointe de la Percée cliff, which, from here, looks very Pointe du Hoc-like (American Army Rangers mistook this cliff for Pointe du

Hoc, costing them time and lives). A local artist made that striking metal sculpture rising from the waves in honor of the liberating forces, and to symbolize the rise of freedom on the wings of hope.

Keep hugging the coastline on D-517 and pull over about 100 yards before the Hôtel Casino to find the two German bunkers just below the hotel—one now transformed into a monument to US National Guard troops who landed on D-Day. Anti-tank guns housed in these bunkers were not aimed out to sea, but instead were positioned to fire directly up the beach.

Look out to the ocean. It was here that the Americans assembled their own floating bridge and artificial harbor (à la Arromanches). The harbor functioned for 12 days before being destroyed by an unusually vicious June storm (the artificial port at Arromanches and a makeshift port at Utah Beach were used until November of 1944). Have a seaside drink or lunch at the hotel's view café, and contemplate a stroll toward the jutting Pointe de la Percée.

Drive uphill past Hôtel Casino on D-517. Look to your left to find two small concrete window frames high in the cliff that served German machine gun nests, then notice the pontoon bridge on the right that had been installed at this beach. After the storm, it was moved to Arromanches and used as a second off-loading ramp. It was discovered only a few years ago...in a junkyard.

At the junction with D-514, turn right (west) toward Pointe du Hoc. Along the way, in the hamlet of Englesqueville la Percée, you'll see a 10th-century fortified farm on the left offering **Calvados tastings.** To try some, cross the drawbridge, ring the rope bell, and meet charming owners Souzic and Bernard Lebrec. Start with their cider, move on to Pommeau (a mix of apple juice and Calvados), and finish with Calvados. They also sell various other regional products, including D-Day Honey, which is made by one of the guides I recommend (tel. 09 60 38 60 17, mobile 06 76 37 46 41).

▲▲▲Pointe du Hoc

The intense bombing of the beaches by Allied forces is best imagined here, where US Army Rangers scaled impossibly steep cliffs to disable a German gun battery. Pointe du Hoc's bomb-cratered, lunar-like landscape and remaining bunkers make it one of the most evocative of the D-Day sites.

Cost and Hours: Pointe du Hoc is free and open daily mid-April-mid Sept 9:00-18:00, off-season 9:00-17:00, tel. 02 31 51 62 00.

Getting There: It's off route D-514, 20 minutes west of the American Cemetery.

Visiting Pointe du Hoc: Park near the new visitors center and stop here first for an overview of the heroic efforts to take the Pointe. Relax in the cinema for an eight-minute film on this Mission Impossible assault. Then follow the path toward the sea. Upon entering the site, you'll see an opening on your left that's as wide as a manhole cover and about six feet deep. This was a machine gun nest. Three soldiers would be holed up down there—a commander, a gun loader, and the gunner.

Climb to the **viewing platform** ahead and survey the scene. This point of land was the Germans' most heavily fortified position along the D-Day beaches. It held six 155mm guns that were capable of firing up to 13 miles. The farthest part of Omaha Beach is 9 miles to the east; Utah Beach is only 8 miles to the west. For the American landings to succeed, the Allies had to run the Germans off this cliff. So they bombed it to smithereens, dropping over 1,500 tons of bombs on this one cliff top. That explains the craters. Heavy bombing started in April of 1944, continued into May, and hit its peak on June 6—making this the most intensely bombarded site of the D-Day targets. Even so, only about 5 percent of the bunkers were destroyed. The problem? Multiple direct hits were needed to destroy bunkers like these, which were well-camouflaged and whose thick, dense walls were heavily reinforced.

Walk around. The battle-scarred **German bunkers** and the cratered landscape remain much as the Rangers left them. You can crawl in and out of the bunkers at your own risk, but picnicking is forbidden—the bunkers are considered gravesites. Notice the six large, round open sites with short rusted poles stuck in a concrete center. Each held a gun (picture the 155mm gun you saw by the Omaha Beach Museum). Destroying these was the Rangers' goal.

Walk to the bunker hanging over the ocean with the stone column at its top. This **memorial** symbolizes the Ranger "Dagger," planted firmly in the ground. Read the inscription, then walk below the sculpture to peer into the narrow slit of the bunker. Look over the cliff, and think about the 205 handpicked Rangers who attempted a castle-style assault. They landed to your right, using rocket-propelled grappling hooks connected to 150-foot ropes, and climbed ladders borrowed from London fire departments. With the help of supporting naval fire, the Rangers would take relatively light casualties in the initial attack, partially because the Germans weren't prepared. They regarded their position as nearly impregnable from any attack from the sea.

Timing was critical though; the Rangers had just 30 minutes before the rising tide would overcome the men below. After finally succeeding in their task, the Rangers found that the guns had been moved—the Germans had put telegraph poles in their place. (Commander Erwin Rommel had directed that all coastal guns not under the cover of roofs be pulled back due to air strikes.) The Rangers eventually found the guns stashed a half-mile inland and destroyed them.

Climb down into the bunker, which was the site's communication center, and find the room with the narrow opening. From here, men would direct the firing of the six anti-ship guns via telephone. Also in the bunker are rooms where soldiers ate and slept.

▲German Military Cemetery

To ponder German losses, visit this somber, thought-provoking resting place of 21,000 German soldiers. This was originally the site for one of 15 temporary American cemeteries in Normandy. Compared to the American Cemetery at St. Laurent, which symbolizes hope and victory, this one is a clear symbol of defeat and despair. The site seems appropriately bleak, with two graves per simple marker and dark, basalt crosses in groups of five scattered about. Birth and death dates (day/month/year) on the graves make clear the tragedy of the soldiers' short lives. The circular mound in the middle covers the remains of 207 unknown soldiers and 89 others. Notice the ages of the young soldiers who gave their lives for a cause they couldn't understand. A small visitors center gives more information on this and other German war cemeteries.

Cost and Hours: Free, daily April-Oct 8:00-19:00, off-season generally 9:00-17:00, tel. 02 31 22 70 76.

Getting There: It's on N-13 in the village of La Cambe, 15 minutes south of Pointe du Hoc and 15 minutes west of Bayeux (follow signs reading *Cimetière Militaire Allemand*).

Sleeping near Omaha Beach

With a car, you can find better deals on accommodations and wake up a stone's throw from many landing sites. Besides these recommended spots, you'll pass scads of good-value *chambres d'hôtes* as you prowl the D-Day beaches. The last two places are a few minutes toward Bayeux in the village of Formigny.

$$ Hôtel la Sapinière** is a find just a few steps from the beach at Vierville-sur-Mer. A grassy, beach-bungalow kind of place, it has sharp, crisp rooms, all with private patios, and a lighthearted, good-value restaurant/bar serving €13 omelets and salads, and €16 *plats* (Db-€90, loft Db-€105, Tb/Qb-€130; breakfast-€12, in Le Ruquet in St-Laurent-sur-Mer—10 minutes west of the American Cemetery, take D-517 down to the beach, turn right and keep going; tel. 02 31 92 71 72, www.la-sapiniere.fr, scithierry@wanadoo.fr).

$$ Hôtel du Casino** is a good place to experience Omaha Beach. This average-looking hotel has surprisingly comfortable rooms and sits alone, overlooking the beach in Vierville-sur-Mer, between the American Cemetery and Pointe du Hoc. All rooms have views, but the best face the sea: Ask introverted owner Madame Clémençon for *côté mer* (Db-€90, view Db-€100, extra bed-€16, elevator planned for 2015, view restaurant with *menus* from €27, café/bar on the beach below, tel. 02 31 22 41 02, hotel-du-casino@orange.fr). Don't confuse this with Hôtel du Casino in St-Valery en Caux.

$$ At **Ferme du Mouchel,** animated Odile rents four colorful and good rooms with sweet gardens in a lovely farm setting in the village of Formigny. You won't get lost—this place is well-signed (Db-€65 Tb-€75-90, Qb-€95-110, cash only, includes breakfast, tel. 02 31 22 53 79, mobile 06 15 37 50 20, www.ferme-du-mouchel.com, odile.lenourichel@orange.fr).

$$ La Ferme aux Chats is another good place in Formigny with clean and comfortable rooms at fair prices and welcoming owners (Db-€80, Tb-€93, cash only, includes breakfast, tel. 02 31 51 00 88, www.lafermeauxchats.fr, info@fermeauxchats.fr).

Utah Beach D-Day Sites

These sights are listed in logical order coming from Bayeux or Omaha Beach. For the first two sights, take the Utah Beach exit (D-913) from N-13 and turn right. Serious sightseers can bundle the Utah Beach Landing Museum, the Airborne Museum in Ste-Mère Eglise, and the "Open Sky Museum" GPS driving tour in one combo-ticket (€15, sold only at Ste-Mère Eglise TI).

Church at Angoville-au-Plain

Just five minutes from the N-13 exit, at this simple Romanesque church, two American medics—Kenneth Moore and Robert Wright—treated German and American wounded while battles raged only steps away. On June 6, American paratroopers landed around Angoville-au-Plain, a few miles inland of Utah Beach, and met fierce resistance from German forces. The two medics set up shop in the small church, and treated American and German soldiers for 72 hours straight, saving many lives. German patrols entered the church on a few occasions. The medics insisted that the soldiers leave their guns outside or leave the church—incredibly, they did. In an amazing coincidence, this 12th-century church is dedicated to two martyrs who were doctors as well.

A faded informational display outside the church recounts the events here; an English handout is available inside. Pass through the small cemetery and enter the church. Inside, several wooden pews toward the rear still have visible bloodstains. Find the new window that honors the American medics and another that honors the paratroopers (€3 requested donation for brochure, daily 9:00-18:00, 2 minutes off D-913 toward Utah Beach).

▲▲▲Utah Beach Landing Museum (Musée du Débarquement)

This is the best museum located on the D-Day beaches, and worth the 45-minute drive from Bayeux. For the Allied landings to succeed, many coordinated tasks had to be accomplished: Paratroopers had to be dropped inland, the resistance had to disable bridges and cut communications, bombers had to deliver payloads on target and on time, the infantry had to land safely on the beaches, and supplies had to follow the infantry closely. This thorough yet manageable museum pieces those many parts together in a series of fascinating exhibits and displays.

Cost and Hours: €8, daily June-Sept 9:30-19:00, Oct-Nov and Feb-May 10:00-18:00, closed Dec-Jan, last entry one hour before closing, tel. 02 33 71 53 35, www.utah-beach.com. Guided museum tours are offered (2/day), call ahead for times or ask when you arrive (tours are free, tips appropriate).

Getting There: From Bayeux, travel west toward Cherbourg on N-13 and take the Utah Beach exit (D-913). Turn right at the exit to reach the museum. An American and French flag duo leads to the entry as you approach. The road leaving the museum, the Route de la Liberté, runs all the way from Utah Beach to Cherbourg, and in the other direction, on to Paris and Berlin, with every kilometer identified with historic road markers.

Visiting the Museum: Built around the remains of a concrete German bunker, the museum nestles in the sand dunes on Utah Beach, with floors above and below sea level. Your visit starts with background about the American landings on Utah Beach (20,000 troops landed on the first day alone) and the German defense strategy (Rommel was displeased at what he found two weeks before the invasion). See the good 12-minute film that sets the stage well.

The highlight of the museum is the display of innovative invasion equipment with videos demonstrating how it worked: the remote-controlled Goliath mine, the LVT-2 Water Buffalo and Duck amphibious vehicles, the wooden Higgins landing craft (named for the New Orleans man who invented it), and the best—a fully restored B-26 bomber with its zebra stripes and 11 menacing machine guns, without which the landings would not have been possible (the yellow bomb icons indicate the number of missions a pilot had flown). Enter the simulated briefing room and sense the pilots' nervous energy—would your plane fly *LOW* or *HIGH?* Listen to the many videos as veterans describe how they took the beach and rushed into the interior—including testimony from Richard Winters, the leader of Easy Company in Stephen Ambrose's WWII classic *Band of Brothers*.

The stunning grand finale is the large, glassed-in room overlooking the beach, with Pointe du Hoc looming to your right. From here, you'll peer over re-created German trenches and feel what it must have felt like to have been behind enemy lines. Many German bunkers remain buried in the dunes today. Outside, find the beach access where Americans first broke through Hitler's Atlantic Wall and find a monument to American leadership on the small bluff.

To reach the next sight, follow the coastal route (D-421) and signs to Ste-Mère Eglise.

Ste-Mère Eglise

This celebrated village lies 15 minutes north of Utah Beach and was the first village to be liberated by the Americans, due largely to its strategic location on the Cotentin Peninsula. The area around Ste-Mère Eglise was the center of action for American paratroopers, whose objective was to land behind enemy lines in support of the American landing at Utah Beach.

For *The Longest Day* movie buffs, Ste-Mère Eglise is a necessary pilgrimage. It was around this village that many paratroopers, facing terrible weather and heavy anti-aircraft fire, landed off-target—and many landed in the town. One American paratrooper dangled from the town's church steeple for two hours (a parachute has been reinstalled on the steeple where Private John Steele's became snagged—though not in the correct corner). And though many paratroopers were killed in the first hours of the invasion, the Americans eventually overcame their poor start and managed to take the town (Steele survived his ordeal and the war). They played a critical role in the success of the Utah Beach landings by securing roads and bridges behind enemy lines. Today, the village greets travelers with flag-draped streets and a handful of worthwhile sights.

The **TI** on the square across from the church has loads of information and rents audiovisual guides with GPS, allowing you to discover the town and D-Day sights in the area on your own. It's called the **Open Sky Museum**—but actually it's a three-hour driving tour of the region linking all the D-Day sites together (€8, €250 deposit for GPS unit, may be able to download it for free to your own GPS unit or smartphone, ask at the TI). The TI also sells a combo-ticket good for the Utah Beach Landing Museum, the Airborne Museum, and the Open Sky Museum driving tour (€15, only available at the TI, July-Aug Mon-Sat 9:00-18:00, Sun 10:00-16:00; Sept-June Mon-Sat 9:00-13:00 & 14:00-18:00, Sun 10:00-16:00; 6 Rue Eisenhower, tel. 02 33 21 00 33, www.sainte-mere-eglise.info).

At the center of town, the 700-year-old **medieval church** on the town square was the focus of the action during the invasion. It now holds two contemporary stained-glass windows that acknowledge the heroism of the Allies. The window in the left transept features St. Michael, patron saint of paratroopers (€2 to park in the lots near the church, free on side streets).

The **Airborne Museum** is a must-see sight. Housed in two parachute-shaped structures and one low-slung, hanger-like structure, its collection is dedicated to the daring aerial landings that were essential to the success of D-Day. During the invasion, in the Utah Beach sector alone, 23,000 men were dropped from planes (remarkably, only 197 died), along with 1,700 vehicles and 1,800 tons of supplies.

In the first building, you'll see a Waco glider (104 were flown into Normandy at first light on D-Day) that was used to land supplies in fields to support the paratroopers. Each glider could be used only once. Feel the canvas fuselage and check out the bare-bones interior. The second, larger building holds a Douglas C-47 plane that dropped parachutists, along with many other supplies essential to the successful landings. Here you'll find models of soldiers and their uniforms, displays of their personal possessions and weapons, and two movies: One focuses on the airborne invasion, and the other venerates President Ronald Reagan's 1984 trip to Normandy. Climb to the view platform to appreciate the wingspan of a C-47.

A third structure (labeled *Operation Neptune*) puts you into the paratrooper's experience starting with a night flight and jump, then tracks your progress on the ground past enemy fire using elaborate models and sound effects.

Cost and Hours: €8, daily April-Sept 9:00-18:45, Oct-Dec and Feb-March 10:00-17:00, closed Jan, 14 Rue Eisenhower, tel. 02 33 41 41 35, www.airborne-museum.org.

Canadian D-Day Sites

The Canadians' assignment for the Normandy invasions was to work with British forces to take the city of Caen. They hoped to make quick work of Caen, then move on. That didn't happen. The Germans poured most of their reserves, including tanks, into the city and fought ferociously for two months. The Allies didn't occupy Caen until August of 1944.

Juno Beach Centre

Located on the beachfront in the Canadian sector, this facility is dedicated to teaching travelers about the vital role Canadian forces played in the invasion, and about Canada in general. (Canada declared war on Germany two years before the United States, a fact little recognized by most Americans today.) After at-

tending the 50th anniversary of the D-Day landings, Canadian veterans were saddened by the absence of information on their contribution (after the US and Britain, Canada contributed the largest number of troops—14,000), so they generated funds to build this place (plaques in front honor key donors).

Cost and Hours: €7, €11 with guided tour of Juno Beach—highly recommended, daily April-Sept 9:30-19:00, Oct and March 10:00-18:00, Nov-Dec and Feb 10:00-17:00, closed Jan, tel. 02 31 37 32 17, www.junobeach.org.

Tours: The best way to appreciate this sector of the D-Day beaches is to take a tour with one of the Centre's capable Canadian guides. The tour covers important aspects of the battles and touches on the changes to the sand dunes and beaches since the war (€5.50 for tour alone, €11 with admission, 45 minutes; April-Oct generally at 10:00, 12:00, and 15:00; verify times prior to your visit).

Getting There: It's in Courseulles-sur-Mer, about 15 minutes east of Arromanches off D-514.

Visiting Juno Beach: Your visit to the Centre includes many thoughtful exhibits that bring to life Canada's unique ties with Britain, the US, and France, and explains how the war front affected the home front in Canada. You'll also learn about the heroism of Canadian soldiers and the immense challenges they faced during and after their landings here, which are highlighted in the powerful, 12-minute film that you'll see near the end of your visit.

To better understand the Canadians' role in the invasion, take advantage of the Centre's eager-to-help, red-shirted "exchange students" (young Canadians who work as guides at the Centre for a 4-month period). They are great resources for what to do and see in "their" area. Be sure to ask for the hand-drawn map showing sights of interest.

Nearby: When leaving the Juno Beach Centre, to the left about 400 yards away you'll spot a huge stainless steel cross. This is La Croix de Lorraine, which marks the site where General de Gaulle landed on June 14, 1944. Information plaques describe this important event, which cemented de Gaulle's role as the leader of free France.

Canadian Cemetery

This small, touching cemetery hides a few miles above the Juno Beach Centre and makes a modest statement when compared with other, more grandiose cemeteries in this area. To me, it captures the understated nature of Canadians perfectly. Surrounded by beautiful farmland with distant views to the beaches, you'll find 2,000 graves marked with maple leaves and the soldiers' names and age. Some are engraved with family remembrances; all are decorated with live flowers or plants in their honor. You'll also see a few information plaques between the road and the graves. From Courseulles-sur-Mer, follow signs to *Caen* on D-79. After about 2.5 miles (4 kilometers), follow signs to the cemetery (and Bayeux) at the roundabout.

Caen

Though it was mostly destroyed by WWII bombs, today's Caen (pronounced "kahn," population 115,000) is a thriving, workaday city packed with students and a few tourists. The WWII museum and the vibrant old city are the targets for travelers, though these sights come wrapped in a big city with rough edges. And though Bayeux or Arromanches—which are smaller—make the best base for most D-Day sites, train travelers with limited time might find urban Caen more practical because of its buses to Honfleur, convenient car-rental offices near the train station, and easy access to the Caen Memorial Museum.

Orientation to Caen

The looming château, built by William the Conqueror in 1060, marks the city's center. West of here, modern Rue St. Pierre is a popular shopping area and pedestrian zone. To the east, the more historic Vagueux quarter has many restaurants and cafés in half-timbered buildings. A marathon race in honor of the Normandy invasion is held every June 8 and ends at the Memorial Museum.

TOURIST INFORMATION

The TI is opposite the château on Place St. Pierre, 10 long blocks from the train station (take the tram to the St. Pierre stop). Pick up a map and free visitor's guide filled with practical information (Mon-Sat 9:30-18:30, until 19:00 July-Aug, Sun 10:00-13:00 & 14:00-17:00 except closed Sun Oct-March, drivers follow *Parking Château* signs, tel. 02 31 27 14 14, www.tourisme.caen.fr).

ARRIVAL IN CAEN

These directions assume you're headed for the town's main attraction, the Caen Memorial Museum.

By Car: Finding the memorial is quick and easy. It's a half-mile off the ring-road expressway (*périphérique nord,* take *sortie* #7, look for white *Le Mémorial* signs). When leaving the museum, follow *Toutes Directions* signs back to the ring road.

By Train: Caen is two hours from Paris (12/day) and 20 minutes from Bayeux (20/day). Caen's modern train station is next to the *gare routière,* where buses from Honfleur arrive. Car-rental offices are right across the street. There is no baggage storage at the station, though free baggage storage is available at the Caen Memorial Museum. The efficient tramway runs right in front of both stations, and taxis usually wait in front. For detailed instructions on getting to the Caen Memorial Museum, see "Getting There" in the next section.

By Bus: Caen is one hour from Honfleur by express bus (2-3/day), or two hours by the scenic coastal bus (4/day direct). Buses stop near the train station.

Sights in Caen

▲▲▲Caen Memorial Museum (Le Mémorial de Caen)

Caen, the modern capital of lower Normandy, has the most thorough and by far the priciest WWII museum in France. Located at the site of an important German headquarters during World War II, its official name is The Caen-Normandy Memorial: Center for History and Peace (Le Mémorial de Caen-Normandie: Cité de l'Histoire pour la Paix). With two video presentations and numerous exhibits on the lead-up to World War II, coverage of the war in both Europe and the Pacific, accounts of the Holocaust and Nazi-occupied France, the Cold War aftermath, and more, it effectively puts the Battle of Normandy into a broader context.

Cost and Hours: €19, free for all veterans and kids under 10 (ask about good family rates). Open March-Oct daily 9:00-19:00; Nov-Dec and Feb Tue-Sun 9:30-18:00, closed Mon; closed most of Jan; last entry 75 minutes before closing. An audioguide (€4) streamlines your visit by providing helpful background for each area of the museum (tel. 02 31 06 06 44—as in June 6, 1944, www.memorial-caen.fr).

Getting There by Taxi: Cabs normally wait in front of the train station and are the easiest solution (about €15 one-way, 15 minutes), particularly if you have bags.

Getting There by Public Transit: Allow 30 minutes for the one-way trip via tram and bus. Take the tram right in front of the station; it's the first shelter after you leave the train station—do not cross the tram tracks (line A, direction: Campus 2, or line B, direction: St. Clair; buy €1.30 ticket from machine before boarding). Your ticket is good on both tram and bus for one hour; validate it on tram—white side up—and again on the bus when you transfer. Get off at the third tram stop (Bernières), then transfer to frequent bus #2. To reach the bus stop (which is signed from the tram stop), exit the tram, cross the street to the left in front of the tram, and walk 25 feet up Rue de Bernières until you see the bus shelter for #2. For transit maps, see www.twisto.fr.

Returning from the museum by bus and tram is a snap (taxi there and bus/tram back is a good compromise). Bus #2 waits across from the museum on the street's right side (the museum has the schedule). Buy your ticket from the driver and validate it. The bus whisks you to the Quatrans stop in downtown Caen (follow the stop diagram in the bus as you go), where you'll transfer to the tram next to the bus stop—validate your ticket again when you board. Either line A or line B will take you to the station—get off at the Gare SNCF stop.

Services: The museum provides free baggage storage and free supervised babysitting for children under 10 (for whom exhibits may be too graphic). There's a large gift shop with plenty of books in English, an excellent and reasonable all-day sandwich shop/café above the entry area, and a restaurant with a garden-side terrace (lunch only, located in the Cold War wing). Picnicking in the gardens is also an option.

Minivan Tours: The museum offers good-value minivan tours covering the key sites along the D-Day beaches. Two identical half-day tours leave the museum: one at 9:00 (€66/person) and one at 13:00 or 14:00—depending on the season (€83/person); both include entry to the museum. The all-day "D-Day Tour" package (€116, includes English information book) is designed for day-trippers and includes pick up from the Caen train station (with frequent service from Paris), a tour of the Caen Memorial Museum followed by lunch, then a five-hour tour in English of the American sector. Your day ends with a drop-off at the Caen train station in time to catch a train back to Paris or elsewhere. Canadians have a similar €116 tour option that will take them to Juno Beach. Contact the museum for details, reservations, and advance payment.

Planning Your Museum Time: Allow a minimum of 2.5 hours for your visit, including 50 minutes for the movies. You could easily spend all day here; in fact, tickets purchased after 13:00 are valid for 24 hours, so you can return the next day. The museum is divided into two major wings: the "World Before 1945" (the lead-up to World War II and the battles and related events of the war), and the "World After 1945" (Cold War, the Berlin Wall, cartoonists on world peace, and so on). Though each wing provides stellar exhibits and great learning, I'd spend most of my time on the "World Before 1945."

The museum is amazing, but it overwhelms some with its many interesting exhibits (all well-described in English). Limit your visit to the WWII sections and be sure to read the information boards that give a helpful overview of each sub-area. Then feel free to pick and choose which displays to focus on. The audioguide provides similar context to the exhibits.

My recommended plan of attack: Start your visit with the *Jour J* movie that sets the stage, then tour the WWII sections and finish with the second movie *(Espérance)*.

➲ **Self-Guided Tour:** Begin by watching *Jour J (D-Day)*, a powerful 15-minute film that shows the build-up to D-Day itself (runs every 30 minutes from 10:00 to 18:00, pick up schedule as you enter, works in any language). Although snippets come from the movie *The Longest Day* and German army training films, some footage is of actual battle scenes.

On the opposite side of the entry hall from the theater, find *Début de la Visite* signs and begin your museum tour with a downward-spiral stroll, tracing (almost psychoanalyzing) the path Europe followed from the end of World War I to the rise of fascism to World War II.

The lower level gives a thorough look at how World War II was fought—from General Charles de Gaulle's London radio broadcasts to Hitler's early missiles to wartime fashion to the D-Day landings. Videos, maps, and countless displays relate the war's many side stories, including the Battle of Britain, the French Resistance, Vichy France, German death camps, and the Battle of Stalingrad. To be more comprehensive, the museum has added exhibits about the war in the Pacific as well. Remember to read the information panels in each section, and then be selective about how much detail you want after that. Several powerful exhibits summarize the terrible human costs of World War II (Russia alone saw 21 million of its people die during the war; the US lost 300,000).

A separate exhibit covers just D-Day and the Battle of Normandy—enter on the main level next to the movie theater. Military buffs who expect a huge wing devoted to June 6, 1944, may be disappointed, but there are plenty of other museums in Normandy to satiate their interest (such as the excellent Utah Beach Landing Museum—see page 306).

After exploring the WWII sections, try to see the second movie *(Espérance—"Hope")*, a thrilling sweep through the pains and triumphs of the 20th century (hourly, 20 minutes, good in all languages, shown in the main entry hall).

The Cold War wing sets the scene for this era with audio testimonies and photos of European cities destroyed during World War II. It continues with a helpful overview of the bipolar world that followed the war, with fascinating insights into the psychological battle waged by the Soviet Union and the US for the hearts and minds of their people until the fall of communism. The wing culminates with a major display recounting the division of Berlin and its unification after the fall of the Wall.

An exhibit labeled *Taches d'Opinion* highlights the role of political cartoonists in expressing dissatisfaction with a range of government policies, from military to environmental to human rights issues.

The museum recently restored German General Wilhelm Richter's command bunker next to the main building. As you tour the underground passages, you'll see exhibits on the life of German soldiers stationed along the Atlantic Wall. This wing also explores the struggles of the POWs and French citizens who built the fortifications.

The finale is a walk through the US Armed Forces Memorial Garden (Vallée du Mémorial). On a visit here, I was bothered at first by the seemingly mindless laughing of lighthearted children, unable to appreciate the gravity of their surroundings. Then I read this inscription on the pavement: "From the heart of our land flows the blood of our youth, given to you in the name of freedom." And their laughter made me happy.

Mont St-Michel

For more than a thousand years, the distant silhouette of this island abbey sent pilgrims' spirits soaring. Today, it does the same for tourists. Mont St-Michel, among the top four pilgrimage sites in Christendom through the ages, floats like a mirage on the horizon. Today, several million visitors—far more tourists than pilgrims—flood the single street of the tiny island each year.

The year 2015 is a momentous one for this timeless abbey. This is the last year for the causeway that for more than 100 years has brought tourists to Mont St-Michel's front. (It's supposed to be demolished this year—see "The Causeway and Its Demise" sidebar.)

Orientation to Mont St-Michel

Mont St-Michel is surrounded by a vast mudflat and connected to the mainland by a half-mile causeway. Think of the island as having three parts: the fortified abbey soaring above, the petite village

The Causeway and Its Demise

In 1878, a causeway was built that allowed Mont St-Michel's pilgrims to come and go regardless of the tide (and without hip boots). The causeway increased the flow of visitors, but stopped the flow of water around the island. The result: Much of the bay silted up, and Mont St-Michel is no longer an island.

An ambitious project is well under way to return the island to its original form (the TI located next to the parking lot does a good job of explaining the project). Workers are replacing the causeway with a super-sleek bridge (allowing water to flow underneath). The first phase, completed in 2010, saw the construction of a dam *(barrage)* on the Couesnon River, which traps water at high tide and releases it at low tide, flushing the bay and forcing sediment out to the sea (the dam also provides great views of the abbey from its sleek wood benches). In 2011, parking near the island was removed and the mainland parking lot was built. In 2012, *navettes* (shuttles) began taking visitors from the parking lot to the island and in 2014 the new bridge was completed. The entire project should be done sometime in 2015. For the latest, visit www.projet-montsaintmichel.fr.

squatting in the middle, and the lower-level medieval fortifications. The village has just one main street on which you'll find all the hotels, restaurants, and trinkets. Between 11:00 and 16:00, tourists trample the dreamscape (much like earnest pilgrims did 800 years ago). A ramble on the ramparts offers mudflat views and an escape from the tourist zone. Though several tacky history-in-wax museums tempt visitors, the only worthwhile sights are the abbey at the summit of the island, and views from the ramparts and quieter lanes as you descend.

Daytime Mont St-Michel is a touristy gauntlet—worth a stop, but a short one will do. To avoid crowds, arrive late, sleep on the island or nearby on the mainland, and depart early. To bypass the tacky souvenir shops and human traffic jam on the main drag, follow the detour path up or down the mount (described on page 320). The tourist tide recedes late each afternoon. On nights from autumn through spring, the island stands serene, its floodlit abbey towering above a sleepy village. The abbey interior is open until midnight from mid-July to the end of August (Mon-Sat only).

The "village" on the mainland side of the causeway (called La

Caserne) consists of a lineup of modern hotels and a handful of shops.

TOURIST INFORMATION

An excellent TI with helpful English-speaking staff is in the new wood-and-glass building near the shuttle stop. Find the slick touch-screen monitors describing the various phases of the causeway project (daily April-Sept 9:00-18:00, off-season 10:00-18:00). Free WCs and baggage lockers are available.

When you arrive on the island, the tiny TI is on your left as you enter Mont St-Michel's gates. Since it's so cramped, it's smart to get your information at the TI near the parking lot. Both TIs have listings of *chambres d'hôtes* on the mainland, English tour times for the abbey, tour times for walks outside the island, bus schedules, and the tide table *(Horaires des Marées)*, which is essential if you plan to explore the mudflats outside Mont St-Michel (island TI daily July-Aug 9:00-19:00, March-June and Sept-Oct 9:00-12:30 & 14:00-18:00, Nov-Feb 10:00-12:30 & 14:00-17:00; tel. 02 33 60 14 30, www.ot-montsaintmichel.com). A post office and ATM are 50 yards beyond the TI.

ARRIVAL IN MONT ST-MICHEL

Prepare for lots of walking, particularly if you arrive by car and are not sleeping on the island or in nearby La Caserne.

By Train: The nearest train station is in Pontorson (called Pontorson-Mont St-Michel). The few trains that stop here are met by a bus waiting to take passengers right to the gates of Mont St-Michel (about €3, 12 buses/day July-Aug, 8/day Sept-June, fewer on Sun, 20 minutes). Taxis between Pontorson and Mont St-Michel get you to the *navette* (island shuttle) stop and cost about €20 (€25 after 19:00 and on weekends/holidays; tel. 02 33 60 33 23 or 02 33 60 82 70). If you plan to arrive on Saturday night, beware that Sunday train service from Pontorson is almost nonexistent.

By Bus: Buses from Rennes and St-Malo stop next to the TI at the parking lot (for details, see "Mont St-Michel Connections" at the end of this chapter). From Bayeux, it's faster to arrive on Hôtel Churchill's minivan shuttle (see page 283).

By Car: If you're staying at a hotel on the island, follow signs for *La Caserne* and enter the parking lot on your right. Parking P3 is for you (€12.30). Those staying in La Caserne can drive right to their hotel, but need a code number to open a gate blocking the access road (€4 access fee per entry, subject to change; get code and directions from your hotelier before you arrive).

Day-trippers are directed to a sea of parking (see map). The layout is confusing; follow the parking signs with a car icon. To avoid extra walking, take your parking ticket with you and pay at

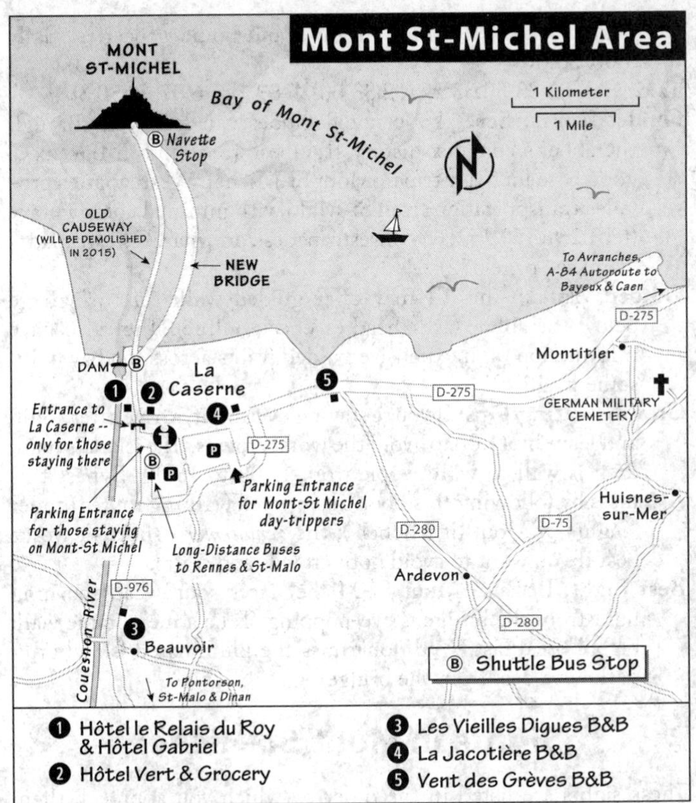

the machines near the TI when you leave (€12.30 flat fee, good for 24 hours, no re-entry privileges—if you leave and return on the same day, you'll pay another €12.30, machines accept cash and US credit cards, parking tel. 02 14 13 20 15). If you arrive after 19:00 and stay only for the evening, parking is free. If you arrive after 19:00 and leave before 11:30 in the morning, the fee is €4.

From the remote parking lot or *La Caserne* village, you can either walk to the island, or take the short ride on the free shuttle (departures every few minutes). You can also ride in the horse-drawn *maringote* (double-decker wagon, €5.20).

HELPFUL HINTS

Tides: The tides here rise above 50 feet—the largest and most dangerous in Europe, and second in the world after the Bay of Fundy between New Brunswick and Nova Scotia, Canada. High tides *(grandes marées)* lap against the TI door, where you should find tide hours posted.

Groceries: Next to **Hôtel Vert** in La Caserne is a misnamed Super

Marché stocked with souvenirs and some groceries (daily 9:00-20:00).

Taxi: Call 02 33 60 33 23, 02 33 60 26 89, or 06 07 96 50 36.

Guided Tours: Several top-notch guides can lead you through the abbey's complex history. The best are found in Bayeux, a good base for a day trip to Mont St-Michel. **Westcapades** provides transportation from St-Malo with minimal commentary (tel. 02 96 39 79 52, www.westcapades.com, marc@westcapades.com; see page 332).

Guided Walks: The **TI** may offer guided walks of the village below the abbey (ask ahead or check online). They also have information on inexpensive guided walks across the bay (with some English).

Crowd-Beating Tips: If you're staying overnight, arrive after 16:00 and leave by 11:00 to avoid the worst crowds. The island's main drag is wall-to-wall people from 11:00 to 16:00. Bypass this mess by following this book's suggested walking routes (under "Sights in Mont St-Michel"); the *gendarmerie* shortcut works best if you want to avoid both crowds and stairs.

Best Light: Because Mont St-Michel faces southwest, morning light from the bridge is eye-popping. Take a memorable walk before breakfast. And don't miss the illuminated island after dark (also best from the bridge).

Sights in Mont St-Michel

These sights are listed in the order by which you approach them from the mainland.

The Bay of Mont St-Michel

The vast Bay of Mont St-Michel has long played a key role. Since the sixth century, hermit-monks in search of solitude lived here. The word "hermit" comes from an ancient Greek word meaning "desert." The next best thing to a desert in this part of Europe was the sea. Imagine the desert this bay provided as the first monk climbed the rock to get close to God. Add to that the mythic tide, which sends the surf speeding eight miles in and out with each tide cycle. Long before the causeway was built, when Mont St-Michel was an island, pilgrims would approach across the mudflat, aware that the tide swept in "at the speed of a galloping horse" (well, maybe a trotting horse—12 mph, or about 18 feet per second at top speed).

Quicksand was another peril. A short stroll onto the sticky sand helps you imagine how easy it would be to get one or both feet stuck as the tide rolled in. The greater danger for adventurers today is the thoroughly disorienting fog and the fact that the sea

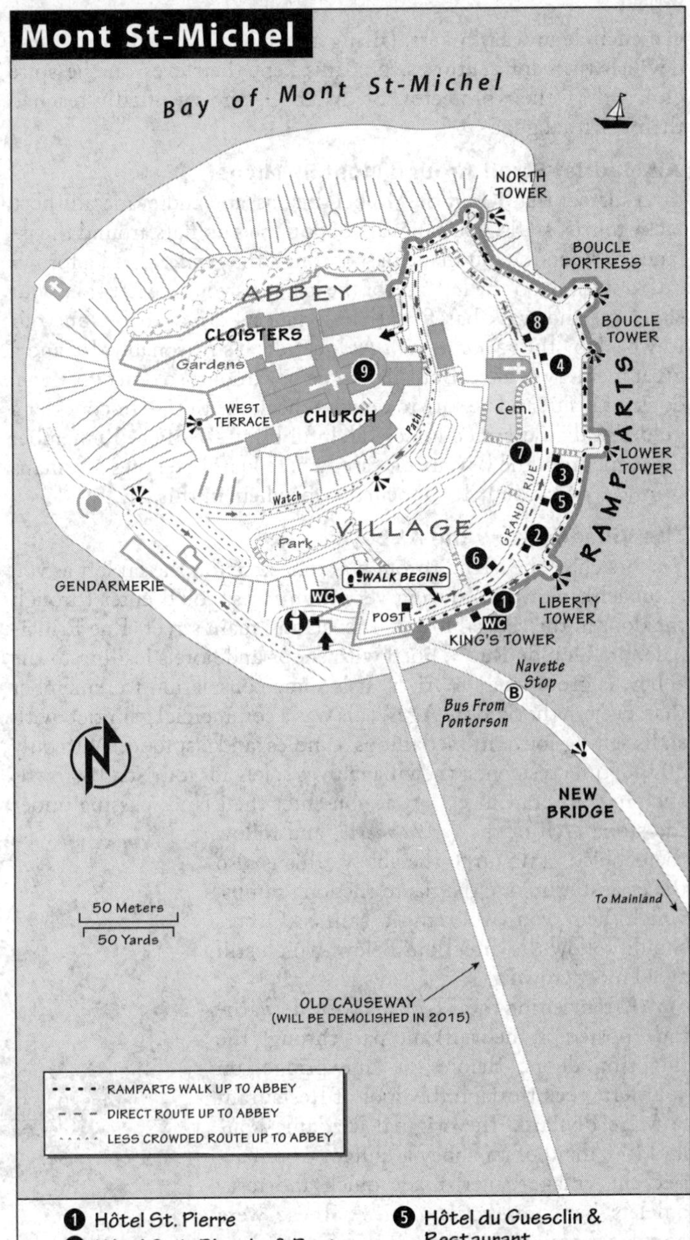

1 Hôtel St. Pierre
2 Hôtel Croix Blanche & Rest.
3 Hôtel le Mouton Blanc & Café Mère Poulard
4 Hôtel la Vieille Auberge & Restaurant
5 Hôtel du Guesclin & Restaurant
6 La Sirene Crêperie
7 Restaurant le St. Michel
8 Les Terrasses Poulard
9 Entry to Abbey

can encircle unwary hikers. (Bring a mobile phone.) Braving these devilish risks for centuries, pilgrims kept their eyes on the spire crowned by their protector, St. Michael, and eventually reached their spiritual goal.

▲▲Mudflat Stroll Around Mont St-Michel

To resurrect that Mont St-Michel dreamscape and evade all those tacky tourist stalls, you can walk out on the mudflats around the island (to reach the mudflats, pass through the *gendarmerie,* a former guard station, on the left side of the island as you face it). Take your shoes off and walk barefoot (handy faucets are available on your way back by the *gendarmerie*). At low tide, it's reasonably dry and a great memory-maker. But this can be hazardous, so don't go alone, don't stray far, and be sure to double-check the tides—or consider a guided walk (described under "Helpful Hints," earlier). Remember the scene from the Bayeux tapestry where Harold rescues Normans from the quicksand? It happened somewhere in this bay.

The Village Below the Abbey

Visitors enter the island through a stone arch (on the far left as you approach). However, during very high tides, you'll enter through the door in the central tower. The island's main street (Rue Principale, or "Grande Rue"), lined with shops and hotels leading to the abbey, is grotesquely touristy. It is some consolation to remember that, even in the Middle Ages, this was a commercial gauntlet, with stalls selling souvenir medallions, candles, and fast food. With only 30 full-time residents, the village lives solely for tourists. If crowds stick in your craw, keep left as you enter the island, passing under the stone arch of the *gendarmerie,* and follow the cobbled ramp up to the abbey. This is also the easiest route up, thanks to the long ramps, which help you avoid most stairs. (Others should follow the directions below, which still avoid most crowds.)

After visiting the TI, check the tide warnings (posted on the wall) and pass through the imposing doors. Before the drawbridge, on your left, peek through the door of Restaurant la Mère Poulard. The original Madame Poulard (the maid of an abbey architect who married the village baker) made quick and tasty omelets here *(omelette tradition).* These were popular for pilgrims, who, in pre-causeway days, needed to beat the tide to get out. They're still a hit with tourists—even at the rip-off price they charge today (they're much cheaper elsewhere). Pop in for a minute, just to enjoy the show as old-time-costumed cooks beat eggs.

You could continue the grueling trudge uphill to the abbey with the masses (all island hotel receptions are located on this street). But if the abbey's your goal, bypass the worst crowds and tourist kitsch by climbing the first steps on your right after the drawbridge and following the ramparts in either direction up and up to the abbey (quieter if you go right; ramparts described on page 325).

Public WCs are next to the island TI at the town entry, after the Mère Poulard Biscuiterie on the right, and partway up the main drag by the tiny St. Pierre church, where you can attend Mass (times posted on the door), opposite Les Terrasses Poulard gift shop.

▲▲Abbey of Mont St-Michel

Mont St-Michel has been an important pilgrimage center since A.D. 708, when the bishop of Avranches heard the voice of Archangel Michael saying, "Build here and build high." With the foresight of a saint, Michael reassured the bishop, "If you build it...they will come." Today's abbey is built on the remains of a Romanesque church, which stands on the remains of a Carolingian church. St. Michael, whose gilded statue decorates the top of the spire, was the patron saint of many French kings, making this a favored site for French royalty through the ages. St. Michael was particularly popular in Counter-Reformation times, as the Church employed his warlike image in the fight against Protestant heresy.

This abbey has 1,200 years of history, though much of its story was lost when its archives were taken to St-Lô for safety during World War II—only to be destroyed during the D-Day fighting. As you climb the stairs, imagine the centuries of pilgrims and monks who have worn down the edges of these same stone steps. Keep to the right, as tour groups can clog the left side of the steps.

Cost and Hours: €9; May-mid-July daily 9:00-19:00; mid-July-Aug Mon-Sat 9:00-24:00, Sun 9:00-19:00; Sept-April daily 9:30-18:00; closed Dec 25, Jan 1, and May 1; last entry one hour before closing, mid-July-Aug ticket office closes from 18:00-18:30; www.mont-saint-michel.monuments-nationaux.fr/en. Buy your ticket to the abbey and keep climbing. Mass is held Mon-Sat at 12:00, Sun at 11:15, in the abbey church (www.abbaye-montsaintmichel.com).

Visiting the Abbey: Allow 20 minutes to hike at a steady pace from the island TI. To avoid crowds, arrive by 10:00 or after 16:00 (the place gets really busy by 11:00). On most summer evenings, when the abbey is open until 24:00 and crowds are gone, visits come with music and mood lighting called *Ballades Nocturnes* (€9, none held Sun). It's worth paying a second admission to see the abbey so peaceful (nighttime program starts at 19:00; daytime tickets aren't valid for re-entry, but you can visit before 19:00 and stay on).

Tours: Get an English leaflet and follow my self-guided tour below. The excellent audioguide gives greater detail (€4.50, €6/2 people). You can also take a 1.25-hour English-language guided tour (free but tip requested, 2-4 tours/day, first and last tours usually around 10:00 and 15:00, confirm times at TI, meet at top terrace in front of church). The guided tours, which can be good, come with big crowds. You can start a tour, then decide if it works for you—but I'd skip it, instead following my directions below.

➲ **Self-Guided Tour:** Visit the abbey by following a one-way route. You'll climb to the ticket office, then climb some more. Stop after you pass a public WC, and look back to the church. That boxy Gothic structure across the steps is one of six cisterns that provided the abbey with water. Inside the room marked *Accueil* you'll find interesting models of the abbey through the ages.

• *Find your way to the big terrace, walk to the round lookout at the far end, and face the church.*

West Terrace: In 1776, a fire destroyed the west end of the church, leaving this grand view terrace. The original extent of the church is outlined with short walls (as well as the stonecutter numbers, generally not exposed like this—a reminder that they were paid by the piece). The buildings of Mont St-Michel are made of granite stones quarried from the Isles of Chausey (visible on a clear day, 20 miles away). Tidal power was ingeniously harnessed to load, unload, and even transport the stones, as barges hitched a ride with each incoming tide.

As you survey the Bay of Mont St-Michel, notice the polder land—farmland reclaimed by Normans in the 19th century with the help of Dutch engineers. The lines of trees mark strips of land used in the process. Today, this reclaimed land is covered by salt-loving plants and grazed by sheep whose salty meat is considered a local treat. You're standing 240 feet above sea level, at the summit of what was an island called "the big tomb." The small island just farther out is "the little tomb."

The bay stretches from Normandy (on the right as you look to the sea) to Brittany (on the left). The Couesnon River below marks the historic border between the two lands. Brittany and Normandy have long vied for Mont St-Michel. In fact, the river used to pass Mont St-Michel on the other side, making the abbey part of Brittany. Today, it's just barely—but definitively—on Norman soil. The new dam across this river (easy to see from here—it looks like a bridge when its gates are open) was built in 2010. Central to the dam is a system of locking gates that retain water upriver during high tide and release it six hours later, in effect flushing the bay and returning it to a mudflat at low tide (see "The Causeway and Its Demise" sidebar on page 315).

• *Now enter the...*

Abbey Church: Sit on a pew near the altar, under the little statue of the Archangel Michael (with the spear to defeat dragons and evil, and the scales to evaluate your soul). Monks built the church on the tip of this rock to be as close to heaven as possible. The downside: There wasn't enough level ground to support a sizable abbey and church. The solution: Four immense crypts were built under the church to create a platform to support each of its wings. While most of the church is Romanesque (round arches, 11th century), the light-filled apse behind the altar was built later, when Gothic arches were the rage. In 1421, the crypt that supported the apse collapsed, taking that end of the church with it. Few of the original windows survive (victims of fires, storms, lightning, and the Revolution).

In the chapel to the right of the altar stands a grim-looking statue of the man with the vision to build the abbey (St. Aubert). Take a spin around the apse, and find the suspended pirate-looking ship and the glass-covered manhole (you'll see it again later from another angle).

• *After the church, enter the...*

Cloisters: A standard feature of an abbey, this was the peaceful zone that connected various rooms, where monks could meditate, read the Bible, and tend their gardens (growing food and herbs for medicine). The great view window is enjoyable today (what's the tide doing?), but it was of no use to the monks. The more secluded a monk could be, the closer he was to God. (A cloister, by definition, is an enclosed place.) Notice how the columns are staggered. This efficient design allowed the cloisters to be supported with less building material (a top priority, given the difficulty of transporting stone this high up). The carvings above the columns feature various plants and heighten the Garden-of-Eden ambience the cloister offered the monks. The statues of various saints, carved among some columns, were de-faced—literally—by French revolutionaries.

• *Continue on to the...*

Refectory: This was the dining hall where the monks consumed both food and the word of God in silence—one monk read in a monotone from the Bible during meals (pulpit on the right near the far end). The monks gathered as a family here in one undivided space under one big arch (an impressive engineering feat in its day). The abbot ate at the head table; guests sat at the table in the middle. The clever columns are thin but very deep, allowing maximum light while offering solid support. From 966 until 2001, this was a Benedictine abbey. In 2001, the last three Benedictine monks checked out, and a new order of monks from Paris took over.

• *Stairs lead down one flight to a...*

Round Stone Relief Sculpture of St. Michael: This scene depicts the legend of Mont St-Michel: The archangel Michael wanted to commemorate a hard-fought victory over the devil with the construction of a monumental abbey on a nearby island. He chose to send his message to the bishop of Avranches (St. Aubert), who saw Michael twice in his dreams. But the bishop did not trust his dreams until the third time, when Michael drove his thumb into the bishop's head, leaving a mark that he could not deny.

• *Continue down the stairs another flight to the...*

Guests' Hall: St. Benedict wrote that guests should be welcomed according to their status. That meant that when kings (or other VIPs) visited, they were wined and dined without a hint of monastic austerity. This room once exploded in color, with gold stars on a blue sky across the ceiling. (The painting of this room was said to be the model for Sainte-Chapelle in Paris.) The floor was composed of glazed red-and-green tiles. The entire space was bathed in glorious sunlight, made divine as it passed through a filter of stained glass. The big double fireplace, kept out of sight by hanging tapestries, served as a kitchen—walk under it and see the light.

• *Hike the stairs through a chapel to the...*

Hall of the Grand Pillars: Perched on a pointy rock, the huge abbey church had four sturdy crypts like this to prop it up. You're standing under the Gothic portion of the abbey church—this was the crypt that collapsed in 1421. Notice the immensity of the columns (15 feet around) in the new crypt, rebuilt with a determination not to let it fall again. Now look up at the round hole in the ceiling and recognize it as the glass manhole cover from the church altar above.

• *To see what kind of crypt collapsed, walk on to the...*

Crypt of St. Martin: This simple 11th-century Romanesque vault has minimal openings, since the walls needed to be solid and fat to support the buildings above. As you leave, notice the thickness of the walls.

• *Next, you'll find the...*

Ossuary (identifiable by its big treadwheel): The monks celebrated death as well as life. This part of the abbey housed the hospital, morgue, and ossuary. Because the abbey graveyard was small, it was routinely emptied, and the bones were stacked here.

During the Revolution, monasticism was abolished. Church property was taken by the atheistic government, and from 1793 to 1863, Mont St-Michel was used as an Alcatraz-type prison. Its first inmates were 300 priests who refused to renounce their vows. (Victor Hugo complained that using such a place as a prison was like keeping a toad in a reliquary.) The big treadwheel—the kind that did heavy lifting for big building projects throughout the Middle Ages—is from the decades when the abbey was a prison. Teams of six prisoners marched two abreast in the wheel—hamster-style—powering two-ton loads of stone and supplies up Mont St-Michel. Spin the rollers of the sled next to the wheel.

Finish your visit by walking through the Promenade of the Monks, under more Gothic vaults, and into the vast **Scriptorium Hall** (a.k.a. Knights Hall), where monks decorated illuminated manuscripts. You'll then spiral down to the gift shop, turn right, and follow signs to the *Jardin*. The room after the shop holds temporary exhibits related to Mont St-Michel.

• *Exit the room and walk out into the rear garden. From here, look up at the miracle of medieval engineering.*

The "Merveille": This was an immense building project—a marvel back in 1220. Three levels of buildings were created: the lower floor for the lower class, the middle floor for VIPs, and the top floor for the clergy. It was a medieval skyscraper, built with the social strata in mind. The vision was even grander—the place where you're standing was to be built up in similar fashion, to support a further expansion of the church. But the money ran out, and the project was abandoned. As you leave the garden, notice the tall narrow windows of the refectory on the top floor.

• *Stairs lead from here back into the village. To avoid the crowds on your descent, turn right when you see the knee-high sign for* Musée Historique *and find your own route down or, at the same place, follow the Chemin des Ramparts to the left and hike down via the...*

Ramparts: Mont St-Michel is ringed by a fine example of 15th-century fortifications. They were built to defend against a new weapon: the cannon. They were low, rather than tall—to make a smaller target—and connected by protected passageways, which enabled soldiers to zip quickly to whichever zone was under attack. The five-sided Boucle Tower (1481, see map on page 319) was crafted with no blind angles, so defenders could protect it and the nearby walls in all directions. And though the English conquered all of Normandy in the early 15th century, they never took this well-fortified island. Because of its stubborn success against the English in the Hundred Years' War, Mont St-Michel became a symbol of French national identity.

After dark, the island is magically floodlit. Views from the ramparts are sublime. For the best view, exit the island and walk out on the bridge a few hundred yards.

NEAR MONT ST-MICHEL

German Military Cemetery (Cimetière Militaire Allemand)

Located three miles from Mont St-Michel, near tiny Huisnes-sur-Mer (well-signed east of Mont St-Michel, off D-275), this somber but thoughtfully presented cemetery-mortuary houses the remains of 12,000 German WWII soldiers brought to this location from all over France. (The stone blocks on the steps up indicate the regions in France from where they came.) A display of letters they sent home (with English translations) offers insights into the soldiers' lives. From the lookout, take in the sensational views over Mont St-Michel.

Sleeping in Mont St-Michel

Sleep on or near the island so that you can visit Mont St-Michel early and late. What matters is being here before or after the crush of tourists. Sleeping on the island—inside the walls—is a great experience for medieval romantics who don't mind the headaches associated with spending a night here, including average rooms and baggage hassles. To reach a room on the island, you'll need to carry your bags 10 minutes uphill from the *navette* (shuttle) stop. Take only what you need for one night in a smaller bag, but don't leave any luggage visible in your car.

Hotels near the island in *La Caserne* are a good deal cheaper and require less walking—you can park right at your hotel. All are a short walk from the free and frequent shuttle to the island, allowing easy access at any time.

ON THE ISLAND

There are eight small hotels on the island, and because most visitors day-trip here, finding a room is generally no problem (but finding an elevator is). Though some pad their profits by requesting that guests buy dinner from their restaurant, *requiring* it is illegal. Higher-priced rooms generally have bay views. Several hotels are closed from November until Easter.

The following hotels are listed in order of altitude; the first hotels are lowest.

$$$ Hôtel St. Pierre*** and **Hôtel Croix Blanche***,** which share the same owners and reception desk, sit side by side (reception at St. Pierre). Each provides comfortable rooms at inflated prices, some with good views. Both have several family loft rooms (non-view Db-€220, view Db-€225, Tb or Qb-€270-300; lower rates for Hôtel Croix Blanche; breakfast-€17, guest computer, Wi-Fi, tel. 02 33 60 14 03, www.auberge-saint-pierre.fr, contact@auberge-saint-pierre.fr).

$$$ Hôtel le Mouton Blanc** delivers a fair midrange value, with 15 rooms split between two buildings. The main building *(bâtiment principal)* is best, with cozy rooms, wood beams, and decent bathrooms; the more modern "annex" has cramped bathrooms (Db-€145, loft Tb-€160, loft Qb-€195, breakfast-€17, tel. 02 33 60 14 08, www.lemoutonblanc.fr, contact@lemoutonblanc.fr).

$$$ Hôtel la Vieille Auberge** is a small place with sharp rooms at fair prices (Db-€130, Tb-€180; spring for one of the four great terrace rooms—Db-€165; breakfast-€17, check in at their restaurant, but book through Hôtel St. Pierre, listed above).

$$ Hôtel du Guesclin** has the cheapest and best-value rooms I list on the island and is the only family-run hotel left there. Rooms have traditional decor and are perfectly comfortable. Check in at reception one floor up; if no one's there, try the bar on the main-street level (Db-€80-95, Tb-€95-105, breakfast-€9, Wi-Fi, tel. 02 33 60 14 10, www.hotelduguesclin.com, hotel.duguesclin@wanadoo.fr).

ON THE MAINLAND

Modern hotels gather in La Caserne on the mainland. These have soulless but cheaper rooms with easy parking (€4 access fee for entering La Caserne) and many tour groups. Remember to call at least a day ahead to get the code allowing you to skip the parking lot and drive to your hotel's front door.

$$$ Hôtel le Relais du Roy*** houses tight but well-configured and plush rooms with small balconies allowing "lean-out" views to the abbey. Most rooms are on the river side and have nice countryside views (Db-€90-115, Wi-Fi, bar, restaurant, breakfast-€10.50, tel. 02 33 60 14 25, www.le-relais-du-roy.com, reservation@le-relais-du-roy.com).

$$$ Hôtel Gabriel*** has modern and bright rooms with flashy colors and fair rates (Db-€105, Tb/Qb-€125, includes breakfast, Wi-Fi, tel. 02 33 60 14 13, www.hotelgabriel-montsaintmichel.com, hotelgabriel@le-mont-saint-michel.com).

$$ Hôtel Vert** provides motel-esque rooms with Wi-Fi at good rates (Db-€67-87, Tb-€81-106, Qb-€98-122, breakfast-€8.20, tel. 02 33 60 09 33, www.hotelvert-montsaintmichel.com, stmichel@le-mont-saint-michel.com).

CHAMBRES D'HOTES

Simply great values, these converted farmhouses are a few minutes' drive from the island.

$$ Les Vieilles Digues, where charming, English-speaking Danielle and Kin will pamper you, is two miles toward Pontorson on the main road (on the left if you're coming from Mont St-Michel). It has a lovely garden and seven nicely furnished and homey rooms with subtle Asian touches, all with showers (but no Mont St-Michel views). Ground-floor rooms have patios on the garden (D-€75, Db-€85, Tb-€105, includes good breakfast, easy parking—and you can walk to the free shuttle at the main parking lot, Wi-Fi, 68 Route du Mont St-Michel, tel. 02 33 58 55 30, www.bnb-normandy.com, danielle.tchen@wanadoo.fr).

$$ La Jacotière is closest to Mont St-Michel and within walking distance of the regional bus stop and the shuttle (allowing you to avoid the €12.30 fee to park). Gérald and Alicia offer six immaculate rooms and views of the island from the backyard (Db-€85, studio with great view from private patio-€90, extra bed-€20, includes breakfast, Wi-Fi, tel. 02 33 60 22 94, www.lajacotiere.fr, la.jacotiere@wanadoo.fr). Drivers coming from Bayeux should turn off the road just prior to the main parking lot. As the road bends to the left away from the bay, look for a regional-products store standing alone on the right. Take the small lane in front of the store signed *sauf véhicule autorisé*—La Jacotière is the next building.

$ Vent des Grèves is about a mile down D-275 from Mont St-Michel (green sign; if arriving from the north, it's just after Auberge de la Baie). Sweet Estelle (who speaks English) offers five bright, big, and modern rooms with good views of Mont St-Michel and a common deck with tables to let you soak it all in (Sb-€40, Db-€50, Tb-€60, Qb-€70, includes breakfast, Wi-Fi, tel. 02 33 48 28 89, www.ventdesgreves.com, ventdesgreves@orange.fr).

Eating in Mont St-Michel

Puffy omelets (*omelette montoise,* or *omelette tradition*) are Mont St-Michel's specialty. Also look for mussels (best with crème fraîche), seafood platters, and locally raised lamb *pré-salé* (a saltwater-grass diet gives the meat a unique taste, but beware of impostor lamb from New Zealand—ask where your dinner was raised). Muscadet wine (dry, white, and cheap) is the local wine and goes well with most regional dishes.

The menus at most of the island's restaurants look like carbon copies of one another (with *menus* from €18 to €28, cheap crêpes, and full à la carte choices). Some places have better views or more appealing decor, and a few have outdoor seating with views along the ramparts walk—ideal when it's sunny. If it's too cool to sit outside, window-shop the places that face the bay from the ramparts walk and arrive early to land a bay-view table. Unless noted otherwise, the listed restaurants are open daily for lunch and dinner.

La Sirene Crêperie offers a good island value and a cozy interior (€9 main-course crêpes, open daily for lunch, open for dinner in summer only, closed Fri off-season, enter through gift shop across from Hôtel St. Pierre, tel. 02 33 60 08 60).

Hôtel du Guesclin is the top place for a traditional meal, with white tablecloths and beautiful views of the bay from its inside-only tables (book a window table in advance; see details under "Sleeping in Mont St-Michel—On the Island," earlier).

Restaurant le St. Michel is lighthearted, reasonable, family-friendly, and run by helpful Patricia (decent omelets, mussels, salads, and pasta; open daily for lunch only, closed Thu-Fri off-season, open for dinner in July-Aug, test its toilet in the rock, across from Hôtel le Mouton Blanc, tel. 02 33 60 14 37).

Café Mère Poulard is a stylish three-story café-*crêperie*-restaurant one door up from Hôtel le Mouton Blanc. It's worth considering for its upstairs terrace, which offers the best outside table views up to the abbey (when their umbrellas don't block it). **La Vieille Auberge** has a broad terrace with the next-best views to the abbey and, so far, no big umbrellas. **La Croix Blanche** owns a small deck with abbey views and window-front tables with bay views, and **Les Terrasses Poulard** has indoor views to the bay.

Picnics: This is the romantic's choice. The small lanes above the main street hide scenic picnic spots, such as the small park at the base of the ancient treadwheel ramp to the upper abbey. You'll catch late sun by following the ramp that leads you through the *gendarmerie* and down behind the island (on the left as you face the main entry to the island). Sandwiches, pizza by the slice, salads, and drinks are all available to go at shops along the main drag. But you'll find a better selection at the modest Super Marché located on the mainland (see "Helpful Hints" on page 317).

NORMANDY

Mont St-Michel Connections

BY TRAIN, BUS, OR TAXI

Bus and train service to Mont St-Michel is a challenge. Depending on where you're coming from, you may find that you're forced to arrive and depart early or late—leaving you with too much or too little time on the island.

From Mont St-Michel to Paris: There are several ways to get to Paris. Most travelers take the regional bus from Mont St-Michel to Rennes or Dol-de-Bretagne and connect directly to the TGV (4/day via Rennes, 1/day via Dol-de-Bretagne, 4 hours total via either route from Mont St-Michel to Paris' Gare Montparnasse; €12.70 for bus to Rennes, €6.60 for bus to Dol-de-Bretagne; not covered by rail pass, buy ticket from driver, all explained in English at www.destination-montsaintmichel.com). You can also take the 20-minute bus ride to Pontorson (see next) and catch one of a very few trains from there (3/day, 5.5 hours, transfer in Caen, St-Malo, or Rennes).

From Mont St-Michel to Pontorson: The nearest train station to Mont St-Michel is five miles away, in Pontorson (called Pontorson/Mont St-Michel). It's connected to Mont St-Michel by a 20-minute bus ride (10/day July-Aug, 7/day Sept-June, tel. 02 14 13 20 15, www.accueilmontsaintmichel.com) or by taxi (€20, €25 at night and on weekends, tel. 02 33 60 33 23 or 02 33 60 82 70).

From Pontorson by Train to: Bayeux (2-3/day, 2 hours; also see Hôtel Churchill's shuttle van service—page 283).

From Mont St-Michel by Bus to: St-Malo (1/day direct usually at 15:45, 1.25 hours, daily July-Aug, less off-season, €20 round-trip fare even if only going one-way, buy from driver; or take 16:10 bus to Dol-de-Bretagne then train to St-Malo, 1.25 hours), **Rennes** (4/day direct, 1.75 hours). Keolis buses provide service to St-Malo, Dol-de-Bretagne, and Rennes (tel. 02 99 19 70 70, www.keolis-emeraude.com/en).

Taxis are more expensive, but are helpful when trains and buses don't cooperate. Figure €90 from Mont St-Michel to St-Malo, and €100 to Dinan (50 percent more on Sun and at night).

BY CAR

From Mont St-Michel to St-Malo, Brittany: The direct (and free) freeway route takes 40 minutes. For a scenic drive into Brittany, take the following route: Head to Pontorson, follow *D-19* signs to St-Malo, then look for *St. Malo par la Côte* and join D-797, which leads along *La Route de la Baie* to D-155 and on to the oyster capital of Cancale. In Cancale, keep tracking *St. Malo par la Côte* and *Route de la Baie* signs. You'll be routed through the town's port (good lunch stop), then emerge on D-201. Take time to savor Pointe du Grouin, then continue west on D-201 as it hugs the coast to St-Malo (see page 357).

From Mont St-Michel to Bayeux: Take the free and zippy A-84 toward Caen, exit at St. Lô, then follow signs to Bayeux.

BRITTANY

Dinan • St-Malo • Fougères

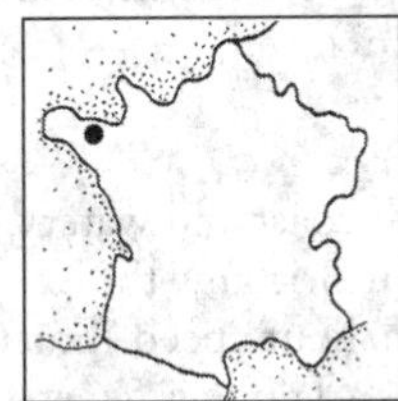

The bulky peninsula of Brittany ("Bretagne" in French; "Breizh" in Breton) is windswept and rugged, with a well-discovered coast, a forgotten interior, strong Celtic ties, and a craving for crêpes. This region of independent-minded locals is linguistically and culturally different from Normandy—and, for that matter, the rest of France. Tradition is everything here, where farmers and fishermen still play a big part in the region's economy.

The Couesnon River skirts the western edge of Mont St-Michel and has long marked the border between Normandy and Brittany. The constant moving of the riverbed made Mont St-Michel at times Norman and at other times Breton. To end the bickering, the border was moved a few miles to the west—making Mont St-Michel a Normandy resident for good.

In 1491, the French King Charles VIII forced Brittany's 14-year-old Duchess Anne to marry him (at Château de Langeais in the Loire Valley). Their union made feisty, independent Brittany a small, unhappy cog in a big country (the Kingdom of France). Brittany lost its freedom but, with Anne as queen, gained certain rights, such as free roads. Even today, more than 500 years later, Brittany's freeways come with no tolls, which is unique in France.

Locals take great pride in their distinct Breton culture. In Brittany, music stores sell more Celtic albums than anything else. It's hard to imagine that this music was forbidden as recently as the 1980s. During that repressive time, many of today's Breton pop stars were underground artists. And not long ago, a child would lose French citizenship if christened with a Celtic name.

But the locals are now free to wave their black-and-white-striped flag, sing their songs, and *parler* their language (there's a Breton TV station and radio station). Look for *Breizh* bumper stickers and flags touting the region's Breton name. Like their Irish counterparts, Bretons are chatty, their music is alive with stories of struggles against an oppressor, and their identities are intrinsically tied to the sea.

PLANNING YOUR TIME

With one full day, spend the morning in Dinan and the afternoon either along the Rance River (walking or biking are best, but driving works) or along Brittany's wild coast, where you can tour Fort la Latte and enjoy the massive views between Sable-d'Or-les-Pins and Cap Fréhel. Try to find a few hours for St-Malo—ideally when connecting Mont St-Michel with Brittany. The coastal route between Mont St-Michel and St-Malo—via the town of Cancale (famous for oysters and a good place for lunch), with a stop at Pointe du Grouin (fabulous ocean views)—gives travelers with limited time a worthwhile glimpse at this photogenic province.

GETTING AROUND BRITTANY

By Car: This is the ideal way to scour the ragged coast and watery towns. While autoroutes do not officially exist in Brittany, the expressways here are free but limited to a 110 km/hour speed limit (unlike the 130 km/hour limit on true autoroutes). Traffic is generally negligible, except in summer along the coast.

By Train and Bus: Trains provide barely enough service to Dinan and St-Malo (on Sun, service all but disappears). Key transfer points by train include the big city of Rennes and the small town of Dol-de-Bretagne. Some trips are more convenient by bus (including Rennes to Dinan and Dinan to St-Malo).

By Minivan Tour: Westcapades runs daylong minivan tours covering Dinan, St-Malo, and Mont St-Michel. Designed for day-trippers from Paris, the tours leave from St-Malo or Rennes. While flexible, these tours are light on information. You can get off at Mont St-Michel (described in the Normandy chapter)—making this tour a convenient way to reach that remote island abbey (€89/day, tel. 02 23 23 01 96, www.westcapades.com, marc@westcapades.com). A different tour option starts at the Rennes TGV Station, includes Mont St-Michel and key parts of the D-Day beaches, and ends at the train station in either Bayeux or Caen.

Another small tour company, **Afoot in France,** provides multiday tours in Brittany and Normandy for small groups or individuals. This service is ideal for people who'd like to have a local tour guide as their personal driver (www.afootinfrance.com, afootinfrance@gmail.com). Both of its guides also lead tours for my company.

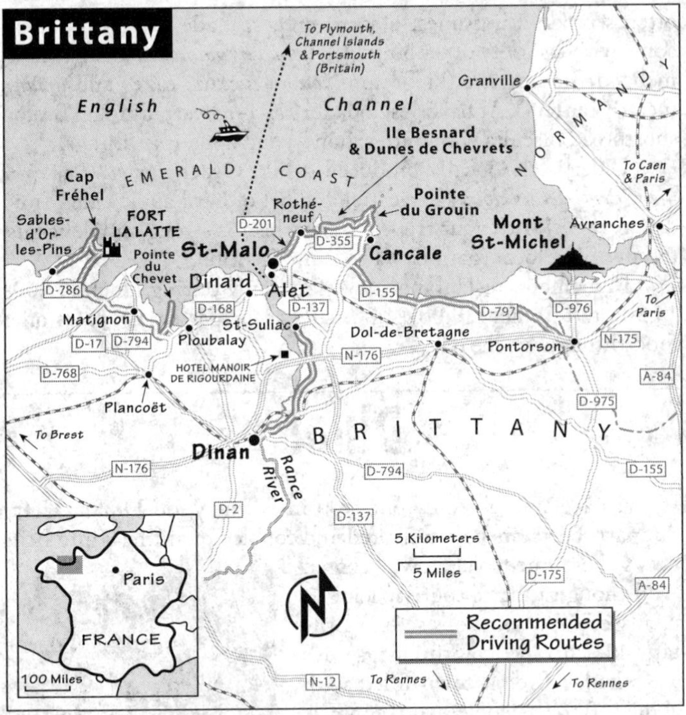

Brittany

English Channel
To Plymouth, Channel Islands & Portsmouth (Britain)
EMERALD COAST
Granville
NORMANDY
Ile Besnard & Dunes de Chevrets
To Caen & Paris
Cap Fréhel
Pointe du Grouin
Sables-d'Or-les-Pins
FORT LA LATTE
Rothéneuf
D-201
Mont St-Michel
Avranches
St-Malo
D-355
Cancale
Pointe du Chevet
Dinard
Alet
D-786
D-155
To Paris
D-168
D-137
D-797
D-976
Matignon
St-Suliac
Dol-de-Bretagne
D-17
D-794
Ploubalay
Pontorson
N-175
HOTEL MANOIR DE RIGOURDAINE
N-176
D-768
A-84
Plancoët
D-975
To Brest
BRITTANY
Dinan
N-176
Rance River
D-794
D-155
D-2
D-137
5 Kilometers
5 Miles
D-175
Paris
FRANCE
A-84
100 Miles
Recommended Driving Routes
N-12
To Rennes
To Rennes

BRITTANY'S CUISINE SCENE

Though the endless coastline suggests otherwise, there is more than seafood in this rugged Celtic land. Crêpes are to Bretons what pasta is to Italians: a basic, reasonably priced, daily necessity. *Galettes* are savory buckwheat crêpes, commonly filled with ham, cheese, eggs, mushrooms, spinach, seafood, or a combination. Purists insist that a *galette* should not have more than three or four fillings—overfilling it masks the flavor (which is the point in certain places).

Oysters *(huîtres)*, the second food of Brittany, are available all year. Mussels, clams, and scallops are often served as main courses, and you can also find *galettes* with scallops and *moules marinières* (mussels steamed in white wine, parsley, and shallots). Farmers compete with fishermen for the hearts of locals by growing fresh vegetables, such as peas, beans, and cauliflower.

For dessert, look for *far breton*, a traditional flan-like cake often served with prunes. Dessert crêpes, made with white flour, come with a variety of toppings. Or try *kouign amann*, a puffy, caramelized Breton cake (in Breton, *kouign* means "cake" and *amann* means "butter"). At bakeries, look for *ker-y-pom*, traditional Breton shortbread biscuits with butter, honey, and apple-pie fillings.

Cider is the locally produced drink. Order *une bolée de cidre brut, demi-sec* or *doux* (a traditional bowl of hard apple cider, from dry to sweet) with your crêpes. Breton beer is strong and delicious; try anything local (Sant Erwann is my favorite).

Remember, restaurants serve food only during lunch (12:00-14:00) and dinner (19:00-21:00, later in bigger cities); cafés offer food throughout the day.

Dinan

If you have time for only one stop in Brittany, do Dinan. Hefty ramparts corral its half-timbered and cobbled quaintness into Brittany's best medieval town center. And though it has a touristy icing—plenty of *crêperies*, shops selling Brittany kitsch, and colorful flags—it's a workaday Breton town filled with about 10,000 people who appreciate the beautiful, peaceful place they call home. This impeccably preserved ancient city escaped the bombs of World War II. It's also conveniently located, about a 45-minute drive from Mont St-Michel. For a memorable day, spend your morning exploring Dinan and your afternoon walking, biking, or boating the Rance River.

BRITTANY

Orientation to Dinan

Dinan's old city, wrapped in its medieval ramparts, gathers on a hill well above the Rance River. Cobbled lanes climb steeply from Dinan's small river port to the vast Place du Guesclin (gek-lahn). There you'll find lots of parking, Château de Dinan, and the TI. Place des Merciers, just north of Place du Guesclin, is the center of most shopping activities.

TOURIST INFORMATION

At the TI, pick up a free map and bus schedules, ask about boat trips on the Rance River, and check your email (July-Aug Mon-Sat 9:30-19:00, Sun 10:00-12:30 & 14:30-18:00; Sept-June Mon-Sat

9:30-12:30 & 14:00-18:00, closed Sun; just off Place du Guesclin near Château de Dinan at 9 Rue du Château, tel. 02 96 87 69 76, www.dinan-tourisme.com).

ARRIVAL IN DINAN

By Train: To get to the town center from Dinan's Old World train station (no lockers or baggage storage), find a taxi (see "Helpful Hints," below) or walk 20 steady minutes (see map on page 338). If walking, head left out of the train station, make a right at Hôtel de la Gare up Rue Carnot, turn right on Rue Thiers following *Centre Historique* signs, and go left across big Place Duclos-Pinot, passing just left of Café de la Mairie. To reach the TI and Place du Guesclin, go to the right of the café (on Rue du Marchix).

By Bus: Dinan's key intercity bus stop is in front of the post office on Place Duclos-Pinot, 10 minutes above the train station and five minutes below Place du Guesclin. To reach the historic core, cross the square, passing to the left of Café de la Mairie (for more bus information, see "Dinan Connections," later).

By Car: Dinan confuses drivers. Slow down, and expect to pay for most street parking. Follow *Centre Historique* signs and park on Place du Guesclin (free parking 19:00-9:00 except July-Sept and on market days on Thu). If you enter Dinan near the train station, drive the route described above (see "By Train"), and keep to the right of Café de la Mairie to reach Place du Guesclin. Check with your hotelier before leaving your car overnight on Place du Guesclin; it will be towed before 8:00 on market or festival days.

HELPFUL HINTS

Market Days: Every Thursday, a big open-air market is held on Place du Guesclin (8:00-13:00). In July and August, there's an art market on Wednesdays on Place St. Sauveur.

Internet Access: The TI has computers (small fee) and Wi-Fi.

Laundry: There's a self-serve launderette a few blocks from Place Duclos-Pinot at 19 Rue de Brest (Mon-Fri 8:30-12:00 & 13:45-19:00, Sat 8:30-18:00, closed Sun).

Supermarkets: Groceries are upstairs in the **Monoprix** (Mon-Sat 9:00-19:30, 7 Rue du Marchix). Or try **Carrefour City** on Place Duclos-Pinot (Mon-Sat 7:00-21:00, Sun 8:00-13:00).

Bike Rental: The TI has up-to-date information on bike-rental places. Try to rent your bike at the port, to avoid riding down and back up a big hill.

Taxi: Call 06 08 00 80 90 (www.taxi-dinan.com). Figure about €50-60 to St-Malo and €100 to Mont St-Michel.

Tourist Train: This *petit train* runs a circuit connecting the port and upper old town (€6, Easter-Sept 11:00-17:00, runs every

40 minutes, leaves in the old town from in front of Théâtre des Jacobins, a block off Place du Guesclin.

Picnic Park: The small but flowery Jardin Anglais hides behind the Church of St. Sauveur.

Dinan Walk

Frankly, I wouldn't go through a turnstile in Dinan. The attraction is the town itself. Enjoy the old town center, ramble around the ramparts, and explore the old riverfront harbor. Here are some ideas, laced together as a relaxed one-hour walk (not including exploring the port). Start near the TI, and as you wander, notice the pride locals take in their Breton culture.

• *Start in the center of Place du Guesclin, and find the statue of the horseback rider.*

Place du Guesclin: This sprawling town square/parking lot is named after Bertrand du Guesclin, a native 14th-century knight and hero (described as small in stature but big-hearted) who became a great French military leader, famous for his daring victories over England during the Hundred Years' War (like Joan of Arc, he was a key player in defeating the English). On this very square, he beat Sir Thomas of Canterbury in a nail-biter of a joust that locals still talk about to this day. The victory freed his brother, whom Thomas had taken prisoner in violation of a truce. For 700 years, merchants have filled this square to sell their produce and crafts (in modern times, it's Thu 8:00-13:00).

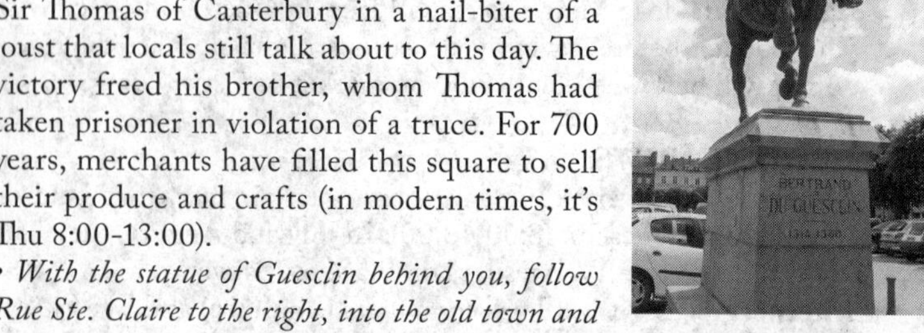

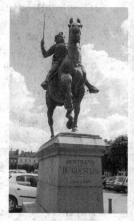

• *With the statue of Guesclin behind you, follow Rue Ste. Claire to the right, into the old town and to the...*

Théâtre des Jacobins: Fronting a pleasant little square, the theater was once one of the many convents that dominated the town. In fact, in medieval times, a third of Dinan consisted of convents. They're still common in Brittany, which remains the most Catholic part of France. The theater today offers a full schedule of events.

• *Turn left and walk down Rue de l'Horloge ("Clock Street") toward the clock tower. On the way, on your left, you'll see...*

Anybody's Tombstone: The tombstone without a head is a town mascot. It's actually a prefab tombstone, made during the Hundred Years' War, when there was more death than money in France. A portrait bust would be attached to this generic body for a proper, yet economical, burial.

• *On your right, before the clock tower, enter...*

La Craquanterie: This shop specializes in Breton cookies and treats. Look for *caramels au beurre salé* (salted butter caramels), *kouign amann* (extremely rich butter cake), *gâteau breton* (traditional cake), *craquants* (crisp cookies with salted butter), and the Breton answer to Nutella—*Craquamel.* Smiling Sam offers tastes of her goodies (Mon-Sat 10:00-19:00, closes at 18:00 off-season, closed Sun year-round, 12 Rue de l'Horloge, tel. 02 96 85 10 05).

• *Continue to the...*

Clock Tower: The old town spins around this clock tower, which has long symbolized the power of the town's merchants. The tower's 160 steps (the last few on a ladder) lead to a sweeping city view. Warning: Plug your ears at the quarter-hour, when the bells ring (€4, daily June-Sept 10:00-18:30, May 14:00-18:00, closed Oct-April).

• *At the corner of the street find the store...*

A l'Aise Breizh: This store, with its distinctive name (meaning "take it easy" in Breton), has been riding the wave of Brittany's cultural renewal since 1996. You've probably seen the store's name on bumper stickers throughout the region. Inside the store, you'll find some fun clothing and souvenirs designed in Brittany. Their mugs are based on the traditional Breton bowls that every local kid was raised with—hand-painted designs of costumed Bretons and inscribed with the kid's first name (Mon 14:00-19:00, Tue-Sat 10:00-19:00, closed Sun except July-Aug 10:00-19:00, 8 Rue de l'Apport, tel. 02 96 86 28 08).

• *Take the first left into Dinan's historic commercial center, Place des Merciers. Stop under a porch.*

Old Town Center: The arcaded, half-timbered buildings around you are Dinan's oldest. They date from the time when property taxes were based on the square footage of the ground floor. To provide shelter from both the rain and taxes, buildings started with small ground floors, then expanded outward as they got taller. Notice the stone bases supporting the wood columns. Because trees did not come in standard lengths, it was easier to adjust the size of the pedestals.

Medieval shopkeepers sold goods in front of their homes under the shelter of leaning walls. Most streets are named for the key commerce that took place there. Wander further toward the square and locate picturesque Rue de la Cordonnerie ("Shoe Street," to the left of the pretty restaurant La Mère Pourcel), a good example of a medieval lane, with overhanging buildings whose roofs nearly touch. After a disastrous 18th-century fire, a law required that the traditional thatch be replaced by safer slate.

• *From La Mère Pourcel, go up Rue de la Cordonnerie into a small maze*

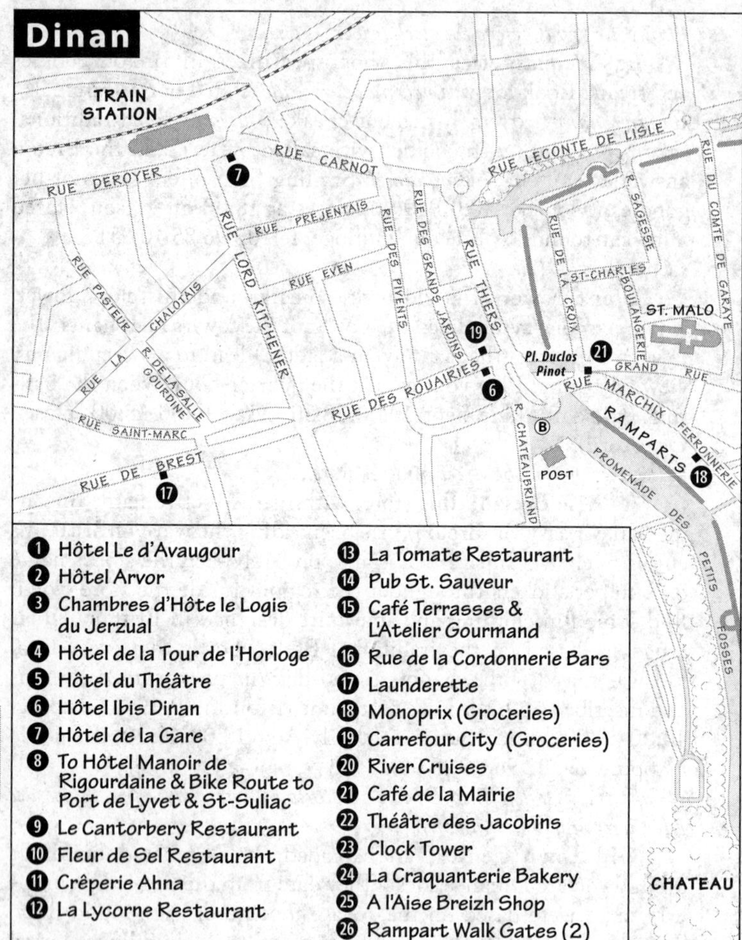

of streets. Walk through this "pub row," turn right, and then right again, climbing a set of stairs leading to a modern market.

La Cohue: If you're looking for a place to gather a picnic lunch, the shiny, renovated market stalls of La Cohue is it. There's been a market here since the 13th century, but the ambience today is very 21st century. It has a produce stand, wine store, cheese shop, bakery, and a rôtisserie where you can pick up a roast chicken to go (Tue-Sun 8:00-14:00, Fri-Sat until 19:00, closed Mon, www.la-cohue.com).

• *If it's open, walk through the market; otherwise you'll need to backtrack to Place des Merciers, where you can go into...*

La Belle Iloise: For three generations, a fishing family has respected the traditions of canning their fresh catch. The factory,

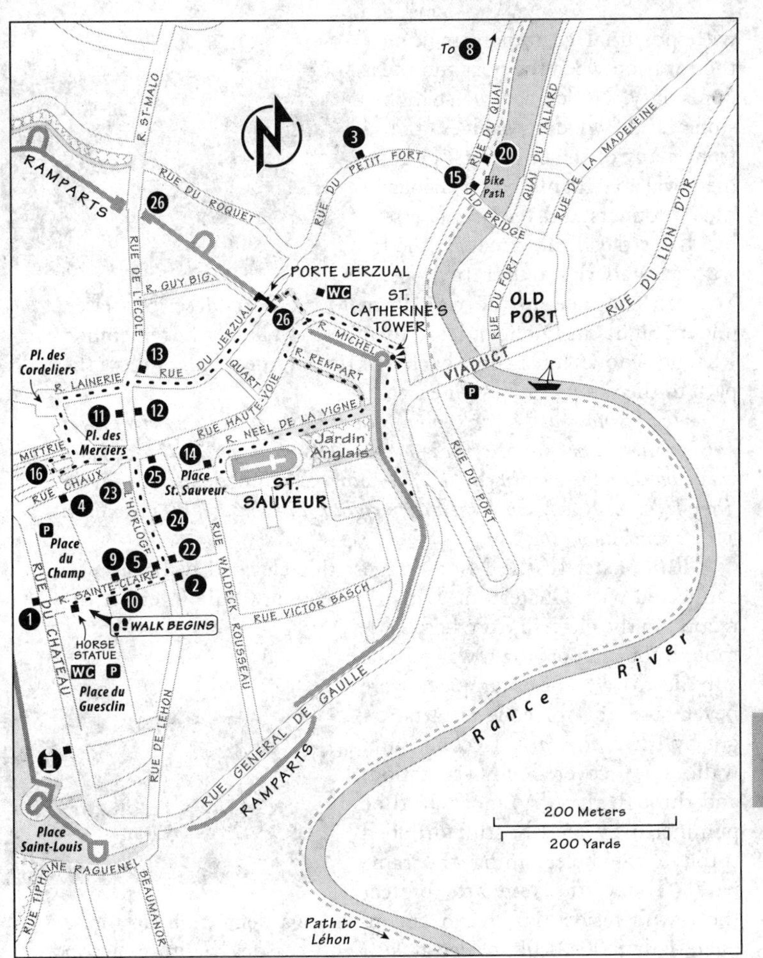

which is based in southern Brittany and has outlets all over France, produces tasty sardine, mackerel, and tuna spreads. Grab a baguette and a few pretty cans for a picnic later in the old harbor or let Fabienne share a quick recipe with you (daily 10:30-13:00 & 14:30-18:30, 1 Place des Merciers, tel. 02 96 39 69 23).

• *Continue working your way through the square. (The building with the arched stone facade at the end of the square—Les Cordeliers—used to be a Franciscan monastery during the Middle Ages; today, it's a middle school...wrap your brain around that change.) Turn right on Rue de la Lainerie ("Street of Wool Shops"), which becomes...*

Rue du Jerzual: This spiraling road was the primary medieval link to the port and the focus of commercial activity in old Dinan. The steep cobbled street (slippery when wet) was chock-a-block

with potential customers making their way between the port and the upper city. Notice the waist-high stone and wooden shelves that front many of the buildings. Here, medieval merchants could display their products and tempt passers-by. These days, the street is lined with art galleries and craft shops. You can continue all the way down to the port (described later, under "Sights in Dinan"); it's a 10-minute walk down (remember, what goes down must come back up). If your knees balk, follow the path to the ramparts, described next.

• *For the best look at Dinan's impressive fortified wall, turn right after passing under the massive medieval gate (Porte du Jerzual) and work your way up the curving road, following* Chemin de Ronde *signs. Turn right on Rue Michel, then turn right again through the green iron gate to walk along the...*

Ramparts: In the Middle Ages, this elevated walkway was connected with Château de Dinan (it's about a mile in either direction to the château from here). Although the old port town was repeatedly destroyed, these ramparts were never taken by force. If an attacker got by the *contrescarpe* (second outer wall, now covered in vegetation) and through the (dry) moat, he'd be pummeled by ghastly stuff dropped through the holes lining the ramparts. Today, the ramparts protect the town's residential charm and private gardens (ramparts gate open daily 8:00-21:00, closes at 17:00 off-season). Venture out on the (second) huge Governor's Tower to see how the cannon slots enabled defenders to shoot in all directions. As you look uphill, the St-Malo Tower is the last one you can see. But our next destination is the tower built into the wall to the right (with your back to the upper old town). The tall church even farther to the right is where our walk ends—the Church of St. Sauveur.

BRITTANY

• *Double back to Rue Michel and turn right. Take the first left, onto Rue du Rempart. Walk to the round tower (in the corner of the park), called...*

St. Catherine's Tower: This part of Dinan's medieval defense system allows strategic views of the river valley and over the old port. Find the medieval bridge below and the path that leads along the river to the right to Léhon (described later, under "Sights in Dinan"). To the left you can follow the Rance River downstream as it meanders toward the sea. The English gardens behind you are picnic-pleasant.

• *Walk through the gardens to the church behind you, and dip into the...*

Church of St. Sauveur: Enter this asymmetrical church (typical in Brittany) to see striking, modern stained-glass windows and a beautifully lit nave. Pick up the simple English explanation and learn the church's raison d'être. The building is a thousand years old—the wood balcony in the entry confirms that, as it heaves under the weight of the organ. When built, the church sat lonely on this hill, as all other activity was focused around the port.

• *Your tour is over. Good lunch cafés are across the square (see "Eating in Dinan," later), and you are a block below the main Rue de l'Horloge.*

Sights in Dinan

Dinan's Old Port

Following the self-guided walk, you can reach Dinan's modest little port by continuing down Rue du Jerzual (which becomes Rue du Petit Fort). Notice the unusual wood-topped building on the left-hand side before the port. This was a leather tannery. Those wooden shutters could open to dry the freshly tanned hides while the nearby river flushed the toxic waste products (happily, swimming was not in vogue then). The last business on the right before the port is a killer bakery with delicious local specialties, including *far breton* and *kouign amann* (you'll also find good picnic fixings and drinks to go). You deserve a baked break.

The port was the birthplace of Dinan a thousand years ago. For centuries, this is where people lived and worked, and today it's a great place for a riverside drink or snack. This once-thriving port is connected to the sea—15 miles away—by the Rance River. By taxing river traffic, the town grew prosperous. The tiny Vieux Pont (Old Bridge) dates to the 15th century. Because the port area was so exposed, the townsfolk retreated to the bluff behind its current fortifications. Notice the viaduct high above, built in 1850 to alleviate congestion and to send traffic around the town. Until then, the main road crossed the tiny Old Bridge, heading up Rue du Jerzual to Dinan.

▲Rance River Valley

The best thing about Dinan's port is the access it provides to lush riverside paths that amble along the gentle Rance River Valley. You can walk, bike, drive, or boat in either interesting direction (perfect for families).

On Foot: For a breath of fresh Brittany air and an easy walk, visit the flower-festooned village of **Léhon.** Trails on both sides of the river take you to the village in 30 minutes. The trail on the far side is more scenic but has been blocked by a landslide for several years and the detour is a rough hike up and down a steep hillside. Ask if the landslide has been cleared—with a new mayor, things might finally change. If you prefer staying on the level, a trail on the old-city side of the river starts in the parking lot under the viaduct.

Arriving in pristine little Léhon—a town of character, as the sign reminds you—visitors are greeted by a beautiful ninth-century abbey that rules the roost (find the cloisters). Explore the village's flowery cobbled lanes, but skip the town-topping castle ruin (free, daily 10:00-19:00 in summer, open only Sat-Sun off-season). Enjoy a meal at the adorable **La Marmite de l'Abbaye** restaurant, with seating inside or out. Your hostess, sweet Breton Madame Borgnic, serves wood-fire grilled meats for lunch and dinner (arrive for the 12:00 or 13:30 service, closed Mon-Tue, tel. 02 96 87 39 39). The trail continues on well past Léhon, but you'll need a bike to make a dent in it. The villages of Evran and Treverien are both reachable by bike (allow 45 minutes from Dinan to Evran, and an additional 25 minutes to Treverien).

By Bike: The Rance River Valley could not be more bike-friendly, as there's nary a foot of elevation gain (for bike rentals, ask at the TI). Here's what I'd do with three hours and a bike: Pedal to Léhon (following the "On Foot" route, above), then double back to Dinan and follow the bike path along the river downstream to the Port de Lyvet.

To reach the Port de Lyvet, ride through Dinan's port, staying on the old-city side of the river. You'll join a parade of ocean-bound boats as the river opens up, becoming more like an inlet of the sea. It's a breezy, level 30-minute ride past rock faces, cornfields, and slate-roofed farms to the tiny **Port de Lyvet** (cross bridge to reach village, trail ends a short distance beyond). **Le Lyvet Gourmand** café/restaurant is well-positioned in the village (open daily for lunch, dinner on weekends only, or a refreshing drink on its wooden deck, closed Wed off-season, tel. 02 96 41 45 48). Serious cyclists should continue on to St-Suliac via La Vicomté (described later, under "By Car").

By Boat: Boats depart from Dinan's port, at the bottom of Rue du Jerzual, 50 feet to the left of the Old Bridge on the Dinan side (schedules depend on tides, get details at TI). The snail-paced, one-hour cruise on the ***Jaman IV*** runs upriver to Léhon (the trip is better on foot or bike), taking you through a lock and past pretty scenery (€13, April-Oct 2-4/day, fewer off-season, tel. 02 96 39 28 41, www.vedettejamaniv.com). A longer cruise with **Compagnie Corsaire**

goes to St-Malo (€32.50 round-trip, €26 one-way, runs April-Sept, 1/day, slow and scenic 2.5 hours one-way, schedule changes with the tide, tel. 08 25 13 81 00, www.compagniecorsaire.com, or ask at TI). Enjoy St-Malo (described later in this chapter), then take the bus or train back (or do the reverse—bus/train to St-Malo, then boat back). Get the bus schedule before leaving Dinan (3-6/day, 1 hour, no buses on Sun except in summer).

By Car: Meandering the Rance River Valley by car requires a good map (orange Michelin #309 worked for me). Drivers connecting Dinan and St-Malo can include this short Rance joyride detour: From Dinan, go down to the port, then follow D-12 with the river to your right toward Taden, then toward Plouër-sur-Rance (Dinan's port-front road is occasionally blocked, in which case you'll join this route beyond the port). Stay straight through La Hisse, then drop down and turn right, following signs to *La Vicomté-sur-Rance.* Cross the Rance on the bridge and find the cute **Port de Lyvet** (lunch café described earlier), then continue to La Vicomté and find D-29 north towards St-Malo. Track your way to **St-Suliac,** a pretty little port town—classified in *les plus beaux villages de France*—with a handful of restaurants, a small grocery store, and a *boulangerie.* Stroll the ancient alleys, find a bench on the grassy waterfront, and contemplate lunch. From here, continue on to St-Malo or return to Dinan.

Sleeping in Dinan

Dinan is popular. Weekends and summers are tight; book ahead if you can. Dinan likes its nightlife, so be wary of rooms over loud bars, particularly on lively weekends.

IN THE OLD CENTER

$$$ Hôtel Le d'Avaugour**** is Dinan's most central four-star hotel, with an efficient staff, stay-awhile lounge areas, full bar, and backyard garden oasis. It faces busy Place du Guesclin, near the town's medieval wall. The wood-furnished rooms have comfortable queen- or king-sized beds and modern hotel amenities. Likable owner Nicolas strongly encourages two-night stays (streetside Db-€120-150, garden-side Db-€120-190, third person-€17, suites available, prices vary greatly by season, rooms over garden are best, good breakfast-€15, elevator, Wi-Fi, bikes available, 1 Place du

Sleep Code

Abbreviations **(€1 = $1.40, country code: 33)**
S = Single, **D** = Double/Twin, **T** = Triple, **Q** = Quad, **b** = bathroom, **s** = shower only, * = French hotel rating (0-5 stars)

Price Rankings

$$$ **Higher Priced**—Most rooms €95 or more
$$ **Moderately Priced**—Most rooms between €60-95
$ **Lower Priced**—Most rooms €60 or less

Unless otherwise noted, credit cards are accepted, English is spoken, and Wi-Fi is generally free. Prices change; verify current rates online or by email. For the best prices, always book directly with the hotel.

Champ, tel. 02 96 39 07 49, www.avaugourhotel.com, contact@avaugourhotel.com).

$$ Hôtel Arvor* ** is a top-notch place with a fine stone facade, ideally located in the old city a block off Place du Guesclin. It's well-run, with 24 tastefully appointed and comfortable rooms (standard Db-€78-98, Tb-€115-140, family suite for up to 6 people-€145 , breakfast-€9.80, elevator, Wi-Fi, parking-€6/day, 5 Rue Pavie, tel. 02 96 39 21 22, www.hotelarvordinan.com, contact@hotelarvordinan.com).

$$ Chambres d'Hôte le Logis du Jerzual is just about as cozy as it gets, with five warmly decorated rooms, period furnishings, and thoughtful touches throughout. Ideal hostess Sylvie Ronserray welcomes guests. Enjoy the terraced yard in this haven of calm close to the action: It's just up from the port but a long, steep walk below the main town (Db-€85-98, Db suite-€118, extra bed-€25, includes breakfast, Wi-Fi, 25 Rue du Petit Fort, tel. 02 96 85 46 54, www.logis-du-jerzual.com, sylvie.logis@laposte.net). To drop your bags, drive up the steep, narrow, and bumpy Rue du Petit Fort from the port (ignore the pedestrian zone warnings and follow the hotel signs). Parking is nearby.

$$ Hôtel de la Tour de l'Horloge** is a good two-star bet burrowed deep in the town's center, with 12 imaginatively decorated and impeccably maintained rooms fronting the bar-lined Rue de la Chaux (some rooms can be noisy on weekends). Gentle Catherine speaks English and gives a warm welcome; her goal is to connect travelers to Dinan and Brittany (Db-€69-78, Tb-€82-87, Qb-€92-105, prices higher in Aug, Wi-Fi in public areas, 5 Rue de la Chaux, tel. 02 96 39 96 92, www.hotel-dinan.com, hotel.pbdelatour@orange.fr).

$ Hôtel du Théâtre is ideal for budget travelers, with six central, simple, and clean rooms above a luminous café/bar, across from Hôtel Arvor (Db-€45, Tb-€65, prices higher July-Aug, breakfast-€6, Wi-Fi, 2 Rue Ste. Claire, tel. 02 96 39 06 91, owner Mickael speaks some English).

CLOSER TO THE TRAIN STATION

$$$ Hôtel Ibis Dinan*,** with its shiny, predictable comfort, stands tall between Place du Guesclin and the train station. It works especially well for bus and train travelers, as it's central, reasonably priced, and next to the bus stop—convenient for hitting regional destinations such as St-Malo. They may have rooms when others don't (Db-€90-110, extra bed-€10, breakfast-€9.50, 1 Place Duclos-Pinot, tel. 02 96 39 46 15, www.ibishotel.com, h5977@accor.com).

$ Hôtel de la Gare* faces the station and offers the full Breton Monty, with *charmant* Laurence and Claude (who both love Americans), a local-as-it-gets café hangout, and surprisingly quiet, clean, and comfy rooms for a bargain. The hotel has no email of its own and you won't find it on Booking.com, but it does offer free Wi-Fi—thanks to the owners' teenage son. Be sure to reserve in advance, as this hotel may close in 2015 (Ds-€37, Db-€50, Tb/Qb-€50-65, breakfast-€6, Place de la Gare, tel. 02 96 39 04 57).

NEAR DINAN

To locate this place, see the map on page 338.

$$$ Hôtel Manoir de Rigourdaine*** is *the* place to stay if you have a car and two nights to savor Brittany. Overlooking a splendid scene of green meadows and turquoise water, this well-renovated farmhouse comes with wood beams, comfy public spaces, immaculate grounds, and three-star rooms (many with views) for two-star prices (Db-€97-105, extra person-€20, breakfast-€9.50, guest computer, Wi-Fi, 15-minute drive north of Dinan, tel. 02 96 86 89 96, www.hotel-rigourdaine.fr, hotel.rigourdaine@wanadoo.fr). From Dinan, drop down to the port and follow D-12 toward Taden, then follow signs to *Plouër-sur-Rance,* then *Langrolay,* and look for signs to the hotel. If coming from the St-Malo area, take D-137 toward Rennes, then N-176 toward Dinan. Take the Rance Plouër exit, and follow signs to *Langrolay* until you see hotel signs. If coming from Rennes, take D-137 toward St-Malo, then N-176 toward Saint-Brieuc, take the Plouër-sur-Rance exit, and look for signs to *Langrolay* and then the hotel.

Eating in Dinan

Dinan has good restaurants for every budget. Since *galettes* (savory crêpes) are the specialty, *crêperies* are a nice, inexpensive choice—and available on every corner. Be daring and try the crêpes with scallops and cream, or go for the egg-and-cheese crêpes. Ham-filled crêpes can be salty. For a good dinner, book Le Cantorbery a day ahead if you can, and think hard about walking, riding, or driving to nearby Léhon for a charming village experience (see "Rance River Valley—On Foot," earlier).

Le Cantorbery is a warm place (literally), where meats are grilled in the cozy dining-room fireplace *à la tradition.* The seafood is *très* tasty (*menus* from €31, lunch from €14, closed Wed except July-Aug, just off Place du Guesclin at 6 Rue Ste. Claire, indoor dining only, two floors, tel. 02 96 39 02 52, well-run by sincere Madame Touchais).

Fleur de Sel, run by welcoming Monsieur Guillo, is where locals go for fish (meat dishes also served). The decor is appealing and the choices are varied. You'll find traditional food served with a modern twist (*menus* from €26-46, lunch *menu* €18, closed Sun eve and on Mon, 7 Rue Ste. Claire, tel. 02 96 85 15 14).

Crêperie Ahna rocks Dinan. Locals jam the place: The price is right, the dishes are excellent, and owner Gregory sets the tone for a fun experience. His vanilla rum is excellent. The cuisine goes well beyond crêpes; the do-it-yourself *pierrades*—where you cook your meat or fish on a hot stone at your table—are a treat (inside seating only, closed Sun, reservations recommended, 7 Rue de la Poissonnerie, tel. 02 96 39 09 13).

BRITTANY

La Lycorne is Dinan's place to go for a healthy serving of mussels prepared 20 different ways. The cook-at-your-table *pierrades* are a good deal (€14 mussels—served with fries of course, €15-18 *pierrade*). The ambience is medieval, especially if you order *Potence Flambée*—meat or fish served on mini-gallows (€18/person, minimum 2 orders). It's situated on a traffic-free street (closed Mon except July-Aug, 6 Rue de la Poissonnerie, tel. 02 96 39 08 13, www.restaurant-lycorne-dinan.com).

La Tomate dishes up pizza and pasta for €12-15 with appealing indoor or outdoor seating (April-Sept open daily, Oct-March closed Sun-Mon, 4 Rue de l'Ecole, tel. 02 96 39 96 12).

Pub St. Sauveur is a local watering hole/café with good prices and a hard-to-beat setting...when it's sunny (€7 for lunch salads and *plats,* Oct-March closed Sun, across from the church at 21 Place St. Sauveur, tel. 02 96 85 30 20). The café next door offers a similar menu and prices.

At the Old Port: You'll find several restaurants at the old port.

Have a before-dinner drink—or a meal if the waterfront setting matters more than the cuisine—at one of the places on the river. **Café Terrasses** is decent, with nice outdoor seating by the river (*menus* from €17, daily March-Oct, tel. 02 96 39 09 60).

L'Atelier Gourmand is revered by locals. Enjoy homemade French fare cooked by Christine and served by her husband Fabrice in an indoor seating or in the half-covered, river-view room. The daily specials have an exotic touch (€11 *salades* and *tartines*, €15 *plats*, closed Mon year-round, off-season closed Sun and Tue eve, tel. 02 96 85 14 18).

Nightlife: So many lively pub-like bars line the narrow, pedestrian-friendly **Rue de la Cordonnerie** that the street is nicknamed "Rue de la Soif" ("Street of Thirst"). When the weather is good, you can sit outside at a picnic table and strike up a conversation with a friendly, tattooed Breton.

Dinan Connections

Locals take the bus to Dol-de-Bretagne or to Rennes, then catch trains from there (trains from Dinan require several changes, take longer than buses for regional destinations, and barely run on Sundays). Regional bus service is provided by Tibus (www.tibus.fr) or Illenoo (www.illenoo-services.fr).

From Dinan by Train to: Paris' Gare Montparnasse (2/day, 3.5 hours, change in Dol-de-Bretagne, more with transfers in Dol and Rennes), **Pontorson/Mont St-Michel** (2/day, 1.5-2.5 hours, change in Dol, then bus or taxi from Pontorson, see "Mont St-Michel Connections" on page 329, **St-Malo** (6/day, 1-2 hours, transfer in Dol, bus is better—see below), **Amboise** (1/day, 6 hours, via Dol, Le Mans, and Tours or via Paris).

By Bus to: Rennes (with good train connections to many destinations, 7/day, 1 hour), **St-Malo** (3-6/day, none on Sun except in summer, 1 hour; faster, cheaper, and better than train, as bus stops are more central), **Mont St-Michel** (3/day, 3.5 hours, transfer in Rennes), **Dinard** (7/day, fewer on Sun, 45 minutes). All buses depart from Place Duclos-Pinot (near the main post office), and most make a stop at the train station, too.

St-Malo

Come here to experience a true Breton beach resort. The old city (called Intra Muros) is your target, with pretty beaches, powerful ramparts that hug the entire town, and island fortifications that litter the bay. The inner city has an eerie, almost claustrophobic feeling, thanks to the concentration of tall, dark stone buildings hemmed in by the towering ramparts (though a few pedestrian streets buck that sensation). The town feels better up top on the walls, which are *the* sight here. St-Malo is packed in July and August, when the 8,000 people who call the old city home are joined by 12,000 additional daily "residents." But if you're willing to brave the crowds, it's an easy 45-minute drive—or a manageable bus or train ride—from Mont St-Michel or Dinan. (However, there's no baggage storage anywhere.) If you have a whole day here, circumnavigate St-Malo along its walls, take the walk to Alet, and visit Fort du Petit Bé.

Orientation to St-Malo

TOURIST INFORMATION

St-Malo's TI is across from the main city gate (Porte St. Vincent) on Esplanade St. Vincent (Mon-Sat 9:00-19:30, Sun 10:00-18:00; closed at lunchtime April-June and Sept; shorter hours and closed Sun in off-season; tel. 08 25 13 52 00, www.saint-malo-tourisme.com). Pick up the helpful city map, along with schedules for the bus, train, or ferry (to Dinard). Downloadable walking tours of the city are available through the TI website.

ARRIVAL IN ST-MALO

By Train: The modern TGV Station is a five-minute bus ride on the #C-1, #C-2, or #C-3 lines to Porte St. Vincent (€1.25). If you'd rather walk, go for 15 minutes straight out of the station, then track the pointed spire in the distance for another five minutes.

By Bus: The main bus stops are near the Porte St. Vincent and TI (closer to town) and at the train station (confirm which stop your bus uses—some stop at both).

By Car: Follow *Intra-Muros* signs to the old center, and park as close as possible to the Porte St. Vincent (at the merry-go-round).

St-Malo's Seafaring Past

St-Malo has been a sailor's town since its origin as an ancient monastic settlement about 1,500 years ago. After the fall of the Roman Empire, monasteries provided security and stability, allowing communities like this one to grow and evolve into towns—and sometimes into important cities. By the 1100s, St-Malo was a powerful, fortified island guarding access to the Rance River Valley from one direction and the English Channel from the other. St-Malo later became notorious as the home of the corsairs—French mercenaries working for the king of France, and famous for daring raids on ships from other (unfriendly) countries. Unlike other pirates, these swashbuckling sailors were spared from the usual punishment for pillaging (death), as they were considered the king's combatants—a fine legal distinction. The corsairs of St-Malo were immensely profitable to the king (and themselves), and wreaked economic havoc on other countries (such as England) all the way up until the late 1700s. Find the statue of the last and best-known corsair of St-Malo, Robert Surcourf, as you stroll the rampart walls.

A big underground parking lot is opposite the Porte St. Vincent, and smaller surface lots are scattered around the walls.

HELPFUL HINTS

Internet Access: The most central place to get online inside the walls is at **Mokamalo** (Tue-Sat 10:00-13:00 & 15:00-19:00, closed Sun-Mon, 5 Rue de l'Orme, tel. 02 99 56 60 17). To get Wi-Fi for the price of a drink, try **Tam's Kaffé** on Place des Frères Lamennais (tel. 02 23 18 24 14, off-season closed Mon-Tue).

Services: You'll find pay WCs in some gates *(portes)* leading to the old city.

Laundry: Inside the walls, you'll find a launderette on the corner of Rue de la Herse and Halle aux Blés (daily 7:00-21:00).

Bike Rental: There are several places to rent bikes near the train station and TI. Ask at the TI or find **Ty'Boost** bikes near the TI at 49 Quai Duguay-Trouin (tel. 02 99 56 47 18).

Car Rental: Avis (tel. 02 23 18 07 18) and **Europcar** (tel. 02 99 56 75 17) are both inside the train station.

Foot Ferry: A nifty little ferry *(Bus de Mer)* shuttles passengers between St-Malo and Dinard in 10 minutes (€8.10 round-trip, runs 9:30-18:00, later in summer, closed Nov-Jan). Boats depart from the Cale de Dinan on the south side of the old city.

Minivan Tour: Westcapades guarantees minivan departures at least three times a week from St-Malo. Tours include Dinan and Mont St-Michel, and officially end at the Rennes train station so you can connect to Paris (see page 332).

Sights in St-Malo

▲St-Malo's Ramparts

To reach the ramparts, climb the stairs inside Porte St. Thomas and tour the walls counterclockwise. It's a rewarding mile-long romp around the medieval fortifications (the oldest segments date from the 1100s).

Along the way, stairs at several points *(portes)* provide access to the beach and the town. Walk down to the **beaches** if the tides allow (along with Mont St-Michel, St-Malo has Europe's greatest tidal changes). You'll see tree trunks planted like little forests on the sand—these form part of St-Malo's breakwater and must be replaced every 20 years. Storms scream in off the English Channel and bring surges of waves that pound the seawalls.

Those **fortified islands** were built during the wars of Louis XIV (late 1600s) by his military architect, Vauban, to defend the country against England. You can tour the closer forts when tides allow (each costs €5 to enter). **Fort National** is the first you'll come across (but can be visited only with a French-language tour). Farther along, you'll see the more worthwhile **Fort du Petit Bé** (access is often submerged), which sits behind Ile du Grand Bé, where the famous poet Chateaubriand is buried. The island of Grand Bé is worth a romp if the tide agrees, and the views of Fort du Petit Bé will send your imagination soaring. The longer, low-slung island even farther out has no buildings and is off-limits until WWII mines are completely removed. Speaking of World War II, St-Malo was decimated by American bombs during the war as part of the campaign to liberate France. Eighty percent of St-Malo was leveled. Even though they look old, most of the town's buildings date from 1945 or later.

As you walk along the wall, find the **Québec flags** flying in honor of St-Malo's sister city, Québec City. Explorer Jacques Cartier, who visited the future site of Québec City and is credited with discovering Canada, lived in and sailed from St-Malo. Cartier's statue can be found along the ramparts.

A bit after the recommended Le Corps de Garde Crêperie, you'll pass a ***Chiens du Guet*** restaurant sign. At one time, bulldogs were kept in the small, enclosed area behind the restaurant, then let loose late at night to patrol the beaches.

You'll eventually spot a long, concrete **jetty** below that offers good views back to the ramparts. Across the bay is the belle époque resort city of Dinard (described later). Farther along, look for long ***pétanque*** (a.k.a. *boules*) courts below the walls (you may encounter

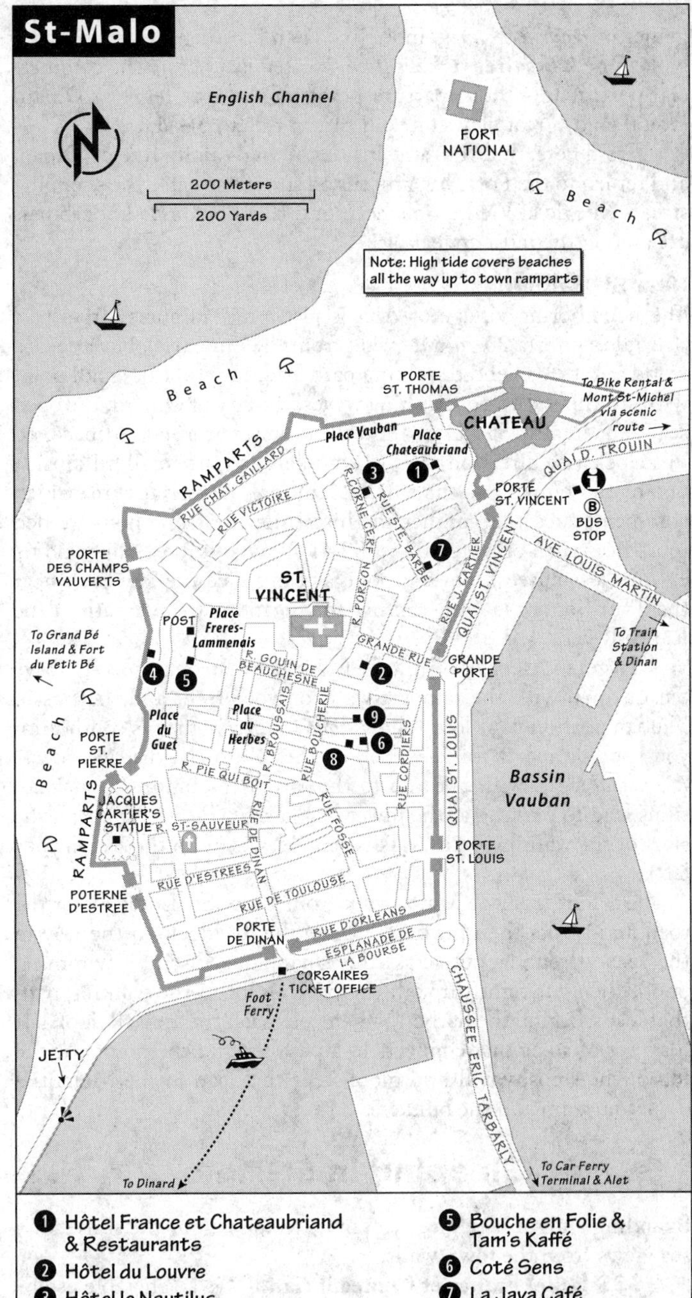

1. Hôtel France et Chateaubriand & Restaurants
2. Hôtel du Louvre
3. Hôtel le Nautilus
4. Le Corps de Garde Crêperie
5. Bouche en Folie & Tam's Kaffé
6. Coté Sens
7. La Java Café
8. Mokamalo (Internet)
9. Launderette

games of *boule bretonne*—more like lawn bowling and with bigger balls). The **Corsaires ticket office,** located just before the commercial port, marks the departure point for the foot ferry to Dinard (you'll enjoy great views on your return ride to St-Malo).

From here, find your way inside the walls along Rue de Dinan, and return to the Porte St. Vincent on surface streets. The shopping streets Rue de la Vieille Boucherie and Rue Porcon de la Barbinais are among the most appealing.

Near St-Malo: Alet

The neighboring village of Alet is just a few minutes' drive past St-Malo's port (a 20-minute walk from the ramparts), but it feels a world apart. A splendid walking path leads around this small point with stunning views of crashing waves, the city of Dinard, the open sea, and, finally, St-Malo (allow 30 minutes at a relaxed pace, go in a clockwise direction). WWII bunkers cap the small hill; inside one of the bunkers is the small Mémorial 39/45 museum, which commemorates the conflict in this region (€6, one-hour guided tours in French only, tel. 02 99 82 41 74, www.ville-saint-malo.fr/culture/les-musees). Several popular cafés face the bay back near the Tour Solidor (a 14th-century fortification at the mouth of the Rance River).

To get to Alet by car from St-Malo (see map on page 351), drive out of town with the rampart walls on your right and the Bassin Vauban port on your left; follow *Toutes Directions* signs south until you spot signposts for *Alet.* Follow these into the district. *Musée Memorial* signs will take you to the top of the bluff; *Tour Solidor* signs lead to parking at the tower or Place St. Pierre. To reach the start of the walking path, walk several blocks (with the sea on your left).

BRITTANY

On foot from St-Malo, walk from Porte St. Louis along the road and across the drawbridge (note the dry dock on the way to the second roundabout). Pass the Olympique Piscine (swimming pool), then cut right through the parking lot to the walking path that leads around the harbor. When you reach the seawall, look left for a set of steps that connects to a path around the point. At the top of the steps, you'll find more steps that lead to the Mémorial 39/45 museum and the bunkers.

Sleeping in St-Malo

Spending a night here gives you more time to enjoy the sunset and sea views from the town walls.

$$$ Hôtel France et Chateaubriand*** is a venerable establishment near the Porte St. Vincent, with 80 rooms at decent rates (Db-€100-190, most rooms around €130, breakfast-€12, secure parking-€15/day, Wi-Fi, 12 Place Chateaubriand, tel. 02 99 56 66 52, www.hotel-chateaubriand-st-malo.com).

$$$ Hôtel du Louvre***, a modern three-star hotel within the city walls has comfortable rooms at fair rates (Db-€82-151, breakfast-€12.50, elevator, guest computer, Wi-Fi, parking-€12/day, 2 Rue des Marins, tel. 02 99 40 86 62, www.hoteldulouvre-saintmalo.com, contact@hoteldulouvre-saintmalo.com).

$$ Hôtel le Nautilus** is a solid value, run by the affable team of Loïck and Jean-Michel. It's conveniently located inside the walls near Porte St. Vincent (Db-€70, Tb-€88, breakfast-€8.50, elevator, guest computer, Wi-Fi, parking-€5.50/day, 9 Rue de la Corne de Cerf, easiest to park outside walls and walk in through Porte St. Vincent, tel. 02 99 40 42 27, www.hotel-lenautilus-saint-malo.com, info@lenautilus.com).

Eating in St-Malo

St-Malo is all about seafood and crêpes. There's no shortage of restaurants, many serving the local specialty of mussels *(moules)* and oysters *(huîtres)*. Look also for bakeries selling *ker-y-pom*, traditional Breton apple-filled shortbread biscuits that are the best-tasting treat in town, especially when warmed.

Le Corps de Garde Crêperie is my favorite lunch stop. It's up on the walls, with St-Malo's cheapest view tables. They serve inventive crêpes at fair prices from 11:30 to 22:00, with a cool ambience indoors or out (daily, 3 Montée Notre Dame, tel. 02 99 40 91 46).

Bouche en Folie matches tasty specialties that change daily with a cozy setting; it's traditional without being kitsch (*menus* from €25, closed Tue-Wed, 14 Rue du Boyer, mobile 06 72 49 08 89).

Coté Sens is my St-Malo mini-splurge. Enthusiastically run by the wife and husband team of Sandrine and Olivier, Coté Sens has a small but delightfully fresh selection that Sandrine happily translates for you (*menus* from €29, open daily, 16 Rue de la Herse, tel. 02 99 20 08 12).

Le Chateaubriand offers two choices. The ground-floor restaurant delivers a grand, Old World aura and a full range of choices at decent prices (*menus* from €16, daily, inside and outdoor dining). Their gourmet restaurant—**Le 5**—is five floors up; you pay for the views (€29 *menu*, €16-28 main dishes, closed Mon-Tue, Place Chateaubriand, tel. 02 99 56 66 52, www.le5-restaurant.com).

Nightlife: The oldest café in St-Malo (open since 1820) also has the longest name (too long to repeat here) and 2,874 dolls along its walls. Locals call it **La Java** and gather here for beer, wine, and *les bons temps*. Even if you won't be staying overnight in St-Malo, it's worth taking a peek at the quirky decor any time of day (near Porte St. Vincent at 3 Rue Ste. Barbe, tel. 02 99 56 41 90, www.lajavacafe.com).

St-Malo Connections

From St-Malo by Train to: Dinan (6/day, 1-2 hours, transfer in Dol-de-Bretagne, bus is better—see below), **Pontorson** (with bus connections to **Mont St-Michel;** 2/day, 2 hours, transfer in Dol), **Rennes** (1 hour, 10/day).

By Bus to: Dinan (3-6/day, none on Sun except in summer, 1 hour; faster and better than train, as bus stops are more central), **Mont St-Michel** (1/day direct bus usually at 9:45, 1.25 hours, daily July-Aug, less off-season, €20 round-trip fare even if only going one-way, buy from driver, tel. 02 99 19 70 70, www.keolis-emeraude.com/en).

Alternative Ways to Mont St-Michel: If you can't take the direct bus, there are a few train-to-bus and bus-to-bus trips that work (at least 2 hours to Mont St-Michel, depending on the time of day). And schedules change like the wind, so let the TI explain your options.

Near St-Malo

Dinard

This upscale-traditional resort comes with a kid-friendly beach and an old-time, Coney Island-style, beach-promenade feel (7 buses/day from Dinan, fewer on Sun, 45 minutes). Its Saturday market is worthwhile, and views from the foot ferry *(Bus de Mer)* to St-Malo are wonderful (€8.10 round-trip, runs 9:30-18:00, later in summer, departs Dinard from below *Promenade du Clair de Lune* at *Embarcadère*). The town has no real sights.

Once you're at the beach, there are attractions in several directions. To reach the promenade and pool, face the ferry-ticket office, turn right, and follow the path that leads to a small cove with a couple of restaurants. Continue following the seaside on the circular *Promenade du Moulinet,* where rich Brits settled during the belle époque. When you reach the beachside swimming pool, go under the elevated road and backtrack to the boat terminal.

To get to the family-friendly beach, face the ferry-ticket office and turn left to reach this quieter beach via the yacht club. Along the way you'll see photogenic trees framing views of St-Malo.

The **TI,** between the casino and Place de la République parking lot, is at 2 Boulevard Féart (July-Aug daily 10:00-12:30 & 14:30-18:00, off-season closed Sun, tel. 02 99 46 94 12, www.ot-dinard.com). To get to the TI from Place de la République, walk toward the water, take the first right, and make another right onto Boulevard Féart.

Dinard is a 10- to 20-minute drive from St-Malo. Leaving St-Malo, follow *Barrage de la Rance* signs through the unappealing port; when you arrive in Dinard, follow *Centre-Ville* signs, and park on Place de la République.

▲▲Scenic Drive on the Western Emerald Coast

For drivers, the western Emerald Coast (*Côte d'Emeraude*) between Cap Fréhel and St-Malo offers sweeping views of sandy beaches with wind-sculpted rocks and immense cliffs overlooking crashing waves (see map on page 333). The highlight is Fort la Latte, a medieval castle built on a rocky spur over the ocean.

Allow a half-day for the entire trip. You'll first drive to the farthest point of the journey—the resort town of Sables-d'Or-les-Pins—and then slowly work your way back toward St-Malo. If you don't have much time and just want to see the fort, it's about an hour's drive from St-Malo or Dinan. During summer or on a weekend, do this drive early to avoid crowds. If it's Saturday and off-season, consider starting at the market in Dinard (described earlier) and then follow my directions.

Getting to Sables-d'Or-les-Pins from St-Malo: Take D-168 west, which becomes D-786 near Ploubalay. Continue toward Matignon and Fréhel, then watch for the turnoff to Sables-d'Or-les-Pins.

Getting to Sables-d'Or-les-Pins from Dinan: Take D-794 to Plancoët. In the town center, follow signs to *St-Brieuc/Toutes directions.* Then follow D-17 to Matignon and D-786 to Fréhel, then turn off to Sables-d'Or-les-Pins.

Turn left just before entering Sables-d'Or-les-Pins (a little before the Fréhel sign). Look for signs marked *la Fleche Dunaire* and park along the road under pine trees. Tracking the Flèche Dunaire trail, walk along the beach. At low tide, you could walk to the small harbor.

Next, drive 15 lovely minutes on D-34 to Cap Fréhel. Use the parking at Plage de la Fosse and explore the rugged coast east from here. Strong hikers can park at Fort la Latte instead (see next page) and take a 75-minute walk to visit Cap Fréhel.

Cap Fréhel: This popular destination lies at the tip of a long peninsula and features walking paths over soaring cliffs with views in all directions. You'll pay €2 to park near Cap Fréhel's stone lighthouse. The place gets jammed on weekends and summer afternoons (if time is tight, skip this stop and head directly to Fort la Latte). Views from the trails are sufficiently expansive, but it is possible to climb the lighthouse each afternoon (€2, Mon-Fri 15:00-17:00, Sat-Sun 14:30-17:30). That's Fort la Latte to the east, your next destination.

Fort la Latte: This mighty fortress, worth ▲▲, is a five-minute drive east of Cap Fréhel. From the parking lot, it's a 10-minute walk to stunning views of a medieval castle hugging a massive rock above the ocean. Pick up the English flier (€0.20) or learn the historical background of the castle by reading the English info panels.

Cost and Hours: €5.20, daily 10:30-18:00, July-Aug until 19:00, tel. 02 96 41 57 11, www.castlelalatte.com.

Visiting the Fort: The first fort on this site was made from wood and built as a lookout for nasty Normans. What you see today dates from the 14th and 15th centuries, when wars between England and France caught Brittany in the middle for well over a hundred years. While the castle was never successfully attacked from the sea, in 1597 its garrison of 25 men was overwhelmed by a force of 2,000 soldiers coming overland. Later, Louis XIV's military architect Vauban oversaw work shoring up the castle's outer defenses. It was used well into the 18th century.

Touring the site, you'll cross two impressive drawbridges (notice the spiked gates), peer into dungeons (one still holds a prisoner), and wander ramparts towering high above the ocean. The guardroom houses a small gift shop (there's a good book about the castle in English for about €5). The small chapel was added in the 18th century, replacing the original chapel, and is dedicated to St. Michael, protector of warriors. The largest structure inside the fort is the governor's lodge (closed to the public because the owners—from the same family that restored the place in the 1930s—live here).

The highlight of a visit to Fort la Latte is the climb to the top of the castle keep, with a magnificent 360-degree view. You'll pass several beautifully vaulted rooms on the way up. Once on top, as you gaze out from this invincible castle, clinging for its life to a rock, think of Fort la Latte as a symbol of Brittany's determination to remain independent from France. It's no surprise that Hollywood used this castle in the 1958 film *The Vikings* with Kirk Douglas.

The low-slung *four à boulets* in the western end served as a kiln to heat cannonballs. The defenders aimed hot shots at ships to set them afire. That's cool. One hundred cannon balls could be heated at a time.

If you want to stretch your legs, a trail behind the ticket kiosk links to Cap Fréhel. A 10-minute walk up this path rewards you with killer views back to the fort; it takes 75 minutes to walk all the way to the cape. There's also a short trail down to a rocky beach, giving you a sea-level perspective of the fortress.

Fort la Latte to St-Malo: Go back to D-786 via Plévenon and head east. A worthwhile detour on the way is **Pointe du Chevet.** From D-786, follow D-62 into the sweet little town of St-Jacut-de-la-Mer, then track signs to *Pointe du Chevet*—and don't park until the road ends. Beautiful views (and far fewer people) surround you. If the tide is out, you can hike to an island and study the impressive rows of wooden piers sunk into the bay. These are used to grow mussels, which cling to the wooden poles; farmers eventually harvest them using a machine that pushes a ring around the poles. From here, return to D-786 heading toward Ploubalay and find signs to *St-Malo* or *Dinan*.

▲▲Scenic Drive Between St-Malo and Mont St-Michel

If you have less time, consider this lovely ride—worth ▲▲▲ if it's clear (see route on map on page 333). This quick taste-of-Brittany driving tour samples a bit of the rugged peninsula's coast, with lots of views but no dramatic forts. Allow two hours for the drive between Mont St-Michel and St-Malo, including stops (a more direct route takes 45 minutes). On a weekend or in summer, the drive will take longer—start early. These directions are from St-Malo to Mont St-Michel, but the drive works just as well in reverse order.

St-Malo to Cancale: From St-Malo, take the scenic road hugging the coast east on D-201 to Pointe du Grouin. To find the road, leave St-Malo following *Paramé/Cancale* signs, then look for *Rothéneuf*, where you'll access D-201 which skirts in and out of camera-worthy views. As you drive towards Cancale, you will be surrounded by fields of cauliflowers, potatoes, and onions, reminding you that tourism and agriculture form the economic base of Brittany.

Fans of quirky sights can make a quick stop at ***Les Rochers Sculptés*** in Rothéneuf. At the end of the 19th century, a Catholic abbot decided to devote his life to sculpture after he became deaf and mute. With a hammer and chisel, he worked for 15 years creating his story out of the rock of a sea cliff (€2.50, daily in summer 9:00-19:00, off-season 10:00-12:00 & 14:00-18:00, short introduction provided in English, www.lesrocherssculptes.com). You could make this stop longer by having lunch right here at **Le Bénétin,** a mod restaurant serving fresh food with panoramic views (lunch *menus* €26, daily April-Sept, tel. 02 99 56 97 64).

Back on the road to Cancale, brown signs lead to short worthwhile detours to the coast; these are my favorites:

Ile Besnard and Dunes de Chevrets: A five-minute detour off D-201 leads to this pretty, sandy beach arcing alongside a crescent bay. There are sea-piercing rocks to scramble on, a nature trail above the beach, and a view restaurant past the campground (**La Perle Noire,** daily except off-season closed Mon, tel. 02 99 89 01 60). From the hamlet of La Guimorais, a 10-minute drive from Rothéneuf, follow signs to *Ile Besnard* and *Dunes de Chevrets* to the very end (past the campground), and park at the far end of the lot.

Pointe du Grouin: This striking rock outcrop yields views from easy trails in all directions. Park near Hôtel Pointe du Grouin (outdoor café with views), and continue on foot. Pass the *sémaphore du Grouin* (signal station), where paths lead everywhere. Breathe in the sea air. Can you spot Mont St-Michel in the distance? The big rock below is Ile des Landes, an island earmarked for a fort during the French Revolution. The fort was never built, and the island remains home to thousands of birds. What fool would build on an island in this bay?

BRITTANY

Cancale: Return to your car and leave Pointe du Grouin, following signs to *Cancale,* Brittany's appealing oyster capital. Follow *le port* signs leading to a quiet harbour and turn left. Slurp oysters at the outdoor stands. There are several types. *Belon* are flat and round—they're finer and pricier than the more common *creuse. Pied de cheval* are older and even more expensive as they are wild, unlike most oysters growing in the seabeds in front of you. Size is rated from #5 (smallest) to #0 (biggest). The port is lined with more than 30 restaurants showing off the label *Site remarquable du goût* (extraordinary place to taste).

My favorite *site remarquable* is **Le Narval.** It serves fine seafood and meat dishes, and is named after the fishing boat of the chef's grandfather. Gégé, *le chef,* greets you first in the painting when you arrive, and then for real at the end of your meal (*menus* from €15 on weekdays, €21 on weekends and holidays, daily except closed Wed off-season, reservations smart, tel. 02 99 89 63 12).

Cancale to Mont St-Michel: Cancale is a 45-minute drive from Mont St-Michel. Head out of Cancale toward Mont St-Michel on D-76/D-155, then D-797, and drive along the *Route de la Baie,* which skirts the bay and passes big-time oyster farming, windmill towers (most lacking their sails), flocks of sheep, and, at low tide, grounded boats waiting for the sea to return. On a clear day, look for Mont St-Michel in the distance. On a foggy day, look harder.

Fougères

The very Breton city of Fougères, worth ▲, is a handy stop for drivers traveling between the Loire châteaux and Mont St-Michel. Fougères has one of Europe's largest medieval castles, a lovely old city center, and a panoramic park viewpoint. Drivers follow *Centre-Ville* signs, then *Château,* and park at the free lot just past the château.

For a memorable loop through new and old Fougères, start at the parking lot near the château. Walk into Fougères with the water-filled moat on your left, then follow the *Château* sign. Stop for a peek in the handsome **Church of St. Sulpice** (English handout inside)—the woodwork is exceptional, especially the choir stalls and altar. Then walk through **Porte Sainte Anne,** the only remaining gate to the walled city. The château is on your left, but there's no reason to visit it unless you need more exercise or want to pick up a town map at the ticket office (€8, includes audioguide, June-Sept daily 10:00-19:00, off-season shorter hours and closed Mon, closed Jan; tel. 02 99 99 79 59, www.chateau-fougeres.com).

Next, walk up Rue de la Pinterie (fine views) to the top of the street, then turn right on Rue Nationale at the TI. You are now in the Haute Ville (modern Fougères). Keep walking towards St. Léonard Church, passing the old belfry on your right. At the church, enter the **Jardin Public** and enjoy its floral panorama. From here all paths lead down to the old town. At the bottom of the garden, find various types of *fougères* (ferns). To finish the loop, exit the Jardin Public following signs to the château and cross the little Nançon River. You'll land in the Basse Ville, the old medieval town with lovely half-timbered houses on Place du Marchix. The château is ahead.

Eating in Fougères: You'll find a gaggle of cafés and *crêperies* near the château with good choices and prices. **Le Bonheur Est Dans le Blé** is a notch above the others, serving tasty crêpes on a lovely little terrace overlooking the valley (June-Aug daily, off-season closed Mon and Tue eve, a block up from the château at 3 Rue Fourchette, tel. 02 99 94 99 72).

THE LOIRE

Amboise • Chinon • Beaucoup de Châteaux

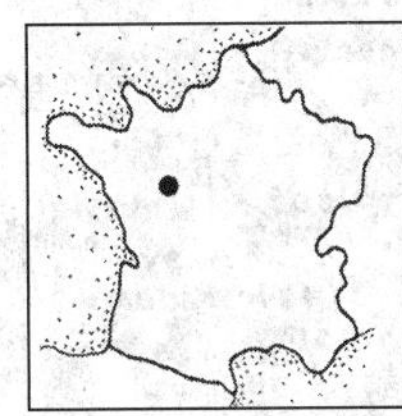

As it glides gently east to west, officially separating northern from southern France, the Loire River has come to define this popular tourist region. The importance of this river and the valley's prime location, in the center of the country just south of Paris, have made the Loire a strategic hot potato for more than a thousand years. The Loire was the high-water mark for the Moors as they pushed into Europe from Morocco. Today, this region is still the dividing line for the country—for example, weather forecasters say, "north of the Loire...and south of the Loire..."

Because of its history, this region is home to more than a thousand castles and palaces of all shapes and sizes. When a "valley address" became a must-have among 16th-century hunting-crazy royalty, rich Renaissance palaces replaced outdated medieval castles. Hundreds of these castles and palaces are open to visitors, and it's castles that you're here to see (you'll find better villages and cities elsewhere). Old-time aristocratic château-owners, struggling with the cost of upkeep, enjoy financial assistance from the government if they open their mansions to the public.

Today's Loire Valley is carpeted with fertile fields, crisscrossed by rivers, and laced with rolling hills. It's one of France's most important agricultural regions. It's also under some development pressure, thanks to TGV bullet trains that link it to Paris in an hour, and cheap flights to England that make it a prime second-home spot for many Brits, including Sir Mick Jagger.

CHOOSING A HOME BASE

This is a big, unwieldy region, so I've divided it into two halves, each centered around a good, manageable town—Amboise and

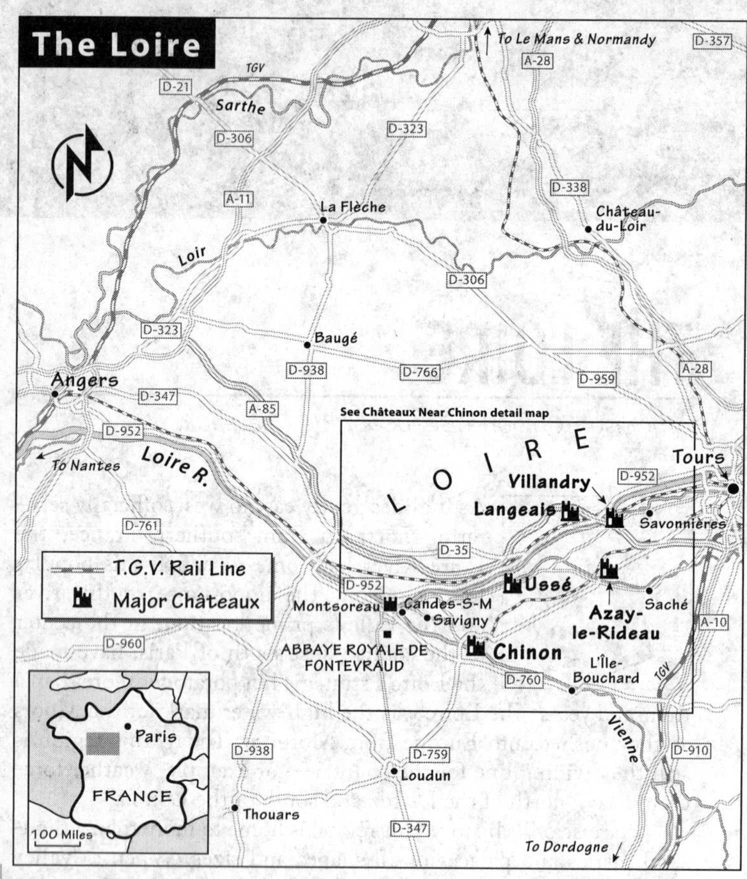

Chinon—to use as a home base for exploring nearby châteaux. Which home base should you choose? That will depend mainly on which châteaux you'd like to visit; for ideas, scan my descriptions in the "Loire Valley Châteaux at a Glance" sidebar on page 366. For many travelers, Amboise is the better choice.

Châteaux-holics and gardeners can stay longer and sleep in both towns. Amboise is east of the big city of Tours, and Chinon lies west of Tours. The drive from Amboise to Chinon takes about 1.5 hours; if you sleep on one side of Tours and intend to visit castles on the other side, you're looking at a long round-trip drive—certainly doable, but not my idea of good travel. Instead, sleep in or near the town nearest the castles you plan to visit, and avoid crossing traffic-laden Tours. The A-85 autoroute (toll) is the quickest way to link Amboise with châteaux near Chinon. Thanks to this uncrowded freeway, sleepy Azay-le-Rideau is another good base for destinations west of Tours; it also works as a base for sights on both sides of Tours.

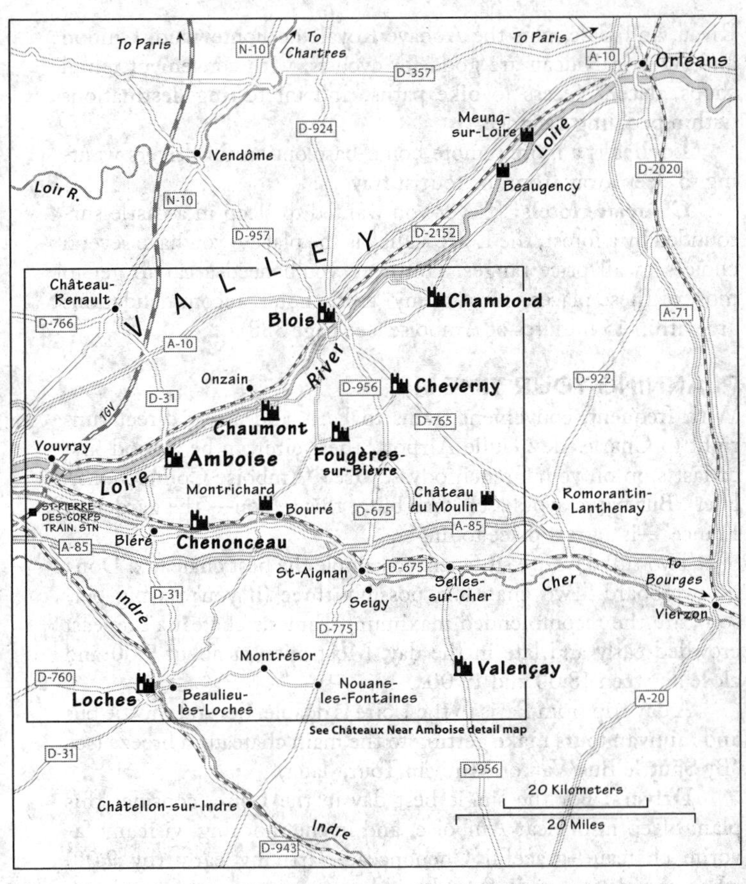

Amboise and, to a lesser extent, **Blois** or **Chenonceaux,** make the best home bases for first-timers. Amboise and Blois have handy car or bus/minivan access to these important châteaux: elegant Chenonceau, urban Blois, epic Chambord, canine-crazy Cheverny, royal Amboise, and garden-showy Chaumont-sur-Loire. Amboise has good minivan service to area sights, and drivers appreciate its small scale and easy parking; Blois has better train connections from Paris and better low-cost transportation options to nearby sights in high season. The town of Chenonceaux works for drivers and hardy bicyclists. Most visitors choose Amboise for its just-right size and more varied tourist appeal.

Chinon, Azay-le-Rideau, and their nearby châteaux don't feel as touristy; these towns appeal to gardeners and road-less-traveled types. The key châteaux in this area include historic Chinon, fairy-tale Azay-le-Rideau, fortress-like Langeais, and garden-lush Villandry. Lesser sights include the châteaux at Chatonnière,

Rivau, and Ussé, plus the Abbaye Royale de Fontevraud. Chinon and Azay-le-Rideau are good for cyclists, with convenient rental shops, decent access to bike paths, and interesting destinations within pedaling distance.

Loches is a more remote home-base option for drivers wanting to sleep away from the tourist fray.

Château Hotels: If ever you wanted to sleep in a castle surrounded by a forest, the Loire Valley is the place—you have several choices in all price ranges. However, you'll need a car to get to most of these places. Most of my "castle hotel" recommendations are within 15 minutes of Amboise (see page 388).

PLANNING YOUR TIME

With frequent, convenient trains to Paris and a few direct runs right to Charles de Gaulle Airport, the Loire can be a good first or last stop on your French odyssey (see "Amboise Connections," later). But try to avoid a château blitz; this region—"the garden of France"—is a great place to linger.

Two full days are sufficient to sample the best châteaux. Don't go overboard. Two châteaux, possibly three (if you're a big person), are the recommended maximum. Famous châteaux are least crowded early and late in the day. Most open at about 9:00 and close between 18:00 and 19:00.

A day trip from Paris to the Loire is doable. Several shuttle bus and minivan tours make getting to the main châteaux a breeze (see "By Shuttle Bus/Van or Minivan Tour," later).

Drivers: For the single best day in the Loire, consider this plan: Sleep in or near Amboise, and in the morning, visit my favorite château—graceful Chenonceau—arriving early (by 9:00) when crowds are small. Spend midday at monumental Chambord, a 30-minute drive from Chenonceau. And if there's time, stop at Cheverny (where the hunting dogs are fed at 17:00) on the way back to your hotel. Allow time to visit Amboise's sights the next morning. With a second full day, you could move to Chinon, visiting Villandry and its gardens en route, then devote your afternoon to the château and old town in Chinon.

Try to see one château on your drive in (for example, if arriving from the north, visit Chambord, Cheverny, or Blois; if coming from the west or the south, see Azay-le-Rideau or Villandry). If you're coming from Burgundy, don't miss the one-of-a-kind Château de Guédelon (see page 878 in the Burgundy chapter). If you're driving to the Dordogne from the Loire, the A-20 autoroute via Limoges (near Oradour-sur-Glane) is fastest and toll-free until Brive-la-Gaillarde.

The best map of the area is Michelin #518, covering all the sights described in this chapter (the TI's free map of Touraine, the area surrounding Tours, is also good).

Without a Car and on a Budget: Sleep in Amboise. The next morning, rent a bike or catch the public bus, shuttle van (high season only), or train from Amboise to the town of Chenonceaux, tour Chenonceau (my must-see château), then return to Amboise in the afternoon to enjoy its château and Leonardo's last stand at Clos-Lucé. With a second day, take the short (and cheap) train ride to Blois, and grab a shuttle bus (runs April-August) to massive Chambord; try to budget time to also visit Blois before returning to Amboise. Other second-day options are the châteaux of Cheverny or Chaumont. (For more train and bus specifics, see "Amboise Connections" on page 392 and "Blois Connections" on page 408.) With more time, those connecting Paris with Amboise or Chinon can layover in Blois en route (free lockers available at Blois château with paid admission).

Budget travelers based in Chinon can bike to Langeais, Ussé, and Villandry, and/or take the train to Azay-le-Rideau and Langeais (but keep in mind that the train trips are long and not a good option for most).

Without a Car but Not Broke (Yet): Take a minivan excursion directly from Amboise or Tours (described in the next section).

GETTING AROUND THE LOIRE VALLEY

Traveling by car is the easiest way to get around, and day rentals are reasonable. Trains, buses, minivan tours, bikes, or taxis help non-drivers reach the well-known châteaux. But even the less-famous châteaux are reachable without a car: Take a taxi, arrange a custom minivan excursion (affordable for small groups), or ride a bike (great option for those with time and stamina).

By Car

You can rent a car most easily at the St-Pierre-des-Corps TGV station just outside Tours; rentals are also available in Amboise (see page 372). I've listed specific driving instructions for each destination covered in this chapter. Parking is free at all châteaux except Chambord.

By Train

With easy access from Amboise and Chinon, the big city of Tours is the transport hub for travelers bent on using trains or buses to explore the Loire (but it has little else to offer visitors—I wouldn't sleep there). Tours has two important train stations and a major bus station (with service to several châteaux). The main train station is Tours SNCF, and the smaller, suburban TGV station (located between Tours and Amboise) is St-Pierre-des-Corps. Check schedules carefully, as service is sparse on some lines. The châteaux of Amboise, Blois, Chenonceau, Chaumont (via the town of Onzain

Loire Valley Châteaux at a Glance

Which châteaux should you visit—and why? Here's a quick summary. Local TIs sell bundled tickets for several châteaux that save you money and time in ticket lines (see page 372).

Châteaux East of Tours

▲▲▲**Chenonceau** For sheer elegance arching over the Cher River, and for its lovely gardens. **Hours:** Daily mid-March-mid-Sept 9:00-19:30, July-Aug until 20:00, closes earlier off-season. See page 396.

▲▲**Blois** For its urban setting, beautiful courtyard, and fun sound-and-light show. **Hours:** Daily July-Aug 9:00-19:00, April-June and Sept 9:00-18:30, Oct 9:00-18:00, Nov-March 9:00-12:30 & 14:30-17:30. See page 402.

▲▲▲**Chambord** For its epic grandeur (440 rooms), fun rooftop views, and evocative setting surrounded by a forest. **Hours:** Daily April-Sept 9:00-18:00, Oct-March 10:00-17:00. See page 409.

▲▲**Cheverny** For its intimate feel, lavishly furnished rooms, and daily feeding of the hunting dogs. **Hours:** Daily July-Aug 9:15-18:45, April-June and Sept 9:15-18:15, Oct 9:45-17:30, Nov-March 9:45-17:00. See page 413.

▲▲**Chaumont-sur-Loire** For its imposing setting over the Loire River, historic connections to America, and impressive Festival of the Gardens. **Hours:** Daily July-Aug 10:00-19:00, May-June and early Sept 10:00-18:00, April and late Sept 10:30-17:30, Oct-March 10:00-17:00. See page 415.

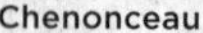

Chenonceau

Chambord

plus a long walk), Langeais, Chinon, and Azay-le-Rideau all have train and/or bus service from Tours' main SNCF station; Amboise, Blois, Chaumont, Chenonceau, and Chinon are also served from the St-Pierre-des-Corps station. Look under each sight for specifics, and seriously consider a minivan excursion (described next).

▲Amboise For terrific views over Amboise and Leonardo da Vinci memories. **Hours:** Daily April-Oct 9:00-18:00, until 19:00 July-Aug, shorter hours off-season. See page 371.

▲Clos-Lucé (in Amboise) For a chance to see Leonardo da Vinci's final home, and to stroll through gardens decorated with models of his creations. **Hours:** Daily Feb-Oct 9:00-19:00, until 20:00 July-Aug; shorter hours off-season. See page 380.

Châteaux West of Tours

▲▲Azay-le-Rideau For its fairy-tale facade and setting on a romantic reflecting pond, and for its beautifully furnished rooms. **Hours:** Daily July-Aug 9:30-19:00, April-June and Sept-Oct 9:30-18:00, Nov-March 10:00-17:15. See page 430.

▲▲Villandry For the best gardens in the Loire Valley—and possibly all of France. **Hours:** Daily April-Sept 9:00-19:00, March and Oct 9:00-18:00, Nov-Feb 9:00-17:00. See page 435.

▲Chinon For its Joan of Arc history. **Hours:** Daily March-Oct 9:30-18:00, until 19:00 May-Aug; Nov-Feb 9:30-17:00. See page 419.

▲Langeais For its fortress-like setting above an appealing little village and its evocative 15th- and 16th-century rooms. **Hours:** Daily July-Aug 9:00-19:00, April-June and Sept-mid-Nov 9:30-18:30, mid-Nov-March 10:00-17:00. See page 433.

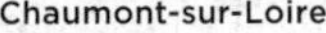

Chaumont-sur-Loire

Azay-le-Rideau

By Shuttle Bus/Van or Minivan Tour

Shuttle services and minivan tours offer affordable transportation to many of the valley's châteaux. Shuttles connect Amboise, Tours, or Blois with key châteaux several times a day (€4-16), and minivan tours combine several châteaux into a painless day tour (€23-37/person for scheduled half-day itineraries from Amboise or Tours,

€55 for all day; figure €230 for custom groups of up to 7 for 4 hours, €400 for 8 hours). Most of these services start from TIs (who can book them for you) and can save you time (in line) and money (on admissions) when you purchase your château ticket at a discounted group rate from the driver.

By Shuttle Bus: In high season, two handy excursion buses depart from the train station in Blois (an easy train ride from Amboise and a good place to bed down). One runs a loop route connecting Blois, Chambord, Cheverny, and (skippable) Beauregard, allowing visits to the châteaux with your pick of return times; another bus goes to the château of Chaumont (see "Blois Connections," page 408). **Public buses** also connect Tours, Amboise, and Chenonceaux (see "Amboise Connections," page 392).

By Shuttle Van: Quart de Tours runs a high-season-only shuttle service between Amboise and the Château de Chenonceau. **Touraine Evasion** runs a similar shuttle linking Amboise with Chambord and Chenonceau (see "Amboise Connections," page 392).

By Minivan Tour: Tour operators **Acco-Dispo, Quart de Tours,** and **Loire Valley Tours** offer half- and full-day itineraries from Amboise and/or Tours that hit all the main châteaux (see "Amboise Connections," page 392).

Minivan excursions also leave from the Tours TI office to many châteaux; some include wine tasting (book online at www.tours-tourisme.fr). The TI is right outside the Tours SNCF train station (easy connections from Amboise, Blois, or Chinon; see "By Train," earlier).

By Taxi

Taxi excursions can be affordable when split among several people, especially from the Blois train station to nearby châteaux, or from Amboise to Chenonceau. For details, see "Blois Connections," page 408, and "Amboise Connections," page 392.

By Bike

Cycling options are endless in the Loire, where the elevation gain is generally manageable. (However, if you have only a day or two, rent a car or stick to the châteaux easily reached by buses and minivans.) Amboise, Chenonceaux, Blois, Azay-le-Rideau, and Chinon all make good biking bases and have rental options (ask at the TI in each city for bike rental shops). A network of nearly 200 miles of bike paths and well-signed country lanes connect many châteaux near Amboise. Pick up the free bike-path map at any TI, buy the more detailed map available at TIs, or study the route options at www.loireavelo.fr. (I also list several accommodations with easy access to these bike paths.)

Hot-Air Balloon Rides

In France's most popular regions, you'll find hot-air balloon companies eager to take you for a ride (Burgundy, the Loire, Dordogne, and Provence are best suited for ballooning). It's not cheap, but it's unforgettable—a once-in-a-lifetime chance to sail serenely over châteaux, canals, vineyards, Romanesque churches, and villages. Balloons don't go above 3,000 feet and usually fly much lower than that, so you get a bird's-eye view of France's sublime landscapes.

Most companies offer similar deals and work this way: Trips range from 45 to 90 minutes of air time, to which you should add two hours for preparation, champagne toast, and transport back to your starting point. Deluxe trips add a gourmet picnic, making it a four-hour event. Allow about €210 for a short tour, and about €300 for longer flights. Departures are, of course, weather-dependent, and are usually scheduled first thing in the morning or in early evening. If you've booked ahead and the weather turns bad, you can reschedule your flight, but you can't get your money back. Most balloon companies charge about €25 more for a bad-weather refund guarantee; unless your itinerary is very loose, it's a good idea.

Flight season is April through October. It's smart to bring a jacket for the breeze, though temperatures in the air won't differ too much from those on the ground. Air sickness is usually not a problem, as the ride is typically slow and even. Baskets have no seating, so count on standing the entire trip. Group (and basket) size can vary from 4 to 16 passengers. Area TIs have brochures. **France Montgolfières** gets good reviews and offers flights in the areas that I recommend (tel. 02 54 32 20 48, www.france-montgolfiere.com). Others are **Aérocom Montgolfière** (tel. 02 54 33 55 00, www.aerocom.fr) and **Touraine Montgolfière** (tel. 02 47 56 42 05, www.touraine-montgolfiere.fr).

About five miles from Chinon, a 30-mile bike path runs along the Loire River, passing by Ussé and Langeais. It meets the Cher River at Villandry and continues along the Cher to Tours and beyond. To follow this route, pick up the *La Loire à Vélo* brochure at any area TI.

Détours de Loire can help you plan your bike route and will deliver rental bikes to most places in the Loire for reasonable rates. They have a full range of bikes from kid-size to tandems, and will shuttle luggage to your next stop. They have shops in Amboise, Blois, and Tours and allow one-way rentals between these and their partner shops at no added charge (www.locationdevelos.com).

TOURS IN THE LOIRE VALLEY

Local Guides

Fabrice Maret is an expert in all things Loire and a great teacher. He lives in Blois but can meet you in Amboise to give an excellent walking tour of the city and its sights, or he'll guide you around the area's châteaux using your rental car (€260/day plus transportation from Blois, tel. 02 54 70 19 59, www.chateauxloire.com, info@chateauxloire.com). Another capable guide is **Charlotte Coignard;** she lives in Tours but can meet you anywhere (charlotte.coignard@gmail.com).

Smartphone Apps

Many of the major châteaux now have free apps that reproduce their rentable audioguides—check château websites for info. The Amboise and Blois TIs also offer free city guide apps. Download these apps before you leave home to save time and money when you get here.

THE LOIRE VALLEY'S CUISINE SCENE

Here in "the garden of France," locally produced food is delicious. Loire Valley rivers yield fresh trout *(truite),* salmon *(saumon),* and smelt *(éperlau),* which are often served fried *(friture). Rillettes,* a stringy pile of cooked and whipped pork, makes for a cheap, mouthwatering sandwich spread (use lots of mustard and add a baby pickle, called a *cornichon).* Locals love their steak in this area; be on the lookout for *pavé* (thick hunk of prime steak), *bavette* (skirt steak), *faux filet* (sirloin), and *entrecôte* (rib-eye steak). Don't be surprised to see snails, *confit de canard,* and seafood on menus—the Loire borrows much from neighboring regions. The area's wonderful goat cheeses include Crottin de Chavignol (*crottin* means horse dung, which is what this cheese, when aged, resembles), Saint-Maure Fermier (soft and creamy), and Selles-sur-Cher (mild). For dessert, try a delicious *tarte tatin* (upside-down caramel-apple tart). Regional pastries include *pithiviers* (puff pastry with almond filling) from Pithiviers and *sablés* (shortbread cookies) from Sablé-sur-Sarthe.

Remember, restaurants serve food only during lunch (11:30-14:00) and dinner (19:00-21:00, later in bigger cities); bigger cafés offer eats throughout the day.

WINES OF THE LOIRE

Loire wines are overlooked, and that's a shame—there is gold in them thar grapes. The Loire is France's third-largest producer of wine and grows the greatest variety of any region. Four main grapes are grown in the Loire: two reds, Gamay and Cabernet Franc, and two whites, Sauvignon Blanc and Chenin Blanc.

The Loire is divided into four subareas, and the name of a wine (its *appellation*) generally refers to where its grapes were grown. The Touraine subarea encompasses the wines of Chinon and Amboise. Using 100 percent cabernet franc grapes, growers in Chinon and Bourgeuil are the main (and best) producers of reds. Thanks to soil variation and climate differences year in and out, wines made from a single grape have a remarkable range in taste. The best and most expensive white wines are the Sancerres, made on the less-touristed eastern edge of the Loire. Less expensive, but still tasty, are Touraine Sauvignons and the sweeter Vouvray, whose grapes are grown near Amboise. Vouvray is also famous for its light and refreshing sparkling wines (called *vins pétillants*)—locals will tell you the only proper way to begin any meal in this region is with a glass of it, and I can't disagree (try the *rosé pétillant* for a fresh sensation). A dry rosé is popular in the Loire in the summer and can be made from a variety of grapes.

You'll pass scattered vineyards as you travel between châteaux, though there's no scenic wine road to speak of (the closest thing is around Bourgeuil). Remember that it's best to call ahead before visiting a winery.

East of Tours

Amboise

Straddling the widest stretch of the Loire River, Amboise is an inviting town with a pleasing old quarter below its hilltop château. A castle has overlooked the Loire from Amboise since Roman times. Leonardo da Vinci retired here...just one more of his many brilliant ideas.

As the royal residence of François I (r. 1515-1547), Amboise wielded far more importance than you'd imagine from a lazy walk through its pleasant, pedestrian-only commercial zone. In fact, its residents are pretty conservative, giving the town an attitude—as if no one told them they're no longer the second capital of France. The locals keep their wealth to themselves; consequently, many grand mansions hide behind nondescript facades.

With or without a car, Amboise is an ideal small-town home base for exploring the best of château country.

Orientation to Amboise

Amboise (pop. 14,000) covers ground on both sides of the Loire, with the "Golden Island" (Ile d'Or) in the middle. The train station is on the north side of the Loire, but nearly everything else is on the south (château) side, including the TI. Pedestrian-friendly Rue Nationale parallels the river a few blocks inland and leads from the base of Château d'Amboise through the town center and past the clock tower—once part of the town wall—to the Romanesque Church of St. Denis.

TOURIST INFORMATION

The information-packed TI is on Quai du Général de Gaulle (May-Sept Mon-Sat 10:00-18:30, Sun 10:00-13:00 & 14:00-17:00; Oct-April Mon-Sat 10:00-13:00 & 14:00-18:00, Sun 10:00-13:00; tel. 02 47 57 09 28, www.amboise-valdeloire.com). Pick up the brochures with self-guided walking tours in and around the city, download their free city guide app, and consider purchasing tickets to key area châteaux (saving time in ticket lines—explained under "Helpful Hints," below). Ask about sound-and-light shows in the region (generally summers only). The TI stores bags (€2.50 each), books local guides, and can reserve a room for you in a hotel or *chambre d'hôte* (€3 fee). They can also help organize tours to the châteaux with a shuttle bus or minivan service.

ARRIVAL IN AMBOISE

By Train: Amboise's train station is birds-chirping peaceful. You can't store bags here, but you can leave them at the TI or at the châteaux (see "Baggage Storage," later). Turn left out of the main station (you may have to cross under the tracks first), make a quick right, and walk down Rue Jules Ferry five minutes to the end, then turn right and cross the long bridge leading over the Loire River to the city center. It's a €7 taxi ride from the station to central Amboise, but taxis seldom wait at the station (taxi tel. 02 47 57 13 53 or 02 47 57 30 39).

By Car: Drivers set their sights on the flag-festooned château that caps the hill. Most recommended accommodations and restaurants either have or can help you locate parking (it's free in the big lot along the river).

HELPFUL HINTS

Save Time and Money: The TI sells tickets in bundles of two or more to sights and châteaux around Amboise and Chinon, which saves you some on entry fees—and, more important, time spent in line at each sight. You can also get discounted tickets if you take a minivan tour (see "Getting Around the Loire Valley" on page 365).

Market Days: Open-air markets are held on Friday (smaller but more local; food only) and Sunday (the big one) in the parking lot behind the TI on the river (both 8:30-13:00).

Regional Products: Galland, at 29 Rue Nationale, sells fine food and wine products from the Loire (daily 9:30-19:00).

Supermarket: Carrefour City is near the TI (Mon-Sat 7:00-21:00, Sun 9:00-13:00), though the shops on pedestrian-only Rue Nationale are infinitely more pleasing.

Internet Access: The **TI** allows 10 minutes of free Wi-Fi and has a public computer terminal; they can also tell you where to find Wi-Fi elsewhere, such as **Café des Arts,** across from the château's Heurtault Tower (32 Rue Victor Hugo).

Bookstore: Maison de la Presse is a good bookstore with a small selection of English novels and a big selection of maps and English guidebooks such as Michelin's Green Guide *Châteaux of the Loire;* they also sell English translations of bike-route books (open Mon 14:00-19:00, Tue-Sat 8:00-19:00, Sun 9:00-13:00, across from the TI at 5 Quai du Général de Gaulle).

Laundry: The nearest launderette is at Supermarket LeClerc, a half-mile from the TI toward Tours on D-751.

Baggage Storage: Besides the Amboise TI, which stores bags for a fee (see earlier), most châteaux offer free storage if you've paid admission.

Bike Rental: You can rent a bike (leave your passport or a photocopy) at any of these reliable places: **Détours de Loire** (allows one-way trips to any of its partner shops May-Sept, in round building across from TI on Quai du Général de Gaulle, tel. 02 47 30 00 55), **Locacycle** (daily, full-day rentals can be returned the next morning, 2 Rue Jean-Jacques Rousseau, tel. 02 47 57 00 28), or **Cycles le Duc** (good bikes, closed Sun-Mon, 5 Rue Joyeuse, tel. 02 47 57 00 17).

Taxi: There is no taxi station in Amboise, so you must call for one. Try 02 47 57 13 53, 06 12 92 70 46, or 06 88 02 44 10 (allow €27 to Chenonceaux, €39 in the evening or on Sun).

Local Guides: Fabrice Maret and **Charlotte Coignard** both enjoy teaching about the cities and castles of the Loire region. They'll meet you at your hotel or the château of your choice; for details, see page 370.

Car Rental: It's easiest to rent cars at the St-Pierre-des-Corps train station (TGV service from Paris), a 15-minute drive from Amboise. On the outskirts of Amboise, **Garage Jourdain** rents cars (roughly €55/day for a small car with 100 kilometers/62 miles free, requires credit card for €600 deposit; office open Mon-Fri 7:45-12:00 & 14:00-18:00, Sat 9:00-12:00 &

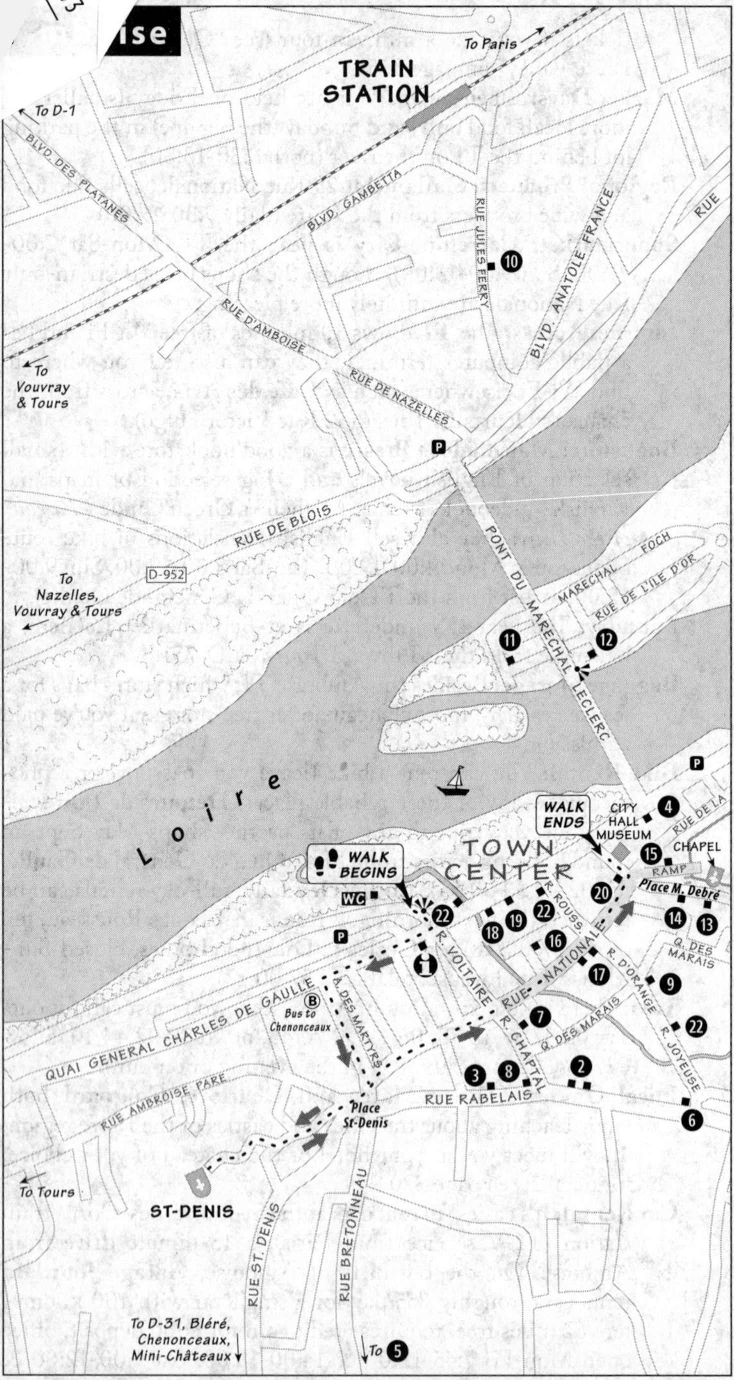

...ise

To Paris
TRAIN STATION
To D-1
BLVD. DES PLATANES
BLVD. GAMBETTA
RUE JULES FERRY
10
BLVD. ANATOLE FRANCE
RUE
RUE D'AMBOISE
RUE DE NAZELLES
To Vouvray & Tours
P
RUE DE BLOIS
D-952
To Nazelles, Vouvray & Tours
PONT DU MARECHAL LECLERC
MARECHAL FOCH
RUE DE L'ILE D'OR
11
12
Loire
P
WALK ENDS
CITY HALL MUSEUM
4
RUE DE LA
15
CHAPEL
RAMP
Place M. Debré
TOWN CENTER
WALK BEGINS
WC
22
R. ROUSS
20
18
19
22
16
14
13
P
R. VOLTAIRE
RUE NATIONALE
R. D'ORANGE
Q. DES MARAIS
17
9
QUAI GENERAL CHARLES DE GAULLE
B Bus to Chenonceaux
R. DES MARTYRS
R. CHAPTAL
7
Q. DES MARAIS
22
R. JOYEUSE
RUE AMBROISE PARE
3
8
2
RUE RABELAIS
6
Place St-Denis
To Tours
ST-DENIS
RUE ST. DENIS
RUE BRETONNEAU
To D-31, Bléré, Chenonceaux, Mini-Châteaux
To 5

LOIRE

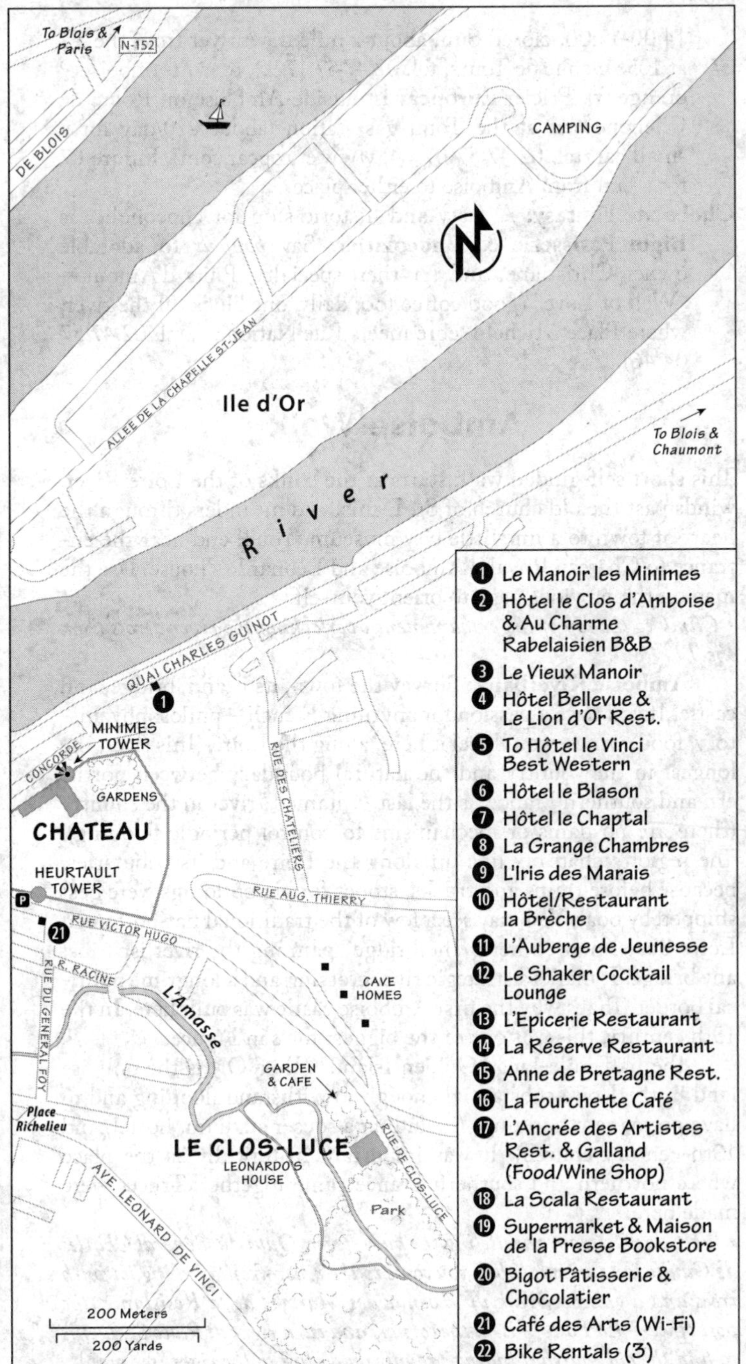
To Blois & Paris
N-152
DE BLOIS
CAMPING
ALLEE DE LA CHAPELLE ST-JEAN
Ile d'Or
River
To Blois & Chaumont
QUAI CHARLES GUINOT
MINIMES TOWER
CONCORDE
GARDENS
CHATEAU
HEURTAULT TOWER
P
RUE DES CHATELIERS
RUE AUG. THIERRY
RUE VICTOR HUGO
R. RACINE
RUE DU GENERAL FOY
L'Amasse
CAVE HOMES
GARDEN & CAFE
Place Richelieu
LE CLOS-LUCE
LEONARDO'S HOUSE
RUE DE CLOS-LUCE
Park
AVE. LEONARD DE VINCI
200 Meters
200 Yards
1 Le Manoir les Minimes
2 Hôtel le Clos d'Amboise & Au Charme Rabelaisien B&B
3 Le Vieux Manoir
4 Hôtel Bellevue & Le Lion d'Or Rest.
5 To Hôtel le Vinci Best Western
6 Hôtel le Blason
7 Hôtel le Chaptal
8 La Grange Chambres
9 L'Iris des Marais
10 Hôtel/Restaurant la Brèche
11 L'Auberge de Jeunesse
12 Le Shaker Cocktail Lounge
13 L'Epicerie Restaurant
14 La Réserve Restaurant
15 Anne de Bretagne Rest.
16 La Fourchette Café
17 L'Ancrée des Artistes Rest. & Galland (Food/Wine Shop)
18 La Scala Restaurant
19 Supermarket & Maison de la Presse Bookstore
20 Bigot Pâtisserie & Chocolatier
21 Café des Arts (Wi-Fi)
22 Bike Rentals (3)

14:00-17:00, closed Sun, about a mile downriver from the TI at 105 Avenue de Tours, tel. 02 47 57 17 92, renault-amboise@orange.fr). Pricier **Europcar** is outside Amboise on Route de Chenonceaux at the Total gas station (about €70/day for a small car, tel. 02 47 57 07 64, www.europcar.com). Figure €7 for a taxi from Amboise to either place.

Chocolate Fantasy: A tasty and historic stop for chocoholics is **Bigot Pâtisserie & Chocolatier.** Say *bonjour* to adorable owner Christiane, and try their specialty, Puits d'Amour—"Well of Love" (good coffee too, daily, one block off the river, where Place Michel Debré meets Rue Nationale, tel. 02 47 57 04 46).

Amboise Walk

This short self-guided walk starts at the banks of the Loire River, winds past the old church of St. Denis, and meanders through the heart of town to a fine little city museum. You'll end near the entrance to Château Royal d'Amboise and Leonardo's house. Use the map on the previous page to orient yourself.

• *Climb to the top of the embankment overlooking the river across from the TI.*

Amboise Riverbank: Survey the town, its island, bridge, and castle. If you have a passion for anything French—philosophy, history, food, wine—you'll feel it here, along the Loire. This river, the longest in the country and the natural boundary between northern and southern France, is the last "untamed" river in the country (there are no dams or mechanisms to control periodic flooding). The region's châteaux line up along the Loire and its tributaries, because before trains and trucks, stones for big buildings were best shipped by boat. You may see a few of the traditional flat-bottomed Loire boats moored here. The bridge spanning the river isn't just any bridge. It marks a strategic river crossing and a longtime political border. That's why the first Amboise castle was built here. In the 15th century, this was one of the biggest forts in France.

The half-mile-long "Golden Island" (Ile d'Or) is the only island in the Loire substantial enough to withstand flooding and to have permanent buildings (including a soccer stadium, hostel, and 13th-century church). It was important historically as the place where northern and southern France came together. Truces were made here.

• *Walk downstream paralleling the busy street, Quai du Général Charles de Gaulle, and cross it when you come to the river-front parking lot with trees and a gazebo. Walk up Avenue des Martyrs de la Résistance (the post office—La Poste—is on the corner) and turn right at Place St. Denis to find the old church standing proudly on a bluff to the right (see map).*

Church of St. Denis (Eglise St. Denis): Ever since ancient Romans erected a Temple of Mars here, this has been a place of worship. According to legend, God sent a bolt of lightning that knocked down the statue of Mars, and Christians took over the spot. The current Romanesque church dates from the 12th century. A cute little statue of St. Denis (above the round arch) greets you as you step in. The delightful carvings capping the columns inside date from Romanesque times. The lovely (but poorly lit) pastel-painted *Deposition* to the right of the choir is restored to its 16th-century brilliance. The medieval stained glass in the windows, likely destroyed in the French Revolution, was replaced with 19th-century glass.

From the steps of the church, look out to the hill-capping Amboise château. For a thousand years, it's been God on this hill and the king on that one. It's interesting to ponder how, throughout French history, the king's power generally trumped the Church's, and how the Church and the king worked to keep people down—setting the stage for the French Revolution.

• *Retrace your steps down from the church and across Place St. Denis, go past Amboise's lone cinema, continue walking straight, and follow Rue Nationale through the heart of town toward the castle.*

Rue Nationale: In France, districts around any castle or church officially classified as historic are preserved. The broad, pedestrianized Rue Nationale, with its narrow intersecting lanes, survives from the 15th century. At that time, when the town spread at the foot of the king's castle, this was the "Champs-Elysées" of Amboise. Supporting the king and his huge entourage was a serious industry. The French king spilled money wherever he stayed.

As you walk along this spine of the town, spot surviving bits of rustic medieval oak in the half-timbered buildings. The homes of wealthy merchants rose from the chaos of this street. Side lanes can be more candid—they often show what's hidden behind modern facades.

Stop when you reach the impressive **clock tower** (Tour de l'Horloge), built into part of the 15th-century town wall. This was once a fortified gate, opening onto the road to the city of Tours. Imagine the hefty wood-and-iron portcullis (fortified door) that dropped from above.

• *At the intersection with Rue François I (where you'll be tempted by the Bigot chocolate shop—see "Helpful Hints," earlier), turn left a couple of steps to the...*

City Hall Museum (Musée de l'Hôtel de Ville): This free museum is worth a quick peek for its romantic interior, town paintings, and historic etchings (Wed-Mon 10:00-12:30 & 14:00-18:00, closed Tue and off-season). In the room dedicated to Leonardo da Vinci, find his busts and the gripping deathbed painting of him with caring King François I at his side. In the Salle des Rois (Kings' Room), find portraits of Charles VIII (who coldcocked himself at Amboise's castle; more on this later) and other kings who called Amboise home; I like to admire their distinct noses.

Upstairs, in the still-functioning city assembly hall (last room), notice how the photo of the current president faces the lady of the Republic. (According to locals, her features change with the taste of the generation, and the bust of France's Lady Liberty is often modeled on famous supermodels of the day.)

• *Your walk ends here, but you can easily continue on to the nearby Château Royal d'Amboise (and beyond that, to Leonardo's last residence): Retrace your steps along Rue François I to Place Michel Debré, at the base of the château. Here, at one of the most touristy spots in the Loire, you can feel how important tourism is to the local economy. Notice the fat, round 15th-century fortified tower, whose interior ramp was built for galloping horses to spiral up to castle level. But to get to the castle without a horse, you'll have to walk up the long ramp.*

Sights in Amboise

CHATEAUX

▲Château Royal d'Amboise

This historic heap became the favored royal residence in the Loire under Charles VIII, who did most of the building in the late 15th century. Charles is famous for accidentally killing himself by walking into a door lintel on his way to a tennis match (seriously). Later, more careful occupants include Louis XII (who moved the royal court to Blois) and François I (who physically brought the Renaissance here in 1516, in the person of Leonardo da Vinci).

Cost and Hours: €10.70, unnecessary audioguide-€4 (kid's version available), daily April-Oct 9:00-18:00, until 19:00 July-Aug, shorter hours off-season, Place Michel Debré, tel. 02 47 57 00 98, www.chateau-amboise.com.

Tours: In summer, daily tours of the château run in English, usually in early afternoon (call to confirm or ask on arrival).

Visiting the Château: Pick up the free and well-done English brochure, which gives all you need to know.

After climbing the long ramp to the ticket booth and picking up the English handout, your first stop is the petite **chapel** where Leonardo da Vinci is supposedly buried. This flamboyant little Gothic chapel is where the king began and ended each day in prayer. It comes with two fireplaces "to comfort the king" and two plaques "evoking the final resting place" of Leonardo (one in French, the other in Italian). Where he's actually buried, no one seems to know. Look up at the ceiling to appreciate the lacy design.

Enter the **castle rooms** across from Leonardo's chapel. The three-floor route takes you chronologically from Gothic-style rooms to those from the early Renaissance and on to the 19th century. The first room, **Salle des Gardes,** shows the château's original, much larger size; drawings in the next room give you a better feel for its original look. Some wings added in the 15th and 16th centuries have disappeared. (The little chapel you just saw was once part of the bigger complex.)

You'll pass **council chambers** where the king would meet with his key staff. King **Henry II's bedroom** is livable. The second son of François I, Henry is remembered as the husband of the ambitious and unscrupulous Catherine de' Medici—and for his tragic death in a jousting tournament.

The rose-colored top-floor rooms are well furnished from the post-Revolutionary 1800s and demonstrate the continued interest among French nobility in this château. Find the classy portrait of King Louis-Philippe, the last Louis to rule France.

Climb to the top of the **Minimes Tower** for grand views. From here, the strategic value of this site is clear: The visibility is great, and the river below provided a natural defense. The bulky tower climbs 130 feet in five spirals—designed for a mounted soldier in a hurry.

Exit into the **gardens.** Each summer, bleachers are set up for sound-and-light spectacles—a faint echo of the extravaganzas Leonardo orchestrated for the court. Modern art decorating the garden reminds visitors of the inquisitive and scientific Renaissance spirit that Leonardo brought to town. The flags are those of France and Brittany—a reminder that, in a sense, modern France was created at the nearby château of Langeais when Charles VIII (who was born here) married Anne of Brittany, adding her domain to the French kingdom.

There are two ways down to Amboise. While you can leave the way you came, it's more interesting to spiral down the **Heurtault Tower** (access through the gift shop near the top of the entry ramp). As with the castle's other tower, this was designed to accommodate a soldier on horseback. As you gallop down to the exit, notice the cute little characters and scenes left by 15th-century stone carvers. While they needed to behave when decorating churches and palaces, here they could be a bit racier and more spirited.

Leaving the Château: The turnstile puts you on the road to Château du Clos-Lucé (described next; turn left and hike straight for 10 minutes). Along the way, you'll pass **troglodyte houses**—both new and old—carved into the hillside stone (a type called *tuffeau*, a sedimentary rock). Originally, poor people resided here—the dwellings didn't require expensive slate roofing, came with natural insulation, and could be dug essentially for free, as builders valued the stone quarried in the process. Today wealthy stone lovers are renovating them into stylish digs worthy of *Better Homes and Caves*. You can see chimneys high above. Unfortunately, none are open to the public.

▲Château du Clos-Lucé and Leonardo da Vinci Park

In 1516, Leonardo da Vinci packed his bags (and several of his favorite paintings, including the *Mona Lisa*) and left an imploding Rome for better wine and working conditions in the Loire Valley. He accepted the position of engineer, architect, and painter to France's Renaissance king, François I. This "House of Light" is the plush palace where Leonardo spent his last three years. (He died on May 2, 1519.) François, only 22 years old, installed the 65-year-old Leonardo here just so he could enjoy his intellectual company.

The house is a kind of fort-château of its own, with a fortified rampart walk and a 16th-century chapel. Two floors of finely decorated rooms are open to the public, but none of the furnishings are original, nor are they particularly compelling (though you can stare face-to-face with a copy of Leonardo's *Mona Lisa*). Come to see well-explained models of Leonardo's inventions, displayed inside the house and out in the huge park.

Leonardo came with disciples who stayed active here, using this house as a kind of workshop and laboratory. The place survived the Revolution because the quick-talking noble who owned it was sympathetic to the cause; he convinced the Revolutionaries that, philosophically, Leonardo would have been on their side.

Cost and Hours: The €14 admission (includes house and park) is worth it for Leonardo fans with two hours to spend taking full advantage of this sight. Skip the garden museum and its €5 supplement. Daily Feb-Oct 9:00-19:00, until 20:00 July-Aug; shorter hours off-season, last entry one hour before closing, follow the helpful free English handout, tel. 02 47 57 00 73, www.vinci-closluce.com. A free app in English includes background information and audio tours of the château and grounds.

Getting There: It's a 10-minute walk uphill from Château Royal d'Amboise, past troglodyte homes (see end of previous listing). If you drive, don't leave valuables visible in your car if you park in the nearby lot.

Eating: Several garden cafés, including one just behind the house and others in the park, are reasonably priced and appropriately meditative. For a view over Amboise, choose the terrace *crêperie*.

Visiting the Château and Gardens: Your visit begins with a tour of Leonardo's elegant yet livable Renaissance **home.** This little residence was built in 1450—just within the protective walls of the town—as a guesthouse for the king's château nearby. Today it re-creates (with Renaissance music) the everyday atmosphere Leonardo enjoyed while he lived here, pursuing his passions to the very end. Find the touching sketch in Leonardo's bedroom of François I comforting his genius pal on his deathbed.

The basement level is filled with **sketches** recording the storm patterns of Leonardo's brain and **models** of his remarkable inventions (inspired by nature and built according to his notes). Leonardo was fascinated by water. All he lacked was steam power. It's hard to imagine that this Roman candle of creativity died nearly 500 years ago. Exit into the rose garden, then find another room with 40 small models of his inventions (with handheld English explanations).

Imagine Leonardo's résumé letter to kings of Europe: "I can help your armies by designing tanks, flying machines, wind-up cars, gear systems, extension ladders, and water pumps." The French considered him a futurist who never really implemented his visions.

Your visit finishes with a stroll through the whimsical, expansive and kid-friendly **park grounds,** with life-size models of Leonardo's inventions (including some that kids can operate), "sound stations" (in English), and translucent replicas of some of his paintings. The models make clear that much of what Leonardo observed and created was based on his intense study of nature.

LOIRE

OTHER SIGHTS AND ACTIVITIES

▲Château Royal d'Amboise Sound-and-Light Show

If you're into S&L, this is considered one of the best shows of its kind in the area. Although it's entirely in French, you can buy the English booklet for €5. Volunteer locals from toddlers to pensioners re-create the life of François I with costumes, juggling, impressive light displays, and fireworks. Dress warmly.

Cost and Hours: Bench-€14, chair-€17, family deals, only about 20 performances a year, 1.5-hour show, Wed and Sat late June-July 22:30-24:00, Aug 22:00-23:30, tel. 02 47 57 14 47, www.renaissance-amboise.com. The ticket window is on the ramp to the château and opens at 20:30.

The Loire and Its Many Châteaux: A Historical Primer

It's hard to overstate the importance of the Loire River to France. Its place in French history goes back to the very foundation of the country. As if to proclaim its storied past, the Loire is the last major wild river in France, with no dams and no regulation of its flow.

Traditional flat-bottomed boats romantically moored along embankments are a reminder of the age before trains and trucks, when river traffic safely and efficiently transported heavy loads of stone and timber. With prevailing winds sweeping east from the Atlantic, barge tenders raised their sails and headed upriver; on the way back, boats flowed downstream with the current.

With this transportation infrastructure providing (relatively) quick access to Paris—and the region's thick forests—offering plenty of timber, firewood, and hunting terrain—it's no wonder that castles were built here in the Middle Ages. The first stone fortresses went up here a thousand years ago, and many of the pleasure palaces you see today rose over the ruins of those original defensive keeps.

The Hundred Years' War—roughly 1336 to 1453—was a desperate time for France. Because of a dynastic dispute, the English had a serious claim to the French throne, and by 1415 they controlled much of the country, including Paris. France was at a low ebb, and its king and court retreated to the Loire Valley to rule what remained of their realm. Chinon was the refuge of the dispirited king, Charles VII. He was famously visited there in 1429 by the charismatic Joan of Arc, who inspired the king to get off his duff and send the English packing.

The French kings continued to live in the Loire region for the next two centuries, having grown comfortable with the château culture of the region. The climate was mild, hunting was good, dreamy rivers made nice reflections, wealthy friends lived in similar luxury nearby, and the location was close enough to Paris—but still far enough away. Charles VII ruled from Chinon, Charles VIII preferred Amboise, Louis XII reigned from Blois, and François I held court in Chambord and Blois.

This was a kind of cultural Golden Age. With peace and stability, there was no need for fortifications. The most famous luxury hunting lodges, masquerading as fortresses, were built during this period—including Chenonceau, Chambord, Chaumont, Amboise, and Azay-le-Rideau. Kings (François I), writers (Rabelais), poets (Ronsard), and artists (Leonardo da Vinci) made the Loire a cultural hub. Many years later, these same châteaux attracted other notables, including Voltaire, Molière, and perhaps Benjamin Franklin.

Because French kings ruled effectively only by being constantly on the move among their subjects, many royal châteaux were used infrequently. The entire court—and its trappings—had to be portable. A castle kept empty and cold 11 months of the year would suddenly become the busy center of attention when the king came to town. As you visit the castles, imagine the royal roadies setting up a kingly room—hanging tapestries, unfolding chairs, wrestling big trunks with handles—in the hours just before the arrival of the royal entourage. The French word for furniture, *mobilier,* literally means "mobile."

When touring the châteaux, you'll notice the impact of Italian culture. From the Renaissance onward, Italian ways were fancy ways. French nobles and court ministers who traveled to Italy returned inspired by the art and architecture they saw. Kings imported Italian artists and architects. It's no wonder that the ultimate French Renaissance king, François I, invited the ultimate Italian artist, Leonardo da Vinci, to join his court in Amboise. Tastes in food, gardens, artists, and women were all influenced by Italian culture.

Women had a big impact on Loire château life. Big personalities like kings tickled more than one tiara. Louis XV famously decorated the palace of Chenonceau with a painting of the Three Graces—featuring his three favorite mistresses.

Châteaux were generally owned by kings, their ministers, or their mistresses. A high-maintenance and powerful mistress often managed to get her own place even when a king's romantic interest shifted elsewhere. In many cases, the king or minister would be away at work or at war for years at a time—leaving home-improvement decisions to the lady of the château, who had unlimited money. That helps explain the emphasis on comfort and the feminine touch you'll enjoy while touring many of the Loire châteaux.

In 1525, François I moved to his newly built super-palace at Fontainebleau, and political power left the Loire. From then on, châteaux were mostly used as vacation and hunting retreats. They became refuges for kings again during the French Wars of Religion (1562-1598)—a sticky set of squabbles over dynastic control that pitted Protestants (Huguenots) against Catholics. Its conclusion marked the end of an active royal presence on the Loire. With the French Revolution in 1789, symbols of the Old Regime, like the fabulous palaces along the Loire, were ransacked. Fast talking saved some châteaux, especially those whose owners had personal relationships with Revolutionary leaders.

Only in the 1840s did the châteaux of the Loire become appreciated for their historic value. The Loire was the first place where treasures of French heritage were officially recognized and protected by the national government. In the 19th century, Romantic Age writers—such as Victor Hugo and Alexander Dumas—visited and celebrated the châteaux. Aristocrats on the Grand Tour stopped here. The Loire Valley and its historic châteaux found a place in our collective hearts and have been treasured to this day.

Mini-Châteaux

This five-acre park on the edge of Amboise (on the route to Chenonceaux) shows the major Loire châteaux in 1:25-scale models, forested with 2,000 bonsai trees and laced together by a model TGV train and river boats. For children, it's a fun introduction to the real châteaux they'll be visiting (and there's a cool toy store). Essential English information is posted throughout the sight.

You'll find other kid-oriented attractions at Mini-Châteaux; consider playing a round of mini-golf and feeding the fish in the moat (a great way to get rid of that old baguette).

Cost and Hours: Adults-€14, kids-€10, daily June-Aug 10:00-19:00, Sept-Oct 10:30-18:00, mid-April-May 10:30-19:00, closed Nov-mid-April, last entry one hour before closing, tel. 02 47 23 44 57, www.decouvrez-levaldeloire.com.

Caveau des Vignerons

This small *cave* offers free tastings of cheeses, pâtés, and regional wines from 10 different vintners (daily mid-March-mid-Nov 10:00-19:00, under Château d'Amboise, across from recommended L'Epicerie restaurant, tel. 02 47 57 23 69).

Biking from Amboise

A signed bike route takes you to Chenonceaux (about 8 miles one-way) in about an hour. Leading past Leonardo's Clos-Lucé, the first two miles are uphill, and the entire ride is on a road with some traffic. Serious cyclists can continue to Chaumont in 1.5 hours, connecting Amboise, Chenonceaux, and Chaumont in an all-day, 37-mile pedal (see "Bike Route" on the map on page 394). The most appealing pedal from Amboise follows the Loire along a dedicated bike path, though you won't see any great castles. The village of Lussault-sur-Loire makes an easy destination (2.5 miles one-way), or keep on pedaling to Montlouis, two miles past Lussault.

Canoe Trips from Amboise or Chenonceaux

Paddling under the Château de Chenonceau is a memorable experience. **Canoe Company** offers canoe rentals on the Loire and Cher rivers (€12-25/person depending on how far you go, mobile 06 70 13 30 61 or 06 37 01 89 92, www.canoe-company.fr).

NEAR AMBOISE

Wine Tasting in Vouvray

In the nearby town of Vouvray, 10 miles toward Tours from Amboise, you'll find wall-to-wall opportunities for wine tasting (but less impressive vineyards than in other parts of France). From Amboise you can take the speedy D-952 there, or joyride on the more appealing D-1 (see map on page 394). Here are two top choices for testing the local sauce:

The big **Cave des Producteurs** is a smart place to start. It has an English-speaking staff, English-language tours of the winery, and a good selection from the 25 producers they represent, including wines from other Loire areas (free wine tasting, cellar tour-€2.40, daily 9:00-19:00 except mid-Sept-mid-May closes daily 12:30-14:00, cellar tours in English at 11:30, 14:30, and 16:30—call ahead to confirm, 38 La Vallée Coquette in Vouvray, tel. 02 47 52 75 03, www.cavedevouvray.com). It's just west of Vouvray in Rochecorbon. Go past the smaller Cave des Producteurs outlet you'll see along D-952 in Vouvray, turn when you see the blue signs to *Moncontour,* then follow the small brown signs to *Cave des Producteurs.*

For a more intimate experience, drop by **Marc Brédif,** where you'll find a top-quality selection of Vouvray wines, as well as red wines from Chinon and Bourgeuil. You can also tour their impressive 1.2 miles of cellars dug into the hillside (free wine tasting, cellar tour-€6, Mon-Sat 10:30-12:00 & 14:30-18:00, Sun 10:30-13:00, tel. 02 47 52 50 07, www.deladoucette.net—select "Brédif" under "Domaines"). Coming from Amboise, you'll pass it on D-952 after Vouvray; it's on the right, just after the Moncontour turn off.

For tips on wine tasting, see "French Wine-Tasting 101" on page 1072.

ZooParc de Beauval

If you need a zoo fix, this is France's biggest and most impressive one, with thousands of animals from the land and sea. It's about 30 minutes southeast of Amboise toward Vierzon—pick up details at the TI (daily from 9:00 to dusk, English audioguides available, tel. 02 54 75 50 00, www.zoobeauval.com).

Sleeping in Amboise

Amboise is busy in the summer, but there are lots of reasonable hotels and *chambres d'hôtes* in and around the city; the TI can help with reservations (for a €3 fee).

IN THE TOWN CENTER

$$$ Le Manoir les Minimes****** is a good place to experience the refined air of château life in a 17th-century mansion, with antique furniture and precious art objects in the public spaces. Its 15 large, modern rooms work for those seeking luxury digs in Amboise. (Tall folks take note: Top-floor attic rooms have low ceilings.) Several rooms have views of Amboise's château (standard Db-€139-156, larger Db-€225, suite-€305, 3- to 4-person suites-€500, continental breakfast-€16, air-con, Wi-Fi, closed late Nov-mid-

Dec, three blocks upriver from bridge at 34 Quai Charles Guinot, tel. 02 47 30 40 40, www.manoirlesminimes.com, reservation@manoirlesminimes.com).

$$$ Hôtel le Clos d'Amboise**** is a smart urban refuge opening onto beautiful gardens and a small, heated swimming pool. It offers stay-awhile lounges, a lovely rear terrace, and well-designed rooms that mix a touch of modern with a classic, traditional look (standard Db-€140, bigger Db-€180, Db suites-€210-310, extra person-€20, check website for deals, good buffet breakfast-€13.50, mini-fridges, air-con, elevator, Wi-Fi, sauna, free parking, 27 Rue Rabelais, tel. 02 47 30 10 20, www.leclosamboise.com, infos@leclosamboise.com, helpful Patricia or Pauline are ever-present).

$$$ Le Vieux Manoir*** is an entirely different high-end splurge. American expats Gloria and Bob Belknap have restored this secluded but central one-time convent with an attention to detail that Martha Stewart would envy. The gardens are lovely—as is the atrium-like breakfast room—and its six bedrooms would make an antique collector drool. Eager-to-help Gloria is a one-person tourist office (Db-€155-200, cottages-€240-300—require 3-night minimum stay, includes superb breakfast, air-con, Wi-Fi in lobby, no room phones or TVs, free parking, 13 Rue Rabelais, tel. 02 47 30 41 27, www.le-vieux-manoir.com, le_vieux_manoir@yahoo.com).

$$$ Hôtel le Vinci Best Western*** delivers modern, pricey-but-reliable comfort a mile from the town center (standard Db-€105-115, superior Db-€120, extra person-€20, breakfast-€13, 12 Avenue Emile Gounin, tel. 02 47 57 10 90, www.vinciloirevalley.com, reservation@vinciloirevalley.com).

$$ Hôtel Bellevue** is a good midrange bet and centrally located, overlooking the river where the bridge hits the town. The 30 modern rooms are well appointed, and its stylish café/wine bar has nightly piano music (standard Db-€75-98, big Db-€115-160, Tb/Qb-€140-170, elevator, Wi-Fi, 12 Quai Charles Guinot, tel. 02 47 57 02 26, www.hotel-bellevue-amboise.com, contact@hotel-bellevue-amboise.com).

$ Hôtel le Blason,** in a 15th-century, half-timbered building on a busy street, is run by helpful Damien and Beranger, who speak English. The rooms—some with ship's-cabin-like bathrooms—are tight and bright, and have double-paned windows (but avoid the rooms fronting the street). There's air-conditioning on the top floor—but these rooms also have sloped ceilings and low beams (Sb-€53, Db-€63, Tb-€78, Qb-€88, quieter rooms in back and on

Sleep Code

Abbreviations **(€1 = about $1.40, country code: 33)**

S = Single, **D** = Double/Twin, **T** = Triple, **Q** = Quad, **b** = bathroom, **s** = shower only, * = French hotel rating (0-5 stars).

Price Rankings

$$$ Higher Priced—Most rooms €100 or more.

$$ Moderately Priced—Most rooms between €70-100.

$ Lower Priced—Most rooms €70 or less.

Unless otherwise noted, credit cards are accepted, English is spoken, and Wi-Fi is generally free. Prices can change; verify current rates online or by email. For the best prices, always book directly with the hotel.

top floor, guest computer, Wi-Fi, secure parking-€3/day, 11 Place Richelieu, tel. 02 47 23 22 41, www.leblason.fr, hotel@leblason.fr).

$ Hôtel le Chaptal** is a plain, modern hotel with small but clean and cheap rooms, making it a favorite for budget travelers (Db-€54-64, Tb-€74, Qb-€84, breakfast-€7.50, Wi-Fi, 11 Rue Chaptal, tel. 02 47 57 14 46, www.hotel-chaptal-amboise.fr, infos@hotel-chaptal-amboise.fr).

CHAMBRES D'HOTES

The heart of Amboise offers several solid bed-and-breakfast options.

$$$ Au Charme Rabelaisien is a lovely place run by charming Madame Viard. Big doors from the street open onto a grand courtyard with manicured gardens, a heated pool, and four sumptuous rooms surrounding it (Sb-€82-92, Db-€145-179, includes breakfast, air-con, Wi-Fi, private parking, closed Nov-March, 25 Rue Rabelais, tel. 02 47 57 53 84, www.au-charme-rabelaisien.com, aucharmerabelaisien@wanadoo.fr).

$$ La Grange Chambres welcomes with an intimate, flowery courtyard and four comfortable rooms, each tastefully restored with modern conveniences and big beds. There's also a common room with a fridge and tables for do-it-yourself dinners (Db-€85, extra person-€25, includes breakfast, credit card to reserve room but pay in cash only, where Rues Châptal and Rabelais meet at 18 Rue Châptal, tel. 02 47 57 57 22, www.la-grange-amboise.com, lagrange-amboise@orange.fr). Adorable Yveline Savin also rents a small two-room cottage (€590/week, 2- to 3-day stays possible) and speaks fluent *franglais*.

$ L'Iris des Marais is a budget B&B with three rooms and a garden courtyard; avoid the tight low-priced double (Sb-€50-60, Db-€55-75, includes breakfast, Wi-Fi, 14 Quai des Marais, tel. 02 47 30 46 51, www.irisdesmarais.com).

NEAR THE TRAIN STATION

$$ Hôtel la Brèche*, a sleepy place near the station, has 14 solid-value rooms and a good restaurant. Many rooms overlook the peaceful graveled garden, while those on the street are generally larger and come with some traffic noise; all are tastefully decorated (Sb-€59, Db-€68-70, Tb-€86, Qb-€99, breakfast-€9.50, Wi-Fi, 15-minute walk from city center and 2-minute walk from station, 26 Rue Jules Ferry, tel. 02 47 57 00 79, www.labreche-amboise.com, info@labreche-amboise.com).

***Hostel:* $ L'Auberge de Jeunesse** (Centre Charles Péguy) is ideally located on the western tip of the "Golden Island," a 10-minute walk from the train station. Open to people of all ages, and popular with student groups (who can fill the place), it's friendly and easy on the wallet. There are a handful of double rooms—some with partial views to the château—so book ahead (D-€36, bunk in 3- to 4-bed room-€20, no surcharge for nonmembers, breakfast-€4.50, reception open daily 15:00-20:00, no curfew, on Ile d'Or, email is useless—call no more than two weeks ahead to book, tel. 02 47 30 60 90).

NEAR AMBOISE

The area around Amboise is peppered with good-value accommodations of every shape, size, and price range. This region offers drivers the best chance to experience château life at affordable rates—and my recommendations justify the detour. For locations, see the map on page 394. Also consider the recommended accommodations in Chenonceaux and the Hôtel du Grand St. Michel at Chambord.

$$$ Château de Pray**** allows you to sleep in a 770-year-old fortified castle with hints of its medieval origins. A few minutes from Amboise, the 14 rooms in the château aren't big or luxurious, but they come with character and wads of history—and with tubs in most bathrooms. There is no lounge, but the backyard terrace compensates well when the weather agrees. A newer annex offers four contemporary rooms (sleeping up to three each), with lofts, terraces, and views of the castle. A big pool and the restaurant's vegetable garden lie below the château (small Db in main building-€140-150, bigger Db-€200-265, Db in annex-€170-230, continental breakfast-€17, no air-con, 3-minute drive upriver from Amboise toward Chaumont on D-751 in the village of Chargé, Route de Chargé, tel. 02 47 57 23 67, www.chateaudepray.fr, contact@chateaudepray.fr). The dining room is splendid and a

relaxing place to splurge...and feel good about it (four-course *menus* from €57, reservations required).

$$$ At **Château de Nazelles Chambres,** gentle owners Veronique and Olivier Fructus offer six rooms in a 16th-century hillside manor house that comes with a cliff-sculpted pool, manicured gardens, a guest kitchen (picnics are encouraged), views over Amboise, and a classy living room with billiards, a guest computer, and Wi-Fi. The bedrooms in the main building are traditional, while the pleasant rooms cut into the hillside come with private terraces and rock-walled bathrooms. They also have a cozy and very comfortable two-room cottage with living area, kitchen, and private garden (Db-€115-130, bigger Db-€140-150, Qb-€260, includes breakfast, cottage-€280-300 for up to 4 guests, extra person-€30, 16 Rue Tue-La-Soif, Nazelles-Négron, tel. 02 47 30 53 79, www.chateau-nazelles.com, info@chateau-nazelles.com). From D-952, take D-5 into Nazelles-Négron, then turn left on D-1 and quickly veer right onto the little lane above and behind the post office (La Poste) to 16 Rue Tue-la-Soif.

$$$ Château de Perreux*** is a renovated 18th-century castle with a stony, tony feel. Here, upscale bed-and-breakfast service meets château-hotel ambience with 11 plush and tastefully designed rooms just a few minutes from Amboise (Db-€165-195, suites-€260, family rooms-€290, includes breakfast, no restaurant, underground parking, tricky to find, on D-1 between Nazelles-Négron and Pocé-sur-Cisse at 36 Rue de Pocé, tel. 02 47 57 27 47, www.chateaudeperreux.fr, info@chateaudeperreux.fr).

$$$ Château des Arpentis*,** a medieval château-hotel centrally located just minutes from Amboise, makes a fun and classy splurge. Flanked by woods and acres of grass, and fronted by a stream and a moat, you'll come as close as you can to château life during the Loire's Golden Age. Rooms are big, with tasteful decor—and the pool is even bigger. There's no restaurant, but picnics on the terrace tables are encouraged. Efficient manager Olivier takes good care of his clients (Db-€170-190, amazing family suites-€305-355, air-con, elevator, Wi-Fi, near St-Règle, tel. 02 47 23 00 00, www.chateaudesarpentis.com, contact@chateaudesarpentis.com). It's on D-31 just southeast of Amboise; from the roundabout above the Leclerc Market, follow *Autrèche* signs, then look for small signs on the right next to a tall flagpole.

$$ L'Auberge de Launay, five miles upriver from Amboise, gets positive reviews for its easy driving access to many châteaux, fair prices, and good restaurant (roadside Db-€73, bigger garden-side Db-€86, guest computer, Wi-Fi, about 4 miles from Amboise, across the river toward Blois, at 9 Rue de la Rivière in Limeray, tel. 02 47 30 16 82, www.aubergedelaunay.com, info@

aubergedelaunay.com). The star of this place is the country-classy restaurant, with *menus* from €25 (closed Sun except for hotel guests).

$$ Le Moulin du Fief Gentil is a lovely 16th-century mill house set on four acres with a backyard pond (fishing possible in summer, dinner picnics anytime, fridge and microwave at your disposal), and the possibility of home-cooked dinners by English-speaking owner Florence (twin Db-€87, bigger Db-€105, 2-room apartment for 2-€140, extra person-€25, includes breakfast, four-course dinner *menu* with wine-€32—must reserve in advance, cash only, 3 Rue de Culoison, tel. 02 47 30 32 51, mobile 06 64 82 37 18, www.fiefgentil.com, contact@fiefgentil.com). It's located on the edge of Bléré, a 15-minute drive from Amboise and 7 minutes from Chenonceaux—from Bléré, follow signs toward *Luzille,* and it's on the right.

$$ Hostellerie du Château de L'Isle is a rustic, lost-in-time place wrapped in a lush park with a pond and acres of grass on the Cher River. Located in Civray-de-Touraine, two minutes from Chenonceaux, it offers 12 sufficiently comfortable rooms with laissez-faire management. Rooms in the main building are better (small Db-€55, standard Db-€73, big Db-€88-105, 1 Rue de l'Écluse, tel. 02 47 23 63 60, www.chateau-delisle.com, chateaudelisle@orange.fr). The gazebo-like restaurant, as lovely as a Monet painting, features the owner's cooking (€26-33 *menus,* limited choices). From the center of Civray-de-Touraine, follow D-81 toward Tours.

$ La Chevalerie owners Ljubisa and Martine Aleksic rent four simple bargain *chambres* that are family-friendly, with a swing set, tiny fishing pond, shared kitchens, and connecting rooms. The spartan setting works best for budget travelers (Sb-€40, Db-€55, Tb-€75, includes basic breakfast, cash only, in La Croix-en-Touraine, tel. 02 47 57 83 64, lyoubisa.aleksic@orange.fr, owners speak French and German—but not English). From Amboise, take D-31 toward Bléré, look for the *Chambres d'Hôte* sign on your left at about three miles, and then turn left onto C-105.

Eating in Amboise

Amboise is filled with inexpensive and forgettable restaurants, but a handful of places are worth your attention. Some offer a good, end-of-meal cheese platter—a rarity in France these days. The epicenter of the city's dining action is on Place Michel Debré, along Rue Victor Hugo, and across from the château entrance. Troll the places here and find a seat if inspired, or consider my suggestions. After dinner, make sure to cross the bridge for floodlit views of the castle, and consider a view drink at **Le Shaker Cocktail Lounge** (daily from 18:00 until later than you're awake, 3 Quai François Tissard). For more after-hours action, try the piano bar at the recommended Hotel Bellevue.

DINING BELOW THE CHATEAU

L'Epicerie, across from the château entry, serves tasty and well-presented traditional cuisine at fair prices. Choose a table outdoors facing the château or in the rustically elegant dining room. The snails are scrumptious, and the sauces are delectable. Several *menus* come with an amazing cheese platter (€27-36 *menus,* July-Sept daily, Oct-June closed Mon-Tue, reserve ahead, 46 Place Michel Debré, tel. 02 47 57 08 94, www.lepicerie-amboise.com).

La Réserve feels like a wine bar-bistro with modern but tasteful decor, fair-enough prices, and a loyal clientele. The €19 *menu* offers a fine value—and the château view is free (€19-35 *menus,* daily, reservations smart, 28 Place Michel Debré, tel. 02 47 57 97 96).

Anne de Bretagne offers typical, inexpensive café fare in a good location with charming ambience—come for the setting, not the cuisine. The outdoor tables are ideal for surveying the street scene (nonstop service daily 12:00-22:00, Place du Château, tel. 02 47 57 05 46).

ELSEWHERE IN AMBOISE

La Fourchette is Amboise's tiny family diner, with simple decor inside and out. Hardworking chef Christine makes everything fresh in her open kitchen, offering a limited selection at good prices. The place is popular, so call ahead—the morning of the same day is fine (€16-27 *menus,* closed Sun-Mon, on a quiet corner near Rue Nationale at 9 Rue Malebranche, mobile 06 11 78 16 98).

Le Lion d'Or has a chef who takes his job seriously and delivers quality regional fare at reasonable prices. His cuisine is more contemporary than many of the tourist-oriented eateries in Amboise—and the desserts are particularly imaginative. You'll dine in a mod indoor setting (€22-32 *menus,* closed Sun-Mon, reservations smart, where the bridge meets the town at 7 Quai Charles Guinel, tel. 02 47 57 00 23, www.leliondor-amboise.com).

L'Ancrée des Artistes is Amboise's reliable and central *crêperie.* It's a young-at-heart place with music to dine by and easygoing servers (€9 dinner crêpes, €20 three-course crêpe *menus,* good meat dishes grilled on stones—*pierres,* 35 Rue Nationale, tel. 02 47 23 18 11).

La Scala is good for inexpensive Italian food with easygoing service and a broad terrace (daily, near the TI at 6 Quai du Général de Gaulle, tel. 02 47 23 09 93).

Hôtel la Brèche serves good-value €22-44 *menus* in their warm, traditional dining room and large garden. Stretch your legs and cross the river to the restaurant, then enjoy floodlit castle views on your walk home (daily; for details, see "Sleeping in Amboise," earlier).

NEAR AMBOISE

These options merit the short drive. For an elegant and exquisite castle dining experience (best on a warm evening), consider making the quick drive to **Château de Pray**—call ahead to reserve (see page 388). In summer, head to **Chenonceaux** village for dinner, then enjoy a floodlit walk through the château grounds (try any of the places listed under "Eating in and near Chenonceaux," later).

Amboise Connections

BY BUS OR MINIVAN

By Public Bus to: Chenonceaux (1-2/day, Mon-Sat only, none on Sun, 20 minutes, departs Amboise about 9:45, returns from Chenonceaux at about 12:15, allowing you about an hour and 20 minutes at the château during its most crowded time; in summer, there's also an afternoon departure at about 15:00 with a return from Chenonceaux at about 17:50; confirm times with the TI; the Amboise stop—called Théâtre—is between Place St. Denis and the river on the west side of Avenue des Martyrs de la Résistance, across from the Théâtre de Beaumarchais; in Chenonceaux, the bus stops across the street from the TI and at the château gate—it's still a 15-minute walk to the château; for more flexibility, consider taking a train back instead—see next page; tel. 02 47 05 30 49, www.tourainefilvert.com—search for "line C"); **Tours** (8/day Mon-Sat, none on Sun, buses are cheaper than trains).

By Shuttle Van to Chenonceau, Chambord, and Cheverny: Quart de Tours runs two round-trips per day (high season only) between Amboise and Chenonceau (€16 round-trip, €10 one-way, includes €2.50 discount for château, 15-minute trip), and excursion trips from Amboise and Tours to various combinations of the top châteaux, including Chambord and Cheverny (half-day-€37/person, allow 5 hours; full-day-€55/person, allow 7 hours). Book ahead, as seats are limited (mobile 06 30 65 52 01, www.chateaux-tours.com). **Touraine Evasion** runs a van from Amboise that stops at Chambord and Chenonceau; they also have many château options out of Tours (daily in season, none in winter, mobile 06 07 39 13 31, www.tourevasion.com). Check with the Amboise TI for details and pickup locations for both companies.

By Minivan Excursion to Nearby Châteaux: Acco-Dispo runs good half- and all-day English tours from Amboise and Tours to all the major châteaux six days a week (Mon-Sat). Costs vary with the itinerary (half-day-€23/person, full-day-€54/person; free hotel pickups, small groups of 2-8 people, mobile 06 82 00 64 51, www.accodispo-tours.com). While on the road, you'll usually get a fun and enthusiastic running commentary—but you're on your own at the sights (discounted tickets available from the driver). Reserve a week ahead by email, or two to three days by phone. (Day-trippers from Paris find this service convenient.) Acco-Dispo also runs multiday tours of the Loire and Brittany.

Another minivan option, **Loire Valley Tours** offers all-day itineraries from Amboise and Tours that are fully guided and include admissions, lunch, and wine-tasting (about €140/person, tel. 02 54 33 99 80, www.loire-valley-tours.com). **Quart de Tours** also offers excursions (see "By Shuttle Van," earlier).

BY TAXI

Most châteaux are too expensive to visit by cab, but a taxi from Amboise to Chenonceau costs about €27 (€39 on Sun and after 19:00, tel. 02 47 57 13 53 or 02 47 57 30 39). The meter doesn't start until you do.

BY TRAIN

Within the Loire

From Amboise by Train to: Chenonceaux (trains are a more frequent, if a slower and pricier, option than the bus; 6/day, most about 1 hour, transfer at St-Pierre-des-Corps—check connections to avoid long waits), **Blois** (14/day, 20 minutes, bus or taxi excursions from there to Chambord, Chaumont, or Cheverny—see "Blois Connections," page 408), **Chaumont** (about 14/day, 35 minutes, take 10-minute train to Onzain on the Amboise-Blois route, 25-minute walk—you can see château from station), **Tours** (12/day, 25 minutes, allows connections to châteaux west of Tours), **Chinon** (7/day, 1.5-2 hours, transfer in Tours), **Azay-le-Rideau** (6/day, 1-2 hours, transfer in Tours).

LOIRE

Beyond the Loire

Twenty 15-minute trains link Amboise daily to the regional train hub of St-Pierre-des-Corps (in suburban Tours). There you'll find reasonable connections to distant points (including the TGV to Paris' Gare Montparnasse). Transferring in Paris can be the fastest way to reach many French destinations, even in the south.

From Amboise by Train to: Paris (8/day, 1.5 hours to Gare Montparnasse with change to TGV at St-Pierre-des-Corps, requires TGV reservation; 3/day, 1.75 hours direct to Gare d'Austerlitz, no reservation required; more to Gare d'Austerlitz

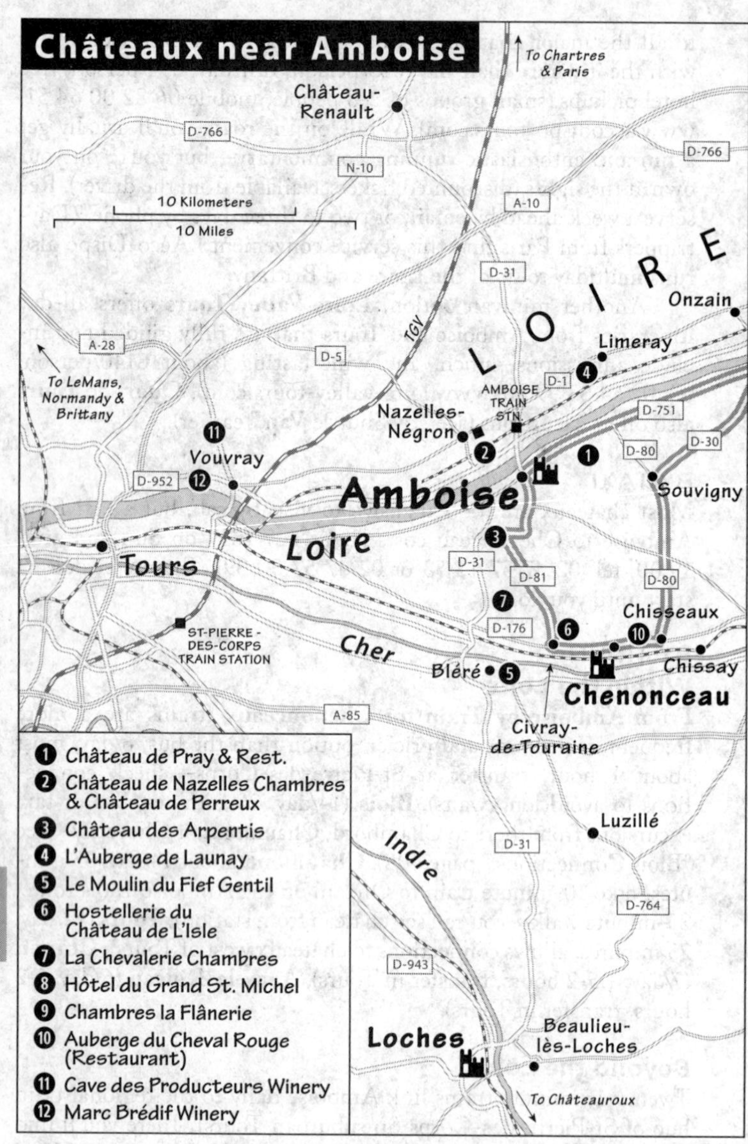

with transfer in Orléans), **Sarlat-la-Canéda** (3/day, 5-7 hours, change at St-Pierre-des-Corps, then TGV to Libourne, then train through Bordeaux vineyards to Sarlat), **Limoges** (near Oradour-sur-Glane, 7/day, about 4 hours, change at St-Pierre-des-Corps, then at Vierzon or Poitiers, then tricky bus connection from Limoges to Oradour-sur-Glane—see page 497), **Pontorson/Mont St-Michel** (1/day, 5.5 hours with transfers at Nantes and Rennes,

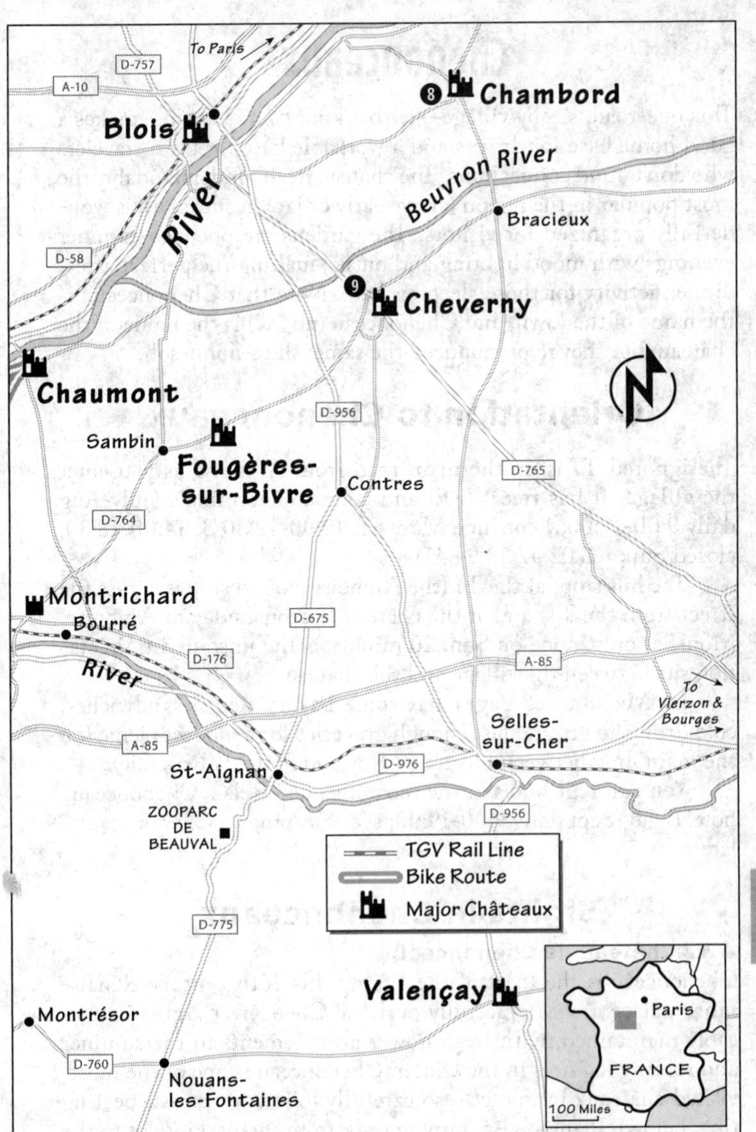

longer connections through Paris), **Bayeux** (2/day, 4.5 hours, transfer at Tours' St-Pierre-des-Corps and Caen, more with transfer in Paris—arrive at Paris' Gare d'Austerlitz, then Métro to Gare St. Lazare), **Beaune** (1/day, 4.5 hours, transfer at St-Pierre-des-Corps, more with additional transfer at Nevers), **Bourges** (roughly hourly—though fewer midday, 2-3 hours, change at St-Pierre-des-Corps).

Chenonceaux

This one-road, sleepy village—with a knockout château—makes a good home base for drivers and a workable base for train travelers who don't mind connections. The château itself, understandably the most popular in the region (arrive early or late in summer), is wonderfully organized for visitors. The gardens are open on summer evenings with mood lighting and music, making the perfect after-dinner activity for those sleeping here. Note that Chenonceaux is the name of the town, and Chenonceau (no "x") is the name of the château, but they're pronounced the same: shuh-nohn-soh.

Orientation to Chenonceaux

The ignored **TI** is on the main road from Amboise as you enter the village. It has free Wi-Fi and computer terminals (July-Aug daily 9:00-19:00; Sept-June Mon-Sat 10:00-12:30 & 14:00-18:30, closed Sun; tel. 02 47 23 94 45).

The **bus** stops at the TI (the Amboise-bound stop is across the street from the TI) and at the château (1-2 buses/day to Amboise, Mon-Sat only, none on Sun, 20 minutes). The unstaffed train station sits between the village and the château.

La Maison des Pages has some bakery items, sandwiches, cold drinks to go, and just enough groceries for a modest picnic (on the main drag between Hostel du Roy and Hôtel la Roseraie).

You can rent **bikes** at the recommended Relais Chenonceaux hotel (May-Sept daily 9:00-19:00; see "Sleeping in Chenonceaux," later).

Sights in Chenonceaux

▲▲▲Château de Chenonceau

Chenonceau is the toast of the Loire. This 16th-century Renaissance palace arches gracefully over the Cher River and is impeccably maintained, with fresh flower arrangements in the summer and roaring log fires in the winter. Chenonceau is one of the most-visited châteaux in France—so carefully follow my crowd-beating tips (below). Plan on a 15-minute walk from the parking lot to the château. Warning: Don't leave any valuables visible in your car.

Cost and Hours: €12.50 includes château and wax museum, kids under 18-€9.50, daily mid-March-mid-Sept 9:00-19:30, July-Aug until 20:00, closes earlier off-season, last entry 30 minutes before closing, tel. 02 47 23 90 07, www.chenonceau.com.

Chenonceau at Night *(Promenade Nocturne)*: On summer nights, floodlights and period music create a romantic after-dinner cap to your Loire day (gardens only). Just stroll over whenever and for as long as you like (€5, daily July-Aug 21:30-23:30, Fri-Sun in June).

Crowd-Beating Tips: Spaces are tight inside the château, so smart travelers plan around Chenonceau's crowds. This place gets slammed in high season, when you should come early (by 9:00) or late (after 17:00). Avoid slow ticket lines by purchasing your ticket in advance (at area TIs) or from the ticket machines at the main entry (just follow the prompts; US credit cards work but instructions in English are hit-and-miss—withdraw your card at the prompt "retirez").

Tours: The interior is fascinating—but only if you take full advantage of the free, excellent 20-page **booklet** (included with entry), or rent the wonderful **video/audioguide** (€4.50; two different versions available—45 or 80 minutes, each with the same stops; request the unhurried 80-minute version to enjoy full coverage). There's also an audioguide for kids. Pay for the audioguide when buying your ticket (before entering the château grounds), then pick it up just inside the château's door. Or, before you visit, download the iTunes-only app—search for "Discover Chenonceau" (free).

Services: WCs are available by the ticket office and behind the wax museum. There's a free bag check at the turnstile.

Wax Museum, Play Area, and Traditional Farm: The wax museum (La Galerie des Dames-Musée de Cires, located in the château stables), while tacky and designed for children, puts a waxy face on the juicy history of the château. Reading the English displays requires a series of deep knee-bends. You can taste the owner's wines in the atmospheric **Cave du Dôme** below. A kids' play area lies just past the wax museum, and a few steps beyond that you can stroll around a traditional farm and imagine the production needed to sustain the château (free, always open).

Eating: A reasonable cafeteria is next door to the wax museum. Fancy meals are served in the *orangerie* behind the stables. There's a cheap *crêperie*/sandwich shop at the entrance gate. While picnics are not allowed on the grounds, there are picnic tables in a park near the parking lot.

Boat Trips: In summer, the château has rental **rowboats**—an idyllic way to savor graceful château views, but not available when the river is low (€6/30 minutes, July-Aug daily 10:00-19:00, 4 people/boat).

Background: Find a riverside view of the château to get oriented. Although earlier châteaux were built for defensive purposes, Chenonceau was the first great pleasure palace. Nicknamed the "château of the ladies," it housed many famous women over the centuries. The original owner, Thomas Bohier, was away on the king's business so much that his wife, Katherine Briçonnet, made most of the design decisions during construction of the main château (1513-1521).

In 1547, King Henry II gave the château to his mistress, Diane de Poitiers, who added an arched bridge across the river to access the hunting grounds. She enjoyed her lovely retreat until Henry II died (pierced in a jousting tournament in Paris); his vengeful wife, Catherine de' Medici, unceremoniously kicked Diane out (and into the château of Chaumont, described on page 415). Catherine added the three-story structure on Diane's bridge. She died before completing her vision of a matching château on the far side of the river, but not before turning Chenonceau into *the* place to see and be seen by the local aristocracy. (Whenever you see a split coat of arms, it belongs to a woman—half her husband's and half her father's.)

➲ **Self-Guided Tour:** Strut like an aristocrat down the tree-canopied path to the château. (There's a fun plant maze partway up on the left.) You'll cross three moats and two bridges, and pass an old round tower, which predates the main building. Notice the tower's fine limestone veneer, added so the top would better fit the new château.

The main château's original **oak door** greets you with the coats of arms of the first owners. The knocker is high enough to be used by visitors on horseback. The smaller door within the large one could be for two purposes: to slip in after curfew, or to enter during winter without letting out all the heat.

Once inside, you'll tour the château in a clockwise direction (turn left upon entering). Take time to appreciate the beautiful brick floor tiles and lavishly decorated ceilings. As you continue, follow your pamphlet or audioguide, and pay attention to these details:

In the **guard room,** the best-surviving original floor tiles are near the walls—imagine the entire room covered with these tiles. And though the tapestries kept the room cozy, they also functioned to tell news or recent history (to the king's liking, of course). You'll see many more tapestries in this château.

The superbly detailed **chapel** survived the vandalism of the Revolution because the fast-thinking lady of the palace filled it with firewood. Angry masses were supplied with mallets and instructions to smash everything royal or religious. While this room was both, all they saw was stacked wood. The hatch door provided a quick path to the kitchen and an escape boat downstairs. The windows, blown out during World War II, are replacements from the 1950s. Look for graffiti in English left behind by the guards who protected Mary, Queen of Scots (who stayed here after her marriage to King François II).

The centerpiece of the **bedroom of Diane de Poitiers** is a severe portrait of her rival, Catherine de' Medici, at 40 years old. After the queen booted out the mistress, she placed her own portrait over the fireplace, but she never used this bedroom. The 16th-century tapestries are among the finest in France. Each one took an average of 60 worker-years to make. Study the complex compositions of the *Triumph of Charity* (over the bed) and the violent *Triumph of Force.*

At 200 feet long, the three-story **Grand Gallery** spans the river. The upper stories house double-decker ballrooms and a small museum. Notice how differently the slate and limestone of the checkered floor wear after 500 years. Imagine grand banquets here. Catherine, a contemporary of Queen Elizabeth I of England, wanted to rule with style. She threw wild parties and employed her ladies to circulate and soak up all the political gossip possible from the well-lubricated Kennedys and Rockefellers of her realm. Parties included grand fireworks displays and mock naval battles on the river. The niches once held statues—Louis XIV took a liking to them, and consequently, they now decorate the palace at Versailles.

In summer and during holidays, you can take a quick walk outside for more good palace **views:** Cross the bridge, pick up a re-entry ticket, then stroll the other bank of the Cher (across the river from the château). During World War I, the Grand Gallery served as a military hospital, where more than 2,200 soldiers were cared for—picture hundreds of beds lining the gallery. And in World War II, the river you crossed marked the border between the collaborationist Vichy government and Nazi-controlled France. Back then, Chenonceau witnessed many prisoner swaps, and at night, château staff would help resistance fighters and Jews cross in secret. Because the gallery was considered a river crossing, the Germans had their artillery aimed at Chenonceau, ready to destroy the "bridge" to block any Allied advance.

Double back through the gallery to find the sensational state-of-the-art (in the 16th century) **kitchen** below. It was built near water (to fight the inevitable kitchen fires) and in the basement; because heat rises, the placement helped heat the palace. Cross the small bridge (watch your head) to find the stove and landing bay for goods to be ferried in and out.

The staircase leading **upstairs** wowed royal guests. It was the first non-spiral staircase they'd seen...quite a treat in the 16th century. The balcony provides lovely views of the gardens—which originally supplied vegetables and herbs. (Diane built the one to the right; Catherine, the prettier one to your left.) The estate is still full of wild boar and deer—the primary dishes of past centuries. You'll see more lavish bedrooms on this floor. Small side rooms show fascinating old architectural sketches of the château. The walls, 20 feet thick, were honeycombed with the flues of 224 fireplaces and passages for servants to do their pleasure-providing work unseen. There was no need for plumbing. Servants fetched, carried, and dumped everything pipes do today.

On top of the Grand Gallery is the **Medici Gallery,** now a mini-museum for the château. Displays in French and English cover the lives of six women who made their mark on Chenonceau (one of them had a young Jean-Jacques Rousseau, who would later become an influential philosopher, as her personal secretary). There's also a timeline of the top 10 events in the history of the château and a cabinet of curiosities.

To end your visit, escape the hordes by touring the **two gardens** with their postcard-perfect views of the château. The upstream garden hasn't changed since Diane de Poitiers first commissioned it in 1547. Designed in the austere Italian style, the forceful jet in its water fountain was revolutionary in its time. The downstream garden of Catherine de' Medici is more relaxed, with tree roses and lavender gracing its lines in high season.

Sleeping in Chenonceaux

Hotels are a good value in Chenonceaux, and there's one for every budget. You'll find them *tous ensemble* on Rue du Dr. Bretonneau, all with free and secure parking.

$$$ Auberge du Bon Laboureur**** turns heads with its ivied facade, lush terraces, and, inside, leathery lounges and bars. The staff acts a tad stiff, but if you get past the formal pleasantries, you have four-star rooms at three-star prices (Db-€134-189, suites-€210-310, breakfast-€16, heated pool, air-con, 6 Rue du Dr. Bretonneau, tel. 02 47 23 90 02, www.bonlaboureur.com, laboureur@wanadoo.fr).

$$ Hôtel la Roseraie*** has a flowery terrace and 22 warmly decorated rooms. Sabine and Jerome run a good show with good prices for three-star comfort, and their big white Alsatian Achilles watches over it all (standard Db-€75-92, big Db-€115-138, Tb-€115-150, buffet breakfast-€11.50, queen- or king-size beds, air-con, Wi-Fi, pool, closed Dec-Feb, 7 Rue du Dr. Bretonneau, tel. 02 47 23 90 09, www.hotel-chenonceau.com, laroseraie-chenonceaux@orange.fr). The traditional dining room and delightful terrace are ideal for a nice dinner

available for guests and non-guests alike who reserve ahead (€25-29 *menus,* closed Tue and mid-Nov-mid-March).

$$ Relais Chenonceaux,** above a restaurant, greets guests with a nice patio and unimaginative, wood-paneled rooms at fair rates. The coziest—and, in summer, hottest—rooms are on the top floor, but watch your head (Db-€79, Tb-€88, Qb-€118, Wi-Fi, rental bikes available, tel. 02 47 23 98 11, 10 Rue du Dr. Bretonneau, www.chenonceaux.com, info@chenonceaux.com).

$ Hostel du Roy** offers 30 spartan but well-priced rooms, some around a garden courtyard, and a mediocre but cheap restaurant. Hardworking Nathalie runs the place with papa's help (Db-€44-55, Tb-€65, two-room Qb-€95-110, room for up to five-€120, breakfast-€7.50, Wi-Fi, 9 Rue du Dr. Bretonneau, tel. 02 47 23 90 17, www.hostelduroy.com, hostelduroy@wanadoo.fr).

Eating in and near Chenonceaux

Reserve ahead to dine in formal style at the country-elegant and Michelin-starred **Auberge du Bon Laboureur** (€52 and €85 *menus*). **Hôtel la Roseraie** serves good fixed-price meals in a lovely dining room or on a garden terrace (*menus* from €29, €5 more buys a cheese course, Mon and Wed-Sun 19:00-21:00, closed Tue and mid-Nov-mid-March). **Relais Chenonceaux** dishes up savory *tartes,* salads, and *plats* at fair prices in a pleasant interior or on its terrace (daily). The price is right for the basic cuisine at **Hostel du Roy,** with a daily *plat du jour* at €9.50 and *menus* from €13. All of these are listed earlier, under "Sleeping in Chenonceaux."

For a French treat, book ahead and drive about a mile to Chisseaux and dine at the *très* traditional **Auberge du Cheval Rouge.** You'll enjoy some of the region's fine cuisine at affordable prices, either inside or on a flower-filled patio (€29-35 *menus,* closed Mon-Tue, 30 Rue Nationale, Chisseaux, tel. 02 47 23 86 67).

LOIRE

Chenonceaux Connections

From Chenonceaux by Train to: Tours (10/day, 30 minutes), with connections to **Chinon, Azay-le-Rideau,** and **Langeais; Amboise** (6/day, 1 hour, transfer at St-Pierre-des-Corps).

By Bus to: Amboise (1-2/day, Mon-Sat only, none on Sun, 20 minutes, departs Chenonceaux at about 12:15, in summer also at about 17:50, catch bus at the château gate or across the street from the TI, tel. 02 47 05 30 49, www.tourainefilvert.com).

By Shuttle Van/Minivan Excursion: Quart de Tours and **Touraine Evasion** run shuttle trips (high season only) from Amboise and Tours that pair different châteaux, including Chenonceau and Chambord or Cheverny. Minivan excursions from Amboise and Tours are also available (see "Amboise Connections" on page 392).

By Taxi to: Amboise (€27, €39 on Sun and after 19:00).

Blois

Bustling Blois (pronounced "blah") feels like the Big Apple after all of those rural villages and castles—its urban vibe can be a shock. Blois owns a rich history, dolled-up pedestrian areas, and a darn impressive château smack in its center. With convenient access to Paris, Blois can make a handy base for train travelers; Chambord, Chaumont, and Cheverny are within reach by excursion bus (cheap, high season only) or taxi (pricey, any season). Frequent train service to Paris and Amboise enables easy stopovers in Blois (luggage lockers available at château with paid entry).

If Blois feels more important than other Loire towns, it was. From this once powerful city, the medieval counts of Blois governed their vast lands and vied with the king of France for dominance. The center of France moved from Amboise to Blois in 1498, when Louis XII inherited the throne (after Charles VIII had his unfortunate head-banging incident in Amboise). The château you see today is living proof of this town's 15 minutes of fame. But there's more to Blois than just its château. Tour the flying-buttressed St. Nicholas Church, find the medieval warren of lanes below St. Louis Cathedral, and relax in a café on Place Louis XII.

Orientation to Blois

Unlike most other Loire châteaux, Blois' Château Royal sits right in the city center, with no forest, pond, moat, or river to call its own. It's an easy walk from the train station, near ample underground parking, and just above the TI. Below the château, Place Louis XII marks the hub of traffic-free Blois, with cafés and shops lining its perimeter. Rue du Commerce, leading up from the river, is Blois' primary shopping street. Atmospheric cafés and restaurants hide in the medieval tangle of lanes below St. Louis Cathedral and around St. Nicholas Church. Blois was heavily bombed in World War II, leaving much of the old town in ruins, but the château survived. Today, the city largely ignores its river and celebrates Saturdays with a great market (until about 13:00) centered on Place Louis XII. Sundays are quiet in Blois.

ARRIVAL IN BLOIS

Train travelers can walk 10 minutes straight out of the station down Avenue du Dr. Jean Laigret to the TI and château (follow small brown *Château* signs), or take a two-minute taxi from in front of the station. Although there's no bag check at the station, you can use the château's large, free **lockers** if you pay for admission—so you can drop off your luggage, visit the château and the town, and even take an excursion or taxi tour to Chambord and Cheverny (provided you're back in Blois to reclaim your bag before the château closes).

Drivers follow *Centre-Ville* and *Château* signs (metered parking along Avenue du Dr. Jean Laigret or inside at Parking du Château—first 30 minutes free, then about €2/2.5 hours).

TOURIST INFORMATION

The cramped TI is across from the château entrance. They sell discounted tickets to many châteaux and offer a pay guest computer and pay Wi-Fi (daily April-Sept 9:00-19:00, Oct-March 10:00-17:00, 23 Place du Château, tel. 02 54 90 41 41, www.bloispaysdechambord.com). You can explore the center of Blois by using the TI's handy walking-tour brochure (€2, brown and purple routes are best), download their free city guide app, or just follow my suggested route below. The TI also has information on bike rentals and routes.

HELPFUL HINTS

Local Guide: Fabrice Maret lives in Blois and is a skilled teacher (see page 370 for details).

Laundry: A self-service launderette is at 6 Rue St. Lubin (daily from 7:00 until late).

Bike Rental: Détours de Loire bike rental is near the train station at 39 Avenue du Dr. Jean Laigret (tel. 02 54 56 07 73). Because they also have a shop in Amboise, you can rent a bike for a one-way ride to Amboise, stopping at garden-rich Chaumont-sur-Loire on the way (26-mile trip). See "Biking from Blois," later, for route ideas.

Sights in Blois

▲▲Château Royal de Blois

A castle has inhabited this site since the 900s. Size up the current one from the big square before entering. Even though parts of the building date from the Middle Ages, notice the complete absence of defensive towers, drawbridges, and other fortifications. Gardens once extended behind the château and up the hill to a forest (where the train station is today). A walk around the building's perimeter (to the right as you face it) reveals more of its beautiful Renaissance facade.

Kings Louis XII and François I built most of the château you see today, each calling it home during their reigns. That's Louis looking good on his horse in the niche. The section on the far right looks like a church but was actually the château's most important meeting room (more on this later).

Cost and Hours: €10, kids under age 18-€5, €15 combo-ticket with House of Magic (described later, under "Other Sights and Activities") or sound-and-light show (see next), €20 covers all three, daily July-Aug 9:00-19:00, April-June and Sept 9:00-18:30, Oct 9:00-18:00, Nov-March 9:00-12:30 & 14:30-17:30, audioguide-€4; free lockers available with entry, tel. 02 54 90 33 33, www.chateaudeblois.fr.

Sound-and-Light Show: This simple "show" takes place in the center courtyard and features projections with a historical narrative of the "loves, dramas, and mysteries" of French royal life. An audioguide provides a simultaneous translation in English (€8, covered by combo-tickets described above, daily April-Sept at about 22:00).

Information: At the ticket office, pick up the helpful English brochure, then read the well-presented English displays in each room. The entertaining audioguide tells the story of the château through the voices of its inhabitants (a nice change of pace from other audioguides).

Tours: In summer, tours of the château are run in English once a day (usually early afternoon).

Visiting the Château: Begin in the **courtyard,** where four different wings—ranging from Gothic to Neoclassical—underscore this château's importance over many centuries. Stand with your back to the entry to get oriented. The medieval parts of the château are the brick-patterned sections (to your left and behind you), both built by Louis XII. While work was under way on Chambord, François I (who apparently was addicted to home renovation) added the elaborate Renaissance wing (to your right; early 16th century), centered on a protruding spiral staircase and slathered with his emblematic salamanders. Gaston d'Orléans inherited the place in the 1600s and wanted to do away with the messy mismatched styles. He demolished a church that stood across from you (the chapel to your left is all that remains) and replaced it with the clean-lined, Neoclassical structure you see today. Luckily, that's as far as he got.

Visit the interior counterclockwise, and focus on the Renaissance wing. Begin in the far-right corner (where you entered the courtyard) and walk under the stone porcupine relief, Louis' symbol, and up the steps into the dazzling **Hall of the Estates-General** (it resembles a church from the outside). This is the oldest surviving part of the château (predating Louis and François), where the Estates-General met twice to deliberate who would inherit the throne from Henry III, who had no male heir. (Keep reading to see how Henry resolved the problem.)

Continue into the small **lapidary museum** (down the steps by the wooden staircase), with an engaging display of statues and architectural fragments from the original château (love the gargoyles).

Stone stairs lead up to the **royal apartments of François I.** Immerse yourself in richly tiled, ornately decorated rooms with some original furnishings (excellent English explanations posted). You'll see busts and portraits of some of the château's most famous residents, and near the end, learn about the dastardly 1588 murder of the duke of Guise, which took place in these apartments. In the late 1500s, the devastating Wars of Religion pitted Protestant against Catholic, and took a huge toll on this politically and religiously divided city—including the powerful Guise brothers. King Henry III (Catherine de' Medici's son) had the devoutly Catholic duke assassinated to keep him off the throne.

Skip the Neoclassical wing (no English and little of interest), and end your visit with a walk through the small **fine-arts museum.** Located just over the château's entry, this 16th-century who's-who portrait gallery lets you put faces to the characters that made this château's history.

OTHER SIGHTS AND ACTIVITIES

House of Magic (Maison de la Magie)

The home of Jean-Eugène Robert-Houdin, the illusionist whose name was adopted by Harry Houdini, offers an interesting but overpriced history of illusion and magic. Kids enjoy the gift shop. Several daily 30-minute shows have no words, so they work in any language.

Cost and Hours: Adults-€9, kids under 18-€5, €15 combo-ticket with château, €20 combo-ticket includes château and sound-and-light show; daily 10:00-12:30 & 14:00-18:30, "séance" schedule posted at entry—usually at 11:15, 14:15 or 15:15, and 17:15; at the opposite end of the square from the château, tel. 02 54 90 33 33, www.maisondelamagie.fr.

Wine Cooperative

Sample wines from a variety of local vintners on the château square, next to Le Marignan café (free, daily 11:00-19:00, closed at lunchtime off-season, tel. 02 54 74 76 66).

A Walk Through the Historic Center

There's little to do along the river except to cross Pont Jacques Gabriel for views back to the city. But Blois' old town is well worth a wander. Although much of the historic center was destroyed by WWII bombs, it has been tastefully rebuilt with traffic-free streets and pleasing squares.

For a taste of medieval Blois, head to Place Louis XII, ground zero in the old city; from here, walk down Rue St. Lubin. Follow along as the street (now called Rue des Trois Marchands) curves to the left; continue until you see the church of **St. Nicholas** on your left. The towering church, with its flying buttresses, dates from the late 1100s, and is worth a peek inside for its beautifully lit apse and its blend of Gothic and Romanesque styles. Find Rue Anne de Bretagne behind the church and track it back to Place Louis XII. From here, pedestrian-friendly streets like Rue St. Martin lead north to Rue du Commerce, the town's main shopping drag, and to peaceful medieval lanes below Blois' other hill, crowned by **St. Louis Cathedral.** Nearby Rue de la Foulerie is headquarters for hip Blois.

Biking from Blois

Blois is well positioned as a starting point for biking forays into the countryside. Cycling from Blois to Chambord is a level, one-hour, one-way ride along a well-marked, 10-mile route, much of it a bike-only lane that follows the river. You can loop back to Blois without repeating the same route, and connect to a good network of other bike paths (the TI's free *Les Châteaux à Vélo* map shows the bike routes in this area). Hardy riders can bike one-way to Amboise via Chaumont by renting at the Détours de Loire bike shop (See "Helpful Hints" for Blois, earlier).

Sleeping in Blois

Blois has a scarcity of worthwhile hotels.

$$$ Hôtel Mercure Blois*** is modern and pricey but reliable, with a riverfront location within a 15-minute walk below the château (Db-€160-210, breakfast-€16, air-con, elevator, Wi-Fi, parking-€9/day, 28 Quai Saint Jean, tel. 02 54 56 66 66, www.mercure.com).

$$$ Best Western Blois Château*** has stylish decor, small-but-sharp rooms, and all the comforts you'd expect from this chain. In summer you can have breakfast on their quiet garden terrace

(Db-€90-150, breakfast-€10, air-con, elevator, Wi-Fi, across from the train station and behind the château at 8 Avenue du Dr. Jean Laigret, tel. 02 54 56 85 10, www.bestwesternblois.com, bwblois-chateau@orange.fr).

$$ La Maison de Thomas is a mod B&B that doubles as a wine-tasting boutique specializing in Loire vintages. It's an old building, but all four rooms have been updated with Euro-chic decor and refinished floors (Db-€90-100, includes breakfast, cash only, Wi-Fi, uphill from the château near the pedestrian main drag at 12 Rue Beauvoir, ask for directions to street parking, tel. 02 54 46 12 10, www.lamaisondethomas.fr, resa@lamaisondethomas.fr, Guillaume).

$ Hôtel Anne de Bretagne** offers top value with 30 comfortable, traditional rooms at good prices, a central location near the château and train station, and a welcoming terrace. Ask for a room on the quiet side of the building facing the terrace. They also rent bikes—best to book in advance. Say hello to the hotel *chien,* Jappy (Db-€60, Tb-€65-75, Qb-€85, breakfast-€8.50, no elevator or air-con, Wi-Fi, 150 yards uphill from Parking du Château, 5-minute walk below the train station at 31 Avenue du Dr. Jean Laigret, tel. 02 54 78 05 38, www.hotelannedebretagne.com, contact@hotelannedebretagne.com).

Eating in Blois

Diners can start off their evening with a glass of wine at welcoming **Chez Laurent,** where locals gather around wine barrels to sip and people-watch (5 Rue St. Martin). Another popular watering hole is **Le St. Lubin,** a café-bar (16 Rue St. Lubin).

If you're stopping in Blois around lunchtime, plan on eating at one of the places on the square in front of the château. **Le Marignan** is a good choice (daily, good salads and crêpes, €19 *menus,* fast service, 5 Place du Château, tel. 02 54 74 73 15). At the top of the hour, you can watch the stately mansion opposite the château become the "dragon house," as monsters crane their long necks out its many windows.

LOIRE

Between the Château and the River: The traffic-free streets between the château and the river are home to many cafés with standard, easy meals. **La Banquette Rouge,** a block above St. Nicholas Church's left transept, is your best bet for foodie-pleasing pleasures. It features fine regional dishes with creative twists—try the roast duck filet or pan-fried veal liver. You'll dine in a long red booth—as the name suggests (€29 and €35 *menus,* closed Sun-Mon, reservations smart, 16 Rue des Trois Marchands, tel. 02 54 78 74 92, www.lesbanquettesrouges.com). **Le Clipper,** dishing up wood-fired pizza and basic café fare, has a favored location on Place

Louis XII with great outdoor seating and Wi-Fi (daily, tel. 02 54 78 22 39). **Le Castelet,** also near St. Nicholas, is simple and cheap with good vegetarian choices (*menus* from €20, closed Sun and Wed, 40 Rue St. Lubin, tel. 02 54 74 66 09).

Between the Cathedral and the River: To dine cheaply on an atmospheric square with no tourists in sight, find Place de Grenier à Sel (a block from the river, below St. Louis Cathedral). You'll find these options nearby: **La Grolle** specializes in tasty fondues, raclettes, and other melted-cheese dishes (closed Mon, 36 Rue de la Foulerie, tel. 02 36 23 64 65), and next door, **Le Vespa** does a Franco-Italian mix (€9-13 pizzas, €13 *rissotto,* closed Mon, 11 Rue Vauvert, tel. 02 54 78 44 97).

Blois Connections

From Blois by Train to: Amboise (14/day, 20 minutes), **Tours** (roughly hourly, 40 minutes), **Chinon** (6/day, 1.75-2.5 hours, transfer in Tours and possibly in St-Pierre-des-Corps), **Azay-le-Rideau** (7/day, 1.75-2.5 hours, transfer in Tours and possibly in St-Pierre-des-Corps), **Paris** (4/day direct to Gare d'Austerlitz, 1.5 hours, more with transfer in St-Pierre-des-Corps or Orléans).

By Bus to Chambord and Cheverny: From April through August, **Transports du Loir-et-Cher** (TLC) excursion buses to Chambord, Cheverny, and (less important) Beauregard leave from the Blois train station—look for them immediately to the left as you leave the station (TLC bus marked *Navette-Châteaux, line #18*). Morning departures from Blois station at 9:30 and 11:30 go to Chambord; from Chambord, departures link Cheverny and Beauregard with various return trips to Blois, allowing you from two to seven hours at a château. Verify these times at a TI or online (€6 bus fare, discounts offered on château entries including the Château Royal in Blois; buy tickets and get schedule from TI or bus driver, www.tlcinfo.net—look for "Navette Châteaux de la Loire"). You can also board these buses at the Blois château (2 minutes later than the train station departure).

By Bus to Chaumont-sur-Loire: This handy service takes travelers from the Blois train station to the garden-rich Château de Chaumont (€4 round-trip, departs at 9:25 and 14:00, returns from Chaumont at 14:55 and 17:10, 30-minute trip, daily July-Aug, Sat-Sun only April-June and Sept-Oct, confirm times at TI or at www.azalys-blois.fr).

By Taxi: Blois taxis wait 30 steps in front of the station and offer excursion fares to **Chambord, Chaumont,** or **Cheverny** (current rates posted in taxi shelter, about €34 one-way from Blois to any of these three châteaux, €110 round-trip to Chambord and Cheverny, €155 for Chambord and Chenonceau, 8-person minivans available, tel. 02 54 78 07 65). These rates are per cab, making the per-person price downright reasonable for groups of three or four.

Château de Chambord

With its huge scale and prickly silhouette, Château de Chambord, worth ▲▲▲, is the granddaddy of the Loire châteaux. It's surrounded by Europe's largest enclosed forest park, a game preserve defined by a 20-mile-long wall and teeming with wild deer and boar. Chambord (shahm-bor) began as a simple hunting lodge for bored Blois counts and became a monument to the royal sport and duty of hunting. (Apparently, hunting was considered important to keep the animal population under control and the vital forests healthy.)

The château's massive architecture is the star attraction—particularly the mind-boggling double-helix staircase. Six times the size of your average Loire castle, the château has 440 rooms and a fireplace for every day of the year. It consists of a keep in the shape of a Greek cross, with four towers and two wings surrounded by stables. Its four floors are each separated by 46 stairs, giving it very high ceilings. The ground floor has reception rooms, the first floor up houses the royal apartments, the second floor up houses temporary exhibits and a hunting museum, and the rooftop offers a hunt-viewing terrace. Special exhibits describing Chambord at key moments in its history help animate the place. Because hunters could see best after autumn leaves fell, Chambord was a winter palace (which helps explain the 365 fireplaces). Only 80 of Chambord's rooms are open to the public—but that's plenty.

If you hate crowds, you'll like Chambord. Because it's so huge, it's relatively easy to escape the hordes. It helps that there's no one-way, mandatory tour route—you're free to roam like a duke surveying his domain.

Cost and Hours: €11, daily April-Sept 9:00-18:00, Oct-March 10:00-17:00, last entry 30 minutes before closing, parking-€4, tel. 02 54 50 40 00, www.chambord.org. There are two ticket offices: one in the village in front of the château, and another (less crowded) inside the actual château.

Getting There: It's a 30-minute drive from Chenonceau. Without a car, the Blois excursion bus is best (€6, two daily departures from Blois station April-Aug, taxis from Blois also available; see "Blois Connections," earlier, for bus and taxi details).

Renovations: Scaffolding will likely cover part of Chambord's roofline.

Information and Tours: This château requires helpful information to make it come alive. The free handout is a start, and most rooms have adequate English explanations, and for many visitors, this is enough. For more, rent an audioguide (€5, two can share one audioguide with volume turned to max) or a videoguide (€6).

Services: The bookshop in the château has a good selection of children's books. Among the collection of shops near the château, you'll find a TI (closed Nov-March, tel. 02 54 33 39 16), an ATM, local souvenirs, a wine-tasting room, and cafés. There's only one WC at the château itself (in a courtyard corner); otherwise use the pay WC in the village.

Biking Around the Park: You can rent bikes to explore the park—a network of leafy lanes crisscrossing the vast expanse contained within its 20-mile-long wall.

Medieval Pageantry on Horseback Show: The 45-minute show, designed for young children, is not worth most people's time or money (€11, July-Aug daily at 11:45 and 18:00, May-June and Sept-early Oct Tue-Sun at 11:45 only, closed Mon, in the stables across the field from the château entry, tel. 02 54 50 50 40).

Views: There are many great views of the château, with the best depending on where the light is on any given day. Walk straight out the main entrance one to two hundred yards for exquisite looks back to the château. On the opposite (parking lot) side, you can cross the small river in front of the château and turn right for terrific frontal views. It's also fun to admire the building while sipping a drink at the recommended Hôtel du Grand St. Michel's terrace.

Background: Starting in 1518, François I created this "weekend retreat," employing 1,800 workmen for 15 years. (You'll see his signature salamander symbol everywhere.) François I was an absolute monarch—with an emphasis on absolute. In 32 years of rule (1515-1547), he never once called the Estates-General to session (a rudimentary parliament in *ancien régime* France). This imposing hunting palace was another way to show off his power. Countless guests, like Charles V—the Holy Roman Emperor and most powerful man of the age—were invited to this pleasure palace of French kings...and were totally wowed.

The grand architectural plan of the château—modeled after an Italian church—feels designed as a place to worship royalty. Each floor of the main structure is essentially the same: four equal arms of a Greek cross branch off of a monumental staircase, which leads up to a cupola. From a practical point of view, the design pushed the usable areas to the four corners. This castle, built while the pope was erecting a new St. Peter's Basilica, is like a secular rival to the Vatican.

Construction started the year Leonardo died, 1519. The architect is unknown, but an eerie Leonardo-esque spirit resides here. The symmetry, balance, and classical proportions combine to reflect a harmonious Renaissance vision that could have been inspired by Leonardo's notebooks.

Typical of royal châteaux, this palace of François I was rarely used. Because any effective king had to be on the road to exercise his power, royal palaces sat empty most of the time. In the 1600s, Louis XIV renovated Chambord, but he visited it only six times (for about two weeks each visit).

➲ **Self-Guided Tour:** This tour covers the highlights, floor by floor.

Ground Floor: This stark level shows off the general plan—four wings, small doors to help heated rooms stay warm, and a massive staircase. In a room just inside the front door, on the left, you can watch a worthwhile 18-minute video—look for a screen on the side wall for viewing with English subtitles.

The attention-grabbing **double-helix staircase** dominates the open vestibules and invites visitors to climb up. Its two spirals are interwoven, so people can climb up and down and never meet. Find the helpful explanation of the staircase posted on the wall. From the staircase, enjoy fine views of the vestibule action, or just marvel at the playful Renaissance capitals carved into its light tuff stone.

First Floor: Here you'll find the most interesting rooms. Starting opposite a big ceramic stove, tour this floor basically clockwise. You'll enter the lavish apartments in the **king's wing** and pass through the grand bedrooms of Louis XIV, his wife Maria Theresa, and, at the far end after the queen's boudoir, François I (follow *Logis de François 1er* signs). These theatrical bedrooms place the royal beds on raised platforms—getting them ready for some nighttime drama. Look for the wooden toilet with removable chamber pot, and notice how the furniture in François' bedroom was designed so it could be easily disassembled and moved with him.

A highlight of the first floor is the fascinating seven-room **Museum of the Count of Chambord** (Musée du Comte de Chambord). The last of the French Bourbons, Henri d'Artois (a.k.a. the count of Chambord) was next in line to be king when France decided it didn't need one. He was raring to rule—you'll see his coronation outfits and even souvenirs from the coronation that never happened. Check out his boyhood collection of little guns and other weapons. The man who believed he should have become King Henry V lived in exile from the age of 10. Although he opened the palace to the public, he actually visited this château only once, in 1871.

The **chapel** tucked off in a side wing is interesting only for how unimpressive and remotely located it is. It's dwarfed by the mass of this imposing château—clearly designed to trumpet the glories not of God, but of the king of France.

Second Floor: Beneath beautiful coffered ceilings (notice the "F" for François) is a series of ballrooms that once hosted post-hunt parties. Today, a quirky hunting museum with plenty of taxidermy and temporary exhibits occupies these rooms. From here, you'll climb up to the rooftop, but first lean to the center of the staircase and look down its spiral.

Rooftop: A pincushion of spires and chimneys decorates the rooftop viewing terrace. From a distance, the roof—with its frilly forest of stone towers—gives the massive château a deceptive lightness. From here, ladies could scan the estate grounds, enjoying the spectacle of their ego-pumping men out hunting. On hunt day, a line of beaters would fan out and work inward from the distant walls, flushing wild game to the center, where the king and his buddies waited. The showy lantern tower of the tallest spire glowed with a nighttime torch when the king was in.

Gaze up at the grandiose tip-top of the tallest tower, capped with the king's fleur-de-lis symbol. It's a royal lily—not a cross—that caps this monument to the power of the French king.

In the Courtyard: In the far corner, next to the summer café, a door leads to the classy **carriage rooms** and the fascinating **lapidary rooms.** Here you'll come face-to-face with original stonework from the roof, including the graceful lantern cupola, with the original palace-capping fleur-de-lis. Imagine having to hoist that load. The volcanic tuff stone used to build the spires was soft and easy to work, but not very durable—particularly when so exposed to the elements. Several displays explain the ongoing renovations to François' stately pleasure dome.

Sleeping near Chambord and Cheverny

$$ Hôtel du Grand St. Michel** lets you wake up with Chambord outside your window. It's an Old World, hunting-lodge kind of place with well-worn hallways, rooms in pretty good shape, and a trophy-festooned dining room (good *menus* from €23). Sleep here and you'll have a chance to roam the château grounds after the peasants have been run out (small Db-€76, Db facing château-€94-110 and worth the extra euros, breakfast-€10, tel. 02 54 20 31 31, on Place Saint Louis, www.saintmichel-chambord.com, hotelsaintmichel@wanadoo.fr).

$ Chambres la Flânerie, on the bike route from Chambord to Cheverny, offers two family rooms in an adorable home. It's riddled with flowers, crawling with ivy, and surrounded by wheat fields and forests. The gentle Delabarres speak enough English and loan bikes to their fortunate guests (Db-€66-70, Tb-€83-87, Qb-€100-104, includes breakfast, Wi-Fi, 25 Rue de Gallerie, tel. 02 54 79 86 28, mobile 06 75 72 28 41, www.laflanerie.com, laflanerie@laflanerie.com). Coming from Blois on D-765, it's before Cheverny in the hamlet of Les Fées. After crossing a small river and continuing beyond the D-77 intersection, turn right where you see wooden bus shelters flanking the road, and follow the *la Flânerie* signs (see map on page 394).

Cheverny

This stately hunting palace, a ▲▲ sight, is one of the more lavishly furnished Loire châteaux. Because the immaculately preserved Cheverny (shuh-vehr-nee) was built and decorated in a relatively short 30 years, from 1604 to 1634, it has a unique architectural harmony and unity of style. From the start, this château has been in the Hurault family, and Hurault pride shows in its flawless preservation and intimate feel (it was opened to the public in 1922). The charming viscount and his family still live on the third floor (not open to the public, but you'll see some family photos). Cheverny was spared by the French Revolution; the owners were popular then, as today, even among the village farmers.

LOIRE

The château sits alongside a pleasant village, with a small grocery, cafés offering good lunch options, and a few hotels.

Cost and Hours: €9, €13.50 combo-ticket includes Tintin "adventure" rooms, family deals, daily July-Aug 9:15-18:45, April-June and Sept 9:15-18:15, Oct 9:45-17:30, Nov-March 9:45-17:00, tel. 02 54 79 96 29, www.chateau-cheverny.fr.

Getting There: You can get to Cheverny by bus from Blois (see "Blois Connections" on page 408), or by shuttle bus or minivan tour from Amboise (see "Amboise Connections" on page 392).

Visiting the Château: As you walk across the manicured grounds toward the gleaming château, the sound of hungry hounds will follow you. Lined up across the facade are sculpted medallions with portraits of Roman emperors, including Julius Caesar (above the others in the center). As you enter the château, pick up the excellent English self-guided tour brochure, which describes the interior beautifully.

Your visit starts in the lavish **dining room,** decorated with leather walls and a sumptuous ceiling. Next, as you climb the stairs to the private apartments, look out the window and spot the *orangerie* across the gardens. It was here that the *Mona Lisa* was hidden (along with other treasures from the Louvre) during World War II.

On the top floor, turn right from the stairs and tour the I-could-live-here **family apartments** with silky bedrooms, kids' rooms, and an intimate dining room. On the other side of this floor is the impressive **Arms Room** with weapons, a sedan chair, and a snare drum from the count of Chambord (who would have been king; see page 409). The **King's Bedchamber** is literally fit for a king. Study the fun ceiling art, especially the "boys will be boys" cupids.

Back down on the ground floor, find a family tree going back to 1490, a grandfather clock with a second-hand that's been ticking for 250 years, and a letter of thanks from George Washington to this family for their help in booting out the English.

Nearby: Barking dogs remind visitors that the viscount still loves to hunt (he goes twice a week year-round). The **kennel** (200 yards in front of the château, look for *Chenil* signs) is especially interesting at dinnertime, when the 70 hounds are fed (April-mid-Sept daily at 17:00, mid-Sept-March Mon and Wed-Fri at 15:00). The dogs—half English foxhound and half French Poitou—are bred to have big feet and bigger stamina. They're given food once a day (two pounds each in winter, half that in summer), and the feeding *(la soupe des chiens)* is a fun spectacle that shows off their strict training. Before chow time, the hungry hounds fill the little kennel rooftop and watch the trainer (who knows every dog's name) bring in troughs stacked with delectable raw meat. He opens the gate, and the dogs gather enthusiastically around the food, yelping hysterically. Only when the trainer says to eat can they dig in. You can see the dogs at any time, but the feeding show is fun to plan for.

Also nearby, **Tintin** comic lovers can enter a series of fun rooms designed to take them into a Tintin adventure (called Les Secrets de Moulinsart, €13.50 combo-ticket with castle); hunters can inspect an antler-filled **trophy room;** and gardeners can prowl the château's fine **kitchen and flower gardens** (free, behind the dog kennel).

Wine Tastings at the Château Gate: Opposite the entry to the château sits a slick wine-tasting room, **La Maison des Vins.** It's run by an association of 32 local vintners. Their mission: to boost the Cheverny reputation for wine (which is fruity, light, dry, and aromatic compared to the heavier, oaky wines made farther downstream). Tasters have two options. In the first, any visitor can have four free tastes from featured bottles of the day, offered with helpful guidance. Or, for a fee, you can sample more freely among the 32 labels, at your own pace, by using modern automated dispensers. Even if just enjoying the free samples, wander among the spouts. Each gives the specs of that wine in English (€6.50 for small tastes of 7 wines, €6-9 bottles, daily 11:00-13:15 & 14:15-19:00, closed in winter, tel. 02 54 79 25 16, www.maisondesvinsdecheverny.fr).

Chaumont-sur-Loire

A castle has been located on this spot since the 11th century; the current version is a ▲▲ sight (▲▲▲ for garden or horse lovers). The first priority at Chaumont (show-mon) was defense. You'll appreciate the strategic location on the long climb up from the village below. (Drivers can avoid the uphill hike except off-season—explained later.) Gardeners will appreciate the elaborate Festival of Gardens that unfolds next to the château every year, and modern-art lovers will enjoy how works have been incorporated into the gardens, château, and stables.

Cost and Hours: Château and stables-€10.50; château open daily July-Aug 10:00-19:00, May-June and early Sept 10:00-18:00, April and late Sept 10:30-17:30, Oct-March 10:00-17:00, last entry 30 minutes before closing; stables close daily 12:00-14:00; audioguide-€4, English handout available, app available in English for iPhone and Android, tel. 02 54 20 99 22, www.domaine-chaumont.fr.

Festival of Gardens: This annual exhibit, with 25 elaborate gardens arranged around a different theme each year, draws rave reviews from international gardeners. It's as impressive as the Chelsea Flower Show in England, but without the crowds—if you love contemporary garden design, don't miss this (Garden Festival only-€12; €4 more for the château and stables; about mid-April to mid-Oct daily 10:00-20:00, in 2015 may be open with special lighting until 24:00 July-Aug, tel. 02 54 20 99 22, www.domaine-chaumont.fr). When the festival is on, you'll find several little cafés and reasonable lunch options scattered about the hamlet (festival ticket not needed).

Getting There: There is no public transport to Chaumont, although the train between Blois and Amboise (14/day) can drop you (and your bike, if you like) in Onzain, a 25-minute roadside walk across the river to the château. Bikes (Chaumont is about 11 level miles from Amboise or Blois), taxis (about €34 from Blois train station), and summertime shuttle buses (€4) also work for non-drivers (see "Blois Connections," page 408).

From May to mid-October, drivers can park up top, at an entrance open only during the Festival of Gardens (you don't need to buy tickets for the garden event). From the river, drive up behind the château (direction: Montrichard), at the first roundabout follow the signs to *Château* and *Festival du Jardins,* and drive to the lot beyond the soccer field.

Background: The Chaumont château you see today was built mostly in the 15th and 16th centuries. Catherine de' Medici forced Diane de Poitiers to swap Chenonceau for Chaumont; you'll see tidbits about both women inside.

There's a special connection to America here. Jacques-Donatien Le Ray, a rich financier who owned Chaumont in the 18th century, was a champion of the American Revolution. He used his wealth to finance loans in the early days of the new republic (and even let Benjamin Franklin use one of his homes in Paris rent-free for 9 years). Unfortunately, the US never repaid the loans in full and eventually Le Ray went bankrupt.

Ironically, the American connection saved Chaumont during the French Revolution. Le Ray's son emigrated to New York and became an American citizen, but returned to France when his father deeded the castle to him. During the Revolution, he was able to turn back the crowds set on destroying Chaumont by declaring that he was now an American—and that all Americans were believers in *liberté, égalité,* and *fraternité.*

Today's château offers a good look at the best defense design in 1500: on a cliff with a dry moat, big and small drawbridges with classic ramparts, loopholes for archers, and handy holes through which to dump hot oil on attackers.

➲ **Self-Guided Tour:** Your walk through the palace—restored mostly in the 19th century—is described by the English flier you'll pick up when you enter. As the château has more rooms than period furniture, your tour includes a few modern-art exhibits that fill otherwise empty spaces. The rooms you'll visit first (in the east wing) show the château as it appeared in the 15th and 16th centuries. Your visit ends in the west wing, which features furnishings from the 19th-century owners.

The castle's medieval **entry** is littered with various coats of arms. As you walk in, take a close look at the two drawbridges (a new mechanism allows the main bridge to be opened with the touch of a button). Once inside, the heavy defensive feel is replaced with palatial luxury. Peek into the courtyard—during the more stable mid-1700s, the fourth wing, which had enclosed the courtyard, was taken down to give the terrace its river-valley view.

Entering the château rooms, signs direct you along a one-way loop path *(suite de la visite)* through the château's three wings. Catherine de' Medici, who missed her native Florence, brought a touch of Italy to all her châteaux, and her astrologer (Ruggieri) was so important that he had his own (plush) room—next to hers. **Catherine's bedroom** has a 16th-century throne—look for unicorns holding a shield. The Renaissance-style bed is a reproduction from the 19th century.

The exquisitely tiled **Salle de Conseil** has a grand fireplace designed to keep this conference room warm. The treasury box in the **guard room** is a fine example of 1600s-era locksmithing. The lord's wealth could be locked up here as safely as possible in those days, with a false keyhole, no handles, and even an extra-secure box inside for diamonds.

Next comes the **Diane de Poitiers room,** which doesn't have much to do with Diane but does have a fascinating collection of medallions. Look for the case of ceramic portrait busts dating from 1772, when Le Ray invited the Italian sculptor Jean-Baptiste Nini to work for him. In addition to Marie Antoinette, Voltaire, and Catherine the Great, you'll find several medallions depicting Benjamin Franklin.

A big spiral staircase leads up through unfurnished rooms and then galleries of contemporary art. After the shock of the 21st century, you go back in time about 150 years to rooms decorated in 19th-century style. The **dining room**'s fanciful limestone fireplace is exquisitely carved. Find the food (frog legs, snails, goats for cheese), the maid with the bellows, and even the sculptor with a hammer and chisel at the top (on the left). Your visit ends with a stroll through the 19th-century library, the billiards room, and the living room.

In the **courtyard,** study the entertaining spouts and decor on the walls, and remember that this space was originally enclosed on all sides. Chaumont has one of the best château views of the Loire River—rivaling Amboise for its panoramic tranquility.

The **stables** *(ecuries)* were entirely rebuilt in the 1880s. The medallion above the gate reads *pour l'avenir* (for the future), which shows off an impressive commitment to horse technology. Inside, circle clockwise—you can almost hear the clip-clop of horses walking. Notice the deluxe horse stalls, padded with bins and bowls for hay, oats, and water, complete with a strategically placed drainage gutter. The horses were named for Greek gods and great châteaux. The Horse Kitchen (Cuisine des Chevaux) produced mash twice weekly for the animals. The "finest tack room in all of France" shows off horse gear. Beyond the covered alcove where the horse and carriage were prepared for the prince, you'll see four carriages parked and ready to go. Finally, the round former kiln was redesigned to be a room for training the horses.

The **estate** is set in a 19th-century landscape, with woodlands and a fine lawn. More English than French, it has rolling open terrain, follies such as a water tower, and a brilliantly designed *potager* (vegetable garden) with an imaginative mix of edible and decorative plants. Its trees were imported from throughout the Mediterranean world to be enjoyed—and to fend off any erosion on this strategic bluff.

Loches and Valençay

Loches

The overlooked town of Loches (lohsh), located about 30 minutes south of Amboise, makes a good base for drivers wanting to visit sights east and west of Tours (in effect triangulating between Amboise and Chinon), but has no easy train or bus connections. This pretty town sits on the region's loveliest river, the Indre, and holds an appealing mix of medieval monuments, stroll-worthy streets, and fewer tourists. Its château dominates the skyline and is worth a short visit. The Wednesday and Saturday street markets are lively; the Saturday market takes over many streets in the old city.

Sleeping in Loches: For an overnight stay, try **$$ Hôtel George Sand*****, located on the river, with a well-respected restaurant, an idyllic terrace, and rustic, comfortable rooms (Db-€64-74, luxury Db-€135, Tb-€95, Wi-Fi, no elevator, 300 yards south of TI at 39 Rue Quintefol, tel. 02 47 59 39 74, www.hotelrestaurant-georgesand.com, contactGS@hotelrestaurant-georgesand.com).

Valençay

The Renaissance château of Valençay (vah-lahn-say) is a massive, luxuriously furnished structure with echoes of its former owner Talleyrand (a famous French diplomat who helped broker the Louisiana Purchase). It has a killer kitchen, lovely gardens, kid-friendly activities and elaborate big toys, and lots of summer events such as fencing demonstrations and candlelit visits.

Cost and Hours: €12 includes audioguide covering château and gardens, ask about family rates, daily June 9:30-18:30, July-Aug 9:30-19:00, April-May and Sept 10:00-18:00, Oct 10:20-17:30, closed Nov-March, tel. 02 54 00 15 69, www.chateau-valencay.fr.

West of Tours

Chinon

This pleasing, sleepy town straddles the Vienne River and hides its ancient streets under a historic royal fortress. Henry II (Henry Plantagenet of England), Eleanor of Aquitaine, Richard the Lionheart, and Joan of Arc all called this town home for a while. Today's Chinon (shee-nohn) is best known for its popular red wines. But for me it's also a top home base for seeing the sights west of Tours: Azay-le-Rideau, Langeais, Villandry, Chatonnière, Rivau, Ussé, and the Abbaye Royale de Fontevraud. Each of these worthwhile sights is no more than a 20-minute drive away. Trains provide access to many châteaux (via Tours) but are time-consuming, so you're better off with your own car or a minivan excursion (see "Chinon Connections," later).

Orientation to Chinon

Chinon stretches out along the Vienne River, and everything of interest to travelers lies between it and the hilltop fortress. Charming Place du Général de Gaulle—ideal for café-lingering—is in the center of town. Rue Rabelais is Chinon's traffic-free shopping street, with restaurants, bars, and cafés—as lively as they can be in peaceful Chinon.

TOURIST INFORMATION

The TI is in the town center, near the base of the hill and a 15-minute walk from the train station. You'll find *chambre d'hôte* listings, wine-tasting and bike-rental information, and an English-language brochure with a self-guided tour of the town (May-Sept daily 10:00-13:30 & 14:00-19:00; shorter hours and closed Sun off-season; in village center on Place Hofheim, tel. 02 47 93 17 85, www.chinon-valdeloire.com). Free public WCs are around the back of the TI.

HELPFUL HINTS

Market Days: A bustling market takes place all day Thursday on Place Jeanne d'Arc (west end of town). There's also a sweet little market on Saturday and Sunday, around Place du Général de Gaulle.

Groceries: Carrefour City is across from the Hôtel de Ville, on Place du Général de Gaulle (Mon-Sat 7:00-21:00, Sun 9:00-13:00).

Laundry: Salon Lavoir is near the bridge at 7 Quai Charles VII (daily 7:00-21:00).

Bike and Canoe Rental: Canoë Kayak & Vélo rents bikes and canoes on the river, next to the campground (bikes-€15/day; canoes-€11/2 hours or €21/half-day, shuttle included; €14-25 to combine bike and canoe in a half/full day; cash only, Quai Danton, mobile 06 23 82 96 33, www.loisirs-nature.fr). For more on biking and canoeing, see page 426.

Taxi: Call 06 83 51 87 88 for an English-speaking taxi driver; tel. 02 47 95 85 48 for other taxi service.

Car Rental: It's best to rent a car at the St-Pierre-des-Corps train station.

Best Views: You'll find terrific rooftop views from the fortress and along Rue du Coteau St. Martin (between St. Mexme Church and the fortress—see map), and rewarding river views to Chinon by crossing the bridge in the center of town and turning right (small riverfront café May-Sept).

Chinon Walk

Chinon offers a peaceful world of quiet cobbled lanes, historic buildings, and few tourists. By following this self-guided walk (or the TI's self-guided tour brochure) and reading plaques at key buildings, you'll gain a good understanding of this city's historic importance.

• *Begin this short walk from the highest point of the bridge that crosses the Vienne River, and enjoy the great view.*

Chinon Riverbank: Chinon is sandwiched between the Vienne River (which flows into the Loire River only a few miles from here) and an abrupt cliff. People have lived along the banks of this river since prehistoric times. The Gallo-Romans built the first defenses in Chinon 1,600 years ago, and there's been a castle up on that hill for over a thousand years—which pretty much predates every other castle you'll visit in the Loire area. The skinny, curved clock tower served as the entrance to the middle section of the fortress during the Middle Ages. Starting in 1044, that fortress-castle became an important outpost for the king of France, and by 1150 Henry II Plantagenet (king of England) made this the center of his continental empire. A few hundred years later, Charles VII took refuge behind those walls during the Hundred Years' War, during which Chinon was France's capital city.

Down on the water, you'll see reproductions of the traditional wooden boats once used to shuttle merchandise up and down the river; some boats ventured as far west as the Atlantic.

• *Walk toward the city, then make a right along the riverbank and find the big statue that honors a famous Renaissance writer and satirist.*

Rabelais Statue: The great French writer François Rabelais was born here in 1494. You'll see many references to him in his proud hometown. His best-known work, *Gargantua and Pantagruel,* describes the amusing adventures of father-and-son giants and was set in Chinon. Rabelais' vivid humor and savage wit are, for many, quintessentially French—there's even a French word for it: *rabelaisien.* In his bawdy tales, Rabelais critiqued society in ways that deflected outright censorship—though the Sorbonne called his work obscene. A monk and a doctor, he's considered the first great French novelist, and his farces were a voice against the power of the Church and the king.

• *Turn your back on Rabelais and follow the cobbled sidewalk leading to the center of Chinon's main square.*

Place du Général de Gaulle: The town wall once sat on the wide swath of land running from this square down to the river, effectively walling the city off from the water. This explains why, even now, Chinon seems to turn its back on its river. In medieval times, the market was here, just outside the wall. The town hall building, originally an arcaded market, was renovated only in the 19th century. Today it flies three flags: Europe, France, and Chinon (with its three castles). From here, you can see the handy elevator that connects the town with its castle.

Turn left down **Rue Voltaire.** If the old wall still stood, you'd be entering town through the east gate. (Note the black info posts here and scattered throughout town.) Walk along a fine strip of 16th-, 17th-, and 18th-century houses to find a trio of fun wine-tasting possibilities. A half-block to the right is the charming little **Musée Animé du Vin;** at the next corner is the laid-back **Cave Voltaire wine shop,** and a right turn on the next small lane leads to **Caves Painctes** and the quarry where the stone for the castle originated (all covered later, under "Sights in Chinon.")

LOIRE

• *Continue walking a few blocks farther into the historic city center.*

Old Town: In the immediate post-WWII years, there was little money or energy to care for beautiful old towns. But in the 1960s, new laws and sensitivities kicked in, and old quarters like this were fixed up and preserved. Study the vernacular architecture. **La Maison Rouge** (at 38-42 Rue Voltaire) is a fine example of the town's medieval structures: a stone foundation and timber frame, filled in with whatever was handy. With dense populations crowding within the protective town walls, buildings swelled wider at the top to avoid blocking congested streets.

Pop into the ancient **bookshop** on the corner. I asked the owner where he got his old prints. He responded, "Did you ever

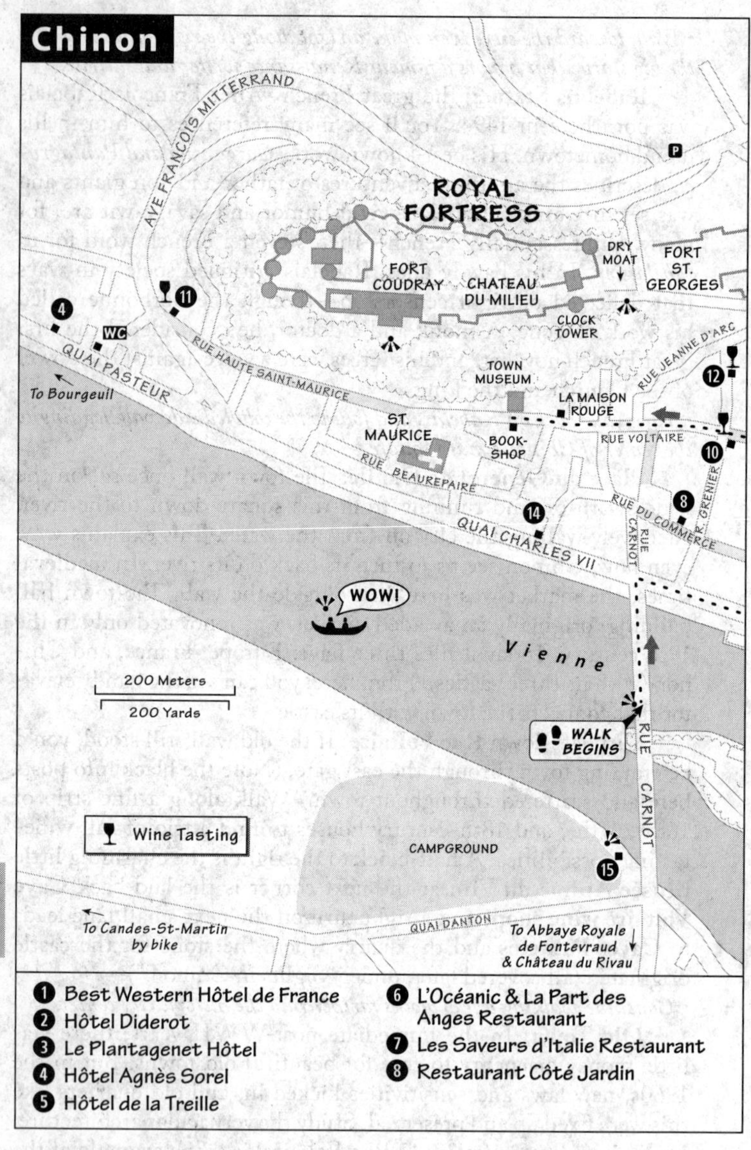

enjoy a friend's mushrooms and ask him where he found them? Did he tell you?"

The **town museum** is across the street. Its plaque recalls that this building housed an Estates-General meeting, convened by Charles VII, in 1428. Just around the corner, find a good tower view (and a public WC).

• *From here the street changes names to Rue Haute St. Maurice. You can*

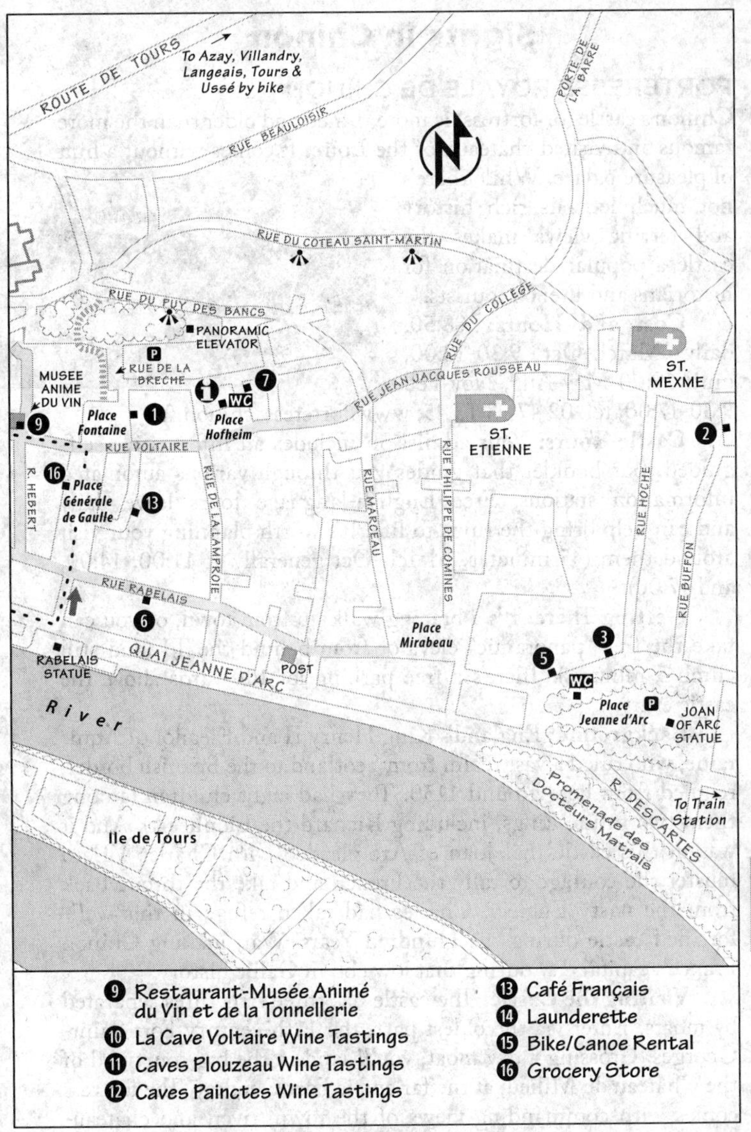

continue in the same direction and find the Caves Plouzeau wine cellars at #94 (described later). If you'd rather visit the castle, turn around, walk back and climb up Rue Jean d'Arc (look for the plaque that tells us that Joan of Arc dismounted her horse at this spot in 1429)—or take the elevator near the TI—to the fortress.

Sights in Chinon

FORTERESSE ROYALE DE CHINON

Chinon's castle (or fortress) is more ruined and older than the more famous and visited châteaux of the Loire. It comes without a hint of pleasure palace. While there's not much left, its rich history and terrific views makes the castle a popular destination for historians and French tourists.

Cost and Hours: €8.50, daily March-Oct 9:30-18:00, until 19:00 May-Aug, Nov-Feb 9:30-17:00, tel. 02 47 93 13 45, www.forteressechinon.fr.

Castle Tours: Your admission includes an informative self-guided tour booklet that guides you through various automated information stations. Free English-language tours leave daily and can help bring the ruins to life. It's worth planning your visit around them (45 minutes, March-Oct generally at 11:00, 14:00, and 17:00).

Getting There: It's a bracing walk up from town, or you can take the free "panoramic" elevator from behind the TI (and still climb 5 minutes). There's a free parking lot 100 yards above the castle entry.

Background: England's King Henry II and Eleanor of Aquitaine, who ruled a vast realm from Scotland to the Spanish border, reigned from here around 1150. They had eight children (among them two future kings, including Richard the Lionheart). And it was in this castle that Joan of Arc pleaded with Charles VII to muster the courage to rally the French and take the throne back from the nasty English. Charles had taken refuge in this well-fortified castle during the Hundred Years' War, making Chinon France's capital city during that low ebb in Gallic history.

Visiting the Castle: The castle has three structures separated by moats. Enter via the oldest part, the 12th-century Fort Saint-Georges. Crossing a dry moat, you'll land in the big courtyard of the Château du Milieu; at the far end is Fort Coudray. The fortress comes with commanding views of the town, river, and château-studded countryside.

Follow the arrows through eight stark and stony rooms, enjoying the clever teaching videos. There's a small museum devoted to the legendary Joan of Arc and her myth, developed through the centuries to inspire the French to pride and greatness. Chinon—both the city and the castle—developed as its political importance grew. It was the seat of French royalty in the 14th century. Most of the stones were quarried directly below the castle and hauled up through a well. The resulting caverns keep stores of local wine cool to this day.

WINE SIGHTS AND TASTINGS IN AND NEAR CHINON

Chinon reds are among the most respected in the Loire, and there are a variety of ways to sample them.

La Cave Voltaire

At the most convenient of Chinon's wine-tasting options, ponytailed, English-speaking sommelier Patrice would love to help you learn about his area's wines. He serves inexpensive appetizers and has wines from all regions of France—the best, of course, are from Chinon. It's a good place to come before dinner. The ambience inside is wine-shop cozy, but the tables outside are hard to resist (daily 10:30-23:30, near Place du Général de Gaulle at 13 Rue Voltaire, tel. 02 47 93 37 68, www.lacavevoltaire.fr).

Caves Plouzeau

This place offers another opportunity to walk through long, atmospheric *caves*—complete with mood lighting—that extend under the château to a (literally) cool tasting room and reasonably priced wines (€6-11/bottle, April-Sept Tue-Sat 11:00-13:00 & 15:00-19:00, closed Sun-Mon and Oct-March, at the western end of town on 94 Rue Haute St-Maurice, tel. 02 47 93 16 34, www.plouzeau.com).

Caves Painctes

At this *cave*, summer travelers can sample Chinon wines and walk through the cool quarry from which stones for the castle and town's houses were cut. This rock (tuff) is soft and easily quarried, and when exposed to oxygen, it hardens. The *caves*, 300 feet directly below the castle, were dug as the castle was built. Its stones were hauled directly up to the building site with a treadmill-powered hoist. Converted to wine cellars in the 15th century, the former quarry is a pilgrimage site of sorts for admirers of Rabelais, who featured it prominently in his writings. To visit, you must sign up for a tour (in English), which takes about an hour and includes a 10-minute video and a tasting of three local wines. Designed to promote Chinon wines, it's run by a local winemakers' association (€3, July-Aug Tue-Sun at 11:00, 15:00, 16:30, and 18:00; closed Mon and Sept-June; off Rue Voltaire on Impasse des Caves Painctes, tel. 02 47 93 30 44).

Restaurant-Musée Animé du Vin et de la Tonnellerie (Wine and Barrel Museum/Restaurant)

This combination museum/restaurant is the life's work of a passionate wine lover, the mustachioed Dédé la Boulange. You'll stroll through a few rooms animated by characters re-creating the production of local wines, and smile at the ingenuity of his handiwork (€4.50, €2.50 if you enjoy dinner at his recommended restaurant on the premises, daily mid-March-mid-Oct 10:00-22:00, closed off-season, 12 Rue Voltaire, tel. 02 47 93 25 63).

Domaine de la Chevalerie

For an authentic winery experience in the thick of the vineyards, drive about 25 minutes from Chinon to Domaine de la Chevalerie. This traditional winery has been run by the same family for 14 generations. If you're lucky, fun-loving and English-speaking daughter Stéphanie (occasionally other English-speaking staff) will take you through the cavernous hillside cellars crammed with 260,000 bottles, then treat you to a tasting of their 100 percent Cabernet Franc reds from seven different plots of land. (free, Mon-Sat 10:00-18:30, shorter hours off-season, call before you visit, off D-35 at 7 Rue du Peu Muleau, Restigné, for location see map on page 432, tel. 02 47 97 46 32, www.domainedelachevalerie.fr).

OTHER CHINON ACTIVITIES

▲Biking from Chinon

A few good options are available from Chinon (be sure to get maps from the TI or your bike rental shop). The easiest ride—thanks to the level terrain—is to the pretty village of Candes-St-Martin, where the Vienne and Loire rivers meet. Some cyclists can manage the longer ride from Chinon to Ussé and back, and some may want to venture even farther to Villandry. To avoid the monumental hill when leaving town, take your bike in the free elevator behind the TI up to the château level (get directions from your bike rental). Connecting these château towns is a full-day, 40-mile round-trip ride that only those in fit condition will enjoy (see "Helpful Hints," earlier, for rental location and costs).

Canoeing/Kayaking from Chinon

From May through mid-October, plastic canoes and kayaks are available to rent next to the campground across the lone bridge in Chinon. The outfitters will shuttle you upriver to tiny Anché for a scenic and fun two-hour, four-mile float back to town—ending with great Chinon fortress views. They also offer a 10-mile, half-day float that starts in Chinon and ends downriver in the sweet little village of Candes-St-Martin. Or do your own biathlon by canoeing one way and biking back (see "Helpful Hints," earlier, for rental location and costs).

Nighttime in Chinon

Café Français, run by Jean François (a.k.a. "Jeff"), is a characteristic local hangout and *the* place for any late-night fun in this sleepy town. It sometimes has live music off-season (open Tue-Sat from 18:00 and Sun from 19:00 until you shut it down, closed Mon year-round and Sun off-season, behind town hall at 37 Rue des Halles, tel. 02 47 93 32 78).

Sleeping in Chinon

Hotels are a good value in Chinon. If you stay overnight here, walk out to the river and cross the bridge for a floodlit view of the château walls.

$$$ Best Western Hôtel de France*** offers good comfort in 28 rooms on Chinon's best square; many have partial views of the fortress (Db-€118-155, Tb/Qb-€165-215, includes breakfast, several rooms have balconies over the square, some have thin walls, air-con, Wi-Fi, parking-€9, 49 Place du Général de Gaulle, tel. 02 47 93 33 91, www.bestwestern-hoteldefrance-chinon.com, elmachinon@aol.com).

$$ Hôtel Diderot,** a handsome 18th-century manor house on the eastern edge of town, is the closest hotel I list to the train station (drivers, look for signs from Place Jeanne d'Arc). It's a family affair, run by spirited Laurent and his equally spirited sisters, Françoise and Martine, who will adopt you into their clan if you're not careful. The hotel surrounds a carefully planted courtyard, and has a small bar with a good selection of area wines. Rooms in the main building vary in size and decor, but all are well-maintained, with personal touches. Ground-floor rooms come with private patios. The four good family rooms have connecting rooms, each with a private bathroom. Breakfast (€9.40) includes a rainbow of Laurent's homemade jams (Sb-€60-86, Db-€69-98, extra bed-€12, Wi-Fi, limited parking-€8/day, 4 Rue de Buffon, tel. 02 47 93 18 87, www.hoteldiderot.com, hoteldiderot@wanadoo.fr).

$$ Le Plantagenet*** has 30 comfortable rooms and may have space when others don't. There's a modest garden courtyard—picnics encouraged if you buy drinks from hotel, onsite washer/dryer, and a great €10.50 breakfast (Db-€70, superior Db-€85, some rooms have balconies, guest computer and Wi-Fi, 12 Place

LOIRE

Jeanne d'Arc, tel. 02 47 93 36 92, www.hotel-plantagenet.com, resa@hotel-plantagenet.com).

$ Hôtel Agnès Sorel, at the western end of town, sits on the river and is handy for drivers, but it's a 30-minute walk from the train station and has some traffic noise. Of its ten sharp rooms, a few have river views, some have balconies, and five surround a small courtyard. Friendly owner Christine speaks English (Db-€58, bigger Db-€65, big Db suite-€110, T/Qb suite-€135, breakfast-€8.50, Wi-Fi, 4 Quai Pasteur, tel. 02 47 93 04 37, www.hotel-agnes-sorel.com, christine.tarre@hotel-agnes-sorel.com).

$ Hôtel de la Treille has five rugged and rustic rooms for budget travelers who won't mind the noise from the restaurant below (D-€34, Db-€44, Tb-€54, breakfast-€7, 4 Place Jeanne d'Arc, tel. 02 47 93 07 71, no email, no overhead).

OUTSIDE CHINON, NEAR LIGRE

$$$ Le Clos de Ligré lets you sleep in farmhouse silence, surrounded by vineyards and farmland. A 10-minute drive from Chinon, it has room to roam, a pool overlooking the vines, and a billiards room with a baby grand piano. English-speaking Martine Descamps spoils her guests with cavernous and creatively decorated rooms (Db-€110, good family rooms, includes breakfast, €35 dinner includes the works, cash only, Wi-Fi, 37500 Ligré, tel. 02 47 93 95 59, mobile 06 61 12 45 55, www.le-clos-de-ligre.com, mdescamps@club-internet.fr). From Chinon, cross the river and go toward Richelieu on D-749, turn right on D-115 at the *Ligré par le vignoble* sign, and continue for about five kilometers (3 miles). Turn left, following signs to *Ligré;* at the Dozon winery turn left and look for signs to *Le Clos de Ligré* (see map on page 432).

Eating in Chinon

For a low-stress meal with ambience, choose one of the cafés on the photogenic Place du Général de Gaulle. Many of these are closed Wednesday: Check before you go.

L'Océanic, in the thick of the pedestrian zone, is where locals go for fish and tasty desserts. It has the best wine list in town, but tends to be a tad stiff for some (*menus* from €26, closed Sun-Mon, 13 Rue Rabelais, tel. 02 47 93 44 55).

Les Saveurs d'Italie is a cheap and cheery deli/diner with a warm greeting and the town's best Italian cuisine (€10 pizzas and pasta, limited outside seating, closed Sun-Mon, next to TI at 3 Impasse J. Macé, tel. 02 47 58 80 62).

Restaurant-Musée Animé du Vin et de la Tonnellerie is a simple, one-man show where jolly Dédé dishes up all the wine you can drink and *fouées* you can eat (little pastry shells filled with garlic paste, cheese, or *rillettes*—that's a meat spread), accompanied by *mâche*-and-walnut salad, green beans, dessert *fouées,* wine, and coffee—all for €19. Let your hair down in this get-to-know-your-neighbor kind of place as you watch Dédé slap the *fouées* in his rustic oven (daily for lunch and dinner, 12 Rue Voltaire, tel. 02 47 93 25 63).

La Part des Anges is a two-person love affair with food in an intimate setting. Virginie creates contemporary cuisine based on timeless French technique while husband Hervé serves with aplomb even when it's packed. The seafood dishes are good here, and the extra touches, such as a carrot soup *amuse-bouche,* add to the experience (*menus* from €22, good lunch options, limited outdoor seating, daily, 5 Rue Rabelais, tel. 02 47 93 99 93).

At **Restaurant Côté Jardin,** you'll dine smartly on traditional French food. Along with regional specialties, there are classics such as *coq au vin, coquilles St. Jacques,* and *rôti de porc.* In summer, linger in the secluded garden courtyard and order one of the best deals in town—the €14 *menu* that includes a starter, the *plat du jour,* and dessert. A French phrase book is a big help here (€14 and €25 *menus,* 30 Rue du Commerce, tel. 02 47 93 10 97).

Near Chinon: For a memorable countryside meal, drive 25 minutes to **Etape Gourmande at Domaine de la Giraudière,** in Villandry (see listing on page 437). A trip here combines well with visits to Villandry and Azay-le-Rideau.

Chinon Connections

BY MINIVAN

From Chinon to Loire Châteaux: Acco-Dispo, Loire Valley Tours, and **Quart de Tours** offer fixed-itinerary minivan excursions from Tours (see "Amboise Connections," page 392). Take the train to Tours from Chinon (see below), or get several travelers together to book your own van from Chinon.

BY TRAIN

Twelve trains and SNCF buses link Chinon daily with the city of Tours (1 hour, connections to other châteaux and minibus excursions from Tours) and to the regional rail hub of St-Pierre-des-Corps in suburban Tours (TGV trains to distant destinations, and the fastest way to Paris). Traveling by train to the nearby châteaux (except for Azay-le-Rideau) requires a transfer in Tours and healthy walks from the stations to the châteaux. Fewer trains run on weekends.

From Chinon to Loire Châteaux: Azay-le-Rideau (7/day, 20 minutes direct, plus long walk to château), **Langeais** (5/day, 1.5-2 hours, transfer in Tours), **Amboise** (7/day, 1.5-2 hours, transfer in

Tours), **Chenonceaux** (4/day, 1.5-2 hours, transfer in Tours), **Blois** (6/day, 1.75-2.5 hours, transfer in Tours and possibly in St-Pierre-des-Corps).

To Destinations Beyond the Loire: Paris' Gare Montparnasse (8/day, 3-2.5 hours, transfer in Tours and sometimes also St-Pierre-des-Corps), **Sarlat-la-Canéda** (3/day, 6-7 hours, change at St-Pierre-des-Corps, then TGV to Libourne or Bordeaux-St. Jean, then train through Bordeaux vineyards to Sarlat), **Pontorson/Mont St-Michel** (3/day, 6-8.5 hours with change at Tours main station, Le Mans, and Rennes, then bus from Rennes), **Bayeux** (2/day, 5-6 hours with change in Tours and Caen, more via Tours, St-Pierre-des-Corps, and Paris' Gare Montparnasse and Gare St. Lazare).

Azay-le-Rideau

About 30 minutes west of Tours, Azay-le-Rideau (ah-zay luh ree-doh) is an endearing little town with a small but lively pedestrian zone and a château that gets all the attention. Azay-le-Rideau works well as a base for visiting sights west of Tours by car or bike (but not by train—the train station is a half-mile walk from the town center). The town is close to the A-85 autoroute, offering drivers reasonable access to châteaux near Amboise. Travelers who bed down here will be tempted by the fun sound-and-light show at the château.

Orientation to Azay-le-Rideau

Tourist Information: Azay-le-Rideau's TI is just below Place de la République, a block to the right of the post office (July-Aug daily 10:00-19:00; Sept-Oct and April-June daily 9:00-13:00 & 14:00-18:00; Nov-March Mon-Sat 9:00-13:00 & 14:00-18:00, closed Sun; 4 Rue du Château, tel. 02 47 45 44 40, www.visitazaylerideau.com). The TI sells reduced-price tickets to all area châteaux, has free Wi-Fi, and is a good place to pick up information on the sound-and-light show. Ask them for bike-rental info, too.

Arrival in Azay-le-Rideau: It's about a 25-minute walk from the station to the town center (taxi mobile 06 60 94 42 00). Walk down from the station, turn left, and follow *Centre-Ville* signs. Drivers can head for the château and park there.

Sights in Azay-le-Rideau

▲▲Château d'Azay-le-Rideau

This charming 16th-century château sparkles on an island in the Indre River, its image romantically reflected in the slow-moving

waters. The building is a prime example of an early-Renaissance château. With no defensive purpose, it was built simply for luxurious living in a luxurious setting. The ornamental facade is perfectly harmonious, and the interior—with its grand staircases and elegant loggias—is Italian-inspired.

The château was built between 1518 and 1527 by a filthy-rich banker—Gilles Berthelot, treasurer to the king of France. The structure has a delightfully feminine touch: Because Gilles was often away for work, his wife, Philippe, supervised the construction. The castle was so lavish that the king, François I, took note, giving it the ultimate compliment: He seized it, causing its owner to flee. Because this château survived the Revolution virtually unscathed, its interior capably demonstrates three centuries of royal styles. The French government purchased it in 1905.

Cost and Hours: €8.50, daily July-Aug 9:30-19:00, April-June and Sept-Oct 9:30-18:00, Nov-March 10:00-17:15, last entry one hour before closing, unnecessary audioguide-€4.50, storage lockers, tel. 02 47 45 42 04, www.azay-le-rideau.monuments-nationaux.fr/en.

Sound-and-Light Show: Meander through the château at night, accompanied by mood lighting and music (€8.50, nightly mid-July-Aug, gates open at 19:00 and close at 23:00).

Visiting the Château: Rooms are very well-described in English (only serious students should consider the audioguide). Cross the water to the island, enter the château, and climb to the top floor. Your visit starts in the castle attic *(comble)*, where you'll wander under a strikingly beautiful roof support cut from 500-year-old oak trees. Then work your way down through sumptuous Renaissance rooms loaded with elaborate tapestries, colossal fireplaces, and intricately carved wood chests. Pause to admire the king's portrait gallery in the "Apartement du XVII Siecle" (three Louis, three Henrys, Catherine de' Medici, and François I).

For many, the highlight of a visit is the romantic garden, designed in the 19th century to show off the already beautiful château. Take a spin on the path around the castle to enjoy romantic views from all sides, especially of the fanciful turrets, gracefully framed by the trees reflected on the water, then have a drink or snack at the tranquil garden café (April-Sept).

Sleeping and Eating in Azay-le-Rideau

LOIRE

The town's appealing center may convince you to set up here.

$$ Hôtel de Biencourt*** is a find. Ideally located on a traffic-free street between Place de la République (easy parking) and the château, this sharp boutique hotel is a former girls school whose gentle owners have completed a masterful renovation. Rooms offer three-star comfort at two-star prices. There's a pleasing garden terrace and a calming lounge area (Db-€69-94, Tb-€102, Qb-€128, breakfast-€10, Wi-Fi, shared fridge, picnics OK on terrace, closed mid-Nov-late March, 7 Rue de Balzac, tel. 02 47 45 20 75, www.hotelbiencourt.com, contact@hotelbiencourt.fr).

Côte Cour is a good place to dine inside or out for fresh and creative cuisine at reasonable prices. Friendly Sandrine offers a few, select choices—local products and mostly organic foods—served in a warm interior or on a great outdoor terrace (€17-23 *menus*, closed Tue-Wed, faces the château gate at 19 Rue Balzac, tel. 02 47 45 30 36). **Crêperie du Roy** is small, central, and cheap (24 Rue Nationale, tel. 02 47 45 91 88). If you have a car, seriously consider

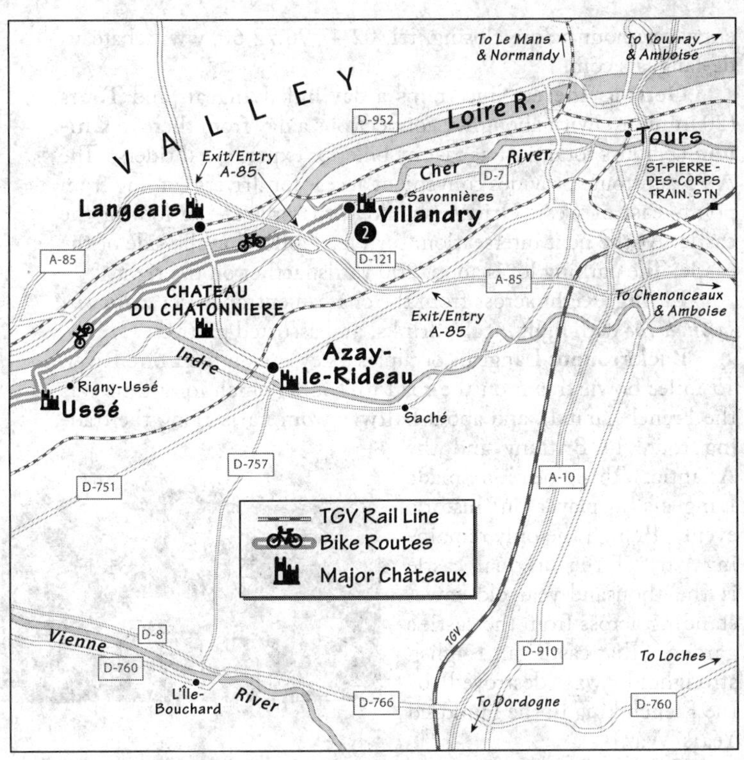

the 15-minute drive to **Domaine de la Giraudière** in Villandry (see page 437).

Azay-le-Rideau Connections

From Azay-le-Rideau, the **train** runs to **Tours** (8/day, 30 minutes, with connections to Amboise, Langeais, and other châteaux), to **Chinon** (7/day, 20 minutes), and to **Blois** (7/day, 1.5 hours, transfer in Tours and possibly in St-Pierre-des-Corps). Summertime **buses** run to Villandry and Langeais twice a day (the TI has bus schedules).

LOIRE

Langeais

One of the most imposing-looking fortresses of the Middle Ages, Langeais—rated ▲—was built mostly for show. Towering above its appealing little village, it comes with a moat, a drawbridge, lavish defenses, and turrets.

Cost and Hours: €9, daily July-Aug 9:00-19:00, April-June and Sept-mid-Nov 9:30-18:30, mid-Nov-March 10:00-17:00, last entry one hour before closing, tel. 02 47 96 72 60, www.chateau-de-langeais.com.

Getting There: Nine trains a day link Langeais and **Tours** (20 minutes), with about five connections a day from there to **Chinon** (2 hours total, just as fast by bike for experienced riders). The A-85 autoroute provides convenient access for drivers coming from points east or west. Drivers should turn right at the foot of the castle. At the next intersection, turn left, following the side of the castle. The parking lot is about 200 yards farther on the right.

Eating: Right across from the château entrance is a *pâtisserie/salon de thé* with light meals, drinks, and assorted pastries.

Background: Langeais occupies a key site on the Loire River, 15 miles downstream on the road to Tours (which for a time was the French capital), and about halfway from Paris along the trading route to Brittany and the Atlantic. This location made Langeais a player in historic events, though the only remaining part of the original castle is the thousand-year-old tower standing across from the castle's garden. (That castle, an English stronghold, was destroyed by the French king in the Hundred Years' War.)

The "new" castle, built in the 15th century, dates from the age of cannons, which would have made quick work of its tough-looking facade. In fact, the imposing walls were mostly for show. This is a transitional piece of architecture: part medieval and part Renaissance. The mullioned windows overlooking the courtyard indicate this was a fancy residence more than a defensive fortress. While Langeais makes a show of its defenses, castles built just 50 years later (such as Azay-le-Rideau) give not a hint of fortification.

Visiting the Château: The interior is late Middle-Ages chic. It's the life's work of a 19th-century owner who was a lover of medieval art. He decorated and furnished the rooms with 15th- and 16th-century artifacts or good facsimiles. Most of what you see is modern-made in 16th-century style.

Langeais tries hard to give visitors a feel for royal life in the 15th century. The palace is decked out as palaces were—designed to impress, and ready to pack and move. The rooms are well-decorated and well-explained in the handy information sheets. In the **bedrooms,** it looks like the master has just left—gloves and other accessories are lying on the bedcovers. There were bedrooms for show, and bedrooms for sleeping.

The **banquet room** table would have groaned with food and

luxury items—but just one long, communal napkin and no forks. Belgian tapestries on the walls still glimmer with 500-year-old silk thread. If you look closely at the astrology tapestry in one room, you'll see that Aurora (Dawn) seems to be wearing headphones.

As you wander, notice how the rooms—with hanging tapestries, foldable chairs, and big chests with handles—could have been set up in a matter of hours. Big-time landowners circulated through their domains, moving every month or so. Also notice how each piece of furniture had multiple uses—such as a throne that doubled as a writing desk.

In the so-called **Wedding Hall,** wax figures re-create the historic marriage that gave Langeais its 15 minutes of château fame in 1491. It was here that King Charles VIII secretly wed 14-year-old Anne (duchess of Brittany), a union that brought independent Brittany into France's fold. The gowns are accurate and impressive, and it's interesting to see how short everyone was in the Middle Ages. An eight-minute sound-and-light show explains the event—usually in English at :15 past each hour.

The top-floor museum has a rare series of 16th-century **tapestries** featuring nine heroes—biblical, Roman, and medieval. This is one of just three such sets in existence, with seven of the original nine scenes surviving.

Finish your visit by enjoying commanding **town views** from the ramparts.

Villandry

Villandry (vee-lahn-dree) is famous for its extensive gardens, considered to be the best in the Loire Valley, and possibly all of France. Its château is just another Loire palace, but the grounds—arranged in elaborate geometric patterns and immaculately maintained—make it a ▲▲ sight (worth ▲▲▲ for gardeners). Still, if you're visiting anyway, it's worth the extra euros to tour the château as well.

Cost and Hours: €10, €6.50 for gardens only, daily April-Sept 9:00-19:00, March and Oct 9:00-18:00, Nov-Feb 9:00-17:00, unnecessary audioguide-€4, storage lockers, tel. 02 47 50 02 09, www.chateauvillandry.fr. You can stay as late as you like in the gardens, though you must enter before the ticket office closes and exit through the back gate after 19:30. Parking is free and easy between the trees across from the entry (hide valuables in your trunk).

Background: Finished in 1536, Villandry was the last great Renaissance château built on the Loire. It's yet another pet project of a fabulously wealthy finance minister of François I—Jean le Breton. While serving as ambassador to Italy, Jean picked up a love of Italian Renaissance gardens. When he took over this property, he razed the 12th-century castle (keeping only the old tower), put up his own château, and installed a huge Italian-style garden. The château was purchased in 1906 by the present owner's great-grandfather, and the garden—a careful reconstruction of what the original might have been—is the result of three generations of passionate dedication.

Visiting the Château and Gardens: The excellent English handout included with your admission leads you through the **château**'s 19th-century rooms. They feel so lived-in that you'll wonder if the family just stepped out to get their poodle bathed. The 15-minute *Four Seasons of Villandry* slideshow, with period music and no narration, offers a look at the gardens throughout the year in a relaxing little theater (ask at the ticket window or you may miss it). The literal high point of your château visit is the spiral climb to the top of the keep—the only surviving part of the medieval castle—where you'll find a 360-degree view of the gardens, village, and surrounding countryside. The extra cost for visiting the château seems worth it when you take in the panorama.

The lovingly tended **gardens** are well described by your handout. Follow its recommended route through the four garden types. The 10-acre Renaissance garden, inspired by the 1530s Italian-style original, is full of symbolism. Even the herb and vegetable sections are put together with artistic flair. The earliest Loire gardens were practical, grown by medieval abbey monks who needed vegetables to feed their community and medicinal herbs to cure their ailments. And those monks liked geometrical patterns. Later Italian influence brought decorative ponds, tunnels, and fountains. Harmonizing the flowers and vegetables was an innovation of 16th-century Loire châteaux. This example is the closest we have to that garden style. Who knew that lentils, chives, and cabbages could look this good?

The 85,000 plants—half of which come from the family greenhouse—are replanted twice a year by 10 full-time gardeners. They use modern organic methods: ladybugs instead of pesticides and a whole lot of hoeing. The place is as manicured as a putting green—just try to find a weed. Stroll under the grapevine trellis, through a good-looking salad zone, and among Anjou pears (from the nearby region of Angers). If all the topiary and straight angles seem too rigid, look for the sun garden in the back of the estate, which has "wilder" perennial borders favored by the Brits. Charts posted throughout identify everything in English.

Bring bread for the piranha-like carp who prowl the fanciful moat. Like the carp swimming around other Loire châteaux, they're so voracious, they'll gather at your feet to frantically eat your spit.

Eating and Sleeping in Villandry

The pleasant little village of Villandry offers several cafés and restaurants, a small grocery store, a bakery, and fair rates at the little **$$ Hôtel-Restaurant le Cheval Rouge***** right on the main drag (Db-€68, extra person-€9, dinner *menus* from €23, Wi-Fi, tel. 02 47 50 02 07, www.lecheval-rouge.com).

Eating near Villandry: **Etape Gourmande at Domaine de la Giraudière** offers a wonderfully rustic farmhouse dining experience. Gentle owner Beatrice takes time with every client, and the country-gourmet cuisine is simply delicious (ask her how she landed here). The *menu* is flexible: Choose just a starter and dessert, a starter and main course, or all three if you're starved. The dining room is *très* cozy, but the outside seating is pleasant, too (€18-39 *menus,* mid-March-mid-Nov daily 12:00-14:30 & 19:30-21:00, closed mid-Nov-mid-March, reservations smart, a half-mile from Villandry's château toward Druye, for location see map on page 432, tel. 02 47 50 08 60, www.letapegourmande.com). This place works best for lunch, as it's well-signed between Villandry and Azay-le-Rideau on D-121. It also works for dinner when combined with a visit to Azay-le-Rideau's sound-and-light show.

More Château Gardens

Gardeners will be tempted by these untouristy "lesser châteaux" because of their pleasing plantings.

Château de Chatonnière

The grounds feature romantic paths through 12 exquisitely tended gardens of various themes. Surrounded by fields of wildflowers (my favorite part), it's a must-visit for gardeners and flower fanatics from May to early July, when the place positively explodes in fragrance and color. At other times, when flowers are few, the entry fee is not worth it for most.

Cost and Hours: €8, cash only, daily mid-March-mid-Nov 10:00-20:00, closed mid-Nov-mid-March, last entry one hour before closing, château interior closed to visitors, between Langeais and Azay-le-Rideau just off D-57, tel. 02 47 45 40 29, www.lachatonniere.fr.

Château du Rivau

Gleaming white and medieval, this château sits wedged between wheat and sunflower fields, and makes for a memorable 15-minute drive from Chinon. Its owners have spared little expense in their decades-long renovation of the 15th-century castle and its extensive gardens. The 14 different flower and vegetable gardens and orchards are kid-friendly (with elf and fairy guides) and lovingly tended with art installations, topiaries, hammocks, birds, a maze, and much more. The stables—with projections about jousting and "Heroic Horses" from history—will delight most kids (English subtitles), but the medieval castle interior is skippable. A good little café serves reasonable meals in a lovely setting.

Cost and Hours: €10, daily April-Oct 10:00-18:00, until 19:00 May-Sept, closed Nov-March, audioguide-€2, in Lémeré on D-759—from Chinon follow *Richelieu* signs, then signs to the château; tel. 02 47 95 77 47, www.chateaudurivau.com.

Ussé

This château, famous as an inspiration for Charles Perrault's classic version of the Sleeping Beauty story, is worth a quick photo stop for its fairy-tale turrets and gardens, but don't bother touring the interior of this pricey pearl. The best view, with reflections and a golden-slipper picnic spot, is from just across the bridge.

Cost and Hours: €14, daily 10:00-18:00 in spring and fall, until 19:00 April-Aug, closed mid-Nov-mid-Feb, tel. 02 47 95 54 05, www.chateaudusse.fr.

Abbaye Royale de Fontevraud

The Royal Abbey of Fontevraud (fohn-tuh-vroh) is a 15-minute journey west from Chinon. This vast 12th-century abbey provides a fascinating look at medieval monastic life. The "abbey" was actually a 12th-century monastic city, the largest such compound in Europe—with four monastic complexes, all within a fortified wall.

Cost and Hours: €9.50; April-Oct daily 9:30-18:30, until 19:00 July-Aug; Nov-Dec and Feb-March Tue-Sun 9:30-17:00, closed Mon; closed Jan, tel. 02 41 51 73 52, www.abbayedefontevraud.com.

Tours: Spring for the helpful €4.50 audioguide (kid version available), as the free English leaflet is short on information and the guided tours are only in French.

Parking: There's free parking 100 yards beyond the abbey entrance; look for a yellow *P* sign and turn right.

Background: The order of Fontevraud, founded in 1101, was an experiment of rare audacity. This was a double monastery, where both men and women lived under the authority of an abbess while observing the rules of St. Benedict (but influenced by the cult of the Virgin Mary). Men and women lived separately and chastely within the abbey walls. The order thrived, and in the 16th century, this was the administrative head of more than 150 monasteries. Four communities lived within these walls until the Revolution. In 1804, Napoleon made the abbey a prison, which actually helped preserve the building. It functioned as a prison for 150 years, until 1963, with five wooden floors filled with cells. Designed to house 800 inmates, the prison was notoriously harsh. Life expectancy here was eight months.

Visiting the Abbey: Thanks to the audioguides for adults and kids, this abbey is well presented for English speakers.

Your visit begins in the bright, 12th-century, Romanesque **abbey church.** Sit on the steps, savor the ethereal light and the cavernous setting, and gaze down the nave. At the end of it are four painted sarcophagi belonging to Eleanor of Aquitaine; her second husband, Henry II, the first of England's Plantagenet kings; their son Richard the Lionheart; and his sister-in-law. These are the tops of the sarcophagi only. Even though we know these Plantagenets were buried here (because they gave lots of money to the abbey), no one knows the fate of the actual bodies.

You'll leave the church through the right transept into the **cloister.** This was the center of the abbey, where the nuns read, exercised, checked their email, and washed their hands. While visiting the abbey, remember that monastic life was extremely simple: nothing but prayers, readings, and work. Daily rations were a loaf of bread and a half-liter of wine per person, plus soup and smoked fish.

Next you'll find the **chapter house,** where the nuns' meetings took place, as well as the **community room**—the only heated room in the abbey, where the nuns embroidered linen. In rooms leading off the cloister, Renaissance paintings feature portraits of the women in black habits who ran this abbey.

The nearby **refectory,** built to feed 400 silent monks at a time, was later the prison work yard, where inmates built wooden chairs.

Your abbey visit ends in the unusual, honeycombed, 12th-century **kitchen,** with five bays covered by 18 chimneys to evacuate smoke. It likely served as a smokehouse for fish farmed in the abbey ponds. Abbeys like this were industrious places, but focused on self-sufficiency rather than trade.

Finish your visit by wandering through the abbey's **medicinal gardens** out back.

Near Fontevraud: Mushroom Caves

For an unusual fungus find close to the abbey of Fontevraud, visit the mushroom caves called **Le Saut aux Loups.** France is the world's third-largest producer of mushrooms (after the US and China), so mushrooms matter. Climb to a cliff ledge and enter 16 chilly rooms bored into limestone to discover everything about the care and nurturing of mushrooms. You'll see them raised in planters, plastic bags, logs, and straw bales, and you'll learn about their incubation, pasteurization, and fermentation. Abandoned limestone quarries like this are fertile homes for mushroom cultivation, and have made the Loire Valley the mushroom capital of France since the 1800s. You'll ogle at the weird shapes and never take your 'shrooms for granted again. The growers harvest a ton of mushrooms a month in these caves; shitakes are their most important crop. Pick up the English booklet and follow the fungus. Many visitors come only for the on-site mushroom restaurant, whose wood-fired *galipettes* (stuffed mushrooms with crème fraîche and herbs) are the kitchen's forté.

Cost and Hours: €6.50, March-mid-Nov daily 10:00-18:00, closed mid-Nov-Feb, dress warmly, lunch served daily, €20-23 *menus,* just north of Fontevraud at Montsoreau's west end along the river, for location see map on page 432, tel. 02 41 51 70 30, www.troglo-sautauxloups.com.

Sleeping and Eating near Abbaye Royale de Fontevraud

$$$ Hôtel la Croix Blanche*,** 10 steps from the abbey, welcomes travelers with open terraces and will have you sleeping and dining in comfort. This ambitious restaurant-hotel combines a hunting-lodge feel with polished service, comfortable open spaces, a pool, and 23 plush rooms with cozy themes (Db-€100-120, Db suites-€135-155, Wi-Fi, Place Plantagenets, tel. 02 41 51 71 11, www.hotel-croixblanche.com, info@hotel-croixblanche.com).

The abbey faces the main square of a cute town with several handy eateries. The ***boulangerie*** opposite the entrance to the abbey serves mouthwatering quiche and sandwiches at impossibly good prices. You'll also find a few *crêperies* and cafés near the abbey.

DORDOGNE

Sarlat-la-Canéda • Dordogne River Valley • Cro-Magnon Caves • Oradour-sur-Glane • St-Emilion • Rocamadour • Lot River Valley

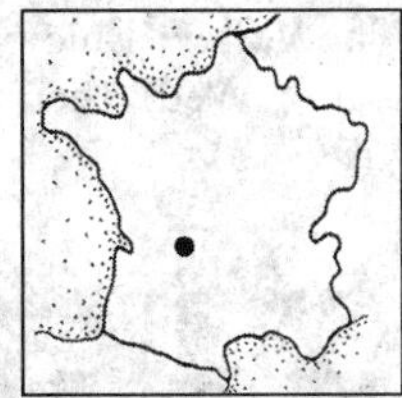

The Dordogne River Valley is a delicious brew, blending natural and man-made beauty. Walnut orchards, tobacco plants, sunflowers, and cornfields carpet the valley, while stone fortresses patrol the cliffs above. During much of the on-again, off-again Hundred Years' War (when this region was called the Périgord), this strategic river—so peaceful today—separated warring Britain and France. Today's Dordogne River carries more travelers than goods, as the region's economy relies heavily on tourism.

The joys of the Dordogne include rock-sculpted villages, fertile farms surrounding I-should-retire-here cottages, memory-card-gobbling vistas, lazy canoe rides, and a local cuisine worth loosening your belt for. But its big draw is its amazing cache of prehistoric artifacts. Limestone caves decorated with prehistoric artwork litter the Dordogne region.

PLANNING YOUR TIME

Although tourists inundate the region in the summer, the Dordogne's charm is protected by its relative inaccessibility. Given the time it takes to get here by car, I'd allow a minimum of two nights (ideally three) and most of two days...or I'd skip it. Whirlwind travelers could consider flying here: Inexpensive flights now connect Paris with the region's main city, Brive-la-Gaillarde (where you can rent a car).

Your sightseeing obligations, in order of priority, are as follows: prehistoric cave art; the Dordogne River Valley, nearby villages, and castles; the town of Sarlat-la-Canéda (often shortened to "Sarlat," pronounced sar-lah); and, if you have a bit more time, the less-traveled Lot River Valley (most efficiently viewed when heading to or from the south). Wine lovers work in a pilgrimage to St-Emilion, two hours west of Sarlat.

If you're connecting the Dordogne with the Loire region by car, the fastest path is via the free A-20 autoroute (exit at Souillac for Sarlat-la-Canéda and nearby villages). Break up your trip from the north by stopping in Oradour-sur-Glane. If you're connecting the Dordogne and Carcassonne, explore the Lot River Valley on your way south. If heading west, taste the Bordeaux wine region's prettiest town, St-Emilion.

Those serious about visiting the Dordogne's best caves (especially with a relatively rare English-speaking tour) need to plan carefully and book ahead when possible (explained on page 486).

The following three-day itinerary is designed for drivers, but it's doable—if you're determined—by taxi rides, a canoe trip (the best way to see the Dordogne regardless of whether you've got a car), and a minivan tour.

Day 1—Sarlat-la-Canéda and the Dordogne Valley: Enjoy a morning in Sarlat (ideally on a market day—Sat or Wed), then spend the afternoon on a canoe trip, with time at the day's end to explore Beynac and Castelnaud. If it's not market day in Sarlat, do the canoe trip, Beynac, and Castelnaud first, and enjoy the late afternoon and evening in Sarlat. (Because the town's essential sights are outdoors, my self-guided Sarlat walk works great after dinner.) The sensational views from Castelnaud's castle and Domme are best in the morning; visit Beynac's castle or viewpoint late in the day for the best light. With a little lead time, some canoe-rental companies can pick up non-drivers in Sarlat. Taxis are reasonable between Sarlat and the river villages.

Day 2—Prehistoric Caves: Start your day in Les Eyzies-de-Tayac at the Prehistory Welcome Center and the National Museum of Prehistory for a solid cave-art introduction. From there your day will depend on the cave(s) you can get an entry for (varies by season, described under each cave later). The Lascaux II replica cave delivers an excellent tour and can be reserved, the Grotte de Font-de-Gaume is the best cave with original art (though getting in is tricky), and the Grotte de Rouffignac makes a good and more reliable substitute. If you visit Lascaux II, follow the scenic Vézère River, stopping for a coffee or lunch in idyllic little St-Léon.

Without a car, this day's full list of activities is only possible by taxi or excursion tour. By train, you can link Sarlat-la-Canéda and Les Eyzies-de-Tayac, though you have to transfer and some connections aren't great.

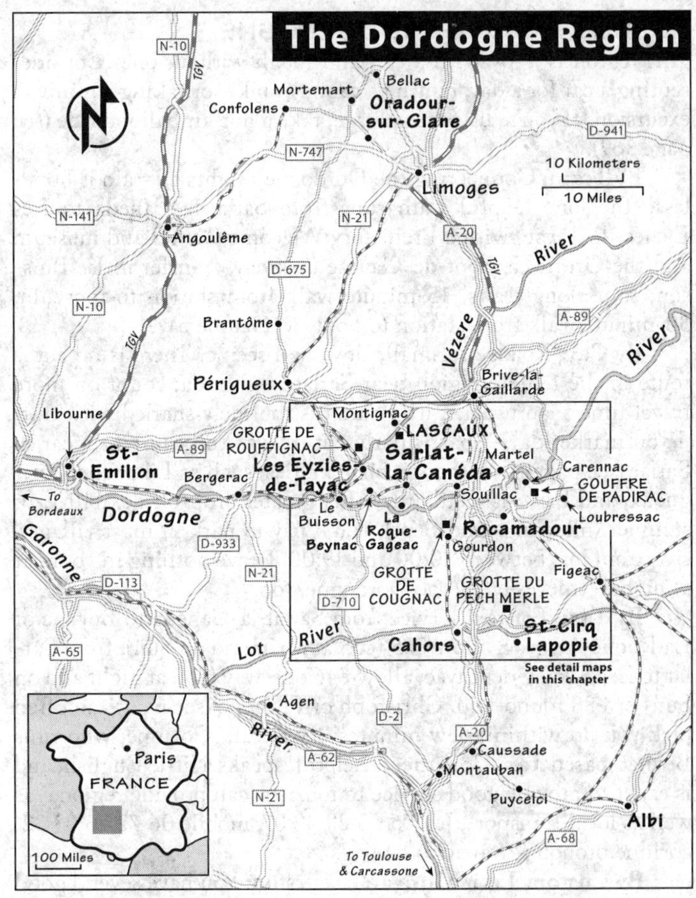

Day 3—Other Sights: Head east and upriver to explore Rocamadour, Gouffre de Padirac, and storybook villages such as Carennac, Autoire, and Loubressac. Though Rocamadour is accessible by train and a short taxi ride, the rest of these places are feasible only with your own wheels, by taxi, or on an excursion tour.

CHOOSING A HOME BASE

Sarlat-la-Canéda is the only viable solution for train travelers, but those with a car should consider sleeping riverside in La Roque-Gageac (a beautiful village with good hotels) or Beynac (a *très* photogenic village with good *chambres d'hôtes* and a so-so hotel). For a grand château hotel experience that won't break the bank, sleep near the Lascaux caves at Château de la Fleunie (30 minutes north of Sarlat; see page 492). For the best view hotel I've found in the area, try Hôtel de l'Esplanade in Domme (see page 468).

GETTING AROUND THE DORDOGNE

This region is a joy with a car, and tough without one. Consider renting a car for a day, renting a canoe or bike, or taking a minivan excursion. If you're up for a splurge, take a hot-air balloon ride (see page 369).

By Train: Connecting the Dordogne's sights by train is hopeless. The lone helpful train runs from Sarlat-la-Canéda to Les Eyzies-de-Tayac, with a Prehistory Welcome Center and museum and the Grotte de Font-de-Gaume (3-4/day, transfer in Le Buisson, some long waits, 15-minute walk from station to museum, 30-minute walk from station to Font-de-Gaume cave).

By Car: Roads are small, slow, and scenic. There is no autoroute in the remote region near Sarlat-la-Canéda; count on more travel time than usual. Little Sarlat is routinely snarled with traffic on market days—particularly Saturdays. You can rent a car in Sarlat (see page 450), though bigger cities, such as Libourne, Périgueux, and Brive-la-Gaillarde, offer greater drop-off flexibility. In summer (mid-June-mid-Sept), you'll pay to park in most villages' riverfront lots between 10:00 and 19:00. Leave nothing in your car at night—thieves enjoy the Dordogne, too.

By Taxi: For taxi service from Sarlat-la-Canéda to Beynac or La Roque-Gageac, allow €25 (€35 at night and on Sun); from Sarlat to Les Eyzies-de-Tayac, allow €46 one-way (€66 at night and on Sun) or €88 round-trip. Christoph or Philippe (see next) can often pick you up within a few minutes if you call. Corinne, who runs Beynac-based **Taxi Corinne,** is helpful, speaks a little English, and is eager to provide good service to tourists (can provide regional as well as local transport, tel. 05 53 29 42 07, mobile 06 72 76 03 32, corinne.brouqui@wanadoo.fr).

By Custom Taxi/Minivan Excursion: You have several good options. Gentle **Christoph** and lively **Sarissa Kusters** speak flawless English and provide top service in their Land Rover (6 people) or Tesla (4 people), whether you need a taxi from the train station in Sarlat-la-Canéda to the town center, a pickup in Paris or Oradour-sur-Glane, or a day-long tour. This couple can help organize your trip from soup to nuts and give you a good running commentary as you ride. They offer flexible plans allowing for a fast or slow pace, based on your interests (€40/hour, mobile 06 08 70 61 67, www.taxialacarte.com, taxialacarte@gmail.com).

Allô-Philippe Taxi is run by amiable Philippe, who speaks some English. He will custom-design your tour and can pick you up anywhere. For excursions, he charges €42/hour for up to four people (€63/hour on Sun, tel. 05 53 59 39 65, mobile 06 08 57 30 10, http://allophilippetaxi.monsite.orange.fr, allophilippetaxi@wanadoo.fr).

Ophorus Excursions offers a full range of scheduled half- and full-day trips—for individuals or private groups—to caves, castles, and villages in a comfortable minivan with competent, English-fluent guides and up to 10 fellow travelers (€65-70/half-day, €105-140/day, mobile 06 33 05 10 09, www.ophorus.com, info@ophorus.com).

Caves and Castles is run by a delightful British couple (Steve and Judie Burman) who offer tours to the area's main sights for a day or more. They offer translation services for French-only cave visits, and Steve has plenty of tricks to keep families happy and kids entertained (tel. 05 53 50 31 21, www.cavesandcastles.com, cavesandcastles@gmail.com).

Béatrice Mollart and Bruno Elure, a fun local guide team headquartered in Sarlat-la-Canéda, create tours tailor-made for travelers wanting to dig into Dordogne culture and get off the beaten track (9 Cours des Fontaines, mobile 06 79 63 28 47, www.dordogne-fellow-traveller.com, loeildelagazelle@orange.fr).

By Boat: Non-drivers should rent a canoe, my favorite way to explore a small but gorgeous slice of this region. A canoe offers easy access to the river's sights and villages, and some canoe companies will pick you up in Sarlat-la-Canéda for no extra charge. Since a canoe costs about €18/person (for the trip I recommend, from Vitrac to Beynac), and you can spend all day on and off the river touring sights I cover, this is a swimmingly good deal. For the same scenery with less work (and no ability to visit villages and castles en route), you can also take a boat cruise from Beynac or La Roque-Gageac (€9). Details on all these options are covered later in this chapter.

By Bike: Cyclists find the Dordogne beautiful but really hilly, with lots of traffic on key roads. You can pick up a basic bike for the day in Sarlat-la-Canéda; serious riders will be impressed with **Liberty Bike**'s services and **Aquitaine Bike**'s fleet (see page 450).

By Balloon: The Dordogne is a terrific place to spring for a hot-air balloon trip, taking you high above its gorgeous river and hilly terrain capped with golden stone castles and villages. **Montgolfières du Périgord** is conveniently based in La Roque-Gageac and offers a variety of flights with well-trained pilots (one-hour flight-€200/person, www.montgolfiere-du-perigord.com, tel. 05 53 28 18 58).

THE DORDOGNE'S CUISINE SCENE

Gourmets flock to this area for its geese, ducks, and wild mushrooms. The geese produce (involuntarily) the region's famous foie gras. (They're force-fed, denied exercise during the last weeks of their lives, and slaughtered for their livers, meat, and fluffy down—see sidebar on page 476.) Foie gras tastes like butter and costs like gold. The duck specialty is *confit de canard* (duck meat preserved in its own fat—sounds terrible, but tastes great).

Pommes de terre sarladaises are mouthwatering, thinly sliced potatoes fried in duck fat and commonly served with *confit de canard.* Wild truffles are dirty black tubers that grow underground, generally on the roots of oak trees. Farmers traditionally locate them with sniffing pigs and then charge a fortune for their catch (roughly $250 per pound). Native cheeses are Cabécou (a silver-dollar-size, pungent, nutty-flavored goat cheese) and Echourgnac (made by local Trappist monks). You'll find walnuts *(noix)* in salads, cakes, liqueurs, salad dressings, and more.

Wines to sample are Bergerac (red, white, and rosé), Pecharmant (red, must be at least four years old), Cahors (a full-bodied red), and Monbazillac (sweet dessert wine). The *vin de noix* (sweet walnut liqueur) is delightful before dinner.

Remember, restaurants serve only during lunch (11:30-14:00) and dinner (19:00-21:00, later in bigger cities); bigger cafés serve food throughout the day.

DORDOGNE MARKETS

Markets are a big deal in rural France, and nowhere more so than in the Dordogne. I've listed good markets for every day of the week, so there's no excuse for drivers not to experience one. Here's what to look for:

Strawberries *(fraises):* For the French, the Dordogne is the region famous for the very tastiest strawberries. Available from April to November, they're gorgeous, and they smell even better than they look. Buy *une barquette* (small basket), and suddenly your two-star hotel room is a three-star. Look also for *fraises des bois,* the tiny, sweet, and less visually appealing strawberries found in nearby forests.

Fresh Veggies: Outdoor markets allow you to meet the farmer, and give you a chance to buy direct. (See what's fresh, and look for it on your menu this evening.) Subtly check out the hands of the person helping customers—if they're not gnarled and rough from working the fields, move on.

Cheeses *(fromages):* The region is famous for its Cabécou goat cheese (described earlier), though often you'll also find Auvergne cheeses (St. Nectaire and Cantal are the most common) from just east of the

Dordogne (usually in big rounds), and Tomme and Brébis (sheep cheeses) from the Pyrenees to the south.

Truffles *(truffes):* Only the bigger markets will have these ugly, jet-black tubers on display. Truffle season is our off-season (Nov-Feb), when you'll find them at every market. During summer, the fresh truffles you might see are *truffes d'été,* a less desirable and cheaper, but still tasty species. If you see truffles displayed at other times, they've been sterilized (a preservative measure that can reduce flavor). On Sarlat-la-Canéda market days, there's usually a guy in the center of Place de la Liberté with a photo of his grandfather and his truffle-hunting dog. From November to mid-March there's a truffle market on Saturday mornings on Rue Fénelon (get details at the TI).

Anything with Walnuts *(aux noix): Pain aux noix* is a thick-as-a-brick bread loaf chock-full of walnuts. *Moutarde de noix* is walnut mustard. *Confiture de noix* is a walnut spread for hors d'oeuvres. *Gâteaux de noix* are tasty cakes studded with walnuts. *Liqueur de noix* is a marvelous creamy liqueur, great over ice or blended with a local white wine.

Goose or Duck Livers and Pâté (foie gras): This spread is made from geese (better) and ducks (still good), or from a mix of the two. You'll see two basic forms: *entier* and *bloc.* Both are 100 percent foie gras; *entier* is a piece cut right from the product, whereas *bloc* has been blended to make it easier to spread—*mousse* has been whipped for an even creamier consistency. Foie gras is best accompanied by a sweet white wine (such as the locally produced Monbazillac, or Sauterne from Bordeaux). You can bring the unopened tins back into the US, *pas de problème.* For more on foie gras, see the sidebar on page 476.

Confit de Canard: At butcher stands, look for hunks of duck smothered in white fat, just waiting for someone to take them home and cook them up. If you have kitchen access, try it: Scrape off some of the fat, then sauté the chunks until they're crispy on the outside and heated through. Save some of that fat for roasting potatoes.

Dried Sausages *(saucissons secs):* Long tables piled high with dried sausages covered in herbs or stuffed with local goodies are a common sight in French markets. You'll always be offered a mouth-watering sample. Some of the variations you'll see include *porc, canard* (duck), *fumé* (smoked), *à l'ail* (garlic),

cendré (rolled in ashes), *aux myrtilles* (with blueberries), *sanglier* (wild boar), and even *âne* (donkey)—and, but of course, *aux noix* (with walnuts).

Olive Oil *(huile d'olive):* You'll find stylish bottles of various olive oils, as well as vegetable oils flavored with truffles, walnuts, chestnuts *(châtaignes)*, and hazelnuts *(noisettes)*—good for cooking, ideal on salads, and great as gifts. Pure walnut oil, pressed at local mills from nuts grown in the region, is a local specialty, best on salads. Don't cook with pure walnut oil, as it will burn quickly.

Olives and Nuts *(olives et noix):* These interlopers from Provence find their way to every market in France.

Brandies and Liqueurs: Although they're not made in this region, Armagnac, Cognac, and other southwestern fruit-flavored liquors are often available from a seller or two. Try the *liqueur de pomme verte,* and sample Armagnac in the tiny plastic cups.

Dordogne Market Days

The best markets are in Sarlat-la-Canéda (Sat and Wed, in that order), followed by the markets in Cahors on Saturday, St-Cyprien on Sunday, and Le Bugue on Tuesday. Markets usually shut down by 13:00.

Sunday: St-Cyprien (lively market, 10 minutes west of Beynac, difficult parking), Montignac (near Lascaux), and St-Geniès (a tiny, intimate market with few tourists; halfway between Sarlat and Montignac)

Monday: Les Eyzies-de-Tayac and a tiny one in Beynac

Tuesday: Cénac (you can canoe from here) and Le Bugue (great market 20 minutes west of Beynac)

Wednesday: Sarlat (big market)

Thursday: Domme

Friday: Souillac (transfer point to Cahors, Carcassonne)

Saturday: Sarlat and Cahors (both are excellent), and the little *bastide* village of Belvès (small market)

Sarlat-la-Canéda

Sarlat–la-Canéda is a pedestrian-filled banquet of a town, serenely set amid forested hills. There are no blockbuster sights. Still, Sarlat delivers a seductive tangle of traffic-free, golden cobblestone lanes peppered with beautiful buildings, lined with foie gras shops (geese hate Sarlat), and stuffed with tourists. The town is warmly lit at night and ideal for after-dinner strolls. It's just the right size—large enough to have a theater with four screens, but small enough so that everything is an easy meander from the town center. And though undeniably popular with tourists, it's the handiest home base for those without a car.

Orientation to Sarlat-la-Canéda

Rue de la République slices like an arrow through the circular old town. Sarlat's smaller half has few shops and many quiet lanes. The action lies east of Rue de la République.

TOURIST INFORMATION

The TI is 50 yards to the right of the Cathedral of St. Sacerdos as you face it (July-Aug Mon-Sat 9:00-19:00, Sun 10:00-12:00 & 14:00-18:00; April-June and Sept-Oct Mon-Sat 9:00-12:00 & 14:00-18:00, Sun 10:00-13:00 & 14:00-17:00; shorter hours and closed Sun Nov-March; on Rue Tourny, tel. 05 53 31 45 45, www.sarlat-tourisme.com). Their city map with English information is helpful (small fee). Ask for information on car, bike, and canoe rental (this and other information can also be downloaded from the TI's website). Bikers can purchase route maps in English (€2).

The TI rents audioguides for self-guided tours of the city (€5/person, €7 with two sets of earphones). They also offer guided tours of Sarlat in English (€6, Thu at 11:00, mid-May-July and Sept-mid-Oct, no tours in Aug or off-season), and sell tickets for the panoramic elevator ride in the covered market hall (€5; described later in my self-guided walk).

ARRIVAL IN SARLAT-LA-CANEDA

By Train: The sleepy train station keeps a lonely vigil (without a shop, café, or hotel in sight). It's a mostly downhill, 20-minute walk to the town center (taxis are about €7—see "Helpful Hints"). To walk into town, turn left out of the station and follow Avenue de la Gare as it curves downhill, then turn right at the bottom, on Avenue Thiers, to reach the town center. Some trains (such as those from Limoges and Cahors) arrive at nearby Souillac, which is connected to Sarlat's train station by an SNCF bus.

By Car: The hilly terrain around Sarlat-la-Canéda creates traffic funnels unusual for a town of this size. Metered parking is easy in the center on non-market and non-summer days (about €4/2 hours, free Mon-Sat 12:00-14:00 & 19:00-9:00 and all day Sun). On market days, avoid the center by parking along Avenue Gambetta (at the north end of town), or in one of the signed lots on the ring road. The closest parking to the center is metered.

HELPFUL HINTS

Market Days: Sarlat has been an important market town since the Middle Ages. Outdoor markets still thrive on Wednesday morning and all day Saturday. Saturday's market swallows the entire town and is best in the morning (produce and food vendors leave around noon). Come before 8:00 to watch them set up, and, once the market is under way, plant yourself at a well-positioned café to observe the civilized scene. In summer months, a small organic market enlivens the town's lower (southern) side (Thu 18:30-22:00, Place du 14 Juillet). From November to March, a truffle market takes place on Saturday mornings on Rue Fénelon. For tips on what to look for at the market, see "Dordogne Markets," earlier.

Supermarket: There's a **Petit Casino** grocery at 32 Rue de la République.

Internet Access: Ask the TI where you can get connected. The recommended **Brasserie le Glacier** has free Wi-Fi for customers.

Laundry: Madame Mazzocato runs the launderette across from the recommended Hôtel la Couleuvrine (self-serve daily 24 hours, drop-off/pickup Mon-Fri 9:00-12:00 & 14:00-18:00, Sat 9:00-12:00, none Sun, 10 Place de la Bouquerie). And for Rick Steves readers, she will drop off laundry at your (Sarlat) hotel. Another **self-serve laundry** is near the hotels north of the center (daily 7:00-21:00, 74 Avenue Gambetta).

Biking: Sarlat-la-Canéda is surrounded by beautiful country lanes that would be ideal for biking were it not for all those hills. Villages along the Dordogne River make good biking destinations, though expect some traffic and some serious ups and downs between Sarlat and the river (bike-rental places can advise quieter routes). A 26-kilometer bike-only lane runs from Sarlat to Souillac, but doesn't connect the river villages I describe (get map at TI). **Liberty Cycle** rents bikes and offers short bike tours (open daily, by the canoe rental in Castelnaud, tel. 07 81 24 78 79, www.liberty-cycle.com). **Aquitaine Bike,**

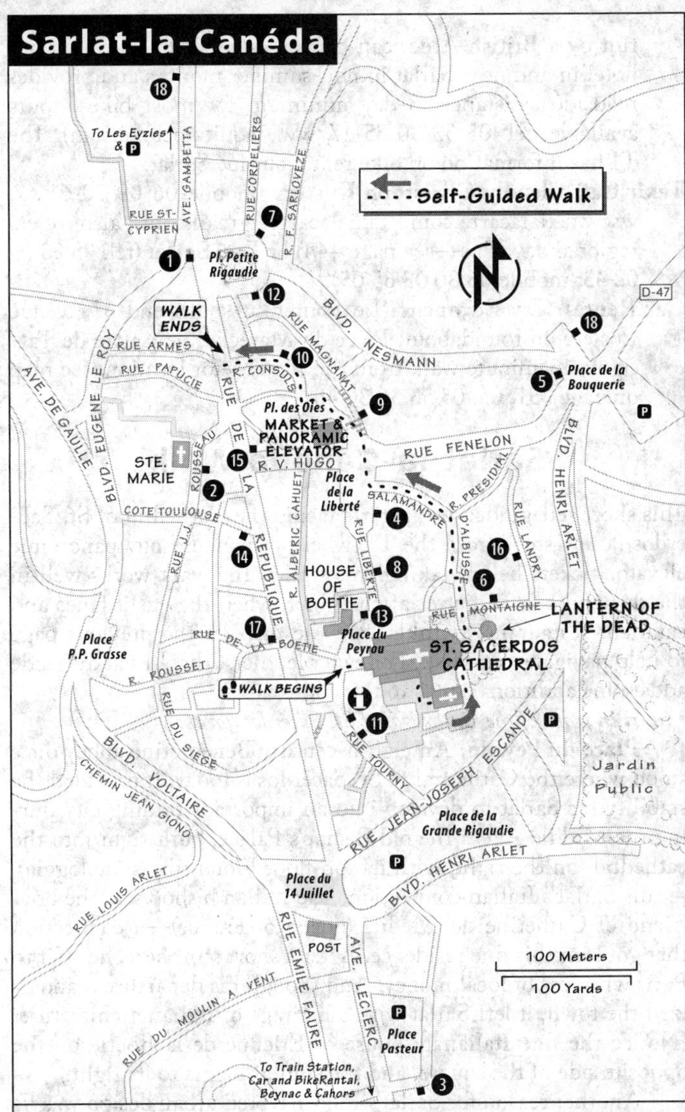

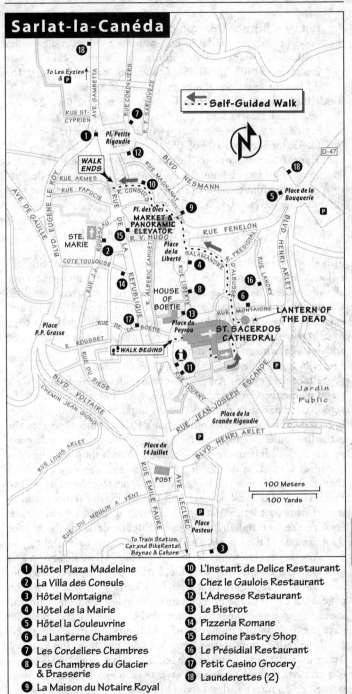

1. Hôtel Plaza Madeleine
2. La Villa des Consuls
3. Hôtel Montaigne
4. Hôtel de la Mairie
5. Hôtel la Couleuvrine
6. La Lanterne Chambres
7. Les Cordeliers Chambres
8. Les Chambres du Glacier & Brasserie
9. La Maison du Notaire Royal
10. L'Instant de Delice Restaurant
11. Chez le Gaulois Restaurant
12. L'Adresse Restaurant
13. Le Bistrot
14. Pizzeria Romane
15. Lemoine Pastry Shop
16. Le Présidial Restaurant
17. Petit Casino Grocery
18. Launderettes (2)

run by a British-American couple, can deliver bikes to your hotel in and near Sarlat in non-summer months and provides roadside assistance (3-day minimum for most bikes, tours available, tel. 05 53 30 35 17, www.aquitainebike.com). The TI has information on bike rental outside Sarlat.

Taxi: Call friendly **Christoph Kusters** (mobile 06 08 70 61 67, www.taxialacarte.com, taxialacarte@gmail.com, also offers regional day trips—see page 444) or **Taxi Sarlat** (tel. 05 53 59 02 43, mobile 06 80 08 65 05).

Car Rental: Try **Europcar** (Le Pontet, at south end of Avenue Leclerc on roundabout, Place du Maréchal de Lattre de Tassigny, 15-minute walk from the center—for location, see map on page 451, tel. 05 53 30 30 40).

Sarlat-la-Canéda Walk

This short self-guided walk starts facing the Cathedral of St. Sacerdos (a few steps from the TI, where you should buy panoramic elevator tickets before taking this walk). The walk works well in the day and is even better after dinner, when the gaslit lanes and candlelit restaurants twinkle. See the map on the previous page to help navigate this walk. For eager learners, the TI's audioguide adds some additional stops to this tour.

• *Start in front of the Cathedral of St. Sacerdos, on the...*

Place du Peyrou: An eighth-century Benedictine abbey once stood where the Cathedral of St. Sacerdos is today. It provided the stability for Sarlat to develop into an important trading city during the Middle Ages. The old Bishop's Palace, built right into the cathedral (on the right, with its top-floor Florentine-style loggia), recalls Sarlat's Italian connection. The Italian bishop was the boyfriend of Catherine de' Medici (queen of France)—a connection that got him this fine residence. After a short stint here, he split to Paris with lots of local money. And though his departure scandalized the town, it left Sarlat with a heritage of Italian architecture. (Notice the fine Italianate house of Etienne de la Boëtie on the opposite side of the square, and the similar loggia to its right.)

Another reason for Sarlat's Italo-flavored urban design was its loyalty to the king during wartime. Sarlat's glory century was from about 1450 to 1550, after the Hundred Years' War (see sidebar on page 241). Loyal to the French cause—through thick and thin and a century of war—Sarlat was rewarded by the French king, who gave the town lots of money to rebuild itself in stone. Sarlat's new nobility needed fancy houses, complete with ego-boosting features. Many of Sarlat's most impressive buildings date from this prosperous era, when the Renaissance style was in vogue, and everyone wanted an architect with an Italian résumé.

• *Take a closer look (opposite the cathedral) at...*

The House of Etienne de la Boëtie: This house was a typical 16th-century merchant's home—family upstairs and open ground floor (its stone arch now filled in) with big, fat sills to display retail goods. Pan up, scanning the crude-but-still-Renaissance carved reliefs. It was a time when anything Italian was trendy (when yokels "stuck a feather in their cap and called it macaroni"). La Boëtie (lah bow-ess-ee), a 16th-century bleeding-heart liberal who spoke and wrote against the rule of tyrannical kings, remains a local favorite.

Notice how the house just to the left arches over the small street. This was a common practice to maximize buildable space in the Middle Ages. Sarlat enjoyed a population boom in the mid-15th century after the Hundred Years' War ended.

• *If you're doing this walk during the day, head into the cathedral now. If it's after hours, skip ahead to the Lantern of the Dead: Face the cathedral, walk around it to the left, up the lane, and through the little door in the wall to the rocket-shaped building on a bluff 30 yards behind the church.*

Cathedral of St. Sacerdos: Though the cathedral's facade has a few well-worn 12th-century carvings, most of it dates from the 18th and 19th centuries. Step inside this historic Sarlat interior. The faithful believed that Mary delivered them from the great plague of 1348, so you'll find a full complement of Virgin Marys here and throughout the town. The Gothic interiors in this part of France are simple, with clean lines and nothing extravagant. The first chapel on the left is the baptistery. Locals would come here to give thanks after they made the pilgrimage to Lourdes for healing and returned satisfied. A column on the right side of the nave shows a long list of hometown boys who gave their lives for France in World War I.

• *Exit the cathedral from the right transept (through a padded brown door) into what was once the abbey's cloisters. Snoop through two quiet courtyards, then turn left, making your way around and around to the back of the church, where you'll climb steps (above the monks' graveyard) to a bluff behind the church. You'll find a bullet-shaped building ready for some kind of medieval takeoff, known as the...*

Lantern of the Dead (Lanterne des Morts): Dating from 1147, this is the oldest monument in town. In four horrible days, a quarter of Sarlat's population died in a plague (1,000 out of 4,000). People prayed to St. Bernard of Clairvaux for help. He blessed their bread—and instituted hygiene standards while he was at it, stopping the disease. This lantern was built in gratitude.

• *Facing the church, exit downhill and to the right, toward an adorable house with its own tiny tower. Cross one street and keep straight, turn left a block later on Impasse de la Vieille Poste, make a quick right on Rue d'Albusse, and then take a left onto...*

Rue de la Salamandre: The salamander—unfazed by fire or water—was Sarlat's mascot. Befitting its favorite animal, Sarlat was also unfazed by fire (from war) and water (from floods). Walk several steps down this "Street of the Salamander" and find the Gothic-framed doorway just below on your right. Step back and notice the tower that housed the staircase. Staircase towers like this (Sarlat has about 20) date from about 1600 (after the wars of religion between the Catholics and Protestants), when the new nobility needed to show off.

• *Continue downhill, passing under the salamander-capped arch, and pause near (or better, sit down at) the café on the...*

Place de la Liberté: This has been Sarlat's main market square since the Middle Ages, though it was expanded in the 18th century. Sarlat's patriotic town hall stands behind you (with a café perfectly situated for people-watching). You can't miss the dark **stone roofs** topping the buildings across the square. They're typical of this region: Called *lauzes* in French, the flat limestone rocks were originally gathered by farmers clearing their fields, then made into cheap, durable roofing material (today few people can afford them). The unusually steep pitch of the *lauzes* roofs—which last up to 300 years—helps distribute the weight of the roof (about 160 pounds per square foot) over a greater area. Although most *lauzes* roofs have been replaced by roofs made from more affordable materials, a great number remain. The small window is critical: It provides air circulation, allowing the lichen that coat the porous stone to grow—sealing gaps between the stones and effectively waterproofing the roof. Without that layer, the stone would crumble after repeated freeze-and-thaw cycles.

• *Walk right, to the "upper" end of the square. The bulky Church of Ste. Marie, right across from you, today serves as Sarlat's...*

Covered Market and Panoramic Elevator: Once a parish church dedicated to St. Marie, with a massive *lauzes* roof and a soaring bell tower, this building was converted into a gunpowder factory and then a post office before becoming today's **indoor market** (daily 8:30-13:00). Marvel at its tall, strangely modern, seven-ton doors. Wander through the market, and turn right to find a modern, glass-sided **panoramic elevator,** which whisks tourists up through the center of the ancient church's bell tower for bird's-eye views over the rooftops (€5, buy tickets at TI, 5/hour, visit lasts 12 minutes, April-Dec daily 9:00-19:00, dependent on good weather and daylight, shorter

hours off-season—check with TI for times). Your elevator operator doubles as a guide, who gives a quick but effective history of Sarlat at the top (in English, if the group is mostly English-speaking; if your visit is in French, use the good English handout).

• *When you've returned to earth, double back into Place de la Liberté and climb the small lane opposite the market's big doors to meet the "Boy of Sarlat"—a statue marking the best view over Place de la Liberté. Notice the cathedral's tower, with a salamander swinging happily from its spire. Turn around and find...*

Foie Gras and Beyond: Tourist-pleasing stores like **La Boutique du Badaud** line the streets of Sarlat and are filled with the finest local products. This quiet shop sells it all, from truffles to foie gras to walnut wine to truffle liqueur. They also offer tastings *(dégustations)* of local liquors. To better understand what you're looking at, read the foie gras sidebar on page 476.

• *Turn left (behind the boy statue) and trickle like medieval rainwater down the ramp into an inviting square. Here you'll find a little gaggle of geese.*

Place des Oies: Feathers fly when geese are traded on this "Square of the Geese" on market days (Nov-March). The birds have been serious business here since the Middle Ages. Trophy homes surround this cute little square on all sides. Check out the wealthy merchant's home to the right as you enter the square—the **Manoir de Gisson**—with a tower built big enough to match his ego. The owner was the town counsel, a position that arose as cities like Sarlat outgrew the Middle Ages. Town counsels replaced priests in resolving civil conflicts and performing other civic duties. Touring the interior of the manor shows you how the wealthy lived in Sarlat (study the big poster next to the entry). It's carefully decorated with authentic 16th- to 18th-century furniture, and offers a peek at the inside of its impressive *lauzes* roof (€7, daily April-Sept 10:00-19:00, closes earlier off-season, English handout, tel. 05 53 28 70 55, www.manoirdegisson.com).

• *Walk to the right along Rue des Consuls. Just before Le Mirandol restaurant, turn right toward a...*

Fourteenth-Century Vault and Fountain: For generations, this was the town's only source of water, protected by the Virgin Mary (find her at the end of the fountain). Opposite the restaurant and fountain, find the wooden doorway (open late June-Aug only) that houses a massive Renaissance stairway. These showy stairways, which replaced more space-efficient spiral ones, required a big house and a bigger income. Impressive.

• *Follow the curve along Rue des Consuls, and enter the straight-as-an-arrow...*

Rue de la République: This "modern" thoroughfare, known as *La Traverse* to locals, dates from the mid-1800s, when blasting big roads through medieval cities was standard operating procedure. It wasn't until 1963 that Sarlat's other streets would become off-limits to cars, thanks to France's forward-thinking minister of culture, André Malraux. The law that bears his name has served to preserve and restore important monuments and neighborhoods throughout France. Eager to protect the country's architectural heritage, private investors, cities, and regions worked together to create traffic-free zones, rebuild crumbling buildings, and make sure that no cables or ugly wiring marred the ambience of towns like this. Without the Malraux Law, Sarlat might well have more "efficient" roads like Rue de la République slicing through its once-charming old town center.

Your tour is over, but make sure you take time for a poetic ramble through the town's quiet side—or, better yet, stroll any of Sarlat's lanes after dark. This is the only town in France illuminated by gas lamps, which cause the warm limestone to glow, turning the romance of Sarlat up even higher. Now may also be a good time to find a café and raise a toast to Monsieur Malraux.

Sleeping in Sarlat-la-Canéda

Even with summer crowds, Sarlat-la-Canéda is the train traveler's best home base. Note that in July and August, some hotels require half-pension, and hotels in downtown Sarlat book up first. Parking can be a headache—drivers will find rooms and parking more easily just outside the town (see "Near Sarlat-la-Canéda" on page 460) or in the nearby villages and destinations described later, under "The Best of the Dordogne River Valley" (most are a 15-minute drive away).

HOTELS IN THE TOWN CENTER

$$$ Hôtel Plaza Madeleine**** is a central and upscale value with formal service, a handsome pub/wine-bar, and 39 very sharp rooms with every comfort. You'll find a pool out back, a sauna, and a Jacuzzi—all free for guests (standard Db-€130-155, most at €130, bigger Db-€170-215; extra person-€25, several connecting rooms for families, great €14 breakfast buffet, air-con, elevator, guest computer, Wi-Fi, garage parking-€12/day, at north end of ring road at 1 Place de la Petite Rigaudie, tel. 05 53 59 10 41, www.plaza-madeleine.com, contact@plaza-madeleine.com).

DORDOGNE

$$ La Villa des Consuls*,** a cross between a B&B and a hotel, occupies a 17th-century home buried on Sarlat's quiet side with 13 lovely, spacious rooms with microwave ovens and refrigerators; most also have a kitchen and a living room. The rooms surround a small courtyard and come with wood floors, private decks, and high ceilings. English-fluent owner David prices his rooms

Sleep Code

Abbreviations **(€1 = about $1.40, country code: 33)**
S = Single, **D** = Double/Twin, **T** = Triple, **Q** = Quad, **b** = bathroom, **s** = shower only, * = French hotel rating (0-5 stars)

Price Rankings

$$$ Higher Priced—Most rooms €120 or more
$$ Moderately Priced—Most rooms between €70-120
$ Lower Priced—Most rooms €70 or less

Unless otherwise noted, credit cards are accepted, English is spoken, and Wi-Fi is generally free. Prices change; verify current rates online or by email. For the best prices, always book directly with the hotel.

to encourage longer stays; these rates are for stays of two to six nights (Db-€98-115, big Db/Tb/Qb-€142-175, 10 percent more for 1-night stays, less for 7 or more days, air-con, guest computer, Wi-Fi, free use of washers and dryers, garage parking-€9/day, train station pickup-€7, 3 Rue Jean-Jacques Rousseau, tel. 05 53 31 90 05, www.villaconsuls.fr, villadesconsuls@yahoo.fr).

$$ Hôtel Montaigne***, a good value located a block south of the pedestrian zone, is run by the smiling Martinats (Mama, Papa, and daughter). The rooms are simple, spotless, comfortable, and air-conditioned. Of the hotels I list, this is the one nearest to the train station (Db-€69-90, extra person-€15, two-room family suites-€110-125, good breakfast buffet-€10, air-con, elevator, guest computer, Wi-Fi, easy parking nearby, Place Pasteur, tel. 05 53 31 93 88, www.hotelmontaigne.fr, contact@hotelmontaigne.fr).

$ Hôtel de la Mairie's** quirky rooms are located above its namesake café, smack dab on the main square (ideal for market days). The rooms provide basic comfort at fair prices, and most have beamed ceilings; rooms #3 and #6 have the best views. The management is *très* laissez faire (Db-€70, Tb-€75-90, Qb-€100, reception in café, Wi-Fi, Place de la Liberté, tel. 05 53 59 05 71, www.hotel-mairie-sarlat.com, hoteldelamairie@orange.fr).

$ Hôtel la Couleuvrine** offers simple rooms with character at good rates in a historic building with a handy location—across from the launderette and with easy parking (for Sarlat). Families enjoy *les chambres familles* (several in the tower). Some rooms have tight bathrooms, some could use new carpets, and a few have private terraces (Db-€50-85, Db suite-€95, family rooms-€95-115, elevator, Wi-Fi, on ring road at 1 Place de la Bouquerie, tel. 05 53

59 27 80, www.la-couleuvrine.com, contact@la-couleuvrine.com). Half-pension is encouraged during busy periods and in the summer—figure €70 per person for room, breakfast, and a good dinner in the classy restaurant.

HOTELS NORTH OF TOWN

The following hotels are a 10-minute walk north of the old town on Avenue de Selves. All have easy parking. For locations, see map on next page.

$$$ Hôtel de Selves**** feels *très* American, with a big lobby, professional staff, and 40 (pricey for Sarlat) rooms in a modern shell with a year-round swimming pool (Db-€120-165, Db with balcony-€180-200, extra person-€35, all rooms non-smoking, big breakfast-€14, 10 percent discount on room and breakfast for Rick Steves readers, air-con, elevator, guest computer, Wi-Fi, outside parking-€8/day, garage parking-€13/day, 93 Avenue de Selves, tel. 05 53 31 50 00, www.selves-sarlat.com, hotel@selves-sarlat.com).

$$ Hôtel de Compostelle*** features a cheery, spacious lobby and well-maintained, generously sized, and air-conditioned rooms, including several good family rooms (Db-€88-108, Tb-€150, family room-€170 for 4-6 people, elevator is one floor up, Wi-Fi, sweet backyard terrace, parking-€7/day, 64 Avenue de Selves, tel. 05 53 59 08 53, www.hotel-compostelle-sarlat.com, info@hotel-compostelle-sarlat.com).

$$ Hôtel le Madrigal,** one block past Hôtel de Compostelle, is a charming nine-room hotel with good two-star rooms and rates, all with queen-size beds, air-conditioning, and smallish bathrooms. Check in at the Hôtel de Compostelle a few doors down (Db-€70, Tb-€90, Qb-€100, Wi-Fi, fitness room, parking-€7, 50 Avenue de Selves, tel. 05 53 59 21 98, www.hotel-madrigal-sarlat.com, info@hotel-madrigal-sarlat.com).

CHAMBRES D'HOTES

These *chambres d'hôtes* are central and compare well with the hotels listed earlier.

$$ La Lanterne, named for the monument it faces, occupies a 500-year-old building that could not be more central nor more welcoming. British Terri Bowen (and dogs Frodo and Fibi) deliver cozy public spaces and thoughtfully appointed, quiet rooms that surround a sweet little courtyard (Db-€85-95, Tb studio-€105, breakfast-€9, cash or PayPal only, Wi-Fi, 9 bis Rue Montaigne, tel. 05 53 59 17 79, mobile 06 33 38 89 11, www.sarlat.biz, info@sarlat.biz).

$$ Les Cordeliers, owned by gentle Brits Chris and Amanda Johnson, offers four-star comfort at two-star prices. Most of the seven cushy rooms are huge; all are air-conditioned and well-

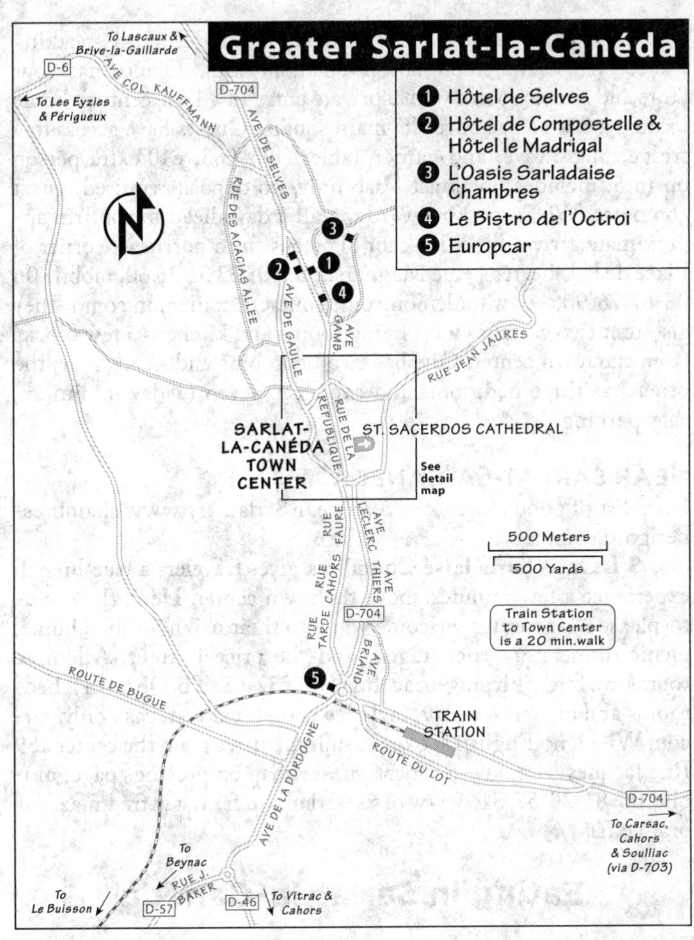

furnished; and a small kitchen is at your disposal with serve-yourself snacks and drinks (Db-€98, extra bed-€20, big breakfast with fresh fruit and eggs-€7, closed Nov-Feb, Wi-Fi, 51 Rue des Cordeliers, tel. 06 76 78 04 01, www.hotelsarlat.com, info@hotelsarlat.com).

$ Les Chambres du Glacier, where kind Monsieur Da Costa and son Bruno offer four cavernous and surprisingly classy rooms above an outdoor café, is in the thick of Sarlat's pedestrian zone (perfect for market days). Rooms come with sky-high ceilings, big and well-insulated windows over Sarlat's world, polished wood floors, and bathrooms you can get lost in (Db-€85, Tb-€110, Qb-€135, includes breakfast, Wi-Fi, Place de la Liberté, tel. 05 53 29 99 99, www.chambres-du-glacier-sarlat.com, carlos.da.costa.24@wanadoo.fr).

$ La Maison du Notaire Royal, run by English-speaking Pierre-Henri Toulemon and French-speaking Diane, has four large and simple rooms with a private entry in a 17th-century home located a few steps above the main square. Guests have access to a fridge, microwave, and garden tables (Db-€63, €10/extra person up to 5, includes breakfast, cash only, no deposit required, guest computer, Wi-Fi, parking-€1/day, call a day ahead to confirm approximate arrival time, look for big steps from northeast corner of Place de la Liberté, 4 Rue Magnanat, tel. 05 53 31 26 60, mobile 06 08 67 76 90, www.toulemon.com, contact@toulemon.com). They also rent two cottages with living rooms and kitchens a few blocks from the town center. One has two bedrooms and sleeps four; the other has three bedrooms and can sleep seven (3-day minimum, easy parking).

NEAR SARLAT-LA-CANEDA

For a list of good *chambres d'hôtes* near Sarlat, try www.chambres-perigord.com.

$ L'Oasis Sarladaise Chambres gives travelers a true French experience a few minutes above the town center. Here, the eager-to-please Mazzocatos welcome you into their neighborhood home, picnic dinners are encouraged, and the price is right. All three rooms are bird-chirping-peaceful (Db-€52-65, Tb/Qb with 2 bedrooms and big terrace-€99, includes good breakfast, cash only, air-con, Wi-Fi, no English spoken, 5-minute drive from the center at 9 Rue Jacques Monod—for location, see map on previous page; mobile 06 81 30 57 81, www.oasis-sarladaise.fr, www.fred.mazzo@orange.fr).

Eating in Sarlat-la-Canéda

Sarlat is stuffed with restaurants that cater to tourists, but you can still dine well and cheaply. The following places have been reliable; the last is the most formal. If you have a car, consider driving to Beynac (see page 473) or La Roque-Gageac (page 469) for a riverfront dining experience. Wherever you dine, sample a glass of sweet Monbazillac wine with your foie gras.

L'Instant de Delice, with tables lining a cobbled lane, is a popular place for budget cuisine, with reasonably priced salads, *plats du jour,* and €18-32 *menus* (daily, a block off Rue de la République at 5 Rue des Consuls, tel. 05 53 59 28 67).

Chez le Gaulois is a change from the traditional places that line Sarlat's lanes. Pyrenees-raised Olivier and his wife Nora serve a hearty mountain cuisine featuring fondue, raclette, *tartiflette* (roasted potatoes mixed with ham and cheese—comes with a good salad for €14), and thinly sliced ham (Olivier spends all evening slicing away). The *cassolette des légumes* (a ratatouille-like dish) is also tasty (€11). They have a few sidewalk tables, but the fun is inside and the service is English-fluent. The ceiling is cluttered with ham hocks, and the soundtrack is jazz (good salads, try *la tarte au figues* (fig tart) for dessert, daily April-Oct, Nov-March closed Sun-Mon, near the TI at 1 Rue Tourny, tel. 05 53 59 50 64).

Le Bistro de l'Octroi, a few blocks north of the old town, has to provide top cuisine and competitive prices to draw locals—and it does. Quality bistro fare (mostly meat dishes) is served on a generous terrace and within the pleasant interior (€20-30 three-course *menus* offering many options; order two starters if you prefer, daily, 111 Avenue des Selves—for location see map on page 459, tel. 05 53 30 83 40).

L'Adresse, a sweet little bistro, serves regional specialties with a creative twist—ideal for foodies. It gets rave reviews from locals so try to book ahead, particularly if you want a table on the front or back terrace (€21-33 *menus* with good choices, closed Sun, 8 Place d la Petite Rigaudie, tel. 05 53 30 56 19).

Le Bistrot has marvelous outside seating across from the cathedral, plus a cozy interior. The traditional cuisine is served at affordable prices (€18-28 *menus*, closed Sun-Mon, 14 Place du Peyrou, tel. 05 53 28 28 40).

Brasserie le Glacier offers main-square views from its outdoor tables and good café fare at reasonable prices nonstop from 11:00-22:00. Come here for good service (Filomena has the big smile); a big salad for €11 (the *salade paysanne*—peasant salad—works for me), pizza (€10), or *plat* (€13); and a view of the lights warming the town buildings (daily, Place de la Liberté, tel. 05 53 29 99 99, also rents rooms—see "Sleeping in Sarlat-la-Canéda," earlier).

Pizzeria Romane is a cheap, spacious, and family-friendly eatery where you can watch your pizza cook (€10 pizza, lots of salads, daily July-Aug, otherwise closed Sun-Mon, on the quiet side of Sarlat at 3 Côte de Toulouse, tel. 05 53 59 23 88).

At **Lemoine,** a classy pastry shop with a line of sidewalk tables, you can enjoy rich chocolate cake (chocolate decadence) with a hot drink, or pick from a selection of savory treats at lunchtime (daily, 13 Rue de la République, tel. 05 53 59 20 77).

Le Présidial is a lovely place for a refined meal in a historic mansion. The setting is exceptional—you're greeted with beautiful gardens (where you can dine in good weather), and the interior comes with high ceilings, stone walls, rich wood floors, and formal service (€20-42 *menus,* closed Sun, Rue Landry, tel. 05 53 28 92 47).

Sarlat-la-Canéda Connections

Sarlat's TI has train schedules. Souillac and Périgueux are the train hubs for points within the greater region. For all the following destinations, you can go west, on the Libourne/Bordeaux line (transferring in either city, depending on your connection), or east, by SNCF bus to Souillac (covered by rail pass, bus leaves from Sarlat train station). I've listed the fastest path in each case. Sarlat train info: tel. 05 53 59 00 21.

From Sarlat-la-Canéda **by Train to: Les Eyzies-de-Tayac** (3/day, 1-3 hours, transfer in Le Buisson), **Paris** (4/day, allow 6 hours: 3/day with change in Libourne or Bordeaux-St-Jean, then TGV; and 1/day by bus to Souillac, then train with possible change in Brive-la-Gaillarde), **Amboise** (3/day, 5-7 hours, via Libourne, then TGV to Tours' St-Pierre-des-Corps, then local train to Amboise), **Bourges** (4/day, 6-7 hours, 2-4 changes), **Limoges/Oradour-sur-Glane** (slow and difficult trip with lots of changes, 5/day, 3-4 hours: 3/day by bus to Souillac and train to Limoges, then 15-minute walk to catch bus to Oradour-sur-Glane—and 2/day to Limoges with change in Le Buisson and Périgueux), **Cahors** (5/day, 3 hours, bus to Souillac or Siorac, then train to Cahors), **Albi** (6/day, 6 hours with 2-3 changes, some require bus from Sarlat to Souillac), **Carcassonne** (5/day, 5.5-7 hours, 1-3 changes, some require bus from Sarlat to Souillac), **St-Emilion** (3-4/day, 2 hours, no transfer, or 3/day to nearby Libourne, then bus or taxi to St-Emilion).

To Beynac, La Roque-Gageac, Castelnaud, and Domme: These are accessible only by taxi or bike (best rented in Sarlat). See Sarlat's "Helpful Hints" on page 450 for specifics.

The Best of the Dordogne River Valley

DORDOGNE

The most striking stretch of the Dordogne lies between Carsac and Beynac. Traveling by canoe is the best way to savor the highlights of the Dordogne River Valley, though several scenic sights lie off the river and require a car or bike. Following my "Dordogne Scenic Loop" directions (next page), you can easily link Sarlat-la-Canéda with La Roque-Gageac, Beynac and its château, and Castelnaud before returning to Sarlat.

PLANNING YOUR TIME

Drivers should allow a minimum of a half-day to sample the river valley (a full day if they toss in a cave visit). Drive slowly to savor the scenery and to stay out of trouble (these are narrow, cliff-hanging roads). The area is picnic-perfect, but buy your supplies before leaving Sarlat; pickings are slim in the villages (though view cafés are in full supply). Vitrac (near Sarlat) is the best place to park for a canoe ride down the river. La Roque-Gageac, Beynac, and Domme have good restaurants. There are a few good places to witness the *gavage* (feeding of the geese and ducks to make foie gras) between Beynac and Sarlat—their dinnertime is generally about 18:00.

You'll pay €3 for all-day parking in riverfront villages (display your parking chit on your dashboard; cars are checked).

I've given distances in kilometers for drivers to match up with your rental car's odometer.

Self-Guided Tours Along the Dordogne

▲▲DORDOGNE SCENIC LOOP

Following these directions, beginning and ending in Sarlat-la-Canéda, you can see this area by car or bike (27 hilly miles). Cyclists can cut seven miles off this distance and still see most of the highlights by following D-704 from Sarlat toward Cahors, then taking the Montfort turn off (well-signed after the big Leclerc grocery store) and tracking signs to Montfort—see the map on page 466. Once in Montfort, follow the river downstream to La Roque-Gageac.

Key villages along this route are described in detail later in this chapter, under "Dordogne Towns and Sights."

The Tour Begins: From Sarlat, follow signs on D-704 toward *Cahors.* Not long after leaving Sarlat, you'll pass the Rougie foie gras outlet store, then the limestone quarry that gives the houses in this area their lemony color.

In about five minutes, be on the lookout for the little signposted turn off on the right to the *Eglise de Carsac* (Church of Carsac). Set peacefully among cornfields, with its WWI monument, bonsai-like plane trees, and simple, bulky Romanesque exterior, the **Eglise de Carsac** church is part of a vivid rural French scene. Take a break here and enter the church (usually open, find English handout). The stone capitals behind the altar are exquisitely medieval. Back outside, the small cornfields nearby are busy growing food for ducks and geese—locals are appalled that humans would eat the stuff.

From here, continue on, following signs to *Montfort*. About a kilometer west of Carsac, pull over to enjoy the scenic viewpoint (overlooking a bend in the river known as Cingle de Montfort). Across the Dordogne River, fields of walnut trees stretch to distant castles, and the nearby hills are covered in oak trees. This region of the Périgord is nicknamed "black Périgord" for its thick blanket of oaks, which stay leafy throughout the winter. The fairy-tale castle you see is **Montfort,** which was once the medieval home of Simon de Montfort, who led the Cathar Crusades in the early 13th century. Today it's considered mysterious by locals. (The hometown rumor is that the castle is now the home of a brother of the emir of Kuwait.) A plaque on the rock near where you parked honors those who fought the Nazi occupiers in this area in 1943.

Continue on, passing under Montfort's castle (which you can't tour; its cute little village has a few cafés). If you're combining a canoe trip with this drive, cross the river following signs to *Domme,* and find my recommended canoe rental on the right side (see "Dordogne Canoe Trip," next). The touristy *bastide* (fortified village) of **Domme** is well worth a side-trip from Vitrac or La Roque-Gageac for its sensational views (best early in the day), though the town itself is skippable. Our driving route continues to the more important riverfront villages of **La Roque-Gageac,** then on to **Castelnaud,** and finally to **Beynac** (all described later in this chapter). From Beynac, it's a quick run back to Sarlat.

▲▲▲DORDOGNE CANOE TRIP

For a refreshing break from the car or train, explore the riverside castles and villages of the Dordogne by canoe.

Renting a Canoe (or Kayak): You can rent plastic boats—which are hard, light, and indestructible—from many outfits in this area. Whether a one-person kayak or a two-person canoe, they're stable enough for beginners. Many rental places will pick you up at an agreed-upon spot (even in Sarlat, provided that your group is big enough, and they aren't too busy). All companies let you put in anytime between 9:30 and 16:00 (start no later than 15:00 to allow time to linger when the mood strikes; they'll pick you up at about 18:00). They all charge about the same and typically accept cash only (€14-18/person for two-person canoes, €17-24 for one-person kayaks). You'll get a life vest and, for a few extra euros, a watertight bucket in which to store your belongings. (The bucket is bigger than you'd need for just a camera, watch, wallet, and cell phone, so bring a resealable plastic

baggie or something similar for dry storage in the canoe.) You must have shoes that stay on your feet; travelers wearing flip-flops will be invited to purchase more appropriate footwear (sold at most boat launches for around €9).

The trip is fun even in light rain (if you don't mind getting wet)—but heavy rains can make the current too fast to handle, so be sure to check on river levels. If you don't see many other canoes in the river, the river is probably too high—ask before you rent.

Beach your boat wherever it works to take a break—it's light enough that you can drag it up high and dry to go explore. (The canoes aren't worth stealing, as they're cheap and clearly color-coded for their parent company.) It's OK if you're a complete novice—the only whitewater you'll encounter will be the rare wake of passing tour boats...and your travel partner frothing at the views.

Of the region's many canoe companies, only **Copeyre Canoë** (also called **Périgord-Aventure et Loisirs**) has a pullout arrangement in Beynac (to get to their Vitrac put-in base, from the main roundabout in the town of Vitrac, cross the Dordogne, and turn right). Readers of this book get a 10 percent discount in 2015, and they'll even pick you up in Sarlat for free if you arrange it in advance (this allows non-drivers a chance to explore the riverfront villages for the price of a canoe trip—tip the driver a few euros for this helpful service; tel. 05 53 28 23 82, mobile 06 83 27 30 06, www.canoe-copeyre.com). Allow time to explore Beynac after your river paddle and before the return shuttle trip. Copeyre Canoë also arranges a longer 14-mile trip from Carsac to Beynac, adding the gorgeous Montfort loop *(Cingle de Montfort)*. Ask about their canoe-hike-bike option that starts with the canoe trip to Beynac, continues with a walk along a riverside trail to Castlenaud, and ends with a bike ride back to your starting point in Vitrac (€30).

The Nine-Mile Paddle from Vitrac to Beynac: This is the most interesting, scenic, and handy trip if you're based in or near Sarlat. Vitrac, on the river close to Sarlat, is a good starting point. And, with its mighty castle and pleasant hotels and restaurants, Beynac delivers the perfect finale to your journey. Allow 2 hours for this paddle at a relaxed pace in spring and fall, and up to 2.5 hours in summer when the river is usually at its lowest flow.

Here's a rundown of the two-hour Vitrac-Beynac adventure: Leave **Vitrac,** paddling at an easy pace through lush, forested land. The fortified hill town of Domme will be dead ahead. Pass through Heron Gulch, and after about an hour you'll come to **La Roque-Gageac** (one of two easy and worthwhile stops before Beynac).

Paddle past La Roque-Gageac's wooden docks (with the tour boats) to the stone ramp leading up to the town. Do a 180-degree turn and beach thyself, dragging the boat high and dry. From there you're in La Roque-Gageac's tiny town center (described on page

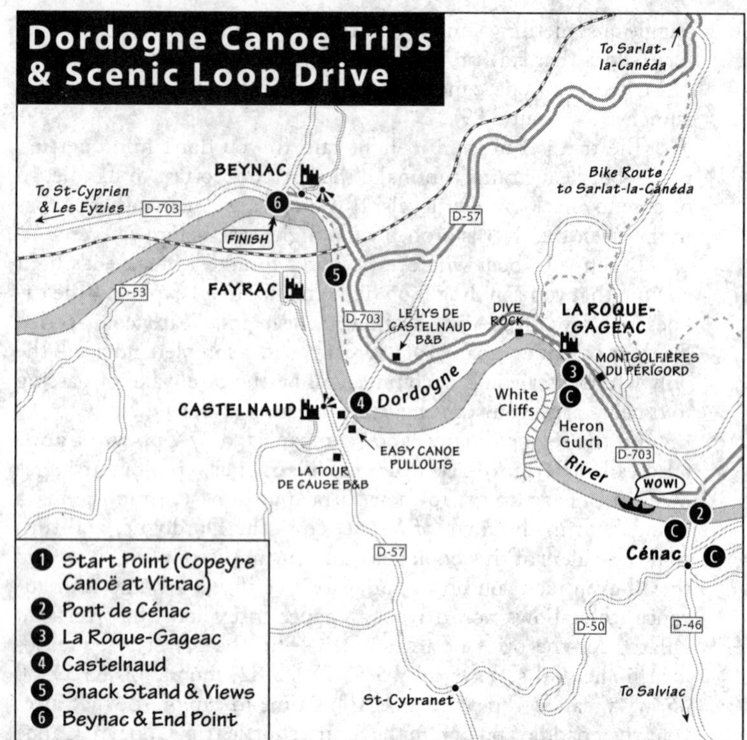

469), with a TI and plenty of cafés, snacks, and ice-cream options. Enjoy the town before heading back to your canoe and into the water.

When leaving La Roque-Gageac, float backward to enjoy the village view. About 15 minutes farther downstream, you'll approach views of the feudal village and castle of **Castelnaud.** Look for the castle's huge model of medieval catapults silhouetted menacingly against the sky (it's a steep but worthwhile climb to tour this castle—see page 472). About 15 minutes after you first spot the castle, you'll find two grassy pullouts flanking the bridge below the castle, and the bridge arches make terrific frames for castle views. Just past the grass there's a small market and charcuterie with all you need for a picnic. La Plage Café serves good café fare with views (near where you pull out).

Another 15 minutes downstream brings views of **Château de Fayrac** on your left. The lords of Castelnaud built this to spy on Beynac during the Hundred Years' War (1336-1453). It's another 15 minutes to your last stop: **Beynac** (described on page 473). The awesome Beynac castle—looming high above the town—gets better and better as you approach. Slow down and enjoy the ride (sometimes there's a snack stand with the same views at the bridge

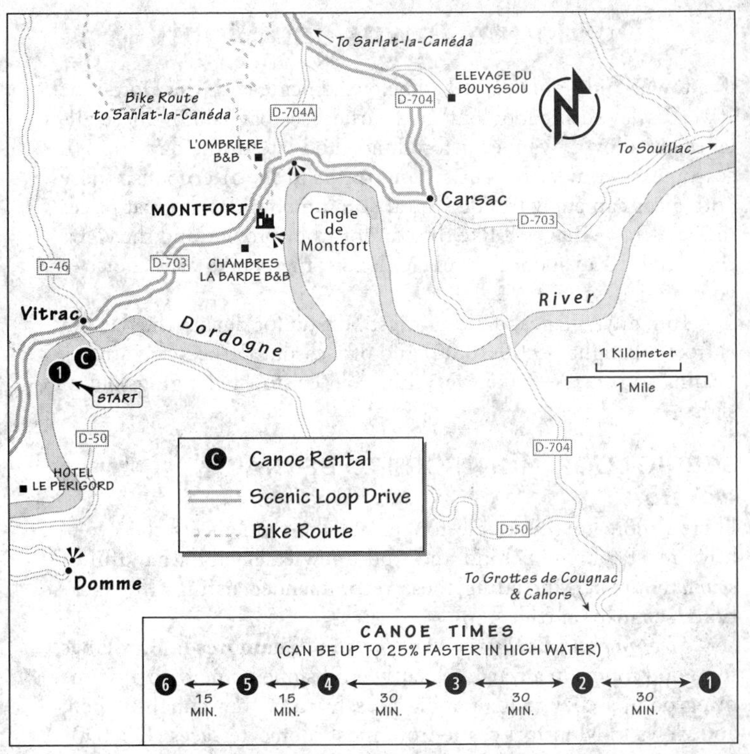

on the right). Keep to the right as you approach the Copeyre Canoë depot. You'll see the ramp just before the parking lot and wooden dock (where the tour boats generally tie up). Do another 180-degree turn, and beach yourself hard. The office is right there. Return your boat, and explore Beynac.

Other Canoe Options: All along the river you'll see canoe companies, each with stacks of plastic canoes. Depending on their location and relations with places to pull out, each one works best on a particular stretch of the river. All have essentially the same policies. Below Domme in Cénac, **Dordogne Randonnées** has canoes and kayaks for the scenic two-hour stretch to a pullout just past Beynac (to reach their office coming from Sarlat or Beynac, take the first left after crossing the bridge to Cénac, tel. 05 53 28 22 01, randodordogne@wanadoo.fr). In La Roque-Gageac, **Canoe-Dordogne** rents canoes for the worthwhile two-hour float to Château des Milandes, allowing canoers to stop in Beynac along the way (tel. 05 53 29 58 50). For a lazier no-paddle alternative, try a boat cruise on the river to Castelnaud and back, either from Beynac or La Roque-Gageac (€8-9, 50-60 minutes, both options are great for landlubbers and described in the next section).

Dordogne Towns and Sights

The towns and sights described below coincide with the Dordogne River Valley scenic loop outlined earlier (see page 463). These villages are a joy to wander before lunch and late in the day. In high season expect mobs of tourists and traffic in the afternoons. Those with a car can enjoy tranquil rural accommodations at great prices in these cozy villages. I like the comfort they provide and the views they offer. Read about the villages below, then make your choice—you can't go wrong.

In many villages, parking must be paid for during the day but is free overnight (19:00-10:00) and off-season. Parked cars are appealing to thieves—take everything out or stow belongings out of sight.

SCENIC LOOP: MONTFORT TO BEYNAC

Montfort

There's more to this castle-topped village than meets the eye—leave most tourists behind and find a few cafés and a handful of *chambres d'hôtes,* including these recommended listings (for locations, see map on page 466).

Sleeping and Eating in Montfort: **$$ Chambres la Barde** has five good rooms in a warm, recently built stone home with a swimming pool, a cozy lounge, a big grass yard, a communal kitchen, and views to Montfort castle from most rooms' terraces (Db-€90-110, extra person-€20, 2-room suite sleeps 5, cash only, Wi-Fi, below Montfort castle—green signs guide you there, tel. 05 53 28 24 34, mobile 06 86 88 60 93, www.labardemontfort.com, labardemontfort@gmail.com).

$$ L'Ombriere, with four elegant rooms and caring Italian hosts Andrea and Barbara, is a calm B&B overlooking a walnut grove (Db-€82-96, some rooms have air-con, Wi-Fi, on east edge of Montfort village—watch for signs, tel. 05 53 28 11 38, www.lombriere.com, info@lombriere.com).

▲▲Domme

This busy little town merits a stop for its stunning view and is ideal early in the day. Otherwise, come late, when crowds recede and the light is best. If you come for lunch or dinner, arrive early enough to savor the cliff-capping setting, and if you come on market day (Thu) expect to hoof it up from a parking lot well below (cars not allowed in old town until the market is over). On other days, follow signs up to *La Bastide de Domme,* and drive right through the narrow gate of the fortified town walls. Park at the pay lot near the view *(Panorama).* You'll find picnic-perfect benches, cafés, and a view you won't soon forget. I'd ignore the village center and escape after enjoying the view.

Sleeping and Eating in Domme: The town has many forgettable restaurants, but a few places stand out.

$$$ Hôtel de l'Esplanade delivers the valley's most sensational views from many of its comfortable and traditional bedrooms and restaurant tables. If you come for the restaurant (€40-70 *menus*), book ahead for view seating (Db-€98-140, view Db-€145-165, air-con, tel. 05 53 28 31 41, www.esplanade-perigord.com, esplanade.domme@wanadoo.fr).

Chabanoix et Châtaigne is a small bistro serving delicious Dordogne fare blended with international flavors. Enjoy the sunset from Domme's viewpoint, then come here for dinner, but book a table ahead—local foodies are all over this place (daily for lunch and dinner, July-Aug closed Sat; from the viewpoint, walk past the church several blocks down Grand Rue to 3 Rue Geoffroy de Vivans; tel. 05 53 31 07 11).

Belvédère Café owns a privileged position at the viewpoint and serves café fare at good prices with million-dollar views from its outside tables (daily for lunch and dinner, closed Oct-March, at *Le Panorama,* tel. 05 53 31 12 01)

▲▲▲La Roque-Gageac

Whether you're joyriding, paddling the Dordogne or taking a hot-air balloon ride, La Roque-Gageac (lah rohk-gah-zhahk) is an essential stop—and a strong contender on all the "cutest towns in France" lists. Called by most simply "La Roque" ("The Rock"), it looks sculpted out of the rock between the river and the cliffs. It also makes a fine base for touring the region.

Orientation: At the upstream end of town, you'll find plenty of parking and an ATM; the **TI** (Easter-Sept daily 10:00-12:00 & 14:00-17:00, open later in summer, closed off-season, tel. 05 53 29 17 01); a WC; swings and slides for kids; canoe rental; and *pétanque (boules)* courts, which are lively on summer evenings (17:00-21:00). A small market brightens La Roque-Gageac on Friday mornings in summer. Though busy with day-trippers, the town is tranquil at night.

La Roque-Gageac Town

Stand along the river near the TI and survey La Roque-Gageac: It's a one-street town stretching along the river. The highest stone

work (on the far right) was home to the town's earliest inhabitants in the 10th century. High above (about center), 12th-century cave dwellers built a settlement during the era of Norman (Viking) river raids. Long after the Vikings were tamed, French soldiers used this lofty perch as a barracks while fighting against England in the Hundred Years' War.

Now locate the exotic foliage around the church on the right. Tropical gardens (bamboo, bananas, lemons, cactus, and so on) are a village forte, because limestone absorbs heat.

Those wooden boats on the river are modeled after boats called *gabarres,* originally built here to take prized oak barrels filled with local wine down to Bordeaux. Unable to return against the river current, those boats were routinely taken apart for their lumber. Today, tourists, rather than barrels, fill the boats on river cruises (described later). If you're experiencing a movie-based déjà vu, it's because these actual boats (dolled up, of course) were used by Johnny Depp, who delighted viewers and Juliette Binoche alike in the movie *Chocolat*.

La Roque-Gageac frequently endures winter floods that would leave you (standing where you are now) underwater. When there's a big rain in central France, La Roque-Gageac floods two days later. The first floors of all the riverfront buildings are vacated off-season. The new riverfront wall, finished in 2014, was pushed out into the river, adding 13 feet of width to the street. Notice the openings at sidewalk level allowing water to flow through in heavy rains. Walk on the main drag to get a closer look. A house about five buildings downriver from Hôtel la Belle Etoile shows various high-water marks (*inondation* means "flood"). Looking farther downstream, notice the fanciful castle built in the 19th century by a British aristocrat (whose family still nurtures Joan of Arc dreams in its turrets). The old building just beyond that (downstream end of town) actually is historic—it's the quarantine house, where lepers and out-of-town visitors who dropped by in times of plague would be kept (after their boats were burned).

Climb into the town by strolling up the cobbled lane to the right of Hôtel la Belle Etoile. Where the stepped path ends, veer right to find the exotic plants and viewpoint (in front of the simple church). From here you can make out Château de Castlenaud downriver. A left turn at the end of the stepped path takes you to more views and the privately owned Fort Troglodytique (closed to the public). For a terrific medieval fort experience, visit the prehistoric La Roque St-Christophe (described on page 495).

Boat Tours: Tour boats make one-hour cruises from La Roque-Gageac to Castelnaud and back (€9, 2/hour, April-Nov daily, tel. 05 53 29 40 44).

Hot-Air Balloon Rides: Remember that **Montgolfières du Périgord,** located in La Roque-Gageac, offers a range of flights with well-qualified pilots (one-hour flight-€200/person, www.montgolfiere-du-perigord.com, tel. 05 53 28 18 58).

Sleeping and Eating in and near La Roque-Gageac: Along with Beynac, this is one of the region's most beautiful villages. Park in the lot at the eastern end of town if you're staying in La Roque-Gageac, and take everything of value out of your car.

$$$ Manoir de la Malatrie is a wonderful splurge with five country-classy rooms and one family-ideal apartment with oak-meets-leather public areas, all surrounding a big, heated pool and terraced gardens (begging for a picnic). Your gentle hostess Ouaffa manages her place with elegance (Db-€140-160, several rooms with air-con, large apartment, barely downstream from the village, tel. 06 18 61 61 18, www.chambresdhotes-lamalartrie.com, lamalatire@orange.fr).

$$ Hôtel la Belle Etoile,** a well-managed hotel-restaurant in the center of La Roque-Gageac, is a terrific value. Hostess Danielle and chef Régis (ray-geez) offer good rooms, most overlooking the river, a nice terrace, and a fine restaurant (non-riverview Db-€56, riverview Db-€67 or €77, gorgeous suite-€120-150, air-con, free parking, closed Dec-March, tel. 05 53 29 51 44, www.belleetoile.fr, hotel.belle-etoile@wanadoo.fr). Régis is third generation of his family to be chef here and he takes his job seriously. Come for a memorable dinner of classic French cuisine with modern accents in a romantic setting. The *oeufs cocottes* are, well, really good (*menus* from €31, closed for lunch Wed and all day Mon; book a few days ahead).

$$ Hôtel le Périgord,** a modern hotel across the river from the hill town of Domme, offers good rooms at fair rates with nice gardens, a view pool, tennis courts, a game room, and a restaurant (Db-€65-75, Db with balcony and view-€85, Tb-€104, dinner *menus* from €25, free parking, Port de Domme, tel. 05 53 28 36 55, www.hotelleperigord.eu, bienvenue@hotelleperigord.eu).

$$ L'Auberge des Platanes,** across from La Roque-Gageac's TI and parking lot, rents 13 rooms above a sprawling café—guests take a backseat to café clients. Half the rooms are basic and traditional; the other half are modern and pricier (small Db-€65, standard Db-€85, Tb-€75-119, a few rooms have air-con, tel. 05 53 29 51 58, www.aubergedesplatanes.com, contact@aubergedesplatanes.com).

▲▲Château de Castelnaud

This castle may look a tad less mighty than Château de Beynac (down the river), but it packs a powerful medieval punch. The well-done English handout escorts you room by room through the castle-museum.

Cost and Hours: €8.60, €7.40 before 13:00 in summer; open daily July-Aug 9:00-20:00, April-June and Sept 10:00-19:00, Oct and Feb-March 10:00-18:00, Nov-Jan 14:00-17:00, last entry one hour before closing; daily demonstrations of medieval warfare and guided visits in English mid-July-Aug, call for exact times (tel. 05 53 31 30 00, www.castelnaud.com.)

Getting There: From the river, it's a steep 25-minute hike through the village to the castle. Drivers must park in the €3 lot (5-minute walk uphill from there). You can stop at Castelnaud on your canoe trip, or hike an hour from Beynac along a riverside path (though it's tricky to follow in parts—it hugs the river as it passes through campgrounds and farms—determined walkers do fine).

Visiting the Castle: After passing the ticket booth, read your essential handout and follow the *suite de la visite* signs. Start by climbing through the tower. Every room has a story to tell, and many have displays of costumed mannequins, weaponry (including the biggest and most artistic crossbows I've ever seen), and artifacts from the Hundred Years' War. Other rooms show informative videos (with English subtitles)—don't miss the catapult video where you'll learn that the big ones could fire only two shots per hour and required up to 250 men to manage. Kids eat it up, in part thanks to the children's guide with fun puzzles. The upper courtyard has a 150-foot-deep well (drop a pebble). The rampart views are as unbeatable as the four siege machines are formidable. A few cafés and fun medieval shops await at the foot of the castle.

Sleeping near Castelnaud: This village, ideally situated between La Roque-Gageac and Beynac, has two excellent B&B choices nearby (see map on page 466).

$$ La Tour de Cause is where California refugees Albert and Caitlin have found their heaven, amid their renovated farmhouse with five top-quality rooms, a big pool, and, best of all, a *pétanque* court (Sb-€75, Db-€93, includes breakfast, cash only, 2-night minimum, en-suite bathrooms—some with immense walk-in showers, closed Nov-April, guest computer, Wi-Fi, tel. 05 53 30 30 51, US tel. Nov-March 707/527-5051, www.latourdecause.com, info@latourdecause.com). From the Dordogne River, cross the bridge to Castelnaud, follow signs toward *Daglan,* then make a hard right turn in the hamlet of Pont de Cause and park near their gate.

$ Le Lys de Castelnaud is run by French medieval enthusiasts and travel fanatics Nathalys and Dominique. Nathalys is a Joan of Arc fanatic who adores her home's namesake castle and loves helping travelers. Public areas are steeped in the Middle Ages, with knights in armor, tapestries, and more. The four lovely rooms are a great value (three have Castelnaud views), and there's a well-designed one-bedroom apartment below with a kitchen (Db-€68, Tb/Qb-€90-110, Db apartment-€90, cash only, Wi-Fi, tel. 05 53 28 20 27, mobile 06 09 57 21 97, www.chambres-dordogne.com, contact@chambres-dordogne.com). It's well-signed at the foot of the road that leads across the river to Castelnaud.

▲▲▲Beynac

Four miles downstream from La Roque-Gageac, Beynac (bay-nak) is the other must-see Dordogne village. It's also home to one of the most imposing castles in France.

This well-preserved medieval village winds like a sepia-tone film set, from the castle above to the river below (easy parking at the top avoids the steep climb). The stone village—with cobbled lanes that retain their Occitan (old French) names—is just plain pretty, best late in the afternoon and downright dreamy after dark. For the best light, tour the castle late, or at least walk out to the sensational viewpoint, then have a dinner at the recommended Taverne des Remparts or La Petite Tonelle (both described later).

Orientation: The **TI** is near the river, across from Hôtel du Château (daily 10:00-13:00 & 14:00-17:30, tel. 05 53 29 43 08). Pick up the *Plan de Beynac* in English for a simple self-guided walking tour, get information on hiking and canoes, and even get change for the parking meters (€10 or lower denomination notes only). A few steps down from the TI is the post office (ATM outside). If you need a lift, call Beynac-based **Taxi Corinne** (see page 444). From June to September, there's a cute little market on Monday mornings in the riverfront parking lot. Drivers can park at pay lots located on the river, way up at the castle (follow signs to Château de Beynac), or halfway between. The same parking ticket works up at the château if you decide against the climb.

Château de Beynac: Beynac's brooding, cliff-clinging château, worth ▲▲, soars 500 feet above the Dordogne River. During the Hundred Years' War (see sidebar on page 241), the castle of Beynac housed the French, while the British set up camp across the river at Castelnaud. This sparsely furnished castle is best for its valley views, but it still manages to evoke a memorable medieval feel. (These castles never had much furniture in any case.) When buying your ticket, notice the list showing the barons of Beynac *(Beynac et Ses Barons)*—Richard the Lionhearted *(Coeur de Lion)* spent 10 years here (€8, daily May-Oct 10:00-18:00, Nov-April closes at 17:00, last entry 45 minutes before closing, tel. 05 53 29 50 40).

You're free to wander on your own, though occasional tours are available in English. Pick up the English explanations (small fee) or spring for the excellent €5 pamphlet, and don't miss the nearby viewpoint (described next). As you tour the castle, swords, spears, and crossbows keep you honest, and the two stone WCs keep kids entertained. I like the soldiers' party room best—park your sword at the door and hang your crossbow on the hooks above, s'il vous plaît. Authentic-looking wooden stockades were installed for the 1998 filming of the movie *The Messenger: The Story of Joan of Arc*.

Walks and Viewpoints: A too-busy road separates Beynac from its river, making walks along the river unappealing in the village center. Traffic-free lanes climb steeply uphill from the river to the château—the farther you get from the road, the more medieval the village feels. A riverfront trail begins across from Hôtel Bonnet at the eastern end of town and follows the river toward Castelnaud, with great views back toward Beynac and—for able route-finders—a level one-hour hike to the village of Castelnaud. Make time to walk at least a few hundred yards along this trail to enjoy the view to Beynac.

One of the Dordogne's most commanding views lies a short walk from the castle at the top of the village (easy parking). Walk outside the village at the top, passing to the right of the little cemetery, and stroll uphill until the view opens up. Castelnaud's castle hangs on the hill in the distance straight ahead; Château de Fayrac (owned by a Texan) is just right of the rail bridge; it was originally constructed by the lords of Castelnaud to keep a closer eye on the castle of Beynac. The Château de Marqueyssac, on a hill to the left, was built by the barons of Beynac to keep a closer eye on the boys at Castelnaud—touché. More than a thousand such castles were erected in the Dordogne alone during the Hundred Years' War. That's right: 1,000 castles in this area alone.

Boat Trips: Boats leave from Beynac's riverside parking lot for relaxing, 50-minute river cruises to Castelnaud and back (€9, nearly hourly, departures Easter-Oct daily 10:00-12:30 & 14:00-18:00, more frequent trips July-Aug, written English explanations, tel. 05 53 28 51 15).

Sleeping near Beynac: **$ Le Petit Versailles** does its name justice, with five immaculate rooms that Louis would have appreciated. The place has a quiet terrace and garden, and—best of all—the welcoming Fleurys, Jean-Claude and Françoise (Db-€75, 2-night minimum, 3 rooms have fine views, all have big beds, includes large English breakfast, cash only, no smoking anywhere, guest computer, Wi-Fi, laundry facilities, Route du Château, mobile 06 71 88 59 72, www.lepetitversailles.fr, info@lepetitversailles.fr). With the river on your right, take the small road—wedged between the hill and Hôtel Bonnet—for a half-mile, turn right when you see the Résidence de Versailles sign and continue 100 yards, then take a right down a steep driveway.

Eating in Beynac: Beynac has two worthwhile places to eat and a bakery with handy picnic-ready lunch items (across from the TI). Have a drink up high at the café opposite the castle entry, or down below at the (recommended) café that hides right on the river (walk down the steps across from Hôtel du Château); stay for dinner if the spirit moves you.

Taverne/Café des Remparts, Beynac's scenic eatery, faces the castle at the top of the town and serves copious salads, good omelets, and *plats.* I can't imagine leaving Beynac without relaxing at their view-perfect café for at least a drink. Sophie promises a free apéritif with this book in 2015 and usually keeps the place open to at least 20:00—plenty late for most Americans to have dinner. Call ahead to be sure they're open (daily, closed in winter, across from castle, tel. 05 53 29 57 76).

La Petite Tonnelle, cut into the rock, has a romantic interior, welcoming service and a fine terrace out front. Locals love it for its tasty cuisine served at fair prices. It's a block up from Hôtel du Château (€18-33 *menus,* on the road to the castle, tel. 05 53 29 95 18).

BEYOND THE SCENIC LOOP

Foie Gras Farms

During the evenings, many farms in this area let you witness the force-feeding of geese for the "ultimate pleasure" of foie gras. Look

Foie Gras and Force-Feeding the Geese and Ducks

Force-feeding geese and ducks has the result of quickly fattening their livers, the principal ingredient of the Dordogne specialty foie gras. The practice is as controversial as bullfighting among animal-rights activists. And though some view these birds as tortured prisoners, here's the (politically incorrect) perspective of those who produce and consume such farm-raised animals.

French enthusiasts of *la gavage* (as the force-feeding process is called) say the animals are calm, in no pain, and are designed to take in food in this manner because of their massive gullets and expandable livers (used to store lots of fat for their long migrations). Geese and ducks do not have a gag reflex, and the linings of their throats are tough (they swallow rocks to store in their gizzards for grinding the food they eat). They can eat lots of food easily, without choking. They live lives at least as comfy as the chickens, cows, and pigs that many people have no problem eating, and are slaughtered as humanely as any nonhuman can expect in this food-chain existence.

The quality of foie gras depends on a stress-free environment; the birds do best with the same human feeder and a steady flow of good corn. These mostly free-range geese and ducks live six months (most of our factory-farmed chickens in the US live less than two months, and are plumped with hormones). Their "golden weeks" are the last three or four, when they go into the

for *Gavage* signs, but beware: It's hard for the squeamish to watch (read the sidebar for a description before you visit).

Elevage du Bouyssou

This big, homey goose farm a short drive from Sarlat is run by a couple who enjoy their work. Denis Mazet (the latest in a long line of goose farmers here) spends five hours a day feeding his gaggle of geese. His wife, Nathalie—clearly in love with country life—speaks wonderful English and enthusiastically shows guests around their idyllic farm. Each evening, she leads a one-hour, kid-friendly tour. You'll meet the goslings, do a little unforced feeding, and hear how every

pen to have their livers fattened. With two or three feedings a day, their liver grows from about a quarter-pound to nearly two pounds. A goose with a fattened liver looks like he's waddling around with a full diaper under his feathers. (Signs and placards in the towns of the region show geese with this unique and, for foie-gras lovers, mouthwatering shape.) The same process is applied to ducks to get the marginally less exquisite and less expensive duck-liver foie gras.

The varieties of product you'll be tempted to buy (or order in restaurants) can be confusing. Here's a primer: first, *foie gras* means "fattened liver"; *foie gras d'oie* is from a goose, and *foie gras de canard* is from a duck (you'll also see a blend of the two). *Pâté de foie gras* is a "paste" of foie gras combined with other meats, fats, and seasonings (think of liverwurst). Most American consumers get the chance to eat foie gras only in the form of pâtés.

The *foie gras d'oie entier* (a solid chunk of pure goose liver) is the most expensive and prized version of canned foie gras, costing about €18 for 130 grams (about a tuna-can-size tin). The *bloc de foie gras d'oie* is made of chunks of pure goose liver that have been pressed together; it's more easily spreadable (figure €14 for 130 grams). The *medaillons de foie gras d'oie* must be at least 50 percent foie gras (the rest will be a pâté filler, about €8 for 130 grams). A small tin of blended duck-and-goose foie gras costs about €5. When choosing, look for a "*production locale*" label to be assured that your foie gras is indeed locally made. Note: Airport security may require you to carry these in your checked baggage, not your carry-on.

After a week in the Dordogne, I leave feeling a strong need for foie gras detox.

part of the goose (except heads and feet) is used—even feathers (for pillows). Nathalie explains why locals see force-feeding as humane (comparable to raising any other animal for human consumption) before you step into the dark barn where about a hundred geese await another dinner. The tour finishes in the little shop. They raise and slaughter a thousand geese annually, producing about 1,500 pounds of foie gras—most of which is sold directly to visitors at good prices.

DORDOGNE

Cost and Hours: Free, tours July-Aug daily at 18:30, Sept-June Mon-Sat at 18:30, groups welcome, English tour on request at any time by reservation (tel. 05 53 31 12 31, elevage.bouyssou@wanadoo.fr).

Getting There: Leave Sarlat on the Cahors-bound road (D-704), go about seven kilometers, turn left at the cement plant (where you see the *Camping Aqua-Viva* sign), and follow *Bouyssou* signs until you reach the farm (the last section winds up several curves—keep going—you'll hear the geese).

▲Château de Commarque

This mystical medieval castle ruin is ripe for hikers wanting to get away from it all. From the remote and secluded parking lot, it's a 20-minute walk down through a forest of chestnut trees to a clearing, where the mostly ruined castle appears...like a mirage. Pick up the English brochure, and you're free to scour the sight. Owner Hubert de Commarque bought the castle in 1968 and has been digging it out of the forest ever since.

Cost and Hours: €7, daily May-Sept 10:00-19:00, April and Oct 10:30-18:00, closed Nov-March, last entry one hour before closing, WCs back at the parking lot, off D-47 and D-6 between Sarlat and Les Eyzies-de-Tayac—see map on page 480, www.commarque.com.

Getting There: From Sarlat, follow signs to *Les Eyzies,* then follow the D-6 to Marquay. As you pass through Marquay, keep right, following *Commarque* signs, then go about two kilometers and turn right. Hearty hikers can walk from Abri du Cap Blanc (see page 491) to the castle in 25 minutes (ask for trail conditions at the site). Signs also direct drivers from here.

Maison Forte de Reignac

For over 700 years, a powerful lord ruled from this unusual home carved from a rock face high above the Vézère River. After a short but steep hike to the entry, you'll climb through several floors of well-furnished rooms, some with lit fireplaces. Kids love this tree house of a place. Your tour concludes in a room that houses torture devices and highlights man's creative abilities to inflict unthinkable pain...and a slow death. The loaner English handout provides good context.

Cost and Hours: €7.50, May-Sept daily 10:00-19:00, April until 18:00, Oct-Nov until 17:00, closed Dec-March, just north of the village of Tursac, tel. 05 53 50 69 54, www.maison-forte-reignac.com.

Getting There: From Les Eyzies-de-Tayac, it's a twisty 10-minute drive up D-706 (direction: La Roque St-Christophe).

Cro-Magnon Caves

The towns and sights of the Dordogne region—including Les Eyzies-de-Tayac, Grotte de Font-de-Gaume, Abri du Cap Blanc, Grotte de Rouffignac, Lascaux II, and Grottes de Cougnac—have a rich history of prehistoric cave art. The paintings you'll see here are famous throughout the world for their remarkably modern-looking technique, beauty, and mystery. To fully appreciate them, take time to read the following information, written by Gene Openshaw, on the purpose of the art and the Cro-Magnon style of painting.

CAVE ART 101

From 18,000 to 10,000 B.C., long before Stonehenge, before the pyramids, before metalworking, farming, and domesticated dogs, back when mammoths and saber-toothed cats still roamed the earth, prehistoric people painted deep inside limestone caverns in southern France and northern Spain. These are not crude doodles with a charcoal-tipped stick. They're sophisticated, costly, and time-consuming engineering projects planned and executed by dedicated artists supported by a unified and stable culture—the Magdalenians.

The Magdalenians (c. 18,000-10,000 B.C.): These hunter-gatherers of the Upper Paleolithic period (40,000-10,000 B.C.) were driven south by the Second Ice Age. (Historians named them after the Madeleine archaeological site near Les Eyzies-de-Tayac.) The Magdalenians flourished in southern France and northern Spain for eight millennia—long enough to chronicle the evolution and extinction of several animal species. (Think: Egypt lasted a mere 3,000 years; Rome lasted 1,000; America fewer than 250 so far.)

DORDOGNE

Physically, the people were Cro-Magnons. Unlike hulking, beetle-browed Neanderthals, Cro-Magnons were fully developed *Homo sapiens* who could blend in to our modern population. We know these people by the possessions found in their settlements: stone axes, flint arrowheads, bone needles for making clothes, musical instruments, grease lamps (without their juniper wicks), and cave paintings and sculpture. Many objects are beautifully decorated.

The Magdalenians did not live in the deep limestone caverns they painted (which are cold and difficult to access). But many did

Cro-Magnon Caves near Sarlat-la-Canéda

To Perigueux & St-Emilion via A-89
D-45
D-32
2 Kilometers
2 Miles
GROTTE DE ROUFFIGNAC
St-Léon
D-706
LA ROQUE ST-CHRISTOPHE
MAISON FORTE DE REIGNAC
D-710
D-47
River
D-65
ABRI DU CAP BLANC
D-48
Les Eyzies-de-Tayac
GROTTE DE FONT-DE-GAUME
CHATEAU DE COMMARQUE
D-703
Le Bugue
Vézère
(WELCOME CENTER & MUSEUM)
D-47
D-35
D-48
LE CHEVREFEUILLE CHAMBRES
DORDOGNE
D-703
St-Cyprien
River
Le Buisson
D-51
D-29
D-25
D-703
To Bergerac & St-Emilion
Dordogne
D-25
D-703
D-53
Siorac-en-Périgord
CHATEAU DES MILANDES
D-710
D-53
Belvès
D-53
Paris
FRANCE
100 Miles
Prehistoric Sites
Foie Gras Farm
Scenic Loop

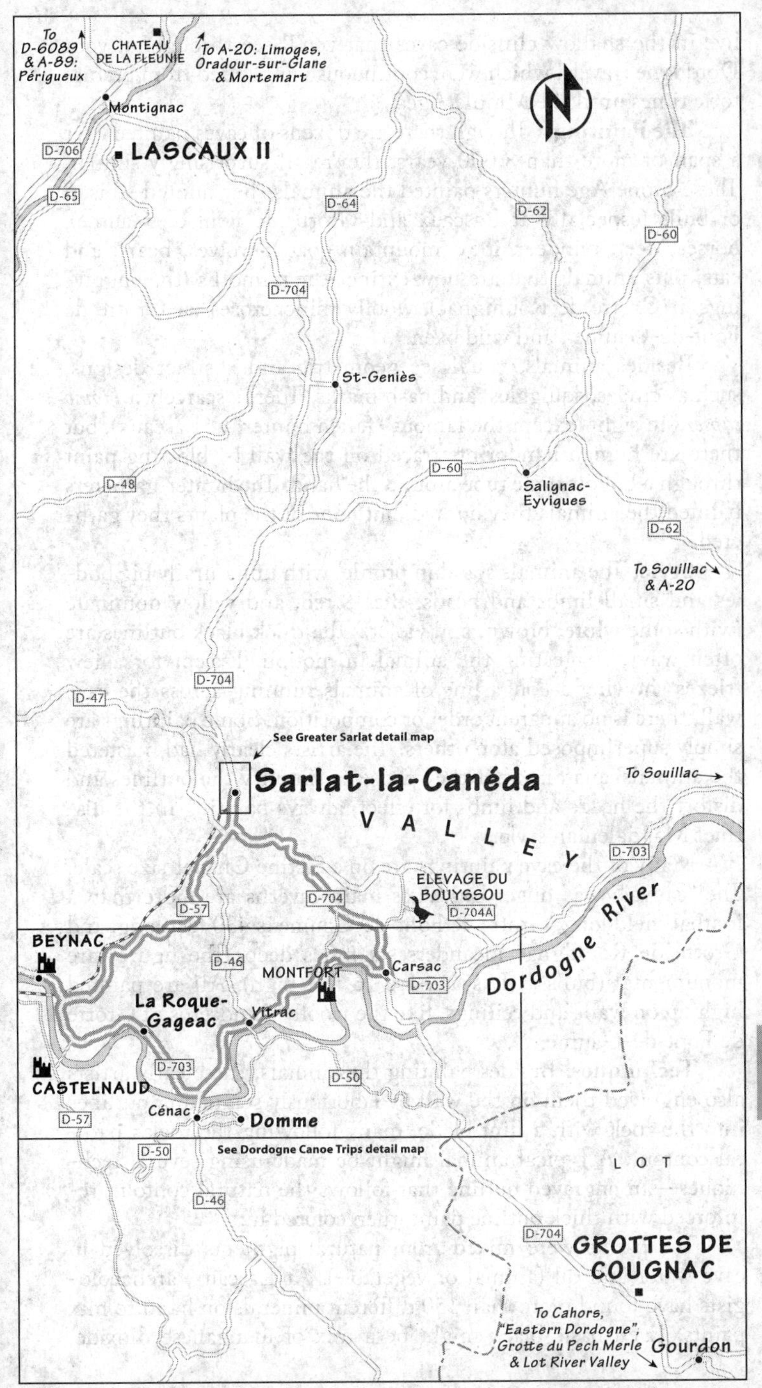
To D-6089 & A-89: Périgueux
CHATEAU DE LA FLEUNIE
To A-20: Limoges, Oradour-sur-Glane & Mortemart
Montignac
LASCAUX II
D-706
D-65
D-64
D-62
D-60
D-704
St-Geniès
D-60
Salignac-Eyvigues
D-48
D-62
To Souillac & A-20
D-704
D-47
See Greater Sarlat detail map
Sarlat-la-Canéda
To Souillac
V A L L E Y
D-703
ELEVAGE DU BOUYSSOU
D-704
D-704A
D-57
Dordogne River
BEYNAC
D-46
MONTFORT
Carsac
D-703
La Roque-Gageac
Vitrac
CASTELNAUD
D-703
D-50
Cénac
Domme
D-57
See Dordogne Canoe Trips detail map
D-50
L O T
D-46
D-704
GROTTES DE COUGNAC
To Cahors, "Eastern Dordogne", Grotte du Pech Merle & Lot River Valley
Gourdon
DORDOGNE

live in the shallow cliffside caves that you'll see throughout your Dordogne travels, which were continuously inhabited from prehistoric times until the Middle Ages.

The Paintings: Though there are dozens of caves painted over a span of more than 8,000 years, they're all surprisingly similar. These Stone Age hunters painted the animals they hunted—bison or bulls (especially at Lascaux and Grotte de Font-de-Gaume), horses, deer, reindeer, ibex (mountain goats), wolves, bears, and cats, plus animals that are now extinct—mammoths (the engravings at Grotte de Rouffignac), woolly rhinoceroses (at Grotte de Font-de-Gaume), and wild oxen.

Besides animals, you'll see geometric and abstract designs, such as circles, squiggles, and hash marks. There's scarcely a *Homo sapiens* in sight (except the famous "fallen hunter" at Lascaux), but there are human handprints traced on the wall by blowing paint through a hollow bone tube around the hand. The hunter-gatherers painted the animals they hunted, but none of the plants they gathered.

Style: The animals stand in profile, with unnaturally big bodies and small limbs and heads. Black, red, and yellow dominate (with some white, brown, and violet). The thick black outlines are often wavy, suggesting the animal in motion. Except for a few friezes showing a conga line of animals running across the cave wall, there is no apparent order or composition. Some paintings are simply superimposed atop others. The artists clearly had mastered the animals' anatomy, but they chose to simplify the outlines and distort the heads and limbs for effect, always painting in the distinct Magdalenian style.

Many of the cave paintings are on a Sistine Chapel-size scale. The "canvas" was huge: Lascaux's main caverns are more than a football field long; Grotte de Font-de-Gaume is 430 feet long; and Grotte de Rouffignac meanders six miles deep. The figures are monumental (bulls at Lascaux are 16 feet high). All are painted high up on walls and ceilings, like the woolly rhinoceros of Grotte de Font-de-Gaume.

Techniques: Besides painting the animals, these early artists also engraved them on the wall by laboriously scratching outlines into the rock with a flint blade, many following the rock's natural contour. A typical animal might be made using several techniques—an engraved outline that follows the natural contour, reinforced with thick outline paint, then colored in.

The paints were mixed from natural pigments dissolved in cave water and oil (animal or vegetable). At Lascaux, archaeologists have found more than 150 different minerals on hand to mix paints. Even basic black might be a mix of manganese dioxide, ground quartz, and a calcium phosphate that had to be made by heating bone to 700 degrees Fahrenheit, then grinding it.

No paintbrushes have been found, so artists probably used a sponge-like material made from animal skin and fat. They may have used moss or hair, or maybe even finger-painted with globs of pure pigment. Once they'd drawn the outlines, they filled everything in with spray paint—either spit out from the mouth or blown through tubes made of hollow bone.

Imagine the engineering problems of painting one of these caves, and you can appreciate how sophisticated these "primitive" people were. First, you'd have to haul all your materials into a cold, pitch-black, hard-to-access place. Assistants erected scaffolding to reach ceilings and high walls, ground up minerals with a mortar and pestle, mixed paints, tended the torches and oil lamps, prepared the "paintbrushes," laid out major outlines with a connect-the-dots series of points...then stepped aside for Magdalenian Michelangelos to ascend the scaffolding and create.

Dating: Determining exactly how old this art is—and whether it's authentic—is tricky. (Because much of the actual paint is mineral-based with no organic material, carbon-dating techniques are often ineffective.) As different caves feature different animals, prehistorians can deduce which caves are relatively older and younger, since climate change caused various animal species to come and go within certain regions. In several cases, experts confirmed the authenticity of a painting because the portrayals of the animals showed anatomical details not previously known—until they were discovered by modern technology. (For instance, in Grotte de Rouffignac, the mammoths are shown with a strange skin flap over their anus, which was only discovered during the 20th century on a preserved mammoth found in Siberian permafrost.) They can also estimate dates by checking the amount of calcium glaze formed over the paint, which can sometimes only be seen by infrared photography.

Why?: No one knows the purpose of the cave paintings. Interestingly, the sites the artists chose were deliberately awe-inspiring, out of the way, and special. They knew their work here would last for untold generations, as had the paintings that came before theirs. Here are some theories of what this first human art might mean.

It's no mystery that hunters would paint animals, the source of their existence. The first scholar to study the caves, Abbé Henri Breuil, thought the painted animals were magic symbols made by

Prehistoric Sights at a Glance

You can reserve ahead only for Lascaux II, Grotte du Pech Merle, Abri du Cap Blanc, and possibly Font-de-Gaume. For the other caves, it's first-come, first-served.

Prehistory Welcome Center Free, good intro to region's important prehistoric sites. **Hours:** May-Sept daily 9:30-18:30; Oct-April Sun-Fri 9:30-17:30, closed Sat. **Reservations:** Not necessary. Allow about 45 minutes to visit on your own. See page 487.

▲National Museum of Prehistory More than 18,000 artifacts with good English explanations—good preparation for your cave visit. **Hours:** July-Aug daily 9:30-18:30; June and Sept Wed-Mon 9:30-18:00, closed Tue; Oct-May Wed-Mon 9:30-12:30 & 14:00-17:30, closed Tue. **Reservations:** Not necessary, but reserve if you want a tour. Allow about 60 minutes to visit. See page 488.

▲▲▲Grotte de Font-de-Gaume Last prehistoric multicolored paintings open to public, with strict limits on the number of daily visitors allowed. **Hours:** Mid-May-mid-Sept Sun-Fri 9:30-17:30, mid-Sept-mid-May Sun-Fri 9:30-12:30 & 14:30-17:30, closed Sat year-round. **Reservations:** May be possible in 2015 (check website). Sans reservation, be in line by 7:00 in summer, by 8:30 in spring and fall and in winter by 9:00. Required 45-minute tour (likely in French). See page 490.

▲Abri du Cap Blanc 14,000-year-old carvings that use natural contours of cave to add dimension. **Hours:** Mid-May-mid-Sept Sun-Fri 10:00-17:00, mid-Sept-mid-May Sun-Fri 10:00-12:30 & 14:00-17:00, closed Sat year-round, last entry at about 16:15. **Reservations:** Call to reserve a tour time or reserve in person at Font-de-Gaume. Required 45-minute tour (usually with some English; usually 6/day); call for times. See page 491.

▲▲Lascaux II Exact replica of the world's most famous cave paintings. **Hours:** July-Aug daily 9:00-20:00, night visits pos-

hunters to increase the supply of game. Or perhaps hunters thought that if you could "master" an animal by painting it, you could later master it in battle. Some scholars think the paintings teach the art of hunting, but there's very little apparent hunting technique shown. Did they worship animals? The paintings definitely depict an animal-centered (rather than a human-centered) universe.

The paintings may have a religious purpose, and some of the caverns are large and special enough that rituals and ceremonies could have been held there. But the paintings show no sacrifices,

sible; April-June and Sept-Oct daily 9:00-18:00; Nov-Dec and mid-Feb-March Tue-Sun 10:00-12:00 & 14:00-17:30, closed Mon; closed Jan-mid-Feb. **Reservations:** Reserve a maximum of 2-5 days ahead for July-Aug. Required 40-minute tour; call for English tour times (2-4/day). See page 492.

▲▲Grotte de Rouffignac Etchings and paintings of prehistoric creatures such as mammoths in a large cave accessible by little train. **Hours:** Daily July-Aug 9:00-11:30 & 14:00-18:00, April-June and Sept-Nov 10:00-11:30 & 14:00-17:00, closed Dec-March. **Reservations:** Not available or necessary, arrive mid-July-Aug by 8:30, otherwise 30 minutes early. Visit lasts 60 minutes. See page 493.

▲La Roque St-Christophe Terraced cliff dwellings where prehistoric people lived. **Hours:** Daily July-Aug 10:00-20:00, Sept-Dec and Feb-June 10:00-18:00, Jan 14:00-17:30. **Reservations:** Not available or necessary. Allow 45 minutes to visit on your own (good English handout). See page 495.

▲▲Grottes de Cougnac Oldest paintings (14,000-25,000 years old) open to public, showing rust-and-black ibex, mammoths, giant deer, and a few humans. **Hours:** July-Aug daily 10:00-18:00; April-June and Sept daily 10:00-11:30 & 14:30-17:00; Oct Mon-Sat 14:00-16:00, closed Sun; closed Nov-March. **Reservations:** Not available. Arrive 10 minutes before it opens. Required 1.5-hour tour (with minimal English explanation). See page 496.

▲▲Grotte du Pech Merle Brilliant cave art of mammoths, bison, and horses, plus Cro-Magnon footprint. **Hours:** Daily March-mid-Nov 9:30-17:00, closes earlier off-season. **Reservations:** Book a week ahead in summer (fewer visitors allowed on weekends), or arrive by 9:30. Allow two hours for a complete visit (good English information). See page 512.

rituals, or ceremonies. Scholars writing on primitive art in other parts of the world speculate that art was made by shamans in a religious or drug-induced trance, but France's paintings are very methodical.

The order of paintings on the walls seems random. Could it be that the caves are a painted collage of the history of the Magdalenians, with each successive generation adding its distinct animal or symbol to the collage, putting it in just the right spot that established their place in history?

The fact that styles and subject matter changed so little over the millennia might imply that the artists purposely chose timeless images to relate their generation with those before and after. Perhaps they simply lived in a stable culture that did not value innovation. Or were these people too primitive to invent new techniques and topics?

Maybe the paintings are simply the result of the universal human drive to create, and these caverns were Europe's first art galleries, bringing the first tourists.

Very likely there is no single meaning that applies to all the paintings in all the caves. Prehistoric art may be as varied in meaning as current art.

Picture yourself as a Magdalenian viewing these paintings: You'd be guided by someone into a cold, echoing, and otherworldly chamber. In the darkness, someone would light torches and lamps, and suddenly the animals would flicker to life, appearing to run around the cave, like a prehistoric movie. In front of you, a bull would appear, behind you a mammoth (which you'd never seen in the flesh), and overhead a symbol that might have tied the whole experience together. You'd be amazed that an artist could capture the real world and reproduce it on a wall. Whatever the purpose—religious, aesthetic, or just plain fun—there's no doubt the effect was (and is) thrilling.

Today, you can visit the caves and share a common experience with a caveman. Feel a bond with these long-gone people...or stand in awe at how different they were from us. Ultimately, the paintings are as mysterious as the human species.

HELPFUL HINTS

Drivers Fare Best: All the prehistoric caves listed here are within a reasonable drive of Sarlat-la-Canéda. Considering the scarcity of public transit, if you don't have a car, you'll be like a caveman without a spear (see page 444 for guided tours that connect some of these sights).

Get Up Early: Only the Lascaux II, Grotte du Pech Merle, Abri du Cap Blanc (and maybe Font-de-Gaume) caves take reservations; for all others it's first-come, first-served. That means it's essential to arrive early to secure a ticket, and then find something to do in the area if you have time to kill. How early you need to arrive varies by cave; I've suggested times for caves where you can't make a reservation. July, August, and holiday weekends are busiest; Saturdays are quieter—but note that Grotte de Font-de-Gaume and Abri du Cap Blanc are closed that day, and from October to April, so is the Prehistory Welcome Center.

Cave Tips: Read "Cave Art 101" (previous section) to gain a better understanding of what you'll see. Dress warmly, even if it's hot outside. Tours can last up to an hour, and the caves are all a steady, chilly 55 degrees Fahrenheit, with 98 or 99 percent humidity. While on tour, lag behind the group to have the paintings to yourself for a few moments. Photos, day packs, big purses, and strollers are not allowed. (You can take your camera—without using it—and check the rest at the site.)

Local Guide: Angelika Siméon is a passionate guide/lecturer eager to teach you about the caves and well worth spending a day with. She handles cave reservations and makes it easy and educational (book ahead; €135/half-day, €225/day, tel. 05 53 35 19 30, mobile 06 24 45 96 28, angelika.simeon@wanadoo.fr).

Les Eyzies-de-Tayac

This single-street town is the touristy hub of a cluster of Cro-Magnon caves, castles, and rivers. It merits a stop for its Prehistory Welcome Center, National Museum of Prehistory, and (maybe) the Grotte de Font-de-Gaume cave (a 15-minute walk outside town; described later, under "Caves near Les Eyzies-de-Tayac"). Les Eyzies-de-Tayac is world-famous because it's where the original Cro-Magnon man was discovered in 1870. That breakthrough set of bones was found just behind the hotel of Monsieur Magnon—Hôtel le Cro-Magnon, which is in business to this day on the western end of the main street. The name "Cro-Magnon" translates as "Mr. Magnon's Hole."

Orientation: Les Eyzies-de-Tayac's **TI** rents bikes and has free Wi-Fi (July-Aug Mon-Sat 9:30-18:30, Sept-June Mon-Sat 9:30-12:30 & 14:00-18:00, closed Sun except June-Sept 10:00-12:00 & 14:00-17:00, tel. 05 53 06 97 05, www.tourisme-vezere.com). The train station is a level 500 yards from the town center (turn right from the station to get into town).

Sights in Les Eyzies-de-Tayac

Prehistory Welcome Center (Pôle International de la Préhistoire)

Start your prehistoric explorations at the Pôle International de la Préhistoire (PIP) at the Sarlat (east) end of town. This glass-and-concrete facility is a helpful resource for planning a visit to the region's important prehistoric sites. The low-slung building houses timelines, slideshows, and exhibits (all in English) that work together to give visitors a primer on the origins of man. The English-speaking staff is happy to provide maps of the region and give suggestions on places to visit. Park here (for free), then walk out the center's back door 200 yards on a pedestrian-only lane to the National Museum of Prehistory.

Cost and Hours: Free; May-Sept daily 9:30-18:30; Oct-April Sun-Fri 9:30-17:30, closed Sat; Wi-Fi, free parking across the street, located east of downtown Les Eyzies-de-Tayac at 30 Rue du Moulin—watch for tall silver *PIP* sign, tel. 05 53 06 06 97, www.pole-prehistoire.com.

▲National Museum of Prehistory (Musée National de Préhistoire)

This modern museum houses more than 18,000 bones, stones, and crude little doodads that were uncovered locally. It takes you through prehistory—starting 400,000 years ago—and is good preparation for your cave visits. The museum does a great job of presenting its exhibits, with ample handheld English explanations throughout. Appropriately located on a cliff inhabited by humans for 35,000 years (above Les Eyzies-de-Tayac's TI), the museum's sleek design is intended to help it blend into the surrounding rock. Inside, you'll see many worthwhile exhibits, including videos demonstrating scratched designs, painting techniques, and how spearheads were made. You'll also see full-size models of Cro-Magnon people and animals that stare at racks of arrowheads.

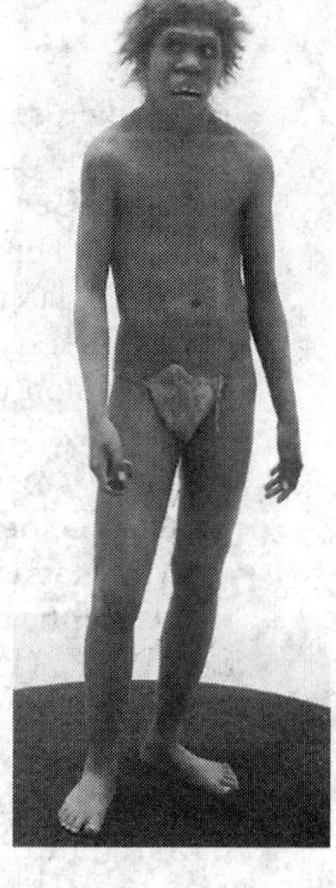

Cost and Hours: €8; July-Aug daily 9:30-18:30; June and Sept Wed-Mon 9:30-18:00, closed Tue; Oct-May Wed-Mon 9:30-12:30 & 14:00-17:30, closed Tue; tel. 05 53 06 45 45, www.musee-prehistoire-eyzies.fr.

Information: For context, read "Cave Art 101," on page 479, before you go.

Tours: To get the most out of your visit, consider a private or semiprivate English-language guided tour; for details, call 05 53 06 45 65 or email reservation.prehistoire@culture.gouv.fr.

Visiting the Museum: Pick up the museum layout with your ticket. Notice the timeline shown on the stone wall starting a mere 7 million years ago. Then enter, walking in the footsteps of your ancestors, and greet the 10-year-old *Turkana Boy,* whose bone fragments were found in Kenya in 1984 by Richard Leakey and date from 1.5 million years ago.

The **first floor** up sets the stage, describing human evolution and the fundamental importance of tools. Find the numbered English info sheets provided (all along the same wall) and match them to exhibit numbers to make sense of what you're seeing. Grab several at a time for efficiency.

The **second floor** up is better, and highlights prehistoric artifacts found in France. Some of the most interesting objects you'll see are displayed in this order: a handheld arrow launcher, a 5,000-year-old flat-bottomed boat (pirogue) made from oak, prehistoric fire pits, amazing cavewoman jewelry (including a necklace, or is that a bracelet?—made of 70 stag teeth—pretty impressive, given that stags only have two teeth each...do the math), engravings on stone (find the unflattering yet impressively realistic female figure), a handheld lamp used to light cave interiors *(lampe à manche),* and beautiful rock sculptures of horses (much like the sculptures at the cave of Abri du Cap Blanc).

Your visit ends on the **cliff edge,** with a Fred Flintstone-style photo op on a stone ledge (through the short tunnel) that some of our ancient ancestors once called home.

Sleeping near Les Eyzies-de-Tayac

$$ Le Chevrefeuille, halfway between Les Eyzies-de-Tayac and St-Cyprien, is a family-friendly place offering modern comfort in a farm setting. Ian and Sara Fisk moved to France from England (via Brazil) to raise their children. Expert cook Ian prepares scrumptious dinners several nights a week in season and offers occasional cooking classes. Five guest rooms and suites in various configurations handle singles to family groups; common areas include a lounge and kitchen area (Db-€75-95, family rooms/suites-€120-180, includes breakfast, pay laundry facilities, cash only, Wi-Fi, swimming pool and play areas, closed Nov-Easter, tel. 05 53 59 47 97, www.lechevrefeuille.com, info@lechevrefeuille.com). From near Les Eyzies, head south on D-48 about six kilometers, turn right into the small hamlet of Pechboutier, and look for their sign.

Caves near Les Eyzies-de-Tayac

▲▲▲Grotte de Font-de-Gaume

Even if you're not a connoisseur of Cro-Magnon art, you'll dig this cave—the last one in France with prehistoric multicolored (polychrome) paintings still open to the public. (Lascaux—45 minutes down the road—has replica caves for visitors instead.) This cave, made millions of years ago—not by a river, but by the geological activity that created the Pyrenees Mountains—is entirely natural. It contains 15,000-year-old paintings of 230 animals, 82 of which are bison.

On a carefully guided and controlled 100-yard walk, you'll see about 20 red-and-black bison—often in elegant motion—painted with a moving sensitivity. When two animals face each other, one is black, and the other is red. Your guide, with a laser pointer and great reverence, will trace the faded outline of the bison and explain how, 15 millennia ago, cave dwellers used local minerals and the rock's natural contours to give the paintings dimension. Some locals knew about the cave long ago, when there was little interest in prehistory, but the paintings were officially discovered in 1901 by the village schoolteacher.

Warning: Access to Font-de-Gaume is extremely restricted. The number of available tickets meets only a small fraction of the demand. The site's ticketing and booking processes change regularly: Some years about a third of the slots can be booked ahead online, while at other times your only option is to get up at the crack of dawn and stand in line. Check the website four to six months in advance of your trip to see if reserved tickets are possible. Otherwise I'd skip this place unless it's solidly off-season. Lining up for hours is a poor use of your precious time, and other good options exist to see original cave art. Drivers who can't get a ticket here should try the other interesting caves I recommend in this chapter.

Cost and Hours: €7.50, 17 and under free, includes required 45-minute tour; open mid-May-mid-Sept Sun-Fri 9:30-17:30, mid-Sept-mid-May Sun-Fri 9:30-12:30 & 14:30-17:30, closed Sat year-round; last tour departs 1.5 hours before closing, no photography or large bags, tel. 05 53 06 86 00, www.eyzies.monuments-nationaux.fr, fontdegaume@monuments-nationaux.fr—don't expect a fast reply. Those planning to also visit the Abri du Cap Blanc cave (described next) can reserve and buy tickets here in July and Aug.

Getting a Ticket: To preserve the precious and fragile art, group size is limited to 12. The number of daily visitors allowed is strictly regulated (180/day in 2011, 96/day in 2012, 80/day in 2013, and possibly fewer in 2015). You may be able to reserve ahead in 2015 (though it's unlikely—check the website well before your trip). Otherwise, tickets are doled out each morning starting at 9:30. In summer, plan to be in line by 7:00, in spring and fall no later than 8:30, and in the winter you should be OK if you arrive by 9:00. You can drop by the sight at any time during opening hours and get the latest on how early you need to show up to get a ticket. You must check in 15 minutes before your tour, or you'll lose your place to the sightseeing vultures waiting to snatch up the spots of late arrivals.

Tours: English tours are available but limited; prepare to visit with a French guide. The English-info flier is useless, but depending on the guide, the actual tour can be either illuminating and enthusiastic, or little more than pointing out legs, eyes, heads, and bellies of the bison. Don't fret if you're not on an English tour—most important is experiencing the art itself.

Getting There: The cave is at the corner of D-47 and D-48, about a two-minute drive (or a 15-minute walk) east of Les Eyzies-de-Tayac (toward Sarlat). There's easy on-site parking. After checking in at the ticket house, walk 400 yards on an uphill path to the cave entrance (where there's a free, safe bag check and a WC).

▲Abri du Cap Blanc

In this prehistoric cave (a 10-minute drive from Grotte de Font-de-Gaume), early artists used the rock's natural contours to add dimension to their sculpture. Your guide spends the 30-minute tour in a single stone room explaining the 14,000-year-old carvings. The small museum (with English explanations) helps prepare you for your visit, and the useful English handout describes what the French-speaking guide is talking about (some guides add English commentary). Look for places where the artists smoothed or roughened the surfaces to add depth. Impressive as these carvings are, their subtle majesty is lost on some.

Cost and Hours: €7.50, 17 and under free; includes required 45-minute tour, 6 tours/day, call for tour times and to reserve. The cave is open mid-May to mid-Sept Sun-Fri 10:00-17:00, mid-Sept-mid-May Sun-Fri 10:00-12:30 & 14:00-17:00, closed Sat year-round, last entry at about 16:15, no photos, tel. 05 53 59 60 30. In July and August, tickets and reservations are also available at the Font-de-Gaume cave (fontdegaume@monuments-nationaux.fr).

Getting a Ticket: Like Font de Gaume, the reservation process is subject to change. In 2014 you could book a tour by phone. Give it a try, or book in person at the more conveniently located Font de Gaume ticket office for this site.

Getting There: Abri du Cap Blanc is well-signed and is located about three kilometers after Grotte de Font-de-Gaume on the road to Sarlat. From the parking lot, walk 200 yards down to the entry. Views of the Château de Commarque (described on page 478) are terrific as you arrive.

Caves North of Les Eyzies-de-Tayac

▲▲Lascaux II

The region's—and the world's—most famous cave paintings are at Lascaux, 14 miles north of Sarlat-la-Canéda and Les Eyzies-de-Tayac. The Lascaux caves were discovered accidentally in 1940 by four kids and their dog. From 1948 to 1963, more than a million people climbed through this prehistoric wonderland—but these visitors tracked in fungus on their shoes and changed the temperature and humidity with their heavy breathing. In just 15 years, the precious art deteriorated more than during the previous 15,000 years, and the caves were closed. A copy cave—accurate to within one centimeter, reproducing the best 40-yard-long stretch, and showing 90 percent of the paintings found in Lascaux—was opened next to the original in 1983. Guides assure visitors that the original is every bit as crisp and has just as much contrast as the facsimile you'll see.

At impressive Lascaux II, the reindeer, horses, and bulls of Lascaux I are painstakingly reproduced by top artists using the same dyes, tools, and techniques their predecessors did 15,000 years ago. Of course, seeing the real thing at the other caves is important, but come here first (taking one of the scheduled English-language tours) for a great introduction to the region's cave art. Although it feels a bit rushed—40 people per tour are hustled through the two-room cave reproductions—the guides are committed to teaching, the paintings are astonishing, and the experience is mystifying. (Forget that they're copies, and enjoy being swept away by the prehistoric majesty of it all.) The cave is a constant 56 degrees year-round, so

dress warmly. Pleasant Montignac is worth a wander if you have time to kill.

Cost and Hours: €10; July-Aug daily 9:00-20:00, night visits possible; April-June and Sept-Oct daily 9:00-18:00; Nov-Dec and mid-Feb-March Tue-Sun 10:00-12:00 & 14:00-17:30, closed Mon; closed Jan-mid-Feb. You'll see Lascaux II with a 40-minute English tour (4/day July-Aug, 2-4 per day May-Sept—usually 1-2 tours in the morning and 1-2 more in the afternoon, www.semitour.com, call 05 53 51 96 23 for ticket availability and estimated English tour times).

Getting Tickets: Unless you're visiting in winter (Oct-March), you must buy your ticket before coming to Lascaux. Reservations are strongly suggested in July and August and accepted only 2-5 days in advance (up to 7 days in advance in person); the ticket office is next to the TI in Montignac, five minutes away by car. Deep-blue signs direct drivers to *La Billetterie* in Montignac (follow signs for *Centre-Ville,* then look for *La Billetterie*—don't double-park); Lascaux is well-signed from there.

Sleeping near Lascaux: **$$ Château de la Fleunie***** allows you to bed down in a medieval castle at peasant prices (well, almost). Built between the 12th and 16th centuries, this castle shares its land with pastures and mountain goats, a big pool (unheated), worn tennis courts, and play toys. Stay-awhile terraces overlook the scene and its riddled-with-character restaurant (€29-45 *menus*). Rooms are located in three buildings: the main château, an attached wing, and the modern pavilion. The château's rooms are old-world-worn with musty and dated bathrooms (many big rooms for families), while the pavilion offers contemporary rooms with private view decks (small Db-€80-120, big Db-€105-136, Tb-€190, Qb-€210, half-pension requested July-Aug, 10-minute drive north of Montignac on road to Brive-la-Gaillarde, in Condat-sur-Vézère, tel. 05 53 51 32 74, www.lafleunie.com, lafleunie@free.fr).

▲▲Grotte de Rouffignac

Rouffignac provides a different experience from other prehistoric caves in this area. Here you'll ride a clunky little train down a giant subterranean riverbed, exploring about half a mile of this six-mile-long gallery. The cave itself was known to locals for decades, but the 13,000-year-old paintings were discovered only in 1956. With a little planning, you'll have no trouble getting a ticket.

Cost and Hours: €6.50, essential videoguide-€1.50, daily July-Aug 9:00-11:30 & 14:00-18:00, April-June and Sept-Nov 10:00-11:30 & 14:00-17:00, closed Dec-March, one-hour guided tours run 2-3/hour, no reservations, tel. 05 53 05 41 71, www.grottederouffignac.fr. Dress warmly. It's really crowded only mid-July-Aug—during these months the ticket office opens at 9:00 and closes when tickets are sold out for the day—usually by noon. Arrive by 8:30 in summer and 30 minutes early at other times of year, and you'll be fine. Weekends tend to be quietest, particularly Sat.

Getting There: Grotte de Rouffignac is well-signed from the route between Les Eyzies-de-Tayac and Périgueux; allow 25 minutes from Les Eyzies-de-Tayac.

Visiting the Cave: Your tour will be in French (with highlights described in caveman English), but the videoguide explains it all. Before the tour begins, read your videoguide's background sections and the informative displays in the cave entry area. Once on the tour it's easy to follow along. Here's the gist of what they're saying on the stops of your train ride:

The cave was created by the underground river. It's entirely natural, but it was much shallower before the train-track bed was excavated. As you travel, imagine the motivation and determination of the painters who crawled more than a half-mile into this dark and mysterious cave. They left behind their art...and the wonder of people who crawled in centuries later to see it all.

You'll ride about five minutes before the first stop. Along the way, you'll see crater-like burrows made by hibernating bears long before the first humans painted here. There are hundreds of them—not because there were so many bears, but because year after year, a few of them would return, preferring to make their own private place to sleep (rather than using some other bear's den). After a long winter nap, bears would have one thing on their mind: Cut those toenails. The walls are scarred with the scratching of bears in need of clippers.

Stop 1: The guide points out bear scratches on the right. On the left, images of woolly mammoths etched into the walls can be seen only when lit from the side (as your guide will demonstrate). As the rock is very soft here, these were simply gouged out by the artists' fingers.

Stop 2: Look for images of finely detailed rhinoceroses outlined in black. Notice how the thicker coloring under their tummies suggests the animals' girth. The rock is harder here, so nothing is engraved. Soon after, your guide will point out graffiti littering the ceiling—made by "modern" visitors who were not aware of the prehistoric drawings around them (with dates going back to the 18th century).

Stop 3: On the left, you'll see woolly mammoths and horses engraved with tools in the harder rock. On the right is the biggest composition of the cave: a herd of 10 peaceful mammoths. A mysterious calcite problem threatens to cover the paintings with ugly white splotches.

Off the Train: When you get off the train, notice how high the original floor was (today's floor was dug out in the 20th century to allow for visitors). Imagine both the prehistoric makers and viewers of this art crawling all the way back here with pretty lousy flashlight-substitutes. The artists lay on their backs while creating these 60 images (unlike at Lascaux, where they built scaffolds).

The ceiling is covered with a remarkable gathering of animals. You'll see a fine 16-foot-long horse, a group of mountain goats, and a grandpa mammoth. Art even decorates the walls far down the big, scary hole. When the group chuckles, it's because the guide is explaining how the mammoth with the fine detail (showing a flap of skin over its anus) helped authenticate the paintings: These paintings couldn't be fakes, because no one knew about this anatomical detail until the preserved remains of an actual mammoth were found in Siberian permafrost in modern times. (The discovery explained the painted skin flap, which had long puzzled French prehistorians.)

▲La Roque St-Christophe

Five fascinating terraces carved by the Vézère River have provided shelter to people here for 50,000 years. Although the terraces were inhabited in prehistoric times, there's no prehistoric art on display—the exhibit (except for one small cave) is entirely medieval. The official recorded history goes back to A.D. 976, when people settled here to steer clear of the Viking raiders who'd routinely sail up the river. (Back then, in this part of Europe, the standard closing of a prayer wasn't "amen," but "and deliver us from the Norseman, amen.")

A clever relay of river watchtowers kept an eye out for raiders. When they came, cave dwellers gathered their kids, hauled up their animals (see the big, re-created winch), and pulled up the ladders. Although there's absolutely nothing old here except for the carved-out rock (with holes for beams, carved out of the soft limestone), it's easy to imagine the entire village—complete with butcher, baker, and candlestick-maker—in this family-friendly exhibit. This place is a dream for kids of any age who hold fond treehouse memories.

It's simple to visit: There's a free parking lot across the stream, with picnic tables, a WC, and, adjacent to the babbling brook, a pondside café (providing good salads, omelets, and drinks—the nearby pretty village of St-Léon provides more lunch choices). Grab the English booklet at the turnstile; stop to take in the picture showing its medieval buildings; and climb through the one-way circuit, which is slippery when damp. Allow at least 45 minutes for your visit.

Cost and Hours: €8, daily July-Aug 10:00-20:00, Sept-Dec and Feb-June 10:00-18:00, Jan 14:00-17:30, last entry 45 minutes before closing, lots of steps, eight kilometers north of Les Eyzies-de-Tayac, follow signs to *Montignac*, tel. 05 53 50 70 45. Note that this sight is very near the Maison Forte de Reignac (described on page 478).

▲▲Grottes de Cougnac

Located 23 kilometers south of Sarlat-la-Canéda (allow 30 minutes) and three well-signed kilometers north of Gourdon on D-704, this cave holds fascinating rock formations and the oldest (14,000-25,000-year-old) paintings open to the public. Less touristy than other sites, it provides a more intimate look at cave art, as guides take more time to explain the caves and paintings (your guide should give some explanations in English—ask if he or she doesn't).

Cost and Hours: €7.50; these hours correspond to first/last tour times: July-Aug daily 10:00-18:00; April-June and Sept daily 10:00-11:30 & 14:30-17:00; Oct Mon-Sat 14:00-16:00, closed Sun; closed Nov-March; free WCs, beverages sold on-site, tel. 05 65 41 47 54, www.grottesdecougnac.com.

Visiting the Cave: The 1.5-hour tour, likely in French, begins in a cave where the guide explains the geological formations (you'll learn that it takes 70 years for water to make it from the earth's surface into the cave). From this first cave, you'll return to the fresh air and walk 15 minutes to a second cave—and the paintings you came to see. They are worth the wait. Vivid depictions (about 10) of ibex, mammoths, and giant deer *(Megaloceros)*, as well as a few nifty representations of humans, are outlined in rust or black. The rendering of the giant deer's antlers is exquisite, and many paintings use the cave's form to add depth and movement.

Because access is first-come, first-served (and groups are limited to 25), try to arrive first thing (ideally 10 minutes before opening). In the off-season, be careful not to arrive too close to the last tour before lunch (11:30)—if that tour is full, you'll have to wait for the 14:30 departure. The caves are damp, so expect a few drops on your head (hats or hoods help). English-only tours happen on occasion (call ahead to check times); you can also buy a €5 English booklet about the site.

Oradour-sur-Glane

Lost in lush countryside, two hours north of Sarlat-la-Canéda, Oradour-sur-Glane is a powerful experience—worth ▲▲▲. French children know this town well, as most come here on school trips. **Village des Martyrs,** as it is known, was machine-gunned and burned on June 10, 1944, by Nazi troops. With cool attention to detail, the Nazis methodically rounded up the entire population of 642 townspeople, of whom 200 were children. The women and children were herded into the town church, where they were tear-gassed and machine-gunned as they tried to escape the burning chapel. Oradour's men were tortured and executed. The town was then set on fire, its victims left under a blanket of ashes.

The reason for the mass killings remains unclear today. Some believe that the Nazis wanted revenge for the kidnapping of one of their officers, some believe they wanted to teach locals a lesson for stealing a large amount of gold, and still others believe that the Nazis were simply terrorizing the populace in preparation for the upcoming Allied invasion (this was four days after D-Day). Today, the ghost town, left untouched for 70 years (by order of President Charles de Gaulle), greets every pilgrim who enters with only one English word: Remember.

Cost and Hours: Entering the village is free, but the museum costs €8 (audioguide-€2). Both are open daily mid-May-mid-Sept 9:00-19:00, off-season until 17:00 or 18:00, last visit one hour before closing, tel. 05 55 43 04 30, www.oradour.org. Allow two hours for your visit.

Getting There: For **drivers** coming from the south, Oradour-sur-Glane is well-signed off the (free) A-20. Those driving from the north should take A-10 to Poitiers, then follow signs toward *Limoges* and turn south at Bellac. **Bus #12** links Oradour-sur-Glane with the train station in Limoges (3/day, 40 minutes, consider taking the bus one way to Oradour and taxi the other); Limoges is a stop on an alternative train route between Amboise and Sarlat (Limoges TI tel. 05 55 34 46 87). Those without a car should consider hiring a **taxi;** Christoph Kusters can pick you up in Limoges and take you to Oradour and other sights on the way to your Dordogne hotel (reverse this plan if leaving the Dordogne; see listing under "Getting Around the Dordogne" on page 444).

Visiting Oradour-sur-Glane: Follow *Village des Martyrs* signs and enter at the rust-colored **underground museum** (Centre de la

Mémoire). The pricey-for-what-it-offers museum gives a standard timeline of WWII events and describes Oradour before and after the attack. While thorough English explanations are posted for every exhibit and the 12-minute movie adds drama, the museum as a whole is skippable for some.

From the museum, join other hushed visitors to walk the length of Oradour's **main street,** past gutted, charred buildings and along lonely streetcar tracks. *Lieu de Supplice* signs show where the townsmen were tormented and murdered. The plaques on the buildings provide the names and occupations of the people who lived there (*laine* means wool, *sabotier* is a maker of wooden shoes, *couturier* is a tailor, *quincaillerie* is a hardware store, *cordonnier* is shoe repair, *menuisier* is a carpenter, and *tissus* are fabrics).

You'll pass several cafés and butcher shops, and a hôtel-restaurant. This village was not so different from many you have seen on your trip. Visit the modest **church,** with its bullet-pocked altar, and walk into the **cemetery.** The names of all who died in the massacre on that June day are etched into the rear wall of the cemetery and on stone plaques inside the **underground memorial** (before the cemetery), where you'll also see displays of people's possessions found after the attack.

Nearby: The adorable village of Mortemart lies 10 minutes south of Bellac with a good café (closed Mon) wedged between its ancient market hall and low-slung chateau (wander behind for a sweet scene).

St-Emilion

Two hours due west of Sarlat-la-Canéda and just 40 minutes from Bordeaux, pretty St-Emilion is carved like an amphitheater into the bowl of a limestone hill. Its tidy streets connect a few inviting squares with heavy cobbles and scads of well-stocked wine shops. There's little to do in this well-heeled town other than enjoy the setting and sample the local sauce. Sunday is market day.

They've been making wine in St-Emilion for more than 1,800 years—making it the oldest wine producer in the Bordeaux region (though it accounts for barely 5 percent of Bordeaux's famous red wine). Blending cabernet franc and merlot grapes, St-Emilion wines are also the most robust in Bordeaux. About 60 percent of the grapes you see are merlot.

The helpful **TI** is located at the top of the town on Place des Créneaux, across from the town's highest bell tower (open daily year-round, Place Pioceau, tel. 05 57 55 28 28, www.saint-emilion-tourisme.com, st-emilion.tourisme@wanadoo.fr). The TI rents bikes and has helpful English-language handouts outlining self-guided cycling routes as well as themed, well-marked walking routes through the vineyards. Ask also about their English-language guided tours (see "Tours and Views," below).

Getting There: It's a 20-minute walk from St-Emilion's train station into town; taxis don't wait at the station, but you can call one from there (6 trains/day Mon-Fri from Bordeaux, 4/day Sat-Sun). You can also get off in Libourne (5 miles away, with better train service, easy car rental, taxis, and 3 buses/day to St-Emilion).

Drivers will find pay parking in lots at the upper end of the town or along the wall.

Wine Tasting and Wine Shops: Located next to the TI, **Maison du Vin** is a fair starting point for an introduction to wine (free, daily, tel. 05 57 55 50 55, www.maisonduvinsaintemilion.com, maisonduvin@vins-saint-emilion.com). They also offer wine-tasting classes (usually mid-July–mid-Sept, register in advance).

Keepers of small shops greet visitors in flawless English, with a free tasting table, maps of the vineyards, and several open bottles. Americans may represent only about 15 percent of the visitors, but we buy 40 percent of their wine. **Cercle des Oenophiles** is an easygoing place where you can taste wines and tour nearby cellars storing more than 400,000 bottles (free, daily, 12 Rue Guadat, tel. 05 57 74 45 55).

Château Visits and Minivan Excursions: The TI can send you to a tasting at selected châteaux (no charge, but a tasting fee may apply) and offers a minivan tour through the vineyards—in English and French—that includes a tasting at one château (two hours, usually May-mid Sept only; verify times on website).

Tours and Views: You can climb the bell tower in front of the TI for a good view (small fee, ask at TI for key, open daily), but the view is best from the Tour du Roy several blocks below (small fee, open daily).

The TI offers two guided tours in St-Emilion (fees for both). The interesting 45-minute underground tour makes three stops at sights that otherwise aren't open to visitors: the catacombs (sorry, no bones), monolithic church, and Trinity Chapel (English tour daily, usually at 14:00, more in French, thorough English handout given on French tours). The city walking tour takes 1.5 hours and covers aboveground sights and the back streets of St-Emilion.

Quickie Vineyard Loop by Car or Bike: This 10-kilometer

loop can be done in 20 minutes if driving, and in 2 hours if pedaling. Leave the upper end of St-Emilion on D-243E-1 and head to St-Christophe des Bardes. Pass through the village (direction: St-Genès), then follow signs to the right to *St. Laurent des Combes.* Joyride your way down through hillsides of vines, then find signs looping back to St-Emilion's lower end via D-245 and D-122.

If you need a driver, local guide **Robert Faustin** drives a comfortable station wagon, speaks enough English, and arranges visits to wineries—he knows them all (tel. 05 57 25 17 59, mobile 06 77 75 36 64, www.taxi-lussac-winetour-stemilion.com, robert.faustin@wanadoo.fr).

Sleeping in St-Emilion: There are no cheap hotels in St-Emilion. *Chambres d'hôtes,* hidden among the surrounding vineyards, offer a better value—ask at the TI for a list. Hotel prices skyrocket during the VinExpo festival at the end of June and during harvest time (late Sept).

$$$ Au Logis des Remparts*** offers top comfort, a pool, and a tranquil garden with vineyards (tel. 05 57 24 70 43, www.logisdesremparts.com, contact@logisdesremparts.com).

$$ L'Auberge de la Commanderie** has 16 well-maintained rooms at midrange prices (closed Jan-Feb, free parking, tel. 05 57 24 70 19, www.aubergedelacommanderie.com, contact@aubergedelacommanderie.com).

$$ At **Moulin la Grangère,** Marie-Annick and Alain Noel rent three rooms at good prices in a 19th-century mill with manicured gardens, a big pool, and a *pétanque* court (cash only, tel. 05 57 24 72 51, www.moulin-la-grangere.com, alain.noel25@orange.fr).

Eating in St-Emilion: Skip most of the cafés lining the street by the TI and instead head to the melt-in-your-chair square, Place du Marché.

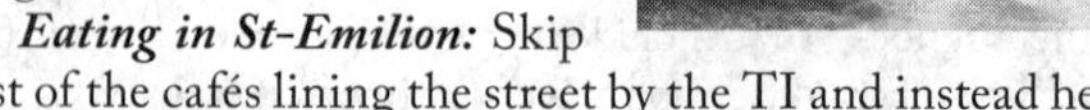

Amelia-Canta Café is *the* happening spot on Place du Marché with café fare, salads, and veggie options (daily March-Nov, 2 Place de l'Eglise Monolithe, tel. 05 57 74 48 03).

L'Envers du Décor wine bar-bistro is about fun, wine, and food—in that order. Meat dishes are their forte (daily, a few doors from the TI at 11 Rue du Clocher, tel. 05 57 74 48 31).

Logis de la Cadène has street appeal with a pleasing patio terrace, a warm interior, and fine, traditional cuisine (closed Sun-Mon, just above Amelia-Canta Café at 3 Place du Marché du Bois, tel. 05 57 24 71 40).

The Overlooked Eastern Dordogne

Many find this remote, less-visited section of the Dordogne (Quercy *région*) even more beautiful than the countryside around Sarlat-la-Canéda. Its undisputed highlight is the pilgrimage town of Rocamadour, but there's so much more to see. For a good introduction to this area, follow this self-guided driving tour connecting Sarlat and Rocamadour.

Eastern Dordogne Driving Tour

For the most scenic route from Sarlat to Rocamadour, follow this self-guided tour along the Dordogne River heading east, driving about an hour upriver from Souillac, to connect these worthwhile stops: Martel, Carennac, Château de Castelnau-Bretenoux, Loubressac, and Autoire. Rocamadour lies a short hop south of this area, as do the Tom Sawyer-like Gouffre de Padirac caves (both described later in this chapter). Allow 45 minutes from Sarlat to Souillac, then 15 minutes to Martel, and 20 minutes to Carennac (Château de Castelnau-Bretenoux and Loubressac are within 10 minutes of Carennac). From Carennac, it's 25 minutes south to Rocamadour. On Mondays, these towns are very quiet, and most shops are closed.

• *From Souillac's center, take D-803 east to...*

Martel: This well-preserved medieval town of 1,500 souls and seven towers offers a good chance to stretch your legs and stock up on picnic items (market days are Wed and Sat on the atmospheric Place des Consuls). Lacking a riverfront or a hilltop setting, Martel is largely overlooked by tourists. Pick up a copy of the TI's well-done walking-tour pamphlet (in English, TI closed 12:00-13:00 and Sun), and enjoy the handsome pedestrian area lined with historic buildings. The walking tour starts at Martel's terrific main square (Place des Consuls)—with a medieval covered market and reasonable lunch cafés—and connects the town's seven towers and the fortress-like church of St. Maur. The town is said to be named for Charles Martel, Charlemagne's grandfather and role model, who stopped the Moors' advance into northern France in 732.

• *From Martel, continue east on D-803 toward Vayrac and Bétaille, then cross the Dordogne on D-20 to find...*

Carennac: This jumble of peaked roofs and half-timbered walls, lassoed between the river and D-20, begs to be photographed. Park along D-20 and wander the village to the river on foot. Find the fortified Prieuré St.-Pierre, explore its evocative

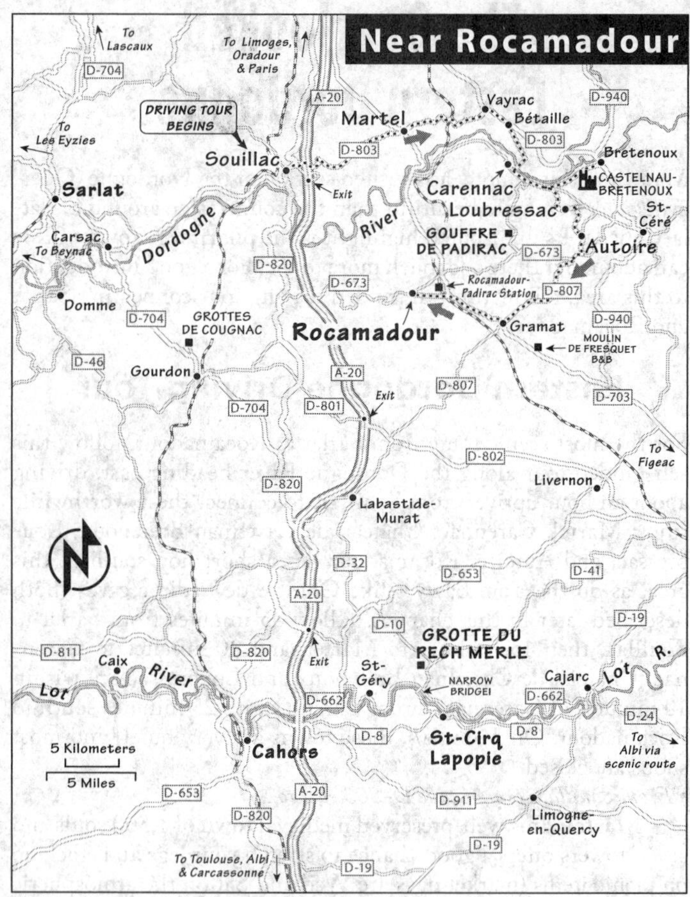

church, and examine its exquisitely carved tympanum. It was built as an outpost of the Cluny Abbey in the 10th century, and then fortified in the 1500s during the French Wars of Religion (a series of civil wars between Catholic and Protestant factions). Cross the small bridge behind the restaurant for more village views.

• *From here, head east on D-30, tracking the Dordogne River. On the left you'll pass the splendidly situated and once-powerful military castle called...*

Château de Castelnau-Bretenoux: This château has views in all directions and a few well-furnished rooms. The reddish-golden stone and massive 12th-century walls make an impression, as does its height—almost 800 feet. Consider detouring for a closer look, but skip the interior. The village of Bretenoux has good markets on Tuesday and Saturday mornings.

• *From D-30, turn right on D-14 and then left on D-118. You'll come to...*

Loubressac: Mystical Loubressac hangs atop a beefy ridge, with outlandish views and a gaggle of adorable homes at its eastern end. If this is not the most beautiful village in France, I'd like to see the one that is. Park along the central green (with a small grocery store), take a loop stroll through the village, and consider a *café* or meal at the *très* traditional and reasonable **$ Hôtel Lou Cantou**.** Or, if you're really on vacation, spend the night, have dinner (restaurant closed Fri and Sun nights), and let owner Marie-Claude take good care of you (Db-€62-76, half with valley views, Wi-Fi, tel. 05 65 38 20 58, www.loucantou.com, lou_cantou@orange.fr).

• *From here it's a short hop on D-118 to lovely little...*

Autoire: The *other* most beautiful village in France, this one lies a few minutes beyond Loubressac. Visit and decide which village is fairest of them all.

• *From here you can follow signs to Gramat, then on to Rocamadour.*

Rocamadour

An hour east of Sarlat-la-Canéda, this historic town with its dramatic rock-face setting is a ▲▲ sight after dark. Once one of Europe's top pilgrimage sites, today it feels more tacky than spiritual. Still, if you can get into the medieval mindset, its peaceful and dramatic setting—combined with the memory of the countless thousands of faithful who trekked from all over Europe to worship here—overwhelms the kitschy tourism, and it becomes a nice (short) stop.

Those who visit only during the day might wonder why they bothered, as there's little to do here except climb the pilgrims' steps (with scads of people who aren't pilgrims) to a few churches, and then stare at the view. Travelers who arrive late and spend the night enjoy fewer crowds—and a floodlit spectacle. To scenically connect Rocamadour and Sarlat, follow the driving tour outlined in the previous section.

Orientation to Rocamadour

Rocamadour has three basic levels, connected by steps or elevators. The bottom level (La Cité Médiévale, or simply La Cité) is a long, single pedestrian street lined with shops and restaurants. The sanctuary level (Cité Religieuse) is up 223 holy steps from La Cité. Its centerpiece is a church with seven chapels gathered around a small square. A switchback trail, the Way of the Cross (Chemin de la Croix), leads from the sanctuary to the top level (called L'Hospitalet) and château (public access to ramparts only) that crowns the cliff and offers a great view and free parking. For most, the goal is the sanctuary at midlevel.

TOURIST INFORMATION

There are two TIs in Rocamadour (www.rocamadour.com): the glassy TI that most drivers come to first, in the village of **L'Hospitalet** above Rocamadour (daily July-Aug 9:30-19:00, April-June and Sept-Oct 10:00-12:30 & 14:00-18:00, closed Nov-March); and another on the level pedestrian street in **La Cité Médiévale** (roughly same hours but open Nov-March until 17:00, tel. 05 65 33 22 00). On the same pedestrian street, you'll find an ATM next to the post office.

ARRIVAL IN ROCAMADOUR

By Train: Five daily trains (transfer in Brive-la-Gaillarde) leave you 2.5 miles from the village at an unstaffed station. It's about a €12 taxi ride to Rocamadour (see "Helpful Hints—Taxi," next page).

By Car: Drivers can park above or below the town for free, but I prefer the upper lot, which is easier and cheaper. From the upper town, follow *P Château* signs and drive all the way to the western end of town until you see the *ascenseur incliné* (elevator), where the parking is free. Walk or take the elevator down (see below).

To park below the town, follow signs to *La Cité* and park at *Parking de la Vallée*. Walk 15 minutes into La Cité Médiévale, or take the little tourist train (4/hour, €4 round-trip); then either climb the stairs or take the elevator to the sanctuary level.

HELPFUL HINTS

Elevators: This vertical town has two handy elevators. From top to bottom, the *ascenseur incliné* (€2.60 one-way, €4.20 round-trip) connects the sanctuary with the château and parking lot at the top. The *ascenseur cité* (€2 one-way, €3 round-trip) links the lower town with the sanctuary. If you buy a round-trip, keep the receipt for your return ride, and if no one is staffing the ticket window, pay as you exit. Each elevator is run like any other: on demand (push the button if no one is there). Managed by two different companies, they're within 50 yards of one another at the sanctuary level.

Views After Dark: If you're staying overnight, don't miss the views of a floodlit Rocamadour from the opposite side of the valley (doable by car, on foot, or by tourist train; see next). It's best as a half-hour (round-trip) stroll. From the town's southeast end (Porte du Figuier), follow the quiet road down, cross the bridge, and head up the far side of the gorge opposite the town. Leave before it gets dark, as the floodlighting is best at twilight. Wear light-colored or reflective clothing, or take a flashlight—it's a dark road with no shoulder. Within the town, climb the steps to just below the sanctuary, and consider a drink with a view at the Hôtel Sainte Marie.

Tourist Train: You can take the cheesy but convenient *petit train* to enjoy the view after dark (runs evenings only April-Sept), complete with 50 other travelers, a bad sound system blaring worthless commentary in four languages, a flashing yellow light, and a rooftop crimping your view (€5, 30-minute round-trip, 2 trips/evening, departures starting at twilight—the first one is by far the best, check at the TI or call 05 65 33 67 84). Or you can walk the same route in 30 minutes (see above), and take much better photos.

Small Grocery Store: It's on Place de l'Europe in the upper city (open daily 8:00-20:00).

Taxi: Call 06 73 44 79 98 or 06 86 18 71 55.

Sights in Rocamadour

IN THE UPPER TOWN (L'HOSPITALET)

If you're coming from Sarlat or from the north, your first view of Rocamadour is the same as the one seen by medieval pilgrims—at the top of the gorge from the hamlet of **L'Hospitalet,** named for the hospitality it gave pilgrims. Stop here for the sweeping views: A right turn takes you to the *Château* parking lot described earlier (for most this is the best place to explore from); a left leads to the glassy TI and the lower Cité. Imagine the impact of this sight in the 13th century, as awestruck pilgrims first gazed on the sanctuary cut from the limestone cliffs. It was through L'Hospitalet's fortified gate that medieval pilgrims gained access to the "Holy Way," the path leading from L'Hospitalet to Rocamadour.

Château

Dating from the 14th century, the original château fortified a bluff that was an easy base for bandits to attack the wealthy church below. Today's structure is a 19th-century private house that was transformed into a reception spot for pilgrims. It's *privé* unless you are a pilgrim (in which case you can sleep here). All it offers tourists is a short rampart walk for a grand view (not worth the €2 fee; turnstile requires exact change).

The zigzag **Way of the Cross** (Chemin de la Croix—a path marked with 14 Stations of the Cross, with a chapel for each station) gives religious purpose to the 15-minute hike between the château and the sanctuary below.

Rocamadour's Religious History

Rocamadour was once one of Europe's top pilgrimage sights. Today tourists replace the pilgrims, enjoying a dramatically situated one-street town under a pretty forgettable church—all because of a crude little thousand-year-old black statue of the Virgin Mary.

Of France's roughly 200 "Black Virgins," this was perhaps the most venerated. Black Virgins date to the end of the pagan era—when Europe was forcefully being Christianized. In Europe's pagan religions, black typically symbolized fertility and motherhood. For newly converted (and still reluctant) pagans, it was easier to embrace the Virgin if she was black.

A thousand years ago, many Europeans expected the world to end, and pilgrimages became immensely popular. About that time, the first pilgrims came here—to a little cave in a cliff over a gorge created by the Alzou River—to pray to a crude statue of a Black Virgin. Then, in 1166, a remarkably intact body was found beneath the threshold of the troglodyte chapel. People assumed this could only be a hermit (certainly a saintly hermit) who had lived in this cave. He was given the name Amadour (servant of Mary), and the place was named Rocamadour (the rock of the servant of Mary).

Suddenly, this humble site was on the map. The Benedictines moved in to develop the spot, building a church over the cave. Like Mont St-Michel, a single-street town sprouted at its base to

Grotte Préhistorique des Merveilles

This cave, located next to the upper TI, has the usual geological formations and a handful of small, blurred cave paintings. It's of no interest if you have seen or will see other prehistoric caves—its sole advantages are that it requires little effort to visit (with only about 10 steps down), and the guide can answer questions in English on the 40-minute tour.

Cost and Hours: €7, daily July-Aug 9:30-19:00, April-June and Sept 10:00-12:00 & 14:00-18:00, Oct until 17:00, closed Nov-March, decent handout available, tel. 05 65 33 67 92, www.grottes-des-merveilles.com.

BETWEEN THE UPPER AND LOWER TOWNS (LA CITE RELIGIEUSE)

These sights form the heart of your vertical sightseeing. To reach the sights from the château's parking lot in the **upper town,** descend the paved Way of the Cross path or take the elevator and walk downhill. If you're coming from the **lower town,** ride the elevator up or climb the Grand Escalier steps (like a good pilgrim), passing a plaque listing key medieval pilgrims, such as St. Bernard,

handle the needs of its growing pilgrim hordes. During Europe's great age of pilgrimages (12th and 13th centuries), the greatest of pilgrims (St. Louis, St. Dominique, Richard the Lionhearted, and so on) all trekked to this spot to pray. Rocamadour became a powerful symbol of faith and hope.

During the 14th century, up to 8,000 people lived in Rocamadour, earning their living off the pilgrims—who arrived in numbers of up to 20,000 a day. But with the 16th-century Wars of Religion and the Age of Enlightenment (in the 18th century), pilgrimages declined...and so did Rocamadour.

During the Romantic Age of the 19th century, pilgrimages were again in vogue, and Rocamadour rebounded. Local bishops rebuilt the château above the sanctuary, making it a pilgrims' reception center, and connecting it to the church with the Way of the Cross. (Most of the current buildings in the Sanctuary of Our Lady of Rocamadour date from the 19th century.) But there hasn't been a bona fide miracle here for eight centuries...and that's not good for the pilgrimage business.

Since the mid-20th century, Rocamadour has become more a tourist attraction, and today, its 650 inhabitants earn a living off its million visitors a year. The vast majority of those who climb the holy steps to the sanctuary are tourists—more interested in burning calories than incense.

St. Dominique, and St. Louis (the only French king to become a saint; he brought the Crown of Thorns to Paris and had Sainte-Chapelle constructed to house it). Either way, your destination will be signed *Sanctuaires* (free, open daily generally 8:00-19:00).

▲▲Sanctuary of Our Lady of Rocamadour

Find the concrete bench on the small square facing the cliff, and look up to the open door of the Church of St. Saveur. Though the buildings originated much earlier, most of what you see was rebuilt in the 19th century. Crammed onto a ledge on a cliff, the church couldn't follow the standard floor plan, so its seven chapels surround the square (called the *parvis*) rather than the church. The bishop's palace is behind you and to your left, and houses a gift shop selling various pilgrimage mementos, including modern versions of the medallions that pilgrims prized centuries ago as proof of their visit (about €11 for a tiny one). The two most historic chapels are straight ahead on either side of the steps.

• *Walk up the flight of steps to the cliff, where a tomb is cut into the rock.*

This is where the miraculously preserved body of St. Amadour was found in 1166. Places of pilgrimage do better with multiple miracles, so, along with its Black Virgin and the miracle of St. Amadour's body (see sidebar on page 506), Rocamadour has the **Sword of Roland.** The rusty sword of Charlemagne's nephew sticks in the cliffside, above Amadour's tomb (to the right, about where the church roof meets the cliff). According to medieval sources, Roland was about to die in battle, but the great warrior didn't want his sword to fall into enemy hands. He hurled it from the far south of France, and it landed here—stuck miraculously into the Rocamadour cliffs just above the Black Virgin. (The sword is clearly from the 18th century, but never mind.)

St. Michael's Chapel is built around the original cave to your left (open only to pilgrims, with little to see inside). A few steps farther along, the tiny **Chapel of St-Louis** is sculpted into the rock with a view terrace just beyond. Backtrack to the **Chapel of the Virgin** (Chapelle Notre-Dame), the focal point for pilgrims. Step inside. Sitting above the altar is the much-venerated Black Virgin, a 12th-century statue (covered with a thin plating of blackened silver—see sidebar on page 506) that depicts Mary presenting Jesus to the world. The oldest thing in the sanctuary—from the ninth century—is a simple rusted bell hanging from the ceiling. The suspended sailboat models are a reminder that sailors relied on Mary for safe passage.

The adjacent **Church of St. Saveur** is the sanctuary's main place of worship. You can't miss the dazzling new organ, installed in 2013. The rebuilt wooden balcony overhead was for the monks. Imagine attending a Mass here in centuries past, when pilgrims filled the church and monks lined the balconies. While Rocamadour's church seems more like a tourist attraction, it remains a sacred place of worship. A sign reminds tourists "to admire, to contemplate, to pray. You're welcome to respectfully visit." A bulletin board on the wall usually displays fliers for pilgrimages to Lourdes or Santiago de Compostela. Rocamadour has been both a key destination and staging point for pilgrims for centuries.

• *From here you can walk down the Grand Escalier to the lower town or walk under the Church of St. Saveur and find the Way of the Cross (Chemin de la Croix) and elevators up* (Château par ascenseur) *or down* (La Cité par ascenseur).

IN THE LOWER TOWN (LA CITE MEDIEVALE)

Rocamadour's town is basically one long street traversing the cliff below the sanctuary. For eight centuries it has housed, fed, and sold souvenirs to the site's countless visitors. There's precious little here other than tacky trinket shops, but I enjoy popping into the **Galerie le Vieux Pressoir** (named for its 13th-century walnut millstone). It fills a medieval vaulted room with the fine art of a talented couple: Richard Begyn and Veronique Guinard (about 50 yards up from the elevator).

Of Rocamadour's 11 original **gates,** 7 survive (designed to control the pilgrim crowds). In the 14th century, as many as 20,000 people a day from all over Europe would converge on this spot. From the western end of town, 223 steps lead up to the church at the sanctuary level. Traditionally, pilgrims kneel on each and pray an "Ave Maria" to Our Lady.

NEAR ROCAMADOUR

▲Gouffre de Padirac

A 20-minute drive northeast of Rocamadour is the huge sinkhole of Padirac, with its underground river and miles of stalagmites and stalactites (but no cave art). Though it's an impressive cave, if you've seen caves already, it may feel slow in comparison (and there's little English). But the mechanics of the visit are easy, and there's not much to communicate anyway. Here's the drill: After paying, hike the stairs (with big views of the sinkhole—a round shaft about 100 yards wide and deep), or ride the elevator to the river level. Line up and wait for your boat. Pack into the boat with about a dozen others for the slow row past a fantasy world of hanging cave formations. Get out and hike a big circle with your group and guide, enjoying lots of caverns, underground lakes, and mighty stalagmites and stalactites. Get back on the boat and retrace your course. Two elevators zip you back to the sunlight. The visit takes 1.5 hours (crowds make it take longer in summer). Dress warmly.

Cost and Hours: €10, reserve online at least 48 hours ahead and save lots of waiting, daily mid-July-Aug 9:30-20:30, April-mid-July and Sept-early Nov 9:30-18:00, closed mid-Nov-March, tel. 05 65 33 64 56, www.gouffre-de-padirac.com. For a knick-knack Padirac, don't miss the shop.

Sleeping in Rocamadour

Hotels are a deal here. Those in the upper La Cité (near L'Hospitalet) have views down to Rocamadour and easier parking, but the spirit of St. Amadour is more present below, in the medieval city (which I prefer). Every hotel—including the ones I recommend—has a restaurant where they'd like you to dine.

$ Hôtel Belvédère,** in the upper city (L'Hospitalet) has 17 well-maintained, modern, and appealing rooms. Five rooms have views over Rocamadour, and seven have valley views (rooms #14-18 have best views, Db with no view-€69, Db with view-€80, tel. 05 65 33 63 25, www.hotel-le-belvedere.fr, lebelvedere-rocamadour@orange.fr).

$ Hôtel-Restaurant le Terminus des Pèlerins,** at the western end of the pedestrian street in La Cité Medievale, has immaculate, comfortable rooms with wood furnishings; the best have balconies and face the valley. Reserved owner Geneviève was born in this hotel (Db-€64, Db with view and balcony-€84, Tb/Qb-€90, Wi-Fi, tel. 05 65 33 62 14, www.terminus-des-pelerins.com, contact@terminus-des-pelerins.com).

Near Rocamadour: **$$ Moulin de Fresquet** is simply idyllic. Here gracious Gérard and his wife, Claude, have lovingly restored an ancient mill in a lush, park-like setting. The five antique-furnished rooms come with wood beams, oodles of character, lovely terraces, chaise lounges, and a duck pond (with at least 50 ducks for pets, not for dinner). Book well ahead (Db-€83-99, Db suite-€120, Tb suite-€143, includes big breakfast, cash only, Wi-Fi, closed Nov-March, in Gramat, tel. 05 65 38 70 60, mobile 06 08 85 09 21, www.moulindefresquet.com, info@moulindefresquet.com). Go to Gramat, then follow signs toward *Figeac.* The *chambres d'hôte* is well-signed at the east end of Gramat, at a big roundabout.

Eating in Rocamadour

Hôtel Belvédère, in the upper town, has the best interior view from its modern dining room. Book ahead for a window-side table, ideally for a meal just before sunset (*menus* from €19, daily, tel. 05 65 33 63 25; also recommended under "Sleeping in Rocamadour," earlier).

The **Bar l'Esplanade** hunkers cliffside below Hôtel Belvédère and owns unobstructed views from the tables in its garden café. It's open for lunch, dinner, drinks, and snacks (daily, tel. 05 65 33 18 45).

Lot River Valley

An hour and a half south of the Dordogne, the overlooked Lot River meanders through a strikingly beautiful valley under stubborn cliffs and past tempting villages. If you have a car, the fortified bridge at Cahors, the prehistoric cave paintings at Grotte du Pech Merle, and the breathtaking town of St-Cirq Lapopie are worthwhile sights in this valley. These sights can be combined to make a terrific day for drivers willing to invest the time (doable as a long day trip from the Sarlat area). They also work well as a day trip from Rocamadour, but

are best to visit when connecting the Dordogne with Albi, Puycelci, or Carcassonne. (If you're going to or coming from the south, you can scenically connect this area with Albi via Villefranche-de-Rouergue and Cordes-sur-Ciel.)

St-Cirq Lapopie

This spectacularly situated village, clinging to a ledge sailing above the Lot River, knows only two directions—straight up and way down. In St-Cirq Lapopie, there's little to do but wander the rambling footpaths, inspect the flowers and stones, and thrill over the vistas. You'll find picnic perches, a gaggle of galleries and restaurants, and views from the bottom and top of the village that justify the pain. Leave no stone unturned in your quest to find the village's best view (the overlook from the rocky monolith across from the TI makes a good start). In this town, every building seems historic. You'll lose most tourists by wandering downhill from the church.

The **TI** is located across from the recommended Auberge du Sombral (May-Sept daily 10:00-13:00 & 14:00-18:00 except July-Aug 10:00-19:00, Oct-April until 17:00 and closed Sun, tel. 05 65 31 31 31). Pick up the visitor's guide in English, with brief descriptions of 22 historic buildings, and ask for information on hikes in the area.

St-Cirq Lapopie is slammed on weekends and in high season (mid-June-mid Sept), but is peaceful early and after-hours in any season. Come early and spend a few hours, or arrive late and spend the night—your first views of St-Cirq Lapopie are eye-popping enough to convince you to stay. The lanes are steep—those with imperfect knees but still wanting a lovely village retreat should sleep an hour south in the level, quiet hilltop village of Puycelci (see page 529).

Getting There: St-Cirq Lapopie is well-signed 40 minutes east of Cahors, 75 minutes south of Rocamadour, and just 20 minutes from the cave paintings of Grotte du Pech Merle.

Arriving by car from the west, you'll pass the town across the Lot River, then cross a narrow bridge and climb. There are five **parking lots** (€3-5) from well below the village to the top; unless it's high season, keep climbing and park at lot closest to the town center near the post office (in high season you'll be directed to lower lots, leaving you a good climb to the center). Pull over for photo stops as you climb.

Sleeping and Eating in St-Cirq Lapopie: The village has all of 18 rooms, none of which are open off-season (mid-Nov-March).

$$ Auberge du Sombral,** run by English-speaking Marion is a good value in the town center below the TI. She'll welcome you with an oh-so-cozy lobby area and eight comfortable rooms in various sizes above, most with double beds (small Sb-€60, Db-€77-82, breakfast-€9, tel. 05 65 31 26 08, www.lesombral.com, aubergesombral@gmail.com). The good restaurant serves reliable lunches (every day but Thu) and dinners (Fri-Sat only) in its lovely dining room or out front on a photogenic terrace (€17 lunch *menus*, €24-30 dinner *menus*).

As restaurants go, **Lou Boulat Brasserie** works for me. It serves low-risk lighter meals (salads, crêpes, pizza, and *plats*) in a low-stress setting, with good views from the pleasant side terrace (daily for lunch and dinner June-Sept, otherwise lunch only, at the upper end of town, off the main road by the post office, tel. 05 65 30 29 04).

L'Oustal is the most traditional restaurant in town, with a handful of cozy tables inside and out on a little terrace (*menus* from €18, €15 *plats du jour*, beneath the towering church, tel. 05 65 31 20 17).

Picnicking: This town was made for picnics; consider picking up dinner fixings in the hamlet of La Tour de Faure. There's a small grocery store on the other side of the river just west of the bridge to St-Cirq Lapopie, and a bakery a short way east of the bridge.

▲▲Grotte du Pech Merle

This cave, about 30 minutes east of Cahors, has prehistoric paintings of mammoths, bison, and horses—rivaling the better-known cave art at Grotte de Font-de-Gaume. Although this cave is easier to view, as more people per day are allowed in (700), that also makes the cave a bit less special. Still, it has brilliant cave art and interesting stalactite and stalagmite formations. I like the mud-preserved Cro-Magnon footprint. Allow a total of two hours for your visit, starting at the small museum, continuing with a 20-minute film subtitled in English, and finishing with the caves. If you can't join an English tour, ask for the English booklet.

Cost and Hours: €10, daily March-mid-Nov 9:30-17:00, closes earlier off-season, fewer visitors on weekends, tel. 05 65 31 27 05, www.pechmerle.com. Before you visit, read "Cave Art 101" on page 479.

Getting Tickets: It's smart to reserve your spot in advance (by phone or online), as private groups can fill the cave's quota. Book a week ahead in summer; if you visit without a reservation, arrive by 9:30 and line up.

▲Cahors and the Pont Valentré

Cahors is home to one of Europe's best medieval monuments. This massive fortified bridge was built in 1308 to keep the English out of Cahors. It worked. Learn the story of the devil on the center tower, then cross the bridge and have a view drink at the riverside café. Consider walking up the trail across the road: A short, steep hike leads to terrific views (the rock is dangerous if the trail is wet). This trail was once part of the pilgrimage route to Santiago de Compostela in northwest Spain. Imagine that cars were allowed to cross this bridge until recently.

To find the bridge as you're approaching Cahors, follow signs to *Centre-Ville, Gare SNCF,* then Pont *Valentré.* Turn left at the river and find parking lots a few blocks down and a fine riverside promenade to the bridge.

On the city side, Cahors' small **TI** is at the foot of the bridge. Across the street, **Le Cèdre** boutique offers a good selection of Cahors wines at fair prices (daily 10:00-18:00).

If you need an urban fix, walk for 10 minutes on the street that continues straight from the bridge (Rue de Président Wilson) and find the old city *(Vielle Ville)* after crossing Boulevard Gambetta. Cahors' thriving, pedestrian-friendly center is filled with good lunch options, cafes, cool gardens, and riverside parkways. To find this area by car, follow *Centre-Ville* and *St. Urcisse Eglise* signs, and park where you can.

LANGUEDOC-ROUSSILLON

Albi • Carcassonne • Collioure

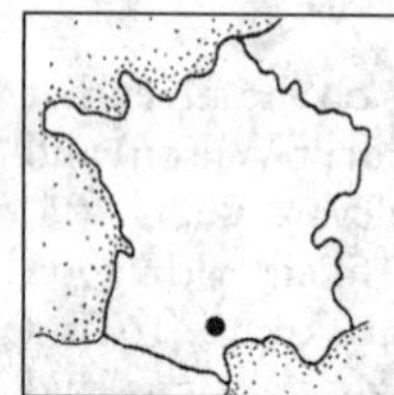

From the 10th to the 13th century, this mighty and independent region controlled most of southern France. The ultimate in mean-spirited crusades against the Cathars (or Albigensians) began here in 1208, igniting Languedoc-Roussillon's meltdown and eventual incorporation into the state of France.

The name *languedoc* comes from the *langue* (language) that its people spoke: *Langue d'oc* ("language of Oc," *Oc* for the way they said "yes") was the dialect of southern France; *langue d'oïl* was the dialect of northern France (where *oïl* later became *oui,* or "yes"). Languedoc-Roussillon's language faded with its power.

The Moors, Charlemagne, and the Spanish have all called this area home, with the Roussillon part corresponding closely with its Catalan corner, near the border with Spain. The Spanish influence is still *muy* present, particularly in the south, where restaurants serve paella and the siesta is still respected.

While sharing many of the same attributes as Provence (climate, wind, grapes, and sea), this sunny, intoxicating, southwesternmost region of France is allocated little time by most travelers. Lacking Provence's cachet and sophistication, Languedoc-Roussillon (long-dohk roo-see-yohn) feels more real. Pay homage to Henri de Toulouse-Lautrec in Albi; spend a night in Europe's greatest fortress city, Carcassonne; scamper up to a remote Cathar castle; and sift through sand in Collioure. That wind you feel is called *la tramontane* (trah-mohn-tahn-yuh), this region's version of Provence's mistral wind.

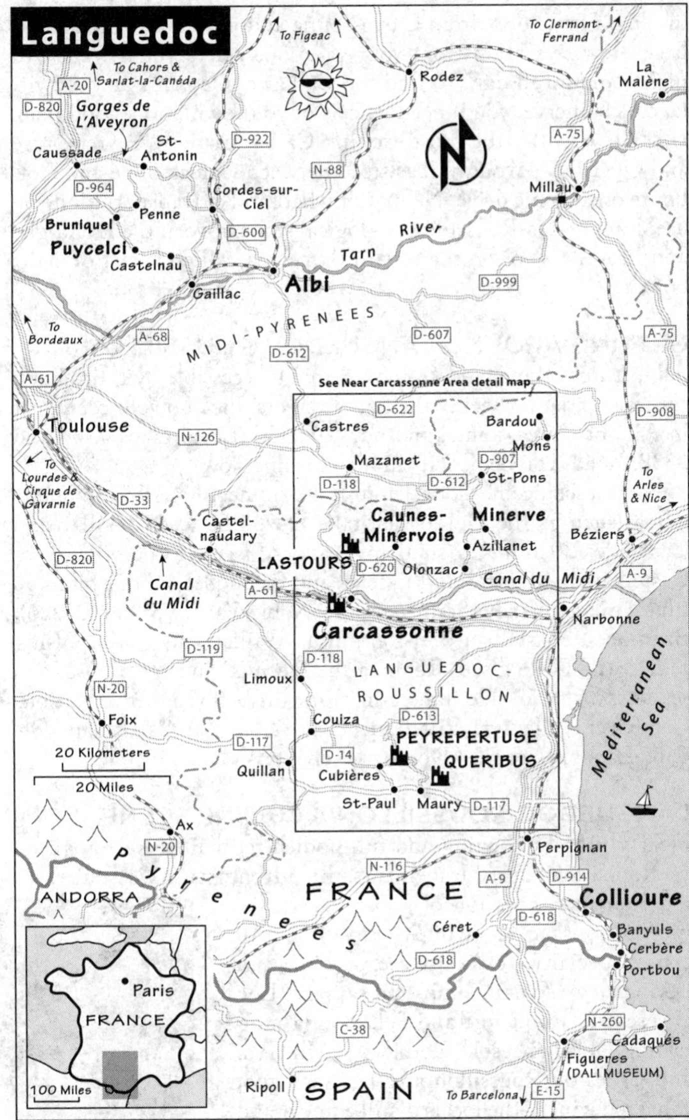

PLANNING YOUR TIME

Albi or Puycelci make a good day or overnight stop between the Dordogne region and Carcassonne (figure about two autoroute hours from Albi to either place; Puycelci is 40 minutes closer to the Dordogne. Plan your arrival in popular Carcassonne carefully: Get there late in the afternoon, spend the night, and leave no later than 11:00 the next morning to miss most day-trippers. Collioure lies a few hours from Carcassonne and is your Mediterranean beach-town vacation from your vacation, where you'll want two nights and a full day. To find the Cathar castle ruins and the village of Minerve, you'll need wheels of your own and a good map. If you're driving, the most exciting Cathar castles—Peyrepertuse and Quéribus—work well as stops between Carcassonne and Collioure on a scenic drive. No matter what kind of transportation you use, Languedoc-Roussillon is a logical stop between the Dordogne and Provence—or on the way to Barcelona, which is just over the border.

GETTING AROUND LANGUEDOC-ROUSSILLON

Albi, Carcassonne, and Collioure are all accessible by train, but a car is essential for seeing the remote sights. Pick up your rental car in Albi or Carcassonne, and buy Michelin Local maps #344 and #338. Roads can be pencil-thin, and traffic slow.

For a scenic one-hour detour route connecting Albi and points north (such as the Dordogne), take D-964 between Gaillac and Caussade (30 minutes south of Cahors), passing the villages of Castelnau de Montmiral, Puycelci, and Bruniquel. With a bit more time, link Caussade, Saint-Antonin-Noble-Val (D-5 and D-926), Bruniquel, Castelnau-de-Montmiral, Gaillac, and Albi (using D-115 and D-964; see "Route of the *Bastides*" on page 528). If you really want to joyride, take a half-day drive through the glorious Lot River Valley via Villefranche-de-Rouergue, Cajarc, and St-Cirq-Lapopie (see the "Dordogne" chapter).

LANGUEDOC-ROUSSILLON'S CUISINE SCENE

Hearty peasant cooking and full-bodied red wines are Languedoc-Roussillon's tasty trademarks. Be adventurous. Cassoulet, an old Roman concoction of goose, duck, pork, mutton, sausage, and white beans, is the main-course specialty. You'll also see *cargolade*, a satisfying stew of snail, lamb, and sausage. Local cheeses are Roquefort and Pelardon (a nutty-tasting goat cheese). Corbières, Minervois, and Côtes du Roussillon are the area's good-value red wines. The locals distill a fine brandy, Armagnac, which tastes just like cognac and costs less.

Remember, restaurants serve only during lunch (11:30-14:00) and dinner (19:00-21:00, later in bigger cities); some cafés serve food throughout the day.

Albi

Albi, an enjoyable river city of sienna-tone bricks, half-timbered buildings, and a marvelous traffic-free center, is worth a stop for two world-class sights: its towering cathedral and the Toulouse-Lautrec Museum. Lost in the Dordogne-to-Carcassonne shuffle and overshadowed by its big brother Toulouse, unpretentious Albi rewards the stray tourist well. For most, Albi works best as a day stop, though some will be smitten by its red-brick charm and lured into spending a night.

Orientation to Albi

Albi's cathedral is home base. For our purposes, all sights, pedestrian streets, and hotels fan out from here and are less than a five-minute walk away. The Tarn River hides below and behind the cathedral. The best city view is from the 22 Août 1944 bridge. Albi is dead quiet on Sundays and Monday mornings. The city is ambitiously renovating parts of the city center—expect some construction detours.

TOURIST INFORMATION

There are two TIs in Albi. The main TI is on the square in front of the cathedral, next to the Toulouse-Lautrec Museum (mid-June-Sept Mon-Sat 9:00-19:00, Sun 10:00-12:30 & 14:30-18:30; Oct-mid-June Mon-Sat 9:00-12:30 & 14:30-18:00, Sun 10:00-12:30 & 14:30-17:00; free Wi-Fi, tel. 05 63 49 48 80, www.albi-tourisme.fr). A second TI is just off Place Lapérouse on Avenue du Général de Gaulle (you can't miss the wild bronze screen; daily 10:00-18:00). Both sell a combo-ticket that includes the Toulouse-Lautrec museum and the cathedral choir for €9 (saves €1). Ask about concerts, and pick up a map of the city center, the walking-tour brochure, and the map of *La Route des Bastides Albigeoises* (hill towns near Albi). You can download a free, 19-minute English audiotour of the city's monuments and old town from the TI website.

ARRIVAL IN ALBI

By Train: There are two stations in Albi; you want Albi-Ville (see "Helpful Hints" for baggage storage). It's a level 15-minute walk to

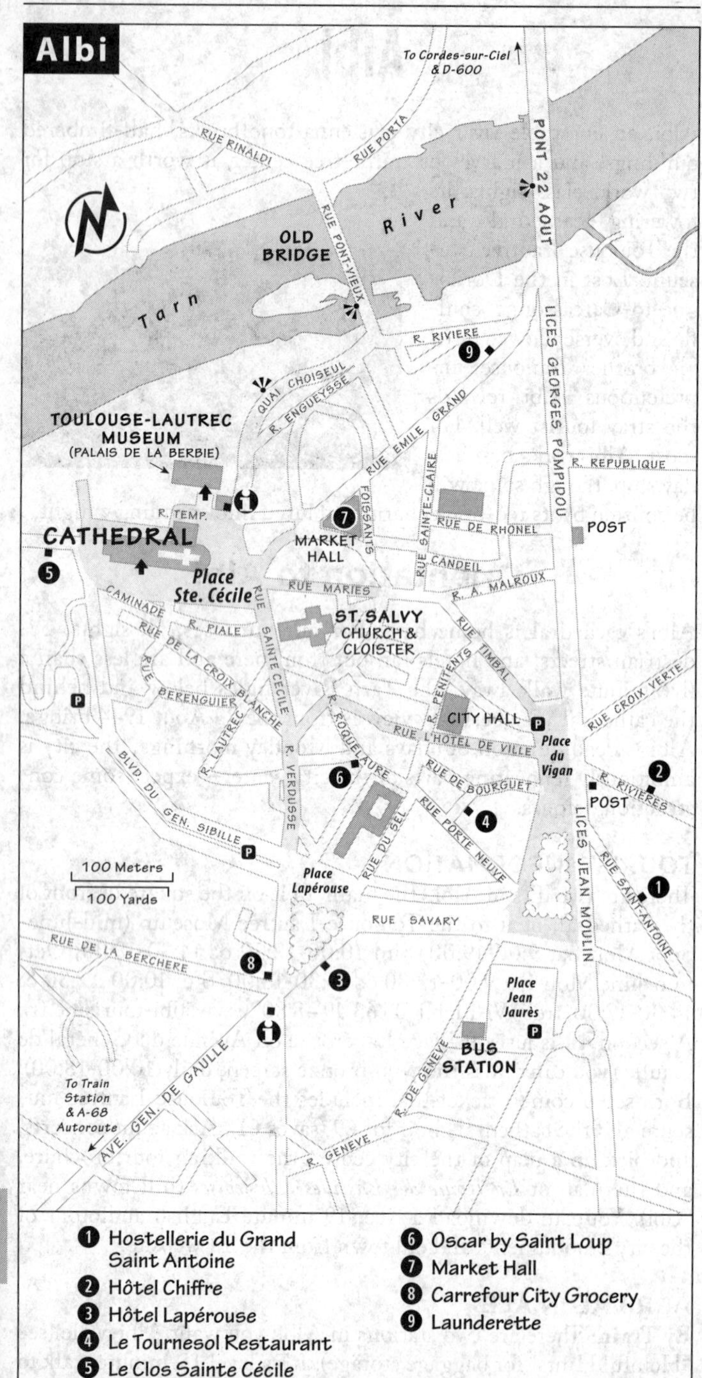
Albi
To Cordes-sur-Ciel & D-600
RUE RINALDI
RUE PORTA
PONT 22 AOUT
River
Tarn
OLD BRIDGE
RUE PONT-VIEUX
R. RIVIERE
LICES GEORGES POMPIDOU
QUAI CHOISEUL
R. ENGUEYSSE
RUE EMILE GRAND
TOULOUSE-LAUTREC MUSEUM
(PALAIS DE LA BERBIE)
R. REPUBLIQUE
R. TEMP.
FOISSANTS
RUE SAINTE-CLAIRE
RUE DE RHONEL
POST
CATHEDRAL
MARKET HALL
CANDEIL
R. A. MALROUX
Place Ste. Cécile
RUE MARIES
CAMINADE
R. PIALE
RUE SAINTE CECILE
ST. SALVY CHURCH & CLOISTER
RUE TIMBAL
RUE DE LA CROIX BLANCHE
RUE PENITENTS
RUE CROIX VERTE
RUE BERENGUIER
R. ROQUELAURE
CITY HALL
RUE L'HOTEL DE VILLE
Place du Vigan
R. LAUTREC
R. VERDUSSE
RUE DE BOURGUET
R. RIVIERES
POST
BLVD. DU GEN. SIBILLE
RUE DU SEL
RUE PORTE NEUVE
LICES JEAN MOULIN
RUE SAINT-ANTOINE
100 Meters
100 Yards
Place Lapérouse
RUE SAVARY
RUE DE LA BERCHERE
Place Jean Jaurès
BUS STATION
R. DE GENEVE
To Train Station & A-68 Autoroute
AVE. GEN. DE GAULLE
R. GENEVE
1 Hostellerie du Grand Saint Antoine
2 Hôtel Chiffre
3 Hôtel Lapérouse
4 Le Tournesol Restaurant
5 Le Clos Sainte Cécile
6 Oscar by Saint Loup
7 Market Hall
8 Carrefour City Grocery
9 Launderette

the town center: Exit the station, take the second left onto Avenue Maréchal Joffre, and then take another left on Avenue du Général de Gaulle. Go straight across Place Lapérouse and find the traffic-free street to the left that leads into the city center. This turns into Rue Ste. Cécile, which takes you to my recommended hotels and the cathedral.

By Car: Follow *Centre-Ville* and *Cathédrale* signs (if you lose your way, follow the tall church tower). For the lot closest to the old city, follow signs for *Cathédrale* parking along Boulevard Général Sibille. If you find a spot on the street, remember parking meters are free 12:00-14:00 & 19:00-8:00, and all day Sunday; otherwise pay by the hour with coins.

HELPFUL HINTS

Market Days: The beautiful Art Nouveau market hall, a block past the cathedral square, hosts a market daily except Monday (8:00-14:00). A farmers' market is held Saturdays outside the market hall.

Internet Access: The main TI has free Wi-Fi, as do many cafés.

Baggage Storage: The **Toulouse-Lautrec Museum** has large lockers (€1) accessible only during the museum's open hours.

Groceries: Carrefour City is across from the recommended Hôtel Lapérouse (Mon-Sat 8:00-21:00, Sun 9:00-13:00, 14 Place Lapérouse).

Laundry: Do your washing at **Lavomatique,** above the river at 10 Rue Emile Grand (daily 7:00-21:00).

Taxi: Call **Albi Taxi Radio** at 06 12 99 42 46.

Tourist Train: Le Petit Train leaves from Place Ste. Cécile in front of the cathedral and makes a 45-minute scenic loop around Albi (€6).

Sights in Albi

Everything of sightseeing interest is within a few blocks of the towering cathedral. (I've included walking directions to connect some of the key sights.) Get oriented in the main square (see map on facing page; remember that you can download a free audiotour from the TI's website).

Place Ste. Cécile

Grab a bench on the far side of Place Ste. Cécile. With the church directly in front of you, the bishop's palace (along with the Toulouse-Lautrec Museum, river view, and TI) is a bit to the right. The market hall is a block behind you on your right.

Why the big church? At its peak, Albi was the administrative center for 465 churches. Back when tithes were essentially legally required taxes, everyone gave their 10 percent, or "*dime*" (pron. "deem"), to the church. The local bishop was filthy rich, and with all those *dimes,* he had money to build a dandy church. In medieval times, there was no interest in making a space so people could step back and get a perspective on such a beautiful building. A clutter of houses snuggled right up to the church's stout walls, and only in the 19th century were things cleared away. Just in the last few years the cars were also cleared out (another triumph for pedestrians).

Why so many bricks? Because there were no stone quarries nearby. Albi is part of a swath of red-brick towns from here to Toulouse (nicknamed "the pink city" for the way its bricks dominate that townscape). Notice on this square the buffed brick addresses next to the sluggish stucco ones. As late as the 1960s, the town's brickwork was considered low-class and was covered by stucco. Today, the stucco is being peeled away, and Albi has that brick pride back.

▲▲Ste. Cécile Cathedral (Cathédrale Ste. Cécile)

When the heretical Cathars were defeated in the 13th century, this massive cathedral was the final nail in their coffin. Big and bold, it made it clear who was in charge. The imposing exterior and the stunning interior drive home the message of the Catholic (read: "universal") Church in a way that would have stuck with any medieval worshipper. This place oozes power—get on board, or get run over.

Cost and Hours: Free, daily June-Sept 9:00-18:30, Oct-May 9:00-12:00 & 14:00-18:30. Once inside, you'll pay €2 to enter the choir (worthwhile). The treasury (a single room of reliquaries and church art) is not worth the €2 fee or the climb (€3 for both with audioguide).

Organ Concerts: The cathedral and St. Salvy Church host frequent concerts (the TI has a schedule), most often in July and August (Wed, Fri, and Sun at 16:00).

➲ Self-Guided Tour: Visit the cathedral using the following commentary.

• *Begin facing the...*

Exterior: The cathedral looks less like a church and more like a fortress. That's because it was a central feature of the town's defensive walls. Notice how high the windows are (out of stone-tossing range). The simple Gothic style was typical of this region—designed to be sensitive to the anti-materialistic tastes of the local Cathars.

The top (from the gargoyles and newer, brighter bricks up-

The Cathars

The Cathars were a heretical group of Christians who grew in numbers from the 11th through the 13th century under tolerant rule in Languedoc-Roussillon. They saw life as a battle between good (the spiritual) and bad (the material), and they considered material things evil and of the devil. Although others called them "Cathars" (from the Greek word for "pure") or "Albigensians" (for their main city, Albi), they called themselves simply "friends of God." Cathars focused on the teachings of St. John, and recognized only baptism as a sacrament. Because they believed in reincarnation, they were vegetarians.

Travelers encounter traces of the Cathars in their Languedoc sightseeing because of the Albigensian Crusades (1209-1240s). The king of France wanted to consolidate his grip on southern France. The pope needed to make a strong point that the only acceptable Christianity was Roman style. They found self-serving reasons to wage a genocidal war together against the Cathars, who never amounted to more than 10 percent of the local population and coexisted happily with their non-Cathar neighbors. After a terrible generation of torture and mass burnings, the Cathars were wiped out. The last Cathar was burned in 1321.

Today, tourists find haunting castle ruins (once Cathar strongholds) high in the Pyrenees, and eat meaty, if misnamed, *salades Cathar.*

ward) is a fanciful, 19th-century, Romantic-era renovation. The church was originally as plain and austere as the bishop's palace (the similar, bold brick building to the right, now housing the Toulouse-Lautrec Museum). Imagine the church with a rooftop more like that of the bishop's palace.

• *Climb up to the extravagant Flamboyant Gothic...*

Entry Porch: The entry was built about two centuries after the original plain church (1494), when concerns about Cathar sensitivities were long passé. Originally colorfully painted, it provided one fancy entry.

• *Head into the cathedral's...*

Interior: The inside of the church—also far from plain—looks essentially as it did in 1500. The highlights are the vast *Last Judgment* painting (west wall, under the organ) and the ornate choir (east end).

• *Walk to the front of the altar and face the...*

Last Judgment: The oldest art in the church (1474), this is also the biggest Last Judgment painting from the Middle Ages. The dead come out of the ground, then line up (above) with a printed accounting of their good and bad deeds displayed in ledgers on their chests. Judgment, here we come. Those on the left (God's right) look confident and comfortable. Those on the right—the hedonists—look edgy. Get closer. Below, on both sides of the arch, are seven frames illustrating a wonderland of gruesome punishments sinners could suffer through while attempting to earn a second chance at salvation. Those who fail end up in the black clouds of Hell (upper right).

But where's Jesus—the key figure in any Judgment Day painting? The missing arch in the middle (cut out in late-Renaissance times to open the way to a new chapel) once featured Christ overseeing the action. Go back to the last pew and find the black-and-white image on a small stand. The picture provides a good guess at how this painting would have looked—though no one knows for sure. The assembly above (on the left) shows the heavenly hierarchy: The pope and bishops sit closest to (the missing) Jesus; then more bishops and priests—before kings—followed by monks; and then, finally, commoners like you and me. To learn more about the *Last Judgment*, tour the choir (described below), which includes an audioguide with commentary on the painting.

The **altar** is the newest art in the church. But this is not the front of the church at all—you're facing west. Turn 180 degrees and head east, for Jerusalem (where most medieval churches point).

• *Stop first at the choir—a fancy, more intimate room within the finely carved stone "screen."*

The Choir: In the Middle Ages, nearly all cathedrals had ornate Gothic choir screens like this one. These highly decorated walls divided the church into a private place for clergy and a general zone for the common rabble. The screen enclosed the altar and added mystery to the Mass. In the 16th century, with the success of the Protestant movement and the Catholic Church's Counter-Reformation, choir screens were removed. (In the 20th century, the Church took things one step further, and priests actually turned and faced their parishioners.) Later, French Revolutionary atheists destroyed most of the choir screens that remained—Albi's is a rare survivor.

Pay €2 to stroll around the choir (excellent audioguide included, follow the English diagram). You'll see colorful Old Testament figures along the Dark Ages exterior columns and New Testament figures in the enlightened interior. Stepping inside the choir, marvel at the fine limestone carving. Scan each of the 72 unique little angels just above the wood-paneled choir stalls. Check out the brilliant ceiling, which hasn't been touched or restored in 500 years. A bishop, impressed by the fresco technique of the Italian Renaissance, invited seven Florentine artists to do the work. Good call.

• *Exit through the side door, next to where you paid for the choir. You'll pass a WC on your way to the...*

▲▲Toulouse-Lautrece Museum (Musée Toulouse-Lautrec)

The Palais de la Berbie (once the fortified home of Albi's archbishop) has the world's largest collection of Henri de Toulouse-Lautrec's paintings, posters, and sketches.

Cost and Hours: €8, €10 during special exhibits; July-Sept daily 9:00-18:00; June daily 9:00-12:00 & 14:00-18:00; April-May and Oct daily 10:00-12:00 & 14:00-18:00—but closed Tue in Oct; Nov-March Wed-Mon 10:00-12:00 & 14:00-17:30, closed Tue; audioguide-€4 (for most, the printed English explanations are sufficient), lockers for day packs-€1; Place Ste. Cécile, tel. 05 63 49 48 70, www.museetoulouselautrec.net.

Background: Henri de Toulouse-Lautrec, born here in 1864, was crippled from youth. After he broke his right leg at age 13 and then his left leg the next year (probably due to a genetic disorder), the lower half of his body stopped growing. His father, once very engaged in parenting, lost interest in his son. Henri moved to the fringes of society, where he gained an affinity for people who didn't quite fit in. He later made his mark painting the dregs of the Parisian underclass with an intimacy only made possible by a man with his life experience.

Visiting the Museum: From the turnstile, walk down a few steps and enter the main floor collection. Every room has information sheets in English.

The first room is filled with **portraits** of Henri de Toulouse-Lautrec painted by other artists. In the next sections we see his earliest classical paintings, horses, and his boyhood doodles. I especially like the dictionary he scribbled all over as a schoolkid. In the 1880s, Henri was stuck in Albi, far from any artistic action. During these years, he found inspiration in nature, in the pages of magazines, and by observing people. This was his Impressionistic stage—find *Cheval de Trait à Céleyran* for a good example.

Next, go down a few more steps and see his most famous stuff, the paintings of the prostitutes and brothels of **Paris.** In 1882, Henri moved to the big city to pursue his passion. In these early Paris works, we see his trademark shocking colors; down-and-dirty, street-life scenes emerge. Compare his art-school work and his street work: Henri augmented his classical training with vivid life experience. His subjects were from bars, brothels, and cabarets...Toto, we're not in Albi anymore. Henri was fascinated by cancan dancers (whose legs moved with an agility he'd never experience), and he captured them expertly. In these exploratory years, he dabbled in any style he encountered. The naked body emerged as one of his fascinations.

Henri started making money in the 1890s by selling illustrations to magazines and newspapers. Back then, his daily happy hour included brothel visits—1892-1894 was his prostitution period. He respected the ladies, feeling both fascination and empathy toward them. The **prostitutes** accepted him the way he was and let him into their world...which he sketched brilliantly. Notice how he shows the prostitutes as real humans—they are neither glorified nor vulgarized in his works.

In the next room, find the big ***Au Salon de la Rue des Moulins*** (1894). There are two versions: the quick sketch, then the finished studio version. With this piece, Toulouse-Lautrec arrived—no more sampling. The artist has established his unique style, oblivious to society's norms: colors (strong), subject matter (hidden worlds), and moralism (none). Henri's trademark use of cardboard was simply his quick, snapshot way of working: He'd capture these slice-of-life impressions on the fly on cheap, disposable material, intending to convert them to finer canvas paintings later, in his studio. But the cardboard quickies survive as Toulouse-Lautrec masterpieces.

Now, spiral up two flights through a room showing off a rare, 13th-century terra-cotta tile floor original to the building. You'll soon come to Toulouse-Lautrec's famous **advertising posters,** which were his bread and butter. He was an innovative advertiser, creating simple, bold, and powerful lithographic images. Look for displays of his original lithograph blocks (simply prepare the stone with a backward image, apply ink—which sticks chemically to the black points—and print posters). Four-color posters meant creating four different blocks. Many of the displayed works show different stages of the printing process—first with black ink, then the red layer, then the finished poster. The **Moulin Rouge** poster established his business reputation in Paris—strong symbols, bold and simple: just what, where, and when. Cabaret singer and club owner Aristide Bruant (*dans son cabaret*—"in his cabaret") is portrayed as bold and dashing.

Next, move on to other portraits of Parisian notables and misfits and finally the darker works he painted before his death.

Toulouse-Lautrec's **cane** offers more insight into this tortured artistic genius (often away on loan). To protect him from his self-destructive lifestyle, loved ones had him locked up in a psychiatric hospital. But, with the help of this clever hollow cane, he still got his booze. Friends would drop by with hallucinogenic absinthe, his drink of choice—also popular among many other artists of the time. With these special deliveries, he'd restock his cane, which even came equipped with a fancy little glass.

In 1901, at age 37, alcoholic, paranoid, depressed, and syphilitic, Henri de Toulouse-Lautrec returned to his mother—the only woman who ever really loved him—and died in her arms. The art world didn't mourn. Obituaries, speaking for the art establishment, basically said good riddance to Toulouse-Lautrec and his ugly art. Although no one in the art world wanted Henri's pieces, his mother and his best friend—a boyhood pal and art dealer named Maurice Joyant—recognized his genius and saved his work. They first offered it to the Louvre, which refused. Finally, in 1922, the mayor of Albi accepted the collection and hung Toulouse-Lautrec's work here in what, for more than a century, had been a boring museum of archaeology.

Your visit ends with a few rooms showing off the one-time grandeur of the Palais de la Berbie and two captivating paintings by 17th-century master Georges de La Tour.

▲Albi Town View

Albi was situated here because of its river access to Bordeaux (which connected the town to the global market). In medieval times, the fastest, most economical way to transport goods was down rivers like this. The lower, older bridge (Pont Vieux) was first built in 1020. Prior to its construction, the weir (look just beyond this first bridge) provided a series of stepping stones that enabled people to cross the river. Look at the bishop's palace. The garden below dates from the 17th century (when the palace at Versailles inspired the French to create fancy gardens). The palace itself grew from the 13th century until 1789, when the French Revolution ended the power of the bishops and the state confiscated the building. Since 1905, it's been a museum.

• *The last two sights are in the town center, roughly behind the cathedral.*

St. Salvy Church and Cloister (Eglise St. Salvi et Cloître)

Although this church (the oldest in town) is nothing special, the cloister creates a delightful space centered around an ancient well and modern garden. Delicate arches surround an enclosed courtyard (open 8:00-20:00), providing a peaceful interlude from the shoppers that fill the pedestrian streets. Notice the church wall from the courtyard. It was the only stone building in Albi in the 11th century; the taller parts, added later, are made of brick. This is one of many little hidden courtyards throughout town. In the rough-and-tumble Middle Ages, most buildings faced inward. If doors are open, you're welcome to pop in to courtyards.

• *Leave the cloister, go up the steps, and find a sweet square with quiet cafés.*

Market Hall (Marché Couvert)

Albi's elegant Art Nouveau market is good for picnic-gathering and people-watching—and has a grocery store in its lower level (Tue-Sun 8:00-14:00, closed Mon, 2 blocks from cathedral). On Saturday, a farmers' market sets up outside the market hall.

Sleeping in Albi

$$$ Hostellerie du Grand Saint Antoine**** is Albi's oldest hotel (established in 1784) and the most comfortable and traditional place I list. Guests enter an inviting, spacious lobby that opens onto an enclosed garden. Some rooms are Old World cozy, others have a modern flare (Db-€130-150, big Db-€170-200, suites-€190-260, Wi-Fi, parking-€10/day, a block above big Place du Vigan at 17 Rue Saint-Antoine, tel. 05 63 54 04 04, www.hotel-saint-antoine-albi.com, courriel@hotel-saint-antoine-albi.com).

$$ Hôtel Chiffre*** is a safe bet, with 38 well-appointed rooms (Db-€78, bigger Db-€98-128, family rooms-€145, some with queen-size beds, check website for deals, air-con, elevator, Wi-Fi, garage-€9/day, traditional restaurant, near Place du Vigan at 50 Rue Séré de Rivières, tel. 05 63 48 58 48, www.hotelchiffre.com, contact@hotelchiffre.com).

$ Hôtel Lapérouse** is a work in progress, one block from the old city and a 10-minute walk to the train station. This family-run hotel offers simple rooms and enthusiastic owners. Spring for a room with a balcony over the quiet garden and big pool (Db-€55-75, Db with deck-€80, Tb-€70-85, reception closed 12:00-15:00 and after 20:00, Wi-Fi, 21 Place Lapérouse, tel. 05 63 54 69 22, www.hotel-laperouse.com, contact@hotel-laperouse.com).

Eating in Albi

Albi is filled with reasonable restaurants that serve a rich local cuisine. Be warned: "Going local" here is likely to get you tripes (cow intestines), andouillette (sausages made from pig intestines), *foie de veau* (calf liver), and *tête de veau* (calf's head). Choose a restaurant or select one of the many tempting cafés on a traffic-free lane or on a quiet square (the squares behind St. Salvy's cloister and in front of the market hall are two good choices).

Le Tournesol is a good lunch option for vegetarians, since that's all they do. The food is organic and delicious, the setting is bright with many windows, and the service is friendly. Try the wonderful homemade tarts (€10 *plats,* open for lunch only, closed Sun, 11 Rue de l'Ort en Salvy, tel. 05 63 38 38 14).

Le Clos Sainte Cécile, a short block behind the cathedral, is

Sleep Code

Abbreviations **(€1 = about $1.40, country code: 33)**

S = Single, **D** = Double/Twin, **T** = Triple, **Q** = Quad, **b** = bathroom, **s** = shower only, * = French hotel rating (0-5 stars)

Price Rankings

$$$ **Higher Priced**—Most rooms €90 or more

$$ **Moderately Priced**—Most rooms between €60-90

$ **Lower Priced**—Most rooms €60 or less

Unless otherwise noted, credit cards are accepted, English is spoken, and Wi-Fi is generally free. Prices change; verify current rates online or by email. For the best prices, always book directly with the hotel.

an old school transformed into a delightful family-run restaurant. Friendly waiters serve delicious dishes in their large, shady garden—at a French pace (€18-26 *menus,* closed Tue-Wed, 3 Rue du Castelviel, tel. 05 63 38 19 74).

Oscar by Saint Loup may intimidate some with its fine stemware and chandeliers, but beyond the formal dining room lies an inviting courtyard full of happy eaters enjoying well-priced Mediterranean cuisine (€13 lunch *menus* come with a *plat,* dessert, and choice of coffee or wine, good-value dinner *menus* from €19, open for lunch Tue-Fri, for dinner Thu-Sat, 8 Rue Roquelaure, tel. 05 67 67 42 96).

Albi Connections

You'll connect to just about any destination through Toulouse.

From Albi by Train to: Toulouse (11/day, 70 minutes), **Carcassonne** (12/day, 3 hours, change in Toulouse), **Sarlat-la-Canéda** (6/day, 6 hours with 2-3 changes, some require bus from Souillac to Sarlat), **Paris** (6/day, 7-8.5 hours, change in Toulouse, also night train).

Near Albi

▲ROUTE OF THE BASTIDES

The hilly terrain north of Albi was tailor-made for medieval villages to organize around for defensive purposes. Here, along the Route of the Bastides (La Route des Bastides Albigeoises), scores of fortified villages *(bastides)* spill over hilltops, above rivers, and between wheat fields, creating a worthwhile detour for drivers. These planned communities were the medieval product of community efforts organized by local religious or military leaders. Most *bastides* were built during the Hundred Years' War (see sidebar on page 241) to establish a foothold for French or English rule in this hotly contested region, and to provide stability to benefit trade. Unlike other French hill towns, *bastides* were not safe havens provided by a castle. Instead, they were a premeditated effort by a community to collectively construct houses as a planned defensive unit, *sans* castle.

Connect these *bastides* as a day trip from Albi, or as you drive between Albi and the Dordogne. I've described the top *bastides* in the order you'll reach them on these driving routes.

Day Trip from Albi: For a good loop route northwest from Albi, cross the 22 Août 1944 bridge and follow signs to *Cordes-sur-Ciel* (allow 30 minutes). The view of Cordes as you approach is memorable. From Cordes, follow signs to *Saint-Antonin-Noble-Val,* an appealing, flat "hill town" on the river, with few tourists. Then pass vertical little Penne, Bruniquel (signed from Saint-Antonin-Noble-Val), Larroque, Puycelci (my favorite), and, finally, Castelnau-de-Montmiral (with a lovely main square), before returning to Albi. Each of these places is worth exploring if you have the time.

On the Way to the Dordogne: For a one-way scenic route north to the Dordogne that includes many of the same *bastides,* leave Albi, head toward Toulouse, and make time on the free A-68. Exit at Gaillac, go to its center, and track D-964 to Castelnau-de-Montmiral, Puycelci, and on to Bruniquel. From here you can head directly to Caussade on D-118 and D-964, then to Cahors on the free A-20 (and on to Sarlat-la-Canéda if that or the river villages are your destination).

Cordes-sur-Ciel

It's hard to resist this brilliantly situated hill town just 15 miles north of Albi, but I would (in high season, at least). Enjoy the fantastic view on the road from Albi, and consider a detour up into town only if the coast looks clear (read: off-season). Cordes, once an important Cathar base, has slipped over the boutique-filled edge to the point where it's hard for me to find the medieval town. But it's a dramatic setting filled with steep streets, beautiful half-timbered buildings, and great views. A rubber-tired train shuttles visitors to the top from near the TI (tel. 05 63 56 00 52, www.cordessurciel.fr).

Bruniquel

This overlooked, *très* photogenic, but less-tended village will test your thighs as you climb the lanes upward to the château (€3, April-Sept daily 10:00-12:30 & 14:00-18:00, closed Oct-March). Don't miss the dramatic view up to the village from the river below as you drive along D-964.

▲Puycelci

Forty minutes north of Albi, this town crowns a high bluff overlooking thick forests and sweeping pastures. Drive to the top, where you'll find easy parking and an unspoiled, level village with a couple of cafés, a bistro with a view, a small grocery, a bakery, a few *chambres d'hôtes,* and one sharp little hotel.

Stroll through the village, passing the Puycelci Roc Café, and make your way through town. At the opposite side of the village, a rampart walk circles counterclockwise back to the parking lot, reminding us of the village's history as a *bastide.* The park-like ramparts come with picnic benches and grand vistas (ideal at sunset). It's a good place to listen to the birds and feel the wind. Cut back through the village to appreciate the fine collection of buildings with lovingly tended flowerbeds.

As you wander, consider the recent history of an ancient town like this. In 1900, 2,000 people lived here with neither running water nor electricity. Then things changed. Millions of French men lost their lives in World War I; Puycelci didn't escape this fate, as the monument (by the parking lot) attests. World War II added to the exodus and by 1968 the village was down to three families. But then running water replaced the venerable cisterns, and things started looking up. Today, there is just enough commercial activity to keep locals happy. The town has a stable population of 110, all marveling at how lucky they are to live here.

Sleeping in Puycelci: An overnight here is my idea of vacation. Church bells keep a vigil, ringing on the hour throughout the night.

$$ L'Ancienne Auberge is *the* place to sleep, with eight surprisingly smart and comfortable rooms, some with sublime views. Owner/chef Dorothy moved here from New Jersey many moons ago and is eager to share her passion for this region (Db-€70-125, air-con in some rooms, Wi-Fi in the lobby, Place de l'Eglise, tel. 05 63 33 65 90, www.ancienne-auberge.com, contact@ancienne-auberge.com). Ask about their self-catering apartments that can accommodate up to five people (€550/week), and consider dinner at their view bistro Jardin de Lys (described below).

$$ Delphine de Laveleye Chambres is another great choice just behind L'Ancienne Auberge, with everything from a small romantic room for two to a three-bedroom suite with a kitchen, all hovering above a small garden and pool (Db-€64-76, Tb-€90-110, Qb-€145, cash only, Wi-Fi, tel. 05 63 33 13 65, mobile 06 72 92 69 59, www.chezdelphine.com).

***Eating in Puycelci*:** The **Jardin de Lys** bistro-café clings to the hillside, offering breathtaking views and all-day service. Come for a drink at least, or better for a fine dinner based on original recipes and cooked with fresh products (€21 *menus,* €16 *plats,* daily 10:00-23:00, tel. 05 63 33 65 90). **Puycelci Roc Café,** at the parking lot, has standard café fare, a warm interior, and pleasant outdoor tables (July-Aug daily for dinner and Sat-Wed for lunch, reduced hours in winter, tel. 05 63 33 13 67).

Castelnau-de-Montmiral

This overlooked village has quiet lanes leading to a perfectly preserved *bastide* square surrounded by fine arcades and filled with brick half-timbered facades. Ditch your car below and wander up to the square, where a TI, a restaurant, a café, and a small *pâtisserie* await. Have a drink or lunch on the square either at the simple **Auberge des Arcades** café (open daily, tel. 05 63 33 20 88) or the slightly more upscale **La Table des Consuls**—worth the extra euro or two if you have time to linger (May-Sept, closed Mon, tel. 05 63 40 63 55).

Carcassonne

Medieval Carcassonne is a 13th-century world of towers, turrets, and cobblestones. Europe's ultimate walled fortress city, it's also stuffed with tourists. At 10:00, salespeople stand at the doors of their main-street shops, a gaunt-

let of tacky temptations poised and ready for their daily ration of customers—consider yourself warned. But early, late, or off-season, a quieter Carcassonne is an evocative playground for any medievalist. Forget midday—spend the night.

Locals like to believe that Carcassonne got its name this way: 1,200 years ago, Charlemagne and his troops besieged this fortress-town (then called La Cité) for several years. A cunning townsperson named Madame Carcas saved the town. Just as food was running out, she fed the last few bits of grain to the last pig and tossed him over the wall. Splat. Charlemagne's bored and frustrated forces, amazed that the town still had enough food to throw fat party pigs over the wall, decided they would never succeed in starving the people out. They ended the siege, and the city was saved. Madame Carcas *sonne*-d (sounded) the long-awaited victory bells, and La Cité had a new name: Carcas-sonne. It's a cute story... but historians suspect that Carcassonne is a Frenchified version of the town's original name (Carcas).

As a teenager on my first visit to Carcassonne, I wrote this in my journal: "Before me lies Carcassonne, the perfect medieval city. Like a fish that everyone thought was extinct, somehow Europe's greatest Romanesque fortress city has survived the centuries. I was supposed to be gone yesterday, but here I sit imprisoned by choice—curled in a cranny on top of the wall. The wind blows away the sounds of today, and my imagination 'medievals' me. The moat is one foot over and 100 feet down. Small plants and moss upholster my throne."

Avoid the midday mobs and let this place make you a kid on a rampart.

Orientation to Carcassonne

Contemporary Carcassonne is neatly divided into two cities: the magnificent La Cité (the fortified old city, with 200 full-time residents taking care of lots more tourists) and the lively Ville Basse (modern lower city). Two bridges, the busy Pont Neuf and the traffic-free Pont Vieux, both with great views, connect the two parts.

TOURIST INFORMATION

Carcassonne's TI has three locations. The main TI, in **Ville Basse,** is useful only if you're walking to La Cité (28 Rue de Verdun). A far more convenient branch is in **La Cité,** to your right as you enter the main gate (Narbonne Gate—or Porte Narbonnaise). Both TIs

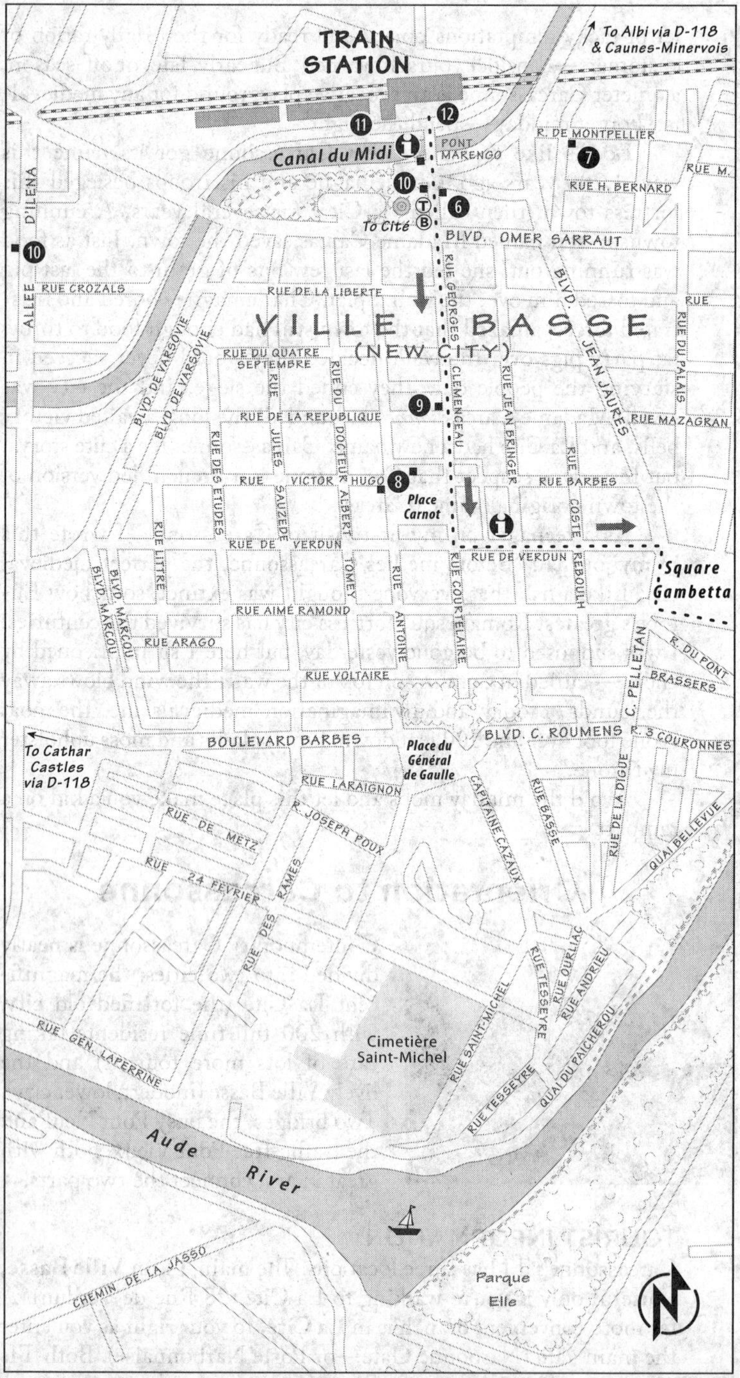

TRAIN STATION

To Albi via D-118 & Caunes-Minervois

Canal du Midi

PONT MARENGO

R. DE MONTPELLIER

RUE M.

RUE H. BERNARD

To Cité

BLVD. OMER SARRAUT

ALLEE D'ILENA

RUE CROZALS

RUE DE LA LIBERTE

RUE GEORGES CLEMENCEAU

VILLE BASSE (NEW CITY)

RUE

RUE DU PALAIS

BLVD. JEAN JAURES

RUE DU QUATRE SEPTEMBRE

BLVD. DE VARSOVIE

RUE DU DOCTEUR ALBERT

RUE JULES SAUZEDE

RUE JEAN BRINGER

RUE DE LA REPUBLIQUE

RUE MAZAGRAN

RUE DES ETUDES

RUE VICTOR HUGO

Place Carnot

RUE BARBES

RUE COSTE REBOULH

RUE DE VERDUN

Square Gambetta

RUE LITTRE

BLVD. MARCOU

RUE TOMEY

RUE ANTOINE

RUE COURTELAIRE

RUE AIMÉ RAMOND

RUE ARAGO

RUE VOLTAIRE

C. PELLETAN

R. DU PONT

BRASSERS

To Cathar Castles via D-118

BOULEVARD BARBES

Place du Général de Gaulle

BLVD. C. ROUMENS

R. 3 COURONNES

RUE LARAIGNON

CAPITAINE CAZAUX

RUE BASSE

RUE DE LA DIGUE

QUAI BELLEVUE

RUE DE METZ

R. JOSEPH POUX

RUE 24 FEVRIER

RUE DES RAMES

RUE OURLIAC

RUE TESSEYRE

RUE ANDRIEU

RUE GEN. LAPERRINE

Cimetière Saint-Michel

RUE SAINT-MICHEL

RUE TESSEYRE

QUAI DU PAICHEROU

Aude River

CHEMIN DE LA JASSO

Parque Elle

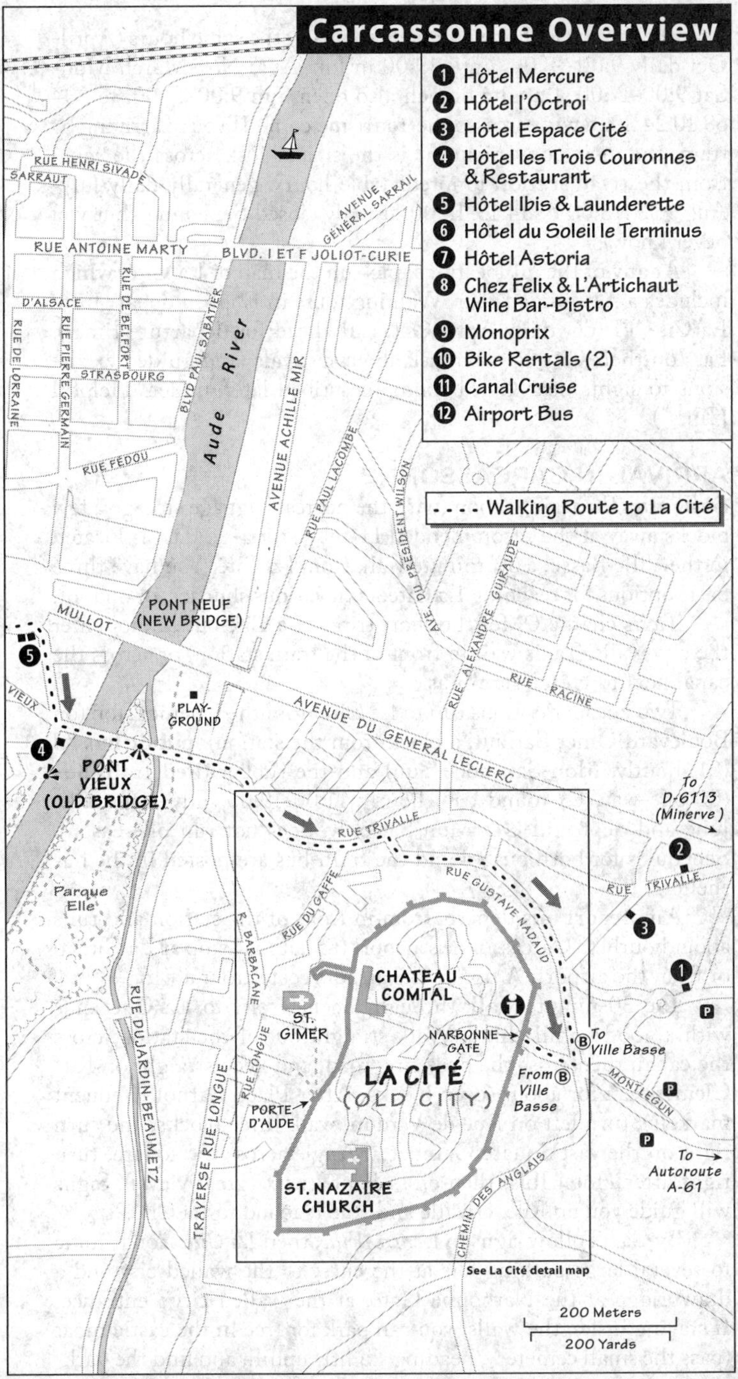

Carcassonne Overview

1. Hôtel Mercure
2. Hôtel l'Octroi
3. Hôtel Espace Cité
4. Hôtel les Trois Couronnes & Restaurant
5. Hôtel Ibis & Launderette
6. Hôtel du Soleil le Terminus
7. Hôtel Astoria
8. Chez Felix & L'Artichaut Wine Bar-Bistro
9. Monoprix
10. Bike Rentals (2)
11. Canal Cruise
12. Airport Bus

Walking Route to La Cité

RUE HENRI SIVADE
SARRAUT
AVENUE GÉNÉRAL SARRAIL
RUE ANTOINE MARTY
BLVD. I ET F JOLIOT-CURIE
D'ALSACE
RUE DE BELFORT
BLVD PAUL SABATIER
Aude River
RUE DE LORRAINE
RUE PIERRE GERMAIN
STRASBOURG
AVENUE ACHILLE MIR
RUE FEDOU
RUE PAUL LACOMBE
RUE PRESIDENT WILSON
AVE DU PRESIDENT WILSON
RUE ALEXANDRE GUIRAUDE
PONT NEUF (NEW BRIDGE)
MULLOT
RUE RACINE
VIEUX
PLAY-GROUND
AVENUE DU GENERAL LECLERC
PONT VIEUX (OLD BRIDGE)
To D-6113 (Minerve)
RUE TRIVALLE
RUE GUSTAVE NADAUD
Parque Elle
RUE DU GAFFE
R. BARBACANE
CHATEAU COMTAL
ST. GIMER
NARBONNE GATE
To Ville Basse
From Ville Basse
MONTLEGUN
RUE DUJARDIN-BEAUMETZ
RUE LONGUE
TRAVERSE RUE LONGUE
LA CITÉ (OLD CITY)
PORTE D'AUDE
To Autoroute A-61
CHEMIN DES ANGLAIS
ST. NAZAIRE CHURCH

See La Cité detail map

200 Meters
200 Yards

have the same telephone number and nearly the same hours (April-Oct daily 9:00-18:00, until 19:00 in July-Aug; Nov-March Mon-Sat 9:00-17:00, La Cité branch also open Sun 9:00-17:00; tel. 04 68 10 24 30, www.carcassonne-tourisme.com). If you're arriving by train, the most convenient TI is the small kiosk across the canal from the **train station** (unpredictable hours, generally daily July-Aug 9:15-13:00 & 14:15-18:00, usually closed Sept-June...but you never know).

At any of the TI locations, pick up the map of La Cité, which includes a self-guided tour. Walking tours in English depart from La Cité TI (€6, daily April-Oct, call ahead for departure times). Pass on their City Pass but ask about festivals (and guided excursions to sights near Carcassonne (described later, under "Helpful Hints").

ARRIVAL IN CARCASSONNE

By Train: The train station (with the nearest baggage storage a few blocks away at the recommended Hôtel Astoria-€2/day) is located in the Ville Basse, a 30-minute walk from La Cité. You have three basic options for reaching La Cité: taxi, various shuttles, or on foot.

Taxis charge €9 for the short trip to La Cité but cannot enter the city walls. Taxis wait in front of the train station, or across the canal next to Hôtel Terminus.

Two cheaper options run to La Cité from the Chénier stop (on Boulevard Omer Sarraut, a block from the station): **public bus #4** (€1, hourly, Mon-Sat, none Sun) and the rubber-tired **train-bus** (€2 one-way, €3 round-trip, hourly 11:00-19:00, July-Aug daily, June and Sept-mid-Oct Mon-Sat only, does not run off-season). Schedules for both bus #4 and the train-bus are posted in the bus shelter.

An **airport bus** departs from in front of the station and runs about hourly to Carcassonne's airport (€5); it may stop at La Cité to or from the airport. A taxi to the airport costs around €15.

The 30-minute **walk** through the new city to La Cité ends with a good uphill climb. Walk straight out of the station, cross the canal, then cross the busy ring road, and keep straight on Rue Clemenceau for about seven blocks. After Place Carnot (frequent markets), turn left on Rue de Verdun, walk three blocks, and turn right on the vast Square Gambetta. Angle across the square, turn right after Hôtel Ibis, then cross Pont Vieux (great views). Signs will guide you up Rue Trivalle and Rue Nadaud to La Cité.

By Car: Follow signs to *Centre-Ville*, then *La Cité*. You'll come to several large parking lots at the entry to the walled city and a drawbridge at the Narbonne Gate, at the walled city's entrance. If staying inside the walls, you can park for free in the castle moat (pass the small cemetery, heading slightly uphill, and find the parking access). You must show your reservation or have the attendant call your hotel. (Verbal assurances won't do.) Allow 15 minutes on foot over uneven surfaces to hotels (the recommended Hôtels le Donjon and de la Cité will pick you up). Theft is common—leave nothing in your car at night.

HELPFUL HINTS

Market Days: Pleasing Place Carnot in Ville Basse hosts a non-touristy open market (Tue, Thu, and Sat mornings until 13:00; Sat is the biggest).

Summer Festivals: Carcassonne becomes colorfully medieval during many special events each July and August. Highlights are the *spectacle équestre* (jousting matches) and July 14 (Bastille Day) fireworks. The TI has details on these and other events.

Internet Access: Several cafés on Place Marcou have Wi-Fi for customers.

Laundry: Try **Laverie Express** (daily 8:00-22:00, 5 Square Gambetta at Hôtel Ibis; from La Cité, cross Pont Vieux and turn right).

Grocery Stores: There's one in the train station. You'll also find a **Monoprix**—a department store with grocery section—where Rues Clemenceau and de la République cross, a few blocks from the train station.

Bike Rental: Bike riding is very popular thanks to the scenic towpath that follows the canal (at the train station). **Génération VTT** rents bikes (get the free English map, daily 9:30-18:00, across the canal from the train station TI kiosk, mobile 06 09 59 30 85, www.generation-vtt.com). **Evasion 2 Roues** also rents bikes, and has tandems (closed Sun-Mon, 85 Allée d'Iéna, tel. 04 68 11 90 40, www.evasion2roues.eu).

Taxi: Call 04 68 71 50 50 or 04 68 71 36 36.

Car Rental: Avis is at the train station (tel. 04 68 25 05 84). The airport has all the rental companies, but it's 30 minutes from Carcassonne.

Guided Excursions from Carcassonne: Vin en Vacances runs day-long vineyard tours that mix wine tasting with local food, sightseeing, and cultural experiences. It's run by Wendy Gedney and her team of wine experts. Prices range from €110 to €135 per person and include visits to two wineries, a fine lunch, and visits to key sights such as the Cathar castles (mobile 06 42 33 34 09, www.vinenvacances.com, wendy@vinenvacances.com).

Minivan Service: Friendly Didier provides comfortable transportation for up to eight passengers to all area châteaux and sights. He's not a guide and speaks just a little English, though he's full of smiles (for 4 passengers plan on about €170/half-day, €300/day, or just €24/person for the Châteaux of Lastours, mobile 06 03 18 39 95, www.catharexcursions.com, bod.aude11@orange.fr).

Tourist Train: Hop on at the Narbonne Gate for a 20-minute loop around La Cité (€7).

Carcassonne Walk

While the tourists shuffle up the main street, this self-guided walk, rated ▲▲▲, introduces you to the city with history and wonder, rather than tour groups and plastic swords. We'll sneak into the town on the other side of the wall...through the back door (see map on the next page). This walk is wonderfully peaceful and scenic early or late in the day, when the sun is low.

Start on the asphalt outside La Cité's main entrance, the Narbonne Gate (Porte Narbonnaise). You're welcomed by a contemporary-looking bust of Madame Carcas—which is actually modeled after a 16th-century original of the town's legendary first lady (for her story, see page 530).

• *Cross the bridge toward the...*

Narbonne Gate: Pause at the drawbridge and survey this immense fortification. When forces from northern France finally conquered Carcassonne, it was a strategic prize. Not taking any chances, they evicted the residents, whom they allowed to settle in the lower town (Ville Basse)—as long as they stayed across the river. (Though it's called "new," this lower town actually dates from the 13th century.) La Cité remained a French military garrison until the 18th century.

The drawbridge was made crooked to slow attackers' rush to the main gate and has a similar effect on tourists today.

• *After crossing the drawbridge, lose the crowds and walk left between the walls. At the first short set of stairs, climb to the outer-wall walkway and linger while facing the inner walls.*

Wall View: The Romans built Carcassonne's first wall, upon which the bigger medieval wall was constructed. Identify the ancient Roman bits by looking about one-third of the way up and finding the smaller rocks mixed with narrow stripes of red bricks (and no arrow slits). The outer wall that you're on was not built until the 1300s, more than a thousand years after the Roman walls went up. The massive walls you see today—nearly two miles around, with 52 towers—defended an important site near the intersection of north-south and east-west trade routes.

Look over the wall and down at the moat below (now mostly used for parking). Like most medieval moats, it was never filled with water (or even alligators). A ditch like this—which was originally even deeper—effectively stopped attacking forces from rolling

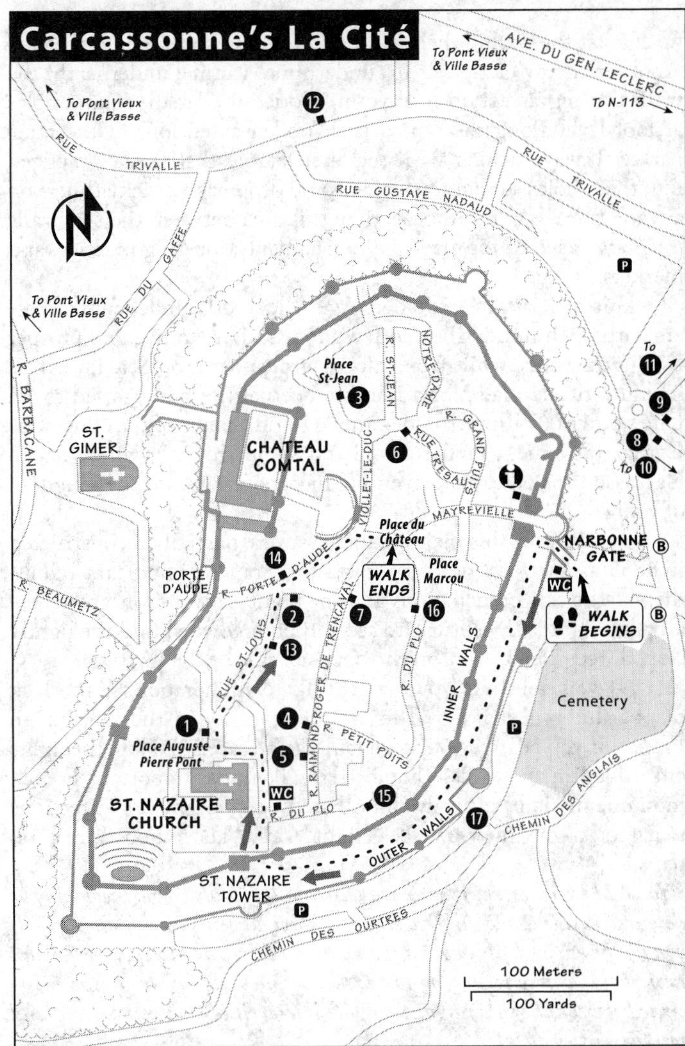

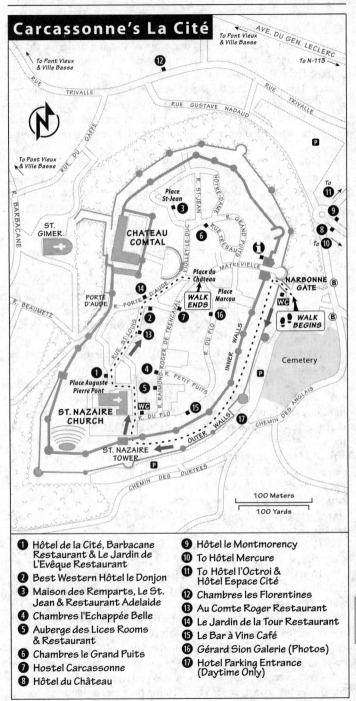

1 Hôtel de la Cité, Barbacane Restaurant & Le Jardin de L'Evêque Restaurant
2 Best Western Hôtel le Donjon
3 Maison des Remparts, Le St. Jean & Restaurant Adelaide
4 Chambres l'Echappée Belle
5 Auberge des Lices Rooms & Restaurant
6 Chambres le Grand Puits
7 Hostel Carcassonne
8 Hôtel du Château
9 Hôtel le Montmorency
10 To Hôtel Mercure
11 To Hôtel l'Octroi & Hôtel Espace Cité
12 Chambres les Florentines
13 Au Comte Roger Restaurant
14 Le Jardin de la Tour Restaurant
15 Le Bar à Vins Café
16 Gérard Sion Galerie (Photos)
17 Hotel Parking Entrance (Daytime Only)

up against the wall in their mobile towers and spilling into the city. Another enemy tactic was to "undermine" (tunnel underneath) the wall, causing a section to cave in. Notice the small, square holes at foot level along the ramparts. Wooden extensions of the rampart walkways (which we'll see later, at the castle) once plugged into these holes so that townsfolk could drop nasty, sticky things on anyone tunneling in. In peacetime this area between the two walls *(les lices)* was used for medieval tournaments, jousting practice, and markets.

During La Cité's Golden Age, the 1100s, independent rulers with open minds allowed Jews and Cathars to live and prosper within the walls, while troubadours wrote poems of ideal love. This liberal attitude made for a rich intellectual life but also led to La Cité's downfall. The Crusades aimed to rid France of the dangerous Cathar movement (and their liberal sympathizers), which led to Carcassonne's defeat and eventual incorporation into the kingdom of France.

The walls of this majestic fortress were partially reconstructed in 1855 as part of a program to restore France's important monuments. The tidy crenellations and the pointy tower roofs are generally from the 19th century (to see authentic towers, find the lightly sloped, red-tiled towers on the opposite side of the fortress).

As you continue your wall walk to higher points, the lack of guardrails is striking. This would never fly in the US, but in France, if you fall, it's your own fault (so be careful). Note the lights embedded in the walls. This fortress, like most important French monuments, is beautifully illuminated every night (for directions to a good nighttime view, see "Night Wall Walk to Pont Vieux" on page 540).

• *You could keep working your way around the walls (though you may be detoured inside the walls for a stretch if special events block your path). If you do the entire walk around the walls, you'll see five authentic Roman towers just before returning to the Narbonne Gate. Walking the entire circle between the inner and outer gate is a terrific 30-minute stroll (and fantastic after dark).*

But for this tour, we'll stop at the first entrance possible into La Cité, the...

Inner Wall Gate: The wall has the same four gates it had in Roman times. Before entering, notice the squat tower on the outer wall—this was a "barbican" (placed opposite each inner gate for extra protection). Barbicans were always semicircular—open on the inside to expose anyone who breached the outer defenses. Invading today is far easier than in the good old days. Notice the holes in the barbican for supporting a wooden catwalk. Breach the walls and enter the square gate—look up to see a slot for the portcullis (the big iron grate) and the frame for a heavy wooden door.

Once safely inside, look back up at the inner wall tower to view *beaucoup de* narrow arrow slits facing inside La Cité—even if enemies made it past the walls, they still weren't home free.

• *Opposite the tower, work your way around to the entry of the...*

St. Nazaire Church (Basilique St. Nazaire): This was a cathedral until the 18th century, when the bishop moved to the lower town. Today, due to the depopulation of the basically dead-except-for-tourism Cité, it's not even a functioning parish church. Notice the Romanesque arches of the nave and the delicately vaulted Gothic arches over the altar and transepts. After its successful conquest of this region in the 13th-century Albigensian Crusades, France set out to destroy all the Romanesque churches and replace them with Gothic ones—symbolically asserting its northern rule with this more northern style of church. With the start of the Hundred Years' War in 1337, the expensive demolition was abandoned. Today, the Romanesque remainder survives, and the destroyed section has been rebuilt Gothic, which makes it one of the best examples of Gothic architecture in southern France. When the lights are off, the interior—lit only by candles and 14th-century stained glass—is evocatively medieval. A plaque near the door tells that St. Dominique (founder of the Dominican order) preached at this church in 1213 (Mon-Sat 9:00-11:45 & 13:45-18:00, Sun 9:00-10:45 & 14:00-18:00, Sun Mass at 11:00).

Hôtel de la Cité: Located 50 steps from St. Nazaire Church, this luxury hotel sits where the Bishop's Palace did 700 years ago. Today, it's a worthwhile detour to see how the privileged few travel. You're free to wander, so find the library-cozy bar (€8 beer and wine), then find the rear garden and turn right for super wall views that you can't see from anywhere else.

• *From here, follow Rue St. Louis for several blocks, merge right onto Rue Port d'Aude, then look for a small castle-view terrace on your left a block up.*

Château Comtal: Originally built in 1125, Carcassonne's third layer of defense was completely redesigned in later reconstructions. From this impressive viewpoint you can see the wooden rampart extensions that once circled the entire city wall. (Notice the empty peg holes to the left of the bridge.) During sieges, these would be covered with wet animal skins as a fire retardant. When *Robin Hood: Prince of Thieves,* starring Kevin Costner, was filmed here in 1990, the entire city was turned into a film set. Locals enjoyed playing bit parts and seeing their château labeled "Nottingham Castle" in the fanciful film.

Château Comtal is a worthwhile visit for those with time and interest. Grab the basic flyer in English and climb to the top of the stairs. A well-done film with booming sound sets the stage for your visit. Next is a room-size model of La Cité—find the black-

and-white images of old Carcassonne on the walkway above. From here, a self-guided tour with posted English explanations leads you around the inner ramparts of Carcassonne's castle. You'll see the underpinnings of the towers and of the catwalks that hung from the walls and learn all about medieval defense systems. The views are terrific. Your visit ends with a museum showing bits of St. Nazaire Church and fragments from important homes (€8.50, daily April-Sept 9:30-18:30, shorter hours off-season, last entry 45 minutes before closing, unnecessary audioguide-€4.50 or €6/2 people).

• *Fifty yards away, opposite the entrance to the castle, is...*

Place du Château: This busy little square sports a modest statue honoring the man who saved the city from deterioration and neglect in the 19th century. The bronze model circling the base of the statue shows Carcassonne's walls as they looked before the 1855 reconstruction by Eugène Viollet-le-Duc.

• *Facing the château entry, Place du Grand Puits lies a block to your right. This huge well is the oldest of Carcassonne's 22 wells.*

Sights in Carcassonne

▲▲▲Night Wall Walk to Pont Vieux

Save some post-dinner energy for a don't-miss walk around the same walls you visited today (great dinner picnic sites as well). The effect at night is mesmerizing: The embedded lights become torches and unfamiliar voices become the enemy. End at Pont Vieux for a floodlit fantasy. The best route is a partial circumnavigation clockwise between the walls. Start at the Narbonne Gate, and follow my self-guided walk (described earlier) to the Inner Wall Gate. Don't enter La Cité through this gate; instead, continue your walk between the walls (this section is occasionally closed; if so, you'll have to make your way through the village and out the rear along Rue de la Porte d'Aude to meet up with the route described from here).

The path narrows as you walk behind Château Comtal. When you come to a ramp leading down (after about five minutes), make a U-turn to the left, just before the path rises back up. This ramp leads down the hill; make a left when you come to the church (St. Gimer), then a right on Rue de la Barbacane (follow the *Centre-Ville* sign). Go straight to reach Pont Vieux and exceptional views of floodlit Carcassonne. Return from the bridge the same way you came, and complete your clockwise walk between the walls back to the Narbonne Gate, or take Rue Trivalle to Rue Gustave Nadaud for a quicker return.

Riverside Walk

Two scenic paths running southwest along each side of the Aude River below La Cité offer occasional views to the fortress and a verdant escape for runners and walkers. Both paths can be accessed from below the Pont Vieux.

Canal du Midi

Completed in 1681, this sleepy 155-mile canal connects France's Mediterranean and Atlantic coasts and, at about its midpoint, runs directly in front of the train station in Carcassonne. Before railways, Canal du Midi was clogged with commercial traffic; today, it entertains only pleasure craft. Small boats that ferry tourists along the canal leave from in front of the train station (€10/1.5 hours, €13/2.5 hours, 3-5/day, April-Oct, closed Mon, mobile 06 80 47 54 33, www.carcassonne-croisiere.com). A better way to experience the canal is on a relaxed bike ride along the level towpath (for bike rental, see "Helpful Hints," earlier).

Gérard Sion Galerie

Duck into this impressive photo gallery before selecting which Cathar castles you want to visit (brilliant shots of many monuments in Languedoc-Roussillon, generally open daily 10:00-19:00, just up from Place Marcou at 27 Rue du Plô).

Nightlife in Carcassonne

For relief from all the medieval kitsch, savor a drink in four-star, library-meets-bar ambience at the **Hôtel de la Cité** bar (€8 beer and wine, Place de l'Eglise). To taste the liveliest square, with loads of tourists and strolling musicians, sip a drink or nibble a dessert on **Place Marcou.** To be a medieval poet, share a bottle of wine in your own private niche somewhere remote on the ramparts.

Le Bar à Vins (also recommended later, under "Eating in Carcassonne") offers lively music, good wines by the glass for €2.50, and a young crowd enjoying a garden in the moonshadow of the wall...without any tourists (open daily until 2:00 in the morning during high season).

For a fine before- or after-dinner drink and floodlit wall views, stop by the recommended **Hotel du Château**'s broad terrace, below the Narbonne Gate (2 Rue Camille Saint-Saëns).

Sleeping in Carcassonne

Sleep within or near the old walls, in La Cité. I've also listed a pair of hotels near the train station. In the summer, when La Cité is jammed with tourists, think of sleeping in quieter Caunes-Minervois (you'll find my suggestions on page 545). Top prices listed are for July and August, when the town is packed. At other times of the year, prices drop and there are generally plenty of rooms.

IN LA CITÉ

Pricey hotels, good B&Bs, and an excellent youth hostel offer a full range of rooms inside the walls.

$$$ Hôtel de la Cité***** offers 61 rooms with deluxe everything in a beautiful building next to St. Nazaire Church. Peaceful gardens, a swimming pool, royal public spaces, the elegant Barbacane restaurant, and reliable luxury are yours—for a price (deluxe Db-€350-480, suites-€600-950, extra adult-€80, breakfast-€28, air-con, Wi-Fi, garage-€21/day, Place Auguste-Pierre Pont, tel. 04 68 71 98 71, www.hoteldelacite.com, reservations@hoteldelacite.com).

$$$ Best Western Hôtel le Donjon**** has 62 well-appointed rooms, a polished lobby with a full bar, and a great location inside the walls. Rooms are split between three buildings in La Cité (the main building, a look-alike annex across the street, and the cheaper Maison des Remparts a few blocks away). The main building is most appealing, and the rooms with terraces on the garden are delightful (main building and annex: Db-€150-185, Db suite-€180-400, extra person-€20; Maison des Remparts: Db-€125-170; check website for deals, air-con, elevator, guest computer, Wi-Fi, private parking-€15/day, 2 Rue Comte Roger, tel. 04 68 11 23 00, www.hotel-donjon.fr, info@bestwestern-donjon.com).

$$$ Chambres l'Echappée Belle, in the center of La Cité, is run by cheery Australian Jackie who has four traditional units with wood floors and jet showers. There's air-conditioning in most rooms (Db-€85-150, includes breakfast, check-in between 16:00 and 19:00, Wi-Fi, near St. Nazaire Church, just off Rue du Plô at 5 Rue Raymond Roger Trencavel, tel. 04 68 25 33 40, mobile 06 40 44 63 18, www.lechappeebelle.co.uk, infolechappeebelle@orange.fr).

$$ Auberge des Lices hides two lovely rooms above its restaurant, with high ceilings, exposed beams, and stone walls (Db with basilica views-€80-100, larger Db with rampart views-€140-200, air-con, 3 Rue Raymond Roger Trencavel, tel. 04 68 72 34 07, mobile 06 73 69 36 22, www.blasco.fr, leslices@blasco.fr).

$$ Chambres le Grand Puits, across from Maison des Remparts, is a splendid value. It has one cute double room and two cavernous apartment-like rooms that could sleep five, with kitchenette, private terrace, and sweet personal touches. Inquire in the small boutique, and say *bonjour* to happy-go-lucky Nicole (Db-€55-65, larger apartment-like Db-€65-85, €10-extra person, includes self-serve breakfast, cash only, 8 Place du Grand Puits, tel. 04 68 25 16 67, mobile 06 20 47 02 31, http://legrandpuits.free.fr, nicole.trucco@club-internet.fr).

$ Hostel Carcassonne is big, clean, and well-run, with an outdoor garden courtyard, a self-service kitchen, a TV room, bar, a washer/dryer, bike rental, pay Internet access, Wi-Fi, and a welcoming ambience. If you ever wanted to bunk down in a hostel, do it here—all ages are welcome. Only summer is tight; reserve ahead (bunk in 4- to 6-bed dorm-€25/bed, 2-bed private room-€52, includes sheets and breakfast but no towels, open all day, Rue du Vicomte Trencavel, tel. 04 68 25 23 16, www.fuaj.org or www.hihostels.com, carcassonne@hifrance.org).

JUST OUTSIDE LA CITE

Sleeping just outside La Cité offers the best of both worlds: quick access to the ramparts, less claustrophobic surroundings, and easy parking.

$$$ Hôtel du Château**** and **$$$ Hôtel le Montmorency***** are adjacent hotels that lie barely below La Cité's main gate and are run by the same family. They offer travelers a full range of price options, an easy walk to La Cité, air-conditioning, €15 breakfasts, and €10 parking. They also share a snazzy pool (heated from Easter to November), a Jacuzzi (heated all year), view terraces to the walls of Carcassonne, two lazy hounds, and a sweet cat (free guest computer, Wi-Fi, www.hotels-carcassonne.net, contact@hotels-carcassonne.net). Both hotels offer frequent discounts online. Rick Steves readers receive a 5 percent discount off the best available price through 2015 (use code RICKSTEVES). Hôtel du Château gives four-star comfort with 17 sumptuous rooms (Db-€175-255, extra person-€25, 2 Rue Camille Saint-Saëns, tel. 04 68 11 38 38). Hôtel Montmorency, a block behind Hôtel du Château, has a split personality. Half the rooms are neon-colored-mod (Db-€135-195, extra person-€20), and half are purely *Provençal* and a bit smaller (Db-€100-130, extra person-€20). Several rooms have views to the ramparts, and many come with private decks or terraces (2 Rue Camille Saint-Saëns, tel. 04 68 11 96 70, www.lemontmorency.com).

$$$ Hôtel Mercure*** hides a block behind the Hôtel le Montmorency, a five-minute walk to La Cité. It rents 80, snug-but-comfy, air-conditioned rooms and has a refreshing garden, a good-sized pool, big elevators, and a warm bar-lounge. A few rooms have views of La Cité (small Db-€130-170, bigger Db-€140-220, breakfast-€15, guest computer, Wi-Fi, free parking, 18 Rue Camille Saint-Saëns, tel. 04 68 11 92 82, www.mercure.com, h1622@accor.com).

CLOSE TO LA CITE ON RUE TRIVALLE

These places are 10 minutes below La Cité and 20 minutes from the train station on foot.

$$$ Hôtel l'Octroi*** delivers colorful, contemporary comfort, efficient service, and a young vibe from its full-service bar to its small, stylish pool (Db-€95-145, extra person-€15, several family suites for up to 6-€255, frequent online deals, 5 percent discount off best available price in 2015—use code RICKSTEVES, air-con, Wi-Fi, 143 Rue Trivalle, tel. 04 68 25 29 08, www.hoteloctroi.com).

$$ Hôtel Espace Cité,** two blocks downhill from Hôtel le Montmorency (described earlier), is a good value, with 48 small but sharp rooms (Db-€73-98, Tb-€85-120, Qb-€95-140, breakfast-€9, air-con, guest computer, limited free parking—otherwise €7/day in garage, Wi-Fi, 132 Rue Trivalle, tel. 04 68 25 24 24, www.hotelespacecite.fr, espace-cite@inter-hotel-carcassonne.fr).

$$ Chambres les Florentines is a good-value bed-and-breakfast run by charming Madame Mistler. The five rooms are spacious and homey, one room comes with a big deck and million-dollar views of La Cité (Db-€75-90, view Db-€110, Tb-€110, Qb-€130, includes breakfast, Wi-Fi, parking-€4/day, 71 Rue Trivalle, tel. 04 68 71 51 07, mobile 06 88 89 33 42, www.lesflorentines.net, lesflorentines11@gmail.com).

BETWEEN LA CITE AND THE TRAIN STATION

These hotels are close to Pont Vieux, a 15-minute walk below La Cité, and 15 minutes on foot from the train station.

$$$ Hôtel les Trois Couronnes*,** a modern hotel in a concrete shell, offers 44 rooms with terrific views up to La Cité—and 26 non-view rooms that you don't want (Db with view-€140-165, €20 less for no view, air-con, elevator, Wi-Fi, indoor pool with views, garage-€9/day, 2 Rue des Trois Couronnes, tel. 04 68 25 36 10, www.hotel-destroiscouronnes.com, hotel3couronnes@wanadoo.fr). Their reasonably priced restaurant also has a good view (see "Eating in Carcassonne," later).

$$ Hôtel Ibis,** on Square Gambetta, delivers reliable two-star comfort at fair prices (Db-€80-100, request a room off the square, air-con, guest computer, Wi-Fi, 5 Square Gambetta, tel. 04 68 72 37 37, www.ibishotel.com, ibiscentre.carcassonne@wanadoo.fr).

NEAR THE TRAIN STATION

$$$ Hôtel du Soleil le Terminus*,** across from the train station, is turn-of-the-century faded-grand. The lobby reminds me of a train-station waiting hall. Rooms are big and comfortable, with high ceilings and prices (Db-€125-150, pricier rooms have better views, check website for deals, air-con, elevator, guest computer, Wi-Fi, basement pool, secure parking-€10/day, lots of groups, 2 Avenue Maréchal Joffre, tel. 04 68 25 25 00, www.soleilvacances.com, reservation@soleilvacances.com).

$$ Hôtel Astoria**, run by delightful Marc and Sevrine, offers some of the cheapest hotel beds that I list in town, divided between a main hotel and an annex across the street. The shiny, tiled, and colorful rooms are modern, clean, and air-conditioned. Book ahead; it's popular (D-€35-49, Ds-€47-62, Db-€57-72, Tb/Qb-€67-96, 5-person room-€88-106, Wi-Fi, bike rentals, parking-€5/day; from the train station, walk across the canal, turn left, and go two blocks to 18 Rue Tourtel; tel. 04 68 25 31 38, www.astoriacarcassonne.com, hotel-astoria@wanadoo.fr).

IN CAUNES-MINERVOIS

To experience unspoiled, tranquil Languedoc-Roussillon, sleep surrounded by vineyards in the characteristic village of Caunes-Minervois. Comfortably nestled in the foothills of the Montagne Noire, Caunes-Minervois is a 25-minute drive from Carcassonne. Take route D-118 or follow signs toward *Mazamet* to a big roundabout and find D-620. The town offers an eighth-century abbey, two cafés, two good restaurants, a pizzeria, a handful of wineries, and no other tourists. The friendly staff at the town's TI (in the abbey) is eager to help you explore the region. Caunes-Minervois makes an ideal base for exploring area wine roads.

$$$ Hôtel d'Alibert**, in a 15th-century home with ambience galore, sits in the heart of the village. It has a mix of nicely renovated, Old World traditional rooms. It's managed with a relaxed *je ne sais quoi* by Frédéric "call me Fredo" Dalibert and his daughter Mathilde (standard Db-€90, huge Db-€100, extra person-€10, includes breakfast and bottle of local wine on arrival, Wi-Fi in lobby, Place de la Mairie, tel. 04 68 78 00 54, www.hoteldalibert.com, frederic.dalibert@wanadoo.fr). Eat lunch or dinner in his cozy restaurant with great courtyard tables and let Fredo plan your wine-tasting excursion (closed Sun dinner and Mon).

Nearby, in Le Somail: Drivers who want to experience the Canal du Midi boating scene sleep in Le Somail, a picturesque hamlet that has changed little since the construction of the canal in the 1600s. The town has an impressive bookshop, three art galleries, and two restaurants. Sleep at **$$ La Maison des Escalliers,** where Tina and Ruud have created a beautiful B&B with five stylish and comfortable rooms in their restored 19th-century house. Breakfast is served by the pool with views of the vineyards (D-€70, Db-€80-90, whole house-€2,000-2,600, 6 Rue Paul Riquet, tel. 04 68 48 44 23, mobile 06 79 55 33 37, www.patiasses.com, mail@patiasses.com).

Eating in Carcassonne

For a social outing in La Cité, take your pick from a food circus of basic eateries on a leafy courtyard—often with strolling musicians in the summer—on lively **Place Marcou.** If rubbing elbows with too many tourists gives you hives, go local and dine below in La Ville Basse (the new city). Cassoulet (described on page 516) is the traditional must (tip: a dash of vinegar helps the digestion); big salads provide a lighter alternative. For a local before-dinner drink, try a glass of Muscat de Saint-Jean-de-Minervois.

On Place St. Jean: My favorite area for dinner in La Cité is on Place St. Jean, where three eateries compete for your business, with view tables from their outside terraces to the floodlit Château Comtal. **Restaurant Adelaide** is the best, with a lively, loyal following and well-presented bistro fare at reasonable prices; they serve a good €16, three-course *menu* with cassoulet, as well as good €12-18 *plats* and big €15 salads in an orange-walled, beamed interior or at great outside tables (daily June-Aug, closed Mon Sept-May, tel. 04 68 47 66 61). **Le St. Jean,** next door, is a less-reliable runner-up, with similar prices and choices (€16-26 *menus,* €8 kid *menu,* daily, tel. 04 68 47 42 43).

Hôtel de la Cité's **Barbacane Restaurant** owns La Cité's only Michelin star (€85-160 *menus*), but even better is their summer-only restaurant **Le Jardin de L'Evêque,** where you can linger at a lovely garden table for much less (€16 starters, €25-30 main courses); see "Sleeping in Carcassonne," earlier).

Elsewhere in La Cité: **Au Comte Roger**'s quiet elegance seems out of place in this touristy town. For half the price of the Barbacane, you can celebrate a special occasion with Chef Pierre's fresh Mediterranean cuisine. Ask for a table on the vine-covered patio, or eat inside in their stylish dining room. Book ahead in high season (€21 lunch *menus,* €39 dinner *menus,* massive cassoulet-€22, closed Sun-Mon, 14 Rue St. Louis, tel. 04 68 11 93 40, www.comteroger.com).

Auberge des Lices, a good-value restaurant hidden down a quiet lane, has a courtyard with cathedral views. It manages a delicate balance of price and quality for traditional cuisine (€20-42 *menus,* daily July-Aug, closed Tue-Wed Sept-June, 3 Rue Raymond Roger Trencavel, tel. 04 68 72 34 07).

Le Jardin de la Tour, run with panache by Elodie for more than 20 years, has cool, windproof seating in the rear park-like garden and cozy indoor tables (€20 *menu,* excellent cassoulet-€16, open Tue-Sat, closed Sun-Mon, 11 Rue Porte-d'Aude, tel. 04 68 25 71 24).

Le Bar à Vins, popular with the twenty- and thirtysomething set at night, is tucked away in a big garden just inside the wall but away from the crowds. It serves an enticing selection of open wines (€2.50 a glass), €9-13 appetizers and tapas, and €6 sandwiches (daily 10:00-2:00 in the morning, closes earlier off-season, closed Nov-Jan, 6 Rue du Plô, tel. 04 68 47 38 38).

Elsewhere in Carcassonne: **Restaurant les Trois Couronnes,** just outside La Cité in Hôtel les Trois Couronnes (described earlier, under "Sleeping in Carcassonne"), gives you a panorama of Carcassonne from the top floor of a concrete hotel (€31 *menus,* open daily for dinner only, closed Jan, call ahead, 2 Rue des Trois Couronnes, tel. 04 68 25 36 10).

Chez Felix has good seats on the main square, is family-run, and serves traditional cuisine (closed Sun, 11 Place Carnot, tel. 04 68 25 17 01). Nearby, snazzy **L'Artichaut Wine Bar-Bistro** serves good-value cuisine and wines (closed Sun-Mon, 14 Place Carnot, tel. 09 52 15 65 14).

Picnics: Basic supplies can be gathered at the shops along the main drag (generally open until at least 19:30, better to buy outside La Cité). For your beggar's banquet, picnic on the city walls.

Carcassonne Connections

From Carcassonne by Train to: Albi (12/day, 3 hours, change in Toulouse), **Collioure** (8/day, 2 hours, most require change in Narbonne), **Sarlat-la-Canéda** (5/day, 5.5-7 hours, 1-3 changes, some require bus from Souillac to Sarlat), **Arles** (4/day direct, 2.5 hours, more with transfer in Narbonne), **Nice** (3/day, 6-7 hours), **Paris** (Gare de Lyon: 8/day, 5.5 hours, 1 change; Gare d'Austerlitz: 1/day direct, 7.5 hours; 1 night train, 8.5 hours), **Toulouse** (nearly hourly, 1 hour), **Barcelona** (1/day direct, 2.5 hours, 4/day with change in Narbonne, 2-3 hours).

Near Carcassonne

The land around Carcassonne is carpeted with vineyards and littered with romantically ruined castles, ancient abbeys, and photogenic villages. The castle remains of Peyrepertuse and Quéribus make terrific stops between Carcassonne and Collioure (allow 2 hours from Carcassonne on narrow, winding roads). You can also link them on a fine loop trip from Carcassonne. The gorge-sculpted village of Minerve, 45 minutes northeast of Carcassonne, works well for Provence-bound travelers.

Getting There: Public transportation is hopeless; taxis for up to six people cost €300 for a day-long excursion (taxi tel. 04 68 71 50 50). See page 535 for excursion bus and minivan tours to these places.

▲▲▲CHATEAUX OF HAUTES CORBIERES

About two hours south of Carcassonne, in the scenic foothills of the Pyrenees, you'll find a series of surreal, mountain-capping castle ruins. Like a Maginot Line of the 13th century, these cloud-piercing castles were strategically located between France and the Spanish kingdom of Roussillon. As you can see by flipping through the picture books in Carcassonne's tourist shops, these castles' crumbled ruins are an impressive contrast to the restored walls of La Cité. If you go, bring a hat (there's no shade) and sturdy walking shoes—and prepare for a vigorous climb.

Connect these castles (ultimately with Collioure if you want) along this incredibly scenic, two-hour drive: From Carcassonne drive to Limoux, then Couiza. At Couiza follow little D-14 to Bugarach (passing through Languedoc's only spa town, Rennes-le-Château). Near Bugarach, views open to rocky ridgelines hovering above dense forests. You'll soon see signs leading the way to Peyrepertuse. At Cubières, canyon lovers can detour to the **Gorges de Galamus,** driving partway into the teeth of white-rock slabs that seem to get closer the farther in you go (those looping back to Carcassonne can do the whole canyon on their way back). **Peyrepertuse** is a short hop from Cubières; you'll pass snack stands and view cafés on the twisty drive up. After visiting this Cathar castle, your next destination—**Quéribus**—is a well-signed, 15-minute drive away. From Quéribus it's a 90-minute drive to the seaside village of Collioure (follow signs in direction: Maury, then direction: Perpignan). If returning to Carcassonne, follow signs for Maury, then St-Paul-de-Fenouillet, then drive through the Gorges de Galamus and track D-14 to Bugarach, Couiza, Limoux, and Carcassonne.

Peyrepertuse

The most spectacular Cathar castle is Peyrepertuse (pay-ruh-pair-twos), where the ruins rise from a splinter of cliff: Try to spot it on your drive up from the village. The views are sensational in all directions, but what's most amazing is that they could build this place at all. This was a lookout in the Middle Ages, staffed with 25 very lonely men. Today, it's a scamperer's paradise with weed-infested structures in varying states of ruin. Let your imagination soar, but watch your step as you try to reconstruct this eagle's nest—the footing is tricky. Don't miss the St. Louis stairway to the upper castle

ruins, and be prepared for a 10-minute uphill hike from the ticket office to reach the castle's base.

Cost and Hours: €6.50, €8.50 in July-Aug, daily April-Sept 9:00-19:00, until 20:00 July-Aug, shorter hours off-season, closed Jan, theatrical audioguide-€4 (narrated from the perspective of a French captain posted here), free handout gives plenty of background for most, tel. 04 82 53 24 07, www.chateau-peyrepertuse.com.

Quéribus

While Peyrepertuse rides along a high ridge, this bulky castle caps a mountain top and delivers more amazing views (find the snow-covered peaks of the Pyrenees). It owns a similar history to Peyrepertuse but has an easier (but still uphill) footpath to access the site and gentler climbing within the ruins. It's famous as the last Cathar castle to fall, and was abandoned after 1659, when the border between France and Spain was moved farther south into the high Pyrenees.

Cost and Hours: €6, daily April-Sept 9:30-19:00, until 20:00 July-Aug, shorter hours off-season, same audioguide concept as at Peyrepertuse-€4, good handout, tel. 04 68 45 03 69, www.cucugnan.fr).

Sleeping near Peyrepertuse and Quéribus: To really get away (and I mean really), sleep in the lovely little village of Cucugnan, located between the castles. **$$ L'Ecurie de Cucugnan** is a friendly bed-and-breakfast with five comfortable rooms at great rates, a view pool, and a shady garden, but the staff doesn't speak English (Sb-€58, Db-€68, includes breakfast, Wi-Fi, 2-room house-€550/week, 18 Rue Achille Mir, tel. 04 68 33 37 42, mobile 06 76 86 38 52, ecurie.cucugnan@orange.fr).

CATHAR SIGHTS NEAR CAUNES-MINERVOIS

The next two Cathar sights tie in well with a visit to Caunes-Minervois (where I recommend accommodations—see page 545) and provide an easy excursion from Carcassonne, offering you a taste of this area's appealing countryside.

Châteaux of Lastours

Ten miles north of Carcassonne, these four ruined castles cap a barren hilltop and give drivers a handy (if less dramatic) look at the region's Cathar castles. From Carcassonne, follow signs to *Mazamet,* then *Conques-sur-Orbiel,* then *Lastours.* In Lastours you can hike to the castle or drive to a viewpoint.

Hikers park at the lot as they enter the village, walk five minutes upriver to the glass entry, then walk 20 minutes uphill to the castles (allow at least an hour for a reasonable tour, wear sturdy walking shoes). The castles, which once surrounded a fortified village, date from the 11th century. The village welcomed Cathars (becoming a bishop's seat at one point) but paid for this tolerance with destruction by French troops in 1227. Everyone should make the short drive to the belvedere for a smashing panorama over the castles.

Cost and Hours: €6 for castles and belvedere viewpoint, €2 for viewpoint only; daily July-Aug 9:00-20:00, April-June and Sept 10:00-18:00, Oct 10:00-17:00; off-season generally Sat only 10:00-17:00, closed Jan-Feb; tel. 04 68 77 56 02.

Eating: An idyllic lunch awaits near the lower entry at **Le Moulin de Lastours,** where a small bakery has arranged a few tables serenely overlooking the river (good quiche, sandwiches, drinks, closed Tue off-season, tel. 04 68 25 23 14).

▲Minerve

A onetime Cathar hideout with Celtic origins, the spectacular village of Minerve is sculpted out of a swirling canyon that provided a natural defense. Strong as it was, it couldn't keep out the Pope's armies, and the village was razed during the vicious Albigensian Crusades of the early 1200s.

Getting There: Located between Carcassonne and Béziers, Minerve is seven miles north of Olonzac and 45 minutes by car from Carcassonne. It makes for a good stop between Provence and Carcassonne.

Visiting Minerve: As you arrive, follow the *P* signs to the parking lot above the village (€3). Take in the views from the cliff at the parking lot, then enter the village and find the **TI** on the same street (Rue des Martyrs, tel. 04 68 91 81 43, www.minerve-tourisme.fr). Pick up the brochure with a simple self-guided tour of the village describing Minerve's history, and ask about hiking into the canyon below (not difficult).

Minerve has cool cafés (**Café de la Place** is my favorite), one hotel, a nifty little bookshop, a few wine shops, and a smattering of art galleries. You'll also find two small museums: a prehistory museum and the compact **Hurepel de Minerve,** with models from the Cathar era that effectively describe this terrible time (€3, free for children under 14, excellent English explanations, interesting for kids, daily April-Oct 10:00-13:00 & 14:00-18:00, closed Nov-March, Rue des Martyrs, tel. 04 68 91 12 26).

After your village stroll, explore the canyon below by walking down to the riverbed: Look for a path by the ruined tower near the parking lot, or follow *Access Remparts* signs from below Café de la Place. A path across the riverbed leads to a catapult and views back to Minerve.

Sleeping and Eating in Minerve: Stay here and melt into southern France (almost literally, if it's summer). **$ Relais Chantovent**'s unpretentious and spotless rooms are designed for those who come to get away from it all, with no phones or TV...and ample quiet. All rooms have queen-size beds (Sb-€46, Db-€55, breakfast-€8, Wi-Fi, tel. 04 68 91 14 18, www.relaischantovent-minerve.fr, relaischantovent@orange.fr). Its sharp restaurant has a marvelous view from its deck and deserves your business; it's popular, so reserve ahead (*menus* from €23, closed Wed year-round, closed Sun-Tue for dinner in winter).

Collioure

Surrounded by less-appealing resorts, lovely Collioure is blessed with a privileged climate and a romantic setting. By Mediterranean standards, this seaside village should be slammed with tourists—it has everything. Like an ice-cream shop, Collioure offers 31 flavors of pastel houses and six petite, scooped-out, pebbled beaches sprinkled with visitors. This sweet scene, capped by a winking lighthouse, sits under a once-mighty castle in the shade of the Pyrenees.

Just 15 miles from the Spanish border, Collioure (Cotlliure in Catalan) shares a common history and independent attitude with its Catalan siblings across the border. Undeniably French yet proudly Catalan, it flies the yellow-and-red flag of Catalunya, displays street names in French and Catalan, and sports business names with *el* and *els,* rather than *le* and *les.* Sixty years ago, most villagers spoke Catalan; today that language is enjoying a resurgence as Collioure rediscovers its roots.

Come here to unwind and regroup. Even with its crowds of vacationers in peak season (July and August are busy), Collioure is what many look for when they head to the Riviera—a sunny, relaxing splash in the Mediterranean.

PLANNING YOUR TIME

Check your ambition at the station. Enjoy a slow coffee on *le Med,* lose yourself in the old town's streets, compare the *gelati* shops on Rue Vauban, sample the fine local wines, and relax on a pebble-sand beach (waterproof shoes are helpful). And if you have a car, don't miss a drive into the hills above Collioure.

Orientation to Collioure

Most of Collioure's shopping, sights, and hotels are in the old town, near the Château Royal. There are good views of the old town from across the bay near the recommended Hôtel Boramar and brilliant views from the hills above. You can walk from one end of Collioure to the other in 20 minutes.

TOURIST INFORMATION

The TI hides behind the main beachfront cafés at 5 Place du 18 Juin (July-Aug Mon-Sat 9:00-20:00, Sun 10:00-18:00; April-June and Sept Mon-Sat 9:00-12:00 & 14:00-19:00, Sun 10:00-12:30 & 14:30-18:00; Oct-March Mon-Sat until 18:00 and closed Sun; tel. 04 68 82 15 47, www.collioure.com).

ARRIVAL IN COLLIOURE

By Train: Walk out of the station (no baggage storage), turn right, and follow Rue Aristide Maillol downhill for about 10 minutes until you see Hôtel Fregate (directions to hotels are listed from this reference point—see "Sleeping in Collioure," later). Pick up a schedule for Spanish side-trips or for your next destination (station staffed 9:00-13:30 & 14:40-18:00).

By Car: Collioure is 16 miles south of Perpignan. Take the *Perpignan-Sud Sortie* exit from the autoroute and follow signs to *Argelès-sur-Mer* (also called *Argelès*), then *Collioure par la Corniche.* Parking is a challenge and almost impossible in summer—arrive early or late. To reach the center, follow *Collioure Centre-Ville* signs, turn left onto Rue de la République, and look for any available spots. There's a big pay lot (Parking Glacis) accessed from the intersection of Rue de la République and Avenue du Général de Gaulle; you can also access it from the bottom of Rue de la République (see map; €12/24 hours). I often find a space at Parking Douy, as you drop downhill toward the city center (5-minute walk to the center, €12/24 hours). The best deal is Parking du Stade, a 15-minute walk from the center past Fort Miradou (on Route du Pla de las Fourques, €2/24 hours year-round). In high season, it's easiest to park at the remote Parking Cap Dourats on the Route de Madeloc (€6/24 hours) and take the free shuttle bus into town (3/hour, 10:00-24:00). Once parked, make sure to take everything of value out of the car.

HELPFUL HINTS

Market Days: Markets are held on Wednesday and Sunday mornings on Place Général Leclerc, across from Hôtel Fregate.

Internet Access: The lighthearted **Café Sola,** next to the recommended Hôtel Casa Pairal, offers free Wi-Fi if you buy a

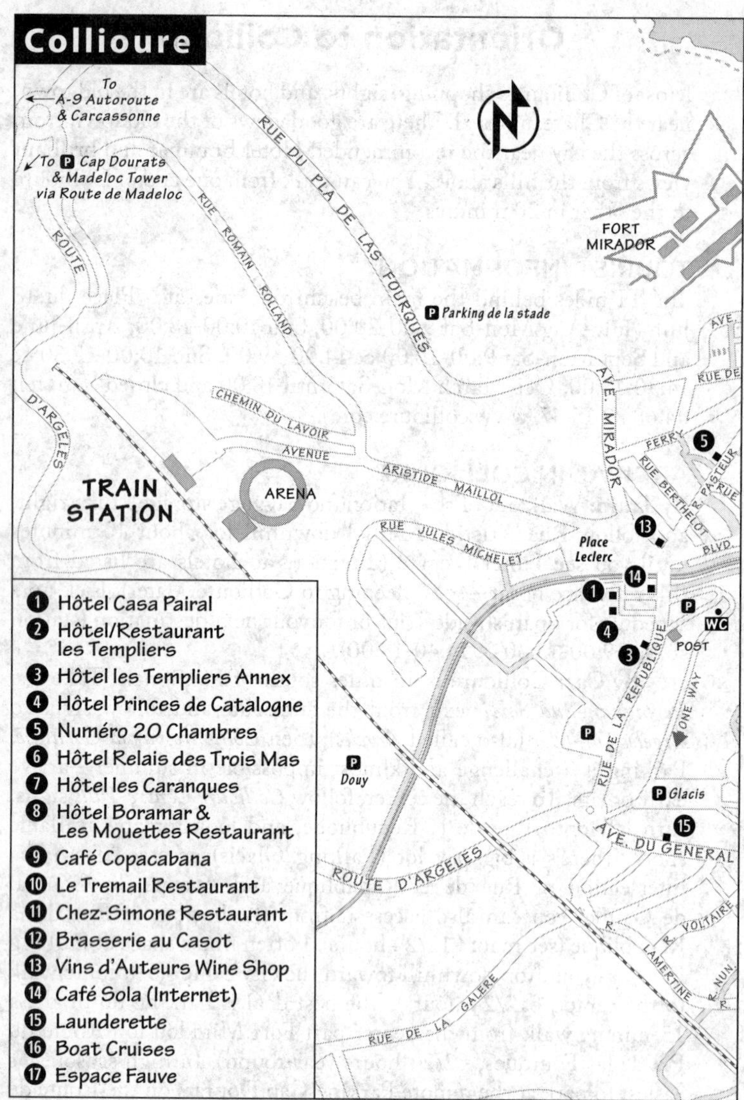

drink (daily, about 7:00-21:00 or later, 2 Rue de la République, tel. 04 68 82 55 02).

Laundry: A self-serve **launderette** is at 8 Avenue du Général de Gaulle (daily 7:00-21:00, mobile 06 74 57 17 39).

Taxi: Call 04 68 82 27 80 or mobile 07 62 12 68 68.

Tourist Train: Collioure's ***petit train*** leaves from the post office at the bottom of Rue de la République and toots you to Port

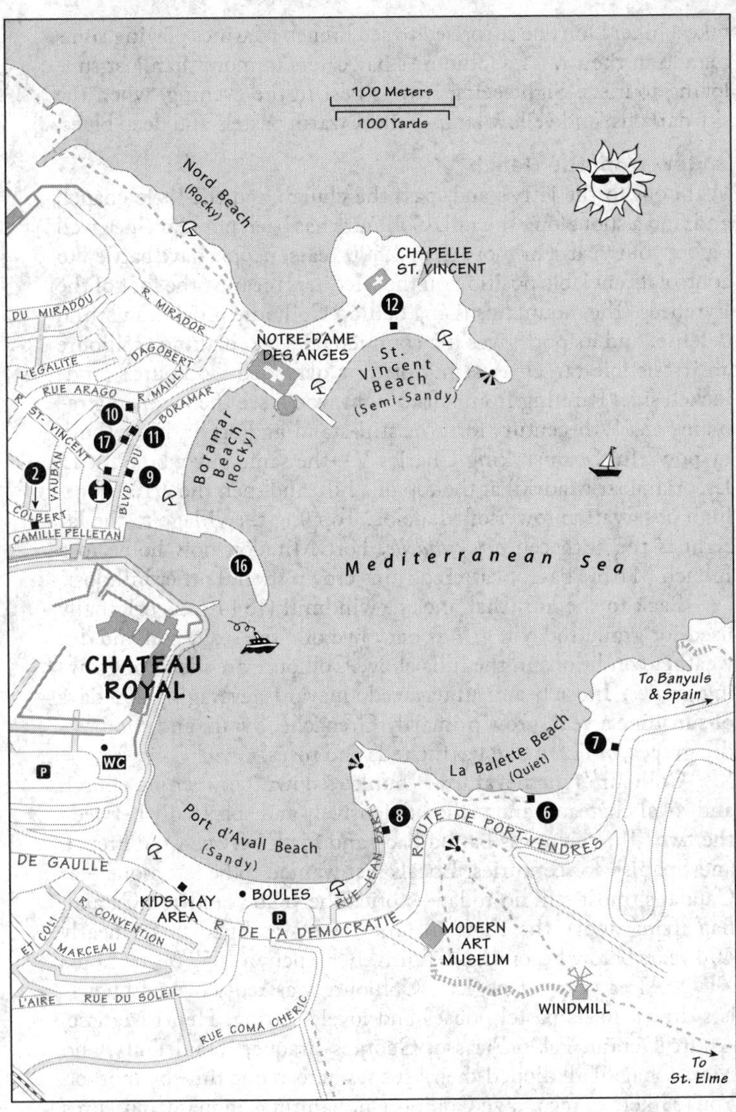

Vendres and up to Fort St. Elme for brilliant views, sans sweat (€7 round-trip).

Sights in Collioure

There's no important sight here except what lies on the beach and the views over Collioure. Indulge in a long seaside lunch, inspect the colorful art galleries, catch up on your postcards, and maybe take a hike. Don't be surprised to see French Marines playing commando in their rafts; Collioure's bay caters to more than just sun-loving tourists. Sightseeing here is best in the evening, when the sky darkens, and yellow lamps reflect warm pastels and deep blues.

▲View from the Beach

Walk out to the jetty's end, past the church and the little chapel, and find a spot along the rail. Collioure has been popular since well before your visit. For more than 2,500 years, people have battled to control its enviable position on the Mediterranean at the foot of the Pyrenees. The mountains rising behind Collioure provide a natural defense, and its port gives it a commercial edge, making Collioure an irresistible target. A string of forts defended Collioure's landlocked side. Panning from left to right, you'll see the low-slung remains of a 17th-century fort, the still-standing Fort St. Elme (built by powerful Spanish king Charles V—the same guy who built El Escorial near Madrid) at the top of a hill, and then the 2,100-foot-high observation tower of Madeloc. Topping the village to the far right is the 18th-century *citadelle,* Fort Mirador, now home to a French Marine base. Scattered ruins crown several other hilltops.

Back to the left, that ancient windmill (1344) was originally used for grain; today it grinds out olive oil. The stony soil and dry weather conditions in the hills above Collioure are ideal for growing grapes. Those beautiful terraced vineyards, averaging 250 days of sunshine a year, grow primarily Grenache, Syrah, and Mourvèdre grapes, which make terrific reds and rosés.

Collioure's medieval town hunkers down between its church and royal château, sandwiched defensively and spiritually between the two. The town was batted back and forth between the French and Spanish for centuries. Locals just wanted to be left alone—as Catalans (most still do today—notice the yellow-and-red Catalan flag flying above the château). The town was Spanish for nearly 400 years before becoming definitively French in 1659 (*merci* Louis XIV). After years of neglect, Collioure was rediscovered by artists drawn to its pastel houses and lovely setting. Henri Matisse, André Derain, Pablo Picasso, Georges Braque, Raoul Dufy, and Marc Chagall all dipped their brushes here at one time or another. You're likely to recognize Collioure in paintings in many museums across Europe.

Château Royal (Royal Castle)

The 800-year-old castle, built over Roman ruins, served as home over the years to Majorcan kings, Crusaders, Dominican monks, and Louis XIV (who had the final say on the appearance we see now). Today it serves tourists, offering great rampart walks, views, and mildly interesting local history exhibits.

Cost and Hours: €4, daily June-Sept 10:00-17:45, Oct-May 9:00-16:15, tel. 04 68 82 06 43.

Notre-Dame des Anges (Our Lady of the Angels Church)

This waterfront church is worth a gander (daily 9:00-18:00). Find a pew and listen to the waves while searching your soul. Supporting a guiding light (in more than one way), the church's foundations are built into the sea, and its one-of-a-kind lighthouse-bell tower helped sailors return home safely. The highlight is its over-the-top golden altar, unusual in France but typical of Catalan churches across the border. Drop €1 in the box to the left of the altar: lights, cameras, reaction—ooh la la!

Path of Fauvism (Chemin du Fauvisme)

As you stroll Collioure's lanes, you'll occasionally see faded prints hanging on the walls. You're on the "Chemin du Fauvisme," where you'll find 20 copies of Derain's and Matisse's works, inspired by their stays in Collioure in 1905. The **Espace Fauve** office (behind the TI at 10 Rue de la Prud'homie) has French-only fliers for sale that identify where the copies are mounted in Collioure. As with Arles and Vincent van Gogh, there are no original paintings by Derain or Matisse here for the public to enjoy. However, the museum in Céret has a good collection (see page 559), as does the recommended Hôtel les Templiers.

Beaches *(Plages)*

You'll usually find the best sand-to-stone ratio at Plage de Port d'Avall or Plage St. Vincent (chaise lounge rental-€10/day, paddleboat/kayak rentals-€14-20/hour, summer only). The tiny Plage de la Balette is quietest but rocky, with brilliant views of Collioure.

Wine Tasting

Collioure and the surrounding area produce well-respected wines, and many shops offer informal tastings of the sweet Banyuls and Collioure reds and rosés. Try **Vins d'Auteurs,** with a good selection from many wineries and fair prices (next to Hôtel Fregate at 6 Place Maréchal Leclerc, tel. 04 68 55 45 22).

Cruise

Mildly interesting **Promenade sur Mer** boat excursions provide views of Collioure from the Mediterranean as they cruise toward Spain and back (€12-16, 3-5/day, 1 hour, Easter-Sept weather permitting, leaves from breakwater near château, commentary in

French only, mobile 06 10 73 51 77, www.roussillon-croisieres.com).

HIKES

The three views described here offer different perspectives of this splendid area.

▲Views Below the Stone Windmill

Stone steps lead 10 minutes up behind Collioure's modern art museum to fine views that are positively peachy at sunset. Find the museum behind Hôtel Triton, walk through its stony backyard, keep left—hugging its back, then come to steps that lead up to a small, square structure with fine views (just below the windmill).

▲Hike to Fort St. Elme

This vertical hike is best done early or late (there's no shade) and is worth the sweat, even if you don't make it to the top (trail starts from windmill described above, allow 30 minutes from there each way). You can't miss the square castle lurking high above Collioure. The privately owned castle has a rich history (built in 1552 by Holy Roman Emperor Charles V) and medieval exhibits—pick up the English booklet that explains them (€6, daily April-Sept 10:30-19:00, shorter hours off-season, closed mid-Nov-mid-Feb, mobile 06 64 61 82 42, www.fortsaintelme.com).

Cheaters can drive there via Port Vendres or take Collioure's *petit train* up (see "Helpful Hints," earlier).

▲▲▲Drive/Hike Through Vineyards to Madeloc Tower (Tour de Madeloc)

Check your vertigo at the hotel, fasten your seatbelt, and take this drive-and-hike combination high above Collioure. The narrow road, hairpin turns, and absence of guardrails only add to the experience, as Collioure shrinks to Lego-size and the clouds become your neighbors. Drive as far as you like on this route—the views get exceptional fast and turnouts allow for panorama appreciation and easy turnarounds.

Leave Collioure, heading toward Perpignan, and look for signs reading *Tour de Madeloc* at the roundabout just above the town. Climb through steep and rocky terraced vineyards, following *Tour* signs and negotiating countless hairpin turns. About six kilometers past the roundabout, you'll pass a rocky trail leading to *Tour de Madeloc.* In 10 kilometers (about 20 minutes), you'll come to a fork in the road with a paved path (marked by a "no entry" symbol that applies to cars) and a road leading downhill. Park at the fork, and walk up the paved path. The views everywhere are magnificent—the Pyrenees on one side, and the beach towns of Port Vendres and Collioure on the other. Allow 40 minutes at a slow-yet-steady pace along the splintered ridgetop to reach the eagle's-nest setting of the ancient tower (La Tour), now fitted with communication devices. Here you can commune with the gods, but beware—there's no shade, so do this hike early or late in the day.

NEAR COLLIOURE

Day Trip to Spain

The 15-mile, 40-minute coastal drive via the Col de Banyuls into Spain is beautiful and well worth the countless curves, even if you don't venture past the border.

To visit the wild **Salvador Dalí Theater-Museum,** take the autoroute to Figueres, which takes about an hour each way (museum: €12; July-Sept daily 9:00-20:00; March-June and Oct Tue-Sun 9:30-18:00, closed Mon; Nov-Feb Tue-Sun 10:30-18:00, closed Mon; last entry 45 minutes before closing, Spanish tel. 972-677-500, www.salvador-dali.org).

Train travelers can also day-trip to Spain, either to Barcelona (9/day, 2-4 hours, transfer in Perpignan or Portbou) or to the closer Figueres (6/day, 2 hours, transfer in Portbou). Get train schedules at the station.

Céret

To see the art that Collioure inspired, you'll have to drive 25 windy miles inland to this pleasing town, featuring fountains and mountains at its doorstep. Céret's claim to fame is its **modern-art museum,** with works by some of Collioure's more famous visitors, including Picasso, Joan Miró, Chagall, and Matisse (€8, daily July-mid-Sept 10:00-19:00, mid-Sept-June 10:00-18:00, closed Tue Oct-March, tel. 04 68 87 27 76, www.musee-ceret.com). Allow 40 minutes to Céret by car, or ride the bus—ask at Collioure's TI.

Sleeping in Collioure

Collioure has a fair range of hotels at favorable rates. You have two good choices for your hotel's location: central, in the old town (closer to train station); or across the bay, with views of the old town (10-minute walk from the central zone, with easier parking).

IN THE OLD TOWN

Directions to the following places are given from the big Hôtel Fregate, at the edge of the old town, a 10-minute walk down from the train station. Price ranges reflect low versus high season.

$$$ Hôtel Casa Pairal*,** opposite Hôtel Fregate and hiding down a short alley (behind Café Sola), is Mediterranean-elegant. Enter to the sounds of a fountain gurgling in the flowery courtyard. Reclining lounges await in the garden and by the pool. The rooms are quiet and tastefully designed. "Privilege" rooms, on the first floor, have high ceilings and small balconies over a courtyard (standard Db-€100-130, "privilege" Db-€145-195, big Db suite with terrace-€195-295, breakfast-€16, air-con, Wi-Fi, parking-€16/day, Impasse des Palmiers, tel. 04 68 82 05 81, www.hotel-casa-pairal.com, contact@hotel-casa-pairal.com, reserve ahead for room and parking).

$$ Hôtel les Templiers,** in the heart of the old town, has wall-to-wall paintings squeezed in every available space in its main building, a perennially popular café-bar, low-key management, and good-value rooms. The paintings are payments in kind and thank-yous from artists who have stayed here—find the black-and-white photo in the bar of the hotel's owner with Picasso. The rooms—some of which have views—are either new and modern, or older and charming. Those in the main building (where you check in) are best. There are two annex buildings with less character but cheaper rates (figure €10 less per room); one is across from the main building and the other is on Rue de la République (standard Db-€72-99, bigger Db-€92-135, basic breakfast-€6.50, air-con and Wi-Fi in main building only, a block toward beach from Hôtel Fregate along drainage canal at 12 Quai de l'Amirauté, tel. 04 68 98 31 10, www.hotel-templiers.com, info@hotel-templiers.com).

$$ Hôtel Princes de Catalogne*** offers 30 comfortable, spacious, contemporary rooms. Get a room on the mountain side, or *côté montagne* (koh-tay mon-tan-yah), for maximum quiet (Db without mountain view-€70-80, superior Db with view-€80-90, air-con, Wi-Fi, limited free parking, next to Casa Pairal, Rue des Palmiers, tel. 04 68 98 30 00, www.hotel-princescatalogne.com, contact@hotel-princescatalogne.com).

$ Numéro 20 Chambres, with eager-to-help hosts Véronique and Noel, is a good budget value. The rooms are simple, clean, spacious, and suitable for families, with Wi-Fi, small fridges, coffeemakers, and microwaves (Db-€60, Tb-€80, Qb-€100, cash only, on the pedestrian street two blocks past Hôtel Fregate at 20 Rue Pasteur, tel. 04 68 82 15 31, mobile 06 17 50 16 89, www.collioure-chambre-peroneille.fr, numero20ruepasteur@gmail.com).

ACROSS THE BAY

$$$ Hôtel Relais des Trois Mas**** clings to the hill below the main road in Collioure and delivers comfortable, colorful rooms, many with killer views. They have the best view pool and Jacuzzi in Collioure (standard Db-€150-175, bigger Db with view-€210-280, suites-€230-455, breakfast-€18, air-con, Wi-Fi, free parking, fine restaurant with *menus* from €48, Route de Port Vendres, tel. 04 68 82 05 07, www.relaisdestroismas.com, contact@relaisdes3mas.com).

$$$ Hôtel les Caranques**, a few curves toward Spain from Collioure's center, tumbles down the cliffs and showcases million-dollar sea views from each of its rooms, which all have balconies. Enjoy the sensational view decks scattered about and the stylish bar (smallish Db-€135-160, razzle-dazzle Db-suite-€250, Wi-Fi, Route de Port Vendres, 30-minute walk from train station, 15 minutes from town center, tel. 04 68 82 06 68, www.les-caranques.com, contact@les-caranques.com). For a scenic walk to Collioure's center, follow the sidewalk, then turn right down the steps just after the *Relais des Trois Mas* sign.

$$ Hôtel Boramar**, across the bay from Collioure's center, is understated and modest (like its owner Thierry), but well-maintained (also like Thierry) and a terrific value. Ten of their 14 rooms face the water, many with balconies (Db without view-€65, Db with view-€80, Tb with view-€85, breakfast-€7, Rue Jean Bart, tel. 04 68 82 07 06, www.hotel-boramar.fr, hotelboramar.collioure@orange.fr).

Eating in Collioure

Test the local wine and eat anything Catalan, including the fish and anchovies (hand-filleted, as no machine has ever been able to accomplish this precise task). Consistency is elusive with restaurants in Collioure, but those listed below have been reliable. All of my recommended restaurants have indoor and outdoor tables, and most are in the old town. Your task is to decide whether you want to eat well or with a view. Several delicious *gelati* shops and a Grand Marnier crêpe stand next to the Café Copacabana fuel after-dinner strollers with the perfect last course. If you're traveling off-season, call ahead—many restaurants here are closed December through February.

Café Copacabana, on the main beach (Boramar), offers big salads and a few seafood dishes in its sandy café. Skip their sidewalk-bound restaurant (which has a bigger selection but smaller view) and find a chair beachside. The quality is good enough, considering the view, and it's family-friendly—kids can play on the beach while you dine (daily mid-March-mid-Dec, Plage Boramar, tel. 04 68 82 06 74, best at sunset).

Le Tremail is good for contemporary seafood and Catalan specialties served outside or in. It's a small and cozy place one block from the bay, where Rue Arago and Rue Mailly meet (€27 *menus,* open daily year-round, 16 bis Rue Mailly, tel. 04 68 82 16 10).

The restaurant at the recommended **Hôtel les Templiers** is popular with locals and dishes up reliable value (daily, 12 Quai de l'Amirauté, tel. 04 68 98 31 10).

Chez-Simone, a lighthearted and *très* popular budget place, serves €3-5 tapas, cheap *tartines,* and €12 *plats* with sea views and smiles (daily for lunch, Thu-Sun for dinner, Boulevard Boramar, tel. 04 68 82 12 56).

Les Mouettes, a 10-minute stroll around the bay, is a simple seaside place with a local following, reliable seafood-focused cuisine, and terrific views (€15-20 *plats,* daily, next to the recommended Hôtel Boramar at 17 Rue Jean Bart, tel. 04 68 88 86 65).

Brasserie au Casot owns the best setting away from the crowds, past the church on Plage St. Vincent, and serves salads and *plats* with views for a fair price. Matisse would dig the decor. Ask owner Alix about his homemade sangria (€13-16 *plats,* generally June-Sept daily 11:00-20:00 weather permitting, lunch only Oct and May, Plage St. Vincent, tel. 04 68 22 42 46).

Eating Cheaply: Small places sell a variety of meals to go (*à emporter;* ah em-pohr-tay) for budget-minded romantics wanting to dine on the bay.

Collioure Connections

Collioure's tiny station is staffed from 9:00-13:30 and 14:40-18:00. If you need to buy tickets, do so during those hours (tel. 04 68 82 05 89).

From Collioure by Train to: Carcassonne (8/day, 2 hours, most require change in Narbonne), **Paris** (8/day, 6-7 hours, 1-2 changes, one direct night train to Gare d'Austerlitz in 12 hours), **Barcelona,** Spain (6/day, 3-4 hours, most change in Perpignan or Portbou), **Figueres,** Spain (6/day, 1-2 hours, most change in Perpignan), **Avignon/Arles** (8/day, 3.5-4.5 hours, several transfer points possible).

PROVENCE

Arles • Avignon • Pont du Gard • Les Baux • Orange • Villages of the Côtes du Rhône • Hill Towns of the Luberon

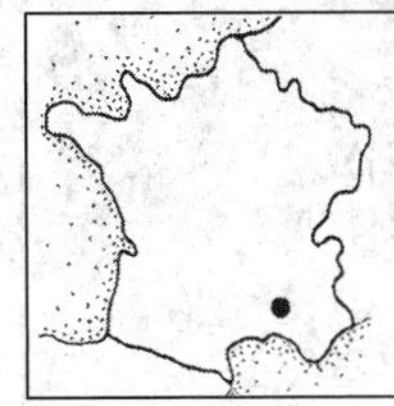

This magnificent region is shaped like a giant wedge of quiche. From its sunburned crust, fanning out along the Mediterranean coast from the Camargue to Marseille, it stretches north along the Rhône Valley to Orange. The Romans were here in force and left many ruins—some of the best anywhere. Seven popes, artists such as Vincent van Gogh and Paul Cézanne, and author Peter Mayle all enjoyed their years in Provence. This destination features a splendid recipe of arid climate, oceans of vineyards, dramatic scenery, lively cities, and adorable hill-capping villages.

Explore the ghost town that is ancient Les Baux, and see France's greatest Roman ruins, the Pont du Gard aqueduct and the theater in Orange. Admire the skill of ball-tossing *boules* players in small squares in every Provençal village and city. Spend a few Van Gogh-inspired starry, starry nights in Arles. Youthful but classy Avignon bustles in the shadow of its brooding Palace of the Popes. It's a short hop from Arles or Avignon into the splendid scenery and villages of the Côtes du Rhône and Luberon regions.

PLANNING YOUR TIME

Make Arles or Avignon your sightseeing base—particularly if you have no car. Italophiles prefer smaller Arles, while poodles pick urban Avignon. Arles has a blue-collar quality; the entire city feels like Van Gogh's bedroom. Avignon—double the size of Arles—feels sophisticated, with more nightlife and shopping, and makes a good base for non-drivers thanks to its convenient public-transit options. To measure the pulse of rural Provence, spend at least one night in a smaller town (such as Vaison la Romaine or Roussillon),

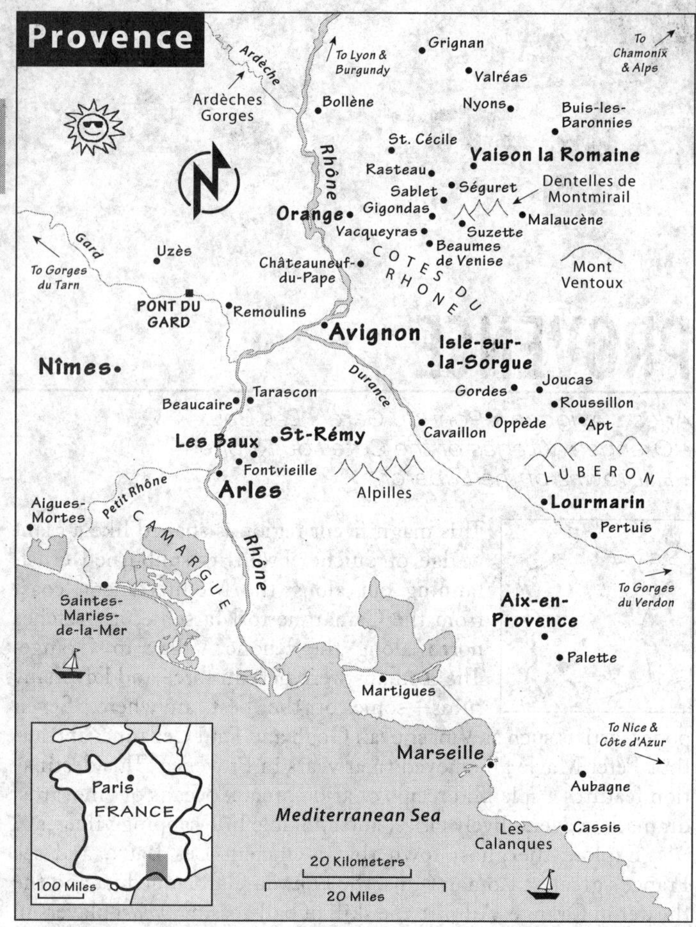

or in the countryside. These villages can be terminally quiet from mid-October to Easter.

When budgeting your time, you'll want a full day for sightseeing in Arles and Les Baux (for example, spend most of the day in Arles—best on Wed or Sat, when it's market day—and visit Les Baux in the late afternoon or early evening); a half-day for Avignon; and a day or two for the villages and sights in the countryside.

Pont du Gard is a short hop west of Avignon and on the way to/from Languedoc-Roussillon for drivers. Les Baux works well by car from Avignon or Arles, and in summer by bus from Arles (daily July-Aug, Sat–Sun only June and Sept). The town of Orange ties in tidily with a trip to the Côtes du Rhône villages. The Côtes du Rhône is ideal for wine connoisseurs and an easy stop for those heading to or from the north. Vaison la Romaine is also ideal for those heading to/from the north, and Isle-sur-la-Sorgue (the most accessible small town by train) is conveniently located between Avignon and the Luberon.

GETTING AROUND PROVENCE

By Bus or Train: Public transit is good between cities and decent to some towns, but marginal at best to the smaller villages. Frequent trains link Avignon and Arles (no more than 30 minutes between each). Avignon has good train connections with Orange and adequate service to Isle-sur-la-Sorgue.

Buses connect many smaller towns, though service can be sporadic. From Avignon you can bus to Pont du Gard, Isle-sur-la-Sorgue (also by train), and to some Côtes du Rhône villages. While a tour of the villages of the Côtes du Rhône or Luberon is best on your own by car, a variety of minivan tours and basic bus excursions are available. (TIs in Arles and Avignon also have information on bus excursions to regional sights that are hard to reach *sans* car; see "Tours of Provence," below.)

By Car: The region is made to order for a car, though travel time between some sights will surprise you—thanks, in part, to narrow roads and endless roundabouts (for example, figure an hour from Les Baux to Pont du Gard, and two hours from Arles to Vaison la Romaine). The yellow Michelin maps #332 (Luberon and Côtes du Rhône) and #340 (Arles area) are worth considering; the larger-scale orange Michelin map #527 also includes the Riviera. Avignon (pop. 110,000) is a headache for drivers. Arles (pop. 52,000) is easier but still challenging. Be wary of thieves—this is France's worst area for car break-ins (whether in cities, out-of-the-way sights, and everywhere in between). Park only in well-monitored spaces and leave nothing valuable in your car. If you're heading north from Provence, consider a half-day detour through the spectacular Ardèche Gorges (for route tips, see page 923).

TOURS OF PROVENCE

Wine Safari

Dutchman **Mike Rijken** runs a one-man show, taking travelers through the region he adopted more than 20 years ago. Mike came to France to train as a chef, later became a wine steward, and has now found his calling as a driver/guide. His English is fluent, and though his focus is on wine and wine villages, Mike knows the region thoroughly and is a good teacher of its history (€75/half-day, €130/day, priced per person, group size varies from 2 to 6; pickups possible in Arles, Avignon, Lyon, Marseille, or Aix-en-Provence; tel. 04 90 35 59 21, mobile 06 19 29 50 81, www.winesafari.net, mikeswinesafari@orange.fr).

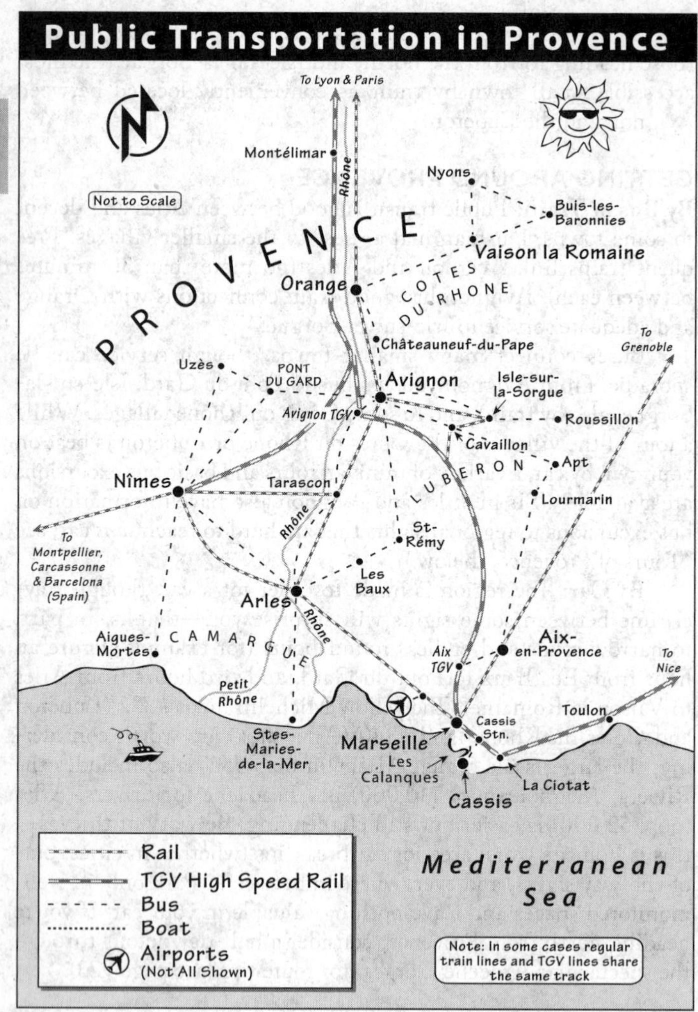

Le Vin à la Bouche

Celine Viany, a wine *sommelier* and charming tour guide, is an easy-to-be-with expert on her region and its chief product (from €75/half-day per person, from €90/day for up to 6 people, tel. 04 90 46 90 80, mobile 06 76 59 56 30, www.levinalabouche.com, contact@degustation-levinalabouche.com).

Discover Provence

Discover Provence was founded by English-born **Sarah Pernet,** who has lived in France since 1990. Based in Aix-en-Provence, she offers a variety of well-organized and easygoing small-group tours to local sites of interest, including Luberon villages, Cassis, Arles, and St-Rémy (per person from €90/half-day, €150/day, tel. 06 16 86 40 24, www.discover-provence.net, discoverprovence@hotmail.com).

Treasure-Europe

Art historian and photographer **Daniela Wedel** moved from Germany to Provence after falling in love with southern France. She and her team of guides eagerly share their passion for the history, food, wine, and people of Provence (€180/half-day, €460/day, price varies depending on itinerary and number of people, tel. 06 43 86 30 83, www.treasure-europe.com, daniela@treasure-europe.com).

Avignon Wine Tour

For a playful and distinctly French perspective on wines of the Côtes du Rhône region, contact François Marcou, who runs his tours with passion and energy, offering different itineraries every day (€110/person for all-day wine tours that include 4 tastings, €80/person for half-day tours, €350 for private groups, less in winter, mobile 06 28 05 33 84, www.avignon-wine-tour.com, avignon.wine.tour@modulonet.fr).

Imagine Tours

Unlike most tour operators, this nonprofit organization focuses on cultural excursions, offering low-key, personalized tours that allow visitors to discover the "true heart of Provence and Occitania." The itineraries are adapted to your interests, and the guides will meet you at your hotel or the departure point of your choice (€190/half-day, €315/day, prices are for up to 4 people starting from the region around Avignon or Arles, mobile 06 89 22 19 87, www.imagine-tours.net, imagine.tours@gmail.com). They are also happy to help you plan your itinerary, book hotel rooms, or address other traveler issues.

Wine Uncovered

Passionate and engaging Englishman Olivier Hickman takes small groups on focused tours of selected wineries in Châteauneuf-du-Pape and in the villages near Vaison la Romaine. Olivier is serious about wine and knows his subject matter inside and out. His in-depth tastings include a half-day tour of two or three wineries—the Châteauneuf-du-Pape tour is especially popular. He also offers multiday tours with food and wine tastings, and can help arrange transportation (€35-70/person for half-day to full-day tours, prices subject to minimum tour fees, mobile 06 75 10 10 01, www.wine-uncovered.com, olivier.hickman@orange.fr).

Tours du Rhône

American Doug Graves, who owns a small wine *domaine* in the Côtes du Rhône, shares his passion for his adopted region, its people, and its wines on his custom tours of Châteauneuf-du-Pape, the villages of the Côtes du Rhône, and the Luberon Valley (€125/person for a full-day tour for up to 4 people, mobile 06 37 16 04 56, www.toursdurhone.com, doug@masdelalionne.com).

Promo Vinum

Experienced guide and wine connoisseur Joe McLean offers tours focused on the wines of Uzès, Châteauneuf-du-Pape, and the Côtes du Rhône. He also organizes custom tours at fair prices (€65/person half-day, €100/person full-day, tel. 06 73 08 23 97, www.promo-vinum.com/gb/winetours, info@promo-vinum.com).

Visit Provence

This company runs day tours from Avignon and Arles. Tours from Avignon run year-round and include a great variety of destinations; tours from Arles run April through September only and are more limited in scope. While these tours provide introductory commentary to what you'll see, there is no guiding at the actual sights. They use eight-seat, air-conditioned minivans (about €60-80/half-day, €100-120/day; they'll pick you up at your hotel in Avignon or Aix-en-Provence or at the main TI in Arles). Ask about their cheaper big-bus excursions, or consider hiring a van and driver for your private use (plan on €220/half-day, €490/day, tel. 04 90 14 70 00, www.provence-reservation.com).

PROVENCE'S CUISINE SCENE

The almost extravagant use (by French standards) of garlic, olive oil, herbs, and tomatoes makes Provence's cuisine France's liveliest. To sample it, order anything *à la provençale*. Among the area's spicy specialties are ratatouille (a mixture of vegetables in a thick, herb-flavored tomato sauce), aioli (a rich, garlicky mayonnaise spread over vegetables, potatoes, fish, or whatever), tapenade (a paste of pureed olives, capers, anchovies, herbs, and sometimes tuna), *soupe au pistou* (thin yet flavorful vegetable soup with a sauce—called *pistou*—of basil, garlic, and cheese), and *soupe à l'ail* (garlic soup, called *aigo bouido* in the local dialect). Look for *riz de Camargue* (the reddish, chewy, nutty-tasting rice that has taken over the Camargue area) and *taureau* (bull's meat). The native goat cheeses are Banon de Banon or Banon à la Feuille (wrapped in chestnut leaves) and spicy Picodon. Don't miss the region's

prized Cavaillon melons (cantaloupes) or its delicious cherries and apricots, which are often turned into jams and candied fruits.

Provence also produces some of France's great wines at relatively reasonable prices (€5-10/bottle on average). Look for wines from Gigondas, Rasteau, Cairanne, Beaumes de Venise, Vacqueyras, and, of course, Châteauneuf-du-Pape. For the cheapest but still tasty wines, look for labels showing Côtes du Rhône Villages or Côtes de Provence. If you like rosé, you'll be in heaven here. Rosés from Tavel are considered among the best in Provence. For reds, splurge for Châteauneuf-du-Pape or Gigondas, and for a fine apéritif wine or a dessert wine, try the Muscat from Beaumes de Venise.

Remember, restaurants serve only during lunch (12:00-14:00) and dinner (19:00-21:00, later in bigger cities), but some cafés serve food throughout the day.

PROVENCE MARKET DAYS

Provençal market days offer France's most colorful and tantalizing outdoor shopping. The best markets are on Monday in Cavaillon, Tuesday in Vaison la Romaine, Wednesday in St-Rémy, Thursday in Nyons or Orange, Friday in Lourmarin, Saturday in Arles, Uzès, and Apt, and, best of all, Sunday in Isle-sur-la-Sorgue. Crowds and parking problems abound at these popular events—arrive by 9:00, or, even better, sleep in the town the night before.

Monday: Cavaillon, Bedoin (between Vaison la Romaine and Mont Ventoux)
Tuesday: Vaison la Romaine, Gordes, and Lacoste
Wednesday: St-Rémy, Arles, Uzès, Sault, and Malaucène (near Vaison la Romaine)
Thursday: Nyons, Orange, Vacqueyras, Roussillon, and Isle-sur-la-Sorgue
Friday: Lourmarin, Carpentras, Bonnieux, and Châteauneuf-du-Pape
Saturday: Arles, Uzès, Apt, and Sainte-Cécile-les-Vignes (near Vaison la Romaine)
Sunday: Isle-sur-la-Sorgue, Coustellet

HOW ABOUT THEM ROMANS?

Provence is littered with Roman ruins. Many scholars claim the best-preserved ancient Roman buildings are not in Italy, but in France. These ancient stones will compose an important part of your sightseeing agenda in this region, so it's worth learning about how they came to be.

Classical Rome endured from about 500 B.C. through A.D. 500—spending about 500 years growing, 200 years peaking, and

300 years declining. Julius Caesar conquered Gaul—which included Provence—during the Gallic Wars (58-51 B.C.), then crossed the Rubicon River in 49 B.C. to incite civil war within the Roman Republic. He erected a temple to Jupiter on the future site of Paris' Notre-Dame Cathedral.

The concept of one-man rule lived on with his grandnephew, Octavian (whom he had also adopted as his son). Octavian killed Brutus, eliminated his rivals (Mark Antony and Cleopatra), and united Rome's warring factions. He took the title "Augustus" and became the first in a line of emperors who would control Rome for the next 500 years—ruling like a king, with the backing of the army and the rubber-stamp approval of the Senate. Rome morphed from a Republic into an Empire: a collection of many diverse territories ruled by a single man.

Augustus' reign marked the start of 200 years of peace, prosperity, and expansion known as the *Pax Romana.* At its peak (c. A.D. 117), the Roman empire had 54 million people and stretched from Scotland in the north to Egypt in the south, as far west as Spain and as far east as modern-day Iraq. To the northeast, Rome was bounded by the Rhine and Danube Rivers. On Roman maps, the Mediterranean was labeled *Mare Nostrum* ("Our Sea"). At its peak, "Rome" didn't just refer to the city, but to the entire civilized Western world.

The Romans were successful not only because they were good soldiers, but also because they were smart administrators and businessmen. People in conquered territories knew they had joined the winning team and that political stability would replace barbarian invasions. Trade thrived. Conquered peoples were welcomed into the fold of prosperity, linked by roads, education, common laws and gods, and the Latin language.

Provence, with its strategic location, benefited greatly from Rome's global economy and grew to become an important part of its worldwide empire. After Julius Caesar conquered Gaul, Emperor Augustus set out to Romanize it, building and renovating cities in the image of Rome. Most cities had a theater (some had several), baths, and aqueducts; the most important cities had sports arenas. The Romans also erected an elaborate infrastructure of roads, post offices, schools (teaching in Latin), police stations, and water-supply systems.

With a standard language and currency, Roman merchants

Le Mistral

Provence lives with its vicious mistral winds, which blow 30-60 miles per hour, about 100 days out of the year. Locals say it blows in multiples of threes: three, six, or nine days in a row. The mistral clears people off the streets and turns lively cities into ghost towns. You'll likely spend a few hours or days taking refuge. The winds are strongest between noon and 15:00.

When the mistral blows, it's everywhere, and you can't escape. Author Peter Mayle said it could blow the ears off a donkey (I'd include the tail). According to the natives, it ruins crops, shutters, and roofs (look for stones holding tiles in place on many homes). They'll also tell you that this pernicious wind has driven many people crazy (including young Vincent van Gogh). A weak version of the wind is called a *mistralet.*

The mistral starts above the Alps and Massif Central mountains and gathers steam as it heads south, gaining momentum as it screams over the Rhône Valley (which acts like a funnel between the Alps and the Cévennes mountains) before exhausting itself when it hits the Mediterranean. And though this wind rattles shutters everywhere in the Riviera and Provence, it's strongest over the Rhône Valley...so Avignon, Arles, and the Côtes du Rhône villages bear its brunt. While wiping the dust from your eyes, remember the good news: The mistral brings clear skies.

were able to trade wine, salt, and olive oil for foreign goods. The empire invested heavily in cities that were strategic for trade. For example, the Roman-built city of Arles was a crucial link in the trade route from Italy to Spain, so they built a bridge across the Rhône River and fortified the town.

A typical Roman city (such as Arles, Orange, Vaison la Romaine, or Nîmes) was a garrison town, laid out on a grid plan with two main roads: one running north-south (the *cardus*), the other east-west (the *decumanus*). Approaching the city on your chariot, you'd pass by the cemetery, which was located outside of town for hygienic reasons. You'd enter the main gate and speed past warehouses and apartment houses to the town square (forum). Facing the square were the most important temples, dedicated to the patron gods of the city. Nearby, you'd find bathhouses; like today's fitness clubs, these served the almost sacred dedication to personal vigor. Also close by were businesses that catered to the citizens' needs: the marketplace, bakeries, banks, and brothels.

Aqueducts brought fresh water for drinking, filling the baths, and delighting the citizens with bubbling fountains. Men flocked to the stadiums in Arles and Nîmes to bet on gladiator games; eager

couples attended elaborate plays at theaters in Orange, Arles, and Vaison la Romaine. Marketplaces brimmed with exotic fruits, vegetables, and animals from the far reaches of the empire. Some cities in Provence were more urban 2,000 years ago than they are today. For instance, Roman Arles had a population of 100,000—double today's size. Think about that when you visit.

In these cities, you'll see many rounded arches. These were constructed by piling two stacks of heavy stone blocks, connecting them with an arch (supported with wooden scaffolding), then inserting an inverted keystone where the stacks met. *Voilà!* The heavy stones were able to support not only themselves, but also a great deal of weight above the arch. The Romans didn't invent the rounded arch, but they exploited it better than their predecessors, stacking arches to build arenas and theaters, stringing them side by side for aqueducts, stretching out their legs to create barrel-vaulted ceilings, and building freestanding "triumphal" arches to celebrate conquering generals.

When it came to construction, the Romans' magic building ingredient was concrete. A mixture of volcanic ash, lime, water, and small rocks, concrete—easier to work than stone, longer-lasting than wood—served as flooring, roofing, filler, glue, and support. Builders would start with a foundation of brick, then fill it in with poured concrete. They would then cover important structures, such as basilicas, in sheets of expensive marble (held on with nails), or decorate floors and walls with mosaics—proving just how talented the Romans were at turning the functional into art.

Arles

By helping Julius Caesar defeat his archrival Gnaeus Pompey at Marseille, Arles (pronounced "arl") earned the imperial nod and was made an important port city. With the first bridge over the Rhône River, Arles was a key stop on the Roman road from Italy to Spain, the Via Domitia. After reigning as the seat of an important archbishop and a trading center for centuries, the city became a sleepy backwater of little importance in the 1700s. Vincent van Gogh settled here in the late 1800s, but left only a chunk of his ear (now long gone). American bombers destroyed much of Arles in World War II as the townsfolk hid out in its underground Roman galleries. But today Arles thrives again, with its evocative Roman ruins, an eclectic assortment of museums, made-for-ice-cream pedestrian zones, and squares that play hide-and-seek with visitors.

Workaday Arles is not a wealthy city, and compared to its neighbors Avignon and Nîmes, it feels unpolished and even a little dirty. But to me, that's part of its charm.

Orientation to Arles

Arles faces the Mediterranean, turning its back on Paris. And though the town is built along the Rhône, it largely ignores the river. Landmarks hide in Arles' medieval tangle of narrow, winding streets. Virtually everything is close—but first-timers can walk forever to get there. Hotels have good, free city maps, and Arles provides helpful street-corner signs that point you toward sights and hotels. Speeding cars enjoy Arles' medieval lanes, turning sidewalks into tightropes and pedestrians into leaping targets.

TOURIST INFORMATION

The **main TI** is on the ring road Boulevard des Lices, at Esplanade Charles de Gaulle (April-Sept daily 9:00-18:45; Oct-March Mon-Sat 9:00-16:45, Sun 10:00-13:00; tel. 04 90 18 41 20, www.arlestourisme.com). The other TI, at the **train station** (Mon-Fri 9:30-13:00 & 14:00-18:00, closed Sat-Sun), may close in 2015.

At the TI, pick up the city map and bus schedules, and request English information on nearby destinations such as the Camargue wildlife area (described on page 590). Ask about walking tours and "bullgames" in Arles and nearby towns (Provence's more humane version of bullfights—see page 592).

ARRIVAL IN ARLES

By Train: The train station is on the river, a short walk from the town center. Before heading into town, get what you need at the train station TI (if it's open; it may close in 2015). There's no baggage storage at the station, but you can walk 10 minutes to stow it at Hôtel Régence (see "Helpful Hints," later).

To reach the town center or Ancient History Museum from the train station, wait for the free **Envia minibus** at the glass shelter facing away from the station (cross the street and veer left, 2/hour Mon-Sat 7:00-19:00, none Sun). The bus makes a counterclockwise loop around Arles, stopping near most of my recommended hotels (see the bus stops marked on the map in this chapter). It's a 10- to 15-minute **walk** into town; turn left out of the train station. **Taxis** usually wait in front of the station, but if you don't see any, call the posted telephone numbers, or dial 04 90 96 52 76. If the train station TI is open, you can ask them to call. Taxi rates are fixed—allow about €11 to any of my recommended hotels.

By Bus: Most buses serve only the *Centre-Ville* bus station, a few blocks below the main TI, on the ring road at 16-24 Boulevard Georges Clemenceau. But buses to Avignon's TGV Station and Les Baux stop at the train station.

By Car: Most hotels have parking nearby—ask for detailed directions (€3/8 hours at most meters; free Mon-Sat 12:00-14:00 & 19:00-9:00, and all day Sun; some meters limited to 2.5 hours). For most hotels, first follow signs to *Centre-Ville*, then *Gare SNCF* (train station). You'll come to a big roundabout (Place Lamartine) with a Monoprix department store to the right. You can park along the city wall and find your hotel on foot; the hotels I list are no more than a 10-minute walk away (best not to park here overnight due to theft concerns and markets on Wed and Sat). Fearless drivers can plunge into the narrow streets between the two stumpy towers via Rue de la Calade, and follow signs to their hotel. Again, theft is a problem—leave nothing in your car, and trust your hotelier's advice on where to park.

If you can't find parking near your hotel, Parking des Lices (Arles' only parking garage), near the TI on Boulevard des Lices, is a good fallback (€2.30/hour, €16/24 hours).

HELPFUL HINTS

Market Days: The big markets are on Wednesdays and Saturdays. For details, see page 592.

Crowds: An international photo event jams hotels the second weekend of July. The let-'er-rip, twice-yearly Féria draws crowds over Easter and in mid-September (described on page 592).

Internet Access: A cyber café is near Place Voltaire at 31 Rue Augustin Tardieu (daily).

Baggage Storage and Bike Rental: The recommended Hôtel Régence will store your bags for €3 (daily 7:30-22:00 mid-March-mid-Nov, closed in winter, 5 Rue Marius Jouveau). They also rent bikes (€7/half-day, €15/day, reserve ahead for electric bikes, one-way rentals within Provence possible, same hours as baggage storage). From Arles you can ride to Les Baux (25 miles round-trip). It's a darn steep climb going into Les Baux, so consider busing up there (regional buses have bike racks) and gliding back. Those in great shape can consider biking into the Camargue (40 miles round-trip, forget it in the wind).

Laundry: A launderette is at 12 Rue Portagnel (daily 7:00-21:30, you can stay later to finish if you're already inside, English instructions).

Car Rental: Avis is at the train station (Mon-Fri 8:30-12:00 & 15:00-18:30, tel. 04 90 96 82 42); **Europcar** and **Hertz** are downtown (Europcar is at 61 Avenue de Stalingrad, tel. 04 90 93 23 24; Hertz is closer to Place Voltaire at 10 Boulevard Emile Combes, tel. 04 90 96 75 23).

Local Guides: Charming **Agnes Barrier,** who knows Arles and nearby sights intimately, enjoys her work. Her tours cover Van Gogh and Roman history (€130/3 hours, mobile 06 11 23 03 73, agnes.barrier@hotmail.fr). **Alice Vallat** loves her native city and offers a variety of scheduled visits of its key sights (€15/person, otherwise €130/3 hours, tel. 06 74 01 22 54 or 04 90 47 75 68, www.guidearles.com, alice.vallat@voila.fr).

English Book Exchange: A small exchange is available at the recommended **Soleileis** ice-cream shop.

Public Pools: Arles has three pools (indoor and outdoor). Ask at the TI or your hotel.

Boules: The local "*boul*ing alley" is by the river on Place Lamartine. After their afternoon naps, the old boys congregate here for a game of *pétanque* (see page 1044).

GETTING AROUND ARLES

In this flat city, everything's within **walking** distance. Only the Ancient History Museum requires a healthy walk (or you can take a taxi or bus). The elevated riverside promenade provides Rhône views and a direct route to the Ancient History Museum (to the southwest) and the train station (to the northeast). Keep your head up for *Starry Night* memories, but eyes down for doggie droppings.

Arles' **taxis** charge a set fee of about €11, but nothing except the Ancient History Museum is worth a taxi ride. To call a cab, dial 04 90 96 52 76 or 04 90 96 90 03.

The free **Envia minibus** circles the town, useful for access to the train station, hotels, and the Ancient History Museum (see map on page 576, 2/hour, Mon-Sat 7:00-19:00, none Sun).

Sights in Arles

Most sights cost €3.50-7, and though any sight warrants a few minutes, many aren't worth their individual admission price. The TI sells two different monument passes (called Passeports). **Le Passeport Avantage** covers most of Arles' sights except for the Fondation Van Gogh (€13.50, free under age 18). **Le Passeport Liberté**

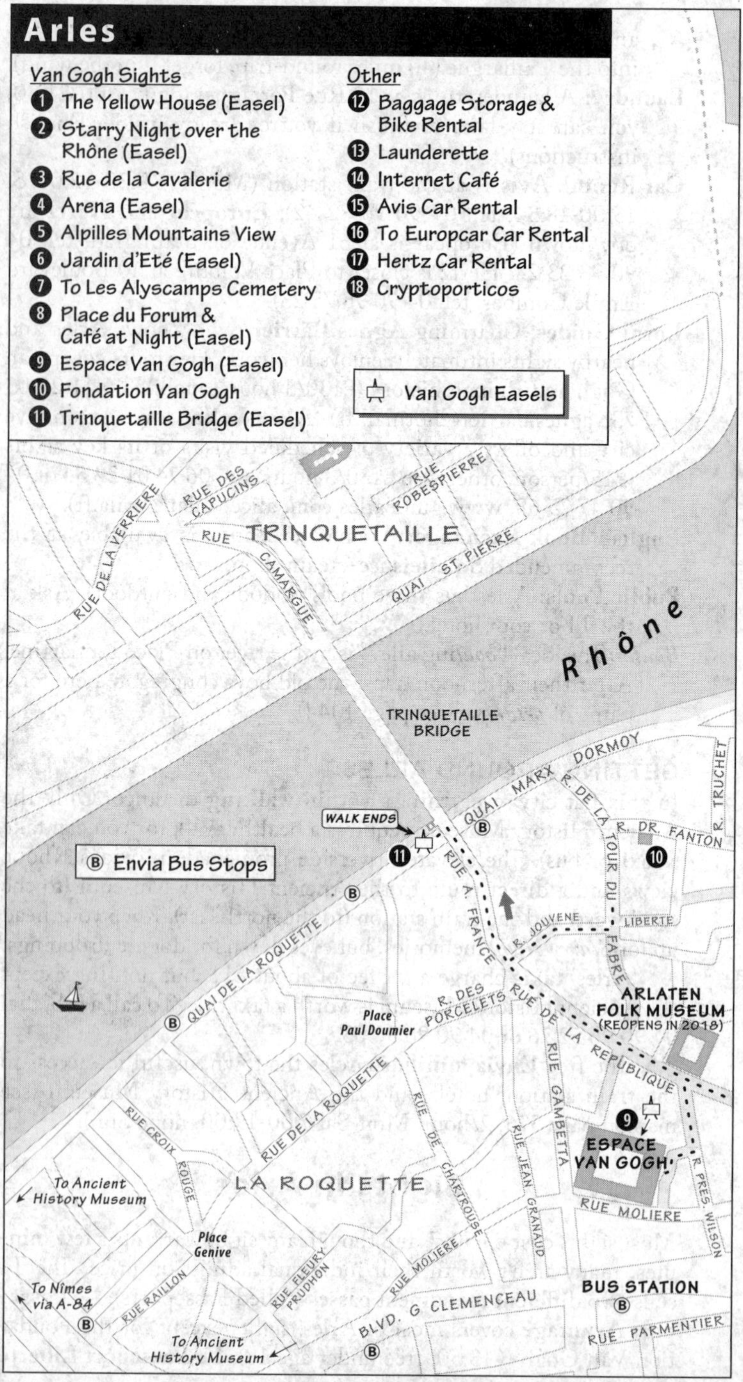

Arles

Van Gogh Sights

1. The Yellow House (Easel)
2. Starry Night over the Rhône (Easel)
3. Rue de la Cavalerie
4. Arena (Easel)
5. Alpilles Mountains View
6. Jardin d'Eté (Easel)
7. To Les Alyscamps Cemetery
8. Place du Forum & Café at Night (Easel)
9. Espace Van Gogh (Easel)
10. Fondation Van Gogh
11. Trinquetaille Bridge (Easel)

Other

12. Baggage Storage & Bike Rental
13. Launderette
14. Internet Café
15. Avis Car Rental
16. To Europcar Car Rental
17. Hertz Car Rental
18. Cryptoporticos

Ⓑ Envia Bus Stops

TRINQUETAILLE
RUE DE LA VERRIERE
RUE DES CAPUCINS
RUE ROBESPIERRE
RUE CAMARGUE
QUAI ST. PIERRE
Rhône
TRINQUETAILLE BRIDGE
QUAI MARX DORMOY
R. DE LA TOUR DU FABRE
R. TRUCHET
R. DR. FANTON
WALK ENDS
RUE A. FRANCE
R. JOUVENE
LIBERTE
QUAI DE LA ROQUETTE
R. DES PORCELETS
Place Paul Doumier
RUE DE LA REPUBLIQUE
ARLATEN FOLK MUSEUM (REOPENS IN 2018)
RUE GAMBETTA
RUE DE LA ROQUETTE
RUE CROIX ROUGE
RUE DE CHARTROUSE
RUE JEAN GRANAUD
ESPACE VAN GOGH
R. PRES. WILSON
LA ROQUETTE
To Ancient History Museum
RUE MOLIERE
Place Genive
To Nîmes via A-84
RUE RAILLON
RUE FLEURY PRUDHON
RUE MOLIERE
BLVD. G CLEMENCEAU
BUS STATION
RUE PARMENTIER
To Ancient History Museum

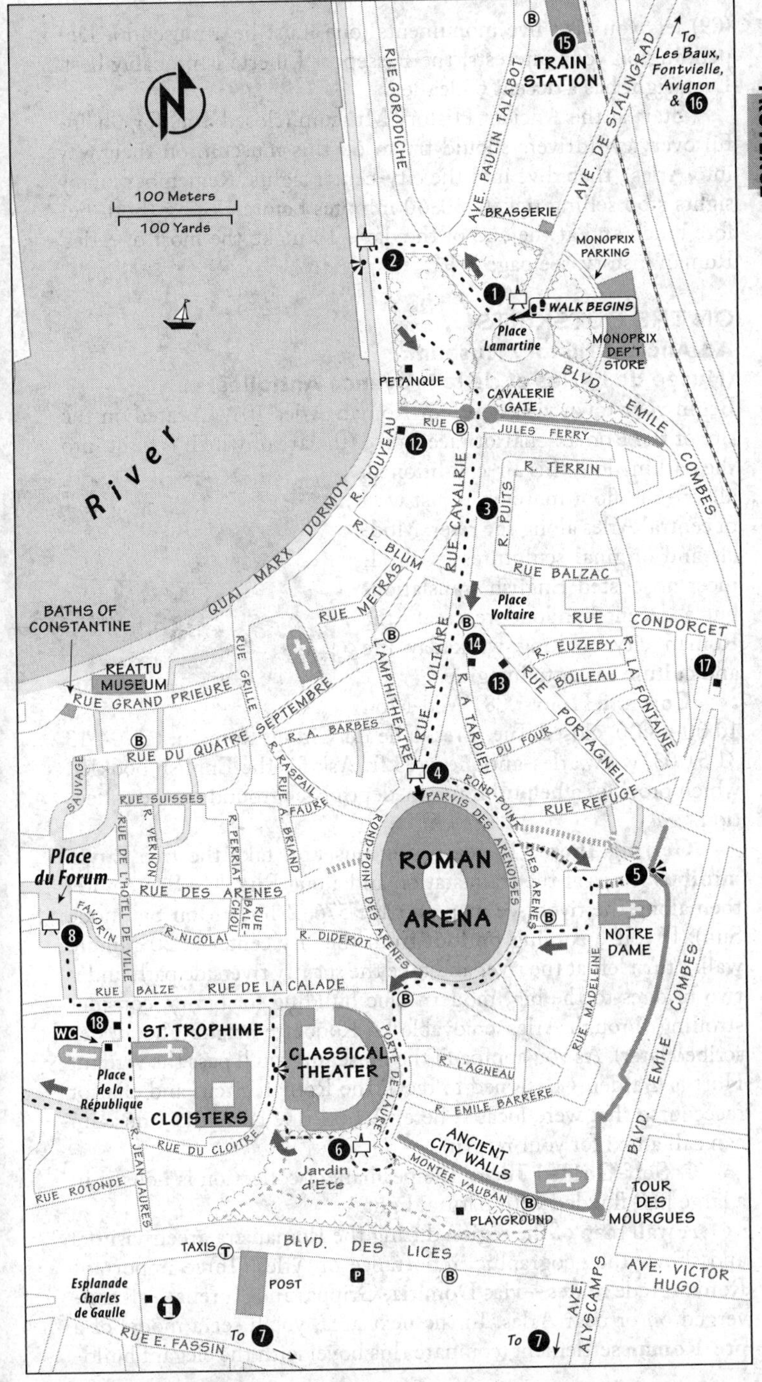
TRAIN STATION
To Les Baux, Fontvielle, Avignon & 16
100 Meters
100 Yards
River
RUE GORODICHE
AVE. PAULIN TALABOT
AVE. DE STALINGRAD
BRASSERIE
MONOPRIX PARKING
WALK BEGINS
Place Lamartine
MONOPRIX DEP'T STORE
PETANQUE
CAVALERIE GATE
BLVD. EMILE COMBES
RUE JULES FERRY
R. TERRIN
R. JOUVEAU
QUAI MARX DORMOY
R. L. BLUM
RUE CAVALRIE
R. PUITS
RUE BALZAC
Place Voltaire
RUE CONDORCET
BATHS OF CONSTANTINE
RUE METRAS
L'AMPHITHEATRE
RUE VOLTAIRE
R. EUZEBY
R. LA FONTAINE
REATTU MUSEUM
RUE GRAND PRIEURE
RUE QUATRE SEPTEMBRE
RUE GRILLE
R. A. TARDIEU
RUE BOILEAU
RUE PORTAGNEL
R. A. BARBES
RUE DU QUATRE SEPTEMBRE
DU FOUR
SAUVAGE
RUE SUISSES
R. RASPAIL
RUE A. BRIAND
RUE FAURE
PARVIS DES ARENES
ROND-POINT DES ARENOISES
RUE REFUGE
ROMAN ARENA
ROND-POINT DES ARENES
Place du Forum
RUE DE L'HOTEL DE VILLE
R. VERNON
R. PERRIAT
RUE DES ARENES
RUE BALECHOU
FAVORIN
R. NICOLAI
R. DIDEROT
NOTRE DAME
RUE MADELEINE
RUE BALZE
RUE DE LA CALADE
WC
ST. TROPHIME
CLASSICAL THEATER
PORTE DE LAURE
R. L'AGNEAU
Place de la République
CLOISTERS
R. EMILE BARRERE
ANCIENT CITY WALLS
RUE DU CLOITRE
R. JEAN JAURES
Jardin d'Ete
MONTEE VAUBAN
TOUR DES MOURGUES
RUE ROTONDE
PLAYGROUND
TAXIS
BLVD. DES LICES
AVE. VICTOR HUGO
POST
AVE. ALYSCAMPS
Esplanade Charles de Gaulle
RUE E. FASSIN
To 7
To 7

(€9) lets you visit five monuments (one must be a museum). Depending on your interests, the Passeport Liberté is probably best. Each sight has a decent €3 leaflet.

Start at the Ancient History Museum (closed Tue) for a helpful overview (drivers should try to do this museum on their way into Arles), then dive into the city-center sights. Remember, many sights stop selling tickets 30-60 minutes before closing (both before lunch and at the end of the day). To make the most of Arles' Roman history, see page 569.

ON THE OUTSKIRTS

▲▲Ancient History Museum (Musée de l'Arles et de la Provence Antiques)

Begin your town visit here, for Roman Arles 101. Located on the site of the Roman chariot racecourse (the arc of which is built into the parking lot), this air-conditioned, all-on-one-floor museum is just west of central Arles along the river. Models and original sculptures (with almost no posted English translations but a decent handout) re-create the Roman city, making workaday life and culture easier to imagine.

Cost and Hours: €8, Wed-Mon 10:00-18:00, closed Tue, Presqu'île du Cirque Romain, tel. 04 13 31 51 03, www.arles-antique.cg13.fr. Ask for the English booklet, which provides a helpful if not in-depth background on the collection.

Getting There: To reach the museum, take the free **Envia minibus** (stops at the train station and along Rue du 4 Septembre, then along the river, see map on page 576, 2/hour Mon-Sat, none Sun). If you're coming **on foot** from the city center (a 20-minute walk), turn left at the river and take the scruffy riverside path under two bridges to the big, modern blue building (or better, consider strolling through Arles' enjoyable La Roquette neighborhood, described later). As you approach the museum, you'll pass the verdant Hortus Garden—designed to recall the Roman circus and chariot racecourse that were located here. A **taxi** ride costs €11 (museum can call a taxi for your return).

➲ **Self-Guided Tour:** The permanent collection is housed in a large hall flooded with natural light.

A wall **map** of the region during the Roman era greets visitors and shows the geographic importance of Arles: Three important Roman trade routes—vias Domitia, Grippa, and Aurelia—all converged on or near Arles. In the next area, you'll see a model of a **pre-Roman** settlement (compare this hovel with the elegant buildings constructed during the Roman period). You'll then pass maps showing Roman Arles' expanding city limits.

Next, you'll see **models** of every Roman structure in (and near) Arles. These are the highlight for me, as they breathe life into the buildings as they looked 2,000 years ago. Start with the model of Roman Arles and ponder the city's splendor over 2,000 years ago when Arles' population was double that of today. That's something to chew on. Find the forum—still the center of town today, though only two columns survive (the smaller section of the forum is where today's Place du Forum is built). Look at the space Romans devoted to their arena and huge racecourse—a reminder that a reverence for sports is not unique to modern civilizations (the museum you're in is at the non-city end of the course). The model also illustrates how little Arles seems to have changed over two millennia, with its houses still clustered around the city center, and warehouses still located on the opposite side of the river.

Prowl the room for individual models of the major buildings shown in the city model: the elaborately elegant forum; the floating wooden bridge that gave Arles a strategic advantage (over the widest, and therefore slowest, part of the river); the theater (with its magnificent stage wall); the arena (with its movable stadium cover to shelter spectators from sun or rain); and the hydraulic mill of Barbegal (with its 16 waterwheels powered by water cascading down a hillside).

You'll also see displays of pottery, jewelry, metal, and glass artifacts, as well as well-crafted mosaic floors that illustrate how Roman Arles was a city of art and culture. The many **statues** are all original, except for the greatest—the *Venus of Arles,* which Louis XIV took a liking to and had moved to Versailles. It's now in the Louvre—and, as locals say, "When it's in Paris...bye-bye." The statue of Caesar Augustus stood in the center of Arles' theater stage wall.

As you enter the next hall, find a large model of the chariot racecourse. Part of the original racecourse was just outside the windows, and though long gone, it likely resembled Rome's Circus Maximus.

The museum's newest and most exciting exhibit is the **Gallo-Roman vessel** and much of its cargo. This almost-100-foot-long Roman barge was hauled out of the Rhône in 2010, along with some 280 amphorae and 3,000 ceramic artifacts. It was typical of flat-bottomed barges used to shuttle goods between Arles and ports along the Mediterranean (vessels were manually towed upriver). At the end of the room, a good 30-minute video (French only) illustrates how the barge was removed from the river.

Just before leaving the museum, you'll come across expertly carved pagan and early-Christian **sarcophagi** (from the second to fifth century A.D.). These would have lined the Via Aurelia outside the town wall. In the early days of the Church, Jesus was often portrayed beardless and as the good shepherd, with a lamb over his shoulder.

IN THE CITY CENTER

Ideally, visit these sights in the order listed below, from Forum Square to the Roman Arena. I've included some walking directions to connect the dots (see the Arles map on page 576).

▲▲Forum Square (Place du Forum)

Named for the Roman forum that once stood here, Place du Forum was the political and religious center of Roman Arles. Still lively, this café-crammed square is a local watering hole and popular for a *pastis* (anise-based apéritif). The bistros on the square, though no place for a fine dinner, can put together a passable salad or *plat du jour*—and when you sprinkle on the ambience, that's €12 well spent.

At the corner of Grand Hôtel Nord-Pinus (a favorite of Pablo Picasso), a plaque shows how the Romans built a foundation of galleries to make the main square level in order to compensate for Arles' slope down to the river. The two columns are all that survive from the upper story of the entry to the forum. Steps leading to the entrance are buried—the Roman street level was about 20 feet below you (you can get a glimpse of it by peeking through the street-level openings under the Hôtel d'Arlatan, two blocks below Place du Forum on Rue du Sauvage; find information panels above the openings).

The statue on the square is of **Frédéric Mistral** (1830-1914). This popular poet, who wrote in the local dialect rather than in French, was a champion of Provençal culture. After receiving the Nobel Prize in Literature in 1904, Mistral used his prize money to preserve and display the folk identity of Provence. He founded the regional folk museum (the Arlaten Folk Museum) at a time when France was rapidly centralizing and regions like Provence were losing their unique identities. (The local mistral wind—literally, "master"—has nothing to do with his name.)

The **bright-yellow café**—called Café la Nuit—was the subject of one of Vincent van Gogh's most famous works in Arles.

Although his painting showed the café in a brilliant yellow from the glow of gas lamps, the facade was bare limestone, just like the other cafés on this square. The café's current owners have painted it to match Van Gogh's version...and to cash in on the Vincent-crazed hordes who pay too much to eat or drink here.

• *With your back to Café la Nuit, walk left one block (past Grand Hôtel Nord Pinus) and turn left. Walk through Hôtel de Ville's vaulted entry (or take the next right if it's closed), and pop out onto the big...*

Republic Square (Place de la République)

This square used to be called "Place Royale"...until the French Revolution. The obelisk was the former centerpiece of Arles' Roman Circus. The lions at its base are the symbol of the city, whose slogan is (roughly) "the gentle lion." Find a seat and watch the peasants—pilgrims, locals, and street musicians. There's nothing new about this scene.

• *Find the exquisitely carved facade of...*

▲▲St. Trophime Church

Named after a third-century bishop of Arles, this church sports the finest Romanesque main entrance I've seen anywhere. The Romanesque-and-Gothic interior, with tapestries and relics, is worth a wander. The cloisters are skippable.

Cost and Hours: Church—free, daily 9:00-12:00 & 14:00-18:30, closes at 17:00 Oct-March; cloisters—€3.50, similar hours as church, but open all day (no lunch break).

➲ **Self-Guided Tour:** Like a Roman triumphal arch, the church facade trumpets the promise of Judgment Day. The tympanum (the semicircular area above the door) is filled with Christian symbolism. Christ sits in majesty, surrounded by symbols of the four evangelists: Matthew (the winged man), Mark (the winged lion), Luke (the ox), and John (the eagle). The 12 apostles are lined up below Jesus. It's Judgment Day...some are saved and others aren't. Notice the condemned (on the right)—a chain gang doing a sad bunny-hop over the fires of hell. For them, the tune trumpeted by the three angels above Christ is not a happy one. Below the chain gang, St. Stephen is being stoned to death, with his soul leaving through his mouth and instantly being welcomed by angels. Ride the exquisite detail back to a simpler age. In an illiterate medieval world, long before the vivid images of our Technicolor time, this was a neon billboard over the town square.

Interior: Just inside the door on the right, a chart locates the interior highlights and helps explain the carvings you just saw on the tympanum.

Tour the church counterclockwise. The tall 12th-century Romanesque nave is decorated by a set of tapestries showing scenes from the life of Mary (17th century, from the French town of Aubusson). Amble around the Gothic apse. Two-thirds of the way around, find the relic chapel behind the ornate wrought iron gate, with its fine golden boxes that hold long-venerated bones of obscure saints. The next chapel houses the skull of St. Anthony of the Desert. Several chapels down, look for the early-Christian sarcophagus from Roman Arles (dated about A.D. 300) under the black columns. The heads were lopped off during the French Revolution.

This church is a stop on the ancient pilgrimage route to Santiago de Compostela in northwest Spain. For 800 years pilgrims on their way to Santiago have paused here...and they still do today. Notice the modern-day pilgrimages advertised on the far right near the church's entry.

Cloisters: Leaving the church, turn left, then left again through a courtyard to enter the adjacent cloisters. The cloisters are worth a look only if you have a pass (big cleaning underway, enter at the far end of the courtyard). The many small columns were scavenged from the ancient Roman theater. Enjoy the sculpted capitals, the rounded 12th-century Romanesque arches, and the pointed 14th-century Gothic ones. The pretty vaulted hall exhibits 17th-century tapestries showing scenes from the First Crusade to the Holy Land. On the second floor, you'll walk along an angled rooftop designed to catch rainwater—notice the slanted gutter that channeled the water into a cistern and the heavy roof slabs covering the tapestry hall below.

• *Return to the square and walk into the Hôtel de Ville to find the entrance to...*

Cryptoporticos (Cryptoportiques)

This dark, drippy underworld of Roman arches was constructed to support the upper half of Forum Square. Two thousand years ago, most of this gallery of arches was at or above street level; modern Arles has buried about 20 feet of its history over the millennia.

Cost and Hours: €3.50, daily May-Sept 9:00-12:00 & 14:00-19:00, March-April and Oct 9:00-12:00 & 14:00-18:00, Nov-Feb 10:00-12:00 & 14:00-17:00.

• *Walk up Rue de la Calade to reach the...*

Classical Theater (Théâtre Antique)

This first-century B.C. Roman theater once seated 10,000...just like the theater in Orange. But unlike Orange, here in Arles there was no hillside to provide structural support. This theater was an elegant, three-level structure with 27 arches radiating out to the street level. From the outside, it looked much like a halved version of Arles' Roman Arena.

Cost and Hours: €6.50 (combo-ticket with the arena), daily May-Sept 9:00-19:00, March-April and Oct 9:00-18:00, Nov-Feb 10:00-17:00. Budget travelers can peek over the fence from Rue du Cloître and see just about everything for free.

Visiting the Theater: Start with the video outside, which provides helpful background information and images that make it easier to put the scattered stones back in place (crouch in front to make out the small English subtitles). You'll also find a large information panel nearby on the grass that adds more context. Walk into the theater and pull up a stone seat in a center aisle. To appreciate the theater's original size, look left (about 9:00) to the upper-left side of the tower and find the protrusion that supported the highest seating level. The structure required 33 rows of seats covering three levels to accommodate demand. During the Middle Ages, the old theater became a convenient town quarry—St. Trophime Church was built from theater rubble. Precious little of the original theater survives—though it still is used for events, with seating for 3,000 spectators.

Two lonely Corinthian columns are all that remain of a three-story stage wall that once featured more than 100 columns and statues painted in vibrant colors. Actors with main roles entered through the central arch, over which a grandiose statue of Caesar Augustus stood (on display at the Ancient History Museum). Bit players entered through side arches. The orchestra section is defined by a semicircular pattern in the stone in front of you. Stepping up onto the left side of the stage, look down to the slender channel that allowed the brilliant-red curtain to disappear below, like magic. The stage, which was built of wood, was about 160 feet across and 20 feet deep. The actors' changing rooms are backstage, down the steps.

• *A block uphill is the...*

▲▲▲Roman Arena (Amphithéâtre)

Nearly 2,000 years ago, gladiators fought wild animals here to the delight of 20,000 screaming fans. Today local daredevils still fight wild animals here—"bullgame" posters around the arena advertise upcoming spectacles (see page 592).

Cost and Hours: €6.50 (combo-ticket with the theater), daily May-Sept 9:00-19:00, March-April and Oct 9:00-18:00, Nov-Feb 10:00-17:00. Rond-point des Arènes, tel. 04 90 49 36 86, www.arenes-arles.com.

Visiting the Arena: After passing the ticket kiosk, find the helpful English information display describing the arena's history

and renovation, then take a seat in the upper deck. In Roman times, games were free (sponsored by city bigwigs), and fans were seated by social class. More than thirty rows of stone bleachers extended all the way to the top of those vacant arches that circle the arena.

There were no gates, just welcoming arches, numbered to allow entertainment-seekers to come and go freely. The purpose was to create a populace that was thoroughly Roman—enjoying the same activities and entertainment, all thinking as one (not unlike Americans' nationwide obsession with the same reality-TV shows). The many passageways you'll see (called *vomitoires*) allowed for rapid dispersal after the games—fights would break out among frenzied fans if they couldn't leave quickly. During medieval times and until the early 1800s, the arches were bricked up and the stadium became a fortified town—with 200 humble homes crammed within its circular defenses. Parts of three of the medieval towns survive (the one above the ticket booth is open and rewards those who climb it with terrific views). To see two still-sealed arches—complete with cute medieval window frames—turn right as you leave, walk to the L'Andaluz Restaurant, and look back to the second floor.

MORE SIGHTS IN ARLES

▲Fondation Van Gogh

This art foundation delivers a refreshing stop for modern-art lovers and Van Gogh fans, with temporary exhibits in which artists pay homage to Vincent through thought-provoking interpretations of his works (for more on Vincent, see "Van Gogh Sights in Arles," later). You'll also see at least one original work by Van Gogh (painted during his time in the region) and examples of the Japanese prints that were so influential to his art. The second-floor terrace gives you a good view of the kaleidoscopic glass rooftop sculpture by Raphael Hefti, and the fourth-floor terrace offers expansive views over Arles' rooftops. A good variety of Van Gogh souvenirs, prints, and postcards is in the gift shop.

Cost and Hours: €9, daily 11:00-19:00, closed between exhibits and likely Mon off-season, audioguide-€3; Hôtel Leautaud de Donines, 35 Rue du Docteur Fanton, tel. 04 90 49 94 04, check website for current exhibit and opening times, www.fondation-vincentvangogh-arles.org.

La Roquette District

To escape the tourist beat in Arles, take a detour into Arles' little-visited western fringe. Find Rue de la Roquette near the Trinquetaille Bridge and stroll several blocks into pleasing Place Paul Doumier, where you'll find a lively assortment of cafés, bakeries, and inexpensive bistros with nary a tourist in sight (see map on page 576). Continue along Rue de la Roquette and turn right on charming Rue Croix Rouge to reach the river. Those walking to or from the Ancient History Museum can use this appealing stroll as a shortcut.

Baths of Constantine (Thermes de Constantin)

These partly intact Roman baths were built in the early fourth century when Emperor Constantine declared Arles an imperial residence. Roman cities such as Arles had several public baths like this, which were used as much for exercising, networking, and chatting with friends as for bathing. These baths were located near the Rhône River for easy water access. You can get a pretty good look at the baths through the fence (€3, daily May-Sept 9:00-12:00 & 14:00-18:30, Oct-April 10:00-12:00 & 14:00-16:30).

Réattu Museum (Musée Réattu)

Housed in the former Grand Priory of the Knights of Malta, this modern-art collection is always changing. The permanent collection usually includes a series of works by homegrown Neoclassical artist Jacques Réattu, along with at least one Picasso painting and a roomful of his drawings (donated by the artist and all done in a flurry of creativity). The museum shuffles its large Picasso collection around regularly (they have more works than space to display them). Most of the three-floor museum houses (usually worthwhile) temporary exhibits of modern artists; check the website to see who's playing.

Cost and Hours: €7, free first Sun of each month, March-Oct Tue-Sun 10:00-18:00, closes at 17:00 Nov-Feb, closed Mon year-round, last entry 30 minutes before closing, 10 Rue du Grand Prieuré, tel. 04 90 49 37 58, www.museereattu.arles.fr.

▲Arlaten Folk Museum (Musée Arlaten/Museon Arlaten)

This museum, which explains the ins and outs of daily Provençal life, is closed for renovation until 2018 (www.museonarlaten.fr, French only).

VAN GOGH SIGHTS IN ARLES

In the dead of winter in 1888, 35-year-old Dutch artist Vincent van Gogh left big-city Paris for Provence, hoping to jump-start his floundering career and social life. He was as inspired as he was lonely. Coming from the gray skies and flat lands of the north,

Vincent was bowled over by everything Provençal—the sun, bright colors, rugged landscape, and raw people. For the next two years he painted furiously, cranking out a masterpiece every few days.

Only a few of the 200-plus paintings that Van Gogh did in the south can be found today in the city that so moved him (see "Fondation Van Gogh," earlier). But here you can walk the same streets he knew and see places he painted, marked by about a dozen steel-and-concrete **"easels,"** with photos of the final paintings for then-and-now comparisons. Small stone markers with yellow accents embedded in the pavement lead to the easels.

• *Take a walk in Vincent's footsteps (roughly north to south through Arles' center) and watch his paintings come to life by putting yourself in his shoes (use the map on page 576). Start at* ***Place Lamartine*** *and find the stone easel by the grass with the big Monoprix to your right.*

❶ **The Yellow House Easel:** Vincent arrived in Arles on February 20, 1888, to a foot of snow. He rented a small house on the north side of Place Lamartine. The house was destroyed in 1944 by an errant bridge-seeking bomb, but the four-story building behind it—where you see the brasserie—still stands (find it in the painting). The house had four rooms, including a small studio and the cramped trapezoid-shaped bedroom made famous in paintings. It was painted yellow inside and out, and Vincent named it..."The Yellow House." In the distance, the painting shows the same bridges you see today, as well as a steam train—which was a rather recent invention in France, allowing people like Vincent to travel greater distances and be jarred by new experiences. (Today's TGV system continues that trend.)

Freezing Arles was buttoned up tight when Vincent arrived, so he was forced to work inside, where he painted still lifes and self-portraits—anything to keep his brush moving. In late March, spring finally arrived. In those days, a short walk from Place Lamartine led to open fields. Donning his straw hat, Vincent set up his easel outdoors and painted quickly, capturing what he saw and felt—the blossoming fruit trees, gnarled olive trees, peasants sowing and reaping, jagged peaks, and windblown fields, all lit by a brilliant sun that drove him to use ever-brighter paints.

• *Walk to the river, passing a monument in honor of two WWII American pilots killed in action during the liberation of Arles. The monument was erected in 2002 as a post-9/11 sign of solidarity with Americans. Find the easel in the wall where ramps lead down to the river (this is also about where the Roman bridge would have crossed the Rhône).*

❷ ***Starry Night over the Rhône* Easel:** One night, Vincent set up shop along the river and painted the stars boiling above the city skyline. Vincent looked to the night sky for the divine and was the first to paint outside after dark, adapting his straw hat to hold candles (which must have blown the minds of locals back then). As his paintings progressed, the stars became larger and more animated (like Vincent himself). The lone couple in the painting pops up again and again in his work. Experts say that Vincent was desperate for a close relationship with another being...someone to stroll the riverbank with under a star-filled sky. (Note: This painting is not the *Starry Night* you're thinking of—that one was painted later in St-Rémy-de-Provence.)

To his sister Wilhelmina, Van Gogh wrote, "At present I absolutely want to paint a starry sky. It often seems to me that night is still more richly colored than the day; having hues of the most intense violets, blues, and greens. If only you pay attention to it, you will see that certain stars are lemon-yellow, others pink or a green, blue, and forget-me-not brilliance." Vincent painted this scene on his last night in Arles. Come back at night to match his painting with today's scene.

• *Turn around and walk through the small park, then go into town between the stumpy stone towers along* ❸ ***Rue de la Cavalerie,*** *which becomes Rue Voltaire.*

Van Gogh walked into town the same way. Arles' 19th-century red light district was just east of Rue de la Cavalerie, and the far-from-home Dutchman spent many lonely nights in its bars and brothels. The street still has some local color—drop in to the down-and-dirty café at Hôtel de Paris for a taste.

• *Keep straight through Place Voltaire, continue walking up Rue Voltaire to the Roman Arena, and then find the easel at the top of the arena steps, to the right.*

❹ **Arena Easel:** All summer long, fueled by sun and alcohol, Vincent painted the town. He loved the bullfights in the arena and sketched the colorful surge of the crowds, spending more time studying the people than watching the bullfights (notice how the bull is barely visible). Vincent had little interest in Arles' antiquity—it was people and nature that fascinated him.

• *Walk clockwise around the arena, then up the cobbled lane next to L'Andaluz Restaurant. Keep left in the parking lot to find a viewpoint.*

❺ **Alpilles Mountains View:** This view (no easel) pretty much matches what Vincent would have seen (be here late in the day for the best light). Vincent was an avid walker. Imagine him hauling his easel into those fields under intense sun, leaning against a ferocious wind, struggling to keep his hat on. He did this about 50 times during his stay in Arles, just to paint the farm workers. Vincent venerated but did not glorify peasants. Wanting to show their lives and their struggles, he reproached Renoir and Monet for elevating them in their works.

Vincent carried his easel as far as the medieval abbey of Montmajour, that bulky structure three miles straight ahead on the hill. The St. Paul Hospital, where he was eventually treated in St-Rémy, is on the other side of the Alpilles mountains, several miles beyond Montmajour. On a clear day, you can make out the hill town of Les Baux at about two o'clock (with Montmajour at high noon).

• *Continue along the upper end of the arena, turn left before the Classical Theater, and walk out Rue de Porte de Laure. Just after the street turns left, go right, down the curved staircase into the park and find the easel on the second path to the right.*

❻ **Jardin d'Eté Easel:** Vincent spent many a sunny day painting the leafy Jardin d'Eté. In another letter to his sister, Vincent wrote, "I don't know whether you can understand that one may make a poem by arranging colors... In a similar manner, the bizarre lines, purposely selected and multiplied, meandering all through the picture may not present a literal image of the garden, but they may present it to our minds as if in a dream."

Vincent never made real friends, though he desperately wanted to. The son of disinterested parents, he never found the social skills necessary to sustain close friendships. He palled around with (and painted) his mailman and a Foreign Legionnaire. (The fact that locals pronounced his name "vahn-saw van gog" had nothing to do with his psychological struggles here.)

Packing his paints and a picnic in a rucksack, he day-tripped to the old Roman cemetery of ❼ **Les Alyscamps,** a worthwhile 10-minute detour from this route (across the busy street and to the left). The walk along the alley of sarcophagi to reach St. Honorat Church feels downright Indiana Jones-esque (€3.50, daily May-Sept 9:00-19:00, closes earlier and for lunch off-season).

• *Continue through the gardens, walking toward the arches of the Classical Theater, and exit the park at the upper-right corner. Turn right on Rue du Cloître, then turn left on Rue de la Calade, and stroll downhill for several blocks. Turn right on Rue du Palais to find* ***Place du Forum;*** *locate an easel one café down from the yellow Café la Nuit.*

❽ ***Café at Night*** **Easel:** In October, lonely Vincent—who dreamed of making Arles a magnet for fellow artists—persuaded his friend Paul Gauguin to come. He decorated Gauguin's room with several humble canvases of sunflowers (now some of the world's priciest paintings), knowing that Gauguin had admired a similar painting he'd done in Paris. Their plan was for Gauguin to be the "dean" of a new art school in Arles, and Vincent its instructor-in-chief. At first, the two got along well. They spent days side by side, rendering the same subject in their two distinct styles. At night they hit the bars and brothels. Van Gogh's well-known *Café at Night* captures the glow of an absinthe buzz at Café la Nuit on Place du Forum.

After two months together, the two artists clashed over art and personality differences (Vincent was a slob around the house, whereas Gauguin was meticulous). The night of December 23, they were drinking absinthe at the café when Vincent suddenly went ballistic. He threw his glass at Gauguin. Gauguin left. Walking through Place Victor Hugo, Gauguin heard footsteps behind him and turned to see Vincent coming at him, brandishing a razor. Gauguin quickly fled town. The local paper reported what happened next: "At 11:30 p.m., Vincent Van Gogh, painter from Holland, appeared at the brothel at no. 1, asked for Rachel, and gave her his cut-off earlobe, saying, 'Treasure this precious object.' Then he vanished." He woke up the next morning at home with his head wrapped in a bloody towel and his earlobe missing. Was Vincent emulating a successful matador, whose prize is cutting off the bull's ear?

• *From here retrace your steps and walk into Place de la République, turn right in the square's far corner (Rue de la République), and walk to the Arlaten Folk Museum. Turn left on Rue Président Wilson, and find Espace Van Gogh (on the right through the arch). There's an easel in the courtyard near the postcard racks.*

❾ **Espace Van Gogh Easel:** Vincent was checked into the local hospital—today's Espace Van Gogh cultural center (the Espace is free, but only the courtyard is open to the public). It surrounds a flowery courtyard that the artist loved and painted when he was being treated for blood loss as well as for hallucinations and severe depression that left him bedridden for a month. The citizens of Arles circulated a petition demanding that the mad Dutchman be kept under medical supervision. Félix Rey, Vincent's kind doctor, worked out a compromise: The artist could leave during the day so that he could continue painting, but he had to sleep at the hospital at night. Look through the postcards sold in the courtyard and find a painting of Vincent's ward showing nuns attending to patients in a gray hall *(Ward of Arles Hospital).*

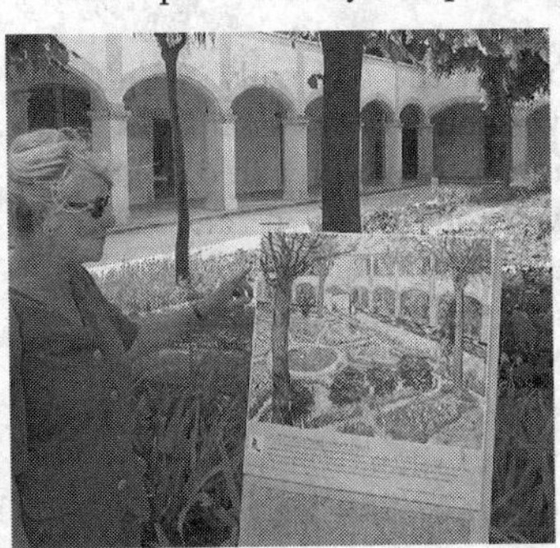

In the spring of 1889, the bipolar genius (a modern diagnosis) admitted himself to the St. Paul Monastery and Hospital in St-

Rémy-de-Provence, where he spent a year, thriving in the care of nurturing doctors and nuns. Painting was part of his therapy, so they gave him a studio to work in, and he produced more than 100 paintings. Alcohol-free and institutionalized, he did some of his wildest work. With thick, swirling brushstrokes and surreal colors, he made his placid surroundings throb with restless energy. Today, at the hospital in St-Rémy, you can see a replica of his room and his studio, plus many scenes like these he painted in situ in Arles—the courtyard, the plane trees, the view out the upstairs window of nearby fields, and the rugged Alpilles mountains.

In the spring of 1890, Vincent left Provence to be cared for by a sympathetic doctor in Auvers-sur-Oise, just north of Paris. On July 27, he wandered into a field and shot himself. He died two days later.

• *To see paintings by artists inspired by Van Gogh, find the* ***Fondation Van Gogh*** *on your map* ❿*; described on page 584.*

Bridge Easels: The ⓫ **Trinquetaille Bridge** is on the river walkway toward the Ancient History Museum (the current bridge is a 1951 replacement). Most famous, the **Langlois Drawbridge** is 1.5 miles south of town, along a Rhône canal (today's bridge is a 1926 duplicate of the original).

NEAR ARLES

The Camargue

Knocking on Arles' doorstep, this is one of the few truly "wild" areas of France, where pink flamingos, wild bulls, nasty boars, nastier mosquitoes (in every season but winter—come prepared), and the famous white horses wander freely through lagoons and tall grass. It's a ▲▲▲ sight for nature-lovers, but underwhelming for others. While possible by public transportation, it's ideal by car. The best route to follow is toward **Salin de Giraud** (see map on page 591): Leave Arles toward Stes-Maries-de-la-Mer and find the D-570. Skip the D-36 turnoff to Salin de Giraud (you'll return along this route). After about six kilometers (3.5 miles), consider a stop at the **Camarguais Museum.** Next, continue along D-570, then turn left on D-37 and follow it as it skirts the Etang de Vaccarès lagoon. The lagoon itself is off-limits, but this area has views and good opportunities to get out of the car and smell the marshes (look for viewing stands, but any dirt turnoff works). Turn right off D-37 onto the tiny road at Villeneuve, following signs for C-134 to La Capelière and La Fiélouse.

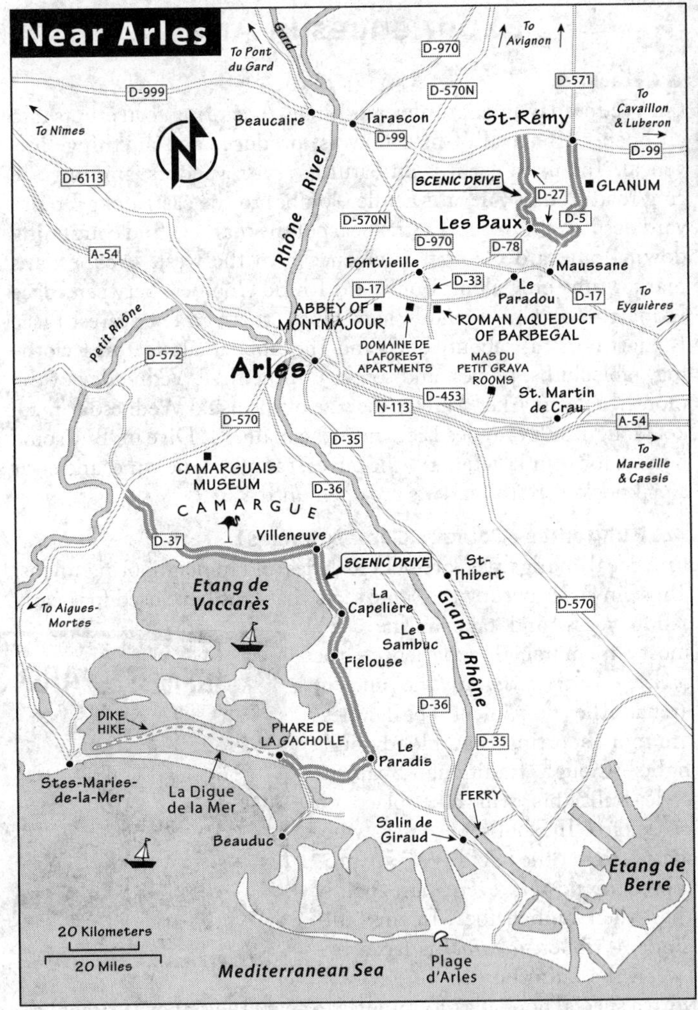

The best part of this drive (particularly in spring) is the next stretch to and around **La Digue de la Mer,** about six scenic miles past La Capelière. At La Digue de la Mer, a rough dirt road greets travelers; it's time to get out of your car and stroll (though you can drive on for about three miles to Phare de la Gacholle). This is a critical reproduction area for flamingos (about 13,000 couples produce 5,000 offspring annually), so it's your best chance to see groups of mamas and papas up close and personal.

Experiences in Arles

▲▲Markets

On Wednesday and Saturday mornings, Arles' ring road erupts into an open-air festival of fish, flowers, produce...and anything Provençal. The main event is on Saturday, with vendors jamming the ring road from Boulevard Emile Combes to the east, along Boulevard des Lices near the TI (the heart of the market), and continuing down Boulevard Georges Clemenceau to the west. Wednesday's market runs only along Boulevard Emile Combes, between Place Lamartine and bis Avenue Victor Hugo; the segment nearest Place Lamartine is all about food, and the upper half features clothing, tablecloths, purses, and so on. On the first Wednesday of the month, a flea market doubles the size of the usual Wednesday market along Boulevard des Lices near the main TI. Dive in: Buy some flowers for your hotelier, try the olives, sample some wine, and swat a pickpocket. Both markets are open until 12:30.

▲▲Bullgames *(Courses Camarguaises)*

Provençal "bullgames" are held in Arles and in neighboring towns. Those in Arles occupy the same seats that fans have used for nearly 2,000 years, and take in the city's most memorable experience—the *courses camarguaises* in the ancient arena. The nonviolent "bullgames" are more sporting than bloody bullfights (though traditional Spanish-style bullfights still take place on occasion). The bulls of Arles (who, locals stress, "die of old age") are promoted in posters even more boldly than their human foes. In the bullgame, a ribbon *(cocarde)* is laced between the bull's horns. The *razeteur,* with a special hook, has 15 minutes to snare the ribbon. Local businessmen encourage a *razeteur* (dressed in white with a red cummerbund) by shouting out how much money they'll pay for the *cocarde.* If the bull pulls a good stunt, the band plays the famous "Toreador" song from *Carmen.* The following day, newspapers report on the games, including how many *Carmens* the bull earned.

Three classes of bullgames—determined by the experience of the *razeteurs*—are advertised in posters: The *course de protection* is for rookies. The *trophée de l'Avenir* comes with more experience. And the *trophée des As* features top professionals. During Easter (Féria de Pâques) and the fall rice-harvest festival (Féria du Riz), the arena hosts traditional Spanish bullfights (look for *corrida*) with outfits, swords, spikes, and the whole gory shebang.

Don't pass on a chance to see *Toro Piscine*, a silly spectacle for warm summer evenings where the bull ends up in a swimming pool (uh-huh...get more details at the TI or check online at www.ffcc.info—French only, click on *Calendrier des Courses* for schedules). Nearby villages stage *courses camarguaises* in small wooden bullrings nearly every weekend; TIs have the latest schedule.

Cost and Hours: Arles' bullgame tickets usually run €5-15; bullfights are pricier (€34-97). Schedules vary (usually July-Aug on Wed and Fri)—ask at the TI or check online at www.arenes-arles.com.

Sleeping in Arles

Hotels are a great value here—many are air-conditioned, though few have elevators. The Calendal, Musée, and Régence hotels offer exceptional value.

$$$ Hôtel le Calendal*** is a seductive place located between the Roman Arena and Classical Theater. Enter an expertly run hotel with airy lounges and a lovely palm-shaded courtyard. Enjoy the elaborate €12 buffet breakfast, have lunch in the courtyard or at the garden café/sandwich bar (daily 8:00-19:00), and take advantage of their four free laptops for guests. You'll also find a Jacuzzi and a spa with a Turkish bath, hot pool, and massages at good rates. The comfortable rooms sport Provençal decor and come in all shapes and sizes (standard Db-€139, larger or balcony Db-€159, Tb/family-€199, air-con, Wi-Fi, reserve ahead for parking-€8, just above arena at 5 Rue Porte de Laure, tel. 04 90 96 11 89, www.lecalendal.com, contact@lecalendal.com). They also run the nearby, budget La Maison du Pelerin, described later.

$$$ Hôtel d'Arlatan*** offers a great location in a 15th-century building on the site of a Roman basilica. It has comfy public spaces, a tranquil terrace, a designer pool, and a range of rooms, many with high, wood-beamed ceilings and stone walls. This once-elegant hotel is being renovated top to bottom, so prices will likely change for 2015 (standard Db-€85-130, bigger Db with terrace or Tb-€170, family rooms-€170-220, excellent buffet breakfast-€15, air-con, ice machines, elevator, Wi-Fi, parking garage-€14, closed Nov-March, a block below Place du Forum at 26 Rue du Sauvage—tough by car, tel. 04 90 93 56 66, www.hotel-arlatan.fr, hotel-arlatan@wanadoo.fr).

$$ Hôtel du Musée** is a quiet, affordable manor-home hideaway tucked deep in Arles (difficult to find by car, ask hotelier for access code to street barrier so you can drop off bags in front). This delightful refuge comes with 28 air-conditioned and wood-floored

Sleep Code

Abbreviations **(€1 = about $1.40, country code: 33)**
S = Single, **D** = Double/Twin, **T** = Triple, **Q** = Quad, **b** = bathroom, **s** = shower only, * = French hotel rating (0-5 stars)
Price Rankings
$$$ Higher Priced—Most rooms €90 or more.
$$ Moderately Priced—Most rooms between €65-90.
$ Lower Priced—Most rooms €65 or less.
Unless otherwise noted, credit cards are accepted, English is spoken, and Wi-Fi is generally free. Prices change; verify current rates online or by email. For the best prices, always book directly with the hotel.

rooms, a flowery two-tiered courtyard, and comfortable lounges. Lighthearted Claude and English-speaking Laurence, the gracious owners, are eager to help (Sb-€65, Db-€70-90, Tb-€95-100, Qb-€130, buffet breakfast-€8.50, no elevator, Wi-Fi, laptop available for guests, garage-€10, follow signs to *Réattu Museum* to 11 Rue du Grand Prieuré, tel. 04 90 93 88 88, www.hoteldumusee.com, contact@hoteldumusee.com).

$$ Hôtel de la Muette**, with reserved owners Brigitte and Alain, is another good choice. Located in a quiet corner of Arles, most rooms come with stone walls, tiled floors, and pebble showers (Db-€81, Tb-€95, family room-€100, buffet breakfast-€9, air-con, no elevator, guest computer, Wi-Fi, private garage-€10, 15 Rue des Suisses, tel. 04 90 96 15 39, www.hotel-muette.com, hotel.muette@wanadoo.fr).

$ Hôtel Régence**, a top budget deal, has a riverfront location, immaculate and comfortable Provençal rooms, safe parking, and easy access to the train station (Db-€55-70, Tb-€70-85, Qb-€80-100, choose river-view or quieter courtyard rooms, good buffet breakfast-€6, air-con, no elevator but only two floors, guest computer, pay Wi-Fi, garage-€7; from Place Lamartine, turn right immediately after passing between towers to reach 5 Rue Marius Jouveau; tel. 04 90 96 39 85, www.hotel-regence.com, contact@hotel-regence.com). The gentle Valérie and Eric speak English.

$$ Hôtel Acacias**, just off Place Lamartine and inside the old city walls, is a modern hotel selling reliable comfort at fair prices. The pretty rooms are on the small side, but the modern elevator makes this a find in Arles (standard Sb-€60, Db-€60-75, Tb-€75-90, breakfast-€8, air-con, Wi-Fi, 2 Rue de la Cavalerie, tel. 04 90 96 37 88, www.hotel-acacias.com, contact@hotel-acacias.com).

$ Hôtel Voltaire rents 12 small, spartan rooms with ceiling fans and nifty balconies overlooking a fun square. A block below the arena, it works for starving artists who aren't particular about cleanliness. Smiling owner "Mr." Ferran (fur-ran) loves the States, and hopes you'll add to his postcard collection (D-€30, Ds-€35, Db-€40, Wi-Fi in restaurant only, 1 Place Voltaire, tel. 04 90 96 49 18, levoltaire13@aol.com). They also serve a good-value lunch and dinner in their recommended restaurant.

$ La Maison du Pelerin offers spotless dorm rooms with three to six beds per room. It's a great value, just above the Roman Arena and Classical Theater, with a shared kitchen and homey living area. Book in advance by phone or email and get the door code. You can also check in next door at the recommended Hôtel le Calendal (they own the place). Sheets are included (€25/person, shared bath, must pay in advance, Wi-Fi, 26 Place Pomme, mobile 06 99 71 11 89, www.arles-pelerins.fr).

NEAR ARLES

Many drivers, particularly those with families, prefer staying outside Arles in the peaceful countryside, with easy access to the area's sights. See also "Sleeping in and near Les Baux," on page 637.

$$$ La Peiriero***, 15 minutes from Arles in the town of Fontvieille, is a pooped parent's dream come true, with a grassy garden, massive heated pool, table tennis, badminton, massage parlor, indoor children's play area, and even a few miniature golf holes. The spacious family-loft rooms, capable of sleeping up to five, have full bathrooms on both levels. This complete retreat also comes with a terrace café and a well-respected restaurant, and helpful owners, the Levys (streetside Sb or Db-€105, gardenside Db-€122, Db with terrace-€142, loft-€220, dinner *menu*-€30, breakfast and dinner-€38, air-con, Wi-Fi, free parking, just east of Fontvieille on road to Les Baux, 34 Avenue des Baux, tel. 04 90 54 76 10, www.hotel-peiriero.com, info@hotel-peiriero.com). Just a short drive from Arles and Les Baux (and 20 minutes from Avignon), little Fontvieille slumbers in the shadows of its big-city cousins—though it has its share of restaurants and boutiques.

$$$ Mas du Petit Grava is a vintage Provençal farmhouse 15 tree-lined minutes east of Arles. Here California refugees Jim and Ike offer four large and well-cared-for rooms with tubs, tiles, and memories of Vincent (Jim is an expert on Van Gogh's life and art—ask him anything). A lovely garden surrounds a generously sized pool, but what draws most here are Jim and Ike. Book this place early (Db-€110-130, includes a fine breakfast, no air-con, Wi-Fi, tel. 04 90 98 35 66, www.masdupetitgrava.net, masdupetitgrava@masdupetitgrava.net). From Arles, drive east on D-453 toward St-Martin de Crau (1.5 miles), then turn left on route St. Hippolyte to the right of the large white-and-blue building.

$$ Domaine de Laforest is ideally located a few minutes

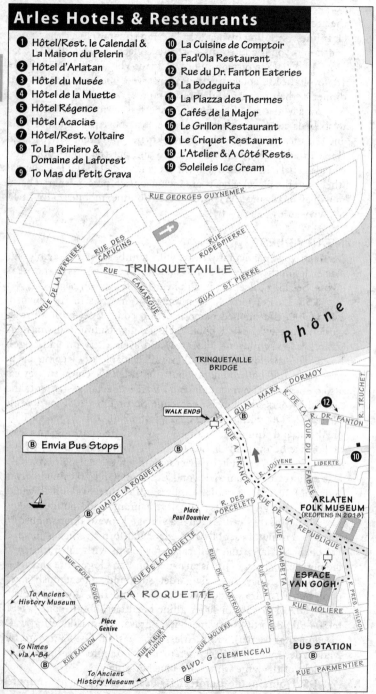

Arles Hotels & Restaurants

1 Hôtel/Rest. le Calendal & La Maison du Pelerin
2 Hôtel d'Arlatan
3 Hôtel du Musée
4 Hôtel de la Muette
5 Hôtel Régence
6 Hôtel Acacias
7 Hôtel/Rest. Voltaire
8 To La Peiriero & Domaine de Laforest
9 To Mas du Petit Grava
10 La Cuisine de Comptoir
11 Fad'Ola Restaurant
12 Rue du Dr. Fanton Eateries
13 La Bodeguita
14 La Piazza des Thermes
15 Cafés de la Major
16 Le Grillon Restaurant
17 Le Criquet Restaurant
18 L'Atelier & A Côté Rests.
19 Soleileis Ice Cream

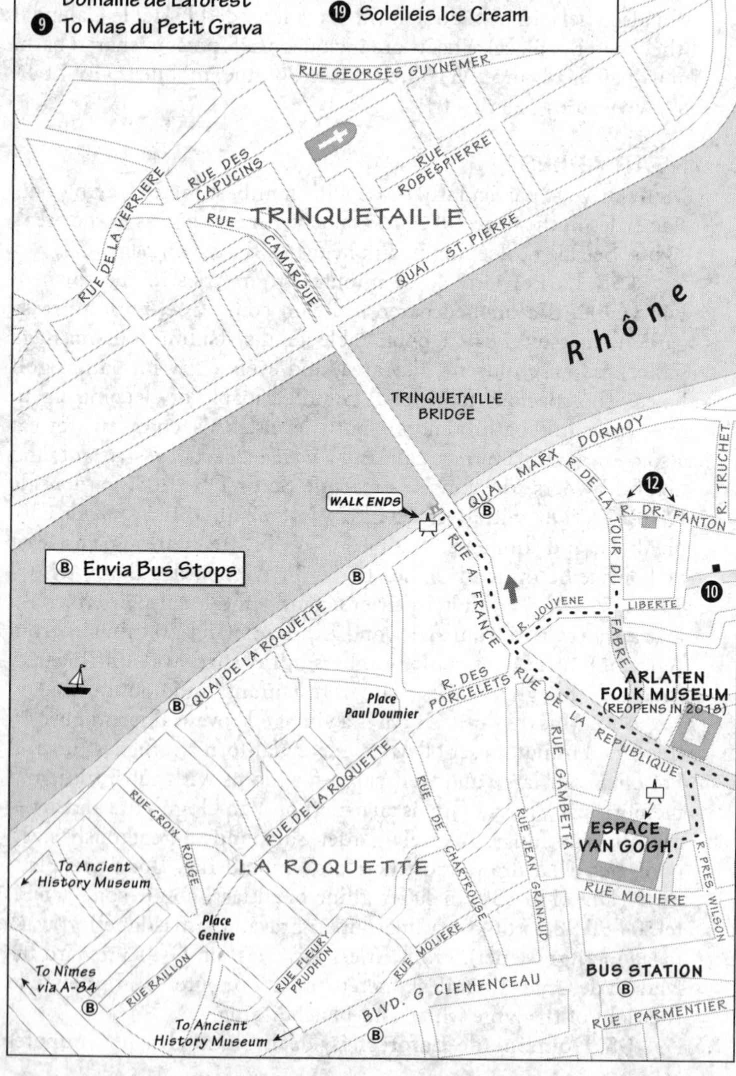

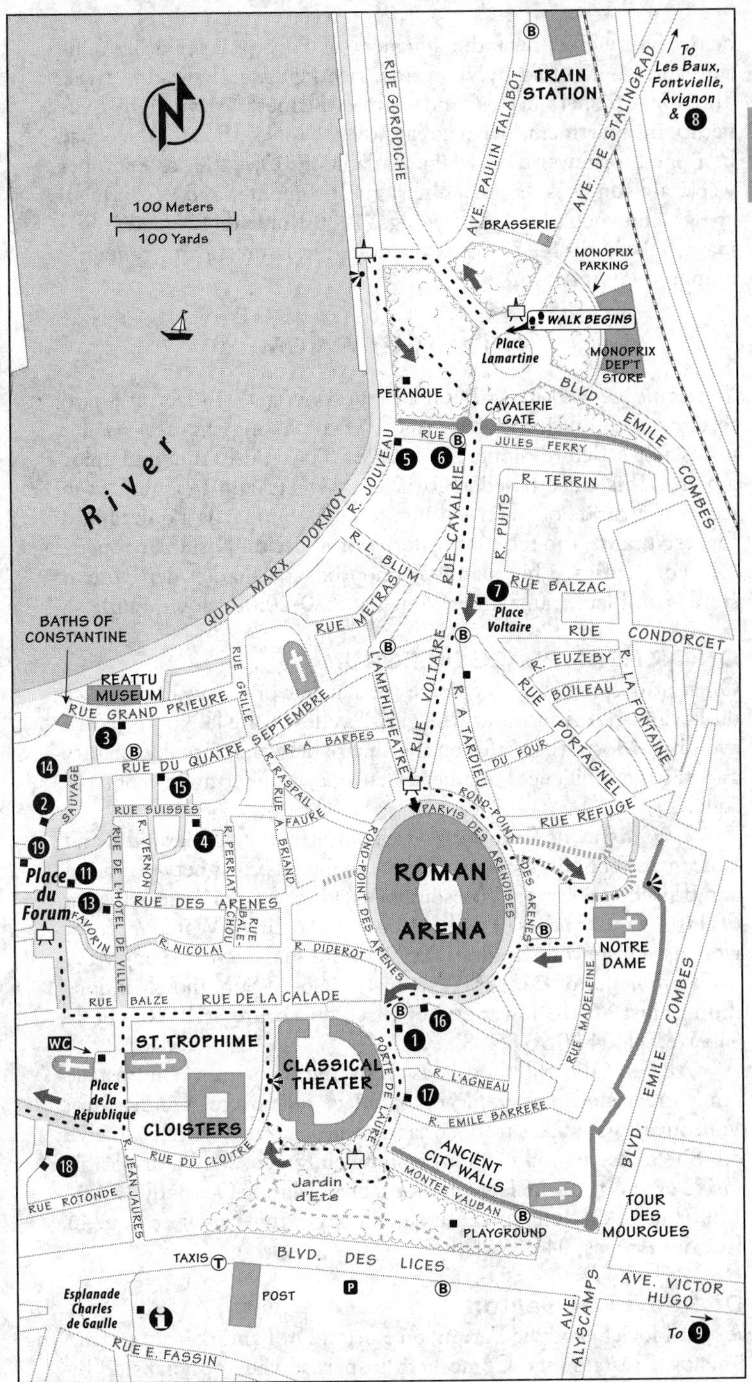

TRAIN STATION
To Les Baux, Fontvielle, Avignon & 8
100 Meters
100 Yards
RUE GORODICHE
AVE. PAULIN TALABOT
AVE. DE STALINGRAD
BRASSERIE
MONOPRIX PARKING
WALK BEGINS
Place Lamartine
MONOPRIX DEP'T STORE
PETANQUE
CAVALERIE GATE
BLVD. EMILE COMBES
RUE JULES FERRY
River
R. JOUVEAU
QUAI MARX DORMOY
R. TERRIN
R. PUITS
RUE CAVALRIE
R. L. BLUM
RUE BALZAC
Place Voltaire
RUE METRAS
RUE CONDORCET
R. EUZEBY
R. LA FONTAINE
RUE BOILEAU
RUE PORTAGNEL
BATHS OF CONSTANTINE
REATTU MUSEUM
RUE GRAND PRIEURE
RUE GRILLE
RUE DU QUATRE SEPTEMBRE
L'AMPHITHEATRE
RUE VOLTAIRE
R. A. TARDIEU
DU FOUR
R. A. BARBES
SAUVAGE
RUE SUISSES
R. VERNON
R. RASPAIL
R. A. FAURE
R. A. BRIAND
RUE REFUGE
ROND-POINT
PARVIS DES ARENOISES
DES ARENES
ROMAN ARENA
ROND-POINT DES ARENES
NOTRE DAME
Place du Forum
RUE DE L'HOTEL DE VILLE
R. PERRIAT
CHOU
RUE BALECHOU
RUE DES ARENES
FAVORIN
R. NICOLAI
R. DIDEROT
RUE MADELEINE
RUE BALZE
RUE DE LA CALADE
WC
ST. TROPHIME
CLASSICAL THEATER
PORTE DE LAURE
R. L'AGNEAU
R. EMILE BARRERE
Place de la République
CLOISTERS
RUE DU CLOITRE
R. JEAN JAURES
Jardin d'Ete
ANCIENT CITY WALLS
MONTEE VAUBAN
TOUR DES MOURGUES
RUE ROTONDE
PLAYGROUND
TAXIS
BLVD. DES LICES
POST
AVE. VICTOR HUGO
Esplanade Charles de Gaulle
AVE ALYSCAMPS
To 9
RUE E. FASSIN

below Fontvieille, near the aqueduct of Barbegal. It's a big 320-acre spread engulfed by vineyards, rice fields, and swaying trees. The sweet owners (Sylvie and mama Marinette) have eight two-bedroom apartments with great weekly rates, though they may be rented for fewer days when available (€310, €400, or €850 per week, air-con, washing machines, guest computer and Wi-Fi in all apartments, pool, big lawn, swings, 1000 Route de l'Aqueduc Romain, tel. 04 90 54 70 25, www.domaine-laforest.com, contact@domaine-laforest.com).

Eating in Arles

You can dine well in Arles on a modest budget—in fact, it's hard to blow a lot on dinner here (most of my listings have *menus* for under €25). Before dinner, go local on Place du Forum and enjoy a *pastis*. This anise-based apéritif is served straight in a glass with ice, plus a carafe of water—dilute to taste. Sunday is a quiet night for restaurants, though most eateries on Place du Forum are open.

For **picnics,** a big, handy Monoprix supermarket/department store is on Place Lamartine (Mon-Sat 8:30-20:00, closed Sun).

ON OR NEAR PLACE DU FORUM

Great atmosphere and mediocre food at fair prices await on Place du Forum. By all accounts, the garish yellow Café la Nuit is worth avoiding. Most other cafés on the square deliver acceptable quality and terrific ambience. For better cuisine, wander away from the square.

La Cuisine de Comptoir's welcoming owners, Alexandre and Vincent, offer light *tartine* dinners—a delicious cross between pizza and bruschetta, served with soup or salad for just €11—a swinging deal (the *brandada*—salt cod—is tasty and filling). Watch *le chef* at work as you sip your €3 glass of rosé in fine glassware and enjoy the lively ambience of this cool little bistro (closed Sun, mostly indoor dining, just off the lower end of Place du Forum at 10 Rue de la Liberté, tel. 04 90 96 86 28).

At **Fad'Ola,** the food is as fresh and colorful as the restaurant's green-and-orange facade on Place du Forum. Cindy, from Vancouver BC, makes tasty €6 sandwiches drizzled with local olive oil. She offers a good €12 deal: sandwich, greens, and a drink. Sit inside or at one of the few outdoor tables (March-Oct daily 12:00-15:00 but all day long July-Aug, lunch only Mon-Fri off-season, 46 Rue des Arènes, 04 90 49 70 73).

On Rue du Dr. Fanton

A half-block below the Forum, on Rue du Dr. Fanton, lies a terrific lineup of restaurants. Come here to peruse your options side by side. You can't go wrong—all offer good value and have appealing indoor and outdoor seating.

Les Filles du 16 is a warm, affordable place to enjoy a fresh salad (€11), or a fine two- or three-course dinner (€21-€27). The choices are limited, so check the selection before sitting down. The *taureau* (bull's meat) in a tasty sauce is a good selection (closed Sat-Sun, 16 Rue du Dr. Fanton, tel. 04 90 93 77 36).

Au Brin de Thym, a few doors down, offers a reliable blend of traditional French and Provençal cuisine at very fair prices. Arrive early for an outdoor table or call ahead, and let hardworking and formal Monsieur and Madame Colombaud and their daughter take care of you. Monsieur does *le cooking* while *les filles* do *le serving* (€15 lunch *menu,* excellent €20 *plats;* closed Tue, 22 Rue du Dr. Fanton, tel. 04 90 97 85 18).

Le Plaza, next to Au Brin, is run by a young couple (Stéphane cooks while Graziela serves) and features tasty Provençal cuisine in a fine setting—inside or out—at good prices (€22 *menu,* daily April-Sept, closed Wed Oct-March, 28 Rue du Dr. Fanton, tel. 04 90 96 33 15).

Le Galoubet is a popular local spot, blending a cozy interior, traditional French cuisine, and service with a smile, thanks to owner Frank. It's the most expensive of the places I list on this street and the least flexible, serving a €29 *menu* only. If it's cold, a roaring fire keeps you toasty (closed Sun-Mon, great fries and desserts, 18 Rue du Dr. Fanton, tel. 04 90 93 18 11).

And for Dessert: Soleileis has Arles' best ice cream, with all-natural ingredients and unusual flavors such as *fadoli*—olive oil mixed with nougatine. There's also a shelf of English books for exchange (daily 14:00-18:30, plus 20:00-22:30 Wed-Sun July-Aug, across from recommended Le 16 restaurant at 9 Rue du Dr. Fanton).

Other Places near Place du Forum

La Bodeguita is ideal if Spanish food and ambience appeal. You can snack on tapas (€4) and enjoy a good selection of wines (by the bottle mainly) and cocktails in a lively setting with friendly service. Their *Délice au Nutella* is to sigh for (19:30 until late, reservation recommended especially on Fri-Sat, closed Sun, 49 Rue des Arènes, 04 90 96 68 59, www.bodeguita.fr).

La Piazza des Thermes, an inviting eatery a few blocks north of Place du Forum, serves good pizza and pasta for €10-15 and has comfortable indoor and outdoor seating (daily except Sun lunch, 6 Rue du Sauvage, tel. 04 90 49 60 64).

Cafés de la Major is *the* place to go to recharge with some serious coffee or tea (Tue-Sat 8:30-19:00, closed Sun-Mon, 7 bis Rue Réattu, tel. 04 90 96 14 15).

NEAR THE ROMAN ARENA

For about the same price as on Place du Forum, you can enjoy regional cuisine with a point-blank view of the arena. Because they change regularly, the handful of (mostly) outdoor eateries that overlook the arena are pretty indistinguishable.

Le Grillon, with the best view above the arena, offers friendly service and good-enough salads (the *camarguaise* is a riot of color), pizza and tasty *tartines* for €10 (including small salad), and *plats du jour* for €11-14 (closed all day Wed and Sun night, at the top of the arena on Rond-point des Arènes, tel. 04 90 96 70 97).

Le Criquet, a sweet little place two blocks above the arena, serves Provençal classics with joy at good prices. If you're really hungry, try the €25 *bourride*—a creamy fish soup thickened with aioli and garlic and stuffed with mussels, clams, calamari, and more (good €24-28 *menus,* indoor and outdoor dining, 21 Rue Porte de Laure, tel. 04 90 96 80 51).

For details on the next two places, see their listings under "Sleeping in Arles," earlier. **Hôtel le Calendal** serves seasonal light food all day in its lovely courtyard or at the café (delicious little sandwiches for €2.50 each, daily 8:00-19:00). **Hôtel Voltaire,** well-situated on a pleasing square, serves simple three-course lunches and dinners at honest prices to a loyal clientele (€13 *menus;* hearty *plats* and filling salads for €10—try the *salade fermière, salade Latine,* or the filling *assiette Provençale;* closed Sun evening except July-Aug).

A GASTRONOMIC DINING EXPERIENCE

One of France's most recognized chefs, Jean-Luc Rabanel, has created a sensation with two very different options 50 yards from Place de la République (at 7 Rue des Carmes). They sit side by side, both offering indoor and terrace seating.

L'Atelier is so intriguing that people travel great distances just for the experience. Diners fork over €125 (at lunch, you'll spoon out €65) and trust the chef to create a memorable meal...which he does—and Monsieur Michelin agrees, having confirmed his second star. There is no menu, just an onslaught of delicious taste sensations served in artsy dishes. Don't plan on a quick dinner, and don't come for a traditional setting; rooms are *très* contemporary. Several outdoor tables are also available. You'll probably see or hear the famous chef. Hint: He has long salt-and-pepper hair and a deep voice (closed Mon-Tue, best to book ahead, friendly servers will hold your hand through this palate-widening experience, tel. 04 90 91 07 69, www.rabanel.com).

A Côté saddles up next door, offering a smart wine bar/bistro ambience and top-quality cuisine for far less. Here you can sample the famous chef's talents with the €29 three-course *menu* (open daily, tel. 04 90 47 61 13, www.bistro-acote.com).

Arles Connections

BY TRAIN

Some trains in and out of Arles require a **reservation.** These include connections with Nice to the east and Bordeaux to the west (including intermediary stops). Ask at the station.

From Arles by Train to: Paris (11/day, 2 direct TGVs—4 hours, 9 with transfer in Avignon—5 hours), **Avignon *Centre-Ville*** (roughly hourly, 20 minutes, less frequent in the afternoon), **Nîmes** (9/day, 30 minutes), **Orange** (4/day direct, 35 minutes, more frequent with transfer in Avignon), **Aix-en-Provence *Centre-Ville*** (10/day, 2.25 hours, transfer in Marseille, train may separate midway—be sure you're in section going to Aix-en-Provence), **Marseille** (11/day, 1 hour), **Cassis** (7/day, 2 hours), **Carcassonne** (4/day direct, 2.5 hours, more with transfer in Narbonne, direct trains may require reservations), **Beaune** (10/day, 4.5-5 hours, 9 with transfer in Lyon and Nîmes or Avignon), **Nice** (11/day, 3.75-4.5 hours, most require transfer in Marseille), **Barcelona** (3/day, 4.5 hours, transfer in Nîmes), **Italy** (3/day, transfer in Marseille and Nice; from Arles, it's 4.5-5 hours to Ventimiglia on the border, 8 hours to Milan, 9.5 hours to Cinque Terre, 11-12 hours to Florence, and 13 hours to Venice or Rome).

BY BUS

The bus station is at 16-24 Boulevard Georges Clemenceau (2 blocks below main TI, next to Café le Wilson). Cartreize buses to St-Rémy, Les Baux, and the Camargue depart from the train station and/or from the downtown bus station. The downtown station is labeled on schedules as Rue Georges Clemenceau (see timetables at www.lepilote.com). Bus info: Tel. 08 10 00 13 26. Ask at the TI for the latest information.

From Arles Train Station to Avignon TGV Station: The direct SNCF bus is easier than the train and leaves only from Arles' train station (8/day, 1 hour, included with rail pass). You can also take the train from Arles to Avignon's *Centre-Ville* Station, then catch the *navette* (shuttle bus) to the TGV Station (2-block walk, see page 603).

From Arles by Bus to: Nîmes (bus #C30, 6/day, 1 hour), **Aix-en-Provence** (faster than trains, from Clémenceau stop only, 5/day

Mon-Sat, 2/day Sun, 1.5 hours), **St-Rémy-de-Provence** (bus #54, 3/day Mon-Sat, none on Sun, 50 minutes; bus #57 also goes to St-Rémy via Les Baux in summer—see below), **Fontvieille** (6/day, 10 minutes), **Camargue/Stes-Maries-de-la-Mer** (bus #20, 6/day including Sun, 1 hour).

From Arles by Bus to Les Baux and St-Rémy: Bus #57 connects Arles to **Les Baux** and **St-Rémy** (6/day daily July-Aug, Sat-Sun only in June and Sept; 35 minutes to Les Baux, 50 minutes to St-Rémy, then runs to Avignon). Bus #54 (see above) also goes to St-Rémy but not via Les Baux.

For other ways to reach Les Baux and St-Rémy, see page 631.

Avignon

Famous for its nursery rhyme, medieval bridge, and brooding Palace of the Popes, contemporary Avignon (ah-veen-yohn) bustles and prospers behind its almighty walls. During the 94 years (1309-1403) that Avignon starred as the *Franco Vaticano* (the temporary residence of the popes) and hosted two antipopes, it grew from a quiet village into a thriving city. With its large student population and fashionable shops, today's Avignon is an intriguing blend of medieval history, youthful energy, and urban sophistication. Street performers entertain the international throngs who fill Avignon's ubiquitous cafés and trendy boutiques. If you're here in July, expect big crowds and higher prices, thanks to the rollicking theater festival. (Reserve your hotel far in advance.) Clean, lively, and popular with tourists, Avignon is more impressive for its outdoor ambience than for its museums and monuments.

Orientation to Avignon

Cours Jean Jaurès, which turns into Rue de la République, runs straight from the *Centre-Ville* train station to Place de l'Horloge and the Palace of the Popes, splitting Avignon in two. The larger eastern half is where the action is. Climb to the Jardin du Rocher des Doms for the town's best view, consider touring the pope's immense palace, lose yourself in Avignon's back streets (follow my self-guided walk on page 613), and find a shady square to call home. Avignon's shopping district fills the traffic-free streets near where Rue de la République meets Place de l'Horloge. As you wander, look for signs in Occitan—the language of the Occitania region; you might see the name of the city written as "Avinhon" or "Avignoun."

TOURIST INFORMATION

The main TI is between the *Centre-Ville* train station and the old town, at 41 Cours Jean Jaurès (April-Oct Mon-Sat 9:00-18:00, Sun 10:00-17:00, daily until 19:00 in July; Nov-March Mon-Fri 9:00-18:00, Sat 9:00-17:00, Sun 10:00-12:00; tel. 04 32 74 32 74, www.avignon-tourisme.com). In summer, a branch TI office opens at the TGV train station (July-Aug Tue-Sat 11:15-14:15 & 15:00-17:15). Get the helpful map, plus the free magazines if you're staying awhile (info on bike rentals, restaurants, hotels, apartment rentals, events, and museums).

Sightseeing Pass: Everyone should pick up the free **Avignon Passion Pass** (valid 15 days, for up to 5 family members). Get the pass stamped when you pay full price at your first sight (choose a cheap one), and then receive price reductions at the others (for example, €2 less at the Palace of the Popes and €3 less at the Petit Palais). The discounts add up—always show your Passion Pass when buying a ticket. The pass comes with the Avignon "Passion" map and guide, which includes several good (but tricky-to-follow) walking tours.

ARRIVAL IN AVIGNON

By Train: Avignon has two train stations: TGV (linked to downtown by frequent shuttle trains) and *Centre-Ville.* While most TGV trains serve only the TGV Station, some also stop at *Centre-Ville*—verify your station in advance.

The shiny new **TGV Station** (*Gare TGV*) on the outskirts of town has a summer-only TI (see above), but no baggage storage. Car rental, buses, and taxis are all out the north exit *(sortie nord).*

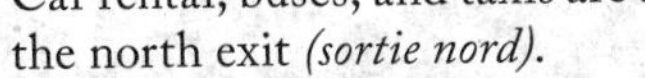

To get from the TGV Station to the city center, take the **shuttle train** from platform A or B to the *Centre-Ville* train station (€1.60, 5 minutes, 2/hour, buy ticket from machine on platform or at desk in main hall). A **taxi** ride between the TGV Station and downtown Avignon costs about €20 (more on Sunday and from 19:00 to 6:00).

If you are connecting onward to Arles, **buses** to Arles' *Centre-Ville* train station stop at the second bus shelter (8/day, 1 hour, €9.10, included with rail pass, schedule posted on the shelter and available at info booths inside the TGV train station).

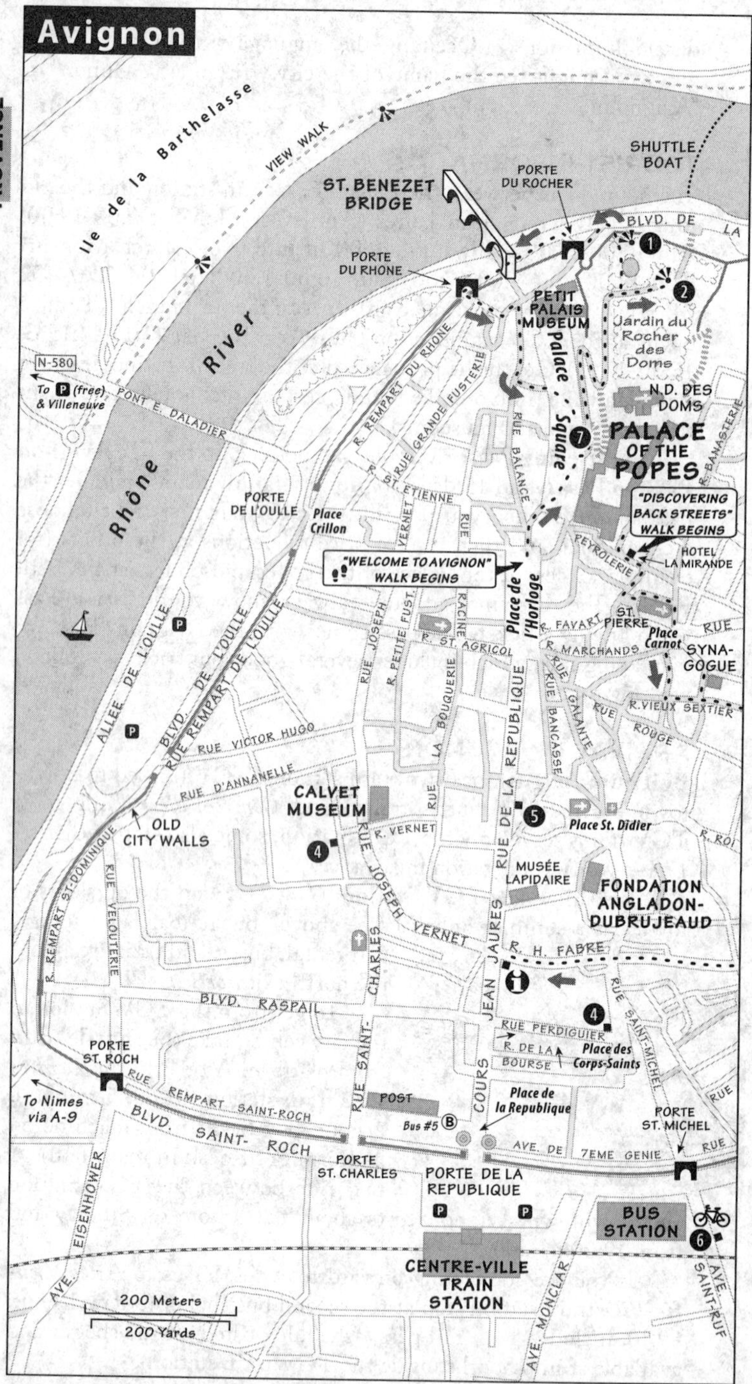
Avignon
Ile de la Barthelasse
VIEW WALK
SHUTTLE BOAT
ST. BENEZET BRIDGE
PORTE DU ROCHER
BLVD. DE LA
PORTE DU RHONE
PETIT PALAIS MUSEUM
Jardin du Rocher des Doms
Rhône River
N-580
To P (free) & Villeneuve
PONT E. DALADIER
R. REMPART DU RHONE
RUE GRANDE FUSTERIE
Palace Square
N.D. DES DOMS
PALACE OF THE POPES
R. BANASTERIE
RUE BALANCE
R. ST. ETIENNE
PORTE DE L'OULLE
Place Crillon
RUE VERNET
RUE
"DISCOVERING BACK STREETS" WALK BEGINS
PEYROLERIE
HOTEL LA MIRANDE
"WELCOME TO AVIGNON" WALK BEGINS
Place de l'Horloge
ST. PIERRE
Place Carnot
RUE
SYNAGOGUE
R. FAVART
R. MARCHANDS
R. ST. AGRICOL
RUE JOSEPH
R. PETITE FUST.
RACINE
ALLEE DE L'OULLE
BLVD. DE L'OULLE
RUE REMPART DE L'OULLE
RUE VICTOR HUGO
RUE D'ANNANELLE
RUE LA BOUQUERIE
RUE DE LA REPUBLIQUE
RUE GALANTE
RUE BANCASSE
R. VIEUX SEXTIER
RUE ROUGE
CALVET MUSEUM
RUE
Place St. Didier
R. ROI
OLD CITY WALLS
R. VERNET
RUE JOSEPH VERNET
MUSÉE LAPIDAIRE
FONDATION ANGLADON-DUBRUJEAUD
R. REMPART ST-DOMINIQUE
RUE VELOUTERIE
RUE SAINT-CHARLES
JEAN JAURES
R. H. FABRE
RUE SAINT-MICHEL
BLVD. RASPAIL
RUE PERDIGUIER
R. DE LA BOURSE
Place des Corps-Saints
COURS
PORTE ST. ROCH
RUE REMPART SAINT-ROCH
To Nimes via A-9
POST
Bus #5
Place de la Republique
BLVD. SAINT-ROCH
PORTE ST. CHARLES
PORTE DE LA REPUBLIQUE
AVE. DE 7EME GENIE
RUE
PORTE ST. MICHEL
BUS STATION
AVE. EISENHOWER
CENTRE-VILLE TRAIN STATION
AVE. MONCLAR
AVE. SAINT-RUF
200 Meters
200 Yards

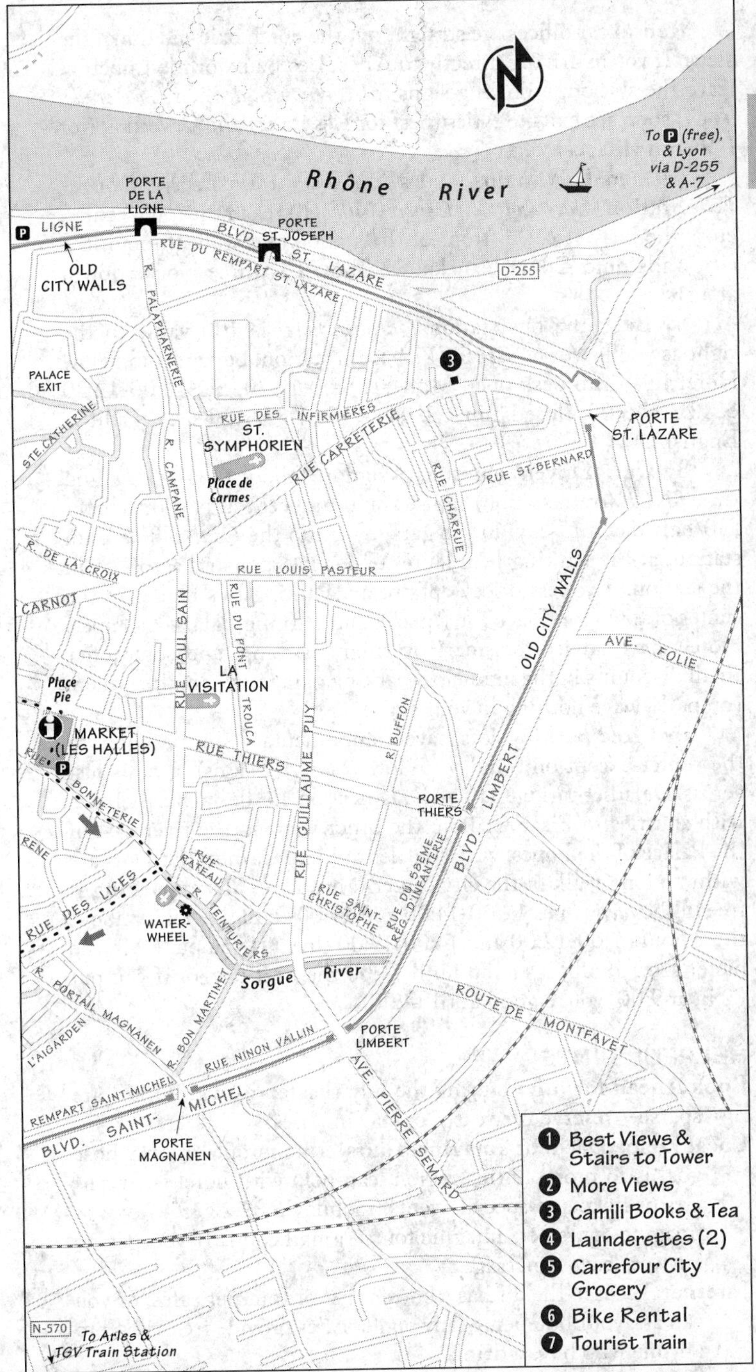

Rhône River
To P (free), & Lyon via D-255 & A-7
PORTE DE LA LIGNE
PORTE ST. JOSEPH
LIGNE
BLVD. ST. LAZARE
RUE DU REMPART ST. LAZARE
D-255
OLD CITY WALLS
R. PALAPHARNERIE
PALACE EXIT
STE. CATHERINE
RUE DES INFIRMIERES
ST. SYMPHORIEN
Place de Carmes
R. CAMPANE
RUE CARRETERIE
RUE CHARRUE
RUE ST-BERNARD
PORTE ST. LAZARE
R. DE LA CROIX
RUE LOUIS PASTEUR
CARNOT
RUE PAUL SAIN
RUE DU PONT TROUCA
OLD CITY WALLS
AVE. FOLIE
Place Pie
LA VISITATION
MARKET (LES HALLES)
RUE THIERS
R. BUFFON
RUE GUILLAUME PUY
PORTE THIERS
BLVD. LIMBERT
BONNETERIE
RENE
RUE RATEAU
R. TEINTURIERS
RUE DES LICES
WATER-WHEEL
RUE SAINT-CHRISTOPHE
RUE DU 58EME REG. D'INFANTERIE
Sorgue River
ROUTE DE MONTFAVET
R. PORTAIL MAGNANEN
L'AIGARDEN
R. BON MARTINET
RUE NINON VALLIN
PORTE LIMBERT
AVE. PIERRE SEMARD
REMPART SAINT-MICHEL
BLVD. SAINT-MICHEL
PORTE MAGNANEN
N-570
To Arles & TGV Train Station
1 Best Views & Stairs to Tower
2 More Views
3 Camili Books & Tea
4 Launderettes (2)
5 Carrefour City Grocery
6 Bike Rental
7 Tourist Train
PROVENCE

Rental car offices are straight out the north exit and down the steps. If you're driving directly to Arles, Les Baux, or the Luberon, leave the station, following signs to *Avignon Sud,* then *La Rocade.* You'll soon see exits to Arles (best for Les Baux) and Cavaillon (for Luberon villages).

All non-TGV trains (and a few TGV trains) serve ***Centre-Ville*** **Station** (*Gare Avignon Centre-Ville*). To reach the town center, cross the busy street in front of the station and walk through the city walls onto Cours Jean Jaurès. The TI is three blocks down, at #41.

By Bus: The bus station *(gare routière)* is 100 yards to the right as you leave the *Centre-Ville* train station, beyond and below Hôtel Ibis (info desk open Mon-Fri 8:00-19:30, Sat 10:00-12:30 & 13:30-18:00, closed Sun, tel. 04 90 82 07 35, staff speaks a little English).

By Car: Drivers entering Avignon follow *Centre-Ville* and *Gare SNCF* (train station) signs. You'll find central pay lots (about €10/half-day, €15/day) in the garage next to the *Centre-Ville* train station, at the Parking Jean Jaurès under the ramparts across from the station. Two less pricey options are Parking Les Halles in the center of town, on Place Pie ("pee"), and Parking Palais des Papes. Hotels have advice for smart overnight parking, and some offer small discounts in the municipal parking garages. No matter where you park, leave nothing in your car.

Two **free parking** lots have complimentary shuttle buses to the center except on Sunday (follow *P Gratuit* signs): One is just across Daladier Bridge (Pont Daladier) on Ile de la Barthelasse, with shuttles to Place Crillon; the other is along the river east of the Palace of the Popes, with shuttles to Place Carnot (both lots are within a long walk of the city center if need be). **Street parking** is free in the *bleu* zones 12:00-14:00 and 19:00-9:00. It's €2 for about three hours 9:00-12:00 and 14:00-19:00 (hint: If you put €2 in the meter after 19:00, it's good until 14:00 the next day, or if you put €2 in at 9:00, you're good until 14:00).

HELPFUL HINTS

Book Ahead for July: During the July theater festival, rooms are sparse—reserve very early, or stay in Arles.

Local Help: David at **Imagine Tours,** a nonprofit group whose goal is to promote this region, can help with hotel emergencies or tickets to special events (mobile 06 89 22 19 87, www.imagine-tours.net, imagine.tours@gmail.com). If you get no answer, leave a message.

Internet Access: The TI has a current list of Internet cafés, or you can ask your hotelier. Many bigger cafés provide free Wi-Fi to anyone who buys a drink.

English Bookstore: Try **Camili Books & Tea,** a secondhand bookshop with a refreshing courtyard and hot drinks (Tue-Sat 12:00-19:00, closed Sun-Mon, Wi-Fi, 155 Rue Carreterie, in Avignon's northeast corner, tel. 04 90 27 38 50, www.camilibooksandtea.com).

Baggage Storage: There is none in Avignon.

Laundry: At **La Blanchisseuse,** you can drop off your laundry and pick it up the same day for about €12 a load (daily 7:00-21:00, a few blocks west of main TI at 24 Rue Lanterne, tel. 04 90 85 58 80). The launderette at 66 Place des Corps-Saints, where Rue Agricol Perdiguier ends, has English instructions and is handy to most hotels (daily 7:00-20:00).

Grocery Store: Carrefour City is central and has long hours (Mon-Sat 7:00-22:00, Sun 9:00-12:00, next to McDonald's, 2 blocks from TI, toward Place de l'Horloge on Rue de la République).

Bike Rental: You can rent bikes and scooters near the train station at **Provence Bike** (April-Oct 9:00-18:30, 7 Avenue St. Ruf, tel. 04 90 27 92 61, www.provence-bike.com). You'll enjoy riding on the Ile de la Barthelasse, but biking is better in Isle-sur-la-Sorgue and Vaison la Romaine.

Car Rental: Both train stations have car-rental agencies (TGV—open long hours daily; *Centre-Ville*—Mon-Sat 9:00-12:00 & 14:00-18:00, closed Sun).

Shuttle Boat: A free shuttle boat, the *Navette Fluviale,* plies back and forth across the river (as it did in the days when the town had no functioning bridge) from near St. Bénezet Bridge (3/hour, daily April-June and Sept 10:00-12:30 & 14:00-18:00, July-Aug 11:00-21:00, Oct-March weekends and Wed afternoon only). It drops you on the peaceful Ile de la Barthelasse, with its recommended riverside restaurant, grassy walks, and bike rides with terrific city views. If you stay on the island for dinner, check the schedule for the last return boat—or be prepared for a taxi ride or a pleasant 25-minute walk back to town.

Commanding City Views: For great views of Avignon and the river, walk or drive across Daladier Bridge, or ferry across the Rhône on the *Navette Fluviale* (described above). I'd take the boat across the river, walk the view path to Daladier Bridge, and then cross back over the bridge (45-minute walk over mostly level ground). You can enjoy other impressive vistas from the top of the Jardin du Rocher des Doms, from the tower in the Palace of the Popes, from the end of the famous, broken St. Bénezet Bridge, and from the entrance to Fort St. André, across the river in Villeneuve-lès-Avignon.

Tours in Avignon

Walking Tours

The TI offers informative English walking tours of Avignon, which include a visit to the Palace of the Popes (€19.50, discounted with Avignon Passion Pass, tours normally April-June on Sat at 15:00, Aug on Fri at 10:00, Sept on Wed and Sat at 15:00, no tours in July or Nov-March). Ask at the TI or check their website to confirm tour times and to reserve (www.avignon-tourisme.com).

Tourist Trains

The little train leaves regularly from in front of the Palace of the Popes and offers a decent overview of the city, including the Jardin du Rocher des Doms and St. Bénezet Bridge (€7, 2/hour, 40 minutes, mid-March-mid-Oct daily 10:00-18:00, until 19:00 July-Aug, English commentary).

Guided Excursions

Several minivan tour companies based in Avignon offer transportation to destinations described in this chapter, including Pont du Gard, the Luberon, and the Camargue (see "Tours of Provence" on page 565).

Self-Guided Walks in Avignon

For a fine overview of the city, combine these two walks. "Welcome to Avignon" covers the major sights, while "Avignon's Back Streets" leads you along the lanes less taken, delving beyond the surface of this historic city.

▲▲WELCOME TO AVIGNON WALK

Before starting this walk—which connects the city's top sights—be sure to pick up the Avignon Passion Pass at the TI, then show it when entering each attraction to receive discounted admission (explained earlier, under "Tourist Information").

• *Start your tour where the Romans did, on Place de l'Horloge, in front of City Hall (Hôtel de Ville).*

Place de l'Horloge

This café square was the town forum during Roman times and the market square through the Middle Ages. (Restaurants here offer good people-watching, but they also have less ambience and low-quality meals—you'll find better squares elsewhere to hang your beret in.) Named for a medieval clock tower mostly hidden behind City Hall (find plaque in English), this square's present popularity arrived with the trains in 1854. Walk a few steps to the center of the square, and look down the main drag, Rue de la République.

When the trains came to Avignon, proud city fathers wanted a direct, impressive way to link the new station to the heart of the city (just like in Paris)—so they plowed over homes to create Rue de la République and widened Place de l'Horloge. This main drag's Parisian feel is intentional—it was built not in the Provençal manner, but in the Haussmann style that is so dominant in Paris (characterized by broad, straight boulevards lined with stately buildings).

• *Walk slightly uphill past the carousel (public WCs behind). Veer right at the Hôtel des Palais des Papes and continue into...*

Palace Square (Place du Palais)

Pull up a concrete stump just past the café. Nicknamed *bites* (slang for the male anatomy), these stumps effectively keep cars from double-parking in areas designed for people. Many of the metal ones slide up and down by remote control to let privileged cars come and go.

Now take in the scene. This grand square is lined with the Palace of the Popes, the Petit Palais, and the cathedral. In the 1300s the entire headquarters of the Catholic Church was moved to Avignon. The Church bought Avignon and gave it a complete makeover. Along with clearing out vast spaces like this square and building this three-acre palace, the Church erected more than three miles of protective wall (with 39 towers), "appropriate" housing for cardinals (read: mansions), and residences for its entire bureaucracy. The city was Europe's largest construction zone. Avignon's population grew from 6,000 to 25,000 in short order. (Today, 13,000 people live within the walls.) The limits of pre-papal Avignon are outlined on your city map: Rues Joseph Vernet, Henri Fabre, des Lices, and Philonarde all follow the route of the city's earlier defensive wall.

The Petit Palais (Little Palace) seals the uphill end of the square and was built for a cardinal; today it houses medieval paintings (museum described later). The church just to the left of the Palace of the Popes is Avignon's cathedral. It predates the Church's purchase of Avignon by 200 years. Its small size reflects Avignon's modest, pre-papal population. The gilded Mary was added in 1854, when the Vatican established the doctrine of her Immaculate Conception. Mary is taller than the Palace of the Popes by design: The Vatican never accepted what it called the "Babylonian Captivity" and had a bad attitude about Avignon long after the pope was definitively back in Rome. There hasn't been a French pope since the Holy See returned to Rome—over 600 years ago. That's what I call holding a grudge.

Right behind you, across the square from the palace's main entry stands a cardinal's residence, built in 1619 (now the Conservatoire National de Musique). Its fancy Baroque facade was a visual counterpoint to the stripped-down Huguenot aesthetic of the age.

During this time, Provence was a hotbed of Protestantism—but, buried within this region, Avignon was a Catholic stronghold.

• *You can visit the massive* ***Palace of the Popes*** *(described on page 612) later, or walk up the square and take in the...*

Petit Palais Museum (Musée du Petit Palais)

This former cardinal's palace now displays the Church's collection of mostly medieval Italian painting (including one delightful Botticelli) and sculpture. All 350 paintings deal with Christian themes. The information is only in French, but a visit here before going to the Palace of the Popes helps furnish and populate that otherwise barren building, and a quick peek into its courtyard (even if you don't tour the museum) shows the importance of cardinal housing. The museum's garden café provides a shady, peaceful refuge.

Cost and Hours: €6, Wed-Mon 10:00-13:00 & 14:00-18:00, closed Tue; at north end of Palace Square, tel. 04 90 86 44 58.

• *From Palace Square we'll head up to the rocky hilltop where Avignon was first settled, then drop down to the river. With this short loop, you can enjoy a small park, hike to a grand river view, and visit Avignon's beloved broken bridge.*

Start by climbing to the church level (you can fill your bottle with cold water here), then take the central switchback ramps up to...

▲▲Jardin du Rocher des Doms

Though the park itself is a delight—with a sweet little café (good prices for food and drinks) and public WCs—don't miss the climax: a panoramic view of the Rhône River Valley and the broken bridge. For the best views (and the favorite make-out spot for local teenagers later in the evening), find the small terrace behind the odd zodiac display across the grass from the pond-side park café. If the green fence is ruining it for you, stand on the short wall behind you, or detour a few minutes through the park (to the right, with the river on your left) to find a bigger terrace.

On a clear day, the tallest peak you see, with its white limestone cap, is Mont Ventoux ("Windy Mountain"). Below and just to the right, you'll spot free passenger ferries shuttling across the river (great views from path on other side of the river), and—tucked amidst the trees on the far side of the river—a fun, recommended restaurant, Le Bercail. The island in the river is the Ile de la Barthelasse, a lush nature preserve where Avignon can breathe. To the left in the distance, the TGV rail bridge floats gracefully above the valley.

Fort St. André (across the river on the hill; see the info plaque to the left) was built by the French in 1360, shortly after the pope moved to Avignon, to counter the papal incursion into this part of Europe. The castle was across the border, in the kingdom of France. Avignon's famous bridge was a key border crossing, with towers on either end—one was French, and the other was the pope's. The French one, across the river, is the Tower of Philip the Fair (described later, under "More Sights in Avignon").

Cost and Hours: Free, park gates open daily April-Sept 7:30-20:00, until 21:00 June-Aug, Oct-March 7:30-18:00 (confirm closing time at entrance).

• *Take the walkway down to the left and find the stairs (closed at dusk) leading down to the tower. You'll catch glimpses of the...*

Ramparts

The only bit of the rampart you can walk on is accessed from St. Bénezet Bridge (pay to enter—see next). Just after the papacy took control of Avignon, the walls were extended to take in the convents and monasteries that had been outside the city. What you see today was restored in the 19th century.

• *When you come out of the tower on street level, exit out of the walls, then turn left along the wall to the old bridge. Pass under the bridge to find its entrance shortly after.*

▲▲St. Bénezet Bridge (Pont St. Bénezet)

This bridge, whose construction and location were inspired by a shepherd's religious vision, is the "Pont d'Avignon" of nursery-rhyme fame. The ditty (which you've probably been humming all day) dates back to the 15th century: *Sur le Pont d'Avignon, on y danse, on y danse, sur le Pont d'Avignon, on y danse tous en rond* ("On the bridge of Avignon, we will dance, we will dance, on the bridge of Avignon, we will dance all in a circle").

But the bridge was a big deal even outside of its kiddie-tune fame. Built between 1171 and 1185, it was the only bridge crossing the mighty Rhône in the Middle Ages—important to pilgrims, merchants, and armies. It was damaged several times by floods and subsequently rebuilt. In 1668 most of it was knocked out for the last time by a disastrous, icy flood. Lacking a government stimulus package, the townsfolk decided not to rebuild this time, and for more than a century, Avignon had no bridge across the Rhône. While only four arches survive today, the original bridge was huge: Imagine a 22-arch,

3,000-foot-long bridge extending from Vatican territory across the island to the lonely Tower of Philip the Fair, which marked the beginning of France (see displays of the bridge's original length).

Cost and Hours: €5, includes audioguide, €13.50 combo-ticket includes Palace of the Popes, same hours as Palace of the Popes (described next), tel. 04 90 27 51 16.

Visiting the Bridge: The ticket booth is housed in what was a medieval hospital for the poor (funded by bridge tolls). Admission includes a small room that displays a 3-D reconstruction of the bridge (through 2015) and your only chance to walk a bit of the ramparts (enter both from the tower). A Romanesque chapel on the bridge is dedicated to St. Bénezet. Though there's not much to see on the bridge, the audioguide included with your ticket tells a good enough story. It's also fun to be in the breezy middle of the river with a sweeping city view.

• *To get to the Palace of the Popes from here, leave via the riverfront exit, turn left, then turn left again back into the walls. Walk to the end of the short street, then turn right following signs to Palais des Papes. Next, look for brown signs leading left under the passageway, then stay the course up the narrow steps to Palace Square.*

▲Palace of the Popes (Palais des Papes)

In 1309 a French pope was elected (Pope Clément V). At the urging of the French king, His Holiness decided that dangerous Italy was no place for a pope, so he moved the whole operation to Avignon for a secure rule under a supportive king. The Catholic Church literally bought Avignon (then a two-bit town), and popes resided here until 1403. Meanwhile, Italians demanded a Roman pope, so from 1378 on, there were twin popes—one in Rome and one in Avignon—causing a schism in the Catholic Church that wasn't fully resolved until 1417.

Cost and Hours: €11 (more for special exhibits), €13.50 combo-ticket includes St. Bénezet Bridge, daily March-June and Sept-Oct 9:00-19:00, July-Aug 9:00-20:00, Nov-Feb 9:30-17:45, last entry one hour before closing, essential audioguide-€2, tel. 04 90 27 50 00, www.palais-des-papes.com.

Visiting the Palace: Spring for the slick multimedia audioguide, which leads you along a one-way route and does a decent job of overcoming the palace's complete lack of furnishings. It teaches the basic history while allowing you to tour at your own pace. A small room inside the palace with videos and displays adds context.

Still, touring the palace is pretty anticlimactic, given its historic importance.

As you wander, ponder that this palace—the largest surviving Gothic palace in Europe—was built to accommodate 500 people as the administrative center of the Holy See and home of the pope. This was the most fortified palace of the age (remember, the pope left Rome to be more secure). Nine popes ruled from here, making this the center of Christianity for nearly 100 years. You'll walk through the pope's personal quarters (frescoed with happy hunting scenes), see many models of how the various popes added to the building, and learn about its state-of-the-art plumbing. The rooms are huge. The "pope's chapel" is twice the size of the adjacent Avignon cathedral.

The last pope (or, technically, antipope, since by then Rome also had its own rival pope) checked out in 1403 (escaping a siege), but the Church owned Avignon until the French Revolution in 1789. During this interim period, the pope's "legate" (official representative, normally a nephew) ruled Avignon from this palace. Avignon residents, many of whom had come from Rome, spoke Italian for a century after the pope left, making it a linguistic ghetto within France. In the Napoleonic age, the palace was a barracks, housing 1,800 soldiers. You can see cuts in the wall where high ceilings gave way to floor beams. Climb the tower (Tour de la Gâche) for grand views and a rooftop café with surprisingly good food at very fair prices.

Wine/Herbal Tea Room: The artillery room at the end of the tour is dedicated to papal herbal teas (one for each pope), and to the region's wines, of which they claim the pope was a fan. The nearby village of Châteauneuf-du-Pape is where the pope summered in the 1320s. Its famous wine is a direct descendant of his wine.

• *You'll exit at the rear of the palace, where my "Back Streets" walking tour begins (described next). Or, to return to Palace Square, make two rights after exiting the palace.*

▲▲AVIGNON'S BACK STREETS WALK

Use the map in this chapter or the TI map to navigate this easy, level, 30-minute walk. This self-guided tour begins in the small square (Place de la Mirande) behind the Palace of the Popes. If you've toured the palace, this is where you exit. Otherwise, from the front of the palace, follow the narrow, cobbled Rue de la Peyrolerie—carved out of the rock—around the palace on the right side as you face it.

• *Our walk begins at the...*

Hôtel La Mirande: Located on the square, Avignon's finest hotel welcomes visitors. Find the atrium lounge and consider a coffee break amid the understated luxury (€14.50 afternoon tea served daily 15:00-18:00, includes a generous selection of pastries). Inspect the royal lounge and dining room; cooking demos are offered in the basement below (www.la-mirande.fr). Rooms start at about €450 in high season.

• *Turn left out of the hotel and left again on Rue de la Peyrolerie ("Coppersmiths Street"), then take your first right on Rue des Ciseaux d'Or. On the small square ahead you'll find the...*

Church of St. Pierre: The original chestnut doors were carved in 1551, when tales of New World discoveries raced across Europe. (Notice the Indian headdress, top center of left-side door.) The fine Annunciation (eye level on right-side door) shows Gabriel giving Mary the exciting news in impressive Renaissance 3-D. Now take 10 steps back from the door and look way up. The tiny statue breaking the skyline of the church is the pagan god Bacchus, with oodles of grapes. What's he doing sitting atop a Christian church? No one knows. The church's interior holds a beautiful Baroque altar. (For recommended restaurants near the Church of St. Pierre, see "Eating in Avignon," later.)

• *Facing the church door, follow the alley to the left, which was covered and turned into a tunnel during the town's population boom. It leads into...*

Place des Châtaignes: The cloister of St. Pierre is named for the chestnut *(châtaigne)* trees that once stood here (now replaced by plane trees). The practical atheists of the French Revolution destroyed the cloister, leaving only faint traces of the arches along the church side of the square.

• *Continue around the church and cross the busy street to the Banque Chaix. Across little Rue des Fourbisseurs find the classy...*

15th-Century Building: With its original beamed eaves showing, this is a rare vestige from the Middle Ages. Notice how this building widens the higher it gets. A medieval loophole based taxes on ground-floor square footage—everything above was tax-free. Walking down Rue des Fourbisseurs ("Street of the Animal Furriers"), notice how the top floors almost touch. Fire was a constant danger in the Middle Ages, as flames leapt easily from one home to the next. In fact, the lookout guard's primary responsibility was watching for fires, not the enemy. Virtually all of Avignon's medieval homes have been replaced by safer structures.

• *Walk down Rue des Fourbisseurs and turn left onto the traffic-free Rue du Vieux Sextier ("Street of the Old Balance," for weighing items); another left under the first arch leads 10 yards to Avignon's...*

Synagogue: Jews first arrived in Avignon with the Diaspora (exile) of the first century. Avignon's Jews were nicknamed "the Pope's Jews" because of the protection that the Vatican offered to Jews expelled from France. Although the original synagogue dates from the 1220s, in the mid-19th century it was completely rebuilt in a Neoclassical Greek-temple style by a non-Jewish architect. This is the only synagogue under a rotunda that you'll see anywhere. It's an intimate, classy place dressed with white colonnades and walnut furnishings. To enter the synagogue, you'll have to email in advance of your visit (free, closed Sat-Sun, 2 Place Jerusalem, tel. 04 90 85 21 24, rabinacia@hotmail.fr).

• *Retrace your steps to Rue du Vieux Sextier and turn left, then continue to the big square and find the big, boxy...*

Market (Les Halles): In 1970, the town's open-air market was replaced by this modern one. The market's jungle-like green wall reflects the changes of seasons and helps mitigate its otherwise stark exterior (open Tue-Sun until 13:00, closed Mon). Step inside for a sensual experience of organic breads, olives, and festival-of-mold cheeses. The Rue des Temptations cuts down the center. Cafés and cheese shops are on the right—as far as possible from the stinky fish stalls on the left. Follow your nose away from the fish and have a coffee with the locals. Every Saturday at 11:00 (except in Aug) in the *Petite Cuisine des Halles,* local chefs demonstrate a recipe that you can sample.

• *Exit out the back door of Les Halles, turn left on Rue de la Bonneterie ("Street of Hosiery"), and track the street for five minutes to the plane trees, where it becomes...*

Rue des Teinturiers: This "Street of the Dyers" is a tie-dyed, tree- and stream-lined lane, home to earthy cafés and galleries. This was the cloth industry's dyeing and textile center in the 1800s. The stream is a branch of the Sorgue River. Those stylish Provençal fabrics and patterns you see for sale everywhere were first made here, after a pattern imported from India.

About three small bridges down, you'll pass the Grey Penitents chapel on the right. The upper facade shows the GPs, who dressed up in robes and pointy hoods to do their anonymous good deeds back in the 13th century (long before the KKK dressed this way).

As you stroll on, you'll see the work of amateur sculptors, who have carved whimsical car barriers out of limestone. Fun restaurants on this atmospheric street are recommended later, under "Eating in Avignon."

• *Farther down Rue des Teinturiers, you'll come to the...*

Waterwheel: Standing here, imagine the Sorgue River—which hits the mighty Rhône in Avignon—being broken into several canals in order to turn 23 such wheels. Starting in about 1800, waterwheels powered the town's industries. The little cogwheel above the big one could be shoved into place, kicking another machine into gear behind the wall.

• *To return to the real world, double back on Rue des Teinturiers and turn left on Rue des Lices, which traces the first medieval wall. (*Lice *is the no-man's-land along a protective wall.) After a long block you'll pass a striking four-story building that was a home for the poor in the 1600s, an army barracks in the 1800s, a fine-arts school in the 1900s, and is a deluxe condominium today (much of this neighborhood is going high-class residential). Eventually you'll return to Rue de la République, Avignon's main drag.*

More Sights in and near Avignon

Most of Avignon's top sights are covered earlier by my self-guided walks. With more time, consider these options.

Fondation Angladon-Dubrujeaud

Visiting this museum is like being invited into the elegant home of a rich and passionate art collector. It mixes a small but enjoyable collection of art from Post-Impressionists to Cubists (including Paul Cézanne, Vincent van Gogh, Honoré Daumier, Edgar Degas, and Pablo Picasso), with re-created art studios and furnishings from many periods. It's a quiet place with a few superb paintings.

Cost and Hours: €6.50, Tue-Sun 13:00-18:00 except closed Tue Nov-March, closed Mon year-round, 5 Rue Laboureur, tel. 04 90 82 29 03, www.angladon.com.

Calvet Museum (Musée Calvet)

This fine-arts museum, ignored by most, impressively displays its collection, highlighting French Baroque works and several by Northern masters such as Hieronymus Bosch and Pieter Bruegel. You'll find a few diamonds upstairs: one painting each from Manet, Sisley, Géricault, and David. And on the ground floor is a room dedicated to more modern artists, with works by Soutine, Bonnard, and Vlaminck.

Cost and Hours: €6, includes audioguide, Wed-Mon 10:00-13:00 & 14:00-18:00, closed Tue, in the quieter western half of town at 65 Rue Joseph Vernet. Its antiquities collection, **Le Musée Lapidaire,** is hosted in a church a few blocks away at 27 Rue de la République—same ticket and hours (but closed on Mon), tel. 04 90 86 33 84, www.musee-calvet.org.

▲Tower of Philip the Fair (Tour Philippe-le-Bel)

Built to protect access to St. Bénezet Bridge in 1307, this hulking tower, located in nearby Villeneuve-lès-Avignon, offers a terrific view over Avignon and the Rhône basin. It's best late in the day.

Cost and Hours: €2.30; Tue-Sun May-Oct 10:00-12:30 & 14:00-18:00, Feb-April 14:00-17:00, closed Nov-Jan and Mon year-round.

Getting There: To reach the tower from Avignon, drive five minutes (cross Daladier Bridge, follow signs to *Villeneuve-lès-Avignon*), or take bus #5 (2/hour, catch bus in front of post office on Cours Président Kennedy—see map on page 604).

Sleeping in Avignon

Hotel values are better in Arles, though I've found some pretty good deals in Avignon. Avignon is crazy during its July festival, when you must book long ahead (expect inflated prices). Drivers should ask about parking deals as most hotels offer 20 percent off on pay lots.

NEAR CENTRE-VILLE STATION

These listings are a five-to-ten-minute walk from the *Centre-Ville* train station.

$$$ Hôtel Bristol*** is a big, professionally run place on the main drag, offering predictable "American" comforts, including spacious public spaces, large rooms decorated in neutral tones, duvets on the beds, an elevator, air-conditioning, and a generous buffet breakfast (standard Db-€117, bigger Db-€143, Tb/Qb-€173, breakfast-€13, parking-€13, 44 Cours Jean Jaurès, tel. 04 90 16 48 48, www.bristol-hotel-avignon.com, contact@bristol-avignon.com).

$$ Hôtel Colbert** is a solid two-star hotel and a good mid-range bet, with richly colored, comfortable rooms in many sizes. Your serious hosts—Patrice, Annie, and *le chien* Brittany—care for this restored manor house, with its warm public spaces and sweet little patio. It's a popular place, so it's best to book in advance (Sb-€74, small Db-€80, bigger Db-€90, some tight bathrooms, no triples, rooms off the patio can be musty, air-con, Wi-Fi, no elevator, closed Nov-mid-March, turn right off Cours Jean Jaurès on Rue Agricol Perdiguier to #7, tel. 04 90 86 20 20, www.lecolbert-hotel.com, contact@avignon-hotel-colbert.com).

$$ Hôtel Ibis Centre Gare*** offers no surprises—just predictable comfort at the central train and bus stations. This well-priced place offers generous public spaces, a big café, an elevator, and a bar (Db-€99, guest computer, Wi-Fi, 42 Boulevard St. Roch, tel. 04 90 85 38 38, www.ibishotel.com, h0944@accor.com).

Avignon Hotels & Restaurants

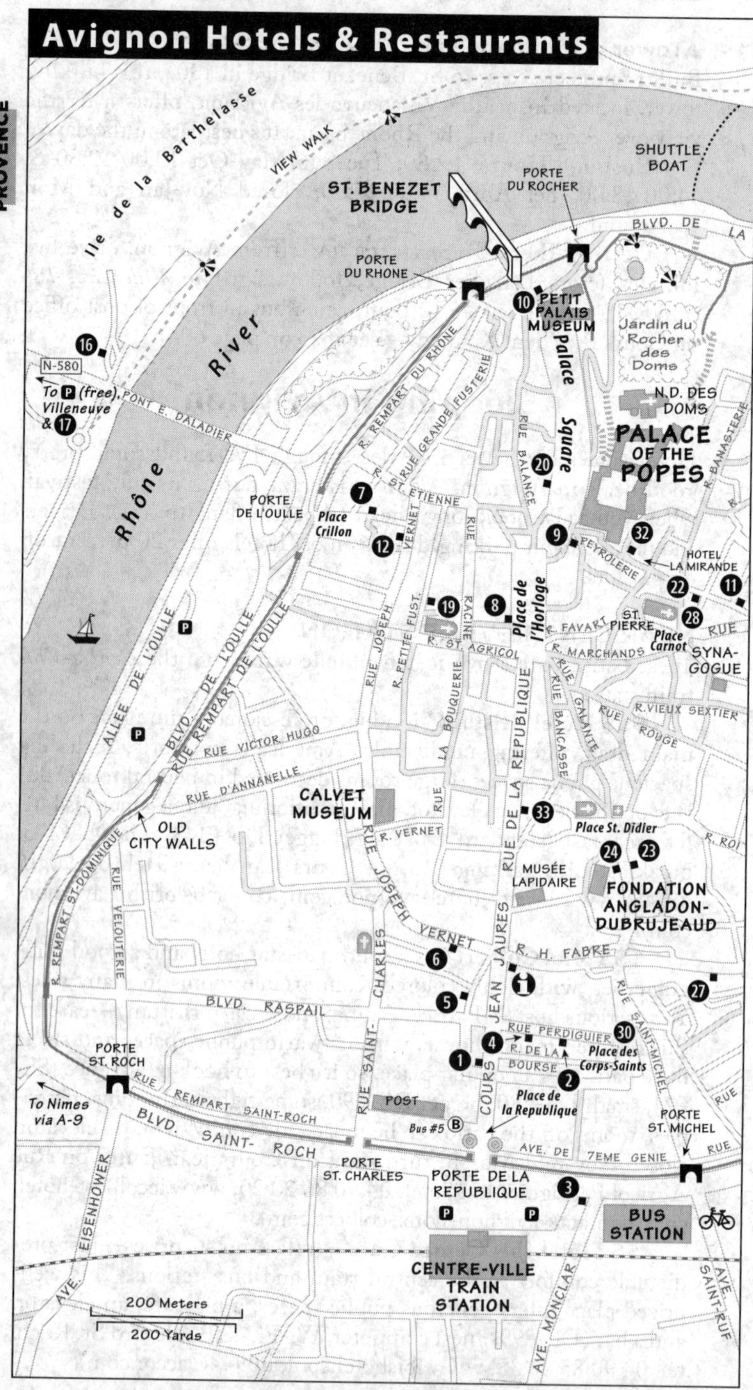

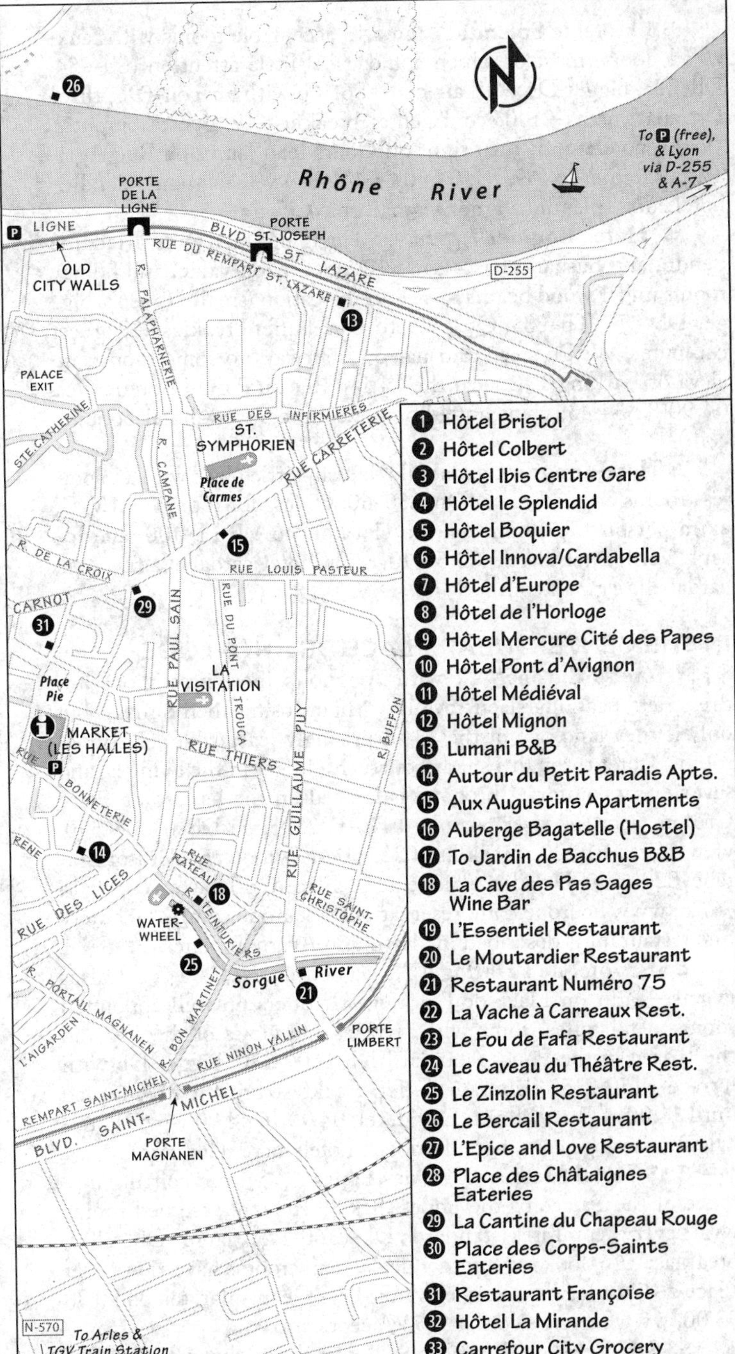
Rhône River
To P (free), & Lyon via D-255 & A-7
PORTE DE LA LIGNE
PORTE ST. JOSEPH
LIGNE
BLVD ST. LAZARE
RUE DU REMPART ST. LAZARE
D-255
OLD CITY WALLS
R. PALAPHARNERIE
PALACE EXIT
RUE DES INFIRMIERES
ST. SYMPHORIEN
STE. CATHERINE
RUE CARRETERIE
R. CAMPANE
Place de Carmes
R. DE LA CROIX
RUE LOUIS PASTEUR
CARNOT
RUE PAUL SAIN
RUE DU PONT
Place Pie
LA VISITATION
TROUCA
RUE GUILLAUME PUY
R. BUFFON
MARKET (LES HALLES)
RUE THIERS
RUE BONNETERIE
RENE
RUE RATEAU
RUE DES LICES
R. TEINTURIERS
RUE SAINT-CHRISTOPHE
WATER-WHEEL
Sorgue River
R. PORTAIL MAGNANEN
R. BON MARTINET
L'AIGARDEN
RUE NINON VALLIN
PORTE LIMBERT
REMPART SAINT-MICHEL
BLVD. SAINT-MICHEL
PORTE MAGNANEN
N-570
To Arles & TGV Train Station
PROVENCE
1 Hôtel Bristol
2 Hôtel Colbert
3 Hôtel Ibis Centre Gare
4 Hôtel le Splendid
5 Hôtel Boquier
6 Hôtel Innova/Cardabella
7 Hôtel d'Europe
8 Hôtel de l'Horloge
9 Hôtel Mercure Cité des Papes
10 Hôtel Pont d'Avignon
11 Hôtel Médiéval
12 Hôtel Mignon
13 Lumani B&B
14 Autour du Petit Paradis Apts.
15 Aux Augustins Apartments
16 Auberge Bagatelle (Hostel)
17 To Jardin de Bacchus B&B
18 La Cave des Pas Sages Wine Bar
19 L'Essentiel Restaurant
20 Le Moutardier Restaurant
21 Restaurant Numéro 75
22 La Vache à Carreaux Rest.
23 Le Fou de Fafa Restaurant
24 Le Caveau du Théâtre Rest.
25 Le Zinzolin Restaurant
26 Le Bercail Restaurant
27 L'Epice and Love Restaurant
28 Place des Châtaignes Eateries
29 La Cantine du Chapeau Rouge
30 Place des Corps-Saints Eateries
31 Restaurant Françoise
32 Hôtel La Mirande
33 Carrefour City Grocery

$$ Hôtel le Splendid** rents 16 acceptable rooms with faux-wood floors, most of which could use a little attention (Sb-€54, Db-€76, bigger Db with air-con-€86, Tb with air-con-€96, three Db apartments-€100, continental breakfast-€9, guest computer, Wi-Fi, no elevator, turn right off Cours Jean Jaurès on Rue Agricol Perdiguier to #17, tel. 04 90 86 14 46, www.avignon-splendid-hotel.com, splendidavignon@gmail.com).

$ Hôtel Boquier**, run by engaging managers Madame Sendra and husband Pascal, has 12 quiet, good-value, and homey rooms under wood beams in a central location (small Db-€63, bigger Db-€76, Tb-€85, Qb-€99, air-con, buffet breakfast-€9, guest computer, Wi-Fi, steep and narrow stairways to some rooms, no elevator, parking-€12, near the TI at 6 Rue du Portail Boquier, tel. 04 90 82 34 43, www.hotel-boquier.com, contact@hotel-boquier.com).

$ Hôtel Innova/Cardabella* is a shy little place with 11 spotless rooms at good rates (Db-€50-60, €8 less for rooms *sans* WC, extra person-€7, no air-con, no elevator, no Wi-Fi, 100 Rue Joseph Vernet, tel. 04 90 82 54 10, www.hotel-cardabella.fr, hotel.cardabella@gmail.com).

IN THE CENTER, NEAR PLACE DE L'HORLOGE

$$$ Hôtel d'Europe*****, with Avignon's most prestigious address, lets peasants sleep royally without losing their shirts—but only if they land one of the 13 surprisingly reasonable "classique" rooms. Enter through a shady courtyard, linger in the lounges, and savor every comfort. The hotel is located on the handsome Place Crillon, near the river (standard Db-€225, large Db-€380-€590, view suites-€1,100, breakfast-€22, guest computer, elevator, garage-€20, near Daladier Bridge at 12 Place Crillon, tel. 04 90 14 76 76, www.heurope.com, reservations@heurope.com). The hotel's fine restaurant is described in "Eating in Avignon," later.

$$$ Hôtel de l'Horloge****, a good choice, is as central as it gets—right on Place de l'Horloge. It offers 66 well-appointed rooms at fair rates, some with terraces and views of the city and the Palace of the Popes (standard Db-€100-120, bigger Db with terrace-€150-215, elaborate buffet breakfast/brunch-€18, served until 11:00, 1 Rue Félicien David, tel. 04 90 16 42 00, www.hotel-avignon-horloge.com, hotel.horloge@hotels-ocre-azur.com).

$$$ Hôtel Mercure Cité des Papes****, within spitting distance of the Palace of the Popes, has 89 smartly designed rooms with every comfort (standard Db-€160-175, large Db-€200, breakfast-€16, look for Internet deals, many rooms have views over Place de l'Horloge, air-con, elevator, 1 Rue Jean Vilar, tel. 04 90 80 93 00, www.mercure.com, h1952@accor.com).

$$$ Hôtel Pont d'Avignon****, just inside the walls near St.

Bénezet Bridge, is part of the same chain as Hôtel Mercure Cité des Papes, with the same prices for its 87 rooms. There's a smart atrium breakfast room and small garden terrace (direct access to a garage makes parking easier than at the other Mercure hotel, both hotels offer a 20 percent discount on parking, elevator, on Rue Ferruce, tel. 04 90 80 93 93, www.mercure.com, h0549@accor.com).

$$ Hôtel Médiéval** is burrowed deep a few blocks from the Church of St. Pierre. Built as a cardinal's home, this stone mansion has a small garden and 35 pastel, air-conditioned rooms, with helpful Régis and Mike manning the ship (Sb-€60, Db-€75-92, Tb-€120, kitchenettes available but require 3-night minimum stay, Wi-Fi, no elevator, 5 blocks east of Place de l'Horloge, behind Church of St. Pierre at 15 Rue Petite Saunerie, tel. 04 90 86 11 06, www.hotelmedieval.com, hotel.medieval@wanadoo.fr).

$$ Hôtel Mignon* is a good-enough, one-star place with fair comfort, air-conditioning, and tiny bathrooms. The rooms are nicer than the hallways suggest (Sb-€60, Db-€70-75, Tb-€87, Qb-€100, guest computer, Wi-Fi, 12 Rue Joseph Vernet, tel. 04 90 82 17 30, www.hotel-mignon.com, reservation@hotel-mignon.fr).

CHAMBRES D'HOTES AND APARTMENTS

$$$ Lumani provides the ultimate urban refuge just inside the city walls, a 15-minute walk from the Palace of the Popes. In this graceful old manor house, gentle Elisabeth and Jean welcome guests to their art-gallery-cum-bed-and-breakfast that surrounds a fountain-filled courtyard with elbow room. She paints, he designs buildings, and both care about your experience in Avignon. The five rooms are decorated with flair; no two are alike, and all overlook the shady garden (small Db-€110, big Db-€150, Db suites-€170, extra person-€30, includes organic breakfast, guest computer, Wi-Fi, music studio, parking-€10 or easy on street, 37 Rue de Rempart St. Lazare, tel. 04 90 82 94 11, www.avignon-lumani.com, lux@avignon-lumani.com).

$$$ Autour du Petit Paradis Apartments and Aux Augustins, run by Sabine and Patrick, offer 22 contemporary, well-furnished apartments spread over two locations, both conveniently located in the city center (€550-850/week, Db-€180 with 3-night minimum, 5 Rue Noël Biret and 16 Rue Carreterie, tel. 04 90 81 00 42, www.autourdupetitparadis.com, contact@autourdupetitparadis.com).

ON THE OUTSKIRTS OF TOWN

$ Auberge Bagatelle offers dirt-cheap beds in two buildings—a budget hotel and a youth hostel—and has a young and lively vibe, café, grocery store, launderette, great views of Avignon, and campers for neighbors (Ds-€48, Db-€68, Tb-€97, Qb-€100, dorm bed-€18, breakfast-€5, across Daladier Bridge on Ile de la Barthelasse, bus #5 from main post office, tel. 04 90 86 30 39, www.campingbagatelle.fr, auberge.bagatelle@wanadoo.fr).

$$$ At **Jardin de Bacchus,** a 15-minute drive northwest of Avignon by car and convenient to Pont du Gard, enthusiastic and English-speaking Christine and Erik offer three double rooms in their village home, overlooking the rocky outcroppings and famous rosé vineyards of Tavel (Db-€90-120, includes breakfast, lower prices for longer stays, fine dinner possible-€30, Wi-Fi, swimming pool, great patio, ask about bike rentals, tel. 04 66 90 28 62, www.jardindebacchus.fr, jardindebacchus@gmail.com). Check their website to learn about their small-group food and wine tours. By car, it's just off the A-9 autoroute (exit 22); by bus, it's a 30-minute ride from Avignon (www.edgard-transport.fr).

Eating in Avignon

Avignon offers a good range of dining experiences and settings from lively squares to atmospheric streets. Skip the overpriced, underwhelming restaurants on Place de l'Horloge and find a more intimate location for your dinner. Avignon is riddled with delightful squares and backstreets with tables ready to seat you.

Wherever you dine, start or end your evening on atmospheric Rue des Teinturiers at **La Cave des Pas Sages** for a cheap glass of regional wine. Choose from the blackboard by the bar that lists all the open bottles, then join the gang outside by the canal. In the evening, this place is a hit with the young local crowd for its wine and weekend concerts (Mon-Sat 10:00-1:00 in the morning, closed Sun, no food in evening, across from waterwheel at 41 Rue des Teinturiers).

WORTHWHILE FOR A SPLURGE

Book a few days ahead for these places:

L'Essentiel is where in-the-know locals go for a fine meal at reasonable prices. The setting is classy-contemporary, the wine list is extensive, the cuisine is classic French, and gentle owner Dominique makes timid diners feel at ease (inside and outdoor seating, €31-45 *menus,* closed Sun-Mon, 2 Rue Petite Fusterie, tel. 04 90 85 87 12, www.restaurantlessentiel.com).

Le Moutardier serves fine meals with a mesmerizing, full-monty view of the floodlit Palace of the Popes. Book ahead for the terrace tables, but skip it if you can't dine outside (€35-49 *menus,* daily, 15 Place du Palais, tel. 04 90 85 34 76).

Hôtel d'Europe's restaurant, **La Vieille Fontaine,** earned a Michelin star and serves a surprisingly reasonable menu in its lovely dining room and courtyard terrace (€68 *menu,* inexpensive quality champagne, €38 lunch *menu,* see "Sleeping in Avignon," earlier, for details).

Restaurant Numéro 75 is worth the walk. It fills the Pernod mansion (of *pastis* liquor fame) and a large, romantic courtyard with outdoor tables. The selection is limited to Mediterranean cuisine, but everything's *très* tasty (€32 lunch *menu,* dinner *menus:* €29 two-course and €36 three-course, Mon-Sat 12:00-14:00 & 19:45-22:00, closed Sun, 75 Rue Guillaume Puy, tel. 04 90 27 16 00, www.numero75.com).

GOOD FOR MODERATE BUDGETS

La Vache à Carreaux venerates cheese and wine, while offering a full range of cuisine. It's a lively place to spend an evening, with colorful decor and an extensive and reasonable wine list. This place is a hit with locals, who gather around outside sipping €4 glasses of good wine, reluctant to leave. Try the *poulet au Comté* (chicken with Comté cheese) or a *tartiflette* (tasty potatoes with bacon and melted cheese; best in winter), and say *bonsoir* to welcoming owner Ludovic (inside dining only, €10 starters, €12-16 *plats,* open daily, just off atmospheric Place des Châtaignes at 14 Rue de la Peyrolerie, tel. 04 90 80 09 05).

Le Fou de Fafa's friendly British owners are making a splash with locals, serving tasty, fresh, creative cuisine at good prices. Delightful Antonia runs the entire room alone while her husband cooks (inside dining only, book ahead or arrive early, open at 18:30, closed Mon-Tue, €24-30 *menus,* 17 Rue des Trois Faucons, tel. 04 32 76 35 13).

Le Caveau du Théâtre is a convivial place where Richard invites diners to have a glass of wine or dinner at a sidewalk table, or inside in one of four carefree rooms (€17 *plats,* €22-26 *menus,* fun ambience for free, closed for lunch Sat and all day Sun, 16 Rue des Trois Faucons, tel. 04 90 82 60 91).

Rue des Teinturiers: This street has a fun concentration of midrange eateries popular with the locals, and justifies the walk. It's a trendy, youthful area, spiffed up with a canalside ambience and little hint of tourism. **Le Zinzolin,** enjoyable and artsy, serves international cuisine to a younger crowd at fair prices with good vegetarian options (meal-size salads-€14, *plats*-€15, desserts-€5, closed Mon evening and Sun, 22 Rue des Teinturiers, tel. 04 90 82 41 55). (Note that Restaurant Numéro 75 and La Cave des Pas Sages, both listed earlier, are on this street.)

On the Rhône River: **Le Bercail** offers a fun opportunity to get out of town (barely) and take in *le fresh air* with a terrific riverfront view of Avignon, all while enjoying big portions of Provençal cooking (*menus* from €28, daily April-Oct, serves late, reservation recommended, tel. 04 90 82 20 22). Take the free shuttle boat (located near St. Bénezet Bridge) to the Ile de la Barthelasse, turn right, and walk five minutes. As the boat usually stops running at about 18:00 (except in July-Aug, when it runs until 21:00), you can either taxi home or walk 25 minutes along the pleasant riverside path and over Daladier Bridge.

GOOD BUDGET PLACES

At **L'Epice and Love** (the name is a fun French-English play on words, pronounced "lay peace and love"), English-speaking owner Marie creates a playful atmosphere in her inviting restaurant, where the few colorfully decorated tables (inside only) greet the hungry traveler. The selection changes weekly, and Marie cooks it all: tasty meat, fish, and vegetarian dishes, some with a North African touch, all served at good prices (€17-20 *menus,* closed Sun, 30 Rue des Lices, tel. 04 90 82 45 96).

Place des Châtaignes: This square offers cheap meals and a fun commotion of tables. The intimate **Chez Lulu** is the best of the lot, with a handful of tables inside and out and a limited menu that assures quality cuisine. Their gourmet burger is a treat (€16 *plats,* closed Tue-Wed, 6 Place des Châtaignes, tel. 04 90 85 69 44). The **Crêperie du Cloître** makes cheap, mediocre dinner crêpes and salads, but has the best seating on the square (daily).

At **La Cantine du Chapeau Rouge,** a small and unpretentious place, chef Julien surveys the dining room from his colorful open kitchen. He cooks with fresh, organic ingredients and is famous for his fish dishes (€11-15.50 *menus,* Tue-Sat lunch, Thu-Sat dinner, cash only, reservations recommended, 36 Rue du Chapeau Rouge, tel. 06 95 50 82 73).

Place des Corps-Saints: This untouristy yet welcoming square is my favorite place for simple outdoor dining in Avignon. You'll find several reasonable eateries with tables sprawling under big plane trees. **Bistrot à Tartines** does its namesake justice, serving big slices of toast smothered with a variety of toppings, and has the coziest interior and best desserts on the square (€7 *tartines* and salads, daily, tel. 04 90 85 58 70). **Zeste** is a friendly, modern deli offering fresh soups, pasta salads, wraps, smoothies, and more for lunch. Get it to go, or eat inside or on the scenic square—all at unbeatable prices (closed Sun, tel. 09 51 49 05 62). **Boulangerie Olivero** makes a fine setting for a budget breakfast, lunch, or a light (and early) dinner. Monsieur Olivero makes a mean baguette and offers anyone showing this book a free croissant with any purchase. Enjoy your coffee, croissant, sandwich, or quiche at the outside tables (on the square near Rue des Lices, daily until 20:00).

Place Pie: On this big square filled with cafés, Avignon's youth make their home. **Restaurant Françoise** is a pleasant café and tea salon, where fresh-baked tarts—savory and sweet—and a variety of salads and soups make a healthful meal, and vegetarian options are plentiful (€7-10 dishes, Mon-Sat 8:00-19:00, closed Sun, Wi-Fi, a block off Place Pie at 6 Rue Général Leclerc, tel. 04 32 76 24 77).

Avignon Connections

BY TRAIN

Remember, there are two train stations in Avignon: the suburban TGV Station and the *Centre-Ville* Station in the city center (€1.60 shuttle trains connect the stations, buy ticket from machine on platforms or at a counter, 2/hour, 5 minutes). TGV trains usually serve the TGV Station only, though a few depart from *Centre-Ville* station (check your ticket).

From Avignon's *Centre-Ville* Station to: Arles (roughly hourly, 20 minutes, less frequent in the afternoon), **Orange** (15/day, 20 minutes), **Nîmes** (12/day, 30 minutes), **Isle-sur-la-Sorgue** (10/day on weekdays, 5/day on weekends, 30 minutes), **Lyon** (10/day, 2 hours, also from TGV Station in 70 min—see below), **Carcassonne** (8/day, 7 with transfer in Narbonne or Nîmes, 3 hours), **Barcelona** (2/day, 5.75 hours with changes in Nîmes and Figueres-Vilafant; more frequent but slower with a change in Cerbère).

From Avignon's TGV Station to: Nice (10/day, most by TGV, 4 hours, many require transfer in Marseille), **Marseille** (10/day, 35 minutes), **Cassis** (7/day, with transfer in Marseille, 1.5 hours), **Aix-en-Provence TGV** (12/day, 25 minutes), **Lyon** (12/day, 70 min, also from *Centre-Ville* Station—see above), **Paris**' Gare de Lyon (10/day direct, 2.5 hours; more connections with transfer, 3-4 hours), **Paris**' Charles de Gaulle airport (7/day, 3.25 hours).

BY BUS

The bus station *(gare routière)* is just past and below Hôtel Ibis, to the right as you exit the train station. Nearly all buses leave from this station (a few leave from the ring road outside the station—ask, buy tickets on bus, small bills only, explained on page 603).

From Avignon to Pont du Gard: Buses go to this famous Roman aqueduct (3/day, 50 minutes, departs from bus station, ask about round-trip ticket that includes Pont du Gard entry, see page 626).

By Bus to Other Regional Destinations: Arles (8/day, 1 hour, leaves from TGV Station); **Aix-en-Provence** (6/day Mon-Sat, 2/day Sun, 75 minutes, faster and easier than train), **Uzès** (3-5/day, 60-80 minutes, stops at Pont du Gard); **St-Rémy-de-Provence** (Cartreize #57 bus, 6/day, 50 minutes, stall #2, handy way to visit its Wed market); **Orange** (Mon-Sat hourly, 5/day Sun, 1 hour—take the train instead); **Isle-sur-la-Sorgue** (6-8/day Mon-Sat, 3-4/day Sun, 45 minutes, stall #13, some leave from ring road). For the **Côtes du Rhône** area, the bus runs to **Vaison la Romaine, Nyons, Sablet,** and **Séguret** (5/day during the school year—called *période scolaire,* 3/day otherwise, and 1/day from TGV Station; 1.5 hours, all buses pass through Orange—faster to take train to Orange, and transfer to bus there). For the **Luberon** area—including **Lourmarin, Roussillon,** and **Gordes**—take the bus to Cavaillon, then take bus #8 toward Pertuis for Lourmarin (3/day) or bus #15 for Gordes/Roussillon (only 1/day); you must reserve a day ahead for buses from Cavaillon (tel. 04 90 74 20 21).

Pont du Gard

Throughout the ancient world, aqueducts were like flags of stone that heralded the greatness of Rome. A visit to this sight still works to proclaim the wonders of that age. This perfectly preserved Roman aqueduct was built in about 19 B.C. as the critical link of a 30-mile canal that, by dropping one inch for every 350 feet, supplied nine million gallons of water per day (about 100 gallons per second) to Nîmes—one of ancient Europe's largest cities. Though most of the aqueduct is on or below the ground, at Pont du Gard it spans a canyon on a massive bridge—one of the most remarkable surviving Roman ruins anywhere. Wear sturdy shoes if you want to climb around the aqueduct (footing is tricky), and bring swimwear and flip-flops if you plan to backstroke with views of the monument.

GETTING TO PONT DU GARD

The famous aqueduct is between Remoulins and Vers-Pont du Gard on D-981, and 13 miles from Avignon.

By Car: Pont du Gard is a 25-minute drive due west of Avignon (follow N-100 from Avignon, tracking signs to *Nîmes* and *Remoulins,* then *Pont du Gard* and *Rive Gauche*), and 45 minutes northwest of Arles (via Tarascon on D-6113). If going to Arles from Pont du Gard, follow signs to *Nîmes* (not *Avignon*), then D-6113, or A-54 (autoroute) to Arles.

By Bus: Buses run to Pont du Gard (on the Rive Gauche side) from Avignon (3/day, 50 minutes), Nîmes, and Uzès. Consider this plan: Take a morning bus from Avignon's bus station (8:45 or 11:40), then hop on the early-afternoon (13:17) or evening (17:28) bus back to Avignon. Confirm all of these times at a TI or at www.edgard-transport.fr (line A15). The 8:45 trip out and 13:17 trip

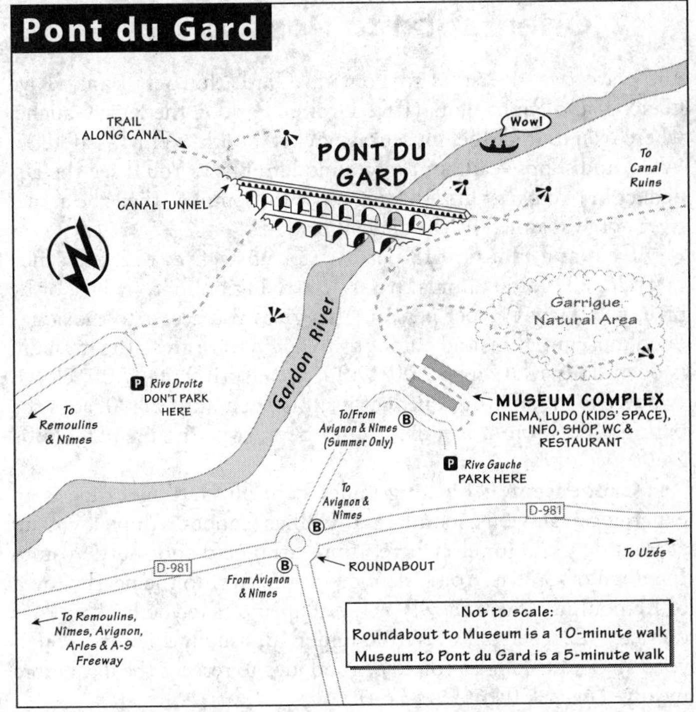

back works best for most. Allow about four or five hours for visiting Pont du Gard, including transportation time from Avignon.

Buses stop at the traffic roundabout 400 yards from the museum (stop name: Rond Point Pont du Gard; see Pont du Gard map). In July and August, however, buses usually drive into the Pont du Gard site and stop at the parking lot's ticket booth. Confirm where the bus stops at the parking booth inside the Pont du Gard site.

At the roundabout, the stop for buses coming from Avignon and Nîmes (and going to Uzès) is on the side opposite Pont du Gard; the stop for buses to Nîmes and to Avignon is on the same side as Pont du Gard (a block to your left as you exit Pont du Gard onto the main road). Make sure you're waiting for the bus on the correct side of the traffic circle (stops have schedules posted), and wave your hand to signal the bus to stop for you (otherwise, it'll chug on by). Buy your ticket when you get on and verify your destination with the driver.

By Taxi: From Avignon, it's about €60 for a taxi to Pont du Gard (around €80 after 19:00 and on Sun, tel. 04 90 82 20 20). If you're staying in Avignon and only want to see Pont du Gard, consider splurging on a taxi to the aqueduct in the morning, then take the early-afternoon bus back.

Orientation to Pont du Gard

There are two riversides to Pont du Gard: the Left Bank (Rive Gauche) and Right Bank (Rive Droite). Park on the Rive Gauche, where you'll find the museums, ticket booth, ATM, cafeteria, WCs, and shops—all built into a modern plaza. You'll see the aqueduct in two parts: first the fine museum complex, then the actual river gorge spanned by the ancient bridge.

Cost and Hours: €18 per car (for up to five; €12 for a motorcycle, €23 for an annual pass). If arriving on foot, by bus, or by bike, you'll pay €10 per person. This gives you access to the aqueduct, museum, film, and outdoor *garrigue* nature area. The museum is open daily May-Sept 9:00-19:00, Oct-April 9:00-17:00, closed two weeks in Jan. The aqueduct itself is open until 24:00, as is the parking lot. From mid-June to mid-Sept, it is illuminated 22:00-24:00.

Canoe Rental: Floating under Pont du Gard by canoe is an experience you won't soon forget. Collias Canoes will pick you up at Pont du Gard (or elsewhere, if pre-arranged) and shuttle you to the town of Collias. You'll float down the river to the nearby town of Remoulins, where they'll pick you up and take you back to Pont du Gard (€21/person, €12/child under 12, usually 2 hours, though you can take as long as you like, good idea to reserve the day before in July-Aug, tel. 04 66 22 85 54).

Plan Ahead for Swimming and Hiking: Pont du Gard is perhaps best enjoyed on your back and in the water—bring along a swimsuit and flip-flops for the rocks. The best Pont du Gard viewpoints are up steep hills with uneven footing—bring good shoes.

Sights at Pont du Gard

▲Museum

In this state-of-the-art museum (well-presented in English), you'll enter to the sound of water and understand the critical role fresh water played in the Roman "art of living." You'll see copies of lead pipes, faucets, and siphons; walk through a mock rock quarry; and learn how they moved those huge rocks into place and how those massive arches were made. A wooden model shows how Roman engineers determined the proper slope. While actual artifacts from the aqueduct are few, the exhibit shows the immensity of the undertaking as well as the payoff. Imagine the excitement as this extravagant supply of water finally tumbled into Nîmes. A relaxing highlight is the scenic video of a helicopter ride along the entire 30-mile course of the structure, from its start at Uzès all the way to the Castellum in Nîmes.

Other Activities

Several additional attractions are designed to give the sight more meaning—and they do (but for most visitors, the museum is sufficient). A corny, romancing-the-aqueduct 25-minute film plays in the same building as the museum and offers good information in a flirtatious French-Mediterranean style...and a cool, entertaining, and cushy break. The nearby kids' museum, called *Ludo,* offers a scratch-and-sniff teaching experience (in English) of various aspects of Roman life and the importance of water. The extensive outdoor *garrigue* natural area, closer to the aqueduct, features historic crops and landscapes of the Mediterranean.

▲▲▲Viewing the Aqueduct

A park-like path leads to the aqueduct. Until a few years ago, this was an actual road—adjacent to the aqueduct—that had spanned the river since 1743. Before you cross the bridge, walk to this riverside viewpoint: Pass under the bridge and aqueduct and hike about 300 feet along the riverbank to the concrete steps leading down to a grand view of the world's second-highest standing Roman structure. (Rome's Colosseum is only 6 feet taller.)

This was the biggest bridge in the whole 30-mile-long aqueduct. It seems exceptional because it is: The arches are twice the width of standard aqueducts, and the main arch is the largest the Romans ever built—80 feet (so it wouldn't get its feet wet). The bridge is about 160 feet high and was originally about 1,200 feet long. Today, 12 arches are missing, reducing the length to 900 feet.

Though the distance from the source (in Uzès, on the museum side of the site) to Nîmes was only 12 miles as the eagle flew, engineers chose the most economical route, winding and zigzagging 30 miles. The water made the trip in 24 hours with a drop of only 40 feet. Ninety percent of the aqueduct is on or under the ground, but a few river canyons like this required bridges. A stone lid hides a four-foot-wide, six-foot-tall chamber lined with waterproof mortar that carried the stream for more than 400 years. For 150 years, this system provided Nîmes with good drinking water. Expert as the Romans were, they miscalculated the backup caused by a downstream corner, and had to add the thin extra layer you can see just under the lid to make the channel deeper.

The bridge and the river below provide great fun for holiday-goers. While parents suntan on rocks, kids splash into the gorge from under the aqueduct. Some daredevils actually jump from the aqueduct's lower bridge—not knowing that crazy winds scrambled by the structure cause painful belly flops (and sometimes even accidental deaths). For the most refreshing view, float flat on your back underneath the structure.

The appearance of the entire gorge changed in 2002, when a huge flood flushed lots of greenery downstream. Those floodwaters put Roman provisions to the test. Notice the triangular-shaped buttresses at the lower level—designed to split and divert the force of any flood *around* the feet of the arches rather than *into* them. The 2002 floodwaters reached the top of those buttresses. Anxious park rangers winced at the sounds of trees crashing onto the ancient stones...but the arches stood strong.

The stones that jut out—giving the aqueduct a rough, unfinished appearance—supported the original scaffolding. The protuberances were left, rather than cut off, in anticipation of future repair needs. The lips under the arches supported wooden templates that allowed the stones in the round arches to rest on something until the all-important keystone was dropped into place. Each stone weighs four to six tons. The structure stands with no mortar (except at the very top, where the water flowed)—taking full advantage of the innovative Roman arch, made strong by gravity.

Hike over the bridge for a closer look and the best views. Steps lead up a high trail (marked *view point/panorama*) to a superb vista (go right at the top; best views are soon after the trail starts descending). You'll also see where the aqueduct meets a rock tunnel built in the 1800s to try to reuse the aqueduct to provide water to Nîmes (it failed). Notice how the aqueduct curves left before the tunnel.

Back on the museum side, steps lead up to the Rive Gauche side of the aqueduct, where you can follow the canal path along a trail (marked with red-and-white horizontal lines) to find some remains of the Roman canal. You'll soon reach another *panorama* with more great views of the aqueduct. Hikers can continue along the path, following the red-and-white markings that lead through a forest, after which you'll come across more remains of the canal (much of which are covered by vegetation). There's not much left to see because of medieval cannibalization—frugal builders couldn't resist the precut stones as they constructed area churches (stones along the canal were smaller and easier to retrieve than the massive blocks high on the aqueduct). The path continues for about 15 miles, but there's little reason to go farther. However, there is talk of opening the ancient quarry...someday.

Les Baux

The hilltop town of Les Baux crowns the rugged Alpilles (ahl-pee) mountains, evoking a tumultuous medieval history. Here, you can imagine the struggles of a strong community that lived a rough-and-tumble life—thankful more for their top-notch fortifications than for their dramatic views. It's mobbed with tourists most of the day, but Les Baux rewards those who arrive by 9:00 or after 17:30. (Although the hilltop citadel's entry closes at the end of the day, once you're inside, you're welcome to live out your medieval fantasies all night long, even with a picnic.) Sunsets are dramatic, the castle is brilliantly illuminated after dark, and nights in Les Baux are pin-drop peaceful.

GETTING TO LES BAUX

By Car: Les Baux is a 20-minute drive from Arles: Follow signs for *Avignon,* then *Les Baux.*

By Bus: From Arles, **Cartreize** bus #57 runs to Les Baux (daily July-Aug, in June and Sept Sat-Sun only, 6/day, 35 minutes, via Abbey of Montmajour, Fontvieille, and Le Paradou, destination: St-Rémy, see timetables at www.lepilote.com).

The appealing town of St-Rémy, about seven miles north of Les Baux, is a workable transit point for those home-basing in Avignon: Ride the Cartreize #57 bus from Avignon to St-Rémy (6/day, 45 minutes); on weekends in June or September or daily July-August, you can continue to Les Baux on the same bus (see above website for timetables). Or travel from St-Rémy to Les Baux by taxi (see next).

By Taxi: If buses aren't running to Les Baux, you can taxi there from St-Rémy, then take another taxi to return to St-Rémy or to your home base. Figure €40 for a taxi one-way from Arles to Les Baux (€50 after 19:00), and allow €18 one-way from St-Rémy (mobile 06 80 27 60 92).

By Minivan Tour: A good option for many is a minivan tour, which can be both efficient and economical (easiest from Avignon; see "Tours of Provence," page 565).

Orientation to Les Baux

Les Baux is actually two visits in one: castle ruins perched on an almost lunar landscape, and a medieval town below. Savor the castle, then tour—or blitz—the lower streets on your way out. While the town, which lives entirely off tourism, is packed with shops, cafés, and tourist knickknacks, the castle above stays manageable because crowds are dispersed over a big area. The lower town's polished-stone gauntlet of boutiques is a Provençal dream come true for shoppers.

TOURIST INFORMATION

The TI is immediately on the left as you enter the village (April-Oct Mon-Fri 9:00-18:00, Sat-Sun 10:00-17:30; off-season Mon-Sat 9:30-17:00, closed Sun). Consider purchasing their "Passes," which can save you money if you visit all the sights. You'll also see deals combining Les Baux with other sights in the region (such as the theater in Orange). The TI has free Wi-Fi and can call a cab for you.

ARRIVAL IN LES BAUX

Drivers pay €5 to park near the village (behind the barrier), or €4 to park several blocks below (you'll pass the parking lot on your way in; the ticket is good for the day). Pay at the machine just below the town entry (next to the pay phone, WC, and bakery) before you return to your car—you'll need the validated ticket to exit the lot. You can park for free at the Carrières de Lumières (described later) and walk along the road to Les Baux (narrow road with blind curves, so be careful).

Walk up the cobbled street into town, where you're greeted first by the TI. From here the main drag leads directly to the castle—just keep going uphill (a 10-minute walk).

Sights in Les Baux

▲▲▲THE CASTLE RUINS (THE "DEAD CITY")

The sun-bleached ruins of the "dead city" of Les Baux are carved into, out of, and on top of a rock 650 feet above the valley floor. Many of the ancient walls of this striking castle still stand as a testament to the proud past of this once-feisty village.

Cost and Hours: €8, €10 if there's "entertainment," mentioned below (ask about family rates), €15 combo-ticket with Carrières de Lumières (described later), includes excellent audioguide available up to one hour before closing, daily Easter-June and Sept 9:00-19:15, July-Aug 9:00-20:15, March and Oct 9:30-18:30,

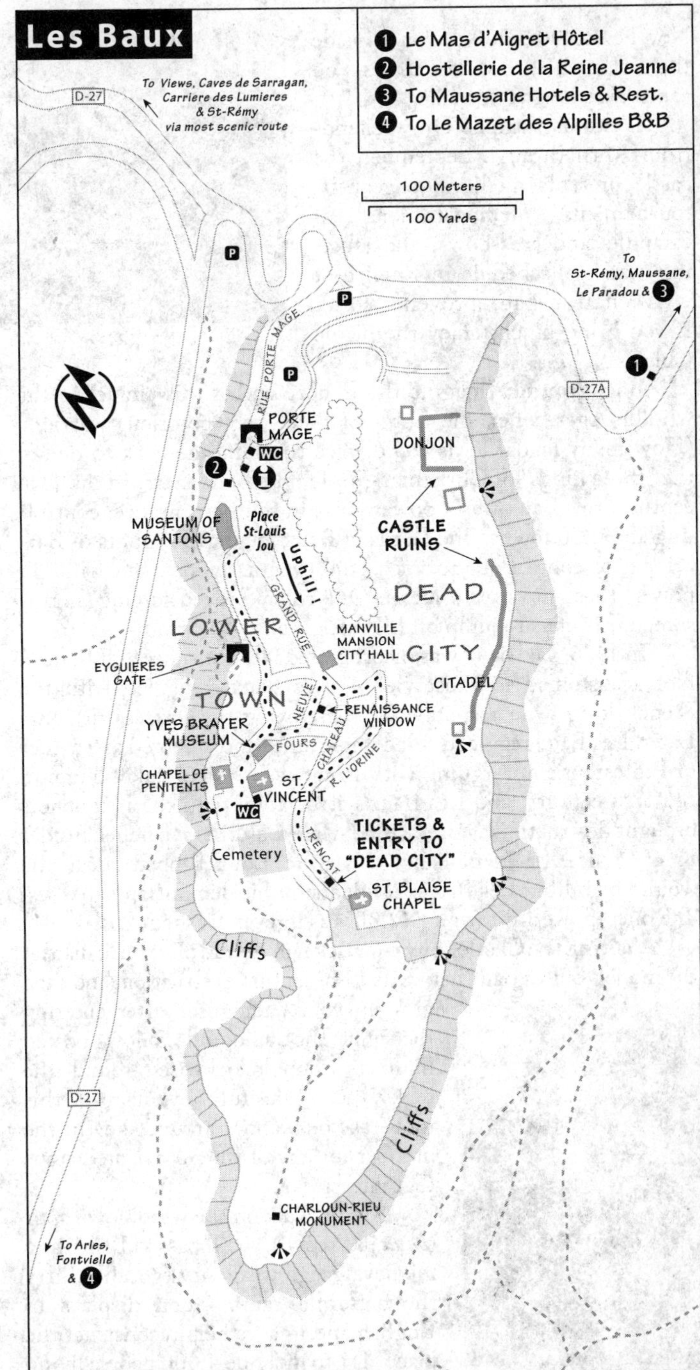
Les Baux
1 Le Mas d'Aigret Hôtel
2 Hostellerie de la Reine Jeanne
3 To Maussane Hotels & Rest.
4 To Le Mazet des Alpilles B&B
100 Meters
100 Yards
D-27
To Views, Caves de Sarragan, Carriere des Lumieres & St-Rémy via most scenic route
To St-Rémy, Maussane, Le Paradou & 3
D-27A
RUE PORTE MAGE
PORTE MAGE
WC
DONJON
CASTLE RUINS
MUSEUM OF SANTONS
Place St-Louis - Jou
Uphill !
GRAND RUE
DEAD CITY
LOWER TOWN
EYGUIERES GATE
MANVILLE MANSION CITY HALL
CITADEL
NEUVE
RENAISSANCE WINDOW
YVES BRAYER MUSEUM
FOURS
CHATEAU
R. L'ORINE
CHAPEL OF PENITENTS
ST. VINCENT
TICKETS & ENTRY TO "DEAD CITY"
Cemetery
TRENCAT
ST. BLAISE CHAPEL
Cliffs
Cliffs
CHARLOUN-RIEU MONUMENT
To Arles, Fontvielle & 4

Nov-Feb 10:00-17:00. If you're inside the castle when the entry closes, you can stay as long as you like.

Demonstrations: On weekends from April through September, the castle presents medieval pageantry, tournaments, demonstrations of catapults and crossbows, and jousting matches (schedule in English at www.chateau-baux-provence.com). If you bring lunch, enjoy the picnic tables.

Background: Imagine the importance of this citadel in the Middle Ages, when the Lords of Baux were notorious warriors. (How many feudal lords could trace their lineage back to one of the "three kings" of Christmas-carol fame, Balthazar?) In the 11th century, Les Baux was a powerhouse in southern France, controlling about 80 towns. The Lords of Baux fought the counts of Barcelona for control of Provence...and eventually lost. But while in power, these guys were mean. One ruler enjoyed forcing unransomed prisoners to jump off his castle walls.

In 1426, Les Baux was incorporated into Provence and France. Not accustomed to subservience, Les Baux struggled with the French king, who responded by destroying the fortress in 1483. Later, Les Baux regained some importance and emerged as a center of Protestantism. Arguing with Rome was a high-stakes game in the 17th century, and Les Baux's association with the Huguenots brought destruction again in 1632 when Cardinal Richelieu (under King Louis XIII) demolished the castle. Louis rubbed salt in the wound by billing Les Baux's residents for his demolition expenses. The once-powerful town of 4,000 was forever crushed.

Visiting the Castle: Buy your ticket in the old olive mill, inspect the models of Les Baux before its 17th-century destruction, and then pick up your audioguide after entering the sight. The audioguide follows posted numbers counterclockwise around the rocky spur. Take full advantage of this tool—as you wander around, key in the number for any of the 30 narrated stops that interest you.

As you walk on the windblown spur (*baux* in French), you'll pass kid-thrilling medieval siege weaponry (go ahead, try the battering ram). Good displays in English and images help reconstruct the place. Try to imagine 4,000 people living up here. Notice the water-catchment system (a slanted field that caught rainwater and drained it into cisterns—necessary during a siege) and find the reservoir cut into the rock below the castle's highest point. Look for post holes throughout the stone walls that reveal where beams once supported floors.

For the most sensational views, climb to the blustery top of the citadel. Hang on. The mistral wind just might blow you away.

The St. Blaise chapel across from the entry/exit runs videos with Provençal themes (plays continuously; just images and music, no words).

Picnicking: While there is no food or drink sold inside the castle grounds, you are welcome to bring your own and use one of the several picnic tables (best view table is at the edge near the siege weaponry). Sunset dinner picnics are memorable.

▲LOWER TOWN

After your castle visit, you can shop and eat your way back through the new town. Or you can escape some of the crowds by following my short walking tour, below, which covers these minor but worthwhile sights as you descend (all stay open at lunch except the Yves Brayer Museum).

• *Take the first right, on quieter Rue de Lorme, below the castle exit, then get back to the main street, Grand Rue/Château, and find flags on the...*

Manville Mansion City Hall

The 15th-century city hall occasionally flies the red-and-white flag of Monaco amid several others, a reminder that the Grimaldi family (which has long ruled the tiny principality of Monaco) owned Les Baux until the French Revolution (1789). In fact, in 1982, Princess Grace Kelly and her royal husband, Prince Rainier Grimaldi, came to Les Baux to receive the key to the city.

Exit left out of the city hall and walk uphill to the empty 1571 **Renaissance window frame,** marking the site of a future Calvinist museum. This beautiful stone frame stands as a reminder of this town's Protestant history. This was probably a place of Huguenot worship—the words carved into the lintel, *Post tenebras lux,* were a popular Calvinist slogan: "After the shadow comes the light."

• *Continue walking uphill, and turn right on Rue des Fours to find the...*

Yves Brayer Museum (Musée Yves Brayer)

This enjoyable museum lets you peruse three floors of paintings (Van Gogh-like Expressionism, without the tumult) by Yves Brayer (1907-1990), who spent his final years here in Les Baux. Like Van Gogh, Brayer was inspired by all that surrounded him, and by his travels through Morocco, Spain, and the rest of the Mediterranean world. Pick up the descriptive English sheet at the entry.

Cost and Hours: €5, daily April-Sept 10:00-12:30 & 14:00-

18:30, Oct-Dec and March Wed-Mon 11:00-12:30 & 14:00-17:00, closed Jan-Feb, tel. 04 90 54 36 99, www.yvesbrayer.com.

• *Next door is...*

St. Vincent Church

This 12th-century Romanesque church was built short and wide to fit the terrain. The center chapel on the right (partially carved out of the rock) houses the town's traditional Provençal processional chariot. Each Christmas Eve, a ram pulled this cart—holding a lamb, symbolizing Jesus, and surrounded by candles—through town to the church.

• *As you leave the church, WCs are to the left and up the stairs. Directly in front of the church is a vast view, making clear the strategic value of this rocky bluff's natural fortifications. A few steps away is the...*

Chapel of Penitents

Inside, notice the nativity scene painted by Yves Brayer, illustrating the local legend that says Jesus was born in Les Baux. On the opposite wall, find his version of a starry night. Leaving the chapel, turn left.

• *As you leave the church, wash your shirt in the old town "laundry"—with a pig-snout faucet and 14th-century stone washing surface designed for short women.*

Continue down steep Rue de la Calade, passing cafés with wonderful views, the town's fortified wall, and one of its two gates. Before long, you'll run into the...

Museum of Santons

This free and worthwhile "museum" displays a collection of *santons* ("little saints"), popular folk figurines that decorate local Christmas mangers. Notice how the Nativity scene "proves" once again that Jesus was born in Les Baux. These painted clay dolls show off local dress and traditions (with good English descriptions). Find the old couple leaning heroically into the mistral.

NEAR LES BAUX

A half-mile beyond Les Baux, D-27 (toward Maillane) leads to dramatic views of the hill town. There are pullouts with great vistas, and cavernous caves in former limestone quarries dating back to the Middle Ages. (The limestone is easy to cut, but gets hard and nicely polished when exposed to the weather.) Speaking of quarries, in 1821, the rocks and soil of this area were found to contain an important mineral for making aluminum. It was named after the town: bauxite.

You'll enjoy superb views of Les Baux from the Caves de Sarragan parking lot, once occupied by the Sarragan Winery. For still better views, continue driving up. After several switchbacks you'll reach the top—turn right on the paved lane where you see a red kilometer marker and find the views. You'll see walking trails nearby (ask at TIs for info on hikes in the Alpilles; Les Baux to St-Rémy is a 2.5-hour hike).

▲▲Carrières de Lumières

This nearby cave offers a mesmerizing sound-and-slide show, with 48 projectors flashing countless images on expansive quarry walls, accompanied by music. The show lasts 40 minutes (dress warmly, as the cave is cool), and there's a different program every year (the 2015 show is titled "Leonardo da Vinci, Michelangelo, Raphael: The Giants of the Renaissance"). You can also visit part of the quarries.

Cost and Hours: €10, €15 combo-ticket with Les Baux castle, daily April-Sept 9:30-19:30, March and Oct-Dec 10:00-18:00, closed Jan-Feb, tel. 04 90 54 47 37, www.carrieres-lumieres.com.

Sleeping in and near Les Baux

IN LES BAUX

$$$ Le Mas d'Aigret***, a 10-minute walk east of the town on the road to St-Rémy (D-27), is a lovely refuge that crouches under Les Baux. Lie on your back and stare up at the castle walls rising beyond the heated swimming pool, or enjoy valley views from the groomed terraces. The rooms are simple and slightly worn, but you can't beat the location (viewless Db-€100-125, larger Db with balcony and view-€125-160, Tb/Qb-€190-250, two cool troglodyte rooms-€215, breakfast-€14, convenient half-pension dinner and breakfast option-€46/person, air-con, Wi-Fi, rooms have some daytime road noise, tel. 04 90 54 20 00, www.masdaigret.com, contact@masdaigret.com, Dutch Marieke and French Eric are wonderful hosts).

$$ Hostellerie de la Reine Jeanne**, warmly run by Gaelle (speaks English) and Marc (speaks French), offers a handful of rooms above a busy, handy restaurant. The good-value rooms are tastefully decorated (standard Db-€56, Db with view deck-€70, Tb-€80, cavernous family suite-€100, air-con in some rooms, for view deck ask for *chambre avec terrasse,* good *plats* from €14, 150 feet to your right after entry to the village of Les Baux, tel. 04 90 54 32 06, www.la-reinejeanne.com, marc.braglia@wanadoo.fr).

IN MAUSSANE

The appealing village of Maussane lies a few minutes' drive south of Les Baux. It has some hotels, a handful of restaurants, and an atmospheric square lined with cafés. There's also bike rental and a small TI (tel. 04 90 54 33 60, www.maussane.com). These two accommodations are well worth considering.

$$ Hôtel les Magnanarelles,** in the center of Maussane, gives solid two-star value in its 18 tastefully designed rooms above a handsome restaurant. Enjoy the generously sized pool (Db-€78-82, extra person-€17, breakfast-€7, ask for a room off the street, no air-con, 104 Avenue de la Vallée des Baux, tel. 04 90 54 30 25, www.hotel-magnanarelles.com, hotel.magnanarelles@wanadoo.fr).

$$ Le Mas de l'Esparou *chambres d'hôte* is welcoming and kid-friendly, with four simple-yet-spacious rooms, a big swimming pool, table tennis, swings, and distant views of Les Baux. Jacqueline loves her job, and her lack of English only makes her more animated. She dislikes email though, so you'll have to call (Db-€78, Tb/Qb-€124-149, includes breakfast, cash only, no air-con, between Les Baux and Maussane on D-5, look for white sign with green lettering, close to the *gendarmerie*).

IN LE PARADOU

$ Le Mazet des Alpilles is a small home with three tidy, air-conditioned rooms around a lovely garden, located just outside the sleepy village of Le Paradou (five minutes south of Les Baux). Sweet Annick is happy to share her knowledge of the area with you (Db-€68, ask for largest room, includes breakfast, cash only, air-con, child's bed available, drive into Le Paradou and look for signs, Route de Brunelly, tel. 04 90 54 45 89, or 06 12 14 93 06, www.alpilles.com/mazet.htm, lemazet@wanadoo.fr).

Eating in and near Les Baux

You'll find quiet cafés with views along my self-guided tour route.

The recommended **Hostellerie de la Reine Jeanne** offers friendly service and good-value meals indoors or out (€12 salads, €16 *menus,* try the *salade Estivale,* open daily).

You'll also find several worthwhile places in Maussane, south of Les Baux. Place de la Fontaine, the town's central square, makes a good stop for café fare. **Pizza Brun** has the town's best pizza (closed Mon-Tue, 1 Rue Edouard Foscalina; with your back to Place de la Fontaine, walk to the right for about 10 minutes and look for colored tables in an alleyway; tel. 04 90 54 40 73). **La Place** is a good choice for a real restaurant (*menus* from €21-38, closed Wed off-season, indoor seating and big outside terrace, 65 Avenue de la Vallée des Baux, tel. 04 90 54 23 31).

Orange

Orange, called *Arausio* in Roman times, is notable for its Roman arch and grand Roman Theater. Orange was a thriving city in ancient times—strategically situated on the Via Agrippa, connecting the important Roman cities of Lyon and Arles. It was actually founded as a comfortable place for Roman army officers to enjoy their retirement. Even in Roman times, professional military men retired with time for a second career. Did the emperor want thousands of well-trained, relatively young guys hanging around Rome? No way. What to do? "How about a nice place in the south of France...?"

Today's Orange (oh-rahnzh) is a busy, workaday city with a gritty charm that reminds me of Arles. Leafy café-lined squares, a handful of traffic-free streets, a sensational Hôtel de Ville, and that theater all give the town some street appeal. For some, Orange works well as a base with its quick access to the wine villages by car (slower but OK by bus) and quick rail access to Avignon (that even drivers should consider).

Thursday is **market day** in Orange, and it's a big deal here, with all the town's streets and squares crammed with produce and local goods for sale. I like this market because it focuses on locals' needs and not touristy knick-knacks.

Orientation to Orange

TOURIST INFORMATION

The unnecessary TI is located next to the fountain and parking area at 5 Cours Aristide Briand (April-Sept Mon-Sat 9:00-18:30, Sun 9:00-13:00 & 14:00-18:30; shorter hours and closed Sun off-season; tel. 04 90 34 70 88, www.otorange.fr). A branch TI is across from the theater entrance (summer only, same hours).

ARRIVAL IN ORANGE

By Train: Orange's **train station** is a level 15-minute walk from the Roman Theater (or an €8 taxi ride, mobile 06 09 51 32 25). The recommended Hôtel de Provence, across from the station, will keep your bags for no charge, though it's polite to buy a drink from the café (see "Sleeping and Eating in Orange," later). To walk into town from the train station, head straight out of the station (down Avenue Frédéric Mistral), merge left onto Orange's main shopping street (Rue de la République), then turn left on Rue Caristie; you'll run into the Roman Theater's massive stage wall.

By Bus: Lieutaud buses stop at the train station (Gare SNCF) and at Place Pourtoules, two blocks from the Roman Theater (walk to the hill and turn right to reach the theater, bus station tel. 04 90 34 15 59, www.cars-lieutaud.fr/provence/en/regular-lines). Bus #4 to Vaison la Romaine from Place Pourtoules leaves from across the street and to the right of the main shelter/stop (see map on page 641).

By Car: Follow *Centre-Ville* signs, then *Théâtre Antique* signs, and park as close to the Roman Theater's huge wall as possible—the easiest option is labeled *Parking Office du Tourisme* (by the fountain and the TI). Those coming from the autoroute will land here by following *Centre-Ville* signs; others should follow *Centre-Ville* signs, then *Office du Tourisme* signs, to find this parking lot. To reach the theater, walk to the hill and turn left. If you're arriving on a Thursday morning (market day), you'll encounter lots of traffic and scarce parking; it's better to park on the road leading to the train station (15-minute walk to the theater).

Sights in Orange

▲▲Roman Theater (Théâtre Antique)

Orange's ancient theater is the best-preserved in existence, and the only one in Europe with its acoustic wall still standing. (Two others in Asia Minor also survive.)

Cost and Hours: €10, drops to €9 one hour before closing; ticket includes film, multimedia show, good audioguide (not available if you arrive within an hour of closing), and entry to small museum across the street; daily April-Sept 9:00-18:00, until 19:00 June-Aug; Oct-March 9:30-17:30 except Nov-Feb until 16:30, closing times can sometimes be changed for evening performance or rehearsals, tel. 04 90 51 17 60, www.theatre-antique.com.

Cheap Trick: Vagabonds wanting a partial but free view of the theater can see it from the bluff high above in the Parc de la Colline St-Eutrope. Find the *escalier est* (east staircase) off Rue Pourtoules and start climbing—it's several hundred steps to the top. At the sign for *Promenade Botanique*, keep left, and at the next fork, follow the stairs up to the right. When you see the playground, head to the right to find the view. Benches and grassy areas make this a good picnic spot (but no WCs), and you can scamper about for views of the theater from different angles.

Museum: Pop into the museum across the street (Musée d'Art et d'Histoire, included with ticket, free audioguide) for a quick spin to see a few theater details and a rare marble grid, ordered by Emperor Vespasian in 79 A.D., to be used as the official property-ownership registry—each square represented a 120-acre plot of land.

Eating: The café in the theater, La Grotte d'Auguste, has reasonably priced snacks and lunches plus views (closed Sun year-

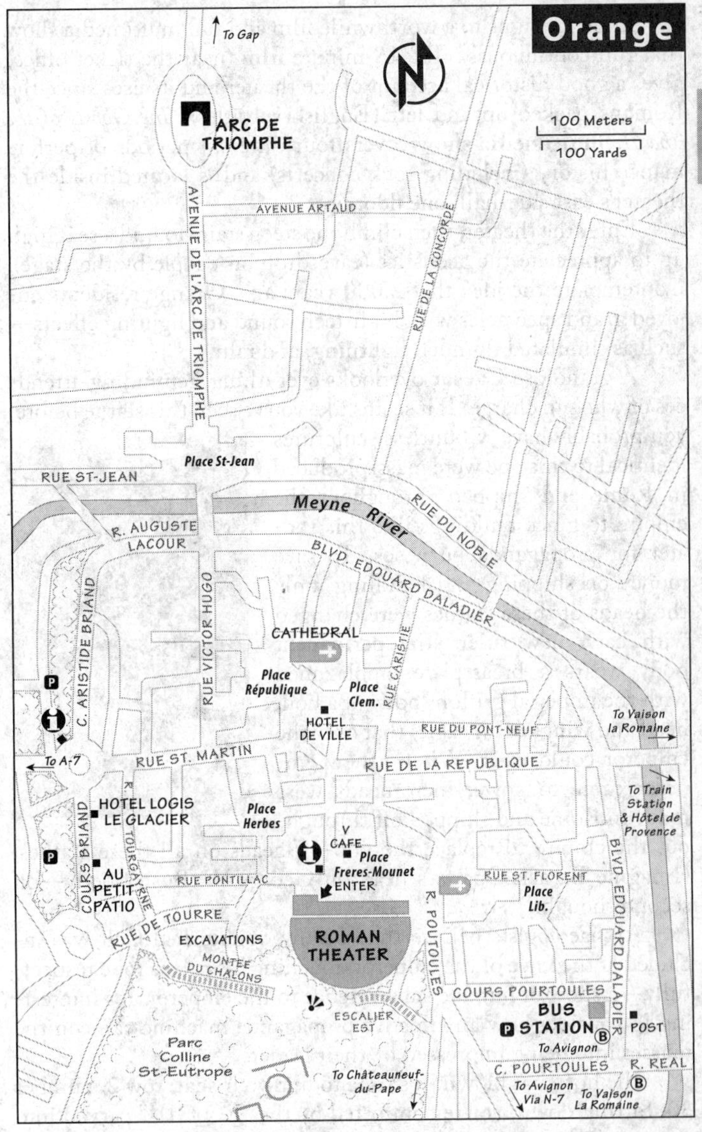

round, closed Mon off-season, tel. 04 90 60 22 54). A shaded, café-filled square, Place de la République, is two blocks from the theater up Rue Ségond Weber.

➲ **Self-Guided Tour:** After you enter (to the right of the actual theater), you'll see a huge dig—the site of the Temple to the Cult of the Emperor (English explanations posted). *Arausio* is the Roman name for the town.

Look for signs to a worthwhile film and fun multimedia show that run continuously. The 15-minute **film** (near the ticket office) gives a good historical account of the theater and its uses since the Romans packed up and left (English subtitles). *The Ghosts of the Theatre* **multimedia show** covers four different periods of performance history (including rock concerts) and is located inside the theater's east side-hall, one floor up.

Enter the theater, then climb the steep stairs to find a seat high up to appreciate the acoustics (eavesdrop on people by the stage). Contemplate the idea that 2,000 years ago, Orange residents enjoyed grand spectacles with high-tech sound and lighting effects—such as simulated thunder, lightning, and rain.

A grandiose **Caesar** overlooks everything, reminding attendees of who's in charge. If it seems like you've seen this statue before, you probably have. Countless sculptures identical to this one were mass-produced in Rome and shipped throughout the empire to grace buildings like this theater for propaganda purposes. To save money on shipping and handling, only the heads of these statues were changed with each new ruler. The permanent body wears a breastplate emblazoned with the imperial griffon (body of a lion, head and wings of an eagle) that only the emperor could wear. When a new emperor came to power, new heads were made in Rome and shipped off throughout the empire to replace the pop-off heads on all these statues. (Imagine Barack Obama's head on George W. Bush's body—on second thought...)

Archaeologists believe that a puny, vanquished Celt was included at the knee of the emperor, touching his ruler's robe respectfully—a show of humble subservience to the emperor. It's interesting to consider how an effective propaganda machine can con the masses into being impressed by their leader.

The horn has blown. It's time to find your **seat:** row 2, number 30. Sitting down, you're comforted by the "EQ GIII" carved into the seat (*Equitas Gradus* #3...three rows for the Equestrian order). You're not comforted by the hard limestone bench (thinking it'll probably last 2,000 years). The theater is filled with 10,000 people. Thankfully, you mix only with your class, the nouveau riche—merchants, tradesmen, and city big shots. The people seated above you are the working class, and way up in the "chicken roost" section is the scum of the earth—slaves, beggars, prostitutes, and youth hostellers. Scanning the orchestra section (where the super-rich sit on real chairs), you notice the town dignitaries hosting some visiting VIPs.

OK, time to worship. They're parading a bust of the emperor from its sacred home in the adjacent temple around the **stage.** Next is the ritual animal sacrifice called *la pompa* (so fancy, future generations will use that word for anything full of such...pomp). Finally, you settle in for an all-day series of spectacles and dramatic entertainment. All eyes are on the big stage door in the middle—where the Angelina Jolies and Brad Pitts of the day will appear. (Lesser actors come out of the side doors.)

The play is good, but many come for the halftime shows—jugglers, acrobats, and striptease dancers. In Roman times, the theater was a festival of immorality. An ancient writer commented, "The vanquished take their revenge on us by giving us their vices through the theater."

With an audience of 10,000 and no amplification, **acoustics** were critical. A roof made of linen (called the velarium) originally covered the stage, somewhat like the glass-and-iron roof you see today (installed to protect the stage wall). The original was designed not to protect the stage from the weather, but to project the voices of the actors into the crowd. For further help, actors wore masks with leather caricature mouths that functioned as megaphones. The theater's side walls originally rose as high as the stage wall and supported a retractable roof that gave the audience some protection from the sun or rain. After leaving the theater, look up to the stage wall from the outside and notice the supports for poles that held the velarium in place, like the masts and sails of a ship.

The Roman Theater was all part of the "give them bread and circuses" approach to winning the support of the masses (not unlike today's philosophy of "give them tax cuts and *American Idol*"). The spectacle grew from 65 days of games per year when the theater was first built (and when Rome was at its height) to about 180 days each year by the time Rome finally fell.

▲Roman "Arc de Triomphe"

This just-cleaned, 60-foot-tall arch is in the center of a big traffic circle, a level 15-minute walk from the theater due north of the city center. Technically the only real Roman arches of triumph are in Rome's Forum, built to commemorate various emperors' victories. But this arch was the model for those in Rome, preceding both the famous arches of Septimius Severus and Constantine. The great Roman arch of Orange is actually a municipal arch erected (in about A.D. 19) to commemorate a general named Germanicus, who protected the town. The facade is covered with reliefs of military exploits, including naval battles and Romans beating up on barbarians and those nasty Gauls.

Hôtel de Ville

Orange owns Provence's most beautiful city hall, worth the short detour to appreciate it (in the heart of the old town on Place Georges Clemenceau).

Sleeping and Eating in Orange

$$ Hôtel de Provence,** at the train station, is air-conditioned, quiet, comfortable, and affordable. Gentle Monsieur Motte runs this traditional place with grace (Db-€55-75, Tb-€75-110, family rooms €80-100, breakfast-€8, small rooftop pool, Wi-Fi, café, parking-€5/day, 60 Avenue Frédéric Mistral, tel. 04 90 34 00 23, www.hotelprovence-orange.com, hoteldeprovence84@orange.fr).

$$ Hôtel Logis Le Glacier*,** across from the TI, is run by English-speaking and affable Philippe. It's a good value, with easy parking, a small bar in a comfortable lobby, and well-designed rooms at good rates (Db-€70-90, bigger Db-€90-130, elevator, air-con, a few parking spaces, 46 Cours Aristide Briand, tel. 04 90 34 02 01, www.le-glacier.com, info@le-glacier.com).

For lunch or dinner, Orange has several inviting squares with ample choices in all price ranges. I like dining across from the theater. **V Café** works well, with a large terrace and €12 *tartines* and *plats* (daily, 2 Place des Frères Mounet, tel. 04 90 66 32 14). For a more refined meal, **Au Petit Patio** delivers elegant dining and fine cuisine at fair rates (€27-37 *menus,* closed Wed-Thu and Sun, 58 Cours Aristide Briand, tel. 04 90 29 69 27).

Orange Connections

From Orange by Train to: Avignon (15/day, 20 minutes), **Arles** (4/day direct, 35 minutes, more frequently with transfer in Avignon), **Lyon** (16/day, 2 hours).

By Bus to: Vaison la Romaine (3-5/day, 45 minutes), **Avignon** (Mon-Sat hourly, 5/Sun, 1 hour—take the train instead). Buses to Vaison la Romaine and other wine villages depart from the Gare SNCF and from Place Pourtoules (turn right out of the Roman Theater, and right again onto Rue Pourtoules).

Villages of the Côtes du Rhône

The sunny Côtes du Rhône wine road—one of France's most engaging—starts at Avignon's doorstep and winds along a mountainous landscape carpeted with vines, studded with warm stone villages, and presided over by the Vesuvius-like Mont Ventoux. The wines of the Côtes du Rhône (grown on the *côtes,* or hillsides, of the Rhône River Valley) are easy on the palate and on your budget. But this hospitable place offers more than wine—its hill-capping villages inspire travel posters, its Roman ruins add a historical perspective, and the locals are, well, welcoming...and often as excited about their region as you are. Yes, you'll have good opportunities for enjoyable wine tasting, but there is also a soul to this area...if you take the time to look and to listen.

PLANNING YOUR TIME

Vaison la Romaine is the handy hub of this region, offering limited bus connections with Avignon and Orange, bike rental, and a mini-Pompeii in the town center. Nearby, you can visit the impressive Roman Theater in Orange (described earlier), follow my self-guided driving tour of Côtes du Rhône villages and wineries, or pedal along small lanes to nearby towns for a breath of fresh air. The vineyards' centerpiece, the Dentelles de Montmirail mountains, are laced with a variety of trails ideal for hikers.

To explore this area, allow two nights for a decent dabble. Drivers should head for the hills. Those without wheels find that Vaison la Romaine or Orange make the only practical home bases (consider a minivan tour for this area).

GETTING AROUND THE COTES DU RHONE

By Car: Pick up Michelin maps #332 or #527 to navigate your way around the Côtes du Rhône. (Landmarks like the Dentelles de Montmirail and Mont Ventoux make it easy to get your bearings.) I've described my favorite driving route on page 655.

By Bus: Lieutaud buses run to Vaison la Romaine from Orange and Avignon (5/day, 45 minutes from Orange, 1.5 hours from Avignon) and connect several wine villages with Vaison la Romaine and Nyons to the north. (From Avignon, you can save time by taking the 15-minute train to Orange, then connecting by bus to Vaison la Romaine.) Another bus line runs from Vaison la Romaine to Carpentras, serving Crestet, Malaucène, and Le Barroux (3/day Mon-Sat, none on Sun, tel. 04 90 36 09 90, www.cars-lieutaud.fr/provence/en/regular-lines). Both routes provide scenic rides through this area.

By Train: Trains get you as far as Orange (from Avignon: 15/day, 15 minutes), from there, buses run to Vaison la Romaine.

By Minivan Tour: There's no shortage of people willing to take you for a ride through this marvelous region—so buyer beware. For a wine-focused tour, I recommend several individuals who can expertly guide you through the area. For more general tours and private guides to this area, see "Tours of Provence" on page 565.

Vaison la Romaine

With quick access to vineyards, villages, and Mont Ventoux, this lively little town of 6,000 makes a good base for exploring the Côtes du Rhône region by car, by bike, or on foot. You get two villages for the price of one: Vaison la Romaine's "modern" lower city has Roman ruins, a lone pedestrian street, and a lively main square—café-lined Place Montfort. The car-free medieval hill town looms above, with meandering cobbled lanes, a dash of art galleries and cafés, and a ruined castle with a fine view from its base. (Vaison la Romaine is also a good place to have your hair done, since there are more than 20 hairdressers in this small town.)

Orientation to Vaison la Romaine

The city is split in two by the Ouvèze River. The Roman Bridge connects the more modern lower town (Ville-Basse) with the hill-capping medieval upper town (Ville-Haute).

TOURIST INFORMATION

The superb TI is in the lower city, between the two Roman ruin sites, at Place du Chanoine Sautel (June-Aug Mon-Fri 9:00-18:45, Sat-Sun 9:00-12:30 & 14:00-18:45; Sept-May Mon-Sat 9:30-12:00 & 14:00-17:45, Sun 9:00-12:00—except closed Sun mid-Oct-March; tel. 04 90 36 02 11, www.vaison-ventoux-tourisme.com). Say *bonjour* to *charmante* and ever-so-patient Valerie. Use the free Wi-Fi, ask about festivals and other events in the area, and pick up infor-

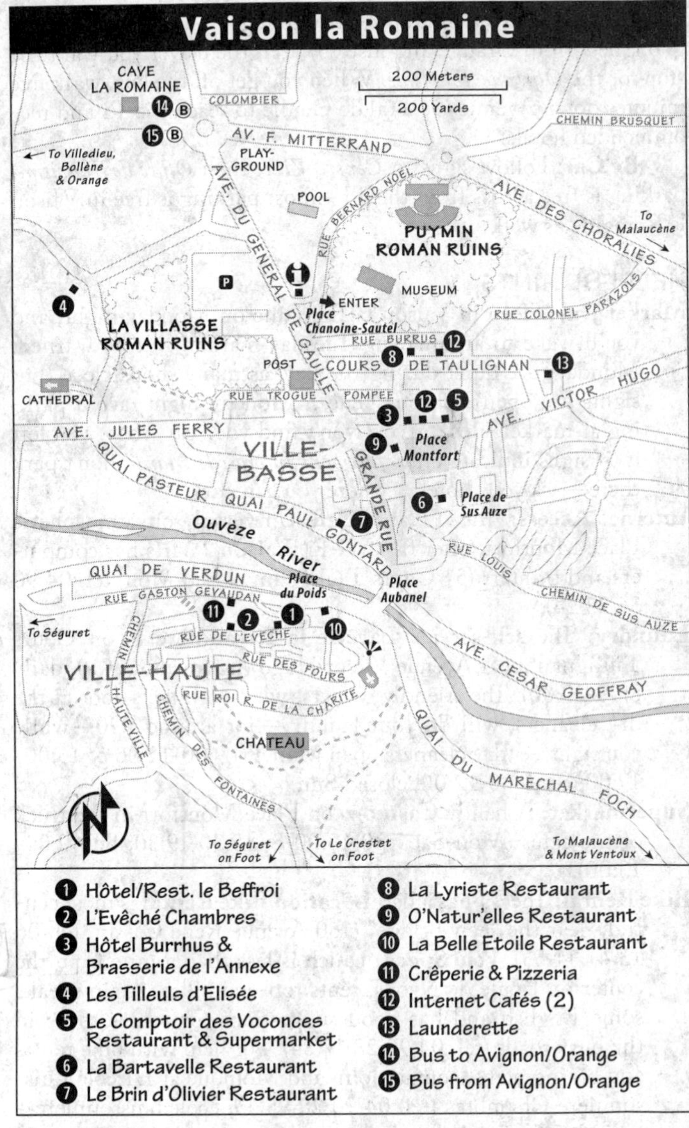

PROVENCE

mation on walks and bike rides from Vaison la Romaine. Find the big wall map showing hiking trails in the area.

ARRIVAL IN VAISON LA ROMAINE

By Bus: The unmarked bus stop to Orange and Avignon is in front of the Cave la Romaine winery (by the driveway closer to the roundabout). Buses from Orange or Avignon drop you across the street (3-5/day, 45 minutes from Orange, 1.5 hours from Avignon, best from Orange and just €3). Tell the driver you want the stop for the *Office de Tourisme*. When you get off the bus, walk five minutes down Avenue Général de Gaulle to reach the TI and recommended hotels.

By Car: Follow signs to *Centre-Ville,* then *Office de Tourisme;* parking is free across from the TI—most parking is free in Vaison la Romaine as well.

HELPFUL HINTS

Market Day: Sleep in Vaison la Romaine on Monday night, and you'll wake to an amazing Tuesday market. But be warned: Mondays are quiet during the day, as many shops close (but sights are open). If you spend a Monday night, avoid parking at market sites, or you won't find your car where you left it (if signs indicate *Stationnement Interdit le Mardi,* don't park there—ask your hotelier where you can park).

Internet Access: The TI and **Café Universal,** on atmospheric Place Montfort, offer free Wi-Fi. **Vaison 2 Mils** has computers and printers (51 Cours Taulignan, closed Mon, tel. 04 90 36 23 24).

Laundry: The self-service **Laverie la Lavandière** is on Cours Taulignan, near Avenue Victor Hugo (figure about €10, daily 8:00-22:00). The friendly owners, who work next door at the dry cleaners, will do your laundry—for around €20—while you sightsee (dry cleaners open Mon-Fri 9:00-12:00 & 15:00-19:00, Sat 9:00-12:00, closed Sun).

Supermarket: A handy **Casino** is on Place Montfort in the thick of the cafés (Mon-Sat 7:30-13:00 & 15:30-19:30, Sun 9:00-13:00).

Bike Rental: The TI has a list. **Location Bike Rental** is most central, near the "new bridge" (160 Avenue René Cassin, tel. 06 13 41 11 53). **Vélo Speed,** which is less than a mile from the center on Route de Nyons, rents top-end bikes. Alain speaks some English and has good suggestions for routes to avoid the busy roads (tel. 04 90 28 17 84). For help with bike rental and biking plans, contact John and Monique at L'Ecole Buissonnière Chambres (tel. 04 90 28 95 19, ecole.buissonniere@wanadoo.fr; for details, see "Sleeping in and near Vaison la Romaine," later).

Taxi: Call 04 90 36 00 04 or 06 22 28 24 49.

Car Rental: You can rent cars by the day, though they must be returned to Vaison la Romaine; ask at the TI for locations.

Local Guide: Let sincere and knowledgeable **Anna-Marie Melard** bring those Roman ruins to life for you (tel. 04 90 36 50 48). Scottish by birth and attorney by career, **Janet Hen-**

derson offers in-depth historic walks of Vaison la Romaine for €25 per person (allow 2 hours, 3-person or €75 minimum, mailto:janet.henderson@wandoo.fr).

Cooking Classes: Charming **Barbara Schuerenberg** offers reasonably priced cooking classes from her view home in Vaison la Romaine, where you'll pick herbs from the garden to use in the recipes (€80, includes lunch, 4-person maximum, tel. 04 90 35 68 43, www.cuisinedeprovence.com, barbara@cuisinedeprovence.com).

Sights in Vaison la Romaine

Roman Ruins

Ancient Vaison la Romaine had a treaty that gave it the preferred "federated" relationship with Rome (rather than simply being a colony). This, along with a healthy farming economy (olives and vineyards), made it a most prosperous place...as a close look at its sprawling ruins demonstrates. About 6,000 people called Vaison la Romaine home 2,000 years ago. When the barbarians arrived, the Romans were forced out, and the townspeople fled into the hills. The town has only recently reached the same population it had during its Roman era.

Cost and Hours: €8 Roman ruins combo-ticket includes both ruins and helpful audioguide; daily April-May 9:30-18:00, June-Sept 9:30-18:30, Oct-March 10:00-12:00 & 14:00-17:00, Oct and March until 17:30.

Visiting the Ruins: Vaison la Romaine's Roman ruins are split by a modern road into two sites: Puymin and La Villasse. Each is well-presented, thanks to the audioguide and occasional English information panels, offering a good look at life during the Roman Empire. The Roman town extended all the way from here to the river, and its main square (forum) still lies under today's main square, Place Montfort. What you can see is only a small fraction of the Roman town's extent—most is still buried under today's city. For helpful background about Roman civilization, read "How About Them Romans" on page 569.

Visit **Puymin** first. Nearest the entry are the scant but impressive ruins of a sprawling mansion. Find the faint remains of a colorful frescoed wall. Climb the hill to the good little **museum** (pick up your audioguide here; exhibits also explained in English loaner booklet). Be sure to see the **3-D film** that takes you inside the home of a wealthy Vaison resident and explores daily life some 2,000 years ago. Behind the museum is a 6,000-seat theater that's still well-used, with just enough seats for the whole town (of yesterday and today).

Back across the modern road in **La Villasse,** you'll explore a "street of shops" and the foundations of more houses. You'll also see a few wells, used before Vaison's two aqueducts were built.

Lower Town (Ville-Basse)

Vaison la Romaine's modern town centers on café-friendly Place Montfort. Tables grab the north side of the square, conveniently sheltered from the prevailing mistral wind while enjoying the generous shade of the ubiquitous plane *(platane)* trees. The trees are cut way back each year to form a leafy canopy.

A 10-minute walk below Place Montfort, the stout **Notre-Dame de Nazareth Cathedral,** which dates from the 11th century and sports an evocative cloister and fine stone carvings, is a good example of Provençal Romanesque. It was the seat of a bishop until 1801 (free, daily April-Sept 10:00-12:00 & 14:00-17:00, closed Oct-March). The pedestrian-only **Grand Rue** is a lively shopping street leading to the small river gorge and the Roman Bridge.

Roman Bridge

The Romans cut this sturdy, no-nonsense vault into the canyon rock 2,000 years ago, and it has survived ever since. Find the information panel at the new town end of the bridge. Until the 20th century, this was the only way to cross the Ouvèze River. See the stone plaque *(Septembre 22-92...)* on the wall to the left as you approach the bridge, showing the high-water mark of the record flood that killed 30 people. The flood swept the modern top of this bridge—and several other modern bridges—downstream, but couldn't budge the 55-foot Roman arch.

Upper Town (Ville-Haute)

Although there's nothing of particular importance to see in the fortified medieval old town atop the hill, the cobbled lanes and enchanting fountains make you want to break out a sketchpad. Vaison la Romaine had had a prince-bishop since the fourth century. He came under attack by the Count of Toulouse in the 12th century. Anticipating a struggle, the prince-bishop abandoned the lower town and built a château on this rocky outcrop (about 1195). Over time, the rest of the townspeople followed, vacating the lower town and building their homes at the base of the château behind the upper town's fortified wall.

To reach the upper town, hike up from the Roman Bridge (passing memorials for both world wars) through the medieval gate, under the lone tower crowned by an 18th-century wrought-iron bell cage. Look for occasional English information plaques as you meander. The château is closed, but a steep, uneven trail to its base rewards hikers with a sweeping view.

▲▲Market Day

In the 16th century, the pope gave Vaison la Romaine market-town status. Each Tuesday morning since then, the town has hosted a farmers' market. Today merchants turn the entire place into a festival of produce and Provençal products. This market is one of France's best, but it can challenge claustrophobes. Be warned that parking is a real headache unless you arrive early (see "Helpful Hints," earlier, and "Market Day" sidebar, page 1059.)

Wine Tasting

Cave la Romaine, a five-minute walk up Avenue Général de Gaulle from the TI, offers a big variety of good-value wines from nearby villages in a pleasant, well-organized tasting room (free tastes, Mon-Sat 8:30-18:30, Sun 9:00-12:00, Avenue St. Quenin, tel. 04 90 36 55 90, www.cave-la-romaine.com).

Biking

This area is not particularly flat, and if it's hot and windy, bike-riding is a dicey option. But if the air's calm and cool, the five-mile ride to cute little Villedieu (with the recommended La Maison Bleue restaurant, listed on page 655, is a delight. Options for renting an electric bike make this an easier outing (see "Helpful Hints," earlier). The bike route is signed along small roads; you'll find signs from Vaison la Romaine to Villedieu at the roundabout past Cave La Romaine, and then turn right on the D-51 (see map on page 647). With a bit more energy, you can pedal beyond Villedieu on the lovely road to Mirabel (from Villedieu, follow signs to Nyons). Make a detour to Piegon (to avoid that busy section of road between Mirabel and Vaison), then rejoin the D-938 to reach Vaison (figure about 18 miles total). Alternatively, get a good map and connect the following villages for an enjoyable 11-mile loop ride through a typical Provencal landscape: Vaison la Romaine, St-Romain-en-Viennois, Puyméras (with the recommended Le

Girocedre restaurant—see page 655), then toward Merindol, Faucon, and back to Vaison la Romaine.

▲Hiking

The TI has information on relatively easy hikes into the hills above Vaison la Romaine. It's about 1.25 hours to the quiet hill town of Crestet, though views begin immediately. To find this trail, drive or walk on the road past the upper town (with the rock base and castle just on your left), continue on Chemin des Fontaines (blue signs), and stay the course as far as you like (follow yellow *Crestet* signs). Cars are not allowed on the road after about a mile. To find the five-mile trail to Séguret (allow two hours), take the same road above the upper town and look for a yellow sign to the right. For either hike, consider the value of hiking one way and taking a taxi back (see "Helpful Hints," earlier, for taxi contact info).

Sleeping in and near Vaison la Romaine

Hotels in Vaison la Romaine are a good value and are split between the lower main town (with all the services) and the upper medieval village (with all the steps). Those in the upper town (Ville-Haute) are quieter, cozier, cooler, and give you the feeling of sleeping in a hilltop (some come with views), with all the services of a real town steps away. But they require a 10-minute walk to the town center and Roman ruins. If staying at one of the first three places, follow signs to Cité Médiévale and park just outside the upper village entry (driving into the Cité Médiévale itself is a challenge, with tiny lanes and nearly impossible parking). If you have a car, think about staying in one of the Côtes du Rhône villages near Vaison la Romaine (see the recommendations I've listed in "Villages and Wineries along the Côtes du Rhône Wine Road," later).

$$$ Hôtel le Beffroi*** hides deep in the upper town, just above a demonstrative bell tower (you'll hear what I mean). It offers 16th-century red-tile-and-wood-beamed-cozy lodgings with nary a level surface. The rooms—split between two buildings a few doors apart—are Old World comfy, and some have views. You'll also find antique-filled public spaces, a garden with view tables (light meals available in the summer), a small pool with more views, and animated Nathalie at the reception (standard Db-€100-130, superior Db-€165, Tb-€190, several good family rooms, Rue de l'Evêché, tel. 04 90 36 04 71, www.le-beffroi.com, info@le-beffroi.com). The hotel's restaurant offers *menus* from €29 (closed for lunch weekdays and all day Tue).

$$$ L'Evêché Chambres, almost next door to Hôtel le Beffroi in the upper town (look for the ivy), is a five-room, melt-in-your-chair B&B. The owners (the Verdiers) have an exquisite sense of interior design and are passionate about books, making this place feel like a cross between a library and an art gallery (Sb-€78-85, standard Db-€85-95, Db suite-€120-145, the *solanum* suite is worth every euro, Tb-€120-145, guest computer, Wi-Fi, Rue de l'Evêché, tel. 04 90 36 13 46, http://eveche.free.fr, eveche@aol.com).

$$ Hôtel Burrhus*** is part art gallery, part simple, funky hotel—and the best value in the lower town. It's a central, laid-back, go-with-the-flow place, with a broad terrace over the raucous Place Montfort (the double-paned windows are effective, but for maximum quiet, request a back room). Its floor plan will confound even the ablest navigator (Db-€63-80, larger Db-€86-105, Qb apartment-€145, extra bed-€15, air-con, guest computer, Wi-Fi, 1 Place Montfort, tel. 04 90 36 00 11, www.burrhus.com, info@burrhus.com).

$$Les Tilleuls d'Elisée is a terrific *chambres d'hôte* in a big stone, blue-shuttered home near Notre-Dame de Nazareth Cathedral, a few minutes' walk below the TI. Enthusiastic Anne and Laurent Viau run this traditional, five-room place with grace and offer great rates (Db-€75, 1 avenue Jules Mazen, tel. 04 90 35 63 04, www.vaisonchambres.info, anne.viau@vaisonchambres.info).

$$ L'Ecole Buissonnière Chambres is run by an engaging Anglo-French team, John and Monique, who share their peace and quiet 10 minutes north of Vaison la Romaine. This creatively restored farmhouse has three character-filled, half-timbered rooms and comfy public spaces. Getting to know John, who has lived all over the south of France, is worth the price of the room. The outdoor kitchen allows guests to picnic in high fashion in the tranquil garden (Db-€62-74, Tb-€78-89, Qb-€94-99, cash only, includes breakfast, Wi-Fi; between Villedieu and Buisson on D-75—leave Vaison following signs to *Villedieu,* then follow D-51 toward Buisson and turn left onto D-75; tel. 04 90 28 95 19, www.buissonniere-provence.com, ecole.buissonniere@wanadoo.fr).

Eating in Vaison la Romaine

Vaison la Romaine offers a handful of terrific dining experiences—arrive by 19:30 in summer or reserve ahead, particularly on weekends. And while you can eat very well on a moderate budget in Vaison, it's well worth venturing to nearby Côtes du Rhône villages to eat (see "Eating near Vaison la Romaine" later).

Dining on Place Monfort: Come here for lighter café fare and to observe the daily flow of life in Vaison la Romaine. Dine here only if you can sit outside. Reliable **Brasserie l'Annexe** has

€12 meals (open daily), and **Le Comptoir des Voconces** is the happening hangout with a pub-like ambience.

La Bartavelle, run by friendly Berenger, is a good place to savor traditional French cuisine in the lower town, with a tourist-friendly mix-and-match choice of local options. Her €30 *menu* gets you four courses; the €23 *menu* gives you access to all the top-end main-course selections and dessert (closed Mon, Fri at lunch, and off-season on Sun; small terrace outside, air-con interior, 12 Place de Sus Auze, tel. 04 90 36 02 16).

Le Brin d'Olivier is the most romantic place I list, with soft lighting, hushed conversations, earth tones, and a semi-gastronomic range of food that celebrates Provence (€32 and €46 three-course *menus,* closed Wed except July-Aug, 4 Rue du Ventoux, tel. 04 90 28 74 79, www.restaurant-lebrindolivier.com, owner Patrick speaks a little English).

La Lyriste, named for the loudest "singing" *cigale* (cicada), puts cuisine above decor. Marie serves what hubby Benoît cooks. Both are shy, yet proud of their restaurant. There's a fine *menu* for €21, but go for the slightly pricier €29 *menus,* which are inventive and *très delectable* (closed Mon, vegetarian options, indoor and outdoor seating, 45 Cours Taulignan, tel. 04 90 36 04 67).

O'Natur'elles is ideal for vegetarians; the all-organic dishes can be served with or without meat. Locals love this place, though service can be slow. It's small, so reservations are smart (€14-20 *plats,* closed Mon, 36 Place Montfort, tel. 04 90 65 81 67.

Eating in the Upper Town: The recommended **Hôtel le Beffroi's** garden is just right for a light dinner in the summer (*menus* from €29, closed at lunch weekdays and all day Tue).

La Belle Etoile is where locals go for simple, fresh, and good-value meals. The outside tables come with views over the lower town (open irregular days April-Sept, closes when they run out of food; it's the first place you pass when coming from the lower town, 1 Rue du Pont Romain, tel. 04 90 37 31 45).

You'll also find a simple ***crêperie*** and a **pizzeria** on the main street leading up to the old town. Both have decks with views over the river, plastic chairs, and cheap food (good for families).

Eating near Vaison la Romaine

Auberge d'Anaïs, at the end of a dirt road 10 minutes from Vaison la Romaine, is another find—and a true Provençal experience. Outdoor tables gather under cheery lights with views and reliable cuisine. Ask for a table *sur la terrasse* (€13 lunch *menu,* good three-course dinner *menus* from €19, closed Mon, tel. 04 90 36 20 06). Heading east of Vaison la Romaine, follow signs to *Carpentras,* then *St-Marcellin,* and signs will guide you from there.

La Girocedre, easiest for drivers, is an enchanting place to eat lunch or dinner if the weather's nice. Just three picturesque miles north of Vaison la Romaine in the village of Puyméras, this eatery offers a complete country-Provençal package: outdoor tables in a lush garden, warm interior decor, and real Provençal cuisine (€18-23 lunch *menus,* €23-28 dinner *menus,* closed all day Mon and for lunch Tue, off-season closed all day Tue, reservations smart; take road into Puyméras, then turn right toward Mirabel; tel. 04 90 46 50 67, www.legirocedre.fr).

La Maison Bleue, about four miles north of Vaison la Romaine on Villedieu's delightful little square, serves pizzas and salads with great outdoor ambience. Skip it if the weather forces you inside (March-Oct Thu-Sun open for lunch and dinner, closed Mon-Wed, except July-Aug closed Mon only, tel. 04 90 28 97 02).

Vaison la Romaine Connections

The most central **bus stop** is a few blocks up Avenue Général de Gaulle from the TI at the main winery, Cave la Romaine.

From Vaison la Romaine by Bus to: Avignon (5/day during school year—called *période scolaire,* otherwise 3/day, all buses pass through Orange, 1.5 hours; faster to bus to Orange and train from there), **Orange** (3-5/day, 45 minutes), **Nyons** (3-5/day, 45 minutes), **Crestet** (lower village below Le Crestet, 2/day, 5 minutes), **Carpentras** (2/day, 45 minutes).

Côtes du Rhône Wine Road

To experience the best of the Côtes du Rhône vineyards and villages, take this ▲▲▲ loop around the rugged Dentelles de Montmirail mountain peaks. You'll experience the finest this region has to offer: natural beauty, glowing limestone villages, inviting wineries, and rolling hills of vineyards.

There are good places to sleep and eat along the way—more highlights of the route. I've listed some of my favorites. Allow a half-day to do this tour.

Start just south of Vaison la Romaine in little **Séguret.** This town is best for a visit early or late, when it's quieter. Explore the village (ideal for a morning coffee break), then drive up and up to the *Domaine de Mourchon* winery (described later). From here return to Vaison la Romaine and follow signs toward *Carpentras/Malaucène,* pass through Crestet, then follow signs leading up to *Le Village* (D-76).

After ambling the quiet village of **Crestet,** follow signs to

Malaucène and turn right on D-90 (direction: Suzette) just before the gas station. The D-90 is the scenic highlight of this loop, which follows the back side of the Dentelles de Montmirail past mountain views, remote villages, and beautifully situated wineries (**Domaine de Coyeux** is best). Take your time for this drive: You'll pass trailheads, scenic pullouts, and good picnic spots. Consider lunch along the way (restaurants listed later).

The D-90 ends in Beaumes de Venise. Follow signs back toward *Vaison la Romaine* to Gigondas and explore this village.

Villages and Wineries along the Côtes du Rhône Wine Road

❶ Séguret

Séguret's name comes from the Latin word securitas (meaning "security"). The bulky entry arch came with a massive gate, which drilled in the message of the village's name. In the Middle Ages, Séguret was patrolled 24/7—they never took their securitas for granted. Walk through the arch. To appreciate how the homes' outer walls provided security in those days, drop down the first passage on your right (near the fountain). These exit passages, or poternes, were needed in periods of peace to allow the town to expand below. Wander deep. Rue Calade leads up to the bulky 12th-century St. Denis Church for views (the circular village you see below is Sablet). Make your way down to the main drag and a café, and return to parking along Rue des Poternes.

Sleeping and Eating in Séguret: **$$$ Domaine de Cabasse***** is a lovely spread flanked by vineyards below Séguret (with a walking path to the village). Winemaking is their primary business—free tastings are offered every evening at 18:30 from April through September (off-season open weekends only, for non-guests, too). Most of the 23 rooms have sharp, contemporary decor, air-conditioning, and nice views; some have balconies. Four Old World rooms have view terraces but no air-conditioning (traditional Db-€105, renovated Db-€125–210, Wi-Fi, elevator, big pool, on D-23 between Sablet and Séguret, entry gate opens automatically...and slowly, tel. 04 90 46 91 12, www.cabasse.fr, hotel@cabasse.fr). The restaurant offers fine, though limited, €32-42 dinner *menus*.

❷ Domaine de Mourchon Winery

This high-flying winery blends state-of-the-art technology with traditional winemaking methods (a shiny

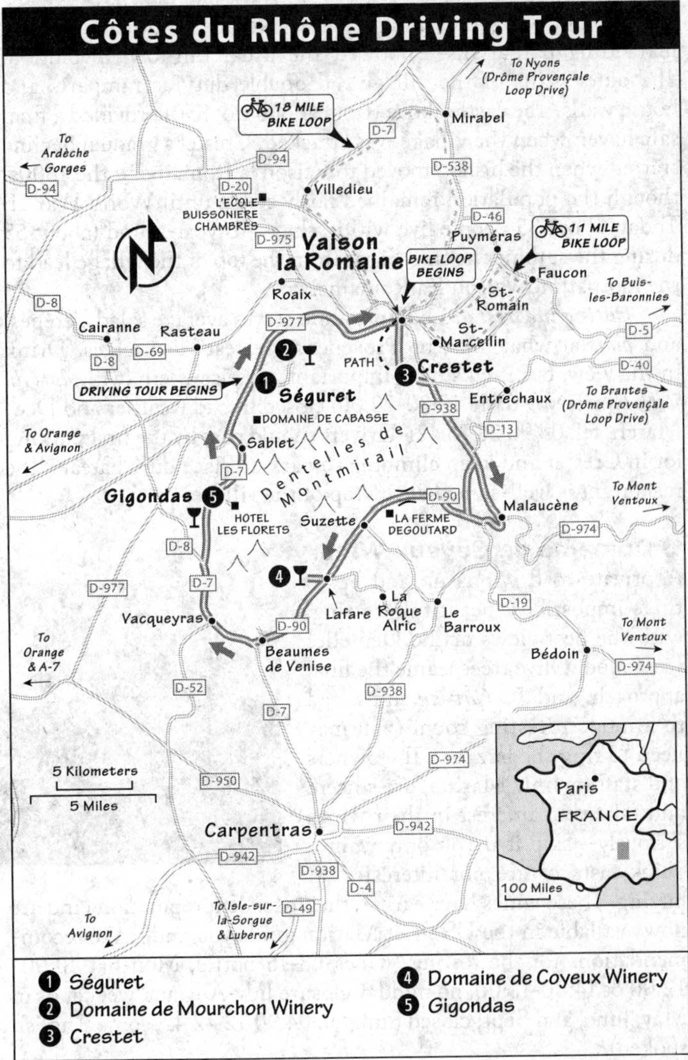

ring of stainless-steel vats holds grapes grown on land plowed by horses). The wines are winning the respect of international critics (prices range from €8-33/bottle, Mon-Sat 9:00-18:00, Sun by appointment only; from Easter-Sept, free English tour and tasting offered usually on Wed at 17:00, call to verify; well-signed above Séguret, tel. 04 90 46 70 30, www.domainedemourchon.com).

❸ Crestet

This village—founded after the fall of the Roman Empire, when people banded together in high places like this for protection from marauding barbarians—followed the usual hill-town evolution. The outer walls of the village did double duty as ramparts and house walls. The castle above (from about A.D. 850) provided a final safe haven when the village was attacked. Crestet's gradual decline started when the bishop moved to Vaison la Romaine in the 1600s, though the population remained fairly stable until World War II. Today, about 35 people live within the walls year-round (about 55 during the summer boom.) Signs from the top of the village lead to the footpath to Vaison La Romaine.

Eating in Crestet: **Le Panoramic** serves average salads, crêpes, and *plats* at what must be Provence's greatest view tables. Drink in the view, but if cuisine is important, eat elsewhere (€13 *plats du jour,* April-Nov daily 10:30-22:00, closed in bad weather and Dec-March, tel. 04 90 28 76 42). Drivers should pass by the first parking lot in Crestet and keep climbing to park at Place du Château. The restaurant is well-signed at the top of the village.

❹ Domaine de Coyeux Winery

A private road winds up and up to this impossibly beautiful setting, with the best views of the Dentelles I've found. Olive trees frame the final approach, and *Le Caveau* signs lead to a modern tasting room (you may need to ring the buzzer). The owners and staff (mainly Marion) are sincere and take your interest in their wines seriously—skip it if you only want a quick taste or are not interested in buying. These wines have earned their excellent reputation (and are now available in the US). Let Marion guide you and make recommendations for the tasting (wines-€8-16/bottle, Mon-Sat 10:00-12:00 & 14:00-18:00, no midday closure July-Aug and weekends in May, June, and Sept, closed Sun, tel. 04 90 12 42 42, some English spoken).

❺ Gigondas

This town produces some of the region's best reds and is ideally situated for hiking, mountain-biking, and driving into the mountains. The **TI** has Wi-Fi, a list of wineries, *chambres d'hôtes,* rental bikes, and tips for good hikes or drives (Mon-Sat 10:00-12:30 & 14:00-18:00, closed Sun, Place du Portail, tel. 04 90 65 85 46, www.gigondas-dm.fr). Take a short walk through the village lanes above the TI—the church is an easy destination with good views over the heart of the Côtes du Rhône vineyards.

You'll find several good tasting opportunities on the main square. **Le Caveau de Gigondas** is the best, where Sandra and Barbara await your visit in a handsome tasting room with a large and free selection of tiny bottles for sampling, filled directly from the barrel (daily 10:00-12:00 & 14:00-18:30, close to the TI on the main town square, tel. 04 90 65 82 29, www.caveaudugigondas.com). Here you can compare wines from 75 private producers in an intimate, low-key surrounding.

Sleeping and Eating in Gigondas: **$$$ Hôtel les Florets****, with tastefully designed rooms, is a half-mile above Gigondas, buried in the foothills of the Dentelles de Montmirail. It comes with an excellent restaurant, a vast terrace with views, and hiking trails into the mountains (standard Db-€120-140, superior Db-€150-180, several good family rooms, breakfast-€16, annex rooms by the pool have front patios, tel. 04 90 65 85 01, www.hotel-lesflorets.com, accueil@hotel-lesflorets.com).

The **restaurant** at Hôtel les Florets is a traditional, family-run place that's well worth it—particularly if you dine on the magnificent terrace. Dinners are a blend of classic French cuisine and Provençal accents, served with class by English-speaking Thierry. The weighty wine list is literally encyclopedic (*menus* from €37, closed Wed except for hotel clients, service can be slow).

The shaded red tables of **Du Verre à l'Assiette** ("From Glass to Plate") entice lunchtime eaters (also good interior ambience, €16 for two-course *menus,* open Thu-Tue for lunch and Fri-Sat nights for dinner, closed Wed year-round and Nov-March, located diagonally across from TI, Place du Village, tel. 04 90 12 36 64).

Hill Towns of the Luberon

Just 30 miles east of Avignon, the Luberon region hides some of France's most captivating hill towns and sensuous landscapes. Those intrigued by Peter Mayle's books love joyriding through the region, connecting I-could-live-here villages, crumbled castles, and meditative abbeys. Mayle's best-selling *A Year in Provence* will mark its 25th anniversary in 2015. The book describes the ruddy local culture from an Englishman's perspective as he buys a stone farmhouse, fixes it up, and adopts the region as his new home. *A Year in Provence* is a great read while you're here—or, better, get it as an audiobook and listen while you drive.

The Luberon terrain in general (much of which is a French

regional natural park) is as enticing as its villages. Gnarled vineyards and wind-sculpted trees separate tidy stone structures from abandoned buildings—little more than rock piles—that challenge city slickers to fix them up. Mountains of limestone bend along vast ridges, while colorful hot-air balloons survey the scene from above.

There are no obligatory museums, monuments, or vineyards in the Luberon. Treat this area like a vacation from your vacation. Downshift your engine. Brake for the views, and lose your car to take a walk. Get on a first-name basis with a village.

What follows is a rundown of my favorite villages and stops in this beautiful area. The D-900 highway cuts the Luberon in half like an arrow. The first four villages I describe are north of it; the last three sit south of it (see map on page 662).

GETTING AROUND THE LUBERON

By Car: Luberon roads are scenic and narrow. With no major landmarks, it's easy to get lost in this area—and you will get lost—but getting lost is the point. Consider buying the Michelin map #332 or #527 to navigate, and look for a copy of the free *Carte Touristique du Pays d'Apt* at local TIs.

By Bus: Isle-sur-la-Sorgue is connected with Avignon's town center by the Raoux-TransVaucluse bus line #6 (€2 one-way, 6-8/day Mon-Sat, 3-4/day Sun, 45 minutes, central stop near post office in Isle-sur-la-Sorgue, ask for schedule info at TI or download French-only schedule from www.voyages-raoux.fr/lignes/index.php). Three to four buses daily connect the Avignon TGV Station to Isle-sur-la-Sorgue (same line and prices). Without a car or minivan tour, skip the more famous hill towns of the Luberon.

By Train: Trains get you to Isle-sur-la-Sorgue (station called "L'Isle-Fontaine de Vaucluse") from Avignon (10/day on weekdays, 5/day on weekends, 30 minutes). If you're day-tripping by train, check return times before leaving the station.

By Minivan Tour: Dutchman Mike Rijken, who runs **Wine Safari,** offers tours of this area, as do several other Avignon-based companies (see "Tours of Provence" on page 565).

By Taxi: Contact **Luberon Taxi** (based in Maubec off D-3, mobile 06 08 49 40 57, www.luberontaxi.com, contact@luberontaxi.com).

By Bike: Hardy bikers can ride from Isle-sur-la-Sorgue to Gordes, then to Roussillon, connecting other villages in a full-day loop ride (30 miles round-trip to Roussillon and back, with lots of hills). Many appealing villages are closer to Isle-sur-la-Sorgue and offer easier biking options.

Isle-sur-la-Sorgue

This sturdy market town—literally, "Island on the Sorgue River"—sits within a split in its crisp, happy little river. It's a workaday town that feels refreshingly real after so many adorable villages. It's also one of the only smaller towns in this region easily accessible by train and bus.

In Isle-sur-la-Sorgue—called the "Venice of Provence"—the Sorgue River's extraordinarily clear and shallow flow divides like cells, producing water, water everywhere. The river has long nourished the region's economy. Today, antique shops power the town's economy—every other shop seems to sell some kind of antique. Although Isle-sur-la-Sorgue is renowned for its market days (Sun and Thu), it's an otherwise pleasantly average town with no important sights and a steady trickle of tourism. It's lively on weekends, calm most weeknights, and dead on Mondays.

Navigate by the town's splintered streams and nine mossy **waterwheels,** which, while still turning, power only memories of the town's wool and silk industries. At its peak, Isle-sur-la-Sorgue had 70 waterwheels; in the 1800s, the town competed with Avignon as Provence's cloth-dyeing and textile center. Find **Le Bassin,** where the Sorgue River crashes into the town and separates into many branches (carefully placed lights make this a beautiful sight after dark). With its source (a spring) a mere five miles away, the Sorgue River never floods and has a constant flow and temperature in all seasons. Despite its exposed (flat) location, Isle-sur-la-Sorgue prospered in the Middle Ages, thanks to the natural protection this river provided.

The town erupts into a carnival-like **market** frenzy each Sunday and Thursday, with hardy crafts and local produce. The Sunday market is astounding and famous for its antiques; the Thursday market is more intimate. Find a table across from the church at the **Café de France** and enjoy the scene.

The **TI** has information on hiking, biking itineraries, Wi-Fi, and a line on rooms in private homes, all of which are outside town (July-Aug only, Mon-Sat 9:00-12:30 & 14:30-18:00, Sun 9:30-13:00, in town center next to church, tel. 04 90 38 04 78, www.oti-delasorgue.fr).

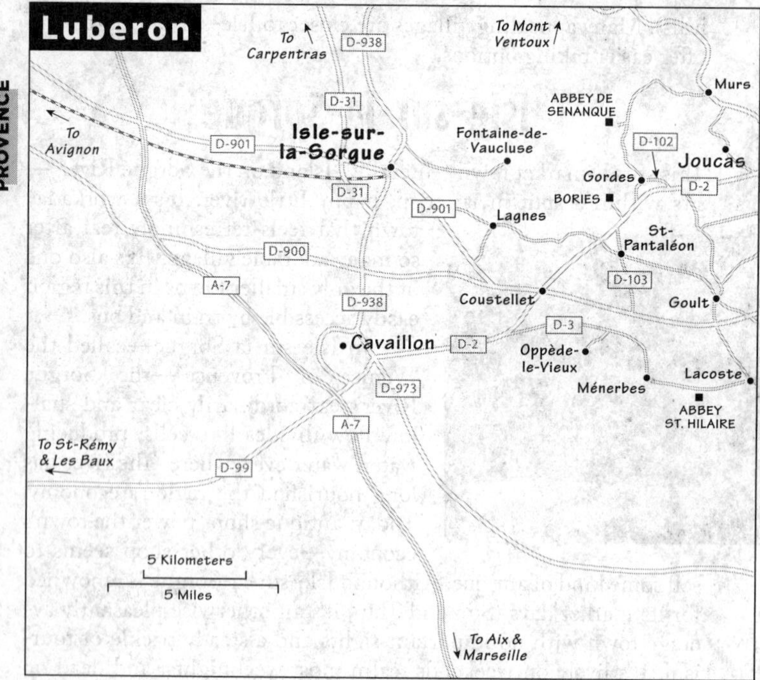

Isle-sur-la-Sorgue is ideally situated for short biking forays into the mostly level terrain. Pick up a biking itinerary at the TI, or consult with David at **Vélo Services** (€10-20/day depending on bike, open daily, 3 Rue Docteur Tallet—but he can deliver bikes about anywhere, mobile 06 38 14 49 50, www.veloservices.jimdo.com).

Sleeping in and near Isle-sur-la-Sorgue

Pickings are slim for good sleeps in Isle-sur-la-Sorgue, though the few I've listed provide solid values. A self-service launderette *(laverie automatique)* is just off Rue de la République on Impasse de l'Hôtel de Palerme.

$$$ La Prévôté*** has the town's highest-priced digs. Its five meticulously decorated rooms—located above a classy restaurant—are adorned in earth tones, with high ceilings, a few exposed beams, and carefully selected furnishings. Séverine manages the hotel while chef-hubby Jean-Marie controls the kitchen (standard Db-€170, larger Db-€195, suite Db-€235, cheaper for longer stays, no elevator, Wi-Fi, rooftop deck with Jacuzzi, no parking, one block from the church at 4 Rue J. J. Rousseau, tel. 04 90 38 57 29, www.la-prevote.fr, contact@la-prevote.fr).

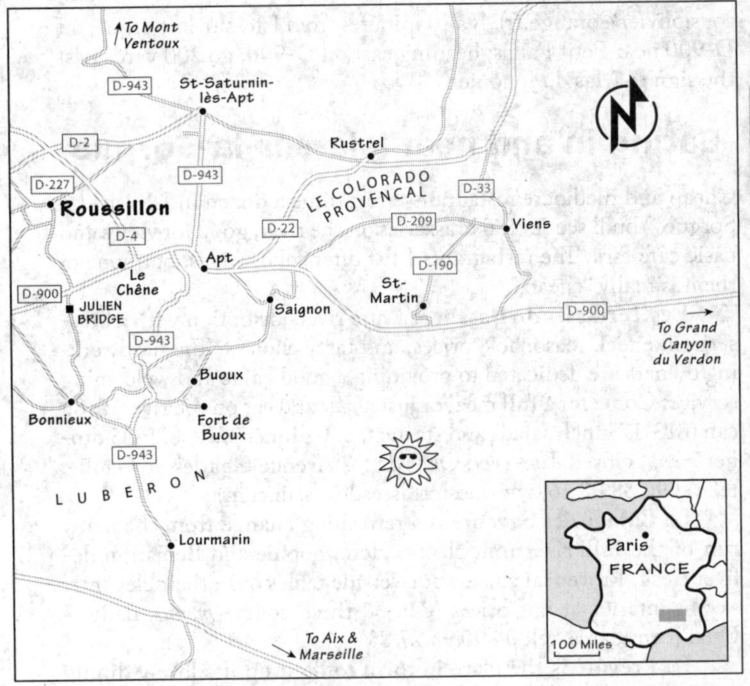

$$ Hôtel les Névons**, two blocks from the center (behind the post office), is concrete motel-modern outside, but has well-priced, comfortable rooms within and a roof deck with a small pool (standard Db-€75, Db with balcony-€90, big Db with terrace-€110, Tb-€140, Qb-160, air-con, Wi-Fi, elevator, easy and safe parking, 205 Chemin des Névons, push and hold the gate button a bit on entry, tel. 04 90 20 72 00, www.hotel-les-nevons.com, hotel-les-nevons@orange.fr).

$$ Hôtel les Terrasses du Bassin's friendly owners Corinne and Gilles rent nine good-value rooms over a pleasant restaurant right on Le Bassin. Several rooms look out over the river, most have a little traffic noise, and a few have queen-size beds (Db-€64-87, Tb-€97, air-con, Wi-Fi in restaurant only, 2 Avenue Charles de Gaulle, tel. 04 90 38 03 16, www.lesterrassesdubassin.com, corinne@lesterrassesdubassin.com).

At **Les Chambres Sous l'Olivier,** big Julien, quiet Carole, and sons Hugo and Clovis adopt you into their sprawling old stone farmhouse, with grass to burn, a big pool, yards of chairs and lounges, and views to the Luberon range. The six rooms are big but lack air-conditioning. Dinner is a family affair, worth every euro (Db-€120-140, Tb-€150-190, three apartments available, dinner-€34, cash only, tel. 04 90 20 33 90, www.chambresdhotesprovence.com, souslolivier@orange.fr). It's 10 minutes from Isle-sur-la-Sorgue, off D-900 near Petit Palais; heading east on D-900, go 200 yards past the sign to Mas du Jonquier.

Eating in and near Isle-sur-la-Sorgue

Cheap and mediocre restaurants are a dime a dozen in Isle-sur-la-Sorgue. You'll see several brasseries on the river, good for views and basic café fare. The restaurants I list offer solid values, but none of them is really "cheap."

Les Terrasses du Bassin is a sure riverside option with a brasserie-like feel, reasonable prices, and tasty choices. The hardworking owners are dedicated to providing a good value and welcoming service. Come for a full meal or just a *plat* and eat on the river if you can (€13-17 lunch salads and starters, €20 dinner *plats,* €25-35 dinner *menu,* closed Tue-Wed Oct-May, 2 Avenue Charles de Gaulle, tel. 04 90 38 03 16, www.lesterrassesdubassin.com).

La Balade des Saveurs is a refreshing change from the many run-of-the-mill riverfront places. Here, Sophie and Benjamin deliver fresh, Provençal cuisine at riverside tables or in their elegantly sky-lit interior at fair prices (€26-37 three-course *menus,* daily, 3 Quai Jean Juares, tel. 04 90 95 27 85).

La Prévôté is the place in town to do it up. Its lovely dining room is country-classy but not stuffy. A stream runs under the restaurant, visible through glass windows (€47-70 *menus,* closed Tue-Wed, 4 Rue J. J. Rousseau, on narrow street that runs along left side of church as you face it, tel. 04 90 38 57 29, www.la-prevote.fr).

The **Fromenterie** bakery next to the post office sells decadent quiche, monster sandwiches, prepared salads, desserts, wine and other drinks, and even plastic cutlery and cups—in other words, everything you need to picnic (open daily until 20:00, 19 Avenue des Quatre Otages).

Roussillon

With all the trendy charm of Santa Fe on a hilltop, photogenic Roussillon requires serious camera and café time. An enormous deposit of ochre gives the earth and its buildings that distinctive reddish color. Climb from any parking lot to the village center, cross the adorable square, and then pass under the bell tower and past the church to find the orientation table and the **viewpoint** at the top of the village. Roussillon sits atop appropriately named Mont Rouge ("Red Mountain") at about 1,000 feet above sea level. During the Middle Ages, a castle occupied this space. On your way down, duck into the pretty 11th-century Church of St. Michel (originally with-

in the castle walls), then linger over *un café,* or—if it's later in the day—*un pastis,* in what must be the most picturesque village square in Provence **(Place de la Mairie).** This is sightseeing in Provence—savor it. While Roussillon receives its share of day-trippers, mornings and evenings are romantically peaceful on this square.

Roussillon was Europe's capital for ochre production until World War II. A stroll to the south end of town, beyond the upper parking lot, shows you why: Roussillon sits on the world's largest known ochre deposit. A radiant orange path—the **Ochre Trail** (Le Sentier des Ocres)—leads around the richly colored, Bryce Canyon-like cliffs (€2.50, €7.50 combo-ticket with Ochre Conservatory—described next; March-April and Oct 10:00-17:30, May-June and Sept 9:30-18:30, July-Aug 9:00-19:30, Nov-Dec 11:00-15:30, closed Jan-Feb. Beware: Light-colored clothing (especially shoes) and orange powder don't mix.

For a good introduction to the history and uses of ochre, visit the **Ochre Conservatory** (Conservatoire des Ocres et Pigments Appliqués), a reconstructed ochre factory. Grab a pamphlet to follow their well-done self-guided tour, which shows how ochre is converted from an ore to a pigment—allow 45 minutes (€6, €7.50 combo-ticket with Ochre Trail, daily 9:00-18:00, July-Aug until 19:00, until 13:00-14:00 in low season, about a half-mile below Roussillon toward Apt on D-104, tel. 04 90 05 66 69, www.okhra.com).

The most central **parking** lot is Pasquier (€3). Sablons parking (€2) usually has space when other lots are full. The little **TI** is in the center, across from the Chez David restaurant. If in need of accommodations, leaf through their informative binders describing area hotels and *chambres d'hôtes.* Walkers should get info on trails from Roussillon to nearby villages (TI open usually April-Oct Mon-Sat 9:30-12:00 & 13:30-18:00, closed Sun except afternoons in July-Aug; Nov-March Mon-Sat 14:00-17:30, closed Sun; Place de la Poste, tel. 04 90 05 60 25, www.roussillon-provence.com). For free **Wi-Fi** find the Croq La Vie bookshop on the little square (Place de la Mairie), and for **groceries** find the Casino market on Avenue de La Burlière, a block from Pasquier parking (Mon-Sat 8:15-12:30 & 15:30-19:00, Sun 8:15-12:30).

PROVENCE

Sleeping in and near Roussillon

The TI posts a list of hotels and *chambres d'hôtes.*

$$$ Le Clos de la Glycine*** delivers Roussillon's plushest accommodations, with nine lovely rooms located dead-center in the village (Db-€160-190, loft suite with deck and view-€275, off-season deals, breakfast-€14, guest computer, Wi-Fi, air-con, across from the TI on Place de la Poste, tel. 04 90 05 60 13, www.luberon-hotel.com, contact@luberon-hotel.fr).

$$$La Ferme de la Huppe*,** a small, farmhouse-elegant hacienda, makes an excellent splurge. Eleven rooms gather on two levels behind the stylish pool. The decor is tasteful, understated, and rustic (Db-€145-177, much bigger Db-€207-225, includes good breakfast buffet, mini-fridges, air-con, Wi-Fi; between Joucas and Gordes on D-156 to Goult, just off D-2; tel. 04 90 72 12 25, www.lafermedelahuppe.com, info@lafermedelahuppe.com). The restaurant has an excellent reputation; notice the shelf of French cookery books at reception. Dine poolside or in the smart dining room (lunch-€17-29, dinner-€39-45 for seasonal three-course *menu* or €62 five-course tasting *menu,* closed all day Sun and Mon at lunch).

$$$ At **Le Mas d'Estonge,** charming Christiane and Robert (call me Bob) welcome you into their little Provençal paradise in a small neighborhood close by Roussillon. Their four well-furnished and comfy rooms share a sweet patio, a common kitchen, and a pool (Db-€95-135, suites-€165-190, 10 minutes from Roussillon on D-227, tel. 04 90 05 63 13, www.destonge.com, destonge@gmail.com).

$$ Le Clos des Cigales is a good refuge run by friendly Philippe and his wife, Brigitte. Of their five blue-shuttered, stylish bungalows, two are doubles and three are two-room suites with tiny kitchenettes; all have private patios facing a big pool (Db-€80-95, Tb/Qb suite-€100-125, includes breakfast, table tennis, hammock, 5 minutes from Roussillon toward Goult on D-104, tel. 04 90 05 73 72, www.leclosdescigales.com, philippe.lherbeil@wanadoo.fr).

$$ Hostellerie des Commandeurs** has simple, good-value rooms in the center of lovely little Joucas. It's kid-friendly, with a big pool and a sports field/play area next door. Ask for a south-facing room *(coté sud)* for the best views. All rooms have showers and air-conditioning (Db-€72-78, extra bed-€16, mini-fridges, tel. 04 90 05 78 01, www.lescommandeurs.com, hostellerie@lescommandeurs.com). The simple restaurant offers Provençal cuisine at fair prices (three-course *menus* from €24).

$$ Hôtel Rêves d'Ocres** provides a good two-star value in Roussillon. Rooms are tastefully decorated, though bathrooms could use updating. Eight smaller rooms under the roof have low ceilings and small terraces; I prefer the larger rooms on the second floor (Db without balcony-€75-85, Db with balcony-€80-95, Tb-€115, Qb-€140, meek air-con, Wi-Fi in lobby only, Route de Gordes, tel. 04 90 05 60 50, www.hotel-revesdocres.com, hotelrevesdocres@wanadoo.fr). Coming from Gordes and Joucas, it's the first building you pass in Roussillon.

$ Madame Cherel rents bare-bones rooms with firm beds and a shared view terrace at fair rates in Roussillon (D-€46, family suite available, cash only, includes basic breakfast, Wi-Fi, access to kitchenette, 3 blocks from upper parking lot, between Casino store and school, La Burlière, tel. 04 90 05 71 71, mulhanc@hotmail.com). Chatty and sincere Cherel speaks English and is a wealth of regional travel tips.

Eating in or near Roussillon

Choose ambience over cuisine if dining in Roussillon, and enjoy any of the eateries on the main square. Restaurants change with the mistral here—what's good one year disappoints the next. Consider my suggestions and go with what looks best.

On Place de la Poste: **Chez David,** at the recommended hotel Le Clos de la Glycine (described earlier), is a good place to splurge. You can enjoy a fine meal on the terrace or from an interior window table with point-blank views over the ochre cliffs (€35-55 *menus,* closed all day Wed and Sun evening, Place de la Poste, tel. 04 90 05 60 13).

La Grappe de Raisin is a top choice, with a fine selection of salads and a house specialty of a simple but tasty plate of vegetables and fish served with aioli (€16.50 aioli plate, lunch daily, dinner available only May-Sept, next to TI, tel. 04 90 71 38 06).

Le Comptoir des Arts offers fair prices and a fine view. Try the aioli platter smothered with veggies and fish, or the Provençal burger topped with ratatouille (Place du Pasquier, tel. 04 90 74 11 92).

On Place de la Mairie: These places on an atmospheric square offer similar ambience and values. At least one should be open.

Le Bistrot de Roussillon offers decent salads and *plats* for the right price. There's a breezy terrace in back and a comfy interior (€16 for a filling salad and dessert, €13-18 *plats,* daily, tel. 04 90 05 74 45). Or try **Café Couleur** and **Le Castrum,** which flank Le Bistrot de Roussillon.

Near Roussillon: **Le Petit Ecole** makes for a tasty stop a few minutes' drive below Roussillon (just off D-900). The charming outdoor seating area is shady in the afternoon and twinkles in the evening. The young owners use local, fresh ingredients (€18 lunch special, €25-€35 dinner *menus,* closed Sun evening and all day Mon, in Le Chêne, tel. 04 32 52 16 41).

More Luberon Hill Towns and Sights

Gordes

The Luberon's most impressively situated hill town is worth a quick stop to admire its setting. As you approach Gordes, make a hard right at the impressive viewpoint. Get out and consider this: In the 1960s Gordes was a virtual ghost town of derelict buildings, but now it has been renovated from top to bottom and filled with people who live in a world without calluses. Many Parisian big-shots and monied foreigners invested heavily, restoring dream homes and putting property values and café prices out of sight for locals. Between the village's natural beauty and the boutiques that followed the money, expect gridlock and parking headaches in high season (arrive early and pay €4 to park a 10- to 15-minute walk from the village). Beyond its viewpoint, the village has little of interest except for its Tuesday market (ends at 13:00) and its 11th-century castle, which houses contemporary art exhibits. The more interesting Abbey Notre-Dame de Sénanque is nearby and well-marked from Gordes.

Abbey Notre-Dame de Sénanque

This still-functioning and beautifully situated Cistercian abbey was built in 1148 as a back-to-basics reaction to the excesses of Benedictine abbeys. The abbey is worth the trip for its splendid and remote setting alone. Come first thing, or linger later and stop at a pullout for a bird's-eye view as you descend, then wander the abbey's perimeter. The abbey church (Eglise Abbatiale) is always open (except during Mass, but you're welcome to attend), and highlights the utter simplicity sought by these monks. In late June through much of July, the five hectares of lavender fields that surround the abbey make for breathtaking pictures and draw loads of visitors. Those arriving just when it opens find a peaceful place they can tour on their own (good English handout). Those arriving after 11:00 must visit the abbey on a 50-minute, French-only

tour (English booklet with translations available). I'd skip the tour and just wander the grounds.

Cost and Hours: €7, with or without the French-only tour (mandatory Feb-Oct after 11:00, tours offered Mon-Sat usually at 10:10, 10:30, 14:30, 15:30, and 16:30; Sun at 14:30, 15:30, and 16:30; more tours June-Sept; tel. 04 90 72 05 72, www.senanque.fr. Appropriate clothing is required for entry—shoulders and knees must be covered. You can also attend Mass (Mon-Sat at 11:45, Sun at 10:00, check website or call to confirm).

Julien Bridge (Pont Julien)

Due south of Roussillon, just below D-900 (see map on page 662), this delicate, three-arched bridge survives as a testimony to Roman engineers—and to the importance of this rural area 2,000 years ago. It's the only surviving bridge on what was the main road from northern Italy to Provence—the primary route used by Roman armies. The 215-foot-long Roman bridge was under construction from 27 B.C. to A.D. 14. Mortar had not yet been invented, so (as with Pont du Gard) the stones were carefully set in place. Amazingly, the bridge survives today, having outlived Roman marches, hundreds of floods, and decades of automobile traffic. A new bridge finally rerouted traffic from this beautiful structure in 2005.

Bonnieux

This village looks better from a distance. The center has no pedestrian focus—skip it.

Lacoste

This town is worth a stop to wander its pretty lanes to the base of the castle for views and to stop for a meal at **Bar/Restaurant de France**'s outdoor tables overlooking Bonnieux (€10-13 omelets and *plats,* daily, lunch only off-season, tel. 04 90 75 82 25). A small *épicerie* near the church has just enough fixings to make a picnic.

Ménerbes

Ménerbes, (in)famous as the village that drew author Peter Mayle's attention to this region, has an upscale but welcoming feel in its center. Wine bars, cafés, and a few galleries gather where key lanes intersect. To explore the old town, walk to both ends of the linear rock that extends from the small commercial area. Find **La Maison de la Truffe et du Vin,** with a nice shop and a cute tasting room representing all 180 of the Luberon's wines (sold here for the same price you'd pay at the winery, daily 12:30-17:00, tel. 04 90 72 38 37, www.vin-truffe-luberon.com).

▲Oppède-le-Vieux

This off-the-beaten-path, fixer-upper of a village was completely abandoned in 1910, and today has a ghost town-like feel. Climb the 20-minute path up to the small church and castle ruins for views. **Le Petit Café** hangs below (€12-15 salads, €25-lunch *menu,* closed Tue-Wed eves, all day Thu, and mid-Dec-April). They also have simple but comfy rooms, all with nice views (Db-€65-75, big Db-€95, extra bed-€15, includes breakfast, air-con, indoor Jacuzzi and sauna-€10, rooftop terrace, tel. 04 90 76 74 01, www.petitcafe.fr).

THE FRENCH RIVIERA

La Côte d'Azur: Nice • Villefranche-sur-Mer • The Three Corniches • Monaco • Antibes • Inland Riviera

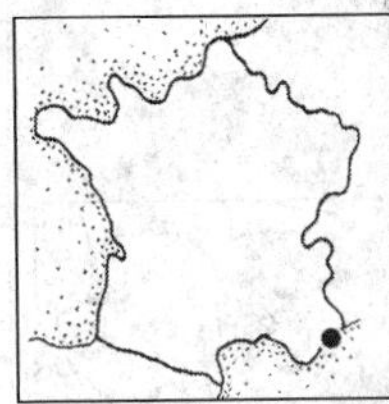

A hundred years ago, celebrities from London to Moscow flocked to the French Riviera to socialize, gamble, and escape the dreary weather at home. Today, budget vacationers and heat-seeking Europeans fill belle-époque resorts at France's most sought-after fun-in-the-sun destination.

Some of the Continent's most stunning scenery and intriguing museums lie along this strip of land—as do millions of sun-worshipping tourists. Nice has world-class museums, a splendid beachfront promenade, a seductive old town, and all the drawbacks of a major city (traffic, crime, pollution, and so on). The day-trip possibilities are easy and exciting: Monaco offers a royal welcome and a fairytale past; Antibes has a thriving port and silky sand beaches; and the inland hill towns present a rocky and photogenic alternative to the beach scene. Evenings on the Riviera, a.k.a. la Côte d'Azur, were made for a promenade and outdoor dining.

CHOOSE A HOME BASE

My favorite home bases are Nice, Antibes, and Villefranche-sur-Mer.

Nice is the region's capital and France's fifth-largest city. With convenient train and bus connections to most regional sights, this is the most practical base for train travelers. Urban Nice also has a full palette of museums, a beach scene that rocks, the best selection of hotels in all price ranges, and good nightlife options. A car is a headache in Nice, though it's easily stored at one of the many pricey parking garages or for free at an outer tram station.

Nearby **Antibes** is smaller, with a bustling center, a lively night scene, great sandy beaches, grand vistas, good walking trails,

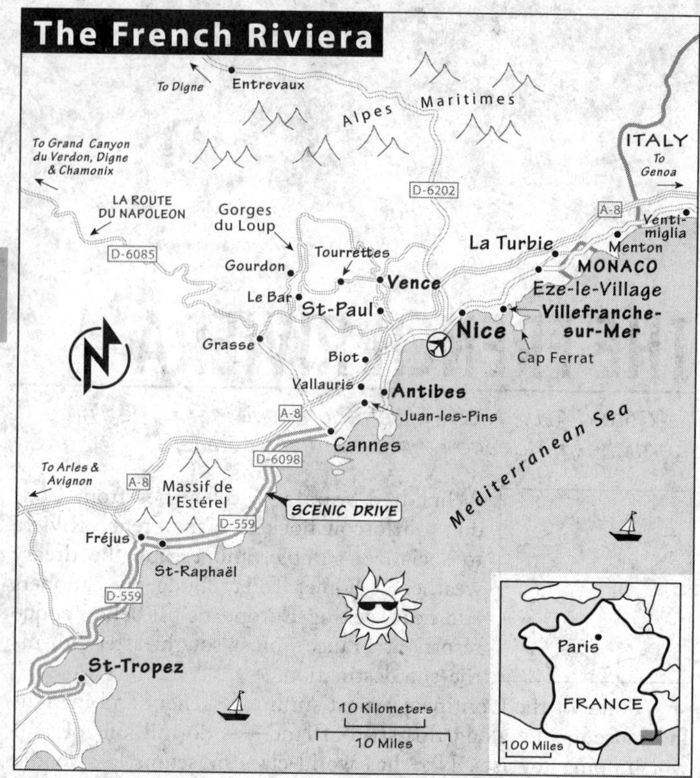

and a much-admired Picasso Museum. Antibes has frequent train service to Nice and Monaco, and it's easy for drivers, with light traffic and easy hotel parking.

Villefranche-sur-Mer is the romantic's choice, with a serene setting and small-town warmth. It has finely ground pebble beaches, quick public transportation to Nice and Monaco, easy parking, and a small selection of hotels in most price ranges.

PLANNING YOUR TIME

Ideally, allow a full day for Nice, a day for Monaco and the Corniche route that connects it with Nice, and a half-day for Villefranche-sur-Mer or Antibes. Monaco and Villefranche-sur-Mer are radiant at night (sights are closed, but crowds are few; consider dinner there), and Antibes works well by day (good beaches and hiking) and night (fine choice of restaurants and a lively after-hours scene). Hill-town-loving naturalists should allow a day to explore the hill-capping hamlets near Vence.

HELPFUL HINTS

Medical Help: Riviera Medical Services has a list of English-speaking physicians all along the Riviera. They can help you make an appointment or call an ambulance (tel. 04 93 26 12 70, www.rivieramedical.com).

Canadian Consulate in Nice: Tel. 04 93 92 93 22, fax 04 93 92 55 51 (2 Place Franklin, consulat.canada-nice@amb-canada.fr).

Closed Days: The following sights are closed on Mondays: the Modern and Contemporary Art Museum, Fine Arts Museum, and Cours Saleya market in Nice, along with Antibes' Picasso Museum and Marché Provençal market (Sept-June). On Tuesdays these museums are closed: the Chagall, Matisse, Masséna, and Archaeological museums in Nice and the Renoir Museum in Cagnes-sur-Mer. On Fridays Matisse's Chapel of the Rosary in Vence is closed.

Events: The Riviera is famous for staging major events. Unless you're actually taking part in the festivities, these occasions give you only room shortages and traffic jams. Here are the three biggies for 2015: **Nice Carnival** (Feb 13-March 1); Festival de Cannes, better known as the **Cannes Film Festival** (May 15-26, www.festival-cannes.com); and the **Grand Prix of Monaco** (May 21-24, www.grand-prix-monaco.com).

Local Guides: Agnès Dumartin, a top guide for the region, is a good teacher who understands Nice particularly well and loves all forms of art. Agnès doesn't drive, but she's ideal for walks in Nice and is happy to join your car for regional sights (€210/half-day, €295/day, mobile 06 81 82 17 67, agnes.dumartin@orange.fr). **Sylvie Di Cristo** offers terrific full-day tours throughout the French Riviera in a car or minivan. She adores educating people about this area's culture and history and adapts her tour to your interests—from quiet hill towns to wine, cuisine, art, or outdoor activities, including rafting, biking, and hiking (€520/day for 2 people, €600/day for 3-8 people, 2-person minimum, mobile 06 09 88 83 83, www.frenchrivieraguides.net, dicristosylvie@gmail.com). **Ingrid Schmucker** is passionate about her adopted region, a good teacher of its history and art, and brings a lovely personality to her work (€490/day for 4 people or €550/day for 5-7 people in her minivan; €180/half-day or €285/day if you don't need transportation, tel. 06 14 83 03 33, www.kultours.fr, info@kultours.fr). **Sofia Villavicencio** is a pleasant guide who makes the Riviera's art come alive (€145/half-day, €200/day, mobile 06 68 51 55 52, sofia.villavicencio@laposte.net).

Cooking Tour and Classes: Charming Canadian Francophile Rosa Jackson, a food journalist, Cordon Bleu-trained cook, and longtime resident of France, runs **Les Petits Farcis,** which offers a variety of food-and-wine oriented walking tours in Nice (€80-150/person). She also teaches popular cooking classes in Vieux Nice, which include a morning trip to the open-air market on Cours Saleya to pick up ingredients and an afternoon session spent creating an authentic Niçois meal from your purchases (€195/person, mobile 06 81 67 41 22, www.petitsfarcis.com).

Minivan Tours: The TI and most hotels have information on minivan excursions from Nice (roughly €50-70/half-day, €80-120/day).

Longer-Stay Rentals: Renting an apartment, house, or villa can be a cost-effective way to explore the Côte d'Azur. Rentals are typically by the week, giving you time to take advantage of day-trip possibilities. **Riviera Pebbles** offers a wide range of rental apartments throughout the Riviera (www.rivierapebbles.com). VRBO, an international network of vacation rentals (houses, apartments, and *gîtes*), cuts out the middleman and puts you directly in touch with the owner (www.vrbo.com).

Cruise-Ship Sightseeing: The French Riviera is a popular cruise destination. Arriving ships are divided about evenly between three ports: Nice, Villefranche-sur-Mer, and Monaco. I've provided arrival instructions in the "Connections" section for these ports. If your cruise includes destinations beyond the French Riviera, consider my guidebook, *Rick Steves Mediterranean Cruise Ports.*

Updates to This Book: For updates to this book, check ricksteves.com/update.

GETTING AROUND THE RIVIERA

If taking the train or bus, have coins handy. Ticket machines don't take US credit cards or euro bills, smaller train stations may be unstaffed, and bus drivers can't make change for large bills.

By Public Transportation: Trains and buses do a good job of connecting places along the coast, with bonus views along many routes. Buses also provide reasonable service to some inland hill towns. Choose the bus for convenience and economy, or the pricier but faster train when you want to save time.

Buses are an amazing deal in the Riviera. Any one-way bus or tram ride costs €1.50 (€10 for 10 tickets) whether you're riding just within Nice, 20 minutes to Villefranche-sur-Mer, 45 minutes to Monaco, or an hour to Antibes. The €1.50 ticket is good for 74 minutes of travel in one direction anywhere within the bus sys-

tem except for airport buses (and can't be used for a round-trip). Buy your bus ticket from the driver (be sure to carry small bills or coins) or from the machines at stops, and validate your ticket in the machine on board. You can even transfer between the buses of the Lignes d'Azur (the region's main bus company, www.lignesdazur.com) and the TAM (Transports Alpes-Maritimes); if you board a TAM bus and need a transfer, ask for *un ticket correspondance*. A €5 all-day ticket is good on Nice's city buses, tramway, and airport express bus, plus selected buses serving nearby destinations (such as Villefranche and Eze-le-Village). The general rule of thumb is this: If the bus number has one or two digits, it's covered with the all-day ticket; with three digits it's not.

The **train** is more expensive but still a good deal (for example, from Nice to Monaco by train is €3, versus €1.50 by bus), and there's no quicker way to move about the Riviera (http://en.voyages-sncf.com). Speedy trains link the Riviera's beachfront destinations—Cannes, Antibes, Nice, Villefranche-sur-Mer, Monaco, and Men-

Public Transportation in the French Riviera

From	To Cannes	To Antibes	To Nice
Cannes by Train	N/A	2/hr, 15 min	2/hr, 30-40 min
Cannes by Bus	N/A	#200, 2-4/hr, 35 min	#200, 2-4/hr, 1.5-1.75 hrs
Antibes by Train	2/hr, 15 min	N/A	2/hr, 15-30 min
Antibes by Bus	#200, 2-4/hr, 35 min	N/A	#200, 2-4/hr, 1-1.5 hrs
Nice by Train	2/hr, 30-40 min	2/hr, 15-30 min	N/A
Nice by Bus	#200, 2-4/hr, 1.5-1.75 hrs	#200, 2-4/hr, 1-1.5 hrs	N/A
Villefranche-sur-Mer by Train	2/hr, 50 min	2/hr, 40 min	2/hr, 10 min
Villefranche-sur-Mer by Bus	Not recommended	Not recommended	#100, 3-4/hr, 20 min; also #81, 2-3/hr, 20 min
Cap Ferrat by Train	Bus #81 to Beaulieu-sur-Mer (2-3/hr, 10 min), then train to Cannes (2/hr, 1 hr)	Bus #81 to Beaulieu-sur-Mer (2-3/hr, 10 min), then train to Antibes (2/hr, 40 min)	N/A
Cap Ferrat by Bus	Not recommended	#81 to Nice (2-3/hr, 35 min), then #200 to Antibes (3-4/hr, 1-1.5 hrs)	#81, 2-3 /hr, 35 min

Note: Bus frequencies are given for Monday-Saturday. Sunday often has limited or no bus service.

To Villefranche-sur-Mer	To Cap Ferrat	To Eze-le-Village	To Monaco
2/hr, 50 min	2/hr, 1 hr to Beaulieu-sur-Mer, then bus #81 to Cap Ferrat (2-3/hr, 10 min)	2/hr, 1 hr to Eze-Bord-de-Mer, then bus #83 to Eze (8/day, 15 min)	2/hr, 70 min
Not recommended	Not recommended	Not recommended	Not recommended
2/hr, 40 min	2/hr, 40 min to Beaulieu-sur-Mer, then bus #81 to Cap Ferrat (2-3/hr, 10 min)	2/hr, 45 min to Eze-Bord-de-Mer, then bus #83 to Eze (8/day, 15 min)	2/hr, 50 min
Not recommended	#200 to Nice (2-4/hr, 1-1.5 hrs), then #81 to Cap Ferrat (2-3/hr, 35 min)	Not recommended	Not recommended
2/hr, 10 min	Not recommended	2/hr, 15 min to Eze-Bord-de-Mer, then bus #83 to Eze (8/day, 15 min)	2/hr, 20 min
#100, 3-4/hr, 20 min; also #81, 2-3/hr, 20 min	#81, 2-3/hr, 35 min	#82/#112, 8-16/day, 40 min	#100, 3-4/hr, 45 min
N/A	N/A	2/hr, 10 min to Eze-Bord-de-Mer, then bus #83 to Eze (8/day, 15 min)	2/hr, 10 min
N/A	#81, 2-3/hr, 20 min	#80 to upper Villefranche (hourly), then bus #82/#112, 8-16/day, 20 min	#100, 3-4/hr, 25 min
N/A	N/A	N/A	N/A
#81, 2-3/hr, 20 min	N/A	#100 direction: Monaco to Gare d'Eze stop (3-4/hr, 30 min), then bus #83 to village (8/day, 15 min)	#100, 3-4/hr, 20 min

(continued on next page)

Public Transportation in the French Riviera

(continued from previous page)

From	To Cannes	To Antibes	To Nice
Eze-le-Village by Train	Bus #83 to Eze-Bord-de-Mer, 8/day, 15 min, then train to Cannes (2/hr, 1 hr)	Bus #83 to Eze-Bord-de-Mer, 8/day, 15 min, then train to Antibes (2/hr, 45 min)	Bus #83 to Eze-Bord-de-Mer, 8/day, 15 min, then train to Nice (2/hr, 15 min)
Eze-le-Village by Bus	Not recommended	Not recommended	#82/#112, 8-16/day, 40 min
Monaco by Train	2/hr, 70 min	2/hr, 50 min	2/hr, 20 min
Monaco by Bus	Not recommended	Not recommended	#100, 3-4/hr, 45 min

ton. Never board a train without a ticket or valid pass—fare inspectors don't accept any excuses, and the minimum fine is €70.

Nice makes the most convenient base for day trips, though public transport also works well from Riviera towns such as Antibes and Villefranche-sur-Mer. Details are provided under each destination's "Connections" section. For a scenic inland train ride, take the narrow-gauge train into the Alps (see 772).

For an overview of many Riviera train and bus connections, see the "Public Transportation in the French Riviera" chart on pages 676-679.

By Boat: Trans Côte d'Azur offers boat service from Nice to Monaco or to St-Tropez from June into September (tel. 04 92 98 71 30, www.trans-cote-azur.com). For details, see "Getting Around the Riviera from Nice" (page 687).

THE RIVIERA'S ART SCENE

The list of artists who have painted the Riviera reads like a Who's Who of 20th-century art. Pierre-Auguste Renoir, Henri Matisse, Marc Chagall, Georges Braque, Raoul Dufy, Fernand Léger, and Pablo Picasso all lived and worked here—and raved about the region's wonderful light. Their simple, semi-abstract, and—most importantly—colorful works reflect the pleasurable atmosphere of the Riviera. You'll experience the same landscapes they painted in this

To Villefranche-sur-Mer	To Cap Ferrat	To Eze-le-Village	To Monaco
Bus #83 to Eze-Bord-de-Mer, 8/day, 15 min, then train to Villefranche (2/hr, 10 min)	N/A	N/A	N/A
#82/#112 to upper Villefranche (8-16/day, 20 min), then bus #80 to Villefranche (hourly)	#83 to Gare d'Eze stop (8/day, 15 min), then bus #100 direction: Nice (3-4/hr, 30 min)	N/A	#112, 6/day Mon-Sat, none on Sun, 20 min
2/hr, 10 min	N/A	N/A	N/A
#100, 3-4/hr, 25 min	#100, 3-4/hr, 20 min	#112, 6/day Mon-Sat, none on Sun, 20 min	N/A

bright, sun-drenched region, punctuated with views of the "azure sea." Try to imagine the Riviera with a fraction of the people and development you see today.

But the artists were mostly drawn to the uncomplicated lifestyle of fishermen and farmers that has reigned here since time began. As the artists grew older, they retired in the sun, turned their backs on modern art's "isms," and painted with the wide-eyed wonder of children, using bright primary colors, basic outlines, and simple subjects.

A dynamic concentration of well-organized modern- and contemporary-art museums (many described in this book) litter the Riviera, allowing art lovers to appreciate these masters' works while immersed in the same sun and culture that inspired them. Many of the museums were designed to blend pieces with the surrounding views, gardens, and fountains, thus highlighting that modern art is not only stimulating, but sometimes simply beautiful.

THE RIVIERA'S CUISINE SCENE

The Riviera adds an Italian-Mediterranean flair to the food of Provence. While many of the same dishes served in Provence are available throughout the Riviera (see "Provence's Cuisine Scene" on page 568), there are differences, especially if you look for anything Italian or from the sea.

Local specialties are bouillabaisse (the spicy seafood stew that seems worth the cost only for those with a seafood fetish), *bourride* (a creamy fish soup thickened with aioli, a garlic sauce), and *salade niçoise* (nee-swaz). This salad has many variations, though most include a base of green salad topped with green beans, boiled potatoes (sometimes rice), tomatoes (sometimes corn), anchovies, olives, hard-boiled eggs, and lots of tuna. You'll also find these tasty bread treats: *pan bagnat* (like a *salade niçoise* stuffed into a hollowed-out soft roll), *pissaladière* (bread dough topped with onions, olives, and anchovies), *fougasse* (a spindly, lace-like bread sometimes flavored with nuts, herbs, olives, or ham), and *socca* (a thin chickpea crêpe, seasoned with pepper and olive oil and often served in a paper cone by street vendors).

Italian cuisine is native (ravioli was first made in Nice), easy to find, and generally a good value (*pâtes fraîches* means "fresh pasta"). For wine, Bandol (red) and Cassis (white) are popular and from a region nearly on the Riviera. The only wines made in the Riviera are Bellet rosé and white.

Remember, restaurants serve only during lunch (11:30-14:00) and dinner (19:00-21:00, later in bigger cities); cafés—except for the smaller ones—serve food throughout the day.

Nice

Nice (sounds like "niece"), with its spectacular Alps-to-Mediterranean surroundings, is the big-city highlight of the Riviera. Its traffic-free old city mixes Italian and French flavors to create a spicy Mediterranean dressing, while its big squares, broad seaside walkways, and long beaches invite lounging and people-watching. Nice may be nice, but it's hot and jammed in July and August—reserve ahead and get a room with air-conditioning. Everything you'll want to see in Nice is either within walking distance or a short bike, bus, or tram ride away.

Orientation to Nice

The main points of interest lie between the beach and the train tracks (about 15 blocks apart—see map on page 682). The city revolves around its grand Place Masséna, where pedestrian-friendly Avenue Jean Médecin meets Vieux (Old) Nice and the Albert 1er parkway (with quick access to the beaches). It's a 20-minute walk (or about €18 by taxi) from the train station to the beach, and a 20-minute walk along the promenade from the fancy Hôtel Negresco to the heart of Vieux Nice.

A 10-minute ride on the smooth-as-silk tramway through the center of the city connects the train station, Place Masséna, Vieux Nice, and the port (from nearby Place Garibaldi). The tram and all city and regional buses cost only €1.50 per trip (see "Getting Around Nice," later). Work is under way on a new tramway line—much of which will be underground—that will parallel the Promenade des Anglais (should be completed in 2017).

TOURIST INFORMATION

Nice's helpful TIs share a phone number and website (tel. 08 92 70 74 07, www.nicetourisme.com). There are TI branches at the **airport** (desks in both terminals, typically quiet, daily 9:00-18:00, until 20:00 April-Sept); next to the **train station** (busy but open early, summer Mon-Sat 8:00-20:00, Sun 9:00-19:00, rest of year Mon-Sat 9:00-19:00, Sun 10:00-17:00); facing the **beach** at 5 Promenade des Anglais (moderately busy, daily 9:00-18:00, until 20:00 July-Aug, closed Sun off-season); and in a kiosk at the south end of **Place Masséna** (less busy, mid-June-Sept only, typically daily 10:00-19:00). Pick up the thorough *Practical Guide to Nice* and a free Nice map, but skip the Riviera Pass. You can also get day-trip information at any TI (including maps of Monaco or Antibes, details on boat excursions, and bus schedules to Eze-le-Village, La Turbie, Vence, and other destinations).

ARRIVAL IN NICE

By Train: All trains stop at Nice's main station, called Nice-Ville (you don't want the suburban Nice Riquier station). With your back to the tracks, baggage storage and car rentals are to the right, and airport bus #99 stops in front. The station area is always busy: Never leave your bags unattended and don't linger.

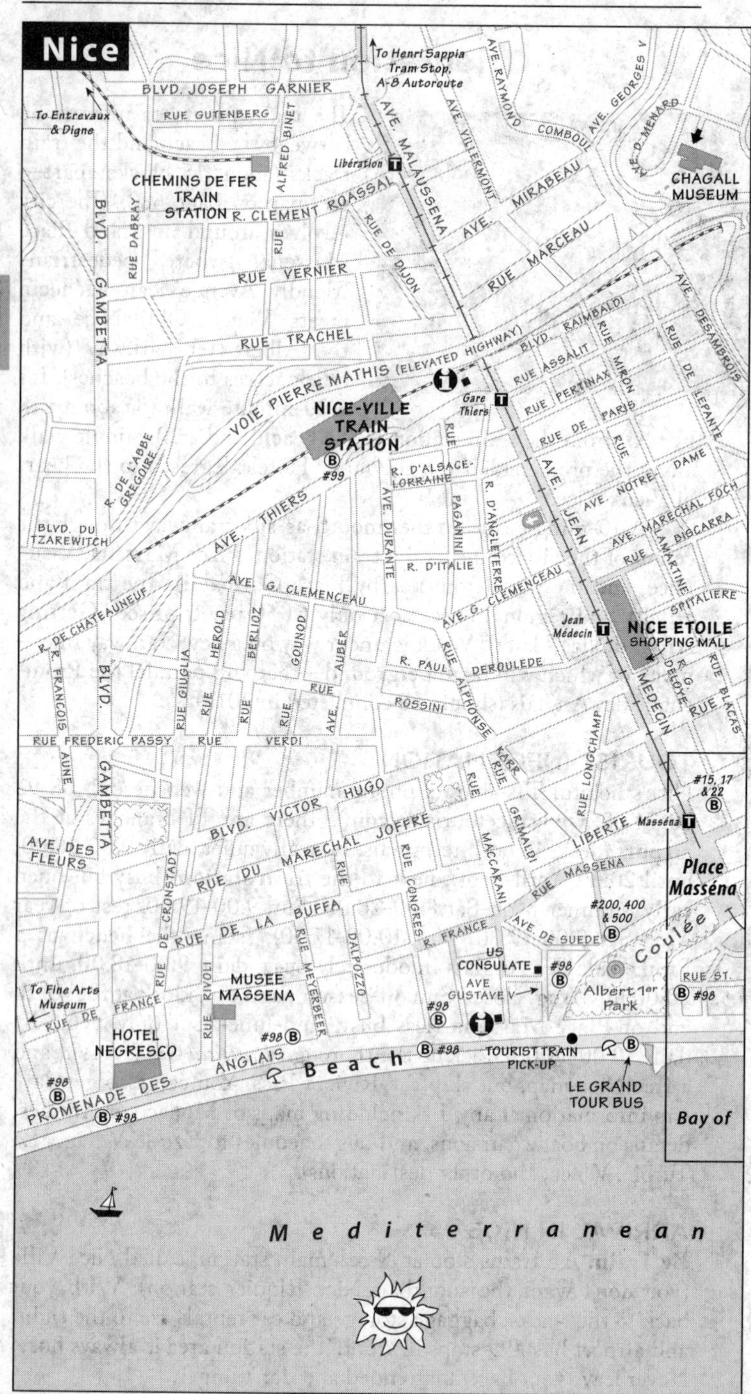
Nice
To Henri Sappia Tram Stop, A-8 Autoroute
To Entrevaux & Digne
BLVD. JOSEPH GARNIER
RUE GUTENBERG
ALFRED BINET
AVE. MALAUSSENA
AVE. VILLERMONT
AVE. RAYMOND COMBOUL
AVE. GEORGES V
AVE. D. MENARD
Libération
CHAGALL MUSEUM
CHEMINS DE FER TRAIN STATION
R. CLEMENT ROASSAL
AVE. MIRABEAU
BLVD. GAMBETTA
RUE DABRAY
RUE DE DIJON
RUE VERNIER
RUE MARCEAU
AVE. DESAMBROIS
RUE TRACHEL
BLVD. RAIMBALDI
VOIE PIERRE MATHIS (ELEVATED HIGHWAY)
RUE ASSALIT
RUE MIRON
RUE DE LEPANTE
Gare Thiers
RUE PERTINAX
NICE-VILLE TRAIN STATION
#99
RUE DE PARIS
R. DE L'ABBE GREGOIRE
R. D'ALSACE-LORRAINE
AVE. NOTRE-DAME
AVE. JEAN MEDECIN
AVE. THIERS
AVE. DURANTE
PAGANINI
R. D'ANGLETERRE
AVE. MARECHAL FOCH
BLVD. DU TZAREWITCH
R. D'ITALIE
RUE BISCARRA
LAMARTINE
AVE. G. CLEMENCEAU
SPITALIERE
R. DE CHATEAUNEUF
HEROLD
BERLIOZ
GOUNOD
AUBER
Jean Médecin
NICE ETOILE SHOPPING MALL
R. G. DELOYE
R. PAUL DEROULEDE
RUE ALPHONSE KARR
R. FRANCOIS AUNE
RUE GIUGLIA
RUE ROSSINI
RUE BLACAS
RUE FREDERIC PASSY
RUE VERDI
BLVD. VICTOR HUGO
RUE LONGCHAMP
#15, 17 & 22
AVE. DES FLEURS
RUE DU MARECHAL JOFFRE
RUE GRIMALDI
LIBERTE
Masséna
Place Masséna
RUE DE CRONSTADT
RUE CONGRES
MACCARANI
RUE MASSENA
RUE DE LA BUFFA
#200, 400 & 500
AVE. DE SUEDE
R. FRANCE
Coulée
US CONSULATE
#98
AVE GUSTAVE V
RUE ST.
Albert 1er Park
To Fine Arts Museum
RUE DE FRANCE
RUE RIVOLI
MUSEE MASSENA
RUE MEYERBEER
DALPOZZO
HOTEL NEGRESCO
TOURIST TRAIN PICK-UP
PROMENADE DES ANGLAIS
Beach
LE GRAND TOUR BUS
Bay of
Mediterranean

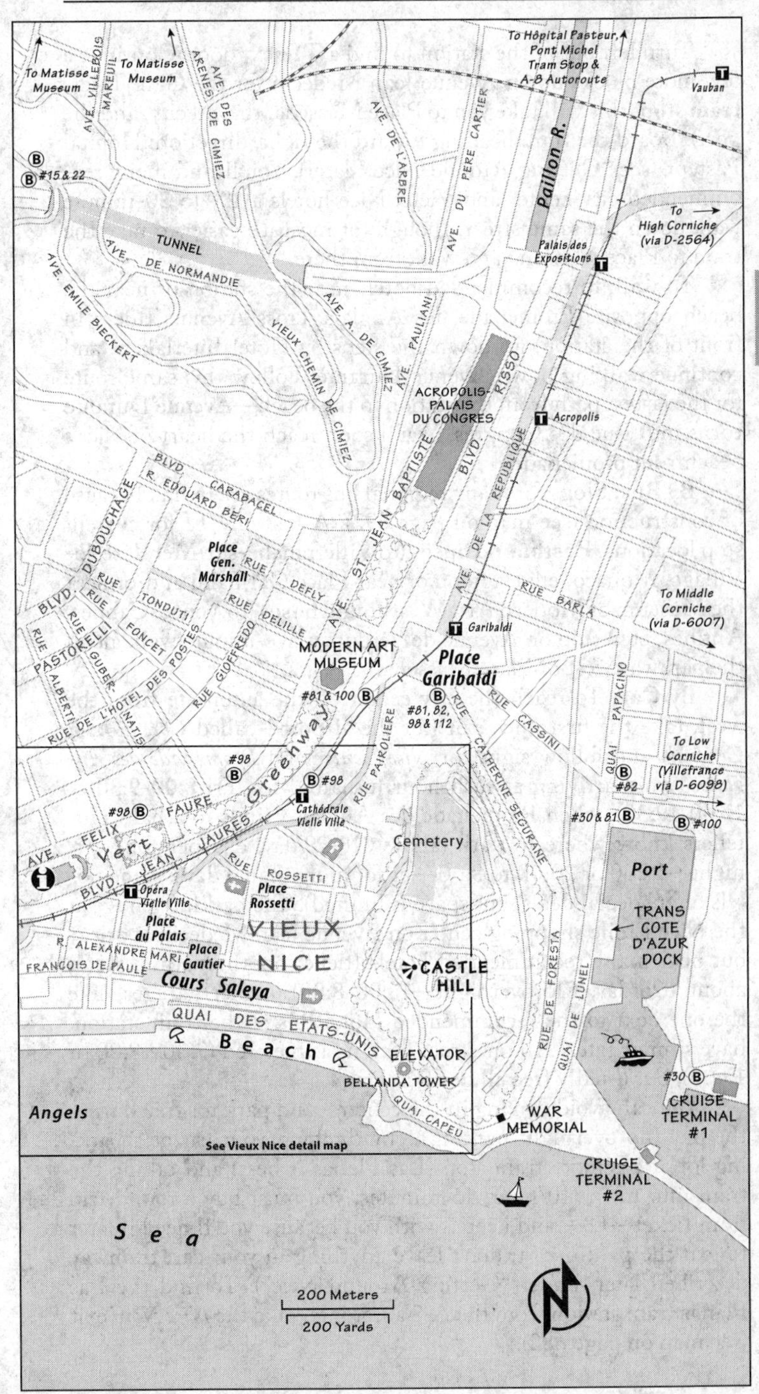
To Matisse Museum
To Matisse Museum
To Hôpital Pasteur, Pont Michel Tram Stop & A-8 Autoroute
Vauban
#15 & 22
Paillon R.
To High Corniche (via D-2564)
TUNNEL
Palais des Expositions
ACROPOLIS-PALAIS DU CONGRES
Acropolis
Place Gen. Marshall
To Middle Corniche (via D-6007)
MODERN ART MUSEUM
Garibaldi
Place Garibaldi
#81 & 100
#81, 82, 98 & 112
To Low Corniche (Villefrance via D-6098)
#98
#98
#82
#98
Cathédrale Vielle Ville
#30 & 81
#100
Greenway
Vert
Cemetery
Port
Opéra Vielle Ville
Place Rossetti
TRANS COTE D'AZUR DOCK
Place du Palais
VIEUX NICE
Place Gautier
CASTLE HILL
Cours Saleya
Beach
ELEVATOR
BELLANDA TOWER
#30
CRUISE TERMINAL #1
Angels
WAR MEMORIAL
See Vieux Nice detail map
CRUISE TERMINAL #2
Sea
200 Meters
200 Yards
AVE. VILLEBOIS MAREUIL
AVE. DES ARENES DE CIMIEZ
AVE. DE L'ARBRE
AVE. DU PERE CARTIER
AVE. DE NORMANDIE
AVE. EMILE BIECKERT
VIEUX CHEMIN DE CIMIEZ
AVE. A. DE CIMIEZ
AVE. PAULIANI
BLVD. RISSO
AVE. ST. JEAN BAPTISTE
AVE. DE LA REPUBLIQUE
BLVD. CARABACEL
R. EDOUARD BERI
BLVD. DUBOUCHAGE
RUE DEFLY
RUE TONDUTI
RUE DELILLE
RUE BARLA
RUE FONCET
RUE PASTORELLI
RUE GUBERNATIS
RUE ALBERTI
RUE DE L'HOTEL DES POSTES
RUE GIOFFREDO
RUE CASSINI
QUAI PAPACINO
RUE CATHERINE SEGURANE
RUE PAIROLIERE
AVE. FELIX FAURE
BLVD. JEAN JAURES
RUE ROSSETTI
R. ALEXANDRE MARI
FRANCOIS DE PAULE
QUAI DES ETATS-UNIS
QUAI CAPEU
RUE DE FORESTA
QUAI DE LUNEL

Turn left out of the station to find a **TI** next door. Continue a few more blocks down Avenue Jean Médecin for the Gare Thiers **tram stop** (this will take you to Place Masséna, the old city, and the port). Board the tram heading toward the right, direction: Hôpital Pasteur (see "Getting Around Nice," later). You'll find many recommended city-center and Vieux Nice hotels a 10- to 20-minute walk down the same street, though for most it's easier to take the tram to Place Masséna and walk from there.

To walk to recommended hotels near the station or near the beach opposite Promenade des Anglais, cross Avenue Thiers in front of the station, go down the steps by Hôtel Interlaken, and continue walking down Avenue Durante. Follow this same route for the fastest path from the station to the beach—Avenue Durante turns into Rue des Congrés. You'll soon reach the heart of Nice's beachfront promenade.

By Bus: Stops for many regional bus routes are in flux because of construction (see map on page 692). Ask at any TI for current stop locations. **Eastbound buses** (to Villefranche-sur-Mer, Eze-le-Village, Monaco, etc.) stop on or near Place Garibaldi and/or near the Museum of Modern Art. **Westbound buses** (to Vence, Cannes, Antibes, etc.) stop on Avenue de Verdun, a five-minute walk along the parkway west of Place Masséna.

By Car: To reach the city center on the autoroute from the west, take the first Nice exit (for the airport—called *Côte d'Azur, Central*) and follow signs for *Nice Centre* and *Promenade des Anglais.* Avoid arriving at rush hour (usually Mon-Fri 8:00-9:30 & 17:00-19:30), when Promenade des Anglais grinds to a halt. Hoteliers know where to park (allow €16-29/day, cheaper for overnight—19:00 or 20:00 to 8:00—or for more than 3 days; some hotels offer special deals, but space is limited). The parking garage at the Nice Etoile shopping center on Avenue Jean Médecin is pricey but near many recommended hotels (ticket booth on third floor, about €26/day, €15/overnight—18:00-8:00). Other garages, like the one next to the recommended Hôtel Ibis at the train station, have similar rates. All on-street parking is metered (9:00-18:00 or 19:00), but usually free all day Sunday.

You can avoid driving in the center—and park for free during the day (no overnight parking)—by ditching your car at a parking lot at a remote tram stop (Las Planas is best) and taking the tram into town (10/hour, 15 minutes, you must buy a round-trip tram ticket—€3—and keep it with you because you'll need it later to exit the parking lot; don't leave anything in your car; tramway described later, under "Getting Around Nice"). To find the Las Planas tram station from the A-8 autoroute, take the *Nice Nord* exit (see map on page 682).

By Plane or Cruise Ship: For information on Nice's airport and cruise-ship port, see "Nice Connections" on page 719.

HELPFUL HINTS

Theft Alert: Nice has its share of pickpockets. Thieves target fanny packs: Have nothing important on or around your waist, unless it's in a money belt tucked out of sight. Don't leave things unattended on the beach while swimming, and stick to main streets in Vieux Nice after dark.

Sightseeing Tips: The following sights are closed on Mondays: the Modern and Contemporary Art Museum, the Fine Arts Museum, and the Cours Saleya market. On Tuesdays the Chagall, Matisse, Masséna, and Archaeological museums are closed.

Free Museum Entry Ends: Nice's longstanding policy of free admission to city museums likely ends in 2015. Be prepared to pay an entry fee.

Internet Access and Wi-Fi: The city offers free Wi-Fi in several public areas, including La Coulée Verte parkway, Place Masséna, and along the Cours Saleya in Old Nice (network: Spot Wifi Nice). Almost all of the hotels I list have free Wi-Fi, and some have guest computers.

Laundry: Ask your hotelier for the nearest one.

Grocery Store: The big **Monoprix** on Avenue Jean Médecin and Rue Biscarra has it all, including a deli counter, bakery, and cold drinks (Mon-Sat 8:30-20:45, Sun 9:00-12:45, see map on page 716). You'll also find small grocery stores (some open Sun and/or until late hours) near my recommended hotels.

Boutique Shopping: The chic streets where Rue Alphonse Karr meets Rue de la Liberté and then Rue de Paradis are known as the "Golden Square." If you need pricey stuff, shop here.

SNCF Boutique: There's a handy French rail ticket office a half-block west of Avenue Jean Médecin at 2 Rue de la Liberté (Mon-Fri 10:00-17:50, closed Sat-Sun).

Renting a Bike (and Other Wheels): Bike rental shops are easy to find in Nice. **Holiday Bikes** has several locations, including across from the train station, and they have electric bikes (www.holiday-bikes.com). **Roller Station** is nicely situated near the sea and rents bikes (*vélos,* can be taken on trains, €5/hour, €10/half-day, €15/day), rollerblades, skateboards, and Razor-style scooters (*trotinettes,* €7/half-day, €9/day). Leave your ID as a deposit (daily, next to yellow awnings of Pailin's Asian restaurant at 49 Quai des Etats-Unis—see map on page 692, tel. 04 93 62 99 05). If you need more power, the TI has a list of places renting electric scooters.

You'll notice blue bikes **(Vélos Bleu)** stationed at various points in the city. A thousand of these bikes, available for locals to use when running errands, rent cheaply for short-term use (first 30 minutes free, European-style chip-and-PIN credit card or American Express card required).

Car Rental: Renting a car is easiest at Nice's airport, which has offices for all the major companies. You'll also find most companies represented at Nice's train station and near Albert 1er Park.

English Radio: Tune in to Riviera-Radio at FM 106.5.

Views: For panoramic views, climb Castle Hill (see page 697), or take a one-hour boat trip (described later, under "Tours in Nice").

Beach Gear: To make life tolerable on the rocks, swimmers should buy a pair of the cheap plastic beach shoes sold at many shops (flip-flops fall off in the water). **Go Sport** at #13 on Place Masséna sells beach shoes, flip-flops, and cheap sunglasses (Mon-Sat 9:30-19:30, Sun 10:30-19:00—see map on page 692).

Updates to This Book: For updates to this book, check ricksteves.com/update.

GETTING AROUND NICE

Although you can walk to most attractions in Nice, smart travelers make good use of the buses and tram. Both are covered by the same €1.50 single-ride ticket (€5 day pass, €10 for 10 tickets that can be shared, good for 74 minutes in one direction, including transfers between bus and tram; single-ride ticket can't be used for a round-trip or airport express bus). The **bus** is particularly handy for reaching the Chagall and Matisse museums and the Russian Cathedral (closed in 2015). Pick up timetables at Nice's TIs (or view them online at www.lignesdazur.com) and buy tickets from the driver. Make sure to validate your ticket in the machine just behind the driver—watch locals do it and imitate. Route diagrams in the buses identify each stop.

The €5 all-day pass is valid on city buses and trams, as well as suburban buses to some nearby destinations. The all-day ticket makes sense if you plan to take the bus to museums or the beach, or to use the tramway several times. Express buses to and from the airport (#98 and #99) require a separate €6 ticket, which is valid for transfers to other buses and the tramway (74-minute ride limit).

Nice's **tramway** makes an "*L*" along Avenue Jean Médecin and Boulevard Jean Jaurès, and connects the main train station (Gare Thiers stop), Place Masséna (Masséna stop, near many regional bus stops and a few blocks' walk from the sea), Vieux

Nice (Opéra-Vieille Ville, Cathédrale-Vieille Ville), and the Modern and Contemporary Art Museum and port (Place Garibaldi). It also comes within a few blocks of the Chemins de Fer de Provence train station (Libération stop)—the departure point for the scenic narrow-gauge rail journey (see page 772).

Boarding the tram in the direction of Hôpital Pasteur takes you from the train station toward the beach and Vieux Nice (direction: Henri Sappia goes the other way). Buy tickets at the machines on the platforms (coins only, no credit cards). Choose the English flag to change the display language, turn the round knob and push the center button to select your ticket, press it twice at the end to get your ticket, or press the red button to cancel. Once you're on the tram, validate your ticket by inserting it into the top of the white box, then reclaiming it (http://tramway.nice.fr).

Taxis are useful for getting to Nice's less-central sights, and worth it if you're nowhere near a bus or tram stop (figure €15 from Promenade des Anglais). Cabbies normally pick up only at taxi stands *(tête de station)*, or you can call 04 93 13 78 78.

The hokey **tourist train** gets you up Castle Hill (see "Tours in Nice," later).

GETTING AROUND THE RIVIERA FROM NICE

By Train and Bus: Nice is perfectly situated for exploring the Riviera by public transport. Monaco, Eze-le-Village, Villefranche-sur-Mer, Antibes, Vence, and St-Paul-de-Vence are all within about a one-hour bus or train ride (see tables on pages 676-679). The train is pricier (fares range from about €2 for nearby Villefranche-sur-Mer to €9 for farther-away Grasse) than the bus (€1.50 for most destinations), but usually saves you time.

All trains serving Nice arrive at and depart from Nice-Ville Station. Remember that eastbound buses (to Villefranche-sur-Mer, Eze-le-Village, Monaco, etc.) stop on or near Place Garibaldi and/or near the Museum of Modern Art; westbound buses (to Vence, Cannes, Antibes, etc.) stop on Avenue de Verdun, a five-minute walk along the parkway west of Place Masséna (see map on page 682 for stop locations, www.lignesdazur.com).

With a little planning, you can link key destinations in an all-day circuit. For example, you can triangulate Nice, Monaco, and Eze-le-Village or La Turbie in a loop that ends up back in Nice (see page 750 for details). For a summary of train and bus connections, see the "Public Transportation in the French Riviera" sidebar on pages 676-679; see also "Nice Connections" on page 719.

By Boat: From June to mid-September, **Trans Côte d'Azur** offers scenic trips several days a week from Nice to Monaco and Nice to St-Tropez. Boats leave in the morning and return in the evening, giving you all day to explore your destination. Drinks and WCs are available on board.

Boats to **Monaco** depart at 9:30 and 16:00, and return at 11:00 and 18:00 (€37 round-trip, €30 if you don't get off in Monaco, 45 minutes each way, June-mid-Sept Tue, Thu, and Sat only).

Boats to **St-Tropez** depart at 9:00 and return at 19:00 (€65 round-trip, 2.5 hours each way; mid-July-Aug Tue-Sun, no boats Mon; June-mid-July and Sept Tue, Thu, and Sat-Sun only).

Reservations are required for both boats, and tickets for St-Tropez often sell out, so book a few days ahead (tel. 04 92 98 71 30 or 04 92 00 42 30, www.trans-cote-azur.com, croisieres@trans-cote-azur.com). The boats leave from Nice's port, Bassin des Amiraux, just below Castle Hill—look for the ticket booth *(billeterie)* on Quai de Lunel (see map on page 682). The same company also runs cruises along the coast to Cap Ferrat (see "Tours in Nice," next).

Tours in Nice

Bus Tours

Le Grand Tour Bus provides a 14-stop, hop-on, hop-off service on an open-deck bus with headphone commentary (2/hour, 1.5-hour loop) that includes the Promenade des Anglais, the old port, Cap de Nice, and the Chagall and Matisse museums on Cimiez Hill (€23/1-day pass, €26/2-day pass, cheaper for seniors and students, some hotels offer small discounts, buy tickets on bus, main stop near where Promenade des Anglais and Quai des Etats-Unis meet—across from the Plage Beau Rivage lounge, tel. 04 92 29 17 00, www.nicelegrandtour.com). This bus tour is a pricey way to get to the Chagall and Matisse museums and the Russian Cathedral, but it's an acceptable option if you also want a city overview.

A night version runs twice a week (June-Sept Wed and Sat at 21:00; €15, €30 for day and night).

Tourist Train

For €8 (€4 for children under age 9), you can spend 45 embarrassing minutes on the tourist train tooting along the promenade, through the old city, and up to Castle Hill (2/hour, daily 10:00-18:00, June-Aug until 19:00, recorded English commentary, meet train near Le Grand Tour Bus stop on Quai des Etats-Unis, tel. 02 99 88 47 07, www.ttdf.com).

▲Boat Cruise

Here's your chance to view Nice from the water. On this one-hour star-studded tour run by Trans Côte d'Azur, you'll cruise in a comfortable yacht-size vessel to Cap Ferrat and past Villefranche-sur-Mer, then return to Nice with a final lap along Promenade des

Nice at a Glance

▲▲▲Chagall Museum The world's largest collection of Marc Chagall's work, popular even with people who don't like modern art. **Hours:** Wed-Mon 10:00-17:00, May-Oct until 18:00, closed Tue year-round. See page 698.

▲▲▲Promenade des Anglais Nice's four-mile, sun-struck seafront promenade. **Hours:** Always open. See page 694.

▲▲Vieux Nice Charming old city offering enjoyable atmosphere and a look at Nice's French-Italian cultural blend. **Hours:** Always open. See page 690.

▲Matisse Museum Modest collection of Henri Matisse's paintings, sketches, paper cutouts, and more. **Hours:** Wed-Mon 10:00-18:00, closed Tue. See page 700.

▲Modern and Contemporary Art Museum Ultramodern museum with enjoyable collection from the 1960s-1970s, including Warhol and Lichtenstein. **Hours:** Tue-Sun 10:00-18:00, closed Mon. See page 702.

▲Russian Cathedral Finest Orthodox church outside Russia (closed for renovation through 2015). See page 703.

▲Castle Hill Site of an ancient fort boasting great views—especially in early mornings and evenings. **Hours:** Park closes at 20:00 in summer, earlier off-season. Elevator runs daily 10:00-19:00, until 20:00 in summer. See page 697.

Fine Arts Museum Lush villa shows off impressive paintings by Monet, Sisley, Bonnard, and Raoul Dufy. **Hours:** Tue-Sun 10:00-18:00, closed Mon. See page 702.

Masséna Museum Lavish beachfront mansion houses museum of city history, including exhibits of Napoleonic paraphernalia and images of Nice over the years. **Hours:** Wed-Mon 10:00-18:00, closed Tue. See page 704.

Molinard Perfume Museum Two-room museum in a storefront boutique tracing the history of perfume. **Hours:** Daily April-Sept 10:00-19:00, Oct-March 10:00-13:00 & 14:00-18:00, sometimes closed Sun off-season. See page 703.

Anglais. It's a scenic trip (the best views are from the seats on top), and worthwhile if you won't be hiking along the Cap Ferrat trails that provide similar views.

French guides play Robin Leach (in French and English), pointing out mansions owned by some pretty famous people, including Elton John (just as you leave Nice, it's the soft-yellow square-shaped place right on the water), Sean Connery (on the hill above Elton, with rounded arches and tower), and Microsoft co-founder Paul Allen (in the saddle of Cap Ferrat hill—look above the umbrellas of Plage de Passable beach and find the house with a sloping red-tile roof). I wonder if this gang ever hangs out together. Guides also like to point out the mansion between Villefranche-sur-Mer and Cap Ferrat where the Rolling Stones recorded *Exile on Main Street* (€18; April-Oct Tue-Sun 2/day, usually at 11:00 and 15:00, no boats Mon or in off-season; call ahead to verify schedule, arrive 30 minutes early to get best seats, WCs on board; for directions to the dock and contact information, see "Getting Around the Riviera from Nice—By Boat," earlier.

Walking Tours

The TI on Promenade des Anglais organizes weekly walking tours of Vieux Nice in French and English (€12, May-Oct only, usually Sat morning at 9:30, 2.5 hours, reservations necessary, depart from TI, tel. 08 92 70 74 07). They also have evening art walks on Fridays at 19:00.

Local Guides and Cooking Classes

See page 673 for a list of guides for Nice and other regional destinations, plus "Taste of Nice" food tours and Vieux Nice cooking classes.

Old Nice Walk

This approximately hour-long, scratch-and-sniff self-guided walk (worth ▲▲) leads you through the delights of Vieux (Old) Nice.

• *See the map on page 692, and start at Nice's main market square...*

Cours Saleya (koor sah-lay-yuh): Named for its broad exposure to the sun *(soleil)*, this commotion of color, sights, smells, and people has been Nice's main market square since the Middle Ages (produce market held Tue-Sun until 13:00—on Mon, an antiques market takes center stage). Amazingly, part of this square was a parking lot until 1980, when the mayor of Nice had an underground garage built.

The first section is devoted to the Riviera's largest flower market (all day Tue-Sun and in operation since the 19th century). Here you'll find plants and flowers that grow effortlessly and ubiquitously in this climate, including the local favorites: carnations, roses, and jasmine. Not long ago, this region supplied all of France with its flowers; today, many are imported from Africa (the glorious orchids are from Kenya). Still, fresh flowers are perhaps the best value in this city.

The boisterous produce section trumpets the season with mushrooms, strawberries, white asparagus, zucchini flowers, and more—whatever's fresh gets top billing. Find your way down the center and buy something healthy.

The market opens up at Place Pierre Gautier (also called Plassa dou Gouvernou—bilingual street signs include the old Niçois language, an Italian dialect). This is where farmers set up stalls to sell their produce and herbs directly.

• *Continue down Cours Saleya. The fine golden building that seals the end of the square is where Henri Matisse spent 17 years with a brilliant view onto Nice's world. The Café les Ponchettes is perfectly positioned for a people-watching break. Turn at the café onto...*

Rue de la Poissonnerie: Look up at the first floor of the first building on your right. **Adam and Eve** are squaring off, each holding a zucchini-like gourd. This scene (post-apple) represents the annual rapprochement in Nice to make up for the sins of a too-much-fun Carnival (Mardi Gras, the pre-Lenten festival). Residents of Nice have partied hard during Carnival for more than 700 years.

A few steps ahead, check out the small **Baroque church** (Notre-Dame-de-l'Annonciation) dedicated to Ste. Rita, the patron saint of desperate causes. She holds a special place in locals' hearts, making this the most popular church in Nice.

• *Turn right on the next street, where you'll pass Vieux Nice's most happening café/bar* ***(Distilleries Ideales)****, with a lively happy hour (18:00-21:00) and a* Pirates of the Caribbean*-style interior. Now turn left on "Right" Street (Rue Droite), and enter an area that feels like a Little Naples.*

Rue Droite: In the Middle Ages, this straight, skinny street provided the most direct route from wall to wall, or river to sea. Stop at **Espuno's bakery** (at Place du Jésus, closed Mon-Tue) and say *bonjour* to the friendly folks. Decades ago, this baker was voted the best in France—the trophies you see were earned for bread-making, not bowling. His son now runs the place. Notice the firewood stacked behind the oven. Try the house specialty, *tourte aux blettes*—a Swiss chard tart. It's traditionally made with jam (a sweet, tasty breakfast treat), but there's also a savory version, stuffed with pine nuts, raisins, and white beets (my favorite for lunch).

RIVIERA

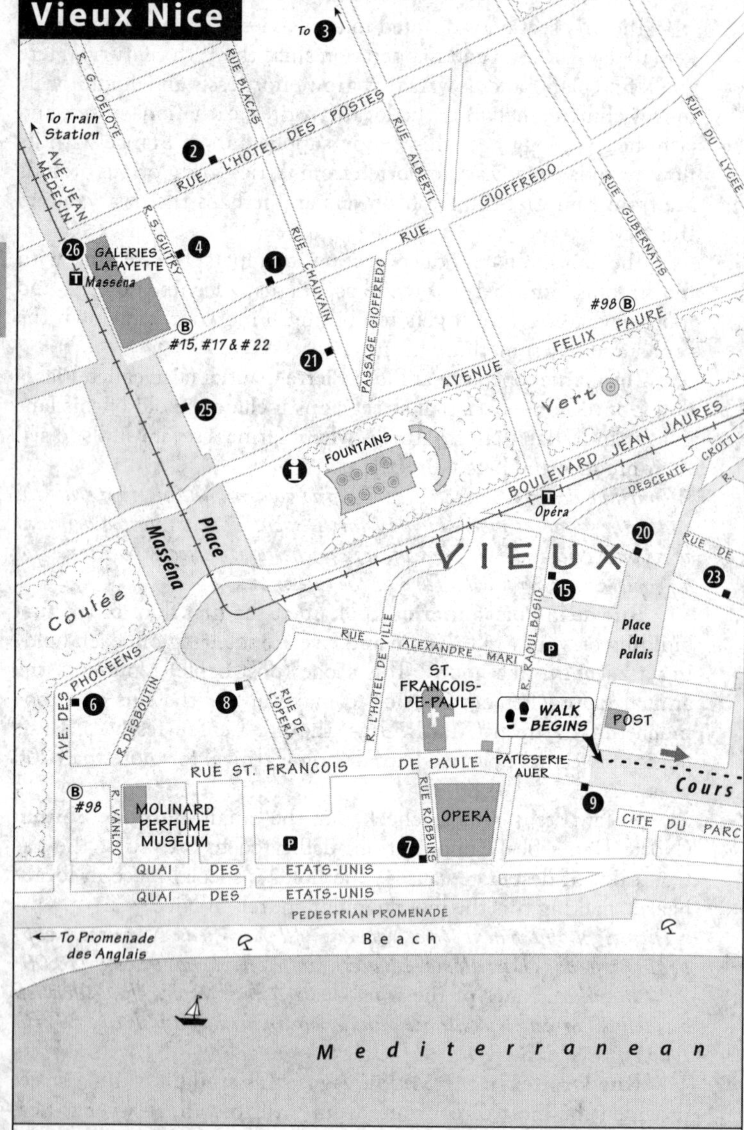

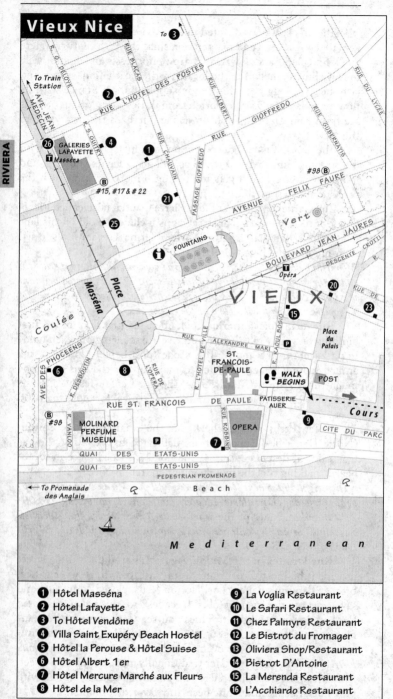

1. Hôtel Masséna
2. Hôtel Lafayette
3. To Hôtel Vendôme
4. Villa Saint Exupéry Beach Hostel
5. Hôtel la Perouse & Hôtel Suisse
6. Hôtel Albert 1er
7. Hôtel Mercure Marché aux Fleurs
8. Hôtel de la Mer
9. La Voglia Restaurant
10. Le Safari Restaurant
11. Chez Palmyre Restaurant
12. Le Bistrot du Fromager
13. Oliviera Shop/Restaurant
14. Bistrot D'Antoine
15. La Merenda Restaurant
16. L'Acchiardo Restaurant

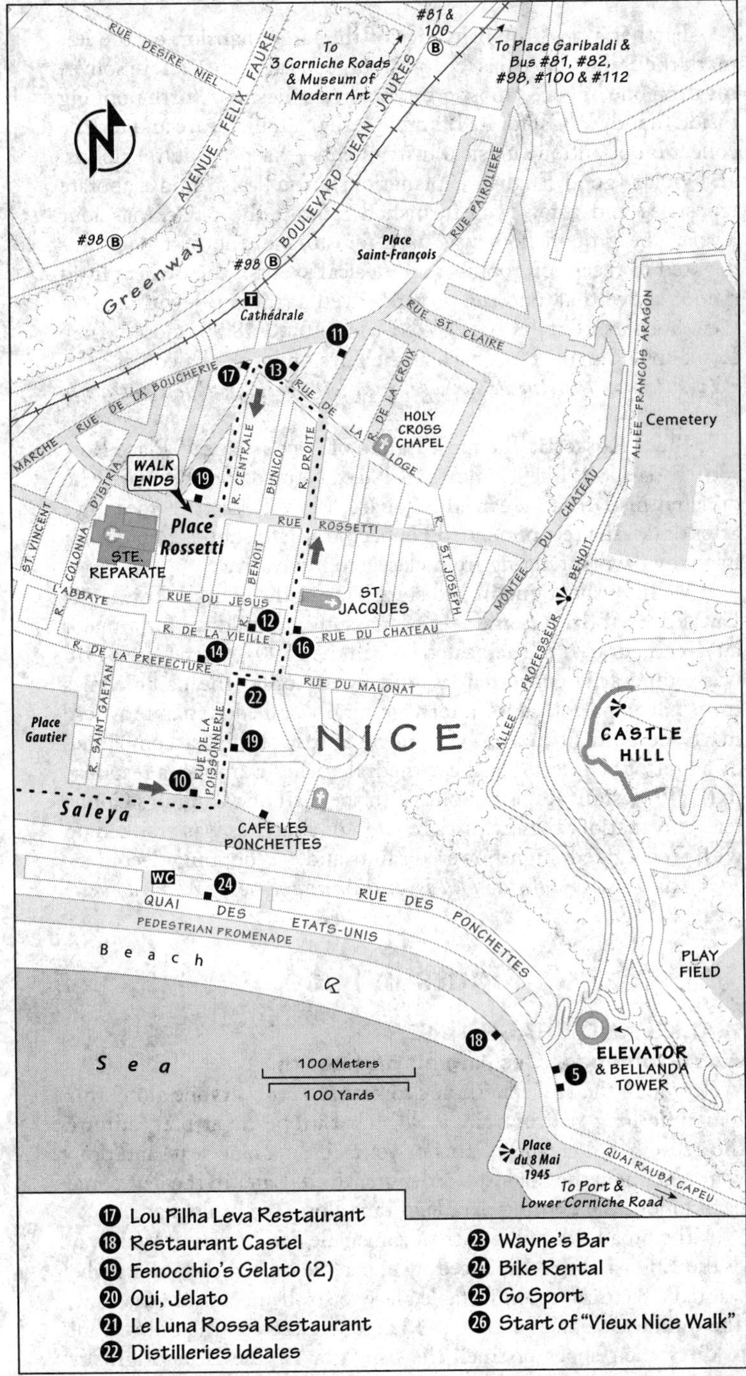

RUE DESIRE NIEL
AVENUE FELIX FAURE
To 3 Corniche Roads & Museum of Modern Art
#81 & 100
To Place Garibaldi & Bus #81, #82, #98, #100 & #112
BOULEVARD JEAN JAURES
RUE PAIROLIERE
#98
Greenway
#98
Place Saint-François
Cathédrale
RUE ST. CLAIRE
RUE DE LA BOUCHERIE
MARCHE
RUE DE LA LOGE
R. DE LA CROIX
HOLY CROSS CHAPEL
ALLEE FRANCOIS ARAGON
Cemetery
WALK ENDS
R. CENTRALE
BUNICO
R. DROITE
Place Rossetti
RUE ROSSETTI
STE. REPARATE
ST. VINCENT
COLONNA D'ISTRIA
BENOIT
R. ST. JOSEPH
MONTEE DU CHATEAU
PROFESSEUR BENOIT
L'ABBAYE
RUE DU JESUS
ST. JACQUES
R. DE LA VIEILLE
RUE DU CHATEAU
R. DE LA PREFECTURE
RUE DU MALONAT
Place Gautier
R. SAINT GAETAN
RUE DE LA POISSONNERIE
NICE
ALLEE
CASTLE HILL
Saleya
CAFE LES PONCHETTES
WC
QUAI DES ETATS-UNIS
RUE DES PONCHETTES
PEDESTRIAN PROMENADE
Beach
PLAY FIELD
ELEVATOR & BELLANDA TOWER
Sea
100 Meters
100 Yards
Place du 8 Mai 1945
QUAI RAUBA CAPEU
To Port & Lower Corniche Road
17 Lou Pilha Leva Restaurant
18 Restaurant Castel
19 Fenocchio's Gelato (2)
20 Oui, Jelato
21 Le Luna Rossa Restaurant
22 Distilleries Ideales
23 Wayne's Bar
24 Bike Rental
25 Go Sport
26 Start of "Vieux Nice Walk"

Farther along, the balconies of the large mansion on the left mark the **Palais Lascaris** (c. 1647, gorgeous at night), a rare souvenir from one of Nice's most prestigious families. It's worth popping inside (handy WCs) for its Baroque Italian architecture and terrific collection of antique musical instruments—harps, guitars, violins, and violas (good English explanations). You'll also find elaborate tapestries and a few well-furnished rooms. The palace has four levels: The ground floor was used for storage, the first floor was devoted to reception rooms (and musical events), the owners lived a floor above that, and the servants lived at the top—with a good view but lots of stairs (free, Wed-Mon 10:00-18:00, closed Tue). Look up and make faces back at the guys under the balconies.

• *Turn left on the Rue de la Loge, then left again on Rue Centrale to reach...*

Place Rossetti: The most Italian of Nice's piazzas, Place Rossetti feels more like Rome than Nice. Named for the man who donated his land to create this square, Place Rossetti comes alive after dark. The recommended Fenocchio gelato shop is popular for its many flavors, ranging from classic to innovative.

Walk to the fountain and stare back at the church. This is the **Cathedral of St. Réparate**—an unassuming building for a major city's cathedral. It was relocated here in the 1500s, when Castle Hill was temporarily converted to military use only. The name comes from Nice's patron saint, a teenage virgin named Réparate whose martyred body floated to Nice in the fourth century accompanied by angels. The interior of the cathedral gushes Baroque, a response to the Protestant Reformation. With the Catholic Church's Counter-Reformation, the theatrical energy of churches was cranked up with reenergized, high-powered saints and eye-popping decor.

• *Our walk is over. Castle Hill is straight up the stepped lane opposite the cathedral.*

Sights in Nice

WALKS AND BEACH TIME

▲▲▲Promenade des Anglais and Beach

Welcome to the Riviera. There's something for everyone along this four-mile-long seafront circus. Watch Europeans at play, admire the azure Mediterranean, anchor yourself on a blue seat, and prop your feet up on the made-to-order guardrail. Later in the day, come back to join the evening parade of tans along the promenade.

The broad sidewalks of the Promenade des Anglais ("Walkway of the English") were financed by upper-crust English tourists who wanted a secure and comfortable place to stroll and admire the view. The walk was done in marble in 1822 for aristocrats who didn't want to dirty their shoes or smell the fishy gravel. The Brits originally

came to Nice seeking relief from tuberculosis; both the dry climate and the salt air helped ease their suffering. It was an era when tanned bodies were frowned upon (Brits didn't want to resemble the lower-class Italians)—visitors wouldn't swim in the Mediterranean for another hundred years, when the region took off as a tourist destination.

Stroll like the belle-époque English aristocrats for whom the promenade was paved. Start at the pink-domed Hôtel Negresco, then cross to the sea and end your promenade at Castle Hill. The following sights are listed in the order you'll pass them. This walk is ideally done at sunset (as a pre-dinner stroll).

Hôtel Negresco

Nice's finest hotel is also a historic monument, offering up the city's most expensive beds (see page 711) and a museum-like interior that, sadly, has been made off-limits to non-guests—at least in high season. But, it's worth a try to enter—dress well, appear confident, and march in. (Or, you can always get in by patronizing the hotel's Le Relais bar, which opens at 15:00.)

The exquisite **Salon Royal** lounge is an elegant place for a drink and frequently hosts modern art exhibits (opens at 11:00). The chandelier hanging from the Eiffel-built dome is made of 16,000 pieces of crystal. It was built in France for the Russian czar's Moscow palace...but thanks to the Bolshevik Revolution in 1917, he couldn't take delivery (portraits of Czar Alexander III and his wife, Maria Feodorovna—who returned to her native Denmark after the Revolution—are to the right, under the dome). Saunter around the perimeter counterclockwise.

If the **Le Relais bar** door is open (after about 15:00), wander up the marble steps for a look. Farther along, nip into the toilets for either an early 20th-century powder room or a Battle of Waterloo experience. The chairs nearby were typical of the age (cones of silence for an afternoon nap sitting up).

Bay of Angels (Baie des Anges)

Grab a blue chair and face the sea. The body of Nice's patron saint, Réparate, was supposedly escorted into this bay by angels in the fourth century. To your right is where you might have been escorted into France—Nice's airport, built on a massive landfill. On that tip of land way beyond the runway is Cap d'Antibes. Until 1860, Antibes and Nice were in different countries—Antibes was French, but Nice was a protectorate of the Italian kingdom of Savoy-Piedmont, a.k.a. the Kingdom of Sardinia. (During that period, the Var River—just west of Nice—was the geographic border between these two peoples.) In 1850 the people here spoke Italian and ate pasta. As Italy was uniting, the region was given a choice: Join the new country of Italy or join good old France (which was enjoying good times under the rule of Napoleon III). The vast majority voted in 1860 to go French...and voilà!

The lower green hill to your left (Castle Hill) marks the end of this walk. Farther left lies Villefranche-sur-Mer (marked by the tower at land's end, and home to lots of millionaires), then Monaco (which you can't see, with more millionaires), then Italy (with lots of, uh, Italians). Behind you are the foothills of the Alps (Alpes-Maritimes), which trap threatening clouds, ensuring that the Côte d'Azur enjoys sunshine more than 300 days each year. While half a million people live here, pollution is carefully treated—the water is routinely tested and very clean.

Stroll the promenade with the sea starboard, and contemplate beach time (see next) on your way to the Albert 1er Park.

Beaches

Settle in on the smooth rocks or find a section with imported sand, and consider your options: You can play beach volleyball, table tennis, or *boules;* rent paddleboats, personal watercraft, or windsurfing equipment; explore ways to use your zoom lens for some revealing people-watching; or snooze on a comfy beach bed.

To rent a spot on the beach, compare rates, as prices vary—beaches on the east end of the bay are usually cheaper (chair and mattress—*chaise longue* and *transat*—about €15, umbrella-€5, towel-€4). Some hotels have special deals with certain beaches for discounted rentals (check with your hotel for details). Have lunch in your bathing suit (€12 salads and pizzas in bars and restaurants all along the beach). Or, for a peaceful café au lait on the Mediterranean, stop here first thing in the morning before the crowds hit. *Plage Publique* signs explain the 15 beach no-nos (translated into English).

Albert 1er Park and La Coulée Verte Parkway

The park is named for the Belgian king who enjoyed wintering here—these were his private gardens. While the English came first, the Belgians and Russians were also big fans of 19th-century Nice. That tall statue at the edge of the park commemorates the 100-year anniversary of Nice's union with France.

If you detour from the promenade through Albert 1er Park and continue down the center of the grassy strip—La Coulée Verte—you'll be walking over Nice's river, the Paillon (covered since the 1800s). For centuries, this river was Nice's natural defense to the north and west (the sea protected the south, and Castle Hill defended the east). Imagine the fortified wall that ran along its length from the hills behind you to the sea. With the arrival of tourism in the 1800s, Nice expanded over and beyond the river. And thanks to today's progressive mayor, the fountain-filled parkway has been extended east past Place Masséna and the old city. Locals refer to it as "Nice's lung." Its elaborate play toys and mist-spraying fountains are heavenly for kids.

▲Castle Hill (Colline du Château)

This hill—in an otherwise flat city center—offers sweeping views over Nice, the port (to the east), the Alps, and the Mediterranean. The views are best early or at sunset, or whenever the weather's clear (park closes at 20:00 in summer, earlier off-season). The city of Nice was first settled here by the Greeks in about 400 B.C. In the Middle Ages, a massive castle stood here, with turrets, high walls, and soldiers at the ready. With the river guarding one side and the sea the other, this mountain fortress seemed strong—until Louis XIV leveled it in 1706. Find the seam that separates the red-tile roofs of Old Nice from the long, more modern buildings located across the now-covered river. Today you'll find a waterfall, a playground, two cafés (with fair prices), and a cemetery—but no castle—on Castle Hill. Nice's port is just below on the east edge of Castle Hill. You can climb to the top of Castle Hill by foot, use the free elevator (daily 10:00-19:00, until 20:00 in summer, next to beachfront Hôtel Suisse), or take the pricey tourist train (described earlier, under "Tours in Nice").

Bike Routes

Meandering along Nice's promenade on foot or by bike is an essential Riviera experience. To rev up the pace of your saunter, rent a bike and glide along the coast in either or both directions (about 30 minutes each way; for rental info see "Helpful Hints," earlier). Both of the following paths start along Promenade des Anglais.

The path to the **west** stops just before the airport at perhaps the most scenic *boules* courts in France. Pause here to watch the old-timers while away the afternoon tossing shiny metal balls (for more on this game, see page 1044). If you take the path heading **east,** you'll round the hill—passing a scenic cape and the town's memorial to both world wars—to the harbor of Nice, with a chance to survey some fancy yachts. Walk or pedal around the harbor and follow the coast past the Corsica ferry terminal (you'll need to carry your bike up a flight of steps). From there the path leads to an appealing tree-lined residential district.

MUSEUMS AND MONUMENTS

You'll find a great variety of museums and monuments in Nice.

The first two museums (Chagall and Matisse) are a long walk northeast of Nice's city center. Because they're in the same direction and served by the same bus line (buses #15 and #22 stop at both museums), it makes sense to visit them on the same trip. From Place Masséna, the Chagall Museum is a 10-minute bus ride or a 30-minute walk, and the Matisse Museum is a 20-minute bus ride or a one-hour walk.

▲▲▲Chagall Museum (Musée National March Chagall)

Even if you're suspicious of modern art, this museum—with the world's largest collection of Marc Chagall's work in captivity—is a delight. After World War II, Chagall returned from the United States to settle in Vence, not far from Nice. Between 1954 and 1967 he painted a cycle of 17 large murals designed for, and donated to, this museum. These paintings, inspired by the biblical books of Genesis, Exodus, and the Song of Songs, make up the "nave," or core, of what Chagall called the "House of Brotherhood."

Each painting is a lighter-than-air collage of images that draws from Chagall's Russian folk-village youth, his Jewish heritage, biblical themes, and his feeling that he existed somewhere between heaven and earth. He believed that the Bible was a synonym for nature, and that color and biblical themes were key for understanding God's love for his creation. Chagall's brilliant blues and reds celebrate nature, as do his spiritual and folk themes. Notice the focus on couples. To Chagall, humans loving each other mirrored God's love of creation.

Don't miss the auditorium, where you'll find three stained-glass windows by Chagall on the themes of the creation of light, elements, and planets; the creation of animals, plants, man, and woman; and the ordering of the solar system.

Although Chagall would suggest that you explore his works without help, the free audioguide gives you detailed explanations of his works and covers temporary exhibits. The free *Plan du Musée* helps you locate the rooms, though you can do without, as the museum is pretty simple.

Cost and Hours: €8, €1-2 more with (frequent) special exhibits, free first Sun of the month (but crowded), open Wed-Mon 10:00-17:00, May-Oct until 18:00, closed Tue year-round, Avenue

Chagall's Style

Chagall uses a deceptively simple, almost childlike style to paint a world that's hidden to the eye—the magical, mystical world below the surface. Here are some of the characteristics of his paintings:

- **Deep, radiant colors,** inspired by Expressionism and Fauvism (an art movement pioneered by Matisse and other French painters).
- **Personal imagery,** particularly from his childhood in Russia—smiling barnyard animals, fiddlers on the roof, flower bouquets, huts, and blissful sweethearts.
- **A Hasidic Jewish perspective,** the idea that God is everywhere, appearing in everyday things like nature, animals, and humdrum activities.
- **A fragmented Cubist style,** multifaceted and multidimensional, a perfect style to mirror the complexity of God's creation.
- **Overlapping images,** like double-exposure photography, with faint imagery that bleeds through, suggesting there's more to life under the surface.
- **Stained-glass-esque technique** of dark, deep, earthy, "potent" colors, and simplified, iconic, symbolic figures.
- **Gravity-defying compositions,** with lovers, animals, and angels twirling blissfully in midair.
- **Happy (not tragic) mood** depicting a world of personal joy, despite the violence and turmoil of world wars and revolution.
- **Childlike simplicity,** drawn with simple, heavy outlines, filled in with Crayola colors that often spill over the lines. Major characters in a scene are bigger than the lesser characters. The grinning barnyard animals, the bright colors, the magical events presented as literal truth...Was Chagall a lightweight? Or a lighter-than-air-weight?

Docteur Ménard, tel. 04 93 53 87 20, www.musees-nationaux-alpesmaritimes.fr/chagall.

Getting to the Chagall Museum: You can reach the museum, located on Avenue Docteur Ménard, by bus or on foot.

Buses #15 and #22 serve the Chagall Museum from the Masséna Guitry stop, near Place Masséna (6/hour Mon-Sat, 3/hour Sun, €1.50, immediately behind Galeries Lafayette department store—see map on page 692). The museum's bus stop (called Musée

Chagall, shown on the bus shelter) is on Boulevard de Cimiez (walk uphill from the stop and cross the street to find the museum).

To **walk** from central Nice to the Chagall Museum (30 minutes), go to the train-station end of Avenue Jean Médecin and turn right onto Boulevard Raimbaldi. Walk four long blocks along the elevated road, then turn left onto Avenue Raymond Comboul, and follow *Musée Chagall* signs.

Cuisine Art and Services: An idyllic café (€10 salads and *plats*) awaits in the corner of the garden. A spick-and-span WC is next to the ticket desk. Another WC is inside.

Leaving the Museum: To take **buses** #15 or #22 back to downtown Nice, turn right out of the museum, then make another right down Boulevard de Cimiez, and catch the bus heading downhill. To continue on to the Matisse Museum, catch buses #15 or #22 using the uphill stop located across the street. **Taxis** usually wait in front of the museum. It's about €12 for a ride to the city center.

To **walk** to the train station area from the museum (20 minutes), turn left out of the museum grounds on Avenue Docteur Ménard, and follow the street as it turns to the left at the first intersection, continuing to hug the museum grounds. Where the street curves right (by #32), take the ramps and staircases down on your left, turn left at the bottom, cross under the freeway and the train tracks, then turn right on Boulevard Raimbaldi to reach the station.

▲Matisse Museum (Musée Matisse)

This small museum contains a sampling of works from the various periods of Henri Matisse's long artistic career. The museum offers a painless introduction to the artist's many styles and materials, both shaped by Mediterranean light and by fellow Côte d'Azur artists Pablo Picasso and Pierre-Auguste Renoir. The collection is scattered throughout several rooms with a few worthwhile works, though it lacks a certain *je ne sais quoi* when compared to the Chagall Museum.

Cost and Hours: Possible entry fee, Wed-Mon 10:00-18:00, closed Tue, 164 Avenue des Arènes de Cimiez, tel. 04 93 81 08 08, www.musee-matisse-nice.org. The museum is housed in a beautiful Mediterranean mansion set in an olive grove amid the ruins of the ancient Roman city of Cemenelum.

Getting to the Matisse Museum: It's a long uphill walk from the city center. Take the bus (details follow) or a cab (€20 from Promenade des Anglais). Once here, walk into the park to find the pink villa. **Buses #15, #17,** and **#22** offer regular service to the Matisse Museum from just off Place Masséna on Rue Sacha Guitry (Masséna Guitry stop, at the east end of the Galeries Lafayette department store—see map on page 692, 20 minutes; note that bus #17 stops at the main train station but does not stop at the Chagall Museum). **Bus #20** connects the port to the museum. On any bus, get off at the Arènes-Matisse bus stop (look for the crumbling Roman wall).

Background: Henri Matisse (1869-1954), the master of leaving things out, could suggest a woman's body with a single curvy line—letting the viewer's mind fill in the rest. Ignoring traditional 3-D perspective, he expressed his passion for life through simplified but recognizable scenes in which dark outlines and saturated, bright blocks of color create an overall decorative pattern. You don't look "through" a Matisse canvas, like you do a window; you look "at" it, as though it were wallpaper.

Matisse understood how colors and shapes affect us emotionally. He could create either shocking, clashing works (early Fauvism) or geometrical, balanced, harmonious ones (later cutouts). Whereas other modern artists reveled in purely abstract design, Matisse (almost) always kept the subject matter at least vaguely recognizable. He used unreal colors and distorted lines not just to portray what an object looks like, but to express its inner nature (even inanimate objects). Meditating on his paintings helps you connect with life—or so Matisse hoped.

As you tour the museum, look for Matisse's favorite motifs—including fruit, flowers, wallpaper, and sunny rooms—often with a window opening onto a sunny landscape. Another favorite subject is the *odalisque* (harem concubine), usually shown sprawled in a seductive pose and with a simplified, masklike face. You'll also see a few souvenirs from his travels, which influenced much of his work.

Visiting the Museum: Enter the museum at park level from the door opposite the olive grove (not the basement entry). The museum features temporary exhibits about Matisse that change frequently.

Rooms on the entry level usually house paintings from Matisse's formative years as a student (1890s). Notice how quickly his work evolves: from dark still lifes *(nature mortes),* to colorful Impressionist scenes, to more abstract pieces, all in a matter of a few years. A beige banner describes his "Découverte de la Lumière" (discovery of light), which the Riviera (and his various travels to sun-soaked places like Corsica, Collioure, and Tahiti) brought to his art. You may see photographs of his apartment on Cours Saleya, which is described in my "Old Nice Walk," earlier.

Other rooms on this floor highlight Matisse's fascination with dance and the female body (these subjects may be upstairs). You'll see pencil and charcoal drawings, and a handful of bronze busts; he was fascinated by sculpture. *The Acrobat*—painted only two years before Matisse's death—shows the artist at his minimalist best. A room devoted to two 25-foot-long watery cutouts for an uncompleted pool project *(La Piscine)* for the city of Nice shows his abiding love of deep blue.

The floor above features sketches and models of Matisse's famous Chapel of the Rosary, located in nearby Vence, and related religious works. On the same floor, you may find paper cutouts from his *Jazz* series, more bronze sculptures, various personal objects, and linen embroideries inspired by his travels to Polynesia.

The bookshop, WCs, and additional temporary exhibits are on the basement level. The fantastic wall-hanging near the bookshop—Matisse's colorful paper cutout *Flowers and Fruits*—shouts, "Riviera!"

Leaving the Museum: When leaving the museum, find the stop for buses #15 and #22 (frequent service to downtown, stops en route at the Chagall Museum): Turn left from the Matisse Museum into the park and keep straight on Allée Barney Wilen, exiting the park at the Archaeological Museum, then turn right. Pass the bus stop across the street (#17 goes to the city center and train station but not the Chagall Museum; #20 goes to the port), and walk to the small roundabout. Cross the roundabout to find the shelter (facing downhill) for buses #15 and #22.

▲Modern and Contemporary Art Museum (Musée d'Art Moderne et d'Art Contemporain)

This ultramodern museum features an explosively colorful, far-out, yet manageable collection focused on American and European-American artists from the 1960s and 1970s (Pop Art and New Realism styles are highlighted). The exhibits cover three floors and include a few works by Andy Warhol, Roy Lichtenstein, and Jean Tinguely, and images of Christo's famous wrappings. You'll find rooms dedicated to Robert Indiana, Yves Klein, and Niki de Saint Phalle (my favorite). The temporary exhibits can be as appealing to modern-art lovers as the permanent collection: Check the museum website for what's playing. Don't leave without exploring the views from the rooftop terrace.

Cost and Hours: Possible entry fee, Tue-Sun 10:00-18:00, closed Mon, about a 15-minute walk from Place Masséna, near Vieux Nice on Promenade des Arts, tel. 04 93 62 61 62, www.mamac-nice.org.

Fine Arts Museum (Musée des Beaux-Arts)

Housed in a sumptuous Riviera villa with lovely gardens, this museum holds 6,000 artworks from the 17th to 20th centuries. Start on the ground floor and work your way up to experience an appealing array of paintings by Bonnard, Van Dongen, and Raoul Dufy, as well as a few sculptures by Rodin and Carpeaux.

Cost and Hours: Possible entry fee, Tue-Sun 10:00-18:00, closed Mon; inconveniently located at the western end of Nice, take bus #12 from the train station or bus #3, #9, #10, or #22 to the Rosa Bonheur stop and walk to 3 Avenue des Baumettes, tel. 04 92 15 28 28, www.musee-beaux-arts-nice.org.

Molinard Perfume Museum

The Molinard family has been making perfume in Grasse (about an hour's drive from Nice) since 1849. Their Nice store has a small museum in the rear that illustrates the story of their industry. Back when people believed water spread the plague (Louis XIV supposedly bathed less than once a year), doctors advised people to rub fragrances into their skin and then powder their bodies. At that time, perfume was a necessity of everyday life.

Cost and Hours: Free, daily April-Sept 10:00-19:00, Oct-March 10:00-13:00 & 14:00-18:00, sometimes closed Sun off-season, just between beach and Place Masséna at 20 Rue St. François de Paule, see map on page 692, tel. 04 93 62 90 50, www.molinard.com.

Visiting the Museum: The tiny first room shows photos of the local flowers, roots, and other plant parts used in perfume production. The second, main room explains the earliest (18th-century) production method. Petals were laid out in the sun on a bed of animal fat, which would absorb the essence of the flowers as they baked. For two months, the petals were replaced daily, until the fat was saturated. Models and old photos show the later distillation process (660 pounds of lavender produced only a quarter-gallon of essence). Perfume is "distilled like cognac and then aged like wine." The bottles on the tables demonstrate the role of the "blender" and the perfume mastermind called the "nose" (who knows best); clients are allowed to try their hand at mixing scents. Of the 150 real "noses" in the world, more than 100 are French. Notice the photos of these lab-coat-wearing perfectionists. You are welcome to enjoy the testing bottles.

▲Russian Cathedral (Cathédrale Russe)

Nice's Russian Orthodox church—claimed by some to be the finest outside Russia—is closed through 2015 for renovation. When open, it's worth a visit. Five hundred rich Russian families wintered in Nice in the late 19th century, and they needed a worthy Orthodox house of worship. Czar Nicholas I's widow provided the land (which required tearing down her house), and Czar Nicholas II gave this church to the Russian community in 1912. (A few years later, Russian comrades who *didn't* winter on the Riviera assassinated him.)

Here in the land of olives and anchovies, these proud onion domes seem odd. But, I imagine, so did those old Russians.

Archaeological Museum (Musée Archéologique)

This museum displays various objects from the Romans' occupation of this region. It's convenient—just below the Matisse Museum—but has little of interest to anyone but ancient Rome aficionados. You also get access to the Roman bath ruins...which are, sadly, overgrown with weeds.

Cost and Hours: Possible entry fee, very limited information in English, Wed-Mon 10:00-18:00, closed Tue, near Matisse Museum at 160 Avenue des Arènes de Cimiez, tel. 04 93 81 59 57).

Masséna Museum (Musée Masséna)

Like Nice's main square, this museum was named in honor of Jean-André Masséna, a highly regarded commander during France's Revolutionary and Napoleonic wars. The beachfront mansion is worth a gander for its lavish decor and lovely gardens alone (pick up your free ticket at the boutique just outside; no English labels in museum, but a €3 booklet in English is available for true fans).

Cost and Hours: Possible entry fee, Wed-Mon 10:00-18:00, closed Tue, last entry 30 minutes before closing, 35 Promenade des Anglais, tel. 04 93 91 19 10, www.massena-nice.org.

Visiting the Museum: There are three levels. The elaborate reception rooms on the ground floor host occasional exhibits and give the best feeling for aristocratic Nice at the turn of the 19th century (find Masséna's portrait to the right after entering). The first floor up, offering a folk-museum-like look at Nice through the years, deserves most of your time. Moving counterclockwise around the floor, you'll find Napoleonic paraphernalia, Josephine's impressive cape and tiara, and Napoleon's dapper vest. Next, antique posters promote vacations in Nice—look for the model and photos of the long-gone La Jetée Promenade and its casino, Nice's first. You'll see paintings of the Russian and British nobility who appreciated Nice's climate, and images of the city before the Promenade des Anglais was built and the town's river was covered over by Place Masséna. You'll also find paintings honoring Italian patriot and Nice favorite Giuseppe Garibaldi. The top-floor painting gallery is devoted to the Riviera before World War II, with scenes of rural Villefranche-sur-Mer and other bucolic spots showing how the area looked before the tourist boom.

Nightlife in Nice

Promenade des Anglais, Cours Saleya, and Rue Masséna are all worth an evening walk. Nice's bars play host to a happening late-night scene, filled with jazz, rock, and trolling singles. Most activity focuses on Vieux Nice. Rue de la Préfecture and Place du Palais are ground zero for bar life, though Place Rossetti and Rue Droite are also good targets. **Distilleries Ideales** is a good place to start or end your evening, with a lively international crowd and a fun interior (where Rue de la Poissonnerie and Rue Barillerie meet, happy hour 18:00-21:00). **Wayne's Bar** is a happening spot for the younger, English-speaking backpacker crowd (15 Rue Préfecture). Along the Promenade des Anglais, the plush bar at **Hôtel Negresco** is fancy-cigar old English.

Plan on a cover charge or expensive drinks where music is involved. If you're out very late, avoid walking alone. Nice is well known for its lively after-dark action, but if you need even more action, head for the town of Juan-les-Pins (page 762). For more relaxed and accessible nightlife, consider nearby Antibes (page 753).

Sleeping in Nice

Don't look for charm in Nice. Go for modern and clean, with a central location and, in summer, air-conditioning.

The rates listed here are for April through October. Prices generally drop €15-30 November through March, but will go sky-high in 2015 during the Nice Carnival (Feb 13-March 1, www.nicecarnaval.com), the Cannes Film Festival (May 15-26, www.festival-cannes.com), and Monaco's Grand Prix (May 21-24, www.acm.mc). Between the film festival and the Grand Prix, the second half of May is very tight every year. Nice is also one of Europe's top convention cities, and June is convention month here. Reserve early if visiting from May through August, especially during these times. For parking, ask your hotelier (several hotels offer deals for stashing your car or have limited private parking; reserve early), or see "Arrival in Nice—By Car" on page 684.

I've divided my sleeping recommendations into three areas: in the city center, between the train station and Place Masséna (easy access to the train station and Vieux Nice via the tramway, 20-minute walk to Promenade des Anglais); in the heart of Vieux Nice between Nice Etoile and the sea (east of Avenue Jean Médecin, good access to the sea at Quai des Etats-Unis); and near the beach, between Boulevard Victor Hugo and the sea (a somewhat classier and quieter area, offering better access to the Promenade des Anglais but longer walks to the train station and Vieux Nice). I've also listed hotels and a hostel on the outskirts. Before reserving, check hotel

Sleep Code

Abbreviations **(€1 = about $1.40, country code: 33)**
S = Single, **D** = Double/Twin, **T** = Triple, **Q** = Quad, **b** = bathroom, **s** = shower only, * = French hotel rating (0-5 stars)

Price Rankings

$$$ Higher Priced—Most rooms €200 or more
$$ Moderately Priced—Most rooms between €100-200
$ Lower Priced—Most rooms €100 or less

Unless otherwise noted, credit cards are accepted, English is spoken, elevators are available, and Wi-Fi is generally free. Prices change; verify current rates online or by email. For the best prices, always book directly with the hotel.

websites for deals (more common at larger hotels). Book directly with the hotel to get any special discounts for Rick Steves readers.

IN THE CITY CENTER

The train station area offers Nice's cheapest sleeps, though most hotels near the station ghetto are overrun, overpriced, and loud. The following hotels are the pleasant exceptions (most are near Avenue Jean Médecin). For locations, see the map on page 708 unless otherwise noted.

$$$ Hôtel Masséna**,** in a classy building two blocks from Place Masséna, is a "professional" hotel (popular with tour groups) with 110 rooms and gaudy public spaces. It's worth it only if you get a discounted rate (small Db-€199, larger Db-€289, still larger Db-€339, skip the €18 breakfast, call same-day for special rates—prices drop big time when hotel is not full, sixth-floor rooms have balconies, Wi-Fi, parking-€25/day—book ahead, 58 Rue Gioffredo, tel. 04 92 47 88 88, www.hotel-massena-nice.com, info@hotel-massena-nice.com). See map on page 692.

$$ At **Hôtel Durante***,** you know you're on the Mediterranean as soon as you enter this cheery, way-orange building with rooms wrapped around a flowery courtyard. Every one of its quiet rooms overlooks a spacious, well-maintained patio/garden. The rooms are good enough (mostly big beds), the price is right enough, and the parking (limited spaces) is free (Sb-€85-110, Db-€100-125, Tb-€155-180, Qb-€190-210, breakfast-€10, air-con, Wi-Fi, 16 Avenue Durante, tel. 04 93 88 84 40, www.hotel-durante.com, info@hotel-durante.com).

$$ Hôtel Lafayette*,** in a handy location a block behind the Galeries Lafayette department store, is a good value. Though rated three stars, it offers two-star value and prices, with 17 mostly spacious, homey, and modest rooms (some with thin walls), all one floor up from the street. You'll hear light traffic noise from many rooms, but be thankful for the great location. It's family-run by Kiril and George (standard Db-€105-120, spacious Db-€115-130, preferential rates for Rick Steves readers if booked directly with the hotel, breakfast-€10, in-room coffee service, air-con, no elevator, guest computer, Wi-Fi, 32 Rue de l'Hôtel des Postes, tel. 04 93 85 17 84, www.hotellafayettenice.com, info@hotellafayettenice.com). See map on page 692.

$$ Hôtel St. Georges,** five blocks from the station toward the sea, offers a handy location, fair rates, a nice backyard patio, and friendly Houssein at the reception. Rooms are simple but fairly priced; look for great Internet deals on their website (Sb-€95, Db-€125, Tb with 3 beds-€150, extra bed-€20, breakfast-€9, air-con, Wi-Fi, 7 Avenue Georges Clemenceau, tel. 04 93 88 79 21, www.hotelsaintgeorges.fr, contact@hotelsaintgeorges.fr).

$$ Hôtel Vendôme*** gives you a whiff of the belle époque, with pink pastels, high ceilings, and grand staircases in a mansion set off the street. The rooms are modern and come in all sizes; many have balconies (Db-€140-180, Tb-€180-200, check website for deals, breakfast-€15, air-con, guest computer, Wi-Fi, limited parking-€15/day—book ahead, 26 Rue Pastorelli at the corner of Rue Alberti, tel. 04 93 62 00 77, www.hotel-vendome-nice.com, contact@vendome-hotel-nice.com).

$ Hôtel Ibis Nice Centre Gare*,** 100 yards to the right as you leave the station, gives those in need of train station access a secure refuge in this seedy area. It's big (200 rooms) and modern, but a good value with well-configured rooms, a refreshing pool, and cheap €10 overnight parking (Db-€90-125, breakfast-€10, air-con, guest computer, Wi-Fi, bar, café, 14 Avenue Thiers, tel. 04 93 88 85 85, www.ibishotel.com, h1396@accor.com).

$ Hôtel Belle Meunière*, in a fine old mansion built for Napoleon III's mistress, offers cheap beds and private rooms a block below the train station. This simple but well-kept place attracts budget-minded travelers of all ages with basic-but-adequate rooms and charismatic Mademoiselle Marie-Pierre presiding with her perfect English (bunk in 4-bed dorm-€28 with private bath, less with shared bath; Db-€58-78, Tb-€84-95, Qb-€116-124, breakfast-€6—free if you book directly with hotel, Wi-Fi, laundry service, limited parking-€10/day, 21 Avenue Durante, tel. 04 93 88 66 15, www.bellemeuniere.com, hotel.belle.meuniere@cegetel.net).

$ Auberge de Jeunesse les Camélias is a fun, laid-back youth hostel with a great location, modern facilities, and a fun evening atmosphere. Rooms accommodate four to eight people of all ages in bunk beds (136 beds in all) and come with showers and sinks—WCs are down the hall. Reservations must be made on the website at least 3 days in advance. If you don't have a reservation, call by 10:00—or, better, try to snag a bunk in person. The place is popular

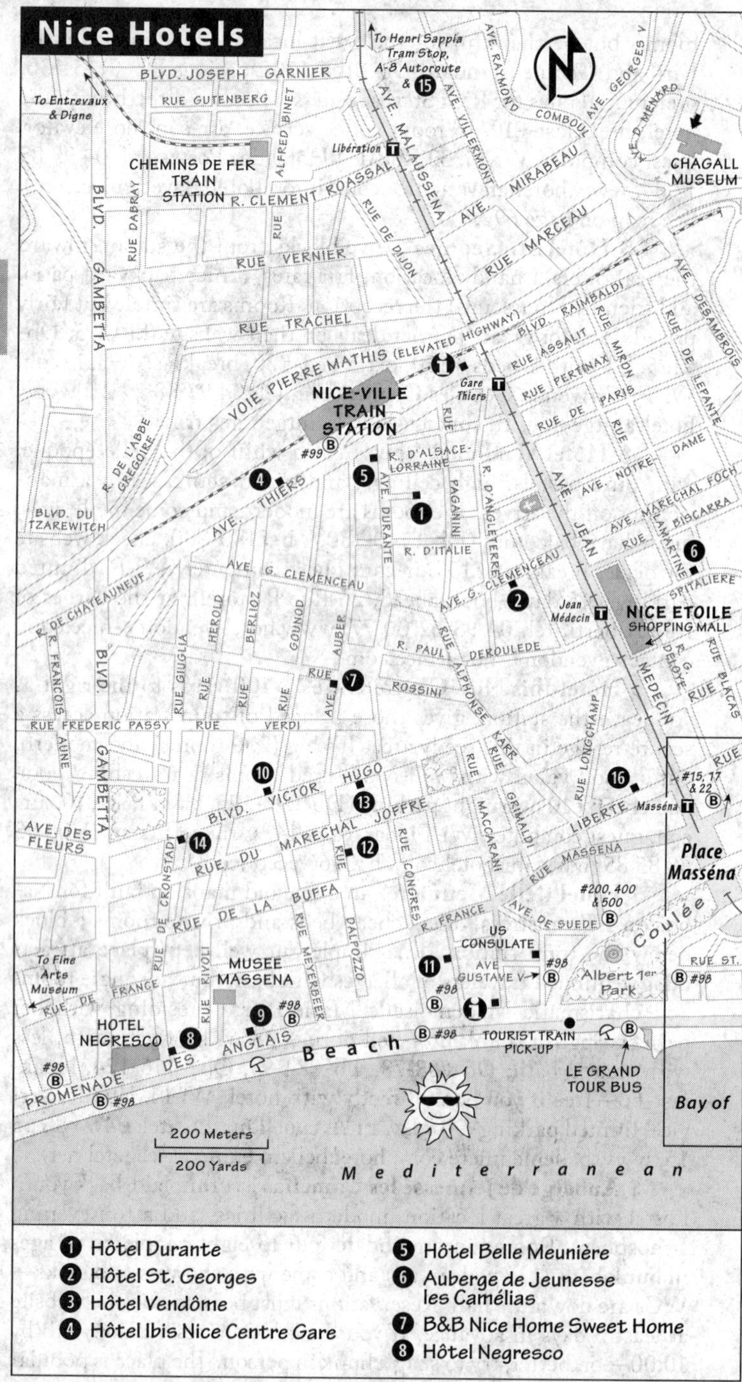

1 Hôtel Durante
2 Hôtel St. Georges
3 Hôtel Vendôme
4 Hôtel Ibis Nice Centre Gare
5 Hôtel Belle Meunière
6 Auberge de Jeunesse les Camélias
7 B&B Nice Home Sweet Home
8 Hôtel Negresco

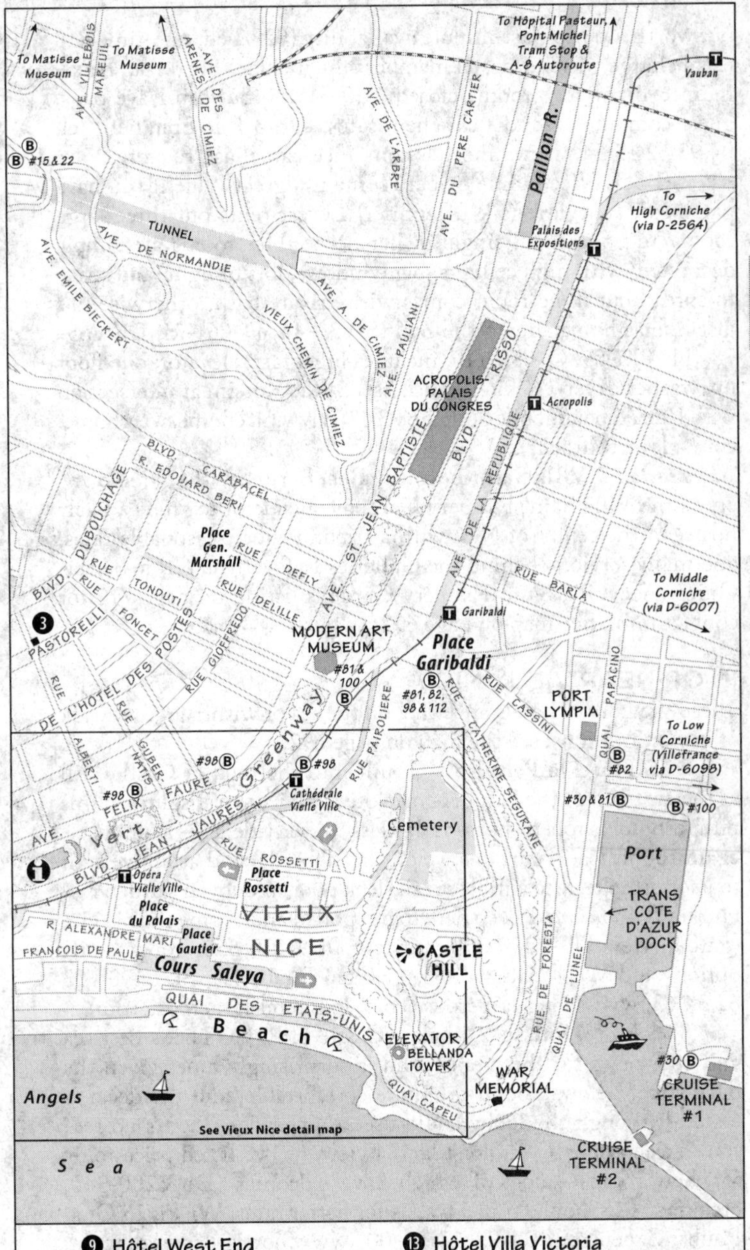

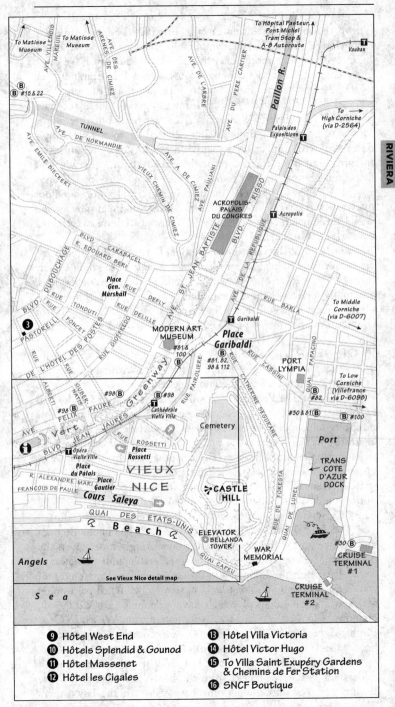

❾ Hôtel West End
❿ Hôtels Splendid & Gounod
⓫ Hôtel Massenet
⓬ Hôtel les Cigales
⓭ Hôtel Villa Victoria
⓮ Hôtel Victor Hugo
⓯ To Villa Saint Exupéry Gardens & Chemins de Fer Station
⓰ SNCF Boutique

but worth a try for last-minute availability (€28/bed, one-time €18 extra charge without hostel membership, includes breakfast, maximum 6-night stay, rooms closed 11:00-15:00 but can leave bags, guest computer, laundry, kitchen, safes, bar, 3 Rue Spitalieri, tel. 04 93 62 15 54, www.hihostels.com, nice-camelias@fuaj.org).

$ B&B Nice Home Sweet Home is a great value if you have patience. Genevieve (a.k.a. Jennifer) Levert rents out three large rooms and one small single in her home. Her rooms are simply decorated, with high ceilings, big windows, lots of light, and space to spread out. One room comes with private bath; otherwise, it's just like at home...down the hall (S-€35-44, D-€61-75, Db-€65-78, Tb-€75-85, Q-€80-110, includes breakfast, elevator, one floor up, washer/dryer-€6, kitchen access, 35 Rue Rossini at intersection with Rue Auber, mobile 06 19 66 03 63, www.nicehomesweethome.com, glevert@free.fr).

Hostel: **$ Villa Saint Exupéry Beach,** run by the same owners as the Villa Saint Exupéry Gardens outside of town, is a lively hostel in the center of Nice with a friendly vibe, reasonable rates, and many services (behind the Galleries Lafayette at 6 Rue Sacha-Guitry; see Villa Saint Exupéry Gardens listing on page 712 for contact info). See map on page 692.

IN OR NEAR VIEUX NICE

These Vieux Nice hotels are either on the sea or within an easy walk of it. For locations, see the map on page 692.

$$$ Hôtel la Perouse****, built into the rock of Castle Hill at the east end of the bay, gets my vote for Nice's best splurge. This refuge-hotel is top-to-bottom flawless in every detail—from its elegant rooms (satin curtains, velour headboards) and attentive staff to its rooftop terrace with Jacuzzi, sleek pool, and lovely garden restaurant (€40 *menus*). Sleep here to be spoiled and escape the big city (garden-view Db-€280-360, seaview Db-€400-550, good family options and Web deals, Wi-Fi, 11 Quai Rauba Capeu, tel. 04 93 62 34 63, www.hotel-la-perouse.com, lp@hotel-la-perouse.com).

$$$ Hôtel Suisse****, below Castle Hill, has Nice's best sea and city views for the money, and is surprisingly quiet given the busy street below. Rooms are quite comfortable, and the decor is tasteful (though the lobby could use an upgrade). There's no reason to sleep here if you don't land a view, so I've listed prices only for view rooms—most of which have balconies (Db-€200-340, breakfast-€18, book far in advance for better rates, Wi-Fi, 15 Quai Rauba Capeu, tel. 04 92 17 39 00, www.hotels-ocre-azur.com, hotel.suisse@hotels-ocre-azur.com).

$$ Hôtel Albert 1er*** is a fair deal in a great location on Albert 1er Park, two blocks from the beach and Place Masséna. Rooms are well appointed; some have views of the bay, others overlook the park (standard Db-€169-189, sea- or park-view Db-€179-199, Tb-€189-209, breakfast-€12, air-con, Wi-Fi, 4 Avenue des Phocéens, tel. 04 93 85 74 01, www.hotelalbert-1er.com, info@hotel-albert1er.com).

$$ Hôtel Mercure Marché aux Fleurs**** is a top choice, ideally situated near the sea and Cours Saleya. Rooms are tastefully designed and prices are usually reasonable—check their website for deals. Don't confuse this Mercure with the four other branches in Nice (standard Db-€180, superior Db-€225-260 and worth the extra euros, sea view-€50 extra and smaller room, air-con, Wi-Fi, 91 Quai des Etats-Unis, tel. 04 93 85 74 19, www.hotelmercure.com, h0962@accor.com).

$$ Hôtel de la Mer** is a tiny place with an enviable location overlooking Place Masséna, just steps from Vieux Nice (it's among the closest of my listings to the old town). The hotel was being renovated at press time so these prices may change (Db-€110-145, Tb-€145-160, breakfast-€7, air-con, Wi-Fi, 4 Place Masséna, tel. 04 93 92 09 10, www.hoteldelamernice.com, hotel.mer@wanadoo.fr).

NEAR THE BEACH

These hotels are close to the Promenade des Anglais (and most are far from Vieux Nice). The Negresco, West End, and le Royal are big, vintage Nice hotels that open onto the sea from the heart of the Promenade des Anglais. For locations, see the map on page 708.

$$$ Hôtel Negresco***** owns Nice's most prestigious address on Promenade des Anglais and knows it. Still, it's the kind of place that if you were to splurge just once in your life...Rooms are opulent (see page 695 for more description), and tips are expected (viewless Db-€380-560, seaview Db-€450-700, view suite-€890-2,900, Old World bar, 37 Promenade des Anglais, tel. 04 93 16 64 00, www.hotel-negresco-nice.com, reservations@hotel-negresco.com).

$$$ Hôtel West End**** opens onto the Promenade des Anglais with formal service and décor, classy public spaces, and high prices. Its smart rooms come with effective blinds and all the comforts (viewless Db-€310, seaview Db-€350, check website for deals, guest computer, Wi-Fi, 31 Promenade des Anglais, tel. 04 92 14 44 00, www.westendnice.com, reservation@westsendnice.com).

$$$ Hôtel Splendid**** is a worthwhile splurge if you miss your Marriott. The panoramic rooftop pool, bar/restaurant, and breakfast room almost justify the cost...but throw in plush rooms (all seven floors are non-smoking), a free gym, spa services, and air-conditioning, and you're as good as at home (Db-€230—some with decks, deluxe Db with terrace-€270, suites-€355-410, breakfast-€20, better prices available on website, parking-€24/day, 50

Boulevard Victor Hugo, tel. 04 93 16 41 00, www.splendid-nice.com, info@splendid-nice.com).

$$ Hôtel Massenet*** is a fine value tucked away a block off the Promenade des Anglais in a pedestrian zone. It has 29 comfortable and mostly spacious rooms (love the shag carpet) at good rates (small Db-€95, standard Db-€140-155, larger Db-€175, some rooms with decks, breakfast-€8, parking-€10/day, 11 Rue Massenet, tel. 04 93 87 11 31, www.hotelmassenet.com, hotelmassenet@wanadoo.fr).

$$ Hôtel les Cigales*,** a few blocks from the Promenade des Anglais, is a smart little pastel place with tasteful decor, 19 sharp rooms (those with showers are a tad small, most have tub-showers and are standard size), air-conditioning, and a nifty upstairs terrace, all well managed by friendly Mr. Valentino, with Veronique and Elaine. Rick Steves readers who book directly through the hotel get a 7 percent discount by typing this code: RICK (standard Db-€110-160, Tb-€130-180, Wi-Fi, 16 Rue Dalpozzo, tel. 04 97 03 10 70, www.hotel-lescigales.com, info@hotel-lescigales.com).

$$ Hôtel Gounod*** is behind Hôtel Splendid. Because the two share the same owners, Gounod's guests are allowed free access to Splendid's pool, Jacuzzi, and other amenities. Most rooms are comfortable and quiet, with high ceilings but tired bathrooms (Db-€140-180, palatial 4-person suites-€280, breakfast-€11, air-con, Wi-Fi, parking-€18/day, 3 Rue Gounod, tel. 04 93 16 42 00, www.gounod-nice.com, info@gounod-nice.com).

$$ Hôtel Villa Victoria**** is a fine place managed by cheery Marlena, who welcomes travelers into her spotless, classy old building with an open, attractive lobby overlooking a sprawling garden-courtyard. Rooms are comfortable and well kept, with space to stretch out (streetside Db-€160, garden-side Db-€175, Tb-€190, suites-€210, 4-night minimum in some seasons, breakfast-€15, air-con, minibar, Wi-Fi, parking-€18/day, 33 Boulevard Victor Hugo, tel. 04 93 88 39 60, www.villa-victoria.com, contact@villa-victoria.com).

$ Hôtel Victor Hugo delivers simple, good value in a fine turn-of-the-century building a short walk from the Promenade des Anglais. All seven rooms come with kitchenettes; sheets are changed every three days (Db-€90-120, includes breakfast, 59 Boulevard Victor Hugo, tel. 04 93 88 12 39, www.hotel-victor-hugo-nice.com).

BARELY BEYOND NICE

$ Villa Saint Exupéry Gardens, a service-oriented hostel (they answer the phone in English), is a haven two miles north of the city center. Its amenities and 60 comfortable, spick-and-span rooms create a friendly climate for budget-minded travelers of any age.

Often filled with energetic youth, the place can be noisy. There are units for one, two, and up to six people. Many have private bathrooms and views of the Mediterranean—some come with balconies. You'll also find a laundry room, complete kitchen facilities, a lively bar, a wall of guest computers in the lobby, and Wi-Fi (bed in dorm-€40/person, S-€50-70, Db-€100-120, Tb-€120-160, includes big breakfast, discounts in low season, no curfew, 22 Avenue Gravier, tel. 04 93 84 42 83, toll-free tel. 08 00 30 74 09—works only within France, www.villahostels.com, reservations@vsaint.com). From the center of town, ride the tram (direction: Henri Sappia) to the Compte de Falicon stop, then either walk 10 minutes or take the free shuttle from the Casino supermarket by the tram stop (no service 12:00-17:00).

NEAR THE AIRPORT

Several airport hotels offer a handy and cheap port in the storm for those with early flights or who are just stopping in for a single night: Hôtel Première Classe (www.premiereclasse.com) and Hôtel Ibis Budget Nice Aéroport (www.ibis.com). Free shuttles connect these hotels with both airport terminals.

You'll find greater comfort at the airport for a bit more (and free private shuttle vans) at these hotels: Novotel (www.novotel.com), Holiday Inn (www.holidayinn.com), and Campanile (www.campanile.fr).

Eating in Nice

Remember, you're in a resort. Seek ambience and fun, and lower your palate's standards. Italian is a low-risk and regional cuisine. The listed restaurants are concentrated in neighborhoods close to my recommended hotels. Promenade des Anglais is ideal for picnic dinners on warm, languid evenings. Vieux Nice has the best and busiest dining atmosphere (and best range of choices), while the Nice Etoile area is more local, convenient, and also offers a good range of choices. To feast cheaply, check out my suggestions in Vieux Nice, or explore the area around the train station. For a more peaceful meal, head for nearby Villefranche-sur-Mer (see page 728). Allow yourself one dinner at a beachfront restaurant in Nice, and for terribly touristy trolling, wander the wall-to-wall eateries lining Rue Masséna. Yuck.

IN VIEUX NICE

Nice's dinner scene converges on Cours Saleya (koor sah-lay-yuh), which is entertaining enough in itself to make the generally mediocre food a good deal. It's a fun, festive spot to compare tans and mussels. Even if you're eating elsewhere, wander through here in the evening. For locations, see the map on page 692.

La Voglia has figured out a winning formula: Good food + ample servings + fair prices = good business. Come here early or late for top-value Italian cuisine, or plan on waiting for a table. Outside seating is best, as the inside ambience is modern and loud (€12-14 pizza and pasta, €15-25 *plats,* open daily, at the western edge of Cours Saleya at 2 Rue St. Francois de Paule, tel. 04 93 80 99 16).

Le Safari is a fair option for Niçois cuisine and outdoor dining on Cours Saleya. The place is packed with locals and tourists, and staffed with hurried waiters (€18-30 *plats,* open daily, 1 Cours Saleya, tel. 04 93 80 18 44, www.restaurantsafari.fr).

Chez Palmyre is the place to eat on a budget in the old town. It's tiny and popular, so arrive by 19:15 or book ahead. The ambience is rustic and fun, with people squeezed into every square inch. The €17 *menu* changes every two weeks, and the food could not be more homemade (closed Sun, cash only, 5 Rue Droite, tel. 04 93 85 72 32).

Bistrot du Fromager's owner, Hugo, is crazy about cheese and wine. Come here to escape the heat and dine in cozy, cool, vaulted cellars surrounded by shelves of wine. All dishes use cheese as their base ingredient, although you'll also find pasta, ham, and salmon (with cheese, of course). This is a good choice for vegetarians (€10-15 starters, €15-22 *plats,* €6 desserts, closed Sun for dinner, just off Place du Jésus at 29 Rue Benoît Bunico, tel. 04 93 13 07 83).

Oliviera venerates the French olive. This shop/restaurant sells a variety of oils, offers free tastings, and serves a menu of dishes paired with specific oils (think of a wine pairing). Welcoming owner Nadim speaks excellent English, knows all his producers, and provides "Olive Oil 101" explanations with his tastings (best if you buy something afterward or have a meal). You'll learn how passionate he is about his products, and once you've had a taste, you'll want to stay and eat—so go early or reserve ahead (allow €40 with wine, €16-26 main dishes, Tue-Sat 10:00-22:00, closed Sun-Mon, indoor seating only, 8 bis Rue du Collet, tel. 04 93 13 06 45).

Bistrot D'Antoine is a welcoming, vine-draped option whose delightful menu emphasizes Niçois cuisine and good grilled selections. The food is delicious and the prices are reasonable, so call ahead to reserve a table (€7-10 starters, €13-19 *plats,* €6 desserts, closed Sun-Mon, 27 Rue de la Préfecture, tel. 04 93 85 29 57).

La Merenda is a shoebox where you'll sit on small stools and dine on simple, home-style dishes in a communal environment. The menu changes with the season, but the hardworking owner, Dominique, does not. This place fills fast, so arrive early or, better yet, drop by during the day to reserve (€10 starters, €14 *plats,* €6 desserts, closed Sat-Sun, cash only, 4 Rue Raoul Bosio, no telephone, www.lamerenda.net).

L'Acchiardo, buried in the heart of Vieux Nice, is a homey eatery that mixes loyal clientele with hungry tourists. Its simple, hearty Niçois cuisine is served at fair prices by gentle Monsieur Acchiardo. The small plaque under the menu outside says the restaurant has been run by father and son since 1927 (€9 starters, €16 *plats,* €7 desserts, closed Sat-Sun, indoor seating only, 38 Rue Droite, tel. 04 93 85 51 16).

Lou Pilha Leva delivers fun and cheap lunch or dinner options with Niçois specialties and always-busy, outdoor-only picnic-table dining (daily, located where Rue de la Loge and Rue Centrale meet in Vieux Nice).

Restaurant Castel is a fine eat-on-the-beach option, thanks to its location at the very east end of Nice looking over the bay. Lose the city bustle by dropping down the steps below Castle Hill. The views are unforgettable even if the cuisine is not; you can even have lunch at your beach chair if you've rented one here (€15/half-day, €19/day). Dinner here is best: Arrive before sunset and find a waterfront table perfectly positioned to watch evening swimmers get in their last laps as the sky turns pink and city lights flicker on. Linger long enough to justify the few extra euros the place charges (€18 salads and pastas, €20-28 main courses, open for dinner May-Sept, 8 Quai des Etats-Unis, tel. 04 93 85 22 66, www.castelplage.com).

AND FOR DESSERT...

Gelato lovers should save room for the tempting ice-cream stands in Vieux Nice. **Fenocchio** is the city's favorite, with mouthwatering displays of 86 flavors ranging from tomato to lavender to avocado—all of which are surprisingly good (daily March-Nov, until 24:00 in summer, two locations: 2 Place Rossetti and 6 Rue de la Poissonnerie). Gelato connoisseurs should head for **Oui, Jelato,** where the selection may be a fraction of Fenocchio's but the quality is superior (daily until late, 5 Rue de la Préfecture, on the Place du Palais).

EATING NEAR NICE ETOILE

If you're not up for eating in Vieux Nice, try one of these spots around the Nice Etoile shopping mall.

On Rue Biscarra: An appealing lineup of bistros overflowing with outdoor tables stretches along the broad sidewalk on Rue Biscarra (just east of Avenue Jean Médecin behind Nice Etoile, all closed Sun). Come here to dine with area residents away from the tourists. These two places are both good choices, with pleasant interior and exterior seating: **L'Authentic** has creative cuisine and

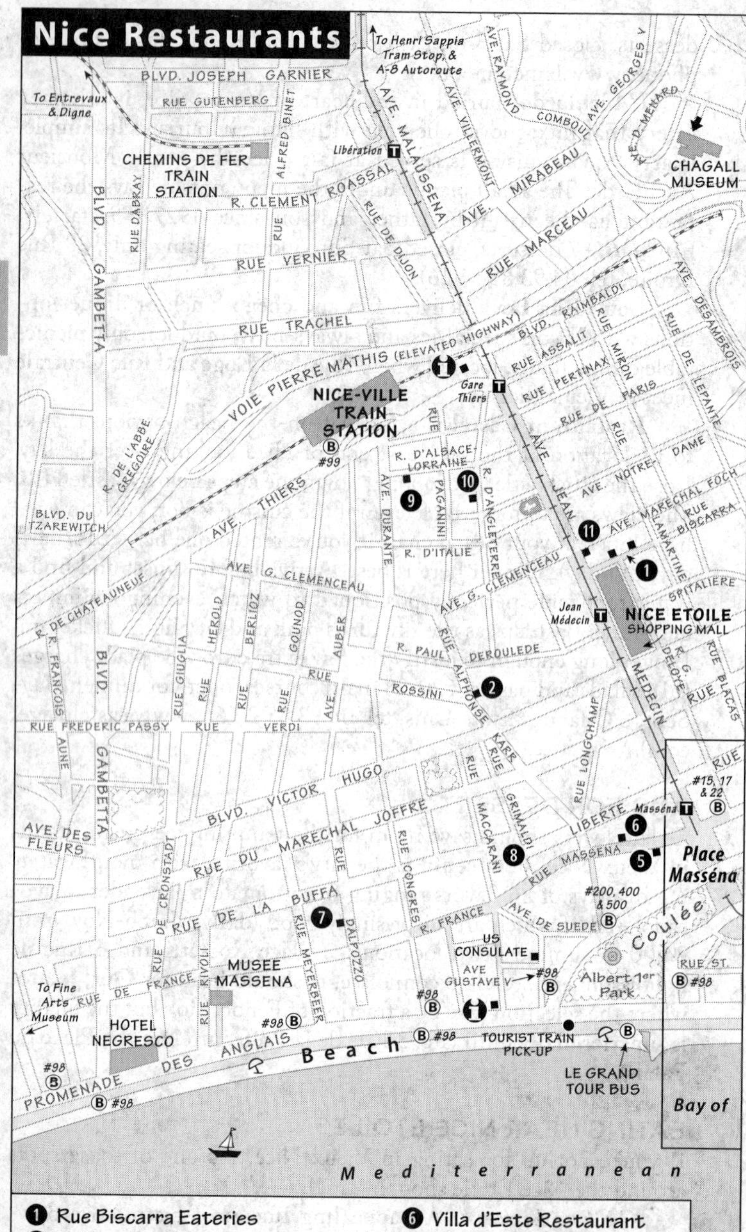

❶ Rue Biscarra Eateries
❷ Rolancy's Restaurant & Bistrot des Viviers
❸ L'Ovale Restaurant
❹ Le Luna Rossa Restaurant
❺ La Maison de Marie Rest.
❻ Villa d'Este Restaurant
❼ Coco & Rico Bistro
❽ Place Grimaldi Eateries
❾ Voyageur Nissart Rest.
❿ Zen Restaurant
⓫ Monoprix Grocery Store

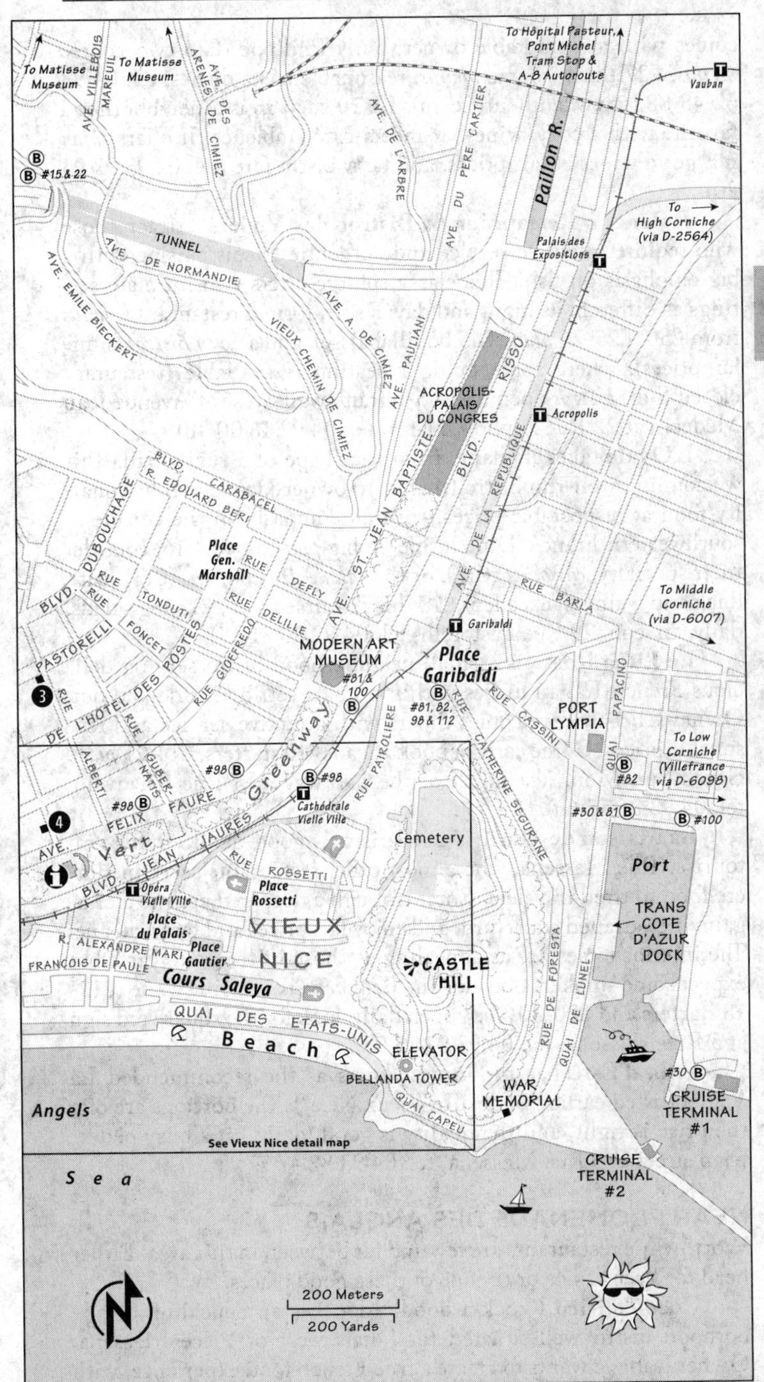

To Matisse Museum
To Matisse Museum
To Hôpital Pasteur, Pont Michel Tram Stop & A-8 Autoroute
Vauban
Paillon R.
To High Corniche (via D-2564)
Palais des Expositions
TUNNEL
AVE. DE NORMANDIE
AVE. EMILE BIECKERT
ACROPOLIS-PALAIS DU CONGRES
Acropolis
Place Gen. Marshall
To Middle Corniche (via D-6007)
Garibaldi
MODERN ART MUSEUM
Place Garibaldi
PORT LYMPIA
To Low Corniche (Villefrance via D-6098)
Greenway
Cathédrale Vielle Ville
Cemetery
Vert
Port
TRANS COTE D'AZUR DOCK
Opéra Vielle Ville
Place Rossetti
Place du Palais
VIEUX NICE
Place Gautier
Cours Saleya
CASTLE HILL
QUAI DES ETATS-UNIS
Beach
ELEVATOR
BELLANDA TOWER
WAR MEMORIAL
CRUISE TERMINAL #1
CRUISE TERMINAL #2
Angels
Sea
See Vieux Nice detail map
200 Meters
200 Yards

comes with a memorable owner, burly Philippe (€23 two-course *menus,* €27 three-course *menus,* reasonable pasta dishes, tel. 04 93 62 48 88, www.lauthentic.com). **Le 20 sur Vin** is a neighborhood favorite with a cozy, wine-bar-meets-café ambience. It offers *(bien sûr)* good wines at fair prices, and tasty bistro fare (tel. 04 93 92 93 20).

Rolancy's Restaurant & Bistrot des Viviers attract those who require attentive service and authentic Niçois cuisine with a big emphasis on fish. This classy splurge offers two intimate settings as different as night and day: a soft, formal restaurant (*menus* from €50, €25-26 *plats,* €45 bouillabaisse), and a cozy *bistrot* (similar prices), where some outdoor seating is available (restaurant closed Sun, *bistrot* open daily, 5-minute walk west of Avenue Jean Médecin at 22 Rue Alphonse Karr, tel. 04 93 16 00 48).

L'Ovale takes its name from the shape of a rugby ball. This welcoming, well-run bistro (thanks to owner Jacqueline) has quality food at respectable prices, with an emphasis on the cuisine of southwestern France. Dine inside on big *plats* for €12-16; consider their specialty, *cassoulet* (€17), or the *salade de manchons* (€13), with duck and walnuts (excellent €18 three-course *menu,* €13 big salads, daily, air-con, 29 Rue Pastorelli, tel. 04 93 80 31 65).

Le Luna Rossa is a small neighborhood bistro serving delicious French-Italian dishes within a smart setting inside and out. Owner Christine welcomes diners with attentive service and reasonable prices. Come early or book ahead (€10 starters, €14-27 *plats,* closed Sun-Mon, just north of the parkway at 3 Rue Chauvain, tel. 04 93 85 55 66).

La Maison de Marie is a surprisingly good-quality refuge off touristy Rue Masséna, where most other restaurants serve mediocre food to tired travelers. Enter through a deep-red arch to a bougainvillea-draped courtyard, and enjoy fair prices and tasty cuisine. The interior tables are as appealing as those in the courtyard, but expect some smokers outside. The €24 *menu* is a terrific value (€12-18 starters and €20-30 *plats,* open daily, look for the square red sign at 5 Rue Masséna, tel. 04 93 82 15 93).

Villa d'Este has the same owners as the recommended La Voglia (listed earlier, under "In Vieux Nice"). The portions are big, the price is right, and the quality is good (daily, on a busy pedestrian street at 6 Rue Masséna, tel. 04 93 82 47 77).

NEAR PROMENADE DES ANGLAIS

Worthwhile restaurants are few and far between in this area. Either head for Vieux Nice or try one of these good places.

Coco & Rico ("cock-a-doodle-doo") is an appealing neighborhood bistro well-situated for hotels west of Place Masséna. Owner Isabelle wants to create a true French food experience, with inventive cuisine based on the classics, a fine wine selection, and good prices (€9 starters, €16-22 *plats,* €7 desserts, closed Sun and sometimes Mon, 3 Rue Dalpozzo, tel. 04 83 50 09 60).

On Place Grimaldi: This square nurtures a lineup of appealing restaurants with good indoor and outdoor seating along a broad sidewalk under tall, leafy sycamore trees. **Crêperie Bretonne** is the only *crêperie* I list in Nice (€11 dinner crêpes, closed Sun, 3 Place Grimaldi, tel. 04 93 82 28 47). **Le Grimaldi** delivers basic café fare (€17 pasta, €15-25 *plats,* closed Sun, 1 Place Grimaldi, tel. 04 93 87 98 13).

NEAR THE TRAIN STATION

Both of the following restaurants, a block below the train station, provide good indoor and outdoor seating as well as excellent value.

Voyageur Nissart has blended good-value cuisine with friendly service since 1908. Kind owner Max is a great host, and the quality of his cuisine makes his place both very popular and a good choice for travelers on any budget (best to book ahead, same day is fine, leave a message in English). Try anything *à la niçoise* or the fine €8 *salade niçoise* (€16 three-course *menus,* good *plats* from €11, cheap wines, closed Mon, 19 Rue d'Alsace-Lorraine, tel. 04 93 82 19 60).

Zen provides a Japanese break from French cuisine. Interior seating is arranged around the chef's stove, and the tasty specialties draw a strong following (€16 three-course *menu,* €8-15 sushi, open daily, 27 Rue d'Angleterre, tel. 04 93 82 41 20).

Nice Connections

BY TRAIN AND BUS

For a comparison of train and bus connections from Nice to nearby coastal towns, see the "Public Transportation in the French Riviera" sidebar on pages 676-679.

Note that most long-distance train connections to other French cities require a change in Marseille. The Grande Ligne train to Bordeaux (serving Antibes, Cannes, Toulon, and Marseille—and connecting from there to Arles, Nîmes, and Carcassonne) requires a reservation. Remember that on regional buses (except on express airport buses), many one-way rides cost €1.50—regardless of length (the €1.50 ticket is good for up to 74 minutes of travel in one direction, including transfers).

From Nice by Train to: Cannes (2/hour, 30-40 minutes), **Antibes** (2/hour, 15-30 minutes), **Villefranche-sur-Mer** (2/hour, 10 minutes), **Eze-le-Village** (2/hour, 15 minutes to Eze-Bord-de-Mer, then bus #83 to Eze, 8/day), **Monaco** (2/hour, 20 minutes), **Menton** (2/hour, 25 minutes), **Grasse** (15/day, 1.25 hours),

Marseille (18/day, 2.5 hours), **Cassis** (14/day, 3 hours, transfer in Toulon or Marseille), **Arles** (11/day, 3.75-4.5 hours, most require transfer in Marseille or Avignon), **Avignon** (10/day, most by TGV, 4 hours, many require transfer in Marseille), **Paris**' Gare de Lyon (hourly, 5.75 hours, may require change; 11.5-hour night train goes to Paris' Gare d'Austerlitz), **Aix-en-Provence** TGV Station (10/day, 2-3.5 hours, usually changes in Marseille), **Chamonix** (4/day, 10 hours, many change in St-Gervais and Lyon), **Beaune** (7/day, 7 hours, 1-2 changes), **Munich** (4/day, 12.5-14 hours with 2-4 transfers, longer night trains possible, some via Italy), **Interlaken** (6/day, 9-10 hours, 2-5 transfers), **Florence** (6/day, 7-9 hours, 1-3 transfers), **Milan** (7/day, 5-5.5 hours, all require transfers), **Venice** (5/day, 8-9 hours, all require transfers), **Barcelona** (1/day via Montpellier, 10 hours, more with multiple changes).

From Nice by Bus to: Cannes (#200, 4/hour Mon-Sat, 2-3/hour Sun, 1.5-1.75 hours), **Antibes** (#200, 4/hour Mon-Sat, 2-3/hour Sun, 1-1.5 hours), **Villefranche-sur-Mer** (#100, 3-4/hour Mon-Sat, 3-4/hour Sun, 20 minutes; or #81, 2-3/hour, 20 minutes), **St-Jean-Cap-Ferrat** (#81, 2-3/hour, 35 minutes), **Eze-le-Village** (#82 or #112, 16/day Mon-Sat, 8/day Sun, 40 minutes), **La Turbie** (#116 or #T-66, 5/day Mon-Sat, 7/day Sun, 45 minutes), **Monaco** (#100, 3-4/hour, 45 minutes), **Menton** (#100, 3-4/hour, 1.25 hours), **St-Paul-de-Vence** (#400, every 30-45 minutes, 45 minutes), **Vence** (#400, every 30-45 minutes, 50 minutes), **Grasse** (#500, every 30-45 minutes, 1.25 hours).

BY PLANE

Nice's easy-to-navigate airport (Aéroport de Nice Côte d'Azur; airport code: NCE) is on the Mediterranean, a 20- to 30-minute drive west of the city center. Planes leave roughly hourly for Paris (one-hour flight, about the same price as a train ticket, check www.easyjet.com for the cheapest flights to Paris' Orly airport). The two terminals (Terminal 1 and Terminal 2) are connected by frequent shuttle buses *(navettes)*. Both terminals have TIs (and Terminal 1 has an info desk just for Monaco), banks, ATMs, taxis, baggage storage (open daily 5:45-23:00), and buses to Nice (tel. 04 89 88 98 28, www.nice.aeroport.fr).

Getting from the Airport to the City Center

Taxis into the center are expensive considering the short distance (figure €35 to Nice hotels, €60 to Villefranche-sur-Mer, €70 to Antibes, 10 percent more 19:00-7:00 and all day Sun). Taxis stop outside door *(Porte)* A-1 at Terminal 1 and outside *Porte* A-3 at Terminal 2. Notorious for overcharging, Nice taxis are not always so nice. If your fare for a ride into town is much higher than €35 (or €40 at night or on Sun), refuse to pay the overage. If this doesn't work, tell the cabbie to call a *gendarme* (police officer). It's always a good idea to ask for a receipt *(reçu)*.

Airport shuttle vans work with some of my recommended hotels, but they make sense only when going *to* the airport, not when arriving on an international flight. Unlike taxis, shuttle vans offer a fixed price that doesn't rise on Sundays, early mornings, or evenings. Prices are best for groups (figure €30 for one person, and only a little more for additional people; keep in mind that taxis to the airport cost roughly €35, so be wary of services that charge much more). **Nice Airport Shuttle** is one option (1-2 people-€32, additional person-€14, mobile 06 60 33 20 54, www.nice-airport-shuttle.com). **Med-Tour,** in addition to sightseeing tours, also offers airport transfers for similar rates (tel. 04 93 82 92 58, mobile 06 73 82 04 10, www.med-tour.com). Ask your hotelier for other recommendations.

Three bus lines connect the airport with the city center. **Bus #99** (airport express) runs from both terminals to Nice's main train station (€6, 2/hour, 8:00-21:00, 30 minutes, transfers OK to city center and tramway, drops you within a 10-minute walk of many recommended hotels). To take this bus *to* the airport, catch it right in front of the train station (departs on the half-hour). If your hotel is within walking distance of the station, #99 is a breeze.

Bus #98 serves both terminals, and runs along Promenade des Anglais to the edge of Vieux Nice (€6, 3/hour, from the airport 6:00-23:00, to the airport until 21:00, 30 minutes, see map on page 708 for stops). The slower, cheaper local **bus #23** serves only Terminal 1, and makes every stop between the airport and Avenue Gambetta in the city center—a 10-minute walk to the train station (€1.50, 5/hour, runs 6:00-20:00, 40 minutes, direction: St. Maurice).

For all buses, buy tickets in the information office just outside either terminal or from the driver. To reach the bus information office and stops at Terminal 1, turn left after passing customs and exit the doors at the far end. Buses serving Terminal 2 stop across the street from the airport exit (information kiosk and ticket sales to the right as you exit).

Getting from the Airport to Nearby Destinations

To get to **Villefranche-sur-Mer** from the airport, take bus #98 to Place Garibaldi, then use the same ticket to transfer to bus #81 or #100 (3-4/hour on #100; 2-3/hour on #81; 20 minutes; see map on page 708 for stop location).

To reach **Antibes,** take bus #250 from either terminal (about 2/hour, 40 minutes, €10). For **Cannes,** take bus #210 from either terminal (2/hour, 50 minutes on freeway, €20). Express bus #110 runs from the airport directly to **Monaco** (2/hour, 50 minutes,

€20); it's cheaper (€6)—but more time-consuming—to take bus #99 or #98 to Nice, then transfer to a Monaco-bound bus or train.

BY CRUISE SHIP

Nice's port is at the eastern edge of the town center, separated from the old town and best beaches by Castle Hill. Cruise ships dock at either end of the mouth of this port: **Terminal 1** to the east (along the embankment called Quai du Commerce), or **Terminal 2** to the west (along Quai Infernet). At both terminals, TI kiosks (under pointy white tents) are timed to be open when cruises arrive.

A street called Place Ile de Beauté runs along the top of the port; here you'll find bus stops (including stops for the bus to Villefranche-sur-Mer and Monaco) and easy access to Place Garibaldi, where you can hop on Nice's tramway (which you can ride to the train station). From either terminal, it's about a 10-minute walk to the top of the port, or you can ride the free shuttle bus *(navette)*.

Taxis at the terminals charge about €25-30 to points within Nice (for example, to the train station or the Matisse or Chagall museums), €35-40 one-way to Villefranche-sur-Mer, or €80-90 one-way to Monaco. **Le Grand Tour Bus** hop-on, hop-off bus circuit has a stop at the top of the port (see "Tours in Nice," earlier).

Getting from the Port to the City Center

Nice's main promenade and old town are just on the other side of Castle Hill from the port. If your ship docks at Terminal 2, just walk around the base of the castle-topped hill (with the sea on your left), and you'll be at Vieux Nice in about 10-15 minutes. Terminal 1 is at the far end of the port from the old town. If you arrive here, it's slightly faster to circle around the back of Castle Hill: Walk or ride the shuttle bus to the top of the port, take the angled Rue Cassini to Place Garibaldi (described next), then walk into the old town from there (total walk: about 20-25 minutes).

The square called **Place Garibaldi** serves as a gateway between the port of Nice and the rest of the city. It's about a 15- to 20-minute walk from either cruise terminal: First, walk (or ride the shuttle bus) to the top-left corner of the port area, and head up the angled Rue Cassini toward the square with the palm trees. After three short blocks, you'll pop out at Place Garibaldi.

Once in Place Garibaldi, to reach Vieux Nice, walk straight through the middle of the square and out the other side, then turn left and walk down the broad Boulevard Jean Jaurès; the old town sprawls to your left. To reach the tram stop from Place Garibaldi, walk along the right side of the square, then turn right on Avenue de la République and walk a half-block. From here, you can ride the tram to Place Masséna (where you can catch bus #15 or #22 to the Chagall or Matisse museums, or #17 to the Matisse Museum) and the train station (Gare Thiers stop).

Getting from the Port to Nearby Destinations

To go from Nice to Villefranche-sur-Mer, Monaco, or other destinations, you can take either a train or a bus. The train is faster, but the bus stop is closer to Nice's port. For specifics on bus and train connections, see the "Public Transportation in the French Riviera" sidebar on pages 676-679.

From Nice's cruise port, you can get to the **train station** by bus (#30, 2/hour, 15 minutes to Gare SNCF stop; catch it at the top-left corner of the port along Place Ile de Beauté; from Terminal 1, you can also catch it along Boulevard de Stalingrad, up the stairs) or by tram (follow directions to Place Garibaldi, earlier, then ride the tramway to the Gare Thiers stop, cross the tracks, and walk straight one long block on Avenue Thiers).

Handy **bus #100**—which connects to points eastward including Villefranche-sur-Mer and Monaco—stops along the top of the port (near the right end of Place Ile de Beauté).

In summer, a **boat** to Monaco departs from near the cruise terminals, but it's slow and inconvenient if you're short on time (see page 687).

Villefranche-sur-Mer

In the glitzy world of the Riviera, Villefranche-sur-Mer offers travelers an easygoing slice of small-town Mediterranean life. From

here convenient day trips allow you to gamble in style in Monaco, saunter the Promenade des Anglais in Nice, or drink in immense views from Eze-le-Village and the Grande Corniche. Villefranche-sur-Mer feels Italian, with soft-orange buildings; steep, narrow streets spilling into the sea; and pasta on most menus. Luxury sailing yachts glisten in the bay—an inspiration to those lazing along the harborfront to start saving when their trips are over. Cruise ships make regular calls to Villefranche-sur-Mer's famously deep harbor, creating periodic rush hours of frenetic shoppers and happy boutique owners. Sand-pebble beaches and a handful of interesting sights keep other visitors just busy enough.

Orientation to Villefranche-sur-Mer

TOURIST INFORMATION

The main TI is in the park named Jardin François Binon, below the main bus stop, labeled *Octroi* (mid-June-mid-Sept daily 9:00-18:00; mid-Sept-mid-June Mon-Sat 9:00-12:00 & 14:00-17:00, closed Sun; 20-minute walk or €10 taxi ride from train station, tel. 04 93 01 73 68, www.villefranche-sur-mer.com). Pick up regional bus schedules here (buses #80, #81, #82, #83, #100, and #112) and information on boat rides (usually mid-June-Sept). A smaller TI is on the port (mid-May-mid-Sept Mon-Fri 10:00-17:00, Sat-Sun 10:00-16:00, closed off-season).

ARRIVAL IN VILLEFRANCHE-SUR-MER

By Bus: Whether you've taken bus #100 or #81 from Nice, or bus #100 from Monaco, hop off at the Octroi stop, at the Jardin François Binon, just above the TI. To reach the old town, walk past the TI down Avenue Général de Gaulle, take the first stairway on the left, then make a right at the street's end.

By Train: Not all trains stop in Villefranche-sur-Mer (you may need to transfer to a local train in Nice or Monaco). Villefranche-sur-Mer's train station is a 15-minute walk along the water from the old town and many of my recommended hotels. Find your way down toward the water, and turn right to walk into town. Taxis to my listed hotels cost €15, but they don't wait here, and they prefer longer trips—call instead, and—if you don't have a mobile phone—pray that the pay phone outside the station is working (for taxi telephone numbers, see the next page).

By Car: From Nice's port, follow signs for *Menton, Monaco,* and *Basse Corniche.* In Villefranche-sur-Mer, turn right at the TI (first signal after Hôtel la Flore) for parking and hotels. For a quick visit to the TI, park at the pay lot just below the TI. A bit farther down, you may find parking in the small lot off Avenue Verdun. There's a secure pay lot on the water across from Hôtel Welcome, and some hotels have their own parking.

By Plane: Allow an hour from Nice's airport to Villefranche-sur-Mer (for details, see page 721).

By Cruise Ship: See "Villefranche-sur-Mer Connections" on page 733.

HELPFUL HINTS

Market Day: A fun bric-a-brac market enlivens Villefranche-sur-Mer on Sundays (on Place Amélie Pollonnais by Hôtel Welcome, and in Jardin François Binon by the TI). On Saturday mornings, a small food market sets up near the TI (only in Jardin François Binon). A small trinket market springs to action on Place Amélie Pollonnais whenever cruise ships grace the harbor.

Last Call: Villefranche-sur-Mer makes a great base for day trips, but the last bus back from Nice or Monaco is at about 20:00. After that, take the train or a cab.

Internet Access: Two options sit side by side on Place du Marché. **Chez Net,** an "Australian International Sports Bar Internet Café," has American keyboards, whereas **L'X Café** has French keyboards. Both are open daily, have Wi-Fi, and let you enjoy a late-night drink while surfing the Internet.

Laundry: The town has two launderettes, both owned by Laura and located just below the main road on Avenue Sadi Carnot. At the upper *pressing moderne,* Laura does your wash for you—for a price (Tue-Sat 9:00-12:30 & 15:00-19:00, closed Sun-Mon, next to Hôtel Riviera, tel. 04 93 01 73 71). The lower *laverie* is self-service only (daily 7:00-20:00, opposite 6 Avenue Sadi Carnot).

Electric Bike Rental: The adventurous can try **Eco-Loc** electric bikes as an alternative to taking the bus to Cap Ferrat, Eze-le-Village, or even Nice (although the road to Nice is awfully busy). You get about 25 miles on a fully charged battery (less on hilly terrain—after that you're pedaling; €20/half-day, €30/day, early April-Sept daily 9:00-17:00, deposit and ID required, best to call for reservations 24 hours in advance; helmets, locks, baskets, and child seats available; pick up bike across from small TI on the port, mobile 06 66 92 72 41, www.ecoloc06.fr).

Taxi: For a reliable taxi in Villefranche-sur-Mer, call or email **Didier** (mobile 06 15 15 39 15, taxididier.villefranchesurmer@orange.fr). If he's busy, beware of taxi drivers who overcharge—the normal weekday, daytime rate to central Nice is about €40; to the airport, figure €60; one-way to Cap Ferrat is about €25, to Eze-le-Village is about €40, and to Monaco is €60. The five-minute trip from the waterfront up to the main street level (to bus stops on the Low Corniche) should be about €10. Ask your driver to write down the price before you get in, and get a receipt when you pay (general taxi tel. 04 93 55 55 55).

Minibus: Little **minibus #80** will save you the sweat of going from the harbor up the hill, but it runs only once per hour (daily 7:00-19:00, €1.50, schedule posted at stops and on www.lignedazur.com). It travels from the port to the top of the hill, stopping near Hôtel la Fiancée du Pirate and the Col de Villefranche stop for buses #82 and #112 to Eze-le-Village, before going to the outlying suburban Nice Riquier train station (only convenient if you're already on minibus, must transfer to train to downtown Nice).

Tourist Train: Skip the useless white *petit train,* which goes nowhere interesting (€7, 20-minute ride).

Spectator Sports: Lively *boules* action takes place each evening just below the TI and the huge soccer field (see page 1044).

Sights in Villefranche-sur-Mer

The Harbor

Browse Villefranche-sur-Mer's minuscule harbor. Although the town was once an important fishing community, only a few families still fish here to make money. Find the footpath that leads beneath the citadel to the sea (by the port parking lot). Stop where the path hits the sea and marvel at the scene: a bay filled with beautiful sailing yachts. (You might see well-coiffed captains being ferried in by dutiful mates to pick up their statuesque call girls.) Local guides keep a list of the world's 100 biggest yachts and talk about some of them as if they're part of the neighborhood.

At 2,100 feet deep, this is the deepest natural harbor on the Riviera and was the region's most important port until Nice built its own in the 18th century. Greek, Roman, and American ships appreciated the setting, as do cruise ships today. The citadel and hilltop castle (both described later) were built to defend the port, Villefranche's greatest asset.

Looking far to the right, that last apartment building on the sea was the headquarters for the US Navy's Sixth Fleet following World War II, and remained so until 1966, when de Gaulle pulled France out of the military wing of NATO. (The Sixth Fleet has been based in Naples ever since.) Two wall plaques at the bottom of Rue de l'Eglise commemorate the US Navy's presence in Villefranche-sur-Mer. Many remember with great regret the day the Americans left, as they had been great for business and livened up this small town during the otherwise quiet 1960s.

Citadel

The town's mammoth castle was built in the 1500s by the Duke of Savoy to defend against the French. When the region joined France in 1860, the castle became just a barracks. In the 20th century, the city had no military use for the space, and started using the citadel to house its police station, city hall, a summer outdoor theater, and two art galleries. There's still only one fortified entry to this huge complex.

Chapel of St. Pierre (Chapelle Cocteau)

This chapel, decorated by artist Jean Cocteau, is the town's cultural highlight. Cocteau was a Parisian transplant who adored little Villefranche-sur-Mer and whose career was distinguished by his work as an artist, poet, novelist, playwright, and filmmaker. Influenced by his pals Marcel Proust, André Gide, Edith Piaf, and Pablo Picasso, Cocteau was a leader among 20th-century avant-garde intellectuals. At the door, Marie-France—who is passionate about Cocteau's art—collects a donation for a fishermen's charity. She then sets you free to enjoy the chapel's small but intriguing interior. She's happy to give some explanations if you ask.

In 1955 Jean Cocteau covered the barrel-vaulted chapel with heavy black lines and pastels. Each of Cocteau's surrealist works—the Roma (Gypsies) of Stes-Maries-de-la-Mer who dance and sing to honor the Virgin, girls wearing traditional outfits, and three scenes from the life of St. Peter—is explained in English. Is that Villefranche-sur-Mer's citadel in the scene above the altar?

Cost and Hours: €3 donation requested, Wed-Mon 10:00-12:00 & 15:00-19:00, usually closed Tue (varies with cruise-ship traffic) and when Marie-France is tired, below Hôtel Welcome, tel. 04 93 76 90 70.

Nearby: A few blocks north along the harbor (past Hôtel Welcome), Rue de May leads to the mysterious **Rue Obscure**—a covered lane running 400 feet along the medieval rampart. This street served as an air-raid shelter during World War II. Much of the lane is closed indefinitely for repair.

Boat Rides (Promenades en Mer)

Consider treating yourself to a seaborne perspective of this beautiful area. A relatively inexpensive option is to take a **cruise** (€12 for one-hour cruise around Cap Ferrat, €20 for two-hour cruise as far as Monaco—but doesn't actually stop there, boats depart at 15:00 from the harbor across from Hôtel Welcome, June-Sept Wed and Sat, also Thu in July-Aug, no trips Oct-May, call to confirm ever-changing schedule, reservations a must, tel. 04 93 76 65 65, www.amv-sirenes.com). Or, to be your own skipper, rent a **motor boat** through Dark Pelican (€110/half-day, €180/day, deposit required, on the harbor at the Gare Maritime, tel. 04 93 01 76 54, www.darkpelican.com).

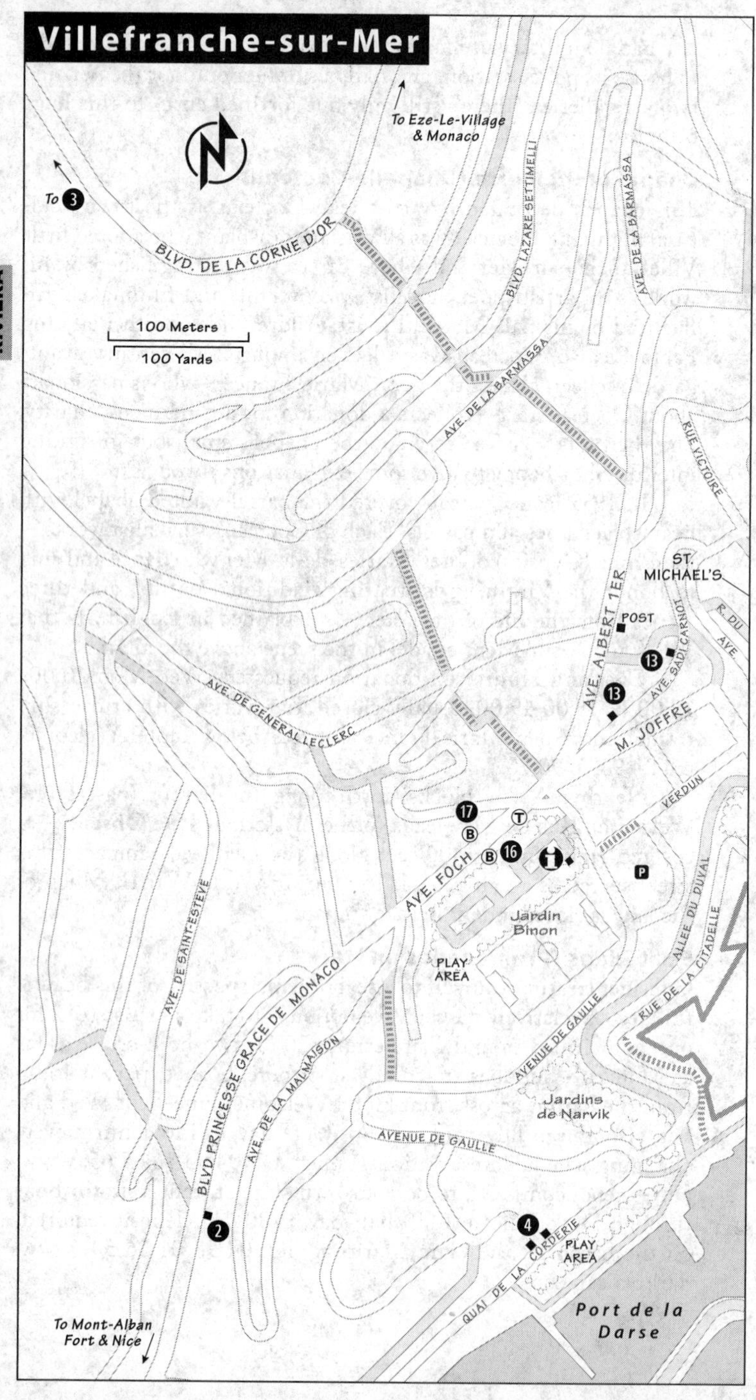
Villefranche-sur-Mer
To Eze-Le-Village & Monaco
To 3
BLVD. DE LA CORNE D'OR
BLVD. LAZARE SETTIMELLI
AVE. DE LA BARMASSA
100 Meters
100 Yards
AVE. DE LA BARMASSA
RUE VICTOIRE
ST. MICHAEL'S
POST
AVE. ALBERT 1ER
AVE. SADI CARNOT
R. DU
AVE
AVE. DE GENERAL LECLERC
M. JOFFRE
VERDUN
AVE. FOCH
Jardin Binon
PLAY AREA
AVE. DE SAINT-ESTEVE
BLVD PRINCESSE GRACE DE MONACO
AVE. DE LA MALMAISON
AVENUE DE GAULLE
ALLEE DU DUVAL
RUE DE LA CITADELLE
Jardins de Narvik
AVENUE DE GAULLE
QUAI DE LA CORDERIE
PLAY AREA
Port de la Darse
To Mont-Alban Fort & Nice

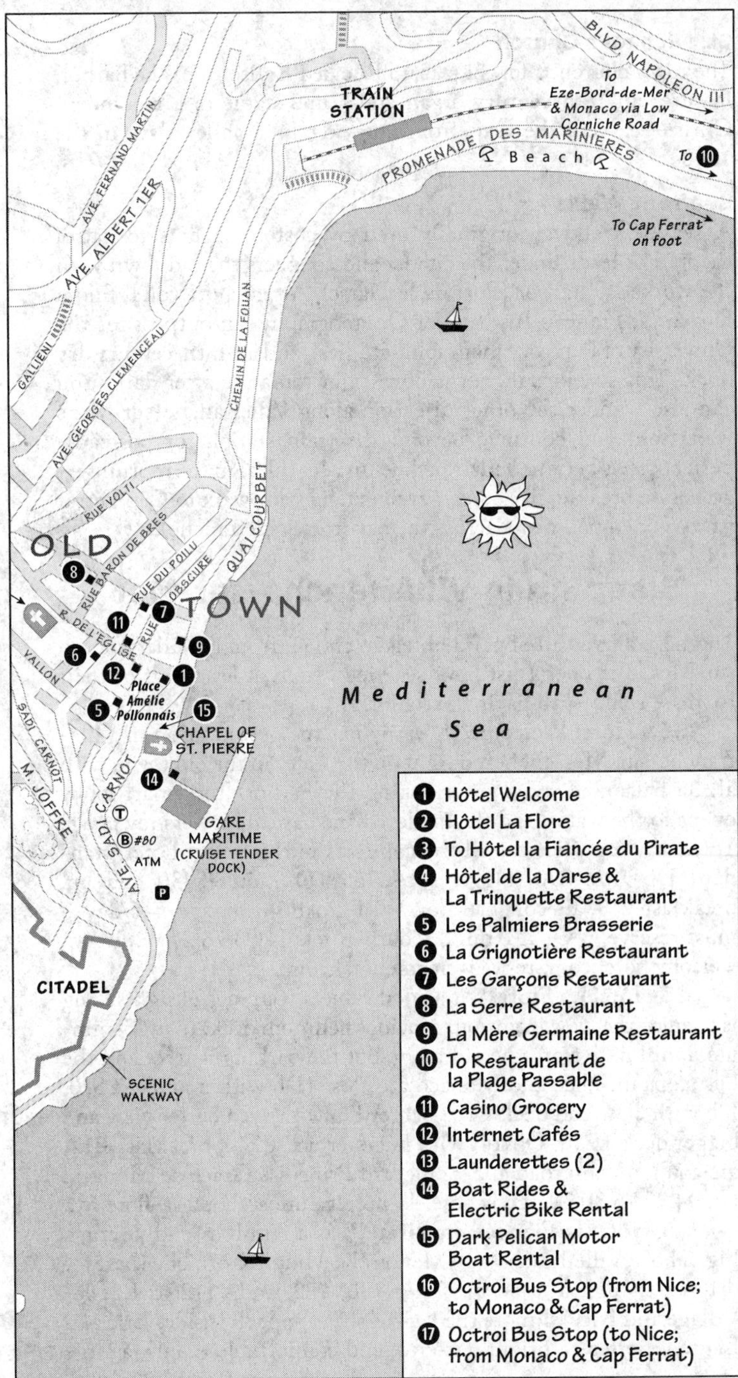
BLVD. NAPOLEON III
To Eze-Bord-de-Mer & Monaco via Low Corniche Road
TRAIN STATION
PROMENADE DES MARINIERES
Beach
To 10
To Cap Ferrat on foot
AVE. FERNAND MARTIN
AVE. ALBERT 1ER
GALLIENI
AVE. GEORGES CLEMENCEAU
CHEMIN DE LA FOUAN
QUAI COURBET
RUE VOLTI
OLD TOWN
RUE BARON DE BRES
RUE DU POILU
RUE OBSCURE
R. DE L'EGLISE
VALLON
Place Amélie Pollonnais
CHAPEL OF ST. PIERRE
SADI CARNOT
M. JOFFRE
AVE. SADI CARNOT
GARE MARITIME (CRUISE TENDER DOCK)
#80
ATM
CITADEL
SCENIC WALKWAY
Mediterranean Sea
1 Hôtel Welcome
2 Hôtel La Flore
3 To Hôtel la Fiancée du Pirate
4 Hôtel de la Darse & La Trinquette Restaurant
5 Les Palmiers Brasserie
6 La Grignotière Restaurant
7 Les Garçons Restaurant
8 La Serre Restaurant
9 La Mère Germaine Restaurant
10 To Restaurant de la Plage Passable
11 Casino Grocery
12 Internet Cafés
13 Launderettes (2)
14 Boat Rides & Electric Bike Rental
15 Dark Pelican Motor Boat Rental
16 Octroi Bus Stop (from Nice; to Monaco & Cap Ferrat)
17 Octroi Bus Stop (to Nice; from Monaco & Cap Ferrat)

St. Michael's Church

The town church, a few blocks up Rue de l'Eglise from the harbor, features an 18th-century organ and a fine statue of a recumbent Christ—carved, they say, from a fig tree by a galley slave in the 1600s.

Seafront Walks

A seaside walkway originally used by customs agents to patrol the harbor leads under the citadel and connects the old town with the workaday harbor (Port de la Darse). At the port you'll find a few cafés, France's Institute of Oceanography (an outpost for the University of Paris oceanographic studies), and an 18th-century dry dock. This scenic walk turns downright romantic after dark. You can also wander the other direction along Villefranche-sur-Mer's waterfront and continue beyond the train station for postcard-perfect views back to Villefranche-sur-Mer (ideal in the morning—go before breakfast). You can even extend your walk to Cap Ferrat (the wooded peninsula across the bay from Villefranche).

Sleeping in Villefranche-sur-Mer

You have a handful of good hotels to choose from in Villefranche-sur-Mer. The ones I list have sea views from at least half of their rooms—well worth paying extra for.

$$$ Hôtel Welcome**** easily has the best location in Villefranche-sur-Mer, anchored right on the water in the old town, with all 35 balconied rooms overlooking the harbor. The smart lobby opens to the water, and the mellow wine bar/café lowers my pulse. You'll pay top price for all the comforts in this smart hotel (standard Db-€215-290, bigger Db-€265-370, suites-€430 and up, breakfast-€18, air-con, elevator, Wi-Fi, parking garage-€45/day—must reserve, 3 Quai Amiral Courbet, tel. 04 93 76 27 62, www.welcomehotel.com, resa@welcomehotel.com).

$$ Hôtel La Flore*** is a good value if your idea of sightseeing is to enjoy the view from your spacious bedroom deck. It's a 15-minute uphill hike from the old town, but the parking is free, and the bus stops for Nice and Monaco are close (Db with no view-€120, Db with view and deck-€170, larger Db with even better view and bigger deck-€230, Qb loft with huge terrace-€240, breakfast-€12, air-con; on main road at 5 Boulevard Princesse Grace de Monaco; tel. 04 93 76 30 30, www.hotel-la-flore.fr, infos@hotel-la-flore.fr).

$$ Hôtel la Fiancée du Pirate*** is a family-friendly refuge high above Villefranche-sur-Mer on the Middle Corniche (best for drivers, though it is on bus lines #80, #82, and #112 to Eze-le-Village and Nice). Ignore the lack of street appeal: Inside, Eric and Laurence offer 15 bright, tasteful, and comfortable rooms, a large pool, a nice garden, and a view lounge area. The big breakfast features homemade crêpes (Db-€140-160, Tb-€160-195, Qb-€210-250, air-con, Wi-Fi, breakfast-€12, laundry service, free parking, 8 Boulevard de la Corne d'Or, Moyenne Corniche/N-7, tel. 04 93 76 67 40, www.fianceedupirate.com, info@fianceedupirate.com).

$ Hôtel de la Darse** is a shy little hotel burrowed in the shadow of its highbrow neighbors and a great budget option. It's less central—figure 10 scenic minutes of level walking to the harbor, and a steep 15-minute walk up to the main road and buses (minibus #80 stops in front, but runs only hourly). Sea-view rooms are worth the few extra euros (Db-€91-101, view Tb-€101-115, garden-side rooms are about €15 less, breakfast-€9.50, no elevator—though planned for late 2015, Wi-Fi); from TI, walk or drive down Avenue Général de Gaulle; walkers should turn left on Allée du Colonel Duval into the Jardins de Narvik and follow steps to bottom, then turn right at the old Port de la Darse; parking usually available nearby, tel. 04 93 01 72 54, www.hoteldeladarse.com, info@hoteldeladarse.com).

Eating in Villefranche-sur-Mer

Comparison-shopping is half the fun of dining in Villefranche-sur-Mer. Make an event out of a pre-dinner stroll through the old city. Check what looks good on the lively Place Amélie Pollonnais (next to Hôtel Welcome), where the whole village seems to converge at night; saunter the string of pricey candlelit places lining the waterfront; and consider the smaller, wallet-friendlier eateries embedded in the old city's walking streets. Arm yourself with a gelato from any ice-cream shop and enjoy a floodlit, post-dinner stroll along the sea.

Les Palimiers serves good-enough brasserie fare on the town's appealing main square (daily, Place Amélie Pollonnais, tel. 04 93 01 71 63).

Disappear into Villefranche-sur-Mer's walking streets and find cute little **La Grignotière,** serving generous and delicious *plats,* and plenty of other options. Gregarious Michel speaks English fluently and runs the place with his sidekick, Brigitte. The mixed-seafood grill is a smart order, as are the spaghetti and *gambas* (shrimp) and Michel's personal-recipe bouillabaisse (€23). They also offer a hearty €33 *menu,* but good luck finding room for it. Dining is primarily inside, making this a good choice for cooler days (daily except closed Wed Nov-April, 3 Rue du Poilu, tel. 04 93 76 79 83).

Les Garcons is where locals go to savor a fine meal at fair prices. Dine in a wood-floor-meets-leather-chair interior or in the small square out front (€20-26 *plats,* closed Tue-Wed, 18 Rue du Poilu, tel. 04 93 76 62 40).

La Serre, nestled in the old town below St. Michael's Church, is a simple place with a hardworking owner. Sylvie serves well-priced dinners to a loyal local clientele, always with a smile. Choose from the many pizzas (all named after US states and €10 or less), salads, and meats; or try the good-value, €17 three-course *menu* (open daily, evenings only, cheap house wine, 16 Rue de May, tel. 04 93 76 79 91).

La Mère Germaine, right on the harbor, is the only place in town classy enough to lure a yachter ashore. It's dressy, with formal service and a price list to match. The name commemorates the current owner's grandmother, who fed hungry GIs during World War II. Try the bouillabaisse, served with panache (€77/person with 2-person minimum, €51 mini-version for one, €45 *menu,* open daily, reserve harborfront table, 9 Quai de l'Amiral Courbet, tel. 04 93 01 71 39, www.meregermaine.com).

La Trinquette is a relaxed, low-key place away from the fray on the "other port," next to the recommended Hôtel de la Darse (a lovely 10-minute walk from the other recommended restaurants). The cuisine is good and weekends bring a cool live-music scene (€11-20 *plats,* daily in summer, closed Wed off-season, 30 Avenue Général de Gaulle, tel. 04 93 16 92 48).

There's a handy **Casino supermarket/grocery store** a few blocks above Hôtel Welcome at 12 Rue du Poilu (Mon-Tue and Thu-Sat 7:30-12:30 & 15:30-19:00, Sun 7:30-12:30 only, closed Wed).

For Drivers: If you have a car and are staying a few nights, take the short drive up to Eze-le-Village or, better still, La Turbie. If it's summer (June-Sept), the best option of all is to go across to Cap Ferrat's **Restaurant de la Plage de Passable** for a before-dinner drink or a dinner you won't soon forget (50-minute walk, 10-minute drive, follow signs from near Villa Rothschild). Enjoy a surprisingly elegant dining experience to the sounds of children still at play on the beach. Notice the streetlights that illuminate the path of the Low and Middle Corniches (€12-16 starters, €18-30 *plats,* open for dinner daily late May-early Sept, tel. 04 93 76 06 17, www.plage-de-passable.com).

Villefranche-sur-Mer Connections

For a comparison of connections by train and bus, see the "Public Transportation in the French Riviera" sidebar on pages 676–679.

BY TRAIN

Trains run later than buses (until 24:00) but leave you a 15-minute walk from the town center.

From Villefranche-sur-Mer by Train to: Monaco (2/hour, 10 minutes), **Nice** (2/hour, 10 minutes), **Antibes** (2/hour, 40 minutes).

BY BUS

All buses in this area cost €1.50 per ride, regardless of your destination (buy ticket from driver). Tickets are good for 74 minutes in one direction and for transfers, but not round-trips. In Villefranche-sur-Mer, all bus stops are along the main drag; the most convenient is the Octroi stop, just above the TI.

These are the key routes: **Bus #81** follows a circular route from Nice through Villefranche-sur-Mer, Beaulieu-sur-Mer, then to all Cap Ferrat stops, ending at the port in the village of St-Jean (2-3/hour daily 6:35-20:15 from Nice, last return trip from St-Jean at 20:50, earlier on Sun). **Bus #100** runs along the coastal road between Nice and Menton, just beyond Monaco (3-4/hour). The last bus leaves Nice for Villefranche-sur-Mer at about 20:00; the last bus from Villefranche-sur-Mer to Nice departs at about 20:45.

From Villefranche-sur-Mer by Bus to: Monaco (#100, 25 minutes), **Nice** (#81 or #100, 20 minutes).

BY CRUISE SHIP

Villefranche-sur-Mer hustles to impress its cruise passengers. Tenders deposit passengers at a slick terminal building (Gare Maritime) at the Port de la Santé, right in front of Villefranche-sur-Mer's old town. At the terminal TI, pick up the free town map that's tailor-made for arriving cruise passengers. The main road (with the main TI and bus stop) is a steep hike above, and the train station is a short stroll along the beach.

Taxis wait in front of the cruise terminal. Their exorbitant rates start with a minimum €10-20 charge for a ride to the train station, but many drivers will flat-out refuse such a short ride. For farther-flung trips, see the price estimates on page 725. For an all-day trip, you can try negotiating a flat fee (e.g., €300 for a 4-hour tour).

It's easy to **walk** to various points in Villefranche-sur-Mer. If you want to see the town itself, just walk straight ahead from the terminal into Villefranche-sur-Mer's charming, restaurant-lined square and start poking into its twisty back lanes.

Little **minibus #80,** which departs from in front of the cruise terminal, saves you some hiking up to the main road and bus stop (see page 725).

To connect to other towns, choose between the **bus** (slower but more scenic) or the **train** (fast). Leaving the terminal, you'll see directional sights pointing left, to *Town center/bus* (a 10- to 15-minute, steeply uphill walk to the Octroi bus stop with connections west to Nice or east to Monaco, both on bus #100 or #81); and right, to *Gare SNCF/train station* (a 10-minute, mostly level stroll with some stairs up at the end—just turn right and walk along the beach, with the sea on your right, until you see stairs up to the station on your left).

The Three Corniches

Nice, Villefranche-sur-Mer, and Monaco are linked by three coastal routes: the Low, Middle, and High Corniches. The roads are nicknamed after the decorative frieze that runs along the top of a building (cornice). Each Corniche (kor-neesh) offers sensational views and a different perspective. You can find the three routes from Nice by driving up Boulevard Jean Jaurès past Vieux Nice. For the Low Corniche, follow signs to N-98 *(Monaco par la Basse Corniche)*, which leads past Nice's port. Shortly after the turnoff to the Low Corniche, you'll see signs for N-7 *(Moyenne Corniche)*, which leads to the Middle Corniche. Signs for the High *(Grande)* Corniche appear a bit after that; follow D-2564 to *Col des 4 Chemins* and the *Grande Corniche.*

Low Corniche: The Basse Corniche (also called "Corniche Inférieure") strings ports, beaches, and seaside villages together for a traffic-filled ground-floor view. It was built in the 1860s (along with the train line) to bring people to the casino in Monte Carlo. When this Low Corniche was finished, many hill-town villagers descended to the shore and started the communities that now line the sea. Before 1860, the population of the coast between Villefranche-sur-Mer and Monte Carlo was zero. Think about that as you make the trip today.

Middle Corniche: The Moyenne Corniche is higher, quieter, and far more impressive. It runs through Eze-le-Village and provides breathtaking views over the Mediterranean, with several scenic pullouts. (The ones above Villefranche-sur-Mer are the best.)

High Corniche: Napoleon's crowning road-construction achievement, the Grande Corniche caps the cliffs with staggering views from almost 1,600 feet above the sea. It is actually the Via Aurelia, used by the Romans to conquer the West.

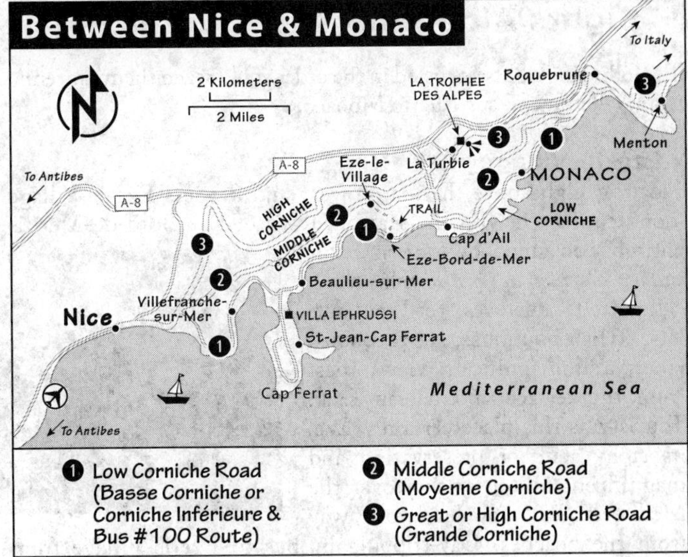

Villas: Driving from Villefranche-sur-Mer to Monaco, you'll come upon impressive villas. A particularly grand entry leads to "La Leopolda," the sprawling estate named for previous owner King Leopold II of Belgium in the 1930s (who owned the entire peninsula of Cap Ferrat in addition to this estate). Those driving up to the Middle Corniche from Villefranche-sur-Mer can look down on this yellow mansion and its lush garden, which fill an entire hilltop. The property was later owned by the Agnelli family (of Fiat fame and fortune), and then by the Safra family (Brazilian bankers). Its current value is somewhere north of $500 million.

The Best Route: For a ▲▲▲ route, **drivers** should take the Middle Corniche from Nice or Villefranche-sur-Mer to Eze-le-Village; from there, follow signs to the *Grande Corniche* and *La Turbie (La Trophée d'Auguste)*, keeping an eye out for brilliant views back over Eze-le-Village, then finish by dropping down into Monaco. **Buses** travel each route; the higher the Corniche, the less frequent the buses (3-4/hour on Low, 12/day on Middle, and 5/day on High; get details at TIs, or check www.lignedazur.com). There are no buses between Eze-le-Village and La Turbie (45-minute walk), though buses do connect Nice and Monaco with La Turbie.

Sights Along the Three Corniches

The following sights are listed in the order you'll reach them, traveling from Villefranche-sur-Mer to Monaco.

▲Eze-le-Village

Floating high above the sea, flowery and flawless Eze-le-Village (don't confuse it with the seafront town of Eze-Bord-de-Mer) is entirely consumed by tourism. This *village d'art et de gastronomie* (as it calls itself) nurtures perfume outlets, stylish boutiques, steep cobbled lanes, and magnificent views (best from the terrace at Château Eza). Touristy as this place certainly Eze, its stony state of preservation and magnificent hilltop setting over the Mediterranean may lure you away from the beaches. Day-tripping by bus to Eze-le-Village from Nice, Monaco, or Villefranche-sur-Mer works well, provided you know the bus schedules (ask at TIs or check www.lignedazur.com; Villefranche-sur-Mer requires a transfer). Arrive by 9:00 to experience a tranquil Eze, or prepare to do battle with the masses.

Bus stops and parking lots weld the town to the highway (Middle Corniche) that passes under its lowest wall. Eze-le-Village's main parking lot is a block below the town's entry. The stop for buses to Nice is across the road by the Avia gas station, and the stops for buses to Eze-Bord-de-Mer and Monaco are on the village side of the main road, near the Casino grocery. The helpful **TI** is adjacent to Eze-le-Village's main parking lot. Ask here for bus schedules. Call in advance to arrange €8 English-language tours of the village and its gardens (TI open April-Oct daily 9:00-18:00, July-Aug until 19:00; Nov-March Mon-Sat 9:00-17:00, closed Sun; Place de Gaulle, tel. 04 93 41 26 00, www.eze-tourisme.com). Public WCs are just behind the TI and in the village behind the church, though the cleanest and best-smelling are at the perfume showrooms.

As you wander up the narrow lanes, stop to read the information plaques (in English) and contemplate the change this village has witnessed in the last 90 years. Eze-le-Village was off any traveler's radar until well after World War II (running water was made available only in the 1930s), yet today hotel rooms outnumber local residents two to one (66 to 33).

Exotic Garden of Eze (Jardin Exotique d'Eze)

You'll find this prickly festival of cactus and exotic plants suspended between the sea and sky at the top of Eze-le-Village. Since 1949, the ruins of an old château have been home to 400 different plants 1,300 feet above the sea (€6, open daily, hours can change but usually July-Sept 9:00-19:00, Oct-June until dusk, well-described in English, tel. 04 93 41 10 30). At the top, you'll be treated to a commanding 360-degree view, with a helpful *table d'orientation.* On a crystal-clear day (they say...), you can see Corsica.

Fragonard Perfume Factory (Parfumerie Fragonard)

Located 350 feet below Eze-le-Village, this spot is designed for tour groups, and cranks them through all day long. Drop in for an informative and free tour. You'll see how the perfume and scented soaps are made, before being herded into the gift shop (daily 8:30-18:30 except closed 12:00-14:00 Nov-Jan, tel. 04 93 41 05 05). For a more personal and intimate (but unguided) look at perfume, cross the main road in Eze-le-Village to visit the **Gallimard** shop.

Trail to Eze-Bord-de-Mer

This steep trail leaves Eze-le-Village from the foot of the hill-town entry, near the fancy hotel gate (60 yards up from the main road), and descends 1,300 feet to the sea along a no-shade, all-view trail. The trail is easy to follow, but uneven—allow 45 minutes at a steady but manageable pace (good walking shoes are essential; expect to crawl on all fours in certain sections). Once in Eze-Bord-de-Mer, you can catch a bus or train to all destinations between Nice and Monaco. While walking this trail in the late 1800s, Friedrich Nietzsche was moved to write his unconventionally spiritual novel, *Thus Spoke Zarathustra.*

Eating in Eze-le-Village: To enjoy Eze-le-Village in relative peace, visit early, when the light is best over the sea, or come at sunset and stay for dinner. There's a handy **Casino** grocery at the foot of the village by the bus stop (Mon-Sat 8:00-19:30, Sun 8:00-19:00) and a sensational picnic spot at the beginning of the trail to Eze-Bord-de-Mer. **Le Cactus** serves good and cheap crêpes, salads, and sandwiches at outdoor tables near the entry to the old town and in a cozy, vaulted-ceiling dining room inside (daily, tel. 04 93 41 19 02). For a real splurge, dine at **Château Eza.** Its sensational view terrace is also home to an expensive-but-excellent restaurant. Reserve well ahead for dinner (€7 teas, €10 beers and glasses of wine, €64 lunch *menus,* allow €130 for dinner, open daily, tel. 04 93 41 12 24, www.chateaueza.com, info@chateaueza.com).

Getting to Eze-le-Village: There are two Ezes: Eze-le-Village (the spectacular hill town) and Eze-Bord-de-Mer (a modern beach resort far below Eze-le-Village). Eze-le-Village is about 20 minutes east of Villefranche-sur-Mer on the Middle Corniche. Get schedules for all buses at www.lignesdazur.com).

From Nice and upper Villefranche-sur-Mer, buses #82 and #112 provide 16 buses per day to Eze-le-Village (8 on Sun, 20 minutes from Villefranche). Take the hourly minibus #80 from the center of Villefranche-sur-Mer uphill to the Col de Villefranche stop near Hôtel la Fiancée du Pirate to make this connection.

From Nice, Villefranche-sur-Mer, or Monaco, you can also take the train or the Nice-Monaco bus to Eze-Bord-de-Mer, getting off at the Gare d'Eze stop. From here, take the #83 shuttle bus straight up to Eze-le-Village (8/day, daily about 9:00-18:00, schedule is posted at the stop, but it's best to know the schedule before you go). From Monaco, it's easiest to connect by direct bus (described next).

To connect Eze-le-Village directly with Monte Carlo in Monaco, take bus #112 (6/day Mon-Sat, none on Sun, 20 minutes).

There are no direct buses from Villefranche-sur-Mer's center to Eze-le-Village, and there are no buses between La Turbie (La Trophée d'Auguste) and Eze-le-Village (40-minute walk).

You could take a pricey taxi between the two Ezes or from Eze-le-Village to La Turbie (allow €25 one-way, mobile 06 09 84 17 84).

▲▲La Trophée d'Auguste (in La Turbie)

High above Monaco, on the Grande (High) Corniche in the overlooked village of La Turbie, lies one of this region's most evocative historical sights (with dramatic views over the entire country of Monaco as a bonus). Rising well above all other buildings, this massive Roman monument commemorates Augustus Caesar's conquest of the Alps and its 44 hostile tribes. It's exciting to think that, in a way, La Trophée d'Auguste celebrates a victory that kicked off the Pax Romana—joining Gaul and Germania, freeing up the main artery of the Roman Empire, and linking Spain and Italy. (It's depressing to think that it's closed on Mondays, if that's your only chance to visit.)

You'll enter through a small park that offers grand views over Monaco and allows you to appreciate the remarkable setting selected by the Romans for this monument. Walk around and notice how the Romans built a fine, quarried-stone exterior, filled in with rubble and coarse concrete. Flanked by the vanquished in chains, the towering inscription tells the story: It was erected "by the senate and the people to honor the emperor." The monument later became a quarry before being restored in the 1930s and 1940s with money from the Tuck family of New Hampshire. The site is not accessible except during open hours.

The one-room **museum** shows a reconstruction and translation of the dramatic inscription, which lists all the feisty alpine tribes that put up such a fight. Recently upgraded, it has good English explanations and modern exhibits (an audioguide is available). Escorts from the museum take people up to the monument, but they're not worth waiting for.

Cost and Hours: €5.50, Tue-Sun mid-May-mid-Sept 9:30-13:00 & 14:30-18:30, off-season 10:00-13:30 & 14:30-17:00, closed Mon year-round, audioguide-€3.50, tel. 04 93 41 20 84.

Eating in La Turbie: The sweet old village of La Turbie sees almost no tourists, but it has plenty of cafés and restaurants. To stroll the old village, park in the main lot on Place Neuve (follow *Monaco* signs one block from the main road to find it), then walk behind the post office and find brick footpaths—they lead through a village with nary a shop. To eat well, find **La Terrasse,** the Riviera's most welcoming restaurant (I'm not kidding—free calls are encouraged from their phone anywhere, anytime; there's also a computer at your disposal, and the Wi-Fi is free). Tables gather under sunshades and everyone seems to be on a first-name basis. Let Helen and Jacques tempt you to return for dinner at sunset—book ahead for a table with a view (€8-12 salads, great €14 *plats du jour,* €20 three-course *menu* includes glass of wine, steak *tartare* is a specialty, daily, near the post office at the main parking lot, 17 Place Neuve, tel. 04 93 41 21 84).

Getting to and from La Trophée d'Auguste and La Turbie: By **car,** take the High Corniche to La Turbie, ideally from Eze-le-Village (La Turbie is 10 minutes east of, and above, Eze-le-Village), then look for signs to *La Trophée d'Auguste.* Once in La Turbie, park in the lot in the center of town (Place Neuve, follow *Monaco* signs for a short block) and walk from there (walk 5 minutes around the old village, with the village on your right); or drive to the site by turning right in front of La Régence Café. Those coming from farther afield can take the efficient A-8 to the La Turbie exit. To reach Eze-le-Village from La Turbie, follow signs to *Nice,* and then look for signs to *Eze-le-Village.*

From Nice, you can also get here on **bus** #T66 from the Pont St. Michel tram stop (7/day, 45 minutes, last bus returns to Nice at about 18:00), or on bus #116 from the Vauban tram stop (6/day, 45 minutes). From Monaco, bus #11 connects to La Turbie (8/day Mon-Sat, 5/day Sun, 30 minutes). La Turbie's bus stop is near the post office on Place Neuve (to reach La Trophée d'Auguste from here, walk 5 minutes around the old village, with the village on your right).

Monaco

Despite high prices, wall-to-wall daytime tourists, and a Disney-esque atmosphere, Monaco is a Riviera must. Monaco is on the go. Since 1929, cars have raced around the port and in front of the casino in one of the world's most famous auto races, the Grand Prix de Monaco. The modern breakwater—constructed elsewhere and towed in by sea—enables big cruise ships to dock here, while the district of Fontvieille, reclaimed from the sea, bristles with luxury high-rise condos. But don't look for anything too deep in this glittering tax haven. Three-fourths of its 36,000 residents live here because there's no income tax—leaving about 6,000 true Monegasques.

This minuscule principality (0.75 square mile) borders only France and the Mediterranean. The country has always been tiny, but it used to be...less tiny. In an 1860 plebiscite, Monaco lost two-thirds of its territory when the region of Menton voted to join France. To compensate, France suggested that Monaco build a fancy casino and promised to connect it to the world with a road (the Low Corniche) and a train line. This started a high-class tourist boom that has yet to let up.

Although "independent," Monaco is run as a piece of France. A French civil servant appointed by the French president—with the blessing of Monaco's prince—serves as state minister and manages the place. Monaco's phone system, electricity, water, and so on, are all French.

The glamorous romance and marriage of the American actress Grace Kelly to Prince Rainier added to Monaco's fairy-tale mystique. Princess Grace (Prince Albert's mother) first came to Monaco to star in the 1955 Hitchcock movie *To Catch a Thief,* in which she was filmed racing along the Corniches. She married the prince in 1956 and adopted the country, but tragically, the much-loved princess died in 1982 after suffering a stroke while driving on one of those same scenic roads. She was just 52 years old.

The death of Prince Rainier in 2005 ended his 56-year career of enlightened rule. Today Monaco is ruled by Prince Rainier's unassuming son, Prince Albert Alexandre Louis Pierre, Marquis of Baux. Prince Albert had long been considered Europe's most eligible bachelor—until he finally married on July 2, 2011, at age 53. His bride, known as Princess Charlene, is a South African commoner twenty years his junior.

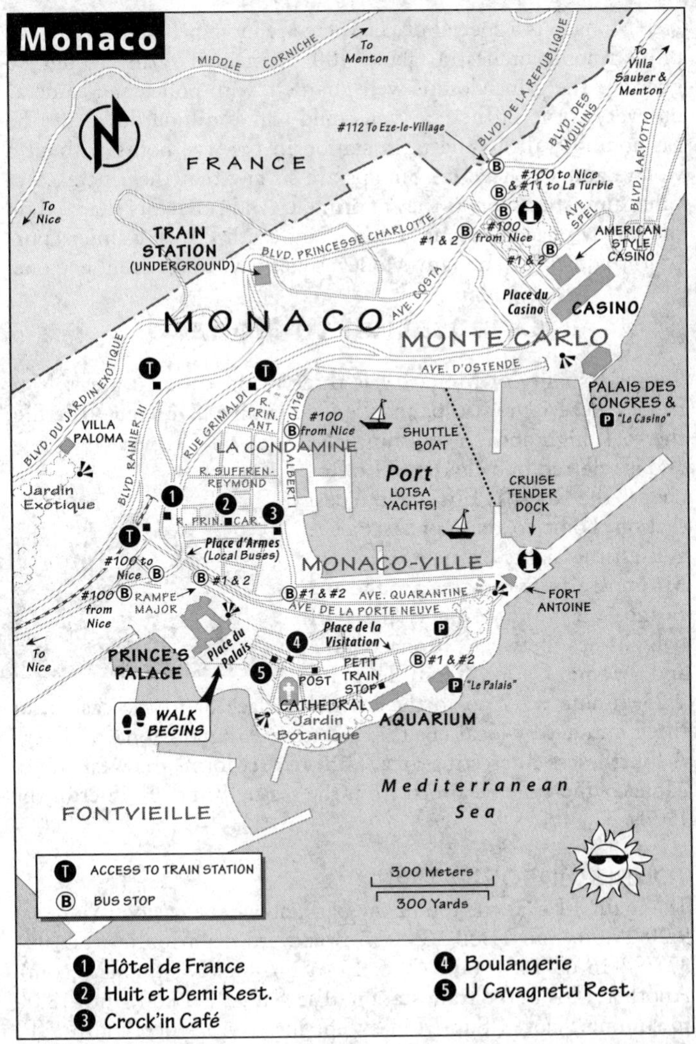

A graduate of Amherst College, Albert is a bobsled enthusiast who raced in several Olympics, and an avid environmentalist who seems determined to clean up Monaco's tarnished tax-haven, money-laundering image. (Monaco is infamously known as a "sunny place for shady people.") Monaco is big business, and Prince Albert is its CEO. Its famous casino contributes only 5 percent of the state's revenue, whereas its 43 banks—which offer an attractive way to hide your money—are hugely profitable. The prince also makes money with a value-added tax (19.6 percent, the same as in France), plus real estate and corporate taxes.

Monaco is a special place: There are more people in Monaco's philharmonic orchestra (about 100) than in its army (about 80 guards). The princedom is well-guarded, with police and cameras on every corner. (They say you could win a million dollars at the casino and walk to the train station in the wee hours without a worry...and I believe it.) Stamps are so few that they increase in value almost as soon as they're printed. And collectors snapped up the rare Monaco versions of euro coins (with Prince Rainier's portrait) so quickly that many Monegasques have never even seen one.

Orientation to Monaco

The principality of Monaco has three distinct tourist areas: Monaco-Ville, Monte Carlo, and La Condamine. **Monaco-Ville** fills the rock high above everything else and is referred to by locals as Le Rocher ("The Rock"). This is the oldest section, home to the Prince's Palace and all the sights except the casino. **Monte Carlo** is the area around the casino. **La Condamine** is the port (which lies between Monaco-Ville and Monte Carlo). From here it's a 25-minute walk up to the Prince's Palace or to the casino, or three minutes by local bus (see "Getting Around Monaco," later). A fourth, less-interesting area, **Fontvieille,** forms the west end of Monaco and was reclaimed from the sea by Prince Rainier in the 1970s.

TOURIST INFORMATION

The main TI is at the top of the park, above the casino (Mon-Sat 9:00-19:00, Sun 11:00-13:00, 2 Boulevard des Moulins, tel. 00-377/92 16 61 16 or 00-377/92 16 61 66, www.visitmonaco.com). Another TI is in the train station (Tue-Sat 9:00-17:00, until 18:00 in summer, closed Sun-Mon except July-Aug). There's also a TI desk for Monaco in Terminal 1 of Nice's airport.

ARRIVAL IN MONACO

By Bus from Nice and Villefranche-sur-Mer: Bus riders need to pay attention, since stops are not announced. Cap d'Ail is the town before Monaco, so be on the lookout after that (the last stop before Monaco is called Cimetière). You'll enter Monaco through the modern cityscape of high-rises of the Fontvieille district. When you see the rocky outcrop of old Monaco, be ready to get off.

There are three stops in Monaco. Listed in order from Nice, they are Place d'Armes (in front of a tunnel at the base of Monaco-

Ville's rock), Princesse Antoinette (on the port), and Office de Tourisme (near the casino and the TI on Boulevard des Moulins). The Place d'Armes stop is the best starting point for most, and is the only signed stop (otherwise, verify with locals that you're at the right stop). From the Place d'Armes stop, you can walk up to Monaco-Ville and the palace (10-15 minutes straight up), or catch a quick local bus (line #1 or #2—see "Getting Around Monaco," later). To reach the bus stop and steps up to Monaco-Ville, cross the street right in front of the tunnel and walk with the rock on your right for about 200 feet (good WCs at the local-bus stop). To begin nearest the casino, pass through the port, and get off the bus at the Office de Tourisme stop.

For directions on returning to Nice by bus, see "Monaco Connections," later.

By Train from Nice: This looooong underground train station is in central Monaco, about a 15-minute walk to the casino or to the port, and about 25 minutes to the palace. The TI, ticket windows, WCs, and bag storage are all up the escalator at the Italy end of the station.

There are three exits from the train platform level (one at each end and one in the middle). To reach Monaco-Ville and the palace, take the platform-level exit at the Nice end of the tracks (signed *Sortie Fontvieille/Le Rocher*), which leads through a long tunnel (TI annex at end); as you emerge from the tunnel, walk to the base of Monaco-Ville at Place d'Armes. From here, it's about a 15-minute hike up to the palace, or take the bus (#1 or #2).

To reach Monaco's port and the casino, take the mid-platform exit, closer to the Italy end of the tracks. Follow *Sortie Port Hercule* signs down the steps and escalators, then follow *Accès Port* signs until you pop out at the port, where you'll see the stop for buses #1 and #2. It's a 25-minute walk from the port to the palace (to your right) or 20 minutes to the casino (up Avenue d'Ostende to your left), or a short trip via buses #1 or #2 to either.

If you plan to return to Nice by train after 20:30, when ticket windows close, buy your return tickets now or be sure to have about €4 in coins (the ticket machines only take coins).

By Car: Follow *Centre-Ville* signs into Monaco (warning: traffic can be a problem), then watch for the red-letter signs to parking garages at *Le Casino* (for Monte Carlo) or *Le Palais* (for Monaco-Ville). You'll pay about €10 for four hours.

By Cruise Ship: For information on arrival by cruise ship, see "Monaco Connections," near the end of this section.

HELPFUL HINTS

Combo-Ticket: If you plan to see Monaco's two big sights (Prince's Palace and the Cousteau Aquarium), buy the €19 combo-ticket at the first sight you visit.

Changing of the Guard: This popular event takes place daily at 11:55 at the Prince's Palace. Arrive by 11:30 to get a good viewing spot.

Telephone Tip: To call Monaco from France, dial 00, then 377 (Monaco's country code) and the eight-digit number. Within Monaco, simply dial the eight-digit number.

Wi-Fi Access: You should be able to connect for free at the main TI and on Place des Moulins near the TI. Ask at the TI for details.

Bus #100 back to Nice: To have a better chance of securing a seat on the often crowded bus #100, board it at the stop across the street from the TI on Boulevard des Moulins.

Loop Trip by Bus or Train: You can get to Monaco by bus or train, then take a bus from Monaco directly to Eze-le-Village (#112, none on Sun) or La Turbie (#11), and then from there return to Nice by bus. For details and stop locations, see "Monaco Connections."

Minivan Tours from Nice: Several companies offer daytime and nighttime tours of Monaco, allowing you freedom to gamble without worrying about catching the last train or bus home (see "Helpful Hints" on page 673).

Evening Events: Monaco's Philharmonic Orchestra (tel. 00-377/98 06 28 28, www.opmc.mc) and Monte Carlo Ballet (tel. 00-377/99 99 30 00, www.balletsdemontecarlo.com) offer performances at reasonable prices.

Passport Stamp: If you want an official memento of your visit, you can get your passport stamped at the main TI (listed earlier).

GETTING AROUND MONACO

By Local Bus: Buses #1 and #2 link all areas with fast and frequent service (single ticket-€2, 6 tickets-€10, day pass-€5, pay driver, slightly cheaper if bought from machine, 10/hour, fewer on Sun, buses run until 21:00). You can split a six-ride ticket with your travel partners (which is handy, since you're unlikely to take more than two or three rides in Monaco). Bus tickets are good for a free transfer if used within 30 minutes.

By Open Bus Tour: You could pay €21 for a hop-on, hop-off open-deck bus tour that makes 12 stops in Monaco, but I wouldn't. This tour doesn't go to the best view spot in the Jardin Exotique (described on page 747) and, besides, most of Monaco is walkable. If you want a scenic tour of the principality that includes its best views, pay €2 to take local bus #2, and stay on board for a full loop (or hop on and off as you please).

By Tourist Train: "Monaco Tour" tourist trains are an efficient way to enjoy a blitz tour of Monaco. They begin at the aquarium and pass by the port, casino, and palace (€9, 2/hour, 40 minutes, recorded English commentary).

By Taxi: If you've lost all track of time at the casino, you can call the 24-hour taxi service (tel. 08 20 20 98 98)...provided you still have enough money to pay for the cab home.

Monaco-Ville Walk

All of Monaco's sights (except the casino) are in Monaco-Ville, packed within a few cheerfully tidy blocks. This self-guided walk makes a tight little loop, starting from the palace square.

• *To get from anywhere in Monaco to the palace square (Monaco-Ville's sightseeing center, home of the palace), take bus #1 or #2 to the end of the line at Place de la Visitation. Turn right as you step off the bus and walk five minutes down Rue Emile de Loth. You'll pass the post office, a worthwhile stop for its collection of valuable Monegasque stamps (Mon-Fri 8:00-19:00).*

If you're walking up from the port, the well-marked lane leads you directly to the palace.

Palace Square (Place du Palais): This square is the best place to get oriented to Monaco. Facing the palace, go to the right and look out over the city (er...principality). This rock gave birth to the little pastel Hong Kong look-alike in 1215, and it's managed to remain an independent country for most of its nearly 800 years. Looking beyond the glitzy port, notice the faded green roof above and to the right: It belongs to the casino that put Monaco on the map in the 1800s. It was located away from Monaco-Ville because Prince Charles III (r. 1856-1889) wanted to shield his people from low-life gamblers.

The modern buildings just past the casino mark the eastern limit of Monaco. The famous Grand Prix runs along the port, and then up the ramp to the casino (at top speeds of 180 mph). Italy is so close, you can almost smell the pesto. Just beyond the casino is France again (which flanks Monaco on both sides)—you could walk one-way from France to France, passing through Monaco in about 60 minutes.

The odd statue of a woman with a fishing net is dedicated to **Prince Albert I's** glorious reign (1889-1922). The son of Charles III, Albert was a Renaissance man with varied skills and interests. He had a Jacques Cousteau-like fascination with the sea (and built Monaco's famous aquarium), and was a determined pacifist who made many attempts to dissuade Germany's Kaiser Wilhelm II from becoming involved in World War I.

• *Now walk toward the palace and find the statue of the monk grasping a sword.*

Meet **François Grimaldi,** a renegade Italian dressed as a monk, who captured Monaco in 1297 and began the dynasty that still rules the principality. Prince Albert is his great-great-great... grandson, which gives Monaco's royal family the distinction of being the longest-lasting dynasty in Europe.

• *Make your way to the...*

Prince's Palace (Palais Princier): A medieval castle sat where Monaco's palace is today. Its strategic setting has had a lot to do with Monaco's ability to resist attackers. Today, Prince Albert and his wife live in the palace, while poor Princesses Stephanie and Caroline live down the street. The palace guards protect the prince 24/7 and still stage a **Changing of the Guard** ceremony with all the pageantry of an important nation (daily at 11:55, fun to watch but jam-packed, arrive by 11:30). Audioguide tours take you through part of the prince's lavish palace in 30 minutes. The rooms are well-furnished and impressive, but interesting only if you haven't seen a château lately (€8, includes audioguide, €19 combo-ticket includes Cousteau Aquarium; hours vary but generally April-Oct daily 10:00-18:00, closed Nov-March, last entry 30 minutes before closing; tel. 00-377/93 25 18 31).

• *With your back to the palace, leave the square through the arch and go to the right corner of the square (under the most beautiful police station I've ever seen—that's where the guards come from during the changing of the guard) and find the...*

Cathedral of Monaco (Cathédrale de Monaco): The somber but beautifully lit cathedral, rebuilt in 1878, shows that Monaco cared for more than just its new casino. It's where centuries of Grimaldis are buried, and where Princess Grace and Prince Rainier were married. Circle slowly behind the altar (counterclockwise). The second tomb is that of Albert I, who did much to put Monaco on the world stage. The second-to-last tomb—inscribed *"Gratia Patricia, MCMLXXXII"*—is where Princess Grace was buried in 1982. Prince Rainier's tomb lies next to Princess Grace's (daily 8:30-19:15).

• *As you leave the cathedral, find the 1956 wedding photo of Princess Grace and Prince Rainier (keep an eye out for other photos of the couple as you walk), then dip into the immaculately maintained Jardin Bota-*

nique, with more fine views. In the gardens, turn left. Eventually you'll find the impressive building housing the...

Cousteau Aquarium (Musée Océanographique): Prince Albert I built this impressive, cliff-hanging aquarium in 1910 as a monument to his enthusiasm for things from the sea. The aquarium, which Captain Jacques Cousteau directed for 32 years, has 2,000 different specimens, representing 250 species. The bottom floor features Mediterranean fish and colorful tropical species (all nicely described in English). My favorite is the zebra lionfish, though I'm keen on eels, too. Rotating exhibits occupy the entry floor. Upstairs, the fancy Albert I Hall houses a museum (included in entry fee, very little English information) and features ship models, whale skeletons, oceanographic instruments and tools, and scenes of Albert and his beachcombers hard at work. Find the display on Christopher Columbus with English explanations.

Don't miss the elevator to the rooftop terrace view, where you'll also find convenient WCs and a reasonable café (aquarium-€14, kids-€7, €19 combo-ticket includes Prince's Palace; daily July-Aug 10:00-19:30, April-June and Sept 10:00-19:00, Oct-March 10:00-18:00; down the steps from Monaco-Ville bus stop, at the opposite end of Monaco-Ville from the palace; tel. 00-377/93 15 36 00, www.oceano.mc).

• *The red-brick steps, across from the aquarium and a bit to the right, lead up to stops for buses #1 and #2, both of which run to the port, the casino, and the train station. To walk back to the palace and through the old city, turn left at the top of the brick steps.*

Sights in Monaco

ABOVE MONACO-VILLE

Jardin Exotique

This cliffside municipal garden, located above Monaco-Ville, has eye-popping views from France to Italy. It's home to more than a thousand species of cacti (some giant) and other succulent plants, but worth the entry only for view-loving botanists (some posted English explanations provided). Your ticket includes entry to a skippable natural cave and an anthropological museum, as well as a not-to-be-missed view snack bar/café. Bus #2 runs here from any stop in Monaco, and makes a worthwhile mini-tour of the country, even if you don't visit the gardens. You can get similar views over Monaco for free from behind the souvenir stand at the Jardin's bus stop; or, for even grander vistas, cross the street and hike toward La Turbie.

Cost and Hours: €7.20, daily May-Sept 9:00-19:00, Oct-April 9:00-18:00 or until dusk, tel. 00-377/93 15 29 80, www.jardin-exotique.com.

IN MONTE CARLO

▲Casino

Monte Carlo, which means "Charles' Hill" in Spanish, is named for the prince who presided over Monaco's 19th-century makeover. Begin your visit opposite Europe's most famous casino, in the park above the pedestrian-unfriendly traffic circle. In the mid-1800s, olive groves stood here. Then, with the construction of casino and spas, and easy road and train access, one of Europe's poorest countries was on the Grand Tour map—*the* place for the vacationing aristocracy to play. Today, Monaco has the world's highest per-capita income.

The casino is intended to make you feel comfortable while losing money. Charles Garnier designed the place (with an opera house inside) in 1878, in part to thank the prince for his financial help in completing Paris' Opéra Garnier (which the architect also designed). The central doors provide access to slot machines, private gaming rooms, and the opera house. The private gaming rooms occupy the left wing of the building.

The scene, flooded with camera-toting tourists during the day, is great at night—and downright James Bond-like in the private rooms. This is your chance to rub elbows with some high rollers—provided you're 18 or older (bring your passport as proof). You can also gamble in the American-style casino, adjacent to the old casino.

Cost and Hours: Entry is free, opens daily 9:00-12:00 for visits to the lobby areas, then reopens at 14:00 for gambling and stays open until the wee hours. The **first gaming rooms** (Salle Renaissance, Salon de l'Europe, and Salle des Amériques) have European and English roulette, blackjack, craps, and slot machines. The more glamorous **private game rooms** (Salons Touzet, Salle Medecin, and Terrasse Salle Blanche) have the same games as above, plus Trente et Quarante, Ultimate Texas Hold 'Em poker, and Punto Banco—a version of baccarat.

Information: Tel. 00-377/92 16 20 00, www.montecarlocasinos.com.

Dress Code: During gambling hours, it is preferred that men wear a jacket and slacks, and that women dress appropriately. Shorts and tennis shoes are not permitted.

Take the Money and Run: The stop for buses returning to Nice and Villefranche-sur-Mer is at the top of the park across the street from the TI on Boulevard des Moulins; the stop for buses #1 and #2 is nearby on Avenue de la Costa (under the arcade). To get back to the train station from the casino, take bus #1 or #2 from this stop, or walk about 15 minutes down Avenue d'Ostende (just outside the casino) toward the port, and follow signs to *Gare SNCF* (see map on page 741).

Sleeping and Eating in Monaco

Sleeping in Monaco: **$$ Hôtel de France****, run by friendly Sylvie, is a centrally located, reasonably priced place—for Monaco (Sb-€115, Db-about €135, Tb-about €160, all rooms with showers, includes breakfast, air-con, Wi-Fi, near west exit from train station at 6 Rue de la Turbie, tel. 00-377/93 30 24 64, www.monte-carlo.mc/france, hotel-france@monte-carlo.mc).

Eating in Monaco: Several cafés serve basic, inexpensive fare (day and night) on the port. I prefer the eateries that line the flowery and traffic-free Rue de la Princesse Caroline, which runs between Rue Grimaldi and the port. The best this street has to offer is **Huit et Demi.** It has a white-tablecloth-meets-director's-chair ambience, mostly outdoor tables, and cuisine worth returning for (€15 pizzas and pastas, €18-24 *plats,* closed Sun, 7 Rue de la Princesse Caroline, tel. 00-377/93 50 97 02). For a simple and cheap salad or sandwich, find the **Crock'in** café farther down at 2 Rue de la Princesse Caroline (closed Sat, tel. 00-377/93 15 02 78).

In Monaco-Ville, you'll find incredible *pan bagnat* (*salade niçoise* sandwich), quiche, and sandwiches at the yellow-bannered **Boulangerie,** a block off Place du Palais (open daily until 21:00, 8 Rue Basse). Try a *barbajuan* (a spring roll-size beignet with wheat, rice, and Parmesan), the *tourta de bléa* (pastry stuffed with pine nuts, raisins, and white beets), or the focaccia sandwich (salted bread with herbs, mozzarella, basil, and tomatoes, all drenched in olive oil). For dessert, order the *fougasse monégasque* (a soft-bread pastry topped with sliced almonds and anise candies). The best-value restaurant in Monaco-Ville is **U Cavagnetu**—and it's no secret. You'll dine cheaply on specialties from Monaco just a block from Albert's palace (€11-12 pasta and pizza, €26 *menu,* daily, 14 Rue Comte Félix Gastaldi, tel. 00-377/97 98 20 40). Monaco-Ville has other pizzerias, *crêperies,* and sandwich stands, but the neighborhood is dead at night.

Monaco Connections

BY TRAIN AND BUS

For a comparison of train and bus connections, see the "Public Transportation in the French Riviera" sidebar on pages 676–679.

From Monaco by Train to: Nice (2/hour, 20 minutes), **Villefranche-sur-Mer** (2/hour, 10 minutes), **Antibes** (2/hour, 50 minutes), **Cannes** (2/hour, 70 minutes).

By Bus to: Nice (#100, 3-4/hour, 45 minutes), **Nice Airport** (#110 express on the freeway, 2/hour, 50 minutes, €20), **Villefranche-sur-Mer** (#100, 3-4/hour, 25 minutes), **Eze-le-Village** (#112, 6/day Mon-Sat, none on Sun, 20 minutes), **Cap Ferrat** (#100, 3-4/hour 20 minutes plus 20-minute walk), **La Turbie** (#11, 8/day Mon-Sat, 5/day Sun, 30 minutes), **Menton** (#100, 3-4/hour 40 minutes).

The Monaco-to-Nice bus (#100) is not identified at most stops—verify with a local by asking, *"A Nice?"* One stop is below Monaco-Ville at Place d'Armes (on the main road to Nice in front of the Brasserie Monte Carlo), and another is a few blocks above the casino in front of the TI. To get a seat on the crowded bus back to Nice, board it at the TI stop.

Bus #112 to Eze-le-Village departs Monaco from Place de la Crémaillère, one block above the main TI and casino park. Walk up Rue Iris with Barclays Bank to your left, curve right, and find the bus shelter across the street at the green Costa à la Crémaillère café (bus number not posted). **Bus #11** runs to **La Turbie** from in front of the TI.

Last Call: The last bus leaves Monaco for Villefranche-sur-Mer and Nice at about 20:00. For night owls going to Nice (not Villefranche-sur-Mer) on Thursday through Saturday, a bus leaves from Place d'Armes every 90 minutes from 23:45-3:45; the last train leaves Monaco for Villefranche-sur-Mer and Nice at about 23:30. If you plan to leave Monaco by a late train, buy your tickets in advance (since the window will be closed), or bring enough coins for the machines.

BY CRUISE SHIP

Cruise ships tender passengers to the end of Monaco's yacht harbor, a short walk from downtown. *Très elegant!* A seasonal **TI** is right next to the tender dock (open on busy days May-Sept). To summon a **taxi** (assuming none are waiting when you disembark), look for the gray taxi call box near the tender dock—just press the button and wait for your cab to arrive.

Whether visiting the sights in Monaco, or heading to outlying destinations, your first step for most journeys is to walk from the cruise port to the little market square called **Place d'Armes.** It's an easy and level stroll: Head straight along the yacht harbor until you reach the busy street, which is Boulevard Albert 1er. Use the white overpass (with an elevator) to cross the street, then follow green *Gare SNCF/Ferroviare* signs through a maze of skyscrapers, across the street, and up a charming lane lined with motorcycle shops. Continue straight into the peach-and-yellow building, and ride the free public elevator up to *Marché Place d'Armes* (level 0). You'll pop out into Place d'Armes. At the far end of this square is a roundabout and the busy Rue Grimaldi.

Getting into Town: To reach the cliff-top old town of **Monaco-Ville,** you can either hike steeply up to the top of the hill next to the harbor, or ride a bus up. By **foot,** the fastest, steepest ascent (with an elevator option partway) is near the tip of the Monaco-Ville peninsula, just above where the tenders arrive: Climb up the stairs next to the Yacht Club de Monaco to the base of the hill, turn left, then curl around the tip of land (with the water on your left side), following signs for *Palais/Musées.* At the parking garage, you can either keep hiking up through the manicured park or enter the garage and ride up the elevator, then the escalator; either way, you'll emerge near the Cousteau Aquarium, close to the end of my self-guided walk. (It's a five-minute walk through town to Palace Square and the start of the walk.) To ride **bus #1** or **#2** up to Monaco-Ville, first walk to the bus stop near Place d'Armes (described earlier). As you exit the elevator into Place d'Armes, turn left and cross the street, then continue up to the second, uphill street (which leads up to the hilltop). Cross this second street and bear right to find the bus stop.

The ritzy skyscraper zone of **Monte Carlo** is basically across the harbor from the tender dock (casino opens for gambling at 14:00). You can walk to the casino area in about 25 minutes—just go all the way around the harbor. To shave some time off the hike, ride the little "bateau bus" shuttle boat across the mouth of the harbor (to find the dock from your tender, walk toward town, then go right along the pier extending into the harbor; €2, €5/day pass, 3/hour). To reach the upper part of Monte Carlo—with the TI, views down over the casino gardens, and handy bus stops (including the one for Eze-le-Village)—catch bus #1 or #2 at the top of the yacht harbor, along Boulevard Albert 1er.

Getting to Sights Beyond Monaco: Monaco is connected to most nearby sights by both train and bus. Monaco's **train station** is about a 20-minute walk from the tender harbor. From Place d'Armes (described earlier), head up to the far end, cross the busy Rue Grimaldi, and take the narrow, angled, red-asphalt lane (Rue de la Turbie) in the middle of the block across the street. Go up the stairs (or ride the elevator) into the little plaza, where you'll see a small TI kiosk (open only in peak season). Turn left, walk up more stairs, and enter the train station (the big, pink building on your right; the easy-to-miss entrance is at the far end—look for *Acces Gare* signs).

The stop for **bus #100**—which conveniently connects Monaco along the Lower Corniche to Villefranche-sur-Mer, Nice, and more—is near Place d'Armes. From Place d'Armes, head up to the far end, along Rue Grimaldi. The bus stop is across the roundabout on the left, on the right side of the street (to get there, cross the street two times in either direction). To ride **bus #112** along the scenic Upper Corniche to Eze-le-Village (6/day Mon-Sat, none on Sun, 20 minutes), first ride bus #1 or #2 to the TI and casino (explained earlier), then follow the directions to the Place de la Crémaillère stop on page 749.

Near Monaco: Menton

If you wish the Riviera were less glitzy and more like a place where humble locals take their families to lick ice cream and make sand castles, visit Menton (15 minutes by bus beyond Monaco). Menton feels like a poor man's Nice. It's unrefined and unpretentious, with lower prices, fewer rentable umbrellas, and lots of Italians day-tripping in from just over the border (five miles away). There's not an American in sight.

Though a bit rough around the edges, the Menton beach is a joy. An inviting promenade lines the beach, and seaside cafés serve light meals and salads (much cheaper than in Nice). A snooze or stroll here is a lovely Riviera experience. From the promenade, a pedestrian street leads through town. Small squares are alive with jazz bands playing crowd-pleasers under palm trees.

Stepping into the old town—which blankets a hill capped by a fascinating cemetery—you're immersed in a pastel-painted, yet dark and tangled Old World scene with (strangely) almost no commerce. A few elegant restaurants dig in at the base of the towering, centuries-old apartment flats. The richly decorated Baroque St. Michael's Church (midway up the hill, Mon-Fri 10:00-12:00 & 15:00-17:15, closed to visitors Sat-Sun) is a reminder that, until 1860, Menton was a thriving part of the larger state of Monaco. Climbing past sun-grabbing flower boxes and people who don't get out much anymore, the steep stepped lanes finally deposit you at the ornate gate of a grand cemetery that fills the old castle walls. Explore the cemetery, which is the final resting place of many aristocratic Russians (buried here in the early 1900s) and offers breathtaking Mediterranean views.

Getting to Menton: While trains serve Menton regularly, the station is a 15-minute walk from the action. Buses are more convenient, as they drop visitors right on the beach promenade (#100, 3-4/hour, 1.25 hours from Nice, 40 minutes past Monaco). To return to Monaco or Nice, catch bus #100 on Avenue Thiers, just off Avenue de Verdun.

Antibes

Antibes has a down-to-earth, easygoing ambience that's rare in this area. Its old town is a maze of narrow streets and red-tile roofs rising above the blue Med, protected by twin medieval towers and wrapped in extensive ramparts. Visitors making the short trip from Nice can browse Europe's biggest yacht harbor, snooze on a sandy beach, loiter through an enjoyable old town, and hike along a sea-swept trail. The town's cultural claim to fame, the Picasso Museum, shows off its great collection in a fine old building.

Though much smaller than Nice, Antibes has a history that dates back just as far. Both towns were founded by Greek traders in the fifth century B.C. To the Greeks, Antibes was "Antipolis"—the town *(polis)* opposite *(anti)* Nice. For the next several centuries, Antibes remained in the shadow of its neighbor. By the turn of the 20th century, the town was a military base—so the rich and famous partied elsewhere. But when the army checked out after World War I, Antibes was "discovered" and enjoyed a particularly roaring '20s—with the help of party animals like Rudolph Valentino and the rowdy (yet silent) Charlie Chaplin. Fun-seekers even invented water-skiing right here in the 1920s.

Orientation to Antibes

Antibes' old town lies between the port and Boulevard Albert 1er and Avenue Robert Soleau. Place Nationale is the old town's hub of activity. The restaurant-lined Rue Aubernon connects the port and the old town. Stroll along the sea between the old port and Place Albert 1er (where Boulevard Albert 1er meets the water). The best beaches lie just beyond Place Albert 1er, and the walk is beautiful. Good play areas for children are along this path and on Place des Martyrs de la Résistance (close to recommended Hôtel Relais du Postillon).

TOURIST INFORMATION

The TI is a few blocks from the station at 42 Avenue Robert Soleau (July-Aug daily 9:00-19:00; Sept-June Mon-Fri 9:00-12:30 & 13:30-18:00, Sat 9:00-12:00 & 14:00-18:00, Sun 9:00-13:00; tel. 04 97 23 11 11, www.antibesjuanlespins.com). Pick up the excellent city map and the self-guided walking tour of old Antibes.

The Nice TI has Antibes maps and the Antibes TI has Nice maps—plan ahead.

ARRIVAL IN ANTIBES

By Train: Bus #14 runs every 30 minutes from the train station (none on Sun, bus stop 50 yards to right as you exit station) to the *gare routière* (bus station; near the main TI and old town), and continues to the fine Plage de la Salis, with quick access to the Phare de la Garoupe trail. Taxis are usually waiting in front of the train station.

To walk to the port, the old town, and the Picasso Museum (15-20 minutes), cross the street in front of the station, skirting left of the café, and follow Avenue de la Libération downhill as it bends left. At the end of the street, head right along the port, and continue until you reach the end of the parking lots, then turn right into the old town.

To walk directly to my hotels and to the main TI (5-minute walk to TI), cross the street to the café, turn right, and stay the course for about eight blocks on Avenue Robert Soleau to Place Général de Gaulle (you'll pass the TI on the way).

The last train back to Nice leaves at about midnight.

By Bus: The airport bus (#250) drops you behind the train station (see "Helpful Hints," below). Buses from other destinations use the bus station at the edge of the old town on Place Guynemer, a block below Place Général de Gaulle (info desk open Mon-Fri 7:30-19:00, Sat 8:30-12:00 & 14:30-17:30, closed Sun, www.envibus.fr).

By Car: Day-trippers follow signs to *Centre-Ville,* then *Port Vauban,* and park in the underground lot. Walk into the old town through the last arch on the right. Street parking is free Monday through Saturday from 12:00-14:00 and 19:00-8:00, and all day Sunday. If you're sleeping here, follow *Centre-Ville* signs, then signs to your hotel, and ask your hotelier where to park (hotels outside the town center have free parking.) The most appealing hotels in Antibes are easiest by car. Antibes works well for drivers—compared with Nice, parking is easy, it's a breeze to navigate, and it's a convenient springboard for the Inland Riviera. Pay parking is available at Antibes' train station, so drivers can ditch their cars here and day-trip from Antibes by train.

HELPFUL HINTS

Monday, Monday: Avoid Antibes on Mondays, when all sights are closed.

Internet Access: Centrally located **l'Outil du Web** is two blocks from Place Général de Gaulle—walk toward the train station

(Mon-Fri 9:30-18:00, closed Sat-Sun, 11 Avenue Robert Soleau, tel. 04 93 74 11 86).

English Bookstore: Heidi's English Bookshop has a welcoming vibe and a great selection of new and used books, with many guidebooks—including mine (Tue-Sat 9:00-19:00, Sun-Mon 11:00-18:00, 24 Rue Aubernon, tel. 04 93 34 74 11).

Laundry: There's a launderette at 19 Avenue du Grand Cavalier (daily).

Grocery Stores: Picnickers will appreciate **L'Épicerie du Marché** at 3 Cours Masséna, up the hill as you exit the Marché Provençal (daily until 23:00). **L'Épicerie de la Place** has a smaller selection (daily until 22:00 in summer, until 21:00 off-season, where Rue Sade meets Place Nationale). A large **Monoprix** is located on Place Général de Gaulle (Mon-Sat 8:30-20:30, Sun 9:00-12:30).

Taxi: For a taxi, call tel. 04 93 67 67 67.

Car Rental: The big-name agencies have offices in Antibes (all close Mon-Sat 12:00-14:00 and all day Sun). The most central are **Avis** (at the train station, tel. 04 93 34 65 15) and **Hertz** (across from the train station at 46 Avenue Robert Soleau, tel. 04 92 91 28 00). **Europcar** is about 1.5 miles northwest of town at 106 Route de Grasse (tel. 04 93 34 79 79).

Boat Rental: You can motor your own seven-person yacht, thanks to **Antibes Bateaux Services** (€100-300/half-day, at the small fish market on the port, mobile 06 15 75 44 36, www.antibes-bateaux.com).

Airport Bus: Bus #250 runs from near the train station to Nice's airport (€10, 2/hour, 40 minutes; cross over the tracks on the pedestrian bridge—it's the last shelter to the right, stop from the airport is labeled *Vautrin,* stop going to the airport is labeled *Passerelle*).

GETTING AROUND ANTIBES

Though most sights and activities are walkable, buses are a great value in Antibes, allowing one hour of travel for €1 (one-way or round-trip, unlimited transfers, www.envibus.fr). **Bus #2** provides access to the best beaches, the path to La Phare de la Garoupe, and the Cap d'Antibes trail. It runs from the bus station down Boulevard Albert 1er, with stops every few blocks (daily 7:00-19:00, every 40 minutes). **Bus #14** is also useful, linking the train station, bus station, old town, and Plage de la Salis. Pick up a schedule for return times for these and other regional buses at the bus station (for more on buses, see "Arrival in Antibes," earlier).

A **tourist train** offers 40-minute circuits around old Antibes, the port, the ramparts, and to Juan-les-Pins (€8, departs from pedestrian-only Rue de la République, mobile 06 15 77 67 47).

Antibes Walk

This 40-minute self-guided walk will help you get your bearings, and works well day or night.

• *Begin at the old port (Vieux Port) at the southern end of Avenue de Verdun. Stand at the port, across from the archway with the clock.*

Old Port: Locals claim that this is Europe's first and biggest pleasure-boat harbor, with 1,600 stalls. The port was enlarged in the 1970s to accommodate ever-expanding yacht dimensions. The work was financed by wealthy yacht owners (mostly Saudi Arabian) eager for a place to park their aircraft carriers. That stone four-pointed structure crowning the opposite end of the port is **Fort Carré,** which protected Antibes from foreigners for more than 500 years. (For information on visiting the fort, see "Sights in Antibes," next page.)

The pathetic remains of a once-hearty **fishing fleet** are moored in front of you. The Mediterranean is pretty much fished out. Most of the seafood you'll eat here comes from fish farms or the Atlantic.

Pass the sorry fleet and duck under the arches to the shell-shaped **Plage de la Gravette,** a normally quiet public beach tucked right in the middle of old Antibes. Wander up the ramp to the massive round lookout to better appreciate the scale of the ramparts that protected this town. Because Antibes was the last fort before the Italian border, the French king made sure the ramparts were top-notch. Those twin towers crowning the old town are the church's bell tower and the tower topping Château Grimaldi (today's Picasso Museum). As you face the old town, forested Cap d'Antibes is the point of land in the distance to the left.

For a quick glimpse at the epitome of conspicuous consumption, take a three-block detour to the right as you leave the beach and enter a restricted area to find yachts the size of my elementary school. Locals call this the ***Quai des Milliardaires*** ("billionaire's dock"). The Union Jacks fluttering above the boats show that they're registered in the Cayman Islands (can you say tax dodge?)

Backtrack and enter Antibes' **old town** through the arch under the clock. Today, the town is the haunt of a large community of English, Irish, and Aussie boaters who help crew those giant yachts. (That explains the Irish pubs and English bookstores.) Continue straight and uphill (halfway up on the right, you'll pass Rue Clemenceau, which leads to the heart of the old town), and you'll arrive at Antibes' **market hall.** This hall does double duty—market by day, restaurants by night (a fun place for dinner).

Go left where the market starts (Rue Chessel) and find Antibes' pretty, pastel **Church of the Immaculate Conception,** built on the site of a Greek temple (worth a peek inside). A church has stood on this site since the 12th century. This one served as the area's cathedral until the mid-1200s.

Looming above the church on prime real estate is the white-stone **Château Grimaldi,** where you'll find Antibes' prized **Picasso Museum** (described later). This site has been home to the acropolis of the Greek city of Antipolis, a Roman fort, and a medieval bishop's palace (once connected to the cathedral below). Later still, the château was the residence of the Grimaldi family (which still rules Monaco; think Prince Rainier and now Prince Albert). Its proximity to the cathedral symbolized the sometimes too-cozy relationship between society's two dominant landowning classes: the Church and the nobility. (In 1789, the French Revolution changed all that.)

Find your way to the water and—heading right—follow the ramparts and views to the **History and Archaeology Museum** (described later). From the terrace above the museum, you'll get a clear view of **Cap d'Antibes,** crowned by its lighthouse and studded with mansions (a good place for a hike, described under "Walks and Hikes," later). The Cap was long the refuge of Antibes' rich and famous, and a favorite haunt of F. Scott Fitzgerald and Ernest Hemingway.

After taking a quick spin through the museum, continue hugging the shore past Place Albert 1er until you see the views back to old Antibes. Benches and soft sand await (a few copies of famous artists' paintings of Antibes are placed on bronze displays along the beach walkway). You're on your own from here—energetic walkers can continue to the view from the Phare de la Garoupe (see page 762); others can return to old Antibes and wander around in its peaceful back lanes.

Sights in Antibes

▲▲Picasso Museum (Musée Picasso)

Sitting serenely where the old town meets the sea, this compact three-floor museum offers a manageable collection of Picasso's paintings, sketches, and ceramics.

Cost and Hours: €6; mid-June-mid-Sept Tue-Sun 10:00-18:00, July-Aug Wed and Fri until 20:00; mid-Sept-mid-June Tue-Sun 10:00-12:00 & 14:00-18:00, closed Mon year-round, last entry 30 minutes before closing, tel. 04 92 90 54 20, www.antibes-juanlespins.com.

Visiting the Museum: Picasso lived in this castle for four months in 1946, when he cranked out an amazing amount of art. He was elated by the end of World War II, and his works show a celebration of color and a rediscovery of light after France's long nightmare of war. Picasso was also reenergized by his young and lovely companion, Françoise Gilot (with whom he would father two children). The resulting collection (donated by Picasso) put Antibes on the tourist map. You'll see many of his ceramics: plates with faces, bird-shaped vases, woman-shaped bottles, bull-shaped statues, and colorful tiles. But the highlight is his lively, frolicking, and big-breasted *La Joie de Vivre* painting (from 1946). This Greek bacchanal sums up the newfound freedom in a just-liberated France and sets the tone for the rest of the collection. You'll also see the colorless three-paneled *Satyr, Faun and Centaur with Trident* and several ceramic creations (the bull rocks).

As you tour the museum, you'll see both black-and-white and colorful ink sketches that challenge the imagination—these show off Picasso's skill as a cartoonist and caricaturist. Look also for the Basque fishermen and several Cubist-style nudes *(nus couchés),* one painted on plywood—Picasso loved experimenting with materials and different surfaces (I particularly like the crayon sketches). *Nature mort* means "still life," and you'll see plenty of these in this collection.

History and Archaeology Museum (Musée d'Histoire et d'Archéologie)

More than 2,000 years ago, Antibes was the center of a thriving maritime culture. It was an important Roman city with aqueducts, theaters, baths, and so on. This museum—the only place to get a sense of the city's ancient roots—displays Greek, Roman, and Etruscan odds and ends in two simple halls (no English descriptions, though the small museum brochure offers some background in English). Your visit starts at an 1894 model of Antibes and continues past displays of Roman coins, cups, plates, and scads of amphorae. The lanky lead pipe connected to a center box was used as a bilge pump; nearby is a good display of Roman anchors made out of lead.

Cost and Hours: €3; mid-June-mid-Sept Tue-Sun 10:00-12:00 & 14:00-18:00; mid-Sept-mid-June Tue-Sun 10:00-13:00 & 14:00-17:00, closed Mon year-round, on the water between Picasso Museum and Place Albert 1er, tel. 04 92 90 54 37.

▲Market Hall (Marché Provençal)

The daily market bustles under a 19th-century canopy, with flowers, produce, Provençal products, and beach accessories. The mar-

ket wears many hats: produce daily until 13:30, handicrafts Thursday through Sunday in the afternoon, and fun outdoor dining in the evenings (Sept-June until 12:30, closed Mon) behind Picasso Museum on Cours Masséna.

Other Markets and Squares

Antibes' lively antiques/flea market fills Place Nationale and Place Audiberti (next to the port) on Thursdays and Saturdays (7:00-18:00). Its clothing market winds through the streets around the post office (Rue Lacan) on Thursdays (9:00-18:00). Place Général de Gaulle, a pleasing, palm-studded, and fountain-flowing square in Antibes' modern city, is the trendy place to be seen.

Fort Carré

This impressively situated citadel, dating from 1487, was the last fort inside France. It protected Antibes from Nice, which until 1860 was part of Italy. You can tour this unusual four-pointed fort for the fantastic views over Antibes, but there's little to see inside.

Cost and Hours: €3, includes tour in French, mid-June-mid-Sept Tue-Sun 11:00-17:30, mid-Sept-mid-June Tue-Sun 10:00-16:00, closed Mon year-round, 30-minute walk from Antibes along Avenue du 11 Novembre, easy parking nearby.

▲Beaches *(Plages)*

The best beaches stretch between Antibes' port and Cap d'Antibes. The first you'll cross is Plage Publique (no rentals required). Next are the groomed Plage de la Salis and Plage du Ponteil (with mattress, umbrella, and towel rental). All are busy but manageable in summer and on weekends, with cheap snack stands and exceptional views of the old town. The closest beach to the old town is at the port (Plage de la Gravette), which seems calm in any season.

WALKS AND HIKES

From Place Albert 1er (where Boulevard Albert 1er meets the beach), you get a good view of Plage de la Salis and Cap d'Antibes. That tower on the hill is your destination for the first walk listed. The longer Cap d'Antibes hike begins on the next beach, just over that hill. The two hikes are easy to combine by bus, bike, or car.

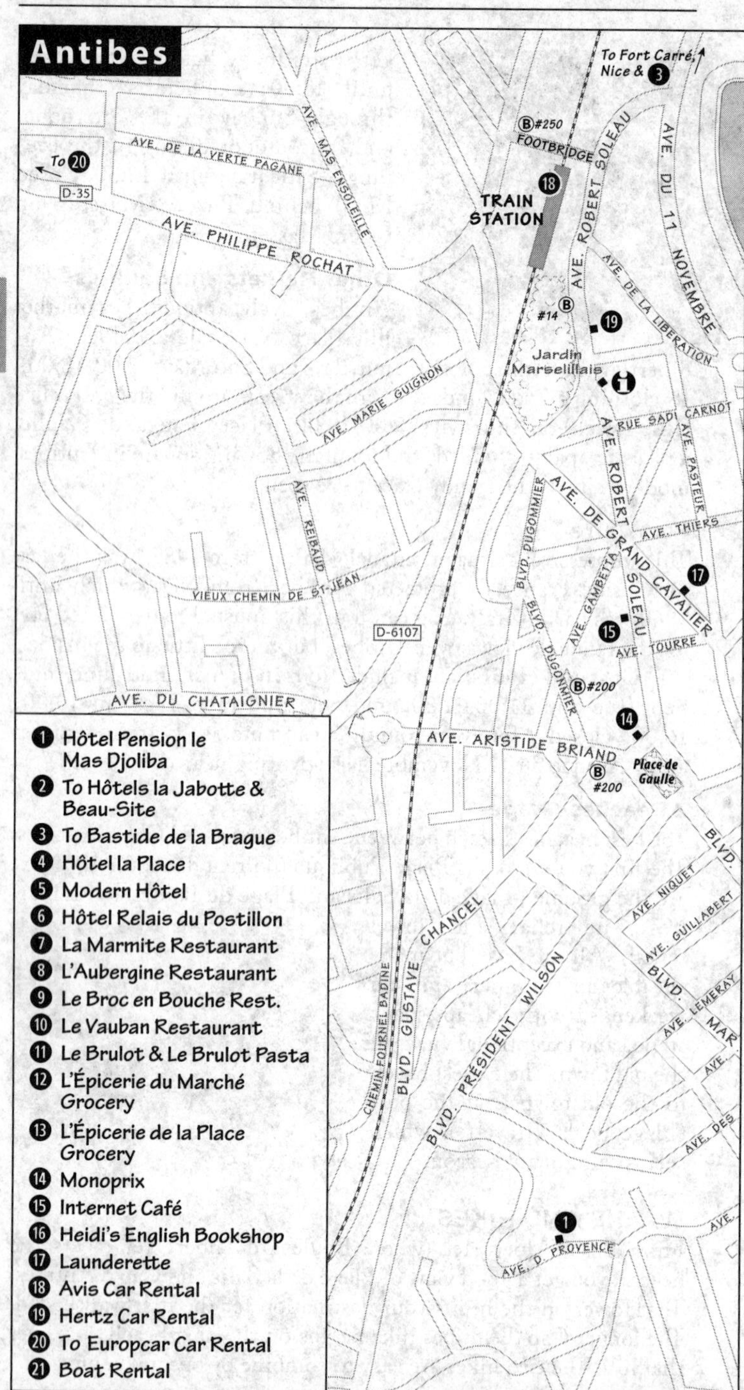
Antibes
To Fort Carré, Nice & 3
To 20
D-35
AVE. DE LA VERTE PAGANE
AVE. MAS ENSOLEILLE
AVE. PHILIPPE ROCHAT
B #250
FOOTBRIDGE
18
TRAIN STATION
AVE. ROBERT SOLEAU
AVE. DU 11 NOVEMBRE
AVE. DE LA LIBERATION
B #14
19
Jardin Marseilllais
AVE. MARIE GUIGNON
RUE SADI CARNOT
AVE. PASTEUR
AVE. REIBAUD
BLVD. DUGOMMIER
AVE. DE GRAND CAVALIER
AVE. ROBERT SOLEAU
AVE. THIERS
17
AVE. GAMBETTA
15
AVE. TOURRE
VIEUX CHEMIN DE ST-JEAN
D-6107
B #200
14
AVE. DU CHATAIGNIER
AVE. ARISTIDE BRIAND
B #200
Place de Gaulle
BLVD.
AVE. NIQUET
AVE. GUILLABERT
CHANCEL
BLVD. GUSTAVE
CHEMIN FOURNEL BADINE
BLVD. PRESIDENT WILSON
BLVD. MAR
AVE. LEMERAY
AVE.
AVE. DES
1
AVE. D. PROVENCE
AVE.
1 Hôtel Pension le Mas Djoliba
2 To Hôtels la Jabotte & Beau-Site
3 To Bastide de la Brague
4 Hôtel la Place
5 Modern Hôtel
6 Hôtel Relais du Postillon
7 La Marmite Restaurant
8 L'Aubergine Restaurant
9 Le Broc en Bouche Rest.
10 Le Vauban Restaurant
11 Le Brulot & Le Brulot Pasta
12 L'Épicerie du Marché Grocery
13 L'Épicerie de la Place Grocery
14 Monoprix
15 Internet Café
16 Heidi's English Bookshop
17 Launderette
18 Avis Car Rental
19 Hertz Car Rental
20 To Europcar Car Rental
21 Boat Rental

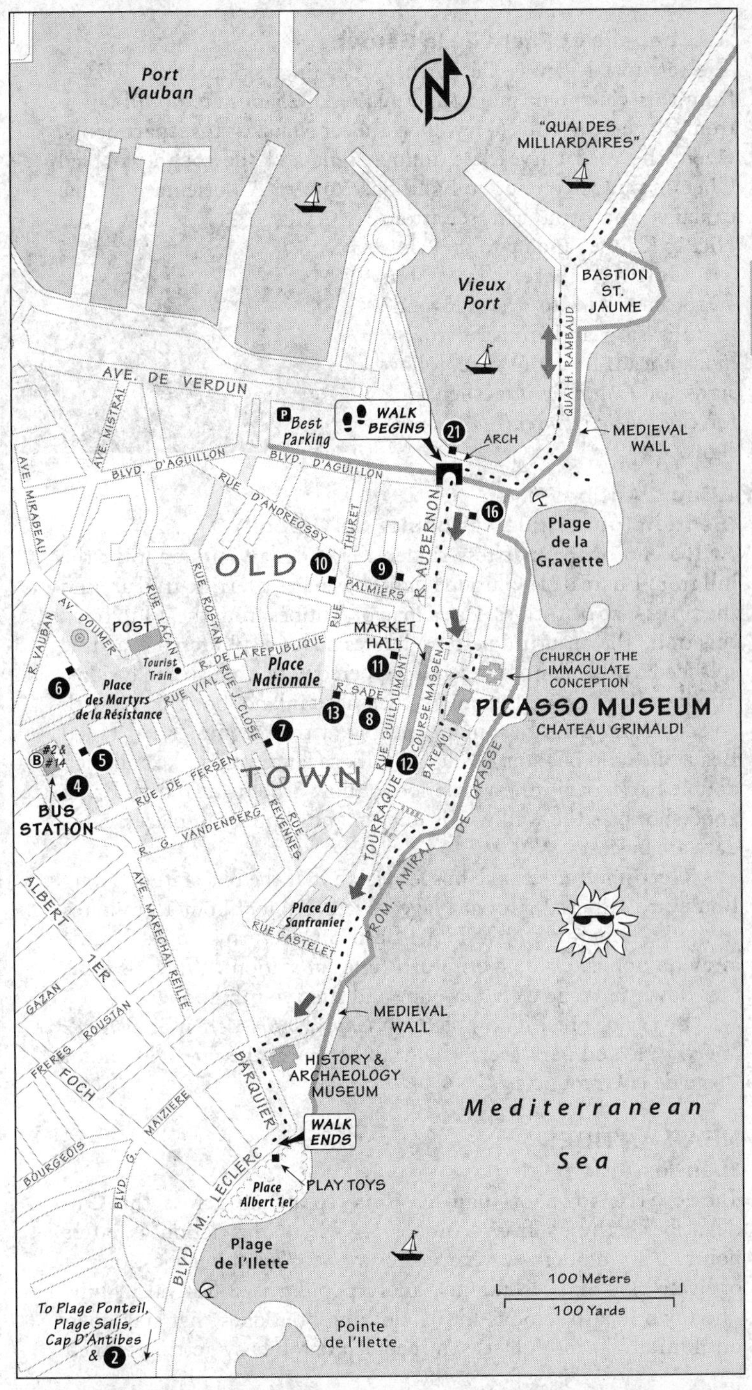
Port
Vauban
"QUAI DES
MILLIARDAIRES"
Vieux
Port
BASTION
ST.
JAUME
QUAI H. RAMBAUD
AVE. DE VERDUN
Best
Parking
WALK
BEGINS
21
ARCH
MEDIEVAL
WALL
BLVD. D'AGUILLON
BLVD. D'AGUILLON
AVE. MISTRAL
AVE. MIRABEAU
RUE D'ANDREOSSY
THURET
16
Plage
de la
Gravette
OLD
10
9
PALMIERS
R. AUBERNON
RUE LACAN
RUE ROSTAN
AV. DOUMER
R. VAUBAN
POST
MARKET
HALL
11
CHURCH OF THE
IMMACULATE
CONCEPTION
Tourist
Train
R. DE LA REPUBLIQUE
Place
Nationale
RUE VIAL
RUE J. CLOSE
R. SADE
COURSE MASSENA
PICASSO MUSEUM
CHATEAU GRIMALDI
6
Place
des Martyrs
de la Résistance
13
8
7
RUE GUILLAUMONT
BATEAU
#2 &
#14
5
12
4
BUS
STATION
RUE DE FERSEN
TOWN
R. G. VANDENBERG
RUE REVENNES
TOURRAQUE
PROM. AMIRAL DE GRASSE
ALBERT
1ER
AVE. MARECHAL REILLE
Place du
Sanfranier
RUE CASTELET
GAZAN
ROUSTAN
FRERES
FOCH
MEDIEVAL
WALL
HISTORY &
ARCHAEOLOGY
MUSEUM
BARQUIER
MAIZIERE
Mediterranean
Sea
WALK
ENDS
BOURGEOIS
BLVD. G.
BLVD. M. LECLERC
PLAY TOYS
Place
Albert 1er
Plage
de l'Ilette
100 Meters
100 Yards
Pointe
de l'Ilette
To Plage Ponteil,
Plage Salis,
Cap D'Antibes
& 2

▲▲Chapelle et Phare de la Garoupe

The territorial views—best in the morning, skippable if hazy—from this viewpoint more than merit the 25-minute uphill climb from Plage de la Salis (a few blocks after Maupassant Apartments, where the road curves left, follow signs and the rough, cobbled Chemin du Calvaire up to lighthouse tower). An orientation table explains that you can see from Nice to Cannes and up to the Alps.

Getting There: Take bus #2 or bus #14 to the Plage de la Salis stop and find the trail a block ahead. By car or bike, follow signs for *Cap d'Antibes,* then look for *Chapelle et Phare de la Garoupe* signs.

▲Cap d'Antibes Hike (Sentier Touristique Piétonnier de Tirepoil)

At the end of the mattress-ridden Plage de la Garoupe (over the hill from Phare de la Garoupe lighthouse) lies a terrific trail around the tip of Cap d'Antibes. Use a map of Antibes from the TI to track this trail. The beautiful path undulates above a splintered coastline splashed by turquoise water and peppered with exclusive mansions. You'll walk for about two miles, then head inland, hooking up with Avenue Mrs. L.D. Beaumont, ending at the recommended Hôtel Beau-Site (and bus stop). You can walk as far as you'd like and then double back, or do the whole loop (allow 3 hours at most). Bring good shoes, as the walkway is uneven and slippery in places. Sundays are busiest.

Getting There: Take bus #2 (catch it at the bus station, along Boulevard Albert 1er, or at Plage de la Salis) for about 15 minutes to the La Fontaine stop at Hôtel Beau-Site (return stop is 50 yards away on opposite side, get return times at station). Walk 10 minutes down to Plage de la Garoupe and start your hike there.

By car or bike, follow signs to *Cap d'Antibes,* then to *Plage de la Garoupe,* and park there. The trail begins at the far-right end of Plage de la Garoupe.

NEAR ANTIBES

Juan-les-Pins

The low-rise town of **Juan-les-Pins,** sprawling across the Cap d'Antibes isthmus from Antibes, is where the action is...after hours. It's a modern waterfront resort with good beaches, plenty of lively bars and restaurants, and a popular jazz festival in July. The town is also famous for its clothing boutiques that stay open until midnight in high season (people are too busy getting tanned to shop at normal hours). As locals say, "Party, sleep in, shop late, party more."

Buses, trains, and even a tourist train (see "Getting Around Antibes" earlier) make the 10-minute trip to and from Antibes constantly.

Sleeping in Antibes

My favorite Antibes hotels are best by car or taxi, though walkers and bus users can manage as well. Pickings are slim when it comes to centrally located hotels in this city, where restaurants are a dime a dozen but hotels play hard to get.

OUTSIDE THE TOWN CENTER

$$$ Hôtel Pension le Mas Djoliba*** is a fair splurge that's better for drivers but also workable for walkers (10-minute walk to Plage de la Salis, 15 minutes to old Antibes, 30 minutes to the train station). Reserve early for this traditional, bird-chirping, flower-filled manor house. Young and English-fluent Delphine runs the place with grace. Some rooms are small, the bigger rooms are well worth the additional cost, and several rooms come with small decks (Db-€145-190 depending on size, several good family rooms-€280, breakfast-€14, air-con, Wi-Fi, *boules* court and loaner balls; 29 Avenue de Provence—from Boulevard Albert 1er, look for gray signs two blocks before the sea, turn right onto Boulevard Général Maizière and follow signs; tel. 04 93 34 02 48, www.hotel-djoliba.com, contact@hotel-djoliba.com).

$$ Hôtel la Jabotte**, hidden along an ignored alley a block from the famous beaches and a 15-minute walk from the old town, is a cozy place that defies the rules. Nathalie runs this adorable beach villa turned boutique hotel with panache: The colors are rich and the decor shows a personal touch. While the cozy rooms have tight bathrooms, they also have individual terraces facing a small, central garden where you'll get to know your neighbor (Db-€140-160, Db suite-€200, includes good breakfast and a few free parking spots, air-con, Wi-Fi, 13 Avenue Max Maurey, take the third right after passing the big Hôtel Josse, tel. 04 93 61 45 89, www.jabotte.com, info@jabotte.com).

$$ Hôtel Beau-Site***, my only listing on Cap d'Antibes, is a 10-minute drive from the old town. It's a terrific value if you want to get away...but not *too* far away. (Without a car, you'll feel isolated.) This place is a sanctuary. Helpful Nathalie and Francine welcome you with a pool, a comfy patio garden, and free, secure parking. Rooms are spacious, modern, and comfortable, and several have balconies (standard Db-€95, bigger Db-€120-180, junior suites-€240; extra bed-€25, huge breakfast-€13, continental breakfast-€8, air-con, Wi-Fi, may have a few bikes available, 141 Boulevard Kennedy, tel. 04 93 61 53 43, www.hotelbeausite.net, info@hotelbeausite.net). From the hotel, it's a 10-minute walk down to Plage de la Garoupe and a nearby hiking trail (described earlier, under "Walks and Hikes").

$ Bastide de la Brague is an easygoing, bed-and-breakfast hacienda up a dirt road above Marineland (10-minute drive east of Antibes). It's run by a fun-loving family (wife Isabelle, who speaks English, and hubby Franck). All seven rooms are comfortable, air-conditioned, and affordable; several are made for families. Request the tasty €29 home-cooked dinner (less for kids; adult meal includes apéritif, wine, and coffee) and enjoy a family dining experience (Db-€88-110, Tb/Qb-€117-135, includes breakfast, Wi-Fi, computer with printer for guests, 55 Avenue No. 6, tel. 04 93 65 73 78, www.bbchambreantibes.com, bastidebb06@gmail.com). From Antibes, follow signs that read *Nice par Bord de la Mer,* turn left toward Marineland, then right at the roundabout (toward Groules), then take the first left and follow the green signs. Antibes bus #10 drops you five minutes away, and the Biot train station and buses #200 or #250 are a 15-minute walk away (ask for details when you book). If arranged in advance, they can pick you up at the train station in Antibes or Biot.

RIVIERA

IN THE TOWN CENTER

$$ Hôtel la Place*** is a central find near the bus station, with tastefully designed rooms at fair rates and a charming patio (Db-€100-155, bigger Db-€140-180, no elevator, Wi-Fi, 1 Avenue 24 Août, tel. 04 97 21 03 11, www.la-place-hotel.com).

$ Modern Hôtel,** in the pedestrian zone below the bus station, is a solid value for budget-conscious travelers. The 17 standard-size rooms—each with air-conditioning, bright decor, and Wi-Fi—are simple and spick-and-span (Db-€75-85, breakfast-€7, 1 Rue Fourmillière, tel. 04 92 90 59 05, www.modernhotel06.com, modern-hotel@wanadoo.fr).

$ Hôtel Relais du Postillon,** with cute rooms at good rates, is a mellow place above a peaceful café on a central square. There are a few cheap true singles and 13 well-designed doubles with small balconies (Sb-€65-75, Db-€80-90, larger Db-132-150, air-con, price varies with room size, most have tight bathrooms, Wi-Fi, 8 Rue Championnet, tel. 04 93 34 20 77, www.relaisdupostillon.com, relais@relaisdupostillon.com).

Eating in Antibes

Antibes is a fun place to dine out. You can eat on a budget, enjoy a good meal at an acceptable price, or join the party just inside the walls on Boulevard d'Aguillon, on Place Nationale, or—my favorite—under the festive Marché Provençal (all are filled with tables and tourists). The options are endless. Take a walk and judge for yourself, and be tempted by these suggestions. Romantics should picnic at the beach (**L'Épicerie du Marché** is open late; see "Helpful Hints" on page 754). Everyone should stroll along the ramparts after dinner.

At **La Marmite,** owner Patrick offers diners an honest, unpretentious budget value in old Antibes, with eight tables, charming decor, helpful service, and delicious seafood choices but no air-conditioning (*menus* from €17, closed Mon, 20 Rue James Close, tel. 04 93 34 56 79).

L'Aubergine's owner Jenny delivers fine cuisine at fair prices—including good vegetarian options—served with no hurry in an intimate room rich with color. Arrive early to get a table (*menus* from €25, opens at 18:30, closed Wed, opens early for lunch on Sun only, 7 Rue Sade, tel. 04 93 34 55 93).

Le Broc en Bouche is part cozy wine bar, part bistro, and part collector's shop. Come early to get a seat at this cool little place, where you'll enjoy well-prepared dishes from a selective list (*tartines,* €20-30 *plats,* closed Tue-Wed, 8 Rue des Palmiers, tel. 04 93 34 75 60).

Le Vauban is run by a young couple who draw a local following in search of delectable seafood (€36 three-course *menu,* closed for lunch Mon and Wed, closed all day Tue, opposite 4 Rue Thuret, tel. 04 93 34 33 05).

Le Brulot is an Antibes institution with two restaurants—Le Brulot and Le Brulot Pasta—that sit almost side-by-side a short block below Marché Provençal on Rue Frédéric Isnard. Join Antibes residents at the **Le Brulot,** known for its Provençal cuisine and meats cooked on an open fire. It's a small place, overflowing onto the street, with a few outside tables and a dining room below. Try the aioli (*menus* from €23, closed Sun, at #2, tel. 04 93 34 17 76). **Le Brulot Pasta** is family-friendly, with excellent pizza (the €13 *printanière* is tasty and huge) and big portions of pasta, served in air-conditioned comfort under stone arches (daily, dinners only, at #3, tel. 04 93 34 19 19).

Antibes Connections

For a comparison of train and bus connections, see the "Public Transportation in the French Riviera" sidebar on pages 676–679.

From Antibes by Train: TGV and local trains serve Antibes' little station. Trains go to **Cannes** (2/hour, 15 minutes), **Nice** (2/hour, 15-30 minutes, €4), **Grasse** (1/hour, 40 minutes), **Villefranche-sur-Mer** (2/hour, 40 minutes), **Monaco** (2/hour, 50 minutes), and **Marseille** (16/day, 2.5 hours).

By Bus: Handy bus #200 ties everything together, but runs at a snail's pace when traffic is bad (Mon-Sat 4/hour, Sun 2-3/hour, any ride costs €1.50). This bus goes west to **Cannes** (35 minutes); and east to **Nice** (1-1.5 hours). Bus #250 links to **Nice Airport** (2/hour, 40 minutes, €10).

Inland Riviera

For a verdant, rocky, fresh escape from the beaches, head inland and upward. Some of France's most perfectly perched hill towns and splendid scenery hang overlooked in this region that's more famous for beaches and bikinis. Driving is the easiest way to get around, though the bus gets you to many of the places described. Vence and St-Paul-de-Vence are well-served by bus from Nice every 30-45 minutes (see "Nice Connections," page 719).

Vence

Vence is a well-discovered yet appealing town set high above the Riviera. While growth has sprawled beyond Vence's old walls, and cars jam its roundabouts, the mountains are front and center and the breeze is fresh. Vence bubbles with workaday life and ample tourist activity in the day but is restful at night, with few visitors and cooler temperatures than along the coast. Vence makes a handy base for travelers wanting the best of both worlds: a hill-town refuge near the sea.

Orientation to Vence

TOURIST INFORMATION

Vence's fully loaded and eager-to-help TI faces the main square at 8 Place du Grand Jardin, across from the merry-go-round. It offers free Wi-Fi, bus schedules, brochures on the cathedral, and a city map with a well-devised self-guided walking tour (25 stops, incorporates informative wall plaques). The TI also publishes a list of Vence art galleries with English descriptions of the collections. To properly engage you in French culture, the staff can help you find French-language classes and—even better—*pétanque* instructions with *boules* to rent. Ask about guided walking tours in English (TI open July-Aug Mon-Sat 9:00-19:00, Sun 10:00-18:00; March-June and Sept-Oct Mon-Sat 9:00-18:00; Nov-Feb 10:00-17:00; closed Sun Sept-June; free Wi-Fi, tel. 04 93 58 06 38, www.ville-vence.fr).

Market day in the *cité historique* (old town) is on Friday mornings on Place Clemenceau. A big all-day antiques market is on Place du Grand Jardin every Wednesday. If you miss market day, a **Monoprix** is on Avenue de la Résistance, across from the entrance to the Marie Antoinette parking lot (grocery store upstairs, Mon-Sat 8:30-20:00, Sun 8:30-12:30).

ARRIVAL IN VENCE

By Bus: Buses #94 and #400 (from Nice, Cagnes-sur-Mer, and St-Paul-de-Vence) drop you at the bus stop labeled *Halte Routière de l'Ara,* which is on a roundabout at Place Maréchal Juin. It's a 10-minute walk to the town center along Avenue Henri Isnard or Avenue de la Résistance.

By Car: Follow signs to *cité historique,* then look for blue *P* signs and park in one of two lots: **Marie Antoinette** or the underground **Grand Jardin.** Both are a five-minute walk from the town center and have the same rates (about €15/day, €2/overnight 20:00-8:00). Some hotels offer discounted rates.

Sights in Vence

Explore the narrow lanes of the old town using the TI's worthwhile self-guided tour map. Connect the picturesque streets, enjoy a drink on a quiet square, inspect an art gallery, and find the small 11th-century cathedral with its colorful Chagall mosaic of Moses. If you're here later in the day, enjoy the *boules* action across from the TI (rent a set from the TI and join in).

Château de Villeneuve

This 17th-century mansion, adjoining an imposing 12th-century watchtower, bills itself as "one of the Riviera's high temples of modern art," with a rotating collection. Check with the TI to see what's playing in the temple.

Cost and Hours: €5, Tue-Sun 10:00-12:30 & 14:00-18:00, closed Mon, tel. 04 93 58 15 78.

▲Chapel of the Rosary (Chapelle du Rosaire)

The chapel, a short drive or 20-minute walk from town, was designed by an elderly and ailing Henri Matisse as thanks to the Dominican sister who had taken care of him (he was 81 when the chapel was completed). The modest chapel holds a simple series of charcoal black-on-white tile sketches and uses three symbolic colors as accents: yellow (sunlight and the light of God), green (na-

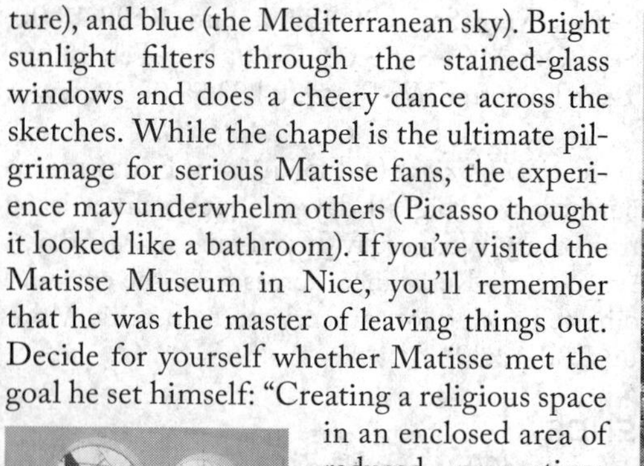

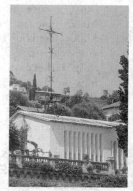

ture), and blue (the Mediterranean sky). Bright sunlight filters through the stained-glass windows and does a cheery dance across the sketches. While the chapel is the ultimate pilgrimage for serious Matisse fans, the experience may underwhelm others (Picasso thought it looked like a bathroom). If you've visited the Matisse Museum in Nice, you'll remember that he was the master of leaving things out. Decide for yourself whether Matisse met the goal he set himself: "Creating a religious space in an enclosed area of reduced proportions and to give it, solely by the play of colors and lines, the dimension of infinity."

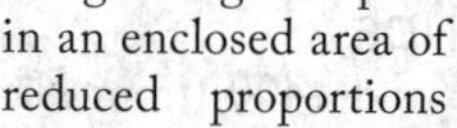

Your entry ticket includes a 20-minute tour from one of the kind nuns who speaks English. Downstairs you'll find displays of the vestments Matisse designed for the priests, his models of the chapel, and sketches. Photography is not allowed.

Cost and Hours: €5; Mon, Wed, and Sat 14:00-17:30, Tue and Thu 10:00-11:30 & 14:00-17:30, Sun only open for Mass at 10:00 followed by tour of chapel, closed Fri and mid-Nov-mid-Dec; 466 Avenue Henri Matisse, tel. 04 93 58 03 26.

Getting There: It's about a 20-minute walk from the TI. After turning right out of the TI, take your first right and then a quick left to get onto Avenue Henri Isnard. Take this street all the way to the traffic circle (notice the colorful tiled roof of the Pénitents Blancs Chapel to your left). At the intersection, turn right across the one-lane bridge on Avenue Henri Matisse, following signs to *St-Jeannet.*

Sleeping in Vence

These accommodations may close their reception desks between 12:00 and 16:00. Make arrangements in advance if you plan to arrive during this time.

$$$ La Maison du Frêne is a modern, art-packed B&B with four sumptuous and spacious suites centrally located behind the TI. Energetic Thierry, who was born in Vence, and kind Guy combine their passions for contemporary art and hosting travelers in this lovingly restored manor house. This place is worth the splurge (Db-€165-190, higher price is for peak times, includes good breakfast, kids sleep free, in-room coffee/tea service, fridges, air-con, Wi-Fi; next to the Château de Villeneuve at 1 Place du Frêne—turn right out of the TI, then right again, then left; tel. 04 93 24 37 83, www.lamaisondufrene.com, contact@lamaisondufrene.com).

$$ Auberge des Seigneurs feels medieval. It's a funky, dark-wooded place in a 17th-century building with six simple but spacious rooms over a restaurant in a good location. It can be hard to find the staff when reception closes at midday and all day Sun-Mon (when the restaurant isn't open)—just ring the bell (small Db in back-€90, Db-€100, Wi-Fi in lobby, includes €10 parking voucher, 1 Rue du Dr. Binet, tel. 04 93 58 04 24, www.auberge-seigneurs.com, sandrine.rodi@wanadoo.fr).

$$ Hôtel Miramar*** is a laid-back, 18-room Mediterranean villa perched on a ledge with grand panoramas, a 10-minute walk above the old town. Old World rooms come with soothing, Provençal colors, worn furnishings, and owners who could use a course in customer service. (Hint: Don't arrive at lunchtime.) The pool and view terrace could make you late for dinner, or seduce you into skipping it altogether—picnics are allowed. Access is a challenge for drivers (standard Db-€78-108, Db with balcony-€98-128, Db with great view and balcony-€160, family suite-€180, some rooms have air-con, bar, table tennis, parking, turn left out of the TI and follow the brown signs to 167 Avenue Bougearel—behind the soccer field, tel. 04 93 58 01 32, www.hotel-miramar-vence.com, resa@hotel-miramar-vence.com).

Eating in Vence

Tempting outdoor eateries litter the old town. Lights embedded in the cobbles illuminate the way after dark. The first three restaurants serve tasty Provençal cuisine in the center of the old town and are my top choices.

La Cassolette, at 10 Place du Clemenceau, is an intimate place with reasonable prices and a romantic terrace across from the floodlit church (€32-35 *menus,* €15-22 *plats,* closed Tue-Wed except July-Aug, tel. 04 93 58 84 15, www.restaurant-lacassolette-vence.com).

Nearby, **La Litote** is lauded by locals as a good value, with outdoor tables on a quiet, hidden square (€26-32 two- and three-course meals, closed Mon-Tue and Sun evening, 7 Rue de l'Evêché, tel. 04 93 24 27 82).

Hiding just behind the TI, on an unassuming street, **La Farigoule** circles a flowery courtyard and serves gourmet meals with limited choices. This is a good splurge (€30-45 *menus,* €23-28 *plats,* closed Tue May-mid-Sept, closed Mon-Tue mid-Sept-April, 15 Avenue Henri Isnard, tel. 04 93 58 01 27).

For less expensive, casual dining, head to Place du Peyra, where you'll find ample outdoor seating and early dinner service. At **Bistro du Peyra,** enjoy a relaxed dinner salad or pasta dish outdoors to the sound of the town's main fountain (€15-20 *plats,* daily April-Oct, off-season closed Wed-Thu at lunch, closed Jan-Feb, 13 Place du Peyra, tel. 04 93 58 67 63).

Near Vence

St-Paul-de-Vence

This most famous of Riviera hill towns is also the most-visited village in France. And it feels that way—like an overrun and over-restored artist-shopping-mall. Its attraction is understandable, as every cobble and flower seems just-so, and the setting is postcard-perfect. Avoid visiting between 11:00 and 18:00, particularly on weekends. Arrive early to park near the village (cars are not allowed inside St-Paul). Beat the crowds by skipping breakfast at your hotel and eating it in St-Paul-de-Vence, or come for dinner and experience the village at its tranquil best.

The helpful **TI,** just through the gate into the old city on Rue Grande, has maps with minimal explanations of key buildings (daily 10:00-18:00, until 19:00 June-Sept, closed some days 13:00-14:00). The TI offers five different themed walking tours with English translations, including tours focused on history, art, and *pétanque (boules).* Call or email in advance to reserve (€5, tel. 04 93 32 86 95, www.saint-pauldevence.com, serviceguide@saint-pauldevence.com). If the traffic-free lane leading to the old city is jammed, walk along the road that veers up and left just after Café de la Place, and enter the town through its side door. Meander deep into St-Paul-de-Vence's quieter streets to find panoramic views. See if you can locate the hill town of Vence at the foot of an impressive mountain.

Fondation Maeght

This inviting, pricey, and far-out private museum is situated a steep walk or short drive above St-Paul-de-Vence. Fondation Maeght (fohn-dah-shown mahg) offers an excellent introduction to modern Mediterranean art by gathering many of the Riviera's most famous artists under one roof.

Cost and Hours: €15, €5 to take photos (you'll get a small button to wear as proof of payment), daily July-Sept 10:00-19:00, Oct-June 10:00-18:00, tel. 04 93 32 81 63, www.fondation-maeght.com.

Getting There: The museum is a steep, uphill-but-doable 20-minute walk from St-Paul-de-Vence and the bus stop. Signs indicate the way (parking is usually available at the upper lot). From the lower lot, signed *Parking Conseille,* a shortcut on a steep, dirt path through the trees leads directly to the green gate in front of the ticket booth.

Visiting the Museum: The founder, Aimé Maeght, long envisioned the perfect exhibition space for the artists he supported and befriended as an art dealer. He purchased this arid hilltop, planted more than 35,000 plants, and hired an architect (José Luis Sert) with the same vision.

A sweeping lawn laced with amusing sculptures and bending pine trees greets visitors. On the right, a chapel designed by Georges Braque—in memory of the Maeghts' young son, who died of leukemia—features a moving purple stained-glass work over the altar. The unusual museum building is purposely low profile, to let its world-class modern-art collection take center stage. Works by Fernand Léger, Joan Miró, Alexander Calder, Georges Braque, and Marc Chagall are thoughtfully arranged in well-lit rooms. The backyard of the museum has views, a Gaudí-esque sculpture labyrinth by Miró, and a courtyard filled with the wispy works of Alberto Giacometti. The only permanent collection in the museum consists of the sculptures, though the museum tries to keep a good selection of paintings by the famous artists here year-round. For a review of modern art, see "The Riviera's Art Scene" on page 678. There's also a great gift shop and cafeteria.

La Route Napoléon: North to the Alps

After getting bored in his toy Elba empire, Napoleon gathered his entourage, landed on the Riviera, bared his breast, and told his fellow Frenchmen, "Strike me down or follow me." France followed. But just in case, he took the high road, returning to Paris along the route known today as La Route Napoléon. (Waterloo followed shortly afterward.)

By Car: The route between the Riviera and the Alps is beautiful (from south to north, follow signs: *Digne, Sisteron,* and *Grenoble*). An assortment of pleasant villages with inexpensive hotels lies along this route, making an overnight easy. Little Entrevaux feels forgotten and still stuck in its medieval shell. Cross the bridge, meet someone friendly, and consider the steep hike up to the citadel (€3, TI tel. 04 93 05 46 73). Sisteron's Romanesque church and view from the citadel above make this town worth a quick leg-stretch.

By Narrow-Gauge Train (Chemins de Fer de Provence): Leave the tourists behind and take the scenic train-bus-train combination that runs between Nice and Digne through canyons, along whitewater rivers, and through many tempting villages (4/day, 25 percent discount with rail pass, departs Nice from Chemins de Fer de Provence Station—about 10 blocks behind the main train station, two blocks from the Libération tram stop, 4 Rue Alfred Binet, tel. 04 97 03 80 80, www.trainprovence.com). Ongoing track work may affect the schedule; be sure to double-check all departures, arrivals, and connections.

Start with an early morning departure (look for an 8:30 train) and go as far as you want. One good destination is **Entrevaux** (€10, 1.5 scenic hours from Nice). Climb high to the citadel for great views and appreciate the unspoiled character of the town. The train ends in **Digne-les-Bains** (a.k.a. simply Digne; €19, 3.5 hours), where you can catch a bus (covered by rail passes) to other destinations such as Aix-en-Provence (6/day, 2 hours). Mainline rail service to Digne was recently eliminated, leaving travelers with few options other than limited bus connections. Most return to Nice by making a round-trip on the narrow-gauge train.

THE FRENCH ALPS

Annecy • Chamonix

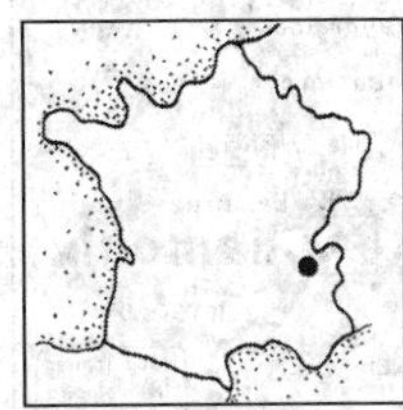

The Savoie region grows Europe's highest mountains and is the penthouse of the French Alps (the lower Alpes-Dauphiné lie to the south). More than just a pretty-peaked face, stubborn Savoie maintained its independence from France until 1860, when mountains became targets, rather than obstacles, for travelers. Savoie's borders once stretched south to the Riviera and far west across the Rhône River Valley. Home to the very first winter Olympics (1924, in Chamonix), today's Savoie is France's mountain-sports capital, featuring 15,771-foot Mont Blanc as its centerpiece. Boasting wooden chalets overflowing with geraniums and cheese fondue in every restaurant, Savoie feels more Swiss than French.

The scenery is drop-dead spectacular. Serenely self-confident Annecy is a postcard-perfect blend of natural and man-made beauty. In Chamonix, it's just you and Madame Nature—there's not a museum or important building in sight. Take Europe's ultimate cable-car ride to the 12,600-foot Aiguille du Midi in Chamonix.

PLANNING YOUR TIME

Lakefront Annecy has boats, bikes, and hikes with mountain views for all tastes and abilities. Its arcaded walking streets and good transportation connections (most trains to Chamonix pass through Annecy) make it a convenient stopover, but if you're pressed for time and

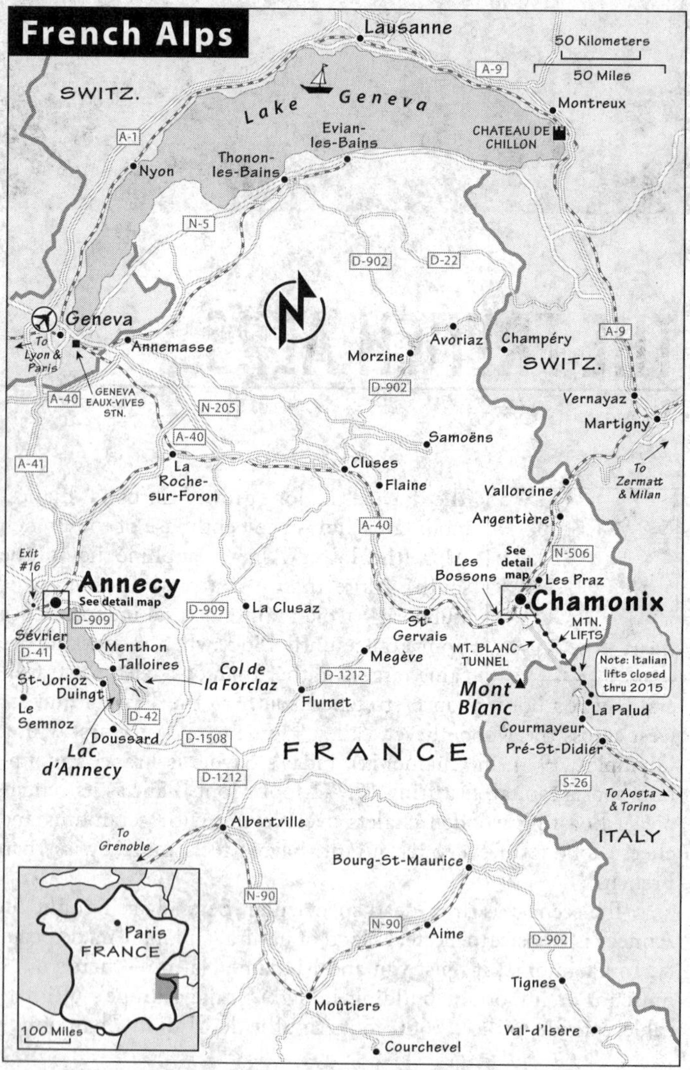

French Alps

antsy for Alps, slide your sled to Chamonix. There you can skip along alpine ridges, glide over mountain meadows, zip down the mountain on a luge (wheeled bobsled), or meander riverside paths on a mountain bike. Plan a minimum of two nights and one day in Chamonix, and try to work in an additional night in Annecy. Because weather is everything in this area, get the forecast by calling Chamonix's TI or checking online. If it looks good, make haste to Chamonix; if it's gloomy, Annecy offers more distraction. Both towns are mobbed with tourists in summer.

The Alps have twin peaks: the summer and winter seasons, when hotels and trails or slopes are slammed. June and November are dead quiet in Chamonix (many hotels and restaurants close) as locals recover from one high season and prepare for the next.

GETTING AROUND THE ALPS

Annecy and Chamonix are well-connected by trains. Buses run from Chamonix to nearby villages, and the Aiguille du Midi lift takes travelers from Chamonix up, up, up, and over to Europe's most scenic border crossing. If you have a car, autoroutes make the going easy, and scenic drives near Annecy allow you to savor remarkable views.

Entering Switzerland by Car: Drivers passing through Switzerland need a "vignette" decal to use Swiss autoroutes (about €33, valid one calendar year)—even if only to reach Geneva's airport from bordering France (skipping the autoroute via local roads through Geneva is possible but a headache). You can buy Swiss vignettes in Annecy (ask at the TI) or on the autoroute at the border crossing.

SAVOIE'S CUISINE SCENE

Savoie cuisine is mountain-hearty. Its Swiss-similar specialties include *fondue savoyarde* (melted Beaufort and Comté cheeses and local white wine, sometimes with a dash of Cognac), raclette (chunks of semi-melted cheese served with potatoes, pickles, sausage, and bread), *tartiflettes* (hearty scalloped potatoes with melted cheese), *poulet de Bresse* (the best chicken in France), Morteau (smoked pork sausage), *gratin savoyard* (a potato dish with cream, cheese, and garlic), and fresh fish. Local cheeses are Morbier (look for a charcoal streak down the middle), Comté (like Gruyère), Beaufort (aged for two years, hard and strong), Reblochon (mild and creamy), and Tomme de Savoie (mild and semi-hard). Evian water comes from Savoie, as does Chartreuse liqueur. Apremont and Crépy are two of the area's surprisingly good white wines. The local beer, Baton de Feu, is more robust than other French beers.

Restaurants serve only during lunch (11:30-14:00) and dinner (19:00-21:00, later in bigger cities and resorts like Chamonix); some cafés serve food throughout the day.

Annecy

There's something for everyone in this lakefront city that knows how to be popular: mountain views, romantic canals, a hovering château, and swimming in—or boating on, or biking around—the translucent lake. Sophisticated yet outdoors-oriented and bike-crazy, Annecy (ahn-see) is France's answer to Switzerland's Luzern, and, though you may not have glaciers knocking at your door as in nearby Chamonix, the distant peaks paint a darn pretty picture with Annecy's lakefront setting. Annecy has a few museums, but none worth your time: You're here for the stunning setting and outdoor activities. During the winter holidays, Christmas markets and festive decorations animate the city. Annecy is a joy before noon in any season, but high-season weekend afternoons will try your patience. Spend your mornings in the old city and afternoons around the lake.

Orientation to Annecy

Modern Annecy (pop. 50,000) sprawls for miles, but we're interested only in its compact old town, on the northwest corner of the lake. The old town is split by the Thiou River and bounded by the château to the south, and the TI and Rue Royale to the north.

TOURIST INFORMATION

The TI is a few blocks from the old town, across from the big grass field, inside the Bonlieu shopping center (June-mid-Sept daily 9:00-18:30 except closed Sun 12:00-13:45; mid-Sept-June Mon-Sat 9:00-12:30 & 13:45-18:00, Sun 10:00-13:00 except closed Sun mid-Nov-March; 1 Rue Jean Jaurès, tel. 04 50 45 00 33, www.lac-annecy.com). Get a city map, the *Town Walks* walking-tour brochure (describes four mildly interesting walks), the map of the lake showing the bike trail, and, if you're staying a while, the helpful *Annecy Guide*, with everything a traveler needs to know. Ask about walking tours in English (€6.50, July-Aug only, normally Tue and Fri at 16:00). You'll also find TIs in most villages on the lake.

ARRIVAL IN ANNECY

By Train and Bus: The stations sit side by side. To reach the old town and TI, cross the street in front of the stations, and turn left toward the pinkish Hôtel des Alpes. Turn right on Rue de la Poste, then left on Rue Royale to reach the TI and some hotels, or continue straight to more recommended hotels. There is no baggage storage in Annecy, but day-trippers who rent bikes can leave their bags at the bike-rental shop while they ride (except at Véloncey, which doesn't offer this service; for more on bike-rental see "Helpful Hints," below).

By Car: Annecy is a traffic mess; in high season (July-Aug), arrive early, during lunch, or late. Avoid most of the snarls by taking exit #16 from the autoroute (headed north, it's signed *Annecy-Centre;* headed south, the sign reads *Albertville).* Avoid exit #17, the other Annecy option, which results in a long stretch of arduous surface-street driving. From exit #16, follow *Annecy/Albertville* signs. Upon entering Annecy, follow signs to *Le Lac* or *Le Château* depending on the location of your hotel. (Don't follow signs for *Annecy-le-Vieux.*)

Refer to the map of Annecy in this chapter for parking lots. The first 30 minutes are free; after that figure €1.30 per hour (about €16/24 hours). If you're staying at a hotel in town, you can park overnight for free at a public lot—but only if you ask at your hotel. Upon arrival, ditch your car at the first lot that is reasonably close, then get advice from your hotel for more convenient parking. Parking Ste. Claire and Parking du Château work for the hotels I list that are away from the lake. On the lake, you can park near the big boat docks at the underground Hôtel de Ville lot or at Parking La Tournette, or a block farther along at Parking Stade Nautique.

By Plane: From Geneva's airport (GVA, www.gva.ch), Annecy is a 45-minute autoroute drive/taxi ride (Swiss vignette required; see page 775); it's a 2.5-hour trip by bus and train. From Lyon's St-Exupéry airport (LYS, www.lyonaeroports.com), allow 1.5 hours by car—all autoroute—or 2.5 hours by train.

HELPFUL HINTS

Market Days: A thriving outdoor food market occupies much of the old town center on Tuesday, Friday, and Sunday mornings until about 12:30. The biggest market in Annecy is on Saturday, but it's less central (food, clothes, and crafts; until 12:30, around Boulevard Taine—several blocks behind the TI).

Supermarkets: The **Monoprix** is at the corner of Rue du Lac and Rue Notre-Dame (Mon-Sat 8:30-19:50, closed Sun, supermarket upstairs). A smaller **Franprix** is on Rue de l'Annexion just off Rue Royale (Mon-Sat 8:00-20:30, Sun 9:00-13:00 but open until 20:30 in summer).

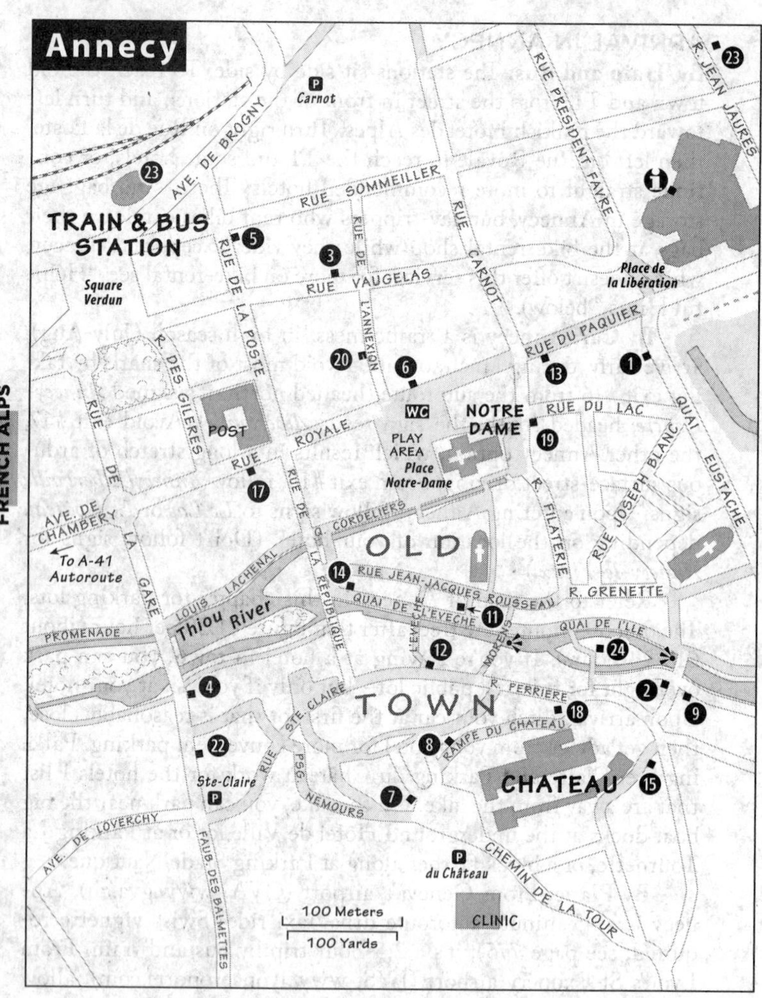

Internet Access: The **TI** has free Wi-Fi, and there's an **Internet café** behind the TI at 4 Rue Jean Jaurès (Mon-Sat 10:00-19:00, Sun 14:30-19:00, tel. 04 50 33 92 60). Many Annecy cafés have Wi-Fi.

Laundry: The launderette is at the western edge of the old town near where Rue de la Gare meets Rue Ste. Claire (daily 7:00-21:00, 6 Rue de la Gare).

Bike Rental: Several places rent electric bikes for about €50/day and standard bikes for about €20/day (leave ID as deposit, includes helmet and basket, half-day rentals and kids' bikes also possible, hours generally 9:00-12:30 & 14:00-18:30). All but Véloncey can keep your bags while you ride (handy for day-trippers).

Roul' ma Poule, near the lakefront bike path across from the lake steamers, rents rollerblades, scooters, and bikes (open mid-May–mid-Oct daily, 4 Rue Marquisats, tel. 04 50 27 86 83, www.annecy-location-velo.com). **Cyclable** has two locations: behind the TI (6 Rue de Bonlieu) and near the lake on Place aux Bois (tel. 04 56 73 97 71, www.cyclable.com). **Véloncey Bikes** is at the train station (student and senior discounts, closed Sun, tel. 04 50 51 38 90).

Car Rental: Avis is at the train station (tel. 08 20 61 16 68).

Taxi: Call 04 50 45 05 67.

Bad Weather: If it's raining, consider a day trip to Lyon (10 trains/day, 2 hours, some change in Chambéry, some by bus; see

Brief History of Annecy

People have called Annecy home for more than 5,000 years. The city has had its ups and downs over the millennia (more ups than downs) and has thrived thanks to its proximity to Geneva's powerful counts and its easy access to routes over the Alps to Italy. In Roman times, Annecy was an important city of about 2,000 people, complete with a forum, temples, and thermal baths. After the Roman Empire fell, locals headed for the hills and occupied the area around the château. A few centuries later, they moved down to the banks of the Thiou River at the lake's mouth. The medieval town then spread to both sides of the river and was protected by the castle you see today. In 1401, Annecy became part of the Savoie region, eventually serving as capital of a large slice of the House of Savoie. The 1800s saw the rise of hydroelectric power in Annecy and the establishment of a strong industrial base. The 1900s brought tourism to the lake, and today, tourism still drives the economy.

Lyon chapter). The last train back to Annecy usually leaves Lyon at about 20:00, allowing a full day in the big city.

Sights in Annecy

▲▲Boating

This is one of Europe's cleanest, clearest lakes, and the water is warmer than you'd think (average summer water temperature is 72 degrees Fahrenheit).

On Your Own: To tool around the lake, rent a **paddleboat** (*pédalos,* some equipped with a slide, 2 people-about €12/30 minutes or €18/hour; some boats can handle 6 passengers) or a **motorboat** (*hors-bord,* no license needed; 2 people-about €33/30 minutes, €50/hour; each extra person-about €1, up to 7 people, several companies all have the same rates).

Lake Cruises: Compagnie des Bateaux du Lac d'Annecy offers several worthwhile lake cruises. The **one-hour cruise** makes no stops but has frequent departures (€14, 8-10/day May-Aug, 6-8/day April and Sept-mid-Oct, generally 1/day Feb-March and mid-Oct-Dec). The **two-hour cruises,** called Circuit Omnibus, make stops at several villages on a clockwise loop around the lake (€18 for entire loop, 3-5/day late April-Sept); these are

ideal for hikers and cyclists (see next two listings). The elaborate dinner and dancing cruises (€56-90) look like fun. Get schedules and prices for all boat trips at the TI or on the lake behind Hôtel de Ville (tel. 04 50 51 08 40, www.annecy-croisieres.com).

▲Scenic Strolls and Hikes near the Lake

Lakeside paths and short, steep hikes up hillsides offer rewarding views, even with clouds. Here are a few ideas.

Old Town: Most of the old city is wonderfully traffic-free. The river, canals, and arcaded streets are made for ambling. The TI's *Town Walks* brochure describes Annecy with basic historical information. Get lost—surrender to the luscious ice-cream shops and waterfront cafés.

Annecy's Waterfront: Stroll the bike/walking path in either direction for lake and mountain views. The best views are found walking toward Annecy-le-Vieux (with the lake on your right). Join the festival of walkers on this popular section that passes grassy beaches and views all the way down the lake.

Duingt: The quiet village of Duingt is a 20-30-minute drive from Annecy; it's also reachable by boat or bike (see "Biking," next page, for a route). It has a short, steep, and beautiful trail leading up to glorious lake views. Park behind Duingt's church, walk along the asphalt lane past the little TI and the old rail tunnel (now the bike path), and find the ramp leading up in 100 yards. Follow signs to *Grotte N-D du Lac,* passing the Stations of the Cross. At the end of the paved walkway (great views with benches), a steep dirt trail continues up for even better vistas (some rocky, uneven sections).

If you arrive by boat, from the dock, walk with the lake on your right into the village; find the church, and then follow the directions given above.

Talloires: From this upscale and charming village (allow 30 minutes from Annecy by car), you can hike (and I mean hike) up to jaw-dropping views over the village and the Golf de Talloires. From here, you can either double back down or continue on the Roc de Chère dirt trail to the village of Menthon-St-Bernard, where you can catch a boat back to Annecy (allow two hours from Talloires to Menthon-St-Bernard). To find the Roc de Chère trail, leave Talloires along the main road (D-909) with the lake on your left (narrow sidewalk available); after the curve, find the short staircase leading left into the trees. The trail climbs for 20 extremely steep minutes up a rocky path with some very uneven footing. You'll pass a map of the trails that crisscross the Roc de Chère and come to benches with views. Follow *Liaison Menthon-St-Bernard* signs to continue to that village. You can reverse this route, but locating the trail from Menthon-St-Bernard's boat dock takes patience: Turn right off the boat, walk to the big hotel/palace, turn left and walk

200 yards up the road, then take a right on a path marked *Roc de Chère*. This leads to a small road (turn right again), taking you up to the trail. If you need lunch in Talloires, find **Café de la Place** (€15-20 *plats,* daily, tel. 04 50 64 40 74).

▲▲Biking

Annecy was made for biking. It's an ain't-it-great-to-be-alive way to poke around the lake (sun or clouds) and test waterfront cafés and grassy parks. A popular bike trail runs along the southwest side of the lake (look for the green bike icon on white signs). Even a short ride on the bike path is worth the effort. Expect big crowds on weekends; wear sunglasses and bring water. Ride as far as your legs take you, break for a lakefront café, then return to Annecy (the path is best after the town of Sévrier, where it leaves the roadside). The **Nautic-Café** in Sévrier-Centre makes a fine lakefront drink stop. It's next to the Le Bistro du Port, a short pedal after passing Sevrier's vertical church (look for banners on the port).

The small village of **Duingt** (cafés and a bakery with good sandwiches) is seven level miles from Annecy and makes a fine destination (see "Scenic Strolls and Hikes," earlier). Steady pedalers make it in 45 minutes; smell-the-roses cyclists need at least an hour. You can ride to Duingt and take the Omnibus boat back to Annecy (€7.60, 3 departures/day from Duingt; normally at 11:45, 15:30, and 18:00; more in summer, verify at boat dock or TI, bikes allowed).

To get to Duingt, leave Annecy on the main road toward Albertville (D-1508). Once the painted bike lane ends, you'll see a sign for the trail *(piste cyclable)* on the left. Follow it to Duingt (to reach the boat dock in Duingt, exit the trail just after passing through the tunnel, coast down to the main road and turn left, then find the small, green boat-dock shelter in the park before the little castle—keep going for cafés and bakery). If you stay on the trail beyond Duingt, the path is beautiful, with views opening up to the south end of the lake. The next village with boats back to Annecy is Doussard (figure a 20-minute pedal from Duingt). This route works even better in reverse, as you don't need to coordinate with the boat back from Duingt or Doussard: Take the Omnibus boat to Duingt or Doussard and pedal back.

Serious cyclists can make it all the way around the lake in about three to four hours (narrow roads and no bike path on most of the opposite side of the lake, with one good hill).

Museum of Annecy (Palais de l'Isle)

This serenely situated 13th-century building cuts like the prow of a ship through the heart of the Thiou River. Once a prison, it held French Resistance fighters during World War II. Today, you can still see several of the prison cells, but most of the museum is taken up with exhibits on local architecture since the war.

Cost and Hours: €3.70, €7 combo-ticket includes Château Museum, June-Sept Wed-Mon 10:30-18:00, Oct-May Wed-Mon 10:00-12:00 & 14:00-17:00, closed Tue year-round, free English leaflet.

Château Museum (Musée-Château d'Annecy)

The castle, built in the late 1100s by aristocrats from nearby Geneva, makes an impressive figure as it hangs above the lake in the old city. But inside, the château has little to offer. Many rooms house modern-art collections that rotate regularly, with a few rooms devoted to local folklore, anthropology, and natural history. Skip it.

Cost and Hours: €5.50, €7 combo-ticket includes Museum of Annecy, same hours as Museum of Annecy.

Driving Around the Lake

The busy roads that link villages along the lake (D-1508 on east side; D-909 on west side) deliver modest lake views for most of the way, but lead to a scenic route to Chamonix and access to fantastic view drives (described next).

Nearby Views

Several roads off D-1508 lead to remarkable views of this gorgeous area. Go early for clearest skies, go late for sunsets, and skip it if it's hazy. Both of the views below are worth ▲▲ in clear weather.

Le Semnoz: For majestic mountain panoramas near Annecy that include Mont Blanc, take the summer-only bus or drive up... and up...and up to Le Semnoz (about 5,000 feet). Allow about 30 minutes one-way and expect lots of bicycles on weekends. To **drive,** follow D-41 from near the lake (see map on page 778). After leaving the city, you'll pass through Annecy's forest and climb past tree level to grandiose views over the high Alps, featuring Monsieur Blanc. Just before the top, you'll pass a great summer luge (Luge d'Eté, about €4/ride in summer, less in other months and with 5 or more rides, July-Aug daily, May-June and Sept-Oct Wed, Sat-Sun, and holidays). Carry on, climbing above the luge area, pass the hotel, and park when you see the chalet-café **Le Courant d'Ere** (fun place for a drink, snacks, or a meal; open daily for lunch, tel. 04 50 01 23 17). Climb to the chairlift station above the café for a magnificent panorama in all directions. You can also take a **bus** to this viewpoint. Ligne d'Eté buses to Le Semnoz leave from the Annecy train station (€5.50 round-trip, 6/day, daily July-Aug, Sat-Sun only in June, none Sept-May, 40 minutes, stops at the luge, details at TI and www.sibra.fr/ligne-dete).

Col de la Forclaz: For drop-dead gorgeous views that take in the entire lake, drive 18 miles from Annecy (allow 45 minutes one-way) to Col de la Forclaz. Start by taking D-1508 south toward Albertville. Three kilometers (about one mile) after leaving the lake at Doussard, turn left on D-42 (signed *Col de la Forclaz*), then wind your way up a narrow lane for five miles past lovely scenery to the Col de la Forclaz (3,600 feet). Look out for cyclists on this climb. At the top, you'll find a sensational viewpoint, cafés and restaurants, and paragliders galore. Several outfits offer a chance to jump off a cliff and sail over the lake, including the appropriately named Adrenaline Parapente (www.annecy-parapente.com). This trip ties in well with the scenic route to Chamonix via D-1508; it also works as a loop back to Annecy (follow D-42 down to Menthon-St-Bernard from the Col de la Forclaz).

Sleeping in Annecy

Annecy is popular, particularly on weekends and during the summer. Hotel rates drop from about mid-October through late April and increase in summer. Most hotels can help you find free overnight parking (in lots, usually after 19:00 until 9:00 in the morning). Unless otherwise noted, these hotels do not have elevators, but they all have free Wi-Fi. For more hotel listings, try Annecy's TI website: www.lac-annecy.com.

IN THE TOWN CENTER

This part of town is pedestrian-friendly and comes with some noise.

$$$ Splendid Hôtel*** decorates Annecy's busy, parkfront street and makes an impression with its grand, American-style facade. Inside, rooms are well-appointed and public spaces are comfy (Db-€145—but a few at €125, suites-€165, extra person-€16, breakfast-€14, air-con, elevator, big beds, guest computer, Wi-Fi, bar, terrace, 4 Quai Eustache Chappuis, tel. 04 50 45 20 00, www.splendidhotel.fr, info@splendidhotel.fr).

$$$ Hôtel du Palais de l'Isle*** offers a romantic canalside location in the thick of the old town and 33 contemporary rooms—several with canal or rooftop views and little fridges. The wine bar/TV room doubles as a nice lounge (true Sb-€85, Db-€127-148, grand suites-€238-295, breakfast-€14, air-con, elevator, guest computer, Wi-Fi, 13 Rue Perrière, tel. 04 50 45 86 87, www.palaisannecy.com, palisle@wanadoo.fr).

$$$ Hotel Mercure*,** well-located near the train station, has predictable comfort (Db-€175-210, frequent and big discounts on website, Wi-Fi, 26 Rue Vaugelas, tel. 04 50 45 59 80 www.mercure.com, H2812@accor.com).

$$$ Hôtel Ibis** is a solid option, with updated, well-configured rooms (all with queen-size beds), a canalside lounge, and easy underground parking. It's well-situated on the edge of the old

Sleep Code

Abbreviations **(€1 = about $1.40, country code: 33)**

S = Single, **D** = Double/Twin, **T** = Triple, **Q** = Quad, **b** = bathroom, **s** = shower only, * = French hotel rating (0-5 stars)

Price Rankings

$$$ Higher Priced—Most rooms €100 or more

$$ Moderately Priced—Most rooms between €75-100

$ Lower Priced—Most rooms €75 or less

Unless otherwise noted, credit cards are accepted, English is spoken, and Wi-Fi is generally free. Prices change without notice; verify current rates online or by email. For the best prices, always book directly with the hotel.

town, a few blocks from the train station (Sb/Db-€110-142, check website for best deals, extra bed-€10, buffet breakfast-€10, air-con, elevator, guest computer, Wi-Fi, 12 Rue de la Gare, tel. 04 50 45 43 21, www.ibishotel.com, h0538@accor.com).

$$ Hôtel des Alpes**, a good value, has 32 comfortable and attractive rooms at a busy intersection just across from the train station. Rooms on the courtyard are quieter, but those on the street have effective double-pane windows (Sb-€65, Db-€70-85, Tb-€96-106, Qb-€108-140, Wi-Fi, 12 Rue de la Poste, tel. 04 50 45 04 56, www.hotelannecy.com, info@hotelannecy.com).

$ Hôtel Central* is just that and more. Run by your Annecy mother, Corinne, this modest, homey, and hyper-decorated place makes a fun stay. Every well-maintained room has a different theme, from Sevilla to India. It's located in the rear of a modest, ivy-covered courtyard (Db-€65-75, Tb-€90, Qb-€110, breakfast-€6, Wi-Fi, 6 bis Rue Royale, tel. 04 50 45 05 37, www.hotelcentralannecy.com, hotelcentralannecy@orange.fr).

AT THE FOOT OF THE CHATEAU

These places are in a quiet area, a steep five-minute walk up from the old town on Rampe du Château.

$$ Residences les Jardins du Château is an urban refuge above the fray near the château entry. It has a small garden and a view terrace, along with eight simple but comfy rooms—there are no phones or TVs, but all come with kitchenettes (Db-€70-120 depending on room size and season, good family rooms, cash only, no refunds, Wi-Fi, 1 Place du Château, tel. 06 67 91 94 23, www.jardinduchateau.sitew.com, rent74@free.fr).

$$ Hôtel du Château**, an unpretentious place run by unpretentious Roman and Amelie, sits barely below the château. It comes with a view terrace and 15 simple, deep yellow, spotless rooms—about half have views. It's first-come, first-get for the precious few free parking spots (small Db-€78, standard Db-€88, Tb-€98, Qb-€114, continental breakfast-€9, Wi-Fi, 16 Rampe du Château, tel. 04 50 45 27 66, www.annecy-hotel.com, hotelduchateau@noos.fr).

Eating in Annecy

Although the touristy old city is well-stocked with forgettable restaurants, I've found a few worthy places. And though you'll pay more to eat with views of the river or canal, the experience is uniquely Annecy. The ubiquitous and sumptuous *gelati* shops remind you how close Italy is. If it's sunny, assemble a gourmet picnic at the arcaded stores and dine lakeside.

Le Cochon à l'Oreille ("The Pig's Ear") is a meat lover's nirvana. Just off the Thiou canal, it welcomes you with a leafy courtyard and a raucous, higgledy-piggledy interior. Amicable owners "Fred" and Jean speak enough English (and fluent pig) and are serious about their cooking (ask to see their pig collection). The accent is on fresh products and meat dishes (particularly ham and pork), though fish options are available. Melted cheese is not their thing (€19 two-course *menu* changes weekly, open daily for lunch and dinner, Quai du Perrière, tel. 04 50 45 92 51).

L'Escargot sits near the lake and offers classic bistro fare at decent prices. It's a welcoming place with indoor and outside seating and a good selection of wines by the glass (€15 two-course *menu* on weekdays, €9-12 good *plats du jour,* closed Mon-Tue, 12 Faubourg des Annonciades, tel. 04 50 51 08 41).

Le Chalet, ideally located along the river, features French and Italian classics. Sit in the cozy, wood-paneled interior or choose canalfront outdoor seating (€28-43 *menus*, closed Sun, Quai de l'Evêché, tel. 04 50 51 82 55).

Le Freti, is a reliable restaurant for local cuisine at fair prices. It's *the* place to go for good fondue, raclette, or anything with cheese. Each booth comes with its own outlet for melting raclette (€14 fondue, €8 salads and onion soup, cheap wine, air-con, open daily, walk through door at 12 Rue Ste. Claire and go upstairs, tel. 04 50 51 29 52).

If Le Freti sounds too cheesy, go next door to **Café l'Estaminet** for some pub grub. You'll get a cozy interior with a few waterside tables on the back terrace, a fun bar area, and salads, omelets, pasta, mussels, fries, and more for fair prices (daily in summer, closed Sun evening and Mon off-season, 8 Rue Ste. Claire, tel. 04 50 45 88 83).

L'Etage is a good choice if you can't decide what you want. Regional specialties and a good range of standard brasserie fare are served at respectable prices. Dine along the pedestrian street terrace or upstairs under wood beams around a big fireplace (€15 fondue, €16 raclette, €20 three-course *menus,* daily, 13 Rue du Pâquier, tel. 04 50 51 03 28).

Auberge du Lyonnais is a classy, well-respected riverfront eatery that specializes in seafood (indoor and outdoor seating). The outgoing owners love Americans; ask Dominique about his many trips to the States, and about his Ford pickup (€27-44 *menus,* cheaper on weeknights, daily, 9 Rue de la République, tel. 04 50 51 26 10).

La Crêperie Perrière, a good budget option in a quiet spot, has €9-10 crêpes and salads, a small terrace, and pleasant interior seating (daily, below the château at 3 Côte Perrière, tel. 04 50 51 76 36).

Lakefront Dining: Many cafés and restaurants ring Annecy's postcard-perfect lake. If you have a car and want views, prowl the many waterfront villages. **Le Bistro du Port,** a nautical place five minutes from Annecy by car, is beautifully situated on the boat dock at the southern end of Sévrier-Centre (€15 lunch *menu,* €36 dinner *menu,* €25 *plats,* daily, Port de Sévrier, turn off D-1508 at the McDonald's, tel. 04 50 52 45 00).

Dessert: Wherever you eat, don't miss an ice-cream-licking stroll along the lake after dark. But if it's chocolate you crave, head for **La Folie-Royale** (closed Sun, 13 Rue Royale, tel. 04 50 52 28 58).

Drinks: Start or end your evening at one of these local and different-as-night-and-day places. At the cozy wine bar, **Les Caves du Château,** you'll escape the crowds by heading just 20 steps up the Rampe du Château from busy Rue Ste. Claire. They offer a huge choice of wines by the glass from throughout France and serve appetizers (June-Sept daily, 6 Rampe du Château, Oct-May closed Monday, tel. 09 51 17 29 98). **Café des Arts** is Annecy's most atmospheric café, marooned on the island at the Palais de l'Ile. With good prices, it attracts a mix of local hipsters and the odd tourist (daily from early to late, 4 Passage de l'Isle, tel. 04 50 51 56 40).

Annecy Connections

From Annecy by Train to: Chamonix (11/day, 2.5 hours, change in St-Gervais), **Lyon** (10/day, 2 hours, most change in Aix-les-Bains, some by bus), **Beaune** (7/day, 4-6 hours, change in Lyon), **Nice** (8/day, 7-9 hours, at least 3 changes, overnight option), **Paris'** Gare de Lyon (hourly, 4 hours, many with change in Lyon), **Geneva** (about hourly, 2 hours; bus-and-train options available from Geneva's airport in 2.5 hours).

Chamonix

Showered with snow-dipped peaks, bullied by menacing glaciers, and blanketed with hiking trails, the resort of Chamonix (shah-moh-nee) is France's best base for alpine exploration. Officially called Chamonix-Mont Blanc, it's the largest of five villages at the base of Mont Blanc, with about 10,000 residents and nearly as many mountain lifts (well, almost). Chamonix's purpose in life has always been to dazzle visitors with some of Europe's top alpine thrills. But you'll also learn a thing or two about glaciers and get an insight into the wild world of mountain climbing. Chamonix is a busy place from early July through late August and during winter holidays, but it's plenty peaceful at other times. Chamonix's sister city is Aspen, Colorado. Perfect.

PLANNING YOUR TIME

Summers bring huge crowds and long lift lines. You won't regret planning your trip to avoid the summer school break *(vacances scolaires),* usually early July to late August. Ride the lifts early (crowds and clouds roll in later in the morning) and save your afternoons for lower altitudes.

If you have one sunny day, spend it this way: Start with the Aiguille du Midi lift (go early, reservations possible and recommended July-Aug), take it all the way to Helbronner (linger around the rock needle longer if you can't get to Helbronner), double back to Plan de l'Aiguille, hike to Montenvers and its Mer de Glace (only with good shoes and snow level permitting), explore there, then take the train down to Chamonix. End your day with a well-deserved drink at a view café in town. If the weather disappoints or the snow line's too low, hike the Petit Balcon Sud or Arve River trails.

Orientation to Chamonix

Eternally white Mont Blanc is Chamonix's southeastern limit; the Aiguilles Rouges mountains form the northwestern border and the frothy Arve River splits linear Chamonix in two. The thriving pedestrian zone, above and west of the river along Rues du Docteur Paccard and Joseph Vallot, forms Chamonix's core. The TI is just above the pedestrian zone, and the train station is two long blocks below and east of the river. To get your mountain bearings, head to the TI and find the big photo in front. With Switzerland and Italy as next-door neighbors, this town has always drawn an international crowd. Today about half of its foreign visitors are British—many have stayed and found jobs in hotels and restaurants.

TOURIST INFORMATION

Visit the TI to prepare your attack. Get the weather forecast, pick up the free town and valley map and the "panorama" map of all the valley lifts, and maybe the €4.50 hiking map called *Carte des Sentiers* (see "Chamonix Area Hikes" on page 802). Ask about snow levels, hours of lifts and trains (critical), the Multipass for lifts, which is described later under "Getting Around (and Up and Down) the Valley," biking information (the TI rents electric bikes for cheap), and help with hotel reservations. Their helpful website has updated sightseeing info, weather forecasts, and more (July-Aug daily 9:00-19:00; Sept-June Mon-Sat 9:00-12:30 & 14:00-18:00, Sun 9:00-12:30; tel. 04 50 53 00 24, www.chamonix.com, info@chamonix.com).

Pull up a beachy sling chair outside the TI and plan your hike, or check your email using their 24-hour Wi-Fi (free access outside, plus small cubicles inside to hole up in).

ARRIVAL IN CHAMONIX

By Train: Walk straight out of the station (no baggage check or WCs) and up Avenue Michel Croz (see the map on page 814). In three blocks, you'll reach the town center; turn left at the big clock, then right for the TI.

By Bus: The long-distance bus station is at the train station.

By Car: For many of my recommended hotels and the TI, take the Chamonix Nord turnoff—coming from Annecy and Geneva, it's the second exit after you pass under the Aiguille du Midi cable car—and follow signs to *Centre-Ville.* Take the exit before the Aiguille du Midi lift station for hotels south of the TI. Most parking is metered and well-signed; your hotel can direct you to free parking. From mid-July to late August, traffic is a mess in Chamonix, and finding parking is messier—plan ahead or arrive before 10:00 to get a spot.

The Mont Blanc tunnel (7.2 miles long, about a 12-minute drive) allows quick access between Chamonix and Italy (one-way-€44, round-trip-€55 with return valid for 1 week, about €400 if you're driving a big truck, www.tunnelmb.com).

By Plane: The nearest international airports are in Lyon (St-Exupéry airport, airport code: LYS, www.lyonaeroports.com; linked by 6 trains/day, 4 hours; 3 hours by car) and Geneva, Switzerland (Genève airport, airport code: GVA, www.gva.ch; hourly

Chamonix: A Quick History

1091 Chamonix is first mentioned in local documents.

1786 Jacques Balmat and Michel-Gabriel Paccard are the first to climb Mont Blanc (find the statue in Chamonix's pedestrian zone).

1818 First ascent of Aiguille du Midi.

1860 The Savoie region (including Chamonix) becomes part of France. After a visit by Napoleon III, the trickle of nature-loving visitors to Chamonix turns to a gush.

1901 Train service reaches Chamonix, unleashing its tourist appeal forever.

1908 The cogwheel train to Montenvers is completed.

1924 First Winter Olympics held in Chamonix.

1930 Le Brévent *téléphérique* (gondola lift) opens to tourists.

1955 Aiguille du Midi *téléphérique* opens to tourists.

1965 The Mont Blanc tunnel is built.

2015 You visit Chamonix.

trains, 3.5-5 hours with two changes; 2 hours by car; best by airport shuttle van or bus—see "Chamonix Connections" on page 820).

HELPFUL HINTS

Crowd-Beating Tips: In high season, take the first lift to beat the crowds and afternoon clouds. Have a view breakfast at *le* top.

Plan Ahead: Bright snow abounds up high, so bring sunglasses. Be sure your camera has enough battery power. For Chamonix's weather, check at your hotel, the TI, or online at www.chamonix.com or www.chamonix-meteo.com. For current lift information and to book the Aiguille du Midi lift, head to the Compagnie du Mont Blanc website (www.compagniedumontblanc.com).

Open-Air Market: Chamonix's market is held Saturdays and fills big Place Mont Blanc (until about 13:00).

Supermarkets: Little **Casino** markets are omnipresent in Chamonix. The **Super-U** is central and big (next to the recommended Hôtel les Crêtes Blanches on Rue Joseph Vallot). Supplement your run-of-the-mill groceries with gourmet local specialties from **Le Refuge Payot** (two locations: 166 Rue Joseph Vallot and 255 Rue du Docteur Paccard).

Inexpensive Mountain Gear: The best deals on sunglasses, lightweight gloves, daypacks, and the like are at **Technique Extrême** (daily 9:00-19:00, 200 Avenue de l'Aiguille du Midi).

Internet Access: The TI has free Wi-Fi and a good list of Internet cafés.

English Books: Small collections are kept at **Librarie Landru** (open daily, 74 Rue Joseph Vallot) and at **Maison de la Presse** (daily, 93 Rue du Docteur Paccard).

Laundry: A self-service *laverie* is one block up from the Aiguille du Midi lift at 174 Avenue de l'Aiguille du Midi (daily 8:00-22:00, instructions in English).

Taxis: There's usually one at the train station. If not, try Alp Taxi (tel. 06 81 78 79 51, www.alp-taxi.com) or Taxi Michel Buton (tel. 06 07 19 70 36, www.taxi-buton-chamonix.com).

Car Rental: Europcar, the only game in town, is across from the train station and offers free airport pickup (36 Place de la Gare, tel. 04 50 53 63 40).

Tours: Chamexpress runs tours of the area in high season (tel. 04 80 96 50 08, www.chamexpress.com).

GETTING AROUND (AND UP AND DOWN) THE VALLEY

Lifts and cogwheel trains are named for their highest destination (for example, Aiguille du Midi, Montenvers, and Le Brévent). More details on individual lifts are described under "Sights in Chamonix," later. You can find current lift information and book the Aiguille du Midi lift on the Compagnie du Mont Blanc website, though it's a little clunky to use (www.compagniedumontblanc.com).

By Lift: Gondolas *(téléphériques)* climb mountains all along the valley, but the best one—Aiguille du Midi—leaves from Chamonix. Though sightseeing is optimal from the Aiguille du Midi gondola, there are more hiking options from the Le Brévent and La Flégère gondolas.

The lift to Aiguille du Midi is open summer and winter (short closures possible in May and June, longer closures late Oct-early Dec). The *télécabines* on the Panoramic Mont Blanc lift to Helbronner (atop the Italian border) run only from about mid-June to mid-September, and even then only in good weather. (The lift on the Italian side of the mountain, from Helbronner down to La Palud, is closed through 2015.) Other area lifts are generally open from January to mid-April and from mid-June to late September. Because maintenance closures can occur anytime, verify schedules for all lifts at the TI.

The **Multipass** ticket option saves time and money for most, particularly if you're spending two or more days in the Chamonix valley. It allows unlimited access to all the lifts and trains (except

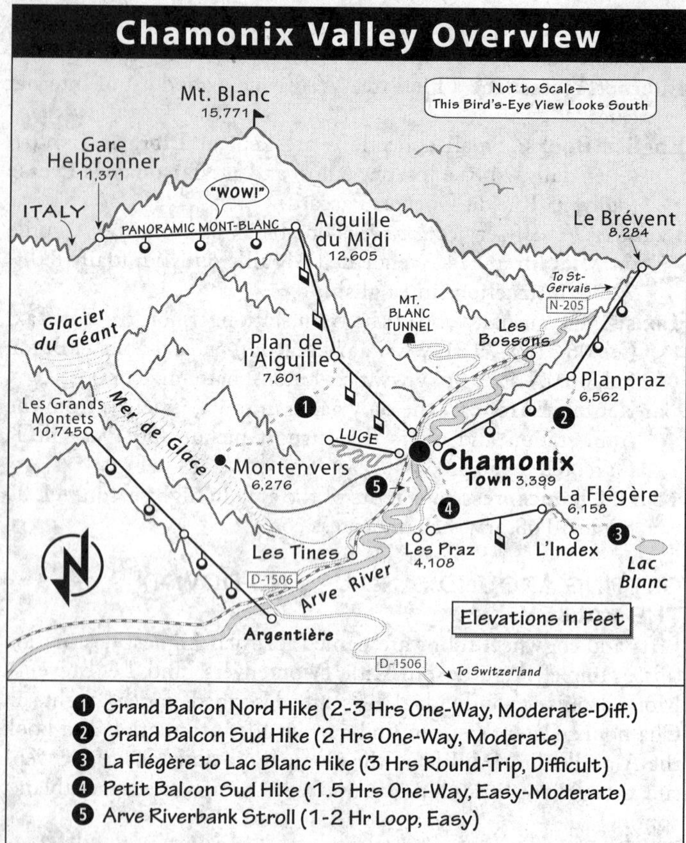

the Helbronner gondola to Italy), and includes all reservation fees (both Aiguille du Midi and Montenvers) and the elevator at the top of Aiguille du Midi. You also get discounts for various activities in Chamonix, such as the Parc de Loisirs des Planards.

Best of all, it lets you bypass lift-ticket lines after your first purchase. Your pass is a smart card, valid all day, that allows you to scan your way to the top and to ride lifts you'd otherwise skip. You could hop on a lift just to have a drink from a view café at the top (€58/1 day, €72/2 days, €83/3 days, €98/4 days, €108/5 days, available for up to 15 days; days are consecutive, though you can buy a more expensive pass for nonconsecutive days; kids ages 4-15—and kids over 64—pay about 15 percent less for two-day and longer passes, kids under 4 may not be allowed). The one-day pass is a good value if you plan to do the round-trip lift from Chamonix to Aiguille du Midi plus the round-trip train from Chamonix to Montenvers (and not hike between the two). Families can benefit from reduced

Chamonix Activities at a Glance

▲▲▲Aiguille du Midi Gondola The valley's most spectacular and popular lift, taking you to magnificent views at 12,600 feet. From here you can ride the cute *télécabines* over the Alps to the Italian border and back, take Chamonix's greatest hike to the Mer de Glace (from the halfway-up stop at Plan de l'Aiguille), or just enjoy the views.

▲▲▲Train to Montenvers Cogwheel train to the Mer de Glace, an eight-mile-long glacier where you can walk inside the glacier, admire jagged mountain peaks, have lunch with a view (or sleep) at the Montenvers hotel, and hike to the Aiguille du Midi lift (though the hike is best done in the other direction).

▲▲▲Le Brévent Gondola Second-most-spectacular lift from Chamonix, allowing access to the mountain range on the opposite side of the valley from Mont Blanc (closed late April-mid-June and Oct). Get off halfway at the Planpraz station for the Grand Balcon Sud hike to the La Flégère lift, or go all the way to Le Brévent for sky-high views and a restaurant.

▲▲▲La Flégère Lift Starting point for hikes to Lac Blanc and to the Grand Balcon Sud trail back to Planpraz (on the Le Brévent gondola). Refuge-Hôtel La Flégère, at the station, offers drinks, snacks, and accommodations, all with a view.

Arve Riverbank Stroll Several trails allow a level walk or bike ride in the woods between Chamonix and Les Praz. See paragliders make dramatic landings and enjoy mountain views outside Chamonix to the sound of the Arve River.

fares. The pass is sold online (www.compagniedumontblanc.com), at participating lift stations, and at some hotels for no added cost. Passes are nonrefundable unless purchased through a hotel.

By Foot: See "Chamonix Area Hikes" on page 802.

By Bike: The peaceful river valley trail is ideal for bikes (and pedestrians). The TI has a brochure showing bike-rental shops and the best biking routes.

By Bus or Train: One road and one scenic rail line lace together the valley's towns and lifts. To help reduce traffic and pollution, your hotel will give you a free **Chamonix Guest Card** good for free travel during your stay. The cards are valid on all Chamonix-area buses (except the night bus) and the scenic valley train between Servoz and Vallorcine, and also give small discounts on a handful of area sights. This is a great value for those with time to explore the valley.

Local buses #1, #2, and #21 run to valley villages (1-2/hour,

#21 runs only mid-June-early September, details in English at www.chamonix-bus.com). The main stops are 200 yards to the right when you leave the TI (past Hôtel Mont Blanc—look for the bus shelters) and on Rue Joseph Vallot where it crosses Avenue du Mont Blanc. Direction "Le Tour" on bus #1, "Les Praz/Flégère" on bus #2, or "Col des Montets" on bus #21 will take you toward Les Praz (for Hikes #2 and #3) and Switzerland (see map on page 806).

Le Mulet minibuses circulate around Chamonix village and are lifesavers for pooped hikers; they're especially handy to or from the Aiguille du Midi lift, which is a 15-minute walk from many hotels (free, every 10 minutes late June-early Sept, otherwise every 20 minutes, 8:30-18:30).

The train ride toward **Martigny** in Switzerland is gorgeous, and villages such as Les Praz and Tines (10 minutes by bus) offer quiet escapes from busy Chamonix.

Sights in Chamonix

MOUNTAIN LIFTS, GONDOLAS, AND TRAINS

▲▲▲Aiguille du Midi

The Aiguille du Midi (ay-gwee doo mee-dee) is easily the valley's (and, arguably, Europe's) most spectacular and popular lift. If the weather's clear, the price doesn't matter. Take an early lift and have breakfast above 12,000 feet.

Cost: From Chamonix to Plan de l'Aiguille—round-trip-€30 (one-way-€15); Aiguille du Midi—round-trip-€56 (one-way-€46, not including parachute); the Panoramic Mont Blanc *télécabine* to Helbronner—round-trip-€84. If you are planning to stop at Plan de l'Aiguille on the way back down and hike to Montenvers, ask about a *spécial randonée* ticket for about €48. Tickets for the *télécabines* from Aiguille du Midi to Helbronner are sold at both base and summit lift stations with no difference in price (round-trip-€25).

Discounts: The prices listed above are for ages 16 and over; kids ages 4-15 cost about 15 percent less (family rates for 2 adults and 2 children ages 15 and under are also available).

Hours: Lifts are weather- and crowd-dependent, but generally run daily July-Aug 6:00 or 7:00-16:30, late May-June and Sept 7:00 or 8:00-16:30 or 17:00, and Oct-late May 8:00-15:30. Gondolas run every 10 minutes during busy times; the last return from Aiguille du Midi is generally one hour after the last ascent. The last *télécabine* departure to Helbronner Point is about 14:00-15:00, and

Alpine Crossing from France to Italy

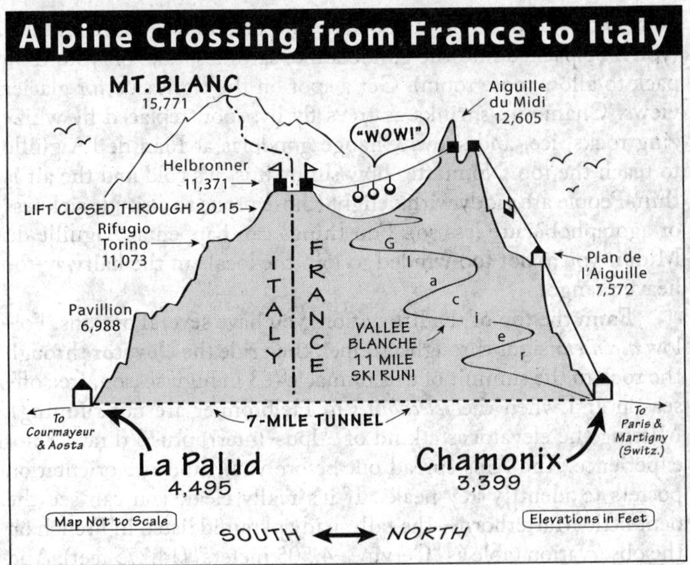

the last train down from Montenvers (for hikers) is about 17:00-18:00.

Crowd-Beating Strategies: To beat the hordes and clouds, ride the Aiguille du Midi lift (up and down) as early as you can. To beat major delays in summer, leave no later than 7:00 or reserve ahead (first lift departs at 6:00 or 7:00, verify in advance). If the weather has been bad and turns good, expect big crowds in any season. If it's clear, don't dillydally. If you arrive after 9:00 in summer your ticket will likely include an assigned gondola time (usually within 30 minutes).

From July to August, smart travelers reserve the Aiguille du Midi lift in advance (€2 fee). You can reserve at the information booth next to the lift (open mid-June-mid-Sept), online at www.compagniedumontblanc.com, or by phone (year-round, tel. 04 50 53 22 75, automated reservations in English). Reservations are taken from one to seven days in advance (not same day); pick tickets up at the lift station at least 20 minutes before departure (the information booth at the Aiguille du Midi lift tells you which window to use for priority access). Reservations are free with a Multipass (see page 791) and are not possible for the *télécabines* to Helbronner.

Time to Allow: Chamonix to Aiguille du Midi—20 minutes one-way, 2 hours round-trip, 3 hours in peak season; Chamonix to Helbronner—1.5 hours one-way, 3-4 hours round-trip, longer in peak season. On busy days, minimize delays by making a reservation for your return lift time upon arrival at the top.

Visiting the Aiguille du Midi: Pile into the *téléphérique* (gondola) and soar to the tip of a rock needle 12,600 feet above sea level (you'll be packed into the gondola like sardines; take off your daypack to allow more room). Get a spot on the right side for glacier views. Chamonix shrinks as trees fly by, soon replaced by whizzing rocks, ice, and snow. Change gondolas at Plan de l'Aiguille to reach the top. No matter how sunny it is, it's cold and the air is thin. People are giddy with delight (those prone to altitude sickness or agoraphobia are less so). Fun things can happen at Aiguille du Midi if you're not too winded to join the locals in the halfway-to-heaven tango.

From the top of the lift station, you have several options. Follow *ascenseur* signs through a tunnel, then ride the **elevator** through the rock to the summit of this pinnacle (€3 in high season, free off-season and when the *télécabines* to Helbronner are not running). Missing the elevator is a kind of Alpus-Interruptus I'd rather not experience. The Alps spread out before you. Find the orientation posters to identify key peaks. If it's really clear, you can see the bent little Matterhorn—the tall, shady pyramid listed in French on the observation table as "Cervin—4,505 meters" (14,775 feet). And looming on the other side is Mont Blanc, the Alps' highest point, at 4,810 meters (15,771 feet). Mont Blanc and the Matterhorn were first connected by intrepid backcountry skiers in 1903 via La Route Haute (The High Route). Today, it's one of the most popular ski trails (not difficult from a technical point of view). Skiers cover approximately 180 kilometers (112 miles) over about eight days, sleeping in hiking huts overnight.

Use the **telescopes** to spot mountain climbers; more than 2,000 scale this mountain each year. A long but not technically challenging climb, it was first scaled in 1786, more than 170 years before this lift was built (are you kidding?). Find the giant's tooth, spot the *télécabines* to Italy, and identify lift stations of the Aiguilles Rouges mountain range on the other side of Chamonix. That rusty tin-can needle above you serves as a communications tower. Check the temperature next to the elevator. Plan on 32 degrees Fahrenheit, even on a sunny day. Sunglasses are essential. Don't miss the chance to step into the void *(Pas dans le Vide)* and stand on a glass platform staring down some 3,000 feet to glaciers below. *Ooh la la.*

Back down, explore Europe's tallest **lift station.** More than 150 yards of tunnels *(galeries)* lead to an enclosed view room, a free and worthwhile exhibit on the extreme sport of mountain climbing, a cafeteria (fair prices—have lunch or coffee with a view), a restaurant (not such fair prices), WCs, a gift shop, and an icicle-covered gateway to the glacial world. A right turn out of the elevator leads you through a tunnel to the Mont Blanc Terrace, a small deck with more views. Interview a mountain climber (many are British) to get an insight into their sport.

Follow *la Vallée Blanche* signs to a drippy **"ice tunnel"** where skiers and mountain climbers make their exit. The views are sensational; merely observing is exhilarating. Peek down the icy cliff and ponder the value of an ice ax. Skiers make the 11-mile run to the Mer de Glace (described later) in about half a day (in winter they can ski 13 miles all the way back to the valley at Argentière). The Access Belvedere walkway leads to bird's-eye views of the *télécabines* to Helbronner and to more amazing mountain views.

Go back through the tunnel to the main building, where gondolas return to Chamonix, and climb metal stairs to more view terraces, WCs, and the cafeteria/gift shop. Inside you'll see posters describing the 1950s construction of the lift station and the gondola line (the first cable was destroyed during construction by an avalanche). The photos are fascinating.

For your private glacial dream world, get into the little red *télécabine* (called Panoramic Mont Blanc) and sail south to **Helbronner Point,** the Italian border station (typically open late June-early Sept). This line stretches three miles with no solid pylon. (It's propped by a "suspended pylon," a line stretched between two peaks 1,300 feet from the Italian end.) In a gondola for four, you'll dangle silently for 40 minutes as you glide over glaciers and past a forest of peaks to Italy. Hang your head out the window and explore every corner of your view. From Helbronner Point, you'll turn around and return to Aiguille du Midi (construction currently prevents access down into Italy from Helbronner Point).

From Aiguille du Midi, you can ride all the way back to Chamonix; or—way, way better—get off halfway down at **Plan de l'Aiguille,** where you'll find a scenic café with sandwiches, drinks, cheap sunglasses, outdoor tables, and paragliders jumping off cliffs (except in July-Aug). But the best reason to get off here is to follow the wonderful trail to the Mer de Glace, then catch the train back into Chamonix (for details, see "Chamonix Area Hikes—Hike #1" on page 802).

Even if you don't do the hike, take a 35-minute round-trip walk below the lift station to the ignored and peaceful **Refuge-Plan de l'Aiguille** for reasonable meals (good omelets, pastas, and salads for €10 made by welcoming manager Claude—no English, no problem) and drinks inside or out (open daily May-late Oct, tel. 06 65 64 27 53). This makes an easy mini-hike for hurried travelers (or a great overnight for a steal—see "Sleeping in Chamonix," later). The short but steep climb back up to the lift will be your exercise for the day (if snow hides the top of the trail, walk under the gondola cables down to the refuge—but ask first to be sure it's safe).

Don't hike all the way down to Chamonix from Plan de l'Aiguille or Montenvers-Mer de Glace; it's a long, steep walk through thick forests with few views.

▲▲▲Mer de Glace (Montenvers)

From Gare de Montenvers (the little station over the tracks from Chamonix's main train station), the cute cogwheel Train du Montenvers toots you up to tiny Montenvers (mohn-tuh-vehr). There you'll see a dirty, rapidly receding glacier called the Mer de Glace (mayr duh glahs, "Sea of Ice") and fantastic views up the white valley (Vallée Blanche) of splintered, snow-capped peaks.

Cost and Hours: Round-trip-€30, one-way-€25, family rates available, prices include gondola and ice caves entry, daily 8:30-17:00, July-Aug 8:00-18:00, last trip down at 16:30, 2-3/hour, 20 minutes, confirm times with TI or call 04 50 53 12 54.

Visiting the Glacier: Find the **view deck** across from the train station. France's largest glacier, at eight miles long, is impressive from above and below. The swirling glacier extends under the dirt about a half-mile downhill to the left. Imagine that it recently reached as high as the vegetation below (see the dirt cliffs—called moraines—left behind in its retreat). In 1860, this glacier stretched all the way down to the valley floor. Some say this fast-moving glacier is just doing its cyclical thing, growing and shrinking—a thousand years ago, cows grazed on grassy fields here. Al Gore thinks people are speeding up the process. Either way, it's an in-your-face lesson about global climate change (see the "Understanding the Alps" sidebar on page 800).

Use an **orientation table** as you look up to the peaks. **Aiguille du Dru**'s powerful spire, at about 11,700 feet, makes an irresistible target for climbers. It was first scaled in 1860 (long before the train you took here was built) and was recently free-climbed (no ropes, belays, etc.); see the colored lines indicating different routes taken—one by an *Américain.* Those guys are nuts. The smooth snow field to the left of Dru's spire (Les Grands Montets) is the top of Chamonix's most challenging ski run, with a vertical drop of about 6,500 feet (down the opposite side). The path to the right (as you face the glacier) leads to a fine view café and a reconstruction of a crystal cave.

The glacier's **ice caves** are beneath you. Take the free, small gondola down and prepare to walk about 450 steps each way. Several years ago, it was 280 steps. This glacier is beating a hasty retreat—as you walk down you'll pass signs that bring this point home by showing the level of the glacier over the years. The ice cave, a hypnotizing shade of blue-green, is actually a long tunnel dug about 75 yards into the glacier. Informative panels describe the digging of the cave. This is also where skiers end their run from the Aiguille du Midi (you might recognize someone if you rode that lift earlier).

The **Refuge-Hôtel du Montenvers,** a few minutes' walk toward Chamonix, offers a full-service restaurant, view tables (fair prices, limited selection), and a warm interior (you can even bunk here—see "Sleeping in Chamonix," later). The five-room museum upstairs describes the history of the Montenvers train (no English but good exhibits). The hotel was built in 1880, when "tourists" arrived on foot or by mule.

The three-hour trail to **Plan de l'Aiguille** (see page 803 for a description) begins across from the hotel. Walk above the two stone buildings and follow the trail as it rises just above the Mer de Glace valley (follow *sentier gauche* signs toward *Signal Montenvers*). For terrific views, hike toward Plan de l'Aiguille—even just a short distance. The views get better fast, and the higher you climb, the better they get as the peaks of the Aiguilles Rouges come into sight behind you. Bring a picnic.

A **Glaciorium** lies fifty yards behind the hotel along the main walkway. It houses a small but worthwhile exhibit on glaciers of the world with dioramas, interactive displays, and terrific images that explain the life of a glacier and where they are headed (free, daily 9:00-16:30).

▲▲▲Gondola Lifts to le Brévent and La Flégère

Though Aiguille du Midi gives a more spectacular ride, the Le Brévent and La Flégère lifts (téléphériques) offer worthwhile hiking and viewing options, with unobstructed panoramas across to the Mont Blanc range and fewer crowds. The Le Brévent (luh bray-vahn) lift is in Chamonix; the La Flégère (lah flay-zhair) lift is in nearby Les Praz (lay prah). The lifts are connected by a scenic hike, or by bus along the valley floor (free with Chamonix Guest Card, see Hike #2 in the next section); both have sensational view cafés. Both lifts are closed from late April to mid-June and again by mid-October (reopening when ski season starts, usually sometime in November).

Le Brévent: This lift is a steep 10-minute walk up the road

Understanding the Alps

The Alps were formed about 100 million years ago by the collision of two continents: the African plate pushing north against the stable plates of Europe and Asia. In the process, the sediments of the ancient Tethys Ocean (which occupied the general real estate of the modern Mediterranean) became smooshed between the landmasses. Shoving all this material together made the rocks and sediments fold, shatter, and pile on top of each other; over millennia, this growing jumble built itself up into today's Alps. Up in the mountains, look for folds and faults in the rocks that hint at this immense compression, which is still happening today: The Alps continue to rise by at least a millimeter each year (while erosion wears them down at about the same rate).

The current shape of the mountains and valleys is the handiwork of at least five ice ages over the last two million years. Glaciers flowed down the mountain valleys, scooped out beautiful alpine lakes, and carried rocks far away from where they formed. The Alps were the first mountains extensively studied by geologists, and many of the geological terms that describe mountains originated here. Once you learn how to recognize a few of the landforms shaped by glaciers, you can easily spot these features when you visit other alpine areas. Study glacier exhibits to train your eye to recognize what you're seeing.

Glaciers are big and blunt, so they make simple, large-scale marks on the landscape. If a valley is U-shaped, like Chamonix's (with steep sides and a rounded base), it's probably been scoured out by a glacier. (California's Yosemite Valley is another classic example.)

A **cirque** (French for "circus") is the amphitheater-like depression carved out at the upper part of a valley by a glacier. If two adjacent cirques erode back close to each other, a sharp, steep-sided ridge forms, called an **arête** (French for "fishbone"). Cirques and

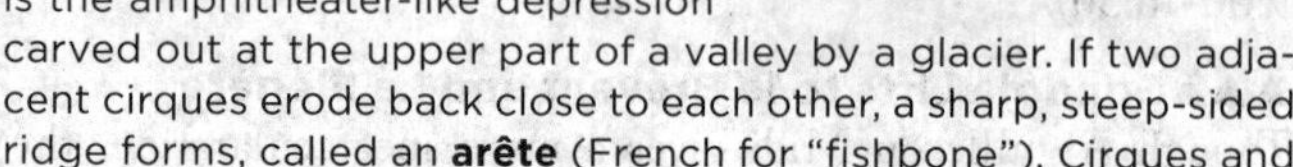

above Chamonix's TI. It takes two lifts to reach Le Brévent's top. The first lift to Planpraz, with automated eight-person *télécabines,* runs every minute. Sit backward and watch Chamonix shrink below (round-trip to Planpraz-€17, one-way-€14, pleasant restaurant, great views and good hiking options, see Hike #2 in the next section).

The second gondola to Le Brévent station leaves from Planpraz and runs every 20-30 minutes. At the top, you get 360-degree views, more hikes, and a view restaurant. For most, Planpraz is

arêtes are common in mountains that have had glaciers. More rarely, when three or more cirques erode toward one another, a pyramidal peak is created—called a **horn.** Switzerland's Matterhorn (visible—barely—from the Aiguille du Midi) is the world's most famous example. Glaciers flowed down all sides of this mountain, scooping material away as they went to leave its distinctive sharp peak.

A common feature left behind by retreating glaciers is a **moraine,** a pile of dirt and rocks that was carried along on the glacier as it advanced, then was dumped as the glacier melted (plainly visible around the Mer de Glace).

Alpine glaciers can only originate above the snowline, so if you see any of these landforms (U-shaped valleys, cirques, horns, or moraines) in lower elevations, you know that the climate there used to be colder. The effects of a warming climate have profoundly hit the glaciers of the Alps, which have lost at least a third of their volume since the 1950s. At that rate, some studies project that most here could virtually disappear by the end of the 21st century, affecting water storage and hydroelectric power generation, and making mountainsides less stable.

Another consequence of the warming climate is that winter weather no longer reliably produces snow at altitudes that it did in the past—which is bad news for Europe's huge ski industry. Seeing a future of ever-warmer winters, alpine resorts are putting their ingenuity to the test. This goes beyond snow machines: Many resorts are investing hugely in new spas, convention centers, and other attractions that don't require snow. Meanwhile, European governments strive to invest in environmentally friendly technologies in hopes of keeping their mountains white and their valleys green.

plenty high (round-trip from Chamonix to Le Brévent-€30, one-way-€22; daily 8:45-17:00, July-Aug 8:15-18:00, last return from Planpraz one hour after last ascent, closed late April-mid-June and Oct, tel. 04 50 53 13 18).

La Flégère: This lift runs from the neighboring village of Les Praz to La Flégère station; to go higher, take the lift to L'Index (La Flégère round-trip-€17, one-way-€14; L'Index round-trip-€27, one-way-€22; daily 8:15-16:45, summer 8:00-17:30, last return from La Flégère 15 minutes after last ascent, closed late April-mid-

Kids' Activities

Chamonix provides a wealth of fun opportunities for kids. The TI can suggest family-friendly hikes and activities (such as mini-golf, swimming pools with big slides, and more). Here are a few kid-pleasing activities to consider.

Parc de Loisirs des Planards—Chamonix's fun park for kids of all ages. It includes a luge (summer only) and a Parc d'Aventure with tree courses, Tarzan swings, trampolines, electric motorbikes, Jet Skis, and more (for details, see "Luge" listing on page 808).

Piscine du Centre Sportif Richard Bozon—A large pool complex with a big waterslide, water garden, Jacuzzi, and more (€7 for adults, €5.50 for those under age 18, open June-early-Sept Mon-Sat in the afternoon and all day Sun, closed early Sept-May).

Parc de Merlet—Animal sanctuary with trails that let you discover mountain animals (marmots, mountain goats, llamas, deer, and more). It's located in Coupeau above Les Houches, and comes with exceptional views (so parents get some scenery while kids get to see animals). You can get there by car (20-minute drive) or hike for two beautiful hours from Chamonix. If you drive, head to the very top parking lot, as you'll be hiking uphill for 20-30 minutes just to reach the entry. There's a lot more walking inside the park to find the animals—bring good shoes and water (€7, €4 for kids ages 4-14, view café with salads and regional dishes, no picnics allowed; July-Aug daily 9:30-19:30; May-June and Sept Tue-Sun 10:00-18:00, closed Mon; tel. 04 50 53 47 89, www.parcdemerlet.com).

June and mid-Sept-Oct, tel. 04 50 53 18 58). Hikes to Planpraz and Lac Blanc leave from the top of this station (see Hikes #2 and #3 in the next section).

CHAMONIX AREA HIKES

A good first stop is the full-service **Maison de la Montagne** across from the TI. On the second floor, the **Office de Haute-Montagne** (High Mountain Office) can help you plan your hikes and tell you about trail and snow conditions (daily 9:00-12:00 & 15:00-18:00, tel. 04 50 53 22 08, www.chamoniarde.com). The staff speaks enough English and has vital weather reports and maps, as well as some English hiking guidebooks (you can photocopy key pages). Ask to look at the trail guidebook (sold in many stores and at the TI but not here, includes the helpful €4.50 *Carte des Sentiers,* the region's hiking map). You can also use the WC here on the second floor.

At **Compagnie des Guides de Chamonix** on the ground floor, you can hire a guide to take you hiking (about €200/half-day,

€320/day, less per person for groups), help you scale Mont Blanc, or hike to the Matterhorn and Zermatt (open daily 9:00-12:00 & 15:30-19:00, closed Sun-Mon off-season, tel. 04 50 53 00 88, www.chamonix-guides.com).

In this chapter, I describe three fairly strenuous hikes and two easier scrambles (see the map on page 806). These hikes give nature lovers of any ability good options in most seasons. Start early, when the weather's generally best. This is critical in summer—if you don't get to the lifts by 8:30, you'll meet a conveyor belt of hikers. If starting later or walking longer, confirm lift closing hours, or prepare for a long, steep hike down. Be prepared to wait it out if the weather gets rough—lifts don't run during electrical storms.

For your hike, pack sunglasses, sunscreen, rain gear, water, snacks, and maybe light gloves. Bring warm layers (mountain weather can change in a moment) and good shoes (trails are rocky and uneven). Take your time, watch your footing, don't take shortcuts, and say "*Bonjour!*" to your fellow hikers. Note that there's no shade on Hikes #1, #2, and #3.

▲▲Hike #1
Plan de l'Aiguille to Montenvers-Mer de Glace (Grand Balcon Nord)

This is the most efficient way to incorporate a high-country hike into your ride down from the valley's greatest lift, and check out a world-class glacier to boot. The well-used trail rises but mostly falls (dropping 1,500 feet from Plan de l'Aiguille to Montenvers and the Mer de Glace) and is moderately difficult, provided the snow is melted (generally covered by snow until June; get trail details at the Office de Haute-Montagne, listed earlier). Some stretches are steep and strenuous, with uneven footing and slippery rocks. Note the last train time from Montenvers-Mer de Glace back to Chamonix, or you'll be hiking another hour and a half straight down.

Here is an overview of this 2.5-hour hike: From the Aiguille du Midi lift, get off halfway down at Plan de l'Aiguille, *sortie* to the café, then find signs leading down to *Montenvers-Mer de Glace*. You'll drop steadily for 15 minutes down to a small refuge (good prices for meals and drinks), then go right, hiking the spectacularly scenic, undulating, and (for short periods) strenuous trail to Montenvers (overlooking the Mer de Glace glacier). Plan on lots of boulder-stepping and occasional stream crossings.

After about an hour at a steady pace, the trail splits. Follow signs up the steep trail to *Le Signal* (more scenic and easier), rather

than to the left toward *Montenvers* (looks easier, but becomes very difficult). At this point, you'll grind it out up switchbacks for about 30 minutes to the best views of the trail at Le Signal. Savor the views you worked so hard to reach. From here, it's a long, sometimes steep, but always memorable drop to Montenvers and the Mer de Glace. In Montenvers, take the train back to Chamonix. Don't walk the rest of the trail down from Montenvers (long, steep, disappointing views).

▲▲Hike #2
La Flégère to Planpraz (Grand Balcon Sud)

This lovely hike undulates for two hours above Chamonix Valley, with staggering views of Mont Blanc and countless other peaks, glaciers, and wildflowers. There's just 370 feet of difference in elevation between the La Flégère and Planpraz lift stations—so this hike, though not without its ups and downs, is doable (but still requires serious stamina and appropriate shoes). The trail is a mix of dirt paths, ankle-twisting rocky sections, and short stretches of service roads. You'll pass by winter lifts and walk through meadows and along small sections of forest. Keep your eyes out for green-lettered signs to *La Flégère* or *Planpraz,* depending on your direction; red-and-white markers also help identify the trail.

You can hike the trail in either direction. If you start at La Flégère, Mont Blanc stays in your sights the entire walk. Ask for the round-trip rate when you combine La Flégère and Planpraz (Le Brévent) lifts, available at either lift (saves about €6). Remember that these lifts are closed from late April to mid-June and again by mid-October.

To start at La Flégère, take free bus #1, #2, or #21 (all buses use Chamonix Sud and Centre stops, get departure times and stop locations to Les Praz/La Flégère at TI or at www.chamonix-bus.com; see page 793), or walk 40 minutes along the Arve River to Les Praz (see Hike #5, described later). Take the lift up to La Flégère, and walk out the back (to near the snack stand) and get your bearings. Find the dirt path of the Mer de Glace glacier and the cliff-hanging Hôtel du Montenvers on the opposite side of Chamonix's valley. To find the trail for your hike, walk down to the refuge just below the lift station and turn right, crossing under the gondola cables to *Planpraz* (you don't want *Les Praz-Chamonix*—that's straight down). Signage is inconsistent, so expect to do some route-finding along the way. End your hike at Planpraz station, the midway stop on the Le Brévent lift line, and return to Chamonix from there.

If starting from the Le Brévent lift, take the *télécabine* up to Planpraz (automated cars leave every minute). As you ride up with your back to Mont Blanc, you may spot your destination lift station (La Flégère) off to the right. From the Planpraz lift station, leave the station, walking behind it (not past La Bergerie Restaurant), then climb above, following green-lettered signs to *La Flégère.* When you reach the La Flégère lift, ride it down to Les Praz (the hike down is not worth the trouble), then walk back to Chamonix following Hike #5 (described later), or take any of the free Chamonix buses that stop on the main road at the entrance to the La Flégère lift station (about 4/hour, 10-minute ride; see page 793 for bus details).

▲▲Hike #3
La Flégère to Lac Blanc

This is the most demanding hiking trail of those I list; it climbs steeply and steadily over a rough, boulder-strewn trail for 1.5 hours to snowy Lac Blanc (pronounced "lock blah"). Some footing is tricky, and good shoes or boots are a must. I like this trail, as it gets you away from the valley edge and opens views to peaks you don't see from other hikes.

The destination is a snow-white lake framed by peaks and the nifty Refuge-Hôtel du Luc Blanc, which offers good lunches (and dinners, if you stay the night, summers only). The views on the return trip are breathtaking. Check for snow conditions on the trail (often a problem until July) and go early (particularly in summer), as there is no shade and this trail is popular.

Follow the directions for Hike #2 to La Flégère station, then walk out the station's rear door past the snack stand to get oriented. Track the trail as it drops way down to that winter chairlift station, then hooks hard left back up a steep hill. You can avoid this considerable down-and-up by taking the L'Index chairlift behind you (about €9 one-way, €11 round-trip, €27 from the base). Make sure the trail from L'Index is free of snow, as this shortcut can be dicey, especially for kids. However you start, the trail is well-signed to Lac Blanc, and its surface improves as you climb.

▲Hike #4
Petit Balcon Sud to Chalet de la Floria and Les Praz

This trail runs above the valley on the Brévent side from the village of Servoz to Argentière, passing Chamonix about halfway, and is handy when snow or poor weather makes other hikes problematic. No lifts are required—just firm thighs to climb up and down. Access paths link the trail to villages below. Once you're up, the trail rises and falls with some steep segments and uneven footing. The

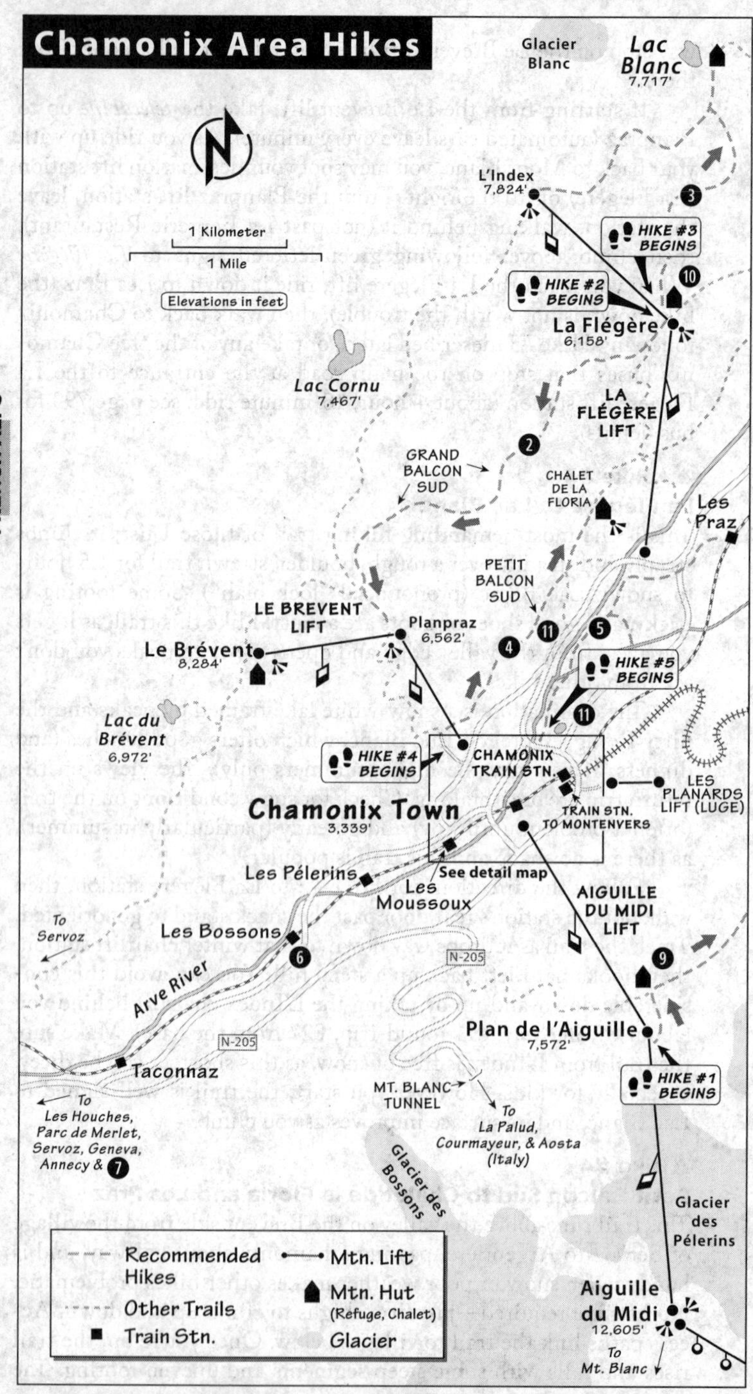
Chamonix Area Hikes
Glacier Blanc
Lac Blanc
7,717'
L'Index
7,824'
1 Kilometer
1 Mile
Elevations in feet
HIKE #3 BEGINS
HIKE #2 BEGINS
La Flégère
6,158'
Lac Cornu
7,467'
LA FLÉGÈRE LIFT
GRAND BALCON SUD
CHALET DE LA FLORIA
Les Praz
PETIT BALCON SUD
LE BREVENT LIFT
Planpraz
6,562'
Le Brévent
8,284'
HIKE #5 BEGINS
Lac du Brévent
6,972'
HIKE #4 BEGINS
CHAMONIX TRAIN STN.
LES PLANARDS LIFT (LUGE)
Chamonix Town
3,339'
TRAIN STN. TO MONTENVERS
Les Pélerins
See detail map
Les Moussoux
AIGUILLE DU MIDI LIFT
To Servoz
Les Bossons
N-205
Arve River
Plan de l'Aiguille
7,572'
N-205
Taconnaz
HIKE #1 BEGINS
MT. BLANC TUNNEL
To La Palud, Courmayeur, & Aosta (Italy)
To Les Houches, Parc de Merlet, Servoz, Geneva, Annecy & 7
Glacier des Bossons
Glacier des Pélerins
Recommended Hikes
Other Trails
Train Stn.
Mtn. Lift
Mtn. Hut (Refuge, Chalet)
Glacier
Aiguille du Midi
12,605'
To Mt. Blanc

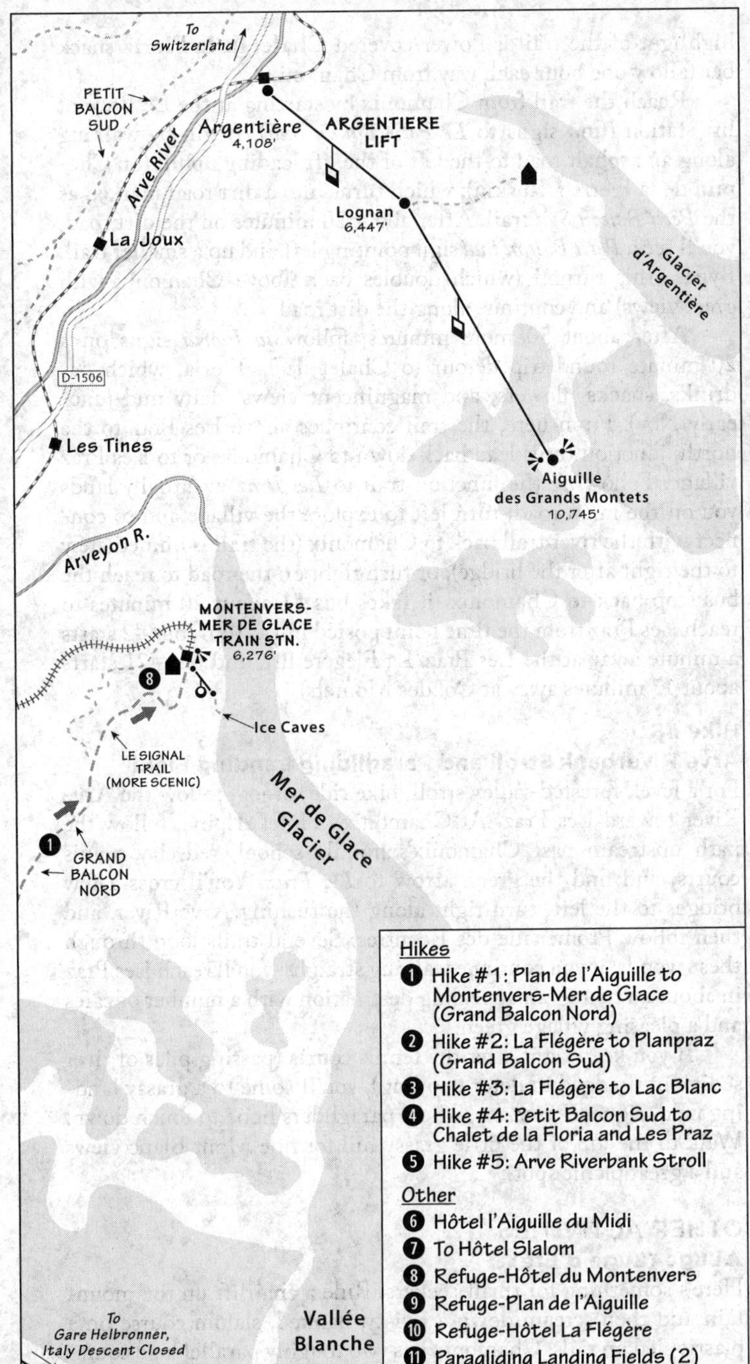
To Switzerland
PETIT BALCON SUD
Arve River
Argentière 4,108'
ARGENTIERE LIFT
Lognan 6,447'
Glacier d'Argentière
La Joux
D-1506
Les Tines
Aiguille des Grands Montets 10,745'
Arveyon R.
MONTENVERS-MER DE GLACE TRAIN STN. 6,276'
8
Ice Caves
LE SIGNAL TRAIL (MORE SCENIC)
Mer de Glace Glacier
1
GRAND BALCON NORD
To Gare Helbronner, Italy Descent Closed
Vallée Blanche
Hikes
1 Hike #1: Plan de l'Aiguille to Montenvers-Mer de Glace (Grand Balcon Nord)
2 Hike #2: La Flégère to Planpraz (Grand Balcon Sud)
3 Hike #3: La Flégère to Lac Blanc
4 Hike #4: Petit Balcon Sud to Chalet de la Floria and Les Praz
5 Hike #5: Arve Riverbank Stroll
Other
6 Hôtel l'Aiguille du Midi
7 To Hôtel Slalom
8 Refuge-Hôtel du Montenvers
9 Refuge-Plan de l'Aiguille
10 Refuge-Hôtel La Flégère
11 Paragliding Landing Fields (2)

FRENCH ALPS

highlight of the trail is flower-covered **Chalet de la Floria** snack bar (allow one hour each way from Chamonix).

Reach the trail from Chamonix by starting at the Le Brévent lift station (find signs to *Le Petit Balcon Sud*). Begin by walking along an asphalt road to the left of the lift leading uphill (on Chemin de la Pierre à Ruskin), which turns into a dirt road marked as the *Petit Balcon Sud* trail. After about 20 minutes on the dirt road, you'll see a *Petit Balcon Sud* sign pointing left and up a smaller trail. Bypass this turnoff (which doubles back above Chamonix with great views) and continue along the dirt road.

After about 30 more minutes, follow *la Floria* signs on a 20-minute round-trip detour to Chalet de la Floria, which has drinks, snacks, flowers, and magnificent views (daily mid-June-early Nov). From here, the trail continues above Les Praz to the north; junction trails lead back down to Chamonix or to Les Praz village. Following the junction trail to *Les Praz* eventually lands you on the main road; turn left to explore the village and to connect with the river trail back to Chamonix (the trail is immediately to the right after the bridge), or turn right on the road to reach the bus stop back to Chamonix (it takes bus #1 about 20 minutes to reach Les Praz from the time point posted in Le Tour; bus #2 starts a minute away at the Les Praz/La Flégère lift, and bus #21 starts about 17 minutes away at Col des Montets).

Hike #5
Arve Riverbank Stroll and Paragliding Landing Field

For a level, forested-valley stroll, bike ride, or jog, follow the Arve River toward Les Praz. At Chamonix's Hôtel Alpina, follow the path upstream past Chamonix's middle school, red-clay tennis courts, and find the green arrow to *Les Praz*. You'll cross a few bridges to the left, turn right along the rushing Arve River, and then follow Promenade des Econtres. Several trails loop through these woods; if you continue walking straight, you'll reach Les Praz in about an hour—an appealing destination with a number of cafés and a pleasing village green.

If you keep right after the tennis courts (passing piles of river sediment dredged to deter flooding), you'll come to a grassy landing field, signed *Parapente,* where paragliders hope to touch down. Walk to the top of the little grassy hill for fine Mont Blanc views and a great picnic spot.

OTHER ACTIVITIES

▲Luge (Luge d'Eté)

Here's something for thrill-seekers: Ride a chairlift up the mountain and then scream down a twisty, banked, slalom course on a plastic sled on rails. Chamonix has two roughly parallel luge courses: While each course is just longer than a half-mile and about the same speed, one is marked for slower sledders, the other for speed demons. Young or old, hare or tortoise, any fit person can manage a luge. *Freinez* signs tell you when to brake. The luge courses are set in a grassy park with kids' play areas.

Cost and Hours: One ride-€5.50, €7.50 for double sled; six rides-€31, €40 for double sled; kids under age 8 must ride with adult, entry includes all activities in Parc de Loisirs des Planards—see "Kids' Activities" on page 802; generally July-Aug daily 10:00-19:00, mid-April-June and Sept-Oct Sat-Sun and select weekdays 14:00-18:00, check website for hours; 15-minute walk from town center, over the tracks from train station and past Montenvers train station; tel. 04 50 53 08 97, www.chamonixparc.com.

▲▲▲Paragliding (Parapente)

When it's sunny and clear, the skies above Chamonix sparkle with colorful parachute-like sails that circle the valley like birds of prey. For about €100 plus the cost of the lift up to Plan de l'Aiguille, Planpraz station, or Le Brévent (€230 from the Aiguille du Midi for true thrill-seekers), you can launch yourself off a mountain in a tandem paraglider with a trained, experienced pilot and fly like a bird for about 20 minutes (40 minutes from Aiguille du Midi). Most pilots will meet you at the lift station in Chamonix (usually from Le Brévent side, though you can ask them to fly you from Plan de l'Aiguille if you'll be there anyway and are pressed for time—not possible July-Aug). **Sean Potts** is English (no language barrier) and easy to work with (info@fly-chamonix.com). You can also try **Summits Parapente** (smart to reserve a day ahead, open year-round, tel. 04 50 53 50 14, mobile 06 84 01 26 00, www.summits.fr).

For a sneak preview, walk to one of the two main landing areas and watch paragliders perfect their landings (see "Chamonix Area Hikes—Hike #5," earlier).

RAINY-DAY OPTIONS

If the weather disagrees with your plans, stay cool and check out the following options.

Alpine Museum (Musée Alpin)

Situated in one of Chamonix's oldest "palaces," this place has good exhibits about Chamonix's evolution from a farming area to one focused on skiing. The museum shows off Chamonix's mountaineering, skiing, and mineralogical history (explanations in French only) and has exhibits on the first Winter Olympics, held right here.

Cost and Hours: €6, includes Crystal Museum, daily 10:00-18:00 in summer, otherwise from 14:00, 89 Avenue Michel Croz, tel. 04 50 53 25 93.

Winter Sports in Chamonix

Chamonix offers some of the best expert-level skiing in the world, a huge choice of terrain at reasonable prices (cheaper than Switzerland), access to lots of high-elevation runs (which means good snow and views), and great nightlife. Ski here for jaw-dropping views and a good balance between true mountaineer culture and touristy glitz.

The slopes are strung out along the valley for about 10 miles, so you must drive or catch the often-crowded shuttle buses to ski more than one area. There's also limitless *off-piste* (ungroomed) skiing, best explored with an experienced guide.

Non-skiers won't be bored. The lifts described in this chapter lead to top-notch views. Swimming, saunas, tennis, skating, and climbing are available at Chamonix's Centre Sportif. You can also relax in a spa, go bowling or dog-sledding, and hike along groomed winter footpaths.

When to Go

High season is usually from December to mid-May. Chamonix is packed from Christmas through New Year's Day and busy in February and March (during European winter and spring breaks). It's quieter in early December, in January after New Year's, the second half of March, and in April (but Easter can be busy). Thanks to easy access to high-elevation runs, you'll usually find good powder in April and May, when it's less crowded. Chamonix is one of the great resorts for spring skiing, and you can usually find special spring package deals.

Tickets

Adult lift tickets covering Chamonix's three main areas, including the lower-elevation beginner areas, are €48/1 day, €90/2 days, €130/3 days, €170/4 days, €215/5 days (about 15 percent less for skiers older than 64 or younger than 16). Or consider the Mont Blanc Unlimited pass—covering all the areas in the Chamonix Valley (details on the websites listed later, under "Information").

Ski Rentals

Prices don't vary much, so go with something convenient to where you're staying and ask your hotel for deals with nearby shops. You'll pay about €14-24/day for skis and about €8-12/day for boots. **Technique Extrême** has the best deals on rentals and gear (tel. 04 50 53 38 25, 200 Avenue de l'Aiguille du Midi, www.technique-extreme.com). **Snell Sports** is a respected shop that's been around for many years (tel. 04 50 53 02 17, 104 Rue du Docteur Paccard, www.cham3s.com). **Sports Alpins** provides great service (tel. 04 50 53 13 60, 7 Place Edmond Désailloud, Chamonix Sud).

Where to Go

It's tough to find one area in Chamonix that offers a perfect mix of terrain for every level of skier, but here's a rundown of Chamonix's key ski areas:

Le Brévent/La Flégère—A 10-minute walk from Chamonix's center, this area has one of the valley's better mixes of terrain. If you're staying in Chamonix and have just a day, ski Le Brévent/La Flégère. Runs are good for intermediates, with some expert options, but not great for beginners. You'll enjoy fantastic views of Mont Blanc.

Les Grands Montets—Above the village of Argentière (about 10 minutes from Chamonix by bus), this area is internationally renowned for its expert terrain (and killer views from the observation deck). Part of Les Grands Montets lies on the Argentière glacier, and there's plenty of vertical. Hire a local guide to explore the *off-piste* options.

Les Houches—A five-minute bus or train ride from Chamonix, Les Houches covers a large area with a variety of runs for most skill levels (good for families), but it has fewer expert options. This area is less crowded than other Chamonix Valley areas, and the tree skiing is good.

Domaine de Balme—The area above the nearby town of Le Tour offers good options for beginners, intermediates, and those looking for mellow cruising runs.

Lower Areas Good for Beginners—Le Savoy is at the bottom of Le Brévent, near Chamonix's center, with scads of kids and a few rope-tows. Les Planards is a short walk from the town center and the largest area for kids and beginners. These areas depend on good snow conditions.

The Vallée Blanche—This unique-to-Chamonix run starts on the sky-high Aiguille du Midi lift and takes you 13 miles down a glacier past astounding views and terrain to Montenvers (easy train back to Chamonix). It requires a lift ticket and hiring a guide or joining a group tour (figure about €320 for a private tour of up to 4 people, €25/additional person, maximum 6 people).

Ski Guides

You can hire a private guide for about €300 for your group or join another group. The Compagnie des Guides de Chamonix (CGC) puts together small groups for about €80/person (tel. 04 50 53 00 88, www.chamonix-guides.com, info@chamonix-guides.com). Groups can accommodate strong intermediate through advanced skiers. Guides also give experts the option to ski even more difficult terrain.

Information

For general information about Chamonix and lift rates, check www.chamonix.com, www.leshouches.com, and www.compagniedumontblanc.fr, or contact the Chamonix TI.

Crystal Museum (Musée des Cristaux-Espace Tairraz)

This fascinating collection features crystals from the region in every color, shape, and size as well as an exhibit on the life of a mountain climber. My kids loved it. Pick up the basic brochure in English for some background.

Cost and Hours: €6, includes Alpine Museum, daily 14:00-19:00 plus 10:00-12:00 in summer, 615 Allée Recteur Payot, tel. 04 50 55 53 93.

Galerie Mario Colonel

Chamonix's most celebrated nature photographer displays his mesmerizing photographs of the scenery high above you. These are so good you may not miss seeing the real thing.

Cost and Hours: Free, daily 9:00-12:30 & 15:00-19:00, a block from the train station at 19 Rue Whymper, tel. 04 50 91 40 20, www.mario-colonel.com.

Day Trips near Chamonix

A Day in French-Speaking Switzerland

Plenty of tempting alpine and cultural thrills await just an hour or two away in Switzerland. A scenic road and rail route sneaks you from Chamonix to the Swiss town of Martigny. Train travelers cross without formalities, but drivers are charged a one-time fee of 40 Swiss francs (about €33) for a permit, known as a vignette, to use Swiss autobahns.

A Little Italy

The remote Valle d'Aosta and its historic capital city of Aosta offer a serious change of culture. Though you won't be able to take the lift over the Alps into *bella Italia* (because of construction at the Helbronner station), you can take the bus from Chamonix to Aosta (about €18 one-way, €28 round-trip, reservation required in summer, 4/day July-mid-Sept, 2/day mid-Sept-June, 2-3 hours). Get schedules at Chamonix's bus station (located at train station, tel. 04 50 53 01 15, www.sat-montblanc.com). For buses using the Mont Blanc tunnel, it's a two-hour trip to Aosta (otherwise it's at least three hours via Martigny). Drivers can travel straight through the Mont Blanc toll tunnel (one-way-€44, round-trip-€55 with return valid for 1 week, www.tunnelmb.com).

Sleeping in Chamonix

Reasonable hotels and dorm-like chalets abound in Chamonix, with easy parking and quick access from the train station. The TI can help you find budget accommodations anytime—either in person or by email (reservation@chamonix.com). Outside winter, mid-

July to mid-August is most difficult, when some hotels have five-day minimum-stay requirements. Very few hotels offer air-conditioning but most have elevators. Prices tumble off-season (outside July-Aug and Dec-Jan). Many hotels and restaurants are closed in April, June, and November, but you'll still find a room and a meal. If you want a view of Mont Blanc, ask for *côté Mont Blanc* (coat-ay mohn blah). Travelers who visit June through September should contemplate a night high above in a refuge-hotel.

All hoteliers speak English, and Wi-Fi is free unless otherwise noted. Price ranges usually reflect low-to-high season rates (low season is roughly March-June and Sept-Nov). Ask at your hotel about the free Chamonix Guest Card, which provides complimentary use of most buses and trains during your stay (described on page 793).

IN THE CITY CENTER

$$$ Hôtel Hermitage****, a 10-minute walk from the town center, is a gorgeous chalet hotel with the coziest lounges in Chamonix and a lovely garden with good kids' areas (swings, slides, ping-pong). It has a small bar (great stools) and 30 alpine-elegant rooms, all with balconies and reasonable prices considering the quality (standard Db-€116-134, larger rooms with Mont Blanc view-€155-250, Tb-€165-190, big family rooms and suites-€275-365, guest computer, Wi-Fi, easy parking, near train station at 63 Chemin du Cé, tel. 04 50 53 13 87, www.hermitage-paccard.com, info@hermitage-paccard.com).

$$$ Hôtel l'Oustalet*** is a chalet hotel that makes me feel like I'm in Austria. It's warmly run by two sisters (Véronique and Agnes), who understand the importance of good service. The place is family-friendly, with lots of grass, a big pool, and six family suites. All rooms are wood-paneled, with views and balconies (standard Db-€142, bigger Db with terrace-€160, Qb family rooms-€198, terrific breakfast-€14, try the *teurgoule* rice pudding, Wi-Fi, free and secure parking, near Aiguille du Midi lift at 330 Rue du Lyret, tel. 04 50 55 54 99, www.hotel-oustalet.com, infos@hotel-oustalet.com).

$$$ Hôtel Gourmets et Italy*** is a 37-room place with comfy public spaces, a cool riverfront terrace, balcony views from many of its appealing rooms, and a small pool (standard Db with shower-€110-130, larger Db with bath and Mont Blanc view-€130-160, a few good family rooms, extra person-€16, closed late April-early June and Nov, guest computer, Wi-Fi, 2 blocks from casino on Mont Blanc side of river, 96 Rue du Lyret, tel. 04 50 53 01 38, www.hotelgourmets-chamonix.com, info@hotelgourmets-chamonix.com).

$$ Hôtel Faucigny*** is a peaceful, polished place with a Scandinavian feel and a welcoming vibe. This full-service hotel

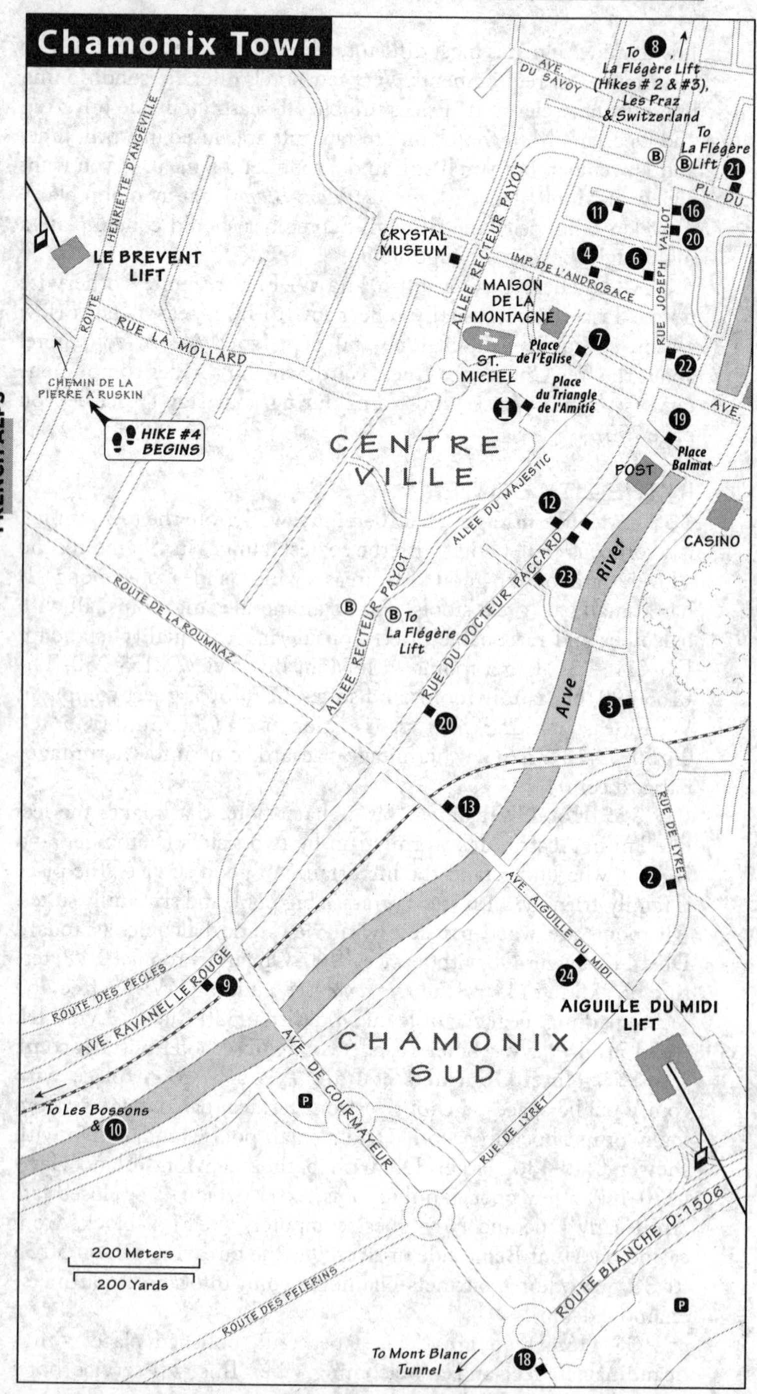
Chamonix Town
To 8, La Flégère Lift (Hikes # 2 & #3), Les Praz & Switzerland
To La Flégère Lift
AVE. DU SAVOY
PL. DU
RUE HENRIETTE D'ANGEVILLE
LE BREVENT LIFT
CRYSTAL MUSEUM
ALLEE RECTEUR PAYOT
IMP. DE L'ANDROSACE
RUE JOSEPH VALLOT
MAISON DE LA MONTAGNE
Place de l'Eglise
ST. MICHEL
Place du Triangle de l'Amitié
ROUTE
RUE LA MOLLARD
CHEMIN DE LA PIERRE A RUSKIN
HIKE #4 BEGINS
AVE.
CENTRE VILLE
POST
Place Balmat
CASINO
ALLEE DU MAJESTIC
RUE DU DOCTEUR PACCARD
Arve River
ROUTE DE LA ROUMNAZ
To La Flégère Lift
RUE DE LYRET
AVE. AIGUILLE DU MIDI
AIGUILLE DU MIDI LIFT
ROUTE DES PECLES
AVE. RAVANEL LE ROUGE
CHAMONIX SUD
AVE. DE COURMAYEUR
To Les Bossons & 10
RUE DE LYRET
ROUTE BLANCHE D-1506
200 Meters
200 Yards
ROUTE DES PELERINS
To Mont Blanc Tunnel

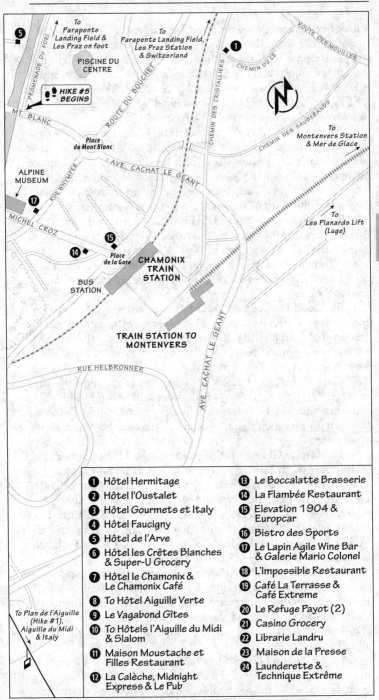

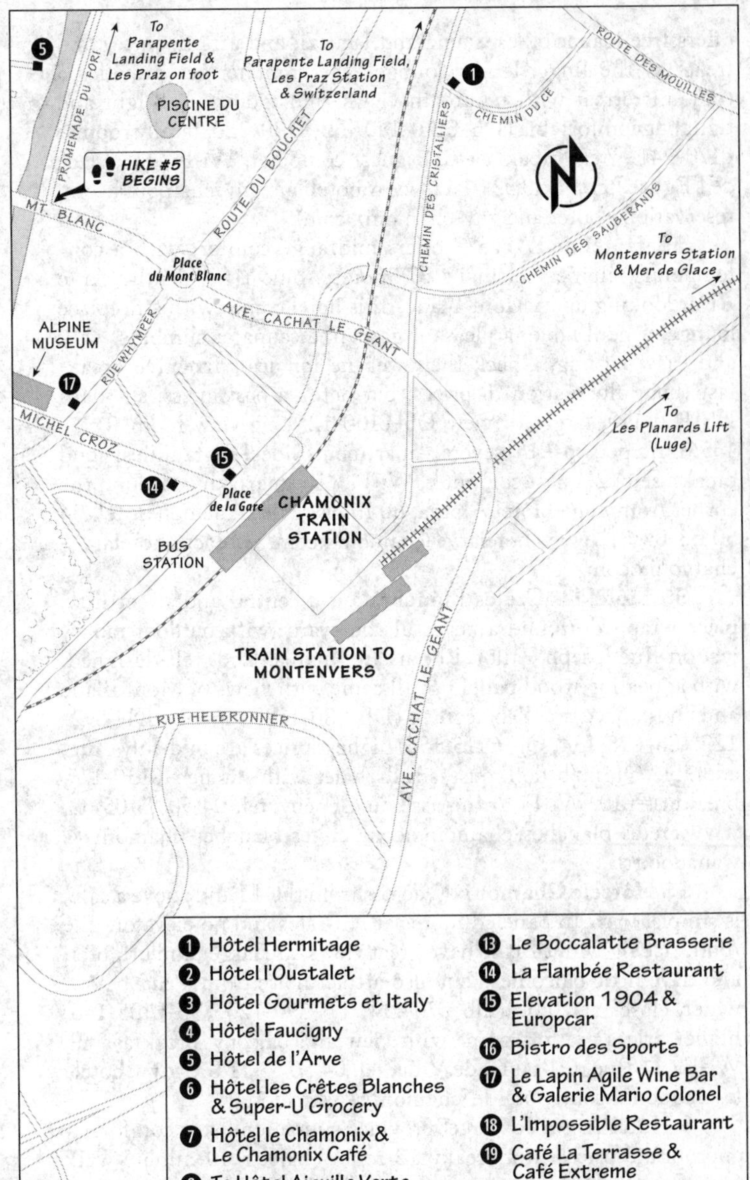
To Parapente Landing Field & Les Praz on foot
To Parapente Landing Field, Les Praz Station & Switzerland
ROUTE DES MOUILLES
CHEMIN DU CE
PROMENADE DU FORI
PISCINE DU CENTRE
HIKE #5 BEGINS
ROUTE DU BOUCHET
CHEMIN DES CRISTALLIERS
MT. BLANC
CHEMIN DES SAUBERANDS
To Montenvers Station & Mer de Glace
Place du Mont Blanc
AVE. CACHAT LE GEANT
ALPINE MUSEUM
RUE WHYMPER
MICHEL CROZ
To Les Planards Lift (Luge)
Place de la Gare
CHAMONIX TRAIN STATION
BUS STATION
TRAIN STATION TO MONTENVERS
RUE HELBRONNER
AVE. CACHAT LE GEANT
To Plan de l'Aiguille (Hike #1), Aiguille du Midi & Italy
1 Hôtel Hermitage
2 Hôtel l'Oustalet
3 Hôtel Gourmets et Italy
4 Hôtel Faucigny
5 Hôtel de l'Arve
6 Hôtel les Crêtes Blanches & Super-U Grocery
7 Hôtel le Chamonix & Le Chamonix Café
8 To Hôtel Aiguille Verte
9 Le Vagabond Gîtes
10 To Hôtels l'Aiguille du Midi & Slalom
11 Maison Moustache et Filles Restaurant
12 La Calèche, Midnight Express & Le Pub
13 Le Boccalatte Brasserie
14 La Flambée Restaurant
15 Elevation 1904 & Europcar
16 Bistro des Sports
17 Le Lapin Agile Wine Bar & Galerie Mario Colonel
18 L'Impossible Restaurant
19 Café La Terrasse & Café Extreme
20 Le Refuge Payot (2)
21 Casino Grocery
22 Librarie Landru
23 Maison de la Presse
24 Launderette & Technique Extrême

offers free loaner bikes, sauna and Jacuzzi, and afternoon tea and treats in the linger-longer lounge. The front terrace provides a tranquil retreat with mountain views, and rooms are bright and tight but comfortable (Db-€110-180, Tb-€130-220, family rooms-€170-240, great breakfast-€11, guest computer, Wi-Fi, 118 Place de l'Eglise, tel. 04 50 53 01 17, www.hotelfaucigny-chamonix.com, reservation@hotelfaucigny-chamonix.com).

$$ Hôtel de l'Arve*** offers midrange comfort with a contemporary alpine feel in its 37 rooms, some right on the Arve River looking up at Mont Blanc. This hotel comes with a fireplace lounge, a pool table, a pleasant garden, a sauna, a climbing wall, and easy parking. Check their website for deals like free breakfast (huge fluctuation in prices, but here's a best guess: standard Db-€80-110, larger or view Db-€100-125, big view room-€125-155, extra person-€15, several "apartments" ideal for families, good breakfast-€12, guest computer, Wi-Fi, private parking, around the corner from huge Hôtel Alpina, 60 Impasse des Anémones, tel. 04 50 53 02 31, www.hotelarve-chamonix.com, contact@hotelarve-chamonix.com).

$$ Hôtel les Crêtes Blanches** is a central and sweet little place wrapped around a peaceful courtyard (with outdoor tables) just off Rue Joseph Vallot. Rooms are smallish and well-designed, with appealing wood paneling; all come with views of Mont Blanc and most have small balconies (Db-€80-112, superior Db-€92-122, Tb-€98-134, Qb-€115-156, highest prices are mid-July-Aug, adorable Quint/b dollhouse-sized chalet with kitchen-€130-175, breakfast-€10, Wi-Fi, 6 Impasse du Génépy, tel. 04 50 53 05 62, www.cretes-blanches-chamonix.com, cretes-blanches-chamonix@wanadoo.fr).

$$ Hôtel le Chamonix,** across from the TI and above a café, is simple, with 16 paneled rooms at fair rates and no elevator. The rooms facing Mont Blanc have great views, are larger and brighter, and have little balconies...but also attract noise from *le café* below, which closes at 20:00 (Db-€70-114, Tb-€90-126, Qb-€105-146, higher prices are for rooms with view and balcony, breakfast-€9, Wi-Fi, 11 Rue de l'Hôtel de Ville, tel. 04 50 53 11 07, www.hotel-le-chamonix.com, hotel-le-chamonix@wanadoo.fr).

$ Hôtel Aiguille Verte* provides simple one-star comfort at appropriate prices in a creaky 12-room chalet a 10-minute walk from the center of town, toward the village of Les Praz. Rooms are clean and cheery; there's no elevator but only two floors to navigate (Db-€69-80, 633 Rue Joseph Vallot, tel. 04 50 53 01 73, hotel-aiguilleverte@orange.fr).

$ Le Vagabond Gîtes offers the best cheap digs in Chamonix in a fun chalet just south of the town center. Most rooms have four to six bunks, while the top floor is one big dorm with twenty beds.

All rooms have sinks. The owner is Welsh, the staff is a mix of other British expats, and the feel is relaxed, with a bar and outside terrace (€30-35/person, includes breakfast, one-time €5.50 charge for linens, reception closed 10:00-16:30, 305 Avenue Ravanel le Rouge, tel. 04 50 53 15 43, www.vaga.eu, info@vaga.eu).

NEAR CHAMONIX

If Chamonix overwhelms you, spend the night in one of the valley's often-overlooked, lower-profile villages.

$$$ Hôtel l'Aiguille du Midi*,** a mountain retreat, lies in the village of Les Bossons, about two miles from Chamonix toward Annecy. It's run by the English-speaking Farini family in a park-like setting with point-blank views of Mont Blanc and the Bossons Glacier. This family-friendly place has a swimming pool, a clay tennis court, table tennis, a massage room, and a laundry room to boot. The alpine-comfortable rooms come with Old World bathrooms, many have decks with views, and several are good for families. The classy restaurant offers à la carte and *menu* options, with *menus* from €26 (Db-€100-156, Tb-€136, Qb-from €150, ask for these special Rick Steves rates when you reserve, elevator, guest computer, Wi-Fi, easy by train, get off at Les Bossons, tel. 04 50 53 00 65, www.hotel-aiguilledumidi.com, info@hotel-aiguilledumidi.com).

$$ Hôtel Slalom*** in nearby little Les Houches makes a lovely, contemporary mountain base. The rooms and public spaces are stylish, and the owners are welcoming (Db-€100, 44 Rue de Bellevue, tel. 04 50 54 40 60, www.hotelslalom.net).

FRENCH ALPS

REFUGES AND REFUGE-HOTELS NEAR CHAMONIX

Chamonix has the answer for hikers who want to sleep high above, but aren't into packing it in: refuge-hotels (generally open mid-June to mid- or late September, depending on snow levels). Refuge-hotels usually have some private rooms (but mostly dorm rooms), hot showers down the hall, and restaurants. Most expect you to take dinner and breakfast there (a great value). Reserve in advance (a few days is generally enough), then pack a small bag for a memorable night among new international friends. The **Office de Haute-Montagne** in Chamonix can explain your options (see page 802).

$ Refuge-Hôtel du Montenvers, Chamonix's oldest refuge, delivers an Old World experience at the Montenvers train stop. It was built in 1880 as a climbing base for mountain guides before the train went there, so materials had to be gathered from nearby. The five simple wood-cozy rooms, top-floor dorm room (35 beds), and dining room feel as though they haven't been modified since then (open July-Aug only, half-pension in a double room-€63/person, in a dorm room-€44/person, good showers down the hall for all, tel. 04 50 53 14 14). For directions, see "Hike #1" on page 803.

$ Refuge-Plan de l'Aiguille is my favorite refuge experience near Chamonix. It's a small, welcoming, easy-to-reach refuge a 15-minute walk below the Plan de l'Aiguille lift, right on the trail between the Aiguille du Midi and Montenvers-Mer de Glace. It has a warm interior and a killer view café. The cook and guardian Claude is a retired pastry chef, so the meals are good and the desserts heavenly (open May-Oct only, €20/bed, half-pension-€46/person, towel-€2, cash only, mobile 06 65 64 27 53, claudius74@hotmail.com).

$ Refuge-Hôtel La Flégère hangs on the edge right at the La Flégère lift station. It's simple and big, but ideally located for hiking to Lac Blanc or Planpraz (open mid-June-mid-Sept only, 4 private rooms with 5 beds, big dorm room with 30 beds, required half-pension-€53/person, fireplace, cool bar-café, mobile 06 03 58 28 14, bellay.catherine@wanadoo.fr). For directions, see "Hike #2" on page 804.

Eating in Chamonix

You have two basic dining options in Chamonix—cozy, traditional *savoyarde* restaurants serving fondue, raclette, and the like, or cafés in central locations serving a wide variety of dishes (including regional specialties) that allow you to watch rivers of hikers return from a full day in the mountains. Prices are roughly the same. If it's a beautiful day, take an outdoor table at a central café (see the "View Cafés" section); if you're dining inside, go local and consider a place in or near the town center (most are closed between lunch and dinner). The regional cuisine is hearty and filling, as restaurants seek to satisfy ravenous hikers.

IN THE TOWN CENTER

Maison Moustache et Filles is named for the mustachioed owner whose daughter *(fille)* runs the place. It boasts a fun, ski-festooned interior, terrific outdoor patio, and delicious cuisine at reasonable prices. Locals love it, and the duck is delectable (€14-24 *plats,* €30 *menu,* €10 kid's menu with good burgers, closed Mon, 37 Impasse des Rhododendrons, tel. 04 50 93 49 68).

La Calèche presents tasty regional dishes in a warm, hyper-decorated alpine setting (pass on the outside seating). You'll dine amid antique dolls, cuckoo clocks, copper pots, animal trophies, and more (find the luge sled from the 1924 Olympic Games). Try the *potée savoyarde* (sausages with melted cheese) or meats grilled at your table on hot stones *(sur la pierre).* Don't leave without a visit to the WCs (€25 *menu,* the €30 *menu* is much better, daily, centrally located just off Place Balmat at 18 Rue du Docteur Paccard, tel. 04 50 55 94 68).

Le Boccalatte Brasserie, with a convivial atmosphere inside and out, serves a good-value lunch or dinner a few blocks above the Aiguille du Midi lift. The place is family-friendly and easygoing. The €16 *tartiflette* with salad will fill your belly, or choose from a large selection of other local specialties, big €11 salads, good pizzas, and 20 kinds of beer. It's run by English-speaking Thierry, a friendly Alsatian (daily 12:00-22:00, 59 Avenue de l'Aiguille du Midi, tel. 04 50 53 52 14).

La Flambée offers reasonable prices in a lively mosh pit of alpine paraphernalia served by a lighthearted staff. They cook up everything from burgers to pizza to fondue to steaks (€15-20 *plats,* €10-14 pizza or pasta dishes, closed Mon, a block from the train station at 232 Avenue Michel Croz, tel. 04 50 54 12 96).

Budget Meals: **Elevation 1904** is a down-and-dirty climbers' haunt across from the train station, serving cheap and tasty sandwiches, burgers, pasta, and salads (daily until about 22:30, Wi-Fi, 263 Avenue Michel Croz). **Bistro des Sports** dishes cheap *plats du jour* and *menus* amid a cacophony of noise in the back of their lively bar (daily, 176 Rue Joseph Vallot). **Midnight Express** serves good sandwiches until late and has a few outside tables across from the recommended La Calèche restaurant. Try a *pain en rond* (round-bread rustic sandwich), served hot *(chaud)* or cold *(froid).*

Drinks: If a pre-dinner glass of wine from anywhere in the world sounds appealing, hop on into little **Le Lapin Agile** for cozy ambience and a happy-hour buffet of finger foods—free if you purchase a drink (closed Mon, a block from the train station at 11 Rue Whymper, tel. 04 50 53 33 25).

FRENCH ALPS

AWAY FROM THE PEDESTRIAN CENTER

L'Impossible, housed in a beautiful farmhouse a 10-20-minute walk from most recommended hotels, is *the* place to go for refined organic cuisine with an Italian bias. Bring your food allergies: This place offers gluten-free, lactose-free, and fat-free (well, maybe not that) dishes without sacrificing flavor. Even if eating healthfully doesn't boost your boots, you'll appreciate the exquisite meals and attention to detail. Papa (who hails from Tuscany) cooks, while Mama and daughter Martha serve (€18-28 *plats,* €30-48 *menus,* daily, 5-minute walk from Aiguille du Midi lift on Route des Pélerins, tel. 04 50 53 20 36).

Après Hike: The **Bistro des Sports** is where locals hang their ice picks after a hard day in the mountains. Drinks are cheap, the crowd is loud, and the ambience works (see "Budget Meals," earlier). **Le Pub** is a good spot to raise a glass with the British crowd (225 Rue du Docteur Paccard, tel. 04 50 55 92 88).

View Cafés: High above Chamonix, many cafés excel in outdoor views, but here are several that I think stand above the rest. **La Bergerie,** at Planpraz station on Le Brévent, is hard to beat and offers surprisingly affordable drinks, snacks, and meals, as does the **Refuge-Plan de l'Aiguille** below Mont Blanc (15-minute walk from Plan de l'Aiguille lift station, described earlier under "Sleeping in Chamonix"). Back down in Chamonix, facing the TI a block off the action-packed pedestrian core, scenic **Le Chamonix Café** sits below Chamonix's pretty little church and has terrific views of both mountain ranges (daily until 20:00, Place de l'Eglise). **Café La Terrasse** has a cool location (literally) above the rush of the Arve River and is well-positioned for Mont Blanc views (daily until late, across from the casino on Place Balmat). **Café Extreme** is a relaxed place for cheap food and lovely views of the main square and mountains (daily, 31 Place du Joseph Balmat, tel. 04 50 21 99 45).

Chamonix Connections

Bus and train service to Chamonix is surprisingly good (information desks for both at the train station). Some train routes pass through Switzerland to reach Chamonix (such as from Paris and Colmar) and require supplements if you have a France-only rail pass. You can avoid passing through Switzerland if you plan ahead, but it usually takes longer, and you miss some great scenery. The **route to Colmar** (via Bern and Basel) is beautiful and costs roughly €60 for the Swiss segment. You'll get a fun taste of Switzerland's charms, and, though you'll make many transfers en route, they all work like a Swiss clock.

From Chamonix by Train to: Annecy (11/day, 2.5 hours, change in St-Gervais), **Beaune** and **Dijon** (7/day, 6-7 hours, change in St-Gervais and Lyon, some require additional changes), **Nice** (4/day, 10 hours, change in St-Gervais and Lyon), **Arles** (5/day, 7-8 hours, change in St-Gervais and Lyon), **Paris'** Gare de Lyon (7/day, more in summer and winter, 5.5-7 hours, some change in Switzerland), **Colmar** (hourly, 6 hours via Switzerland with 3-6 changes), **Martigny,** Switzerland (nearly hourly, 2 hours, scenic trip), **Geneva,** Switzerland, and its airport (roughly hourly, 3.5-5 hours, 2 changes).

From Chamonix by Bus to: Geneva Airport, Switzerland (3/day, about 3 hours), **Courmayeur,** Italy (4/day, 45 minutes), **Aosta,** Italy (4/day July-mid-Sept, 2/day mid-Sept-June, 2-3 hours). Long-distance buses depart from the train station—get information at the TI or at the bus station (tel. 04 50 53 01 15, www.sat-montblanc.com). For more on buses to Italy, see "Day Trips near Chamonix" on page 812.

Airport shuttles also provide service between Chamonix's city center and the airport in **Geneva,** Switzerland (2 hours). **Chamexpress** is British-run and easy to work with (€35/person, €26 if booked in advance online, desk near arrival gate, www.chamexpress.com). You can also try **Chamonix Taxis** (www.chamonix-transfer.com).

BURGUNDY

Beaune • Châteauneuf-en-Auxois • Semur-en-Auxois • Abbey of Fontenay • Flavigny-sur-Ozerain • Alise Ste-Reine • Vézelay • Château de Guédelon • Bourges • Cluny • Taizé

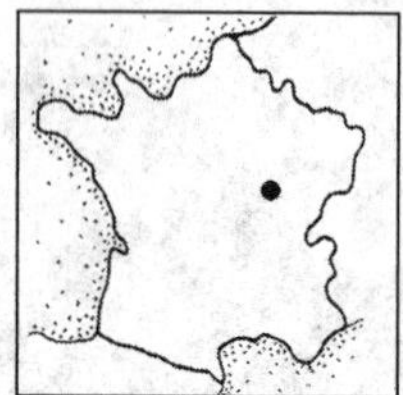

The rolling hills of Burgundy gave birth to superior wine, fine cuisine, spicy mustard, and sleepy villages smothered in luscious landscapes. This deceptively peaceful region witnessed Julius Caesar's defeat of the Gauls, then saw the Abbey of Cluny rise from the ashes of the Roman Empire to vie with Rome for religious influence in the 12th century. Burgundy's last hurrah came in the 15th century, when its powerful dukes controlled an immense area stretching north to Holland.

Today, bucolic Burgundy (roughly the size of Belgium) runs from about Auxerre in the north to near Lyon in the south, and it's crisscrossed with canals and dotted with quiet farming villages. It's also the transportation funnel for eastern France and makes a convenient stopover for travelers (car or train), with easy access north to Paris or Alsace, east to the Alps, and south to Provence.

Traditions are strong. In Burgundy, both the soil and the farmers who work it are venerated. Although many of the farms you see are growing grapes, only a small part of Burgundy is actually covered by vineyards.

This is a calm, cultivated, and serene region, where nature is as sophisticated as the people. If you're looking for quintessential French culture, you'll find it in Burgundy.

PLANNING YOUR TIME

With limited time, stay in or near Beaune. Plan on a half-day in Beaune and a half-day for the vineyards and countryside at its doorstep: Spend the morning in Beaune and the afternoon ex-

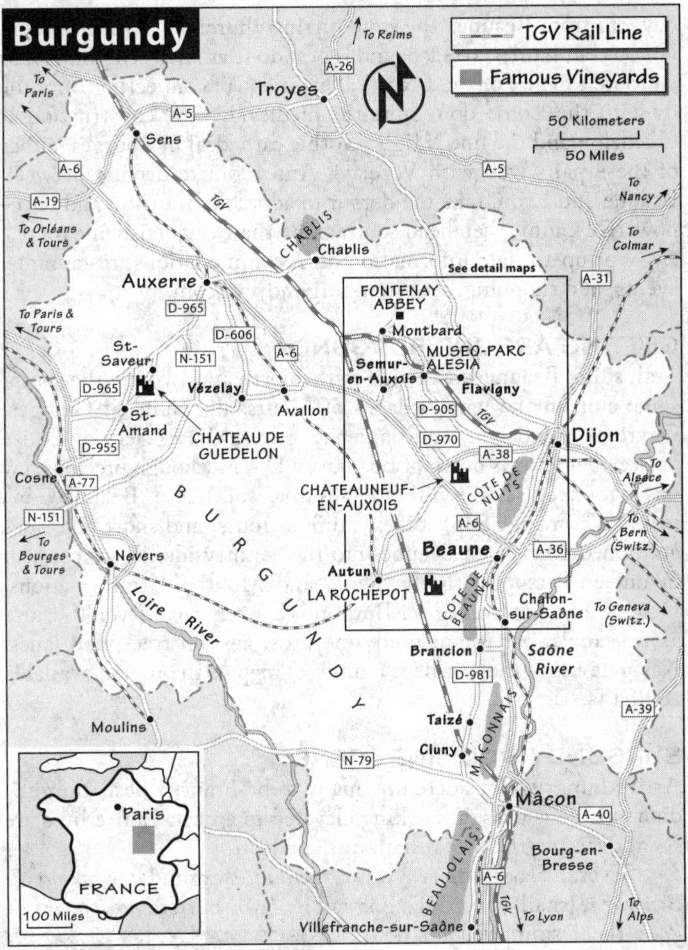

Burgundy

TGV Rail Line
Famous Vineyards
50 Kilometers
50 Miles
To Reims
A-26
Troyes
To Paris
A-5
Sens
A-6
A-19
To Orléans & Tours
TGV
CHABLIS
Chablis
To Nancy
To Colmar
See detail maps
A-31
Auxerre
D-965
To Paris & Tours
D-606
FONTENAY ABBEY
Montbard
St-Saveur
N-151
A-6
Semur-en-Auxois
MUSEO-PARC ALESIA
Flavigny
D-965
Vézelay
Avallon
D-905
St-Amand
CHATEAU DE GUEDELON
D-970
Dijon
D-955
A-38
Cosne
A-77
CHATEAUNEUF-EN-AUXOIS
COTE DE NUITS
To Alsace
N-151
BURGUNDY
A-6
To Bern (Switz.)
To Bourges & Tours
Nevers
Beaune
A-36
Autun
LA ROCHEPOT
Loire River
COTE DE BEAUNE
Chalon-sur-Saône
To Geneva (Switz.)
Brancion
Saône River
D-981
A-39
Moulins
Taizé
MACONNAIS
Cluny
N-79
Paris
Mâcon
A-40
FRANCE
Bourg-en-Bresse
100 Miles
BEAUJOLAIS
A-6
TGV
To Lyon
To Alps
Villefranche-sur-Saône

ploring the surrounding vineyards and wine villages (good by bike, car, or minibus tour). If you have a car (cheap rentals are available), or good legs and a bike, the best way to spend your afternoon is by following my scenic vineyard drive to Château de la Rochepot.

To explore off-the-beaten-path Burgundy, visit unspoiled Semur-en-Auxois or Flavigny-sur-Ozerain, the museum dedicated to the historic victory that won Gaul for Julius Caesar (in Alise Ste-Reine), and France's best-preserved medieval abbey complex at Fontenay. These are all close to each other and on the way to Paris, or doable as a long day trip from Beaune. The soul-stirring church at Vézelay is more famous but harder to reach, and is best done as an overnight trip, or en route to Paris or the Loire Valley. If you're connecting Burgundy with the Loire, don't miss the medieval castle construction at Guédelon and the fine "High" Gothic cathedral in Bourges (either of these pairs well with Vézelay). And if you're driving between Beaune and Lyon, take the detour to adorable Brancion and once-powerful Cluny, then head south along the Beaujolais wine route.

For up-to-date information on accommodations, restaurants, events, and shopping, see www.burgundyeye.com.

GETTING AROUND BURGUNDY

Trains link Beaune with Dijon to the north and Lyon to the south; some stop in the wine villages of Meursault, Nuits St-Georges, Gevrey-Chambertin, and Santenay. Several buses per day cruise between vineyards north of Beaune on D-974, though precious few buses connect Beaune with villages to its south (see "Beaune Connections" on page 848). Bikes, minibus tours, and short taxi rides get non-drivers from Beaune into the countryside. Buses connect Semur-en-Auxois with the Dijon and Montbard train stations. Drivers enjoy motoring on Burgundy's lovely roads; you'll cruise along canals, past manicured vineyards, and on tree-lined lanes. Navigate using the excellent (and free) map of the region available at all TIs.

BURGUNDY'S CUISINE SCENE

Arrive hungry. Considered by many to be France's best, Burgundian cuisine is peasant cooking elevated to an art. Entire lives are spent debating the best restaurants and bistros.

Several classic dishes were born in Burgundy: *escargots de Bourgogne* (snails served sizzling hot in garlic butter), *bœuf bourguignon* (beef simmered for hours in red wine with onions and mushrooms), coq au vin (rooster stewed in red wine), and *œufs en meurette* (poached eggs in a red wine sauce, often served on a large crouton), as well as the famous Dijon mustards. Look also for delicious *jambon persillé* (cold ham layered in a garlic-parsley gelatin), *pain d'épices* (spice bread), and *gougères* (light, puffy cheese pastries). Those white cows (called Charolais) dotting the green pastures are Burgundian and make France's best steak and *bœuf bourguignon*.

Native cheeses are Époisses and Langres (both mushy and great) and my favorite, Montrachet (a tasty goat cheese). Crème de cassis (black currant liqueur) is another Burgundian specialty; look for it in desserts and snazzy drinks (try a *kir*).

Remember, restaurants serve only during lunch (11:30-14:00) and dinner (19:00-21:00, later in bigger cities); some cafés serve food throughout the day.

BURGUNDY'S WINES

Along with Bordeaux, Burgundy is why France is famous for wine. From Chablis to Beaujolais, you'll find great fruity reds, dry whites, and crisp rosés. The three key grapes are chardonnay (dry white wines), pinot noir (medium-bodied red wines), and gamay (light, fruity red wines, such as Beaujolais). Sixty percent of the wines are white, thanks to the white-only impact of the Chablis and Mâcon regions.

The Romans brought winemaking knowledge with them to Burgundy more than 2,000 years ago, but it was medieval monks who perfected the art a thousand years later, establishing the foundations for Burgundy's famous wines. Those monks determined that pinot noir and chardonnay grapes grew best with the soil and climate in this region, a lesson that is followed to the letter by winemakers today. The French Revolution put capitalists in charge of the vineyards (no longer a monkish labor of love), which led to quantity over quality and a loss of Burgundy's esteemed status. Phylloxera insects destroyed most of Burgundy's vines in the late 1800s, and forced growers to rethink how and where to best cultivate grapes in Burgundy. This led to a return of the monks' approach, with the veneration of pinot noir and chardonnay grapes, a focus on quality over quantity, and a big reduction in the land area devoted to vines.

Today the government controls how much farmers can produce (to sustain high quality). This has a huge effect—in Burgundy, the average yield is only about 40 hectoliters per hectare (about 1,000 gallons), whereas in California it's more than double that. There are about 4,200 wineries in 44 villages in Burgundy. (I describe about a third of them in this chapter—it's a dirty job...) The wineries are tiny here (12-15 acres on average) thanks to Napoleon, who determined that land should be equally divided among a family's children when parents died. In many cases a farmer owns just a few rows in a vineyard and pieces together enough parcels to make a go of it.

In Burgundy, location is everything, and winery names take a back seat to the place where the grape is grown. Every village produces its own distinctive wine, from Chablis to Meursault to Chassagne-Montrachet. Road maps read like fine-wine lists. If the wine village has a hyphenated name, the second half usually comes from the town's most important vineyard (such as Gevrey-Chambertin, Aloxe-Corton, and Vosne-Romanée).

Burgundy wines are divided into four classifications: From top to bottom you'll find *grand cru, premier cru* (or *1er cru*), *village,* and *Bourgogne.* Each level allows buyers to better pinpoint the quality and origin of the grapes in their wine. With *Bourgogne* wines, the grapes can come from anywhere in Burgundy; *village* identifies the exact village where they were grown; and *grand cru* and *premier cru* locate the actual plots of land. As you drop from top to bottom, production increases—there is far more *Bourgogne* made than *grand cru.* In general, the less wine a vine produces, the higher the quality.

Look for *Dégustation Gratuite* (free tasting) signs, and prepare for serious wine-tasting—and steep prices, if you're not careful. For a more easygoing tasting experience, head for the hills: The less prestigious Hautes-Côtes (upper slopes) produce some terrific, inexpensive, and overlooked wines. The least expensive wines are Bourgogne and Passetoutgrain (both red) and whites from the Mâcon and Chalon areas (St-Véran whites are also a good value). If you like rosé, try Marsannay, considered one of France's best. And *les famous* Pouilly-Fuissé grapes are grown near the city of Mâcon. For tips on tasting, see the sidebar on page 1072.

Beaune

You'll feel comfortable right away in this prosperous, popular, and perfectly French little wine capital, where life centers on the production and consumption of the prestigious Côte d'Or wines. *Côte d'Or* means "Gold Coast" (from when the sea covered the valley in the Jurassic era), and the "coast" here is a spectacle to enjoy in late October as the leaves turn.

Medieval monks and powerful dukes of Burgundy laid the groundwork that established this town's prosperity. The monks cultivated wine and cheese, and the dukes cultivated power. A ring road (with a bike path) follows the foundations of the medieval walls, and parking lots just outside keep most traffic from seeping into the historic center. One of the world's most important wine auctions takes place here every year on the third weekend of November.

Orientation to Beaune

Beaune is compact (pop. 25,000), with a handful of interesting monuments and vineyards knocking at its door. Limit your Beaune ramblings to the town center, lassoed within its medieval walls and circled by a one-way ring road, and leave time to stroll into the vineyards. All roads and activities converge on the town's two squares, Place Carnot and Place de la Halle. Beaune is quiet on Sundays and Monday mornings. The city's monuments are beautifully lit at night, making Beaune ideal for a post-dinner stroll.

TOURIST INFORMATION

The main TI is located across from the post office on the ring road's southeastern corner (look for the *Porte Marie de Bourgogne* sign above the doorway; daily 9:00-19:00, closes at 18:00 on Sun and from 12:00-13:00 Nov-March, tel. 03 80 26 21 30, www.beaune-tourism.com). A small TI annex (called "Point-I") is housed in the market hall, across from Hôtel Dieu, and has similar hours. The main TI offers free Wi-Fi and rents audioguides for visiting Beaune (€5, 1.5 hours); both TIs have extensive information on wine tasting in the area, a room-finding service, a list of *chambres d'hôtes,* bus schedules, and an excellent, free road map of the region. They can also arrange a local guide (€144/2 hours, €196/4 hours, €340/all day). Skip the TI's €3 bike map; you'll get what you need for free from your bike rental shop.

Ambitious sightseers may benefit by buying the **Pass Beaune,** which gets you a discount at most key sights in Burgundy (including Hôtel Dieu and the wine museum in Beaune, Abbey of Fontenay, the site of the Cluny Abbey, the museum at Alésia, and Château of Clos Vougeot) and most major wine cellars (including the recommended Patriarche Père et Fils and Sensation Vin wine-tastings). The catch: You have to decide what you're going to see when you buy the pass, so you're committed to visiting those attractions (5 percent off 2 sights, 10 percent off 3 sights, 15 percent off 4 or more sights; buy at the TI).

For a shortcut into Beaune's center from the main TI, walk out the back door, cross a small street, continue straight through a long courtyard, and land on Place Carnot.

ARRIVAL IN BEAUNE

By Train: To reach the city center from the train station (no baggage storage), walk straight out of the station up Avenue du 8 Septembre, cross the busy ring road, and continue up Rue du Château. Follow it as it angles left and pass the mural, veering right onto Rue des Tonneliers. A left on Rue de l'Enfant leads to Beaune's pedestrian zone and Place Carnot.

Beaune's Best Wine and Food Stores

Beaune overflows with wine boutiques eager to convince you that their food products or wines are best. Here are a few to look for (to locate these, see the map on page 830).

The wine shop **Denis Perret,** which has a helpful English-speaking staff managed by friendly Alain, offers a good selection in all price ranges, though most are from large merchants *(négociants)*. They can chill a white for your picnic (Mon-Sat 9:00-12:00 & 14:00-19:00, closed Sun afternoon, 40 Place Carnot, tel. 03 80 22 35 47, www.denisperret.fr).

For an exquisite selection of fruit liqueurs (such as crème de cassis—a Burgundian treat), fruit syrups, and Burgundian brandy, find **Védrenne** at 28 Rue Carnot (closed Sun).

For food, **Alain Hess** offers an elegant display of local cheeses, mustards, and other gourmet food products (7 Place Carnot). At the corner, **Mulot-Petitjean Pain d'Epices** shows off exquisite packages of this tasty local spice bread, also handy as gifts (1 Place Carnot).

By Bus: Beaune has no bus station—only several stops along the ring road (see map on page 830 for stop locations). Ask the driver for *le Centre-Ville.* The Jules Ferry (zhul fair-ee) stop is central and closest to the train station. (For details on bus service, see "Getting Around the Beaune Region" on page 848.)

By Car: Follow *Centre-Ville* signs to the ring road. Once on the ring road, turn right at the first signal after the modern post office (Rue d'Alsace), and park for free a block away in Place Madeleine. If the lot is full—which it often is—spaces usually open up before long. The free Parking du Jardin Anglais at the north end of the ring road (see map on page 830) usually has spaces, and there's parking all along the ring road. Parking inside Beaune's ring road is metered from 9:00-12:30 and 14:00-19:00; there's a convenient parking garage next to the main TI on the ring road.

HELPFUL HINTS

Market Days: Beaune hosts a smashing Saturday market and a smaller Wednesday market. Both are centered on Place de la Halle and are open until 12:30. The Saturday market fires up much of the old town and is worth planning ahead for. For either market, watch the action from the **Baltard Café** on Place de la Halle, then do as the locals do and have lunch at an outdoor café (many good choices—see "Eating in Beaune," later, for ideas; sit down by 12:30 or forget it).

Supermarkets: Supermarché Casino has several small shops in Beaune, a store in the town center on Rue Carnot, and a mother-ship store located through the arch off Place Madeleine (Mon-Sat 8:30-20:00, closed Sun except summer mornings).

Internet Access: The **main TI** offers free Wi-Fi, as does **Dix Carnot Café**—provided you consume (daily 8:00-19:00, on Place Carnot next to the Athenaeum's back-door entrance). The recommended **Bistrot Bourguignon** offers Wi-Fi with wine.

Post Office: The main post office is at 7 Boulevard St Jacques. A handy Poste annex sells stamps and Colissimo boxes for international shipping (see page 1087), as well as credit for any mobile phone (Tue-Fri 13:00-17:00, closed Sat-Mon, 37 Rue Carnot).

Laundry: Beaune's lone launderette is open daily 7:00-21:00 (65 Rue Lorraine).

Bike Rental: See "Getting Around the Beaune Region—By Bike" on page 848.

Taxi: Call 06 11 83 06 10 or 06 09 35 63 12.

Car Rental: ADA is cheap and close to the train station (allow €60/day for a small car that includes 100 kilometers—about 60 miles, Mon-Sat 8:00-12:00 & 14:00-18:00, closed Sun, 26 Avenue du 8 Septembre, tel. 03 80 22 72 90). **Avis** is at the train station (tel. 03 80 24 96 46), and **Europcar** is less centrally located (53 Route de Pommard, tel. 03 80 22 32 24).

Cooking Experience: Enthusiastic American chef **Marjorie Taylor** invites traveling foodies to her beautifully appointed, light-filled boutique for a pricey but fun food experience. Marjorie offers a market-day tour of Beaune, followed by a cooking demonstration (there's little cooking instruction) and a five-course lunch with basic wine (€250/person, Sat and Wed best for the market-day experience, www.thecooksatelier.com, marjorie@thecooksatelier.com).

Best Souvenir Shopping: The **Athenaeum** has a great variety of souvenirs, including wine and cookbooks in English, with a good children's section. They also offer wine tastings—for three wines, figure €15 (daily 10:00-19:00, across from Hôtel Dieu at 7 Rue de l'Hôtel Dieu). **Le Vigneron,** at 6 Rue d'Alsace, is crammed with wine-related stuff, French knives, and more.

Tours in and Around Beaune

Tourist Train

A TGV-esque little "Visiotrain" will show you Beaune and nearby vineyards (€7.50, runs April-Oct 11:00-17:00, almost hourly departures from Hôtel Dieu, no morning trips on Wed and Sat market days, 45 minutes).

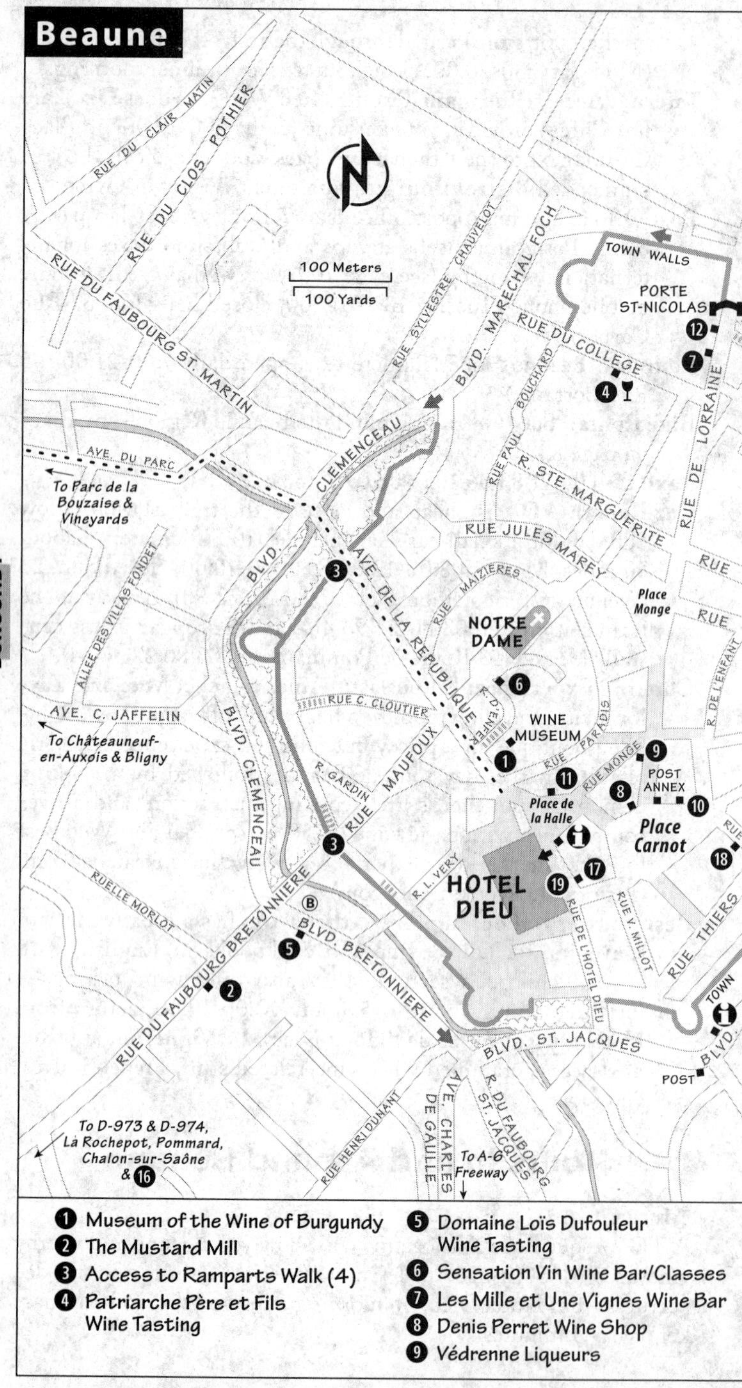
Beaune
100 Meters
100 Yards
RUE DU CLAIR MATIN
RUE DU CLOS POTHIER
RUE DU FAUBOURG ST. MARTIN
RUE SYLVESTRE CHAUVELOT
BLVD. MARECHAL FOCH
TOWN WALLS
PORTE ST-NICOLAS
RUE DU COLLEGE
RUE PAUL BOUCHARD
R. STE. MARGUERITE
RUE DE LORRAINE
RUE JULES MAREY
AVE. DU PARC
To Parc de la Bouzaise & Vineyards
BLVD. CLEMENCEAU
AVE. DE LA REPUBLIQUE
RUE MAIZIERES
NOTRE DAME
Place Monge
RUE
RUE
R. DE L'ENFANT
ALLEE DES VILLAS FONDET
AVE. C. JAFFELIN
To Châteauneuf-en-Auxois & Bligny
RUE C. CLOUTIER
F. D'ENFER
WINE MUSEUM
RUE PARADIS
RUE MONGE
POST ANNEX
Place de la Halle
Place Carnot
R. GARDIN
RUE MAUFOUX
BLVD. CLEMENCEAU
RUELLE MORLOT
R. L. VERY
HOTEL DIEU
RUE V. MILLOT
RUE THIERS
RUE DE L'HOTEL DIEU
TOWN
RUE DU FAUBOURG BRETONNIERE
BLVD. BRETONNIERE
BLVD. ST. JACQUES
BLVD.
POST
To D-973 & D-974, La Rochepot, Pommard, Chalon-sur-Saône & 16
RUE HENRI DUNANT
AVE. CHARLES DE GAULLE
To A-6 Freeway
R. DU FAUBOURG ST. JACQUES
1 Museum of the Wine of Burgundy
2 The Mustard Mill
3 Access to Ramparts Walk (4)
4 Patriarche Père et Fils Wine Tasting
5 Domaine Loïs Dufouleur Wine Tasting
6 Sensation Vin Wine Bar/Classes
7 Les Mille et Une Vignes Wine Bar
8 Denis Perret Wine Shop
9 Védrenne Liqueurs

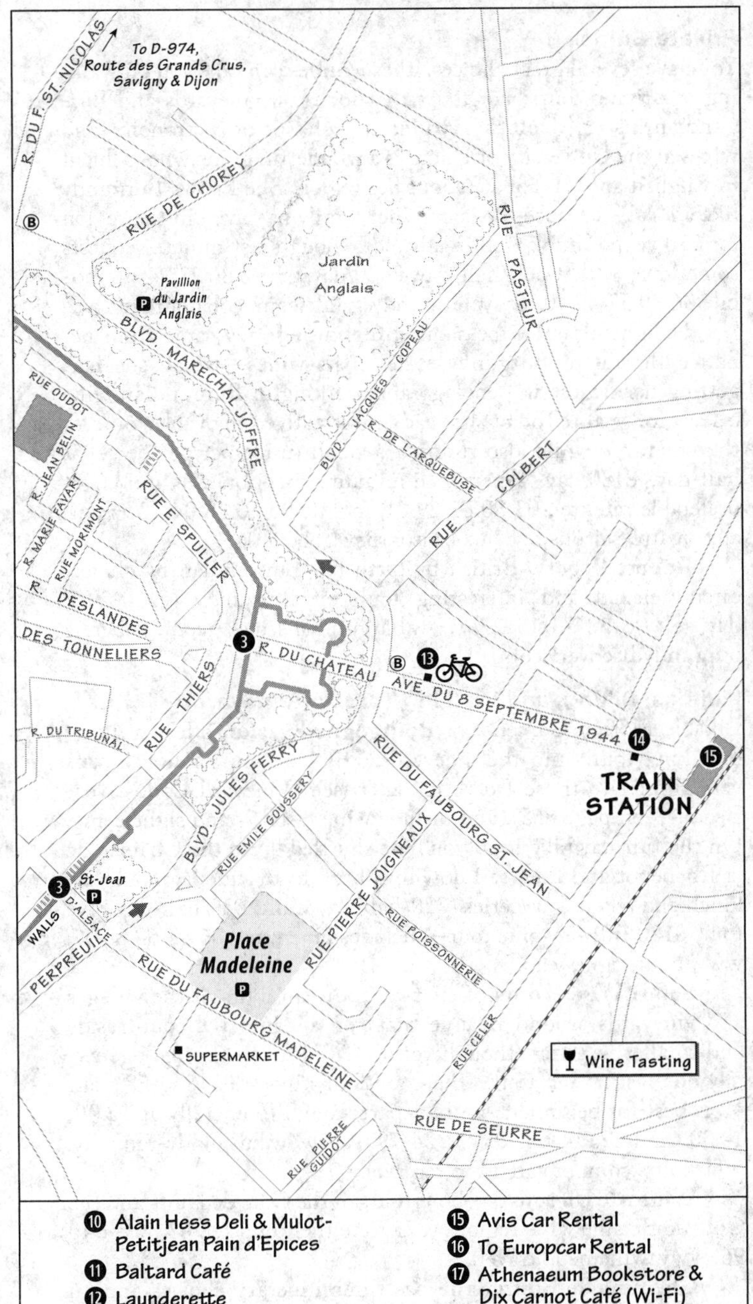

- ❿ Alain Hess Deli & Mulot-Petitjean Pain d'Epices
- ⓫ Baltard Café
- ⓬ Launderette
- ⓭ Bike Rental
- ⓮ ADA Car Rental
- ⓯ Avis Car Rental
- ⓰ To Europcar Rental
- ⓱ Athenaeum Bookstore & Dix Carnot Café (Wi-Fi)
- ⓲ Le Vigneron Shop
- ⓳ Tourist Train Departures

Private Guides

You have several great choices. These guides can take you on walking or driving tours. For tours that focus on vineyards and Burgundian history, **Colette Barbier,** a professor of gastronomy and wines at the University of Dijon, is a wonderful guide who is fluent in English and passionate about her region. She knows Burgundy like a local—because she is one (her family has lived in the region for 250 years). Book well in advance, though last-minute requests sometimes work (€260/half-day, €420/day, tel. 03 80 23 94 34, mobile 06 80 57 47 40, www.burgundy-guide.com, cobatour@sfr.fr).

Delightful and wine-smart **Stephanie Jones** came from her native Britain to Burgundy to learn its wines—which she has, getting her degree in oenology and working in Burgundian wine cellars for years. Today she leads informative, enjoyable tours of the vineyards while also running a B&B (price per person: €95/half-day, €180/day, 2-person minimum, mention this guide for preferable rate, tel. 03 80 61 29 61, mobile 06 10 18 04 12, www.aux-quatre-saisons.net, aux4saisons35@aol.com).

Robert Pygott, British by birth but Burgundian by choice, offers relaxed and interesting tours of Burgundy (€210-240/day, tel. 06 38 53 15 27, www.burgundydiscovery.com, robert@burgundydiscovery.com).

Minibus, Biking, and Walking Tours of Vineyards

Likable Florian Garcenot at **Bourgogne Evasion** offers walking or biking tours into the vineyards. His bike tours follow routes very similar to those I describe later (see "Vineyard Loops Near Beaune," on page 855), and include wine tastings and sightseeing. On the full-day bike tour, you'll be shuttled up to the Château de la Rochepot and then sail downhill back to Beaune, stopping for lunch and at a few wineries (€20/half-day walk, €29/half-day bike tour, €120/full-day bike tour—includes lunch, tel. 06 64 68 83 57, www.bourgogne-velo.fr).

Safari Wine Tours offers two-hour van tours of the villages and vineyards around Beaune that get you into the countryside and smaller wineries (though you won't do much tasting—generally one tasting per tour). There are four itineraries (€40-58, tour #2 is best for beginners; tours depart from TI generally at 12:00, 14:30, and 17:00; tel. 03 80 24 79 12, www.burgundy-tourism-safaritours.com, or call TI to reserve).

Wine Me Up runs 3.5-hour tours of the Côte de Nuits and the Côte de Beaune wine regions (€75 for either tour, tel. 03 80 24 40 96, www.winemeup.travel).

Chemins de Bourgogne has three itinerary choices and an SUV to get you off the beaten path (€50-60/half-day, €115/all-day, tel. 06 60 43 68 86, www.chemins-de-bourgogne.com).

Sights in Beaune

▲▲▲Hôtel Dieu des Hospices de Beaune

This medieval charity hospital is now a museum. The Hundred Years' War and the plague (a.k.a. the Black Death) devastated Beaune, leaving three-quarters of its population destitute. Nicholas Rolin, chancellor of Burgundy (enriched, in part, by his power to collect taxes), had to do something for "his people" (or, more likely, was getting old and wanted to close out his life on a philanthropic, rather than a greedy, note). So, in 1443 Rolin paid to build this place. It was completed in just eight years and served as a hospital until 1971, when the last patient checked out. You'll notice Hospices de Beaune on wine labels in fine shops—they are Burgundy's largest landowner of precious vineyards, thanks to donations made by patients over the centuries (and still happening today). Besides its magnificently decorated exterior, the Hôtel Dieu is famous for Rogier van der Weyden's superb *Last Judgment* altarpiece, which Rolin commissioned.

Cost and Hours: €7, includes audiovisual guide, daily April-mid-Nov 9:00-18:30, mid-Nov-March 9:00-11:30 & 14:00-17:30, last entry one hour before closing; it's dead center in Beaune, dominating Place de la Halle; tel. 03 80 24 45 00, www.hospices-de-beaune.com.

➲ **Self-Guided Tour:** While the audiovisual guide delivers key facts and good information, this self-guided tour will give your visit more meaning. Tour the rooms, which circle the courtyard, in a clockwise direction (following *Sens de la Visite* signs). To start your visit, enter the courtyard and find the stone bench.

Courtyard of Honor: Honor meant power, and this was all about showing off. The exterior of the hospital and the town side of the courtyard are intentionally solemn, so as not to attract pesky 15th-century brigands and looters. The dazzling inner courtyard features a colorful glazed tile roof, establishing what became a style recognized in France as typically "Burgundian." The sturdy tiles, which last 300 years, are fired three times: once to harden, again to burn in the color, and finally for the glaze. They were redone in 1902. The building is lacy Flamboyant Gothic with lots of decor—and boasts more weathervanes than any other building in France. Now enter the hospice halfway down the courtyard on the left.

Paupers' Ward: This grandest room of the hospital was the ward for the poorest patients. The vault, typical of big medieval rooms, was constructed like the hull of a ship. The screen separates the ward from the chapel at the front. Every three hours, the door was opened, and patients could experience Mass from their beds. Study the ceiling. Crossbeams are held by the mouths of creatively carved monsters—each mouth is stretched realistically, and each face has individual characteristics. Between the crossbars are busts of real 15th-century townsfolk—leading citizens, with animals humorously indicating their foibles (for example, a round-faced glutton next to a pig).

The carved wooden statue over the door you just entered shows a bound Christ—demonstrating graphically to patients that their Savior suffered and was able to empathize with their ordeal. Its realism shows that Gothic art had moved beyond the stiff formality of Romanesque carving. Behind the little window next to the statue was the nuns' dorm. The sisters (who were the first nurses) would check on patients from here. Notice the scrawny candleholder; if a patient died in the night, the candle was extinguished.

Find the small tables near the beds on the right. Rolin, who believed every patient deserved dignity, provided each patient with a pewter jug, mug, bowl, and plate. A painting on an easel at the left shows patients being treated in this room in 1949, 500 years after the hospital's founding. During epidemics, there were two to a bed. The ward didn't get heat until the 19th century (notice the heating grates on the floor), and the staff didn't get the concept of infection (and the basic practices of hand-washing) until the late 19th century (thanks to Louis Pasteur). Before then, most patients would have been better off left in a ditch outside.

Chapel: The hospice was not a place of hope. People came here to die. Care was more for the soul than the body. (Local guides are routinely instructed in writing by American tour companies not to use the word "hospice," because it turns off their clients. But this was a hospice, plain and simple, and back then, death was apparently less disturbing.) The stained glass shows Nicolas Rolin (lower left) and his wife, Guigone (lower right), dressed as a nun to show her devotion. Nicolas' feudal superior, the Duke of Burgundy, is portrayed above him. Notice the action on Golgotha. As Jesus is crucified, the souls of the two criminals crucified with him (portrayed as miniature naked humans) are being snatched up—one by an angel and the other by a red devil. At the bottom, Mary cradles the dead body of Christ. You're standing on tiles with the love symbol (or "gallant device") designed by Nicolas and Guigone to celebrate their love (as noble couples often did). The letters *N* and *G* are entwined in an oak branch, meaning that their love was strong. The word *seule* ("only one") and the lone star declare that Guigone is the only star in Nicolas' cosmos.

St. Hugue Ward: In the 17th century, this smaller ward was established for wealthy patients (who could afford Cadillac insurance plans). They were more likely to survive, and the decor displays themes of hope, rather than resignation: The series of Baroque paintings lining the walls shows the biblical miracles that Jesus performed. As the wealthy would lie in their beds, they'd stare at the ceiling—a painting with the bottom of an angel's foot, surrounded by the sick waiting to be healed by Jesus in his scarlet robe. An exhibit describes the hospital's gradual transition to modern practices.

St. Nicolas Room: Originally divided into smaller rooms—one used for "surgery" (a.k.a. bloodletting and amputation), the other as an extension of the kitchen that you'll see next—this room now holds a model of the steep roof support and more tools of the doctoring trade (amputation saws, pans for bloodletting, and so on). The glass panel in the floor's center shows the stream running below; the hole provided a primitive but convenient disposal system after dinner or surgery. Living downstream from the hospital was a bad idea. Notice the display case showing the *Vente aux Enchères des Hospices de Beaune.* Operation of the hospice was primarily funded through auctioning its great wines (made from land donated by grateful patients over the years). Today, the auction of Hospices de Beaune wines is an internationally followed event, and gives the first indication of prices for the previous year's wines. Proceeds from the auction still support the "modern" hospital in Beaune.

Kitchen: The kitchen display shows a 16th-century rotisserie. When fully wound, the cute robot would crank away, and the spit would spin slowly for 45 minutes. The 19th-century stove provided running hot water, which spewed from the beaks of swans. A five-minute, French-only sound-and-light show runs every 15 minutes.

Pharmacy: The nuns grew herbs out back, and strange and wondrous concoctions were mixed, cooked, and then stored in pottery jars. The biggest jar (by the window in the second room) was for *theriaca* ("panacea," or cure-all). The most commonly used medicine back then, it was a syrup of herbs, wine, and opium.

St. Louis Ward: A maternity ward until 1969, this room is lined with fine 16th- and 17th-century tapestries illustrating mostly Old Testament stories. Dukes traveled with tapestries to cozy up the humble places they stayed in while on the road. The 16th-century pieces have better colors but inferior perspective. (The most precious 15th-century tapestries are displayed in the next room, where everyone is enthralled by the great Van der Weyden painting.)

Rogier van der Weyden's *Last Judgment:* This exquisite painting, the treasure of the Hôtel Dieu, was commissioned by Rolin in 1450 for the altar of the Paupers' Ward. He spared no cost, hiring the leading Flemish artist of his time. The entire altarpiece survives.

Burgundian Wine Quality, 2005-2013

2005 The makings of a great vintage: The harvest was healthy and balanced, with great natural sugar. A local magazine called 2005 "the vintage of dreams." The reds are superb—rich, plain, concentrated, full-bodied, and intense. They will age magnificently.

2006 The whites are fresh and fruity with considerable richness. The reds are excellent across the board, with beautiful, intense color.

2007 A hot spring, combined with the worst Burgundian summer in 30 years, meant a light vintage for the reds. I'd skip this vintage.

2008 Another tricky year for grapes. Those who waited longest to harvest came out with the best wines, as September was a warm, dry month. The wines of Chablis are excellent, but other wines are less consistent.

The back side (on right wall) was sliced off so everything could be viewed at the same time. The painting is full of symbolism. Christ presides over Judgment Day. The lily is mercy, the sword is judgment, the rainbow promises salvation, and the jeweled globe at Jesus' feet symbolizes the universality of Christianity's message. As four angels blow their trumpets, St. Michael the archangel—very much in control—determines which souls are heavy with sin. Mary and the apostles pray for the souls of the dead as they emerge from their graves. But notice how both Michael and Jesus are expressionless—at this point, the cries of the damned and their loved ones are useless. In the back row are real people of the day.

The intricate detail, painted with a three-haired brush, is typical of Flemish art from this period. While Renaissance artists employed mathematical tricks of perspective, these artists captured a sense of reality by painting minute detail upon detail. (The attendant is dying to be asked to move the magnifying glass—*le loup*—into position to help you appreciate the exquisite detail in the painting.) Stare at Michael's robe and wings. Check out John's delicate feet and hands. Study the faces of the damned; you can almost hear the gnashing of teeth. The feet of the damned show the pull of a terrible force. On the far left, notice those happily entering the pearly gates. On the far right, it's the flames of hell (no, this has nothing to do with politics).

Except for Sundays and holidays, the painting was kept closed and people saw only the panels that now hang on the right wall:

2009 This was a banner year for Burgundies. The harvest provided beautiful grapes, so the expectations were sky-high after two tough years.

2010 With lots of rain in late spring, the quantity harvested was about half the usual amount—but with good concentration.

2011 This was yet another vintage with tricky weather—the harvest was completed before the grapes could enjoy their usual September sun. Don't keep these wines for too long.

2012 Looks to be much like 2010, with below-average production but good quality for reds and whites. Because quantity is low, prices are likely to be high.

2013 Another tough year—a vicious summer hailstorm ruined as much as 60 percent of some vineyards. With the quantity of wine produced well below normal, many fear big price increases.

Nicolas and Guigone piously at the feet of St. Sebastian—invoked to fight the plague—and St. Anthony, whom patients called upon for help in combating burning skin diseases.

The unusual 15th-century tapestry *A Thousand Flowers,* hanging on the left wall, tells the medieval story of St. Eligius.

Collégiale Notre-Dame

Built in the 12th and 13th centuries, during the transition from Romanesque to Gothic architecture, Beaune's cathedral was a "daughter of Cluny" (built in the style of the Cluny Abbey, described on page 888). The church features a mix of both styles: Its foundation is decidedly Romanesque (notice the small windows and thick walls of the apse), while much of the rest is Gothic.

Enter the second chapel on the left to see the vivid remains of frescoes depicting the life of Lazarus, and then, behind the altar, find five vibrant, 15th-century tapestries illustrating the life of the Virgin Mary (buy the €2 English explanation for frame-by-frame descriptions).

Cost and Hours: Free, tapestries on view daily 11:00-18:00.

Museum of the Wine of Burgundy (Musée du Vin de Bourgogne)

From this well-organized folk-wine museum, which fills the old residence of the Dukes of Burgundy, it's clear that the history and culture of Burgundy and its wine were fermented in the same bottle. Wander into the free courtyard for a look at the striking palace, antique wine presses (in the *cuverie,* or vatting shed; good English explanations), and a concrete model of Beaune's 15th-century street plan (a good chance to appreciate the town's once-impressive fortified wall). Inside the museum, you'll see a model of the region's topography, along with tools, costumes, and scenes of Burgundian wine history—but no tasting. Each room has helpful English explanations.

Cost and Hours: €5.70, ticket also includes the Musée des Beaux-Arts; April-Sept daily 10:00-18:00; Oct-March Wed-Sun 11:00-17:00, closed Mon-Tue; in the Hôtel des Ducs on Rue d'Enfer, tel. 03 80 22 08 19.

Getting There: With your back to the cathedral, turn left down the cobbled alley called Rue d'Enfer ("Hell Street," named for the fires of the Duke's kitchens once located on this street), keep left, and enter the courtyard of Hôtel des Ducs. There's also an entrance off Rue Paradis, opposite Le Petit Paradis restaurant.

The Mustard Mill (La Moutarderie Fallot)

The last of the independent mustard mills in Burgundy opens its doors for guided tours in French (with a little English). The tour is long yet informative—you'll learn why Burgundy was the birthplace of mustard (it's about wine juice), and where they get their grains today (Canada). It takes over an hour to explain what could be explained in half that time—you'll see a short film, learn about the key machines used in processing mustard (with the help of audioguides), and finish with a tasting.

Cost and Hours: €10, tours daily at 10:00 and 11:30, Mon-Sat mid-June-mid-Sept also at 15:30; must call TI to reserve or book online, as space is limited; across ring road in the appropriately yellow building at 31 Rue du Faubourg Bretonnière, tel. 03 80 22 10 02, www.fallot.com.

Park and Vineyard Walk

Stroll across the ring road, through a pleasant Impressionist-like park, and into Beaune's beautiful vineyards. This walk is ideal for those lacking a car, families (good play toys in park), and vine enthusiasts. The vine-covered landscape is crisscrossed with narrow lanes and stubby stone walls and provides memorable early-morning and sunset views.

Follow Avenue de la République west from the center, cross the ring road, and parallel the stream along a few grassy blocks for about five minutes, then angle right into the serene park (Parc de la Bouzaise, opens at 8:00). Walk through the park with the pond to your right and pop out at the right rear (northwest) corner (find the small opening near the house-like building in the park). Turn left on the small road, and enter the Côte de Beaune vineyards. Find the big poster showing how the land is sliced and diced among different plots (called *clos*, for "enclosure"). Each *clos* is named; look for the stone marker identifying the area behind the poster as Clos Les Teurons *(1er cru)*.

Poke about Clos Les Teurons, noticing the rocky soil (wine grapes need to struggle). As you wander, keep in mind that subtle differences of soil and drainage between adjacent plots of land can be enough to create very different-tasting wines—from grapes grown only feet apart. *Vive la différence.* (Read "Wine Tasting in Burgundy" on page 840 to learn more.) A perfectly situated picnic table awaits under that lone tree up Chemin des Tilleuls.

Ramparts Walk

You can wander along sections of the medieval walls that protected Beaune from bad guys. Much of the way is a paved lane used for parking, storage, and access to homes built into the wall, but you'll still get a feel for the ramparts' size and see vestiges of defensive towers. Find the path just inside the ring road that stretches counterclockwise from Avenue de la République to Rue de Lorraine (see map on page 859). You can enter or exit at any cross street (free, always open).

WINE TASTING IN BEAUNE

Here are a couple of good places to learn about Burgundy wines without leaving Beaune. For tastings in nearby wine villages, see page 849.

Patriarche Père et Fils

Home to Burgundy's largest and most impressive wine cellar, this is the best of the big wineries to visit in the city. With helpful video presentations at key points, you'll tour some of their three miles of underground passages and finish in the atmospheric tasting room, where you'll try 13 Burgundian classics (3 whites and 10 reds); each bottle sits on top of its own wine barrel. The long walk back to *la sortie* helps sober you up.

Cost and Hours: €16, daily 9:30-11:30 & 14:00-17:30, 5 Rue du Collège, tel. 03 80 24 53 78, www.patriarche.com.

Sensation Vin

For a good introduction to Burgundy wines, try the informative wine classes given by Céline or Damien. You'll gather around a small counter in the comfortable wine bar/classroom and learn while you taste. Since the young owners do not make wine, you'll get an objective education (with blind tastings) and sample from a variety of producers. Call or email ahead to arrange a class/tasting.

Cost and Hours: Class length and wines tasted vary by season (€35 for 1.5-hour class with 9 wines—4 whites, 5 reds; €70 for half-day tastings covering 10 wines, 2-person minimum—aspirin and

Wine Tasting in Burgundy

Countless opportunities exist for you to learn the finer points of Burgundy's wines. Many shops and wineries in the region offer informal and informative tastings (with the expectation that you'll buy something or pay a tasting fee). You can taste directly at the *domaine* (winery) or at a *caveau* representing a variety of wineries (I list several options for both). To sample older vintages you'll have to visit a winery because *caveaux* usually stock only younger wines. When visiting a cellar, don't mind the mossy ceilings. Many cellars have spent centuries growing this "angel's hair"—the result of humidity created by the evaporation of the wines stored there. For tips on wine tasting, see the sidebar on page 1072.

The limits on our ability to bring wines back to North America can lead to tricky dynamics, particularly at smaller places. Busy winemakers naturally prefer to spend their time with folks who can buy enough wine to make it worth their while—and in most cases, that's not you (as nice as you are). They hope you'll like their wines, buy several bottles or a dozen, and ask for them at your shop back home. Most places now charge an entry fee, allowing you to taste a variety of wines (with less expectation that you'll buy). If you're not serious about buying at least a few bottles, look for places that charge for tastings.

pillow provided). Ask about their tastings-in-the-vineyards class (3-4 hours, very small groups only, €190/person). Open daily, near Collégiale Notre-Dame at 1 Rue d'Enfer, tel. 03 80 22 17 57, www.sensation-vin.com, contact@sensation-vin.com.

Sleeping in Beaune

Beaune has accommodations with all levels of comfort in all price ranges. To sleep peacefully (and usually for less), choose one of the nearby wine villages (see page 849).

IN THE CENTER

$$$ Hôtel le Cep**** is *the* venerable place to stay in Beaune, if you have the means. Buried in the town center, this historic building comes with fine public spaces inside and out, and 64 gorgeous wood-beamed, traditionally decorated rooms in all sizes (standard Sb-€150, Db-€190, deluxe Db-€265, suites-€360-550, continental breakfast-€21, air-con, king-size beds, guest computer, Wi-Fi, fitness center, parking-€18/day, 27 Rue Maufoux, tel. 03 80 22 35 48, www.hotel-cep-beaune.com, resa@hotel-cep-beaune.com).

$$$ Hôtel des Remparts*** is a peaceful oasis in a rustic manor house built around a calming courtyard. It features faded

Taking Wine Home: Some shops and wineries can arrange shipping (about €15 per bottle to ship a case, though you save about 20 percent on the VAT tax when shipping—so expensive wines are worth the shipping cost). To learn more about shipping wine, **Côte d'Or Imports** works with many sellers in Burgundy and has earned a reputation for safe and reliable shipping (US tel. 503-449-2538, www.cotedorpdx.com). The simplest solution for bringing six or so bottles back is to pack them well and check the box on the plane with you. Good packing boxes are available, or you can wrap them well and put them in a hard-sided suitcase. US customs allows one bottle duty-free, but the duty on additional bottles is only 10 percent.

Tasting in Beaune: Visit the cellars listed under "Wine Tasting in Beaune" on page 839.

Visiting Vineyards by Car: Follow one of my two self-guided routes (starting on page 855), which also work well for bikes.

Visiting Vineyards Without Your Own Wheels: Rent a bike, take a taxi, or ride a train (long walks to villages from most stations) to nearby villages (see "Wine Villages and Sights near Beaune," page 849), or take Transco bus #44 to wine villages on La Route des Grand Crus (see page 861). You can also book a minibus tour or hire a recommended local guide (see page 832).

Old World comfort, many rooms with beamed ceilings, big beds, and a few good family suites (standard Db-€120, Db suite-€160, extra person-€20, ask for Rick Steves discount, top-floor rooms have air-con, guest computer, Wi-Fi, laundry service, bike rental, garage-€10/day, just inside ring road between train station and main square at 48 Rue Thiers, tel. 03 80 24 94 94, www.hotel-remparts-beaune.com, hotel.des.remparts@wanadoo.fr, run by the formal Epaillys).

$$$ Les Jardins de Loïs****, run by welcoming winemakers Philippe and Anne-Marie, is a four-star B&B. The five big rooms all overlook large gardens and show a no-expense-spared attention to comfort (Db-€150, big Db-€190, Tb-€200, includes custom-order breakfasts, air-con, Wi-Fi, on the ring road a block after Hôtel de la Poste at 8 Boulevard Bretonnière, tel. 03 80 22 41 97, mobile 06 73 85 11 06, www.jardinsdelois.com, contact@jardinsdelois.com). Their atmospheric wine cellar, Domaine Loïs Dufouleur, also offers tastings (€8 for 4 wines, free for guests, arrange ahead).

$$$ Hôtel Athanor*** is a good choice with a privileged location—a block from the cathedral—and offers a nice mix of modern comfort with a touch of old Beaune. The atmospheric lounge sports a pool table and a full-service bar (standard Db without air-con-€100, *superieure* Db—most with air-con-€140, deluxe Db-€162,

Beaune Hotels & Restaurants

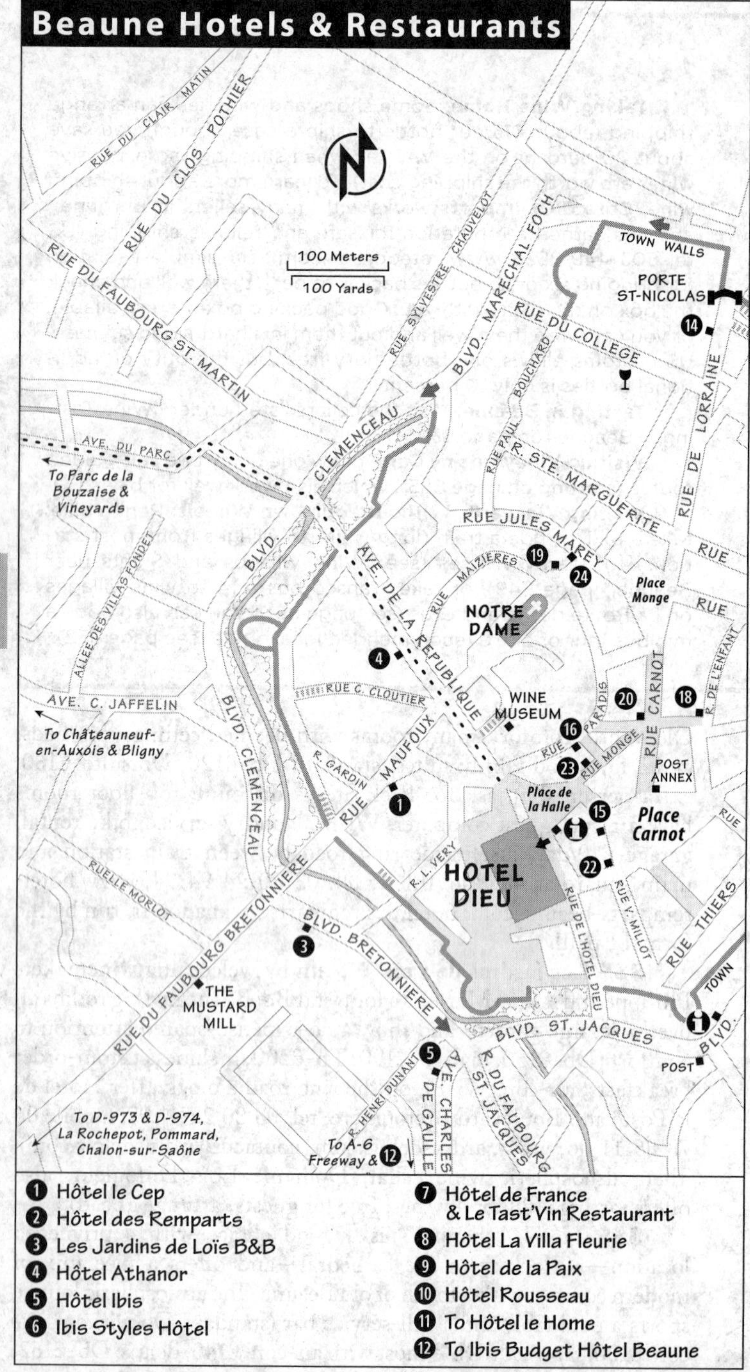

1. Hôtel le Cep
2. Hôtel des Remparts
3. Les Jardins de Loïs B&B
4. Hôtel Athanor
5. Hôtel Ibis
6. Ibis Styles Hôtel
7. Hôtel de France & Le Tast'Vin Restaurant
8. Hôtel La Villa Fleurie
9. Hôtel de la Paix
10. Hôtel Rousseau
11. To Hôtel le Home
12. To Ibis Budget Hôtel Beaune

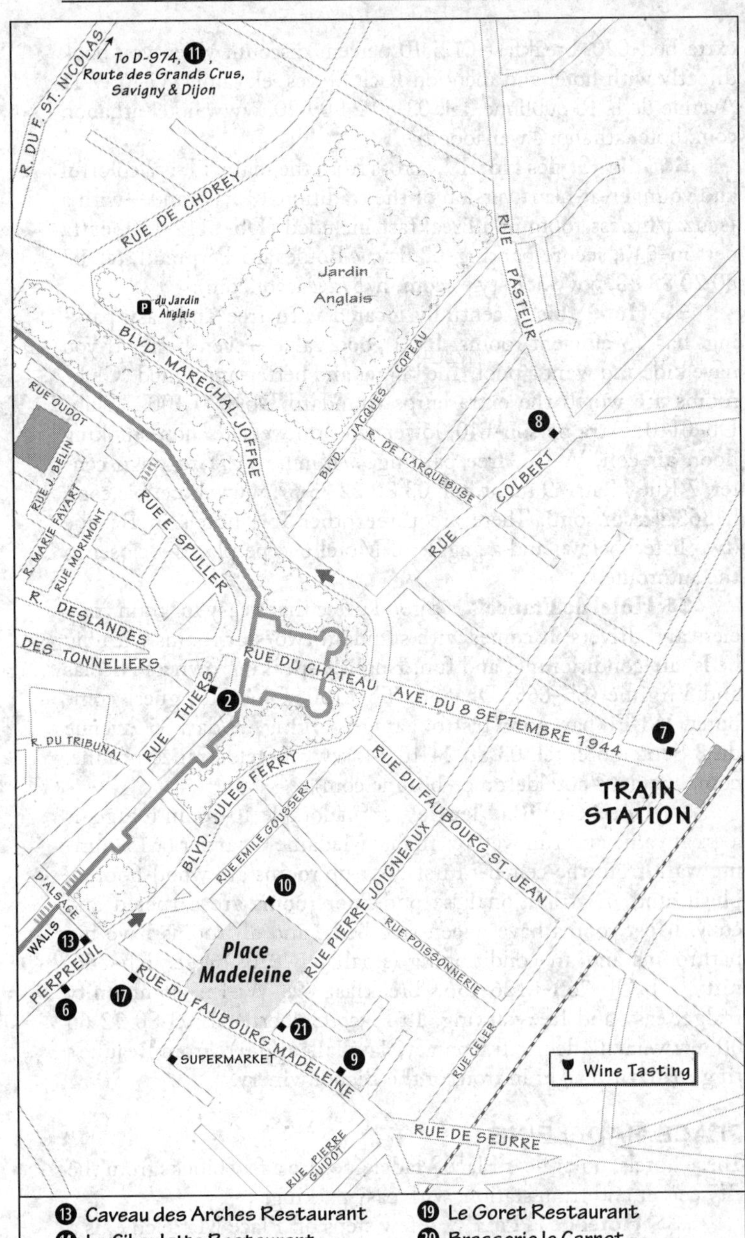

- 13 Caveau des Arches Restaurant
- 14 La Ciboulette Restaurant
- 15 Le Gourmandin Restaurant
- 16 Le Petit Paradis Restaurant
- 17 Les Caves Madeleine Rest.
- 18 Le Conty Restaurant
- 19 Le Goret Restaurant
- 20 Brasserie le Carnot
- 21 L'Auberge Bourguignonne Rest.
- 22 Palais des Gourmets' Salon de Thé
- 23 Bistrot Bourguignon
- 24 Pickwicks Pub

extra bed-€20, breakfast-€12, 10 percent discount when you book directly with hotel and mention Rick Steves, elevator, Wi-Fi, 9-11 Avenue de la République, tel. 03 80 24 09 20, www.hotel-athanor.com, hotel.athanor@wanadoo.fr).

$$$ Ibis Styles Hôtel,** across from the main TI, is a colorful and younger-at-heart version of the traditional Ibis brand—with a Jacuzzi/fitness room and breakfast included (Db-€112-130, extra person-€40, secure parking-€8/day, 7 Boulevard Perpreuil, tel. 03 80 20 88 88, www.ibisstyles.com, h7572@accor.com).

$$ Hôtel Ibis,** centrally located with free and easy parking, has 73 efficient rooms. It's a good value—even better if you have kids and want a pool. The bigger and better-appointed "Club" rooms are worth the extra euros (standard Db-€90-100, "Club" Db-€110, extra person-€10, lower rates on website, non-smoking floor, air-con, Wi-Fi, free parking, 5-minute walk to town center, 7 Rue Henri Dunant, tel. 03 80 22 75 67, www.hotelibis.com, h1363@accor.com). There are three other Ibis hotels in Beaune (two listed below) and a gaggle of Motel 6-type places—closer to the autoroute.

$$ Hôtel de France** is a good place that's easy for train travelers and drivers. It comes with standard two-star rooms with big beds, air-conditioning, and fun, English-speaking owners Nicolas and Virginie (Sb-€65, Db-€86, Tb-€100, Qb-€115, guest computer, Wi-Fi, bar, good bistro, garage parking-€9/day, 35 Avenue du 8 Septembre, tel. 03 80 24 10 34, www.hoteldefrance-beaune.com, contact@hoteldefrance-beaune.com).

$$ Hôtel La Villa Fleurie*,** an adorable 10-room refuge, is a great value and run well by affable Madame Chartier (a 15-minute walk from the center). First-floor-up rooms are wood-floored, plush, and *très* traditional; second-floor rooms are carpeted and cozy. Most rooms have queen-size beds, and all rooms have big bathrooms and air-conditioning (small Db-€76, bigger Db-€86, nifty Tb/Qb loft-€126-136, breakfast-€9, Wi-Fi, community fridge, easy and free parking, 19 Place Colbert, tel. 03 80 22 66 00, www.lavillafleurie.fr, contact@lavillafleurie.fr). From Beaune's ring road, turn right in front of the Bichot winery.

PLACE MADELEINE

These hotels, on or near Place Madeleine, are a few blocks from the city center and train station, with easy parking.

$$$ Hôtel de la Paix*,** a few steps off Place Madeleine, is a top choice, with rooms in two buildings. In the main building (with reception, breakfast room, bar, and comfy lounges), there are 24 three-star, handsome, and well-appointed rooms, including several good family rooms (Db-€120-135, bigger Db/Tb-€140-180, Qb-€150-230. In an annex two blocks away, above the recommended

Sleep Code

Abbreviations **(€1 = about $1.40, country code: 33)**
S = Single, **D** = Double/Twin, **T** = Triple, **Q** = Quad, **b** = bathroom, **s** = shower only, * = French hotel rating (0-5 stars)

Price Rankings

$$$ Higher Priced—Most rooms €100 or more

$$ Moderately Priced—Most rooms between €70-100

$ Lower Priced—Most rooms €70 or less

Unless otherwise noted, credit cards are accepted, English is spoken, and Wi-Fi is generally free. Prices change; verify current rates online or by email. For the best prices, always book directly with the hotel.

L'Auberge Bourguignonne restaurant, are eight traditional and comfortable two-star rooms and two fine family rooms with kitchenettes and small living areas, all at good prices (Db-€90, Tb/Qb-€130, apartments-€175). All rooms have air-conditioning (guest computer and Wi-Fi, private parking-€6/day, 45 Rue du Faubourg Madeleine, tel. 03 80 24 78 08, www.hotelpaix.com, contact@hotelpaix.com).

BURGUNDY

$ Hôtel Rousseau is a good-value, no-frills, frumpy manor house that turns its back on Beaune's sophistication. Cheerful, quirky, and elusive owner Madame Rousseau, her pet birds, and the quiet garden will make you smile, and the tranquility will help you sleep. The cheapest rooms are a godsend for budget travelers. The rooms with showers are like Grandma's, with enough comfort (S-€39, D-€47, D with toilet-€54, Db-€66, T with toilet-€62, Tb-€74, Q-€66, Qb-€79, showers down the hall-€3, includes breakfast, cash only, reservations preferred by email, free and easy parking, 11 Place Madeleine, tel. 03 80 22 13 59, hotelrousseaubeaune@orange.fr). Check-ins after 19:00 and morning departures before 7:30 must be arranged in advance.

JUST OUTSIDE BEAUNE

For listings farther outside town in the nearby wine villages, see page 849.

$$ Hôtel le Home**, off busy D-974 a half-mile north of Beaune, works well for drivers, with comfy rooms in an old mansion. The rooms in the main building come in soft pastels (top-floor rooms have the most character, and the most heat). Rooms on the parking courtyard come with stone floors, simple terraces, and bright colors, but can be a bit musty (standard Db-€75-95, bigger Db-€110, Tb-€115, breakfast-€9-16, Wi-Fi, includes parking, 138 Route de Dijon, tel. 03 80 22 16 43, www.lehome.fr, info@lehome.fr).

$ Ibis Budget Hôtel Beaune is efficient, basic but clean, and a bargain just a five-minute drive from Beaune's center toward the A-6 autoroute (Db-€50, Wi-Fi, easy and free parking, 16 Rue du Moulin Noizé, tel. 08 92 68 32 71, www.ibis.com, h2524@accor.com).

Eating in Beaune

For a small town, Beaune offers a wide range of reasonably priced restaurants. Review my suggestions carefully before setting out, and reserve at least a day ahead to avoid frustration (especially on weekends). Many places are closed Sunday and Monday. This region offers a bounty of worthwhile upscale dining options (I've listed a few), but before you book, check their wine lists (easiest to do online)—the prices may double your total dinner cost. For eating recommendations in the wine villages near Beaune, see page 849.

Caveau des Arches is a good choice if you want to dine on Burgundian specialties at fair prices in romantic stone cellars (€26 *menu* with the classics, €33 *menu* with greater choices, €52 gourmand *menu,* portions can be small, closed Sun-Mon, where the ring road crosses Rue d'Alsace—which leads to Place Madeleine—at 10 Boulevard Perpreuil, tel. 03 80 22 10 37).

La Ciboulette, intimate and family-run with petite Hélène as your hostess, offers reliable cuisine that mixes traditional Burgundian flavors with creative dishes and lovely presentation. It's worth the longer walk—and you can do your laundry next door while you dine (€20 and €38 *menus,* indoor seating only, closed Mon-Tue; from Place Carnot, walk out Rue Carnot to 69 Rue Lorraine; tel. 03 80 24 70 72).

Le Gourmandin is for foodies willing to fork over a tad more. The vintage decor and refined cuisine let you feel you're somewhere special (€20-26 *plats,* daily, 8 Place Carnot, tel. 03 80 24 07 88).

Le Petit Paradis does its name justice, with 10 tables crowding a sharp little room and another 10 outside if the weather agrees. Chef Jean-Marie's menu is inventive and ever-changing—and not traditional Burgundian (*plats*-€18, *menus* from €29, closed Sun-Mon, book ahead, just outside Museum of the Wine of Burgundy at 25 Rue de Paradis, tel. 03 80 24 91 00).

Le Tast'Vin, across from the train station at the recommended Hôtel de France, has a good-value €25 *menu* and fun cheeseburgers with Burgundian cheese (closed Sun-Mon, 35 Avenue du 8 Septembre, tel. 03 80 24 10 34).

At **Les Caves Madeleine,** step down into the warm little dining room and choose a private table—or, better, join the communal table, where good food and wine kindle conversation and new friendships. Owner/chef Martial enjoys sharing his passion for cooking with travelers (€15-26 *plats,* closed Wed and Sun, near Place Madeleine at 8 Rue du Faubourg Madeleine, tel. 03 80 22 93 30).

Le Conty is a small bistro with a prized position at the junction of two pedestrian lanes, with great outdoor seating and refined cuisine (€18 lunch *menus* on weekdays, €34 at dinner, closed Sun-Mon, 5 Rue Ziem, tel. 03 80 22 63 94).

Le Goret turns its back on Beaune's sophistication, serving farmer-sized portions of regional dishes. Pork is their thing, and dietary concerns are not. This is the place to experience down-and-dirty Burgundy (€16-24 *plats,* closed Sun-Mon and Thu, behind Collégiale Notre-Dame at 10 Place Notre-Dame, tel. 03 80 22 05 94, inside tables only).

Brasserie le Carnot is a perennially popular café with good interior seating and better exterior tables in the thick of the pedestrian zone. It serves excellent pizza, good salads, pasta dishes (all about €14) as well as the usual café offerings (open daily, where Rue Carnot and Rue Monge meet).

L'Auberge Bourguignonne is decidedly Burgundian, with a solid reputation among locals (some say they make the best beef Burgundy in Beaune). It's also open on Sundays, when many other places are not. Choose from two traditional dining rooms, or eat outside (basic €28 *menu,* good Burgundian *menu* at €36, air-con, 4 Place Madeleine, tel. 03 80 22 23 53).

At **Palais des Gourmets' Salon de Thé,** Stephanie provides a great value breakfast or lunch outdoors on Place Carnot, with delicious quiche, omelets, and crêpes (from €5-9)—and memorable desserts (Tue-Sun until 18:00, fewer choices after 14:00, closed Mon, next to Athenaeum's back-door entrance at 14 Place Carnot, tel. 03 80 22 13 39).

Bistrot Bourguignon is a laid-back wine bar-bistro with a lengthy wine list and 15 types of *vin* available by the glass (order by number from display behind bar). Come for a glass of wine and Wi-Fi or for a light dinner. Dine at the counter, the sidewalk tables, or in the casually comfortable interior (€11 starters, €18 *plats,* €16 lunch *menu,* closed Sun-Mon, on a pedestrian-only street at 8 Rue Monge, tel. 03 80 22 23 24).

Before Dinner: Consider a glass of wine at **Bistrot Bourguignon** (listed above) or escape the tourists at **Les Mille et Une Vignes** wine bar, which reeks with old-time ambience and local characters. Young, spirited owner Marine serves a good selection of wines by the glass at fair prices and good, splittable appetizers (Tue-Sat 11:00 until late, closed Sun-Mon, next door to launderette at 61 Rue de Lorraine, tel. 03 80 22 03 02).

After Dinner: If you're tired of speaking French, pop into the late-night-lively **Pickwicks Pub** (Mon-Sat 18:00-very late, closed Sun, behind church at 2 Rue Notre-Dame).

Beaune Connections

From Beaune by Train to: Meursault (hourly, 5-30 minutes, 15-minute walk into town), **Gevrey-Chambertin** (hourly, 20 minutes, 15-minute walk into town), **Dijon** (15/day, 25-55 minutes), **Paris** Gare de Lyon (nearly hourly, 2.5 hours, most require reservation and easy change in Dijon; more via Dijon to Paris' Gare de Bercy, no reservation required, 3.5 hours), **Bourges** (7/day, 2.5 hours, transfer in Nevers), **Colmar** (10/day, 2.5-4 hours via TGV between Dijon and Mulhouse, reserve well ahead, changes in Dijon and Mulhouse or Belfort), **Arles** (10/day, 4.5-5 hours, 9 with transfer in Lyon and Nîmes or Avignon), **Chamonix** (7/day, 7 hours, change in Lyon and St-Gervais, some require additional changes), **Annecy** (7/day, 4-6 hours, change in Lyon), **Amboise** (1/day, 4.5 hours, transfer at St-Pierre-des-Corps; also possible with changes at St-Pierre-des-Corps and Nevers).

Touring Burgundy's Wine Villages

Exploring the villages and vineyards in the region near Beaune, by car or by bike, is a delight.

GETTING AROUND THE BEAUNE REGION

By Car: Driving provides the ultimate flexibility for touring the vineyards, though drivers should prepare for narrow lanes in the vineyards and use the handy buckets to spit back after tasting.

By Bike: Pedaling on a bike from Beaune takes you into the world-famous vineyards of the Côte d'Or within minutes. The many quiet service roads and bike-only lanes make this area wonderful for biking. (Beware of loose gravel on the shoulders and along the small roads.) A signed bike route runs south from Beaune all the way to Cluny, and a new route from Beaune north to Dijon may be in place by your visit. My favorite rides are described in detail in "Vineyard Loops near Beaune" (see page 855).

Well-organized, English-speaking Florian and Cedric at **Bourgogne Randonnées** offer excellent bikes of all types, bike racks, kid bikes and kid trailers, maps, and detailed itineraries. Ask about their favorite routes that follow only small roads and dedicated bike paths. They can deliver your bike to your hotel anywhere in France (bikes-€6/hour, €18/day, electric bikes-€35/day, helmets-€1, daily 9:00-12:00 & 13:30-18:00, near Beaune train station at 7 Avenue du 8 Septembre, tel. 03 80 22 06 03, www.bourgogne-randonnees.fr, helloinfobr@aol.com).

By Bus: Transco bus #44 links Beaune with all the important wine villages to the north along the famous Route des Grands Crus, and runs to Dijon's train station (7/day; www.mobigo-bourgogne.eu—click on English flag, then "Transco"). Bus stops are along Beaune's ring road (look for Transco decals). Bus service south of Beaune to villages like Meursault and Puligny-Montrachet is hopeless—take a taxi, hop a train (limited options), or rent a bike.

By Train: Hourly trains stop in the wine villages of Meursault and Santenay to the south of Beaune, and Nuits St-Georges, Vougeot (10-minute walk to Château de Clos Vougeot), and **Gevrey-**Chambertin to the north. Most of these stations require a 15-minute walk to the town center.

By Minibus Tour: Try **Safari Wine Tours, Wine Me Up,** or **Chemins de Bourgogne** (see page 832).

By Taxi: Call **Gerard Rebillard** (mobile 06 11 83 06 10); for another taxi, see page 829.

Wine Villages and Sights near Beaune

You'll find exceptional tasting, eating, and sleeping values in the workaday villages and towns within a 10- to 15-minute drive of Beaune. The Côte d'Or has scads of *chambres d'hôtes;* get a list at the TI and reserve ahead in summer. See also the suggestions along the Route des Grands Crus (page 861).

For driving/biking loops that tie these villages together, see page 855; for the Route des Grands Crus, see page 861.

SOUTH OF BEAUNE

Pommard

The small village of Pommard lies on the bike path just two miles south of Beaune. Walkers can follow the bike path and make it here in 40 minutes. Pommard has cafés, restaurants, and many tasting opportunities.

Domaine Patrick Clémencet offers traditional tastings in a small room with minimal English. You need to know what you want to taste and have the patience to navigate the language barrier. There's a big selection of reasonably priced wines (€6-40/bottle) from most of the famous wine villages, and *bien sûr,* plenty of Pommard (generally open Mon-Sat 10:00-12:00 & 13:30-19:00, closed Sun; 1 Place de l'Europe—enter Pommard when you see Hôtel du Pont and find the winery's green sign a block down, arcing over its entry, push the *sonnez* button if no one is there; tel. 03 80 22 59 11, domaine-clemencet@orange.fr).

Eating in Pommard: Facing Pommard's big church, **Auprès du Clocher** has stylish, contemporary decor one floor up with windows on the village, a formal atmosphere, and a focus on *la cuisine.* Book ahead, as chef Jean-Christophe Moutet has been discovered by locals (€32, €48, and €72 *menus;* closed Tue-Wed, 1 Rue Nackenheim, tel. 03 80 22 21 79).

Meursault

This appealing town 10 minutes south of Beaune is like a mini-Beaune, with a marvelous square, cafés, shops, and a good selection of hotels and restaurants in its compact center. Eat or sleep here for that small-town feel and quick access to Beaune, vineyards, and villages. The train station is a 15-minute walk from the town center.

Sleeping in Meursault: **$$$ Hôtel les Charmes***,** in the heart of town, is a sweet place with fine, traditional rooms and a homey Old World feel, thanks to the easygoing owners. There's a veritable park in the back and a big pool (standard Db-€110, bigger Db-€130, Tb-€150, Wi-Fi, 10 Place du Murger, tel. 03 80 21 63 53, www.hotellescharmes.com, contact@hotellescharmes.com).

$ Hôtel les Arts,** smack in the town center, has seven modest, inexpensive, but comfortable rooms above a good restaurant—described next (Db-€60-70, Wi-Fi, 4 Place de l'Hôtel de Ville, tel. 03 80 21 2098, www.hotel-restaurant-les-arts.fr, contact@hotel-restaurant-les-arts.fr).

Eating in Meursault: Two good places serving top Burgundian cuisine at fair prices face each other on Place de l'Hôtel de Ville. **Restaurant les Arts** mixes old with new, serving fine cuisine including excellent escargot and *oeufs en meurette* (€10-12 lunch salads and *plats,* dinner *menus* from €24, nice terrace in front, closed Mon-Tue, tel. 03 80 21 20 28). **Hôtel du Centre** offers a slightly more refined menu and a sweet courtyard (dinner *menus* from €28, open daily, 4 Rue de Lattre de Tassigny, tel. 03 80 21 20 75).

Puligny-Montrachet

This village of about 400 persons is situated about a 15-minute drive (or 60 minutes by bike) south of Beaune, on the scenic route to Château de la Rochepot (see page 856). It has just enough commercial activity to keep travelers well fed and housed.

Located on the village's central roundabout, the user-friendly **Caveau de Puligny-Montrachet** has a convivial wine-bar-like tasting room, a smart outdoor terrace, and no pressure to buy. Knowledgeable owner Julien is happy to answer your every question. He has wines from 200 quality Burgundian vintners, from

Chablis to Pouilly-Fuissé, but his forte is Puligny-Montrachet and Meursault whites, which is why I taste here. His reds are young and less ready to drink (€15 for 6 wines, free if you buy 6 bottles, can ship to the US; March-Oct daily 9:30-19:00, sometimes closes at lunch; Nov-Feb Tue-Sat 10:00-12:00 & 15:00-18:00, closed Mon; tel. 03 80 21 96 78, www.caveau-puligny.com).

If you're looking for an upscale wine château experience, visit **Château de Chassagne-Montrachet** (just a few minutes south of town). In this elegant mansion, an informative tour takes you through gorgeous cellars—some dating to the 11th century. You'll taste five of Michel Picard's impressive wines from throughout Burgundy (€16 includes tour, €11 without tour, allow at least an hour with tour, daily 10:00-18:00, best to call ahead, tel. 03 80 21 98 57, www.chateaudechassagnemontrachet.com).

Sleeping in Puligny-Montrachet: **$$$ Domaine des Anges** is a lovely place run by a British couple (John and Celine) who pamper their guests with the Queen's English, lovely rooms, linger-longer lounges inside and out, laundry service, fine dinners with drinks (€40, book ahead), and afternoon tea every day. It's also ideally located in the center of Puligny-Montrachet (Db-€80-145, includes a smashing breakfast, no children under 16, Place des Marronniers, tel. 03 80 21 38 28, mobile 06 23 86 63 91, www.domainedesangespuligny.com, domainedesanges@yahoo.fr).

$ Chambres les Gagères is a swinging deal with four cozy and spotless rooms—some with vineyard views, and all with a common kitchen and view terraces overlooking vineyards. Adorable Maria is your hostess (Db-€60-70, Tb-€90, includes breakfast, 17 Rue Drouhin, tel. 03 80 21 97 46, mobile 06 15 97 64 71, maria.adao2@orange.fr).

Eating in Puligny-Montrachet: At **Le Montrachet,** settle in for a truly traditional Burgundian experience—a justifiable splurge if you want a refined and classy dining experience without stuffiness. This is a good choice for a gourmet lunch on a lovely terrace at affordable prices (€32 lunch *menu,* €63-90 dinner *menus,* pricey wine list, open daily, on Puligny-Montrachet's main square at 19 Place des Marronniers, tel. 03 80 21 30 06). Come early for a glass of wine before dinner with Julien at the Caveau de Puligny-Montrachet (described earlier). **L'Estaminet de Meix,** a contemporary wine bar in the heart of the village, serves good brasserie fare at reasonable prices and has fun outdoor seating (€14 lunch *menus,* dinner *menus* from €19, closed Sun evening and all day Mon, Place des Marronniers, tel. 03 80 21 33 01).

▲Château de la Rochepot

Splendid both inside and out, this pint-size, very Burgundian castle rises above its village, eight miles from Beaune.

Cost and Hours: €4.50 to visit on your own, €9 includes 25-minute guided tour, usually possible between 15:00-16:30 only; open April-Sept Wed-Sun 10:00-17:30, shorter hours off-season, closed Mon-Tue year-round.

Information: Tour half on your own and the other half with a French guide (get the English handout; most guides speak some English and can answer questions, tel. 03 80 21 71 37, www.larochepot.com).

Getting There: The highly recommended scenic route from Beaune to the château is described in the "South Vineyard Loop" (see page 856). Or, to reach the château more directly from Beaune, follow signs for *Chalon-sur-Saône* from Beaune's ring road, then follow signs to *Autun* for 15 lovely minutes.

Visiting the Castle: Cross the drawbridge under the Pot family coat of arms and (as instructed) knock three times with the ancient knocker to enter. If no one comes, knock harder, or find a log and ram the gate.

Construction began during the end of the Middle Ages (when castles were built to defend) and was completed during the Renaissance (when castles became luxury homes). So it's neither a purely defensive structure (as in the Dordogne) nor a palace (as in the Loire)—it's a bit of both. The castle was never attacked by foreigners, though the French Revolution laid waste to a good part of it. After being used as a quarry, it was purchased by a local family and rebuilt. The same family owns it today.

The furnishings are surprisingly cushy given the military look of the exterior. Enter through the guard's room, and appreciate the weight of a good suit of armor. I could sleep like a baby in the Captain's Room, surrounded by nine-foot-thick walls. Don't miss the 15th-century alarmed safe. Notice the colorful doorjamb. These same colors were used to paint many buildings (including castles and churches) and remind us that medieval life was not monochromatic. The kitchen will bowl you over; the dining room sports a 15th-century walnut high chair. Look for paintings of the pre-Revolution castle to get a feel for its original appearance.

Climb the tower (fine views) and see the out-of-place Chinese room, sing chants in the resonant chapel, and make ripples in the 240-foot-deep well. (Can you spit a bull's-eye?) Paths outside lead you on a worthwhile walk around the castle. Don't leave without driving, walking, or pedaling up D-33 a few hundred yards toward St-Aubin (behind Hôtel Relais du Château) for a romantic view.

St-Romain

Lovely little St-Romain snuggles in the hills between rocky cliffs and vineyards. You won't find much activity here, but you will find peace and quiet—and views in all directions.

Sleeping in St-Romain: **$$ La Domaine de Corgette** hunkers happily beneath a hillside. Welcoming Véronique has restored an old vintner's home with style. A stay-awhile terrace, private parking, cozy common rooms, and wine tastings are at your disposal (Db-€100-110, Tb-€130, Qb-€150, includes breakfast, cash only, Wi-Fi, 2 blocks below Hôtel les Roches—listed next, look for the *Maison d'Hôte* banner, tel. 03 80 21 68 08, www.domainecorgette.com, accueil@domainecorgette.com).

$ Hôtel les Roches is an unpretentious place offering a handful of simple, clean, and perfectly sleepable rooms snuggled above a restaurant (Db-€50, bigger Db-€70, Wi-Fi, tel. 03 80 21 21 63, www.les-roches.fr, reservation@les-roches.fr).

Chagny

The only reason to come to this unexceptional town 20 minutes south of Beaune is to eat very well (trains allow easy access for non-drivers).

Eating in Chagny: Well known as one of France's finest restaurants, **Maison Lameloise** has Michelin's top rating (three stars). The setting is elegant (as you'd expect), the service is relaxed and patient (which you might not expect), the cuisine is Burgundy's best, and the overall experience is memorable. If you're tempted to dive into the top of the top of French cuisine, book this place well ahead (*menus* from about €180, €80 main courses, very pricey wines, open daily, 36 Place d'Armes, tel. 03 85 87 65 65, www.lameloise.fr). Or consider their nearby contemporary bistro **Pierre et Jean,** where you get the same quality with a simpler menu for less money (around the corner at 2 Rue de la Poste, tel. 03 85 87 08 67).

NORTH OF BEAUNE

Aloxe-Corton

This small, prestigious village has good tasting rooms (and not much more); it's just a 10-minute drive north of Beaune.

At the **Domaines d'Aloxe-Corton** *caveau,* you can sample seven makers of the famous Aloxe-Corton wines in a comfortable and relaxed setting. Prices are affordable, and the easygoing staff speaks enough English (small fee for tasting, free if you buy two bottles, Thu-Mon 10:00-13:00 & 15:00-19:00, usually closed Tue-Wed, tel. 03 80 26 49 85). You'll find the *caveau* a few steps from the little square in Aloxe-Corton.

Mischief and Mayhem is a dream come true for Anglophones serious about Burgundian wine. British-born-and-raised

Fiona and Michael make fine wines and sell them at fair prices (€13-60, but little middle ground). They are thoroughly immersed in Burgundian culture and can help you make sense of this region's wine culture. It's a small operation, so tasting hours vary (generally late mornings and afternoons Thu-Sat, call ahead, a few blocks below the church on D-115d to Ladoix-Serrigny at 10 Impasse du Puits, tel. 03 80 26 47 60, mobile 06 30 01 23 76, www.mischiefandmayhem.com).

Domaine Comte Senard is famous for its prestigious wines and *table d'hôte,* where you get a full lunch with matching wines and thorough explanations from the wine steward as you go (lunch served Tue-Sat 12:00-14:00, €49 with 3 wines, €69 with 6 wines). It's a fun, convivial way to spend two hours learning about the local product—be sure to come early to make the most of the experience. You can also drop by at non-lunch hours to sample their wines (€10 tasting, free if you purchase wine, Tue-Sat 12:00-18:00, closed Sun-Mon, 1 Rue des Chaumes, tel. 03 80 26 41 65, www.table-comte-senard.com).

Sleeping in Aloxe-Corton: **$$$ Hôtel Villa Louise***** is a romantic place burrowed in this wine hamlet. Many of its 13 *très* cozy and tastefully decorated rooms overlook the backyard vineyards, a small covered pool, and a large, grassy garden made for sipping the owner's wine—but, sadly, no picnics are allowed (Db-€100-152—most are about €110-130, Db suite-€150-200, buffet breakfast-€16, guest computer and Wi-Fi, sauna, near the château at 9 Rue Franche, tel. 03 80 26 46 70, www.hotel-villa-louise.fr, hotel-villa-louise@wanadoo.fr).

Magny-les-Villers

This Hautes-Côtes village is located 15 minutes north of Beaune via one of Burgundy's most scenic wine roads (drive up into Pernand Vergeles to find this road signed on the right).

Domaine Naudin-Ferrand is overlooked by most, but makes fine reds and whites at excellent prices, and offers an authentic, small-producer experience (simple tasting room with helpful Claire or Marie who speak enough English). Its best values are wines from the Hautes-Côtes vineyards. Call or email to let them know you are coming and carefully track the faded signs (Mon-Fri 9:00-12:00 & 13:30-17:30, Sat 13:00-18:00, closed Sun, Rue du Meix-Grenot, tel. 03 80 62 91 50, www.naudin-ferrand.com, info@naudin-ferrand.com).

Savigny-lès-Beaune

About five minutes from Beaune, Savigny-lès-Beaune is a thriving village with all the services travelers need, but no central square or focal point to make me want to sleep here.

Savigny-lès-Beaune is home to **Henri de Villamont,** a big-time enterprise with a huge range of wines and a modern, welcoming tasting room. They grow their own grapes and also buy grapes from other vineyards, but make all the wines themselves. This allows them to create a vast selection of wines featuring grapes from virtually all of the famous wine villages, from Pouilly-Fuissé to Chablis (hours vary but generally Tue-Sat 10:00-12:30 & 13:30-18:00, Sun 10:00-13:00, charming Lydie runs the tasting room, Rue du Dr. Guyot, call ahead if you want to visit the cellars, tel. 03 80 21 50 59, www.hdv.fr).

Sights in Savigny-lès-Beaune: The medieval castle **Château de Savigny** comes with a moat and an eclectic collection that includes 100 fighter jets, Abarth antique racing cars, tractor and fire-engines, 300 motorcycles, 2,000 airplane models, and vineyards—but no furnishings (€10, daily mid-April-mid-Oct 9:00-18:30, shorter hours off-season, last entry 1.5 hours before closing, English handout, tel. 03 80 21 55 03, www.chateau-savigny.com).

Eating in Savigny-lès-Beaune: Beyond the château in the village, you'll find the **R. De Famille** café-pizzeria facing a little square with good outdoor seating (closed Mon). A grocery shop and a bakery are a few blocks past the café (grocery usually closed 12:30-15:00).

Vineyard Loops near Beaune

In this section, you'll find two vineyard loops near Beaune and recommendations for touring the Route des Grands Crus between Beaune and Dijon. These drives combine great scenery with some of my favorite wine destinations (for more on these towns, see "Wine Villages and Sights near Beaune," earlier). Certain sections are doable by bike depending on your bike-fitness and determination.

If time is tight and you have a car, drive the beautiful **"South Vineyard Loop"** to Château de la Rochepot (with off-the-beaten-path villages and ample tasting opportunities). This is a tough ride on a bike (unless it's electric), so most bikers will prefer doing just the first section of this route (ideally to Puligny-Montrachet and back—an easy, level ride).

My **"North Vineyard Loop"** takes you to Savigny-lès-Beaune and is good by car or by bike (manageable hills and distances). I also list good stops on the famous **"Route des Grands Crus,"** connecting Burgundy's most prestigious wine villages farther north of Beaune.

Along these routes, I avoid famous wine châteaux (like those in Pommard and Meursault) and look for smaller, more personal places. Although you can drop in unannounced at most wineries (*comme un cheveux sur la soupe*—"like a hair on the soup"), you'll get better service by calling ahead and letting them know you're coming (no need to call ahead for a *caveau* representing multiple wineries). Remember that at free tastings, you're expected to buy at least a bottle or two, unless you're on a group tour.

Before heading out, read the section on Burgundian wines (page 825). You'll almost certainly see workers tending the vines. In winter, plants are pruned way back (determining the yield during grape harvest in the fall). Starting in spring, plants are trimmed to get rid of extraneous growth, allowing just the right amount of sun to reach the grapes. The arrival date of good weather in spring determines the date of harvest (100 days later).

South Vineyard Loop

Beaune to Château de la Rochepot

Take this pretty, peaceful route, worth ▲▲, for the best approach to La Rochepot's romantic castle, and to glide through several of Burgundy's most reputed vineyards. Read ahead and note the open hours of wineries and sights along the route (you can do this loop in reverse). There are wonderful picnic spots along the way; you'll find my favorite one just before entering Puligny-Montrachet from the north (past the first picnic spot by 100 yards, closer to the hills).

Bikers can follow the first part of this route to Puligny-Montrachet, along Burgundy's best bike path (departs from Beaune's Parc de la Bouzaise and connects the wine villages of Pommard, Meursault, Volnay, and Puligny-Montrachet for a level, 18-mile loop; allow two hours round trip). All but power riders should avoid the hills to La Rochepot.

➲ **Self-Guided Tour:** Drivers leave Beaune's ring road, following signs for *Chalon-sur-Saône* (often abbreviated "Chalon-s/S.," first turnoff after Auxerre exit), then follow signs to *Pommard/Autun*. Cyclists take the vineyard bike path by leaving the ring road toward Auxerre and Bligny-sur-Ouche, and turning left at the signal after Lycée Viticole de Beaune (look for bike-route icons).

Whether on a bike or in car, when you come to Pommard, you'll pass many wine-tasting opportunities, including **Patrick Clémencet** (see page 849).

South of Pommard, the road gradually climbs past Volnay and terrific views (bikers take their own parallel path, following bike

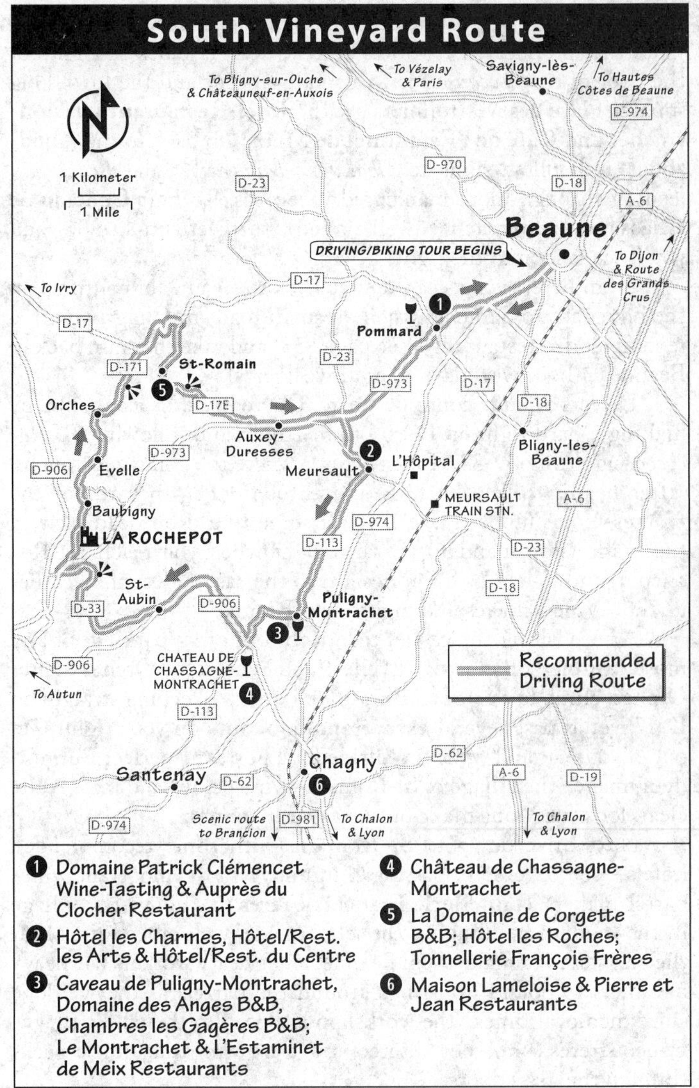

icons). From here, follow signs into **Meursault** (fine square, bakeries, grocery shops, and good restaurants; see page 850).

Follow *Toutes Directions* (and D-974) around the village, turn right on D-113b, and follow signs for *Puligny-Montrachet.* You'll pass through low-slung vineyards south of Meursault, then enter **Puligny-Montrachet** (town and wineries described on page 850)—with good picnic spots on the right as you enter. At the big roundabout with a bronze sculpture of vineyard workers, find the **Caveau de Puligny-Montrachet** and a chance to sample from vines that produce "the world's best whites." A block straight out the door of the *caveau* leads to a small grocery and the town's big square (Place des Marronniers), with **Hôtel-Restaurant Le Montrachet** and **Café de l'Estaminet de Meix.** Go back to the roundabout and follow signs to *Chassagne-Montrachet* and *St. Aubin,* leading through more manicured vineyards. To tour **Château de Chassagne-Montrachet** (well-signed), turn left on D-906, and you'll see it soon to the right.

From here, cyclists can double back to Beaune or continue on the bike path to Santenay, then on small roads to **Chagny** (with a recommended restaurant—see page 853) and take the train back to Beaune (2/hour weekdays, 1/hour weekends).

Drivers should continue on to **Château de la Rochepot** by making a hard right on D-906 to St-Aubin and following *La Rochepot* signs onto D-33. (Bikers, this is where the going gets tough.) After heading over the hills and through the vineyards of the Hautes-Côtes (upper slopes), you'll come to a drop-dead view of the castle (stop mandatory). Turn right when you reach La Rochepot, and follow *Le Château* signs to the castle (described earlier under "Wine Villages and Sights near Beaune").

After visiting the castle, turn right out of its parking lot and mosey through Baubigny, Evelles, and rock-solid Orches. After Orches, climb to the top of Burgundy's world—keeping straight on D-17, you'll pass several **exceptional lookouts** on your right. Get out of your car and wander cliffside for a postcard-perfect Burgundian image. The village of St-Romain swirls below, and if it's really clear, look for Mont Blanc on the eastern horizon.

Next drive down to **St-Romain** (with some recommended hotels—see page 853), passing Burgundy's most important wine-barrel maker, **Tonnellerie Francois Frères** (it's above the village in the modern building on the left). Inside, well-stoked fires heat the oak staves to make them flexible, and sweaty workers use heavy hammers to pound iron rings around the barrels as they've done since medieval times. The workshop is closed to the public (www.francoisfreres.com), but discreet travelers can take quick peeks through the glass doors.

Next, follow signs for *Auxey-Duresses,* and then *Beaune* for a scenic finale to your journey.

North Vineyard Loop

Beaune to Savigny-lès-Beaune

For an easy and rewarding spin by car—or ideally by bike—through waves of vineyards that smother traditional villages, follow this relatively level 12-mile loop from Beaune, worth ▲ (with stops,

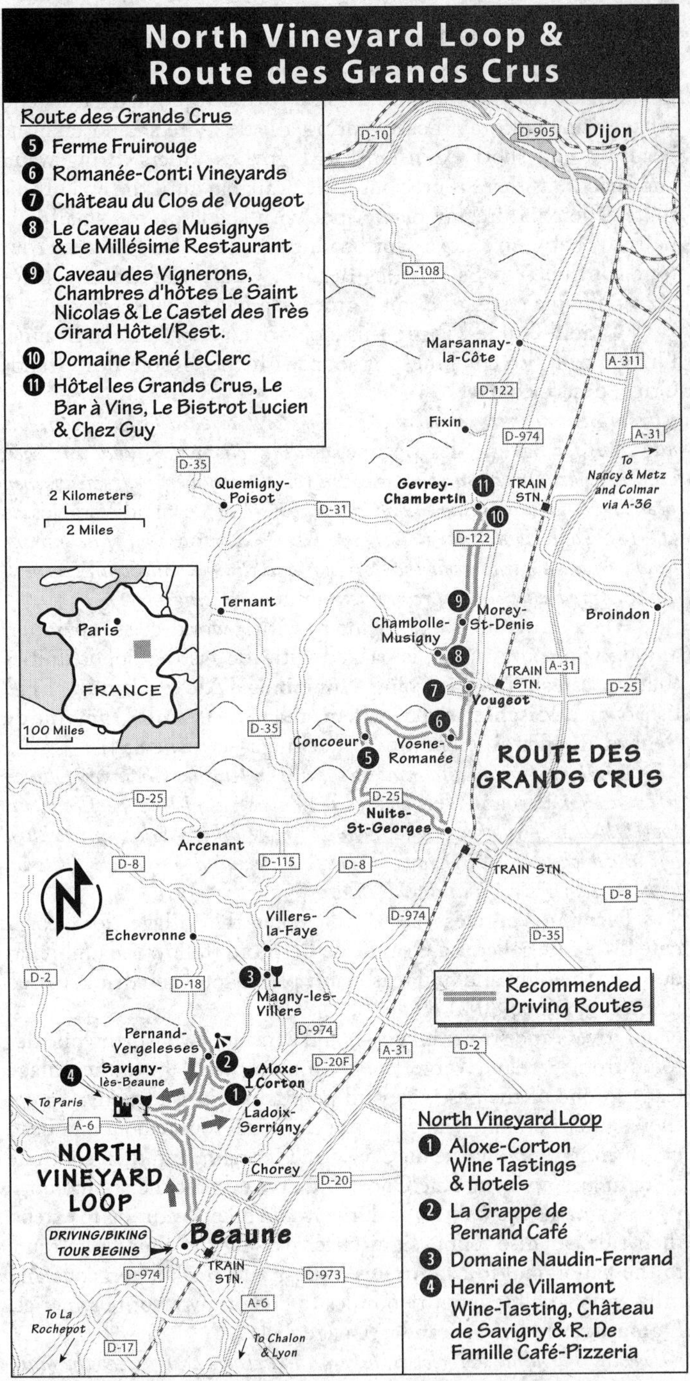

North Vineyard Loop & Route des Grands Crus

Route des Grands Crus

5 Ferme Fruirouge
6 Romanée-Conti Vineyards
7 Château du Clos de Vougeot
8 Le Caveau des Musignys & Le Millésime Restaurant
9 Caveau des Vignerons, Chambres d'hôtes Le Saint Nicolas & Le Castel des Très Girard Hôtel/Rest.
10 Domaine René LeClerc
11 Hôtel les Grands Crus, Le Bar à Vins, Le Bistrot Lucien & Chez Guy

North Vineyard Loop

1 Aloxe-Corton Wine Tastings & Hotels
2 La Grappe de Pernand Café
3 Domaine Naudin-Ferrand
4 Henri de Villamont Wine-Tasting, Château de Savigny & R. De Famille Café-Pizzeria

allow a half-day by bike or 1.5 hours by car). It laces together three renowned wine villages—Aloxe-Corton, Pernand-Vergelesses, and Savigny-lès-Beaune—connecting you with Burgundian nature and village wine culture. Those wanting a little more should take the beautiful and short extension to Magny-les-Villers. Bring water and snacks, as there is precious little available until the end of this route. There's a dreamy picnic spot with shade on the small lane halfway between Aloxe-Corton and Pernand-Vergelesses. Your tour concludes in Savigny-lès-Beaune, where you'll find a café-pizzeria, wine tastings, a small grocery, and a unique château.

➲ **Self-Guided Tour:** This loop drive/pedal starts in Beaune. Drivers can also combine this loop with the "Route des Grands Crus," described next.

• *From Beaune's ring road, take D-974 north toward Dijon. Soon, follow signs for* Savigny-lès-Beaune, *leading left at the signal and then quickly right. On the outskirts of town you'll cross over the freeway, then veer right, following the second signs you see to* Pernand-Vergelesses *(D-18). Turn right at the first sign to* Aloxe-Corton, *and glide into the town. Make a hard left at the stop sign and climb uphill to find a small parking area with several recommended wine-tastings close by).*

Aloxe-Corton: This tiny town, with a world-class reputation among wine enthusiasts, is packed with top tasting opportunities (but no cafés). The easygoing **Domaines d'Aloxe-Corton,** English-owned **Mischief and Mayhem,** and more upscale **Domaine de Senard** all offer different kinds of tastings (see page 854).

• *Leave Aloxe-Corton and head up the hill on Rue des Chaumes, following signs for* Pernand-Vergelesses *(you'll pass a picture-perfect picnic spot). At the T-intersection with D-18, most bikers will want to turn left and pick up the directions for leaving Pernand-Vergelesses (below). Otherwise, turn right and head into...*

Pernand-Vergelesses: As you enter the village, look for a cute little café called **La Grappe de Pernand** (follow the umbrellas down to the right and find reasonably priced food and drink, closed Mon-Tue, tel. 03 80 21 59 46).

Drivers and strong bikers should consider two worthwhile detours from Pernand-Vergelesses: Climbing well above the village leads to one of the best vineyard panoramas in Burgundy. To get there, enter Pernand-Vergelesses at the small roundabout and head up, turning right on Rue du Creux St. Germain, and then continue straight and up along Rue Copeau. Curve up past the church until you see small *Panorama* signs. Drivers and bikers wanting to extend their ride can also follow signs (after passing the church, en route to the panorama) to **Magny-les-Villers** and track a gorgeous and hilly wine lane for about two miles to one of my favorite wineries, **Domaine Naudin-Ferrand** (see page 854).

• *Leaving Pernand-Vergelesses, bikers and drivers both follow the main road (D-18) back toward Beaune, and turn right into the vineyards on the first lane (about 400 yards from Pernand-Vergelesses). Keep left at the first fork and rise gently to lovely views. Drop down and turn right when you come to a T, then joyride along the vine service lanes (bikers should watch for loose gravel). To reach Savigny-lès-Beaune, keep going until you see a* 5T *sign. Turn left just before the sign, then take the first right, and right again when you reach the T-intersection at the bottom. Merge onto the larger road; you'll soon come to a three-way intersection in...*

Savigny-lès-Beaune: The left fork leads back to Beaune, the middle fork leads to *Centre-Ville,* and the road to the right leads to a good wine tasting at **Henri de Villamont.** Follow the middle fork to find the four-towered **Château de Savigny** and the **R. De Famille** café-pizzeria (all described on 855).

• *From Savigny-lès-Beaune, drive or pedal back into Beaune. Those with a car can continue along the "Route des Grands Crus," next.*

Route des Grands Crus

While I prefer the areas south and west of Beaune, a more northern stretch of the Route des Grands Crus is a ▲ must for wine connoisseurs with a car, as it passes through Burgundy's most fabled vineyards.

The first part, between Aloxe-Corton and Nuits St-Georges, forces you onto the busy highway (D-974). But from Vougeot north, the route improves noticeably if you stick to D-122. Locals call this section the "Champs-Elysées of Burgundy." Between Vosne-Romanée and Gevrey-Chambertin, the road runs past 24 *grand cru* wineries of the Côte de Nuits—Pinot Noir paradise, where 95 percent of the wines are red. The path of today's busy D-974 road was established by monks in the 12th century to delineate the easternmost limit of land on which good wine could be grown. (Land to the east of this road is good for other crops but not for wine.) For lunch fixings, you'll find grocery stores in Nuits St-Georges and in Gevrey-Chambertin.

Riders are best off taking their bikes on the train from Beaune to Vougeot (nearly hourly departures, 15-minute trip, bikes are free on trains) and riding from there, skipping the hilly Ferme Fruirouge detour.

Here's a rundown of my favorite places on the northern Route des Grands Crus, listed from Beaune toward Dijon (for locations, see the map on page 859).

Concoeur

Come to this little village high above the wine route (northwest of Nuits St-Georges), for a Back Door stop at the shop called **Ferme**

Fruirouge. Adorable owners Sylvain and Isabelle grow cherries, raspberries, and black currants, and make crème de cassis, vinegars, mustards, and jams with passion. They (or their equally adorable staff) will explain their time-honored process for crafting these products. You can sample everything—including their one-of-a-kind cassis-ketchup—and get free recipe cards in French (Thu-Mon 9:00-12:00 & 14:00-19:00, closed Tue-Wed, 2 Place de l'Eglise, tel. 03 80 62 36 25, www.fruirouge.fr, call ahead to arrange for a good explanation of their operation).

Vosne-Romanée

The fabled Romanée-Conti vineyards of this tiny hamlet produce the priciest wines in Burgundy (figure $6,000 per bottle minimum; sorry, all bottles are presold).

Vougeot

In many ways, this is the birthplace of great Burgundian wines. In the 12th century, monks from the abbey of Cîteaux (8 miles southeast from here) built the magnificent stone **Château du Clos de Vougeot** to store equipment and make their wines. Their careful study of winemaking was the foundation for the world-famous reputation of Burgundian wines. It was here that monks discovered that pinot noir and chardonnay grapes were best suited to the local soil and climate. There's little to see inside except for the fine stone construction, four ancient and massive wine presses, and the room where the Confrérie des Chevaliers Tastevin (a Burgundian brotherhood of wine-tasters) meets to celebrate their legacy—and to apply their label of quality to area wines, called *le Tastevinage*. You can see the historic courtyard and cellar where bottles of each *Tastevinage* are stored and enter the classy gift shop before having to pay admission (which is enough for many). The château has a good English handout and posted information, but no tastings (€5, daily April-Oct 9:00-18:30 except Sat until 17:00, Nov-March 10:00-17:00, tel. 03 80 62 86 09, well-signed just outside town, www.closdevougeot.fr).

Chambolle-Musigny

Le Caveau des Musignys is a fine place to sample Burgundy's rich variety of wines. Say bonjour to sweet Annie, who will introduce you to the region's wines in a cool, vaulted tasting room. Representing 40 producers (recent vintages only for tasting), she has wines in all price ranges from throughout Burgundy. The whites from the Côte Challonaise are a good value, as are the midrange reds from Chambolle-Musigny and Vosne-Romanée (free tasting, Wed-Sun 9:00-18:00, closed Mon-Tue, a block north of the church at 1 Rue Traversière, tel. 03 80 62 84 01). You can eat upstairs in an elegant setting, where modern blends with tradition, at the lovely **Le Millésime** (€20 lunch *menus* except Sat, €29-52 dinner *menus*, indoor seating only, dazzling wine shelves, closed Sun-Mon, tel. 03 80 62 80 37).

Morey-St-Denis

This village houses more vineyards, a café, a bakery, and another worthwhile tasting stop at the **Caveau des Vignerons,** with reasonably priced wines from 13 small producers (each too small to have its own tasting room). Gentle Catherine speaks enough English to welcome you to her free tasting room, where you can sample wines from the Côtes de Nuits (good selection of wines from Gevrey-Chambertin, though I prefer those from Morey-St-Denis, Wed-Mon 10:00-13:00 & 14:00-19:00, closed Tue, next to the church, tel. 03 80 51 86 79).

Sleeping and Eating in Morey-St-Denis: Sleep very well for cheap nearby at **$ Chambres d'Hôte Le Saint Nicolas,** buried in the village but well-signed, where Madame Beaumont rents four traditional rooms and a spacious apartment at the vineyard's edge for a steal (Db-€65-78, Tb-€95, Qb-€112, includes breakfast, credit cards OK, Wi-Fi, wine tastings available, tel. 03 80 58 51 83, www.le-saint-nicolas.com, contact@le-saint-nicolas.com.

At the bottom end of the village lies an intimate, upscale hotel-restaurant, **$$$ Le Castel des Très Girard****.** This eight-room hotel delivers top service and classy comfort, including cozy lounges, a pool, and a restaurant that locals go out of their way for (Db-€190, big suites with two double beds-€270, breakfast-€15, air-con, dinner *menus* from €46, poolside tables, tel. 03 80 34 33 09, www.castel-tres-girard.com, info@castel-tres-girard.com).

Gevrey-Chambertin

For many pinot-noir lovers, a visit to this flowery village is the pinnacle of their Burgundian pilgrimage. The appealing village has a TI (daily, 1 Rue Gaston Roupnel, tel. 03 80 34 38 40), a small grocery, a café, a pizzeria, two restaurants, and a good-value hotel.

Gevrey-Chambertin produces nine of the 32 *grand cru* wines from Burgundy. All are pinot noirs (no whites in sight), and all use the suffix "Chambertin" ("Gevrey" is the historic name of the village; "Chambertin" is its most important vineyard). As you drive through the countryside south of the village, look for signs identifying the famous vineyards.

Domaine René LeClerc is a good place to sample the village's prestigious product. Happy-go-lucky Francois speaks enough English to explain his approach to winemaking (bottles from €28, daily 10:00-19:00, on D-974 at the north end of town opposite the Hôtel Arts et Terroirs, 29 Route de Dijon, tel. 06 31 05 68 50).

Sleeping in Gevrey-Chambertin: You can sleep well at **$$ Hôtel les Grands Crus*****, with simple, spotless, and traditional rooms overlooking vineyards, plus a pleasant patio and free, secure parking (Db-€88-98, €13 buffet breakfast, air-con, Wi-Fi, at the northwest edge of town on Rue de Lavaux, tel. 03 80 34 34 15, www.hoteldesgrandscrus.com, hotel.lesgrandscrus@nerim.net).

Eating in Gevrey-Chambertin: Hang out at the local watering hole, **Le Bar à Vins** café and have a classic Burgundian dinner experience at **Le Bistrot Lucien,** where stone walls meet stone floors inside and out (*menus* from €32, closed Sun-Mon, in the Rotisserie building, tel. 03 80 34 33 20). You can also dine at **Chez Guy,** with snazzy outdoor seating and modern, stylish decor (in the center of the village, *menus* from €30, open daily, 3 Place de la Mairie, tel. 03 80 58 51 51).

Between Beaune and Paris

North of Beaune, you'll find a handful of worthwhile places that string together well for a full-day excursion: towering Châteauneuf-en-Auxois, sleepy Semur-en-Auxois, remote Fontenay's abbey, pretty little Flavigny-sur-Ozerain, and Julius Caesar's victorious battlefield at Alise Ste-Reine (with its good museum, MuséoParc Alésia).

As a bonus, following my driving tour of this area takes you along several stretches of the **Burgundy Canal** (Canal de Bourgogne). As in much of France, Burgundy's canals were dug 200 years ago, in the early Industrial Age, as an affordable way to transport cargo. The Burgundy canal was among the most important, linking Paris with the Mediterranean Sea. The canal is 145 miles long, with 209 locks, and rises over France's continental divide in Pouilly-en-Auxois, just below Châteauneuf-en-Auxois (where the canal runs underground for about two miles). Digging began in 1727 and the canal was completed in 1832—ironically, just in time for the invention of steam engines on rails, which soon eliminated the need for waterway transport.

Back-Door Burgundy Towns and Sights

The towns and sights described below can be connected with my "Back-Door Burgundy Driving Tour" outlined on page 871.

Châteauneuf-en-Auxois

This living hill town hunkers in the shadow of its impressive castle and merits exploring. The perfectly medieval castle once monitored passage between Burgundy and Paris, with hawk-eye views from its 2,000-foot-high setting. *Châteauneuf* means "new castle," so you'll see many in France. This one is in the Auxois area, so it's Châteauneuf-en-Auxois. Park at the lot in the very upper end of the village (where the road ends), and don't miss the **panoramic viewpoint** nearby. The military value of this site is powerfully clear from here. Find the Burgundy Canal and the three reservoirs that have maintained the canal's flow for more than 200 years. The small village below is Châteauneuf's port, Vandenesse-en-Auxois—you'll be there shortly. If not for phylloxera—the vine-loving insect that ravaged France in the late 1800s, killing all of its vineyards—you'd see more vineyards than wheat fields.

Saunter into the village, where every building feels historic and stocky farmers live side by side with tattooed artists. Walk into the courtyard, but skip the **château**'s interior (€5, Tue-Sun 10:00-12:00 & 14:00-18:00, closed Mon, English handout). You'll get better moat views and see the more important castle entry by walking beneath the Hôstellerie du Château, and then turning right, following *Eglise* signs.

Sleeping in Châteauneuf-en-Auxois: You won't break the bank sleeping at the **$$ Hôstellerie du Château****, a simple, cozy place housing an enticing budget-vacation ensemble: nine homey, inexpensive rooms with a rear garden overlooking the brooding floodlit castle at night (Db-€60 for tight bathrooms with showers, Db-€80 for larger rooms with tubs, Tb-€90, Wi-Fi, closed Nov-Feb, tel. 03 80 49 22 00, www.hostellerie-de-chateauneuf.com, contact@hostellerie-de-chateauneuf.com). Their restaurant offers fine regional cuisine and four-course *menus* with a traditional cheese cart for €28 (closed Tue-Wed off-season).

Eating in Châteauneuf-en-Auxois: Châteauneuf has several affordable cafés and restaurants along its main drag. **Orée du Bois** is cozy inside and out, and makes good crêpes, including one stuffed with snails. **Grill du Castel,** across from Hôstellerie du Château, owns a sweet patio and serves big salads and good grilled meats (add a sauce for a few extra euros)—but skip the beef Burgundy.

Alise Ste-Reine

> *A united Gaul forming a single nation animated by the same spirit could defy the universe.*
>
> —Julius Caesar, *The Gallic Wars*

On these lands surrounding the vertical village of Alise Ste-Reine is where historians are convinced that Julius Caesar defeated the Gallic leader Vercingétorix in 52 B.C., thus winning Gaul for the Roman Empire and forever changing France's destiny. Start below with the impressive museum-park and stand where Caesar did, then drive above the village to see things from the Gauls' perspective.

▲MuséoParc Alésia

This circular museum, looking like a modern sports arena, does this important site justice with easy-to-follow exhibits and well-delivered information. The circular structure symbolizes how, more than 2,000 years ago, Caesar ordered his outnumbered forces to surround the Gauls' *oppidum* (hilltop village), starving them out and winning a decisive victory (see sidebar).

Cost and Hours: €9.50, includes essential audioguide (there's also a fun children's version), skip the €2 extra for the archaeological site on the hills above, daily April-Sept 9:00-18:00, until 19:00 July-Aug, shorter hours off-season, closed Feb, tel. 03 80 96 96 23, www.alesia.com.

Visiting the Museum: With the help of a handy audioguide, touchscreens, and posted information, you'll gain a keen understanding of the events that led up to this battle, why it happened here, and how it unfolded. You'll learn much about the two protagonists, Caesar and Vercingétorix, their armies, and their motivations, and be drawn into the conflict with an 18-minute film.

Allow an hour for the museum's single floor of exhibits, then climb to the top floor for views from a Roman perspective. Finally, walk out back to inspect the full-scale reconstruction of a section of the Roman wall and lookouts that pinned the Gauls to that hilltop.

Friendly staff dressed as Romans or Gauls are often present inside or out back to answer your questions and give demonstrations (some English spoken). Pick up the chain-mail suit (30 pounds), and learn that it took a kilometer of metal line to make one. To add more meaning to this sight, read "How About Them Romans" (see page 569).

Nearby: After the museum, drive through the village of Alise Ste-Reine and follow the *Statue de Vercingétorix* signs leading to the park with the huge **statue** of the Gallic warrior overlooking his Waterloo (skip the archaeological site). Stand as he did—imagining yourself trapped on this hilltop—then find the orientation table under the gazebo.

Flavigny-sur-Ozerain

Over the next hill from Alise Ste-Reine, the approach via D-9 to sleepy little Flavigny-sur-Ozerain (flah-veen-yee sur oh-zuh-rain) is picture-perfect. The town had its 15 minutes of fame in 2000,

The Dying Gauls

In 52 B.C., General Julius Caesar and his 60,000 soldiers surrounded Alésia (today's Alise Ste-Reine), hoping to finally end the uprising of free Gaul and establish Roman civilization in central and northern France (they had long controlled southern France). Holed up inside the hilltop fortress were 80,000 die-hard (long-haired, tattooed) Gauls under their rebel chief, Vercingétorix (pronounced something like "verse-an-zhet-or-eex"). Having harassed Caesar for months with guerrilla-war attacks, they now called on their fellow Gauls to converge on Alésia to wipe out the Romans.

Rather than attack the fierce-fighting Gauls, Caesar's soldiers patiently camped at the base of the hill and began building a wall. In six weeks, they completed a 12-foot-tall, stone-and-earth wall all the way around Alésia (11 miles around—blue line on the orientation table at the hilltop site), and then a second, larger one (13 miles around—red line on the orientation table), trapping the rebel leaders with the intention of starving them out. If the Gauls tried to escape, not only would they have to breach the two walls, they'd first have to cross a steep no-man's-land dotted with a ditch, a moat, and booby traps (including sharp stakes in pits and buried iron spikes).

The starving Gauls inside Alésia sent their women and children out to beg for mercy from the Romans. The Romans (with little food themselves) refused. For days, the women and children wandered the unoccupied land, in full view of both armies, until they starved to death.

After months of siege, Vercingétorix's reinforcements finally came riding to save him. With 90,000 screaming Gallic warriors (Caesar says 250,000) converging on Alésia, and 80,000 more atop the hill, Caesar ordered his men to move between the two walls to fight a two-front battle. The Battle of Alésia raged for five days—a classic struggle between the methodical Romans and the impetuous "barbarians." When it became clear the Romans would not budge, the Gauls retreated.

Vercingétorix surrendered, and Gallic culture was finished in France. During the three-year rebellion, one in five Gauls had been killed, enslaved, or driven out. Roman rule was established for the next 500 years, strangling the Gallic/Celtic heritage. Vercingétorix spent his last years as a prisoner, paraded around as a war trophy. In 46 B.C., he was brought to Rome for Caesar's triumphal ascension to power, where he was strangled to death in a public ritual.

when the movie *Chocolat* was filmed here, but otherwise this unassuming and serenely situated village feels permanently stuck in the past, with one café-restaurant, one *crêperie,* and a tiny grocery shop. Flavigny makes a good coffee or lunch stop, as there's little to do here but appreciate the setting (best from the grassy ramparts) and sample the local *anis* (anise) candies. Pick up a map from the TI (in the Maison au Donataire, on Rue de l'Eglise).

Flavigny has been home to an abbey since 719, when the first (Benedictine) abbey of St. Pierre was built. The town thrived during the Middle Ages thanks to its proximity to Vézelay (with its relics of Mary Magdalene) and the flood of pilgrims coming through en route to Santiago de Compostela in northwest Spain. The little town was occupied by the Brits during the Hundred Years' War (15th century), then ever-so-gradually slid into irrelevance. By the time the French Revolution rolled around, it had no religious or defensive importance. The movie *Chocolat* put the town back on the map—at least for a while—and today, Flavigny has been reinvigorated by the return of 50 Benedictine monks at the Abbey of St. Joseph.

You can see the town's *anis* candies being made in the Abbey of St. Pierre—they're sold in pretty tins and make great souvenirs (Mon-Fri 9:00-11:00, on Rue de l'Abbaye, www.anis-flavigny.com). The grassy ramparts are worth a stroll for the view (behind the church, walk down Rue de la Poterne, turn right at the fork, then look for *Petite Ruelle des Remparts*). You'll sleep well at **$$ L'Ange Souriant Chambre d'Hôte** (Sb-€55, Db-€70, Tb-€99, includes breakfast, cash only, €27 home-cooked dinners available if booked ahead, Wi-Fi, a block below the TI on Rue Voltaire, tel. 03 80 96 24 93, mobile 06 11 89 04 66, www.ange-souriant.fr, a.souriant@wanadoo.fr).

Eating in Flavigny-sur-Ozerain: You'll eat for a steal at **La Grange** ("The Barn") on cheap, farm-fresh fare, including luscious quiche, salads, *plats du jour,* fresh cheeses, pâtés, and delicious fruit pies (April-mid-Oct daily 12:30-18:00; open Sun only in off-season and closed Dec-Jan; across from church, look for brown doors and listen for lunchtime dining, tel. 03 80 35 81 78).

▲▲Abbey of Fontenay

The entire ensemble of buildings composing this isolated Cistercian abbey has survived, giving visitors perhaps the best picture of medieval abbey life in France. In the Middle Ages, it was written, "To fully grasp the meaning of Fontenay and the power of its beauty, you must approach it trudging through the forest footpaths...through the brambles and bogs...in an October rain." Those arriving by car will still find Fontenay's secluded setting—blanketed in birdsong and with a garden lovingly used "as a stage set"—truly magical.

Cost and Hours: €10, daily April-mid-Nov 10:00-18:00, mid-Nov-March 10:00-12:00 & 14:00-17:00, tel. 03 80 92 15 00, www.abbayedefontenay.com.

Getting There: The abbey is a 10-minute drive (4 miles) north of Montbard. There's no bus service—allow about €26 round-trip for a taxi from Montbard's train station (taxi mobile 06 08 26 61 55 or 06 08 99 21 13), or rent a bike at Montbard's TI and ride 45 minutes each way (Montbard TI tel. 03 80 92 53 81).

Background: This abbey—one of the oldest Cistercian abbeys in France—was founded in 1118 by St. Bernard as a back-to-basics reaction to the excesses of Benedictine abbeys like Cluny. The Cistercians worked to recapture the simplicity, solitude, and poverty of the early Church. Bernard created "a horrible vast solitude" in the forest, where his monks could live like the desert fathers of the Old Testament. They chose marshland ("Cistercian" is derived from "marshy bogs") and strove to be separate from the world (which required the industrious self-sufficiency these abbeys were so adept at). The movement spread, essentially colonizing Europe religiously. In 1200, there were more than 500 such monasteries and abbeys in Europe.

Like the Cistercian movement in general, Fontenay flourished from the 13th to 15th century. A 14th-century proverb said, "Wherever the wind blows, to Fontenay money flows." Fontenay thrived as a prosperous "mini-city" for nearly 700 years, until the French Revolution, when it became the property of the nation and was eventually sold.

Visiting the Abbey: Like visitors centuries ago, you'll enter through the abbey's **gatehouse.** The main difference: Anyone with a ticket gets in, and there's no watchdog barking angrily at you (through the small hole on the right). Pick up the English self-guided tour flier with your ticket. Your visit follows the route described here (generally clockwise). Arrows keep you on course, and signs tell you which sections of the abbey are private (as its owners still live here).

The **abbey church** is pure Romanesque and built to St. Bernard's specs: Latin cross plan, no fancy stained glass, unadorned columns, nothing to distract from prayer. The lone statue is the 13th-century *Virgin of Fontenay,* a reminder that the church was dedicated to Mary. Enjoy the ethereal light. Quiet your mind and listen carefully to hear the brothers chanting.

Stairs lead from the front of the church to a vast 16th-century, oak-beamed **dormitory** where the monks slept—together, fully dressed, on thin mats. Monastic life was pretty simple: prayer, reading, work, seven services a day, one meal in the winter, two in the summer. Daily rations: a loaf of bread and a quarter-liter of wine.

Back down the stairs, enter the **cloister,** beautiful in its starkness. This was the heart of the community, where monks read, exercised, washed, did small projects—and, I imagine, gave each other those silly haircuts. The shallow alcove (next to the church door) once stored prayer books; notice the slots for shelves. Next to that, the chapter room was where the abbot led discussions and community business was discussed. The adjacent monks' hall was a general-purpose room, likely busy with monks hunched over tables copying sacred texts (a major work of abbeys). The dining hall, or refectory, also faced the cloister (closed to the public).

Across the garden stands the huge abbey **forge.** In the 13th century, the monks at Fontenay ran what many consider Europe's first metalworking plant. Iron ore was melted down in ovens with big bellows. Tools were made and sold for a profit. The hydraulic hammer, which became the basis of industrial manufacturing of iron throughout Europe, was first used here. Leaving the building, walk left around the back to see the stream, which was diverted to power the wheels that operated the forge. Water was vital to abbey life. The pond—originally practical, rather than decorative—was a fish farm (some whopper descendants still swim here). Leave through the gift shop, which was the public chapel in the days when visitors were not allowed inside the abbey grounds.

Semur-en-Auxois

This sleepy town feels real. There are 4,500 residents, few tourists, and no important sights to digest—just a pleasing jumble of Burgundian alleys perched above the meandering Armançon River and behind the town's four massive towers, all beautifully illuminated after dark.

Locals like to believe that Hercules built Semur-en-Auxois (suh-moor-ahn-ohx-wah) on his return from Spain. But Semur's ancient origins date back to Neolithic times, long before Hercules' visit. Today the town works as a base to visit the sights described in this area, or for most, a handy leg-stretching stop. Don't miss the smashing panorama of

Semur from the viewpoint by the Citroën shop, where D-980 and D-954 intersect.

From the TI (across from Hôtel Côte d'Or, at Semur's medieval entry, 2 Place Gaveau, tel. 03 80 97 05 96), pick up a city-walking brochure and tour the town. Enter through the Sauvigny and Guiller gates, then saunter along charming Rue Buffon, Semur's oldest commercial street. You'll come to the 13th-century **Church of Notre-Dame,** the town's main sight, which dominates its small square and is worth a quick look (Mon-Sat 9:00-12:00 & 14:00-18:30, Sun 14:00-18:30, decent English handout). As you leave the church, glance at the second-to-last chapel on your right, with a large plaque honoring American soldiers who died in World War I.

In the Middle Ages, 18 towers were connected by defensive ramparts to protect the center city. Caught in the crossfire between the powerful Dukes of Burgundy and the king of France, Semur's defenses were first destroyed by Louis XI in 1478, then finished off during the Wars of Religion in 1602. For postcard-perfect views, stroll several blocks down from the church along Rue Févret, turn left where it ends (at Rue du Rempart), then turn left again down Rue du Fourneau and amble along the Armançon River.

For fine views over the city, drive or hike downhill from the TI along Rue du Pont Joly, cross the river, then head uphill and turn left at the top roundabout. Across from the Citroën dealership, find the lookout with an orientation table and a memorable view of the red roofs, spires, and towers—especially striking at night. Walkers will find great views just after crossing the bridge.

***Sleeping in Semur-en-Auxois*:** If this quiet town seduces you into spending a night, try **$$ Hôtel les Cymaises**,** with comfortable rooms and big beds in a manor house with a quiet courtyard (Db-€73, Tb-€85, 2-room Qb-€105, Wi-Fi, private parking, 7 Rue du Renaudot, tel. 03 80 97 21 44, www.hotelcymaises.com, contact@hotelcymaises.com).

Eating in Semur-en-Auxois: Cafés along Rue du Buffon offer ambience and average quality. **L'Entract** is where everybody goes for pizza, pasta, salads, and more in a relaxed atmosphere (daily, below the church on 4 Rue Févret, tel. 03 80 96 60 10).

Back-Door Burgundy Driving Tour

This all-day loop links Châteauneuf-en-Auxois, Alise Ste-Reine, and Fontenay, with short stops suggested in Flavigny-sur-Ozerain and Semur-en-Auxois. The trip trades vineyards for wheat fields, canals, and pastoral landscapes. You'll drive along the Burgundy canal and visit a Cistercian abbey, medieval villages, and the site of Gaul's last stand against the Romans. It requires a car and a good

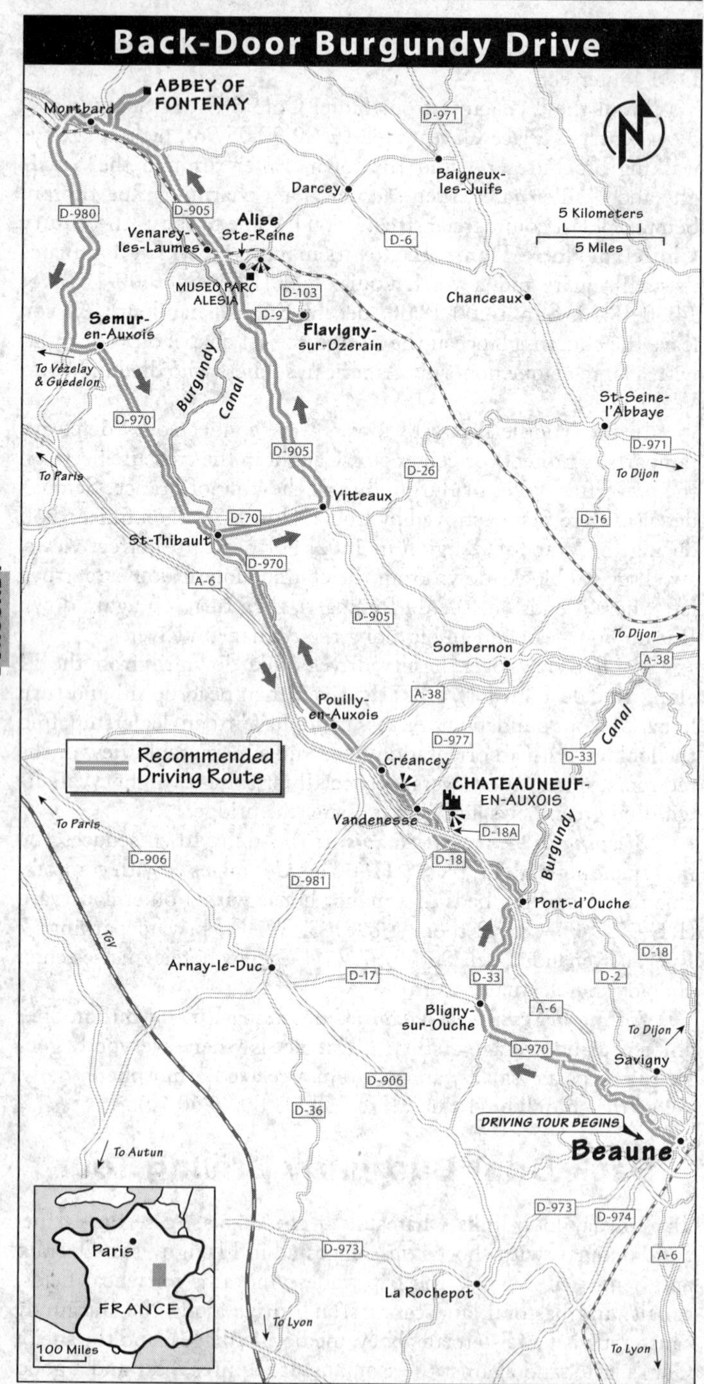
Back-Door Burgundy Drive
ABBEY OF FONTENAY
Montbard
D-971
Baigneux-les-Juifs
Darcey
D-980
D-905
Alise Ste-Reine
Venarey-les-Laumes
D-6
5 Kilometers
5 Miles
MUSEO PARC ALESIA
D-103
Chanceaux
D-9
Flavigny-sur-Ozerain
Semur-en-Auxois
To Vézelay & Guedelon
Burgundy Canal
St-Seine-l'Abbaye
D-970
D-971
D-905
To Dijon
To Paris
D-26
Vitteaux
D-16
D-70
St-Thibault
D-970
A-6
D-905
To Dijon
Sombernon
A-38
A-38
Pouilly-en-Auxois
Canal
D-977
Recommended Driving Route
D-33
Créancey
CHATEAUNEUF-EN-AUXOIS
To Paris
Vandenesse
D-18A
Burgundy
D-906
D-18
D-981
Pont-d'Ouche
TGV
D-18
Arnay-le-Duc
D-17
D-2
D-33
Bligny-sur-Ouche
A-6
To Dijon
D-970
Savigny
D-906
D-36
DRIVING TOUR BEGINS
Beaune
To Autun
D-973
D-974
Paris
D-973
A-6
FRANCE
La Rochepot
To Lyon
100 Miles
To Lyon

BURGUNDY

map (Michelin maps #320 or #519 work well). If you're heading to/from Paris, this tour works well en route or as an overnight stop; I've listed accommodations and described sights along the way in greater detail under "Back-Door Burgundy Towns and Sights," earlier.

Here's how I'd spend this day: Get out early and joyride to MuséoParc Alésia in Alise Ste-Reine (with at least a photo stop for Châteauneuf-en-Auxois), tour the museum and battle site, have lunch a few minutes away in Flavigny, drive to Fontenay and tour the abbey, then consider a stop in Semur-en-Auxois for a stroll on your way home (this plan also works for those continuing to Paris). Energetic sightseers could add Vézelay to this plan by getting on the road no later than 8:00 and focusing on Alise Ste-Reine and Fontenay, then darting over to Vézelay on the way back.

The museum and battlefield at Alise Ste-Reine and the Abbey of Fontenay are your primary goals; allow at least an hour to tour each. With no stops, the one-way drive from Beaune to Fontenay should take about an hour and a half. But you should be stopping—a lot.

➲ **Self-Guided Tour:** Leave Beaune following signs for *Auxerre* and *Bligny-sur-Ouche;* from Bligny-sur-Ouche, take D-33 to Pont d'Ouche (following signs to *Pont du Pany* and *Dijon*), where you'll turn left along the canal (D-18), following signs to *Château de Châteauneuf.* In five minutes, you'll see the castle at **Châteauneuf-en-Auxois** looming above (see page 865). Turn right on D-18a and cross over the canal, then the freeway, for great views of the hill town, even if you're not visiting it. A right on the small lane at the second farm, one kilometer after leaving D-18, leads a short distance up to fine views.

Return back down to the canal, press on to Vandenesse, and turn right, then left toward **Créancey** (still on D-18). There's a nice picnic spot on its "port," with water views of Châteauneuf. Keep following D-18 from Créancey toward Pouilly-en-Auxois. The Burgundy Canal tunnels underground for several miles through Pouilly-en-Auxois, as it passes its highest point between Paris and Dijon (rivers east of here flow to the Mediterranean, those to the west to the Atlantic). You'll go over the canal as you cross Pouilly-en-Auxois.

Go through Pouilly-en-Auxois and follow signs to Vitteaux, where you'll join D-905. Go north toward **Alise Ste-Reine** (described on page 865), where Julius Caesar is said to have defeated the Gauls. Follow signs to *Alésia* and *MuséoParc.* After exploring the museum and battlefield, backtrack a short distance on D-905 and find signs to the quiet village of **Flavigny-sur-Ozerain** (5 minutes away on D-9; see page 868).

From Flavigny-sur-Ozerain, drive back to D-905, turn right

(north), and follow signs to the secluded Cistercian **Abbey of Fontenay** (described on page 868). After the abbey, continue up D-905 to Montbard, then turn onto D-980 and drive south to peaceful and scenic **Semur-en-Auxois** (see page 870). From there, take D-970 via Pouilly-en-Auxois and retrace your route to Beaune. For a quicker option, you can dart from Semur-en-Auxois across to the A-6 autoroute and take it to Beaune (or head north to Paris).

Public Transit Options: Non-drivers can get to Alésia by taking the train from Dijon to Les Laumes-Alésia, and to the Abbey of Fontenay by taking the train to Montbard and a taxi from there (see Abbey of Fontenay listing for details). There are no trains to Semur-en-Auxois, but you can get there by bus (3/day Mon-Sat, 1/day Sun, from Montbard or Dijon—runs early morning, noon, and evening; rail pass gets you a free ticket, ask TI in Semur about where to get bus ticket).

Between Burgundy and the Loire

These three sights—Vézelay, and its Romanesque Basilica of Ste. Madeleine; the under-construction Château de Guédelon; and the underrated, overlooked city of Bourges, with its grand "High" Gothic cathedral—make good stops for drivers connecting Burgundy and the Loire Valley. Squeezing in visits to all three in one day is impossible, so pick two and get an early start (allow six hours of driving from Beaune to the Loire, plus time to stop and visit the sights). The first two sights also work if you're linking Burgundy and Paris (in which case, skip Bourges, which requires a long detour.)

Vézelay

For more than eight centuries, travelers have hoofed it up through this pretty little town to get to the famous hilltop church, the Basilica of Ste. Madeleine. In its 12th-century prime, Vézelay welcomed the medieval masses. Cultists of Mary Magdalene came to file past her (supposed) body. Pilgrims rendezvoused here to march to Spain to venerate St. James' (supposed) relics in Santiago de Compostela. Three Crusades were launched from this hill: the Second Crusade (1146), announced by Bernard of Clairveaux; the Third Crusade (1190), under Richard the Lionhearted and King Philippe Auguste; and the Seventh Crusade (1248), by King (and Saint) Louis IX. Today, tourists flock to Vézelay's basilica, famous for its place in history, its soul-stirring Romanesque architecture—reproduced in countless art books—and for the relics of Mary Magdalene.

Tourist Information: Vézelay's TI is at the lower end of the village (on Rue St. Etienne, which turns into Rue St. Pierre; May-Sept daily 10:00-13:00 & 14:00-18:00, until 19:00 July-Aug; Oct-April Fri-Wed 10:00-13:00 & 14:00-18:00, closed Thu, also closed Sun Nov-March; tel. 03 86 33 23 69). The TI provides free Wi-Fi and pay computer access.

Getting There: Vézelay is about 45 minutes northwest of **Semur-en-Auxois.** Drivers take the Avallon exit from A-6 and follow *Vézelay* signs for about 20 minutes. Train travelers go to **Sermizelles** and take the SNCF shuttle bus (3/day, free with rail pass) or a taxi (6 miles, allow €20 one-way, taxi tel. 03 86 32 31 88 or mobile 06 85 77 89 36). From Paris, Gare de Bercy trains run directly to Sermizelles (6/day, 2.5 hours); if coming from other places, you'll transfer in Auxerre or Avallon).

Sights in Vézelay

▲Basilica of Ste. Madeleine

To accommodate the growing crowds of medieval pilgrims, the abbots of Vézelay enlarged their original church (1104), then rebuilt it after a disastrous 1120 fire. The building we see today—one of the largest and best-preserved Romanesque churches anywhere—was built in stages: nave (1120-1140), narthex (1132-1145), and choir (1215). The construction spanned the century-long transition from the Romanesque style (round barrel arches like the ancient Romans', thick walls, small windows) to Gothic (pointed arches, flying buttresses, high nave, lots of stained glass). Vézelay blends elements of both styles.

Cost and Hours: Free, daily 7:00-20:00; Mass Mon-Fri at 18:30, Sat at 12:30 and 18:30, Sun at 11:00.

Tours: Tours can be arranged by contacting the volunteer coordinator (tel. 03 86 33 39 50, www.basiliquedevezelay.org). Or be your own guide, either by following the route I describe next or buying the €5 guidebook as you enter.

Visiting the Basilica: The **facade**—with one tower missing its original steeple, another that's unfinished, and an inauthentic tympanum—isn't why you came. Step inside.

The **narthex,** or entrance hall, served several functions. Religiously, it was a place to cross from the profane to the sacred. Practically, it gave shelter to overflow pilgrim crowds (even overnight, if necessary) as they shuffled through one of the three doorways. And aesthetically, the dark narthex prepares the visitor for the radiant nave.

The **tympanum** (carved relief) over the central, interior door-

Mary Magdalene

France has a special affection for Mary Magdalene *(La Madeleine),* and Vézelay is one of several churches dedicated to her—a rarity in Europe, where most churches honor Jesus' mother, the Virgin Mary.

The Bible says that Mary Magdalene, one of Jesus' followers, was exorcised of seven demons (Luke 8:2), witnessed the Crucifixion (Matthew 27:56), and was the first mortal to see the resurrected Jesus (Mark 16:9-11)—the other disciples didn't believe her.

Some theologians have fleshed out Mary's reputation by associating her with biblical passages that don't specifically name her—e.g., the sinner who washed Jesus' feet with her hair (Luke 7:36-50), the forgiven adulteress (John 8), or the woman with the alabaster jar who anointed Jesus (Matthew 26:7-13).

In medieval times, legends appeared (especially in France) that, after the Crucifixion, Mary Magdalene fled to southern France, lived in a cave, converted locals, performed miracles, and died in Provence. Renaissance artists portrayed her as a fanciful blend of Bible and legend: a red-headed, long-haired prostitute who was rescued by Jesus, symbolizing the sin of those who love too much.

In recent times, feminists have claimed Mary Magdalene was a victim of male-dominated Catholic suppression. Bible scholars cite passages in two ancient (but noncanonical) gospels that cryptically allude to Mary as Jesus' special "companion." *The Da Vinci Code*—a popular if unhistorical novel—seized on this, slathering it with medieval legend and asserting that Mary Magdalene was actually Jesus' wife who bore him descendants, and that her relics lie not in Vézelay but in a shopping mall in Paris.

way is one of Romanesque's signature pieces. It shows the risen Christ, ascending to heaven in an almond-shaped cloud, shooting Holy Ghost rays at his apostles and telling them to preach the Good News to the ends of the earth. The whole diversity of humanity (appropriate, considering Vézelay's function as a gathering place) appears beneath: hunters, fishermen, farmers, pygmies, and men with long ears, feathers, and dog heads. The signs of the zodiac arch over the scene.

Gaze through the central doorway into the **nave** at the rows and rows of arches that seem to recede into a luminous infinity. The nave is long, high, and narrow (200 feet by 60 feet by 35 feet), creating a tunnel effect formed by 10 columns and arches on each side. Overhead is the church's most famous feature—barrel vaults (wide arches) built of stones alternating between creamy-white and light-brown. The nave rises up between the low-ceilinged side aisles, lined with slender floor-to-ceiling columns that unite both stories. The interior glows with an even light from the unstained glass of the clerestory windows. The absence of distractions or bright colors makes this simple church perfect for meditation.

The capitals of the nave's **columns** are carved masterpieces by several sculptors of saints and Bible scenes. All are worth studying (the guidebook sold at the entry identifies each scene). Here are some you might easily recognize. Start on the right aisle and locate the well-known "Mystical Mill" (fourth column), showing Old Testament Moses and New Testament Paul working together to fill sacks with grain (and, metaphorically, the Bible with words). Cross to the left aisle and find David and Goliath (fourth column), Adam and Eve (ninth column), and Peter Freed from Prison (10th and final column).

The light at the end of the tunnel-like nave is the **choir,** radiating a brighter, blue-gray light. Constructed when Gothic was the rage, the choir has pointed arches and improved engineering, but the feel is monotone and sterile.

In the right transept stands a statue of the woman this church was dedicated to—not the Virgin Mary (Jesus' mother) but one of Jesus' disciples, Mary Magdalene. She cradles an alabaster jar of ointment she used (according to some Bible interpretations) to anoint Jesus.

Go down into the **crypt** for the ultimate medieval experience in one of Europe's greatest medieval churches. You're entering the foundations of the earlier ninth-century church that monks built here on the hilltop after Vikings had twice pillaged their church at the base of the hill. Notice the rough floor, and pause on a pew to reflect on the pure, timeless scene. Notice the utter simplicity of these capitals compared to those you saw earlier. File past the small container with the **relics of Mary Magdalene.** In medieval times, Vézelay claimed to possess Mary's entire body, but the relics were later damaged and scattered by anti-Catholic Huguenots (16th century) and Revolutionaries (18th century), leaving only a few pieces.

Are they really her mortal remains? We only have legends—many different versions—that first appeared in the historical record around A.D. 1000. The most popular says that Mary Magdalene traveled to Provence, where she died, and that her bones were brought here by a monk to save them from Muslim pirates. In the 11th century, the abbots of Vézelay heavily marketed the notion that these were Mary's relics, and when the pope authenticated them in 1058, tourism boomed.

Vézelay prospered until the mid-13th century, when King

Charles of Anjou announced that Mary's body was not in Vézelay, but had been found in another town. Vézelay's relics suddenly looked bogus, and pilgrims stopped coming. For the next five centuries, the church fell into disrepair and then was vandalized by secularists in the Revolution. The church was restored (1840-1860) by a young architect named Eugène Viollet-le-Duc, who would later revamp Notre-Dame in Paris and build the base of the Statue of Liberty.

The chapter house and cloisters are out the right transept, where you'll find small excavations underway to locate remains of the 12th-century cloister.

Sleeping and Eating in Vézelay

You'll find pleasant cafés with reasonable food all along the street leading to the church.

$$$ Hôtel de la Poste et du Lion d'Or has comfortable, country-classy rooms in Vézelay (good Db-€102, bigger Db-€112-149, Wi-Fi, easy parking-€6/day, at the foot of the village, Place du Champ-de-Foire, tel. 03 86 33 21 23, www.laposte-liondor.com, contact@laposte-liondor.com). Dinner in the hotel's country-elegant **restaurant**—indoors or *en plein air*—is a treat (*menus* from €27, closed Mon).

Eating: **La Dent Creuse** has the best terrace tables at the lower end of the village (left side), with salads, pizza, and such (daily until 21:30, Place du Champ-de-Foire, tel. 03 86 33 36 33).

Auberge de la Coquille is a cozy place to eat inside and out, with reasonable prices (€11 salads, €14 *plats, menus* from €16, daily until 21:30, halfway up to the church at 81 Rue St. Pierre, tel. 03 86 33 35 57).

Château de Guédelon

A historian's dream (worth ▲▲, or ▲▲▲ for kids), this castle is being built by 35 enthusiasts using only the tools, techniques, and materials available in the 13th century.

Cost and Hours: €12, kids 5-17-€10, under 5-free, picnic area and good-value lunch café with many options inside; castle open mid-March-early Nov 10:00-17:30, July-Aug daily 10:00-19:00; closed early Nov-mid-March, Wed and weekends in March, the first two Wed in April, and every Wed in Sept (tel. 03 86 45 66 66, www.guedelon.fr).

Tours: There's a good English handout, some posted information, and a downloadable audio tour available (on their website), but this place cries out for a live guide to answer the questions the medieval construction site inspires. Expertly guided tours in English should be available in July and August on Tuesdays, Thursdays, and Saturdays for an additional €2.50 per person; check their website for updated times. Guided private tours are also available throughout the season and are well worth the investment (€150 for your group for a 1.5-hour tour, contact sarah.preston@guedelon.fr).

Getting There: Guédelon lies an hour west of Vézelay on D-955, between St-Amand-en-Puisaye and St-Saveur-en-Puisaye. Finding it requires patient route-finding skills and time. Allow 2.5 hours from Paris or Beaune at a steady pace. Coming from Paris, take exit #18 off the A-6 autoroute (well before Auxerre) and follow D-3 to Toucy; then join D-955 south. Coming from Beaune, exit A-6 at Avallon, then carefully track signs to Vézelay (take a break to visit its basilica), Clamecy, Entrains-sur-Nohain, St-Amand-en-Puisaye, and finally Guédelon. The castle is inaccessible by public transport.

Visiting the Castle: The project is the dream of two individuals who wanted to build a medieval castle (this one is based on plans drafted in 1228). Started in 1997, it will ultimately include four towers surrounding a central courtyard with a bridge and a moat (images of the finished castle are on postcards and in books in the gift shop). The goal of this exciting project is to give visitors a better appreciation of medieval construction, and for the builders to learn about medieval techniques while they work. The castle won't be complete for another 12 years or so, so you still have time to watch the process. When the castle is done, the ambitious owners plan to build a medieval mill and maybe an abbey.

Enter the project to the sound of chisels chipping rock and the sight of people dressed as if it were 800 years ago. Human-powered hamster wheels carefully hoist 440 pounds of stone up tower walls (the largest tower will reach six stories when completed). Carpenters whack away at massive beams, creating supports for stone arches, while weavers demonstrate how clothing was made (a sheep's pen provides raw materials). Thirteen workstations help visitors learn about castle construction, from medieval rope-making to blacksmithing. Ask the workers questions—some speak English, and their job is to answer your questions as best they can. If it's been raining, be prepared for mud—you are, after all, in a construction site.

Kids can't get enough of Guédelon. It's a favorite for local school field trips, so expect lots of children. And if you can't get enough, there's a program for those wanting to join the workers and help (one-week minimum, check the website).

Sleeping near Guédelon: Guédelon is remote. If you need to sleep nearby, try **$$ Hôtel Les Grands Chênes,** where British Rachael and French Alain have restored a pretty manor home among trees, lakes, and waves of grass (Db-€90, Tb-€100, Qb-€115, Quint/b-€135, Wi-Fi, on D-18 between St-Fargeau and St-Amand-en-Puisaye, tel. 03 86 74 04 05, www.hotellesgrandschenes.com, contact@hotellesgrandschenes.com).

Bourges

Nestled between rolling vineyards and thick forests in the geographical center of France, unpretentious Bourges (pronounced "boorzh") is among France's most overlooked and authentic cities. Here you'll uncover a wonderful collection of medieval houses, a Gothic cathedral to rival any you've seen, and a down-to-earth, Midwest-like friendliness. Situated three hours due south of Paris, two hours west of Beaune, and 1.5 hours east of Amboise, Bourges is a handy stopover on the drive through the French heartland between Burgundy and the Loire.

Little-known Bourges has a big story to tell, thanks largely to its strategic location between two once-powerful regions, Burgundy and the Loire. It began as a Celtic city, became one of the first Christian towns in Gaul, and later served as the northern boundary of the sophisticated Kingdom of Aquitaine. Bourges reached its peak in the Middle Ages, when its great cathedral was built. It was home to future King Charles VII (r. 1422-1461), the man who, at Joan of Arc's insistence, rallied the French and drove out the English. During that Hundred Years' War, Bourges was a provisional capital of France, which explains its impressive legacy of medieval architecture.

TOURIST INFORMATION

If the cathedral had a transept, the TI would lie outside the south portal (April-Sept Mon-Sat 9:00-19:00, Sun 10:00-18:00; Oct-March Mon-Sat 9:00-18:00, Sun 14:00-17:00; free Wi-Fi, 21 Rue Victor Hugo, tel. 02 48 23 02 60, www.bourges-tourisme.com). Pick up one of their excellent English walking guides—wine lovers should ask for the *Route des Vignobles* map, and historians the *Route Jacques Cœur* map.

ARRIVAL IN BOURGES

By Train: From the station, it's about a half-mile walk south to the town center and cathedral. Head straight out onto Avenue Henri Laudier and turn left onto Rue du Commerce to find the TI.

By Car: Parking Mairie-Cathédrale is on the south side of the cathedral. The stairs up to the street land you in front of the TI.

HELPFUL HINTS

Street Markets: Bourges is known for its good morning markets (all close by 13:00). The biggest is held on Saturdays on Place de la Nation. A smaller Thursday market takes place near the cathedral on Place des Maronniers, and Place St-Bonnet has a good market on Sundays.

Sound-and-Light Show: Bourges' **Nuits Lumière** starts at sundown every night in July and August, and every Thursday, Friday, and Saturday in May, June, and September. The town's facades, courtyards, and monuments are lit up, accompanied by medieval and Renaissance music.

Music Festival: Every April, Bourges hosts **Printemps de Bourges,** a huge music festival (www.printemps-bourges.com).

Laundry: Try **Laverie Excelclean** (1 Rue Wittelsheim, daily 7:00-21:00, mobile 06 80 24 64 41), or ask at the TI.

Sights in Bourges

The city's medieval lanes, dotted with half-timbered buildings, are best appreciated on foot. The only sights in Bourges that charge admission are the Palais Jacques Cœur and the cathedral tower/crypt (both worth paying for). The handful of municipal museums are all free.

▲▲Cathedral of St. Etienne

One of Europe's great Gothic churches, Bourges' Cathedral of St. Etienne is known for its simple but harmonious design, flying buttresses, stained glass, and mammoth size. A Christian church has stood on this spot since the third century, including a Romanesque cathedral where Eleanor of Aquitaine received her crown in 1137. The present church was started in 1195, and finished just 55 years later—an astonishingly short amount of time for such a large structure. The design was inspired by Paris' Notre-Dame Cathedral, and it was built at the same time as the cathedral in Chartres. These three churches sum up the "High" Gothic style in France, and Bourges is one of the best-preserved, having been spared the ravages of the French Revolution and both world wars.

Cost and Hours: Church interior—free and open daily April-Sept 8:30-19:15, Oct-March 9:00-17:45; tower and crypt—€7.50 for both, €5.50 for tower only, €11 combo-ticket with Palais Jacques Cœur, open Mon-Sat 9:45-11:30 & 14:00-17:30, Sun 14:00-17:30 only, last entry 30 minutes before closing, tel. 02 48 65 49 44, http://cathedrale-bourges.monuments-nationaux.fr.

Visiting the Cathedral: Use this commentary to get oriented, starting with the exterior. The magnificent **west facade** is exceptionally wide (135 feet), dominated by five elaborately carved portals. The five doors reflect the church's unique interior—a central nave, flanked on each side by not one but two aisles. The frightening Last Judgment over the central doorway shows a seated Christ presiding over Judgment Day and deserves your attention.

The church's mismatched **towers** were a problem from the start. In an age of build-'em-high-and-fast, Bourges competed with Chartres to erect the ultimate Gothic cathedral. Bourges arguably won, but at a cost. The hastily built south tower had to be shored up several times—hence the squat tower that sits alongside it. Since the south tower was never strong enough to house any bells, locals call it "The Deaf Tower." The north tower collapsed altogether on New Year's Eve 1506 and had to be rebuilt, financed by donors who were granted an indulgence to eat butter during Lent—hence its nickname, the "Tour de Beurre."

The elegant **flying buttresses** form two rows, supporting both the lower and upper walls. The buttresses slope upward, enfolding the church in a pyramid shape as it rises to the peaked roofline.

Head inside. The view down the **nave** is overwhelming—at 300 feet, this is one of the longest naves in France. It seems even longer because the church has no transept to interrupt the tunnel effect. Notice elements of the "High" Gothic style of the 1200s: The church is tall, filled with light from many windows, and built with slender columns and thin walls (thanks to efficient flying buttresses). It rises up like a three-tiered step-pyramid—the outermost aisles are 30 feet high, the inner aisles are 70 feet, and the central nave is a soaring 120 feet from floor to rib-arched ceiling.

The best **stained glass** (c. 1215) is at the far end of the church, in the apse. Also, the Jacques Cœur Chapel (on the north side near the ambulatory) has a colorful Annunciation in stained glass.

The towering **astronomical clock,** on the south side of the nave, celebrates the most famous wedding the cathedral witnessed: that of hometown boy (and future king) Charles VII and Marie d'Anjou. The old clock, from 1424, still works.

Climbing the Tower: Don't leave the cathedral without climbing the 396 steps up the north tower for terrific views.

Crypt: To see the crypt, you need to join a tour in French... but you don't have to pay attention. Once inside, find the tomb statue of Duke Jean de Berry (1340-1416), the great collector of illuminated manuscripts and patron of this church. He lies on his back atop a black marble slab, dressed in ermine. At his feet sleeps a muzzled bear, representing the duke's quiet ferocity. Nearby, the colorfully painted Holy Sepulchre statues (c. 1530) enact the story of Christ's body being prepared for burial. See how realistic the marble looks as the mourners tug the ends of Christ's shroud—remarkably supple.

Nearby: The Archbishop's Garden (Jardin de l'Archevêché), just behind the cathedral, has a fine classical design and point-blank views of the flying buttresses. On Sundays when the weather agrees, old-school *guinguette* balls (picture a Renoir scene) are held here.

▲Medieval Quarter Stroll

Bourges' old city (Vieille Ville) is lassoed within Rues Bourbonnoux, Mirebeau, Coursarlon, Edouard Branly, and des Arènes. Richly decorated Renaissance mansions, many of which house small museums (worth entering), mix it up with France's greatest concentration of half-timbered homes (more than 500), most of them connected below street level by a labyrinth of underground passages. Look for Hôtel Lallemant (home to the Musée des Arts Décoratifs), Hôtel des Echevins (Musée Estève, with contemporary paintings by Maurice Estève), and Hôtel Cujas (Musée du Berry, with Roman tombstones and the famously expressive mourner statues from the Duke of Berry's elaborate tomb).

▲Palais Jacques Cœur

Bourges matters to travelers because of Jacques Cœur (c. 1395-1456), financier and minister to King Charles VII, who was born in Bourges. Monsieur Cœur helped establish Bourges as a capital for luxury goods and arms manufacturing. He also bankrolled Joan of Arc's call to save France from the English. His extravagant home is an impressive example of a Gothic civil palace, combining all the best elements of a château in an urban mansion. To visit the palace, join a French-only tour or pick up the English handout and go on your own.

Cost and Hours: €7.50, daily 9:45-12:00 & 14:00-17:15, until 18:15 May-June, until 18:30 July-Aug, 10 bis Rue Jacques-Cœur, tel. 02 48 24 79 42, http://palais-jacques-coeur.monuments-nationaux.fr.

Sleeping and Eating in Bourges

Hotels and restaurants are a good value here. Ground zero for dining in Bourges is Place Gordaine and the nearby streets, where you'll find easygoing cafés and *bistrots*.

$$$ Best Western Hôtel d'Angleterre Bourges**** is a fine place and as central as it gets (standard Db-€109, bigger Db-€165, rates include buffet breakfast, air-con, Wi-Fi, 1 Place des Quatre-Piliers, tel. 02 48 24 68 51, www.bestwestern-angleterre-bourges.com, hotel@bestwestern-angleterre-bourges.com).

$$ Hôtel le Christina*** is a good hotel 10 blocks from the cathedral (Db-€70-100, breakfast-€9, air-con, Wi-Fi, 5 Rue de la Halle, tel. 02 48 70 56 50, www.le-christina.com, info@le-christina.com).

La Crêperie des Remparts offers a great range of inexpensive crêpes and salads (closed Sun-Mon, 59 Rue Bourbonnoux, tel. 02 48 24 55 44).

Au Sénat is a local favorite for good-value traditional cuisine (*menus* from €19, closed Wed in summer and Wed-Thu in winter, on Place Gordaine at 8 Rue de la Poissonnerie, tel. 02 48 24 02 56).

Le d'Antan Sancerrois in the old city, boasts a Michelin star, and is a fine place to do it up right (€36-86 *menus,* closed Sun-Mon, 50 Rue Bourbonnoux, tel. 02 48 65 96 26).

Le Bourbonnoux offers good *menus* and fair prices, and copious servings (€13-34 *menus;* closed Fri, Sat for lunch, and Sun evening; 44 Rue Bourbonnoux, tel. 02 48 24 14 76).

Bourges Connections

From Bourges by Train to: Paris (15/day, 2-3 hours, most with 1 change), **Amboise** (roughly hourly—though fewer midday, 2-3 hours, 1 change), **Beaune** (6/day, 2-3 hours, most with transfer in Nevers), **Sarlat-la-Canéda** (4/day, 9 hours, 2 changes).

Between Burgundy and Lyon

Drivers traveling south from Beaune should think about detouring into the lovely, unspoiled Mâconnais countryside. Brancion, Chapaize, Cluny, and Taizé gather a few minutes from one another, about 30 minutes west of the autoroute between Mâcon and Tournus (see map on page 823). For a lovely romp through vineyards and unspoiled villages, drive south of Beaune on D-974 to Chagny, then hook up with D-981 to Cluny (via Givry, Buxy, and Cormatin). South of Buxy, be on the lookout for a surprising château on the west side of the road in cute little Sercy. D-14 heading east to Brancion meets D-981 at Cormatin.

Non-drivers can reach Cluny and Taizé by bus (see info under each listing for details).

Brancion and Chapaize

An hour south of Beaune by car (12 miles west of Tournus on D-14) are two tiny villages, each with "daughters of Cluny"—churches that owe their existence and architectural design to the nearby and once-powerful Cluny Abbey. Between the villages you'll pass a

Stonehenge-era menhir (standing stone) with a cross added on top at a later point—evidence that this was sacred ground long before Christianity (from Brancion, it's on the right just after passing the bulky Château de Nobles).

Brancion

This is a classic feudal village. Back when there were no nations in Europe, control of land was delegated from lord to vassal. The Duke of Burgundy ruled here through his vassal, the Lord of Brancion. His vast domain—much of south Burgundy—was administered from this tiny fortified town.

Within the town's walls, the feudal lord had a castle, a church, and all the necessary administrative buildings to deliver justice, collect taxes, and so on. Strategically perched on a hill between two river valleys, he enjoyed a complete view of his domain. Brancion's population peaked centuries ago at 60. Today, it's home to only four full-time residents.

The **castle,** part of a network of 17 castles in the region, was destroyed in 1576 by Protestant Huguenots. After the French Revolution, it was sold to be used as a quarry and spent most of the 19th century being picked apart. Though the flier gives a brief tour and the audioguide a longer one, the small castle is most enjoyable for its evocative angles and the lush views from the top of its keep (€5, daily April-Sept 10:00-13:00 & 14:00-18:30, Oct-mid-Dec weekends only 10:00-16:00, closed mid-Dec-March, audioguide-€2).

Wandering from the castle to the church, you'll pass the town's lone business (L'Auberge du Vieux Brancion), a 15th-century market hall that was used by farmers from the surrounding countryside until 1900, plus a handful of other buildings from that period.

The 12th-century warm-stone **church** (with faint paintings surviving from 1330) is the town's highlight. Circumnavigate the small building—this is Romanesque at its pure, unadulterated, fortress-of-God best (thick walls, small windows, once colorfully painted interior, no-frills exterior). Notice the stone roof; inside, find the English explanations of the paintings. From its front door, enjoy a lord's view over one glorious Burgundian estate.

Sleeping in Brancion: **$ L'Auberge du Vieux Brancion** serves traditional Burgundian fare (€16 lunch *menu,* €23 dinner *menu*) and also offers a perfectly tranquil place to spend the night. Say *bonjour* to François (very simple and frumpy rooms, Ds-€38, Db-

BURGUNDY

€50-58, family rooms-€55-75, tel. 03 85 51 03 83, fax 03 85 32 17 67, www.brancion.fr, no email—must call or fax to book rooms).

Chapaize

This hamlet, a few miles west of Brancion on D-14, grew up around its Benedictine monastery—only its 11th-century church survives. It's a pristine place (cars park in a lot at the edge of town), peppered with flowers and rustic decay. A ghost-town café faces the village's classic Romanesque church—study the fine stonework by Lombard masons. (Its lean seems designed to challenge the faith of parishioners.) The WWI monument near the entry—with so many names from such a tiny hamlet—is a reminder of the 4.2 million young French men who were wounded or died in the war that *didn't* end all wars. Wander around the back for a view of the belfry, and then ponder Chapaize across the street while sipping a café au lait.

Cluny

People come from great distances to admire Cluny's great abbey that is no more. This mother of all abbeys once vied with the Vatican as the most important power center in Christendom (Cluny's abbot often served as mediator between Europe's kings and the pope). The building was destroyed during the French Revolution, and, frankly, there's not a lot to see today. Still, the abbey makes a worthwhile visit for history buffs and pilgrims looking to get some idea of the scale of this vast complex.

The pleasant little town that grew up around the abbey maintains its medieval street plan, with plenty of original buildings and even the same population it had in its 12th-century heyday (4,500). That's stability. As you wander the town, which claims to be the finest surviving Romanesque town in France, enjoy the architectural details on everyday buildings. Many of the town's fortified walls, gates, and towers survive.

Getting There: Drivers park at designated lots (best is Parking le Rochefort) and follow *Centre-Ville* signs on foot. Bus Céphale provides a few trips to Cluny (4/day from Chalon-sur-Saône, 1.25 hours; 7/day from Mâcon, 40 minutes; toll-free tel. 08 00 07 17 10, www.cg71.fr, French only, click on *Buscéphale horaires*). There is no train station in Cluny.

Orientation to Cluny

Everything of interest is within a few minutes' walk of the **TI** (daily June-Sept 9:30-12:30 & 14:30-19:00, no midday closure July-Aug, until 18:00 May and Oct, until 17:00 Nov-April, 6 Rue Mercière, tel. 03 85 59 05 34, www.cluny-tourisme.com).

The TI is at the base of the **Tour des Fromages**—"Cheese Tower"—so named because it was used to age cheese (or perhaps for the way tourists smell after climbing to the top). The tower offers a sweeping city view (€2, same hours as TI). Facing the abbey's entrance, the TI is 100 yards to the right. There's also a TI branch at Parking le Rochefort (June-Sept only).

A **farmers' market** animates the old town each Saturday.

Sights in Cluny

The first two sights—the museum and the abbey—share the same ticket and schedule (€9.50 ticket covers museum and abbey entrance, both open daily May-Aug 9:30-18:00, Sept-April 9:30-12:00 & 13:30-17:00, tel. 03 85 59 15 93). Historians should invest in *The Abbey of Cluny* guidebook (€7), sold at both sights. English tours should be available on certain days July-Aug; call ahead for times. Start your tour at the museum and finish with the abbey.

Museum of Art and Archaeology (Musée Ochier)

The small abbey museum fills the Palace of the Abbot (Palais de l'Abbée Jean Bourbon). The modest collection features artifacts from the medieval town of Cluny and sets the stage for visiting the abbey site. There's a terrific model of the village and abbey complex and a good short film about the abbey on the first floor up (French only but worth seeing). You'll also see a beautifully carved stone frieze from a mansion in Cluny (first floor up) and fragments of the main entry (Grand Portail) to the abbey church set within a model of the doorway (behind ticket counter).

After touring the museum, cross the lane in front and step into where the abbey church's entry would have been.

Site of Cluny Abbey

The best point from which to appreciate the abbey's awesome dimensions is atop the steps across from the museum. Look out to the remaining tower (there used to be three). You're standing above the end of the nave that stretched all the way to those towers. Down the steps, a marble table shows the original floor plan (*vous êtes ici* means "you are here").

Some of today's old town stands on the site of what was the largest church in Christendom. It was almost two football fields long (555 feet) and crowned with five soaring naves. The whole

History of Cluny and Its (Scant) Abbey

In 1964, St. Benedict (480-547), founder of the first monastery (in Montecassino, south of Rome) from which a great monastic movement sprang, was named the patron saint of Europe. Christians and non-Christians alike recognize the impact that monasteries had in establishing a European civilization out of the dark chaos that followed the fall of Rome.

The Abbey of Cluny was the ruling center of the first great international chain of monasteries in Europe. It was the heart of an upsurge in monasticism, of church reform, and an evangelical revival that spread throughout Europe—a phenomenon that historians call the Age of Faith (11th and 12th centuries). From this springboard came a vast network of abbeys, priories, and other monastic orders that kindled the establishment of modern Europe.

In 910, 12 monks founded a house of prayer at Cluny, vowing to follow the rules of St. Benedict. The cult of saints and relics was enthusiastically promoted, and the order was independent and powerful. From the start, the Abbot of Cluny answered only to the pope (not to the local bishop or secular leader). The abbots of the other Cluniac monasteries were answerable only to the Abbot of Cluny (not to their local bishop or prince). This made the Abbot of Cluny arguably the most powerful person in Europe.

The abbey's success has been attributed to a series of wise leaders. In fact, four of the first six abbots actually became saints. They preached principles of piety (they got people to stop looting the monasteries) and practiced shrewd fundraising (convincing wealthy landowners to will their estates to the monasteries in return for perpetual prayers for the benefit of their needy and frightened souls).

From all this grew the greatest monastic movement of the High Middle Ages. A huge church was built at Cluny, and by 1100 it was the headquarters of 10,000 monks who ran nearly a thousand monasteries and priories across Europe. Cluny peaked in the 12th century, then faded in influence (though monasteries continued to increase in numbers and remain a force until 1789).

complex (church plus monastery) covered 25 acres. Revolutionaries destroyed it in 1790, and today the National Stud Farm and a big school obliterate much of the floor plan of the abbey. Only one tower and part of the transept still stand. The visitor's challenge: Visualize it. Get a sense of its grandeur.

Walk past the nubs that remain of the once-massive columns, work your way down the nave and around the right at the bottom, and climb a stairway to find today's abbey entry. Information displays (in English) designed to introduce the abbey and provide historical context help put the pieces of the ruined building back together. You'll see a 12-minute 3-D film, giving a virtual tour of the 1,100-year-old church that helps you grasp the tragedy of its destruction (French only but you'll get the gist). Use the English flier to tour what little of the abbey still stands. Your visit ends at the flour mill (Tour de Farine); make sure to go upstairs to see the intricate wood roof supports and a display of beautifully carved Romanesque capitals. From here you can loop back along the town's main drag, Rue Mercière (cafés, shops, and the TI line this pedestrian-friendly street).

National Stud Farm (Les Haras Nationaux)

Napoleon (who needed *beaucoup de* horses for his army of 600,000) established this farm in 1806. Today, 50 thoroughbred stallions kill time in their stables. If the stalls are empty, they're out doing their current studly duty...creating strapping racehorses. Since 2010, the complex has been home to the National School of Equestrian Activities. The entry gate is next to Hôtel de Bourgogne.

Cost and Hours: €6, visits by guided tour only (some English spoken), riding demonstrations possible, usually on weekends (check the calendar of "manifestations" on their website); tours available daily April-June and Sept, usually at 14:00 and 16:00, July-Aug at 14:00, 15:30, and 17:00; Oct-April Wed and Sun only at 14:00; call ahead to confirm times, tel. 03 85 59 85 19, www.haras-nationaux.fr.

Sleeping and Eating in Cluny

If you're spending the night, bed down at the homey, traditional, and spotless **$$$ Hôtel de Bourgogne*****, built into the wall of the abbey's right transept and central for enjoying the town. All rooms have queen- or king-size beds (standard Db-€106, bigger Db-€138, parking garage-€10, Place de l'Abbaye, tel. 03 85 59 00 58, www.hotel-cluny.com, contact@hotel-cluny.com). It also has a fine restaurant (*menus* from €26).

Le Nord Brasserie owns the best abbey view from its outdoor tables (skip the mod interior) and serves standard café fare at fair prices, (daily, tel. 03 85 59 09 96, 1 Place du Marché).

Taizé

To experience the latest in European monasticism, drop by the booming Christian community of Taizé (teh-zay), a few miles north of Cluny on the road to Brancion. The normal, uncultlike ambience of this place—with thousands of mostly young, European pilgrims asking each other, "How's your soul today?"—is remarkable. Even

if this sounds a little airy, you might find the 30 minutes it takes to stroll from one end of the compound to the other a worthwhile detour. A visit to Taizé can be a thought-provoking experience, particularly after a visit to Cluny. A thousand years ago, Cluny had a similar power to draw the faithful in search of direction and meaning in life.

Getting There: Drivers follow *La Communauté* signs and park in a dirt lot. SNCF buses (free with rail pass) serve Taizé from Chalon-sur-Saône to the north (4/day, 1 hour) and from Mâcon to the south (6/day, 1 hour).

Tourist Information: At the southern (Cluny) end, the Welcome Office provides an orientation and daily schedule, and makes a good first stop (pick up a copy of the bimonthly *Letter from Taizé* and the single-page information leaflet, *The Taizé Community*).

Visiting Taizé: Taizé is an ecumenical movement—prayer, silence, simplicity—welcoming Protestant as well as Catholic Christians. Though it feels Catholic, it isn't. (But, as some of the brothers are actually Catholic priests, Catholics may take the Eucharist here.) The Taizé style of worship is well known among American Christians for its hauntingly beautiful chants—songbooks and CDs are the most popular souvenirs from here. The Exposition (next to the church) is the thriving community shop, with books, CDs, sheet music, handicrafts, and other souvenirs.

The community welcomes visitors who'd like to spend a few days getting close to God through meditation, singing, and simple living. Although designed primarily for youthful pilgrims in meditative retreat (there are about 5,000 here in a typical week), people of any age are welcome to pop in for a meal or church service. Time your visit for one of the services (Mon-Sat at 8:15, 12:20, and 20:30; Sun at 10:00 and 20:30; Catholic and Protestant communion available daily).

During services, the bells ring and worshippers file into the long, low, simple, and modern Church of Reconciliation. It's dim—candlelit with glowing icons—as the white-robed brothers enter. The service features responsive singing of chants (from well-worn songbooks that list lyrics in 19 languages), reading of biblical passages, and silence, as worshippers on crude kneelers stare into icons. The aim: "Entering together into the

mystery of God's presence." (Secondary aim: Helping Lutherans get over their fear of icons.)

Sleeping and Eating in Taizé: Those on retreat fill their days with worship services; workshops; simple, relaxed meals; and hanging out in an international festival of people searching for meaning in their lives. Visitors are welcome for free. The cost for a real stay is about €20-35 per day (based on a sliding scale; those under 18 stay for less) for monastic-style room and board. Adults (over age 30) are accommodated in a more comfortable zone, but count on simple dorms. Call or email first if you plan to stay overnight (reception open Mon-Fri 10:00-12:00 & 18:00-19:00, tel. 03 85 50 30 02). The Taizé community website explains everything—in 29 languages (www.taize.fr).

The **Oyak** (near the parking lot) is where those in a less monastic mood can get a beer or burger.

LYON

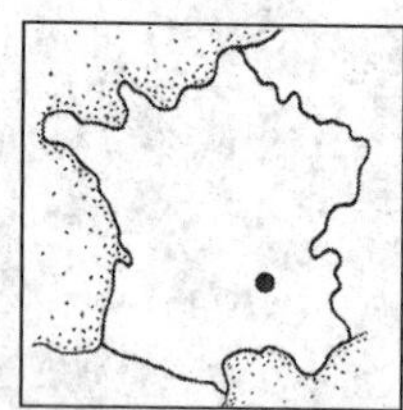

Straddling the mighty Rhône and Saône rivers between Burgundy and Provence, Lyon has been among France's leading cities since Roman times. In spite of its workaday, business-first facade, Lyon is France's most historic and culturally important city after Paris. You'll experience two different-as-night-and-day cities: the Old World cobbled alleys, pastel Renaissance mansions, and colorful shops of Vieux Lyon; and the more staid but classy, Parisian-feeling shopping streets of the Presqu'île. Once you're settled, this big city feels relaxed, welcoming, and surprisingly untouristy. It seems everyone's enjoying the place—and they're all French.

PLANNING YOUR TIME

Just 70 minutes south of Beaune and two hours north of Avignon, Lyon is France's best-kept urban secret. Lyon deserves at least one night and a full day. With frequent and fast service to many regions in France—and baggage storage available—the city makes a handy day-visit for train travelers. But those who spend the night can experience the most renowned cuisine in France at appetizing prices and enjoy one of Europe's most beautifully floodlit cities.

For a full day of sightseeing, take the funicular up to Fourvière Hill, visit the Notre-Dame Basilica, and tour the Roman Theaters and Gallo-Roman Museum. Ride the funicular back down to Vieux Lyon and have a French (read: slow) lunch, then explore the old town and its hidden passageways. Finish your day touring the Museum of Fine Arts, Resistance Center, or Lumière Museum (covering the history of early filmmaking). Most of Lyon's important sights are closed on Mondays or Tuesdays, or both. Dine well in the evening (book ahead if possible; your hotelier is happy to help) and cap your day enjoying a stroll through the best-lit city in France.

Drivers connecting Lyon with southern destinations should contemplate the scenic detour via the Ardèche Gorges (see "Route Tips for Drivers" on page 923).

LYON'S CUISINE SCENE

In Lyon, how well you eat determines how well you live. The best restaurants are all the buzz—a favorite conversation topic likely to generate heated debate. Here, great chefs are more famous than professional soccer players. (Paul Bocuse is the chef MVP.) Restaurants seem to outnumber cars, and all seem busy. With an abundance of cozy, excellent restaurants in every price range, it's hard to go wrong—unless you order tripe (cow intestines, also known as *tablier de sapeur*), *foie de veau* (calf's liver), or *tête de veau* (calf's head). Beware: These questionable dishes are very common in small bistros *(bouchons)* and can be the only choices on cheaper *menus*. Look instead for these classics: St. Marcellin cheese, *salade lyonnaise* (croutons, fried bits of ham, and a poached egg on a bed of lettuce), green lentils *(lentilles)* served on a salad or with sausages, *quenelles de brochet* (fish dumplings in a creamy sauce), and *filet de sandre* (local whitefish).

To secure a table at a popular restaurant, ask your hotelier to book it for you when you reserve your room.

LYON AREA WINES

Fruity and fresh Gamay Beaujolais grapes, which grow in vineyards just north of Lyon, produce a light, fruity, easy-to-drink red wine. Beaujolais vines grow on granite rock slopes, compared to the limestone of nearby Burgundy, giving the wines their distinct flavor. While there are several premier *crus* producing lovely wines, the area is most famous for its simple Beaujolais Nouveau wines, opened just six weeks after bottling. The arrival of the new Beaujolais is cause for lighthearted celebration and mischief in this otherwise hard to impress country. At midnight on the third Thursday of November, the first bottles are opened to great fanfare, road rallies carry the new wine to destinations throughout France, and cafés everywhere post signs announcing its arrival.

Big reds made from mostly Syrah grapes grow to the city's south. Look for Saint-Joseph and Crozes-Hermitage wines. In the village of Condrieu, only Viognier grapes are allowed to grow; they produce a rich and perfumy white wine.

Orientation to Lyon

Despite being France's third-largest city (after Paris and Marseille), with about 1.5 million inhabitants in its metropolitan area, the traveler's Lyon (home to 485,000 people) is peaceful and manageable. Traffic noise is replaced by pedestrian friendliness in the old center—listen to how quiet this big city is. Notice the emphasis on environmentally friendly transport: Electric buses have replaced diesel buses in the historic core, bike lanes run everywhere, and pedal taxis (called *cyclopolitains,* seek-loh-poh-lee-tan) are used instead of traditional taxis for short trips (about €1/kilometer). Lyon's network of more than 5,000 city-owned rental bikes was in place years before Paris' (note that these work only with American Express or chip-and-PIN credit cards).

Lyon provides the organized traveler with a full day of activities. Sightseeing can be enjoyed on foot from any of my recommended hotels, though it's smart to make use of the funiculars, trams, and Métro. Lyon's sights are concentrated in three areas: **Fourvière Hill,** with its white Notre-Dame Basilica glimmering over the city; historic **Vieux Lyon,** which hunkers below on the bank of the Saône River; and the **Presqu'île** (home to my recommended hotels), lassoed by the Saône and Rhone rivers. Huge and curiously empty Place Bellecour, which lies in the middle of the Presqu'île, always seems to be hosting an event.

TOURIST INFORMATION

The well-equipped TI can reserve a hotel for you at no charge (daily 9:00-18:00, tel. 04 72 77 69 69, www.lyon-france.com, corner of Place Bellecour, free public WCs behind the TI building). Pick up the city map (with good enlargements of central Lyon and Vieux Lyon; hotels have similar maps) and an event schedule (ask about concerts in the Roman Theaters during Les Nuits de Fourvière—

early June to early Aug—and events at the Opera House). They also have a brochure on the Beaujolais wine road north of Lyon.

Walking Tours: The TI's **audioguide** (€10/day) offers good, self-guided walking tours of Vieux Lyon. Live **guided walks** of Vieux Lyon are usually offered at 14:30 on weekends and on most days July through early September (€11, 2 hours, usually in French but in English if enough demand, depart from guide office to right of funicular, verify days and times with TI). Other, less-frequent English-language walks include tours of the La Croix-Rousse district and the silk workshops.

Sightseeing Pass: The TI sells a good-value **Lyon City Card** for serious sightseers (€22/1 day, €32/2 consecutive days, €42/3 consecutive days, under 16 half-price). This pass includes all Lyon museums, free use of the Métro/bus/funicular system, a river cruise (April-Oct), a walking tour of Lyon with a live guide, and free use of the TI's audioguide. The one-day pass pays for itself if you visit the Gallo-Roman Museum and the Resistance and Deportation History Center, plus take a guided walking tour and use public transit.

Helpful Website: For useful information in English about visiting Lyon, check out http://lyon.angloinfo.com.

ARRIVAL IN LYON

By Train: Lyon has two train stations—Part-Dieu and Lyon-Perrache. Many trains stop at both, and some through trains connect the two stations but have an inconsistent schedule. Both stations are well-served by Métro, bus, tram, and taxi (figure €15 for a taxi from either station to my recommended hotels near Place Bellecour), and both have the standard car-rental companies. Only Part-Dieu has baggage storage (daily 6:15-23:00), along with free Wi-Fi in the waiting area. The all-day transit ticket is a great value—buy it upon arrival at the station if you plan to do much sightseeing that day (coin machines only), or wait to pick up a Lyon City Card—which covers transit—at the TI (for more on public transportation and tickets, see "Getting Around Lyon," later).

Arriving at Part-Dieu Station: This is where most visitors arrive. There are two exits from the station: *Porte du Rhône* and *Porte des Alpes*. Bag check is near the *Porte des Alpes* exit. To reach Place Bellecour in the **city center** (close to most hotels and the TI), exit by following *Sortie Porte du Rhône* signs, then enter the Métro station and buy your ticket from the machine. Take the blue Métro line B toward Gare d'Oulins, transfer at Saxe-Gambetta to the line D/Gare de Vaise route, and get off at Bellecour. At Bellecour, follow *Sortie Rue République* signs.

The other main exit, *Sortie Porte des Alpes,* offers access to the handy **airport** tram (called Rhône Express, described later under

Illuminated Lyon

The golden statue of Mary above Notre-Dame Basilica was placed atop a 16th-century chapel on December 8, 1852. Spontaneously, the entire city welcomed her with candles in their windows. Each December 8 ever since, the city glows softly with countless candles.

This tradition has spawned an actual industry. Lyon is famous as a model of state-of-the-art floodlighting, and the city hosts conventions on the topic. Each night, more than 200 buildings, sites, and public spaces are gloriously floodlit. Go for an after-dinner stroll and enjoy the view from the Bonaparte Bridge after dark.

"By Plane"; tickets available from machines only, bills and coins accepted, conductors can help). Also out this exit are SNCF buses to Annecy and Grenoble (but train connections are more frequent). Taxis wait outside either exit, though they seem more plentiful at the *Sortie Porte des Alpes*.

Arriving at Perrache Station: This station is within a 20-minute walk of Place Bellecour (no baggage storage). Follow green *Place Carnot* signs out of the station, then cross Place Carnot and walk up pedestrian Rue Victor Hugo to reach the TI and most of my recommended hotels. Or take the Métro (direction: Vaulx-en-Velin) two stops to Bellecour and follow *Sortie Rue République* signs.

By Car: The city center has good signage and is manageable to navigate, though you'll hit traffic on the surrounding freeways. If autoroute A-6 is jammed (not unusual), you'll be directed to bypass freeways (such as A-46). Either way, follow *Centre-Ville* and *Presqu'île* signs, and then follow *Office de Tourisme* and *Place Bellecour* signs. Park in the lots under Place Bellecour or Place des Célestins (yellow *P* means "parking lot") or get advice from your hotel. The TI's map identifies all public parking lots. Overnight parking (generally 19:00-8:00) is only €4.50, but day rates are €2 per hour (figure about €30/24 hours). Garages near Perrache Station are cheaper than those near Bellecour.

By Plane: Lyon's sleek little airport (and TGV station), St-Exupéry, is 15 miles from the city center, and is a breeze to navigate (ATMs, English information booths, airport code: LYS, tel. 08 26 80 08 26, www.lyonaeroports.com). It has air and rail connections to major European cities, including two flights per hour to Paris' Charles de Gaulle Airport and direct TGV service to many French cities. Car rental is a snap. Four **Rhône Express** trams per hour make the 30-minute trip from the airport (follow red tram car icons) to Part-Dieu Station, described earlier (€16 one-way,

€28 round-trip, buy ticket from machine, bills and coins accepted). Allow €65 for a taxi if you have baggage.

HELPFUL HINTS

Market Days: A small market stretches along the Saône River near the Passerelle du Palais de Justice bridge (daily until 12:30). Tuesday through Saturday, it's produce; Sunday morning, it's crafts and contemporary art on the other side of the bridge near the Court of Justice; and Monday, it's textiles. Another bustling morning produce market takes place on Boulevard de la Croix-Rousse (Tue-Sun until 12:30, biggest on Sat, see page 911).

Festivals and Events: Lyon celebrates the Virgin Mary with candlelit windows during the Festival of Lights each year in early December (www.lumieres.lyon.fr). Les Nuits de Fourvière (dance, music, and theater) takes place from early June to early August in the Roman Theaters (www.nuitsdefourviere.com). To browse upcoming performances and events, check youth-oriented magazine *A Nous Lyon*'s website at www.anous.fr and click on "Save the Date"; the site is easy to use even though it's in French.

Internet Access: Raconte Moi La Terre is a traveler's bookstore and resource center; it's also a good place to check your email (Mon 12:00-19:30, Tue-Sat 10:00-19:30, closed Sun, free Wi-Fi if you buy drinks or snacks, air-con, 14 Rue du Plat—see map on page 918, Métro: Bellecour, tel. 04 78 92 60 22, www.racontemoilaterre.com).

Laundry: A launderette is at 7 Rue Mercière on the Presqu'île, near the Alphonse Juin bridge; another is between Place Bellecour and Perrache Station, a few steps off Rue Victor Hugo at 19 Rue Ste. Hélène. Both have long hours daily (see map on page 918 for locations).

SNCF Train Office: The SNCF Boutique at 2 Place Bellecour is handy for train info, reservations, and tickets (Tue-Fri 10:00-18:45, Sat 10:00-17:45, closed Sun-Mon).

Wine Tours and Sightseeing Excursions: Kanpai Tours runs minivan trips to the Beaujolais and northern Rhône Valley wine regions near Lyon (€75/half-day, €85/day for individuals, €400-500/day for private groups, tel. 06 84 52 14 99, www.kanpai-tourisme.com, contact@kanpai-tourisme.com).

Chauffeur Hire: Design your own half-day or full-day tour with a car and driver (mobile 06 65 38 75 08, www.lugdunum-ips.com, contact@lugdunum-ips.com).

Riverside Bike Path and Promenade: A bike path/walkway along the east side of the Rhône River is ideal for adults and children (see map on page 918). For more information on the path and bike rentals, ask at the TI or check http://lyon.angloinfo.com.

Children's Activities: The Parc de la Tête d'Or is vast, with rowboat rentals, a miniature golf course, ponies to ride, and easy access to the riverside bike path described above (across Rhône River from La Croix-Rousse neighborhood, Métro: Masséna, tel. 04 72 69 47 60).

GETTING AROUND LYON

Lyon has a user-friendly public transit system, with five modern streetcar lines (tramways T1-T5 and the Rhône Express line to the airport), four underground Métro lines (A-D), an extensive bus system, and two funiculars to get you up that hill. The subway is similar to Paris' Métro in many ways (e.g., routes are signed by *direction* for the last stop on the line) but is more automated (buy tickets at coin-op machines), cleaner, less crowded, and less rushed (drivers linger longer at stops). Study the wall maps to be sure of your direction; ask a local if you're not certain. Yellow signs lead to transfers, and green signs lead to exits *(Sortie).*

Tickets: You can transfer between Métro and tramway lines with the same ticket (valid one hour), but you can't do round-trips and must revalidate your ticket whenever boarding a tram (€1.70/1 hour, €2.80/2 hours, €5.20/1 day, €15.10/10 rides, all tickets cover funicular). The **one-day ticket** is a great deal (even if you only use the funicular and visit one of the outlying museums—Resistance Center or Lumière Museum) and a great time-saver, as you only have to buy a ticket once. Also remember that the Lyon City Card (described earlier, under "Tourist Information") covers transit.

To use the ticket machines, change the display language to English. Then use the black roller to *selectionner* your ticket, firmly push the top button twice to *confirmer* your request, and then insert coins (no bills, US credit cards won't work). In the Métro, insert your ticket in the turnstile, then reclaim it. If the stop has no turnstile, you must validate your ticket by punching it in a nearby machine (tramway users always validate on the trams).

Bonaparte Bridge Spin-Tour

This central bridge (Pont Bonaparte), just a block from Place Bellecour, is made to order for a day-or-night self-guided spin-tour.

• *Stand on the bridge and face the golden statue of the Virgin Mary marking the Notre-Dame Basilica on Fourvière Hill. (It's actually capping the smaller chapel, which predates the church by 500 years.) The basilica is named for the Roman Forum* (fourvière) *upon which it sits. Now begin to look clockwise.*

The Metallic Tower (called La Tour Métallique—not La Tour Eiffel), like the basilica, was finished just before World War I. It was originally an observation tower but today functions only as a TV tower. The husky, twin-towered church on the riverbank below (St. Jean Cathedral) marks the center of the old town. A block upstream, the Neoclassical columns are part of the Court of Justice (where Klaus Barbie, head of the local Gestapo—a.k.a. "the Butcher of Lyon"—was sentenced to life in prison). Way upstream, the hill covered with tall, pastel-colored houses is the Croix-Rousse district, former home of the city's huge silk industry. With the invention of the Jacquard looms, which required 12-foot-tall ceilings, new factory buildings were needed and the new weaving center grew up on this hill. In 1850, it was churning with 30,000 looms.

You are standing over the Saône River, which, along with the Rhône, makes up Lyon's duo of power rivers. The Saône drains the southern area of the Vosges Mountains in Alsace and runs for about 300 miles before joining the Rhône (barely south of here), which flows to the Mediterranean. The Place Bellecour side of the river (behind you) is the district of Presqu'île. This strip of land is sandwiched by the two rivers, and is home to Lyon's Opera House, City Hall, theater, top-end shopping, banks, and all of my recommended hotels. A morning market sets up daily under the trees (upriver, just beyond the red bridge). The simple riverfront cafés *(buvettes)* are ideal for a drink with a view (best at night).

Speaking of bridges, all of Lyon's bridges—including the one you're standing on—were destroyed by the Nazis as they checked out in 1944. Looking downstream, the stately mansions of Lyon's well-established families line the left side of the river. Across the river, still downstream, the Neo-Gothic St. Georges Church marks the neighborhood of the first silk weavers. The ridge behind St. Georges is dominated by a big, dirty building—once a seminary for priests, now a state high school—and leads us back to Mary.

• *Walk across the bridge and continue two blocks to find the funicular station and ride up Fourvière Hill to the basilica (catch the train marked* Fourvière, *not* St. Just*). Sit up front and admire the funicular's funky old technology (€2.60 round-trip, Métro/tramway tickets valid). Or you can skip Fourvière Hill and go directly into the old town* ***(Vieux Lyon)*** *by turning right at* ***St. Jean Cathedral.***

Sights in Lyon

FOURVIERE HILL

On Fourvière Hill, you can tour the basilica, enjoy a panoramic city view, and visit the Roman Theaters and Gallo-Roman Museum,

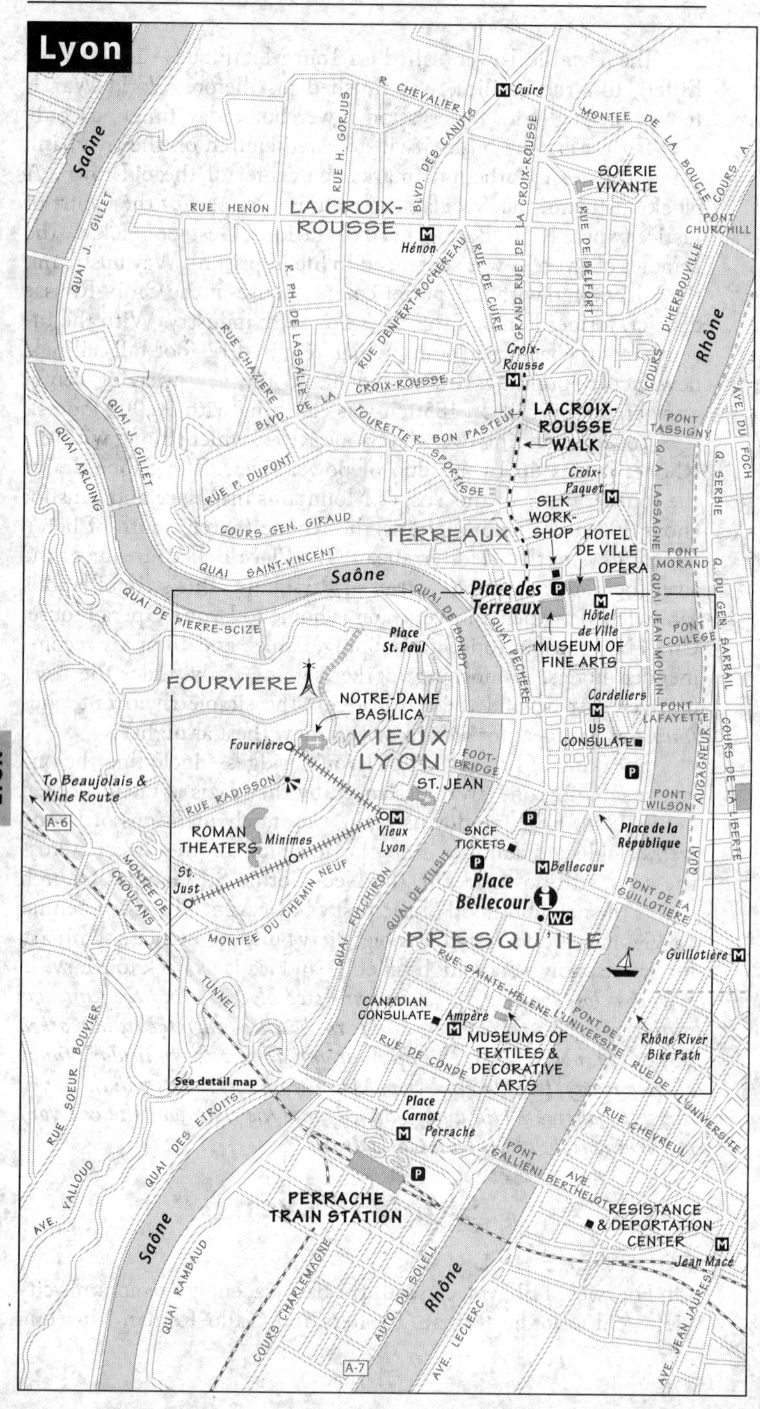
Lyon
Cuire
R. CHEVALIER
MONTEE DE LA BOUCLE
COURS A.
RUE H. GORJUS
BLVD. DES CANUTS
GRAND RUE DE LA CROIX-ROUSSE
SOIERIE VIVANTE
Saône
QUAI J. GILLET
RUE HENON
LA CROIX-ROUSSE
Hénon
R. PH. DE LASSALLE
RUE DENFERT-ROCHEREAU
RUE DE CUIRE
RUE DE BELFORT
PONT CHURCHILL
COURS D'HERBOUVILLE
Rhône
RUE CHAZIERE
Croix-Rousse
BLVD. DE LA CROIX-ROUSSE
COURS
QUAI J. GILLET
QUAI ARLOING
TOURETTE
R. BON PASTEUR
LA CROIX-ROUSSE WALK
PONT TASSIGNY
AVE. DU FOCH
RUE P. DUPONT
SPORTISSE
Croix-Paquet
Q. A. LASSAGNE
Q. SERBIE
COURS GEN. GIRAUD
TERREAUX
SILK WORK-SHOP
HOTEL DE VILLE
OPERA
PONT MORAND
QUAI SAINT-VINCENT
Saône
QUAI DE BONDY
Place des Terreaux
Hôtel de Ville
QUAI DE PIERRE-SCIZE
Place St. Paul
QUAI PECHERE
MUSEUM OF FINE ARTS
QUAI JEAN MOULIN
PONT COLLEGE
Q. DU GEN. SARRAIL
FOURVIERE
NOTRE-DAME BASILICA
Cordeliers
PONT LAFAYETTE
Fourvière
VIEUX LYON
US CONSULATE
COURS DE LA LIBERTE
FOOT-BRIDGE
To Beaujolais & Wine Route
RUE RADISSON
ST. JEAN
PONT WILSON
QUAI AUGAGNEUR
A-6
ROMAN THEATERS
Minimes
Vieux Lyon
SNCF TICKETS
Place de la République
MONTEE DE CHOULANS
St. Just
Bellecour
MONTEE DU CHEMIN NEUF
QUAI FULCHIRON
QUAI DE TILSIT
Place Bellecour
PONT DE LA GUILLOTIERE
WC
MONTEE
PRESQU'ILE
Guillotière
RUE SAINTE-HELENE
TUNNEL
CANADIAN CONSULATE
Ampère
PONT DE L'UNIVERSITE
Rhône River Bike Path
RUE SOEUR BOUVIER
MUSEUMS OF TEXTILES & DECORATIVE ARTS
RUE DE CONDE
See detail map
RUE DE L'UNIVERSITE
Place Carnot
QUAI DES ETROITS
Perrache
RUE CHEVREUL
PONT GALLIENI
AVE. VALLOUD
AVE. BERTHELOT
PERRACHE TRAIN STATION
RESISTANCE & DEPORTATION CENTER
Saône
Jean Macé
QUAI RAMBAUD
COURS CHARLEMAGNE
AUTO. DU SOLEIL
Rhône
AVE. LECLERC
AVE. JEAN JAURES
A-7

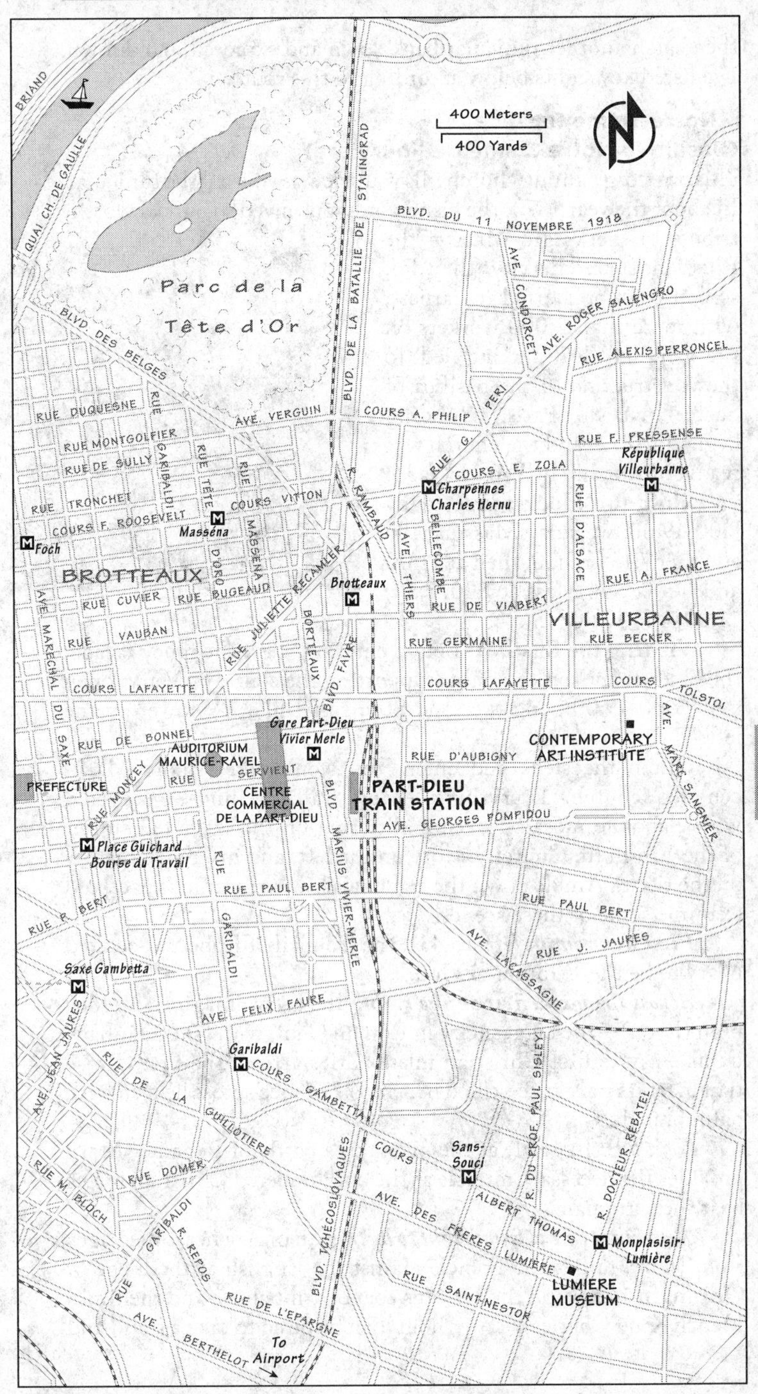
400 Meters
400 Yards
BRIAND
QUAI CH. DE GAULLE
Parc de la
Tête d'Or
BLVD. DE LA BATAILLE DE STALINGRAD
BLVD. DU 11 NOVEMBRE 1918
AVE. CONDORCET
AVE. ROGER SALENGRO
RUE ALEXIS PERRONCEL
BLVD. DES BELGES
RUE DUQUESNE
RUE GARIBALDI
AVE. VERGUIN
COURS A. PHILIP
RUE G. PERI
RUE F. PRESSENSE
République Villeurbanne
RUE MONTGOLFIER
RUE DE SULLY
RUE TÊTE D'OR
RUE MASSÉNA
COURS VITTON
R. RAMBAUD
COURS E. ZOLA
Charpennes Charles Hernu
RUE TRONCHET
COURS F. ROOSEVELT
Masséna
Foch
BROTTEAUX
AVE. THIERS
BELLECOMBE
RUE D'ALSACE
RUE A. FRANCE
Brotteaux
RUE CUVIER
RUE BUGEAUD
RUE JULIETTE RECAMIER
BORTTEAUX
BLVD. FAVRE
RUE DE VIABERT
VILLEURBANNE
RUE BECKER
AVE. MARECHAL DU SAXE
RUE VAUBAN
RUE GERMAINE
COURS LAFAYETTE
COURS LAFAYETTE
COURS TOLSTOI
Gare Part-Dieu Vivier Merle
RUE DE BONNEL
AUDITORIUM MAURICE-RAVEL
RUE SERVIENT
RUE D'AUBIGNY
CONTEMPORARY ART INSTITUTE
AVE. MARC SANGNIER
PREFECTURE
RUE MONCEY
CENTRE COMMERCIAL DE LA PART-DIEU
PART-DIEU TRAIN STATION
AVE. GEORGES POMPIDOU
Place Guichard Bourse du Travail
RUE GARIBALDI
BLVD. MARIUS VIVIER-MERLE
RUE PAUL BERT
RUE PAUL BERT
RUE P. BERT
AVE. LACASSAGNE
RUE J. JAURES
Saxe Gambetta
AVE. FELIX FAURE
Garibaldi
COURS GAMBETTA
AVE. JEAN JAURES
RUE DE LA GUILLOTIERE
R. DU PROF. PAUL SISLEY
R. DOCTEUR REBATEL
Sans-Souci
COURS ALBERT THOMAS
RUE DOMER
BLVD. TCHECOSLOVAQUES
AVE. DES FRERES LUMIERE
Monplaisir-Lumière
RUE M. BLOCH
GARIBALDI
R. REPOS
RUE
RUE SAINT-NESTOR
LUMIERE MUSEUM
RUE DE L'EPARGNE
AVE. BERTHELOT
To Airport

LYON

then catch another funicular back down and explore the old town. I've listed key sights below according to this route.

▲Notre-Dame Basilica (Basilique Notre-Dame de Fourvière)

This ornate, gleaming church fills your view as you exit the funicular. In about the year 1870, the bishop of Lyon vowed to build a worthy tribute to the Virgin Mary if the Prussians spared his city. They did, so construction started in earnest, with more than 2,000 workers on site (similar deal-making led to the construction of the basilica of Sacré-Cœur in Paris.) Building began in 1872, and the church was ready for worship by World War I.

Cost and Hours: Free, daily 8:00-19:00; weekday Mass usually at either 7:15 or 9:30, then at 11:00 and 17:00; Sun Mass at 7:30, 9:30, 11:00, and 17:00.

Visiting the Basilica: Before entering, view the fancy facade, the older chapel on the right (supporting the statue of Mary; open daily 7:00-19:00), and the top of the Eiffel-like TV tower on the left.

Climb the steps and enter. You won't find a more Mary-centered church. Everything—floor, walls, ceiling—is covered with elaborate mosaics. Scenes glittering on the walls tell stories of the Virgin (in Church history on the left, and in French history on the right). Amble down the center aisle at an escargot's pace and examine some of these scenes:

First scene on the left: In 431, the Council of Ephesus declared Mary to be the "Mother of God."

Across the nave, first on the right: The artist imagines Lugdunum (Lyon)—the biggest city in Roman Gaul, with 50,000 inhabitants—as the first Christian missionaries arrive. The first Christian martyrs in France (killed in A.D. 177) dance across heaven with palm branches.

Next left: In 1571, at the pivotal sea battle of Lepanto, Mary provides the necessary miracle as the outnumbered Christian forces beat the Ottomans.

Next right (view from right to left): Joan of Arc hears messages from Mary, rallies the French against the English at the Siege of Orléans in 1429 (find the Orléans coat of arms above and the timid French King Charles VII—whom Joan inspired to take a stand and fight the English—on his horse in the center), and is ultimately burned at the stake in Rouen at age 19 (1431).

Back across the nave on the left: In 1854, Pope Pius I proclaims the dogma of the Immaculate Conception in St. Peter's Square (establishing the belief among Catholics that Mary was born without the "Original Sin" of apple-eating Adam and Eve). To the left of the Pope, angels carry the tower of Fourvière Church; to the right is the image of the Virgin of Lourdes (who miraculously appeared in 1858).

Finally, on the right: Dashing Louis XIII offers the crown of France to the Virgin Mary. (The empty cradle hints that while he had her on the line, he asked, "Could I please have a son?" Louis XIV was born shortly thereafter.) Above marches a parade of pious French kings, from Clovis and Charlemagne to Napoleon (on the far right—with the white cross and red coat). Below are the great Marian churches of France (left to right)—Chartres, Paris' Sacré-Cœur and Notre-Dame, Reims (where most royalty was crowned), and this church. These six scenes in mosaic all lead to the altar where Mary reigns as Queen of Heaven.

Lower Church and Adjacent Chapel: Exit under Joan of Arc and descend to the lower church, dedicated to Mary's earthly husband, Joseph. Priorities here are painfully clear, as money ran out for Joseph's church. Today, it's used as a concert venue (notice the spongy-yellow acoustic material covering the vaulting). Return on the same stairs to the humble 16th-century chapel to the Virgin (push the door); outside, glance up to see the glorious statue of Mary that overlooks Lyon.

Nearby: Just around this chapel (past the church museum and the recommended Restaurant Panoramique) is a commanding **view** of Lyon. You can see parts of both rivers and north from the Croix-Rousse district south to the Bonaparte Bridge, with greater Lyon spread out before you in the distance. The black barrel-vaulted structure to the left is the Opera House, and the rose-colored skyscraper in the distance is called, appropriately, Le Crayon (the pencil). The big green space along the river to the left, across from the Croix-Rousse hill, is Lyon's massive park (La Tête d'Or). On a clear afternoon, you'll get a glimpse of Mont Blanc (the highest point in Europe, just left of the pencil-shaped skyscraper).

• *To get to the Roman Theaters and Gallo-Roman Museum, walk back to the funicular station and turn left down Rue Roger Radisson. The museum hides in the concrete bunker down the steps, where Rue Roger Radisson meets Rue Cléberg. Before entering, get the best overview of the site by taking a few steps left down Rue Cléberg and finding the ramp that leads to the museum's rooftop (open the gate).*

Lyon at a Glance

▲▲Roman Theaters and Gallo-Roman Museum Fine museum covering Roman Lyon. **Hours:** Museum—Tue-Sun 10:00-18:00, closed Mon; theaters—daily until 19:00, May-Sept until 21:00 except during Les Nuits de Fourvière festival in early June-early Aug, when it can close as early as 17:00. See below.

▲▲Vieux Lyon The city's fascinating, traffic-free historic core, with intriguing covered passageways. **Hours:** Passageways usually open daily 8:00-19:30. See page 907.

▲Notre-Dame Basilica Lyon's ornate version of Paris' Sacré-Cœur. **Hours:** Daily 8:00-19:00; weekday Mass usually at either 7:15 or 9:30, then at 11:00 and 17:00; Sun Mass at 7:30, 9:30, 11:00, and 17:00. See page 902.

▲Museum of Fine Arts France's second-most-important fine-arts museum (after the Louvre). **Hours:** Wed-Mon 10:00-18:00, Fri from 10:30, closed Tue. See page 912.

▲Resistance and Deportation History Center Displays and videos telling the inspirational story of the French Resistance. **Hours:** Wed-Sun 10:00-18:00, closed Mon-Tue. See page 913.

▲Lumière Museum Museum of film, dedicated to the Lumière brothers' pivotal contribution. **Hours:** Tue-Sun 10:00-18:30, closed Mon. See page 914.

▲▲Roman Theaters and Gallo-Roman Museum (Musée de la Civilisation Gallo-Romaine)

Founded as Lugdunum in A.D. 43, Lyon was a critical transportation hub for the administration of Roman Gaul (and much of modern-day France—much like today). The city became the central metropolis of the Three Gauls—the integrated Roman provinces of Aquitania (Aquitaine), Belgica (Belgium), and Lugdunensis (Lyon region)—and Emperors Claudius and Caracalla were both born here (for more on the Romans, see "How About Them Romans?" on page 569).

This worthwhile museum—constructed in the hillside with views of the two Roman Theaters—makes clear Lyon's importance in Roman times. Visit the museum first, then tour the theaters.

Cost and Hours: Museum—€4 (includes good audioguide), €7 if special exhibits are on, free on Thu, open Tue-Sun 10:00-18:00, closed Mon; theaters—free, daily until 19:00, May-Sept until 21:00 except during Les Nuits de Fourvière festival early

St. Jean Cathedral Gothic church with 700-year-old astronomical clock (currently under restoration) and lovely stained-glass windows. **Hours:** Mon-Fri 8:15-19:45, Sat-Sun 8:15-19:00. See page 907.

Gadagne Museums Two museums bringing to life Lyon's glory days and the tradition of Guignol puppets, housed in gorgeous Renaissance building. **Hours:** Wed-Sun 11:00-18:30, closed Mon-Tue. See page 910.

Atelier de la Soierie Workshop demonstrating handmade silk printing and screen painting. **Hours:** Mon-Fri 9:30-13:00 & 14:00-18:30, Sat 9:00-13:00 & 14:00-18:00, closed Sun. See page 911.

La Croix-Rousse Fun, avant-garde, historic neighborhood with great morning produce market and vertical pedestrian lanes. **Hours:** Market open Tue-Sun until 12:30; lanes always strollable. See page 911.

Museums of Textiles and Decorative Arts Pair of museums, one tracing the development of textile weaving over 2,000 years, the other featuring 18th-century decor in a mansion. **Hours:** Tue-Sun 10:00-17:30, closed Mon, Museum of Decorative Arts closes 12:00-14:00. See page 912.

June-early Aug, when it can close as early as 17:00; 17 Rue Cléberg, tel. 04 72 38 49 30, www.musees-gallo-romains.com.

➲ **Self-Guided Tour:** The route described below gives an overview of the museum's highlights, while the well-done audioguide, excellent posted English explanations, and helpful staff add as much substance to this museum as you can stomach.

The collection takes you on a chronological stroll down several floors through ancient Lyon. After a brief glimpse at prehistoric objects, dive into the Gallo-Roman rooms. The artifacts you'll see were found locally. The unusual bronze chariot dates from the seventh century B.C. In the next section, the model of Roman Lyon shows a city of 50,000 in its second-century A.D. glory days. Gauls and Romans lived and worked side by side in Roman Lyon. Notice that the forum stands where the basilica does today, hanging on the cliff edge. Find the arena in today's Croix-Rousse neighborhood (you'll see the arena's ruins if you follow my walking route of that area). Look for the white bits of aqueduct sections (with photos of the actual ruins nearby), the network of gray roads leading to Lyon, and the floating bridges across the rivers. The stone Roman pump behind the city model looks like an engine block (read the explanation to find out how it worked).

Those curved stones you pass next were actual seats in an arena—inscribed with the names of big shots who sat there. Soon after, look for a big, black-bronze tablet placed up high. Carved into it is the transcription of a speech given by Emperor Claudius in A.D. 48—his (longwinded) account of how he integrated the Gauls into the empire by declaring them eligible to sit in the Roman Senate (also recorded: the interjections of senators begging him to get to the point already—see the English translation on the wall).

You'll soon come upon displays of Roman coins and tools, and models of a few key Roman buildings in Lyon. A bit farther along, the model of the theater (the original is out the window) demonstrates the mechanics of a Roman theater stage curtain, which was raised instead of lowered. Go ahead...push the button. The last section of the museum shows how Lyon's wealthy merchants built large homes with interior courtyards often tiled with mosaics. Your visit ends with displays on Roman religious life and the onset of Christianity.

• *Exit the museum into the* ***Roman Theaters.***

The closer **big theater** was built under the reign of Emperor Augustus and expanded by Hadrian—at its zenith, it held 10,000 spectators. Today it seats 3,000 for concerts. The **small theater,** an "odeon" (from the Greek "ode" for song), was acoustically designed for speeches and songs. The grounds are peppered with gravestones and sarcophagi. Find a seat in the big theater and read up on Roman theaters (see page 582).

From early June through early August, the theaters host **Les Nuits de Fourvière,** an open-air festival of concerts, theater, dance, and film. Check programs at the TI and purchase tickets here at the theaters (box office at gate exit toward the Minimes funicular station, Mon-Sat 11:00-18:00, closed Sun), or online at www.nuitsdefourviere.com.

• *The ancient road between the Roman Theaters leads down and out, where you'll find the Minimes funicular station (to the right as you leave). Take the funicular to Vieux Lyon (not St. Just), where it deposits you only a few steps from St. Jean Cathedral. Take some time to explore Vieux Lyon. Or, from the Vieux Lyon funicular stop, you can take Métro line D directly to the Lumière Museum or (with an easy transfer) to the Resistance and Deportation History Center (both described later).*

VIEUX LYON (OLD LYON)

St. Jean Cathedral

Stand back in the square for the best view of the cathedral (brilliant at night and worth returning for). This mostly Gothic cathedral took 200 years to build. It doesn't soar as high as its northern French counterparts; influenced by their Italian neighbors, churches in southern France aren't as vertical as those in the north. This cathedral, the seat of the "primate of the Gauls" (as Lyon's bishop is officially titled), serves what's considered the oldest Christian city in France. Its interior houses some beautiful 13th- and 14th-century stained glass above the altar and adorning each transept (look for descriptions of the windows in English, near the altar).

Under the north transept is a medieval astronomical clock (1383); it has survived wars of all kinds, including the French Revolution, but was vandalized in 2013 and is now closed for restoration. Amazingly, its 700-year-old mechanism can compute Catholic holidays (including those that change each year, such as Easter) until 2019.

Cost and Hours: Free, Mon-Fri 8:15-19:45, Sat-Sun 8:15-19:00.

Nearby: Outside (make two right turns as you leave) are the ruins of a mostly 11th-century church, destroyed during the French Revolution (the cathedral was turned into a "temple of reason"). What's left of a baptistery from an early Christian church (c. A.D. 400) is under glass.

▲▲The Heart of Vieux Lyon

Vieux ("Old") Lyon offers the best concentration of well-preserved Renaissance buildings in the country. The city grew rich from its trade fairs and banking, and was the capital of Europe's silk industry from the 16th to 19th centuries. The most prominent vestiges of Lyon's Golden Age are the elegant pastel buildings of the old center, which were inspired by Italy and financed by the silk industry. Rue St. Jean, leading north from the cathedral to Place du Change, is the main drag, flanked by parallel pedestrian streets and punctuated with picturesque squares (Rue de Bœuf is quieter and more appealing than busy Rue St. Jean). The pedestrian-friendly lanes of Vieux Lyon were made for ambling, window-shopping, and café lingering.

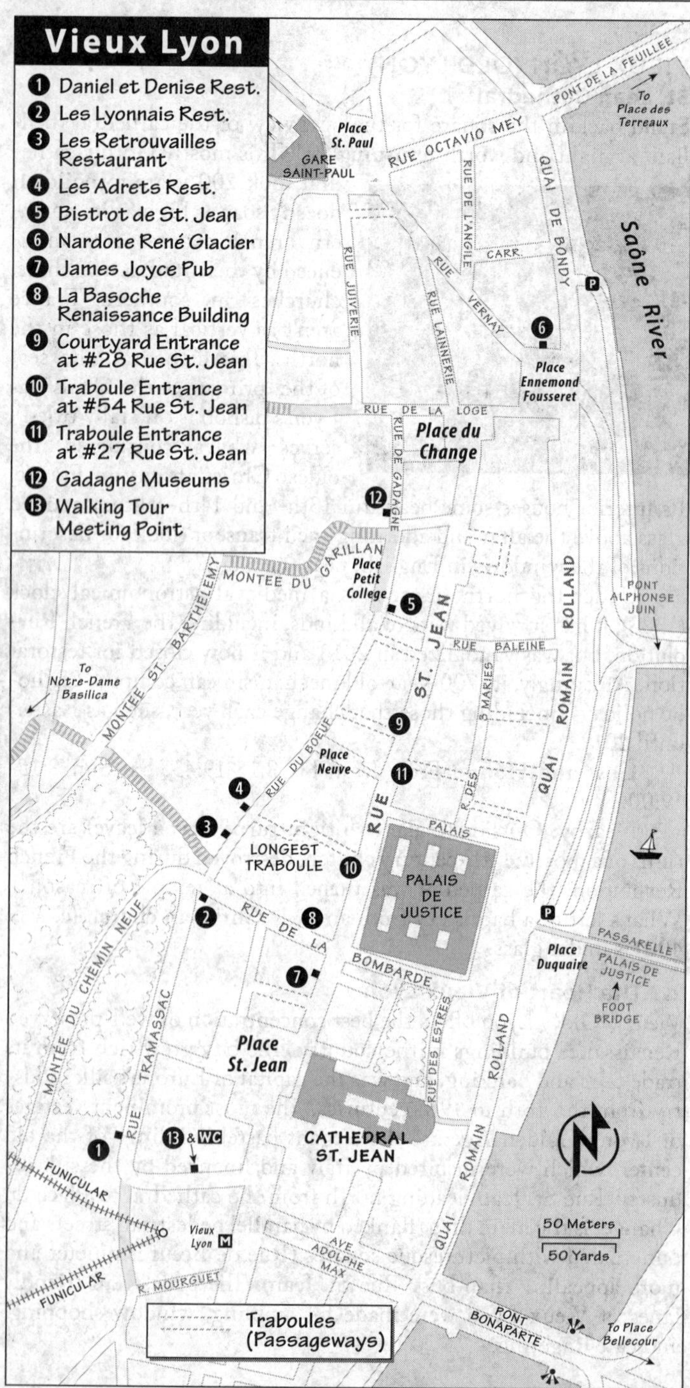
Vieux Lyon
1 Daniel et Denise Rest.
2 Les Lyonnais Rest.
3 Les Retrouvailles Restaurant
4 Les Adrets Rest.
5 Bistrot de St. Jean
6 Nardone René Glacier
7 James Joyce Pub
8 La Basoche Renaissance Building
9 Courtyard Entrance at #28 Rue St. Jean
10 Traboule Entrance at #54 Rue St. Jean
11 Traboule Entrance at #27 Rue St. Jean
12 Gadagne Museums
13 Walking Tour Meeting Point
Place St. Paul
GARE SAINT-PAUL
RUE OCTAVIO MEY
PONT DE LA FEUILLEE
To Place des Terreaux
RUE DE L'ANGILE
QUAI DE BONDY
Saône River
CARR.
RUE VERNAY
RUE JUIVERIE
RUE LAINNERIE
Place Ennemond Fousseret
RUE DE LA LOGE
RUE DE GADAGNE
Place du Change
MONTEE DU GARILLAN
Place Petit College
RUE ST. JEAN
RUE BALEINE
QUAI ROMAIN ROLLAND
PONT ALPHONSE JUIN
MONTEE ST. BARTHELEMY
To Notre-Dame Basilica
3 MARIES
RUE DU BOEUF
Place Neuve
R. DES
PALAIS
LONGEST TRABOULE
PALAIS DE JUSTICE
RUE DE LA BOMBARDE
PASSARELLE PALAIS DE JUSTICE
FOOT BRIDGE
Place Duquaire
MONTÉE DU CHEMIN NEUF
RUE TRAMASSAC
Place St. Jean
RUE DES ESTRES
CATHEDRAL ST. JEAN
13 & WC
FUNICULAR
Vieux Lyon
AVE. ADOLPHE MAX
R. MOURGUET
50 Meters
50 Yards
PONT BONAPARTE
To Place Bellecour
Traboules (Passageways)
LYON

• *Stroll along Rue St. Jean and take a short detour by making a left up Rue de la Bombarde to the colorful courtyard of...*

La Basoche: This beautifully restored Renaissance building gives you a good idea of what hides behind many facades in Vieux Lyon—and a whiff of Lyon's Golden Age. (At the time, the building served as a kind of legal center.) Check out the black-and-white photos that show this structure before its 1968 renovation, and imagine most of Vieux Lyon in this state.

• *Back along Rue St. Jean, notice the heavy doors leading to Lyon's...*

Traboules: The old city's serpentine *traboules* (passageways) worked as shortcuts, linking the old town's three main north-south streets and provided important shelter from the elements when unfinished silk goods were being moved from one stage of production to the next. These hidden paths give visitors a hide-and-seek opportunity to discover pastel courtyards, lovely loggias, and delicate arches. Spiral staircases were often shared by several houses.

Several short *traboules* leading to courtyards are accessible (if a doorway is open, you can wander in—#28 Rue St. Jean is a good example). However, only a few of Vieux Lyon's many *traboules* that connect different streets are open to the public. The longest *traboule* links #54 Rue St. Jean with #27 Rue du Bœuf; another, with gorgeous loggias, leads from #27 Rue St. Jean to #6 Rue de Trois Maries.

Traboules are generally accessible from 8:00 until 19:30. Press the button next to the street-front door to release the door when entering, push the lit buttons to illuminate dark walkways, and slide the door-handle levers when leaving. You're welcome to explore—but please be respectful of the residents, and don't go up any stairs.

While you wander Vieux Lyon, look for door plaques giving a history of each building and *traboule*. After walking through a *traboule*, you'll understand why Lyon's old town was an ideal center for the Resistance fighters to slip in and out of as they confounded the Nazis.

• *At the north end of Rue St. Jean is...*

Place du Change: This was the banking center of medieval Lyon. Its money scene developed after the city was allowed to host trade fairs in 1420. Its centerpiece is France's first stock exchange, Le Loge (now a Reformed Church), which was completely renovated in the 18th century (creating a stark contrast to the Renaissance architecture around it).

• *With your back to the river, head to nearby Place du Petit Collège, where you can peek (for free) into the wonderfully restored courtyard of the...*

Gadagne Museums (Musées Gadagne)

This pair of museums covers two topics (both nicely described in English). The **Lyon History Museum** is overkill for most, taking you from the city's Roman period to the present day—and every era in between (the rooms devoted to its silk industry are interesting, showing looms and sample fabrics). The **Puppets of the World Museum** celebrates Guignol puppetry, the still-vibrant tradition first created in Lyon by an unemployed silk worker. Here you'll see examples of beautifully crafted Guignol puppets from around the world; the fun audioguide narrative may keep some kids engaged for a while. Don't leave the museum without enjoying *un pause* on the rooftop terrace café.

Cost and Hours: €6 for one museum, €8 for both, includes audioguide and English brochure, Wed-Sun 11:00-18:30, closed Mon-Tue, 1 Place du Petit Collège, tel. 04 78 42 03 61, www.gadagne.musees.lyon.fr.

• *A short block down Rue de la Fronde leads to a fun shop selling puppets (and housing its own puppet museum). From here it's a short walk across the river to Place des Terreaux and the Museum of Fine Arts (cross Pont de la Feuillée and continue straight four blocks). Ice-cream connoisseurs must stop at the recommended* ***Nardone René Glacier*** *before crossing the river (on river near Place du Change).*

PRESQU'ILE

This bit of land (French for "peninsula," and literally meaning "almost-an-island") between the two rivers is Lyon's shopping spine, with thriving pedestrian streets. The neighborhood's northern focal point is the...

Place des Terreaux

This grand square hosts the City Hall (Hôtel de Ville), the Museum of Fine Arts, and an action-packed fountain by Frédéric-Auguste Bartholdi (the French sculptor who designed the Statue of Liberty). The fountain features Marianne (the Lady of the Republic) riding a four-horse-powered chariot, symbolically leading Lyon's two great rivers to the sea. It was originally destined for the city of Bordeaux, which (ultimately) realized that it could not afford the price tag, so the sculptor shopped it at the 1889 World Expo in Paris. There, Lyon's mayor fell in love and had to have it. After Bartholdi modified it to fit Lyon's needs, it was installed in 1891. This massive fountain was relocated in 1992 to its current location to make room for access to a parking garage below the square (imagine moving this thing).

The square itself is usually wet, with 69 fountains spurting playfully in a vast grid (designed by Daniel Buren, who did the courtyard of the Palais Royal in Paris).

Atelier de la Soierie

This silk workshop, just off Place des Terreaux on Rue Romarin (behind Café le Moulin Joli, a Resistance hangout during World War II), welcomes the public to drop in to see silk printing and screen painting by hand. Keep in mind that this is a lost art that today has mostly been replaced by machines. Within the shop, you'll see stretched silk canvases, buckets of dye, and artists in action. Friendly staff members speak some English and are happy to field questions while they work. Climb the staircase to visit a boutique selling handmade silk creations. Prices range from €25 to €250.

Cost and Hours: Free entry, Mon-Fri 9:30-13:00 & 14:00-18:30, Sat 9:00-13:00 & 14:00-18:00, closed Sun, tel. 04 72 07 97 83.

La Croix-Rousse

Hilly, untouristy, and SoHo-esque, this neighborhood hummed with some 30,000 silk looms in the 1800s. Today this part of town is popular with Lyon's tie-dye types, drawn here by abandoned, airy apartment spaces (built in the age of the Jacquard loom, which required exceptionally high ceilings).

The smartest way to visit is to take the Métro to the top, then follow a series of scenic slopes and stairs back down (see map on page 900). On the 20-minute stroll from top to bottom, you'll pass bohemian cafés, art galleries, creative graffiti, and used-clothing shops on your way to the Presqu'île. (Or—to burn off last night's *Lyonnaise* feast—follow this suggested route in reverse.)

Begin by exiting Métro line C at the La Croix-Rousse stop. Every day except Monday, until about 12:30, a local produce market stretches across the square and down Boulevard de la Croix-Rousse (much bigger on Saturdays). The statue at the center of the square is Monsieur Jacquard, inventor of the loom that powered Lyon's economy in the mid-1800s.

Start your downhill stroll from behind the Métro stop along Rue des Pierres Plantées. Pause to appreciate the views from the top of the Montée de la Grande Côte, and notice how the small concrete square may be used as a soccer field, a tricycle track, an outdoor café, and any other purpose the neighbors can find for it. Continue down the stairs, through the gardens along the Montée de la Grande Côte. Detour a block to the right on Rue des Tables Claudiennes for a view over the Roman Amphitheater of the Three Gauls. It's hard to imagine that this ruined arena was once the same size as the one in Arles, holding 20,000 spectators. Parts of the arena were destroyed in the 1800s for city development, and serious excavation did not begin until the 1960s. In most other cities, a Roman amphitheater would be big tourist news, but in Lyon it's ignored by most. Backpedal to the hill climb and continue your descent, working your way down to Place des Terreaux via Place des Capucins.

▲Museum of Fine Arts (Musée des Beaux-Arts)

Located in a former abbey, which was secularized by Napoleon in 1803 and made into a public museum, this fine-arts museum has an impressive collection, ranging from Egyptian antiquities to Impressionist paintings. The inner courtyard is a pleasant place to take a peaceful break from city streets. The helpful museum map and free audioguide make touring it a pleasure. Plan your arrival carefully, as several key sections close for lunch. A bar/café with calming terrace seating is on the first floor, next to the bookstore.

Cost and Hours: €7, includes audioguide, Wed-Mon 10:00-18:00 except Fri, when it opens at 10:30, closed Tue, pick up museum map when you enter, picnic-perfect courtyard, 20 Place des Terreaux, Métro: Hôtel de Ville, tel. 04 72 10 17 40, www.mba-lyon.fr.

Visiting the Museum: After passing the ticket taker, walk up a short flight of stairs to the Chapel, a dreamy Orsay-like display of 19th- and 20th-century statues, including works by Auguste Rodin and Bartholdi (sometimes closed between 12:00 and 14:00). The next flight of steps leads to *Les Antiquités* (first floor on map), a fine collection of ancient (especially Egyptian) art, medieval art, and Art Nouveau (furniture). This section closes from 12:30 to 13:15.

The second floor up displays a pretty selection of paintings from the last six centuries (no famous works, but a good Impressionist collection). You'll see Renaissance and Baroque paintings by Veronese, Cranach, Rubens, and Rembrandt, and "modern" works by Monet, Matisse, Pissarro, Gaugin, and Picasso. The highlight is a series of Pre-Raphaelite-type works called *Le Poème de l'Ame* ("The Poem of the Soul"), by Louis Janmot. This cycle of 18 paintings and 16 charcoal drawings traces the story of the souls of a boy and a girl as they journey through childhood, adolescence, and into adulthood. They struggle with fears and secular temptations before gaining spiritual enlightenment on the way to heaven. The boy loses his faith and enjoys a short but delicious hedonistic fling that leads to misery in hell. But a mother's prayers intercede, and he reunites with the girl to enjoy heavenly redemption.

Museums of Textiles and Decorative Arts (Musées des Tissus et des Arts Décoratifs)

These museums, between Place Bellecour and Perrache Station, fill two buildings (sharing a courtyard and connected with an interior hallway). The **Museum of Textiles** was founded in the mid-1800s to "maintain the commercial advantage of Lyon's silk manufacturers by showing their discerning taste for the arrangements and color settings of original motifs." It holds the world's most valuable collection of textiles, going back over 4,000 years and touching all corners of the world. Though packed with fine exhibits, the museum offers spotty information in English (explanations are posted only occasionally, though many objects are labeled in English). Serious fabrics fans can invest in the €19 book *(Collection Guide)* for thorough explanations of the displays. The museum shows off some breathtaking silk work—you'll see tunics, shawls, dresses, coats, capes, and more from around the world and made from a variety of fabrics.

The **Museum of Decorative Arts** fills a luxurious mansion and is decorated to the hilt with 18th-century furniture, textiles, and tapestries in a plush domestic setting. Entire rooms from aristocratic Lyonnaise homes have been re-created, including an 18th-century kitchen. There's plenty of china and a dazzling display of designer teakettles and coffee servers. There is zero, zilch, nada English information in this museum.

Cost and Hours: €10, covers both museums, Tue-Sun 10:00-17:30, closed Mon, Museum of Decorative Arts closes 12:00-14:00, 34 Rue de la Charité, Métro: Bellecour, tel. 04 78 38 42 00, www.mtmad.fr.

Shopping and Eating on the Presqu'île

There's more to this "almost-an-island" than the sights listed here. Join the river of shoppers on sprawling Rue de la République (north of Place Bellecour) and the teeming Rue Victor Hugo pedestrian mall (south of Place Bellecour). Smart clothing boutiques line Rue Président Edouard Herriot. Peruse the *bouchons* (characteristic bistros—especially characteristic in the evening) of Rue Mercière.

Passage de l'Argue is an old-world covered shopping passage from the 1800s that predates shopping malls (78 Rue Président Edouard Herriot).

Grand Café des Négociants is ideal for an indoor break. This *grand café,* which has been in business since 1864, feels like it hasn't changed since then, with its soft leather chairs, painted ceilings, and glass chandeliers (daily, 2 Place Francisque Régaud, near Cordeliers Métro stop, tel. 04 78 42 50 05).

AWAY FROM THE CENTER

▲Resistance and Deportation History Center (Centre d'Histoire de la Résistance et de la Déportation)

Located near Vichy (capital of the French puppet state) and neutral Switzerland, Lyon was the center of the French Resistance from

1942 to 1945. These "underground" Resistance heroes fought the Nazis tooth and nail. Bakers hid radios inside loaves of bread to secretly contact London. Barmaids passed along tips from tipsy Nazis. Communists in black berets cut telephone lines. Farmers hid downed airmen in haystacks. Housewives spread news from the front with their gossip. Printers countered Nazi propaganda with anonymous pamphlets. Without their bravery the liberation of France would not have been possible.

Cost and Hours: €4, Wed-Sun 10:00-18:00, closed Mon-Tue, 14 Avenue Berthelot, tel. 04 78 72 23 11, www.chrd.lyon.fr.

Tours: Free tablets deliver a grand, short, or themed multimedia tour (numbers indicate rooms, letters indicate specific objects). For the best experience, use your own earbuds rather than the headset provided. Printed explanations are also available.

Getting There: For most, the easiest way to reach the museum is to ride the Métro to Perrache Station and transfer to the T2 tramway (cross the tram tracks after exiting the Métro for the right direction for T2 tram). You can also take Métro line B to Jean Macé, exit toward the elevated train line, and transfer to the T2 tramway (going right). Get off the tramway at Centre Berthelot.

Visiting the Museum: Though these days it's dedicated to the history of the Resistance, the center actually served as a Nazi torture chamber and Gestapo headquarters under Klaus Barbie (who was finally tried and convicted in 1987 here in Lyon after extradition from Bolivia). More than 11,000 people were killed or deported to concentration camps during his reign.

This interesting museum gives visitors a thorough understanding of how Lyon became an important city in the Resistance, what life was like for its members, and the clever strategies they employed to fight the Germans. You'll also learn about the fate of the Jews in Lyon during the war. The museum uses interviews with people involved in the fight, reconstructed rooms, and numerous photos and exhibits to tell the inspiring story of the French Resistance.

▲Lumière Museum (Musée Lumière)

Antoine Lumière and his two sons Louis and Auguste—the Eastman-Kodaks of France—ran a huge factory with 260 workers in the 1880s, producing four million glass photographic plates a day. Then, in 1895, they made the first *cinématographe,* or movie. In 1903, they pioneered the "autochrome" process of painting frames to make "color photos." This museum tells their story.

Cost and Hours: €6.50, Tue-Sun 10:00-18:30, closed Mon, essential audioguide-€3, tel. 04 78 78 18 95, www.institut-lumiere.org.

Getting There: Take Métro line D to the Monplaisir-Lumière stop. The museum is in the large mansion with the tiled roof on the square, kitty-corner from the Métro stop at 25 Rue du Premier-Film.

Visiting the Museum: The museum fills Villa Lumière, the family's belle époque mansion, built in 1902. Many interesting displays and the essential audioguide do a great job of explaining the history of filmmaking. After leaving this place, where the laborious yet fascinating process of creating moving images is driven home, you'll never again take the quality of today's movies for granted.

Before your visit, pick up the informative museum plan. The museum's highlights are the many antique cameras and the screens playing the earliest "movies" (located on the ground floor). The first film reels held about 950 frames, which played at 19 per second, so these first movies were only 50 seconds long. About 1,500 Lumière films are catalogued between 1895 and 1907. (Notice that each movie is tagged with its "Catalog Lumière" number.) The very first movie ever made features workers piling out of the Lumière factory at the end of a workday. People attended movies at first not for the plot or the action, but rather to be mesmerized by the technology that allowed them to see moving images. After their initial success, the Lumières sent cameramen to capture scenes from around the world, connecting diverse cultures and people in a way that had never been done before.

Upstairs, the museum features exhibits on still photography and the Lumière living quarters (furnished c. 1900). Across the park from the mansion is a shrine of what's left of the warehouse where the first movie was actually shot. In a wonderful coincidence, *lumière* is the French word for "light."

Nightlife in Lyon

Lyon has France's second-largest cultural budget after Paris, so there are always plenty of theatrical productions and concerts to attend (in French, of course). The TI has the latest information and schedules. From mid-June through mid-September, the terrace-café at the Opera House hosts an outdoor jazz café with free concerts (usually Mon-Sat, www.opera-lyon.com).

After dinner, stroll through Lyon to savor the city's famous illuminations (see sidebar on page 896).

For lively bar and people-watching scenes, prowl Rue de la Monnaie (angles off "restaurant row" Rue Mercière to the south) and the streets between Place des Terreaux and the Opera House. The **James Joyce** Irish pub, in the heart of Vieux Lyon, is a cozy English-speaking place (daily, 68 Rue St. Jean, tel. 04 78 37 84 28).

Sleeping in Lyon

Hotels in Lyon are a steal compared with those in Paris. Weekends are generally discounted (Sundays in particular) in this city that lives off business travelers. Prices rise and rooms disappear when trade fairs are in town, so it's smart to reserve your room in advance. If you have trouble, the TI can help for free in person or by email (resa@lyon-france.com). Most of my listings are on the Presqu'île. Hotels have elevators and free Wi-Fi unless otherwise noted, and air-conditioning is a godsend when it's hot (hottest June-mid-Sept). Expect to push buttons to gain access to many hotels.

ON OR NEAR PLACE DES CELESTINS

Book ahead to sleep in this classy yet unpretentious neighborhood (Métro: Bellecour). Just a block off the central Place Bellecour and a block to the Saône River, this area gives travelers easy access to Lyon's sights. Join shoppers perusing the upscale boutiques, or watch children playing in the small square fronting the Théâtre des Célestins. Warning: Weekend nights can be noisy if you score a room facing Place des Célestins.

$$$ Hôtel Globe et Cecil*** is the most professional and elegant of my listings, with refined comfort on a refined street and a service-oriented staff. Its rooms are tastefully decorated and mostly spacious (Sb-€140, Db-€180, more during festivals, good €7.50 breakfast if you book directly with hotel, air-con, Wi-Fi, 21 Rue Gasparin, tel. 04 78 42 58 95, www.globeetcecilhotel.com, accueil@globeetcecilhotel.com).

$$$ Hôtel des Artistes*,** ideally located on Place des Célestins, is a comfortable, business-class hotel that offers a fair value on weekdays and a good value on weekends (Sb-€97-144, standard Db-€120, larger Db-€144, extra bed-€10, €15 discount Fri-Sat and €25 on Sun, standard rooms are comfortable but tight, breakfast-€13.50, air-con, Wi-Fi, 8 Rue Gaspard-André, tel. 04 78 42 04 88, www.hotel-des-artistes.fr, reservation@hotel-des-artistes.fr). The hotel may close in 2015 for renovation.

$$$ Hôtel des Célestins*,** just off Place des Célestins, is warmly run by Cornell-grad Laurent. Its cheery rooms aren't cheap but are filled with thoughtful touches. Streetside rooms have more light and are bigger (Sb-€74-99, Db-€96-131, bigger Db-€106-151, Tb-€122-191, beautiful suites ideal for families or those in need of room to roam-€175-230, €10 buffet breakfast served 7:00-12:00, completely non-smoking, air-con, guest computer, Wi-Fi, laundry service, 4 Rue des Archers, tel. 04 72 56 08 98, www.hotelcelestins.com, info@hotelcelestins.com).

Sleep Code

Abbreviations **(€1 = about $1.40, country code: 33)**

S = Single, **D** = Double/Twin, **T** = Triple, **Q** = Quad, **b** = bathroom, **s** = shower only, * = French hotel rating (0-5 stars)

Price Rankings

- **$$$** Higher Priced—Most rooms €100 or more
- **$$** **Moderately Priced**—Most rooms between €65-100
- **$** **Lower Priced**—Most rooms €65 or less

Unless otherwise noted, credit cards are accepted, English is spoken, and Wi-Fi is generally free. Prices change; verify current rates online or by email. For the best prices, always book directly with the hotel.

$$ Elysée Hôtel, a few blocks off Place des Célestins, is a simple little hotel with excellent rates and two-star comfort. Gentle Monsieur Larrive is your host (Db-€80-88, breakfast-€8.50, air-con, elevator from first floor up, Wi-Fi, 92 Rue Président Edouard Herriot, tel. 04 78 42 03 15, www.hotel-elysee.fr, accueil@hotel-elysee.fr).

$$ Hôtel du Théâtre** has no air-conditioning and requires stamina to reach the lobby, as it's 40 steps from street level. But the hotel is well-located on Place des Célestins and offers a solid deal. Owners Monsieur and Madame Kuhn run a tight ship, most of the rooms and bathrooms are spacious, and the beds are firm (Db-€69-77, extra bed-€15, continental breakfast-€6, Wi-Fi, no elevator, 10 Rue de Savoie, enter from hotel's rear, tel. 04 78 42 33 32, www.hotel-du-theatre.fr, contact@hotel-du-theatre.fr).

OTHER PLACES ON THE PRESQU'ILE

$$ Le Boulevardier** is a great budget option located a few blocks south of Place des Terreaux. It's particularly fun for jazz lovers, as the 14 rooms sit above a jazz café. Don't let the dumpy facade fool you; the well-priced rooms are full of charm, some with stone walls, antique furniture, and toys; others with sweet church views. Owner Cédric, a bric-a-brac trader with great taste, lives on the top floor (small Db-€69, bigger Db-€79 and worth the extra euros, Tb-€92, 5 Rue de la Fromagerie, tel. 04 78 28 48 22, www.leboulevardier.fr, ccg.bernard@gmail.com).

$$ Hôtel la Residence***, south of Place Bellecour and my closest listing to Perrache Station, has 67 plain but good-value air-conditioned rooms. Most are spacious and have high ceilings and bathtub-showers (Sb/Db-€97, Tb-€110, Qb-€120, breakfast-€8, guest computer, Wi-Fi, 18 Victor Hugo, tel. 04 78 42 63 28, www.hotel-la-residence.com, hotel-la-residence@wanadoo.fr).

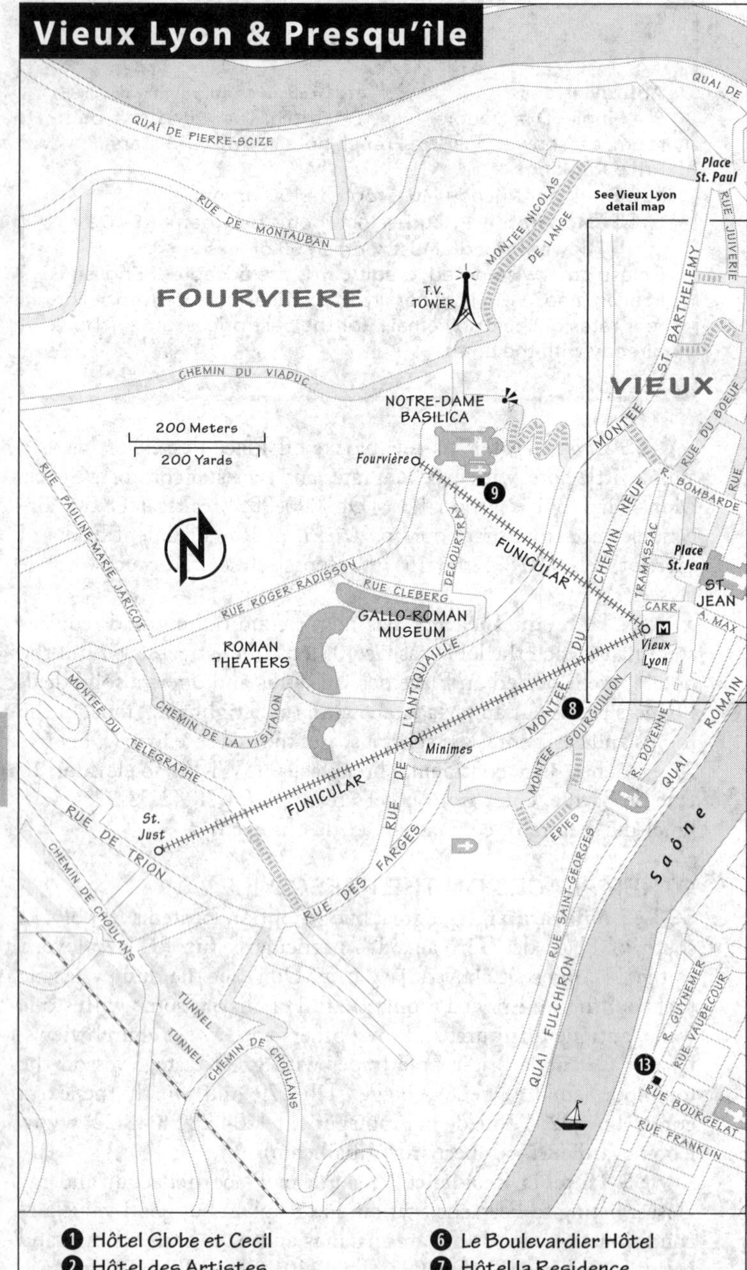
Vieux Lyon & Presqu'île
QUAI DE PIERRE-SCIZE
QUAI DE
Place St. Paul
See Vieux Lyon detail map
RUE DE MONTAUBAN
MONTEE NICOLAS DE LANGE
RUE JUIVERIE
FOURVIERE
T.V. TOWER
ST. BARTHELEMY
CHEMIN DU VIADUC
VIEUX
NOTRE-DAME BASILICA
RUE DU BOEUF
200 Meters
200 Yards
Fourvière
MONTEE
RUE
R. BOMBARDE
RUE PAULINE-MARIE JARICOT
DECOURTRAY
FUNICULAR
CHEMIN NEUF
TRAMASSAC
Place St. Jean
ST. JEAN
RUE ROGER RADISSON
RUE CLEBERG
GALLO-ROMAN MUSEUM
CARR
A. MAX
ROMAN THEATERS
Vieux Lyon
MONTEE DU
MONTEE DU TELEGRAPHE
CHEMIN DE LA VISITAION
RUE DE L'ANTIQUAILLE
MONTEE GOURGUILLON
R. DOYENNE
QUAI ROMAIN
Minimes
FUNICULAR
RUE DE TRION
St. Just
RUE DES FARGES
MONTEE EPIES
RUE SAINT-GEORGES
Saône
CHEMIN DE CHOULANS
TUNNEL
TUNNEL
CHEMIN DE CHOULANS
QUAI FULCHIRON
R. GUYNEMER
RUE VAUBECOUR
RUE BOURGELAT
RUE FRANKLIN
LYON
❶ Hôtel Globe et Cecil
❷ Hôtel des Artistes
❸ Hôtel des Célestins
❹ Elysée Hôtel
❺ Hôtel du Théâtre
❻ Le Boulevardier Hôtel
❼ Hôtel la Residence
❽ Vieux Lyon Youth Hostel
❾ Rest. Panoramique de la Fourvière

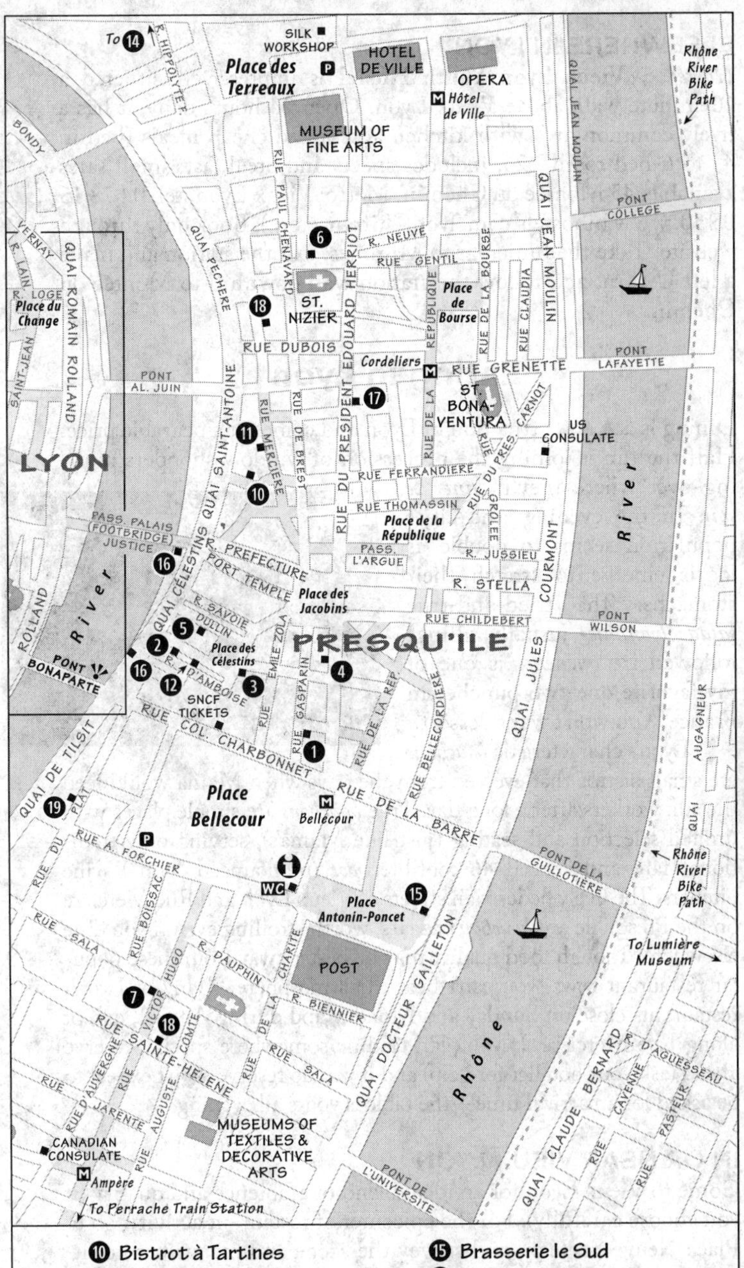

10 Bistrot à Tartines
11 Bistrot de Lyon
12 La Francotte Bistro
13 Café-Comptoir Abel Rest.
14 Archange Restaurant
15 Brasserie le Sud
16 Buvettes (2)
17 Grand Café des Négociants
18 Launderettes (2)
19 Internet Café

ELSEWHERE IN LYON

Hostel: **$ Vieux Lyon Youth Hostel** is impressively situated a 10-minute walk above Vieux Lyon. Open 24 hours daily, it has a lively common area with kitchen access and cheap meals (bed in 4- to 6-bed room-€25, includes sheets and breakfast, small safes available, 45 Montée du Chemin, Métro: Vieux Lyon, tel. 04 78 15 05 50, www.hihostels.com, lyon@hifrance.org). Book only through website. Take the funicular to Minimes, exit the station and make a left U-turn, and follow the station wall downhill to Montée du Chemin.

Eating in Lyon

Dining is a ▲▲▲ attraction in Lyon and comes at a bearable price. Half the fun is joining the procession of window shoppers mulling over where they'll *dîner ce soir.* In the evening, the city's population seems to double as locals emerge to stretch their stomachs. The tried-and-true *salade lyonnaise* (usually filling) followed by *quenelles* is one of my favorite one-two punches in France. You won't want dessert.

Lyon's characteristic *bouchons* are small bistros that evolved from the days when Mama would feed the silk workers after a long day. True *bouchons* are simple places with limited selection and seating (just like Mama's), serving only traditional fare and special 46-centiliter *pot* (pronounced "poh") wine pitchers. The lively pedestrian streets of Vieux Lyon and Rue Mercière on the Presqu'île are *bouchon* bazaars, worth strolling even if you dine elsewhere. Though food quality may be better away from these popular restaurant rows, you can't beat the atmosphere. Many of Lyon's restaurants close on Sunday and Monday and during August, except along Rue Mercière. If you plan to dine somewhere special, reserve ahead (ask your hotelier for help) and if you do reserve, don't expect to be asked for an arrival time—the table is yours all evening.

IN OR NEAR VIEUX LYON

Come to Vieux Lyon for an ideal blend of ambience and quality (if you choose carefully). For the epicenter of restaurant activity, go to Place Neuve St. Jean, and survey the scene and menus before sitting down. All of these places are located on the map on page 908.

Daniel et Denise is worth booking ahead. Reputed chef Joseph Viola has created a buzz by providing wonderful cuisine at affordable prices in a classic *bouchon* setting. His are the best *quenelles*

I have tasted and come with potatoes and a wonderful mac-and-cheese-like side dish (*menus* from €30, €18 *quenelles,* indoor seating only, closed Sun-Mon, 36 Rue Tramassac, tel. 04 78 42 24 62, www.daniel-et-denise-stjean.com).

Les Lyonnais is barely a block off the Rue du Bœuf action, making it a bit quieter. Its lighthearted interior has rich colors, wood tables, and a photo gallery of loyal customers. Sincere Stephane runs the place with grace (good €25 *menu* with *salade lyonnaise* and *quenelles,* fine and filling €14 salads, closed Mon, small terrace, 1 Rue Tramassac, tel. 04 78 37 64 82).

Les Retrouvailles serves tasty but less traditional Lyonnaise cuisine in a charming setting under wood-beam ceilings with an open kitchen. Tables are grouped around a central buffet displaying delectable desserts that inspire diners to eat their vegetables. Here your dining experience is carefully managed by adorable owners Pierre *(le chef)* and Odile (€26 and €32 four-course *menus,* inside dining only, closed Sun evening, 38 Rue du Bœuf, tel. 04 78 42 68 84).

Les Adrets is where *bouchon* meets beer hall. This linear, heavy-beamed place, lined with velvet booths and cheery lights, is crammed with a lively crowd enjoying good-value Lyonnaise cuisine (€27-45 *menus,* €18 lunch *menu,* indoor dining only, closed Sat-Sun and Aug, reservations recommended, 30 Rue du Bœuf, tel. 04 78 38 24 30).

Restaurant Panoramique de la Fourvière, atop Fourvière Hill with a spectacular view overlooking Lyon, serves fine traditional cuisine in a superb setting. Choose from the modern interior or the better, leafy terrace, both with views. Reserve well ahead for a view table (*menus* from €28, €14 lunch *plat du jour,* daily until 22:00, 9 Place de Fourvière, near Notre-Dame Basilica—see map on page 918, tel. 04 78 25 21 15, www.restaurant-fourviere.fr).

Bistrot de St. Jean is a time-warp place with an old-school owner and cheap prices serving basic cuisine. It's cheerfully located on a leafy square with fun seating outside. Bring Gérald a pin to wear on his apron and he will offer you an *apéritif* (€10 *plats,* closed Mon, 3 Place du Petit Collège, tel. 04 78 37 15 81).

Ice Cream: **Nardone René Glacier,** with pleasant outdoor seating on the river near Place du Change, serves up Lyon's best ice cream, made fresh daily next door. Ask Armelle about her peanut ice cream (May-Sept daily 8:30-24:00, off-season 9:00-20:00, 3 Place Ennemond Fousseret).

ON THE PRESQU'ILE

The pedestrian Rue Mercière is the epicenter of *bouchons* on the Presqu'île. Along this street, an entertaining cancan of restaurants stretches four blocks from Place des Jacobins to Rue Grenette.

Enjoy surveying the scene and choose whichever eatery appeals. All of these restaurants appear on the map on page 918.

On or near Rue Mercière

Bistrot à Tartines is a young and fun place for nontraditional cuisine offered at unbeatable prices by a friendly staff. The interior, which feels like an antique general store, has good seating inside and out. Meals are served all day (€7 *tartines,* killer €4 desserts, daily, 2 Rue de la Monnaie, tel. 04 78 37 70 85).

Bistrot de Lyon feels *très* touristy but still bustles with authentic Lyonnaise atmosphere and reliable cuisine. It must be famed chef-owner Jean-Paul Lacombe's least expensive establishment (€21 *quenelles,* €13 *salade lyonnaise,* limited-selection *menus* from €25, open daily, 64 Rue Mercière, tel. 04 78 38 47 47).

On Place des Célestins

La Francotte is a good if slightly pricey choice with a warm interior, a solid zinc-topped bar, and fine outdoor seating on Place des Célestins. Try the excellent fish dishes or anything served with their mouthwatering roasted garlic potatoes (*menus* from €30, closed Sun-Mon, near many recommended hotels at 8 Place des Célestins, tel. 04 78 37 38 64).

Worth a Detour

LYON

Café-Comptoir Abel is an authentic local *bouchon,* far away from restaurant rows and tourists, and catering to one kind of client only: Lyon residents. It has a warm, chalet-like interior, some outside seating, and generous servings—the *quenelle de brochet* is downright massive. Consider a *plat du jour* and maybe a salad. Reserve ahead (€25-39 *menus,* daily from 19:30 except closed Sun evening, about a 15-minute walk south of Place Bellecour, Métro: Ampère, a short block from Saône River, 25 Rue Guynemer, entrance on Rue Bourgelat, tel. 04 78 37 46 18, www.cafecomptoirabel.fr).

Archange is a softly lit, white-tablecloth and fine-glassware place accommodating 26 happy diners, all eager to sample the popular chef's creations that infuse a hint of Japanese influence with classic Lyonnaise cuisine. Ask your hotelier to book your table ahead (€29 *menus,* closed Mon, tricky to find, near Place des Terreaux at 6 Rue Hippolyte, tel. 04 78 28 32 26, www.archangecafe.com).

Brasserie le Sud is one of four places in Lyon where you can sample legendary chef Paul Bocuse's cuisine at affordable prices. His brasseries feature international cuisine from different corners of the world (each named for the corner it represents—north, south, east, and west). Le Sud is the most accessible, with a Mediterranean feel inside and out, but less easygoing service than you'll find at my other recommended restaurants (€26 *menu,* higher prices on Sun, reasonably priced *plats,* daily, 11 Place Antonin-Poncet, a few blocks off Place Bellecour, tel. 04 72 77 80 00).

Lyon Connections

After Paris, Lyon is France's most important rail hub. Train travelers find this gateway to the Alps, Provence, the Riviera, and Burgundy an easy stopover. Two main train stations serve Lyon: Part-Dieu and Perrache. Most trains officially depart from Part-Dieu, though many also stop at Perrache, and trains run between the stations (service can be infrequent). Double-check which station your train departs from.

From Lyon by Train to: Paris (at least hourly, 2 hours), **Annecy** (10/day, 2 hours, some change in Chambéry, some by bus), **Chamonix** (6/day, 4 hours, most change at St-Gervais), **Strasbourg** (4/day, 4 hours), **Dijon** (hourly, 2 hours), **Beaune** (at least hourly, 1.75 hours), **Avignon** (22/day; 12 to TGV Station in 70 min, 10 to center station in 2 hours), **Arles** (14/day, 2.5-3.5 hours, most change in Avignon, Marseille, or Nîmes), **Nice** (6/day, 4.5 hours), **Carcassonne** (4/day, 4 hours), **Venice** (3/day, 9.5-10.5 hours, 2-3 changes, night train), **Rome** (4/day, 10-12 hours, at least one change in Milan, night train), **Florence** (7/day, 8-15 hours), **Geneva** (8/day, 2 hours), **Barcelona** (2 day trains, 7 hours, change in Perpignan; 2 night trains with transfers).

Route Tips for Drivers: En route to Provence, consider a half-day detour through the spectacular Ardèche Gorges: Exit the A-6 autoroute at Privas and follow along through the pleasant villages of Aubenas, Vallon Pont d'Arc (offers kayak trips), and Pont St-Esprit.

Near Lyon: The Rhône Valley

The Rhône Valley is the narrow part of the hourglass that links the areas of Provence and Burgundy. The region is bordered to the west by the soft hills of the Massif Central, and with the rolling foothills of the Alps just to the east, it's the gateway to the high Alps (the region is called Rhône-Alpes). The mighty Rhône River rumbles through the valley from its origin in Lake Geneva to its outlet 500 miles away in the Mediterranean near Arles.

Vineyards blanket the western side of the Rhône Valley, from those of the Beaujolais just north of Lyon to the steep slopes of Tain-Hermitage below Lyon. On the eastern side of the river and closer to Avignon are the vineyards of the famous Côtes du Rhône.

The Rhône Valley has always provided the path of least resistance for access from the Mediterranean to northern Europe, and today, Roman ruins litter the valley between Lyon and Orange.

BEAUJOLAIS WINE ROUTE

Between Mâcon (near Cluny) and Lyon, the Beaujolais region makes for an appealing detour, thanks to its beautiful vineyards and villages and easygoing wine-tasting (for more on Beaujolais wines, see page 893).

The Beaujolais wine road starts 45 minutes north of Lyon and runs from Villefranche-sur-Saône to Mâcon. The *Route du Beaujolais* winds up, down, and around the hills just west of the A-6 autoroute and passes through Beaujolais' most important villages: Chiroubles, Fleurie, Chénas, and Juliénas. Look for *Route du Beaujolais* signs, and expect to get lost more than a few times (Lyon's TI has a route map, and you can check for more information).

Along the wine route, you'll pass Moulin à Vent's famous vineyards and see its trademark windmill. You'll enter the Mâconnais wine region and pass signs to the famous villages of Pouilly and Fuissé as you near Mâcon. Trains running between Lyon and Mâcon stop at several wine villages, including Romanèche-Thorins (described next; 6 trains/day from Lyon). While Villefranche-sur-Saône may be the Beaujolais capital, it's a big, unappealing city that's best avoided. Focus your time on the small villages, and look for *degustation* (tasting) signs.

For a high-priced but thorough introduction to this region's wines, visit **Le Hameau du Vin** in Romanèche-Thorins. The king of Beaujolais, Georges Dubœuf, has constructed a Disney-esque introduction to wine at his museum, which immerses you in the life of a winemaker and features impressive models, exhibits, films, and videos. You'll be escorted from the beginning of the vine to present-day winemaking, with a focus on Beaujolais wines. It also has a lovely garden with fragrant flowers, fruits, herbs, and spices that represent the rich aromas present in wine (€19, includes a small tasting, free English headphones and a *petit train* ride, daily 10:00-18:00; in Romanèche-Thorins, follow signs labeled *Le Hameau du Vin* from D-306—the old N-6, then *La Gare* signs, and look for the old train-station-turned-winery; tel. 03 85 35 22 22, www.hameauduvin.com).

ALSACE

Colmar • Route du Vin • Strasbourg

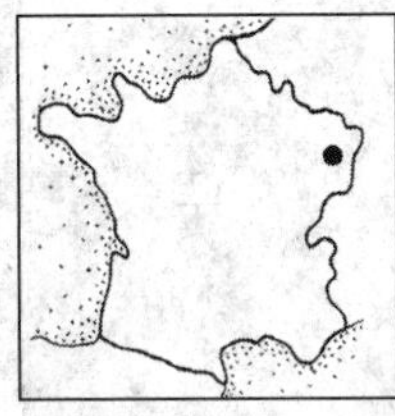

The province of Alsace stands like a flower-child referee between Germany and France. Bounded by the Rhine River on the east and the Vosges Mountains on the west, this is a green region of Hansel-and-Gretel villages, ambitious vineyards, and vibrant cities. Food and wine are the primary industry, topic of conversation, and perfect excuse for countless festivals.

Alsace has changed hands between Germany and France several times because of its location, natural wealth, naked vulnerability—and the fact that Germany considered the mountains the natural border, while the French saw the Rhine as the dividing line.

On a grander scale, Alsace is Europe's cultural divide, with Germanic nations to the north and Romantic ones to the south. The region is a fault line marking the place where cultural tectonic plates collide—it's no wonder the region has been scarred by a history of war.

Through the Middle Ages, Alsace was part of the Holy Roman Empire (in other words, German culture and language ruled). After the devastation of the Thirty Years' War (1618-1648), Alsace started to become integrated into France—revolutionaries took full control in 1792. But in 1871, after France's defeat in the Franco-Prussian War, Alsace "returned" to Germany. Almost five decades later, Germany lost World War I—and Alsace "returned" to France. Except for a miserable stint as part of the Nazi realm from 1940 to 1945, Alsace has been French ever since.

Having been a political pawn for 1,000 years, Alsace has a hybrid culture: Natives who curse do so bilingually, and the local cuisine features sauerkraut with fine wine sauces. In recent years,

Alsace
To Frankfurt
A-62
10 Kilometers
10 Miles
A-8
A-6
Saarbrücken
A-8
A-27
Paris
FRANCE
100 Miles
GERMANY
To Metz, Verdun, Reims & Paris
To Frankfurt
Wissembourg
FRANCE
A-4
To Verdun, Reims & Paris
A-35
TGV
Haguenau
D-1061
Baden-Baden
A-4
Sarrebourg
Saverne
River
To Lunéville
D-1004
A-5
LORRAINE
Strasbourg
Kehl
N-4
28
LE STRUTHOF
Baccarat
D-1420
A-35
D-1083
Rhine
GERMANY
BLACK FOREST
N-59
St-Dié
See detail map
Sélestat
VOSGES MTNS.
ALSACE
A-5
294
D-415
Kaysersberg
Col de Bonhomme
Colmar
Eguisheim
D-415
Breisach
Freiburg
31
To Epinal
A-35
Rhine River
A-5
N-66
D-83
Mulhouse
317
TGV Rail Line
Ronchamp
A-36
A-35
N-19
Belfort
Basel
A-3
A-36
To Zürich
To Besançon, Dijon & Beaune
To Bern
SWITZERLAND

ALSACE

Alsace and its sister German region just across the border have been growing farther apart linguistically—but closer commercially. People routinely cross the border to shop and work. And, while Alsace's mixed German/French dialects are fading, a recent agreement encourages schools on the German side to teach French as the second language and schools on the French side to teach German as the second language.

Of the 1.8 million people living in Alsace, about 270,000 live in Strasbourg (its biggest city) and 70,000 live in Colmar (its best city).

Colmar is one of Europe's most enchanting cities—with a small-town warmth and world-class art. Strasbourg is a big-city version of Colmar, worth a stop for its remarkable cathedral and to feel its high-powered and trendy bustle. The small villages that dot the wine road between them are like petite Colmars, and provide a delightful and charming escape from the two cities.

PLANNING YOUR TIME

The ideal plan: Make Colmar your home base and spend three nights. Take one day to see the town and one day to explore the Route du Vin. To efficiently see the villages and vineyards of the Route du Vin, you'll need a car—or take one of the recommended minibus tours from Colmar. If you have a car and like small towns, think about basing yourself in Eguisheim or Kaysersberg. If you have only one day, spend your morning in Colmar and your afternoon along the Route du Vin. Urban Strasbourg, with its soaring cathedral and vigorous center, is a headache for drivers but a quick 35-minute train ride from Colmar—do it by train as a day trip from Colmar or as a stopover on your way in or out of the region.

The humbling WWI battlefields of Verdun and the bubbly vigor of Reims in northern France (both described in the next chapter) are closer to Paris than to Alsace, and follow logically only if your next destination is Paris. The high-speed TGV-Est train links Paris with Reims, Verdun, Strasbourg, Colmar, and destinations farther east, bringing the Alsace within 2.5 hours of Paris and giving train travelers easy access to Reims or Verdun en route between Paris and Alsace.

GETTING AROUND ALSACE

Frequent trains make the trip between Colmar and Strasbourg a snap (2/hour, 35 minutes). Distances are very short and driving is easy—though a good map helps. Connecting Colmar with neighboring villages is doable via the region's sparse bus service or on a bike if you're in shape. Minivan excursions are ideal for those without cars. And hopping a taxi between towns is an option—if you've got the money. Once in the Route du Vin villages, you can

Early Crockpots

For old-school Alsatian comfort food, order the ubiquitous *Baeckeoffe,* which is still served at your table in traditional pottery. The dish gets its name from where it was cooked—in the "baker's oven." For centuries Alsatian women combined the week's leftover pork, beef, and veal with potatoes, onions, and leeks in a covered clay pot, then added white wine. Carrying the pot on their way to church on Sunday, the women would pass by the bakery and put their pot in one of the large stone ovens, still warm from baking the morning bread. During the three-hour Mass, the meat would simmer and be perfectly stewed in time for lunch. The pottery, which is still produced and sold locally, remains an integral part of every Alsatian household.

also hike or rent bikes to explore (for details on all of these options, see "Alsace's Route du Vin," later).

ALSACE'S CUISINE SCENE

Alsatian cuisine is a major tourist attraction in itself. You can't mistake the German influence: sausages, potatoes, onions, and sauerkraut. Look for *choucroute garnie* (sauerkraut and sausage—although it seems a shame to eat it in a fancy restaurant), the more traditionally Alsatian *Baeckeoffe* (see sidebar), *Rösti* (an oven-baked potato-and-cheese dish), *Spätzle* (soft egg noodles), *quenelles* (dumplings made of pork, beef, or fish), fresh trout, and foie gras. For lighter fare, try the *poulet au Riesling,* chicken cooked ever-so-slowly in Riesling wine (*coq au Riesling* is the same dish done with rooster). At lunch, or for a lighter dinner, try a *tarte à l'oignon* (like an onion quiche, but better) or *tarte flambée* (like a thin-crust pizza with onion and bacon bits). If you're picnicking, buy some stinky Munster cheese. Dessert specialties are *tarte alsacienne* (fruit tart) and *Kuglehopf glacé* (a light cake mixed with raisins, almonds, dried fruit, and cherry liqueur).

Remember, restaurants serve only during lunch (11:30-14:00) and dinner (18:00 or 19:00-21:00, later in bigger cities), but some cafés serve food throughout the day. Many Alsatian restaurants open at 18:00, reflecting the region's Germanic heritage.

ALSATIAN WINES

Thanks to Alsace's Franco-Germanic culture, its wines are a kind of hybrid. The bottle shape, grapes, and much of the wine terminology are inherited from its German past, though wines made today are distinctly French in style (and generally drier than their German sisters). Alsatian wines are named for their grapes—unlike in Burgundy or Provence, where wines are commonly named after villages, or in Bordeaux, where wines are often named after châteaux. White wines rule in Alsace. You'll also come across a local version of Champagne, called Crémant d'Alsace, and several varieties of *eaux-de-vie* (strong fruit-flavored brandy). For a helpful rundown of the regional wines, see "Route du Vin Wines" (page 956).

Colmar

Colmar feels made for wonder-struck tourists—its essentially traffic-free city center is a fantasy of steep pitched roofs, pastel stucco, and aged timbers. Plus, it offers a few heavyweight sights in a comfortable, midsize-town package. Historic beauty was usually a poor excuse for being spared the ravages of World War II, but it worked for Colmar. The American and British military were careful not to bomb the half-timbered old burghers' houses, characteristic red- and green-tiled roofs, and cobbled lanes of Alsace's most beautiful city. The town's distinctly French shutters combined with the ye-olde German half-timbering give Colmar an intriguing ambience.

Today, Colmar is alive with colorful buildings, impressive art treasures, and German tourists. Antiques shops welcome browsers, homeowners fuss over their geraniums, and hoteliers hurry down the sleepy streets to pick up fresh croissants in time for breakfast.

Orientation to Colmar

There isn't a straight street in Colmar—count on getting lost. Thankfully, most streets are pedestrian-only, and it's a lovely town to be lost in. Navigate by church steeples and the helpful signs that seem to pop up whenever you need them (directing visitors to the various sights). For tourists, the town center is Place Unterlinden (a

20-minute walk from the train station), where you'll find Colmar's most important museum, the TI (close by), and a big Monoprix supermarket/department store. City bus routes as well as the touristic mini-trains start near Place Unterlinden.

Colmar is most busy from May through September and during its festive Christmas season (www.noel-colmar.com). Weekends draw crowds all year (best to book lodging ahead). The impressive music festival fills hotels the first two weeks of July (www.festival-colmar.com), and the local wine festival rages in July and August. An open-air market bustles next to the Church of St. Martin on Saturdays.

TOURIST INFORMATION

The TI may move next to the Unterlinden Museum in 2015. If it hasn't moved, look for it hidden behind the Monoprix store, near City Hall at 32 Cours Sainte-Anne (labeled *Mairie de Colmar*). It's signed from the square in front of the Unterlinden Museum (April-Oct Mon-Sat 9:00-18:00, Sun 10:00-13:00; Nov-March Mon-Sat 9:00-12:00 & 14:00-18:00, Sun 10:00-13:00; tel. 03 89 20 68 92, www.tourisme-colmar.com). The TI can reserve hotel rooms for Colmar and the region. Pick up the city map, get information about concerts and festivals in Colmar and in nearby villages, and ask about Colmar's Folklore Evenings held on summer Tuesdays (described later under "Nightlife in Colmar"). The TI has bike maps, a list of launderettes, and places where you can get online. Pick up the free Route du Vin map and get information on bike rental and bus schedules for touring the wine villages.

ARRIVAL IN COLMAR

By Train and Bus: The old and new (TGV) parts of Colmar's train station are connected by an underground passageway. Day-trippers can check their bags at **Colmar Vélo** to the left as you leave the station (donation requested, see "Helpful Hints," next page).

The old train station was built during Prussian rule using the same plans as the station in Danzig (now Gdańsk, Poland). Check out the charming 1991 window that shows two local maidens about to be run over by a train and rescued by an artist. Opposite, he's shown painting their portraits.

Buses to Route du Vin villages arrive and depart from stops to the left and right as you leave the old station (stop locations can change—ask a driver on any bus), as well as from stops closer to the city center (ask at the TI and see "Alsace's Route du Vin," later).

To reach the town center, **walk** straight out past Hôtel Bristol, turn left on Avenue de la République, and keep walking (15 minutes total). For a faster trip, take any **Trace bus** from the station (to the left as you leave the old station) to the Champ de Mars stop

(Place Rapp) or the Théâtre stop, next to the Unterlinden Museum (€1.30, pay driver, infrequent service on Sun, see map on page 934, tel. 03 89 20 80 80, www.trace-colmar.fr). Allow €10 for a **taxi** to any hotel in central Colmar (taxi stand 50 yards on the left as you leave station).

By Car: Follow signs for *Centre-Ville,* then *Place Rapp.* Parking is available at a huge pay-parking garage under Place Rapp. Hotels can advise you where to park (many get deals at pay lots for their guests—ask). There's metered parking along streets in the city center. Half of the spots at Parking de la Vieille Ville near Hôtel St. Martin are free (follow signs from the ring road; during the evening, spaces open up even if full during the day.) Drivers can also find free street parking on residential streets just outside the city center (off Boulevard St-Pierre near the recommended Le Maréchal and Turenne hotels).

When entering or leaving on the Strasbourg side of town (near the Colmar airport), look for the big Statue of Liberty replica erected on July 4, 2004, to commemorate the 100th anniversary of the death of sculptor Frédéric-Auguste Bartholdi. Two traffic circles closer to Colmar (look for a red devil sculpture in the middle) are the imposing army barracks built by the Germans after annexing the region in 1871.

HELPFUL HINTS

Market Days: Markets take place inside the vintage market hall (*marché couvert;* Tue-Sat 8:00-18:00). The Saturday morning market on Place St. Joseph is where locals go for fresh produce and cheese (over the train tracks, 15 minutes on foot from the center, no tourists). Textiles are on sale Thursdays on Place de la Cathédrale (all day) and Saturdays on Place des Dominicains (afternoons only). A flea market happens every Friday from June to August on Place des Dominicains.

Department/Grocery Store: The big **Monoprix,** with a supermarket, is across from the Unterlinden Museum (Mon-Sat 8:00-20:00, closed Sun). A small **Petit Casino** supermarket stands across from the recommended Hôtel St. Martin (Mon-Sat 8:30-19:00, closed Sun).

Internet Access: Try **Cyber Didim,** near the Unterlinden Museum at 9 Rue du Rempart, above a kebab shop (€3/hour, no Wi-Fi; Mon-Sat 10:00-22:00, Sun 14:00-22:00, tel. 03 89 23 90 45).

Laundry: A launderette at 1 Rue Ruest is near the recommended Maison Martin Jund *chambre d'hôte* and just off the pedestrian street Rue Vauban (usually open daily 7:00-21:00). Another, **Laverie Wash Point,** is not far from Parking de la Vieille Ville (daily 7:00-21:00, 49 Rue de l'Est). For more recommendations, ask your hotelier.

Bike Rental: Colmar Vélo rents bikes at the train station (€12/day, behind bike racks on the left as you leave station, Mon-Fri 8:00-12:00 & 14:00-19:00, Sat-Sun 9:00-19:00, shorter weekend hours off-season, tel. 03 89 41 37 90). I prefer renting a bike along the Route du Vin in Eguisheim or Ribeauvillé (suggestions given later in this chapter). If you plan to do much biking, buy a bike map either at the TI or a *librairie* (bookstore).

Taxis: You can find one at the train station (70 yards to your left as you walk out), or call 03 89 23 10 33, mobile 06 14 47 21 80 (William), or mobile 06 72 94 65 55.

Car Rental: Avis is at the train station (tel. 03 89 23 16 89). The TI has a list of other options.

Poodle Care: To give your poodle a shampoo and a haircut (or just watch the action), drop by **Quatt Pattes** (near Hôtel-Restaurant le Rapp at 8 Rue Berthe Molly).

Guided Tours: There are no scheduled city tours in English, but private English-speaking **guides** are available through the TI if you book in advance (€165/3 hours, tel. 03 89 20 68 95, guide@tourisme-colmar.com). See page 955 for my recommended **minivan tour** of the Route du Vin.

Tours in Colmar

Tourist Train

Colmar has two competing choo-choo trains (green and white) that jostle along the cobbles of the old part of town offering visitors a relaxing, narrated tour under a glass roof (departures daily 9:00-18:30). Both trains leave across from the Unterlinden Museum, offer a scant recorded commentary in English, and cost €6.50, or €1 less with an Unterlinden Museum ticket. The green train's is a little shorter (30 minutes, the white train ranges a little farther (40 minutes). In the summer, **horse-drawn carriages** do a similar route.

Canal Cruise

Little flat-bottomed boats glide silently on a straight stretch of the city's canal, making a simple 30-minute lap back and forth with little or no narration (€6, departures every 10 minutes, daily 10:00-12:00 & 13:30-18:30). With eight others, you'll pack onto the boat, gliding peacefully—powered by a silent electric motor—through a lush garden world under willows. While the route is kind of pathetic, the tranquility is enjoyable. Try to sit in front for an unobstructed view. Boats depart from docks near the bridges on Rue de Turenne and Boulevard St. Pierre, both in Petite Venise.

Colmar Old Town Walk

This self-guided walk—good by day, romantic by night—is a handy way to link the city's three worthwhile sights (see this chapter's Colmar map to help navigate). Supplement my commentary by reading the sidewalk information plaques that describe points of interest in the old town. Allow an hour for this walk at a peaceful pace (more if you enter sights). Colmar is wonderfully floodlit after dark on Fridays and Saturdays and during various festivals, when the lighting is changed to give different intensities and colors—and to welcome visiting VIPs.

• *Start in front of the Customs House (where Rue des Marchands hits Grand Rue). Face the old...*

Customs House (Koïfhus): Colmar is so attractive today because of its trading wealth. And that's what its Customs House is all about. The city was an economic powerhouse in the 15th, 16th, and 17th centuries because of its privileged trading status.

In the Middle Ages, most of Europe was fragmented into chaotic little princedoms and dukedoms. Merchant-dominated cities were natural proponents of the formation of large nation-states (proto-globalization). That's why they banded together to form "trading leagues" (the World Trade Organizations of their day). Rather than being ruled by some duke or prince, they worked directly with the emperor.

The Hanseatic League was the super-league of northern Europe. Prosperous Colmar was the leading member of a smaller league of 10 Alsatian cities, called the Decapolis (founded 1354).

This "Alsatian Big Ten" enjoyed special tax and trade privileges, the right to build fortified walls, and to run their internal affairs. As "Imperial" cities they were ruled directly by the Holy Roman Emperor rather than via one of his lesser princes. This was preferable and, by banding together, they negotiated to protect this special status and won the Holy Roman Emperor's promise not to sell them to some other, likely more aggressive, prince. The 10 mostly Alsatian towns of the Decapolis enjoyed this status until the 17th century.

This street—Rue des Marchands—is literally "Merchants Street" and throughout the town you'll notice how street names bear witness to the historic importance of merchants in Colmar. They controlled the power. In fact, right here, in front of the Customs House, find the carved plaque in the wall at #23. This is a "stone of banishment," declaring that the town's merchants kicked a noble family out of Colmar and that family could never live here again.

Get closer to the Customs House. Delegates of the Decapolis would meet here to sort out trade issues, much like the European

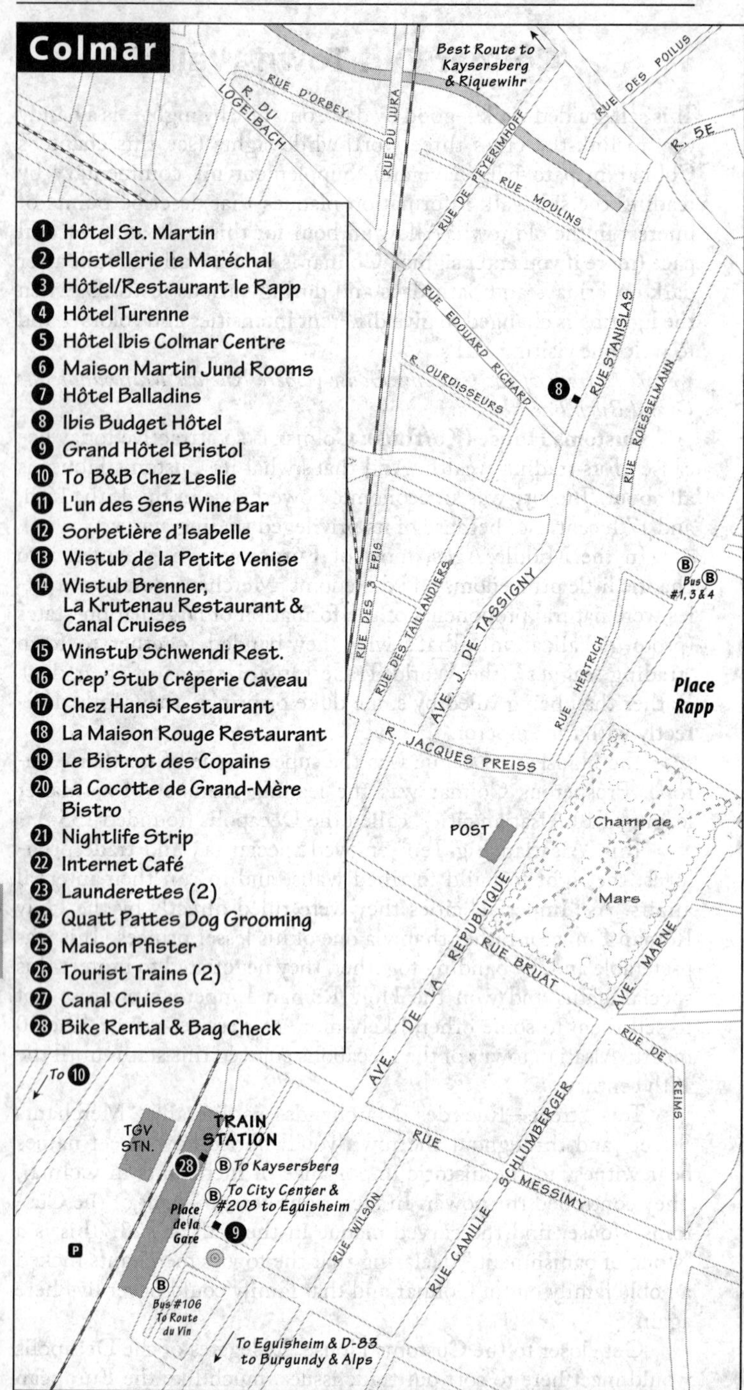
Colmar
1 Hôtel St. Martin
2 Hostellerie le Maréchal
3 Hôtel/Restaurant le Rapp
4 Hôtel Turenne
5 Hôtel Ibis Colmar Centre
6 Maison Martin Jund Rooms
7 Hôtel Balladins
8 Ibis Budget Hôtel
9 Grand Hôtel Bristol
10 To B&B Chez Leslie
11 L'un des Sens Wine Bar
12 Sorbetière d'Isabelle
13 Wistub de la Petite Venise
14 Wistub Brenner, La Krutenau Restaurant & Canal Cruises
15 Winstub Schwendi Rest.
16 Crep' Stub Crêperie Caveau
17 Chez Hansi Restaurant
18 La Maison Rouge Restaurant
19 Le Bistrot des Copains
20 La Cocotte de Grand-Mère Bistro
21 Nightlife Strip
22 Internet Café
23 Launderettes (2)
24 Quatt Pattes Dog Grooming
25 Maison Pfister
26 Tourist Trains (2)
27 Canal Cruises
28 Bike Rental & Bag Check
Best Route to Kaysersberg & Riquewihr
RUE D'ORBEY
R. DU LOGELBACH
RUE DU JURA
RUE DE PEYERIMHOFF
RUE DES POILUS
R. 5E
RUE MOULINS
RUE EDOUARD RICHARD
R. OURDISSEURS
RUE STANISLAS
RUE ROESSELMANN
RUE DES 3 EPIS
RUE DES TAILLANDIERS
AVE. J. DE TASSIGNY
RUE HERTRICH
Bus #1, 3 & 4
Place Rapp
R. JACQUES PREISS
POST
Champ de Mars
AVE. DE LA RÉPUBLIQUE
RUE BRUAT
AVE. MARNE
RUE DE REIMS
To 10
TGV STN.
TRAIN STATION
To Kaysersberg
To City Center & #208 to Eguisheim
Place de la Gare
RUE MESSIMY
RUE SCHLUMBERGER
RUE WILSON
RUE CAMILLE
Bus #106 To Route du Vin
To Eguisheim & D-83 to Burgundy & Alps
P

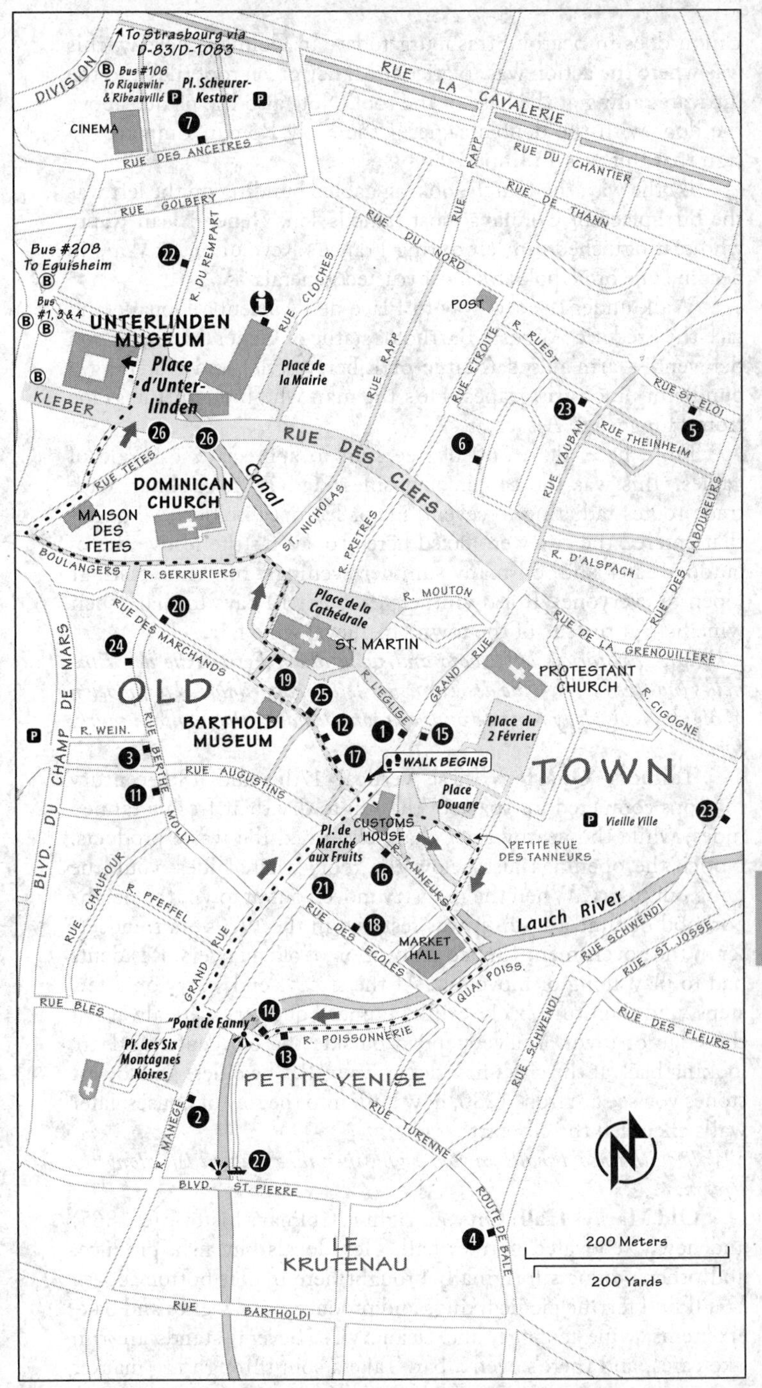
To Strasbourg via D-83/D-1083
DIVISION
Bus #106 To Riquewihr & Ribeauvillé
Pl. Scheurer-Kestner
RUE LA CAVALERIE
CINEMA
RUE DES ANCETRES
RUE DU CHANTIER
RUE DE THANN
RUE GOLBERY
R. DU REMPART
RUE RAPP
RUE DU NORD
Bus #208 To Eguisheim
Bus #1, 3 & 4
UNTERLINDEN MUSEUM
Place d'Unterlinden
RUE CLOCHES
Place de la Mairie
POST
R. RUEST
RUE ETROITE
RUE ST. ELOI
RUE THEINHEIM
RUE VAUBAN
KLEBER
RUE DES CLEFS
Canal
RUE TETES
DOMINICAN CHURCH
MAISON DES TETES
ST. NICHOLAS
R. PRETRES
R. D'ALSPACH
RUE DES LABOUREURS
BOULANGERS
R. SERRURIERS
R. MOUTON
Place de la Cathédrale
ST. MARTIN
RUE DE LA GRENOUILLERE
RUE DES MARCHANDS
OLD
GRAND RUE
PROTESTANT CHURCH
R. L'EGLISE
R. CIGOGNE
BLVD. DU CHAMP DE MARS
R. WEIN.
RUE BERTHE MOLLY
BARTHOLDI MUSEUM
Place du 2 Février
WALK BEGINS
TOWN
RUE AUGUSTINS
Place Douane
CUSTOMS HOUSE
Pl. de Marché aux Fruits
Vieille Ville
PETITE RUE DES TANNEURS
R. TANNEURS
RUE CHAUFOUR
R. PFEFFEL
RUE DES ECOLES
Lauch River
RUE SCHWENDI
RUE ST. JOSSE
MARKET HALL
QUAI POISS.
RUE BLES
"Pont de Fanny"
R. POISSONNERIE
RUE DES FLEURS
Pl. des Six Montagnes Noires
PETITE VENISE
R. MANEGE
RUE TURENNE
BLVD. ST. PIERRE
ROUTE DE BALE
LE KRUTENAU
200 Meters
200 Yards
RUE BARTHOLDI
ALSACE

Union does in nearby Strasbourg today. In Colmar's heyday, this was where the action was. Notice the fancy green roof tiles and the intricate railing at the base of the roof. Note also the plaque above the door with the double eagle of the Holy Roman Emperor—a sign that this was an Imperial city.

By the way, the Dutch-looking gabled building on the left was the birthplace of Colmar's most famous son, General Jean Rapp, who distinguished himself during France's Revolutionary Wars to become one of Napoleon's most trusted generals.

Walk under the archway to Place de l'Ancienne Douane and face the Frédéric-Auguste Bartholdi statue of General Lazarus von Schwendi—arm raised (Statue of Liberty-style) and clutching a bundle of pinot gris grapes. He's the man who brought the grape from Hungary to Alsace.

From here, do a 360-degree spin to appreciate a gaggle of gables. This was the center of business activity in Colmar, with trade routes radiating to several major European cities. All goods that entered the city were taxed here. Today, it's the festive site of outdoor cafés and, on many summer evenings, fun wine tastings (open to everyone). Local vintners each get 10 days to share their wine here at the site of the town's medieval wine fair.

• *Follow the statue's left elbow and walk down Petite Rue des Tanneurs (not the larger "Rue des Tanneurs"). The half-timbered commotion of higgledy-piggledy rooftops on the downhill side of the fountain marks the...*

Tanners' Quarter: These vertical 17th- and 18th-century rooftops competed for space in the sun to dry their freshly tanned hides, while the nearby river channel flushed the waste products. Notice the openings just below the roofs where hides would be hung out to dry. When the industry moved out of town, the neighborhood became a slum. It was restored in the 1970s—a trendsetter in the government-funded renovation of old quarters. Residents had to play along or move out. At the street's end, carry on a few steps, and then turn back. Stinky tanners' quarters were always at the edge of town. You've stepped outside the old center and are looking back at the city's first defensive wall. The oldest and lowest stones you see are from 1230, now built into the row of houses; later walls encircled the city farther out.

• *Walk with the old walls on your right, then take the first left along the stream.*

Old Market Hall: On your right is Colmar's historic (c. 1865) and newly renovated market hall. Here locals buy fish, produce, and other products (originally brought here by flat-bottom boat). You'll find terrific picnic fixings and produce, sandwiches and bakery items, wine tastings, and clean WCs. Several stands are run like cafés, and there's even a bar. Take a spin through the market and see what strikes your fancy (Tue-Sat 8:00-18:00, closed Sun-Mon).

• *Back on the street, cross the canal and turn right on Quai de la Poissonnerie ("Wharf of the Fish Market"), and you'll enter...*

Petite Venise: This neighborhood, a collection of Colmar's most colorful houses lining the small canal, is popular with tourists during the day. But at night it's romantic, with fewer crowds. It lies between the town's first wall (built to defend against arrows) and its later wall (built in the age of gunpowder). Medieval towns needed water. If they weren't on a river, they'd often redirect parts of nearby rivers to power their mills and quench their thirst. Colmar's river was canalized this way for medieval industry—to provide water for the tanners, to allow farmers to barge their goods into town (see the steps leading from docks into the market), and so on.

Walk along the flower-box-lined canal to the end of Rue de la Poissonnerie. At #2, Chez Thierry would love to let you sample their tasty *saucisson*.

Half-Timbered Houses: As you stroll, notice the picturesque houses. The pastel colors are just from this generation—designed to pump up the cuteness of Colmar for tourists. But the houses themselves are historic and real as can be.

Houses of the rich were made of stone, while budget builders made half-timbered structures. The process: Build your frame with pine beams; create a weave of little branches between the beams which you'd fill with mud, straw, and gunk; let it dry; and plaster over it. (This is called "wattle and daub" in England.) Timbers were soaked in vinegar and then treated with ox blood to be waterproof. If you find unrestored timbers (like the house at #8) you can see the faint red tint of ox blood.

When the rich (accustomed to the fine stone buildings of Paris) moved here in the 18th century, they disguised the cheap wattle and daub with a thick layer of plaster. To them, the half-timbers looked cheap...and German. To be French was *à la mode* and that meant no half-timbers. Today, in the 21st century, half-timbered has become charming, so the current owners have peeled away the plaster to reveal the old beams.

Rich or poor, all homes sat on a stone base. There are several explanations: to prevent them from sinking into the marshy ground; to prevent the moist ground from rotting the timbers; and/or to preserve the ground floor in case of a fire—so commonplace back then. You can identify true stone homes by their windowsills:

Wooden sills mean they're half-timbered, stone sills indicate the entire building is built of stone.

As you explore the town, notice how upper floors are cantilevered out. This was a structural support trick and a tax dodge, as real-estate taxes were based on the square footage of the ground floor.

Enjoy the old timbered houses toward the end of Rue de la Poissonnerie. On your right is "Pont de Fanny," a bridge so popular with tourists for its fine views that you see lots of fannies lined up along the railing. Walk to the center of the bridge, and enjoy the scene. To the right you'll see examples of the flat-bottom gondolas used to transport goods on the small river. Today, they give tourists sleepy, scenic, 30-minute canal tours (described earlier).

• *Cross the bridge to find a fountain in the square to your left. Another Bartholdi work, this one was commissioned to honor Jean Roesselmann, a 13th-century town provost who died defending his beloved city when the bishop of Strasbourg tried unsuccessfully to seize it. Take the second right on Grande Rue. Walk for several blocks to the Customs House (green-tiled roof) and land back where you started. With your back to the Customs House, look uphill along Rue des Marchands ("Merchants' Street")—one of the most scenic intersections in town. (The ruler of Malaysia was so charmed by this street that he had it re-created in Kuala Lumpur.)*

Walk up Rue des Marchands, and you'll soon come face-to-face with the...

Maison Pfister (Pfister House): This richly decorated merchant's house dates from 1537. Here the owner displayed his wealth for all to enjoy (and to envy). The external spiral-staircase turret, a fine loggia on the top floor, and the bay windows (called oriels) were pricey add-ons. The painted walls illustrate the city elites' taste for Renaissance humanism.

ALSACE

The cozy wine shop on the ground floor sells fine wines, but they are most proud of their locally made whisky. David enjoys offering tastings, so go ahead—take a hit and see what you think.

Now that you're in a happy mood, stand outside facing the Pfister House for a little review. Find the four main styles of Colmar architecture: the Gothic church (right), local medieval half-timbered structures, Renaissance (that's Mr. Pfister's place), and (behind you) the urbane and elegant shutters and ironwork of Paris from the 19th century.

• *As you stagger on, check out the next building (at #9).*

Meter Man: The man carved into the side of this building was a drapemaker; he's shown holding a bar, Colmar's local measure of about one meter (almost equal to a yard). In the Middle Ages, it was common for cities to have their own units of length; it's one reason that merchants supported the "globalization" efforts of their time to standardize measuring systems.

The building shows off the classic half-timbered design—the beams (upright, cross, angular supports) are grouped in what's called (and looks like) "a man." Typical houses are built with a man in the middle flanked by two "half men." A short block farther up the street on the left is the **Bartholdi Museum** (described later, under "Sights in Colmar"), located in the home where the famous sculptor Frédéric-Auguste Bartholdi lived. Next door (at #28) is Au Croissant Doré, with its charming Art Nouveau facade and interior.

• *A passage opposite (on the right) leads you through the old guards' house to...*

Church of St. Martin: The city's cathedral-like church replaced a smaller Romanesque church that stood here earlier. It was erected in 1235 after Colmar became an Imperial city and needed a bigger place of worship. Colmar's ruler at the time was Burgundian, so the church has a Burgundian-style tiled roof.

The side door (facing the old guard's house) still has the round Romanesque tympanum, starring St. Martin, from the earlier church. Notice how it fits into the pointed Gothic arch. This was the lepers' door—marked by the four totem-like rows of grotesque faces and bodies representing lepers. They could "go to church" but had to stay outside, away from the other people.

Walk left, under expressive gargoyles, to the west portal. Facing the front of the church, notice that the relief over the main door depicts not your typical Last Judgment scene, but the Three Kings who visited Baby Jesus. The Magi, whose remains are nearby in the Rhine city of Cologne, Germany, are popular in this region. The interior is dark, but it holds a few finely carved and beautifully painted altarpieces. The church's beautiful Vosges-stone exterior radiates color in the late afternoon.

• *Walk past the church, go left around Café Jupiler, and wander up the pedestrian-only Rue des Serruriers ("Locksmiths Street") to the...*

Dominican Church: Compare the Church of St. Martin's ornate exterior with this simple Dominican structure. While both churches were built at the same time, they each make different statements. The "High Church" of the 13th century was fancy and corrupt. The Dominican order was all about austerity. It was a time of crisis in the Roman Catholic Church. Monastic orders (as well as heretical movements like the Cathars in southern France) preached a simpler faith and way of life. In the style of St. Dominic and St. Francis, they tried to get Rome back on a Christ-like track. This church houses the exquisite *Virgin in the Rose Bush* by Martin Schongauer (described later) and, until at least late 2015, the popular *Isenheim Altarpiece* while the Unterlinden Museum is undergoing a restoration.

• *Continuing past the Dominican Church, Rue des Serruriers becomes Rue des Boulangers—"Bakers Street." Stop at #16.*

Skyscrapers and Biscuits: The towering six-story house at #16, dating from the 16th century, was one of Colmar's tallest buildings from that age. Notice how it contrasts with the string of buildings to the right, which are lower, French-style structures—likely built after a fire cleared out older, higher buildings.

As this is Bakers Street, check out the one right here at #16. Maison Alsacienne de Biscuiterie sells traditional, home-baked *biscuits* (cookies) including Christmas delights year-round. *Macarons* and *biscuits* are sold by weight.

Turn right on Rue des Têtes (notice the beautiful swan sign over the pharmacie *at the corner). Walk a block to the fancy old house festooned with heads (on the right) and stand in front of the Esprit boutique for the best view.*

Maison des Têtes ("House of Heads"): Colmar's other famous merchant's house, built in 1609 by a big-shot winemaker (see the grapes hanging from the wrought-iron sign and the happy man at the tip-top), is playfully decorated with about 100 faces and masks. On the ground floor, the guy in the window's center has pig's feet.

Look four doors to the right to see a 1947 bakery sign (above the big pretzel), which shows the *boulangerie* basics in Alsace: croissant, *Kugelhopf*, and baguette. Notice the colors of the French flag indicating that this house supported French rule.

Across from the Maison des Têtes, study the early-20th-century store sign trumpeting the tasty wonders of a butcher who once occupied these premises (with the traditional maiden with her goose about to be force-fed, all hanging above or below the beak of a chicken).

• *Angle down Rue de l'Eau ("Water Street") for a shortcut to the TI and the Unterlinden Museum, with its namesake linden trees lining the front yard (popular locally for making the calming "Tilleul" tea). Your walk is over here, at the doorstep of Colmar's top museum.*

Sights in Colmar

▲▲▲Unterlinden Museum

This museum is Colmar's touristic claim to fame. Its extensive yet manageable collection ranges from Roman Colmar to medieval winemaking exhibits, and from traditional wedding dresses to paintings that give vivid insight into the High Middle Ages. The museum is undergoing a thorough restoration—until complete, its highlight, the *Isenheim Altarpiece*, will be displayed in the Dominican Church a block away.

Cost and Hours: €8, includes Dominican Church; May-Oct daily 9:00-18:00; Nov-April Wed-Mon 9:00-12:00 & 14:00-17:00, closed Tue; 1 Rue d'Unterlinden, tel. 03 89 20 15 58, www.musee-unterlinden.com.

➲ **Self-Guided Tour:** As you follow this tour, expect some construction-related changes.

Gothic Statues: The first room features 14th-century Gothic statues from the nearby Church of St. Martin's facade and other area churches. Study the Romanesque detail of the capitals and the faces of the statues. Even though they endured the elements outdoors for more than 500 years, it's still clear that they were sculpted with loving attention to detail. The masons knew their fine stonework would not be seen from below—it was "for God's eyes only." The reddish stone is quarried from the Vosges Mountains, giving these works their unusual coloring. Notice the faint remnants of paint still visible on some statues—then imagine all of these works brightly painted.

Cloister: Step into the soothing cloister (the largest 13th-century cloister in Alsace). This was a Dominican convent founded by (and for) noblewomen in 1230. It functioned until the French Revolution, when the building became a garrison. Rooms with museum exhibits branch off from here.

If it's open, don't miss the wine room (next corner, likely closed during renovation) with its 17th-century oak presses and finely decorated casks. Those huge presses were turned by animals. Wine revenue was used to care for Colmar's poor. The nuns owned many of the best vineyards around, and production was excellent. So was consumption. Notice (on the first cask on left) the Bacchus with the big tummy straddling a keg. The quote from 1781 reads: "My belly's full of juice. It makes me strong. But drink too much and you lose dignity and health."

On the first floor up, the rooms displaying local and folk history are worth a look. You'll see iron signs, massive church bells, and chests with intricate locking systems. There are also ornate armoires, medieval armor, muskets, and antique jewelry boxes.

Painting Gallery: As you enjoy the art, remember that Alsace was historically German and part of the upper Rhine River Valley. (This museum boasts a few paintings by Lucas Cranach. The Three

Kings (of Bethlehem fame) are prominently featured throughout this region, because their heads ended up as relics in Cologne's cathedral (nearby, on the Rhine). You'll also see several worthwhile works by Martin Schongauer (who painted the *Virgin in the Rose Bush* displayed in the Dominican Church).

Throughout the museum you'll see small photos of engravings, illustrating how painters were influenced by other artists' engravings. Most German painters of the time were also engravers (that's how they made money—making lots of copies to sell).

In the last room on the first floor, find a small alcove with 15th-century stained glass. Note the fine details painted into the glass, originally intended for God's eyes only—they were far too tiny for worshippers to see from the floor below. The glass is essentially a jigsaw puzzle connected by lead. Around here, glass this old is rare—most of it was destroyed by rampaging Protestants in the Reformation wars.

The modern-art section (with its small but pleasing collection including a few works by Monet, Renoir, Picasso, Leger, Bonnard, and a wall of Dubuffet) will be closed during much of 2015.

▲▲▲Dominican Church (Eglise des Dominicains)

This beautiful Gothic church is simple—in keeping with the austerity integral to the Dominican style of Christianity. It's plain on the outside and stripped-down on the inside. Instead of gazing at art, worshippers would just listen to the word of God being preached from the pulpit.

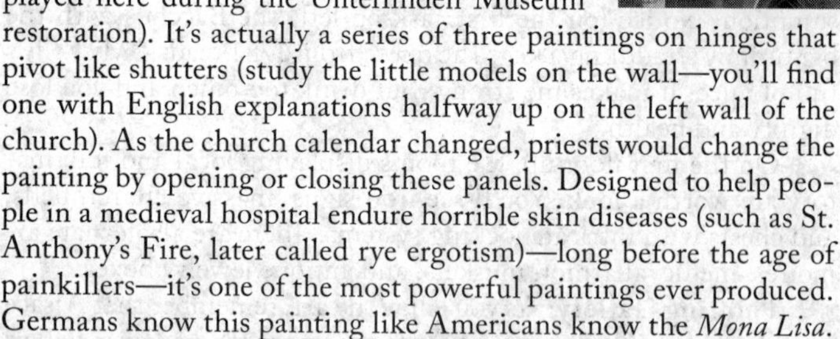

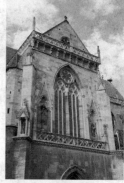

Cost and Hours: €8, includes audioguide and Unterlinden Museum until its renovation is complete; May-Oct daily 9:00-18:00; Nov-April Wed-Mon 9:00-12:00 & 14:00-17:00, closed Tue.

Visiting the Church: For now, the highlight is Matthias Grünewald's gripping *Isenheim Altarpiece* (c. 1515, temporarily displayed here during the Unterlinden Museum restoration). It's actually a series of three paintings on hinges that pivot like shutters (study the little models on the wall—you'll find one with English explanations halfway up on the left wall of the church). As the church calendar changed, priests would change the painting by opening or closing these panels. Designed to help people in a medieval hospital endure horrible skin diseases (such as St. Anthony's Fire, later called rye ergotism)—long before the age of painkillers—it's one of the most powerful paintings ever produced. Germans know this painting like Americans know the *Mona Lisa*.

Stand in front of the altarpiece as if you were a medieval peas-

ant, and feel the agony and suffering of the Crucifixion. It's an intimate drama. The point—Jesus' suffering—is drilled home: The weight of his body bends the crossbar (unrealistically, creating an almost crossbow effect). His elbows are pulled from their sockets by the weight of his dead body. People who are crucified die of asphyxiation, as Jesus' chest illustrates. His mangled feet are swollen with blood. The intended viewers—the hospital's patients—may have felt that Jesus understood their suffering, because he looks like he had a skin disease (though the marks on his skin represent lash marks from whipping). Study the faces and the Christian symbolism. The grief on Mary's face is agonizing. She is wrapped in the white shroud that will cover Jesus' body in the tomb. The sorrowful composition on the left is powerful. On the far left stands St. Sebastian (called upon by those with the plague) and on the right is St. Anthony (called upon by those with ergot poisoning from rotten rye).

The predella (the horizontal painting below) shows a hyper-realistic Entombment of Jesus. Jesus' fingernails are black—as is the case with any corpse, and Mary Magdalene's face is red with anguish.

Walk around to the other side of this panel. The Resurrection scene is unique in art history. (Grünewald was a mysterious artistic genius who had no master and no students.) Jesus rockets out of the tomb as man is transformed into God. As if proclaiming once again, "I am the Light," he is radiant. His shroud is the color of light: Roy G. Biv. Around the rainbow is the "resurrection of the flesh." Jesus' perfect pink flesh would appeal to the patients who meditated on the scene.

The right half of this panel depicts the Annunciation—the angel (accompanied by a translucent dove representing the Holy Spirit) telling Mary she'll give birth to the Messiah. The normally sanguine Mary looks unsettled, as if she's been hit by some unexpected news. She's shown reading the Bible passage that tells of this event.

In the nativity scene on the next panel—set in the Rhineland—the much-adored Mary is tender and loving, true to the Dominican belief that she was the intercessor for all in heaven. The happy ending is a psychedelic explosion of Resurrection joy. The scene on the left is the Concert of Angels. Looking at the last panel, zoom in on the agonizing Temptation of St. Anthony. The other panel shows Anthony's visit to St. Paul, the hermit. The final scene (behind you), carved in wood by Nikolaus Hagenauer, is St. Anthony on his throne.

Patients who meditated on this painting were reminded that they didn't have it so bad. They were also reminded to stay the course (religiously) and to not stray from the path of salvation.

Besides the altarpiece, the church contains another medieval masterpiece. Martin Schongauer's angelically beautiful ***Virgin in the Rosebush*** (1473), looks as if it were painted yesterday. Here, graceful Mary is shown as a welcoming mother. Jesus clings to her, reminding the viewer of the warmth of his relationship with Mary. The Latin on her halo reads, "Pick me also for your child, O very Holy Virgin." Rather than telling a particular Bible story, this is a general scene, designed to meet the personal devotional needs of any worshipper.

Nature is not a backdrop; Mary and Jesus are encircled by it. Schongauer's robins, sparrows, and goldfinches bring extra life to an already impressively natural rosebush. The white rose (over Mary's right shoulder) anticipates Jesus' crucifixion. The frame, with its angelic orchestra, dates only from 1900 and feels to me a bit over-the-top.

The painting was located in the Church of St. Martin until 1972, when it was stolen. After being recovered, it was moved to the better-protected Dominican Church. Detailed English explanations are in the nave to the right of the painting as you face it. The contrast provided by the simple Dominican setting heightens the elegance of this Gothic masterpiece.

As for the rest of the church, the columns are thin to allow worshippers to see the speaker, even if the place is packed. The windows are precious 14th-century originals depicting black-clad Dominican monks busy preaching. Notice how windows face the sun on the south side while the north side is walled against the cloister. If you look at the columns in the rear of the nave, you can see how 14th-century Colmar's street level was about two feet below today's.

▲Bartholdi Museum

This little museum recalls the life and work of the local boy who gained fame by sculpting America's much-loved Statue of Liberty. Frédéric-Auguste Bartholdi (1834-1904) was a dynamic painter/photographer/sculptor with a passion for the defense of liberty and freedom. Although Colmar was his home, he spent most of his career in Paris, refusing to move back here while Alsace was German.

Bartholdi devoted years of his life to realizing the vision of a statue of liberty for America that would stand in New York City's harbor. While Lady Liberty is his most famous work, you'll see several Bartholdi statues gracing Colmar's squares.

Cost and Hours: €5, free on July 4, open March-Dec Wed-Mon 10:00-12:00 & 14:00-18:00, closed Tue and Jan-Feb, in heart of old town at 30 Rue des Marchands, tel. 03 89 41 90 60, www.musee-bartholdi.com. Curiously, even though entry is free on the Fourth of July, there is no English posted in this museum.

➲ **Self-Guided Tour:** The **courtyard** is dominated by a bronze statue, *Les Grands Soutiens du Monde.* It was cast in 1902—two years before Bartholdi died—and shares his personal philosophy. The world is supported by three figures representing patriotism, hard work, and justice. Mr. Hard Work holds a book, symbolizing intellectual endeavors, and a hammer, a sign for physical labor. Ms. Justice has her scales. And Mr. Patriotism holds a flag and a sword—sheathed but ready to be used. All have one foot stepping forward: ahead for progress, the spirit of Industrial Age.

On the **ground floor,** the room to the right of the ticket desk houses temporary exhibits. To the left are exhibits covering Bartholdi's works commissioned in Alsatian cities, commonly dedicated to military heroes.

Climbing the stairs to the middle floor, you pass a portrait of the artist. Rooms re-create Bartholdi's high-society flat in Paris. At the end of the hallway on the left, the dining room is lined with portraits of his aristocratic family.

In the next room hangs a beautiful portrait of the sculptor (by Jean Benner), facing his mother (on a red chair). Bartholdi was very close to his mom, writing her daily letters when he was working in New York. Many see his mother's face in the Statue of Liberty. Scenes on the ceilings represent aspects of Bartholdi's Freemason philosophy.

In the hallway leading right, a room dedicated to Bartholdi's most famous French work, the *Lion of Belfort,* celebrates the Alsatian town that fought so fiercely in 1871 that it was never annexed into Germany. Photos show the red sandstone lion sitting regally below the mighty Vauban fortress of Belfort—a symbol of French spirit standing strong against Germany. Small models give a sense of its gargantuan scale. (If you're linking Burgundy with Alsace by car, you'll pass the city of Belfort and see signs directing you to the *Lion.*)

The rest of the floor shows off Bartholdi's French work. Small wax models let you trace his creative process. A glass case is filled with the tools of his trade. Notice how his patriotic pieces tend to have one arm raised—*Vive la France*...God bless America...Freedom!

The top floor is dedicated to Bartholdi's American works—

the paintings, photos, and statues that Bartholdi made during his many travels to the States. You'll see statues of Columbus pointing as if he knew where he was going, and Lafayette (who was only 19 years old when he came to America's aid) with George Washington.

Two rooms are dedicated to the evolution and completion of Bartholdi's dream of a Statue of Liberty. Fascinating photos show the Eiffel-designed core, the frame being covered with plaster, and then the hand-hammered copper plating, which was ultimately riveted to the frame. The statue was assembled in Paris, then dismantled and shipped to New York, in 1886...10 years late. The big ear in the exhibit is half-size.

Though the statue was a gift from France, the US had to come up with the cash to build a pedestal. This was a tough sell, but Bartholdi was determined to see his statue erected. On 10 trips to the US, he worked to raise funds and lobbied for construction, bringing with him this painting and a full-size model of the torch—which the statue would ultimately hold. (Lucky for Bartholdi and his cause, his cousin was the French ambassador to the US.)

Eventually, the project came together—the pedestal was built, and the Statue of Liberty has welcomed waves of immigrants into New York ever since. Thank you, Frédéric-Auguste Bartholdi.

Nightlife in Colmar

No one would come to Colmar solely for its nightlife. But if you're out after dinner, it does have its charm. Like many French cities, Colmar puts lots of creative energy into its floodlit cityscapes.

Every July and August, five local vintners take 10 days each to show off local wines at a small **wine festival.** It's held under the historic arches of the Customs House (daily 12:00-24:00). It's self-service, there's no food, and glasses are cheap (€1-3). And if you're here on a Tuesday in summer, there's likely Alsatian folk dancing at the town's **Folklore Evening** (Soirée Folklorique, starts at 20:30) to give your wine tasting a little color.

Rue du Conseil Souverain (stretching from the Customs House to the "Pont de Fanny") has a fun line of watering holes—three bars and a cocktail lounge—where you can enjoy mellow outdoor seating with the locals on balmy evenings or characteristic interiors of your choice when it's cold.

Les Incorruptibles has an inviting pubby interior—with just a little Alsatian edginess—and great beers on tap including Chimay, the milkshake of gourmet Belgian monk-made beers (1 Rue des Ecoles).

J. J. Murphy's Irish Pub invites you to share a picnic table on the street or take a trip to Ireland at the bar, where you can enjoy a classic pub vibe and Murphy's Irish Stout on tap (48 Grand Rue).

Sport's Café is a big screen, Red-Bull-and-foosball place. This is *the* place to be if there's a big sporting event on TV and you want to share it with a gang of French enthusiasts. They have Pelforth Blonde, the best French lager, on tap (3 Rue du Conseil Souverain).

Café à l'Ancienne Douane is more of a wine bar with a cleaner, more mature ambience (7 Rue du Conseil Souverain).

Sleeping in Colmar

Hotels are a reasonable value in Colmar. They're busiest on weekends in May, June, September, and October, and every day in July and August. If you have trouble finding a bed, ask the TI for help or look in a nearby village, where small hotels and bed-and-breakfasts are plentiful (see my recommendations in nearby Eguisheim, later).

IN THE CENTER

$$$ Hôtel St. Martin*,** ideally situated near the old Customs House, is a family-run place that began as a coaching inn (since 1361). It has 40 mostly traditional, fairly priced, well-equipped rooms with air-conditioning and big beds. The rooms are woven into its antique frame and joined together by a peaceful courtyard. The 12 units in the back have charming chalet-style decor, but they don't have elevator access (Sb-€95, standard Db-€105, bigger Db-€130, suite Db-€170, Tb/Qb-€150-175, good breakfast-€12, air-con, guest computer, Wi-Fi, free public parking nearby at Parking de la Vieille Ville, 38 Grand Rue, tel. 03 89 24 11 51, www.hotel-saint-martin.com, colmar@hotel-saint-martin.com).

$$$ At **Hostellerie le Maréchal****,** in the heart of La Petite Venise, Colmar's most characteristic digs are surprisingly affordable. Though the rooms are on the small side (three-star quality and prices), the setting is romantic, the decor is cozy, and the service professional (Sb-€95, Db-€115-155, Db with whirlpool tub-€190-225, breakfast-€17, Wi-Fi, garage parking-€15/day, 4 Place des Six Montagnes Noires, tel. 03 89 41 60 32, www.le-marechal.com, info@le-marechal.com). The hotel is more famous for the quality of its well-respected restaurant; many French clients travel to dine here (€34-78 *menus,* reserve ahead).

$$$ Hôtel le Rapp*,** conveniently located off Place Rapp and near a big park, holds rooms for many budgets, a full-service bar, a café, and a good restaurant. The cheapest rooms are tight but smartly configured; the bigger rooms are tastefully designed, usually with queen-size beds. There's also a small basement pool, a sauna, and a Turkish bath. It's well-run and family-friendly (Sb-€79-93, standard Db-€110, bigger Db-€132, junior suite for 2-4

Sleep Code

Abbreviations **(€1 = about $1.40, country code: 33)**
S = Single, **D** = Double/Twin, **T** = Triple, **Q** = Quad, **b** = bathroom, **s** = shower only, * = French hotel rating (0-5 stars)
Price Rankings
$$$ Higher Priced—Most rooms €100 or more
$$ Moderately Priced—Most rooms between €65-100
$ Lower Priced—Most rooms €65 or less
Unless otherwise noted, credit cards are accepted, English is spoken, and Wi-Fi is generally free. Prices change; verify current rates online or by email. For the best prices, always book directly with the hotel.

people-€165, good buffet breakfast-€13, air-con, elevator, guest computer, Wi-Fi, 1 Rue Weinemer, tel. 03 89 41 62 10, www.rapp-hotel.com, rapp-hotel@calixo.net).

$$ Hôtel Turenne*** is a sharp, if less central hotel (a 10-minute walk from the city center) with a *winstub* ambience in its reception area and a welcoming vibe. Rooms vary in size, though all are air-conditioned and well-appointed (standard Db-€80-95, bigger Db-€105-125, Tb-€90-130, Qb-€120-165, breakfast-€9.50, park for free on the street or book ahead to park in their lot-€7/day, elevator for most rooms, guest computer, Wi-Fi, 10 Route de Bâle, tel. 03 89 21 58 58, www.turenne.com, infos@turenne.com).

$$ Hôtel Ibis Colmar Centre***, on the ring road, rents tight rooms with small bathrooms at acceptable rates (Db-€84, bigger Db-€91, breakfast-€9.50, check website for deals, air-con, guest computer, Wi-Fi, 10 Rue St. Eloi, tel. 03 89 41 30 14, www.ibishotel.com, h1377@accor.com).

ALSACE

$ Maison Martin Jund holds my favorite budget beds in Colmar. This ramshackle yet historic half-timbered house—the home of likeable winemakers André and Myriam—feels like a medieval tree house soaked in wine and filled with flowers. The rooms are modest but spacious and comfortable enough. Some have air-conditioning and many are equipped with kitchenettes (Db/Tb-€42-72; big family apartments-€105, breakfast-€7, fun tasting room, guest computer, Wi-Fi, 12 Rue de l'Ange, tel. 03 89 41 58 72, www.martinjund.com, martinjund@hotmail.com). Leave your car at Parking de la Vieille Ville. Train travelers can take any Trace bus from the station to the Unterlinden Museum and walk from there. There is no real reception—though good-natured Myriam seems to be around, somewhere, most of the time (call if you'll arrive after 20:00).

$ Hôtel Balladins**, near the Unterlinden Museum, is a modern, efficient, clean, and cheap place to sleep. They'll hold a room for you until 18:00 if you call ahead. Rooms facing the big square *(grand place)* are quieter (Db-€59, Tb-€69, Qb-€79, breakfast-€8, Wi-Fi, elevator, free parking in big square in front, 5 Rue des Ancêtres, tel. 03 89 24 22 24, www.balladins.com, colmar.centre@balladins.com).

$ Ibis Budget Hôtel offers bright, efficient, all-the–same rooms with three beds—one bed is a bunk—and ship-cabin bathrooms (Db-€44-56, extra person-€9, breakfast-€6, Wi-Fi, secure parking-€7/day or park for free on Place Scheurer-Kestner, 10-minute walk from city center at 15 Rue Stanislas, tel. 08 92 68 09 31, www.ibisbudget.com, h5079@accor.com).

NEAR THE TRAIN STATION

$$$ Grand Hôtel Bristol**** has little personality but works if you want overpriced, four-star comfort at the train station (standard Db-€138-168, big Db-€185-215, breakfast-€17, air-con, Wi-Fi, 7 Place de la Gare, tel. 03 89 23 59 59, www.grand-hotel-bristol.com, reservation@grand-hotel-bristol.com).

$$ Bed-and-Breakfast Chez Leslie is run by engaging Leslie and her Franco-American family (husband Philippe). Located in a neighborhood where "real people live," it's a five-minute walk from the station and a 20-minute walk from the center. The rooms are bright, big, and artfully decorated—plus the backyard is a calming garden. Street parking is free, families will enjoy the big adjacent park, and Leslie has loaner *boules* for anyone wanting to try a little *pétanque* (Sb-€67, Db-€87, family room-€87-120, includes breakfast, 31 Rue de Mulhouse, tel. 03 89 79 98 99, mobile 06 82 58 91 98, www.chezleslie.com, info@chezleslie.com). From the train platform, exit down the stairs into the underground passageway toward Rue du Tir. At the end of the stairs, go left, and then turn right at Rue de Soultz. Continue to the square and turn left on Rue de Mulhouse; find the blue house at #31.

Eating in Colmar

Colmar is full of good restaurants offering traditional Alsatian *menus* for €20-30. (To dine in a smaller town nearby, see "Eating in Eguisheim," later.)

Before Dinner: **L'un des Sens** is a cool little wine bar, good for a glass of wine and an appetizer (long list of wines from many countries) and a short list of foods (meat plates, fancy foie gras, cheese plates, Tue-Thu 15:00-22:00, Fri-Sat 10:00-23:00, closed Sun-Mon, ask about blind tastings, 18 Rue Berthe Molly, tel. 03 89 24 04 37).

After Dinner: **Sorbetière d'Isabelle** sells Colmar's best sorbet to eat in or to go. Ask about her syrup toppings (Mon 14:00-18:30,

Tue-Sun 11:00-18:30, until 22:30 July-Aug, near Maison Pfister at 13 Rue des Marchands, tel. 03 89 41 67 17). If you want lively café and bar action, find **Rue du Conseil Souverain** (described earlier).

IN PETITE VENISE

To dine in Colmar's coziest neighborhood, head into Petite Venise and make your way to the photo-perfect "Pont de Fanny" on Rue Turenne, where you'll find several picturesque places within a couple blocks.

Wistub de la Petite Venise bucks the touristy trend in this area with caring owners Virginie and Julien. It combines a wood-warm, chalet ambience (no outside seating) with the energy of an open kitchen. The service is personal, and the menu is limited in selection—heavy on the meats—but generous in quality. Chef Julien is proud of his *jambonneau,* though his *choucroute* and foie gras are tasty, too (closed at lunch Thu and Sun, closed all day Wed, €14-20 *plats,* 4 Rue de la Poissonnerie, tel. 03 89 41 72 59).

Wistub Brenner is perhaps your best mix of economy, quality cooking, accessible selections, and characteristic ambience. The outside seating is better than inside, but either way you'll enjoy attentive service and seasonal specialties. Their formula is freedom: You can choose any first course to go along with any main course on their €24 *menu* deal (1 Rue Turenne, tel. 03 89 41 42 33).

La Krutenau's picnic tables sprawl along the canal, offering basic *tartes flambées* (just two types: natural-€7.50, garnished-€8.50), plus cheap beer and wine. This is the spot for a low-cost meal with a canalside setting (inside or out, best after dark). Also, consider dropping in for just a dessert or a drink on a warm evening (closed Jan-Feb, 1 Rue de la Poissonnerie, tel. 03 89 41 18 80).

IN THE OLD CITY CENTER

Winstub Schwendi has fun, German pub energy inside with seven beers on tap, lively conversation, and hustling waiters. The big terrace outside is more sedate, but ideal for a warm evening. Choose from a dozen filling, robust Swiss *Rösti* plates (€13 to €17—big enough to split) or *tartes flambées* (€9); I like the *strasbourgeoise flambée* (also good salad and main dish options, daily 12:00-22:30, facing the Customs House at 3 Grand Rue, tel. 03 89 23 66 26). If the Winstub is full, you'll find several similar places with good outdoor seating around Place de l'Ancienne Douane.

Crep' Stub Crêperie Caveau is a good place for crêpes in the old center. Sébastien serves with smiles while Dominique cooks with vigor; there's great outside seating on Place de l'Ancienne Douane or inside in a cute little back room (€10 dinner crêpes, closed Mon, 10 Rue des Tanneurs, tel. 03 89 24 51 88).

Chez Hansi, a half-block up from the Customs House, is where Colmarians go for a traditional meal (served by women in Alsatian dresses). This place feels real, even though it's in the thick of the touristic center. Attentive Annie manages your dining experience; ask her what's good today or try local specialties such as *poulet* or *saumon au Riesling* (chicken or salmon in Riesling sauce) with *Spätzle* (soft egg noodles), or medieval "pub grub" like *choucroute garnie* (€22-42 *menus,* indoor seating only, closed Wed-Thu, 23 Rue des Marchands, tel. 03 89 41 37 84).

La Maison Rouge, with a folk-museum interior and sidewalk seating, has tasty, reasonably priced, beautifully presented Alsatian cuisine and an understandably loyal following. You'll be greeted by manager Cecile and *jambon à l'os*—ham cooking on the bone—but they take their vegetarian plate seriously (€26-43 *menus,* try the veal cordon bleu with Munster or the *tarte flambée au chèvre-basilic,* closed Sun-Mon, 9 Rue des Ecoles, tel. 03 89 23 53 22, http://maison-rouge.net).

Hôtel-Restaurant le Rapp is a traditional place to savor a slow, elegant meal served with grace and fine Alsatian wine. While busy with locals during the day, it may be quiet at dinner. If you want to order high on the menu, this is the perfect place to do it (great *Baeckeoffe* or *choucroute* for €19 that makes a whole meal, three-course *menus* from €30, add €10 for a glass of wine to match each course, good vegetarian options, closed Mon-Tue, air-con, 1 Rue Berthe Molly, tel. 03 89 41 62 10, www.rapp-hotel.com).

Le Bistrot des Copains is a casual, young *bistrot/*café with views of the Church of St. Martin and your choice of indoor or plain outdoor seating. There are lots of traditional French—not just Alsatian—selections (€14-23 main dishes, €18-33 *menus,* daily, 18 Place de Cathédrale, tel. 03 89 29 06 44).

La Cocotte de Grand-Mère offers a break from Alsatian food and decor, with traditional French cuisine fresh from the market. Their €15 "surprise" lunch *menu* is unveiled online every morning. This spot gets busy with locals, so reservations are recommended (€18-23 evening *plats,* closed Sat-Sun, 14 Place de l'Ecole, tel. 03 89 23 32 49, www.lacocottedegrandmere.com).

Colmar Connections

From Colmar by Train to: Strasbourg (about 2/hour, 35 minutes), **Reims** (TGV: 10/day, 3 hours, most change in Strasbourg), **Verdun** (7/day, 4-5.5 hours, 2-3 changes, many with 30-minute bus ride from Gare de Meuse), **Beaune** (10/day, 2.5-4 hours, fastest by TGV via Mulhouse, reserve well ahead, possible changes in Mulhouse or Belfort and Dijon), **Paris**' Gare de l'Est (almost hourly, 3 direct, others change in Strasbourg, 3.5 hours), **Amboise** (13/

day, 5-6 hours, most with transfer in Strasbourg and Paris), **Basel,** Switzerland (hourly, 45 minutes), **Karlsruhe,** Germany (TGV: 7/day, 1.5-2.5 hours, best with change in Strasbourg; non-TGV: hourly, 2-3.5 hours, change in Strasbourg and Appenweier or Offenburg; from Karlsruhe, it's 1.5 hours to Frankfurt, 3 hours to Munich).

Alsace's Route du Vin

Alsace's Route du Vin (Wine Road) is an asphalt ribbon that ties 90 miles of vineyards, villages, and medieval fortress ruins into an understandably popular tourist package. With France's driest climate, this stretch of vine-covered land has made for good wine and happy tourists since Roman days.

This is France's smallest wine region. It's long (75 miles) and skinny (just over a mile wide on average) with vineyards strategically planted to be above the floodline of the marshy plains yet below the frostline of the higher ground. Everyone scrambles for the finest land. The region's 50 *grand cru* vineyards (the highest quality) get the privilege of putting up their names on big signs along the hillsides.

Peppering the landscape are Route du Vin villages, full of quaint half-timbered architecture corralled within medieval walls (for a refresher course, see page 937). The towns with evocative castle ruins are often strategically located at the end of valleys. Their names can reveal their histories—towns ending with "heim" and "wihr" were born as farmsteads (Eguisheim was Egui's farm, Riquewihr was Rick's farm).

Colmar and Eguisheim are well-located for exploring the 30,000 acres of vineyards blanketing the hills from Marlenheim to Thann. As you tour the Route du Vin, you'll see storks' nests on church spires and city halls, thanks to a campaign to reintroduce the birds to this area. (Those nests can weigh over 1,000 pounds, posing a danger if they fall and forcing villagers to shore them up.) Look also for crucifixion monuments scattered about the vineyards—intended to get a little divine intervention for a good harvest.

PLANNING YOUR TIME

If you have only a day, focus on towns within easy striking range of Colmar. World War II hit many Route du Vin villages hard. While some of the towns are amazingly preserved from centuries past, several were entirely rebuilt after the war. It all depended on where the war went in 1944. Villages that emerged from World War II unscathed include Eguisheim, Kaysersberg, Hunawihr, Turckheim, Ribeauvillé, and the *très* popular Riquewihr.

After seeing two or three towns, they start looking the same. Two villages works well for most. If driving, distances are short and you can lace together what you like. If taking a minibus tour, you can see a representative sampling in a half-day or cover the highlights of the entire region in a full day. Those without wheels need to be more selective and deal with the meager-but-workable bus schedules.

Towns are most alive during their weekly morning (until noon) farmers' markets (Mon—Kaysersberg; Tue—Munster; Fri—Turckheim; Sat—Ribeauvillé and Colmar). Riquewihr and Eguisheim have no market days.

GETTING AROUND THE ROUTE DU VIN

By Car: Drivers can pick up a detailed map of the Route du Vin at any area TI. To reach the Route du Vin north of Colmar, leave Colmar following signs to Ingersheim. From here roads fan out northeast to Kaysersberg; north through Sigolsheim to Riquewihr, Hunawihr, Ribeauvillé, and Château du Haut-Kœnigsbourg; or south to Eguisheim. Look for *Route du Vin* signs. For the quickest way to Eguisheim from Colmar, head for the train station and take D-30 and then D-83 south toward Belfort.

Drivers can use some of the scenic wine service lanes known as *sentiers viticoles*—provided they drive at a snail's pace. I've recommended my favorite segments.

By Train: The only Route du Vin village accessible by train from Colmar is pleasant little Turckheim (hourly, 20 minutes, described later).

By Bus: Several bus companies connect Colmar with villages along the Route du Vin (no Sun service), but deciphering schedules and locating bus stops in Colmar is a challenge. I have done this for you (below), but things can change; confirm bus schedules and stop locations by asking at any TI. When reading schedules, note that *année* means the bus runs all year on days listed, *vac* (for *vacances*) means it runs only during summer vacation, and *scol* (for *scolaire*) means buses run only on school days. Trace buses serve the city of Colmar only.

Buses to Route du Vin villages stop in Colmar's city center and at the train station. Here is a rundown of service to key Route du Vin villages from Colmar (see map on page 954 to locate these stops).

Kaysersberg has reasonable service (Kunegel bus #145, direction: Le Bonhomme, 7/day, 30 minutes). The Théâtre stop near Unterlinden Museum is best for most travelers; bus #145 is not signed but uses the same stop as Trace bus #25—it's on the side closest to

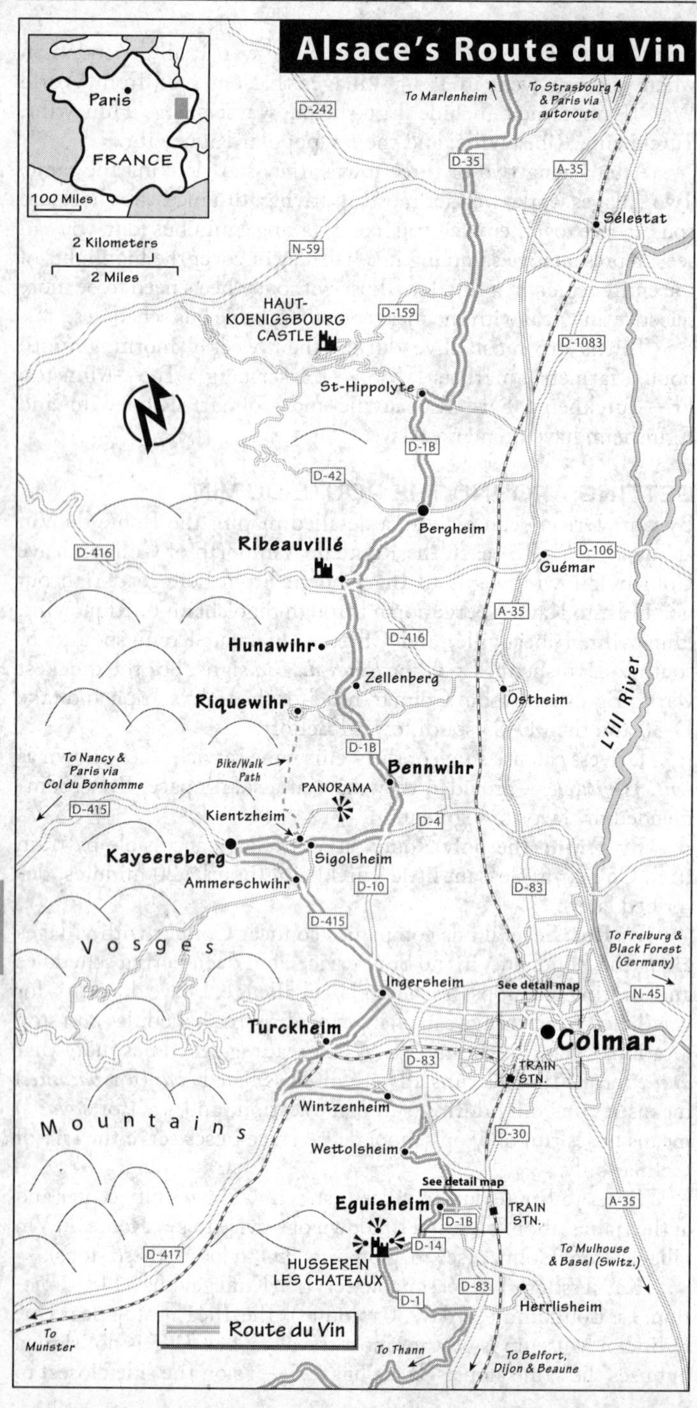
Alsace's Route du Vin
Paris
FRANCE
100 Miles
2 Kilometers
2 Miles
To Marlenheim
To Strasbourg & Paris via autoroute
D-242
D-35
A-35
Sélestat
N-59
HAUT-KOENIGSBOURG CASTLE
D-159
D-1083
St-Hippolyte
D-1B
D-42
Bergheim
Ribeauvillé
D-416
D-106
Guémar
A-35
Hunawihr
D-416
Zellenberg
Ostheim
Riquewihr
L'Ill River
D-1B
To Nancy & Paris via Col du Bonhomme
Bike/Walk Path
Bennwihr
PANORAMA
D-415
Kientzheim
D-4
Kaysersberg
Sigolsheim
Ammerschwihr
D-10
D-83
D-415
Vosges
To Freiburg & Black Forest (Germany)
Ingersheim
See detail map
N-45
Turckheim
Colmar
D-83
TRAIN STN.
Wintzenheim
Mountains
D-30
Wettolsheim
See detail map
Eguisheim
TRAIN STN.
D-1B
A-35
D-417
D-14
HUSSEREN LES CHATEAUX
To Mulhouse & Basel (Switz.)
D-83
D-1
Herrlisheim
To Munster
Route du Vin
To Thann
To Belfort, Dijon & Beaune

ALSACE

the theater. At the train station, find the last stop to the left as you leave the station (signed as *145*).

Riquewihr, Hunawihr, and **Ribeauvillé** have decent service (bus #106, direction: Illhaeusern, 6/day in summer, otherwise 10/day, 30-45 minutes, big midday service gaps in summer). You can also get to Ribeauvillé on Kunegel bus #109 (direction: St-Hippolyte). Buses #106 and #109 leave from the train station (on the right as you exit), but the stop is unsigned—it's best to ask a driver. There's also a signed stop near Place Scheurer-Kestner; it's behind the cinemas on Rue de la 5ème Division.

Eguisheim has minimal service—look for bus #208 (direction: Herrlisheim, 4/day, 15 minutes, leaves from train station or Théâtre stop on side closest to the theater, uses same stop as Trace bus #26 at both locations). Consider biking (described later), or take the bus there and a taxi back.

Château du Haut-Kœnigsbourg has a shuttle bus from the Sélestat train station (explained on page 960).

By Taxi: Allow €15 from Colmar to Eguisheim (€25 round-trip) and €35 from Colmar or Eguisheim to Kaysersberg or Riquewihr. For a group of four with limited time, this is a smart option. For recommendations, see "Taxis" on page 932.

By Minivan Tour: Regioscope delivers a good value in a comfortable vehicle with capable guides. Departures are offered from Colmar with Chloé as your driver-guide and from Strasbourg with Benoit at the helm. Colmar tours are available Tuesday, Thursday, Friday, and Sunday; in the mornings they go to Ribeauvillé and Kaysersberg; in the afternoons, they head to Haut-Kœnigsbourg and Riquewihr, which includes a wine tasting (€50 morning tour, 9:15-12:15; €60 afternoon tour, 13:45-18:30; €105 full-day tour, 9:15-18:30). Excursions from Strasbourg depart every day but Monday. The morning tour includes a wine tasting and Obernai visit; the afternoon tour visits Haut-Kœnigsbourg and Riquewihr, and also includes a wine tasting (€50 morning tour, 9:15-12:30; €70 afternoon tour, 13:45-18:45; €115 full-day tour, 9:15-18:30, entry fees not included, mobile 06 88 21 27 15, www.regioscope.com, info@regioscope.com).

By Bike: With over 2,500 miles of bike-friendly lanes, Alsace is among France's best biking regions. The Route du Vin has an abundance of well-marked trails and *sentier viticole* service roads that run up and down the slopes, offering memorable views and the fewest cars but tough pedaling. Start by getting advice and a good map from a TI or bike shop. Bikers can rent in Colmar, Kaysersberg, Eguisheim, or Ribeauvillé (I've listed rental options for each; Kaysersberg and Eguisheim have electric bikes for rent and make great starting points).

Riding round-trip between Ribeauvillé and Kaysersberg via

Hunawihr and Riquewihr along the upper *sentier viticole* yields sensational views but very hilly terrain (you can reduce some of the climbing by following lower wine-service lanes; details provided later).

From Colmar to Eguisheim, it's a level, five-mile ride on a bike lane through Wintzenheim and Wettolsheim to Eguisheim. Leaving Colmar, go to the far side of the train station on Avenue Général de Gaulle, which becomes Route de Wintzenheim. Keep straight on the bike lane uphill until you find bike signs for *V-11*, leading left toward Wettolsheim and then Eguisheim. Though just the last stretch through vines and towns is scenic, it's a handy option to reach the village. You can loop back to Colmar via Turckheim for a longer but still level ride.

On Foot: Hikers can stroll along *sentier viticole* service roads and paths (explained above) into vineyards from each town on short loop trails (each TI has brochures), or connect the villages on longer walks. Consider taking a bus or taxi from Colmar to one village and hiking to another, then taking a bus or taxi back to Colmar (Ribeauvillé and Riquewihr, or Kaysersberg and Riquewihr make good combinations—see details later in this chapter). Hikers can also climb high to the ruined castles of the Vosges Mountains (Eguisheim and Ribeauvillé are good bases).

ROUTE DU VIN WINES

Romans planted the first grapevines in Alsace over 2,000 years ago. Wine and Rhine worked together to form the backbone of the region's medieval economy. Barrels of wine were shipped along the nearby Rhine to international destinations (Scandinavia, the Low Countries, and Britain were big buyers). This created enormous wealth for Alsatians; their investments financed many of the beautiful buildings and villages we see today. Until the 17th century, Alsace produced more (and better) wine than any other region in the Holy Roman Empire. The Thirty Years' War, French Revolution, and Franco-Prussian War buried Alsace's wine dominance. Two world wars didn't help. Today Alsace is struggling to get its foot back in the door of international wine markets—where the big money is.

To help earn this recognition, they eagerly welcome visitors. Most Route du Vin towns have wineries that give tours (some charge a fee), and scores of small producers open their courtyards with free and fun tastings (remember, it's polite to buy a bottle or two if you like the wines). The cooperatives at Eguisheim, Ben-

nwihr, Hunawihr, and Ribeauvillé, created after the destruction of World War II, provide a good look at modern and efficient methods of production. Before you set off, review "French Wine-Tasting 101" (page 1072).

Learn to recognize the basic grapes and wines of this region. The simplest wines are blended from several grapes and usually called **Edelzwicker.** Despite being cheapest, these wines can be delicious and offer very good value.

Here are the key grapes to look for:

Riesling is the king of Alsatian grapes. It's more robust than sylvaner, but drier than the German style you're probably used to. The name comes from the German word that describes its slightly smoky smell, with a note of *goût petrol* ("gasoline taste").

Sylvaner—fresh and light, fruity and cheap—is a good wine for a hot day.

Pinot blanc is easy to drink as it's a middle-of-the-road but refreshing wine. It's neither too fruity or sweet nor too strong or dry—it's also not too memorable.

Pinot gris was called Tokay d'Alsace until recently, when the term was banned to avoid confusion with Tokaji wines in Hungary (where these grapes originated). These are more full-bodied, spicier, and distinctly different from other pinot gris wines you may have tried.

Muscat is best as a before-dinner wine. Compared with other French muscat wines, the Alsatian version is very dry, usually with a strong floral taste.

Gewürztraminer is "the lady's wine"—its bouquet is like a rosebush, its taste is fruity, and its aftertaste is spicy—as its name implies (*gewürtz* means "spice" in German). Drink this with pâtés and local cheeses.

Pinot noir, the local red wine, is very light and fruity—if you want a red wine with body, look beyond Alsace. Pinot noir is generally served chilled.

Crémant d'Alsace, the Alsatian sparkling wine, is very good—and much cheaper than Champagne.

You'll also see ***eaux-de-vie,*** powerful fruit-flavored brandies—try the *framboise* (raspberry) flavor.

In case you really get "Alsauced," the French term for headache is *mal à la tête.*

Towns and Sights Along the Route du Vin

These sights are listed in the order you'll encounter them if you're heading out from Colmar.

SOUTH OF COLMAR

Eguisheim

This is the most charming village of the region (described on page 961).

Vieil-Armand WWI Memorial (Hartmannswillerkopf)

This powerful memorial evokes the slaughter of the Western Front in World War I, when Germany and France bashed heads for years in a war of attrition. It's up a windy road above Cernay (20 miles south of Colmar). From the parking lot, walk 10 minutes to the vast cemetery, and walk 30 more minutes through trenches to a hilltop with a grand Alsatian view. Here you'll find a stirring memorial statue of French soldiers storming the trenches in 1915-1916—facing near-certain death—and rows of simple crosses marking the graves of those who lost their lives here.

NORTHWEST OF COLMAR

Turckheim

With a picturesque square and a garden-filled moat, this quiet town is refreshingly untouristy, just enough off the beaten path to be overlooked. Its 13th-century walls are some of the oldest in the region. Once upon a time, all foreign commerce entered Turckheim through its France Gate, which faces the train station. Today "foreign commerce" entering the gate includes tourists. Just inside the wall you'll see the **TI,** offering a helpful town map with a suggested stroll (Rue Wickram, tel. 03 89 27 38 44, www.turckheim.com).

Turckheim has a rich history and has long been famous for its wines. It gained town status in 1312, became a member of the Decapolis league of cities in 1354, and was devastated in the Thirty Years' War. In the 18th century it was rebuilt, thanks to the energy of Swiss immigrants. Reviving an old tradition, from May to October there's a town crier's tour each evening at 22:00 (in Alsatian and French).

Turckheim's **"Colmar Pocket" museum,** chronicling the American push to take Alsace from the Nazis, is a hit with WWII buffs (€4, minimal English information; Wed-Sat 14:00-18:00, Sun 10:00-12:00 & 14:00-18:00, closed Mon-Tue except July-Sept 14:00-18:00, closed mid-Oct-mid-April, tel. 03 89 80 86 66, http://musee.turckheim-alsace.com).

Kaysersberg

This is the most historic town outside Colmar in the region. It has a fascinating medieval old center, Dr. Albert Schweitzer's house, and plenty of hiking opportunities (described on page 967).

Bennwihr

After this town was completely destroyed during World War II, the only object left standing was the compelling statue of two girls depicting Alsace and Lorraine (outside its modern church). The war memorials next to the statue list the names of those who died in both world wars. During World War II, 130,000 Alsatian men aged 17-37 were forced into military service under the German army (after fighting against them); most were sent to the deadly Russian front.

Riquewihr

This adorable town is the most touristed on the Route du Vin and understandably so. If you find crowds tiresome, this town is exhausting (described on page 972).

Zellenberg

This place has an impressive setting and is worth a quick stop for the views from either side of its narrow perch.

Hunawihr

This bit of wine-soaked Alsatian cuteness is far less visited than its more famous neighbors, and features a 16th-century fortified church that today is shared by both Catholics and Protestants (the Catholics are buried next to the church; the Protestants are buried outside the church wall). Park at the village washbasin *(lavoir)* and follow the trail up to the church, then loop back through the village. Kids enjoy Hunawihr's small park, **Parc des Cigognes,** where they'll spot otters, over 150 storks, and more (€9.50, kids-€6-8, May-Sept daily 10:00-12:30 & 14:00-18:30, no midday closing June-Aug, until 17:30 in April and Oct, closed Nov-March and Oct mornings, other animals take part in the afternoon shows, tel. 03 89 73 72 62, www.cigogne-loutre.com). A nearby **butterfly exhibit** (Le Jardin des Papillons) houses thousands of the delicate insects from around the world (€8, kids-€5.50, includes audioguide, Easter-Oct daily 10:00-18:00, until 17:00 in April and Oct, closed Nov-Easter, tel. 03 89 73 33 33, www.jardinsdespapillons.fr).

Ribeauvillé

This appealing town, less visited by Americans, is well situated for hiking and biking. It's a linear place with a long pedestrian street (Grande Rue) and feels less tourist-dependent than other towns.

A steep but manageable trail leads from the top of the town into the Vosges Mountains to three castle ruins, and is ideal for hikers wanting a walk in the woods to sweeping views. Follow Grand Rue uphill to the Hôtel aux Trois Châteaux and find the cobbled lane leading up from there. St. Ulrich is the most interesting of the three ruins (allow 2 hours round-trip, or 3 hours to see all three castles, or just climb 10 minutes for a view over the town—get info at TI at 1 Grand Rue, tel. 03 89 73 23 23, www.ribeauville-riquewihr.com). It's a short, sweet, and really hilly bike loop from Ribeauvillé to Hunawihr and Riquewihr (can be extended to Kaysersberg). You can rent a **bike** at Cycles Binder (82 Grand Rue, tel. 03 89 73 65 87) or Ribo Cycles (17 Rue de Landau, tel. 03 89 73 72 94).

▲Château du Haut-Kœnigsbourg

This granddaddy of Alsatian castles tiptoes along on a rocky spur of the Vosges Mountains, 2,500 feet above the flat Rhine plain. Here you'll get an eagle's-nest perspective over the Vosges and villages below.

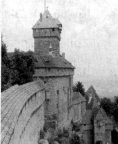

Cost and Hours: €8, under 18 free, audioguide-€4, ticket booth open daily June-Aug 9:15-18:00, April-May and Sept 9:15-17:15, March and Oct 9:30-17:00, Nov-Feb 9:30-12:00 & 13:00-16:30, castle closes 45 minutes after ticket booth, about 15 minutes north of Ribeauvillé above St-Hippolyte, tel. 03 69 33 25 00, www.haut-koenigsbourg.fr.

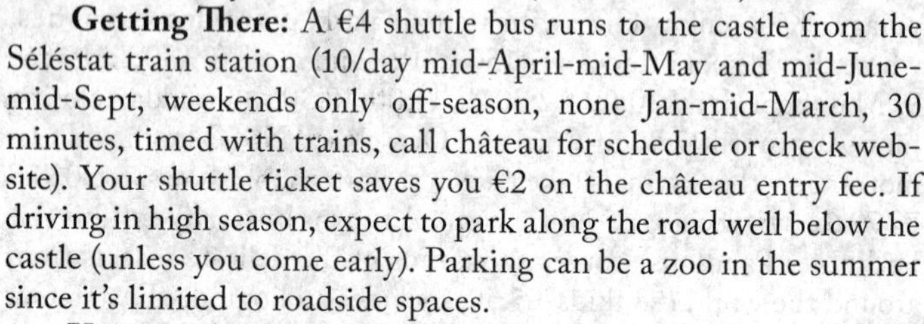

Tours: An English leaflet and posted descriptions give a reasonable overview of key rooms and history, but the one-hour audioguide is a good investment for serious students. There's also an English-language guided tour offered daily at 11:45 in summer (call to confirm).

Getting There: A €4 shuttle bus runs to the castle from the Sélestat train station (10/day mid-April-mid-May and mid-June-mid-Sept, weekends only off-season, none Jan-mid-March, 30 minutes, timed with trains, call château for schedule or check website). Your shuttle ticket saves you €2 on the château entry fee. If driving in high season, expect to park along the road well below the castle (unless you come early). Parking can be a zoo in the summer since it's limited to roadside spaces.

Visiting the Castle: While the elaborate castle was rebuilt barely 100 years ago, it's a romantic's dream, sprawling along its sky-high ridge and providing helpful insight into this 15th-century mountain fortress.

Started in 1147 as an Imperial castle in the extensive network that served the Holy Roman Empire, Haut-Kœnigsbourg was designed to protect valuable trade routes. It was constantly under siege and eventually destroyed by rampaging Swedes in the 17th century. The castle sat in ruins until the early 1900s, when an ambitious restoration campaign began (which you'll learn much about—a model in the castle storeroom shows the castle before its renovation).

Today's castle—well-furnished by medieval standards—highlights Germanic influence in Alsatian history with decorations and weapons from the 15th through 17th centuries. Don't miss the top-floor Grand Bastion with its elaborate wooden roof structure and models showing its construction. There are cannons and magnificent views in all directions.

Eguisheim

Just a few miles south of Colmar's suburbs, this circular, flower-festooned little wine town (pop. 1,600), while often mobbed by tourists, is a delight. In 2013 it was named France's favorite town—and it's gone to its head. Eguisheim ("ay-gush-I'm") is ideal for a relaxing lunch and vineyard walks—and the town is all about welcoming guests. If you have a car, it can make a good small-town base for exploring Alsace. It's a cinch by car (easy parking) and manageable by bike (see "Getting Around the Route du Vin—By Bike," earlier), but barely accessible by bus. Consider taking the bus one way and taxi the other to Colmar or other villages (bus schedules available at TIs and posted at key stops).

Orientation to Eguisheim

The **TI** has free Wi-Fi and information on bus schedules, festivals, vineyard walks, and Vosges Mountain hikes (July-Sept Mon-Sat 9:30-12:30 & 13:30-18:00, Sun 10:30-12:30 & 13:30-16:30; shorter hours and closed Sun off-season, 22 Grand Rue, tel. 03 89 23 40 33, www.ot-eguisheim.fr). They're happy to call a taxi for you (about €15 to Colmar).

Eguisheim's **bus stop** is at the top end of the village close to Place Charles de Gaulle (see map, same stop for both directions).

Just in front of the bus stop, winemaker Jean-Luc Meyer has **bikes for rent** (€7/4 hours, €13/day, daily 8:30-19:00, 4 Rue des Trois Châteaux, tel. 03 89 24 53 66). Alsa Cyclo Tours has rental bikes with GPS and recorded directions in English (electric bike-€25/half-day; €35/day, regular bike-€15/half-day, €25/day; GPS-€3; May-Oct daily 9:00-18:00, 6 Rue Rempart Sud, tel. 07 86 38 80 12 or 06 19 23 53 62).

Public **WCs** are located in the lower pay parking lot, and automatic WC cabins are a few steps from the fountain on Place du Château Saint-Léon, in a courtyard off Cours Unterlinden (hidden on the right).

Eguisheim Walk

Draw a circle and then cut a line straight through it. That's your plan with this inviting little town. The main drag (Grand Rue) cuts through the middle, with gates at either end and a stately town square in the center. And, while Eguisheim's town wall is long gone, it left a circular lane (Rue du Rempart—Nord and Sud) lined with gingerbread-cute houses.

Start your self-guided walk at the bottom of town (near the TI) and circle the former ramparts clockwise, walking up Rue du Rempart Sud. The most enchanting and higgledy-piggledy view in town is right at the start of the loop (at the tight Y in the road; go left and uphill). Rue du Rempart Sud is more picturesque than Rue du Rempart Nord, but I'd walk the entire circle. You'll see that what was once the wall is now lined with 13th- to 17th-century houses—a cancan of half-timbered charm. You're actually walking a lane between the back of fine homes (on the left) and their barns (on the right). Look for emblems of daily life: religious and magical symbols, dates on lintel stones, little hatch doors leading to wine or coal cellars, and so on. (Everything looks sharp because the government subsidizes the work locals do on their exteriors.) Along the way, you may bump into Chez Thierry's *saucisson* stand (plenty of tasty samples) and Frederic Hertzog's farmhouse cheese shop (try the Munster cheese—made in the town of Munster just up the valley). The loop takes a decidedly hip turn along its northern half, as you pass an art gallery, a cool coffee shop, and a trendy bar.

When exploring the town, you may come upon some of its 20 "tithe courtyards." Farmers who worked on land owned by the Church came to these courtyards to pay their tithes (10 percent of their production). With so many of these courtyards, it's safe to conclude that the farming around here was *formidable*.

When you've finished the loop, walk up Grand Rue to Eguisheim's main square—Place du Château Saint-Léon. It's lined with fine Renaissance houses; many were mansions for the managers of wealthy estates and vineyards owned by absentee landowners. The mini-castle is privately owned and closed to the public—its chapel (described below) was built into it more than 100 years ago.

The 19th-century fountain sports a statue of St. Leo IX—the only Alsatian pope. Leo was born, likely in this castle, in 1002. A bishop at 24, he was famed for his pastoral qualities, tending the sick and poor, and working to reform the Church (which had grown corrupt). Made pope in 1048, Leo's pontificate lasted just five years.

Your walk is over. Enjoy sampling the shops, cafés, and fruits of the local vine.

Sights in Eguisheim

Eguisheim Castle and Chapel of St. Leo IX

Fronting the main square, the town castle has an octagonal plan from the 13th century. There's been some kind of castle here for a thousand years—the first was the fortress of a local duke. After the French Revolution, the castle was state-owned and, as the state so often did during that no-nonsense age, it was sold and dismantled. Later, a local bishop purchased it with the intention of honoring his hometown saint. Rather than rebuild the castle keep, he built a chapel dedicated to St. Leo in the Neo-Romanesque style popular in 19th century. Consecrated in 1894, it's of little historic importance. But it's beautiful inside and worth a peek to see how a Romanesque church may have been painted.

As you approach the church, you're welcomed by a statue of Pope Leo IX above the doorway—note the lions supporting him ("Leo" means lion). Inside, the paintings, stained glass, and carvings are all in the Romanesque Revival style. After the paganism of the French Revolution, romantics in the late 1800s used this style to signal a spiritual revival—a new golden age of Christianity.

Linger a while to soak it all in. To the right of the altar is a reliquary with a piece of Leo's jaw. To the left is a statue of Leo. And flanking the altar, two fine stained-glass angels majestically spread their wings (drop any coin into the €0.50 box for light).

Wine Tasting

Don't leave without visiting one of Eguisheim's countless cozy wineries. And please, if you taste for free, purchase at least one bottle.

Paul Schneider's independent winery is located in a one-time hospice, now run by a third-generation family winemaker. They are licensed as a bar, so enjoy a glass (€3-7), or try a few wines in the traditionally furnished tasting room before buying a bottle. Ask Claire to explain the abstract paintings on the walls (also found on the labels of their Grands Crus)—they give a modern twist to some old Alsatian traditions. Call ahead for a short but worthwhile tour of the two cellars (daily 9:00-12:00 & 14:00-18:30, 1 Rue de l'Hôpital, tel. 03 89 41 50 07, vins.paul.schneider@wanadoo.fr).

Views over Eguisheim

If you have a car, follow signs up to *Husseren Les Cinq Châteaux,* then walk 20 minutes to the ruined castle towers for a good view of the Vosges Mountains above and vineyards below.

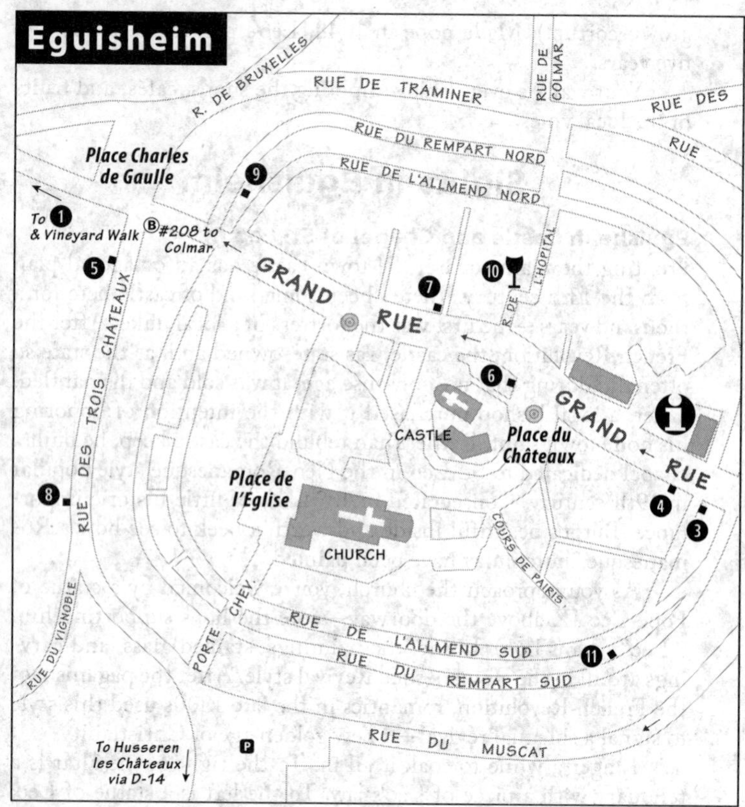

By mountain bike or on foot, find any path through the vineyards above Eguisheim for great views (the TI has a free map). Here's the most direct route: Walk uphill on Grand Rue, cross the ring road and follow *Camping* signs and enter the vineyards past the campground. Orient yourself using the big vineyard-display panel and wander the lanes as high as you like. It's OK to walk on dirt paths between the vines. You'll find occasional vineyard information posted in English and see the five châteaux of Husseren floating above. The TI's map shows a longer walk through the vineyards from the same starting point.

Sleeping in Eguisheim

$$$ Hôtel St. Hubert*** offers 15 spotless rooms with modern, German-hotelesque comfort (and strict management to match), and an indoor pool and sauna. The 10-minute walk from the town center is rewarded with vineyards out your window (Db-€127, Tb-€144, family suite for four-€192, extra bed-€17, four rooms have

patios, free pickup at Colmar's train station if reserved a day in advance and room booked directly through the hotel, reception open 8:00-12:00 & 15:00-21:00, 6 Rue des Trois Pierres, tel. 03 89 41 40 50, www.hotel-st-hubert.com, reservation@hotel-st-hubert.com).

$$ Auberge Alsacienne*** is conveniently located near the lower parking area with reasonably priced, sharp rooms in a picturesque building (Db-€71-94, Tb-€106, breakfast-€9.50, Wi-Fi, 12 Grand Rue, tel. 03 89 41 50 20, www.auberge-alsacienne.net, auberge-alsacienne@wanadoo.fr).

$ Auberge du Rempart is a rockin' deal. It's atmospheric, with bright, airy rooms with big beds and surprisingly elaborate decor above a lively café/restaurant deep inside the town (standard Db-€56, grand Db with air-con-€73-95; great family suite-€122 for 4 people, €142 for 6; Wi-Fi, near TI at 3 Rue du Rempart Sud, tel. 03 89 41 16 87, www.auberge-du-rempart.com, auberge-du-rempart@wanadoo.fr). The reception desk is in the restaurant and is usually open only during lunch and after 18:00.

ALSACE

CHAMBRES D'HOTES

$$ Le Hameau d'Eguisheim, on the grounds of the Pierre Henri Ginglinger organic winery, has five big, bright, tastefully decorated rooms. Stéphanie has transformed the 17th-century place into a cozy cocoon (Db-€70, Tb-€85, Qb-€95, includes breakfast in the old cellar). She also rents two triple-bed studios for up to six people (€130, 3-night minimum, fully equipped kitchen, no breakfast, Wi-Fi, across from TI at 33 Grand Rue, tel. 03 89 24 18 66, www.hameau-eguisheim.com, contact@hameau-eguisheim.com).

$$ Winemaker **Jean-Luc Meyer** rents modern rooms, some with balcony, and apartments for 2 to 12 people at good rates (Db-€60-70 including breakfast in their tasting room, kitchenette studio-€79, good family options, bike rental possible, Wi-Fi at reception only, 4 Rue des Trois Châteaux, tel. 03 89 24 53 66, www.vins-meyer-eguisheim.com, info@vins-meyer-eguisheim.com).

$ Madame Bombenger is sweet, speaks some English, and has a contemporary French home just above Eguisheim with three rooms and nice views into the vineyards and over town (Sb-€40, Db-€50, €2 less for more than one night, includes breakfast, Wi-Fi, across from Hôtel St. Hubert at 3 Rue des Trois Pierres, tel. 03 89 23 71 19, mobile 06 61 94 31 09, bombenger.marie-therese@wanadoo.fr).

Eating in Eguisheim

Charcuterie-Café A Edel, on Place du Château St. Léon IX, has killer quiche "to go" and everything you need for a fun picnic, including small tubs of chopped veggies (daily until 19:00). You can picnic by the fountain, or eat at their adjacent restaurant while listening to the trickling of the square's fountain (restaurant open Thu-Mon until 18:00, closed Tue-Wed, €10-14 *tartes flambées* and quiche served with small salads, 2 Place du Château St. Léon IX, tel. 03 89 41 22 40).

Auberge des Trois Châteaux is very Alsatian, with cozy ambience and traditional cuisine (*menus* from €20, affordable *plats du jour,* closed Tue evening and all day Wed, 26 Grand Rue, tel. 03 89 23 70 61).

Auberge du Rempart is best for outdoor dining in a pleasant courtyard around a big fountain. If you're in town on a summer weekend, good *tartes flambées* go for €11. Come here for less expensive and lighter meals (€14-19 *plats;* closed Mon, Thu, and Sun evenings Sept-June; near TI at 3 Rue du Rempart Sud, tel. 03 89 41 16 87).

Au Vieux Porche is a wood-beamed, white-tablecloth affair serving a blend of regional favorites and cuisine from other areas. It's ideal for a leisurely meal or a special occasion (*menus* from €24, closed Tue-Wed, upper end of town at 16 Rue des Trois Châteaux, tel. 03 89 24 01 90, www.auvieuxporche.fr).

Le Café, a cool hangout morning and night, is run by English-speaking Reiner (drinks and light snacks only, cozy outdoor seating, on Rue Allmend Nord near the top of the village, daily 10:00-22:00).

Kaysersberg

The domain of Germanic princes for much of its history, Kaysersberg ("Emperor's Mountain") was of strategic importance, thanks to its location guarding the important route over the Vosges Mountains that links Colmar with the big city of Nancy. Today, philosopher-physician Albert Schweitzer's hometown offers a cute jumble of 15th-century homes under a romantically ruined castle with easy vineyard trails at its doorstep, and plenty of tourists. Reasonable bus service from Colmar makes Kaysersberg a convenient day trip (7/day, 30 minutes).

Orientation to Kaysersberg

The **TI** is two blocks from the town's main entry, inside Hôtel de Ville at 39 Rue du Général de Gaulle (mid-June-Sept Mon-Sat 9:00-12:30 & 14:00-18:00, Sun 9:30-12:30; mid-Sept-mid-June Mon-Sat 9:30-12:00 & 14:00-17:30, closed Sun; tel. 03 89 78 22 78, www.kaysersberg.com). The TI has a free guest computer, rents audioguides for touring Kaysersberg (€5, €150 deposit, allow 1.5 hours, includes castle ruins), and rents electric bikes (€13/half-day, €20/day, April-Oct only). Pick up town and valley maps, bus schedules, and detailed descriptions of hiking trails between wine villages (€0.50 each; see "Walking/Biking Trails from Kaysersberg," later).

All buses from Colmar serve the Rocade Verte stop at a parking lot on the village's south side, just outside the town walls (best stop for return trip). Drivers will find pay lots (€2/day) along the town's ring road. Porte Basse Parking works best, but all lots offer easy walking access to the center.

Find **WC**s next to the TI and across from the Schweitzer Museum. There's also a fun **Monday morning market** at the top of town, across from the Schweitzer Museum.

Albert Schweitzer
(1875-1965)

I don't know what your destiny will be, but one thing I do know: The only ones among you who will be really happy are those who have sought and found how to serve.

—Albert Schweitzer

Albert Schweitzer—theologian, musician, philosopher, and physician—was an unusually gifted individual who never hesitated to question accepted beliefs and practices. He is probably most famous for his work with sufferers of leprosy and tuberculosis in Africa.

Born to German parents in 1875 in Kaysersberg, he studied philosophy and theology at the University of Strasbourg, eventually becoming a pastor at his church. Not satisfied with that, Schweitzer studied music and soon gained fame as a musical scholar and organist. After trying his hand at writing with *The Quest of the Historical Jesus,* which challenged contemporary secular views of Jesus, he shifted his attention to medicine. After he married Helene Bresslau, the couple left for Africa and founded a missionary hospital in Gabon (then called Lambaréné). During World War I, Schweitzer and his wife were forced by the French out of Africa.

After the war, Schweitzer returned to Gabon on his own, where he remained for most of the rest of his life. He received the 1952 Nobel Peace Prize for his service to humanity, particularly for founding the Albert Schweitzer Hospital in Gabon, where he died in 1965. He was 90 years old.

Kaysersberg Walk

Start your self-guided town stroll in the center of Kaysersberg at the main square, Place de la Mairie. Face Hôtel de Ville and walk along the main drag to its left.

After a few steps, you'll find a round arch from 1604 on the right. Walking through the arch, you'll go past a former gunpowder storehouse (now a hall used for free art exhibits) and a well. Walk into a typical Alsatian courtyard with a wooden gallery and cascades of geraniums. The painting from 1993 celebrates the 700th anniversary of Kayersberg's status as an Imperial city. In 1293, a local prince gave Kaysersberg trade and tax status and the right to build strong city walls. Later, in 1354, the town was a founding member of the Decapolis.

Go back through the arch, turn right, and continue up the main street, Rue de Général de Gaulle. Kaysersberg is known for its handmade glass, and at **Verrerie d'Art de Kaysersberg** (across from the Church of the Holy Cross), you can see glassblowers at work and browse their showroom (workshop generally open Tue-Sat 10:00-12:30 & 14:00-18:00). While the craft almost died out here in the 18th century, it's alive and well now.

Opposite the glassworks (on the side of the church), read some of the names on the **war memorial**—that's a lot of war dead for a small town. We're in France now, but all of this fighting was done for Germany. In World War I they fought on the Western Front. After Hitler annexed Alsace in World War II, local boys were sent to Russia and Poland (far from home, so they couldn't desert). Notice also the noncombatant victims: Some were sent to death camps and others died in bombing raids. In 1944 Allied bombers destroyed 45 percent of Kaysersberg—and that included many of its citizens.

In front of the **Church of the Holy Cross** stands a fountain featuring the Roman Emperor Constantine—holding a cross and honored here because he was the first Christian emperor. Up on the simple Romanesque facade of the church is his mom, Helen. She converted her son to Christianity and, according to Church lore, brought pieces of the True Cross to Rome from Jerusalem.

Before stepping into the church, take a moment to enjoy the vernacular architecture surrounding this square. The church dates from the 13th and 14th centuries (free, daily 9:00-18:00). I know, Gothic was in high gear elsewhere, but back then Alsace was about a hundred years behind the artistic curve. Look at the tympanum (carved relief over the door) and notice how crude and naive it is. The carved red sandstone figures remind me of Archaic Greek statues.

Step inside. The nave is Romanesque but the side aisles, dating from the 15th century when the church was expanded, are more Gothic. The medieval stained glass was destroyed in 1944; what you see is modern. The impressive statue of a crucified Christ is carved out of linden wood and painted. Notice the attempt to manage the perspective by making Jesus' legs shorter than they would have actually been.

Walk up close to the altarpiece (from 1518) and study the finely carved Passion of Christ. These scenes show the events of Jesus' last week—from entering Jerusalem (on the left) to the Resurrection (on the right). The carvings—which are high relief in the center but low relief in the wings so it will all fit when closed—were inspired by 15th-century engravings by Martin Schongauer. You can push the button on the right of the altar for light.

On the right side of the nave (as you leave), check out the statue of the Deposition, showing Christ after his death by crucifixion. A metal hatch on his chest shows where the communion bread was kept back in the 16th century.

Continue walking along this busy street. At #62, the **Kaysersberg History Museum** has a forgettable exhibit of religious and domestic artifacts filling three rooms—without a word of English (€2; July-Aug Wed-Mon 10:00-12:00 & 14:00-18:00, closed Tue; closed off-season; enter from the courtyard between the twin gables). The **Biscuiterie La Table Alsacienne,** tempting visitors with all the traditional baked goods at #70, is more interesting.

Follow the main drag to the top of the town. Just before the bridge, check out a huge house standing at the top of the road—this was an old inn and bathhouse. To its right, a quieter lane leads past a fountain with drinking water, a charming pottery shop, and on to the castle (with a loop path back to the TI).

Maison Herzer, on the right at #101, dates from 1592. Its finely restored ornamentation includes fun faces (could be the owners) and a gargoyle-supported pulley high above to lift hay up to the attic. Look around. Notice how some buildings lining the main drag have settled in the soft ground.

Just before the bridge, walk a few steps up the riverside lane to see where town's canal starts—an example of the importance of water power in the Middle Ages.

Kaysersberg's bridge was fortified on the upstream side to stop enemy boats from entering town. Look downstream; the helter-skelter roofs were for drying the leather and hides of a tannery.

On this 16th-century bridge, find the emblems of the Holy Roman Empire (double eagle) and of Kaysersberg (two bags with a belt to tie goods to the trader's horse). These signs—plus the nearby saint-in-a-cage emblem (Constantine with the Holy Cross and Christ)—meant this bridge offered both political and religious protection for people coming and going.

At the end of World War II, as the Nazis were preparing to retreat, they planned to destroy the bridge. Locals reasoned with the commander, agreeing to dig an anti-tank ditch just beyond the bridge—and the symbol of the town was saved.

Cross the bridge and look back above the bathhouse with its stork nest. (Storks are choosy and often don't like man-made nest cages like this one.) High on the ridge is the town's 12th-century castle and city wall.

Your walk is finished. The castle is an easy climb, and the Albert Schweitzer Museum is a block beyond the bridge.

Sights in Kaysersberg

Wine Tasting

The Caveau des Vignerons de Kaysersberg represents 150 winemakers from around Kaysersberg, including several Grands Crus, and offers free and easy wine tastings with experts who speak "a leetl" English (Wed-Sun 10:30-13:00 & 14:00-18:30, closed Mon except July-Aug, near TI at 20 Rue du Général de Gaulle, tel. 03 89 47 18 43).

Albert Schweitzer Museum

The home of Dr. Albert Schweitzer is a small museum offering two rooms of scattered photos and artifacts from his time in Africa (with English descriptions). Schweitzer was a Renaissance man who opened people's eyes to conditions in the Third World (€2, Easter-Oct Thu-Tue 9:00-12:00 & 14:00-18:00, closed Wed and Nov-Easter, 126 Rue du Général de Gaulle).

Walking/Biking Trails from Kaysersberg

Trails start just outside the TI (get details at the TI). To find the main trail, turn left as you walk out of the TI and walk under the arch. Signs lead hikers up through the vineyards to grand views over the town. It's a worthwhile 10-minute climb to the ruined **castle** (free, always open, more great views and benches, 113 steps up a dark stairway to the top of the tower—worth the climb). Loop back down behind the castle and enter the town near its 16th-century bridge. Or hikers can continue past the castle for more views and trails (TI has detailed map for €0.50). For great views of Kaysersberg sans the climb, follow the trail described next (toward Kientzheim) for about 10 minutes.

For a delightful 2-hour hike—or 40-minute bike ride—along a paved lane over vine-covered hills to **Riquewihr,** turn right on the main trail near the TI. You'll start on a bike path *(piste cyclable)* to **Kientzheim** (well-marked with green crosses and bike icons). In Kientzheim, follow the *sentier viticole* uphill through vineyards to wonderful views and on to Riquewihr. If you get turned around, stop any biker or vineyard worker and ask, *"À Riquewihr?"* (ah reek-veer) Drivers can follow the same signs from Kientzheim to Riquewihr.

NEAR KAYSERSBERG

World War II Sights

The Second World War rolled wildly back and forth through this region. Some towns were entirely destroyed. Others made it through unscathed. Towns with gray rather than red-tiled roofs were rebuilt after 1945. Kientzheim has an American-made tank parked in its front yard (and a wine museum in its castle grounds) and a refreshing network of tiny streams trickling down its streets (as was commonplace around here before World War II). The towns of Sigolsheim (which was the scene of fierce fighting—note its sterile, rebuilt Romanesque church) and nearby Bennwihr are modern, as they were taken and lost a dozen times by the Allies and Nazis, and completely ruined.

The hill just north of Kaysersberg is soaked in soldiers' blood. It houses a **World War II Memorial** and is still called "Bloody Hill" by locals (as it was nicknamed by German troops). The spectacular setting, best at sunset, houses a monument to the American divisions that helped liberate Alsace in World War II (find the American flag). Up the lane, a beautiful cemetery is the final resting place of 1,600 men who fought in the French army (many gravestones are Muslim, for soldiers from France's North African colonies—Morocco, Algeria, and Tunisia). From this brilliant viewpoint you can survey the entire southern section of the Route du Vin and into Germany. The castle hanging high to the north is the Château du Haut-Kœnigsbourg (described earlier).

Riquewihr

This little village, wrapped in vineyards, is so picturesque today because it was so rich centuries ago, thanks to wine exports. You can recognize its old wealth because it has the most stone houses of any place in Alsace. The village is crammed with shops, cafés, galleries, cobblestones, and flowers. Arrive early or visit late if you can, as midday crowds can trample its ample charms.

Orientation to Riquewihr

Buses drop you off at the lower end of the village, opposite the post office (drivers can park in spaces along the ring road for €2). Enter the town under Hôtel de Ville's archway; the main drag runs uphill from here. The **TI** is halfway up at 2 Rue de la 1ère Armée (Mon-Sat 9:30-12:00 & 14:00-18:00, Sun 10:00-12:00 & 14:00-16:00, shorter hours off-season and closed Sun; tel. 03 89 73 23 23, www.ribeauville-riquewihr.com). A good WC is behind the TI. Quieter lanes lead off the main drag. For a taxi, call 03 89 73 73 71 or 06 46 84 40 05.

Riquewihr Walk

Start your self-guided walk at the bottom of town. At the **archway** going through Hôtel de Ville, notice the three flags: Europe, France, and Alsace. Notice also the clever bench just outside designed for ladies with loads on their heads (perhaps baskets of grapes) to sit and take a load off their head. Entering the sleepy (except for tourism) town of 1,300 people, you realize that if there was no wine and no tourism, this place would have no economy. Find the historic map designed to help you imagine Riquewihr in 1644 and appreciate its double wall and moat.

Strolling up Riquewihr's **main street,** Rue de Général de Gaulle, which cuts straight through town, enjoy the architecture. It's fun to remember that before street numbers, each house had a name—often related to an animal—which made it a kind of landmark. Because villages often had only two or three family names, you couldn't say "the Jones house." You'd say, rather, the Unicorn House.

The vineyards surrounding town belonged to absentee princes. The impressive **mansions** all around were the domains of men who managed the estate of a feudal lord and, in return, got a cut of the production. At #14 you can see what would have been considered a skyscraper in the 16th century—the highest Renaissance building in Alsace. At #16, notice the broad arches for wagons of grapes. Venture into the courtyard (filled with restaurant tables) with its traditional Alsatian galleries and evocative old well. The mammoth 1817 wine press drained juice directly into the cellar. At the entry is a collection of 200-year-old iron stove plates. Decorated with old German texts, these were placed behind the fire to both protect the back wall and reflect heat out.

At the town's main intersection is a street leading to two churches (Protestant to the right, Catholic to the left and neither of sightseeing interest). Before the age of private plumbing, public fountains were scattered through town.

Find the sign for the **town gourmet** at #42. The word "gourmet" originated here in France, where each town in winemaking regions had an official wine judge, appraiser, and middleman. The gourmet was instrumental in effectively connecting the vintner with the thirsty market. He facilitated sales and set prices. To judge the wine, he needed to have a little fine food to complement the tasting. The town appointed the gourmet, and the position—quite lucrative as you can see by this fine house—was then handed down from father to son. While the traditional function of the gourmet died out in the 1930s, the concept of the person with the best food in town—the gourmet—survives to this day.

Wander through the gourmet's courtyards. Notice the nails on timbers designed to hold stucco. In the 18th and 19th centuries, half-timbered houses were considered "low class," so owners stuccoed over the wood to make it look like a stone home. Follow the gangly wooden structures to the roofline in back to see a stone wall protruding above the roof tiles—built to stop fires. Back when roofs were made with wood shingles (rather than today's safer terra-cotta), fire was a serious problem.

At the top of town stands one of the most impressive **guard towers** in Alsace (Le Dolder, from 1291). The Dolder Museum, inside the tower, has small rooms covering its history—but doesn't merit the climb or €4 entry fee. Look for the engraving of 13th-century Riquewihr by the fountain opposite the tower's entry.

Older towns were fortified with **walls** built to withstand arrows. When they grew bigger—and war technology advanced to include gunpowder and cannons, the townspeople built a stouter wall outside the original wall. In this case, it left an area in the middle for "newer" 18th-century houses. Notice how homes were built right into the defensive walls.

From the top of town, it's rewarding to turn left and explore the quiet lanes and their picturesque houses. Pass under the bell tower, take a left on Rue des Remparts, and explore. Turn right when you see steps down to the moat (and the big wine press), and double back to the top of the town along the moat.

Sights in Riquewihr

Tourist Train

Within a few yards of the town entry, you'll see the tourist train (€6.50, next departure time posted, 30 minutes). For those without a car, it's handy as it choo-choos into the vineyards, offering terrific views over the village.

Wine Tasting

The vines surrounding Riquewihr produce some of Alsace's most prestigious wines—and the village is lined with good places to sample them. **Caves Dopff et Irion** sits just above Hôtel de Ville and provides a handsome wine-tasting experience with an English-speaking staff (€7-20 bottles, most about €10, special counter for *eau-de-vie* tastings, daily 10:00-18:00, shorter hours in winter, tel. 03 89 49 08 92). **Caves Hugel,** another well-respected producer, has an intimate tasting room on the main drag a bit past the TI (daily 10:00-18:00, tel. 03 89 47 92 15).

Musée de la Communication

This museum, located near the bottom of town (at its château), takes you through the evolution of man's ability to send messages, from mail delivery to mobile phones. The fascinating and substantial museum, with lots of historic artifacts, is by far the most important sight to see in town (€5, some English descriptions, April-Oct and Dec daily 10:00-17:30, closed Nov and Jan-March).

Scenic Routes from Riquewihr

A path with sensational views leads from the north edge of town. Find the *sentier viticole* at the lower end of town (a few blocks to the right as you face Hôtel de Ville) and climb into the vineyards as high as your legs allow.

On the town's south side, another *sentier viticole* leads to Kientzheim (then Kaysersberg), starting from the TI and heading out Rue de la 1ère Armée. Follow blue signs to *Kientzheim* on this beautiful walk or bike ride. The lane rises, then drops into the village—revealing spectacular views all the way (allow 1.75 hours to hike at a steady pace to Kaysersberg, 40 minutes by bike). Drivers can follow the same route and get the same great views, but must go slow and watch out for bikers.

Strasbourg

Strasbourg is urban Alsace at its best—it feels like a giant Colmar with rivers and streetcars. It's a progressive, livable city, with generous space devoted to pedestrians, scads of bikes, mod trams, meandering waterways, and a young, lively mix of university students, Eurocrats, and street people. This city of about 270,000 residents has an Amsterdam-like feel. Bordering the west bank of the Rhine River, Strasbourg provides the ultimate blend of Franco-Germanic culture, architecture, and ambience. A living symbol of the hope for perpetual peace between France and Germany, Strasbourg was selected as home to the European Parliament, the European Council (sharing administrative responsibilities for the European Union with Brussels, Belgium), and the European Court of Human Rights.

PLANNING YOUR TIME

Strasbourg makes a good day trip from Colmar. And, thanks to high-speed TGV-train service, it also makes a handy stop for train travelers en route to or from Paris (baggage storage available). The Alsatian Museum is the only museum worth the admission—you're here to see the cathedral, wander the waterways, and take a bite out of the big city. Plan on three hours to hit the highlights, starting at Strasbourg's dazzling cathedral (arrive in Strasbourg by 10:30 so you can comfortably make the noon cathedral clock performance) and ending with the district called La Petite France (ideally for lunch).

Orientation to Strasbourg

TOURIST INFORMATION

Strasbourg's main TI faces the cathedral (daily 9:00-19:00, 17 Place de la Cathédrale, tel. 03 88 52 28 28, www.otstrasbourg.fr, info@otstrasbourg.fr). Another TI is in the train station's south hall (across from the station's *accueil* office, same hours, sells day passes for the tram). Learn about special events (like the summer sound-and-light show at the cathedral, mentioned in "Sights in Strasbourg" later) and buy the €1.50 city map, which describes a decent walking tour in English, or pay €5.50 to rent an audioguide that covers the cathedral and old city in more detail than most need (available only at the main TI, includes a cute little map of the route, allow 1.5 hours). The TI also has bike maps for the city (€1 with English explanations) and surrounding areas.

The Strasbourg Pass (€17, kids-€8.50), valid three days, is a great value for travelers wanting to do it all. It includes one free museum entry and a half-off coupon for another museum, a discount on the town audioguide, free half-day bike rental, free boat cruise, and free entry to the cathedral narthex view and the astrological clock tour.

ARRIVAL IN STRASBOURG

By Train: TGV trains serve Strasbourg's gleaming train station. Limited baggage storage is available at platform 1 (daily 6:15-21:15, allow time for its airport-type security screening). WCs are across from the stairs to platform 2, and a helpful TI is in the station's south *(sud)* hall.

Rental bikes are available in the lower level of the glass atrium (see "Helpful Hints," next page), and you'll find many budget eating options.

To **walk** to the cathedral in 15 urban minutes, exit straight out of the station, cross the big square (Place de la Gare), and walk past Hôtel Vendôme and up Rue du Maire Kuss. Cross the river, and continue up serpentine, pedestrian-friendly Rue du 22 Novembre all the way to the grand Place Kléber. Angle a bit left through Place Kléber (whose namesake graces the center of the square), then turn right on the broad pedestrian street (Rue des Grandes Arcades). In a few blocks, turn left on Rue Mercière (just after the merry-go-round), then follow that spire.

To get from the train station to the city center by **public transportation,** catch the caterpillar-like tram that leaves from under the station (buy €1.60 one-way ticket or €4.10 day pass from the station TI, or from machines on platforms—coins only (chip cards too), then validate in skinny machines, www.cts-strasbourg.fr). Take tram #A (direction: Illkirch) or tram #D (direction: Aristide Briand) three stops to Langross-Grande Rue, two blocks from the cathedral. (You can return to the station, Gare Centrale, from the same stop.)

By Car: You're better off day-tripping in by train (it's faster and much easier than driving). If you must drive, take sortie #4 from A-35. From this exit you can follow *Centre-Ville* and *Cathédrale* signs to the city center, then park at metered street spaces or in a central lot signed as *La Petite France, Gare Centrale,* or *la Cathédrale* (figure €3/hour).

For less money and stress, follow signs from the same autoroute exit to the *Elsau P+R* (Parking & Relais) lot at the Elsau tram station outside the city center (€3.20/day includes round-trip tram tickets to the center; take green-line "F" tram in direction: *Centre-Ville* and exit at Homme de Fer stop, validate parking ticket at scanner on tram platform both going and returning).

By Plane: The user-friendly Strasbourg-Entzheim airport (tel. 03 88 64 67 67, www.strasbourg.aeroport.fr), with frequent, often inexpensive flights to Paris, is connected by train to the main rail station (€2.30, 10-minute trip).

HELPFUL HINTS

Quiet Transportation: Beware of virtually silent trams and bicycles—look both ways before crossing streets.

Internet Access: Several cybercafés lie on the main street into town from the station, Rue du Maire Kuss (or ask at the TI).

Post Office: It's at the cathedral (Mon-Fri 9:00-18:00, Sat 9:00-17:00, closed Sun).

Laundry: You'll find a handy launderette on Rue des Veaux, near my recommended hotels (daily 7:00-21:00).

Bike Rental: You can rent bikes at **Vélhop,** one level below street level at the train station (€5/day, €150 deposit, Mon-Fri 8:00-19:00, Sat-Sun 9:30-19:00, closed Sun and shorter hours off-season, follow bike signs, Place de la Gare, tel. 09 60 17 74 63, www.velhop.strasbourg.eu).

Taxi: Call 03 88 36 13 13 or 06 80 43 22 25.

Car Rental: All major companies are at or near the train station.

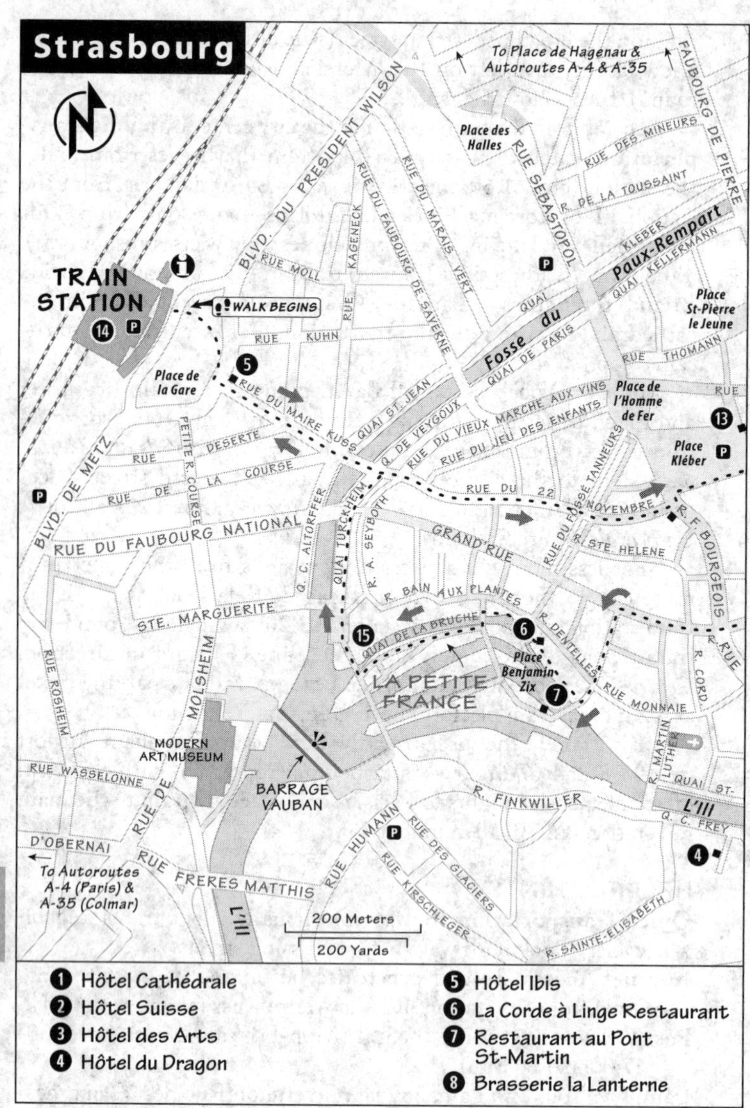

Sights in Strasbourg

▲▲Strasbourg Cathedral (Cathédrale de Notre-Dame)

Stand in front of Hôtel de la Cathédrale and crane your neck way back. If this church, with its cloud-piercing spire and pink sandstone color, drops your jaw today, imagine its impact on medieval tourists. At 466 feet, that spire was the world's tallest until the mid-

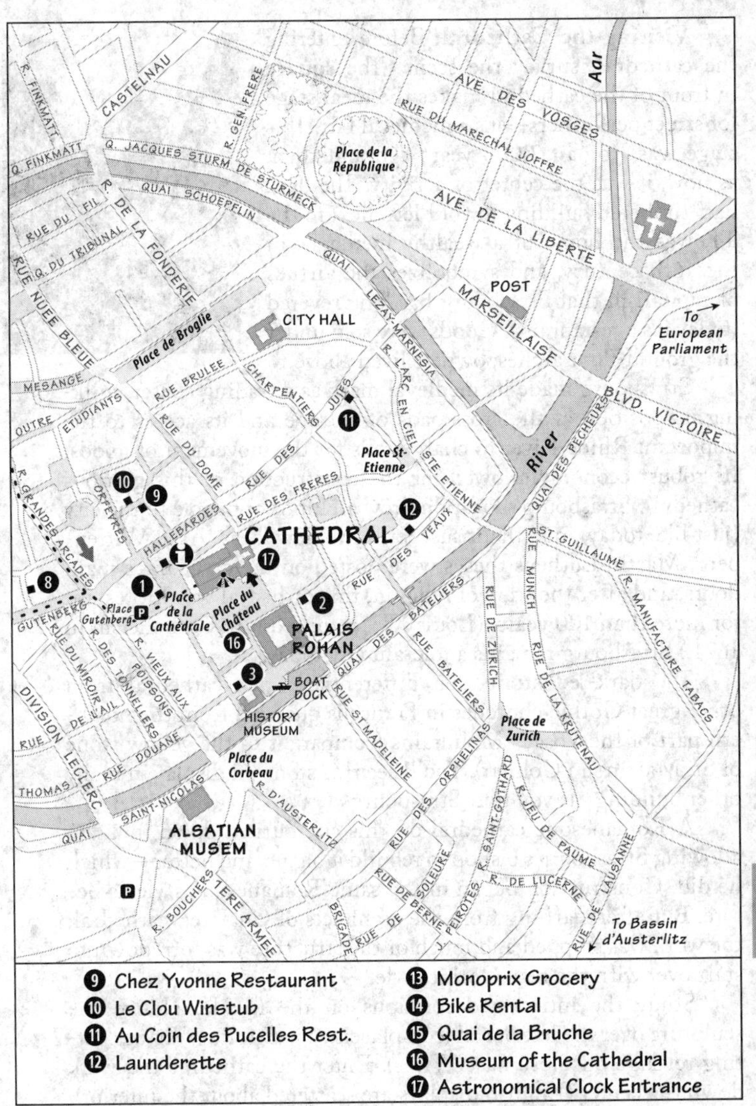

1800s. A matching second tower was planned but never built. The delicate Gothic style of the cathedral (begun in 1176, not finished until 1429) is another Franco-German concoction that somehow survived the French Revolution, the Franco-Prussian War, World War I, and World War II (though it was damaged by British and American bombing raids in World War II).

Cost and Hours: Free, daily 7:00-11:15 & 12:45-19:00. The midday closing is for a special €2 viewing of the astronomical clock (described later).

Visiting the Cathedral: Before entering the cathedral, survey the scene. The **square** in front of the cathedral makes the ideal stage for street performers—it's a medieval fair. This stage was Roman 2,000 years ago and then, as now, it was the center of activity. The dark half-timbered building to your left, next to the TI, was the home of a wealthy merchant in the 16th century, and symbolizes the virtues of capitalism that Strasbourg has long revered (today it's a restaurant). Goods were sold under the ground-floor arches; owners lived above.

Strasbourg made its medieval mark as a trading center, milking its position at the crossroads of Europe and its access to the important Rhine River to charge tolls for the movement of goods. Its robust economy allowed for the construction of this glorious cathedral. Strasbourg's location drew all kinds of people to the city (just like today), making it susceptible to new ideas. As at Wittenberg, Martin Luther's theses were posted on the cathedral's main doors, and after the wars of religion, this cathedral was Protestant for more than 100 years. (Louis XIV returned it to Catholicism in 1621.) Strasbourg remains a tolerant city today.

The dark-red **stone** that differentiates this cathedral from other great Gothic churches in France is quarried from the northern part of the Vosges Mountains (compare it to the yellow stone of St. Martin's in Colmar). You'll see this stone on display in many other buildings as you tour Strasbourg.

A Romanesque cathedral on this site burned down in 1176, allowing Strasbourg's bishop to rebuild it bigger and better—which he did. Construction began in the same Romanesque style as before. But after learning from the architects of Chartres' cathedral, the work was stopped and much of the structure was torn down to start over with the new Gothic style.

Study the intricate decorations on the facade. Notice the sculpture over the left portal (complacent, spear-toting Virtues getting revenge on those nasty Vices). Enter the cathedral and walk down the center (English displays are scattered about the interior). The stained glass on the lower left windows shows various rulers of Strasbourg; the stained glass on your right depicts Bible stories. An exquisite, gold-leafed organ hangs above the second pillars. Admire the elaborately carved stone pulpit. Walk to the choir and find a seat. Gaze into the Byzantine-like scene and find the stained-glass image of Mary with the European Union flag at the top.

Inside the right transept is a high-tech, 15th-century **astronomical clock** (restored in 1883, English explanation below) that gives a ho-hum performance every 15 minutes (keep your eye on the little angel about 15 feet up, slightly left of center). The show is better on the half-hour (angel on the right) and best at 12:30 (everybody gets in the act, including a rooster and 12 apostles—for the 12 hours; this performance is viewable only with a special ticket, described next).

The church is cleared out every day but Sunday between 11:15 and 12:45 for a special presentation of the clock. Visitors pay €2 to enter through the right transept and see a 20-minute movie (with English) that explains the clock's workings, then witness the real event.

For €5 you can climb 332 steps to the **top of the narthex** for an amazing view over Strasbourg, the Alsace, the Rhine, and the Black Forest (free first Sun of the month, access on right side of cathedral, daily April-Sept 9:00-19:15, Oct-March 10:00-17:15, last ascent 30 minutes before closing).

Nearby: Find flying buttress views outside the cathedral's right transept near **Palais Rohan** described later). Before leaving the cathedral area, investigate the network of tidy pedestrian streets that connect the cathedral with the huge Place Kléber. Each street is named for the primary trade that took place there.

▲Alsatian Museum

One of Strasbourg's oldest and most characteristic homes hosts this extensive and well-presented collection of Alsatian folk art. Thanks to its thorough audioguide and printed English explanations, you'll learn much about Alsatian life and traditions from birth to death. Rooms you'd find in traditional homes are beautifully re-created here (including an impressive kitchen), and models explain the ins and outs of half-timbered construction. The tools, pottery, toys, and costumes cover Alsatian culture over the centuries, including a good overview of the life of a winemaker.

Cost and Hours: €7, Wed-Mon 10:00-18:00, closed Tue, across the river and down a block to the right from the boat dock, at 23 Quai St. Nicholas—see map on page 978, tel. 03 88 52 50 01, www.musees.strasbourg.eu.

Other Strasbourg Museums

These four museums lie outside the cathedral's right transept and are interesting only for aficionados with particular interests or who have a full day in Strasbourg. The first three are in **Palais Rohan,** a stately former palace. The **Archaeological Museum,** the best one, has a stellar presentation of Alsatian civilization through the millennia (includes free audioguide). The **Museum of Decorative Arts** feels like the Versailles of Strasbourg, with grand reception rooms, a king's bedroom (where Louis XV and Marie-Antoinette both slept), a big library, and rooms displaying ceramic dishes, ancient clocks, and more—borrow the English booklet. The **Museum**

of Fine Arts holds a small, well-displayed collection of paintings from the Middle Ages to the Baroque period, some by artists you'll recognize. The **Museum of the Cathedral** (Musée de l'Œuvre Notre-Dame) is a well-organized museum near Palais Rohan that has plenty of church artifacts.

Cost and Hours: €6.50 for each smuseum, €12 day pass covers all four, free for those under 18 and on the first Sun of the month; open Wed-Mon 10:00-18:00, closed Tue—except for Museum of the Cathedral, which is closed Mon but open Tue 10:00-18:00; Palais Rohan—2 Place du Château, Museum of the Cathedral—3 Place du Château; tel. 03 88 52 50 00, www.musees.strasbourg.eu.

▲La Petite France

The historic home to Strasbourg's tanners, millers, and fishermen, this charming area is laced with canals, crowned with magnificent half-timbered homes, carpeted with cobblestones, and filled with tourists. As quaint as it looks, keep in mind that this neighborhood was leveled in World War II.

From the cathedral, walk down to Place Gutenberg and continue straight, following Rue Gutenberg (on the square's right side). Cross big Rue des Francs-Bourgeois and keep straight (now on Grande Rue). Turn left on the third little street (Rue du Bouclier, street signs are posted behind you), and make your way to the middle of the bridge (Pont St. Martin) for a good view. Find your way down to the river and follow the walkway over the lock deep into La Petite France. Make friends with a leafy café table on **Place Benjamin Zix,** or find the siesta-friendly parks between the canals across the bridge at Rue des Moulins. Notice the sloping roofs with openings in the roofs where leather hides were dried. Climb the once-fortified grassy wall (Barrage Vauban) for a decent view—the glass structure behind you is the splashy modern-art museum (interesting more for its architecture than its collection).

La Petite France's coziest café tables line the canal on **Quai de la Bruche.** From here it's a 10-minute walk back to the station: With the river on your left, walk along Quai de Turckheim, cross the third bridge, and find Rue du Maire Kuss.

STRASBOURG ACTIVITIES

Boat Ride on the Ill River

To see the cityscape from the water, take a loop cruise around Strasbourg. The glass-topped boats are air-conditioned and sufficiently comfortable—both sides have fine views. You'll pass through two locks as you circle the old city clockwise. The highlight for me was cruising by the European Parliament buildings and the European Court of Human Rights.

Cost and Hours: Adults-€12.50, 70 minutes, good English commentary with live guide or audioguide; April-Oct daily 9:45-19:30, runs later in high season, shorter hours off-season, dock is 2 blocks outside cathedral's right transept, where Rue Rohan meets the river, tel. 03 88 84 13 13, www.batorama.fr.

Traditional Music and Dancing

On Sunday mornings from late June to early September, look for Alsatian folk dancing on Place Gutenberg (starts at about 11:00). During the same season on Mondays, Tuesdays, and Wednesdays at 20:30, listen to traditional music on these squares (Mon—Place des Tripiers, Tue—in La Petite France on Place Benjamin Zix, and Wed—Place du Marché aux Cochons de Lait).

Summer Outdoor Shows

Strasbourg keeps its visitors entertained until the wee hours in summer. Every day from about mid-July to late August, the soaring cathedral is bathed in colorful lights that allow visitors to "contemplate the cathedral and its architecture from a new, contemporary perspective." The **sound-and-light show** is free and runs every 20 minutes until 24:30 (starts at 22:30 in July and 22:10 in Aug). And every day in July and August, a **water-and-light show** explodes over the city featuring fireworks and multimedia effects (free, at 22:30 in July and at 22:00 in Aug, lasts about 30 minutes, location can change—check at TI; in 2014 it was at Barrage Vauban).

Christmas Market

From the last Saturday of November until December 31, the city bustles and sparkles with its delightful Christkindelsmärik, held on several squares in the old town (hotel rates climb).

Sleeping in Strasbourg

Strasbourg is quiet in the summer (July-Aug), when 4,000 Eurocrats leave town and hotel prices fall—and slammed when the parliament is in session, throughout December (thanks to the Christmas market), and during major conferences.

$$$ Hôtel Cathédrale*** is comfortable and contemporary, with a Jack-and-the-beanstalk spiral stairway (elevator begins one floor up) and a hopelessly confusing floor plan. This modern yet atmospheric place lets you stare at the cathedral point-blank from your room (small Db with no view-€100, medium Db with no view-€160, larger Db with view-€190-210, lower prices possible on weekends, frequent Web promotions, buffet breakfast-€13, air-con, Wi-Fi, laundry service, free bicycles for up to 2 hours, book ahead for one of 5 parking spaces-€18/day, 12-13 Place de la Cathédrale, tel. 03 88 22 12 12, toll-free in France 08 00 00 00 84, www.hotel-cathedrale.fr, reserv@hotel-cathedrale.fr).

$$$ Hôtel Ibis*** faces the train station (you can't miss it) and delivers its usual comfort and amenities at fair rates (Db-€120, 10 Place de la Gare, tel. 03 88 23 98 98, www.ibishotel.com, h3018@accor.com).

$$ Hôtel Suisse,** across from the cathedral's right transept and off Place du Château, is a welcoming, central, and solid two-star value (Sb-€70-85, Db-€85-95, extra person-€10, breakfast-€10, elevator, free loaner bikes, Wi-Fi, cozy lounge-café, 2 Rue de la Râpe, tel. 03 88 35 22 11, www.hotel-suisse.com, info@hotel-suisse.com, engaging owner Edith).

$$ Hôtel des Arts,** located in the thick of things above a busy café, is a young-at-heart, simple but comfortable, good-value place with tight bathrooms. Rooms in front are fun but noisy (Sb or Db-€80, cheap breakfast-€6.50, air-con, Wi-Fi, 10 Place du Marché aux Cochons de Lait, tel. 03 88 37 98 37, www.hotel-arts.com, info@hotel-arts.com).

$$ Hôtel du Dragon*** is a tasteful, well-run, and spotless business-class place that's handy for drivers, as they'll park your car for free overnight (standard Db-€98, bigger Db-€119-152, breakfast buffet-€12, 12 Rue du Dragon, tel. 03 88 35 79 80, www.dragon.fr, hotel@dragon.fr).

Eating in Strasbourg

Atmospheric *winstubs* (wine bars) serving affordable salads and *tarte flambée* are a snap to find. If the weather is nice, head for La Petite France and choose ambience over cuisine—dine outside at any café/*winstub* that appeals to you. Stock up on picnic supplies at the Monoprix (Mon-Sat 8:30-20:30) on Place Kléber or for gourmet Alsatian specialties at shops on Rue des Orfèvres and take them to the park near Barrage Vauban.

IN AND NEAR LA PETITE FRANCE

I like the vibe and prices at **La Corde à Linge** on 2 Place Benjamin Zix (big salads, burgers, and several intriguing *Spätzle plats* from €12, tel. 03 88 22 15 17, www.lacordealinge.com).

The touristy **Restaurant au Pont St-Martin** owns a postcard-perfect facade and a fine position on the river, with the best seating on the riverside balcony. It serves good-enough meals at reasonable prices (€10-17 *plats,* 15 Rue des Moulins, tel. 03 88 32 45 13, www.pont-saint-martin.com).

Brasserie la Lanterne, between La Petite France and the cathedral, is a beloved, down-and-dirty, Alsatian microbrewery filled with students and hip locals. This place is famous for its home brews and cheap cuisine (€6-7 *tarte flambée*) and makes me want to plot a revolution (daily 16:00-very late, near Place Kléber at 5 Rue de la Lanterne, tel. 03 88 32 10 10).

NEAR THE CATHEDRAL

For a real meal, skip the touristy restaurants on the cathedral square and along Rue du Maroquin. Consider these nearby places instead; the first two are one block behind the TI (go left out of the TI, then take the first left through the passageway and keep walking).

Chez Yvonne (marked *S'Burjerstuewel* above windows), right out of a Bruegel painting, has a tradition of good food at fair prices. Try the *coq au Riesling* or *choucroute garnie* (€17 each) or the €12 *salade alsacienne* (reservations smart on weekends and holidays, dinner served from 18:00, open late daily, 10 Rue du Sanglier, tel. 03 88 32 84 15, www.restaurant-chez-yvonne.net).

The very cozy **Le Clou Winstub** is half a block left down Rue du Chaudron at #3. This place often looks closed from the outside, but don't be shy (€8-11 salads, €13-20 *plats du jour*, closed Sun, dinner served from 17:30, tel. 03 88 32 11 67, www.le-clou.com).

Au Coin des Pucelles is an institution in the gourmet world of Strasbourg. Roland Rohfritsch and his sister Myriam welcome diners at shared tables in a warm atmosphere and serve generous portions of Alsacian dishes—try the €24 duck *choucroute* (dinner only from 18:30, closed Sun-Mon, reservations recommended, 12 Rue des Pucelles, tel. 03 88 35 35 14).

Strasbourg Connections

Strasbourg makes a good side-trip from Colmar or a stop on the way to or from Paris.

From Strasbourg by Train to: Colmar (2/hour, 35 minutes), **Reims** (10/day, 2 hours, change at Gare Champagne-Ardennes), **Paris'** Gare de l'Est (1-2/hour, 2.5 hours), **Lyon** (4/day direct, 4-5 hours), **Baden-Baden,** Germany (TGV: 1/day direct, 30 minutes; non-TGV train: roughly hourly, 70 minutes, change in Appenweier or Offenburg), **Karlsruhe,** Germany (TGV: 4/day direct, 40 minutes; non-TGV train: hourly, 1-1.5 hours, most with change in Appenweier or Offenburg), **Vienna,** Austria (TGV: 3/day, 5 hours, 2 changes; non-TGV train: 5/day, 6-12 hours, 2-3 changes), **Basel,** Switzerland (regional train: about 2/hour, 1-2 hours).

REIMS AND VERDUN

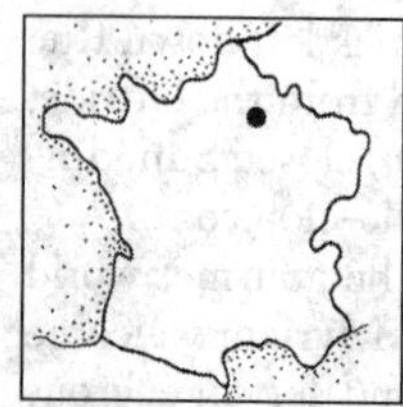

Different as night and day, bubbly Reims and brooding Verdun offer worthwhile stops between Paris and Alsace. The administrative capital of the Champagne region, bustling, modern Reims greets travelers with cellar doors wide open. It features a lively center, a historic cathedral, and, of course, Champagne tasting. Often overlooked, quiet Verdun is famous for the brutal World War I battles that surrounded the city and pummeled the countryside, and offers an exceptional opportunity to learn about the Great War. High-speed TGV trains make both of these destinations easily accessible to travelers (particularly if coming from Paris).

PLANNING YOUR TIME

Organized travelers in a hurry can see Reims and Verdun as they travel between Paris and the Alsace, though most will want an overnight (Reims is the better choice) to best appreciate the sights. Plan on most of a day for Reims and a half-day for Verdun. It's about 70 miles between the two towns, making a day trip from Reims to Verdun worth considering if you have a car—but it's too difficult by train. Day-tripping by train from Paris to Reims is a breeze, but day-tripping to Verdun requires careful planning.

GETTING AROUND REIMS AND VERDUN

Driving is a good option, even in the bigger city of Reims, and many find this a good place to pick up a rental car for a longer trip after leaving Paris (but be aware that all rental agencies are closed 12:00-14:00). Train travelers from Paris will reach Reims before drivers get out of the city.

Reims is easily walkable and offers excellent public transportation, with a tramway and handy buses linking its major sights. In Verdun, those interested in touring the battlefield sights without a car have several options: Ride a hop-on, hop-off bus tour; take a taxi; or take a private tour. Or you could rent a car just for the day.

Frequent high-speed TGV trains link Paris and Reims in 45 minutes, and a few direct TGV trains link Paris and Verdun in 1.5 hours. Most trains between Reims and Verdun are slow, thanks to required transfers.

CHAMPAGNE'S CUISINE SCENE

Because Champagne is not often integrated into meals, cuisine in this region (otherwise without a strong traditional wine) suffers from a lack of originality. Much like Paris, Champagne borrows from the recipe books of other regions. Still, be on the lookout for anything cooked in Champagne, and try the warm dandelion salad with bacon bits *(salade de pissenlit)*. *La potée champenoise* is a blood pudding made from rabbit. Ample rivers make for flavorful trout *(truite)* dishes. *Jambon de Reims,* ham cooked in white wine or Champagne and wrapped in a pastry shell or coated with breadcrumbs, is popular in Reims, as is *andouillette* (tripe sausage). You may also find rooster cooked in the red wine known as Bouzy Rouge *(coq au vin de Bouzy)*. Brie cheese, made on Champagne's border, is a good choice. Other local cheeses include Cendré de Champagne (similar to Brie but the size of a large Camembert, with a thin, edible ash covering), Chaource, Soumaintrain, and Langres. Fruit-flavored brandies are a common way to end an evening.

Reims

With its Roman gate, Gothic cathedral, Champagne *caves,* and vibrant pedestrian zone, Reims feels both historic and youthful. And thanks to the TGV bullet train, it's less than an hour's ride from Paris.

Reims (pronounced like "rance") has a turbulent history: This is where 25 French kings were crowned, where Champagne first bubbled, where WWI devastation met miraculous reconstruction during the Art Deco age, and where the Germans officially surrendered in 1945, bringing World War II to a close in Europe. The town's sights give you an entertaining peek at the entire story.

PLANNING YOUR TIME

You can see Reims' essential sights in an easy day, either as a day trip from Paris or as a stop en route to or from Paris. Frequent

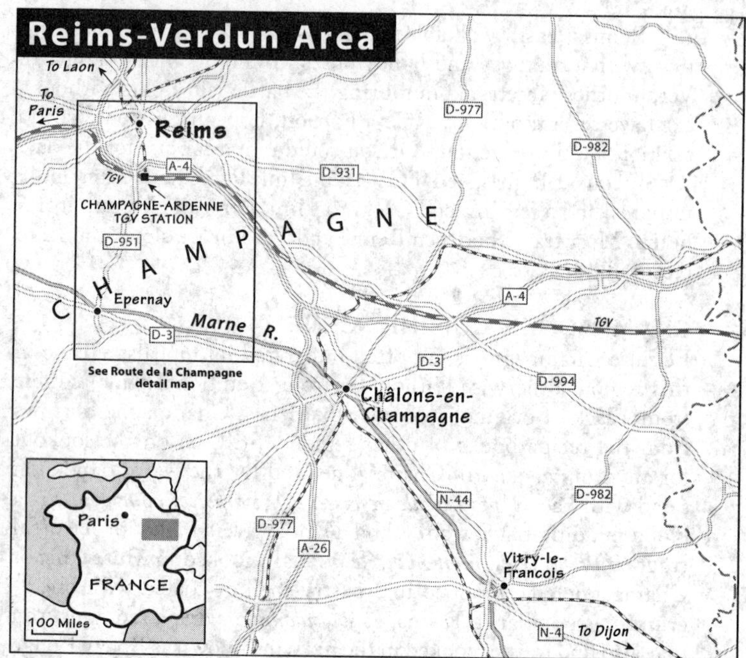

TGV trains make the trip from Paris a breeze (allow about €70 round-trip; if using a rail pass, book your TGV reservations as soon as possible). Take a morning train from Paris and explore the cathedral and city center before lunch, then spend your afternoon below ground, in a cool, chalky Champagne cellar or *cave* (pronounced "kahv"). You can be back at your Parisian hotel by dinner. Those continuing to destinations farther east find Reims a convenient place to rent a car. With a car, it's worth taking a few hours to joyride the Champagne road that leaves from Reims' back step (described later).

To best experience contemporary Reims, explore the busy shopping streets between the cathedral and the Reims-Centre train station. Rue de Vesle, Rue Condorcet, and Place Drouet d'Erlon are most interesting.

Orientation to Reims

Reims' hard-to-miss cathedral marks the city center and makes an easy orientation landmark. Most sights of interest are within a 15-minute walk from the Reims-Centre train station. City buses and taxis connect the harder-to-reach Champagne *caves* with the central train station and cathedral. The city has ambitiously reno-

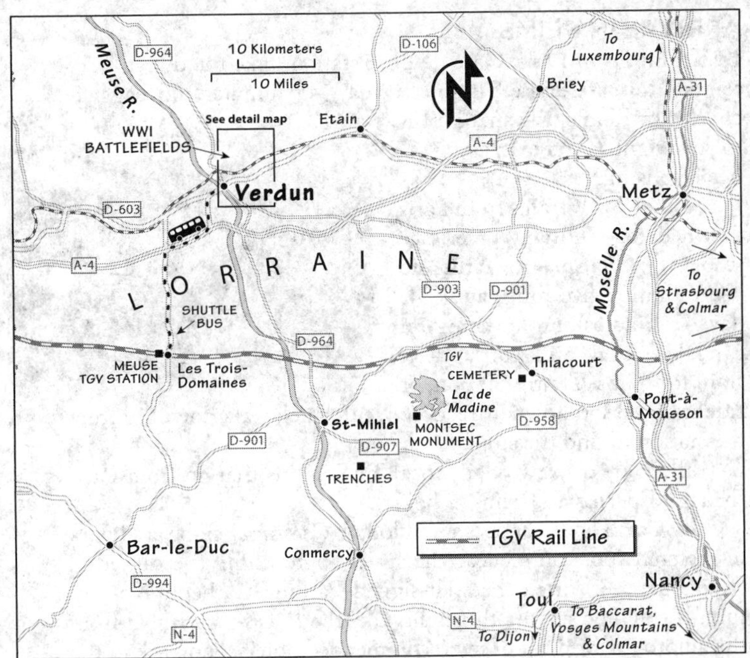

vated its downtown, converting large areas into pedestrian-friendly zones.

TOURIST INFORMATION

The main TI is located outside the **cathedral**'s left (north) transept (TI open Easter-Sept Mon-Sat 9:00-19:00, Sun 10:00-18:00, Oct-Easter Mon-Sat 9:00-18:00, Sun 10:00-16:00; public WCs across street, tel. 03 26 77 45 00, www.reims-tourisme.com). A smaller yet handy TI lies just outside the Reims-Centre **train station** (Mon-Sat 8:30-12:30 & 13:00-18:00—until 19:00 on Fri, Sun 11:00-17:00).

At either TI, pick up free maps of the town center, the bus and tram routes, and the Champagne *caves*. The cathedral TI rents audioguides covering the cathedral, city center, and Art Deco architecture (€6, additional headset-€5, 1-2 hours each, designed to be shared).

Either TI can book a visit to the *caves* at Mumm or Martel (note that most *caves* require advance booking), and they'll call a taxi to get you to any *cave* (about €10). TIs also have information on minivan excursions into the vineyards and Champagne villages. For more information on reservations and reaching the *caves*, see "Champagne Tours and Sights," on page 1002.

ARRIVAL IN REIMS

By Train: From Paris' Gare de l'Est station, take the direct TGV to the **Reims-Centre Station** (12/day, 45 minutes, no baggage check). In Reims, the small TI is to your right as you exit; a taxi office is to your left.

Other TGV trains from Paris destined for Germany or Alsace stop at **Champagne-Ardenne** TGV Station five miles away (4/day, 45 minutes). From there, you can take a local "milk-run" (TER) train to Reims-Centre Station, or ride tram #B into town (direction: Neufchâtel; walk downhill from the station to find the stop).

There are also two daily local TER trains that go from Paris through Epernay to Reims (2 hours).

By Car: Day-trippers should follow *Cathédrale* signs, and park in metered spots on or near the street approaching the cathedral (Rue Libergier) or in the well-signed Parking Cathédrale structure. If you'll be staying the night, take the *Reims-Centre* exit from the autoroute for most of my recommended hotels, and park in the Erlon parking garage.

HELPFUL HINTS

Department Store: Monoprix, inside the Espace Drouet d'Erlon shopping center, provides one-stop shopping for toiletries, cheap clothing, and groceries (Mon-Sat 9:00-20:00, closed Sun, basement level, 53 Place Drouet d'Erlon, follow *FNAC* signs).

Taxi: Taxi offices are at the train station and at 40 Rue Carnot, next to the Opéra. Or you can call 03 26 47 05 05 or 03 26 36 19 88.

Laundry: A convenient launderette is just south of the cathedral (daily 8:00-20:00, 59 Rue Chanzy).

Car Rental: Avis is just outside the central train station at 20 Rue Pingat (tel. 03 26 47 10 08, use the *Clairmarais* exit from the station, turn right, and walk 200 yards). **Europcar** is at 76 Boulevard Lundy (tel. 03 26 88 59 40); **Hertz** is at 26 Boulevard Joffre (tel. 03 26 47 98 78). Rental agencies are usually open Mon-Sat 8:00-12:00 & 14:00-19:00, closed Sun.

City Bus Tours: "Reims Open Tour" takes a one-hour circuit of the city and nearby vineyards with recorded narration and with the top open in good weather (3-5 trips/day, €10, tickets and departure from TI at the cathedral).

GETTING AROUND REIMS

By Bus or Tram: Reims has an integrated network of colorful buses and trams (www.citura.fr, French only). You can purchase tickets onboard the bus from the driver but not on trams; instead, use ticket machines at any tram stop (€1.50/1 hour, €2.50/2 hours, €3.70/24 hours, instructions in English, pay with cash, coins only). Your ticket is valid for unlimited transfers between all buses and trams, even a round-trip on the same line. Each time you board a bus or tram, hold your ticket on the validation machine until you hear a beep.

The tram system's two lines—#A and #B—connect Reims' two train stations and travel on to a few stops in town (about every 10 minutes, fewer on Sun). To get from either station to the cathedral, main TI, and town center, take a tram to the Opéra stop.

A few bus routes are particularly useful for reaching the less central Champagne cellars (listed later in this chapter). These small Citadine buses run along two loop routes (#1 and #2). Key stops are shown on the map on page 992 (€1.50, 3/hour Mon-Sat, none on Sun, don't confuse Citadine buses with regular bus #1). Regular fixed-route buses also cover the city center; the most useful ones are listed under each sight.

BLITZ VISIT FOR TRAIN TRAVELERS

If you're racing through Reims, here's a quick walking plan that follows the order of its main sights (described below in more detail). Reims' highlights can be seen on foot in a three-hour sightseeing stroll from the train station (add another hour if you plan to visit a cellar). Pick up a town map from the TI just outside the train station before you begin.

From the station (which retains its original 1860 facade), walk directly into the park out front. Find the statue of hometown boy Jean-Baptiste Colbert, the finance minister of Louis XIV back in the 17th century.

The **park,** or Grande Allée des Promenades, was originally a garden outside the city walls. In 1848, when it was clear that Reims didn't need a protective wall, the fortifications were demolished to create a three-mile-long circular boulevard. Look at your town map to see the "left-foot"-shaped outline left by the wall.

From Colbert, angle to the right, cross what was the wall, and walk along **Place Drouet d'Erlon.** This long, pedestrianized street-like square marks the commercial center of town. It's Reims' "little Champs-Elysées." The square's centerpiece is a fountain and column crowned by a glistening gold-winged figure of Victory. (The original Victory, from 1906, was melted down by the Nazis—the current one is a recent replacement.) The fountain—with four voluptuous women—celebrates the four major rivers of this district. After one

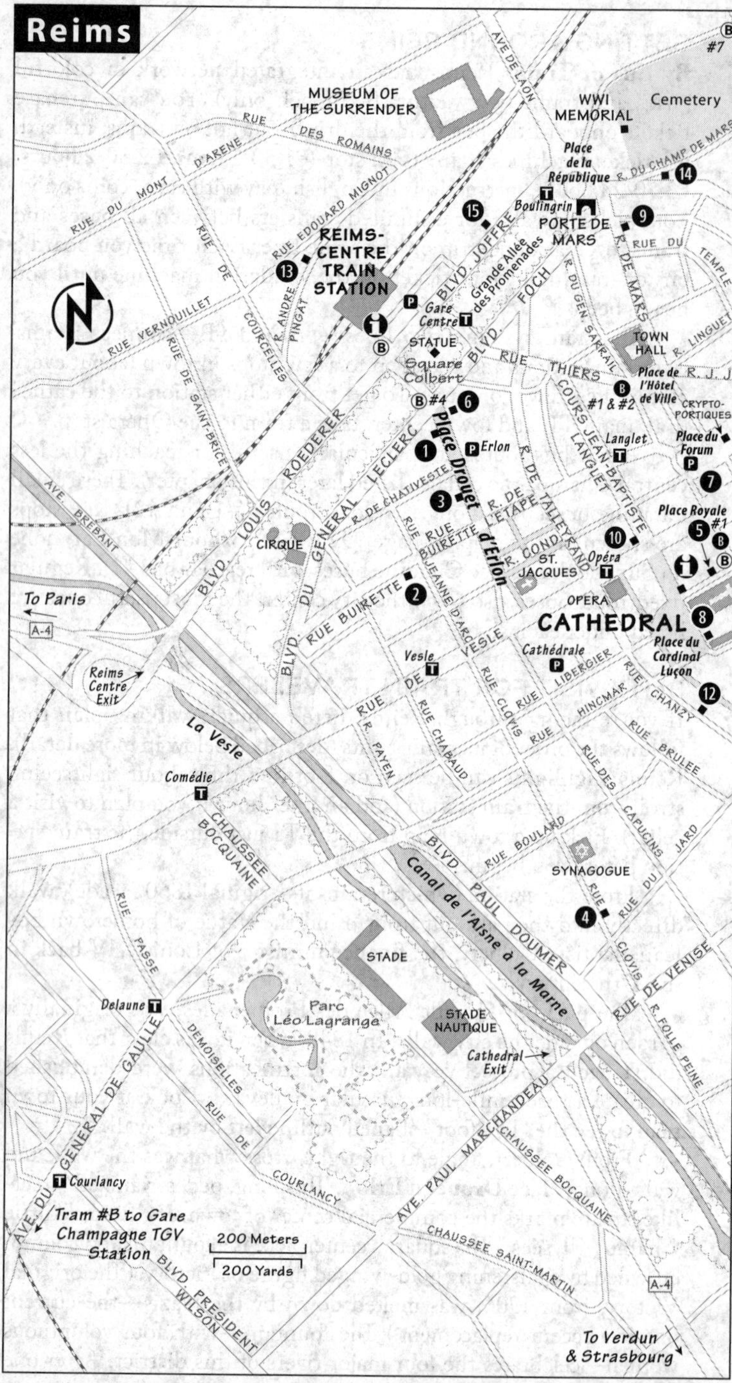
Reims
MUSEUM OF THE SURRENDER
WWI MEMORIAL
Cemetery
Place de la République
R. DU CHAMP DE MARS
Boulingrin
PORTE DE MARS
REIMS-CENTRE TRAIN STATION
Gare Centre
STATUE
Square Colbert
BLVD. JOFFRE
Grande Allée des Promenades
BLVD. FOCH
RUE THIERS
TOWN HALL
Place de l'Hôtel de Ville
#1 & #2
CRYPTO-PORTIQUES
Place du Forum
Langlet
Place Royale
#1
#4
Place Drouet d'Erlon
Erlon
COURS JEAN-BAPTISTE LANGLET
R. DE TALLEYRAND
R. DE L'ETAPE
R. COND
ST. JACQUES
Opéra
OPERA
CATHEDRAL
Place du Cardinal Luçon
Cathédrale
RUE LIBERGIER
RUE HINCMAR
RUE CHANZY
RUE BRULEE
RUE DES CAPUCINS
RUE DU JARD
SYNAGOGUE
RUE CLOVIS
RUE DE VENISE
R. FOLLE PEINE
CIRQUE
BLVD. LOUIS ROEDERER
BLVD. DU GENERAL LECLERC
R. DE CHATIVESTE
RUE BUIRETTE
RUE JEANNE D'ARC
RUE DE VESLE
Vesle
R. PAYEN
RUE CHABAUD
RUE BOULARD
BLVD. PAUL DOUMER
Canal de l'Aisne à la Marne
La Vesle
To Paris
A-4
Reims Centre Exit
AVE. BREBANT
RUE DU MONT D'ARENE
RUE DES ROMAINS
RUE EDOUARD MIGNOT
RUE VERNOUILLET
RUE DE COURCELLES
RUE DE SAINT-BRICE
R. ANDRE PINGAT
AVE DE LAON
RUE DE MARS
RUE DU TEMPLE
R. DU GEN. SARRAIL
R. LINGUET
R. J. J.
Comédie
CHAUSSEE BOCQUAINE
RUE PASSE
Delaune
STADE
STADE NAUTIQUE
Parc Léo Lagrange
Cathedral Exit
AVE. PAUL MARCHANDEAU
RUE DES DEMOISELLES
RUE DE COURLANCY
AVE. DU GENERAL DE GAULLE
Courlancy
Tram #B to Gare Champagne TGV Station
200 Meters
200 Yards
BLVD PRESIDENT WILSON
CHAUSSEE SAINT-MARTIN
A-4
To Verdun & Strasbourg
#7

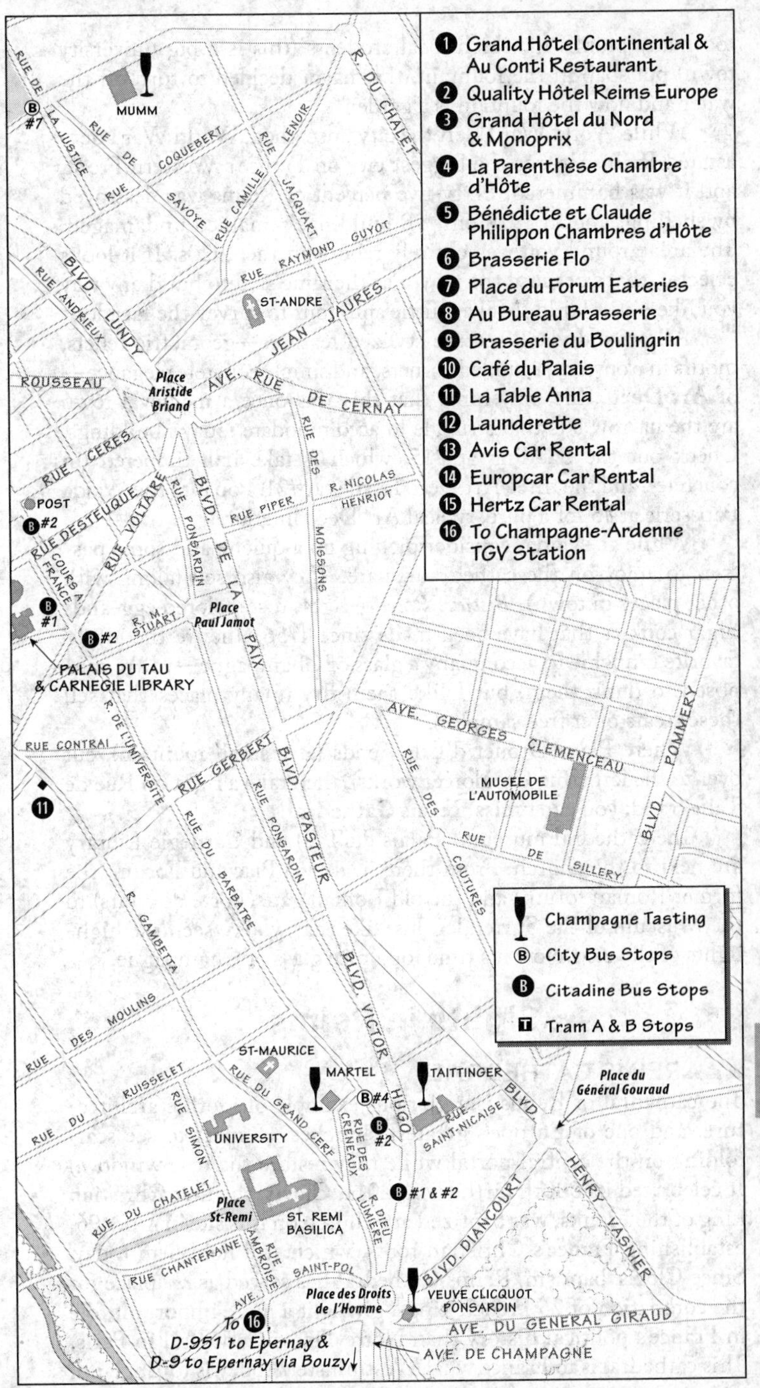

1 Grand Hôtel Continental & Au Conti Restaurant
2 Quality Hôtel Reims Europe
3 Grand Hôtel du Nord & Monoprix
4 La Parenthèse Chambre d'Hôte
5 Bénédicte et Claude Philippon Chambres d'Hôte
6 Brasserie Flo
7 Place du Forum Eateries
8 Au Bureau Brasserie
9 Brasserie du Boulingrin
10 Café du Palais
11 La Table Anna
12 Launderette
13 Avis Car Rental
14 Europcar Car Rental
15 Hertz Car Rental
16 To Champagne-Ardenne TGV Station
Champagne Tasting
City Bus Stops
Citadine Bus Stops
Tram A & B Stops
MUMM
RUE DE LA JUSTICE
RUE DE COQUEBERT
RUE SAVOYE
RUE CAMILLE LENOIR
RUE JACQUART
R. DU CHALET
RUE RAYMOND GUYOT
ST-ANDRE
BLVD. LUNDY
RUE ANDRIEUX
ROUSSEAU
Place Aristide Briand
AVE. JEAN JAURES
RUE DE CERNAY
RUE CERES
POST
RUE DESTEUQUE
RUE VOLTAIRE
RUE PONSARDIN
BLVD. DE LA PAIX
RUE DES MOISSONS
RUE PIPER
R. NICOLAS HENRIOT
COURS A. FRANCE
R. M. STUART
Place Paul Jamot
PALAIS DU TAU & CARNEGIE LIBRARY
R. DE L'UNIVERSITE
RUE CONTRAI
RUE GERBERT
BLVD. PASTEUR
RUE PONSARDIN
RUE DU BARBATRE
AVE. GEORGES CLEMENCEAU
BLVD. POMMERY
MUSEE DE L'AUTOMOBILE
RUE DES COUTURES
RUE DE SILLERY
R. GAMBETTA
RUE DES MOULINS
RUE DU RUISSELET
ST-MAURICE
RUE DU GRAND CERF
MARTEL
BLVD. VICTOR HUGO
TAITTINGER
RUE SAINT-NICAISE
Place du Général Gouraud
RUE SIMON
UNIVERSITY
RUE DES CRENEAUX
R. DIEU LUMIERE
RUE DU CHATELET
Place St-Remi
ST. REMI BASILICA
BLVD. DIANCOURT
BLVD. HENRY VASNIER
RUE CHANTERAINE
RUE AMBROISE
SAINT-POL
AVE.
Place des Droits de l'Homme
VEUVE CLICQUOT PONSARDIN
AVE. DU GENERAL GIRAUD
AVE. DE CHAMPAGNE
To 16, D-951 to Epernay & D-9 to Epernay via Bouzy

too many pranks in which local students (this is a big university town) put soap in the fountain, the mayor decided to turn off the water and now the fountain is a garden.

While World War II left the city unscathed, World War I devastated Reims. It was the biggest city on France's Western Front, and it was hammered. Sixty-five percent of Reims was destroyed by shelling, and in 1918 only 70 buildings remained undamaged. The area around you was entirely rebuilt in the 1920s. If it looks eclectic, that's because the mayor at the time said to build any way you like—just build. Make a little spin tour to survey the facades.

All around you'll see the stylized features—geometric reliefs, motifs in ironwork, rounded corners, and simple concrete elegance—of **Art Deco.** The only hints that this was once a medieval town are the narrow lots that struggle to accommodate today's buildings. Check out the building at #15, which is fake half-timbered (in concrete), and the three Art Deco facades at #21. Pop into the Waida Pâtisserie at #5 for a pure, typical Art Deco interior.

While at Waida, consider picking up a quiche and some pastries to enjoy on the cathedral square. They also sell (along with other places in town) *"Biscuits Roses"*—light, rose-colored egg-and-sugar cookies that have been made since 1756. They're the locals' favorite munchie to accompany a glass of Champagne—you're supposed to dunk them, but I like them dry (many places that sell these treats offer free samples).

Where Place Drouet d'Erlon ends (at a small fountain), cut over to the left (Rue Condorcet works), then take a right on Rue de Talleyrand; you can't miss **Reims Cathedral.**

The cathedral museum (Palais du Tau) and Carnegie Library are next to the church. From there, walk via Place du Forum (the former Roman forum) and the old Roman gate (Porte de Mars) to the Museum of the Surrender. Just like that, you've seen the highlights of the city. Now it's time for a nice glass of Champagne.

Sights in Reims

▲▲▲REIMS CATHEDRAL

The cathedral of Reims is a glorious example of Gothic architecture, and one of Europe's greatest churches. (Expect to see scaffolding on the central portal while they restore the rose window.) It celebrated its 800th birthday in 2011. Clovis, the first Christian king of the Franks, was baptized at a church on this site in A.D. 496, establishing France's Christian roots, which still hold firm today. Since Clovis' baptism, Reims Cathedral has served as *the* place for the coronation of 26 French kings, giving it a more important role in France's political history than Notre-Dame Cathedral in Paris. This cathedral is to France what Westminster Abbey is to England.

And there's lots more history here. A self-assured Joan of Arc led a less-assured Charles VII to be crowned here in 1429. Thanks to Joan, the French rallied around their new king to push the English out of France and finally end the Hundred Years' War. During the French Revolution, the cathedral was converted to a temple of reason (as was Paris' Notre-Dame). After the restoration of the monarchy, the cathedral hosted the crowning of Charles X in 1825—the last coronation here. During World War I about 300 shells hit the cathedral, damaging statues and windows and destroying the roof, but the structure survived. Then, during the 1920s, it was completely rebuilt, thanks in large part to financial support from John D. Rockefeller Jr.

Luckily, World War II spared the church, and since then it has come to symbolize reconciliation. A French plaque set in the pavement just in front recalls the 1962 Mass of Reconciliation between France and Germany. A German version of the marker was added in 2012, commemorating 50 years of friendship and celebrating the fact that another war today between these two nations would be unthinkable.

Cost and Hours: Free, daily 7:30-19:30, helpful information boards in English throughout the church, audioguides are rentable at the adjacent TI (though my self-guided tour below works well for most), www.reims-cathedral.culture.fr.

Getting There: The cathedral is a 15-minute walk from the Reims-Centre Station. Follow *sortie* signs for Place de la Gare, then walk to the TI on the right. Cross the tree-lined parkway and enter the pedestrianized Place Drouet d'Erlon. Turn left on Rue Condorcet, then right on Rue de Talleyrand. Or, to go by tram, find the stop on the square in front of the station (to the left of the statue). Take tram #A (direction: Hôpital Debré) or tram #B (direction: Gare Champagne TGV) two stops to the Opéra stop—the cathedral and TI are behind the Opéra building.

Cathedral Tower: An escorted one-hour tour climbs the 250 steps of the tower for those who'd like to explore the rooftop and enjoy a close-up look at the Gallery of Kings statuary (€7.50, €11 combo-ticket also covers Palais du Tau; tower closed Sun mornings in May-Sept, only open Fri-Sat and Sun afternoons in Oct-April; tours leave about hourly, get tickets and meet escort in the Palais du Tau).

Cathedral Sound and Light Show: For a memorable experience, join the crowd in front of the cathedral for a free, 25-minute sound-and-light show on most summer evenings. The colorful lights and booming sound take you through the ages, evoking the building's design and construction, the original appearance of the statuary, the coronations that occurred here, the faith of the community, and—during the centennial of the Great War—the shelling it absorbed during World War I. Sit directly in front of the cathedral or settle more comfortably into a seat at a café with a clear view through the trees. The show generally starts when it's dark—between 21:30 and 23:00 (nightly except Mon July-Aug, Fri-Sun only in May-June and Sept). Sometimes a second show commences 10 minutes after the first show ends.

➲ **Self-Guided Tour:** Begin your visit by admiring the cathedral's **West Portal.** It's perhaps the best west portal anywhere. Built under the direction of four different architects, it is remarkable for its unity and harmony. The church was started about 1211 and mostly finished just 60 years later. The 260-foot-tall towers were added in the 1400s; the spires intended to top them were never installed for lack of money.

Like the cathedrals in Paris and Chartres, this church is dedicated to **"Our Lady"** (Notre Dame). Statues depicting the crowning of the Virgin take center stage on the facade. For eight centuries Catholics have prayed to the Mother of God, kneeling here to ask her to intervene with God on their behalf. In 1429, Joan of Arc received messages here from Mary encouraging her to rally French troops against the English at the Siege of Orléans (a statue of Joan from 1896 is over your left shoulder as you face the church).

An ornate facade like this comes with a cohesive and carefully designed message. Study the carving. A good percentage of the statues are original and date from around 1250. There are **three main doors,** each with a theme carved into the limestone.

On the left is the **Passion** (the events leading up to and including the Crucifixion). Among the local saints shown below is the famous Smiling Angel, whose jovial expression has served the city well as its marketing icon. The central portal is dedicated to the **Virgin Mary,** featuring the Coronation of Mary with scenes from her life below. And on the right is the **Last Judgment,** with scenes from the apocalypse. Above the great rose window are reliefs of David (with his dog) and Goliath. Notice the fire damage, from 1914, around the rose window (fire melts limestone). Across the top is the **Gallery of Kings,** depicting 56 of France's kings. They flank the country's first Christian king, Clovis, who appears to be wearing a barrel—he's actually kneeling prayerfully at a baptismal font. These anonymous statues, without egos, are unnamed kings whose spiritual mission is to lead their people to God.

Before going inside, step around to the right side and study the exoskeletal nature of the church's structure. Braces on the outside—**flying buttresses**—soar up the sides of the church. These massive "beams" are critical to supporting the building, redirecting the weight of the roof outward (and into the ground), rather than downward on the supporting walls. With the support provided by the columns, arches, and buttresses, the walls—which no longer needed to be so solid and thick—became window holders.

The architects of Reims Cathedral were confident in their building practices. Gothic architects had learned by trial and error—many church roofs caved in as they tested their theories and strove to build ever higher. Work on Reims Cathedral began decades after the Notre-Dame cathedrals in Paris and Chartres, allowing architects to take advantage of what they'd learned from those magnificent earlier structures.

Contemplate the lives of the people in Reims who built this huge building in the 13th century. Construction on a scale like this required a wholesale community effort—all hands on deck. The builders of the Reims Cathedral gave it their all, in part because this was the church of France—where its kings were crowned. Most townsfolk who participated donated their money or their labor knowing that neither they, nor their children, would likely ever see it completed—such was their pride, dedication, and faith. Imagine the effort it took to raise the funds and manage the workforce. Master masons supervised, while the average Jean did much of the sweat work.

Now, step inside and stand at the back of the nearly 500-foot-long **nave.** The weight of the roof is supported by a few towering columns that seem to sprout crisscrossing pointed arches. This load-bearing skeleton of columns, arches, and buttresses allowed the church to grow higher, and liberated the walls to become window frames. Sun pours through the **stained glass,** bathing visitors and worshippers in divine light.

Take a look at the wall of **52 statues** stacked in rectangular blocks inside the door. (Cover the light from the door with this book to see better.) Imagine the 13th-century technology employed to carve each of these blocks in the nearby workshop and then install them so seamlessly here. These blocks continue the stories told by the statues on the outside.

Walk up the central aisle until you find a **plaque in the floor** marking the site of Clovis' baptism in 496. Back then, a much smaller, early Christian Roman church stood here. And back then you couldn't enter a church until you were baptized. Baptisteries stood outside churches, like the one that welcomed Clovis into the Christian faith.

Walk ahead to the **choir.** The set of candlesticks and crucifix at the high altar were given to the church by Charles X on the occasion of his coronation in 1825. Look back at the west wall. The original windows were lost in World War I; these, rebuilt from photographs, date from the 1930s.

Walk into the **south transept.** The WWI-destroyed windows here were replaced in 1954 by the local Champagne makers. The windows' scenes portray the tending of vines (left), the harvest (center), and the time-honored double-fermentation process (right). Notice, around the edges, the churches representing all the grape-producing villages in the area.

Looking high above at the ceiling, you'll see evidence of **bomb damage** from 1917, when the roof took direct hits and collapsed. (The lighter bricks are from the repair job in the 1920s.) The gray/white "grisaille" windows in this transept were installed in the 1970s. Many of the darker, more richly colored medieval glass windows were replaced by clear glass in the 18th and 19th centuries (when tastes called for more light).

The **apse** (east end, behind the altar) holds a luminous set of **Marc Chagall stained-glass windows** from 1974. Chagall's inimitable style lends itself to stained glass, and he enjoyed opportunities to adorn great churches with his windows. The left window illustrates scenes from the Old Testament, with the Tree of Jesse (with Jesse himself sleeping at the bottom) reaching up to Mary with the Christ Child. In the central panels, the cohesion of the Old and New Testament scenes is emphasized by the ladder that connects one to the other. On the right the Tree of Jesse—which is essentially a genealogical diagram of Christ's lineage—is extended to symbolically include the royalty of France, thus affirming the divine power of the monarchs and stressing their responsibility to rule with wisdom and justice. Featured are Clovis (at the bottom, with his bishop), St. Louis XIII (seen at the cathedral, and then dispensing justice), Charles VII (on the right in green), and Joan of Arc, in blue, holding her sword (on the far right).

For the cathedral's 800th anniversary in 2011, six modern, **abstract windows** were installed on either side of the Chagall windows. Just to the left is a 1901 statue of Joan of Arc, her face carved from ivory.

From here, behind the high altar, enjoy the best view of the entire nave. Seen from this distance, the west wall is an ensemble seemingly made entirely of glass. Look at the confidence of the design. Even the corners outside the rose window were glass, made without stone. The architects pulled out all the stops in this triumph of Gothic.

OTHER REIMS SIGHTS

Palais du Tau

This former Archbishop's Palace, named after the Greek letter T *(tau)* for its shape, houses artifacts from the cathedral next door and a pile of royal goodies. You'll look into the weathered eyes of original statues from the cathedral's facade, see precious tapestries, coronation jewels, and more.

Cost and Hours: €7.50, €11 combo-ticket also covers cathedral tower, May-Aug Tue-Sun 9:30-18:30, Sept-April Tue-Sun 9:30-12:30 & 14:00-17:30, closed Mon year-round, scant English information though an audioguide is available at TI for €6, tel. 03 26 47 81 79, www.palais-tau.monuments-nationaux.fr.

Visiting the Palace: The collections are in two distinct parts—the cathedral museum, with statues and tapestries, and the royal chapel and treasury, with jewels and artifacts. Most of the exhibits are on the upper level.

A highlight of the **cathedral museum** is the original centerpiece of the cathedral's west facade: the fire-damaged Coronation of Mary group, carved in the 13th century. In the same room, six figures from the Gallery of Kings stand as if guarding 16th-century tapestries. Originally hung around the choir in the center of the cathedral, the themes of these tapestries illustrating the Virgin's life supported the prayers and preaching of the faithful. Cases show tiny statues with traces of original paint. Admire the amazing detail of the carving.

The **royal chapel** was where the king would spend the night before his coronation, secluded in prayer. Inlaid in the floor are fleurs-de-lis, symbol of the French monarchy. At the altar are six candlesticks used at Napoleon's wedding in 1810.

Flanking the entry to the chapel are **treasury rooms** filled with royal valuables. On the left are examples that survived the melt-it-down mania of the French Revolution. Imagine the fury of the revolutionaries, who would melt down precious crowns and chalices to satisfy their practical need for gold and silver. Very little survived that wasn't buried away—these varied treasures were excavated from royal tombs in the 1920s (and survive in perfect condition). Don't miss the 9th-century talisman worn by Charlemagne and the exquisite chalice used by French royalty in the 12th century.

Another room is filled with gold-plated silver regalia made for the coronation of Charles X in 1825. The new pieces were necessary because the historic regalia had been melted down.

In the next room ponder the royal portraits and the 60-pound mantle of the divine king. Think of the dramatic swings in France's history: A generation after you cut off a king's head, you welcome a new king as if he were divine.

Before leaving, back on the **ground floor,** find the hall dedicated to the rebuilding of the cathedral after WWI bombings and the enlightened philanthropy of John D. Rockefeller Jr. When the roofs of Gothic churches burned, the lead that covered them melted and cascaded down like flowing rivers. Here, the gargoyles with once-molten lead spewing out their storm-drain mouths make that much easier to envision.

▲Carnegie Library (Bibliothèque Carnegie)

The legacy of the Carnegie Library network, funded generously by the 19th-century American millionaire Andrew Carnegie and his steel fortune (notice the American flag above the main entrance on the left), extends even to Reims. Carnegie believed knowledge could put an end to war, and he built several thousand such libraries around the world (he dedicated $200,000 for the one in Reims). Built in 1921 in the flurry of interwar reconstruction, this beautiful Art Deco building still houses the city's public library. Considering that admission is free and it's just behind the cathedral, it's worth a quick look.

Visitors are welcome to poke around but are asked not to enter the reading room. In the onyx-laden entry hall, small marble mosaics celebrate different fields of knowledge, and a chandelier hangs down like the sleek dress of a circa 1920s flapper. Peek through the reading room door to admire the stained-glass windows of this temple of thought. The gorgeous wood-paneled card-catalogue room takes older visitors back to their childhoods. Go ahead, finger the laboriously created typewritten files, and imagine the technology available back in 1928, the year the library was inaugurated.

Cost and Hours: Free; Tue-Wed and Fri-Sat 10:00-13:00 & 14:00-18:00, Thu 14:00-19:00, closed Sun-Mon; Place Carnegie, tel. 03 26 77 81 41.

Getting There: From the station, take tram #A or #B to the Opéra stop and walk five minutes, or take Citadine bus #2 to the Carnegie stop.

Place du Forum

Reims' main square recalls the forum or market that marked the center of the ancient city. Legend has it that Reims was founded by Remus (brother of Romulus), and so the tribe that lived here came to be called "Remes." This old town of 50,000 people was the capital of the Roman province of Gaullia-Belgica. From Place du Forum, you can climb down steps into the **Cryptoportique,** a first-century A.D. Roman gallery. About 10 feet below today's street level, this cool retreat was once the cloister that defined a sacred temple zone in the middle of the Roman Forum (free, daily June-Sept 14:00-18:00 only).

Porte de Mars

The only above-ground monument surviving from ancient Reims is this entry gate to the city (free, always open, at Place du Boulingrin). The Porte de Mars, built in the second century A.D., was one of four principal entrances into the ancient Gallo-Roman town. Inspired by triumphal arches that Rome built to herald war victories, this one was constructed to celebrate the Pax Romana (the period of peace and stability after Rome had vanquished all its foes). Unlike most structures in the rest of town, the gate was undamaged in World War I, but it bears the marks of other eras, such as its integration into the medieval ramparts.

Near the Porte de Mars (on Place de la République) stands a huge WWI memorial. Reims, the biggest city on the Western Front during the Great War, endured 1,051 days of shelling during those four years.

▲Museum of the Surrender (Musée de la Reddition)

WWII buffs enjoy visiting the place where the Germans signed the document of surrender of all German forces on May 7, 1945. The news was announced the next day, turning May 8 into Victory in Europe (V-E) Day. Anyone interested in World War II will find the extensive collection of artifacts fascinating, and it's thrilling to see the war room (or Signing Room), where the Allied operations were managed and the war ultimately was ended.

Start with the 10-minute video (next to the entry). Then climb upstairs to the museum and Signing Room. Imagine running the European Theater of Operation from here, as General Dwight Eisenhower did from February to May 1945 (after the Allies safely controlled the airspace). Covering the walls of the Signing Room are floor-to-ceiling maps showing troop positions, gas supplies, where train lines were functioning, and so on. Progress was painstakingly marked and updated every day. This is where General Eisenhower and the Allies received the unconditional surrender of the Germans. The chairs around the table, with name tags each in its original spot, show where the signatories sat.

Cost and Hours: €4, Wed-Mon 10:00-12:00 & 14:00-18:00, closed Tue, 12 Rue Franklin Roosevelt, tel. 03 26 47 84 19.

Getting There: It's a 10-minute walk from the Reims-Centre train station, or a five-minute ride on tram #A or #B (get off at the Boulingrin stop). Or catch bus #4 in front of the station (direction: La Neuvillette Mairie; go three stops to Mignot, then continue one more block on foot).

▲▲CHAMPAGNE TOURS AND SIGHTS

Reims, the capital of the Champagne region, offers many opportunities to visit its world-famous cellars. All charge entry fees, most have several daily English tours, and most require a reservation (only Taittinger allows drop-in visits). Call or email for the schedule and to secure a spot on a tour. The TI can make reservations for the Mumm and Martel cellars, and they have information on minivan excursions into the nearby vineyards for tastings. **Champagne Tours by Cris** is one you can book directly (€62/person for 4-hour tour, tel. 03 26 88 26 37, www.cristourschampagne-ardenne.com).

Which *cave* should you visit? Martel offers the most personal and best-value tour. Taittinger and Mumm have the most impressive cellars. Veuve Clicquot is popular with Americans and fills up weeks in advance.

All told, Mumm is closest to the city center and train station, and offers one of the best tours in Reims. Without a car, the others involve a long **walk** (40 minutes) or a short **bus** or **taxi** ride (for more, see "Getting There," under "*Caves* Southeast of the Cathedral," later). A **taxi** from either train station to the farthest Champagne *cave* will cost about €10. To return, ask the staff at the *caves* to call a taxi for you. Warning: The meter starts running once they are called, so count on €5 extra for the return trip. Wherever you go, bring a sweater, even in summer, as the *caves* are cool and clammy.

Champagne in the City Center

Mumm

Mumm ("moome") is one of the easiest *caves* to visit, as it's just a short walk from the central train station. Reservations are essential, especially on weekends. You must choose which tasting you want when getting your ticket (the cheapest Cordon Rouge tasting is fine for most, though you can pay more for the same tour with extra "guided" tastings). The tour starts with a good 10-minute promotional video explaining the Champagne-making process. Then a guided walk takes you through the industrial-size chalk cellars, where 25 million bottles are stored (Mumm is Champagne's largest producer), and a museum of old Champagne-making tools and traditions. The tour ends with your tasting choice.

Cost and Hours: €13-28 depending on tasting level, includes one-hour tour; Mon-Sat 9:00-11:00 & 14:00-17:00, closed Sun; 34

Rue du Champ de Mars—go to the end of the courtyard and follow *Visites des Caves* signs; tel. 03 26 49 59 70, www.mumm.com, guides@mumm.com.

Getting There: It's a 15-minute walk from the Reims-Centre train station or from the cathedral. From the station, turn left on Boulevard Joffre and walk to Place de la République; pass through the square, and continue along on Rue du Champ de Mars (to the left of the Europcar office). You can also take bus #7 from the station (direction: Béthany) to the Justice stop, turn right (south) onto Rue de la Justice, and then left onto Rue du Champ de Mars. To return to the station on bus #7, turn left from Mumm and walk a block down Rue du Champ de Mars to the bus shelter (direction: Apollinaire).

Caves Southeast of the Cathedral

Taittinger and Martel, offering contrasting looks at two very different *caves,* are a few blocks apart, and can easily be combined in one visit. Veuve Clicquot Ponsardin is a bit farther out and pricey—but has impressive cellars and that cool name. It's also a big draw for American travelers and must be booked in advance.

Getting There: From the town center, it's a 30-minute **walk** to Taittinger and Martel—starting from behind the cathedral's right transept, it's a straight stroll down Rue de l'Université, then Rue du Barbâtre (see map on page 992). Veuve Clicquot is another 15 minutes farther on foot. If you don't want to walk, use the handy **taxi stand** at 40 Rue Carnot, next to the Opéra (about €10).

To get near any of these *caves* by **bus,** take the small Citadine bus #1 from the Cathédrale stop (behind the cathedral a block to the left—see map on page 992), and ride 10 minutes (direction: Buirette) to the St. Niçaise stop. The bus drops you close to Taittinger and Martel (ask the driver to point you in the right direction). To return to the cathedral, catch Citadine bus #2 (around the corner from where you got off on Rue du Barbâtre, bus stop Salines, direction: Hôtel de Ville), and get off at Royale.

From **Reims-Centre Station** to Taittinger and Martel, catch bus #4 across the parkway from the station TI (6/hour Mon-Sat, 2/hour Sun, direction: Hôpital Debré). Get off at the St. Timothée stop, and ask the driver to point you in the right direction (5-minute walk, return stop is across the street). To get near Veuve Clicquot, take bus #6 from the train station (to the Droits de l'Homme stop, 4/hour, direction: ZI Farman, return stop is on opposite side of the big roundabout on Boulevard Dieu Lumière, bus stop Cimitière du Sud, direction: Gare Centre).

If you're coming from the **Champagne-Ardenne** TGV train station, take the tram to the Opéra stop and walk to the cathedral, then find Citadine bus #1 (described earlier).

Taittinger

One of the biggest, slickest, and most renowned of Reims' *caves,* Taittinger (tay-tan-zhay) runs morning and afternoon tours in English through their vast and historic cellars (call for times, best to show up early, no reservation necessary, about 25 people per tour). After seeing their 10-minute promo-movie (hooray for Taittinger!), descend with your guide for 60 chilly minutes in a chalky underworld of *caves,* the deepest of which were dug by ancient Romans. You'll tour part of the three miles of *caves,* see ruins of an abbey and a Roman chalk quarry, pass some of the three million bottles stored here, and learn all you need to know about the Champagne-making process from your well-informed guide. Popping corks signal that the tour's done and the tasting's begun.

Cost and Hours: €17-41 depending on tasting level, includes one-hour tour; daily mid-March-mid-Nov 9:30-13:00 & 14:00-17:30, open through lunch July-Aug, closed weekends off-season; 9 Place St. Niçaise, tel. 03 26 85 84 33, www.taittinger.fr, visites@taittinger.fr.

Martel

This small operation with less extensive *caves* offers a homey contrast to Taittinger's big-business style, and it's a great deal. Call to set up a visit and expect a small group that might be yours alone. Friendly Emmanuel runs the place with a relaxed manner. Only 20 percent of their product is exported, so you won't find much of their Champagne in the US. Their visit includes an informative 10-minute film, a tour of their small cellars (which are peppered with rusted old wine-making tools), and a tasting of three different Champagnes in a casual living-room atmosphere.

Cost and Hours: €12 includes one-hour tour and tasting, daily 10:00-11:30 & 14:00-17:30, reservations not required but advised, 17 Rue des Créneaux, tel. 03 26 82 70 67, www.champagnemartel.com, boutique@champagnemartel.com.

Veuve Clicquot Ponsardin

Because it's widely exported in the US, Veuve Clicquot is inundated with American travelers. Reservations are required and fill up three weeks in advance, so book early (easy via email) before you start your trip. The basic *cave* visit includes a two-flute tasting; other options add on a glass of "La Grande Dame" or pair tastings with cheese.

Cost and Hours: €20 for one-hour tour and 30-minute tasting, €35 for one-hour tour and "La Grande Dame" Champagne tasting, €90 for 2.5-hour visit that includes cheese pairing; mid-March-mid-Nov Tue-Sat 10:00-12:30 & 13:30-17:30, closed Sun-Mon and rest of year; 1 Place des Droits de l'Homme, tel. 03 26 89 53 90, www.veuve-clicquot.com, visitscenter@veuve-clicquot.fr.

Pop Pop, Fizz Fizz

Like perfume and cognac, Champagne is synonymous with good living and good form in France. When invited to a French home for dinner, your apéritif choice always includes Champagne, as it is the proper way to start an evening with friends. Though many wine-growing regions in France produce sparkling wines (called Crémant), only grapes from this region can be called Champagne. The beverage produced here is commonly regarded as the finest sparkling wine in the world.

Given the notoriety of the Champagne region, surprisingly little of its land is planted in vines (about 60,000 acres), and sparkling wines have little history compared to France's famous wines. While the Romans planted the first grapes here, Champagne was not "invented" until the late 17th century, and then it was by virtue of necessity—the local climate and soil did not produce competitive still wines.

Champagne is made from three grapes: the red pinot noir and pinot Meunier, and the white chardonnay. Most Champagne is roughly an equal blend of these grapes, though some smaller producers will make Champagne from 100 percent of any one of the three grapes.

The rules governing the production of Champagne are the strictest in France; this is done to guarantee quality. The *méthode champenoise* involves two fermentations, the first in casks and the second in bottles (after sugar and yeast are added). As wine turns bubbly, sediment forms in the bottle, which must be removed. In the traditional manner, it's done by hand in a painstaking process of tilting and turning each bottle slightly each day. Nowadays this is mostly done by machines. Most bottles are aged for two to five years, then sold, as Champagne does not improve with age.

Champagnes are classified by their level of sweetness; *brut* and *extra-brut* are dry (and very dry), *demi-sec* is sweeter, and *doux*, the sweetest, is intended for dessert courses. Bottles labeled *tête de cuvée* are as good as it gets; from there, the ranking proceeds to *grand cru* (from top vines), *premier cru* (next best), and *cru* (table champagne). The smaller the bubbles, the better the champagne.

Route de la Champagne

Drivers can joyride through the pretty Montagne de Reims area just south of Reims and experience the chalky soil and rolling hills of vines that produce Champagne's prestigious wines. At the Reims TI, ask for maps of the Route de la Champagne and *The Discovery Guide* for the Marne region. Roads are well-marked: brown *Route Touristique de la Champagne* signs lead along much of our route and take you to some great viewpoints. The only rail-accessible destination along this route is Epernay.

There are thousands of small-scale producers of Champagne in these villages—unknown outside France and producing fine-quality Champagne without the high costs associated with big brand-name houses in Reims and Epernay. These less-famous producers harvest the grapes themselves and make wine only from their own grapes (identified as "*récoltant manipulant*" or just "*RM*" on bottles and elsewhere). It takes a little work to find them, and you must call ahead if you want to tour a cellar rather than just taste, but this usually pays off with a more intimate, rewarding cultural experience. Ask your hotelier or a TI for help, or check in with Les Vignerons Indepéndents de Champagne (Independent Winemakers of Champagne, open-house events and tastings Sat-Sun only April-Oct, usually 3-4 different wineries a day, tel. 03 26 59 55 22, www.vignerons-independants-champagne.com).

If you're doing this drive without reservations, it's easier on a weekend, when more places are open and likely to welcome drop-in tasters. If you plan to picnic, you'll find all you need in the sweet little town of Aÿ. There's also a bakery and a small grocery in Bouzy (unpredictable hours).

➲ **Self-Guided Driving Tour:** For an afternoon ramble over the hills (the Montagne de Reims) and through the vineyards from Reims, try this leisurely loop drive (allow three hours, including stops). If you're pressed for time, you can still sample the vineyard scenery by driving just a few minutes outside Reims, or by working parts of this route into your drive to or from Reims (the best stop is Hautvillers).

• *Leave Reims on A-4 (direction: Châlons-en-Champagne), then exit south to Cormontreuil on D-9, following signs to Louvois (first tasting opportunity). You'll pass through the usual commercial fringe before popping out into lovely scenery just 15 minutes after leaving Reims. Brake for photographs. If you toured Mumm's cellars, you'll notice their hilltop property with a windmill well off in the distance (on the left) as you climb the Montagne de Reims. Remember that the best grapes are grown along the slopes of the Montagne de Reims.*

Louvois: Consider a stop at **Guy de Chassey,** where drop-ins are welcome to enjoy a tasting (assuming the place isn't busy). Call ahead, though, if you want to tour their property (bottles from €15-20, on the roundabout as you enter town at 1 Place de la Demi-Lune, tel. 03 26 57 04 45, www.champagne-guy-de-chassey.com).

• *Continue on D-34. A little after leaving Louvois, look for* Route de la Champagne *signs leading left along a vineyard lane into the appropriately named village of Bouzy. Take the short detour off to the* point de vue *for a fine view over the village and vines.*

Bouzy: There are 30 producers of Champagne in little Bouzy alone, some of whom are famous for their Bouzy Rouge (a red wine made only from Pinot Noir grapes, and not made every year). Most

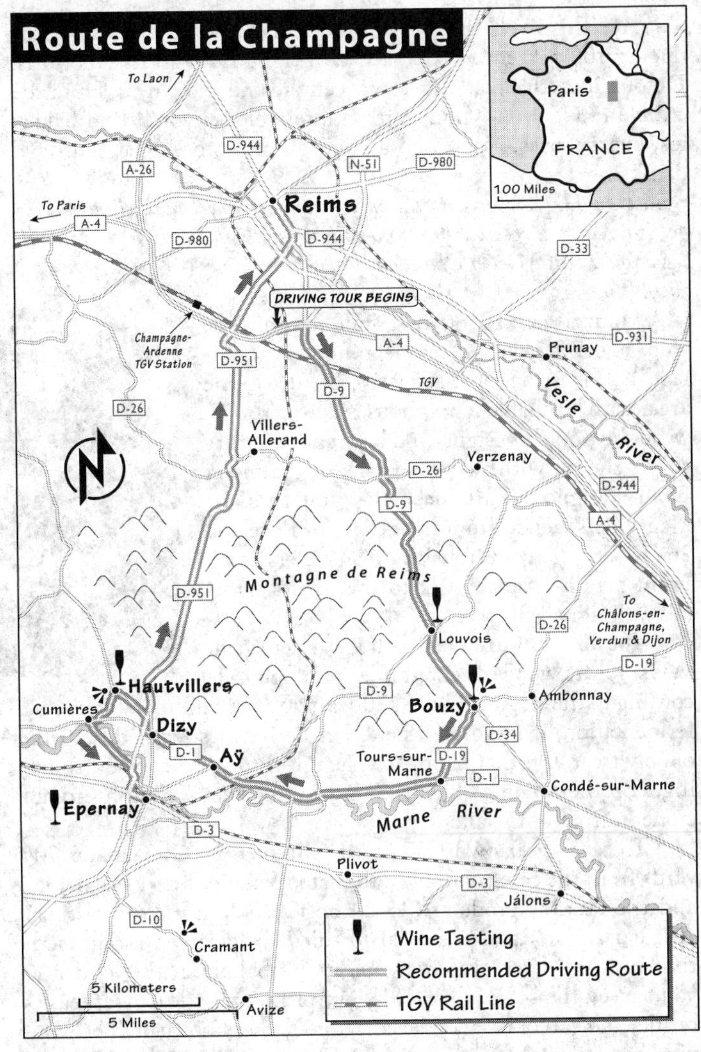

places require reservations to visit, but drop-ins are welcome for the fun tasting at **Champagne Herbert Beaufort.** You'll likely be served by Monsieur Beaufort or his English-speaking son, Ludovic. Arrive at 10:30 or 15:30 for visits to their cellars (free tastings, €17-23 bottles, Mon-Fri 9:30-11:30 & 14:00-17:30, Sat 9:30-12:00 & 14:30-17:00, Sun 10:00-12:00 in summer, closed Sun Sept-Easter, first *domaine* on your left coming from Louvois on D-34 at 32 Rue de Tours, tel. 03 26 57 01 34, www.champagnebeaufort.fr).

• *From Bouzy, leave the vineyards following D-19 to Tours-sur-Marne, then turn right onto D-1 and carefully track signs to Aÿ.*

Aÿ: This lively little town (pronounced "eye") boasts of producing 100 percent *grand cru* Champagne from all its vineyards. Detour into the pleasant town center, and park near Hôtel de Ville and Café du Midi. Within a few blocks you'll find bakeries, charcuteries, cafés, and a good grocery store (that sells cold drinks).

• *Back on D-1, drive into the next town—**Dizy** (which is what you get after too much Bouzy)—and follow signs up the hill to Hautvillers. You'll pass Moët et Chandon vineyards on your way.*

Hautvillers: If you have time for only one stop, make it Hautvillers (meaning "High Village"). This is the most attractive hamlet in the area, with strollable lanes, houses adorned with wrought-iron shop signs, and a seventh-century abbey church with the tombstone of the monk Dom Pérignon. Park near the vintage Café Hautvillers, across from the little TI (TI tel. 03 26 57 06 35, www.tourisme-hautvillers.com). From here it's a nice walk to the town's sights (all well signed).

The **abbey church** is worth a wander (great WCs) for its wood-accented interior alone. According to the story, in about 1700, after much fiddling with double fermentation, it was here that Dom Pérignon stumbled onto the bubbly treat. On that happy day, he ran through the abbey, shouting, "Brothers, come quickly...I'm drinking stars!" Find his tombstone in front of the altar.

To taste your own stars, find **Champagne G. Tribaut** (300 yards from the café), and meet animated Valerie, who loves her job and the family's product (€15-24 bottles, €2/glass for a tasting). Ask her about Ratafia, a local fortified wine served as an apéritif. You can linger over your *coupette* of bubbly in the garden as you survey the sea of vineyards, but please, plan to buy at least a bottle, and call or email a day ahead to let her know you'll be stopping by (daily 9:00-12:00 & 14:00-18:00, tel 03 26 59 40 57, www.champagne.g.tribaut.com, champagne.tribaut@wanadoo.fr).

Another option is **Au 36,** a slick and interesting wine shop/tasting room that represents many producers. The passionate staff will help you understand the differences among grape varieties (€10-15 tastings with 3 contrasting Champagnes, good prices for purchase, Tue-Sun 10:30-18:00, closed Mon, a block from Café Hautvillers at 36 Rue Dom Pérignon, tel. 02 26 51 58 37).

For a simply spectacular picnic spot (with tables and benches, but no WCs) and **sweeping views** over vineyards and the Marne River, drive to the abbey church and follow Rue de l'Eglise past it for three minutes. Get out of the car and wander among the vineyards. That picture-perfect village down below is Cumières.

• *Exit the town or picnic site downhill, toward the river to Cumières, then turn left on D-1 and follow signs home to Reims (about 20 minutes back on the speedy D-951). You could also pass through Cumières and drive two miles into* ***Epernay,*** *home to Moët et Chandon (see below). True connoisseurs can continue along the Route Touristique de Champagne south of Epernay toward Vertus, along the Chardonnay-grape-filled* ***Côte des Blancs.***

Champagne in Epernay

Champagne purists may want to visit Epernay, about 16 miles from Reims (and also well connected to Paris). Epernay is most famously home to Moët et Chandon, which sits along Avenue de Champagne, the Rodeo Drive of grand Champagne houses.

Arrival in Epernay: Trains run frequently between Reims-Centre Station and Epernay (12/day, 30 minutes). From the Epernay station, walk five minutes straight up Rue Gambetta to Place de la République, and take a left to find Avenue de Champagne. Moët et Chandon (described below) is at #20, and the TI is at #7 (mid-April-mid-Oct Mon-Sat 9:30-12:30 & 13:30-19:00, Sun 11:00-16:00; in off-season closes at 17:30 and on Sun; tel. 03 26 53 33 00, www.ot-epernay.fr).

Tasting in Epernay: The granddaddy of Champagne companies, **Moët et Chandon** offers one-hour tours with pricey tasting possibilities (€21-28 for one or two tastes, no reservation needed, kids under 18 can join the tour for €10—but no tasting, daily April-mid-Nov 9:30-11:30 & 14:00-16:30, closed weekends off-season, closed Jan, 20 Avenue de Champagne, tel. 03 26 51 20 20, www.moet.com).

To sip a variety of different Champagnes from smaller producers, stop by the wine bar **C Comme Champagne** (meaning "C like Champagne"). Start with a peek in the wine cellar, then snuggle into an armchair and order by the taste, glass, or bottle. Ask about the ever-changing flight selections—but don't expect great deals (daily 10:00-24:00, 8 Rue Gambetta, tel. 03 26 32 09 55).

Sleeping in Reims

$$ Grand Hôtel Continental*** is a fine, creaky old hotel on lively Place d'Erlon with rooms in every size, shape, and price. Those in the main building come with traditional decor, high ceilings, and big old-style bathrooms; those in the new wing are plush and *très* modern. Helpful Maxence (Max-ahns) runs the place with panache (basic Db-€80, standard Db-€100-120, tradition Db-€150-180, good family options; ask for Rick Steves discount—can be 10-20 percent,

Sleep Code

Abbreviations **(€1 = about $1.40, country code: 33)**
S = Single, **D** = Double/Twin, **T** = Triple, **Q** = Quad, **b** = bathroom, **s** = shower only, * = French hotel rating (0-5 stars)
Price Rankings
$$ Higher Priced—Most rooms more than €100
$ Lower Priced—Most rooms €100 or less
Unless otherwise noted, credit cards are accepted, English is spoken, and Wi-Fi is generally free. Prices change; verify current rates online or by email. For the best prices, always book directly with the hotel.

increases with room price; air-con, elevator, laundry service, Wi-Fi, parking-€9/day, 5-minute walk from central train station at 93 Place Drouet d'Erlon, tel. 03 26 40 39 35, www.grandhotelcontinental.com, reservation@grandhotelcontinental.com).

$$ Quality Hôtel Reims Europe* provides good three-star rooms a block off the big square (Db-€100-140, air-con, Wi-Fi, 26 Rue Buirette, tel. 03 26 47 39 39, www.hotel-europe-reims.com, contact@hotel-europe-reims.com).

$ Grand Hôtel du Nord is a decent two-star value with clean and modern comfort at fair rates in surprisingly quiet rooms, despite being right on the lively square (Db-€75-95, Tb-€115-155, Qb-€150-195, elevator, no air-con, Wi-Fi, 75 Place Drouet d'Erlon, tel. 03 26 47 39 03, www.hotel-nord-reims.com, contact@hotel-nord-reims.com).

$ La Parenthèse, a lovely and well-equipped *chambre d'hôte* with kitchenettes, is situated closer to the river with easy car access and parking (€9/day), welcoming owners, and a pleasant garden and public spaces (Db-€90, 2-night minimum, cash only, less for longer stays, Wi-Fi, 83 Rue Clovis, tel. 03 26 40 39 57, www.laparenthese.fr, contact@laparenthese.fr).

$ Bénédicte et Claude Philippon Chambres d'Hôte is a fine value and a lovely experience. This friendly couple offer two comfortable, homey, and centrally located rooms on Place du Chapitre (#21), 100 yards from the cathedral's north (left) transept. Look for the yellow *Chambres d'Hôte* sign (S-€55, D-€65, T-€80, less for 2-night stays, cash only, includes French breakfast, shared bathroom, third floor with elevator, parking on square, tel. 03 26 91 06 22, mobile 06 77 76 20 13, claude.philippon@sfr.fr).

Eating in Reims

This is a "meaty" city: Most menus will offer *foie gras,* raw *tartares,* lots of beef, and some dishes you may choose to avoid, such as *rognons, ris de veau, tête de veau, pieds de porc,* and *boudin noir* (kidneys, sweetbreads, calf's head, pig's feet, and blood sausage, respectively). Dining in Reims is as much about the area you eat in as the restaurant you choose. I've described areas to troll for dinner as well as a few specific restaurants. If you're just looking for cheap picnic fixings, head to the grocery store at Monoprix (see "Helpful Hints," page 990).

ON PLACE DROUET D'ERLON

This bustling line of cafés and restaurants serves mostly cheap and mediocre meals but has the city's best people-watching and café action. You'll find exceptions to the forgettable offerings at the recommended Grand Hôtel Continental's **Au Conti,** with quiet, inside-only dining, classy decor, and top service thanks to maître' d Frédéric (good €25 three-course *menu* includes a drink or half-bottle of wine, closed Sun evenings, 93 Place Drouet d'Erlon, tel. 03 26 40 39 35), and across the square at **Brasserie Flo,** with an established clientele, a woody brasserie interior, and fine terrace tables outside (€28 two-course *menu,* from €34 for three courses, open daily, 96 Place Drouet d'Erlon, tel. 03 26 91 40 50).

ON OR NEAR PLACE DU FORUM

This quieter but popular spot serves a young professional crowd at several bistros that spill onto the square. Come here for a more wine-focused, intimate meal. Among several appealing options, consider **Bistrot du Forum,** an informal place with small wooden tables, a cool zinc bar, and good terrace seating. They serve hearty salads, bruschetta, and burgers, as well as traditional meat and fish dishes (€13-22 *plats*). You'll also find a good selection of wines (and Champagne, *bien sûr*) by the glass (daily, 6 Place Forum, tel. 03 26 47 56 58). **Le Bouchon du Forum,** a few doors down at #14, offers a similar setting and menu (closed Sun).

Just off the square, on Rue Courmeaux, you'll find **L'Epicerie au Bon Manger,** a foodie refuge whose mantra is "In Good We Trust." They have a handful of tables, stacks of organic local wines, smelly cheese, and charcuterie to go or to enjoy sitting down. It's a handy place if you're eating outside the rigid French lunch hours, because they serve nibbles all day (€10-20 meat-and-cheese platters, €17 *plat du jour,* 7 Rue Courmeaux, tel. 03 26 03 45 29).

ON THE CATHEDRAL SQUARE

The attraction here is to eat outdoors under the towering west facade of the cathedral, where you'll find ample low stone walls—ideal for picnicking while you admire the impressive church. This spot is sensational after dark, when the floodlighting and sound-and-light show make the view a performance. **Au Bureau,** one of a handful of eateries on the square, is worth it only if you grab a table outside and are OK with mediocre café fare (€12-14 salads, €12-16 burgers and *plats,* daily until late, at the cathedral at 9 Place du Cardinal Luçon, tel. 03 26 35 84 83).

DINING ELSEWHERE IN REIMS

Brasserie du Boulingrin is a grand old brasserie. This Reims institution serves traditional French cuisine (including fresh oysters and a seafood platter) at blue-collar prices (€15-22 *plats,* €18-25 *menus,* closed Sun; 10-minute walk from the Reims-Centre train station at 31 Rue de Mars, not far from Porte de Mars and next to the recently renovated Market Halles, tel. 03 26 40 96 22).

Café du Palais is appreciated by older locals who don't mind paying a premium to eat a meal or sip coffee wrapped in 1930s ambience. Reims' most venerable café-bistro stands across from the Opéra (€34 *menus,* €20-30 *plats,* serves hot food during lunch hours and snacks the rest of the day, daily 9:00-20:30, open later for dinner on Sat, 14 Place Myron Herrick, tel. 03 26 47 52 54).

La Table Anna is run by a romantic young couple and is a fine choice for a special meal. *Madame* is in the kitchen and *monsieur* will take your order. The indoors-only dining room is quiet, and their food is traditional and thoughtfully prepared (€15-20 lunch, €30-50 dinner, closed Sun evening and all day Mon, 6 Rue Gambetta, tel. 03 26 89 12 12).

Reims Connections

Reims has two train stations—Reims-Centre and Champagne-Ardennes. Most trains to or from Paris use Reims-Centre, while TGV trains traveling to or from points east (such as Strasbourg or Colmar) use Champagne-Ardennes (5 miles from the center of Reims; frequent connection by tramway to Reims-Centre Station). Trains that stop at Reims-Centre don't stop at Champagne-Ardennes. For more on Reims' train stations, see "Arrival in Reims" on page 990.

From Reims-Centre Station by Train to: Paris Gare de l'Est (via TGV: 12/day, 45 minutes; by local train: 2/day, 2 hours), **Epernay** (12/day, 30 minutes), **Verdun** (8/day, 2-5 hours, most with change in Châlons or Metz).

From Reims Champagne-Ardennes Station by Train to: Paris Gare de l'Est (via TGV: 4/day, 45 minutes), **Strasbourg** (via TGV: 10/day, 2 hours), **Colmar** (via TGV: 10/day, 3 hours, most change in Strasbourg).

Verdun

While World War I was fought a hundred years ago and there are no more survivors to tell its story, the WWI sights and memorials scattered around Europe do their best to keep the devastation from fading from memory.

Perhaps the most powerful WWI sightseeing experience a traveler can have is at the battlefields of Verdun, where, in 1916, roughly 300,000 lives were lost in what is called the "Battle of 300 Days and Nights."

Today, the lunar landscape left by WWI battles is buried under thick forests—all new growth. But there are plenty of rusty remnants of the battle and memorials to the carnage left to be experienced.

A string of Verdun battlefields lines an eight-mile stretch of road outside the town of Verdun. From here (with a tour, rental car, or taxi) you can ride through the eerie moguls left by the incessant shelling, pause at melted-sugar-cube forts, ponder plaques marking spots where towns once existed, and visit a vast cemetery. In as little as three hours you can see the most important sights and appreciate the horrific scale of the battles. While 2014 marked the centennial of the start of World War I, 2016 will mark the centennial of the "Hell of Verdun."

TOURIST INFORMATION

Verdun's official TI (Office de Tourisme) is east of Verdun's city center (just across the river—cross at Pont Chausée, on Avenue du Général Mangin; July-Aug Mon-Sat 9:00-19:00, Sun 10:00-12:00 & 14:30-18:00; Sept-June Mon-Sat 9:30-12:30 & 13:30-18:00, Sun 10:00-12:00 & 14:30-17:00; tel. 03 29 84 55 55, www.tourisme-verdun.fr). Ask for the free Pass Lorraine, which is good for discounts at many sights in the region. The TI also has free Wi-Fi. The pleasant park nearby provides a good picnic setting.

Open-roof bus tours of the battlefield sights depart from the TI (run by Open Tours, tickets sold at TI, see "Getting Around the Verdun Battlefields," later). The TI can also arrange private guides, but you'll need your own car (about €130/2 hours, promotion@tourisme-verdun.fr).

Verdun Tourisme (across from the TI, with the blue roof) is

really a travel agency but offers reasonable visitor information if the real TI is closed, and has a better selection of English books.

ARRIVAL IN VERDUN

By Train: Verdun is served by two train stations: the Meuse TGV Station (18 miles from Verdun) and the Central Train Station (within walking distance of town).

Three daily TGV trains from Paris' Gare de l'Est serve the **Meuse TGV Station;** a 30-minute shuttle bus connects the TGV station with Verdun's central station (free with ticket to Verdun or a rail pass, leaves shortly after train arrives). This high-speed service puts Verdun within 1.5 hours of Paris (compared with 3.5 hours by local train—see "Verdun Connections," later in this section).

Verdun's lonely **Central Train Station,** also called Verdun SNCF, is 15 minutes by foot from the TI. Shuttle buses to the TGV station leave from the building marked *Multimodal* next door. To reach the town center and TI, walk straight out of the station (no baggage check), cross the parking lot and the roundabout, and keep straight down Avenue Garibaldi, then follow *Centre-Ville* signs on Rue St. Paul. Turn left on the first traffic-free street in the old center and walk past the towers and across the river to the TI.

By Car: Drivers can bypass the town center and head straight for the TI or the battlefields. To find the TI, follow signs to *Centre-Ville,* then *Office de Tourisme.* To reach the battlefields, follow signs reading *Verdun Centre-Ville,* then signs toward *Longwy,* then find signs to *Douaumont* and *Champs de Bataille* (battlefields) on D-112, then D-913. Follow signs to *Fort de Douaumont* and *Ossuaire.* The map in this book is adequate for drivers visiting all the basic sights I describe.

Orientation to Verdun Town

While the Battle of Verdun took place in the hills outside town, the town of Verdun itself is worth a look, and is a handy base for exploring the battlefield sights.

With a history going back to Roman times, Verdun's strategic location has left it with a hard-fought history. Locals call it "the most decorated town in France," and war memorials seem to be everywhere. It's a monochrome place, with bullet holes still pocking its stony buildings. And it's small, with only 16,000 people—4,000 fewer than at the start of World War I. Most of the action seems to be along the Meuse River on the Quai de Londres, where you'll find cafés and restaurants, as well as recreational boats from all over this part of Europe.

Along the river, you'll also find the town's mighty 14th-century gate, which still offers visitors a wary greeting and whose state-of-the-art (in the 17th century) fortifications still seem poised to repel foreign armies. Just across the river, a thicker wall—built in 1871 in anticipation of a German attack—supports a mammoth monument to the victims of German invaders in both world wars.

Verdun is crowned by its **Victory Monument,** high above the river, with a cascading fountain connecting it to the pedestrian heart of town. The fountain's centerpiece, a towering warrior, plants his sword in the ground in a declaration of peace. He's flanked by twin cannons—made by the French for the Russians but ultimately used by the Germans against the French at Verdun. While the monument originally honored French and Allied troops, today it honors Germans, too. Now that a century has passed, the varied sights of the Verdun battlefields have risen above national bias and memorialize all victims of that senseless war.

Today the city is a springboard for visitors to the battlefield sights, but in 1916 Verdun was the departure point for the battlefront. The **Citadelle Souterraine** was where French soldiers assembled and had their last good bed, meal, and shower before heading into the shelling zone. The citadel, with 2.5 miles of tunnels cut into a rock, was a teeming military city. How big? Its bakery cranked out 23,000 rations of bread every day. Today, it tries to give the public a glimpse at life on the front with a childish 30-minute ride on a Disneyesque wagon that comes with a recorded narration (€7, open daily). Your Verdun time is better spent at other battlefield sights.

Eating in Verdun: You'll find several inexpensive restaurants in the pedestrian zone and along the river. **Bolzon Charcuterie** on the pedestrian-only Rue Chausée has good salads, quiche, and dishes to go. While the town of Verdun has lots of eateries, there's only one decent café near the battlefields (near the Ossuary, described under "L'Ossuaire de Douaumont" sight listing). If you're short on time, consider assembling a picnic from shops in Verdun or at an autoroute minimart.

Verdun Connections

High-speed TGV trains serve the Verdun area from the Meuse TGV Station, 30 minutes south of Verdun. Regular trains run to Verdun's Central Train Station. For TGV connections listed below, allow an additional 30 minutes to reach Verdun's central station by shuttle bus (included with ticket to Verdun or rail pass).

From Verdun by Train to: Strasbourg (6/day, 3-4 hours, most change in Metz), **Colmar** (7/day, 4-5.5 hours, 2-3 changes), **Reims** (8/day, 2-5 hours, most with a change), **Paris** Gare de l'Est (3/day direct via shuttle bus and TGV, 1.5 hours; by regional train 3.5 hours with transfer in Châlons-en-Champagne).

The Battlefields of Verdun

Verdun's battlefields are littered with monuments and ruined forts. For most travelers, a half-day is enough, though historians could spend days here. We'll concentrate on the two most important sights, the Ossuaire de Douaumont and Fort de Douaumont, and a smattering of smaller nearby sights. If you want to see where American forces fought in World War I under General John Pershing, head to the St-Mihiel area, south of Verdun (for details, see "Other Battlefields Near Verdun" at the end of this chapter).

Information: Sights are adequately described in English (some provide audioguides). If you want more, the TI and all sights sell helpful books in English describing the Battle of Verdun. The simple but adequate booklet *Verdun du Ciel* provides helpful details (in three languages) and black-and-white photos for about €5. More readable is *The Battle of Verdun* by Yves Buffetaut. The best is Alistair Horne's *The Price of Glory*, which sorts through the complex issues surrounding Verdun and offers perspectives from both sides of the conflict—if you can, read it ahead of your visit (available at Verdun Tourisme, the "unofficial" tourist office).

GETTING AROUND THE BATTLEFIELDS

The most interesting battlefield sights all lie along an easy eight-mile stretch of road from the town of Verdun. To lace these sights together, you have four choices:

By Car: Cheap car rental is available a block straight out of Verdun's Central Train Station at **AS Location** (about €44/day with 100 km/60 miles included—that's plenty, Mon-Fri 8:30-12:00 & 14:00-18:00, no office hours Sat-Sun but prebooked rentals possible, 22 Rue Louis Maury, tel. 03 29 86 58 58, fj.location@sfr.fr). I've included basic route tips in my "Verdun Battlefield Driving Tour," later.

By Hop-On, Hop-Off Bus: Open Tours offers a handy hop-on, hop-off open-roof tour bus that circulates around the key sights (except on Mondays). There are five departures per day from the Verdun TI, allowing you 1-2 hours at each monument before the next bus arrives. Sparse commentary is provided (€10, late-April-Nov 11 Tue-Sun; departures at 9:15, 10:45, 13:15, 14:15, and 16:15—but confirm times with TI or online; www.open-tours-lorraine.fr).

By Taxi: For about €50 round-trip, taxis can drop a carload at one sight and pick up at another (walk between sights). Ask to be dropped at Fort de Douaumont and picked up three or so hours later at the Ossuaire de Douaumont; it's 1.3 level miles from the one sight to the other (figure 40 minutes on foot). Taxis normally meet trains at the station; otherwise they park at the TI (taxi mobile 06 07 02 24 16 or 06 80 08 10 09). It's easiest to arrange a taxi with the help of the TI, though you can save the walk from the train station to the TI if you arrange to be picked up at the station in advance.

By Private Guide: It's possible to hire a private guide to join you in your car for a tour. Try Ingrid Ferrand (mobile 06 79 45 30 98, ingrid.ferrand@wanadoo.fr) or Florence Lamousse (tel. 03 29 85 21 83), who are good, English-speaking guides (€200/half-day, €350/day). Or you can have the TI arrange a guide for you—see "Tourist Information," earlier.

BATTLEFIELD BACKGROUND

After the annexation of Alsace and Lorraine following the German victory in the Franco-Prussian War in 1871, Verdun found itself just 25 miles from the German border. This was too close for comfort for the French, who invested mightily in new fortifications ringing Verdun, hoping to discourage German thoughts of invasion. It was as if the French knew they'd be seeing German soldiers again before too long.

The plan failed. World War I erupted in August 1914, and after a lengthy stalemate, in 1916 the Germans elected to strike a powerful knockout punch at the heart of the French defense, to demoralize them and force a quick surrender. They chose Verdun as their target. By defeating the best of the French defenses, the Germans would cripple the French military and morale. The French chose to fight to the bitter end. Three hundred days of nonstop trench warfare ensued. France eventually prevailed, but at a terrible cost. Historically, this is as far as Germany ever got.

World War I introduced modern technology to the age-old business of war. Tanks, chemical weapons, monstrous cannons, rapid communication, and airplanes made their debut, conspiring to kill nearly 10 million people in just four years. In addition, the war ultimately seemed senseless: It started with little provocation, raged on with few decisive battles, and ended with nothing resolved, a situation that sowed the seeds of World War II.

The Battle of Verdun was fought from February through December of 1916. This was one chapter in a horrific "battle of attrition" in which the leaders of Germany and France decided to wage a fierce fight, knowing that they would suffer unprecedented losses. Each side calculated that the other would bleed white and drop first.

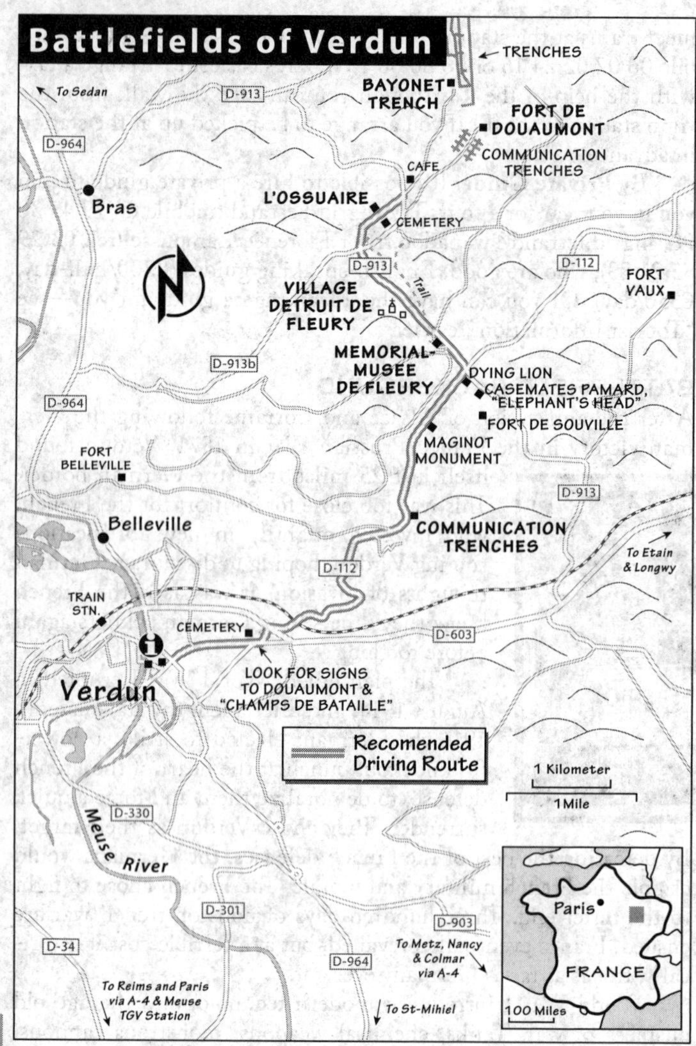

During the "Hell of Verdun" (hell for troops and hell for locals), Germany and France dropped 60 million artillery shells on each other. While we have an image of rifle fire and hand-to-hand combat, most of the casualties were caused by shells bursting into lethal fragments. An estimated 95 percent of the deaths at Verdun were from artillery shrapnel. Shells were fired from as far away as nine miles, with poor accuracy. Death by enemy fire was commonplace...as was death by friendly fire.

Today, soft, forested lands hide the memories of World War I's longest battle. Millions of live munitions are still scattered in vast cordoned-off areas. It's not unusual for French farmers or hikers to be injured by until-now unexploded mines. It's difficult to imagine today's lush terrain as it was just a few generations ago...a gray, treeless, crater-filled landscape, smothered in mud and littered with shattered weaponry and body parts as far as the eye could see. But as you visit, it's good to try.

Verdun Battlefield Driving Tour

Take D-603 from Verdun (direction: Longwy), and then take a left on D-112. As all but a couple of the sights described here are along the same road, and Fort de Douaumont is the most distant stop, simply follow signs for *Douaumont*. With the simple map in this book, you should have no problem. Along the way (within easy view of the road), you'll see the sights described below.

Communication Trenches near the Massif Fortifié de Souville

At this parking and picnic area, find a curving trench and craters, similar to those that mark so much of the land here. A few communication trenches like this remain—they protected reinforcements and supplies being shuttled to the front, and sheltered the wounded being brought back. But the actual trenches defining the front in this area were destroyed during the battles or have since been filled in. The nearby Souville Fort (Massif Fortifié de Souville) is not safe to visit.

Monument to Maginot

André Maginot served as France's minister of war in the 1920s and '30s, when the line of fortifications that later came to bear his name was built. The Maginot Line, which stretches from Belgium to Switzerland, was a series of underground forts and tunnels built after World War I in anticipation of World War II and another German attack. The Germans solved the problem presented by this formidable line of French defense by simply going around it through Belgium. The monument is here because André Maginot's family was from this region, and he was wounded near Verdun.

Monument to the Dying Lion

At the intersection with D-913, where you can turn left to the Ossuary, a statue of a dying lion marks the place where, after giving it their all in an offensive from June through October in 1916, the German forces were stopped. The German military had hoped for a quick victory here so troops could be sent to fight the British in the Somme offensive. The war was dragging on, hunger was setting in among the German citizenry, and the German leadership feared a revolt. They needed a boost—but the offensive failed. This is the site of massive artillery barrages: Imagine no trees here, only a brown lunar-like terrain with shell holes 20 feet deep. A short detour (turn right on D-913 at the intersection) takes you to a small sight signed *Casemates Pamard,* which is an armored machine gun nest nicknamed "Elephant's Head" for the way the 1917 structure looks.

• *Return to the intersection, and continue straight ahead on D-913 (following signs to* Ossuaire *and* Douaumont*). Along the way you'll pass the...*

Mémorial Musée de Fleury

This museum is being rebuilt until 2016. When it reopens it promises to offer the best historic exhibits on the Battle of Verdun anywhere (www.memorial-de-verdun.fr).

Village Détruit (Destroyed Village) de Fleury

Thirty villages caught in the hell of Verdun were destroyed. Six—like this one—were never rebuilt. Though gone, these villages (signposted as *Villages Détruites*) have not been forgotten: One mayor and two adjunct mayors represent the villages and work on preserving their memory.

Park on the roadside and stroll through the cratered former townscape. The rebuilt church stands where the village church once did. Plaques locate the butcher, the baker, and so on. There's also a memorial to two French officers who were executed by the French military because, by leaving the battlefield briefly to take a wounded soldier to safety, they disobeyed the order to "stand your ground until the last drop of blood." Ponder the land around you. Not one square meter was left flat or un-bombed.

• *Drive on, following signs to the tall, missile-like building surrounded by a sea of small white crosses.*

L'Ossuaire de Douaumont (Douaumont Ossuary)

This is the tomb of countless French and German soldiers whose last homes were the muddy trenches of Verdun. In the years after the war, a local bishop wandered through the fields of bones—the bones of an estimated 100,000 French soldiers and even more German soldiers. Concluding there needed to be a decent final resting place, he began the ossuary project in 1920. It was finished in 1932. The unusual artillery shell-shaped **tower** and cross design of this building symbolizes war... and peace (imagine a sword plunged into the ground up to its hilt). Over time, fewer visitors come as pilgrims and more as tourists. Yet even someone who's given little thought to the

human cost of this battle of attrition will be deeply moved by a thoughtful visit to this somber place.

Cost and Hours: Free entry, €5.50 for film and tower; daily April 9:00-18:00, May-Aug 9:00-18:30, Sept 9:00-12:00 & 14:00-18:00, March and Oct-Nov 9:00-12:00 & 14:00-17:00 or 17:30, Dec and Feb 14:00-17:00, closed Jan; tel. 03 29 84 54 81.

Eating: The nearby Café Abri des Pelerins is the only place to eat among all these Verdun monuments (just beyond the Ossuary on the road to Douaumont).

Visiting the Ossuary: Park behind the **theater/shop/tower.** In the back, look through the low windows at the bones of countless unidentified soldiers—probably more German bones than French ones. From there, steps lead down to the shop and theater where you can see the excellent 20-minute film (English-speakers get headphones with adjustable volume) and hike 200 steps up the tower (skippable). While you can visit the interior of the memorial for free, the film and access to the tower require a €6 ticket. The little picture boxes in the gift shop adjacent to the theater are worth a look and worthy of a museum in themselves.

The **Mémorial Ossuaire** is a humbling, moving tribute to the soldiers who believed the propaganda that this, The Great War, would be "the war to end all wars" and that their children would grow up in a world at peace. The building has 22 sections with 46 granite graves, each holding remains from different sectors of the battlefields. The red lettering on the walls lists a soldier's name, rank ("Lt" is lieutenant, "Cal" is corporal, "St" is sergeant), regiment, and dates of birth and death.

Walk through the **cemetery** and reflect on a war that ruined an entire generation, leaving half of all Frenchmen ages 15 to 30 dead or wounded. Rows of 15,000 Christian crosses and Muslim headstones (oriented toward Mecca), all with roses, decorate the cemetery.

Just beyond the main cemetery you'll find memorials to the Muslim and Jewish victims of Verdun. The Muslim memorial (built in 2006, just across the street from the cemetery) recalls the 600,000 "colonial soldiers" who fought for France, most of whom were Muslims from North Africa. These men were often thrown into the most suicidal missions and were considered instrumental in France's ultimate victory at Verdun (a fact often overlooked by anti-immigration, right-wing politicians in France today).

Jews (who were offered French citizenship if they enlisted) also fought and died in great numbers. The Jewish memorial (which you'll pass as you drive out of the Ossuary) survived World War II. That's because the Nazi governor of this part of France, who had fought at Verdun and respected soldiers of any faith, covered it up.

• *Leaving the Ossuary parking lot, follow signs to the...*

Tranchée des Baïonnettes ("Bayonet Trench")

There is a legend that an entire company of French troops was buried in their trench by an artillery bombardment—leaving only their bayonets sticking above the ground to mark their standing graves. The memorial to this "bayonet trench" is a few minutes' drive beyond the Ossuary. The bulky concrete monument, donated by the US and free to enter (notice the inscription reading "*Leurs frères d'Amérique,*" meaning "Brothers from America"), opened in 1920, and was the first such monument at Verdun.

In fact, most of the Third Company of the 137th Infantry Regiment was likely wiped out here because they had no artillery support and died in battle—still tragic, just not quite as vivid as the myth. The notion of the "bayonet trench" could have come from the German habit of making "gun graves"—burying dead French soldiers with their guns sticking up so that their bodies could be found later and given a proper burial. Walking around this monument provides a thought-provoking opportunity to wander into the silent and crater-filled new-growth forest that now blankets the battlefields of Verdun.

• *Backtrack toward the Ossuary, and follow signs to* Fort de Douaumont. *Between the Ossuary and the fort, on either side of the road, you'll pass what remains of the London Communication Trench. This served as a means of communication and resupply for the Fort de Douaumont. Notice the concrete-reinforced sides. You'll see the ruins of several* abris *(shelters) on the hillside above the trench—these provided safe haven for the trench's soldiers.*

Fort de Douaumont

This was the most important stronghold among 38 hilltop fortifications built to protect Verdun after Germany's 1871 annexation of Alsace and the Moselle region of Lorraine. First constructed in 1882, it was built atop and into the hillside and ultimately served as a strategic command center for both sides at various times. Soldiers were protected by a thick layer of sand (to muffle explosions) and a wall of concrete five to seven feet thick. Inside, there are two miles of cold, damp hallways—enlivened by the included audioguide.

Experiencing these corridors will add to your sympathy for the soldiers who were forced to live here like moles. Climb to the bombed-out top of the fort and check out the round, iron-gun emplacements that could rise and revolve. The massive central gun turret was state of the art in 1905, antiquated in 1915, and essentially useless when the war arrived in 1916.

Cost and Hours: €4, includes excellent 45-minute audioguide, daily May-Aug 10:00-18:30, April and Sept until 18:00, Oct until 17:30, Nov-Dec and Feb-March until 17:00, closed Jan.

Other Battlefields near Verdun

St-Mihiel

For a better understanding of the American role in the battles and to see real battle trenches, detour south of Verdun (on D-34 or D-964) to the area known as the St-Mihiel salient (a salient is a territory surrounded on three sides by the enemy). Here, American and French forces joined in 1918 under the command of General John Pershing, in hopes of breaking the Germans' will by gaining the important city of Metz. The joint attack on the St-Mihiel salient caught the Germans by surprise and was initially successful, but later became bogged down by poor roads and related supply problems. The Americans didn't make it to Metz, and the Germans were able to regroup and hunker down.

Today, you can see good examples of WWI trenches (many are reconstructions) and appreciate how close the opposing trenches were. German trenches are generally still in good condition since they were built with concrete. The French ones were built mostly with sandbags—they assumed the war would be short—and thus have not held up as well. Start with the trenches (maps available at Verdun's TI show their locations), then visit the cemetery.

To see the best **trenches,** take D-907 east from St-Mihiel, following signs for *Apremont le Forêt* and *Pont à Mousson,* and drive about five kilometers out of the city. You'll see signs to the right to several trenches (first, *Bois d'Ailly/Tranchées de la Soif,* then *Tranchées des Bavarois et de Roffignac*). Both are interesting and worth a stop. The third set of trenches (to the right) are signed as *Bois Brûlé/Croix des Redoutes.* Here you'll find original German trenches—still in good condition, and French trenches made from sandbags. The French trenches have been rebuilt in their original locations.

The somber **St-Mihiel American Cemetery and Memorial** at Thiaucourt has 4,153 graves (daily 9:00-17:00, 30 kilometers east of St-Mihiel—follow signs to *Pont à Mousson*).

About 19 kilometers farther south, the **Montsec Monument (**Butte de Montsec) marks the conquest of the St-Mihiel salient by the First US Army. From the monument, which offers a fine tribute to American soldiers, you can appreciate views over the battlefields and see the ruins of several forts.

Skip the town of St-Mihiel, which is far from these places of interest.

FRANCE: PAST AND PRESENT

FRENCH HISTORY IN AN ESCARGOT SHELL

About the time of Christ, Romans "Latinized" the land of the Gauls. With the fifth-century fall of Rome, the barbarian Franks and Burgundians invaded. Today's France evolved from this unique mix of Latin and Celtic cultures.

While France wallowed with the rest of Europe in medieval darkness, it got a head start in its development as a nation-state. In 507, Clovis, the king of the Franks, established Paris as the capital of his Christian Merovingian dynasty. Clovis and the Franks would eventually become Louis and the French. The Frankish military leader Charles Martel stopped the spread of Islam by beating the North African Moors at the Battle of Tours (a.k.a. the Battle of Poitiers). And Charlemagne ("Charles the Great"), the most important of the "Dark Age" Frankish kings, was crowned Holy Roman Emperor by the pope in 800. Charlemagne presided over the "Carolingian Renaissance" and effectively ruled an empire that was vast for its time.

The Treaty of Verdun (843), which divided Charlemagne's empire among his grandsons, marks what could be considered the birth of Europe. For the first time, a treaty was signed in vernacular languages (French and German), rather than in Latin. This split established a Franco-Germanic divide, and heralded an age of fragmentation. While petty princes took the reigns, the Frankish king ruled only Ile de France, a small region around Paris.

Vikings, or Norsemen, settled in what became Normandy. Later, in 1066, these "Normans" invaded England. The Norman king, William the Conqueror, consolidated his English domain, accelerating the formation of modern England. But his rule also muddied the political waters between England and France, kicking off a centuries-long struggle between the two nations.

In the 12th century, Eleanor of Aquitaine (a separate country in southwest France) married Louis VII, king of France, bringing Aquitaine under French rule. They divorced, and she married Henry of Normandy (soon to be Henry II of England). This marital union gave England control of a huge swath of land from the English Channel to the Pyrenees. For 300 years, France and England would struggle over control of Aquitaine. Any enemy of the French king would find a natural ally in the English king.

In 1328, the French king Charles IV died without a son. The English king (Edward III), Charles IV's nephew, was interested in the throne, but the French resisted. This quandary pitted France, the biggest and richest country in Europe, against England, which had the biggest army. They fought from 1337 to 1453 in what was modestly called the Hundred Years' War.

Regional powers from within France actually sided with England. Burgundy took Paris, captured the royal family, and recognized the English king as heir to the French throne. England controlled France from the Loire north, and things looked bleak for the French king.

Enter Joan of Arc, a 16-year-old peasant girl driven by religious voices. France's national heroine left home to support Charles VII, the dauphin (boy prince, heir to the throne but too young to rule). Joan rallied the French, ultimately inspiring them to throw out the English. In 1430, Joan was captured by the Burgundians, who sold her to the English, who convicted her of heresy and burned her at the stake in Rouen. But the inspiration of Joan of Arc lived on, and by 1453 English holdings on the Continent had dwindled to the port of Calais. (For more on Joan of Arc, see page 245.)

By 1500, a strong, centralized France had emerged, with borders similar to today's. Its kings (from the Renaissance François I through the Henrys and all those Louises) were model divine monarchs, setting the standards for absolute rule in Europe.

Outrage over the power plays and spending sprees of the kings—coupled with the modern thinking of the Enlightenment (whose leaders were the French *philosophes*)—led to the French Revolution (1789). In France, it was the end of the *ancien régime,* as well as its notion that some are born to rule, while others are born to be ruled.

The excesses of the Revolution in turn led to the rise of Napoleon, who ruled the French empire as a dictator. Eventually, *his* excesses ushered him into a South Atlantic exile, and after another half-century of monarchy and empire, the French settled on a compromise role for their leader. The modern French "king" is ruled by a constitution. Rather than dress in leotards and powdered wigs, France's president goes to work in a suit and carries a briefcase.

The 20th century spelled the end of France's reign as a military

Typical Church Architecture

History comes to life when you visit a centuries-old church. Even if you wouldn't know your apse from a hole in the ground, learning a few simple terms will enrich your experience. Note that not every church has every feature, and a "cathedral" isn't a type of church architecture, but rather a designation for a church that's a governing center for a local bishop.

Aisles: The long, generally low-ceilinged arcades that flank the nave.

Altar: The raised area with a ceremonial table (often adorned with candles or a crucifix), where the priest prepares and serves the bread and wine for Communion.

Apse: The space beyond the altar, often bordered with small chapels.

Barrel Vault: A continuous round-arched ceiling that resembles an extended upside-down U.

Choir: A cozy area, often screened off, located within the church nave and near the high altar where services are sung in a more intimate setting.

Cloister: Covered hallways bordering a square or rectangular open-air courtyard, traditionally where monks and nuns got fresh air.

Facade: The exterior surface of the church's main (west) entrance, usually highly decorated.

Groin Vault: An arched ceiling formed where two equal barrel

and political superpower. Devastating wars with Germany in 1870, 1914, and 1940—and the loss of her colonial holdings—left France with not quite enough land, people, or production to be a top player on a global scale. But the 21st century may see France rise again: Paris is a cultural capital of Europe, and France—under the EU banner—is a key player in integrating Europe as a single, unified economic power. And when Europe is a superpower, Paris may yet be its capital.

FRANCE TODAY

Today, the main political issue in France is—like everywhere—the economy. Initially, France weathered the 2008 downturn better than the US, because it was less invested in risky home loans and the volatile stock market. But now France, along with the rest of Europe, has been struggling. French unemployment remains high (over 10 percent) and growth has flatlined. France has not balanced its books since 1974, and public spending, at 56 percent of GDP, chews up a bigger chunk of output than in any other eurozone country. Abroad, the entire eurozone has been dragged down by countries heavily in debt—Greece, Spain, Portugal, Italy, and Ire-

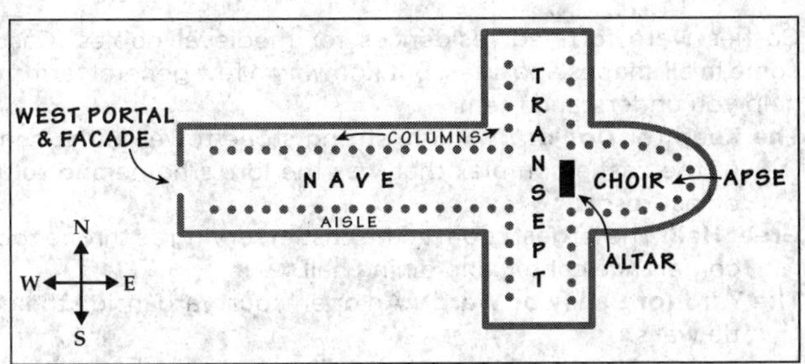

vaults meet at right angles. Less common usage: term for a medieval jock strap.

Narthex: The area (portico or foyer) between the main entry and the nave.

Nave: The long, central section of the church (running west to east, from the entrance to the altar) where the congregation sits or stands through the service.

Transept: In a traditional cross-shaped floor plan, the transept is one of the two parts forming the "arms" of the cross. The transepts run north-south, perpendicularly crossing the east-west nave.

West Portal: The main entry to the church (on the west end, opposite the main altar).

land. The challenge for French leadership is to address its economic problems while maintaining the high level of social services that the French people expect from their government.

France has its economic strengths: a well-educated workforce, an especially robust services sector and high-end manufacturing industry, and more firms big enough to rank in the global Fortune 500 than any other European country. Ironically, while France's economy may be one of the world's largest, the French remain skeptical about the virtues of capitalism and the work ethic. Globalization conflicts in a fundamental way with French virtues—many fear losing what makes their society unique in the quest for a bland, globalized world. Business conversation is generally avoided, as it implies a fascination with money that the French find vulgar. (It's considered gauche even to ask what someone does for a living.) In France, CEOs are not glorified as celebrities—chefs are.

The French believe that the economy should support social good, not vice versa. This has produced a cradle-to-grave social security system of which the French are proud. France's poverty rate is half of that in the US, proof to the French that they are on the right track. On the other hand, if you're considering starting

Typical Castle Architecture

Castles were fortified residences for medieval nobles. Castles come in all shapes and sizes, but knowing a few general terms will help you understand them.

The Keep (or Donjon): A high, strong stone tower in the center of the castle complex that was the lord's home and refuge of last resort.

Great Hall: The largest room in the castle, serving as throne room, conference center, and dining hall.

The Yard (or Bailey or Ward): An open courtyard inside the castle walls.

Loopholes: Narrow slits in the walls (also called embrasures, arrow slits, or arrow loops) through which soldiers could shoot arrows at the enemy.

Towers: Tall structures serving as lookouts, chapels, living quarters, or the dungeon. Towers could be square or round, with either crenellated tops or conical roofs.

Turret: A small lookout tower projecting up from the top of the wall.

Moat: A ditch encircling the wall, often filled with water.

Motte-and-Bailey: A traditional form for early English castles, with a small fort on top of a hill (motte) next to an enclosed and fortified yard (bailey).

Wall Walk (or Allure): A pathway atop the wall where guards could patrol and where soldiers stood to fire at the enemy.

Parapet: Outer railing of the wall walk.

Crenellation: A gap-toothed pattern of stones atop the parapet.

Hoardings (or Gallery or Brattice): Wooden huts built onto the upper parts of the stone walls. They served as watch towers, living quarters, and fighting platforms.

a business in France, think again—taxes are formidable (figure a total small-business tax rate of around 66 percent—and likely to increase). French voters are notorious for their belief in the free market's heartless cruelty, and they tend to see globalization as a threat rather than a potential benefit. France is routinely plagued with strikes, demonstrations, and slowdowns as workers try to preserve their hard-earned rights in the face of a competitive global economy.

France is part of the 28-member European Union, a kind of "United States of Europe" that has successfully dissolved borders and implemented a common currency, the euro. France's governments have been decidedly pro-EU. But many French are Euroskeptics, afraid that EU meddling threatens their job security and social benefits.

The French political scene is complex and fascinating. France is governed by a president (currently François Hollande), elected by

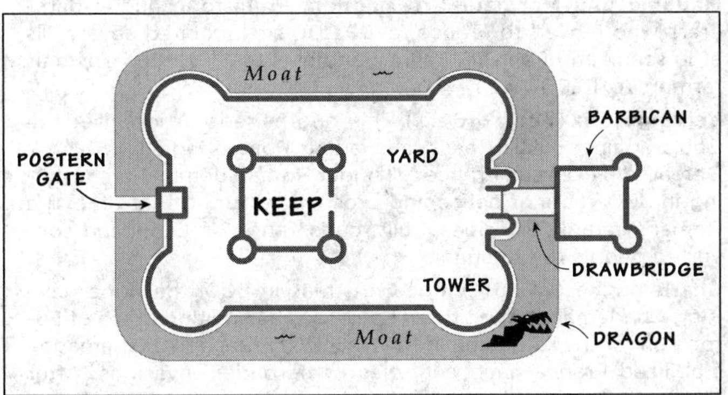

Machicolation: A stone ledge jutting out from the wall, fitted with holes in the bottom. If the enemy was scaling the walls, soldiers could drop rocks or boiling oil down through the holes and onto the enemy below.

Barbican: A fortified gatehouse, sometimes a stand-alone building located outside the main walls.

Drawbridge: A bridge that could be raised or lowered, using counterweights or a chain-and-winch.

Portcullis: A heavy iron grille that could be lowered across the entrance.

Postern Gate: A small, unfortified side or rear entrance used during peacetime. In wartime, it could become a "sally-port" used to launch surprise attacks, or as an escape route.

popular vote every five years. The president then selects the prime minister, who in turn chooses the cabinet ministers. Collectively, this executive branch is known as the *gouvernement*. The parliament consists of a Senate (348 seats) and the 577-seat Assemblée Nationale.

In France, compromise and coalition-building are essential to keeping power. Unlike America's two-party system, France has a half-dozen major political parties, plus more on the fringes. A simple majority is rare. Even the biggest parties rarely get more than a third of the votes. Since the parliament can force the *gouvernement* to resign at any time, it's essential that the *gouvernement* work with them.

For a snapshot of the current political landscape, look no further than the 2012 elections that brought François Hollande to power. He faced incumbent president Nicolas Sarkozy of the center-right Popular Movement Union (UMP)—the man who had

Top French Notables in History

Madame and Monsieur Cro-Magnon: Prehistoric hunter-gatherers who moved to France (c. 30,000 B.C.), painted cave walls at Lascaux and Font-de-Gaume, and eventually settled down as farmers (c. 10,000 B.C.).

Vercingétorix (72 B.C.-46 B.C.): This long-haired warrior rallied the Gauls against Julius Caesar's invading Roman legions (52 B.C.). Defeated by Caesar, France fell under Roman domination, resulting in 500 years of peace and prosperity. During that time, the Romans established cities, built roads, taught in Latin, and converted people to Christianity.

Charlemagne (742-814): For Christmas in 800, the pope gave King Charlemagne the title of Emperor, thus uniting much of Europe under the leadership of the Franks ("France"). Charlemagne stabilized France amid centuries of barbarian invasions. After his death, the empire was split, carving the outlines of modern France and Germany.

Eleanor of Aquitaine (c. 1122-1204): The beautiful, sophisticated ex-wife of the King of France married the King of England, creating an uneasy union between the two countries. During her lifetime, French culture was spread across Europe by roving troubadours, theological scholars, and skilled architects pioneering "the French style"—a.k.a. Gothic.

Joan of Arc (1412-1431): When France and England fought the Hundred Years' War to settle who would rule (1337-1453), teenager Joan of Arc—guided by voices in her head—rallied the French troops. Though Joan was captured and burned as a heretic, the French eventually drove England out of their country for good, establishing the current borders. Over the centuries, the church upgraded Joan's status from heretic to saint (canonized in 1920).

François I (1494-1547): This Renaissance king ruled a united, modern nation, making it a cultural center that hosted the Italian Leonardo da Vinci. François set the tone for future absolute monarchs, punctuating his commands with the phrase, "For such is our pleasure."

Louis XIV (1638-1715): Charismatic and cunning, the "Sun King" ruled Europe's richest, most populous, most powerful nation-state. Every educated European spoke French, dressed in Louis-style leotards and powdered wigs, and built Versailles-like palaces. Though Louis ruled as an absolute monarch (distracting the nobility with courtly games), his reign also fostered the arts and philosophy, sowing the seeds of democracy and revolution.

Marie-Antoinette (1755-1793): As the wife of Louis XVI, she came to symbolize (probably unfairly) the decadence of France's ruling class. When Revolution broke out (1789), she was arrested, imprisoned, and executed—one of thousands who were guillotined on Paris' Place de la Concorde as an enemy of the people.

Napoleon Bonaparte (1769-1821): This daring young military man became a hero during the Revolution, fighting Europe's royalty. He went on to conquer much of the Continent, become leader of France, and eventually rule as a dictator with the title of emperor. In 1815, an allied Europe defeated and exiled Napoleon, reinstating the French monarchy—though future kings and emperors (including Napoleon's nephew, who ruled as Napoleon III) were somewhat subject to democratic constraints.

Claude Monet (1840-1926): Monet's Impressionist paintings captured the soft-focus beauty of the belle époque—middle-class men and women enjoying drinks in cafés, walks in gardens, and picnics along the Seine. At the turn of the 20th century, French culture reigned supreme while its economic and political clout was fading, soon to be shattered by the violence of World War I.

Charles de Gaulle (1890-1970): A career military man, de Gaulle helped France survive occupation by Nazi Germany during World War II with his rousing radio broadcasts and unbending faith in his countrymen. He left politics in the postwar period, but after France's divisive wars in Vietnam and Algeria, he came to the rescue, becoming president of the Fifth Republic in 1959. De Gaulle shocked supporters and allies by granting Algeria its independence, blocking Britain's entry into the Common Market, and withdrawing from the military wing of NATO. The turbulent student riots in the late 1960s eventually led to his resignation in 1969.

Contemporary French: Which recent French people will history remember? President François Mitterrand (1916-1996), the driving force behind La Grande Arche and Opéra Bastille? Marcel Marceau (1923-2007), white-faced mime? Chef Paul Bocuse (b. 1926), inventor of nouvelle cuisine? Brigitte Bardot (b. 1934), film actress, crusader for animal rights, and popularizer of the bikini? Yves Saint Laurent (1936-2008), one of the world's greatest fashion designers? Jean-Marie Le Pen (b. 1928), founder of the far-right Front National party, with staunch anti-immigration policies? Bernard Kouchner (b. 1939), co-founder of Doctors Without Borders and minister of foreign affairs under President Nicolas Sarkozy? Zinédine Zidane (b. 1972), France's greatest soccer player, whose Algerian roots helped raise the status of Arabs in France? Or Dominique Strauss-Kahn (b. 1949), disgraced International Monetary Fund chief? (I hope not.)

cut taxes, reduced the size of government, limited the power of unions, cut workers' benefits, and (most controversially) raised the retirement age from 60 to 62.

Hollande of the Socialist Party (PS) was Sarkozy's main challenger. But other parties were in the mix. The radical Left Front Party (which includes the once-powerful Communists) proposed raising the minimum wage to $2,200 a month, while the environmental Green Party (Les Verts) promised to stimulate the economy with a half-million new green jobs. On the far right was the National Front party (FN), led by Marine Le Pen. She called for expulsion of ethnic minorities, restoration of the French franc as the standard currency, secession from the EU, and broader police powers.

After several months and one TV debate (yes, the French election season is that short), Hollande emerged victorious. And just one month later, his Socialist Party captured more than half of the 577 seats of the Assemblée Nationale. Nevertheless, Hollande has to work closely with legislators, of whom a strong minority are from opposing parties.

François Hollande is politically moderate and personally modest, even boring. Raised in a suburban Parisian middle-class home, he rose quietly through the ranks: assemblyman from a nondescript *département,* small-town mayor, secretary of the Socialist Party. He's never before held a major elected office. Though Hollande is a "Socialist" (a word that spooks Rush Limbaugh), he's in the mainstream of the European political spectrum.

Hollande moved into the Elysée Palace (the French White House) with his "Première Dame" (or first lady), Valerie Trierweiler. Trierweiler is a well-known journalist who writes for the glossy magazine *Paris Match* (the French counterpart to *Time*). She was the first unwed first lady to occupy the Elysée Palace. But in January 2014, it was revealed that Hollande was cheating on his partner (his personal guards drove him on a Vespa to his lover's apartment in the wee hours), which brought the relationship to an end. *Oh-la-la*—imagine this drama in the States. Reaction in France has been predictably understated, as one's personal business is, after all, personal.

But Hollande faces challenges beyond his home life. On the sluggish economy, he favors government expansion and stimulus rather than austerity: hiring thousands of teachers, building hundreds of thousands of homes, and taxing all income above a million euros at 75 percent. Abroad, he's run into trouble working with Germany to shore up weaker members of the eurozone. And he's had to abandon his promise to return the retirement age—at least for some workers—to 60. Hollande's *lune de miel* (honeymoon) has clearly passed, with liberals and conservatives who are furious over his economic policies. By the summer of 2014, his approval rating had dropped to just 18 percent.

An ongoing issue that any French leader must address is immigration, which is shifting the country's ethnic and cultural makeup. Ten percent of France's population is of North African descent, mainly immigrants from former colonies. The increased number of Muslims raises more questions, particularly in tight economic times. The French have (quite controversially) made it illegal for women to wear a full, face-covering veil *(niqāb)* in public. They continue to debate whether banning the veil enforces democracy—or squelches diversity.

Finally, a prominent Socialist whom Hollande must contend with is Ségolène Royal. She lost to Sarkozy in the 2007 presidential election, and lost to Hollande in the 2011 primary. In 2014, she was appointed France's Minister of Ecology. As it happens, Royal and Hollande know each other well: They met in college, lived together for 30 years, and raised four children before splitting up in 2007. They never married. French politics makes strange bedfellows. But that's personal...

For more about French history, consider Europe 101: History and Art for the Traveler *by Rick Steves and Gene Openshaw, available at www.ricksteves.com.*

PRACTICALITIES

Contents

This chapter covers the practical skills of European travel: how to get tourist information, pay for purchases, sightsee efficiently, find good-value accommodations, eat affordably but well, use technology wisely, and get between destinations smoothly. To study ahead and round out your knowledge, check out "Resources" for a summary of recommended books and films.

Tourist Information

The website of the French national tourist office, http://us.rendezvousenfrance.com, is a wealth of information, with particularly good resources for special-interest travel, and plenty of free-to-download brochures. Paris' official tourist-information website, www.parisinfo.com, offers practical information on hotels, special events, museums, children's activities, fashion, nightlife, and more.

Several private companies offer trip-planning services for a fee; Detours in France offers self-drive itinerary packages, hotel bookings, and guided tours of any region in France—ask for helpful Sarah (tel. 09 83 20 71 56, www.detours-in-france.com, sarah@detours-in-france.com). Paris Webservices focuses on Paris-specific assistance (12 Rue de l'Exposition, Mo: Ecole Militaire, RER: Pont de l'Alma, tel. 01 45 56 91 67, www.pariswebservices.com, contactpws@pariswebservices.com).

In France, your best first stop in a new city is generally the tourist information office—except in Paris, where they aren't very necessary. In the rest of France you'll find TIs are well organized, with English-speaking staff. They're good places to get a city map and information on public transit (including bus and train schedules), walking tours, special events, and nightlife. Many TIs have information on the entire country or at least the region, so try to pick up maps for destinations you'll be visiting later in your trip. Towns with a lot of tourism generally have English-speaking guides available for private hire (about €100 for a 2-hour guided town walk).

The French call TIs by different names. *Office de Tourisme* and *Bureau de Tourisme* are used in cities; *Syndicat d'Initiative* or *Information Touristique* are used in small towns. Also look for *Accueil* signs in airports, train stations, and at popular sights. These are information booths staffed with seasonal helpers who provide tourists with limited, though generally sufficient, information. Smaller TIs often close from 12:00 to 14:00 and all day on Sundays.

While TIs can book rooms, use their room-finding service only as a last resort. They are unable to give hard opinions on the relative value of one place over another. Even if there's no "fee," you'll save yourself and your host money by going direct with the listings in this book.

Travel Tips

Emergency and Medical Help: In France, dial 112 for any emergency. For English-speaking police, call 17. To summon an ambulance, call 15. If you get sick, do as the French do and go to a pharmacist for advice. Or ask at your hotel for help—they'll know the nearest medical and emergency services.

Theft or Loss: To replace a passport, you'll need to go in person to an embassy or consulate. You'll find the US embassy in Paris and consulates in Lyon, Marseille, Nice, and Strasbourg (see page 1116; full list at www.usembassy.gov). If your credit and debit cards disappear, cancel and replace them (see "Damage Control for Lost Cards" on page 1040). File a police report either on the spot or within a day or two; you'll need it to submit an insurance claim for lost or stolen rail passes or electronics, and it can help with replacing your passport or credit and debit cards. For more information, see www.ricksteves.com/help. Precautionary measures can minimize the effects of loss—back up your digital photos and other files frequently.

Time Zones: France, like most of continental Europe, is generally six/nine hours ahead of the East/West Coasts of the US. The exceptions are the beginning and end of Daylight Saving Time: Europe "springs forward" the last Sunday in March (two weeks after most of North America), and "falls back" the last Sunday in October (one week before North America). For a handy online time converter, see www.timeanddate.com/worldclock.

Business Hours: You'll find much of rural France closed weekdays from noon to 14:00 (lunch is sacred). On Sunday, most businesses are closed (family is sacred), though some small shops, *boulangeries* (bakeries), and street markets are open until noon, special events and weekly markets pop up, and museums are open all day (but public transportation options are scant). On Mondays, many businesses are closed until 14:00 and possibly all day. Smaller towns are often quiet and downright boring on Sundays and Mondays, unless it's market day. Saturdays are virtually weekdays (without the rush hour).

Watt's Up? Europe's electrical system is 220 volts, instead of North America's 110 volts. Most newer electronics (such as laptops, battery chargers, and hair dryers) convert automatically, so you won't need a converter plug, but you will need an adapter plug with two round prongs, sold inexpensively at travel stores in the US. Avoid bringing older appliances that don't automatically convert voltage; instead, buy a cheap replacement in Europe. You can buy low-cost hair dryers and other small appliances at Darty and Monoprix stores, which you'll find in major cities (ask your hotelier for the closest branch).

Discounts: Discounts aren't always listed in this book. However, many sights offer discounts for youths (up to age 18), students (with proper identification cards, www.isic.org), families, and groups of 10 or more. Always ask, and have passports available at sights for proof. Seniors (age 60 and over) may get the odd discount, though they are often limited to citizens of the European Union (EU). To inquire about a senior discount, ask, *"Réduction troisième âge?"* (ray-dook-see-ohn twah-zee-ehm ahzh).

Online Translation Tip: You can use Google's Chrome browser (available free at www.google.com/chrome) to instantly translate websites. With one click, the page appears in (very rough) English translation. You can also paste the URL of the site into the translation window at www.google.com/translate.

Money

This section offers advice on how to pay for purchases on your trip (including getting cash from ATMs and paying with plastic), dealing with lost or stolen cards, VAT (sales tax) refunds, and tipping.

WHAT TO BRING

Bring both a credit card and a debit card. You'll use the debit card at cash machines (ATMs) to withdraw local cash for most purchases, and the credit card to pay for larger items. Some travelers carry a third card, in case one gets demagnetized or eaten by a temperamental machine.

For an emergency reserve, consider bringing €200 in hard cash in €20 bills. French banks won't exchange dollars, and exchange booths offer lousy rates.

CASH

Cash is just as desirable in Europe as it is at home. Small businesses (B&Bs, mom-and-pop cafés, shops, etc.) prefer that you pay your bills with cash. Some vendors will charge you extra for using a credit card, and some places won't take credit cards at all. Cash is the best—and sometimes only—way to pay for cheap food, bus fare, taxis, and local guides.

Throughout Europe, ATMs are the standard way for travelers to get cash. To withdraw money from an ATM (known as a *distributeur;* dee-stree-bew-tur), you'll need a debit card (ideally with a Visa or MasterCard logo for maximum usability), plus a PIN code. Know your PIN code in numbers; there are only numbers—no letters—on European keypads. For increased security, shield the keypad when entering your PIN code, and don't use an ATM if anything on the front of the machine looks loose or damaged (a sign that someone may have attached a "skimming" device to capture account information). Try to withdraw large sums of money to reduce the number of per-transaction bank fees you'll pay.

When possible, use ATMs located outside banks—a thief is less likely to target a cash machine near surveillance cameras, and if your card is munched by a machine, you can go inside for help. Stay away from "independent" ATMs such as Travelex, Euronet, Moneybox, Cardpoint, and Cashzone, which charge huge commissions, have terrible exchange rates, and may try to trick users with "dynamic currency conversion" (described at the end of "Credit and Debit Cards," next).

Although you can use a credit card for an ATM transaction, it only makes sense in an emergency, because it's considered a cash advance (borrowed at a high interest rate) rather than a withdrawal.

While traveling, if you want to monitor your accounts online

Exchange Rate

1 euro (€) = about $1.40

To convert prices in euros to dollars, add about 40 percent: €20 = about $28, €50 = about $70. (Check www.oanda.com for the latest exchange rates.) Just like the dollar, one euro (€1) is broken down into 100 cents. You'll find coins ranging from €0.01 to €2, and bills from €5 to €500.

to detect any unauthorized transactions, be sure to use a secure connection (see page 1085).

Pickpockets target tourists, particularly those coming in from Paris airports. To safeguard your cash, wear a money belt—a pouch with a strap that you buckle around your waist like a belt and tuck under your clothes. Keep your cash, credit cards, and passport secure in your money belt, and carry only a day's spending money in your front pocket.

CREDIT AND DEBIT CARDS

For purchases, Visa and MasterCard are more commonly accepted than American Express.

Just like at home, credit or debit cards work easily at larger hotels, restaurants, and shops. I typically use my debit card to withdraw cash to pay for most purchases. I use my credit card only in a few specific situations: to book hotel reservations by phone, to cover major expenses (such as car rentals, plane tickets, and hotel stays), and to pay for things near the end of my trip (to avoid another visit to the ATM). While you could use a debit card to make most large purchases, using a credit card offers a greater degree of fraud protection (because debit cards draw funds directly from your account).

Ask Your Credit- or Debit-Card Company: Before your trip, contact the company that issued your debit or credit cards.

• Confirm your **card will work overseas,** and alert them that you'll be using it in Europe; otherwise, they may deny transactions if they perceive unusual spending patterns.

• Ask for the specifics on transaction **fees.** When you use your credit or debit card—either for purchases or ATM withdrawals—you'll typically be charged additional "international transaction" fees of up to 3 percent (1 percent is normal) plus $5 per transaction. If your card's fees seem high, consider getting a different card just for your trip: Capital One (www.capitalone.com) and most credit unions have low to no international fees.

• If you plan to withdraw cash from ATMs, confirm your

daily **withdrawal limit,** and if necessary, ask your bank to adjust it. Some travelers prefer a high limit that allows them to take out more cash at each ATM stop (saving on bank fees), while others prefer to set a lower limit in case their card is stolen. Note that foreign banks also set maximum withdrawal amounts for their ATMs. Also, remember that you're withdrawing euros, not dollars—so if your daily limit is $300, withdraw just €200. Many frustrated travelers walk away from ATMs thinking their cards have been rejected, when actually they were asking for more cash in euros than their daily limit allowed.

• Get your bank's emergency **phone number** in the US (but not its 800 number, which isn't accessible from overseas) to call collect if you have a problem.

• Ask for your credit card's **PIN** in case you need to make an emergency cash withdrawal or encounter Europe's "chip-and-PIN" system; the bank won't tell you your PIN over the phone, so allow time for it to be mailed to you.

Chip and PIN: Europeans are increasingly using chip-and-PIN cards, which are embedded with an electronic security chip (in addition to the magnetic stripe found on American-style cards). To make a purchase with a chip-and-PIN card, the cardholder inserts the card into a slot in the payment machine, then enters a PIN (like using a debit card in the US) while the card stays in the slot. The chip inside the card authorizes the transaction; the cardholder doesn't sign a receipt. Your American-style card might not work at payment machines using this system, such as those at train and subway stations, toll roads, parking garages, luggage lockers, bike-rental kiosks, and self-serve gas pumps.

If you have problems using your American card in a chip-and-PIN machine, here are some suggestions: For either a debit card or a credit card, try entering that card's PIN when prompted. (Note that your credit-card PIN may not be the same as your debit-card PIN; you'll need to ask your bank for your credit-card PIN.) If your cards still don't work, look for a machine that takes cash, seek out a clerk who might be able to process the transaction manually, or ask a local if you can pay them cash to run the transaction on their card.

And don't panic. Most travelers who use only magnetic-stripe cards don't run into problems. Still, it pays to carry plenty of euros, and remember, you can always use an ATM to withdraw cash with your magnetic-stripe debit card.

If you're still concerned, you can apply for a chip card in the US (though I think it's overkill). One option is the no-annual-fee GlobeTrek Visa, offered by Andrews Federal Credit Union in Maryland (open to all US residents; see www.andrewsfcu.org). In the future, chip cards should become standard issue in the US: Visa and MasterCard have asked US banks and merchants to use chip-based cards by late 2015.

Dynamic Currency Conversion: If merchants offer to convert your purchase price into dollars (called dynamic currency conversion, or DCC), refuse this "service." You'll pay even more in fees for the expensive convenience of seeing your charge in dollars. "Independent" ATMs (such as Travelex and Moneybox) may try to confuse customers by presenting DCC in misleading terms. If an ATM offers to "lock in" or "guarantee" your conversion rate, choose "proceed without conversion." Other prompts might state, "You can be charged in dollars: Press YES for dollars, NO for euros." Always choose the local currency in these situations.

Damage Control for Lost Cards

If you lose your credit, debit, or ATM card, you can stop people from using your card by reporting the loss immediately to the respective global customer-assistance centers. Call these 24-hour US numbers collect: Visa (tel. 303/967-1096), MasterCard (tel. 636/722-7111), and American Express (tel. 336/393-1111). In France, to make a collect call to the US, dial 0-800-99-0011, then the number. Press zero or stay on the line for an English-speaking operator. European toll-free numbers (listed by country) can be found at the websites for Visa and MasterCard. For another option (with the same results), you can call these toll-free numbers in France: Visa (tel. 08 00 90 11 79) and MasterCard (tel. 08 00 90 13 87). American Express has a Paris office, but the call isn't free (tel. 01 47 77 70 00, greeting is in French only, dial 1 to speak with someone in English).

Providing the following information will allow for a quicker cancellation of your missing card: full card number, whether you are the primary or secondary cardholder, the cardholder's name exactly as printed on the card, billing address, home phone number, circumstances of the loss or theft, and identification verification (your birthdate, your mother's maiden name, or your Social Security number—memorize this, don't carry a copy). If you are the secondary cardholder, you'll also need to provide the primary cardholder's identification-verification details. You can generally receive a temporary card within two or three business days in Europe (see www.ricksteves.com/help for more).

If you report your loss within two days, you typically won't be responsible for any unauthorized transactions on your account, although many banks charge a liability fee of $50.

TIPPING

Tipping *(donner un pourboire)* in France isn't as automatic and generous as it is in the US. For special service, tips are appreciated, but not expected. As in the US, the proper amount depends on your resources, tipping philosophy, and the circumstances, but some general guidelines apply.

Restaurants: Prices at cafés and restaurants include a 12-15 percent service charge (referred to as *service compris* or *prix net* but generally not broken out on your bill). Most French never tip (credit-card receipts don't even have space to add a tip). But if you feel the service was exceptional, it's kind to tip up to 5 percent extra. If you want the waiter to keep the change when you pay, say, "*C'est bon*" (say bohn), meaning, "It's good." Never feel guilty if you don't leave a tip.

Taxis: For a typical ride, round up your fare a bit (for instance, if the fare is €13, pay €14). If the cabbie hauls your bags and zips you to the airport to help you catch your flight, you might want to toss in a little more. But if you feel like you're being driven in circles or otherwise ripped off, skip the tip.

Services: In general, if someone in the service industry does a super job for you, a small tip of a euro or two is appropriate...but not required. If you're not sure whether (or how much) to tip for a service, ask your hotelier or the TI.

GETTING A VAT REFUND

Wrapped into the purchase price of your French souvenirs is a Value-Added Tax (VAT) of about 20 percent. You're entitled to get most of that tax back if you purchase more than €175 (about $245) worth of goods at a store that participates in the VAT-refund scheme. Typically, you must ring up the minimum at a single retailer—you can't add up your purchases from various shops to reach the required amount.

Getting your refund is straightforward and, if you buy a substantial amount of souvenirs, well worth the hassle. If you're lucky, the merchant will subtract the tax when you make your purchase. (This is more likely to occur if the store ships the goods to your home.) Otherwise, you'll need to:

Get the paperwork. Have the merchant completely fill out the necessary refund document, called a *bordereau de détaxe*. You'll have to present your passport. Get the paperwork done before you leave the store to ensure you'll have everything you need (including your original sales receipt).

Get your stamp at the border or airport. Process your VAT document at your last stop in the European Union (such as at the airport) with the customs agent who deals with VAT refunds. Arrive an additional hour before you need to check in for your flight to allow time to find the local customs office—and to stand in line. It's best to keep your purchases in your carry-on. If they're too large or dangerous to carry on (such as knives), pack them in your checked bags and alert the check-in agent. You'll be sent (with your tagged bag) to a customs desk outside security, which will examine your bag, stamp your paperwork, and put your bag on the belt. You're not supposed to use your purchased goods before you leave. If you show up at customs wearing your chic new shoes, officials might look the other way—or deny you a refund.

Collect your refund. You'll need to return your stamped document to the retailer or its representative. Many merchants work with a service, such as Global Blue or Premier Tax Free, that has offices at major airports, ports, or border crossings (either before or after security, probably strategically located near a duty-free shop). These services, which extract a 4 percent fee, can refund your money immediately in cash or credit your card (within two billing cycles). If the retailer handles VAT refunds directly, it's up to you to contact the merchant for your refund. You can mail the documents from your home, or more quickly, from your point of departure (using an envelope you've prepared in advance or one that's been provided by the merchant). You'll then have to wait—it can take months.

CUSTOMS FOR AMERICAN SHOPPERS

You are allowed to take home $800 worth of items per person duty-free, once every 30 days. You can take home many processed and packaged foods: vacuum-packed cheeses, dried herbs, jams, baked goods, candy, chocolate, oil, vinegar, mustard, and honey. Fresh fruits and vegetables and most meats are not allowed. However, canned meat is allowed if it doesn't contain any beef, veal, lamb, or mutton.

As for alcohol, you can bring in one liter duty-free; it can be packed securely in your checked luggage, along with any other liquid-containing items. To bring alcohol (or any liquid-packed foods) in your carry-on bag on your flight home, buy it at a duty-free shop at the airport. You'll increase your odds of getting it onto a connecting flight if it's packaged in a "STEB"—a secure, tamper-evident bag. But stay away from liquids in opaque, ceramic, or metallic containers, which usually cannot be successfully screened (STEB or no STEB).

To check customs rules and duty rates, visit www.cbp.gov.

Sightseeing

Sightseeing can be hard work. Use these tips to make your visits to France's finest sights meaningful, fun, efficient, and painless.

PLAN AHEAD

Set up an itinerary that allows you to fit in all your must-see sights. For a one-stop look at opening hours, see the "At a Glance" sidebars for Paris, Nice, Lyon, the Loire Valley châteaux, and the Dordogne's prehistoric sights. Most sights keep stable hours, but you can easily confirm the latest by checking with the TI or visiting museum websites.

Don't put off visiting a must-see sight—you never know when a place will close unexpectedly for a holiday, strike, or restoration. Many museums are closed or have reduced hours at least a few days a year, especially on holidays such as Christmas, New Year's, and Labor Day (May 1). A list of holidays is on page 1116; check museum websites for possible closures during your trip. In summer, some sights may stay open late. Off-season, many museums have shorter hours.

Going at the right time helps avoid crowds. This book offers tips on the best times to see specific sights. Try visiting popular sights very early (arrive at least 15 minutes before opening time) or very late. Evening visits are usually peaceful, with fewer crowds. For example, Paris' Louvre and Orsay museums are open selected evenings, and the abbey at Mont St-Michel is open on all summer evenings.

Many French monuments and cities (and some villages) are beautifully lit at night, making evening walks a joy. Sound-and-light shows *(son et lumière)* are outdoor events held at major buildings after dark; you'll take a seat and watch an array of colored lights illuminate the façade (e.g., of the town's cathedral) while a narrator or audioguide melodramatically tells the story of the place. These spectacles, which can cost a fee, can be a fun experience (though once is usually enough for most).

At Mont St-Michel and Carcassonne, it's best to arrive at about 17:00, spend the night, and explore in the morning before the crowds descend. Visit these sights first thing or late in the day: Versailles, Château de Chenonceau, Les Baux, the Dordogne's riverfront villages, St-Cirq Lapopie, and Pont du Gard.

Several cities offer sightseeing passes that are worthwhile values for busy sightseers; do the math to see if they'll save you money.

Study up. To get the most out of the sight descriptions in this book, read them before you visit.

The Rules of *Boules*

Throughout France you'll see people playing *boules* (also known as *pétanque*). Each player starts with three iron balls, with the object of getting them close to the target, a small wooden ball called a *cochonnet* (piglet). The first player tosses the *cochonnet* about 30 feet, then throws the first of his iron balls near the target. The next player takes a turn. As soon as a player's ball is closest, it's the other guy's turn. Once all balls have been thrown, the score is tallied—the player with the closest ball gets one point for each ball closer to the target than his opponent's. The loser gets zero. Games are generally to 15 points.

A regulation *boules* field is 10 feet by 43 feet, but the game is played everywhere—just scratch a throwing circle in the sand, toss the *cochonnet,* and you're off. Strategists can try to knock the opponent's balls out of position, knock the *cochonnet* itself out of position, or guard their best ball with the other two.

AT SIGHTS

Here's what you can typically expect:

Entering: Be warned that you may not be allowed to enter if you arrive 30 to 60 minutes before closing time. And guards start ushering people out well before the actual closing time, so don't save the best for last.

Some important sights have a security check, where you must open your bag or send it through a metal detector. Some sights require you to check daypacks and coats. (If you'd rather not check your daypack, try carrying it tucked under your arm like a purse as you enter.) If you check a bag, the attendant may ask you if it contains anything of value—such as a camera, phone, money, or passport—since these usually cannot be checked.

At churches—which often offer interesting art (usually free) and a cool, welcome seat—a modest dress code (no bare shoulders or shorts) is encouraged though rarely enforced.

Photography: If the museum's photo policy isn't clearly posted, ask a guard. Generally, taking photos without a flash or tripod is allowed. Some sights ban photos altogether.

Temporary Exhibits: Museums may have special exhibits in addition to their permanent collection. Some exhibits are included in the entry price, while others come at an extra cost (which you may have to pay even if you don't want to see the exhibit).

Expect Changes: Artwork can be on tour, on loan, out sick, or shifted at the whim of the curator. To adapt, pick up a floor plan as you enter, and ask the museum staff if you can't find a particular item. Say the title or artist's name, or point to the photograph in this book, and ask for its location by saying, *"Où est?"* (oo ay).

Audioguides: Many sights rent audioguides, which generally offer worthwhile recorded descriptions in English (about €6, sometimes included with admission). If you bring your own earbuds, you can enjoy better sound and avoid holding the device to your ear. To save money, bring a Y-jack and share one audioguide with your travel partner. Many museums and sights offer apps (often free) that you can download to your mobile device (check their websites). I've produced free downloadable audio tours of some of the major sights in Paris; see page 1110.

Services: Important sights may have an on-site café or cafeteria (usually a handy place to rejuvenate during a long visit). The WCs at sights are free and generally clean.

Before Leaving: At the gift shop, scan the postcard rack or thumb through a guidebook to be sure that you haven't overlooked something that you'd like to see.

Every sight or museum offers more than what is covered in this book. Use the information in this book as an introduction—not the final word.

Sleeping

Good-value accommodations in France generally are easy to find. Choose from one- to five-star hotels (two and three stars are my mainstays), bed-and-breakfasts (*chambres d'hôtes,* usually cheaper than hotels), hostels, campgrounds, and even homes (*gîtes,* rented by the week).

I favor hotels and restaurants that are handy to your sightseeing activities. Rather than list hotels scattered throughout a city, I describe two or three favorite neighborhoods and recommend the best accommodations values in each, from dorm beds to fancy doubles with all of the comforts.

A major feature of this book is its extensive and opinionated listing of good-value rooms. I like places that are clean, central, relatively quiet at night, reasonably priced, friendly, small enough to have a hands-on owner and stable staff, and run with a respect for French traditions. (In France, for me, five out of these seven criteria mean it's a keeper.) I'm more impressed by a convenient location and a fun-loving philosophy than flat-screen TVs and a pricey laundry service.

Book your accommodations well in advance, especially if you'll be traveling during busy times. Reserving ahead is particularly important for Paris—the sooner, the better. Wherever you're staying, be ready for crowds during these holiday periods: Easter weekend; Labor Day; Ascension weekend; Pentecost weekend; Bastille Day and the week during which it falls; and the winter holidays (mid-Dec-early Jan). See page 1116 for a list of major holidays and festivals in France; for tips on making reservations, see page 1052.

Some people make reservations as they travel, calling hotels and *chambres d'hôtes* a few days to a week before their arrival. If you'd rather travel without any reservations at all, you'll have greater success snaring rooms if you arrive at your destination early in the day. If you anticipate crowds (weekends are worst), on the day you want to check in, call hotels at about 9:00 or 10:00, when the receptionist knows who'll be checking out and which rooms will be available. If you encounter a language barrier, ask the fluent receptionist at your current hotel to call for you.

RATES AND DEALS

I've described my recommended accommodations using a Sleep Code (see sidebar). Prices listed are for one-night stays in peak season, do not include breakfast (unless noted), and assume you're booking directly with the hotel (not through an online hotel-booking engine or TI). Booking services extract a commission from the hotel, which logically closes the door on special deals. Book direct.

My recommended hotels generally have a website (often with a built-in booking form) and an email address; you can expect a response in English within a day (and often sooner).

If you're on a budget, it's smart to email several hotels to ask for their best price. Comparison-shop and make your choice. This is especially helpful when dealing with the larger hotels that use "dynamic pricing," a computer-generated system that predicts the demand for particular days and sets prices accordingly: High-demand days will often be more than double the price of low-demand days. This makes it impossible for a guidebook to list anything more accurate than a wide range of prices. I regret this trend. While you can assume that hotels listed in this book are good, it's very difficult to say which ones are the better value unless you email to confirm the price.

As you look over the listings, you'll notice that some accommodations promise special prices to Rick Steves readers. To get these rates, you must book direct (that is, not through a booking site like TripAdvisor or Booking.com), mention this book when you reserve, and then show the book upon arrival. Rick Steves discounts apply to readers with ebooks as well as printed books. Because I trust hotels to honor this, please let me know if you don't

Sleep Code

(€1 = about $1.40, country code: 33)

Price Rankings

To help you easily sort through my listings, I've divided the accommodations into three categories, based on the highest price for a standard double room with bath during high season:

$$$	**Higher Priced**
$$	**Moderately Priced**
$	**Lower Priced**

I always rate hostels as $, whether or not they have double rooms, because they have the cheapest beds in town.

Prices can change without notice; verify the hotel's current rates online or by email. For the best prices, always book directly with the hotel.

Abbreviations

To pack maximum information into minimum space, I use the following code to describe the accommodations in this book. Prices listed are per room, not per person. When a price range is given for a type of room (such as double rooms listing for €100-130), it means the price fluctuates with the season, size of room, or length of stay; expect to pay the upper end for peak-season stays.

- **S** = Single room (or price for one person in a double).
- **D** = Double or twin room.
- **T** = Triple (generally a double bed with a single).
- **Q** = Quad (usually two double beds; adding an extra child's bed to a T is usually cheaper).
- **b** = Private bathroom with toilet and shower or tub.
- **s** = Private shower or tub only (the toilet is down the hall).
- ***** = French hotel rating system, ranging from zero to five stars.

According to this code, a couple staying at a "Db-€100" hotel would pay a total of €100 (about $140) for a double room with a private bathroom. Unless otherwise noted, breakfast is not included, hotel staff speak basic English, and credit cards are accepted.

There's almost always free Wi-Fi; guest computers are sometimes available.

receive a listed discount. Note, though, that discounts understandably may not be applied to promotional rates.

In general, prices can soften if you stay at least three nights or mention this book. You can also try asking for a cheaper room or a discount, or offer to skip breakfast.

TYPES OF ACCOMMODATIONS

Hotels

In this book, the price for a double room ranges from €45 (very simple, toilet and shower down the hall) to €400-plus (grand lobbies, maximum plumbing, and the works), with most clustering around €80-110 (with private bathrooms). If I give a single rate for a room, it applies to high season (figure Easter to October); if I give a range, the lower rates are likely available only in winter. Hotels in France must charge a daily tax *(taxe du séjour)* of about €1-2 per person per day. Some hotels include it in the listed prices, but most add it to your bill.

The French have a simple hotel-rating system based on amenities and rated by stars (indicated in this book by asterisks, from * through *****). One star is modest, two has most of the comforts, and three is generally a two-star with a fancier lobby and more elaborately designed rooms. Four-star places give marginally more comfort than those with three. Five stars probably offer more luxury than you'll have time to appreciate. Two- and three-star hotels are required to have an English-speaking staff, though nearly all hotels I recommend have someone who speaks English.

The number of stars doesn't generally reflect room size or guarantee quality. One- and two-star hotels are inexpensive, but some three-star (and even a few four-star) hotels offer good value, justifying the extra cost. Unclassified hotels (no stars) can be bargains or depressing dumps.

Prices vary within each hotel depending on room size and whether the room has a bath or shower, twin beds, or a double bed (tubs and twins cost more than showers and double beds). If you have a preference, ask for it. Hotels often have more rooms with tubs (which the French prefer) and are inclined to give you one by default. You can save as much as €20 per night by finding the increasingly rare room without a private shower or toilet.

Most French hotels now have queen-size beds—to confirm, ask, *"Avez-vous des lits de cent-soixante?"* (ah-vay-voo day lee duh sahn-swah-sahnt). Some hotels push two twins together under king-size-sheets and blankets to make *le king size*. If you'll take

French Hotel-Room Lingo

Study the price list on the hotel's website or posted at the desk, so you know your options. Receptionists often don't mention the cheaper rooms—they assume you want a private bathroom or a bigger room. Here are the types of rooms and beds:

French	Pronounced	English
une chambre avec douche et WC	ewn shahm-bruh ah-vehk doosh ay vay-say	room with private shower and toilet
une chambre avec bain et WC	ewn shahm-bruh ah-vehk ban ay vay-say	room with private bathtub and toilet
une chambre avec cabinet de toilette	ewn shahm-bruh ah-vehk kah-bee-nay duh twah-leht	room with a toilet (shower down the hall)
une chambre sans douche ni WC	ewn shahm-bruh sahn doosh nee vay-say	room without a private shower or toilet
chambres communiquantes	shahm-bruh koh-mew-nee-kahnt	connecting rooms (ideal for families)
une chambre simple, un single	ewn shahm-bruh san-pluh, uhn san-guhl	a true single room
un grand lit	uhn grahn lee	double bed (55 inches wide)
deux petits lits	duh puh-tee lee	twin beds (30-36 inches wide)
un lit de cent-soixante	uhn lee duh sahn-swah-sahnt	queen-size bed (160 cm, or 63 inches wide)
un king size	uhn "king size"	a king-size bed (usually two twins pushed together)
un lit pliant	uhn lee plee-ahn	folding bed
un bérceau	uhn behr-soh	baby crib
un lit d'enfant	uhn lee dahn-fahn	child's bed

Keep Cool

If you're visiting France in the summer, the extra expense of an air-conditioned room can be money well spent, particularly in the south. Most hotel rooms with air-conditioners come with a control stick (like a TV remote) that generally has the similar symbols and features: fan icon (click to toggle through wind power, from light to gale); louver icon (choose steady airflow or waves); snowflake and sunshine icons (cold air or heat, depending on season); clock ("O" setting: run X hours before turning off; "I" setting: wait X hours to start); and the temperature control (21 or 22 degrees Celsius is comfortable; also see the thermometer diagram on page 1121). When you leave your room for the day, turning off the air-conditioning is good form.

either twins or a double, ask for a generic *une chambre pour deux* (room for two) to avoid being needlessly turned away.

Extra pillows and blankets are sometimes in the closet or available on request. To get a pillow, ask for *"Un oreiller, s'il vous plaît"* (un oh-ray-yay, see voo play). Hotel elevators, while becoming more common in big cities, are often very small—pack light, or you may need to take your bags up one at a time.

Hotel lobbies, halls, and breakfast rooms are off-limits to smokers, though they can light up in their rooms. Still, I seldom smell any smoke in the hundreds of rooms I check each year. Some hotels have non-smoking rooms or floors—ask for one if this is important to you.

Most hotels offer some kind of breakfast, but it's rarely included in the room rates—pay attention when comparing rates between hotels. The price of breakfast correlates with the price of the room: The more expensive the room, the more expensive the breakfast. This per-person charge, which increases with the number of stars the hotel has, can add up, particularly for families. While hoteliers hope you'll buy their breakfast, it's optional (for more on breakfast, see page 1060).

Some hoteliers, especially in coastal resort towns, strongly encourage their peak-season guests to take *demi-pension* (half-pension)—that is, breakfast and either lunch or dinner. By law, they can't require you to take half-pension unless you are staying three or more nights, but in practice some do during summer. I've indicated where I think *demi-pension* is a good value.

Hoteliers can be a great help and source of advice. Most know their city well, and can assist you with everything from public transit and airport connections to calling an English-speaking doctor, or finding a good restaurant, Wi-Fi hotspot (*point Wi-Fi*, pwan wee-fee), or self-service launderette (*laverie automatique,* lah-vay-ree oh-to-mah-teek).

If you're arriving early in the morning, your room probably won't be ready. You can drop your bag safely at the hotel and dive right into sightseeing.

Even at the best hotels, mechanical breakdowns occur: Air-conditioning malfunctions, sinks leak, hot water turns cold, and toilets gurgle and smell. Report your concerns clearly and calmly at the front desk. For more complicated problems, don't expect instant results.

It's usually worth asking for a quieter room in the back or on an upper floor. To guard against theft in your room, keep valuables out of sight. Some rooms come with a safe, and other hotels have safes at the front desk. I've never bothered using one.

Checkout can pose problems if surprise charges pop up on your bill. If you settle your bill the day before you leave, you'll have time to discuss and address any points of contention (before 19:00, when the night shift usually arrives).

Some hoteliers will ask you to sign their *Livre d'Or* ("Golden Book," for client comments). They take this seriously and enjoy reading your remarks.

Above all, keep a positive attitude. Remember, you're on vacation. If your hotel is a disappointment, spend more time out enjoying the city you came to see.

Modern Hotel Chains: France is littered with ultramodern hotels, often located on cheap land just outside of town, providing drivers with low-stress accommodations (though you'll find some in city centers as well). The antiseptically clean and cheap Ibis Budget chain (about €45-60/room for up to three people), the more attractive and spacious Ibis hotels (€85-115 for a double), and the cushier Mercure and Novotel hotels (€110-200 for a double) are all run by the same company, Accor (US tel. 800-221-4542, www.accorhotels.com). Though hardly quaint, these can be a good value (look for deals on their website), particularly when they're centrally located; I list many in this book. Another chain, Kyriad, offers moderate prices and good quality, often in central locations (www.kyriad.com). Best Western Hotels are generally reliable and often centrally located (US tel. 800-780-7234, www.bestwestern.com). Château and Hotels Collection has more cushy digs (www.chateauxhotels.com). For a long listing of various hotels throughout France, see www.france.com.

Bed-and-Breakfasts

B&Bs (*chambres d'hôtes,* abbreviated CH) are generally found in smaller towns and rural areas. They're usually a great deal, offering double the cultural intimacy yet costing much less than most hotel

Making Hotel Reservations

Reserve your rooms several weeks in advance—or as soon as you've pinned down your travel dates (for Paris, reserve several months ahead—for any time of year). Note that some national holidays merit your making reservations far in advance (see page 1116).

Requesting a Reservation: It's easiest to book your room through the hotel's website. (For the best rates, always use the hotel's official site and not a booking agency's site.) If there's no reservation form, or for complicated requests, send an email (see below for a sample request). Most recommended hotels take reservations in English.

The hotelier wants to know:

- the number and type of rooms you need
- the number of nights you'll stay
- your date of arrival (use the European style for writing dates: day/month/year)
- your date of departure
- any special needs (such as bathroom in the room or down the hall, cheapest room, twin beds vs. double bed, and so on)

Mention any discounts—for Rick Steves readers or otherwise—when you make the reservation.

Confirming a Reservation: Most places will request a credit-card number to hold your room. If they don't have a secure online reservation form—look for the https—you can email it (I do), but it's safer to share that confidential info via a phone call, two emails (splitting your number between them).

Canceling a Reservation: If you must cancel, it's courteous—and smart—to do so with as much notice as possible, especially

rooms. And though you may lose some hotel conveniences—such as lounges, in-room phones, reliable Wi-Fi, frequent bed-sheet changes, and the ability to pay with a credit card—I happily make the trade-off for the personal touches and lower rates. Your hosts may not speak English, but they will almost always be enthusiastic and pleasant.

You'll find CHs in this book and through local TIs, often listed by the owner's family name. To find small-town TIs online, do a web search for *"office du tourisme"* with the name of town you want (if that doesn't work start with the nearest large city TI and go from there). While most CHs post small *Chambres* or *Chambres d'hôte* signs in their front windows, some are found only through the local TI. If you haven't booked ahead, it's always OK to ask to see the room before you commit.

I recommend reliable CHs that offer a good value and/or unique experience (such as CHs in renovated mills, châteaux, and

From: rick@ricksteves.com
Sent: Today
To: info@hotelcentral.com
Subject: Reservation request for 19-22 July

Dear Hotel Central,

I would like to reserve a room for 2 people for 3 nights, arriving 19 July and departing 22 July. If possible, I would like a quiet room with a double bed and a bathroom inside the room.

Please let me know if you have a room available and the price.

Thank you!
Rick Steves

for smaller family-run places. Be warned that cancellation policies can be strict; read the fine print or ask about these before you book. Internet deals may require prepayment, with no refunds for cancellations.

Reconfirming a Reservation: Always call to reconfirm your room reservation a few days in advance. For smaller hotels and chambres d'hôtes, I call again on my day of arrival to tell my host what time I expect to get there (especially important if arriving late—after 17:00).

Phoning: For tips on how to call hotels overseas, see page 1077.

wine *domaines*). *Chambres d'hôtes* have their own star-rating system, but it doesn't correspond to the hotel rating system. So, to avoid confusion, I don't list stars for CHs. Virtually all of my recommended CHs have private in-room bathrooms, and some have common rooms with refrigerators. Most have Wi-Fi at least in lounge areas. Doubles with breakfast generally cost €60-80 (€100-120 for the fancy ones).

Tables d'hôte are CHs that offer an optional, reasonably priced home-cooked dinner; the meals are almost always worth springing for, and they must be requested in advance.

Hostels

You'll pay about €22-28 per bed to stay at a hostel *(auberge de jeunesse)*. Travelers of any age are welcome if they don't mind dorm-style accommodations and meeting other travelers. Cheap meals are sometimes offered, and most hostels offer kitchen facilities, guest computers, Wi-Fi, and a self-service laundry. Nowadays, concerned about bedbugs, hostels are likely to provide all bedding, including sheets. Family and private rooms may be available on request.

Independent hostels tend to be easygoing, colorful, and informal (no membership required); www.hostelworld.com is the standard way backpackers search and book hostels, but also try www.hostelz.com and www.hostels.com.

Official hostels are part of Hostelling International (HI) and share an online booking site (www.hihostels.com). HI hostels typically require that you either have a membership card or pay extra per night.

Camping

In Europe, camping is more of a social than an environmental experience. It's a great way for American travelers to make European friends. Camping averages about €20 per campsite per night (though most municipal sites cost less), and almost every destination recommended in this book has a campground within a reasonable walk or bus ride from the town center and train station. A tent, pillow, and sleeping bag are all you need. Many campgrounds have small grocery stores and washing machines, and some even come with cafés and miniature golf. French TIs have camping information. You'll find more detailed information in the annually updated *Michelin Camping France,* available in the US and at most French bookstores.

Gîtes, Apartments, and Hotel Barges

Whether you're in a city or the countryside, renting an apartment, house, or villa can be a fun and cost-effective way to go local. Throughout France, you can find reasonably priced rental homes that are ideal for families and small groups wanting to explore a region more closely.

Gîtes (pronounced "zheet") are homes in the countryside (usually urbanites' second homes) rentable by the week, from Saturday to Saturday. The objective of the *gîte* program was to save characteristic rural homes from abandonment and to make it easy and affordable for families to enjoy the French countryside. The government offers subsidies to renovate such homes, then coordinates rentals to make it financially feasible for the owner. Today, France has thousands of *gîtes.* One of your co-authors restored a farmhouse, and even though he and his wife are American, they received the same assistance that French owners get.

With little access to public transit, *gîtes* are best for drivers and ideal for families and small groups (because they can sleep many for a reasonable price). Homes range in comfort from simple cot-

The Good and Bad of Online Reviews

User-generated travel review websites—such as TripAdvisor, Booking.com, and Yelp—have quickly become a huge player in the travel industry. These sites give you access to actual reports—good and bad—from travelers who have experienced the hotel, restaurant, tour, or attraction.

My hotelier friends in Europe are in awe of these sites' influence. Small hoteliers who want to stay in business have no choice but to work with review sites—which often charge fees for good placement or photos, and tack on commissions if users book through the site instead of directly with the hotel.

While these sites work hard to weed out bogus users, my hunch is that a significant percentage of reviews are posted by friends or enemies of the business being reviewed. I've even seen hotels "bribe" guests (for example, offer a free breakfast) in exchange for a positive review. Also, review sites can become an echo chamber, with one or two flashy businesses camped out atop the ratings, while better, more affordable, and more authentic alternatives sit ignored farther down the list. (For example, I find review sites' restaurant recommendations skew to very touristy, obvious options.)

Remember that a user-generated review is based on the experience of one person. That person likely stayed at one hotel and ate at a few restaurants, and doesn't have much of a basis for comparison. A guidebook is the work of a trained researcher who has exhaustively visited many alternatives to assess their relative value. I recently checked out some top-rated TripAdvisor listings in various towns; when stacked up against their competitors, some are gems, while just as many are duds.

Both types of information have their place, and in many ways, they're complementary. If a hotel or restaurant is well-reviewed in a guidebook or two, and also gets good ratings on one of these sites, it's likely a winner.

tages and farmhouses to restored châteaux. Most have at least two bedrooms, a kitchen, a living room, and a bathroom or two—but no sheets or linens (though you can usually rent them for extra). Like hotels, all *gîtes* are rated for comfort from one to four (using ears of corn—*épis*—rather than stars). Two or three *épis* are generally sufficient quality, but I'd lean toward three for more comfort. Prices generally range from €400 to €1,300 per week, depending on house size and amenities such as pools (if it's less than €400 per week, I'd think twice). If your owner does not speak English, be prepared for doing business in French—all the contracts are in French. For more information on *gîtes,* visit www.gites-de-france.com or www.gite.com.

Rental apartments and **homes** are available in cities and in towns

Traveling with Kids

France is kid-friendly for young children, partly because so much of it is rural. (Teenagers, on the other hand, tend to prefer cities.) Both of this book's authors have kids, and we've used our substantial experience traveling with them to improve this book. Our kids have greatly enriched our travels, and we hope the same will be true for you.

My kids' favorite places have been Mont St-Michel, the Alps, Loire châteaux, Carcassonne, and Paris (especially the Eiffel Tower and Seine River boat ride)—and any hotel with a pool. To make your trip fun for everyone in the family, mix heavy-duty sights with kid activities (playing mini-golf, renting bikes, and riding the little tourist trains popular in many towns). And though Disneyland Paris is the predictable draw, my kids had more fun for half the expense by enjoying the rides in the Tuileries Garden in downtown Paris.

Minimize hotel changes by planning three-day stops. Aim for hotels with restaurants, so the older kids can go back to the room while you finish a quiet dinner.

I've listed public pools in many places (especially the south), but be warned: Public pools in France commonly require a small, Speedo-like bathing suit for boys and men (American-style swim trunks won't do)—though they usually have these little suits to loan. At hotel pools, either kind of suit will do.

For breakfast, croissants are a hit, though a good *pain au chocolat* (croissant with chocolate bits) will be appreciated even more. Hot chocolate, fruit, cereals, and yogurt are usually available. For lunch and dinner, it's easy to find fast-food places and restaurants with kids' menus, or *crêperies,* which have a wide variety of crêpes with kid-friendly stuffings, both savory and sweet. In the south of France, pizza is omnipresent.

Kids homesick for friends can keep in touch with cheap texting plans or by email (see page 1078). Hotel guest computers and Wi-Fi hotspots are a godsend for parents with teenagers. Readily available Wi-Fi (at hotels, many TIs, some cafés, and all Starbucks and McDonald's) makes bringing a mobile device worthwhile. Most parents find it worth the peace of mind to buy a supplemental messaging plan for the whole family: Adults can stay connected to teenagers while allowing them maximum independence (see page 1078).

Swap babysitting duties with your partner if one of you

wants to take in an extra sight, or ask at hotels for babysitting services. And for memories that will last long after the trip, keep a family journal. Pack a diary and a glue stick. While relaxing at a café over a *citron-pressé* (lemonade), take turns writing down the day's events, and include mementos such as ticket stubs from museums, postcards, or stalks of lavender.

What to Bring: Children's books in English are scarce and pricey in France. My children read more when traveling in Europe than while at home in the US, so don't skimp here. If your kids love peanut butter, bring it from home (hard to find in France) for food emergencies...or help them acquire a taste for Nutella, the tasty hazelnut-chocolate spread available everywhere.

Choose items that are small and convenient for use on planes, trains, and in your hotel room: compact travel games, a deck of cards, a handheld video game, iPod, and a tablet or lightweight laptop. Bring your own drawing paper, pens, and crayons (expensive in France). For younger kids, Legos are easily packed and practical (it's also fun to purchase kits overseas, as Legos are sometimes different in Europe from those in the US). Budding fashionistas might enjoy traveling with—and buying new outfits for—a Corelle or other doll (the French have wonderful doll clothes).

Car-rental agencies usually rent car seats, though you must reserve one in advance (verify the price ahead of time—you may want to bring your own). According to French law, kids under 10 must be in a car seat in the back seat (unless all other seats are also taken by kids in car seats; if in front, car seats must face backward). And though most hotels have cribs, I didn't regret bringing a portable one.

Cameras are a great investment to get your kids involved. Give younger kids an old digital camera that you don't use anymore. For longer drives, audio books can be fun for the whole family. I recommend Peter Mayle's *A Year in Provence*.

Parenting, French-Style: Famous for topless tanning, French women are equally comfortable with public breastfeeding—no need for shawls or "Hooter Hiders" here. Changing tables are nonexistent, so bring a roll-up changing mat and get comfortable changing your baby on your knees or on a bench.

French grandmothers take their role seriously and won't hesitate to recommend that you put more sunscreen on your child in the summer, or add a layer of clothing if it's breezy. Greet French children with *coucou* (coo-coo) if they are young and *salut* (sal-oo) if they are preteens or older.

For older kids, be aware that the drinking age is 16 for beer and wine and 18 for the hard stuff: Your waiter will assume that your teen will have wine with you at dinner. Teens are also welcome in most bars and lounges (there's no 21-and-older section).

throughout France. **VRBO,** an international rental network (offering apartments as well as houses and *gîtes*), cuts out the middleman by putting you directly in touch with the owners (www.vrbo.com). **France Homestyle** is run by Claudette, a service-oriented French woman from Seattle who handpicks every home and apartment she lists (US tel. 206/325-0132, www.francehomestyle.com, info@francehomestyle.com). Or try **Ville et Village,** which has a bigger selection of high-end places (US tel. 510/559-8080, www.villeetvillage.com, rentals@villeetvillage.com).

Hotel barges are a fun option in canalside towns; I've listed a few in this book. If you're interested in renting one for more than a night or two, try **Papillon Barge** (mobile 06 86 28 11 55, www.hotelbarge.com), the **Saroche Barge** (www.saroche.com), or the cheaper bed-and-breakfast **Barge Nilaya** (May-Sept mobile 06 89 18 80 67, Oct-April UK mobile—from the US dial 00-11-44-7909-151-611, www.bargenilaya.com). For a comprehensive source about enjoying the rivers and canals of France, check www.frenchwaterways.com.

Other Options: Airbnb.com and Roomorama make it reasonably easy to find a place to sleep in someone's home. Beds range from air-mattress-in-living-room basic to plush-B&B-suite posh. If you want a place to sleep that's free, Couchsurfing.org is a vagabond's alternative to Airbnb. It lists millions of outgoing members, who host fellow "surfers" in their homes.

Eating

The French eat long and well. Relaxed lunches, three-hour dinners, and endless hours sitting in outdoor cafés are the norm. Here, chefs are as famous as great athletes, and mamas hope their babies will grow up to be great chefs. Cafés, cuisine, and wines should become a highlight of any French adventure: It's sightseeing for your palate. Even if the rest of you is sleeping in cheap hotels, let your taste buds travel first class in France. (They can go coach in England.)

You can eat well without going broke—but choose carefully: You're just as likely to blow a small fortune on a mediocre meal as you are to dine wonderfully for €20. Carefully read the information that follows, consider my restaurant suggestions in this book, and you'll do fine.

When restaurant-hunting, choose a spot filled with locals, not the place with the big neon signs boasting, "We Speak English and Accept Credit Cards." Venturing even a block or two off the main drag leads to higher-quality food for less than half the price of the tourist-oriented places. Locals eat better at lower-rent locales.

All café and restaurant interiors are smoke-free. Today the only

Market Day *(Jour du Marché)*

Market days are a big deal throughout France. They have been a central feature of life in rural areas since the Middle Ages. No single event better symbolizes the French preoccupation with fresh products, and their strong ties to the soil, than the weekly market. Many locals mark their calendars with the arrival of fresh produce.

Notice the signs as you enter towns indicating the *jours du marché*—essential information to any civilized soul, and a reminder not to park on the streets the night before (*stationnement interdit* means "no parking").

Most *marchés* take place once a week in the town's main square and, if large enough, spill onto nearby streets. Markets combine fresh produce; samples of wine and other locally produced beverages (such as brandies and ciders); and a smattering of nonperishable items, such as knives, berets, kitchen goods, and cheap clothing. The bigger the market, the greater the overall selection—particularly for nonperishable goods. Bigger towns (such as Beaune and Arles) may have two weekly markets. The biggest market days are usually on weekends, so that everyone can go.

Market day is as important socially as it is commercially—it's a weekly chance to resume friendships and get the current gossip. Neighbors catch up on Henri's barn renovation, see photos of Jacqueline's new grandchild, and relax over un café. Dogs are tethered to café tables while friends exchange kisses. Tether yourself to a café table and observe: three cheek-kisses for good friends (left-right-left, a fourth for friends you haven't seen in a while); the appropriate number of kisses varies by region—Paris, Lyon, and Provence all have different standards. It's bad form to be in a hurry on market day. Allow the crowd to set your pace.

Buy most of your picnics at an open-air market. Most perishable items are sold directly from the producers—no middlemen, no Visa cards, just really fresh produce (*du pays* means "grown or made locally"). Space rental is cheap (about €5-10, depending on the size). Most vendors follow a weekly circuit of markets they feel work best for them, showing up in the same spot every week, year in and year out. Notice how much fun they have chatting up their customers and one another. Many vendors speak enough English to assist you in your selection. Markets end by 13:00—in time for lunch, allowing the town to reclaim its streets and squares.

smokers you'll find are at outside tables, which—unfortunately—may be exactly where you want to sit.

Waiters probably won't overwhelm you with friendliness. As their tip is already included in the bill (see "Tipping," page 1040), there's less schmoozing than we're used to at home. Notice how hard they work. They almost never stop. Cozying up to clients (French or foreign) is probably the last thing on their minds. They're often stuck with client overload, too, because the French rarely hire part-time employees, even to help with peak times. To get a waiter's attention, try to make meaningful eye contact, which is a signal that you need something. If this doesn't work, raise your hand and simply say, *"S'il vous plaît"* (see voo play)—"please."

To get the most out of dining—slow down. Allow enough time, engage the waiter, show you care about food, and enjoy the experience as much as the food itself.

BREAKFAST

For about €8-15, you'll almost always have the option of breakfast at your hotel, which is usually pleasant and convenient. A few hotels serve a classic continental breakfast, called *petit déjeuner* (puh-tee day-zhuh-nay). Traditionally, this consisted of a café au lait, hot chocolate, or tea; a roll with butter and marmalade; and a croissant. But these days most hotels put out a buffet breakfast (cereal, yogurt, fruit, cheese, croissants, juice, and hard-boiled eggs).

If all you want is coffee or tea and a croissant, the corner café offers more atmosphere and is less expensive (though you get more coffee at your hotel). Go local at the café and ask for *une tartine* (oon tart-een; baguette slathered with butter or jam) with your café au lait. To keep it cheap, pick up some fruit at a grocery store and pastries at your favorite *boulangerie* (bakery), and have a picnic breakfast, then savor your coffee at the bar *(comptoir)* while standing, like the French do. Some cafés and bakeries offer worthwhile breakfast deals with juice, croissant, and coffee or tea for about €5. If you crave eggs for breakfast, drop into a café and order *une omelette* or *œufs sur le plat* (fried eggs). As a less atmospheric alternative, some fast-food places offer cheap breakfasts.

PICNICS AND SNACKS

Great for lunch or dinner, French picnics can be first-class affairs and adventures in high cuisine. Be daring. Try the smelly cheeses, ugly pâtés, sissy quiches, and minuscule yogurts. Shopkeepers are accustomed to selling small quantities of produce. Get a tasty salad-to-go and ask for a plastic fork *(une fourchette en plastique)*. A small container is *une barquette*. A slice is *une tranche*. If you need a knife *(couteau)* or corkscrew *(tire-bouchon)*, borrow one from your hotelier (but never picnic in your room, as French hoteliers uni-

Picnic Vocabulary

English	French	Pronounced
Please	*s'il vous plaît*	see voo play
a plastic fork	*une fourchette en plastique*	oon foor-sheht ahn plah-steek
a small box	*une barquette*	oon bar-keht
a knife	*un couteau*	uhn koo-toh
Corkscrew	*tire-bouchon*	teer-boo-shohn
Sliced	*tranché*	trahn-shay
a slice	*une tranche*	oon trahnsh
a small slice	*une petite tranche*	oon puh-teet trahnsh
More	*plus*	plew
Less	*moins*	mwah
It's just right.	*C'est bon.*	say bohn
That'll be all.	*C'est tout.*	say too
Thank you.	*Merci.*	mehr-see

formly detest this). Though wine is taboo in public places in the US, it's *pas de problème* in France.

Assembling a Picnic: Visit several small stores to put together a complete meal. Shop early, as many shops close from 12:00 to 15:00 for their lunch break. Say "*Bonjour*" as you enter, then point to what you want and say, "*S'il vous plaît.*" Or visit open-air markets *(marchés),* which are fun and photogenic but shut down around 13:00 (many are listed in this book; French TIs have complete lists).

At the ***boulangerie*** (bakery), buy some bread. A baguette usually does the trick, or choose from the many square loaves of bread on display: *pain aux céréales* (whole grain with seeds), *pain de campagne* (country bread, made with unbleached bread flour), *pain complet* (made with wheat), or *pain de seigle* (rye bread). To ask to have it sliced, say, "*Tranché s'il vous plaît.*" The sales clerk will invariably ask if you would like anything else. If you've ordered all the treats you want, you can reply, "*C'est tout, merci*" (say too, mehr-see), meaning, "That'll be all, thanks."

At the ***pâtisserie*** (pastry shop, which is often the same place you bought the bread), choose a dessert that's easy to eat with your hands. My favorites are *éclairs* (*chocolat* or *café* flavored), individual fruit *tartes* (*framboise* is raspberry, *fraise* is strawberry, *citron* is lemon), and *macarons* (made of flavored cream sandwiched between two meringues, not coconut cookies like in the US).

At the ***crémerie*** or ***fromagerie*** (cheese shop), choose a sampling of cheeses. I usually get one hard cheese (such as Comté, Cantal, or Beaufort), one soft cow's milk (such as Brie or Camembert), one goat's milk cheese (anything that says *chèvre*), and one blue cheese (Roquefort or Bleu d'Auvergne). Goat cheese usually comes in individual portions. For all other large cheeses, point to the cheese you want and ask for *une petite tranche* (a small slice). The shopkeeper will place a knife on the cheese indicating the size of the slice they are about to cut, then look at you for approval. If you'd like more, say, "*Plus.*" If you'd like less, say, "*Moins.*" If it's just right, say, "*C'est bon!*"

At the ***charcuterie*** or ***traiteur*** (for deli items, prepared salads, meats, and pâtés), I like a slice of *pâté de campagne* (country pâté made of pork) and *saucissons sec* (dried sausages, some with pepper crust or garlic—you can ask to have it sliced thin like salami). I get a fresh salad, too. Typical options are *carottes râpées* (shredded carrots in a tangy vinaigrette), *salade de betteraves* (beets in vinaigrette), and *céleri rémoulade* (celery root with a mayonnaise sauce). The food comes in easy-to-carry takeout boxes, and they may supply a plastic fork *(fourchette)*.

At a ***cave à vin,*** you can buy chilled wines that the merchant is usually happy to open and re-cork for you.

At a ***supermarché, épicerie,*** or ***magasin d'alimentation*** (small grocery store or minimart), you'll find plastic cutlery and glasses, paper plates, napkins, drinks, chips, and a display of produce (limited selection at small stores). *Supermarchés* are less colorful than smaller stores, but cheaper, more efficient, and offer adequate quality. Department stores often have supermarkets in the basement. On the outskirts of cities, you'll find the monster *hypermarchés.* Drop in for a glimpse of hyper-France in action.

In stores, unrefrigerated soft drinks, bottled water, and beer are one-third the price of cold drinks. Bottled water and boxed fruit juice are the cheapest drinks. Avoid buying drinks to-go at streetside stands; they cost far less in a shop. Hang on to the half-liter mineral-water bottles (sold everywhere for about €1) and refill. Buy juice in cheap liter boxes, then drink some and store the extra in your water bottle. Of course, water quenches your thirst better and cheaper than anything you'll find in a store or café. I drink tap water throughout France, filling my bottle in hotel rooms as I go.

QUICK BITES

Throughout France you'll find bakeries and small stands selling baguette sandwiches, quiche, and pizza-like items to go for about €4.

Usually filling and tasty, they also streamline the picnic process. Here are some sandwiches you'll see:

Fromage (froh-mahzh): Cheese (white on beige).

Jambon beurre (zhahn-bohn bur): Ham and butter (boring for most, but a French classic).

Jambon crudités (zhahn-bohn krew-dee-tay): Ham with tomatoes, lettuce, cucumbers, and mayonnaise.

Pain salé (pan sah-lay) or ***fougasse*** (foo-gahs): Bread rolled up with salty bits of bacon, cheese, or olives.

Poulet crudités (poo-lay krew-dee-tay): Chicken with tomatoes, lettuce, maybe cucumbers, and always mayonnaise.

Saucisson beurre (saw-see-sohn bur): Thinly sliced sausage and butter.

Thon crudités (tohn krew-dee-tay): Tuna with tomatoes, lettuce, and maybe cucumbers, but definitely mayonnaise.

Anything served ***à la provençale*** (ah lah proh-vehn-sahl) has marinated peppers, tomatoes, and eggplant. A sandwich *à la italienne* is a grilled ***panini.***

Typical **quiches** you'll see at shops and bakeries are *lorraine* (ham and cheese), *fromage* (cheese only), *aux oignons* (with onions), *aux poirreaux* (with leeks—my favorite), *aux champignons* (with mushrooms), *au saumon* (salmon), or *au thon* (tuna).

CREPES

The quintessentially French thin pancake called a crêpe (rhymes with "step," not "grape") is a good budget standby: It's filling, usually inexpensive, and generally quick. A place that sells them is a *crêperie* (krehp-uh-ree).

Crêpes generally come in two types: ***sucrée*** (sweet) and ***salée*** (savory). Technically, a savory crêpe should be made with a heartier buckwheat batter, and is called a *galette.* However, many cheap and lazy *crêperies* use the same sweet batter *(de froment)* for both their sweet-topped and savory-topped crêpes.

For savory crêpes, the standard toppings include *fromage* (cheese, usually Swiss-style Gruyère or Emmentaler), *jambon* (ham), *oeuf* (an egg that's cracked and scrambled right on the hot plate), and *champignons* (mushrooms).

For sweet crêpes, common toppings include *chocolat* (chocolate syrup), Nutella (the delicious milk chocolate-hazelnut spread), jam/jelly, and powdered sugar.

FRENCH CAFES AND BRASSERIES

French cafés and brasseries provide user-friendly meals and a refuge from sightseeing overload. They're not necessarily cheaper than restaurants. Their key advantage is flexibility: they offer long serving hours, and you're welcome to order just a salad, a sandwich, or

Crêpe Lingo

During slow times, the *crêperie* chef might make several crêpes to be stacked up, then reheated later. Don't be surprised if he doesn't make a fresh one for you.

French	Pronounced	English
crêpe (salée)	krehp (sah-lay)	(savory) crêpe
Galette	gah-leht	buckwheat crêpe
au fromage	oh froh-mahzh	with cheese
...jambon	zhahn-bohn	...ham
...oeufs	uhf	...egg
...champignons	shahn-peen-yohn	...mushrooms
crêpe sucrée	krehp sew-kray	sweet crêpe
au sucre	oh sew-kruh	with sugar
...chocolat	shoh-koh-lah	...chocolate
...Nutella	new-teh-lah	...Nutella
...confiture	kohn-fee-tewr	...jam
...chantilly	shahn-tee-yee	...whipped cream
...compote de pommes	kohn-poht duh pohm	...apple jam
...crème de marrons	krehm duh mah-rohn	...chestnut cream
...Grand Marnier	grahn marn-yay	...orange liqueur
Socca	soh-kah	chickpea crêpe

a bowl of soup, even for dinner. It's also OK to split starters and desserts, though not main courses.

Cafés and brasseries usually open by 7:00 in the morning, but closing hours vary. Unlike restaurants, which open only for dinner and sometimes for lunch, some cafés and all brasseries serve food throughout the day (usually with a limited menu), making them the best option for a late lunch or an early dinner. (Note that many cafés in smaller towns close their kitchens from about 14:00 until 18:00.)

If you're a novice, it's easier to sit and feel comfortable when you know the system. Check the price list first, which by law must be posted prominently (if you don't see one, go elsewhere). There are two sets of prices: You'll pay more for the same drink if you're seated at a table *(salle)* than if you're seated or standing at the bar or counter *(comptoir)*. For tips on coffee and tea, see the sidebar.

Coffee and Tea Lingo

By law, the waiter must give you a glass of tap water with your coffee or tea if you request it; ask for "*un verre d'eau, s'il vous plaît*" (uhn vayr doh, see voo play).

Coffee

French	Pronounced	English
un café	uhn kah-fay	shot of espresso
un café allongé (also *café longue*)	uhn kah-fay ah-lohn-zhay (kah-fay lohn)	espresso topped up with hot water—like an Americano
une noisette	oon nwah-zeht	espresso with a dollop of milk (best value for adding milk to your coffee)
café au lait	kah-fay oh lay	espresso mixed with lots of warm milk (used mostly for coffee made at home; in a café, order *café crème*)
café crème	kah-fay krehm	espresso with a sizable pour of steamed milk (closest thing you'll get to an American-style latte)
un grand crème	uhn grahn krehm	double shot of espresso with a bit more steamed milk (and often twice the price)
un décaffiné	uhn day-kah-fee-nay	decaf—available for any of the above

Tea

French	Pronounced	English
un thé nature	uhn tay nah-tour	plain tea
un thé au lait	uhn tay oh lay	tea with milk
un thé citron	uhn tay see-trohn	tea with lemon
une infusion	oon an-few-see-yohn	herbal tea

Standard Menu Items: A ***salad, crêpe, quiche,*** or ***omelet*** is a fairly cheap way to fill up. Each can be made with various extras like ham, cheese, mushrooms, and so on. Popular sandwiches, generally served day and night, are the *croque monsieur* (grilled ham-and-cheese) and *croque madame* (*monsieur* with a fried egg on top). Sandwiches are inexpensive, but most are very plain (*boulangeries* serve better ones). To get more than a piece of ham *(jambon)* on a baguette, order a sandwich *jambon crudités,* which means garnished with veggies. Omelets come lonely on a plate with a basket of bread. The daily special—*plat du jour* (plah dew zhoor), or just *plat*—is your fast, hearty, and garnished hot plate for about €10-16. At most cafés, feel free to order only *entrées* (which in French means the starter course); many find these lighter and more interesting than a main course. A vegetarian can enjoy a tasty, filling meal by ordering two *entrées.* Regardless of what you order, bread is free, but almost never comes with butter; to get more bread, just hold up your bread basket and ask, "*Encore, s'il vous plaît?*"

Salads: They're usually large—one is perfect for lunch or a light dinner. Here are some classics:

Salade niçoise (sah-lahd nee-swahz), a specialty from Nice, usually includes green salad topped with green beans, boiled potatoes, tomatoes, anchovies, olives, hard-boiled eggs, and lots of tuna. It's filling and easy on the budget.

Salade au chèvre chaud is a mixed green salad topped with warm goat cheese on small pieces of toast.

Salade composée is "composed" of any number of ingredients, such as *lardons* (bacon), Comté (a Swiss-style cheese), Roquefort (blue cheese), *œuf* (egg), *noix* (walnuts), and *jambon* (ham, generally thinly sliced).

Salade paysanne generally comes with potatoes *(pommes de terre),* walnuts *(noix),* tomatoes, ham, and egg.

Salade aux gésiers includes chicken gizzards (and often slices of duck).

DINNER

Choose restaurants filled with locals. Consider my suggestions and your hotelier's opinion, but trust your instincts. If a restaurant or café doesn't post its prices outside, move along. Refer to my restaurant recommendations to get a sense of what a reasonable meal should cost.

Tune into the quiet, relaxed pace of French dining. The French don't do dinner and a movie on date nights; they just do dinner. The table is yours for the night. Notice how quietly French diners speak in restaurants and how this improves your overall experience. Out of consideration for others, speak as softly as the locals.

Restaurants usually open for dinner at 19:00 (cafés open earlier), and are typically most crowded at about 20:30 (the early bird gets the table). Last seating is about 21:00 or 22:00 in cities (even later in Paris and on the Riviera), and earlier in small villages during the off-season.

If a restaurant serves lunch, it generally begins at 12:00 and goes until 14:00, with last orders taken at about 13:30. If you're hungry when restaurants are closed (late afternoon), go to a brasserie or café; for more information, see "French Cafés and Brasseries," earlier. Remember that even the fanciest places have affordable lunch *menus* (often called *formules* or *plat de midi*), allowing you to sample the same gourmet cooking for generally about half the cost of dinner.

At a **café** or a **brasserie,** if the table is not set, it's fine to seat yourself and just have a drink. However, if it's set with a placemat and cutlery, you should ask to be seated and plan to order a meal. If you're unsure, ask the server before sitting down.

This is the sequence of a typical restaurant experience: To get the waiter's attention, simply ask, *S'il vous plaît?* The waiter will give you a menu *(carte)* and then ask what you'd like to drink *(Vous voulez quelque choses à boire?),* if you're ready to order *(Vous êtes prêts à commander?)* or what you'd like to eat *(Qu'est-ce que je vous sers?).* At the end of your meal, your waiter might ask, *"Ça vous a plû?"* ("Did you enjoy your meal?"). If you did, say, *"Oui, c'était délicieux!"* (wee, say-tay day-lee-see-uh), meaning, "Yes, it was delicious!"

In restaurants, a waiter will rarely bring you the check unless you request it. For a French person, having the bill dropped off before asking for it is akin to being kicked out—*très* gauche. But busy travelers are often ready for the check sooner rather than later. Here's a tip: When your server comes to clear your plates, he or she will often ask if you would like a post-meal dessert or coffee *(Vous voulez un dessert? Un café?),* and if you're finished *(Vous avez terminé?).* It's the waiter's way of asking, "Are we all done here, folks? Can I get you anything else?" Here's your chance. First, say "*oui*" or "*non*" to the coffee, and then ask for the bill, by saying, "*L'addition, s'il vous plaît.*" If you don't ask now, the wait staff may become scarce as they leave you to digest in peace.

Ordering: In French eateries, there are three ways to order food. First, you can order off the menu, which is called a ***carte.*** Second, you can order a multi-course, fixed-price meal, which is (confusingly) called a ***menu.*** Third, most places have a few special dishes of the day, called ***plat du jour,*** or simply ***plat*** (which means "main course"*).*

So, if you ask for *un menu* (instead of *la carte*), you'll get a fixed-price meal. *Menus,* which usually include two or three courses, are generally a good value and will help you pace your meal like the locals. With a three-course *menu* you'll get your choice of soup, appetizer, or salad; your choice of three or four main courses with vegetables; plus a cheese course and/or a choice of desserts. It sounds like a lot of food, but portions are smaller in France and what we cram onto one large plate they spread out over several courses. Service is included *(service compris)*, but wine and other drinks are extra. Certain premium items add a few euros to the price, clearly noted on the menu (*supplément* or *sup.*). Most restaurants offer less expensive and less filling, two-course *menus*, sometimes called *formules*, featuring an *entrée et plat* (first course and main dish), or *plat et dessert* (main dish and dessert).

If you order *à la carte* (from what we would call the menu), you'll have a wider selection of food. It's traditional to order an *entrée* (a starter—not a main dish) and a *plat principal* (main course). The *plats* are generally more meat-based, while the *entrées* usually include veggies. Multiple course meals, while time-consuming (a positive thing in France) create the appropriate balance of veggies to meat. Elaborate meals may also have *entremets*—tiny dishes served between courses. Wherever you dine, consider the waiter's recommendations and anything *de la maison* (of the house), as long as it's not an organ meat (tripe, *rognons,* or andouillette).

Two people can split an *entrée* or a big salad (since small-size dinner salads are usually not offered á la carte) and then each get a *plat principal.* At restaurants, it's considered inappropriate for two diners to share one main course. If all you want is a salad or soup, go to a café or brasserie. Some restaurants (as well as other types of eateries) offer great-value lunch *menus,* and many restaurants have a reasonable *menu-enfant* (kid's meal).

Galloping gourmets should bring a menu translator. The most complete (and priciest) menu reader around is *A to Z of French Food* by G. de Temmerman. The *Marling Menu-Master* is also good. The *Rick Steves' French Phrase Book & Dictionary,* with a menu decoder, works well for most travelers.

Restaurants are almost always a better value in the countryside than in Paris. If you're driving, look for red-and-blue *Relais Routier* decals on main roads outside cities, indicating that the place is recommended by the truckers' union. These truck-stop cafés offer inexpensive and hearty fare.

VEGETARIANS, ALLERGIES, AND OTHER DIETARY RESTRICTIONS

Many French people think "vegetarian" means "no red meat" or "not much meat." If you're a strict vegetarian, be very specific: Tell your server what you don't eat—and it can be helpful to clarify what you do eat. Write it out on a card and keep it handy. Think of your meal (as the French do) as if it's a finely crafted creation by a trained artist. The chef knows what goes well together, and substitutions are considered an insult to his training. Picky eaters should just take it or leave it. However, French restaurants are willing to accommodate genuine dietary restrictions and other special concerns, or at least point you to an appropriate choice on the menu. These phrases can help: *Je suis végétarien* (zhuh swee vay-zhay-tah-ree-an). A female is a *végétarienne* (vay-zhay-tah-ree-ehn). For the following, fill in the blank with the food you need to avoid: "*Je ne peux pas manger de* ____" (zhuh nuh puh pah mahn-zhay duh) means "I cannot eat ____." "*Je suis allergique à* ____" (zhuh sweez ah-lehr-zheek ah) means "I am allergic to ____."

BEVERAGES

Water: The French are willing to pay for bottled water with their meal (*eau minérale;* oh mee-nay-rahl) because they prefer the taste over tap water. Badoit is my favorite carbonated water (*l'eau gazeuse;* loh gah-zuhz). To get a free pitcher of tap water, ask for *une carafe d'eau* (oon kah-rahf doh). Otherwise, you may unwittingly buy bottled water.

Coffee and Tea: See the "Coffee and Tea Lingo" sidebar.

Wine: Wines are often listed in a separate *carte des vins.* House wine at the bar is generally cheap and good (about €3-5/glass). At a restaurant, a bottle or carafe of house wine costs €8-18. To order inexpensive wine at a restaurant, ask for table wine (*un vin du pays;* uhn van duh pay) in a pitcher (*un pichet;* uhn pee-shay—only available when seated and when ordering food), rather than a bottle. Note, though, that finer restaurants usually offer only bottles of wine.

If all you want is a glass of wine, ask for *un verre de vin rouge* for red wine or *blanc* for white wine (uhn vehr duh van roozh/blahn). A half-carafe of wine is *un demi-pichet* (uhn duh-mee pee-shay); a quarter-carafe (ideal for one) is *un quart* (uhn kar).

Be aware that the legal drinking age is 16 for beer and wine and 18 for the hard stuff—at restaurants it's *normale* for wine to be served with dinner to teens.

Beer: The local beer, which costs about €5 at a restaurant, is cheaper on tap (*une pression;* oon pres-yohn) than in the bottle (*bouteille;* boo-teh-ee). France's better beers are Alsatian; try Kronenbourg or the heavier Pelfort (one of your author's favorites). *Une panaché* (oon pah-nah-shay) is a tasty French shandy (beer and lemon soda). *Un Monaco* is a red drink made with beer, grenadine, and lemonade.

Regional Specialty Drinks: For a refreshing before-dinner drink, order a *kir* (pronounced "keer")—a thumb's level of *crème de cassis* (black currant liqueur) topped with white wine. If you like brandy, try a *marc* (regional brandy, e.g., *marc de Bourgogne*) or an Armagnac, cognac's cheaper twin brother (which I prefer). *Pastis,* the standard southern France apéritif, is a sweet anise (licorice) drink that comes on the rocks with a glass of water. Cut it to taste with lots of water.

Soft Drinks: For a fun, bright, nonalcoholic drink of 7-Up with mint syrup, order *un diabolo menthe* (uhn dee-ah-boh-loh mahnt). For 7-Up with fruit syrup, order *un diabolo grenadine* (think Shirley Temple). Kids love the local orange drink, *Orangina,* a carbonated orange juice with pulp (though it can be pricey). They also like *sirop à l'eau* (see-roh ah loh), flavored syrup mixed with bottled water. In France *limonade* (lee-moh-nahd) is Sprite or 7-Up.

Ordering Beverages: Be clear when ordering drinks—you can easily pay €8 for an oversized Coke and €12 for a supersized beer at some cafés. When you order a drink, state the size in centiliters (don't say "small," "medium," or "large," because the waiter might bring a bigger drink than you want). For something small, ask for 25 *centilitres* (vant-sank sahn-tee-lee-truh; about 8 ounces); for a medium drink, order 33 cl (trahnte-twah; about 12 ounces—a normal can of soda); a large is 50 cl (san-kahnt; about 16 ounces); and a super-size is one liter (lee-truh; about a quart—which is more than I would ever order in France). The ice cubes melted after the last Yankee tour group left.

FRENCH CUISINE

General styles of French cooking include ***haute cuisine*** (classic, elaborately prepared, multi-course meals); ***cuisine bourgeoise*** (the finest-quality home cooking); ***cuisine des provinces*** (traditional dishes of specific regions); and ***nouvelle cuisine*** (a focus on smaller portions and closer attention to the texture and color of the ingredients). Sauces are a huge part of French cooking. In the early 20th century, the legendary French chef Auguste Escoffier identified five French "mother sauces" from which all others are derived: *béchamel* (milk-based white sauce), *espagnole* (veal-based brown sauce), *velouté* (stock-based white sauce), *hollandaise* (egg yolk-based white sauce), and *tomate* (tomato-based red sauce).

The following listing of items found commonly throughout France should help you navigate a typical French menu. For dishes specific to each region, see the "Cuisine Scene" section in every chapter but Paris (which borrows cuisines from all regions).

First Course (Entrée)

Crudités: A mix of raw and lightly cooked fresh vegetables, usually including grated carrots, celery root, tomatoes, and beets, often with a hefty dose of vinaigrette dressing.

Escargots: Snails cooked in parsley-garlic butter. You don't even have to like the snail itself. Just dipping your bread in garlic butter is more than satisfying. Prepared a variety of ways, the classic is *à la bourguignonne* (served in their shells).

Foie gras: Rich and buttery in consistency—and hefty in price—this pâté is made from the swollen livers of force-fed geese (or ducks, in *foie gras de canard*). Spread it on bread with your knife, and never add mustard. For a real French experience, try this dish with some sweet white wine (often offered by the glass for an additional cost). For more on foie gras, see the sidebar on page 476.

Huîtres: Oysters, served raw any month, are particularly popular at Christmas and on New Year's Eve, when every café seems to have overflowing baskets in their window.

Œuf mayo: A simple hard-boiled egg topped with a dollop of flavorful mayonnaise.

Pâtés and *terrines:* Slowly cooked ground meat (usually pork, though game, poultry liver, and rabbit are also common) that is highly seasoned and served in slices with mustard and *cornichons* (little pickles). Pâtés are smoother than the similarly prepared but chunkier *terrines.*

Salades: With the exception of a *salade mixte* (simple green salad, often difficult to find), the French get creative with their *salades*. (See page 1066 for good salad suggestions.)

Soupe à l'oignon: Hot, salty, filling, and hard to find in some parts, French onion soup is a beef broth served with a baked cheese-and-bread crust over the top.

Main Course *(Plat Principal)*

Duck, lamb, and rabbit are popular in France, and each is prepared in a variety of ways. You'll also encounter various stew-like dishes that vary by region. The most common regional specialties are described here.

Bœuf bourguignon: A Burgundian specialty, this classy beef stew is cooked slowly in red wine, then served with onions, potatoes, and mushrooms.

Confit de canard: A favorite from the southwest Dordogne region is duck that has been preserved in its own fat, then cooked in its fat, and often served with potatoes (cooked in the same fat). Not for dieters. (Note that *Magret de canard* is sliced duck breast and very different in taste.)

Coq au vin: This Burgundian dish is rooster marinated ever so slowly in red wine, then cooked until it melts in your mouth. It's served (often family-style) with vegetables.

Daube: Generally made with beef, but sometimes lamb, this is a long and slowly simmered dish, typically paired with noodles or other pasta.

Escalope normande: A favorite from Normandy, this is turkey or veal in a cream sauce.

Gigot d'agneau: A specialty of Provence, this is a leg of lamb often grilled and served with white beans. The best lamb is *pré salé,*

French Wine-Tasting 101

France is peppered with wineries and wine-tasting opportunities. For some people, trying to make sense of the vast range of French wines can be overwhelming, particularly when faced with a no-nonsense winemaker or sommelier. Take a deep breath, do your best to follow the instructions in this sidebar, and don't linger where you don't feel welcome.

Visit several private wineries, or stop by a *cave coopérative* or a *caveau*—an excellent opportunity to taste wines from a number of vintners in a single, less intimidating setting. (I've tried to identify which vineyards are most accepting of wine novices.) You'll have a better experience if you call ahead to let them know you're coming—even if the winery is open all day, it's good form to announce your visit (ask your hotelier for help). Avoid visiting between noon and 14:00, when many places are closed—and those that are open are staffed by people who would rather be at lunch.

Winemakers are happy to work with you...if they can figure out what you want (which they expect you to already know). When you enter a winery, it helps to know what you like (drier or sweeter, lighter or full-bodied, fruity or more tannic, and so on). The people serving you may know those words in English, but you're wise to learn the key words in French (see "French Wine Lingo" on the facing page).

French wines usually have a lower alcohol level than American or Australian wines. Whereas many Americans like a big, full-bodied wine, most French tend to prefer more subtle flavors. They judge a wine by virtue of how well it pairs with a meal—and a big, oaky wine would overwhelm most French cuisine. The French also enjoy sampling younger wines to determine how they will taste in a few years, allowing them to buy at cheaper prices and stash the bottles in their cellars. Americans want it now—for today's picnic.

Remember that the vintner is hoping that you'll buy at least a bottle or two. If you don't buy, you may be asked to pay a small fee for the tasting. They understand that Americans can't take much wine with them, and they don't expect to make a big sale, but they do hope you'll look for their wines in the US. Some of the places I list will ship your purchase home—ask.

French Wine Lingo

Here are some phrases to get you started when wine tasting:

Bonjour, monsieur/madame.
(bohn-zhoor, muhs-yur/mah-dahm)
Hello, sir/madam.

Nous voudrions déguster quelques vins.
(noo voo-dree-ohn day-goo-stay kehl-kuh van)
We would like to taste a few wines.

Nous voudrions un vin ____ et ____.
(noo voo-dree-ohn uhn van ____ ay ____)
We would like a wine that is ____ and ____.

Fill in the blanks with your favorites from this list:

English	French	Pronounced
wine	*vin*	van
red	*rouge*	roozh
white	*blanc*	blahn
rosé	*rosé*	roh-zay
light	*léger*	lay-zhay
full-bodied, heavy	*robuste*	roh-boost
fruity	*fruité*	frwee-tay
sweet	*doux*	doo
tannic	*tannique*	tah-neek
jammy	*confituré*	koh-fee-tuh-ray
fine	*fin, avec finesse*	fahn, ah-vehk fee-nehs
ready to drink	*prêt à boire*	preh ah bwar
not ready to drink	*fermé*	fair-may
oaky	*goût du fût de chêne*	goo dew foo duh sheh-nuh
from old vines	*de vieille vignes*	duh vee-yay-ee veen-yah
sparkling	*pétillant*	pay-tee-yahn

which means the lamb has been raised in salt-marsh lands (like at Mont St-Michel).

Poulet roti: Found everywhere, it's roasted chicken on the bone—French comfort food.

Saumon* and *truite: You'll see salmon dishes served in various styles. The salmon usually comes from the North Sea and is always served with sauce, most commonly a sorrel *(oseille)* sauce. Trout *(truite)* is also fairly routine on menus.

Steak: Referred to as *pavé* (thick hunk of prime steak), *bavette* (skirt steak), *faux fillet* (sirloin), and *entrecôte* (rib steak). French steak is usually thinner and tougher than American steak and is always served with sauces (*au poivre* is a pepper sauce; *une sauce roquefort* is a blue-cheese sauce). Because steak is usually better in North America, I usually avoid it in France (unless the sauce sounds good). You will also see *steak haché,* which is a lean, gourmet hamburger patty served *sans* bun. When it's served as *steak haché à cheval,* it comes with a fried egg on top.

By American standards, the French undercook meats: Their version of rare, *saignant* (seh-nyahn), means "bloody" and is close to raw. What they consider medium, *à point* (ah pwan), is what an American would call rare. Their term for well-done, *bien cuit* (bee-yehn kwee), would translate as medium for Americans.

Steak tartare: This wonderfully French dish is for adventurous types only. It's very lean, raw hamburger served with savory seasonings (usually Tabasco, capers, raw onions, salt, and pepper on the side) and topped with a raw egg yolk. This is not hamburger as we know it, but freshly ground beef. While it can be extremely tasty, it's very rich, and the portions are large.

Cheese Course *(Le Fromage)*

In France, the cheese course is served just before (or instead of) dessert. It not only helps with digestion, it gives you a great opportunity to sample the tasty regional cheeses—and time to finish up your wine. There are more than 400 different French cheeses to try. Some restaurants will offer a cheese platter, from which you select a few different kinds. A good platter has at least four cheeses: a hard cheese (such as Emmentaler—a.k.a. "Swiss cheese"), a flowery cheese (Brie or Camembert), a blue or Roquefort cheese, and a goat cheese.

Those most commonly served are Brie de Meaux (mild and creamy, from just outside Paris), Camembert (semi-creamy and pungent, from Normandy), chèvre (goat cheese with a sharp taste, usually from the Loire), and Roquefort (strong and blue-veined, from south-central France).

If you'd like to sample several types of cheese from the cheese plate, say: *"Un assortiment, s'il vous plaît"* (uhn ah-sor-tee-mahn,

Cooking Classes and Tours

It's easy to hook up with small cooking schools that provide an unthreatening and personal experience, including trips to markets.

L'Atelier des Chefs is a network of cooking schools located in many cities throughout France, with top classes at good rates (half-hour-€15, 1 hour-€36, 2 hours-€72, www.atelierdeschefs.fr).

Both **Le Cordon Bleu** (tel. 01 53 68 22 50, www.lcbparis.com) and **Ritz Escoffier Ecole de Gastronomie** (tel. 01 43 16 30 50, www.ritzparis.com) have pricey demonstration courses in Paris. For a more relaxed (and cheaper) Parisian experience, try **La Cuisine Paris** (great variety of classes in English, reasonable prices, and a beautiful space in central Paris; 2-hour classes-€65-90, 4-hour class with market tour-€150, 89 Boulevard St. Michel, tel. 01 40 51 78 18, www.lacuisineparis.com) or **Cook'n with Class** (convivial cooking and wine-and-cheese classes with a maximum of six students, tasting courses offered as well; 6 Rue Baudelique, Mo: Jules Joffrin or Simplon, mobile 06 31 73 62 77, www.cooknwithclass.com).

Acclaimed chef and author **Susan Herrmann Loomis** offers cooking courses in Paris or at her home in Normandy (www.onruetatin.com). Through **Edible Paris,** friendly Canadian Rosa Jackson puts together personalized "foodie" itineraries and pre-set three-hour "food guru" tours of Paris and Nice (www.edible-paris.com and www.petitsfarcis.com).

In Provence, **Barbara Schuerenberg**'s reasonably priced cooking classes are held at her home in Vaison la Romaine (see listing on page 649).

see voo play). If you serve yourself from the cheese plate, observe French etiquette and keep the shape of the cheese. It's best to politely shave off a slice from the side or cut small wedges.

A glass of good red wine complements your cheese course in a heavenly way.

Dessert *(Le Dessert)*

If you order espresso, it will always come after dessert. To have coffee with dessert, ask for *"café avec le dessert"* (kah-fay ah-vehk luh day-sayr). See the list of coffee terms earlier in this chapter.

Here are the types of treats you'll see:

Baba au rhum: Pound cake drenched in rum, and served with whipped cream.

Café gourmand: An assortment of small desserts selected by the restaurant—a great way to sample several desserts and learn your favorite.

Crème brûlée: A rich, creamy, dense, caramelized custard.

Crème caramel: Flan in a caramel sauce.

Fondant au chocolat: A molten chocolate cake with a runny (not totally cooked) center. Also known as *moelleux au chocolat.*

Fromage blanc: A light dessert similar to plain yogurt (yet different), served with sugar or herbs.

Glace: Ice cream—typically vanilla, chocolate, or strawberry.

Ile flottante: A light dessert consisting of islands of meringue floating on a pond of custard sauce.

Mousse au chocolat: Chocolate mousse.

Profiteroles: Cream puffs filled with vanilla ice cream, smothered in warm chocolate sauce.

Riz au lait: Rice pudding.

Sorbets: Light, flavorful, and fruity ices (known to us as sherbets), sometimes laced with brandy.

Tartes: Narrow strips of fresh fruit, baked in a crust and served in thin slices (without ice cream).

Tarte tatin: Apple pie like grandma never made, with caramelized apples, cooked upside down, but served upright.

Communicating

"How can I stay connected in Europe?"—by phone and online—may be the most common question I hear from travelers. You have three basic options:

1. "Roam" with your US mobile device. This is the easiest option, but likely the most expensive. It works best for people who won't be making very many calls, and who value the convenience of sticking with what's familiar (and their own phone number). In recent years, as data roaming fees have dropped and free Wi-Fi has become easier to find, the majority of travelers are finding this to be the best all-around option.

2. Use an unlocked mobile phone with European SIM cards. This is a much more affordable option if you'll be making lots of calls, since it gives you 24/7 access to low European rates. Although remarkably cheap, this does require a bit of shopping around for the right phone and a prepaid SIM card. Savvy travelers who routinely buy European SIM cards swear by this tactic.

3. Use public phones, and get online with your hotel's guest computer and/or at Internet cafés. These options work particularly well for travelers who simply don't want to hassle with the technology, or want to be (mostly) untethered from their home life while on the road.

Each of these options is explained in greater detail in the following pages. Mixing and matching works well. For example, I routinely bring along my smartphone for Internet chores and Skyping on Wi-Fi, but also carry an unlocked phone and buy SIM cards for affordable calls on the go.

For an even more in-depth explanation of this complicated topic, see **www.ricksteves.com/phoning.**

HOW TO DIAL

Many Americans are intimidated by dialing European phone numbers. You needn't be. It's simple, once you break the code.

Dialing Within France

The following instructions apply whether you're dialing from a French mobile phone or a landline (such as a pay phone or your hotel-room phone). If you're roaming with a US phone number, follow the "Dialing Internationally" directions described later.

France has a direct-dial 10-digit phone system (no area codes). To make domestic calls anywhere within France, just dial the number.

For example, the number of one of my recommended hotels in Nice is 04 97 03 10 70. That's the number you dial whether you're calling it from across the street or across the country.

Understand the various prefixes. All Paris landline numbers start with 01. Any number beginning with 06 or 07 is a mobile phone, and costs more to dial. France's toll-free numbers start with 0800 (like US 800 numbers, though in France you dial a 0 first rather than a 1). In France these 0800 numbers—called *numéro vert* (green number)—can be dialed free from any phone without using a phone card. But you can't call France's toll-free numbers from America, nor can you count on reaching US toll-free numbers from France.

Any 08 number that does not have a 00 directly following is a toll call, generally costing €0.10 to €0.50 per minute. The per-minute cost of the call is announced with a message (in French); you can hang up before being billed.

Dialing Internationally to or from France

Always start with the **international access code**—011 if you're calling from the US or Canada, 00 if you're calling from anywhere in Europe,). If you're dialing from a mobile phone, simply insert a + symbol instead (by holding the 0 key.)

• Dial the **country code** of the country you're calling (33 for France, or 1 for the US or Canada).

• Then dial the local number. If you're calling France, drop the initial zero of the phone number. The European calling chart lists specifics per country.

Calling from the US to France: To call the recommended Nice hotel from the US, dial 011 (US access code), 33 (France's country code), then 4 97 03 10 70 (the hotel's number without its initial zero).

Calling from any European country to the US: To call my office in Edmonds, Washington, from anywhere in Europe, I dial 00 (Europe's access code), 1 (US country code), 425 (Edmonds' area code), and 771-8303.

More Dialing Tips

The chart on the next page shows how to dial per country. For online instructions, see www.countrycallingcodes.com or www.howtocallabroad.com.

Remember, if you're using a mobile phone, dial as if you're in that phone's country of origin. So, when roaming with your US phone number in France, dial as if you're calling from the US. But if you're using a European SIM card, dial as you would from that European country.

Note that calls to a European mobile phone are substantially more expensive than calls to a fixed line. Off-hour calls are generally cheaper.

For tips on communicating over the phone with someone who speaks another language, see page 16.

USING YOUR SMARTPHONE IN EUROPE

Even in this age of email, texting, and near-universal Internet access, smart travelers still use the telephone. I call TIs to smooth out sightseeing plans, hotels to get driving directions, museums to confirm tour schedules, restaurants to check open hours or to book a table, and so on.

Most people enjoy the convenience of bringing their own smartphone. Horror stories about sky-high roaming fees are dated and exaggerated, and major service providers work hard to avoid surprising you with an exorbitant bill. With a little planning, you can use your phone—for voice calls, messaging, and Internet access—without breaking the bank.

Start by figuring out whether your phone works in Europe. Most phones purchased through AT&T and T-Mobile (which use the same technology as Europe) work abroad, while only some phones from Verizon or Sprint do—check your operating manual (look for "tri-band," "quad-band," or "GSM"). If you're not sure, ask your service provider.

Roaming Costs

"Roaming" with your phone—that is, using it outside its home region, such as in Europe—generally comes with extra charges, whether you are making voice calls, sending texts, or reading your email. The fees listed here are for the three major American providers—Verizon, AT&T, and T-Mobile; Sprint's roaming rates tend to be much higher. But policies change fast, so get the latest details before your trip. For example, as of mid-2014, T-Mobile waived voice, texting, and data roaming fees for some plans.

Voice calls are the most expensive. Most US providers charge from $1.29 to $1.99 per minute to make or receive calls in Europe. (As you cross each border, you'll typically get a text message explaining the rates in the new country.) If you plan to make multiple calls, look into a global calling plan to lower the per-minute cost, or buy a package of minutes at a discounted price (such as 30 minutes for $30). Note that you'll be charged for incoming calls whether or not you answer them; to save money ask your friends to stay in contact by texting, and to call you only in case of an emergency.

Text messaging costs 20 to 50 cents per text. To cut that cost, you could sign up for an international messaging plan (for example, $10 for 100 texts). Or consider apps that let you text for free (iMessage for Apple, Google+ Hangouts for Android, or WhatsApp for any device); however, these require you to use Wi-Fi or data roaming. Be aware that Europeans use the term "SMS" ("short message service") to describe text messaging.

Data roaming means accessing data services via a cellular network other than your home carrier's. Prices have dropped dramatically in recent years, making this an affordable way for travelers to bridge gaps between Wi-Fi hotspots. You'll pay far less if you set up an international data roaming plan. Most providers charge $25-30 for 100-120 megabytes of data. That's plenty for basic Internet tasks—100 megabytes lets you view 100 websites or send/receive 1,000 text-based emails, but you'll burn through that amount quickly by streaming videos or music. If your data use exceeds your plan amount, most providers will automatically kick in an additional 100- or 120-megabyte block for the same price. (For more, see "Using Wi-Fi and Data Roaming," later.)

Setting Up (or Disabling) International Service

With most service providers, international roaming (voice, text, and data) is disabled on your account unless you activate it. Before your trip, call your provider (or navigate their website), and cover the following topics:

- Confirm that your phone will work in Europe.
- Verify global roaming rates for voice calls, text messaging, and data.
- Tell them which of those services you'd like to activate.
- Consider add-on plans to bring down the cost of international calls, texts, or data roaming.

When you get home from Europe, be sure to cancel any add-on plans that you activated for your trip.

European Calling Chart

Just smile and dial, using this key:
AC = Area Code, LN = Local Number.

European Country	Calling long distance within...	Calling from the US or Canada to...	Calling from a European country to...
Austria	AC + LN	011 + 43 + AC (without initial zero) + LN	00 + 43 + AC (without initial zero) + LN
Belgium	LN	011 + 32 + LN (without initial zero)	00 + 32 + LN (without initial zero)
Bosnia-Herzegovina	AC + LN	011 + 387 + AC (without initial zero) + LN	00 + 387 + AC (without initial zero) + LN
Croatia	AC + LN	011 + 385 + AC (without initial zero) + LN	00 + 385 + AC (without initial zero) + LN
Czech Republic	LN	011 + 420 + LN	00 + 420 + LN
Denmark	LN	011 + 45 + LN	00 + 45 + LN
Estonia	LN	011 + 372 + LN	00 + 372 + LN
Finland	AC + LN	011 + 358 + AC (without initial zero) + LN	999 (or other 900 number) + 358 + AC (without initial zero) + LN
France	LN	011 + 33 + LN (without initial zero)	00 + 33 + LN (without initial zero)
Germany	AC + LN	011 + 49 + AC (without initial zero) + LN	00 + 49 + AC (without initial zero) + LN
Gibraltar	LN	011 + 350 + LN	00 + 350 + LN
Great Britain & N. Ireland	AC + LN	011 + 44 + AC (without initial zero) + LN	00 + 44 + AC (without initial zero) + LN
Greece	LN	011 + 30 + LN	00 + 30 + LN
Hungary	06 + AC + LN	011 + 36 + AC + LN	00 + 36 + AC + LN
Ireland	AC + LN	011 + 353 + AC (without initial zero) + LN	00 + 353 + AC (without initial zero) + LN
Italy	LN	011 + 39 + LN	00 + 39 + LN

European Country	Calling long distance within...	Calling from the US or Canada to...	Calling from a European country to...
Latvia	LN	011 + 371 + LN	00 + 371 + LN
Montenegro	AC + LN	011 + 382 + AC (without initial zero) + LN	00 + 382 + AC (without initial zero) + LN
Morocco	LN	011 + 212 + LN (without initial zero)	00 + 212 + LN (without initial zero)
Netherlands	AC + LN	011 + 31 + AC (without initial zero) + LN	00 + 31 + AC (without initial zero) + LN
Norway	LN	011 + 47 + LN	00 + 47 + LN
Poland	LN	011 + 48 + LN	00 + 48 + LN
Portugal	LN	011 + 351 + LN	00 + 351 + LN
Russia	8 + AC + LN	011 + 7 + AC + LN	00 + 7 + AC + LN
Slovakia	AC + LN	011 + 421 + AC (without initial zero) + LN	00 + 421 + AC (without initial zero) + LN
Slovenia	AC + LN	011 + 386 + AC (without initial zero) + LN	00 + 386 + AC (without initial zero) + LN
Spain	LN	011 + 34 + LN	00 + 34 + LN
Sweden	AC + LN	011 + 46 + AC (without initial zero) + LN	00 + 46 + AC (without initial zero) + LN
Switzerland	LN	011 + 41 + LN (without initial zero)	00 + 41 + LN (without initial zero)
Turkey	AC (if there's no initial zero, add one) + LN	011 + 90 + AC (without initial zero) + LN	00 + 90 + AC (without initial zero) + LN

- The instructions above apply whether you're calling to or from a European landline or mobile phone.
- If calling from any mobile phone, you can replace the international access code with "+" (press and hold 0 to insert it).
- The international access code is 011 if you're calling from the US or Canada.
- To call the US or Canada from Europe, dial 00, then 1 (country code for US and Canada), then the area code and number. In short, 00 + 1 + AC + LN = Hi, Mom!

Some people would rather use their smartphone exclusively on Wi-Fi, and not worry about either voice or data charges. If that's you, call your provider to be sure that international roaming options are deactivated on your account. To be double-sure, put your phone in "airplane mode," then turn your Wi-Fi back on.

Using Wi-Fi and Data Roaming

A good approach is to use free Wi-Fi wherever possible, and fill in the gaps with data roaming.

Wi-Fi (pronounced "wee-fee" in French) is readily available throughout Europe. At accommodations, access is usually free, but you may have to pay a fee, especially at expensive hotels. At hotels with thick stone walls, the Wi-Fi signal from the lobby may not reach every room. If Wi-Fi is important to you, ask about it when you book—and be specific ("In the rooms?"). Get the password and network name at the front desk when you check in.

When you're out and about, your best bet for finding free Wi-Fi is often at a café. They'll usually tell you the password if you buy something. Or you can stroll down a café-lined street, smartphone in hand, checking for unsecured networks every few steps until you find one that works. Some towns have free public Wi-Fi at TIs and in highly trafficked parks or piazzas. You may have to register before using it, or get a password at the TI. Autoroute stops and fast-food places such as Starbucks and McDonald's also offer free Wi-Fi (handy for drivers as McD's are omnipresent on town outskirts).

Data roaming is handy when you can't find Wi-Fi. Because you'll pay by the megabyte (explained earlier), it's best to limit how much data you use. Save bandwidth-gobbling tasks like Skyping, watching videos, or downloading apps or emails with large attachments until you're on Wi-Fi. Switch your phone's email settings from "push" to "fetch." This means that you can choose to "fetch" (download) your messages when you're on Wi-Fi rather than having them continuously "pushed" to your device. And be aware of apps—such as news, weather, and sports tickers—that automatically update. Check your phone's settings to be sure that none of your apps are set to "use cellular data."

I like the safeguard of manually turning off data roaming on my phone whenever I'm not actively using it. To turn off data and voice roaming, look in your phone's settings menu—try checking under "cellular" or "network," or ask your service provider how to do it. If you need to get online but can't find Wi-Fi, simply turn on data roaming long enough for the task at hand, then turn it off again.

Figure out how to keep track of how much data you've used (in your phone's menu, look for "cellular data usage"; you may have

Internet Calling

To make totally free voice and video calls over the Internet, all you need are a smartphone, tablet, or laptop; a strong Wi-Fi signal; and an account with one of the major Internet calling providers: Skype (www.skype.com), FaceTime (preloaded on most Apple devices), or Google+ Hangouts (www.google.com/hangouts). If the Wi-Fi signal isn't strong enough for video, try sticking with an audio-only call. Or...wait for your next hotel. Many Internet calling programs also work for making calls from your computer to telephones worldwide for a very reasonable fee—generally just a few cents per minute (you'll have to buy some credit before you make your first call).

to reset the counter at the start of your trip). Some companies automatically send you a text message warning if you approach or exceed your limit.

There's yet another option: If you're traveling with an unlocked smartphone (explained later), you can buy a SIM card that also includes data; this can be far cheaper than data roaming through your home provider.

USING EUROPEAN SIM CARDS

While using your American phone in Europe is easy, it's not always cheap. And unreliable Wi-Fi can make keeping in touch frustrating. If you're reasonably technology-savvy, and would like the option of making lots of affordable calls, it's worth getting comfortable with European SIM cards.

Here's the basic idea: With an unlocked phone (which works with different carriers; see below), get a SIM card—the microchip that stores data about your phone—once you get to Europe. Slip in the SIM, turn on the phone, and bingo! You've got a European phone number (and access to cheaper European rates).

Getting an Unlocked Phone

Your basic options are getting your existing phone unlocked, or buying a phone (either at home or in Europe).

Some phones are electronically "locked" so that you can't switch SIM cards (keeping you loyal to your carrier). But in some circumstances it's possible to "unlock" your phone—allowing you to replace the original SIM card with one that will work with a European provider. Note that some US carriers are beginning to offer phones/tablets whose SIM card can't be swapped out in the US but will accept a European SIM without any unlocking process.

You may already have an old, unused mobile phone in a drawer somewhere. Call your service provider and ask if they'll send you the unlock code. Otherwise, you can buy one: Search an online shopping site for an "unlocked quad-band phone," or buy one at a mobile-phone shop in Europe. Either way, a basic model typically costs $40 or less.

Buying and Using SIM Cards

Once you have an unlocked phone, you'll need to buy a SIM card (note that a smaller variation called "micro-SIM" or "nano-SIM" cards—used in most iPhones—is less widely available.)

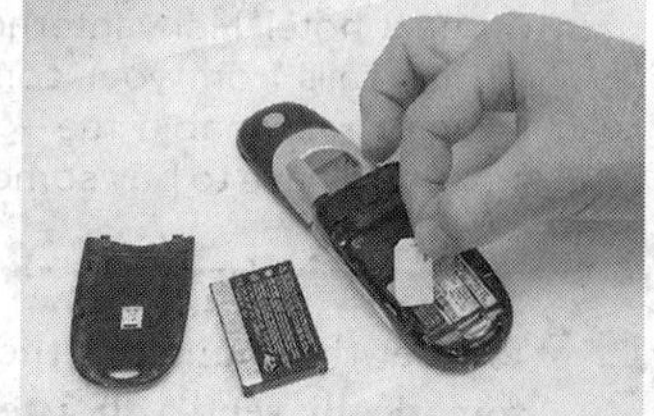

SIM cards are sold at mobile-phone shops, department-store electronics counters, and newsstands for $5–10, and usually include about that much prepaid calling credit (making the card itself virtually free). Because SIM cards are prepaid, there's no contract and no commitment; I routinely buy one even if I'm in a country for only a few days.

However, an increasing number of countries—including France—require you to register the SIM card with your passport (an antiterrorism measure). This takes only a few minutes longer: The shop clerk will ask you to fill out a form, then submit it to the service provider. Sometimes you can register your own SIM card online. Either way, an hour or two after submitting the information, you'll get a text welcoming you to that network.

When using a SIM card in its home country, it's free to receive calls and texts, and it's cheap to make calls—domestic calls average 20 cents per minute. You can also use SIM cards to call the US—sometimes very affordably (Lebara and Lycamobile, which operate in multiple European countries, let you call a US number for less than 10 cents a minute). Rates are higher if you're roaming in another country. But if you bought the SIM card within the European Union, roaming fees are capped no matter where you travel throughout the EU (about 25 cents/minute to make calls, 7 cents/minute to receive calls, and 8 cents for a text message).

While you can buy SIM cards just about anywhere, I like to seek out a mobile-phone shop, where an English-speaking clerk can help explain my options, get my SIM card inserted and set up, and show me how to use it. When you buy your SIM card, ask about rates for domestic and international calls and texting, and about roaming fees. Also find out how to check your credit balance (usually you'll key in a few digits and hit "Send"). You can top up your credit at any newsstand, tobacco shop, mobile-phone shop, or many other businesses (look for the SIM card's logo in the window).

To insert your SIM card into the phone, locate the slot, which is usually on the side of the phone or behind the battery. Turning on the phone, you'll be prompted to enter the "SIM PIN" (a code number that came with your card).

If you have an unlocked smartphone, you can look for a European SIM card that covers both voice and data. This is often much cheaper than paying for data roaming through your home provider.

LANDLINE TELEPHONES AND INTERNET CAFES

If you prefer to travel without a smartphone or tablet, you can still stay in touch using landline telephones, hotel guest computers, and Internet cafés.

Landline Telephones

Phones in your **hotel room** can be great for local calls and for calls using cheap international phone cards (described in the sidebar on the next page). Many hotels charge a fee for local and "toll-free" as well as long-distance or international calls—always ask for the rates before you dial. Since you'll never be charged for receiving calls, it can be more affordable to have someone from the US call you in your room.

While **public pay phones** are on the endangered species list, you'll still see them in post offices and train stations. Pay phones generally come with multilingual instructions. Most public phones work with insertable phone cards (described in the sidebar).

You'll see many cheap **call shops** that advertise low rates to faraway lands, often in train-station neighborhoods. While these target immigrants who want to call home cheaply, tourists can use them, too. Before making your call, be completely clear on the rates.

Internet Cafés and Public Internet Terminals

Finding public Internet terminals in Europe is no problem. Many hotels have a computer in the lobby for guests to use. Otherwise, head for an Internet café, or ask the TI or your hotelier for the nearest place to access the Internet.

European computers typically use non-American keyboards. A few letters are switched around, and command keys are labeled in the local language. Many European keyboards have an "Alt Gr" key (for "Alternate Graphics") to the right of the space bar; press this to insert the extra symbol that appears on some keys. French keyboards are a little different from ours; to type an @ symbol, press the "Alt Gr" key and "à/0" key. If you can't locate a special character (such as the @ symbol), simply copy it from a Web page and paste it into your email message.

Internet Security

Whether you're accessing the Internet with your own device or at a public terminal, using a shared network or computer comes with

Types of Telephone Cards

France uses two different types of telephone cards. Both types are sold at post offices, newsstands, street kiosks, *tabacs* (tobacco shops), and train stations.

Insertable Phone Cards: These cards, called *télécartes* (tay-lay-kart), can only be used at pay phones: Simply take the phone off the hook, insert the card, wait for a dial tone, and dial away. The phone displays your credit ticking down as you talk. They're sold in two denominations—*une petite* costs €8; *une grande* costs €15. Each European country has its own insertable phone card—so your French card won't work in a German phone.

International Phone Cards: These prepaid "code cards" (*cartes à code,* cart ah code) can be used to make inexpensive calls—within Europe, or to the US, for pennies a minute—from nearly any phone, including the one in your hotel room. The cards come with a toll-free number and a scratch-to-reveal PIN code. To make a call, dial the free (usually 4-digit) access number (if that number doesn't work from your hotel-room phone, try the card's 10-digit, toll-free code that starts with 08). A voice in French (followed by English) tells you to enter your (usually 12-digit) code. You may need to press (*touche,* pronounced toosh) the pound key (#, *dièse,* dee-ehz) or the star key (*, *étoile,* ay-twahl). At the next message, dial the number you're calling (again possibly followed by pound or star key).

With the popularization of cell phones you may have to try several places to find one of these cards. Ask the clerk for a *"carte international pour les Etats-Unis"* (for the US; cart an-tehr-nah-see-oh-nahl poor lay-zay-tah-zoo-nee).

the potential for increased security risks. Ask the hotel or café for the specific name of their Wi-Fi network, and make sure you log on to that exact one; hackers sometimes create a bogus hotspot with a similar or vague name (such as "Hotel Europa Free Wi-Fi"). It's better if a network uses a password (especially a hard-to-guess one) rather than being open to the world.

While traveling, you may want to check your online banking or credit-card statements, or to take care of other personal-finance chores, but Internet security experts advise against accessing these sites entirely while traveling. Even if you're using your own computer at a password-protected hotspot, any hacker who's logged on to the same network can see what you're up to. If you need to log on to a banking website, try to do so on a hard-wired connection (i.e., using an Ethernet cable in your hotel room), or if that's not possible, use a secure banking app on a cellular telephone connection.

If using a credit card online, make sure that the site is secure.

Most browsers display a little padlock icon, and the URL begins with *https* instead of *http*. Never send a credit-card number over a website that doesn't begin with *https*.

If you're not convinced a connection is secure, avoid accessing any sites (such as your bank's) that could be vulnerable to fraud.

MAIL

You can mail one package per day to yourself worth up to $200 duty-free from Europe to the US (mark it "personal purchases"). If you're sending a gift to someone, mark it "unsolicited gift." For details, visit www.cbp.gov and search for "Know Before You Go."

The French postal service works fine, but for quick transatlantic delivery (in either direction), consider services such as DHL (www.dhl.com). French post offices are identified as *La Poste*. Hours vary, though most are open weekdays 8:00-19:00 and Saturday morning 8:00-12:00. Stamps and phone cards are also sold at *tabacs*. It costs about €1 to mail a postcard to the US. One convenient, if expensive, way to send packages home is to use La Poste's Colissimo International XL postage-paid mailing box (allow 6 days to reach the US). It costs €36-47 to ship boxes weighing 5-7 kilos (about 11-15 pounds).

Transportation

If you're debating between public transportation and car rental, consider these factors: Cars are best for three or more traveling together (especially families with small kids), those packing heavy, and those scouring the countryside. Trains and buses are best for solo travelers, blitz tourists, city-to-city travelers, those with an ambitious multi-country itinerary, and those who don't want to drive in Europe. While a car gives you more freedom, trains and buses zip you effortlessly and scenically from city to city, usually dropping you in the center, often near a TI. Cars are great in the countryside, but an expensive headache in places like Paris, Nice, and Lyon.

In cities, arriving by train in the middle of town makes hotel-hunting and sightseeing easy. But in France, many of your destinations are likely to be small, remote places far from a station, such as Honfleur, Mont St-Michel, D-Day beaches, Loire châteaux, Dordogne caves, and villages in Provence and Burgundy. In such places, taking trains and buses can require great patience, planning, and time. If you'll be relying on public transportation, focus on fewer destinations, or hire one of the excellent minivan tour guides I recommend.

I've included two sample itineraries—by car and by public

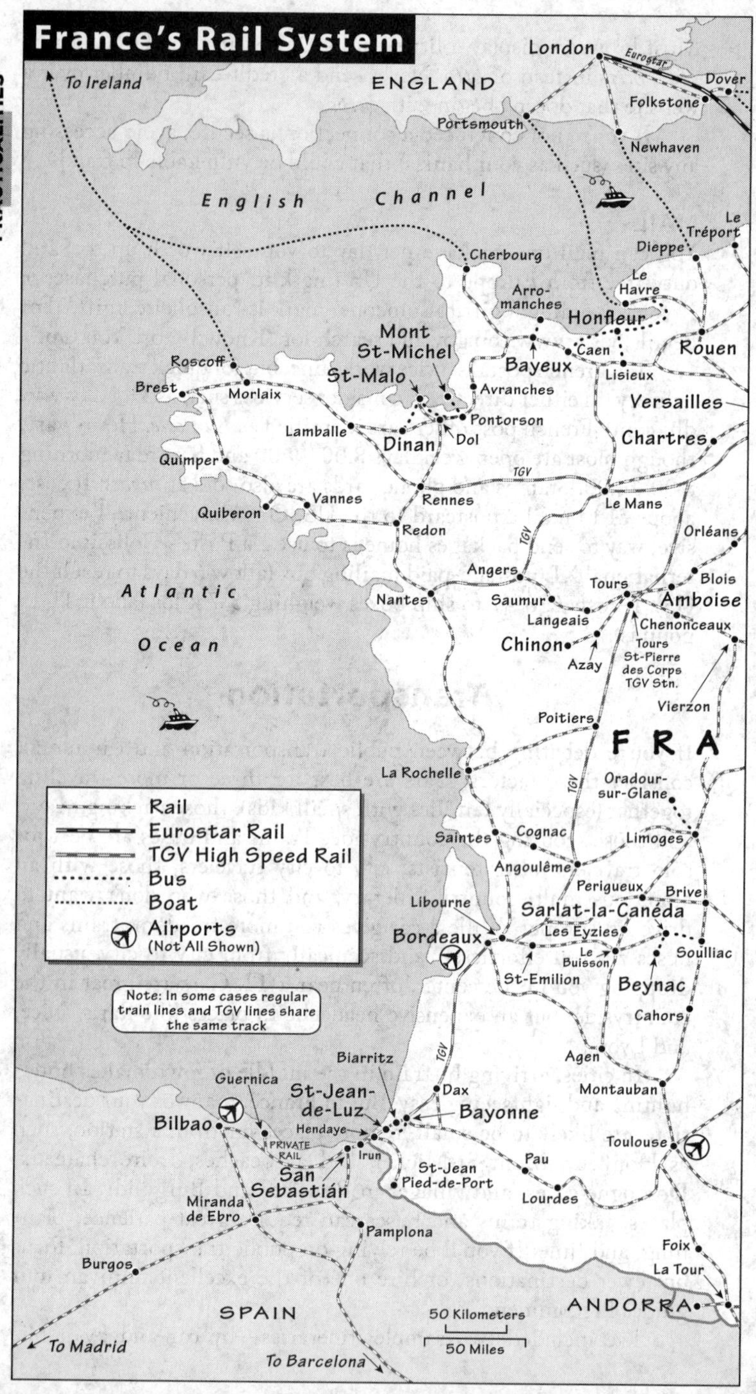
France's Rail System
To Ireland
ENGLAND
London
Eurostar
Dover
Folkstone
Portsmouth
Newhaven
English Channel
Le Tréport
Dieppe
Cherbourg
Le Havre
Arromanches
Honfleur
Rouen
Mont St-Michel
Caen
Bayeux
Lisieux
Roscoff
Brest
Morlaix
St-Malo
Avranches
Versailles
Pontorson
Lamballe
Dinan
Dol
Chartres
Quimper
TGV
Vannes
Rennes
Le Mans
Quiberon
Redon
Orléans
Angers
Blois
Atlantic Ocean
Tours
Nantes
Saumur
Amboise
Langeais
Chenonceaux
Chinon
Tours St-Pierre des Corps TGV Stn.
Azay
Vierzon
Poitiers
FRA
La Rochelle
Oradour-sur-Glane
Rail
Eurostar Rail
TGV High Speed Rail
Bus
Boat
Airports (Not All Shown)
Saintes
Cognac
Limoges
Angoulême
Perigueux
Brive
Libourne
Sarlat-la-Canéda
Les Eyzies
Bordeaux
Le Buisson
Soulliac
St-Emilion
Beynac
Note: In some cases regular train lines and TGV lines share the same track
Cahors
Agen
Biarritz
Guernica
St-Jean-de-Luz
Dax
Montauban
Bilbao
Bayonne
Hendaye
PRIVATE RAIL
Irun
Toulouse
San Sebastián
St-Jean Pied-de-Port
Pau
Miranda de Ebro
Lourdes
Pamplona
Foix
Burgos
La Tour
SPAIN
50 Kilometers
ANDORRA
To Madrid
50 Miles
To Barcelona

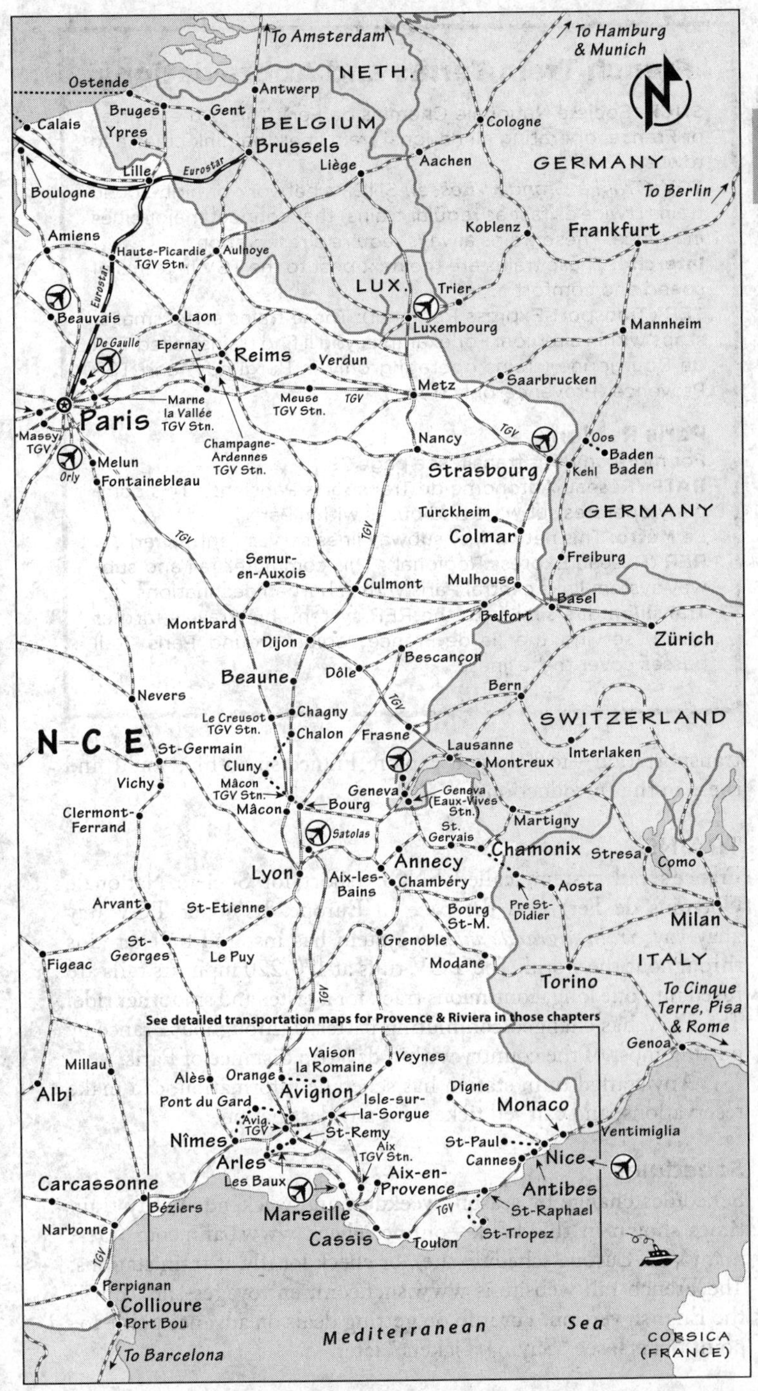
To Amsterdam
To Hamburg & Munich
NETH.
Ostende
Antwerp
Bruges
Gent
BELGIUM
Cologne
Calais
Ypres
Brussels
Aachen
GERMANY
Liège
Lille
Eurostar
Boulogne
To Berlin
Koblenz
Frankfurt
Amiens
Haute-Picardie TGV Stn.
Aulnoye
LUX.
Trier
Eurostar
Beauvais
Laon
Luxembourg
Mannheim
De Gaulle
Epernay
Reims
Verdun
Saarbrucken
Marne la Vallée TGV Stn.
Meuse TGV Stn.
TGV
Metz
Paris
Massy TGV
Champagne-Ardennes TGV Stn.
Nancy
TGV
Oos
Baden Baden
Orly
Melun
Fontainebleau
Strasbourg
Kehl
GERMANY
Turckheim
TGV
TGV
Colmar
Freiburg
Semur-en-Auxois
Culmont
Mulhouse
Basel
Belfort
Montbard
Zürich
Dijon
Bescançon
Beaune
Dôle
Bern
TGV
Nevers
Le Creusot TGV Stn.
Chagny
SWITZERLAND
Chalon
Frasne
N C E
St-Germain
Lausanne
Interlaken
Cluny
Montreux
Vichy
Mâcon TGV Stn.
Geneva
Geneva (Eaux-Vives Stn.)
Mâcon
Bourg
Clermont-Ferrand
Martigny
Satolas
St. Gervais
Chamonix
Stresa
Como
Annecy
Lyon
Aix-les-Bains
Chambéry
Aosta
Arvant
St-Etienne
Bourg St-M.
Pre St-Didier
Milan
St-Georges
Grenoble
Figeac
Le Puy
Modane
ITALY
Torino
TGV
To Cinque Terre, Pisa & Rome
See detailed transportation maps for Provence & Riviera in those chapters
Genoa
Vaison la Romaine
Veynes
Millau
Alès
Orange
Albi
Avignon
Digne
Pont du Gard
Isle-sur-la-Sorgue
Monaco
Avig. TGV
Ventimiglia
St-Remy
Nîmes
Aix TGV Stn.
St-Paul
Arles
Nice
Cannes
Les Baux
Aix-en-Provence
Carcassonne
Antibes
Béziers
Marseille
TGV
St-Raphael
Narbonne
Cassis
Toulon
St-Tropez
TGV
Perpignan
Collioure
Port Bou
Mediterranean Sea
CORSICA (FRANCE)
To Barcelona

French Train Terms and Abbreviations

SNCF (Société Nationale Chemins de Fer): This is the Amtrak of France, operating all national train lines that link cities and towns.
TGV *(Train à Grande Vitesse):* SNCF's network of high-speed trains (twice as fast as regular trains) that connect major cities in France. These trains always require a reservation.
Intercité: These trains are the next best to the TGV in terms of speed and comfort.
TER (Transport Express Régional): These trains serve smaller stops within a region. For example, you'll find trains called TER de Bourgogne (trains operating only in Burgundy) and TER Provence (Provence-only trains).

Paris Region

For more on Paris transit, see page 29.
RATP (Réseau Autonome de Transports Parisiens): This company operates subways and buses within Paris.
Le Métro: This network of subway lines serves central Paris.
RER (Réseau Express Régional): This commuter rail and subway system links central Paris with suburban destinations.
Transilien: It's similar to the RER system, but travels farther afield, serving the Ile-de-France region around Paris. Rail passes cover these lines.

transportation—to help you explore France smoothly; you'll find these in the Introduction.

TRAINS

France's rail system, called SNCF (short for Société Nationale Chemins de Fer), sets the pace in Europe. Its super TGV (tay zhay vay; *train à grande vitesse*) system has inspired bullet trains throughout the world. The TGV runs at 170-220 mph. Its rails are fused into one long, continuous track for a faster and smoother ride. The TGV has changed commuting patterns throughout France by putting most of the country within day-trip distance of Paris.

Any staffed train station has schedule information, can make reservations, and can sell tickets for any destination.

Schedules

Schedules change by season, weekday, and weekend. Verify train times shown in this book—online, check www.bahn.com (Germany's all-Europe schedule site), or check locally at train stations. The French rail website is www.sncf.com; en.voyages-sncf.com is the English version. For info on getting deals on advance point-to-point tickets, see "Buying Tickets," later.

Coping with Strikes

Going on strike (en grève) is a popular pastime in this revolution-happy country. Because bargaining between management and employees is not standard procedure, workers strike to get attention. Truckers and tractors block main roads and autoroutes (they call it Opération Escargot—"Operation Snail's Pace"), baggage handlers bring airports to their knees, and museum workers make Mona Lisa off-limits to tourists. Métro and train personnel seem to strike every year—probably during your trip. What does the traveler do? You could *jeter l'éponge* (throw in the sponge) and go somewhere less strike-prone (Switzerland's nice), or learn to accept certain events as out of your control. Strikes in France generally last no longer than a day or two, and if you're aware of them, you can usually plan around them. Your hotelier will know the latest (or can find out). Make a habit of asking your hotel receptionist about strikes, or check www.americansinfrance.net (look under "Daily Life").

Bigger stations may have helpful information agents roaming the station and at *Accueil* offices or booths. They can answer schedule questions more quickly than staff at the ticket windows. Make use of their help; don't stand in a ticket line if all you need is a train schedule.

Rail Passes

Long-distance travelers can save money with a France Rail Pass, sold only outside Europe (through travel agents or Rick Steves' Europe). For roughly the cost of a full-fare Paris-Avignon-Paris ticket, the France Rail Pass offers three days of travel (within a month) anywhere in France. You can add up to six more days, each for the cost of a two-hour ride. You can save money by getting the second-class instead of the first-class version, but first class gives you more options when reserving popular TGV routes (seats are very limited for passholders, so reserving these fast trains at least several weeks in advance is recommended). The saverpass version gives two or more people traveling together a 15 percent discount.

Each day of use allows you to take as many trips as you want on one calendar day (you could go from Paris to Beaune in Burgundy, enjoy wine tasting, then continue to Avignon, stay a few hours, and end in Nice—though I wouldn't recommend it). Buy second-class tickets in France for shorter trips, and save your valuable pass days for longer trips. Note that if you're connecting the French Alps with Alsace, you might travel through Switzerland, a

PRACTICALITIES

Rail Passes

Prices listed are for 2014 and are subject to change. For the latest prices, details, and train schedules (and easy online ordering), see my comprehensive *Guide to Eurail Passes* at www.ricksteves.com/rail.

"Saver" prices are per person for two or more people traveling together. "Youth" means under age 26. The fare for children 4–11 is half the adult individual fare or Saver fare. Kids under age 4 travel free.

FRANCE PASS

	Adult 1st Class	Adult 2nd Class	Senior 1st Class	Youth 1st Class	Youth 2nd Class
3 days in 1 month	$306	$248	$273	$2221	$187
Extra rail days (max 6)	39-43	30-37	34-38	28-31	24-28

Senior = 60 and up.

FRANCE SAVERPASS

	1st Class	2nd Class
3 days in 1 month	$269	$218
Extra rail days (max 6)	34-38	25-31

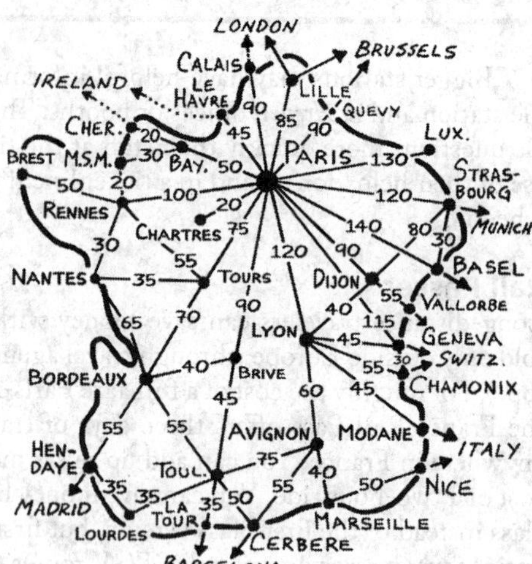

Map key: Approximate point-to-point one-way second-class rail fares in US dollars. First class costs 50 percent more. Add up fares for your itinerary to see if a railpass will save you money.

FRANCE–SPAIN PASS

	Individual 1st Class	Individual 2nd Class	Saver 1st Class	Saver 2nd Class	Youth 2nd Class
4 days in 2 months	$428	$365	$365	$311	$280
Extra rail days (max 6)	45-51	38-44	38-44	33-37	29-33

If you're only dipping into a bit of Spain, you may not need the France-Spain pass. A TGV reservation with a France (only), Spain (only) or France-Spain pass covers the whole trip to/from Barcelona.

FRANCE–ITALY PASS

	Individual 1st Class	Individual 2nd Class	Saver 1st Class	Saver 2nd Class	Youth 2nd Class
4 days in 2 months	$428	$365	$365	$311	$280
Extra rail days (max 6)	45-51	38-44	38-44	33-37	29-33

Paris–Italy overnight trains do not accept rail passes.

FRANCE–GERMANY PASS

	Individual 1st Class	Individual 2nd Class	Saver 1st Class	Saver 2nd Class	Youth 2nd Class
4 days in 2 months	$461	$417	$417	$378	$325
5 days in 2 months	511	459	459	414	357
6 days in 2 months	560	505	505	448	394
8 days in 2 months	655	591	591	514	461
10 days in 2 months	753	678	678	591	532

FRANCE–SWITZERLAND PASS

	Individual 1st Class	Saver 1st Class	Youth 2nd Class
4 days in 2 months	$462	$394	$325
Extra rail days (max 6)	38-58	33-49	26-41

Seat reservation fees can be high for TGV Lyria to Swiss cities, but cheaper to neighboring Strasbourg.

BENELUX–FRANCE PASS

	Individual 1st Class	Individual 2nd Class	Saver 1st Class	Saver 2nd Class	Youth 2nd Class
5 days in 2 months	497	$423	$423	$360	$324
6 days in 2 months	544	463	463	403	355
8 days in 2 months	629	548	548	480	411
10 days in 2 months	711	626	605	545	471

Thalys seat reservations Amsterdam–Paris cost $95 in 1st class or $55 in 2nd class in addition to the pass, similar to prices you could pay by buying tickets months ahead.

SELECTPASS

This pass covers travel in four adjacent countries.

	Individual 1st Class	Saver 1st Class	Youth 2nd Class
5 days in 2 months	$582	$495	$379
6 days in 2 months	635	540	414
8 days in 2 months	739	629	482
10 days in 2 months	845	719	551

Train-Ticket French

Hello, sir (or madam), do you speak English?
Bonjour, monsieur/madame, parlez-vous anglais?
(bohn-zhoor, muhs-yur/mah-dahm, par-lay-voo ahn-glay?)

I would like a departure for Avignon, on 23 May, about 9:00, the most direct way possible.
Je voudrais un départ pour (destination), *pour le* (date), *vers* (general time), *la plus direct possible.*
(zhuh voo-dray uhn day-par poor (destination), poor luh (date), vehr (time), lah plew dee-rehk poh-see-bluh.)

route that requires France Rail Pass holders to buy a ticket for that segment (about €50).

A **Global Pass** can work well throughout most of Europe, but it's a bad value for travel exclusively in France. A cheaper version, the **Select Pass,** allows you to tailor a pass to your trip, provided you're traveling in four adjacent countries directly connected by rail or ferry. For instance, with a four-country pass allowing 10 days of train travel within a two-month period, you could choose France-Switzerland-Italy-Greece or Ireland-France-Spain-Italy.

For more detailed advice on figuring out the smartest rail pass options for your train trip, visit the Trains & Rail Passes section of my website at www.ricksteves.com/rail.

Buying Tickets

Buying Tickets Online: While there's no deadline to buy any train ticket, the fast, reserved TGV trains get booked up. Reserve well ahead for any TGV you cannot afford to miss. Tickets go on sale 90 to 120 days in advance, with a wide range of prices on any one route. The cheapest tickets sell out early and reservations for rail-pass holders also go particularly fast.

To buy the cheapest advance-discount tickets (50 percent less than full fare), visit http://en.voyages-sncf.com, three to four months ahead of your travel date. A pop-up window may ask you to choose between being sent to the Rail Europe website or staying on the SNCF page—click "Stay." Next, choose "Train," then "TGV," and "Book your tickets." When you've picked your travel dates, choose "France" as your ticket collection country. Select the cheapest, non-refundable category of tickets, called "Prems," and be sure that it says "TGV" (avoid iDTGV trains—they're very cheap, but this SNCF subsidiary doesn't accept PayPal). Choose the eticket delivery option (which you can print at home), and pay using a PayPal account. These low-rate tickets may not be available from Rail Europe or other US agents.

After the non-refundable rates are sold out, you can buy other fare types on the French site only if you have set up the "Verified by Visa" or "MasterCard SecureCode" program for your US credit card. Otherwise, US customers have to order through a US agency, such as at www.ricksteves.com/rail, which offers both etickets and home delivery, but may not have access to all of the cheapest rates.

Travelers with smartphones have the option of saving tickets and reservations directly to their phones (choose "m-ticket"). For more details, see http://en.voyages-sncf.com/en/mobile.

Buying Tickets in France: In France, you can buy train tickets at SNCF Boutiques (small offices in city centers) or at any train station, either from a staffed ticket window or from a machine. You can buy tickets on the train for a €4 to €10 surcharge depending on the length of your trip, but you must find the conductor immediately upon boarding; otherwise it's a €35 minimum charge.

The ticket machines available at most stations are great time-savers when other lines are long. The machines won't accept your American credit card unless it has a chip, so be prepared with euro coins. Some machines have English instructions, but for those that don't, here is what you are prompted to do. (The default is usually what you want; turn the dial or move the cursor to your choice, and press "*Validez*" to agree to each step.)

1. *Quelle est votre destination?* (What's your destination?)
2. *Billet Plein Tarif* (Full-fare ticket—yes for most.)
3. *1ère ou 2ème* (First or second class; normally second is fine.)
4. *Aller simple ou aller-retour?* (One-way or round-trip?)
5. *Prix en Euro* (The price should be shown if you get this far.)

Reservations

Reservations are required for any TGV train, *couchettes* (sleeping berths) on night trains, and some other trains when indicated in timetables. You can reserve any train at any station (providing it's more than three days until your departure) or through SNCF Boutiques. If you're buying a point-to-point ticket for a TGV train, you'll reserve your seat when you purchase your ticket.

Popular TGV routes usually fill up quickly, making it a challenge to get reservations (particularly for rail-pass holders, who are allocated a very limited number of seats). It's wise to book well ahead for any TGV, especially on the busy Paris-Avignon-Nice line. Seat reservations cost anywhere from €3 to €26, depending on the kind of train they're for, where you buy them, and if you're using a rail pass. (International trains—such as Eurostar, Thalys, Artesia, and international TGV—have different reservation price ranges.) Rail-pass holders can't book TGV reservations at French stations within three days of departure, but can book them as etickets at www.raileurope.com, if reservations are still available (if lower-priced passholder reservations are sold out, try for the "Easy Access" rate). If the TGV trains you wanted are fully booked, ask about TER trains serving the same destination, as these don't require reservations.

Given the difficulty of getting TGV reservations when traveling with a rail pass, make those reservations online before you go or consider buying separate, advance-discount tickets for key TGV trips (and exclude those legs from your rail pass).

Reservations are generally unnecessary for non-TGV trains (verify ahead, as some Intercité trains require reservations, like the Nice-Bordeaux train), but they are advisable during busy times (for example, Friday and Sunday afternoons, Saturday mornings, weekday rush hours, and holiday weekends; see "Holidays and Festivals" on page 1116).

Validating Tickets, Reservations, and Rail Passes

You are required to validate (*composter*, kohm-poh-stay) all train tickets and reservations before boarding any SNCF train. Look for a yellow machine near the platform or waiting area to stamp your ticket or reservation. If you have a rail pass, validate it at a ticket window before using it the first time; don't stamp it in the yellow machine.

Baggage Check

Baggage check (*consigne* or *Espaces Bagages*) is available only at the biggest train stations (about €5-11 per bag depending on size), and is noted where available in this book (which can depend on current security concerns, so be prepared to keep your bag). For security reasons, all luggage is supposed to carry a tag with the traveler's first and last name and current address (though it's not enforced). This applies to hand luggage as well as bigger bags that are stowed. Free tags are available at train stations in France.

Other baggage-check options in cities are also listed in this book (where available). Here's a tip: Major museums and monuments usually have free baggage check for visitors. Even if the sight is not particularly interesting to you, the entry fee may be worth it if you need to stow your bags for a few hours.

Train Tips

- Arrive at the station with plenty of time before your departure to find your platform (platform numbers are posted about 15 minutes prior to departure), confirm connections, and so on.
- Small stations are minimally staffed; if there is no agent at

the station, go directly to the tracks and look for the overhead sign that confirms your train stops at that track.

• Larger stations have platforms with monitors showing TGV car layouts (numbered forward or backward) so you can figure out where your *voiture* (car) will stop on the long platform and where to board it.

• Check schedules and reservation requirements in advance. Upon arrival at a station, learn your departure possibilities (don't rely exclusively on online schedules). Large stations have a separate information *(accueil)* window or office; at small stations, the ticket office gives information.

• If you have a rail flexipass, write the date on your pass each day you travel (before or immediately after boarding your first train).

• Validate tickets and reservations (not passes) in yellow machines before boarding. If you're traveling with a pass and have a reservation for a certain trip, you must validate the reservation.

• Before getting on a train, confirm that it's going where you think it is. For example, if you want to go to Bayeux, ask the conductor or any local passenger, *"A Bayeux?"* (ah bah-yuh; meaning, "To Bayeux?").

• Some longer trains split cars en route. Make sure your train car is continuing to your destination by asking, for example, *"Cette voiture va à Bayeux?"* (seht vwah-tewr vah ah bah-yuh; meaning, "This car goes to Bayeux?").

• If a non-TGV train seat is reserved, it'll likely be labeled *réservé,* with the cities to and from which it is reserved.

• If you don't understand an announcement (common), ask your neighbor to explain: *"Pardon madame/monsieur, qu'est-ce qui se passe?"* (kehs kee suh pahs; meaning, "Excuse me, what's going on?").

• Verify with the conductor all of the transfers you must make: *"Correspondance à?"*; meaning, "Transfer to where?"

• To guard against theft, keep your bags in sight (directly overhead is ideal but not always possible—the early boarder gets the best storage space). If you must store them in the lower racks by the doors (available in most cars), pay attention at stops. Your bags are most vulnerable to theft before the train takes off and whenever it stops.

• Note your arrival time, so you'll be ready to get off.

REGIONAL BUSES

Regional buses work well for many destinations not served by trains. Buses are almost always comfortable and air-conditioned.

A few bus lines are run by the SNCF rail system and are covered by your rail pass (show rail pass at station to get free bus ticket), but most bus lines are not covered. Bus stations *(gare routière)* are usually located next to train stations. Train stations usually have bus information where train-to-bus connections are important—and vice versa for bus companies.

Bus Tips

• Read the train tips described earlier, and use those that apply (check schedules in advance, arrive at the station early, confirm the destination before you board, find out if you need to transfer, etc.).

• Check out the bus websites listed in this book and use TIs to help plan your trip and verify times (TIs have regional bus schedules).

• Be aware that service is sparse or even nonexistent on Sunday. Wednesday bus schedules often are different during the school year, because school is out this day (and regional buses generally operate school service).

• Confirm a bus stop's location in advance (rural stops are often not signed) and be at bus stops at least five minutes early.

• On schedules *(horaires), en semaine* means Monday through Saturday, *dimanche* is Sunday, and *jours fériés* are holidays. *Année* means the bus runs all year on the days listed, *vac* means it runs only during summer vacations, and *scol (scolaire)* means it runs only when school is in session. *Ligne* means route (or bus line) and *réseau* means network (usually all routes).

REGIONAL MINIVAN EXCURSIONS

Worthwhile day tours generally are available in regions where bus and train service is sparse. For the D-Day beaches, châteaux of the Loire Valley, Dordogne Valley villages and caves, Cathar castles near Carcassonne, Provence's villages and vineyards, the Route du Vin (Wine Road) in Alsace, Brittany sights (including Mont St-Michel), and wine tasting in Burgundy, I list reliable companies that provide this helpful service at fair rates. Some of these minivan excursions simply offer transportation between the sights; others add a running commentary and information on regional history.

RENTING A CAR

If you're renting a car in France, bring your driver's license. Rental companies require you to be at least 21 years old and to have held your license for one year. Drivers under the age of 25 may incur a young-driver surcharge, and some rental companies do not rent to anyone 75 or older. If you're considered too young or old, look into leasing (covered later), which has less-stringent age restrictions.

Research car rentals before you go. It's cheaper to arrange car rentals from the US. Call several companies or look online to compare rates. Most of the major US rental agencies (including Avis, Budget, Enterprise, Hertz, and Thrifty) have offices throughout Europe. Also consider the two major Europe-based agencies,

Europcar and Sixt, and the French agency, ADA (www.ada.fr). It can be cheaper to use a consolidator, such as Auto Europe/Kemwel (www.autoeurope.com) or Europe by Car (www.europebycar.com), which compares rates at several companies to get you the best deal—but because you're working with a middleman, it's especially important to ask in advance about add-on fees and restrictions.

Regardless of the car-rental company you choose, always read the fine print carefully for add-on charges—such as one-way drop-off fees, airport surcharges, or mandatory insurance policies—that aren't included in the "total price." You may need to query rental agents pointedly to find out your actual cost.

For the best deal, rent by the week with unlimited mileage. To save money on fuel, ask for a diesel car. I normally rent the smallest, least-expensive model with a stick shift (generally much cheaper than an automatic). Almost all rentals are manual by default, so if you need an automatic, request one in advance; be aware that these cars are usually larger models. Roads and parking spaces are narrow in France, so you'll do yourself a favor by renting the smallest car that meets your needs.

Figure on paying roughly $200 for a one-week rental. Allow extra for supplemental insurance, fuel, tolls, and parking. For trips of three weeks or more, look into leasing; you'll save money on insurance and taxes. Be warned that international trips—say, picking up in Paris and dropping off in Brussels—can be expensive (it depends partly on distance).

Compare pick-up costs (downtown can be less expensive than the airport or train station) and explore drop-off options. Always check the hours of the location you choose: In France, rental offices tend to close from 12:30-14:00 and on Sunday, although offices at airports and major train stations should be open at these times. Some companies will pick you up from your hotel—inquire when you book.

When selecting a location, don't trust the agency's description of "downtown" or "city center." In some cases, a "downtown" branch can be on the outskirts of the city—a long, costly taxi ride from the center. Before choosing, plug the addresses into a mapping website. You may find that the "train station" location is handier. But returning a car at a big-city train station or downtown agency can be tricky; get precise details on the car drop-off location and hours, and allow ample time to find it.

If you want a car for only a day or two (e.g., for the D-Day beaches or Loire châteaux), you'll likely find it easy to rent on the spot just about anywhere in France. In many cases, this is a worthwhile splurge. All you need is your American driver's license and a major credit card (figure €65-85/day; some include unlimited mileage, others give you 100 kilometers—about 60 miles—for free).

When you pick up the rental car, check it thoroughly and make sure any damage is noted on your rental agreement. Find out how your car's lights, turn signals, wipers, radio, and fuel cap function, and know what kind of fuel the car takes (diesel vs. unleaded). When you return the car, make sure the agent verifies its condition with you. Some drivers take pictures of the returned vehicle as proof of its condition.

Navigation Options

When renting a car in Europe, you have several alternatives for your digital navigator: Use your smartphone's online mapping app, download an offline map app, or rent a GPS device with your rental car (or bring your own GPS device from home).

Online mapping apps used to be prohibitively expensive for overseas travelers—but that was before most carriers started offering affordable international data plans. If you're already getting a data plan for your trip, this is probably the way to go (see "Using Your Smartphone in Europe," earlier).

A number of well-designed apps allow you much of the convenience of online maps without any costly demands on your data plan. City Maps 2Go is one of the most popular of these; OffMaps, Google Maps, and Navfree also all offer good, zoomable offline maps for much of Europe (some are better for driving, while others are better for navigating cities).

Some drivers prefer using a dedicated GPS unit—not only to avoid the data-roaming fees, but because a stand-alone GPS can be easier to operate (important if you're driving solo). The major downside: It's expensive—around $10-30 per day. Your car's GPS unit may only come loaded with maps for its home country—if you need additional maps, ask. Make sure your device's language is set to English before you drive off. If you own a portable GPS device, you can bring that instead. You'll need to buy and download European maps before your trip, but this option is far less expensive than renting.

Car Insurance Options

When you rent a car, you are liable for a very high deductible, sometimes equal to the entire value of the car. Limit your financial risk with one of these three options: Buy Collision Damage Waiver (CDW) coverage from the car-rental company, get coverage through your credit card (free, if your card automatically includes zero-deductible coverage), or get collision insurance as part of a larger travel-insurance policy.

CDW includes a very high deductible (typically $1,000-1,500). Though each rental company has its own variation, the basic CDW costs $10-30 a day (figure roughly 30 percent extra) and reduces your liability, but does not eliminate it. When you pick up the car, you'll be offered the chance to "buy down" the basic deductible to zero (for an additional $10-30/day; this is sometimes called "super CDW" or "zero-deductible coverage").

If you opt for **credit-card coverage,** there's a catch: You'll technically have to decline all coverage offered by the car-rental company, which means they can place a hold on your card (which can be up to the full value of the car). In case of damage, it can be time-consuming to resolve the charges with your credit-card company. Before you decide on this option, quiz your credit-card company about how it works.

If you're already purchasing a **travel-insurance policy** for your trip, adding collision coverage is an option. For example, Travel Guard (www.travelguard.com) sells affordable renter's collision insurance as an add-on to its other policies; it's valid everywhere in Europe except the Republic of Ireland, and some Italian car-rental companies refuse to honor it.

For more on car-rental insurance, see www.ricksteves.com/cdw.

Leasing

For trips of three weeks or more, consider leasing (which automatically includes zero-deductible collision and theft insurance). By technically buying and then selling back the car, you save lots of money on tax and insurance. Leasing provides you a brand-new car with unlimited mileage and a 24-hour emergency assistance program. You can lease for as little as 21 days to as long as five and a half months. Car leases must be arranged from the US.

Anyone age 18 or over with a driver's license is eligible. You can pick up or return cars in major cities outside of France, but you'll have to pay an additional fee.

Four reliable companies offer 21-day lease packages:

• **Auto France** (Peugeot cars only, US tel. 800-572-9655, fax 201/393-7801, www.autofrance.net)

• **Europe by Car** (Peugeot, Citroën, and Renault cars, US tel. 800-223-1516, www.europebycar.com)

• **Idea Merge** (Volkswagen, Citroen, Renault and Peugeot, US and Canada toll-free tel. 888-297-0001, www.ideamerge.com)

• **Auto Europe/Kemwel** (Peugeot cars only, US tel. 877-820-0668, www.kemwel.com).

RV and Campervan Rental

Even given the extra fuel costs, renting your own rolling hotel can be a great way to save money, especially if you're sticking mainly to rural areas. Keep in mind that RVs in France are much smaller than those you see at home. Companies to consider:

• **Van It** (mobile 06 70 43 11 86, www.van-it.com)

• **Idea Merge** (the best resource for small RV rental, see listing in "Leasing," earlier)

• **Origin** (current-model Volkswagen vans fully equipped for 2-3 people, rates less than RVs, mobile 06 80 01 72 77, www.origin-campervans.com).

DRIVING

It's a pleasure to explore France by car, but you need to know the rules.

Road Rules: Seat belts are mandatory for all, and children under age 10 must be in the back seat. In city and town centers, traffic merging from the right (even from tiny side streets) may have the right-of-way *(priorité à droite)*. So even when you're driving on a major road, pay attention to cars merging from the right. In contrast, cars entering the many suburban roundabouts must yield *(cédez le passage)*. U-turns are illegal throughout France, you cannot turn right on red lights, and on expressways it's illegal to pass drivers on the right.

STOP AND LEARN THESE ROAD SIGNS

Speed Limit (km/hr)	Speed Limit No Longer Applies	No Passing	End of No Passing Zone
One Way	Intersection	Main Road	Expressway
Danger	No Entry	Cars Prohibited	All Vehicles Prohibited
No Through Road	Restrictions No Longer Apply	Yield to Oncoming Traffic	No Stopping
Parking	No Parking	Customs	Yield

Be aware of typical European road rules; for example, many countries require headlights to be turned on at all times (in France, they must be used in any case of poor visibility), and it's generally illegal to drive while using your mobile phone without a hands-free device. Ask your car-rental company about these rules, or check the US State Department website (www.travel.state.gov, search for your country in the "Learn about your destination" box, then click on "Travel and Transportation").

Speed Limits: Because speed limits are by road type, they typically aren't posted, so it's best to memorize them:

- Two-lane D and N routes outside cities and towns: 90 km/hour
- When driving on a two-lane road through a village: 50 km/hour (unless posted at 30 km/hour)

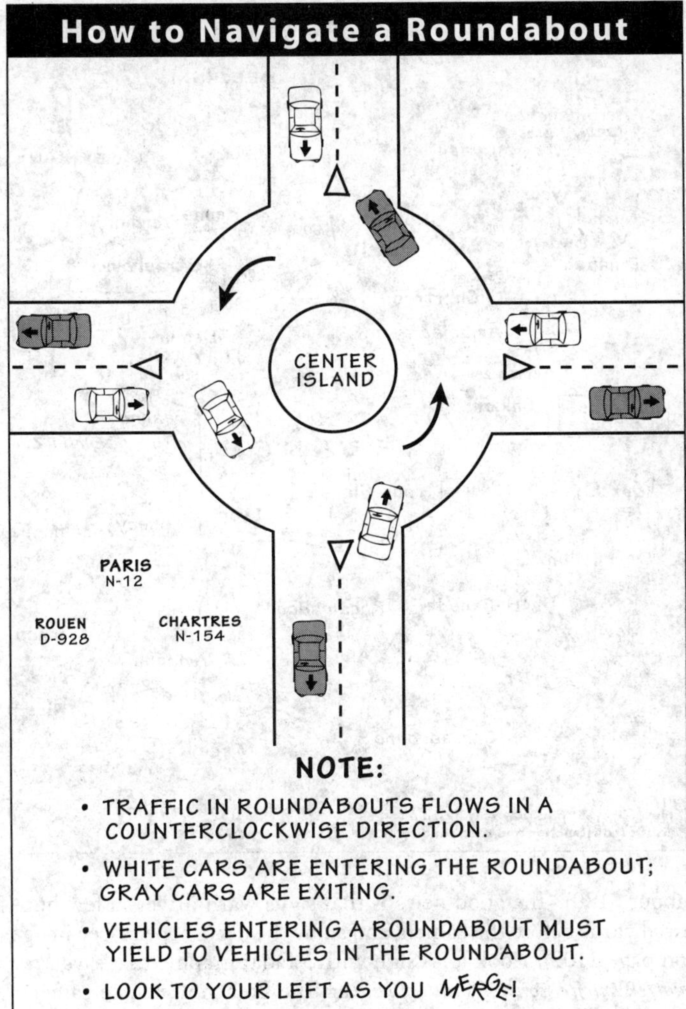

How to Navigate a Roundabout
CENTER ISLAND
PARIS N-12
ROUEN D-928
CHARTRES N-154
NOTE:
• TRAFFIC IN ROUNDABOUTS FLOWS IN A COUNTERCLOCKWISE DIRECTION.
• WHITE CARS ARE ENTERING THE ROUNDABOUT; GRAY CARS ARE EXITING.
• VEHICLES ENTERING A ROUNDABOUT MUST YIELD TO VEHICLES IN THE ROUNDABOUT.
• LOOK TO YOUR LEFT AS YOU MERGE!

- Divided highways outside cities and towns: 110 km/hour
- Autoroutes: 130 km/hour (unless otherwise posted)

If it's raining, subtract 10 km/hour on D and N routes and 20 km/hour on divided highways and autoroutes. Speed-limit signs are a red circle around a number; when you see that same number again in gray with a broken line diagonally across it, this means that limit no longer applies. Speed limits drop to 30-50 km/hour in villages (always posted) and must be respected.

Road speeds are monitored regularly with cameras—a mere two kilometers over the limit yields a pricey ticket (a minimum of

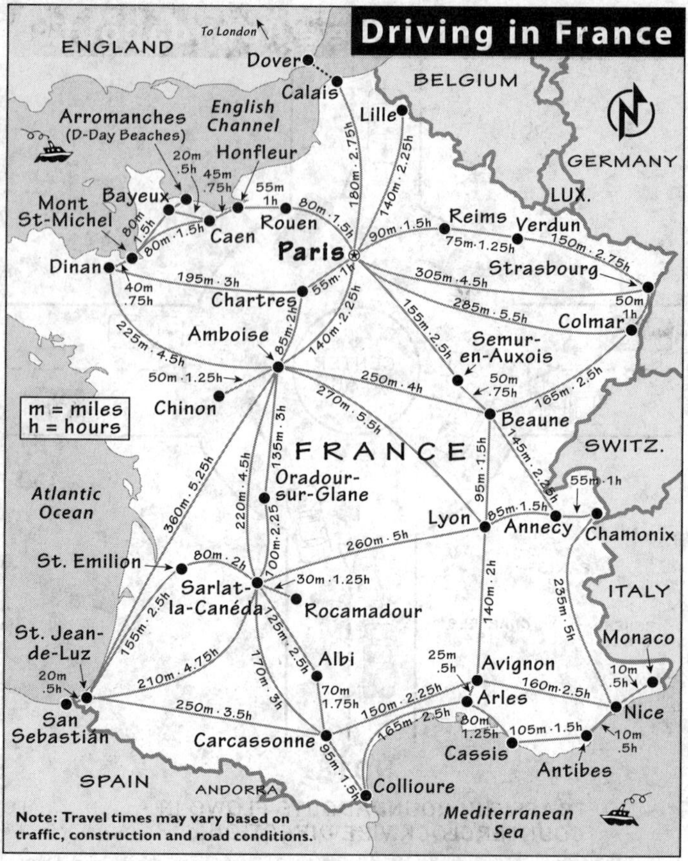

Driving in France

m = miles
h = hours

Note: Travel times may vary based on traffic, construction and road conditions.

about $180). The good news is that signs warn drivers a few hundred yards before the camera and show the proper speed (see image on page 1102). Look for a sign with a radar graphic that says *Pour votre sécurité, contrôles automatiques*. The French use these cameras not to make money but to slow down traffic—and it works.

Don't drink and drive: The French are serious about curbing drunk driving. All motorists, including those in rental cars, are required to have a self-test Breathalyzer on hand so they can tell if they're over the legal blood-alcohol limit (0.05mg/ml—which is lower than in the US—drinker beware). When you pick up your rental car, ask if it has a kit.

Fuel: Gas *(essence)* is expensive—about $8 per gallon. Diesel *(gazole)* costs less—about $7 per gallon. Know what type of fuel your car takes before you fill up. Gas is most expensive on autoroutes and cheapest at big supermarkets. Your US credit and debit cards without a security chip won't work at self-serve pumps—so you'll need to find gas stations with attendants, or get a chip-and-PIN card before your trip (see page 1039).

Plan ahead for Sundays, as most gas stations in town are closed. I fill my tank every Saturday. If stuck, use an autoroute on Sunday, where the gas stations are always staffed.

Autoroutes and Tolls: Autoroute tolls are pricey, but the alternative to these super-"feeways" usually means being marooned in countryside traffic—especially near the Riviera. Autoroutes save enough time, gas, and nausea to justify the cost. Mix high-speed "autorouting" with scenic country-road rambling.

You'll usually take a ticket when entering an autoroute and pay when you leave. Figure roughly €1 in tolls for every 15 kilometers driven on the autoroute (or about €15 for two hours). American credit cards are not accepted unless it's a chip-and-PIN card, but cash is (for more on paying at tollbooths, see the sidebar on page 1108).

Autoroute gas stations are open even on Sundays and usually come with well-stocked mini-marts, clean restrooms, sandwiches, maps, local products, cheap vending-machine coffee (€1.50—I dig the *cappuccino sucré*), and sometimes Wi-Fi. Many have small cafés or more elaborate cafeterias with reasonable prices. For more information, see www.autoroutes.fr.

Highways: Roads are classified into departmental (D), national (N), and autoroutes (A). D routes (usually yellow lines on maps) are often slower but the most scenic. N routes and important D routes (red lines) are the fastest after autoroutes (orange lines on maps). Green road signs are for national routes; blue are for autoroutes. Note that some key roads in France are undergoing letter designation and number changes (mostly N roads converting to D roads). If you are using an older map, the actual route name may differ from what's on your map. Navigate by destination rather than road name...or buy a new map. There are plenty of good facilities, gas stations (most closed Sun), and rest stops along most French roads.

Parking: Finding a parking place can be a headache in larger cities. Ask your hotelier for ideas, and pay to park at well-patrolled lots (blue *P* signs direct you to parking lots in French cities). Parking structures usually require that you take a ticket with you and pay at a machine (called a *caisse*) on your way back to the car. US credit cards won't work in these automated machines, but euro coins (and sometimes bills) will. Overnight parking in lots (usually 19:00-8:00) is generally reasonable, except in Paris and Nice.

Curbside metered parking also works (usually free 12:00-14:00

French Road Signs

Signs You Must Obey

Cédez le Passage	Yield
Priorité à Droite	Right-of-way is for cars
Vous n'avez pas la priorité	You don't have the right-of-way (when merging)
Rappel	Remember to obey the sign
Déviation	Detour
Allumez vos feux	Turn on your lights
Doublage Interdit	No passing
Parking Interdit/ Stationnement Interdit	No parking

Signs for Your Information

Suivre . . . (e.g., *Amboise, suivre Tours*)	Follow. . . (e.g., for Amboise, follow signs for Tours)
Route Barrée	Road blocked
Centre Commercial	Cluster of big-box stores (not city center)
Centre-Ville	City center
Feux	Traffic signal

& 19:00-9:00, and all day and night in Aug). Look for a small machine selling time (called *horadateur*, usually one per block), plug in a few coins (€1.50 buys about an hour, varies by city), push the button, get a receipt showing the amount of time you have, and display it inside your windshield. (Avoid spaces outlined on blue, as they require a special permit.) For cheap overnight parking until the next afternoon, buy three hours' worth of time after 19:00. This gets you until noon the next day, after which two more hours are usually free (12:00-14:00), so you're good until 14:00.

Theft: Theft is a big problem, particularly in southern France. Thieves easily recognize rental cars and assume they are filled with a tourist's gear. Try to make your car look locally owned by hiding the "tourist-owned" rental-company decals and putting a French newspaper in your back window. Be sure all of your valuables are out of sight and locked in the trunk—or, even better, with you or in your room. And don't assume that just because you're parked on a main street that you'll be fine. Thieves work fast.

Horadateur	Parking meter, usually at the end of the block
Parc de Stationnement	Parking lot
Rue Piétonne	Pedestrian-only street
Sauf Riverains	Local access only
Sortie des Camions	Work truck exit
Toutes Directions	All directions (passing through a city)
Autres Directions	Other directions (passing through a city)

Signs Unique to Autoroutes

Aire	Rest stop with WCs, telephones, and sometimes gas stations
Bouchon	Traffic jam ahead
Fluide	No slowing ahead (fluid conditions)
Péage	Toll
Télépéage	Tollbooths—automatic toll payment only
Par Temps de Pluie	When raining (modifies speed limit signs)

Driving Tips

• France is riddled with roundabouts—navigating them is an art. The key is to know your direction and be ready for your turnoff. If you miss it, take another lap (or two).

• At intersections and roundabouts, French road signs use the name of the next destination for directions—the highway number is usually missing. That next destination could be a major city, or it could be the next minor town up the road. Even if you rent a GPS system, it's a good idea to check your map ahead of time and get familiar with the names of towns and cities along your route—and even major cities on the same road beyond your destination.

• When navigating into cities, approach intersections cautiously, stow the map, and follow the signs to *Centre-Ville* (city center). From there, head to the TI *(Office de Tourisme)* or your hotel.

• When leaving or just passing through cities, follow the signs for *Toutes Directions* or *Autres Directions* (meaning "anywhere else") until you see a sign for your specific destination. Look also for

French Tollbooths

For American drivers, getting through the payment stations on France's autoroutes is mostly about knowing which lanes to avoid—and having cash on hand. Skip lanes marked with a lowercase "*t*"—they're reserved for cars using the automatic Télépéage payment system. A pictograph of a credit card (usually a blue sign) means credit or debit cards only—and your US card won't work unless you have a chip-and-PIN card. Look instead for green arrows above the tollbooth and/or icons showing bills or coins, which indicate booths accepting cash (booths often allow more than one payment method). Slow down as you approach tollbooths to study your options, and pull off to the side if you aren't positive of the tollbooth to choose.

Most exits are entirely automated (if you have a problem at the tollbooth, press the red button for help). Have smaller bills ready (payment machines won't accept €50 bills). Shorter autoroute sections have periodic tollbooths, where you can pay by dropping coins into a basket (change is given for bills, but keep a good supply of coins handy to avoid waiting for an attendant).

To figure out how much cash to have on hand for tolls for your route, use the planning tool at ViaMichelin.com.

Suivre signs telling you to follow *(suivre)* signs for the (usually more important) destination listed to continue toward your destination.

• Driving on any roads but autoroutes will take longer than you think, so allow plenty of time for slower traffic (tractors, trucks, and hard-to-decipher signs all deserve blame). First-timers should estimate how long they think a drive will take...then double it. I pretend that kilometers are miles (for distances) and base my time estimates accordingly.

• While locals are eating lunch (12:00-14:00), many sights (and gas stations) are closed, so you can make great time driving—but keep it slow when passing through villages.

• Be very careful when driving on smaller roads—many are narrow, flanked by little ditches that lure inattentive drivers. I've met several readers who "ditched" their cars (and had to be pulled out by local farmers).

• On autoroutes, keep to the right lanes to let fast drivers by, and be careful when merging into a left lane, as cars can be coming at high speeds.

• Motorcycles will scream between cars in traffic. Be ready—they expect you to make space so that they can pass.

• Keep a stash of coins in your ashtray for parking and small autoroute tolls.

BIKING

You'll find areas in France where public transportation is limited and bicycle touring might be a good idea. For many, biking is a romantic notion whose novelty wears off after the first hill or headwind—realistically evaluate your physical condition and be clear on the limitations bikes present. Start with an easy pedal, then decide how ambitious you feel. Most find that two hours on a narrow, hard seat is enough. I've listed bike-rental shops where appropriate and suggested a few of my favorite rides. TIs always have addresses for bike-rental places. For a good touring bike, figure about €12 for a half-day and €18 for a full day. You'll pay more for better equipment; generally the best is available through bike shops, not at train stations or other outlets. French cyclists often do not wear helmets, though most rental outfits have them (for a small fee). Some shops rent electrically assisted bikes.

FLIGHTS

The best comparison search engine for both international and intra-European flights is www.kayak.com. For inexpensive flights within Europe, try www.skyscanner.com or www.hipmunk.com; for inexpensive international flights, try www.vayama.com.

Flying to Europe: Start looking for international flights four to five months before your trip, especially for peak-season travel. Off-season tickets can be purchased a month or so in advance. Depending on your itinerary, it can be efficient to fly into one city and out of another. If your flight requires a connection in Europe, see our hints on navigating Europe's top hub airports at www.ricksteves.com/hub-airports.

Flying within Europe: If you're visiting one or more French cities on a longer European trip—or linking up far-flung French cities (such as Paris and Nice)—a flight can save both time and money. When comparing your options, factor in the time it takes to get to the airport and how early you'll need to arrive to check in.

Well-known cheapo airlines include easyJet (www.easyjet.com) and Ryanair (www.ryanair.com). Also check Air France for specials.

Be aware of the potential drawbacks of flying on the cheap: nonrefundable and nonchangeable tickets, minimal or nonexistent customer service, treks to airports far outside town, and stingy baggage allowances with steep overage fees. If you're traveling with lots of luggage, a cheap flight can quickly become a bad deal. To avoid unpleasant surprises, read the small print before you book.

Resources

RESOURCES FROM RICK STEVES

Rick Steves France 2015 is one of many books in my series on European travel, which includes country guidebooks, city guidebooks (Paris, Rome, Florence, London, etc.), Snapshot guides (excerpted chapters from my country guides), Pocket Guides (full-color little books on big cities, such as Paris), and my budget-travel skills handbook, *Rick Steves Europe Through the Back Door.* Most of my books are available as ebooks. My phrase books—for French, Italian, German, Spanish, and Portuguese—are practical and budget-oriented. My other books include *Europe 101* (a crash course on art and history designed for travelers), *Mediterranean Cruise Ports* and *Northern European Cruise Ports* (how to make the most of your time in port), and *Travel as a Political Act* (a travelogue sprinkled with tips for bringing home a global perspective). A more complete list of my titles appears near the end of this book.

Video: My public television series, *Rick Steves' Europe,* covers European destinations in 100 shows, with 10 episodes on France. To watch full episodes online for free, see www.ricksteves.com/tv. Or to raise your travel I.Q. with video versions of our popular classes, such as France Travel Skills, see www.ricksteves.com/travel-talks.

Audio: My weekly public radio show, *Travel with Rick Steves,* features interviews with travel experts from around the world. I've also produced free, self-guided **audio tours** of the top sights and neighborhoods in Paris. All of this audio content is available for free at Rick Steves Audio Europe, an extensive online library organized by destination. Choose whatever interests you, and download it via the Rick Steves Audio Europe app, www.ricksteves.com/audioeurope, iTunes, or Google Play.

MAPS

The black-and-white maps in this book are concise and simple, designed to help you locate recommended places and get to local TIs, where you can pick up more in-depth maps of cities and regions (usually free). Better maps are sold at newsstands and bookstores.

Begin Your Trip at www.RickSteves.com

My **website** is the place to explore Europe. You'll find thousands of fun articles, videos, photos, and radio interviews on European destinations; money-saving tips for planning your dream trip; monthly travel news; my travel talks and travel blog; my latest guidebook updates (www.ricksteves.com/update); and my free Rick Steves Audio Europe app. You can also follow me on Facebook and Twitter.

Our **Travel Forum** is an immense yet well-groomed collection of message boards, where our travel-savvy community answers questions and shares their personal travel experiences (www.ricksteves.com/forums).

Our **online Travel Store** offers travel bags and accessories that I've designed specifically to help you travel smarter and lighter. These include my popular bags (rolling carry-on and backpack versions), money belts, totes, toiletries kits, adapters, other accessories, and a wide selection of guidebooks, planning maps, and DVDs.

Choosing the right **rail pass** for your trip—amid hundreds of options—can drive you nutty. Our website will help you find the perfect fit for your itinerary and your budget: We offer easy, one-stop shopping for rail passes, seat reservations, and point-to-point tickets.

Want to travel with greater efficiency and less stress? We organize **tours** with more than three dozen itineraries and more than 800 departures reaching the best destinations in this book...and beyond. Our France tours include an 11-day Paris and the Heart of France tour (focusing on the best of the north), a 13-day Loire to the South of France tour, a 14-day Wine Regions of Eastern France tour, and an in-depth seven-day Paris city tour. You'll enjoy great guides, a fun bunch of travel partners (with small groups of 24 to 28 travelers), and plenty of room to spread out in a big, comfy bus when touring between towns. You'll find European adventures to fit every vacation length. For all the details, and to get our Tour Catalog and a free Rick Steves Tour Experience DVD (filmed on location during an actual tour), visit www.ricksteves.com or call us at 425/608-4217.

Before you buy a map, look at it to be sure it has the level of detail you want.

Michelin maps are available throughout France at bookstores, newsstands, and gas stations (about €5 each, cheaper than in the US). The Michelin #721 France map (1:1,000,000 scale) covers this book's destinations with reasonable detail. Drivers should consider the soft-cover Michelin France atlas (the entire country at 1:200,000, well-organized in a €16 book with an index and maps of major cities). Spend a few minutes learning the Michelin key to get the most sightseeing value out of these maps.

Train travelers do fine with a simple rail map (such as the one that comes with a rail pass) and city maps from the TI offices.

RECOMMENDED BOOKS AND MOVIES

To learn more about France past and present, check out a few of these books and films. To learn what's making news in France, you'll find *France 24 News* online at www.France24.com/en.

Nonfiction

For a good introduction to the French culture and people, try *Culture Shock: France* (Sally Adamson Taylor), *French or Foe* (Polly Platt), and/or *Sixty Million Frenchmen Can't Be Wrong* (Jean-Benoit Nadeau and Julie Barlow). The latter is a must-read for anyone serious about understanding French culture, contemporary politics, and what makes the French tick.

For a readable history of the country, try *The Course of French History* (Pierre Goubert). *Portraits of France* (Robert Daley) is an interesting travelogue that roams from Paris to the Pyrenees. A mix of writers explore French culture in *Travelers' Tales: France* (edited by James O'Reilly, Larry Habegger, and Sean O'Reilly).

La Seduction: How the French Play the Game of Life (Elaine Sciolino) gives travelers a fun, insightful, and tantalizing peek into how seduction has been used in all aspects of French life—from small villages to the halls of national government.

Many great memoirs take place in Paris. Consider reading Ernest Hemingway's *A Moveable Feast,* Art Buchwald's *I'll Always Have Paris,* Julia Child's *My Life in France,* and/or *Paris to the Moon* by New Yorker writer Adam Gopnik.

If you'll be visiting Provence, pick up Peter Mayle's memoirs, *A Year in Provence* and *Toujours Provence.* Ina Caro's *The Road from the Past* is filled with enjoyable essays on her travels through France, with an accent on history. *Da Vinci Code* fans will enjoy reading the book that inspired that book—*Holy Blood, Holy Grail* (Michael Baigent, Richard Leigh, and Henry Lincoln)—which takes place mostly in southern France. *Labyrinth* (Kate Mosse) is an intriguing tale, much of which takes place in medieval southern France during the Cathar crusade.

War buffs may want to read these classics before visiting the D-Day Beaches: *The Longest Day* (Cornelius Ryan) and *Wine & War: The French, the Nazis, and the Battle for France's Greatest Treasure* (Donald and Petie Kladstrup). *Is Paris Burning?,* set in the last days of the Nazi occupation, tells the story of the French resistance and how a German general disobeyed Hitler's order to destroy Paris (Larry Collins and Dominique Lapierre).

If you'll be enjoying an extended stay in France, consider *Living Abroad in France* (Terry Link) or *Almost French* (Sarah Turnbull), a funny take on living as a Parisian native. Many appreciate the *Marling Menu-Master for France* (William E. Marling) but the most complete (and priciest) menu reader around is *A to Z of French Food, a French to English Dictionary of Culinary Terms* (G. de Temmerman). Travelers seeking green and vegetarian options in France could consider *Traveling Naturally in France* (Dorian Yates).

Fiction

"It was the best of times, it was the worst of times," begins Charles Dickens' gripping tale of the French Revolution, *A Tale of Two Cities.* Hilary Mantel's *A Place of Greater Safety* is a more recent page-turner about the Revolution. In *Les Misérables* (Victor Hugo), a Frenchman tries to escape his criminal past, fleeing from a determined police captain and becoming wrapped up in the Revolutionary battles between the rich and the starving. Another recommended book set during this time is *City of Darkness, City of Light,* by Marge Piercy.

Ernest Hemingway was a fan of Georges Simenon, a Belgian who wrote mysteries based in Paris, including *The Hotel Majestic.* Other mysteries using Paris as the backdrop are *Murder in Montparnasse* (Howard Engel), *Murder in the Marais* (Cara Black), and *Sandman* (J. Robert Janes).

A Very Long Engagement (Sebastien Japrisot) is a love story set during the bleak years when World War I raged. Using a similar timeframe, *Birdsong* (Sebastian Faulks) follows a 20-year-old Englishman into France, and into the romance that follows.

Chocolat (Joanne Harris)—a book and a 2000 movie with Johnny Depp and Juliette Binoche—charms readers with its story of magic and romance.

Suite Française (Irène Némirovsky) plunges readers into the chaos of the evacuation of Paris during World War II, as well as daily life in a small rural town during the ensuing German occupation. The author, a Russian Jew living in France, wrote her account within weeks of the actual events, and died at Auschwitz in 1942.

Films

In *The Grand Illusion* (1937, directed by Jean Renoir), WWI prisoners of war hatch an escape plan. Considered a masterpiece of French film, the movie was later banned by the Nazis for its anti-fascism message.

Stanley Kubrick's *Paths of Glory* (1957) is a WWI story about the futility and irony of war. François Truffaut, a filmmaker of the French New Wave school, shows the Parisian streets in *Jules and*

Jim (1962). Wander the streets of Paris with a small boy as he chases *The Red Balloon* (1956).

Jean de Florette (1986), a marvelous tale of greed and intolerance, follows a hunchback as he fights for the property he inherited. Its sequel, *Manon of the Spring* (1986), continues with his daughter's story. The hilarious *Dirty Rotten Scoundrels,* with Steve Martin and Michael Caine (1988), was filmed on the Riviera. *Blue/White/Red* (1990s) is a stylish trilogy of films by Krzystof Kieslowski, based on France's national motto—"Liberty, Equality, and Fraternity."

Cyrano de Bergerac (1990) is about a homely, romantic poet who woos his love with the help of another, better-looking man. Fans of crime films—and Robert De Niro—will like *Ronin* (1998), with multiple scenes shot in France. *Saving Private Ryan* (1998) is Steven Spielberg's intense and brilliant story of the D-Day landings.

The Gleaners & I (2000), a quiet, meditative film by Agnès Varda, follows a few working-class men and women as they gather sustenance from what's been thrown away. In *Amélie* (2001), a charming young waitress in Paris searches for love.

If you'll be heading to Versailles, consider seeing *Marie Antoinette* (2006), which stars Kirsten Dunst as the infamous French queen (with a California accent). *La Vie en Rose* (2007) covers the glamorous and turbulent life of the fabled singer Edith Piaf (many scenes shot in Paris).

Woody Allen's *Midnight in Paris* (2011) is a sharp comedy that shifts between today's Paris and the 1920s mecca of Picasso, Hemingway, and Fitzgerald.

APPENDIX

Contents

Useful Contacts

For tips on making calls, including specifics on dialing toll-free service numbers, see "How to Dial" on page 1077.

Emergency Needs

Operators at emergency numbers may speak English, but it's not guaranteed. Calls to 112 and 114 are received by either the Emergency Medical Assistance Service (called "SAMU") or the fire brigade, who will reroute the call if necessary.

Police: Tel. 17
Fire and Accident: Tel. 18
Emergency Medical Assistance (SAMU): Tel. 15
Ambulance for Medical Emergencies: Tel. 15 or 01 45 67 50 50 (message asks for your address and name)
SOS All Services: 112
Hearing-Assisted SOS All Services: 114
Collect Calls to the US: Tel. 00 00 11

EMBASSIES AND CONSULATES

US Consulate and Embassy in Paris: Tel. 01 43 12 22 22, (4 Avenue Gabriel, to the left as you face Hôtel Crillon, Mo: Concorde, http://france.usembassy.gov)

Canadian Consulate and Embassy in Paris: Tel. 01 44 43 29 00 (35 Avenue Montaigne, Mo: Franklin D. Roosevelt, www.amb-canada.fr). For 24/7 emergency assistance call collect to 613/996-8885 or email sos@international.gc.ca.

US Consulate in Lyon: Tel. 04 78 38 36 88 (east of the Cordeliers Métro stop at 1 Quai Jules Courmant, http://lyon.usconsulate.gov, usalyon@state.gov)

Canadian Consulate (Honorary) in Lyon: Tel. 04 72 77 64 07 (21 Rue Bourgelat, www.canadainternational.gc.ca, consulat.canada-lyon@amb-canada.fr)

US Consulate in Marseille: Tel. 04 91 54 90 84 (Place Varian Fry, http://marseille.usconsulate.gov)

US Consulate in Nice: Tel. 04 93 88 89 55 (7 Avenue Gustave V, http://marseille.usconsulate.gov/nice.html, usca.nice@orange.fr)

Canadian Consulate in Nice: Tel. 04 93 92 93 22 (2 Place Franklin, consulat.canada-nice@amb-canada.fr)

US Consulate in Strasbourg: Tel. 03 88 35 31 04 (5 Avenue d'Alsace, http://strasbourg.usconsulate.gov)

US Consulate in Bordeaux: Tel. 05 56 48 63 85 (89 Quai des Chartrons, http://bordeaux.usconsulate.gov, usabordeaux@state.gov)

Holidays and Festivals

This list includes selected festivals in major cities, plus national holidays observed throughout France. Many sights and banks close on national holidays—keep this in mind when planning your itinerary. Before planning a trip around a festival, verify its dates by checking with the festival's website or France's national tourism website (www.franceguide.com). Hotels get booked up on Easter weekend, Labor Day, Ascension Day, Pentecost, Bastille Day, and the winter holidays.

Here is a sampling of events and holidays in 2015:

Jan 1	New Year's Day
Feb-March	Carnival (Mardi Gras) parades and fireworks, Nice (www.nicecarnaval.com)
April 5-6	Easter Sunday/Monday
May-Mid-Oct	International Garden Festival, Chaumont-sur-Loire (www.domaine-chaumont.fr)

2015

JANUARY

S	M	T	W	T	F	S
				1	2	3
4	5	6	7	8	9	10
11	12	13	14	15	16	17
18	19	20	21	22	23	24
25	26	27	28	29	30	31

FEBRUARY

S	M	T	W	T	F	S
1	2	3	4	5	6	7
8	9	10	11	12	13	14
15	16	17	18	19	20	21
22	23	24	25	26	27	28

MARCH

S	M	T	W	T	F	S
1	2	3	4	5	6	7
8	9	10	11	12	13	14
15	16	17	18	19	20	21
22	23	24	25	26	27	28
29	30	31				

APRIL

S	M	T	W	T	F	S
			1	2	3	4
5	6	7	8	9	10	11
12	13	14	15	16	17	18
19	20	21	22	23	24	25
26	27	28	29	30		

MAY

S	M	T	W	T	F	S
					1	2
3	4	5	6	7	8	9
10	11	12	13	14	15	16
17	18	19	20	21	22	23
24/31	25	26	27	28	29	30

JUNE

S	M	T	W	T	F	S
	1	2	3	4	5	6
7	8	9	10	11	12	13
14	15	16	17	18	19	20
21	22	23	24	25	26	27
28	29	30				

JULY

S	M	T	W	T	F	S
			1	2	3	4
5	6	7	8	9	10	11
12	13	14	15	16	17	18
19	20	21	22	23	24	25
26	27	28	29	30	31	

AUGUST

S	M	T	W	T	F	S
						1
2	3	4	5	6	7	8
9	10	11	12	13	14	15
16	17	18	19	20	21	22
23/30	24/31	25	26	27	28	29

SEPTEMBER

S	M	T	W	T	F	S
		1	2	3	4	5
6	7	8	9	10	11	12
13	14	15	16	17	18	19
20	21	22	23	24	25	26
27	28	29	30			

OCTOBER

S	M	T	W	T	F	S
				1	2	3
4	5	6	7	8	9	10
11	12	13	14	15	16	17
18	19	20	21	22	23	24
25	26	27	28	29	30	31

NOVEMBER

S	M	T	W	T	F	S
1	2	3	4	5	6	7
8	9	10	11	12	13	14
15	16	17	18	19	20	21
22	23	24	25	26	27	28
29	30					

DECEMBER

S	M	T	W	T	F	S
		1	2	3	4	5
6	7	8	9	10	11	12
13	14	15	16	17	18	19
20	21	22	23	24	25	26
27	28	29	30	31		

May	Versailles Festival (arts), Versailles
Late May	Festival Jeanne d'Arc (pageants), Rouen
May 1	Labor Day
May 8	VE (Victory in Europe) Day
May 14	Ascension
May 15-26	Cannes Film Festival, Cannes (www.festival-cannes.fr)
May 21-24	Monaco Grand Prix auto race (www.grand-prix-monaco.com)
May 24-25	Pentecost Sunday/Monday
June	Marais Festival (arts), Paris
June 6	Anniversary of D-Day Landing, Normandy

Mid-June	Le Mans Auto Race, Le Mans—near Loire Valley (www.lemans.org)
June 21	Fête de la Musique, concerts and dancing in the streets throughout France
July	Nice Jazz Festival (www.nicejazzfestival.fr); Avignon Festival, theater, dance, music (www.festival-avignon.com); Beaune International Music Festival; Chorégies d'Orange, Orange (performed in Roman theater, www.choregies.asso.fr); "Jazz à Juan" International Jazz Festival, Antibes/Juan-les-Pins (www.jazzajuan.com); Jousting matches and medieval festivities, Carcassonne; Nights of Fourvière, Lyon (theater and music in a Roman theater, www.nuitsdefourviere.org); Colmar International Music Festival (www.festival-colmar.com); International Music and Opera Festival, Aix-en-Provence (www.festival-aix.com)
July 4-26	Tour de France, national bicycle race culminating on the Champs-Elysées in Paris (www.letour.fr)
July 14	Bastille Day (fireworks, dancing, and revelry all over France)
July-Aug	International Fireworks Festival, Cannes (www.festival-pyrotechnique-cannes.com)
Aug 15	Assumption
Late Aug-Sept	Jazz at La Villette Festival, Paris (www.villette.com)
Sept	Fall Arts Festival (Fête d'Automne), Paris; Wine harvest festivals in many towns
Early-Mid-Oct	Grape Harvest Festival in Montmartre, Paris (www.fetedesvendangesdemontmartre.com)
Nov 1	All Saints' Day
Early Nov	Dijon International and Gastronomic Fair, Dijon, Burgundy
Nov 11	Armistice Day
Late Nov	Wine Auction and Festival (Les Trois Glorieuses), Beaune
Late Nov-Dec 24	Christmas Markets, Strasbourg, Colmar, and Sarlat-la-Canéda
Dec 8-11	Festival of Lights (celebration of Virgin Mary, candlelit windows), Lyon (www.fetedeslumieres.lyon.fr)
Dec 25	Christmas Day
Dec 31	New Year's Eve

Conversions and Climate

NUMBERS AND STUMBLERS

- Europeans write a few of their numbers differently than we do: 1 = 1, 4 = 4, 7 = 7.
- In Europe, dates appear as day/month/year, so Christmas 2015 is 25/12/15.
- Commas are decimal points and decimals are commas. A dollar and a half is $1,50, one thousand is 1.000, and there are 5.280 feet in a mile.
- When counting with fingers, start with your thumb. If you hold up your first finger to request one item, you'll probably get two.
- What Americans call the second floor of a building is the first floor in Europe.
- On escalators and moving sidewalks, Europeans keep the left "lane" open for passing. Keep to the right.

METRIC CONVERSIONS

A kilogram is 2.2 pounds, and 1 liter is about a quart, or almost four to a gallon. A kilometer is six-tenths of a mile. I figure kilometers to miles by cutting them in half and adding back 10 percent of the original (120 km: 60 + 12 = 72 miles, 300 km: 150 + 30 = 180 miles).

1 foot = 0.3 meter
1 yard = 0.9 meter
1 mile = 1.6 kilometers
1 centimeter = 0.4 inch
1 meter = 39.4 inches
1 kilometer = 0.62 mile

1 square yard = 0.8 square meter
1 square mile = 2.6 square kilometers
1 ounce = 28 grams
1 quart = 0.95 liter
1 kilogram = 2.2 pounds
32°F = 0°C

CLOTHING SIZES

When shopping for clothing, use these US-to-European comparisons as general guidelines (but note that no conversion is perfect).

- Women's dresses and blouses: Add 30
  (US women's size 10 = European size 40)
- Men's suits and jackets: Add 10
  (US size 40 regular = European size 50)
- Men's shirts: Multiply by 2 and add about 8
  (US men's size 15 collar = European size 38)
- Women's shoes: Add about 31
  (US size 8 = European size 38-39)
- Men's shoes: Add 32-34
  (US size 9 = European size 43; US size 11 = European size 45)

TIRE PRESSURE

In Europe, tire pressure is measured in *bars* of pressure. To convert to PSI (pound per square inch) the formula is: *bar* x 14.5 = PSI (so 2 *bars* would be 2 x 14.5 = 29 PSI. To convert to *bar* pressures from PSI, the formula is: PSI x 0.07 = *bar* (so 30 PSI x 0.07 would = 2.1 *bars*).

FRANCE'S CLIMATE

First line, average daily high; second line, average daily low; third line, average days without rain. For more detailed weather statistics for destinations in this book (as well as the rest of the world), check www.wunderground.com.

	J	F	M	A	M	J	J	A	S	O	N	D
Paris												
	43°	45°	54°	60°	68°	73°	76°	75°	70°	60°	50°	44°
	34°	34°	39°	43°	49°	55°	58°	58°	53°	46°	40°	36°
	14	14	19	17	19	18	19	18	17	18	15	15
Nice												
	50°	53°	59°	64°	71°	79°	84°	83°	77°	68°	58°	52°
	35°	36°	41°	46°	52°	58°	63°	63°	58°	51°	43°	37°
	23	22	24	23	23	26	29	26	24	23	21	21

FAHRENHEIT AND CELSIUS CONVERSION

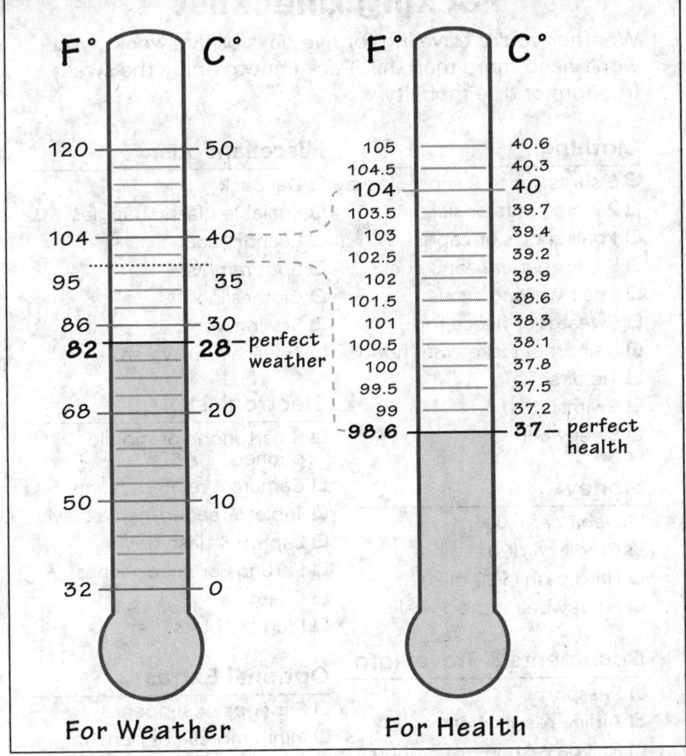

Europe takes its temperature using the Celsius scale, whereas we opt for Fahrenheit. For a rough conversion from Celsius to Fahrenheit, double the number and add 30. For weather, remember that 28°C is 82°F—perfect. For health, 37°C is just right. At a launderette, 30°C is cold, 40°C is warm (usually the default setting), 60°C is hot, and 95°C is boiling.

Packing Checklist

Whether you're traveling for five days or five weeks, you won't need more than this. Pack light to enjoy the sweet freedom of true mobility.

Clothing

- ❑ 5 shirts: long- & short-sleeve
- ❑ 2 pairs pants or skirt
- ❑ 1 pair shorts or capris
- ❑ 5 pairs underwear & socks
- ❑ 1 pair walking shoes
- ❑ Sweater or fleece top
- ❑ Rainproof jacket with hood
- ❑ Tie or scarf
- ❑ Swimsuit
- ❑ Sleepwear

Money

- ❑ Debit card
- ❑ Credit card(s)
- ❑ Hard cash ($20 bills)
- ❑ Money belt or neck wallet

Documents & Travel Info

- ❑ Passport
- ❑ Airline reservations
- ❑ Rail pass/train reservations
- ❑ Car-rental voucher
- ❑ Driver's license
- ❑ Student ID, hostel card, etc.
- ❑ Photocopies of all the above
- ❑ Hotel confirmations
- ❑ Insurance details
- ❑ Guidebooks & maps
- ❑ Notepad & pen
- ❑ Journal

Toiletries Kit

- ❑ Toiletries
- ❑ Medicines & vitamins
- ❑ First-aid kit
- ❑ Glasses/contacts/sunglasses (with prescriptions)
- ❑ Earplugs
- ❑ Packet of tissues (for WC)

Miscellaneous

- ❑ Daypack
- ❑ Sealable plastic baggies
- ❑ Laundry soap
- ❑ Spot remover
- ❑ Clothesline
- ❑ Sewing kit
- ❑ Travel alarm/watch

Electronics

- ❑ Smartphone or mobile phone
- ❑ Camera & related gear
- ❑ Tablet/ereader/media player
- ❑ Laptop & flash drive
- ❑ Earbuds or headphones
- ❑ Chargers
- ❑ Plug adapters

Optional Extras

- ❑ Flipflops or slippers
- ❑ Mini-umbrella or poncho
- ❑ Travel hairdryer
- ❑ Belt
- ❑ Hat (for sun or cold)
- ❑ Picnic supplies
- ❑ Water bottle
- ❑ Fold-up tote bag
- ❑ Small flashlight
- ❑ Small binoculars
- ❑ Insect repellent
- ❑ Small towel or washcloth
- ❑ Inflatable pillow
- ❑ Some duct tape (for repairs)
- ❑ Tiny lock
- ❑ Address list (to mail postcards)
- ❑ Postcards/photos from home
- ❑ Extra passport photos
- ❑ Good book

PRONUNCIATION GUIDE FOR PLACE NAMES

When using the phonetics: Try to nasalize the n sound (let the sound come through your nose). Note that the "ahn" combination uses the "ah" sound in "father," but the "an" combination uses the "a" sound in "sack." Pronounce the "ī" as the long "i" in "light." If your best attempt at pronunciation meets with a puzzled look, just point to the place name on the list.

In Paris

Arc de Triomphe ark duh tree-ohnf
arrondissement ah-rohn-dees-mohn
Bateaux-Mouches bah-toh moosh
Bon Marché bohn mar-shay
Carnavalet kar-nah-vah-lay
Champ de Mars shahn duh mar
Champs-Elysées shahn-zay-lee-zay
Conciergerie kon-see-ehr-zhuh-ree
Ecole Militaire eh-kohl mee-lee-tehr
Egouts ay-goo
Fauchon foh-shohn
Galeries Lafayette gah-luh-ree lah-fay-yet
gare gar
Gare d'Austerlitz gar doh-stehr-leets
Gare de l'Est gar duh less
Gare de Lyon gar duh lee-ohn
Gare du Nord gar dew nor
Gare St. Lazare gar san lah-zar
Garnier gar-nee-ay
Grand Palais grahn pah-lay
Grande Arche de la Défense grahnd arsh duh lah day-fahns
Ile de la Cité eel duh lah see-tay
Ile St. Louis eel san loo-ee
Jacquemart-André zhahk-mar-ahn-dray
Jardin des Plantes zhar-dan day plahnt
Jeu de Paume juh duh pohm
La Madeleine lah mah-duh-lehn
Le Hameau luh ah-moh
Les Halles lay ahl
Les Invalides lay-zan-vah-leed
Orangerie oh-rahn-zhuh-ree
Louvre loov-ruh
Marais mah-ray
Marché aux Puces mar-shay oh poos
Marmottan mar-moh-tahn
Métro may-troh
Monge mohnzh
Montmartre mohn-mart
Montparnasse mohn-par-nahs
Moulin Rouge moo-lan roozh
Musée d'Orsay mew-zay dor-say
Musée de l'Armée mew-zay duh lar-may
Notre-Dame noh-truh-dahm
Opéra Garnier oh-pay-rah gar-nee-ay
Orsay or-say
palais pah-lay
Palais de Justice pah-lay duh zhew-stees
Palais Royal pah-lay roh-yahl
Parc de la Villette park duh la vee-leht
Parc Monceau park mohn-soh
Père Lachaise pehr lah-shehz
Petit Palais puh-tee pah-lay
Pigalle pee-gahl
Place Dauphine plahs doh-feen
Place de la Bastille plahs duh lah bah-steel
Place de la Concorde plahs duh lah kohn-kord
Place de la République plahs duh lah ray-poo-bleek
Place des Vosges plahs day vohzh
Place du Tertre plahs dew tehr-truh
Place St. André-des-Arts plahs san tahn-dray day-zart
Place Vendôme plahs vahn-dohm
Pompidou pohn-pee-doo
pont pohn
Pont Alexandre III pohn ah-leks-ahn-druh twah

Pont Neuf pohn nuhf
Promenade Plantée proh-mehn-ahd plahn-tay
quai kay
Rive Droite reeve dwaht
Rive Gauche reeve gohsh
Rodin roh-dan
rue rew
Rue Cler rew klehr
Rue Daguerre rew dah-gehr
Rue de Rivoli rew duh ree-voh-lee
Rue des Rosiers rew day roz-ee-ay
Rue Montorgueil rew mohn-tor-goy
Rue Mouffetard rew moof-tar
Sacré-Cœur sah-kray-koor
Sainte-Chapelle sant-shah-pehl
Seine sehn
Sèvres-Babylone seh-vruh-bah-bee-lohn
Sorbonne sor-buhn
St. Germain-des-Prés san zhehr-man-day-pray
St. Julien-le-Pauvre san zhew-lee-ehn-luh-poh-vruh
St. Séverin sahn say-vuh-ran
St. Sulpice sahn sool-pees
Tour Eiffel toor ee-fehl
Trianon tree-ahn-ohn
Trocadéro troh-kah-day-roh
Tuileries twee-lay-ree
Venus de Milo vuh-news duh mee-loh

Outside of Paris

Abri du Cap Blanc ah-bree dew cah blahn
Aiguille du Midi ah-gwee dew mee-dee
Aïnhoa an-oh-ah
Albi ahl-bee
Alet ah-lay
Alise Ste-Reine ah-leez sant-rehn
Aloxe-Corton ah-lohx kor-tohn
Alsace ahl-sahs
Amboise ahm-bwahz
Annecy ahn-see
Antibes ahn-teeb
Aosta (Italy) ay-oh-stah
Apt ahp
Aquitaine ah-kee-tehn
Arles arl
Arromanches ah-roh-mahnsh
Autoire oh-twahr
Auvergne oh-vehrn
Avignon ah-veen-yohn
Azay-le-Rideau ah-zay luh ree-doh
Balazuc bah-lah-zook
Bayeux bī-yuh
Bayonne bī-yuhn
Beaucaire boh-kehr
Beaujolais boh-zhoh-lay
Beaune bohn
Bedoin buh-dwan
Bennwihr behn-veer
Beynac bay-nak
Biarritz bee-ah-reetz
Blois blwah
Bonnieux bohn-yuh
Bordeaux bor-doh
Brancion brahn-see-ohn
Brittany bree-tah-nee
Bruniquel brew-nee-kehl
Caen kahn
Cahors kah-or
Cajarc kah-zhark
Calais kah-lay
Camargue kah-marg
Cambord kahn-bor
Cancale kahn-kahl
Carcassonne kar-kah-suhn
Carennac kah-rehn-ahk
Carsac kar-sahk
Castelnaud kah-stehl-noh
Castelnau-de-Montmiral kah-stehl-noh-duh-mohn-mee-rahl
Caussade koh-sahd
Cavaillon kah-vī-ohn
Cénac say-nahk
Céret say-ray
Chambord shahn-bor
Chamonix shah-moh-nee
Champagne shahn-pahn-yuh
Chapaize shah-pehz
Chartres shart
Château de Chatonnière shah-toh duh shah-tuhn-yehr
Château de Rivau shah-toh duh ree-voh
Château du Haut-Kœnigsbourg shah-toh dew oh-koh-neegs-boorg

Châteauneuf-du-Pape shah-toh-nuhf-dew-pahp
Châteauneuf-en-Auxois shah-toh-nuhf-ehn-ohx-wah
Chaumont-sur-Loire shoh-mohn-sewr-lwahr
Chenonceau shuh-nohn-soh
Chenonceaux shuh-nohn-soh
Cherbourg shehr-boor
Cheverny shuh-vehr-nee
Chinon shee-nohn
Cluny klew-nee
Colleville kohl-veel
Collioure kohl-yoor
Collonges-la-Rouge koh-lohnzh-lah-roozh
Colmar kohl-mar
Cordes-sur-Ciel kord-sewr-see-yehl
Côte d'Azur koht dah-zewr
Cougnac koon-yahk
Courseulles-sur-Mer koor-suhl-sewr-mehr
Coustellet koo-stuh-lay
Digne deen-yuh
Dijon dee-zhohn
Dinan dee-nahn
Dinard dee-nar
Domme dohm
Dordogne dor-dohn-yuh
Eguisheim eh-geh-shīm
Entrevaux ahn-truh-voh
Epernay ay-pehr-nay
Espelette eh-speh-leht
Eze-Bord-de-Mer ehz-bor-duh-mehr
Eze-le-Village ehz-luh-vee-lahzh
Faucon foh-kohn
Flavigny-sur-Ozerain flah-veen-yee-sewr-oh-zuh-ran
Font-de-Gaume fohn-duh-gohm
Fontenay fohn-tuh-nay
Fontevraud fohn-tuh-vroh
Fontvieille fohn-vee-yeh-ee
Fougères foo-zher
Fougères-sur-Bièvre foo-zher-sewr-bee-ehv
Gaillac gī-yahk
Gigondas zhee-gohn-dahs
Giverny zhee-vehr-nee
Gordes gord
Gorges de l'Ardèche gorzh duh lar-dehsh
Grenoble gruh-noh-bluh
Grouin groo-an
Guédelon gway-duh-lohn
Hautes Corbières oht kor-bee-yehr
Hendaye ehn-dī
Honfleur ohn-flur
Huisnes-sur-Mer ween-sewr-mehr
Hunawihr uhn-ah-veer
Ile Besnard eel bay-nar
Isle-sur-la-Sorgue eel-sewr-lah-sorg
Juan-les-Pins zhwan-lay-pan
Kaysersberg kī-zehrs-behrg
Kientzheim keentz-īm
La Charente lah shah-rahnt
Lacoste lah-kohst
Langeais lahn-zhay
Languedoc-Roussillon long-dohk roo-see-yohn
La Rhune lah rewn
La Rochepot lah rohsh-poh
La Roque St-Christophe lah rohk san-kree-stohf
La Roque-Gageac lah rohk-gah-zhahk
Lascaux lah-skoh
Lastours lahs-toor
La Trophée des Alpes lah troh-fay dayz ahlp
La Turbie lah tewr-bee
Le Bugue luh bewg
Le Crestet luh kruh-stay
Le Havre luh hah-vruh
Lémeré lay-muh-ray
Le Ruquet luh rew-kay
Les Baux lay boh
Les Eyzies-de-Tayac lay zay-zee-duh-tī-yahk
Les Praz lay prah
Les Vosges lay vohzh
Limoges lee-mohzh
Loches lohsh
Loire lwahr
Longues-sur-Mer long-sewr-mehr
Loubressac loo-bruh-sahk
Lourmarin loo-mah-ran
Luberon lew-beh-rohn
Lyon lee-ohn
Malaucène mah-loh-sehn
Marne-la-Vallée-Chessy marn-lah-vah-lay-shuh-see
Marseille mar-say

Martel mar-tehl
Mausanne moh-sahn
Ménerbes may-nehrb
Millau mee-yoh
Minerve mee-nerv
Mirabel mee-rah-behl
Modreuc mohd-rewk
Mont Blanc mohn blahn
Mont St-Michel mohn san-mee-shehl
Mont Ventoux mohn vehn-too
Montenvers mohn-tuh-vehr
Montfort mohn-for
Montignac mohn-teen-yahk
Mortemart mort-mar
Munster mewn-stehr
Nantes nahnt
Nice nees
Normandy nor-mahn-dee
Nyons nee-yohns
Oradour-sur-Glane oh-rah-door-sewr-glahn
Orange oh-rahnzh
Padirac pah-dee-rahk
Paris pah-ree
Pech Merle pehsh mehrl
Peyrepertuse pay-ruh-per-tewz
Pointe du Hoc pwant dew ohk
Pont du Gard pohn dew gahr
Pontorson pohn-tor-sohn
Provence proh-vahns
Puycelci pwee-suhl-cee
Puyméras pwee-may-rahs
Queribus kehr-ee-bews
Reims rans (rhymes with France)
Remoulins ruh-moo-lan
Rennes rehn
Ribeauvillé ree-boh-vee-yay
Riquewihr reek-veer
Rocamadour roh-kah-mah-door
Rouen roo-ahn
Rouffignac roo-feen-yahk
Roussillon roo-see-yohn
Route du Vin root dew van
Sablet sah-blay
Sare sahr
Sarlat-la-Canéda sar-lah lah cah-nay-duh
Savigny-les-Beaune sah-veen-yee-lay-bohn
Savoie sah-vwah
Séguret say-goo-ray
Semur-en-Auxois suh-moor-ehn-ohx-wah
Sigolsheim see-gohl-shīm
Souillac soo-ee-yahk
St-Cirq Lapopie san-seerk lah-poh-pee
St-Cyprien san-seep-ree-ehn
St-Emilion san-tay-meel-yohn
St-Geniès san-zhuh-nyehs
St-Jean-de-Luz san-zhahn-duh-looz
St-Jean-Pied-de-Port san-zhahn-pee-yay-duh-por
St-Malo san-mah-loh
St-Marcellin-lès-Vaison san-mar-suh-lan-lay-vay-zohn
St-Rémy san-ray-mee
St-Romain-en-Viennois san-roh-man-ehn-vee-ehn-nwah
St-Suliac san-soo-lee-ahk
St-Paul-de-Vence san-pohl-duh-vahns
Ste-Mère Eglise sant-mehr ay-gleez
Stes-Maries-de-la-Mer sant-mah-ree-duh-lah-mehr
Strasbourg strahs-boorg
Suzette soo-zeht
Taizé teh-zay
Tarascon tah-rah-skohn
Tours toor
Turckheim tewrk-hīm
Ussé oo-say
Uzès oo-zehs
Vacqueyras vah-kee-rahs
Vaison la Romaine vay-zohn lah roh-mehn
Valançay vah-lahn-say
Valréas vahl-ray-ahs
Vence vahns
Verdun vehr-duhn
Versailles vehr-sī
Veynes vay-nuh
Vézelay vay-zuh-lay
Vierville-sur-Mer vee-yehr-veel-sewr-mehr
Villandry vee-lahn-dry
Villefranche-de-Rouergue veel-frahnsh-duh-roo-ehrg
Villefranche-sur-Mer veel-frahnsh-sewr-mehr
Villeneuve-lès-Avignon veel-nuhv-lay-zah-veeh-yohn
Vitrac vee-trahk
Vouvray voo-vray
Villedieu vee-luh-dyuh

French Survival Phrases

When using the phonetics, try to nasalize the n sound.

English	French	Pronunciation
Good day.	*Bonjour.*	bohn-zhoor
Mrs. / Mr.	*Madame / Monsieur*	mah-dahm / muhs-yur
Do you speak English?	*Parlez-vous anglais?*	par-lay-voo ahn-glay
Yes. / No.	*Oui. / Non.*	wee / nohn
I understand.	*Je comprends.*	zhuh kohn-prahn
I don't understand.	*Je ne comprends pas.*	zhuh nuh kohn-prahn pah
Please.	*S'il vous plaît.*	see voo play
Thank you.	*Merci.*	mehr-see
I'm sorry.	*Désolé.*	day-zoh-lay
Excuse me.	*Pardon.*	par-dohn
(No) problem.	*(Pas de) problème.*	(pah duh) proh-blehm
It's good.	*C'est bon.*	say bohn
Goodbye.	*Au revoir.*	oh vwahr
one / two	*un / deux*	uhn / duh
three / four	*trois / quatre*	twah / kah-truh
five / six	*cinq / six*	sank / sees
seven / eight	*sept / huit*	seht / weet
nine / ten	*neuf / dix*	nuhf / dees
How much is it?	*Combien?*	kohn-bee-an
Write it?	*Ecrivez?*	ay-kree-vay
Is it free?	*C'est gratuit?*	say grah-twee
Included?	*Inclus?*	an-klew
Where can I buy / find...?	*Où puis-je acheter / trouver...?*	oo pwee-zhuh ah-shuh-tay / troo-vay
I'd like / We'd like...	*Je voudrais / Nous voudrions...*	zhuh voo-dray / noo voo-dree-ohn
...a room.	*...une chambre.*	ewn shahn-bruh
...a ticket to ___.	*...un billet pour ___.*	uhn bee-yay poor ___
Is it possible?	*C'est possible?*	say poh-see-bluh
Where is...?	*Où est...?*	oo ay
...the train station	*...la gare*	lah gar
...the bus station	*...la gare routière*	lah gar root-yehr
...tourist information	*...l'office du tourisme*	loh-fees dew too-reez-muh
Where are the toilets?	*Où sont les toilettes?*	oo sohn lay twah-leht
men	*hommes*	ohm
women	*dames*	dahm
left / right	*à gauche / à droite*	ah gohsh / ah dwaht
straight	*tout droit*	too dwah
When does this open / close?	*Ça ouvre / ferme à quelle heure?*	sah oo-vruh / fehrm ah kehl ur
At what time?	*À quelle heure?*	ah kehl ur
Just a moment.	*Un moment.*	uhn moh-mahn
now / soon / later	*maintenant / bientôt / plus tard*	man-tuh-nahn / bee-an-toh / plew tar
today / tomorrow	*aujourd'hui / demain*	oh-zhoor-dwee / duh-man

In a French Restaurant

English	French	Pronunciation
I'd like / We'd like...	*Je voudrais / Nous voudrions...*	zhuh voo-dray / noo voo-dree-ohn
...to reserve...	*...réserver...*	ray-zehr-vay
...a table for one / two.	*...une table pour un / deux.*	ewn tah-bluh poor uhn / duh
Is this seat free?	*C'est libre?*	say lee-bruh
The menu (in English), please.	*La carte (en anglais), s'il vous plaît.*	lah kart (ahn ahn-glay) see voo play
service (not) included	*service (non) compris*	sehr-vees (nohn) kohn-pree
to go	*à emporter*	ah ahn-por-tay
with / without	*avec / sans*	ah-vehk / sahn
and / or	*et / ou*	ay / oo
special of the day	*plat du jour*	plah dew zhoor
specialty of the house	*spécialité de la maison*	spay-see-ah-lee-tay duh lah may-zohn
appetizers	*hors d'oeuvre*	or duh-vruh
first course (soup, salad)	*entrée*	ahn-tray
main course (meat, fish)	*plat principal*	plah pran-see-pahl
bread	*pain*	pan
cheese	*fromage*	froh-mahzh
sandwich	*sandwich*	sahnd-weech
soup	*soupe*	soop
salad	*salade*	sah-lahd
meat	*viande*	vee-ahnd
chicken	*poulet*	poo-lay
fish	*poisson*	pwah-sohn
seafood	*fruits de mer*	frwee duh mehr
fruit	*fruit*	frwee
vegetables	*légumes*	lay-gewm
dessert	*dessert*	day-sehr
mineral water	*eau minérale*	oh mee-nay-rahl
tap water	*l'eau du robinet*	loh dew roh-bee-nay
milk	*lait*	lay
(orange) juice	*jus (d'orange)*	zhew (doh-rahnzh)
coffee / tea	*café / thé*	kah-fay / tay
wine	*vin*	van
red / white	*rouge / blanc*	roozh / blahn
glass / bottle	*verre / bouteille*	vehr / boo-tay
beer	*bière*	bee-ehr
Cheers!	*Santé!*	sahn-tay
More. / Another.	*Plus. / Un autre.*	plew / uhn oh-truh
The same.	*La même chose.*	lah mehm shohz
The bill, please.	*L'addition, s'il vous plaît.*	lah-dee-see-ohn see voo play
Do you accept credit cards?	*Vous prenez les cartes?*	voo pruh-nay lay kart
tip	*pourboire*	poor-bwahr
Delicious!	*Délicieux!*	day-lee-see-uh

For more user-friendly French phrases, check out *Rick Steves' French Phrase Book and Dictionary* or *Rick Steves' French, Italian & German Phrase Book.*

INDEX

INDEX

C

D

INDEX

INDEX

N

INDEX

INDEX

MAP INDEX

Our website enhances this book and turns

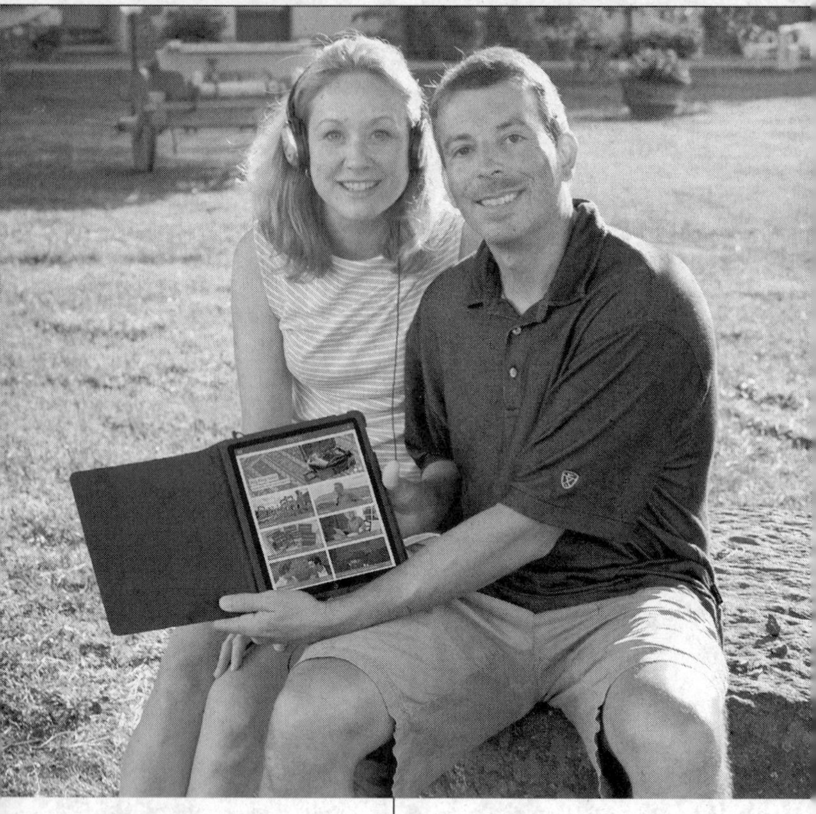

Explore Europe

At ricksteves.com you can browse through thousands of articles, videos, photos and radio interviews, plus find a wealth of money-saving travel tips for planning your dream trip. And with our mobile-friendly website, you can easily access all this great travel information anywhere you go.

TV Shows

Preview the places you'll visit by watching entire half-hour episodes of Rick Steves' Europe (choose from all 100 shows) on-demand, for free.

ricksteves.com

your travel dreams into affordable reality

Radio Interviews

Enjoy ready access to Rick's vast library of radio interviews covering travel

tips and cultural insights that relate specifically to your Europe travel plans.

Travel Forums

Learn, ask, share! Our online community of savvy travelers is a great resource for first-time travelers to Europe, as well as seasoned pros. You'll find forums on each country, plus travel tips and restaurant/hotel reviews. You can even ask one of our well-traveled staff to chime in with an opinion.

Travel News

Subscribe to our free Travel News e-newsletter, and get monthly updates from Rick on what's happening in Europe.

Rick Steves has

Experience maximum Europe

Save time and energy

This guidebook is your independent-travel toolkit. But for all it delivers, it's still up to you to devote the time and energy it takes to manage the preparation and logistics that are essential for a happy trip. If that's a hassle, there's a solution.

Rick Steves Tours

A Rick Steves tour takes you to Europe's most interesting places with great

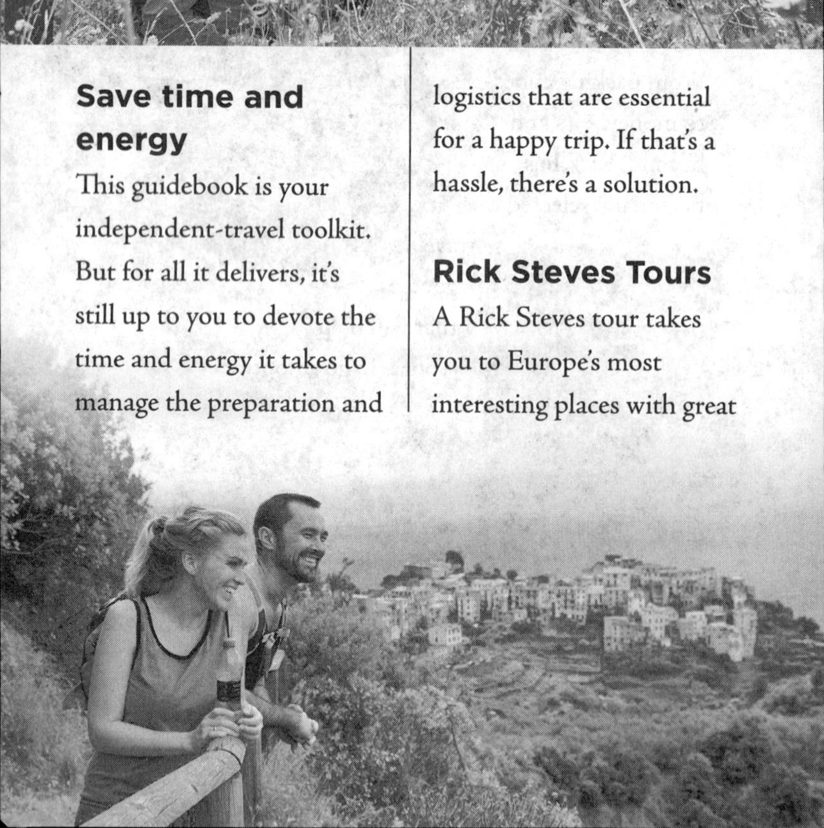

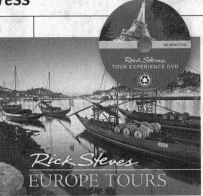

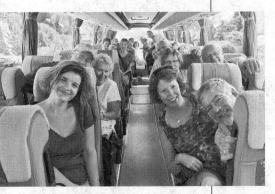

Credits

RESEARCHERS

To help update this book, Rick and Steve relied on...

Mary Bouron

Mary caught the travel bug as a child living in London and as an exchange student in France. Deeply in love with a Frenchman and the mother of three, she's now a proud Parisian. In her free time, she hunts for the city's best baguette and studies delicate differences between our cultures.

Tom Griffin

Tom edits and researches guidebooks for Rick Steves. For this book he traveled to the amazing châteaux of the Loire Valley. Tom has lived and worked in London, Paris, and Germany; he now makes his home in Seattle with his wife, Julie.

Virginie Moré

After living for 10 years in Los Angeles, Montana, and Florida, Virginie has settled in Lyon, France, with her husband, Olivier. When she's not teaching Americans about French culture and history while leading Rick Steves tours, she teaches scuba diving in the Caribbean.

CONTRIBUTOR

Gene Openshaw

Gene is a writer, composer, and lecturer on art and history. Specializing in writing tours of Europe's cultural sights, Gene has co-authored a dozen of Rick's books and contributes to Rick's public television series. As a composer, Gene has written a full-length opera (*Matter*), a violin sonata, and dozens of songs. He lives near Seattle with his daughter, and roots for the Mariners in good times and bad.

ACKNOWLEDGMENTS

Thanks to Steve's wife, Karen Lewis Smith, for her assistance covering French cuisine, and to Steve's children, Travis and Maria, for help with children's activities. Thanks to Rick Steves' video editor and assistant tour guide Aaron Harting for his help with the original "Winter Sports in Chamonix" section. The co-authors would also like to thank David Price, who lives in Avignon and is a fine source of information about key sights in Provence.

Avalon Travel
a member of the Perseus Books Group
1700 Fourth Street
Berkeley, California 94710

Printed in Canada by Friesens. First printing November 2014.

ISBN 978-1-61238-968-4
ISSN 1084-4406

For the latest on Rick's lectures, guidebooks, tours, public radio show, and public television series, contact Rick Steves' Europe, 130 Fourth Avenue North, Edmonds, WA 98020, 425/771-8303, rick@ricksteves.com, www.ricksteves.com.

Rick Steves' Europe
Managing Editor: Risa Laib
Editorial & Production Manager: Jennifer Madison Davis
Editors: Glenn Eriksen, Tom Griffin, Cameron Hewitt, Suzanne Kotz, Cathy Lu, John Pierce, Carrie Shepherd
Editorial & Production Assistant: Jessica Shaw
Editorial Intern: Mallory Presho-Dunne
Researchers: Mary Bouron, Tom Griffin, Virginie Moré
Maps & Graphics: David C. Hoerlein, Sandra Hundacker, Lauren Mills, Mary Rostad

Avalon Travel
Senior Editor and Series Manager: Madhu Prasher
Editor: Jamie Andrade
Associate Editor: Maggie Ryan
Copy Editors: Judith Brown and Rebecca Freed
Proofreader: Kelly Lydick
Indexer: Stephen Callahan
Production & Typesetting: Tabitha Lahr
Cover Design: Kimberly Glyder Design
Maps & Graphics: Kat Bennett, Mike Morgenfeld

Photo Credits
Front Cover: Senanque Abbey, Provence, © Getty Images
Additional Photography: Dominic Bonuccelli, Abe Bringolf, Mary Ann Cameron, Julie Coen, Rich Earl, Barb Geisler, Cameron Hewitt, David C. Hoerlein, Michaelanne Jerome, Lauren Mills, Paul Orcutt, Michael Potter, Carol Ries, Steve Smith, Robyn Stencil, Rick Steves, Gretchen Strauch, Rob Unck, Laura VanDeventer, Wikimedia Commons, Rachel Worthman, Dorian Yates (photos are used by permission and are the property of the original copyright owners)

Want more France?
Maximize the experience with Rick Steves as your guide

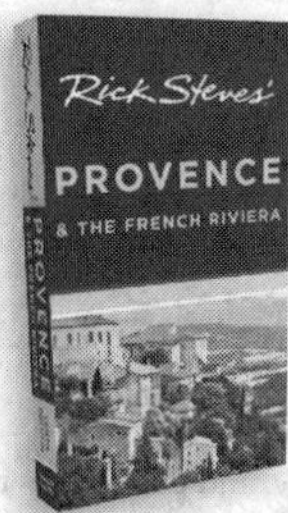

Guidebooks
Provence and Paris guides make side-trips smooth and affordable

Phrase Books
Rely on Rick's French Phrase Book & Dictionary

Rick's TV Shows
Preview your destinations with 11 shows on France

Free! Rick's Audio Europe™ App
Free audio tours for Paris' top sights

Small Group Tours
Rick offers several great itineraries through France

For all the details, visit ricksteves.com